Also by L. S. Stavrianos

The Promise of the Coming Dark Age

The World to 1500

The World Since 1500

A Global History

The Balkans Since 1453

Greece: American Dilemma and Opportunity

Balkan Federation: A History of the Movement Toward
Balkan Unity in Modern Times

Emiliano Zapata, leader of the resistance against the old order in southern Mexico.

Symbol of the old order: Porfirio Díaz, President of Mexico, 1867–1911.

GLOBAL RIFT

The Third World
Comes of Age

by

L. S. Stavrianos

WILLIAM MORROW AND COMPANY, INC.
New York 1981

Library of Congress Cataloging in Publication Data

Stavrianos, Leften Stavros.
  Global rift.

  "Morrow quill paperbacks."

  Bibliography: p.
  Includes index.
  1. Underdeveloped areas. 2. Economic history.
I. Title.
HC59.7.S76   330.9172′4   81-9647
ISBN 0-688-00656-6   AACR2
ISBN 0-688-00657-4 (pbk.)

Printed in the United States of America

First Morrow Quill Paperback Edition

1 2 3 4 5 6 7 8 9 10

BOOK DESIGN BY MICHAEL MAUCERI

Grateful acknowledgment is extended to the following for permission to reproduce pictures:

Aperture, Inc., Millerton, N.Y., for photographs of Chinese rattan factory (no. 12), Canton examination halls (no. 13), from *The Face of China,* by L. C. Goodrich, © 1978.

The Historical Society of Nigeria for illustration of Ethiopian Emperor Theodore's suicide (no. 11), from *Tarikh,* Vol. I, No. 4, p. 24.

Len Lahman and Sharon Myers, 334 South Sixth Avenue, Tucson, Ariz. 85701, for photographs of migrant worker's home (no. 29), breakfast buffet at the Hotel Fiesta (no. 30), residents of hills above Acapulco (no. 31).

The Marine Research Society, Salem, Mass., for illustration of slave ship (no. 5) from *Slave Ships and Slaving,* by George Francis Dow, copyright 1927.

The New York Public Library, Rare Book Division, for illustrations of Indians pouring molten gold down Spaniard's throat (no. 2), the port of Acapulco (no. 3), silver mining at Potosi (no. 4), from *America,* by Theodor de Bry, Frankfurt, 1591 *et seq.* Pt. IV, pl. 20; Pt. XI, Appendix, pl. 13; and Pt. IX, pl. 3, respectively.

The New York Times for photograph of Coca-Cola bottle (no. 22) from a news dispatch of April 15, 1981.

Reynal and Co. for photograph of St. Petersburg forge (no. 6) from *An Illustrated History of Russia,* by Joel Carmichael, © 1960.

The Southeast Asia Research Center, P.O. Box 4000D, Berkeley, Calif. 94704, for photographs of Moro National Liberation Front guerrillas (no. 20), Col. Sanders franchise in Kuala Lumpur (no. 21), Fairchild Electronics in Indonesia (no. 23), National Liberation Front command post at Dien Bien Phu (no. 24), Police Special Forces, Bangkok (no. 25), Thai massage parlor (no. 26).

University of Texas Press for photographs of Mexican peasants taking over haciendas (no. 28), Mexican factory workers (no. 27), from *The Wind That Swept Mexico,* by Anita Brenner, © 1976.

Viking Press for photographs of Shanghai refugees (no. 14), Communist soldiers in Peking (no. 15), Nehru with Lord and Lady Mountbatten (no. 17), iron smelting (no. 18), Ming Tombs Dam construction (no. 19), British couple at the races (no. 16), from *The Face of Asia,* by Henri Cartier-Bresson, © 1972.

Dedicated to Kenneth and Harle Montgomery
who advance principles to
practice

Acknowledgments

With the usual disclaimer about responsibility for facts and interpretation, I take pleasure in acknowledging the generous help of my colleagues at the University of California at San Diego, who read and criticized individual chapters: Allen Lein, Michael P. Monteon, Paul P. Pickowicz, Edward Reynolds and Ramon E. Ruiz. For similar assistance I am indebted also to Marian Daugherty, economist, formerly at Loyola University and the Treasury Department; Elie Schneour, President of Biosystems Associates; and David Mandel, Jerusalem correspondent for American and European newspapers. In particular, I thank Eugene Genovese of Rochester University for reading the entire manuscript and peppering the margins with characteristically pungent and perceptive comments. They are appreciated and cherished despite what must seem as inordinate perversity on my part. Equally appreciated are the encouragement, warm interest and professional guidance afforded from the outset by my editor, Maria Guarnaschelli. Finally, to this book as to earlier ones, my wife has contributed more than she may realize; all are the products of cooperation and comradeship.

GLOBAL RIFT

The Third World Comes of Age

Chapter

Chapter

Chapter

GLOBAL RIFT

The Third World Comes of Age

A Note from the Author

When scores of former colonies won their independence after World War II, Third World historians proceeded to write histories of their individual countries from their individual national viewpoints. This was a natural reaction to the histories of the colonial era, which were written from the angle of vision of London, Berlin or Paris rather than of Lagos, Cairo or Rangoon. The new national histories were much needed and long overdue. Yet by themselves they are not sufficient, for in history as in other fields, the whole is greater than the sum of its parts. In other words, an agglomeration of Third World national histories cannot define the structure and dynamics of the whole. And only the structure and dynamics of the whole brings out and clarifies the common experiences and interests that all Third World peoples share, regardless of their great diversity in history and culture and political commitments.

An integrated Third World history may be needed by Third World peoples, but why should it concern Americans and other Westerners of the developed countries? The answer in the past has been rather condescending. It goes something like this. Since the majority of human beings who live in the Third World are the unfortunates of the earth, it is up to us, the fortunates of the developed world, to be our brother's keeper. It is up to us to understand why the Third World is in its sorry plight and to give a helping hand. This is why past generations of Western children were told: "Don't waste your food. Think of the starving Armenians," and why today's children collect pennies on Halloween for UNESCO to care for the sick and malnourished.

The need for brother's keepers is much greater now than ever before, because the number of starving adults as well as children is correspondingly greater than at any time in the past. Yet charity has become the least significant consideration in the relations between the less than 6 percent of the human race that lives in the United States and the majority that lives in the Third World. Because of the unprecedented impact of modern science and technology, peoples of both the developed and underdeveloped countries find themselves today in the same boat, plagued by similar problems, and confronted with the grim and very real prospect of drowning together.

If this seems preposterous, consider the effect of the Vietnam War on American society, which still has not fully recovered from the political, economic and psychological trauma of that tragedy. Consider also our growing dependence on the Third World as a market for our products, and as a source of raw materials, which are increasingly essential as we deplete our own resources. Consider finally the little-known fact that a growing number of Americans now are beset by problems hitherto considered to be peculiar to the Third World. Our lives are being remolded by the Third Industrial Revolution, which is infinitely more powerful and expansionist than the preceding two Industrial Revolutions. Its impact is worldwide, creating common opportunities but also common problems. Thus if we look about us, and have the eyes to see, we find that much of the Third World is cropping up within our First World.

Example: Unemployment. A high rate of chronic structural unemployment has long been a feature of most Third World countries. Today it is becoming the norm also in the First World, and a basic reason is the exporting of industries as well as of goods from developed to underdeveloped countries. Each time a factory is shipped to an overseas cheap-labor area, there is a corresponding export of jobs, or import of unemployment. The new technology of the Third Industrial Revolution has made possible such a large-scale transplanting of industries to cheap-labor countries that a common global labor market is evolving. The hitherto privileged and highly paid labor force of the West is being forced to share the traditional unemployment and low wages of Third World workers. Martin Gerber, vice president of the United Automobile Workers, was reacting to this fact when he warned his union workers, "In the coming years we're going to have to move from an industrial union perspective to an international perspective. . . . With multinational companies such as Ford, which earns two thirds of its profits overseas, with the interchangeability of parts and the development of products such as the 'world car,' one-nation unionism has become outmoded." [1]

Example: Uprooted Farmers. Capital-intensive agribusiness technology uprooted first the farmers in the United States and then the peasants of the Third World. The new labor-displacing agricultural technology reduced the number of American family farms from a peak of 6.8 million in the mid-1930s to 2.8 million in 1980, to an estimated 1 million in 1985. The displaced farmers drift to the cities, so that two thirds of the Department of Agriculture's 1975 budget was allocated for food programs to feed the urban poor, many of whom were driven off the land by the Department's own agribusiness technology. Likewise, Third World cities are ringed by ghettos filled with displaced peasants who, however, lack the government assistance available in the more affluent United States.

Example: Poverty. Half a billion people are malnourished today, one eighth of the world's total population. Malnourishment is not so widespread in the United States, but it is by no means absent or insignificant. A commonly accepted estimate of the number of malnourished Americans is 20 million. This conforms with the 1980 report of the National Advisory Council on Economic Opportunity, which concludes that "poverty has been little reduced" since the War on Poverty began in the mid-1960s, with the number of officially poor Americans remaining at 25 million.[2] (A family of four is regarded as officially poor if its total annual income is below $7,450.) What this poverty means in terms of human beings was illustrated in Baltimore in September 1980 when a crowd of 26,000 waited for hours in long lines in sweltering heat to apply for 75 government jobs. "I can't think of anything less remarkable," said City Council President Walter Orlinsky. "You'd get the same lines in any other aging American city. It shouldn't come as a surprise to anyone." [3]

Example: Political Prisoners. Andrew Young, United States representative at the United Nations, aroused a storm in July 1978 when he declared that there were political prisoners in the United States as well as in the Soviet Union. In response to demands that he resign, he noted, "There are all varieties of political prisoners. I do think there are some people who are in prison much more because they are poor than because they are bad." [4] In support of this proposition, the Reverend Jesse Jackson, director of Operation PUSH, stated that three hundred thousand of the four hundred thousand inmates of American jails are black or brown. "What I am saying is that three fourths of all American prisoners being black or brown reflects something other than a predisposition on our part to criminal conduct. The fact that so many people are in prison due to the failings of our political system makes them political prisoners in much the same sense as those on whose behalf Carter has invoked the 'human rights' issue." [5]

Example: Ghettoes and Colonies. Distinguished psychologist Kenneth Clark has analyzed the ghettoes of American cities as the "consequence of the imposition of external power and the institutionalization of powerlessness." To support his contention, Clark notes that ghetto political leaders are dependent on the larger power structure, its social agencies rely on outside sources of support, its economy is dominated by small businesses owned mostly by absentee owners, its housing is owned largely by absentee landlords, and its schools are controlled by individuals who live outside the community. Clark concludes that, "ghettoes are in fact social, political, educational, and above all—economic colonies. Those confined within the ghetto walls are subject peoples. . . ." [6]

Example: States and Colonies. Dependent and exploitive relationships in First World countries are not confined to minority peoples. They span color lines and encompass entire regions, as evident in the following reaction by Governor Dick Lamm of Colorado against strip-mining companies: "We have seen what's happened to Kentucky and Tennessee and West Virginia and other states that have been the nation's coal bin, and we're not going to let that happen to us. . . . There are certain things that happen to colonies—whether they are Colorado or the Congo—if there is not some assertiveness on the part of their leaders. And we are not going to be colonized." [7]

Example: Cultural Imperialism. Third World countries protest against what they term the "cultural imperialism" foisted upon them as a result of First World control of global mass media. But the cultural imperialism operates also *within* First World countries, as evident in the following analysis by the *Christian Science Monitor*:

> Today, eight companies control the three television networks, *Time* and *Newsweek* magazines, the *New York Times*, the *Washington Post* and *Washington Star* (the only two newspapers in the nation's capital), the *Wall Street Journal*, the *Los Angeles Times*, television stations covering at least 40% of the TV audience, the leading radio networks and stations, major segments of the cable television industry, leading book publishing companies, a string of newspapers in other key cities across the nation and a bevy of other media and non-media enterprises. [8]

All this is not to say that the United States has become a Third World country. Rather it is to say that the traditional differentiation between affluent developed countries and impoverished underdeveloped countries no longer is clear cut and mutually exclusive. Distinctive Third World conditions and institutions are becoming widespread in the First World. The underlying reason for this dimming of dividing lines is that all regions of the globe are becoming ever more tightly integrated components of the international market economy. This global economy first took shape in the fifteenth century as the new capitalist economy of northwest Europe began expanding abroad, first to Eastern Europe and then to the Americas, Africa and Asia. These overseas lands were made subordinate to, and dependent upon, the industrialized metropolitan centers. In other words, they became the underdeveloped Third World of the periphery as against the developed First World of the center.

The traditional dichotomy between periphery and center now is being undermined. The dynamic technology of the current Third Industrial Revolution is blurring the old distinctions between the hitherto privileged peoples of the First World and the subject peoples of the Third. The inhabitants of all regions now are becoming subject peoples—that is, peoples subject to the imperatives of the global market economy. With Third World conditions sprouting within the metropolitan centers, the history of the Third World no longer is the history of distant and exotic peoples with whom we have only tenuous contact. It is now an integral part of our own history. Hence the need for "A Common Vision," the subject of the concluding chapter.

Part One

EMERGENCE OF THE THIRD WORLD, 1400–1770

The discovery of America, and that of a passage to the East Indies by the Cape of Good Hope, are the two greatest and most important events recorded in the history of mankind. Their consequences have already been very great. . . . By opening a new and inexhaustible market to all the commodities of Europe, it gave occasion to new divisions of labour and improvements of art, which, in the narrow circle of ancient commerce, could never have taken place. . . . To the natives, however, both of the East and West Indies, all the commercial benefits which can have resulted from those events have been sunk and lost in the dreadful misfortunes which they have occasioned.

ADAM SMITH, *The Wealth of Nations*

The Third World emerged in early modern times as the result of a fateful social mutation in northwestern Europe. This was the rise of a dynamic capitalist society that expanded overseas in successive stages, gaining control over widening segments of the globe, until by the nineteenth century it had established a worldwide hegemony. The introductory chapter surveys the main stages of capitalist expansion, and later of capitalist contraction, which constituted the corresponding expansion and contraction of the Third World.

What were the roots of this European expansionism? Why were the early explorers and settlers Europeans rather than Africans or Chinese or Middle Easterners? This central question in Third World history is the subject of the second chapter, analyzing the dynamics of European expansionism.

Although Western expansion is commonly associated with overseas enterprise, the initial impact of the West was on Eastern Europe, and it occurred well before the voyages of Columbus and da Gama. In the third chapter we shall see that it was with Eastern Europe that the burgeoning Western economy first developed a new type of trade that had never before been conducted anywhere in the world. This was a mass trade in necessities rather than the traditional trade in luxuries. In return for Western textiles, hardware and other manufactures, Eastern Europe exported foodstuffs, minerals and naval stores, and in the process became dependent upon, and subordinate to, the Western European economy. In this manner the Third World was born in the fifteenth century in Eastern Europe, for the phrase "Third World" connotes those countries or regions that participated on unequal terms in what eventually became the global market economy.

The next region to come under the domination of the West was the New World. The fourth chapter analyzes the growth of a transatlantic mass trade in which Western manufactures once more were exported, this time in exchange for New World products such as sugar, cotton, tobacco and dyestuffs. And just as the original mass trade had profoundly affected all aspects of East European society, including the imposition of serfdom in order to maximize the profits attainable in the trade with Western Europe, so the new transatlantic trade left its imprint on New World society, including the institution of slavery, which appeared for basically the same reason that serfdom did in Eastern Europe.

During this early modern period between the fifteenth and eighteenth centuries inclusive, the West European economy was not sufficiently developed and powerful to encompass the entire globe. Africa and the Middle East were somewhat infiltrated by the slave trade and by the various Levant companies. Yet even in these regions the Western impact during this period was limited largely to the coastal zones, so that chapters 5 and 6 analyze Africa and the Middle East as "peripheral" areas in relation to the international market economy. As for the old centers of civilization in South and East Asia, they were virtually unaffected by the burgeoning mass trade that was transforming the lands bordering on the Atlantic and the Mediterranean. Thus the concluding chapter of Part One is entitled "Asia: An External Area," for Asia remained beyond the reach of this early market economy until well into the nineteenth century. Only with the Industrial Revolution did the Western economy become sufficiently powerful to exert its sway over all continents, thereby extending the Third World into a global system—the subject of Part Two of this study.

Chapter 1

INTRODUCTION

For the first time since the dawn of civilization about 5000 years ago, the masses have now become alive to the possibility that their traditional way of life might be changed for the better and that this change might be brought about by their own action. This awakening of hope and purpose in the hearts and minds of the hitherto depressed three-fourths of the world's population will, I feel, stand out in retrospect as the epoch-making event of our age. The tapping of atomic energy and its application to the forging of weapons and the exploration of outer space will be seen to have been trifles by comparison.

ARNOLD J. TOYNBEE, *America and the World Revolution*

The phrase "Third World" is of very recent origin. It goes back only to the post-World War II years. Even in this brief period the use of the phrase has shifted from a political to an economic context. During the Cold War following the end of hostilities in 1945, a rigid line was drawn between the capitalist world led by the United States and the socialist world headed by the Soviet Union. At the height of the diplomatic pulling and tugging, it was expected that all countries should line up on one side or the other. Most did so, but a few clung to a precarious neutrality, including Tito's Yugoslavia, Nasser's Egypt, Nehru's India, Nkrumah's Ghana and Sukarno's Indonesia. These maverick states came to be known collectively as the Third World, to distinguish them from the First World of the Western bloc and the Second World of the Soviet bloc.

With the relaxation of the Cold War during the 1950s, the phrase Third World lost its political rationale. Gradually it took on an economic connotation, and was used to refer to the underdeveloped segment of the globe as against the developed capitalist First World (the United States, Japan, Western Europe and the former British dominions) and the developed socialist Second World (the Soviet Union and Eastern Europe). This shift in meaning made the Third World a much more inclusive category, encompassing over one hundred states with roughly three fourths of the world's total population. More specifically, the Third World comprises at present the following portions of the globe: all of Latin America, all of Africa except South Africa, and all of Asia except Japan and Israel.

Before World War II most of that portion of the globe now called the Third World was divided up into colonies of the European powers. The adjective commonly used at that time in describing the colonies was "backward," rather than the more diplomatic term "underdeveloped," or the even more diplomatic, though misleading, term, "developing," currently favored by the United Nations.

The "backwardness" of colonial peoples was taken for granted during those times when the existence and durability of empires also was taken for granted. On those rare occasions when the roots of colonial backwardness were considered, the theories commonly advanced were racist and self-serving. The "natives" were viewed as inherently different from, and inferior to, their European rulers. The "natives" did not respond to opportunities for improving their living standards. They preferred a carefree and leisurely life at subsistence level. They refused to plan or to assume responsibility for their future. If an explanation for such perversity was sought, it was usually attributed to climate or racial inferiority or religious prescriptions and taboos. Colonial rule generally was considered to be not the cause, but the only feasible solution for the prevailing backwardness.

Such apologetics are rarely heard today. Since the end of the Second World War a swelling flood of publications has been devoted to the problems of what were beginning to be called the underdeveloped or developing countries. This was not a spontaneous initiative on the part of Western social scientists. Rather they were responding to the political upheavals of their times: the revolutionary movements in the Third World, the rapid disintegration of imperial structures, and the Cold War, which made the fate of colonies and ex-colonies a matter of concern to policy-makers in Washington and Moscow.

As a result of this research it is beginning to be realized that the underdevelopment of the Third World and the development of the First World are not isolated and discrete phenomena. Rather they are organically and functionally interrelated. Underdevelopment is not a primal or original condition, to be outgrown by following the industrialization course pioneered by Western nations. The latter are overdeveloped today to the same degree that the peripheral lands are underdeveloped. The states of developedness and underdevelopedness are but two sides of the same coin. A recent statement of this proposition has been made by Gerard Chaliand after decades of observing and participating in Third World affairs:

> Underdevelopment is not an internal phenomenon due to the set structures of Third World countries, but a product of the world capitalist system and an integral part of it. There can be no way of overcoming it except by putting an end to dependence itself and to the structures of the dependent relationships. We can better grasp now the extent to which development is not an economic problem to be solved by injections of capital, but rather a *political* problem.[1]

Why is underdevelopedness "a product of the world capitalist system"? The answer is to be found in the unique nature and dynamics of capitalism as a system. The essence of capitalism is the drive for profit from privately owned and privately invested capital, which largely determines what goods are produced and how they are distributed. The uniqueness of this system was not that it used money, but rather that it used it for the first time in history as capital to make profit.

All precapitalist civilizations, whether Indian or Middle Eastern or Roman or Chinese, had developed efficient state mechanisms for siphoning off the agricultural surplus of their peasantries. But the enormous sums thereby accumulated were wasted on unproductive consumption by Roman senators, Indian princes, Confucian literati, Middle Eastern potentates, and their respective ecclesiastical hierarchies; hence the luxurious courts, stately mansions and imposing religious edifices that so impressed Western observers. But the latter did not realize that it was precisely this conspicuous consumption that was to make all these civilizations vulnerable to the new Western society, where accumulated money was used as capital to promote further production rather than to increase consumption. It was the systemic infusion of capital into the economic process that unleashed productive potentialities and enabled modern societies to reach the "take-off stage" into continuous expansion.

This expansionism is the distinguishing feature of capitalism as against earlier social systems. The latter produced primarily for local needs, so that relatively little was exported or imported. The capitalist Western societies, by contrast, extended the range of their economic activities from local scale to national and then to international.

The overseas expansion of European capitalism resulted in the emergence of the Third World through the operation of imperialism. Historian William Langer has defined imperialism as "the rule or control, political or economic, direct or indirect of one state, nation or people over other similar groups. . . ." [2] In the light of this definition, imperialism is as old as human civilization. Certainly the Romans were imperialistic, having conquered and ruled large parts of Europe and the Mediterranean basin. The same is true of the Egyptians in Africa, the Assyrians in the Middle East, the Chinese in the Far East, the Aztecs and Incas in the New World, and so forth. In modern times imperialism has been the inevitable by-product of capitalism as it turned from internal to external markets in its search for profits.

The evolution of imperialism through the centuries shows that the breadth and depth of its operation depended on the technological, economic and political power of the imperialist center. This is why there is a qualitative difference between the invasions of India by Alexander the Great in the fourth century B.C., and by the British East India Company in the eighteenth century A.D. The difference is in the nature of the impact upon the conquered territory. Alexander and other precapitalist conquerors exploited their possessions simply and directly by plundering and by collecting tribute, chiefly in the form of foodstuffs. But this exploitation did not particularly affect the economic life and structure of the subject territories. They continued to produce pretty much the same foodstuffs and handicrafts in the same ways as in the past. To compare this imperialism with the modern version that overran and remade entire continents is like comparing a spade to a steam shovel.

The contrast between the two types of imperialism is evident in the following account of the British impact on India by a distinguished jurist and historian, Sir Henry Maine, who served in India between 1862 and 1869:

> It is by indirect and for the most part unintended influence that the British power [in India] metamorphoses and dissolves the ideas and social forms underneath it, nor is there any expedient by which it can escape the duty of rebuilding upon its own principles that which it unwillingly destroyed . . . we do not innovate or destroy in mere arrogance. We rather change because we cannot help it. Whatever be the nature and value of that bundle of influences which we call Progress, nothing can be more certain than that, when a society is once touched by it, it spreads like a contagion.[3]

Sir Henry's testimony makes clear the distinctive feature of modern imperialism, which remolded the entire globe and in the process engendered the Third World. Precapitalist imperialism involved exploitation but no basic economic and social change. The tribute went to one ruling clique rather than another. Capitalist imperialism, by contrast, forced a thorough transformation of the conquered territories. This was not a matter of deliberate policy, as Sir Henry observed. Rather it was the inevitable "bundle of influences" that dynamic Western capitalism imposed upon the relatively static agrarian societies of Eastern Europe, Asia, Africa and the Americas. Whether the end result should be termed "Progress" depended on whether it was the judgment of conqueror or conquered. But there could be no dispute that the immediate effect of the capitalist intrusion was the absorption of the traditional agrarian societies into the new global market economy. This was a total and all-encompassing process, for the cultures as well as the economies of those societies were profoundly distorted and remolded in order to satisfy the demands of the global market.

Absorption into the international market economy was unavoidable because of the unique mass character of capitalist commerce. During all premodern millennia, trade perforce had been of the luxury variety—small in volume and high in value—because of the long distances involved and the dependence on horses, donkeys, camels and small sailing ships. Articles of trade were limited to spices, jewelry, quality fabrics and other costly artifacts of classical and medieval craftsmen. This traditional commerce served the needs only of the wealthy and powerful —imperial potentates, feudal chieftains, ecclesiastical dignitaries or merchant princes—and therefore it did not substantively influence the economies of the regions involved. The masses of the Eurasian lands were quite unaffected in their daily work and lives during the thousands of years that China exported her silks, India her cottons and Southeast Asia her spices.

In the fifteenth century the historic mutation occurred when Western Europe's capitalist economy generated for the first time a mass trade in necessities that overshadowed the traditional limited trade in luxuries. The new trade, precisely because it was a mass trade, involved entire populations which, willingly or unwillingly, produced for the new global market economy such necessities as foodstuffs, lumber and metals from Eastern Europe, bullion, sugar, tobacco, indigo and cotton from the Americas, slaves from Africa to work the American plantations, and rubber, tea, coffee, tin and jute from Asia. This mass trade inevitably led to the integration of entire societies into the new global economic order.

The commerce between colonies and metropolitan centers, conducted within the context of this global market economy, was hailed for centuries as a "natural" relationship that benefited all the parties involved. David Ricardo in the early nineteenth century worked out the intellectual rationalization for this proposition with his theory of comparative advantage. When the impersonal marketplace regulates global economic affairs, according to this theory, each country will concentrate on making those goods for which it is best suited, and will buy from other countries products for which they are best suited. It follows that each country derived the maximum benefit from participating in the new worldwide trade.

The theory is convincingly logical but it fails to explain what has happened, and is happening, to the Third World. Whereas the discrepancy in average per capita income between the First and Third Worlds was roughly 3 to 1 in 1500, it had increased to 5 to 1 by 1850, to 6 to 1 by 1900, to 10 to 1 by 1960 and to 14 to 1 by 1970. Far from benefiting all parties concerned, the global market economy is widening the gap between poor and rich countries, and at a constantly accelerating pace.

Despite this glaring contradiction between theory and reality, Ricardo's doctrines remained the basis of the economics courses taught in Western universities. Only in recent years has a new generation of economists attempted to square theory with what is actually going on in the Third World. The following passage in Joseph Schumpeter's *Theory of Economic Development* (1949) reflects a break from the traditional comparative-advantage approach: "By 'development,' therefore, we shall understand only such changes in economic life as are not forced upon it from without but arise by its own initiative, from within. Should it turn out . . . that the economy . . . is dragged along by the changes in the surrounding world . . . that the economy continuously adapts itself to them, then we should say that there is no economic development." [4]

Schumpeter here pinpoints the basic difference between the organic, autonomous economic development of the European metropolis and the imposed, externally controlled economic growth (*not* economic development) of the colonial periphery. Europe's Industrial Revolution was preceded by the Agricultural Revolution which, as will be noted in the following chapter, increased rural productivity and provided raw materials, capital and displaced labor for urban industries. The latter consisted of both light industries meeting consumer needs and heavy industries for capital goods. This process was accompanied by social dislocation and unemployment, but it made possible independent industrialization, which expanded enormously the national productive forces and eventually raised living standards for workers as well as entrepreneurs.

In the colonial or semicolonial periphery, by contrast, capital was not generated internally, but rather was brought in by metropolitan investors. Their objective, naturally, was to obtain maximum return on their capital. This could not be realized by promoting local industries because the poverty-stricken peripheral populations lacked purchasing power. The foreign capital therefore was used to finance the production of agri-

cultural and mineral products for the world market. This in turn necessitated the construction of ports, railways and other infrastructure
facilities for exporting the raw materials. Profits naturally went to the
metropolis, where they contributed to the further development of what
was already a developed economy. The native population was reduced
simply to providing cheap, unskilled labor. Thus the peripheral economies became the adjuncts or complements of the metropolitan economies, and could function only within the limits set by this dependent
and subordinate relationship. Hence the continued development of metropolitan economies and the causally related underdevelopment of
peripheral economies.

Other economists, in addition to Schumpeter, have noted the fallacy
of the theory of comparative advantage. Nobel Prize laureate Gunnar
Myrdal states, ". . . the play of the forces in the market normally tends
to increase, rather than to decrease, the inequalities between regions." [5]

Myrdal explains that the integrated world economy led to gross global
inequity because it integrated the weak and the strong. As will be noted
in the following chapter, the new agricultural and industrial technology
of the West, together with its banks, joint stock companies, aggressive
national monarchs and driving capitalist spirit, gave that hitherto retarded Eurasian peninsula superior economic and military power in its
dealings with the rest of the world. The interests of the weak inevitably
were subordinated to those of the strong—by mercantilist regulations in
the earlier centuries, by free trade after the Industrial Revolution, and
by neocolonialism today.

It follows from the above that Third World status involves more than
simple poverty. It does not suffice to draw a line representing a certain
per capita income level and to place the Third World below, and the
First World above, that line. Such a dividing line is by itself inadequate.
Kuwait, with no economic assets other than dwindling oil resources, cannot be considered the leading First World country because its oil royalties provide a per capita income more than double that of the United
States. When the oil wells have dried up a few decades hence, the persisting dependency or Third World status of Kuwait (and of other temporarily affluent oil exporters) will become tragically manifest.

Third World status, then, involves a second distinguishing feature in
addition to low income level, namely, economic growth without economic
development—growth determined by foreign capital and foreign markets
rather than by local needs. Economic growth, as distinct from economic
development, involves vertical economic linkages—that is, links to the
economies of the metropolitan centers—rather than horizontal economic
linkages—those between or among the various domestic sectors of the local
economies. The vertical economic relationships resulted in monoculture

economies that produced mostly mineral resources and agricultural goods for export, that were inherently incapable of overall integrated economic development, and that doomed Third World countries to the dependency and appallingly high unemployment that characterizes them to the present day. In short, the Third World is not a set of countries or a set of statistical criteria but rather a set of relationships—unequal relationships between controlling metropolitan centers and dependent peripheral regions, whether colonies as in the past or neocolonial "independent" states as today.

This view of the world answers Secretary of State Alexander M. Haig, Jr., who, during his nomination hearings, labeled "the so-called third world—a misleading term if there ever was one." He explained that "the communality of conditions, purpose and, by extension, United States foreign policy, implied by that term, third world is a myth—and a dangerous one at that." [6]

What is really dangerous for the United States is not the concept of a Third World, but Haig's interpretation of that concept. "Communality of conditions" obviously cannot be a distinguishing factor for a Third World that includes resource-rich Brazil as well as resource-poor Haiti, and affluent Kuwait as well as debt-ridden Turkey. Nor is "communality of purpose" a distinguishing feature of an agglomeration that includes capitalist Mexico as well as socialist North Korea, and pro-Western Egypt as well as anti-Western Cuba. The Third World concept is indeed a "myth," but only when it is based on static economic and ideological criteria. Which brings us back to the basic point that the nature and significance of the Third World can be understood only if it is viewed as a set of unequal relationships. More specifically, the Third World may be defined as comprising those countries or regions that are economically dependent upon, and subordinate to, the developed First World.

The concept of imperialism also requires elaboration. We noted above that it was the result of capitalism expanding from a national to an international scale of operations, and involved the restructuring of colonial societies to adapt them to the needs of the global market economy. Imperialism, however, did not necessarily lead to colonialism, which is a particular and optional form of imperialism. Colonialism materialized when metropolitan policymakers calculated that direct and formal political control served their interests better than indirect and informal control. The latter type of authority, however, was preferred during those times when the economic power of the metropolis was sufficient to achieve unaided the desired exploitation of the peripheral regions, as during the free-trade imperialism of the nineteenth century, or when peripheral nationalism was so potent that direct outside rule was not feasible, thereby necessitating the neocolonialism that is prevalent today.

Since capitalism is an inherently dynamic system, it has continually changed in character and continually expanded in scope. Profits from the periphery contributed to the development of the metropolitan center, which in turn affected the growth of the periphery. Consequently the Third World was not a frozen or immutable entity. As the West's economic power increased, so did the scope and efficiency of its domination, or imperialism, or if viewed from the periphery, the extent and the subordination of the Third World. Thus the following four stages are recognizable:

Interrelated Evolution of the Metropolitan Center and Its Dependencies

Period	Center	Periphery
1. 1400–1770	Commercial capitalism	Colonialism confined largely to the Americas
2. 1770–1870	Industrial capitalism	Waning colonialism
3. 1870–1914	Monopoly capitalism	Worldwide colonialism
4. 1914–present	Defensive monopoly capitalism	Revolution, decolonization and neocolonialism

The first period, from 1400 to 1770, was the era of commercial capitalism and mercantilism—the era when most capital was invested in commercial enterprises and when merchants organized joint stock companies and secured royal charters granting them trade monopolies and colonization privileges in given overseas territories. Because of the limited technological and economic power of commercial capitalism during those centuries, colonization was confined largely to the Americas, though Eastern Europe, Africa and the Middle East were enmeshed in varying degrees into the emerging world market economy.

The second period, from 1770 to 1870, was the era of industrial capitalism when overseas profits contributed to the advent of the Industrial Revolution in England and later on the Continent. During this century competitive industrial firms exported manufactured goods in return for raw materials from the Third World. Since Britain, as the pioneer industrialized country, enjoyed a head start over all competitors, British firms no longer were interested in charters and monopolies. Rather it was to their interest to promote international free trade which, under prevailing circumstances, meant for them a *de facto* monopoly of global markets. Thus the period of industrial capitalism was the period when monopolistic mercantilism was displaced by what is known as free-trade imperialism. This functioned not only in the Americas but also throughout the world, thanks to the infinitely greater economic and military power of industrial capitalism as against its commercial predecessor. The century from 1770 to 1870 was therefore the century when outright acquisition of colonies lost its attractiveness. It was the century of waning colonialism in the Third World.

About 1870 the combination of industrial capitalism and free-trade imperialism was supplanted by monopoly capitalism and revived colonial imperialism. Giant monopolies replaced the formerly independent and competitive industrial firms, and at the same time newly industrialized states emerged that successfully challenged Britain's lead in industry, finance and world trade. The ensuing conflicts, together with the contemporary vogue of Social Darwinist doctrines, led to the abandonment of free-trade imperialism in favor of the revived colonial imperialism of the late nineteenth century. The end result was the greatest land grab in history, with a handful of European powers literally dividing the globe among themselves as colonies or semicolonies. This resurgent and expanded colonialism made the Third World a truly global system, with the single exception of the small Japanese kingdom on the eastern tip of Eurasia. The worldwide range of the Third World reflected the increased military and economic power of Western capitalism in its monopoly phase.

During the twentieth century, monopoly capitalism was forced on the defensive because of the progressive awakening of colonial peoples and the mounting internal contradictions and conflicts within monopoly capitalism. The latter were reflected by World War I, the Great Depression, World War II, and the post-World War II rivalries among the United States, Western Europe and Japan, as well as their common domestic problem after the 1960s of inflation amid recession and unemployment. This combination of internal tensions and external pressures forced monopoly capitalism to surrender political control over its worldwide empires. The revived colonial imperialism of the late nineteenth century gave way gradually in the twentieth century to a neocolonialism that ceded political independence but retained direct or indirect economic control over former colonial territories. This economic control was exerted effectively with the exponential growth after World War II of the giant multinational corporations, which used new technologies to integrate the peripheries more thoroughly into the international market economy. For the Third World, therefore, the twentieth century is the ambiguous century of decolonization and neocolonialism.

These four stages in the historical evolution of the metropolitan center and the Third World periphery are analyzed in the four parts comprising this study. Each of the four parts consists of a preliminary chapter analyzing the technological and institutional developments in the center, and of following chapters examining the resulting impact and reaction in the various regions of the Third World.

Chapter 2

ERA OF COMMERCIAL CAPITALISM AND NEW WORLD COLONIALISM

The discovery of gold and silver in America, the extirpation, enslavement and entombment in mines of the aboriginal population, the beginning of the conquest and looting of the East Indies, the turning of Africa into a warren for the commercial hunting of black-skins, signalised the rosy dawn of the era of capitalist production. These idyllic proceedings are the chief momenta of primitive accumulation. On their heels treads the commercial war of the European nations, with the globe for a theater.

KARL MARX

In the fifteenth century the Western Europeans began modern world history by starting their great expansion overseas. Why did they take the initiative in this fateful enterprise? Why didn't the Chinese "discover" Europe instead? This is not an insignificant question, for had the Chinese done so, and settled the Americas and Australia and the rest of Oceania, the population of the globe might today be one-half Chinese rather than one-fifth.

A clue to the reason for Europe's leadership is to be found in the fact that the Vikings had stumbled on North America about five hundred years before Columbus, and for a century they had tried unsuccessfully to maintain settlements there. In contrast, Columbus was followed by people from all countries of Europe in a massive and overwhelming penetration of both North and South America. The difference in the reaction between the tenth and fifteenth centuries suggests certain developments in the intervening half millennium that had made Europe willing and able to expand overseas. These developments consisted essentially of the emergence of commercial capitalism, a new and inherently expansionist social order that stimulated the discovery of new lands overseas, the acquisition of colonies in these new lands and the evolution of a body of economic theories and practices known as mercantilism.

If capitalism was responsible for Europe's pioneering in overseas enterprise, then why did this demonic social system appear first in the relatively underdeveloped western tip of Eurasia? The answer, paradoxically, is to be found in the very underdevelopedness of Western Europe. The fall of Rome in the West was not followed by an imperial restoration, as happened repeatedly in other Eurasian regions under similar circumstances. Rather there were repeated and prolonged barbarian invasions, which eventually destroyed irrevocably the imperial classical residuum, thereby clearing the ground for the fateful social mutation known as capitalism.

The fact that the West experienced this mutation because of its backwardness is a significant and recurring phenomenon in world history. In the second millennium B.C. an earlier mutation had occurred with the rise of the new classical civilizations in what were then the peripheral regions of Europe, India and China, rather than in the old core region of the Middle East. Again the reason was precisely that the ancient civilization of the Middle East had survived the invasions of the second millennium B.C., while the peripheral regions had gone under, leaving the way clear for a fresh start—for the emergence of the new classical civilizations.

So it was during the transition from the classical to the medieval and modern capitalist civilizations. But this time the existing classical civilizations survived everywhere except in the West. For this reason the West alone was free to strike out in new directions and to evolve during the medieval centuries a new technology, new institutions and new ideas—in short, the new capitalist civilization.

The fact that the birth of the classical, medieval and capitalist civilizations occurred in peripheral regions suggests that when a social system becomes obsolete and is superseded, the leadership in the transition process is likely to be provided not by the affluent, traditional and sclerotic societies in the center, but by the primitive, poverty-stricken and adaptable societies in the peripheries. The implications of this pattern are obvious for the twentieth-century world: contrary to Marx's expectation, the revolutionary upheavals are occurring in the peripheries, while the center remains capitalist.

ᴥ *I. Commercial Revolution and Commercial Capitalism in the West*

The Roman Empire, out of which the dynamic medieval Western civilization emerged, was not substantively different from other classical Eurasian empires. Certain differences in detail did exist because of distinctive historical backgrounds and cultural traditions. But the overall social structures of all the classical Eurasian civilizations were basically similar. At the head of each was the ruling king or emperor, followed by nobles and top officials, priestly hierarchies, traders, craft enterprisers and moneylenders. At the bottom of the pyramid everywhere, comprising the great majority of the total population, were the workers in agriculture and the crafts. Some were free; others were serfs or slaves, with the proportion varying according to region and period.

Despite this Eurasianwide social homogeneity, a qualitatively different type of civilization emerged in the West in modern times. This was not due merely to the fall of the Roman Empire, for the rise and fall of empires were recurring experiences in all regions of Eurasia. The Han Empire of China, for example, was roughly contemporary with the Roman Empire in the West, and the Han collapsed before barbarian onslaughts as did the Roman. But the Han Dynasty was followed by the Sui, and Chinese civilization continued to flourish relatively unchanged despite the rise and fall of successive dynasties. In Europe, however, Roman civilization did not survive the fall of the Empire, which explains why the West deteriorated to a state of crumbling anarchy.

The unique feature of the medieval Western historical experience was the failure to restore Roman civilization, in contrast to traditional civilizations in China and India, which repeatedly revived after the periodic barbarian invasions. Various factors explain this historic failure of the West. The western provinces of the Roman Empire lacked the financial resources, naval strength and resourceful diplomats of the eastern or Byzantine provinces. They lacked also the agricultural productivity, the administrative efficiency and the cultural homogeneity of the Chinese Empire. Also the West was uniquely vulnerable because it was the terminal point of East to West nomadic migrations. The nomads of the East were lured by the better watered and more fertile lands of the western Eurasian steppes, so that a geographic steppe gradient persisted throughout these centuries. The main invasion route followed the corridor of grassland that stretched across central Eurasia, beginning in the environs of Peking and ending in the Hungarian plains of central Europe. This was the route followed by the Germans and Huns who overthrew the original Roman Empire in the fourth and fifth centuries, by the Avars and Slavs who destroyed the Merovingian Empire in the sixth century, and by the Magyars, Vikings and Muslims who ended the Carolingian Empire in the ninth century.

This prolonged succession of invasions was responsible for the unique historical dénouement in the West. The repeated demolitions ended any possibility of imperial restoration and cleared the ground for something new to take root—a new Western civilization with pluralistic institutions, which gradually replaced the former monolithic imperial structure.

Three institutions personified this pluralism—feudalism in the realm of politics, manorialism in the realm of economics, and the Papacy in the realm of church-state relations. Feudalism meant a congeries of warring feudal kings and lords in place of the former imperial authority. The Papacy meant an independent church in place of dictation by an emperor, so that medieval European history was characterized by struggles between kings and popes as well as between kings and nobles. Finally, manorialism meant the emergence of autonomous local economic units in place of the former slave plantations and integrated imperial economy. A new merchant class emerged later, gradually gaining economic and political strength to challenge the feudal nobles and eventually even the monarchy. It was this pluralism that provided Western society with the dynamism necessary for overseas expansion.

One manifestation of dynamism was the extraordinary technological precocity of the medieval West. In fact, the West made more technological progress than did classical Greece and Rome during their entire histories. One reason was the absence of slavery, a practice that tended to inhibit technological innovation. Another was the prevalence of frontier conditions, which stimulated labor-saving devices and endowed manual labor with a status and respect lacking in slave societies. The traditional gulf between philosopher and artisan began to be bridged. The resulting combination of brainpower and sweat generated the technological spurt forward that propelled Western Europe to world leadership. Finally, Western technology was sparked by the humanitarian ethic of Christianity. The monks in the monasteries insisted that manual labor was an integral part of the spiritual life. Or, as they put it, "to work is to pray"—*laborare est orare*. These monks were historically significant as the first intellectuals to get dirt under their fingernails, and in doing so, they aided technological advance.

Two stages are discernible in the technological progress of the medieval West. The first, between the sixth and eleventh centuries, was in the development of the "three field" rotation system of farming, which raised productivity substantially because only a third of the land lay fallow at any one time instead of the half left by the former "two field" system. Another was the invention of a heavy wheeled plow with a sharp iron point that could cut under the sod six to eight inches or more. This plow made possible the cultivation of the heavy, sodden soils of central and northern Europe, which were invulnerable to the light scratch plow used in the Mediterranean lands. Agriculture was aided also by the invention of horseshoes and by the use of an improved horse harness that enabled the animal to pull four to five times more weight. Finally, note should be made of the all-important watermill and windmill, both of which were little used in Greco-Roman times, because of the abundance of slave labor and the scarcity of streams dependable the year round. With both these obstacles absent in the northern lands, the mill and the miller soon were to be found in almost every manor.

At first the mills were used exclusively for grinding grain, but with the proliferation of cities and of manufacturing after the eleventh century, water power and wind power were applied to an increasing variety of productive processes. These included use for forge hammers and forge bellows, for sawmills and lathes, for fulling mills making cloth, pulping mills making paper and stamping mills crushing ore. Other technological advances in the later Middle Ages contributed directly to Europe's overseas expansion. These included progress in the construction and rigging of ships, in the increasingly effective use of the compass and astrolabe, in the preparation of accurate new maps and in the casting of iron naval guns that by the beginning of the sixteenth century could shoot balls capable of damaging a hull at three hundred yards. Naval tactics now shifted from the traditional boarding and hand-to-hand fighting on decks to broadside firing at increasingly long distances. The new ships and naval artillery gave the Europeans command of the oceans of the world. By 1513 the Portuguese Albuquerque, who had won control of the Indian Ocean, could justifiably boast, "at the rumor of our coming, the native ships all vanished, and even the birds ceased to skim over the water." [1]

Technological advance was matched by corresponding demographic and economic advance. Western Europe's population increased 50 percent between the tenth and fourteenth centuries, a rate that seems insignificant today but that was unmatched at the time. The demographic spurt stimulated improvements in agriculture to support the growth of population, and the increased food supply in turn made further population increase possible. Average gross yields per seed for rye, wheat, barley and oats doubled in England between the thirteenth and sixteenth centuries. Peasants also cultivated unused lands in their midst, and then immigrated into the vast underpopulated regions of Eastern Europe—a medieval European eastward movement comparable to the later American westward movement.

At the same time new mining methods led to rising output of salt, silver, lead, zinc, copper, tin and iron ore in central and northern Europe. Likewise the rich timber and naval stores of Britain, Scandinavia and the Baltic now were exploited more extensively than ever before. The same was true of the northern fisheries, particularly the cod of Iceland and Norway, and the herring of the Baltic.

Rising output in agriculture, mining, fishing and forestry stimulated a corresponding growth of commerce and of cities. Merchants were to be found in tenth-century Europe but they trafficked mostly in luxuries. By the fourteenth century, however, commerce had advanced from the periphery to the center of everyday life. Goods exchanged included raw wool from England, woolen cloth from Flanders made from English wool, iron and timber from Germany, furs from Slavic areas, leather and steel from Spain and luxury goods from the East. Towns appeared to expedite this trade, first in Italy and then along the inland trade routes and along the Baltic coast.

Western European cities were insignificant in medieval times compared to those of China as regards population or volume of trade. But the Western European cities were quite unique because of their growing autonomy and political power. Starting afresh within the framework of a politically fragmented Europe rather than a monolithic empire, they were able to extract charters from the various monarchs. These documents licensed them to act as a corporation and to permit merchants and craftsmen to organize as guilds that regulated manufacturing standards, prices and working hours. Towns came to be recognized as a new element in society, their inhabitants being outside feudal law. In certain regions, groups of cities banded together to form leagues, which became powerful political and economic entities. This was the case with the Lombard League in Italy, which defied the Hohenstaufen emperors, and the Hanseatic League in the Baltic, which pressed for trading privileges in foreign countries and virtually monopolized the trade of northern Europe.

These developments gave the European merchant a status as well as a power that was unique in Eurasia. In China, for example, the merchant was regarded as inferior and undesirable, and suffered restrictions concerning clothing, carrying of weapons, riding in carts and owning land. His function of transporting commodities from place to place was regarded as nonproductive and parasitic, and he was placed at the bottom of the social scale. In Western Europe, by contrast, merchants steadily gained in power and prestige. They were becoming lord mayors in London, senators in the German imperial free cities and grand pensioners in Holland. All this was to prove of prime significance for the future Third World: it meant more consideration and more consistent state support for mercantile interests and for overseas ventures.

Such was the background out of which sprung the new economic order of commercial capitalism. The transition from feudalism, as noted by Eric Hobsbawm, was "a long and by no means uniform process." [2] Feudalism persisted to a large degree in the Iberian peninsula, for example, after the great discoveries and the commercial expansion into the Americas and the East Indies. But the crucial point, so far as Third World history is concerned, is that the triumph of capitalism did occur in Western Europe, and therefore it was that Eurasian peninsula that subsequently transformed the rest of the world.

Symbolic of the new capitalist order was the changing attitude toward charging interest for loans. In the early Middle Ages, churchmen had denounced interest as constituting usury, a mortal sin and "a vice most odious and detestable in the sight of God." But by 1548 the French jurist Charles Dumoulin was pleading for the acceptance of "moderate and acceptable usury." And this modification soon gave way to the cynical attitude, "He who takes usury goes to hell; he who does not goes to the poorhouse."

Acceptance of the taking of interest reflected the gradual shift to an entirely different type of society in Western Europe. Whereas the Roman Empire had the same basic social structure as other contemporary Eurasian civilizations, now the medieval West was making the fateful transition to capitalism. This meant that the money accumulated from technological advances and the increasing commerce within and without Europe was being used as capital to make profit and to finance indefinite expansion.

All past precapitalist civilizations had siphoned off vast amounts of surplus capital from their peasant masses to support the palaces, temples, mansions and the administrative, ecclesiastical and military bureaucracies that were the hallmarks of those civilizations. It follows, then, that the mere accumulation of money did not necessarily lead to the advent of capitalism. Rather it was necessary to have, in addition to the accumulation of capital, the concurrent proletarianization of the peasantry. By this is meant the dissolution of traditional feudal relations, so that the peasants were excluded from their village communities and transformed into a displaced labor force available for trade and the crafts.

Such a change occurred early in England, where specific local factors speeded up the transformation of the countryside. The Wars of the Roses (1455–85) decimated the feudal nobility, while the strong Tudor kings tamed the survivors. The expropriation of church lands by Henry VIII and their distribution among his followers created new landed families more in tune with prevailing economic trends. Also the growth of national and foreign markets for English wool and foodstuffs attracted men with capital who viewed land as a lucrative business investment rather than a means of support for the local population.

These entrepreneurs made profit in various ways. They bought estates and squeezed the maximum revenue from the tenants by disregarding their legal rights as copyholders through sheer force or legal swindling. Also they forced the tenants off the land by various legal and extralegal methods, and then used it for more efficient large-scale farming or for sheep raising. The latter was so remunerative that, according to current saying, "a sheep's foot changes sand into gold."

These changes involved the displacement or proletarianization of the peasants. Some were able to find jobs in the towns. Others fell back on rural crafts such as weaving to support themselves. Many were not able to do either, so that England now experienced the phenomenon of able-bodied vagabonds drifting about the countryside and resorting to any measures to stay alive. All past ages and societies had been accustomed to poverty caused by old age, or the sickness or death of breadwinners. But now England, and later other countries undergoing the transition to capitalism, faced the new problem of able-bodied men deprived of both homes and jobs. The plight of these "beggars" is evident in the nursery rhyme:

> *Hark! Hark! the dogs do bark;*
> *the beggars are coming to town.*
> *Some give them white bread,*
> *and some give them brown.*
> *And some gave them a good horsewhip,*
> *and sent them out of town.*

The provocative contrast between the few engaged in the "money business" and the many who were its victims culminated in class hatred and class warfare. A revealing feature of the urban revolts and peasant uprisings was that they occurred at about the same time in scattered regions, reflecting simultaneous pressure and dispossessions in the countryside, and overproduction and unemployment in the cities. This was the period when the peasants revolted in Flanders and were supported by the workers of Ypres and Bruges, when the textile workers of Florence seized power and the English peasants under Wat Tyler captured London, when the Catalan, German and Bohemian peasants rose in desperate jacqueries, and the miners and peasants of Sweden, Norway, Denmark and Finland also broke out in rebellion.[3]

Nothing like this happened in the other regions of Eurasia, where imperial authority remained intact or was quickly reasserted after brief interregnums. Central authority consequently was able to curb the nobles and merchants, and thus to prevent the proletarianization of the peasants and the workers. The contrast between the class conflicts in

Western Europe and the relative social peace in the rest of Eurasia was strikingly evident along the lengthy common frontier between the Ottoman Empire and Christian Europe. Contemporary travelers frequently reported that the peasants on the Ottoman side of the frontier were generally better off than their counterparts in the Western lands. Even Martin Luther observed that "one finds in German lands those who desire the future of the Turks and their government, as well as those who would rather be under the Turks than under the Emperor and the Princes." [4]

The advent of capitalism was manifestly disruptive and painful. But it was so precisely because of its inherent dynamism, so that it rapidly expanded from local to national and global scale of operation. While Suleiman the Magnificent was besieging Vienna in the heart of Europe (1529), the Christian infidels were becoming the masters of the world with their voyages to the New World and around the Cape to India. Thus it was not Ottoman merchants who journeyed to Western Europe, but rather it was the French, the English and the Dutch who organized their respective Levant companies and exploited the Ottoman Empire. By 1788 the French ambassador in Constantinople could justifiably boast that, "The Ottoman Empire is one of the richest colonies of France." [5] During the following century virtually the entire globe was destined to follow the Ottoman Empire to subordinate and exploited status in relation to the capitalist West.

ꙮ II. Mercantilism and Colonialism in the Third World

European merchants who traded in all corners of the earth provided a striking contrast to the Chinese, who between 1405 and 1433 had conducted by far the most far-reaching overseas expeditions of the time, and then stopped them abruptly. These expeditions were extraordinary in their magnitude and in their achievements. The first comprised sixty-two ships and twenty-eight thousand men, and sailed as far as Java, Ceylon and Calicut. Later expeditions pressed on farther, reaching as far as the eastern coast of Africa and the entrances to the Persian Gulf and the Red Sea. More than thirty ports in the Indian Ocean were visited by the Chinese, and everywhere they persuaded or compelled the local rulers to recognize the suzerainty of the Ming Emperor. And all this at a time when the Portuguese, with much smaller ships and inferior navigation techniques, were just beginning to feel their way down the coast of Africa, not reaching Cape Verde until 1445!

These remarkable Chinese expeditions were suddenly halted by imperial fiat in 1433. The precise reasons why they were halted remains as much a mystery as why they were started in the first place. But the underlying factor is the fundamental difference between the Chinese and Western societies, as reflected in the contrasting nature and conduct of their overseas enterprises. The Chinese voyages were organized and led by a court eunuch rather than a joint stock company. They were designed to secure recognition of the suzerainty of the Celestial Emperor rather than in earning dividends for company shareholders. They returned with zebras, ostriches and giraffes for the titillation of the imperial court rather than with profit-yielding cargoes for a domestic market. And they were terminated completely and irrevocably on imperial order with no effective opposition from Chinese merchants, an outcome that would have been utterly inconceivable in contemporary Europe, with its rival national monarchies and joint stock companies competing ferociously to extract maximum profits from their overseas enterprises.

The reason why Columbus was not Chinese is evident in contemporary European and Chinese writings. "Coming into contact with barbarian peoples," wrote Chang Hsieh in 1618, "you have nothing more to fear than touching the left horn of a snail. The only things one should really be anxious about are the means of mastery of the waves of the sea—and, worst of all dangers, the minds of those avid for profit and greedy of gain." [6] By contrast, Hernando Cortes, the conquistador who overran Mexico, wrote in 1521, "We the Spanish, suffer an affliction of the heart which can only be cured by gold. . . . I came in search of gold and not to work the land like a laborer." And the Portuguese Captain João Ribeiro boasted in 1685, "From the Cape of Good Hope onwards we were unwilling to leave anything outside of our control; we were anxious to lay hands on everything in that huge stretch of over 5000 leagues from Sofala to Japan . . . there was not a corner which we did not occupy or desire to have subject to ourselves." [7]

Two factors explain the remarkable difference between Chinese and Western attitudes toward overseas expansion. One was political—the rise of the European national monarchs who competed vigorously for the riches and self-sufficiency afforded by colonial possessions. Thus when the Spanish and Portuguese monarchs laid claim to all overseas territories, France's King Francis I rejoined: "I should like to see Adam's will, wherein he divided the earth between Spain and Portugal."

This royal competition for overseas territories is most significant, for it meant that the merchants and their joint stock companies enjoyed state support in their global operations. In fact, one reason for the rise of powerful European monarchs such as Henry VIII in England (1509–47), Francis I in France (1515–47) and Ferdinand and Isabella in Spain (1479–1516) was their informal alliance with the growing merchant class. From this class the kings obtained essential financial support and also competent and subservient officials to staff the burgeoning state bureaucracies. In return, the consolidation of royal power aided the burghers by ending the incessant feudal wars and the crazy-quilt pattern of local feudal authorities, each with its own customs, laws, weights and currencies. With the removal of such encumbrances and the enforcement of royal law and order, the merchants were enabled to carry on their operations under much more favorable circumstances than in earlier centuries.

The significance of the large new monarchies for the Third World is that they, and they alone, were able to mobilize the human and natural resources needed for large-scale overseas enterprise. The royal courts issued the charters for the joint stock companies that carried on the exploring, trading and colonizing, and also backed up the companies with royal navies and royal funds. The sums involved seem trivial today, but for the modest economies of the time they were comparable to the billions needed at present for space exploration. It was not accidental that although most of the early explorers were Italians, their sponsors were the new national monarchies rather than their minuscule home city-states. The Spanish and Portuguese courts provided the backing for Columbus and da Gama, and the English and French courts quickly and eagerly followed up with backing for Cabot, Verrazano and many other Italian navigators.

The second reason for the fateful difference between Chinese and Western attitudes toward overseas enterprise was societal. Capitalism monetized all facets of Western society. The essence of the new economic order was the growing use of money, the minting of standard coins that were acceptable everywhere and the development of banks and of credit instruments. How rapidly this financial proliferation occurred is evident in the mounting assets of the leading banking families of Europe. The Peruzzi of Florence in 1300 commanded capital totaling $1.6 million (in 1958 American dollars). By 1440 the Medici of Florence had $15 million, and by 1546 the Fuggers of Augsburg $80 million. The Third World of the future was to feel the impact of these banks, which invested in overseas commercial ventures, plantations and mines.

We have seen how monetization transformed the countryside by uprooting the peasants. Equally disruptive was capitalism's impact on the craft and merchant guilds in the towns. These guilds, with their strict regulation of workmanship and pricing and trading practices, were geared not to making profit but to preserving a traditional way of life. Guild members were committed to the concept of a "just price," and profiteering at the expense of a neighbor was considered ethically reprehensible and definitely un-Christian. But these concepts and practices gave way with the appearance of the entrepreneur, who avoided the guilds by purchasing raw material and taking it to underemployed peasants in the countryside, who worked on it on a piece basis. The rationale of this new "putting out" system was profit rather than "just price." The entrepreneur paid as little as possible for the material and labor, and sold the finished product as dearly as possible in order to secure the maximum return on his capital investment.

The new economic order was reflected also in commerce, with the appearance of joint stock companies, the counterparts in early modern times of the multinational corporations of today. These institutions were unique because their joint stock character limited the responsibility of the investor, separated the function of investing and management and also made possible the mobilization of large amounts of capital for specific ventures. Anyone who wished to speculate risked only the amount he invested in company shares. Details of management were entrusted to directors selected for their responsibility and experience, and these directors in turn could choose dependable individuals to manage company affairs in the field. This arrangement made it attractive for all sorts of scattered individuals—a London wool merchant, a Paris storekeeper, a Haarlem herring fisher, an Antwerp banker, or a Yorkshire landowner—to invest their savings in individual ventures. In this manner it was possible to mobilize European capital easily and simply, and to penetrate the entire globe with the Dutch, English and French East India companies, the various Levant and Africa companies, the Muscovy Company, and the still extant Hudson's Bay Company. No Eastern merchant, limited to his own resources or those of his partners, could hope to compete with the powerful and impersonal joint stock company.

The resulting expansion of European overseas enterprises led to the development between 1500 and 1800 of a body of economic theories and practices known as mercantilism. The objective of mercantilism was to enhance the unity and power of the new monarchies, and this was to be achieved by amassing bullion to pay for the cost of the recurring wars and the proliferating bureaucracies. Hence the efforts to promote a favorable balance of trade and to obtain colonies that produced raw materials needed by the mother country. Hence also the granting of royal charters, which conferred monopoly privileges to joint stock companies in colonizing or trading in specified overseas territories. It follows that the interests of colonies were automatically subordinated to those of the mother country. The purpose of colonies was to provide markets for manufactures, to supply raw materials that could not be produced at home, to support a merchant marine that would be valuable in wartime and to engender a large colonial population that would provide manpower. All Western European nations followed these mercantilist practices, whether it was Portugal obtaining spices in the East Indies, Spain extracting gold and silver in the Americas, Holland developing a worldwide merchant marine or Britain passing the Navigation Acts against Dutch trade and enforcing the British East India Company's tea monopoly, which culminated in the Boston Tea Party.

The fact that Western Europeans first reached the Americas and the East Indies does not explain why their descendants during the following centuries should have become the masters of the entire world, including ancient civilizations in Asia that were much more populous and wealthy than Western Europe. It is true that the Westerners did have superior ships and guns, and did gain control of the oceans and of global commerce. But control of trade routes does not in itself lead to economic and political domination of entire continents, and to the unprecedented division of the globe into the developed, affluent West and the underdeveloped, impoverished Third World. For centuries the Arabs and Italians had controlled and profited from the commerce they carried on around the circumference of the Eurasian land mass, from the British Isles in the West to the Spice Isles and China in the East. Yet this did not give them global mastery, nor did it even save them from Western rule and exploitation.

The roots of Western dominance, then, are to be found not in the global scope of Western commerce, but rather in its unique character. For the first time in history European capitalism generated a mass trade in necessities that soon superseded the traditional limited trade in luxuries. Because of its unprecedented volume, this new trade enveloped entire countries and continents, integrating them into the new international market economy. Adam Smith in the late eighteenth century perceived the significance of this historic development when he noted that the overseas discoveries opened "a new and inexhaustible market to all the commodities of Europe"—a market that encompassed "almost all the different nations of Asia, Africa and America." [8] Adam Smith not only perceived the new global market economy created by capitalist overseas enterprise, but he also noted the adverse effect of the enterprise on the native populations:

> By uniting, in some measure, the most distant parts of the world, by enabling them to relieve one another's wants, to increase one another's enjoyments, and to encourage one another's industry, their general tendency would seem to be beneficial. To the natives, however, both of the East and West Indies, all the commercial benefits which can have resulted from those events have been sunk and lost in the dreadful misfortunes which they have occa-

sioned. . . . The savage injustice of the Europeans rendered an event, which ought to have been beneficial to all, ruinous and destructive to several of those unfortunate countries.[9]

In attributing "dreadful misfortunes" to the "savage injustice of the Europeans," Adam Smith opened a debate that persists to the present day. Some agree with the Scottish economist and hold that centuries of Western imperialist exploitation are responsible for the still persisting "misfortunes" of the Third World. Others consider this to be historical romanticizing of the original overseas societies as "moral" utopias, where in fact there had been at least as much exploitation under native rulers and elites as later under European administrators and businessmen. Both positions are justified, because the effect of Europe's impact on indigenous societies depended on the nature of these extremely disparate societies.

"Moral" societies definitely did exist overseas before the European intrusion. Plentiful testimony was provided by early explorers and observers from all the continents. The Australian aboriginal hunter who brought in game, or the woman who returned from a day of root digging was required to divide the take among all the kin according to strict regulations, thus assuring the sustenance and security of all band members. This tradition of sharing persisted long after the arrival of the Europeans, so that an anthropologist noted: "Give a man a shirt in return for work, and the chances are that you will find a friend of his . . . wearing it the next day." [10] Likewise the nineteenth-century anthropologist Lewis Morgan reported that "the law of hospitality as administered by the American aborigines tended to the final equalization of subsistence. Hunger and destitution could not exist at one end of an Indian village . . . while plenty prevailed elsewhere in the same village." [11] Earlier testimony along these lines has been left by the Jesuit, Fr. Jacob Baegert, who spent seventeen years in the mid-eighteenth century with the Indians of Southern California. On his return to Germany he wrote an account of his experiences, in which he described the Spartan life of the native Californians: "They spend their whole life, day and night, in the open air, the sky above them forming their roof, and the hard soil the couch on which they sleep." But after detailing these rigors he concluded:

> . . . it might be inferred that they are the most unhappy and pitiable of all the children of Adam. Yet such a supposition would be utterly wrong, and I can assure the reader that . . . they live unquestionably much happier than the civilized inhabitants of Europe. . . . Throughout the whole year nothing happens that causes a Californian trouble or vexation, nothing that renders his

life cumbersome and death desirable. . . . Envy, jealousy, and slander embitter not his life, and he is not exposed to the fear of losing what he possesses, nor to the care of increasing it . . . the Californians do not know the meaning of *meum* [mine] and *tuum* [thine], those two ideas which, according to St. Gregory, fill the days of our existence with bitterness and unaccountable evils.

Though the Californians seem to possess nothing, they have, nevertheless, all that they want, for they covet nothing beyond the productions of their poor, ill-favored country, and these are always within their reach. It is no wonder then, that they always exhibit a joyful temper, and constantly indulge in merriment and laughter, showing thus their contentment, which after all, is the real source of happiness.[12]

It is significant that all such accounts refer to "primitive" peoples who had remained at the food-gathering stage of human development. This raises a crucial question underlying all Third World history: Why did the European explorers, when they sailed to all corners of the globe, find people living at most varied levels of development—from food-gathering Australian aborigines, Tierra del Fuegians and African Bushmen, to the highly civilized Chinese, Indians and Middle Easterners, who were regarded by contemporary Westerners with awe as well as envy? The most important reason for this disparity, according to the anthropologist Franz Boas, was not racial but geographic—that is, the varying degrees of accessibility:

The history of mankind proves that advances of culture depend upon the opportunities presented to a social group to learn from the experience of their neighbors. The discoveries of the group spread to others and, the more varied the contacts, the greater the opportunities to learn. The tribes of simplest culture are on the whole those that have been isolated for very long periods and hence could not profit from the cultural achievements of their neighbors.[13]

In other words, if other geographic factors are equal, the key to human progress is accessibility and interaction. The people who are the most accessible and who have the most opportunity to interact with other people are the most likely to forge ahead, at least in the realm of technology, which can be objectively appraised. Those who are isolated and receive no stimulus from the outside are likely to stand still.

The European explorers did in fact find a correlation between degree of isolation and degree of technological retardation. The food-gathering societies were located in isolated regions such as Australia and certain parts of the Americas (northern North America and southern South

America) and of Africa (the deserts and rain forests). Because they were necessarily nomadic, the food gatherers could not accumulate large stores of wealth and develop complex class-differentiated societies. Instead they formed migratory bands of a few families, with a communal type of social organization that so appealed to European observers.

But the technological retardation that generated the "moral" communalism also left the indigenous peoples vulnerable to European penetration. The lower the level of technological development, the lesser the capability for resistance to external intrusion. Retarded technology meant, in the first place, retarded weaponry; spears, bows and arrows, and boomerangs against steel pikes, swords and muskets. Second, it meant a fatal lack of manpower, for the simple reason that only one or two hunters could exist per square mile in favorable environments, and only one every thirty to forty square miles in arid or mountainous regions. In the case of Australia, this added up to a total of three hundred thousand men, women and children when the Europeans arrived—a number that obviously was insufficient for holding an island continent almost as large as all Europe. Finally, technological retardation isolated individual bands from human communities in other regions, and the isolation left them without immunity against the diseases of outside peoples. This was to prove devastating for the Australian aborigines and for the equally isolated American Indians when the Europeans arrived with their smallpox, measles, typhus and other diseases.

The above considerations indicate that Adam Smith's "dreadful misfortunes" were indeed endured by overseas peoples at the food-gathering stage. A Third World history should not overlook the fact that tribal peoples are enduring "dreadful misfortunes" to the present day. At the time of writing (1980), the following poignantly typical barbarities are reported by the press:

• Australian aborigines are being further uprooted following the discovery of uranium, bauxite and manganese on their lands.

• In the Philippines' northern highlands, the existence of eighty thousand tribal people is being threatened by a huge hydroelectric project.

• In Brazil, only two hundred thousand of the original six million Indians survive, and they continue to be decimated by highways, ranges, mines, logging operations and advancing settlers.

• Alaska's Eskimos, according to a University of Pennsylvania study, are "practically committing suicide" by mass alcoholism, the alcoholism rate in Barrow being 72 percent of all adults.[14]

By contrast, those peoples who were technologically more advanced automatically forfeited their social communalism, but at the same time gained in strength to resist external aggression. Where agriculture was practiced at a sufficiently advanced level to yield surplus food, this surplus was used to support a class of administrative, religious and military leaders. They gathered in centers that developed into cities, and gradually expanded into states and empires. Thus the classless communalism of the food gatherers gave way to the class-stratified societies of the agriculture-based civilizations. The latter were in no way "moral," as were the Indians of Father Baegert.

As early as the third millennium B.C. an Egyptian father exhorted his son to attend school and obtain an education, and the reason he gave was the contrast between the affluence of the few at the top and the misery of the many at the bottom. He described vividly the plight of the stonemason—"his arms are worn out . . . his knees and spine are broken"; of the barber—"he shaves from morning till night; he never sits down except to meals"; of the farmer—"he wears the same clothes for all times, his voice is as raucous as the crows, his fingers are always busy, his arms are dried-up by the wind." The scribe, however, "is released from manual tasks; it is he who commands." And so, the father implored his son: "Put writing in your heart that you may protect yourself from hard labor of any kind. . . ." [15]

This inherent inequality of all class-stratified civilizations persisted through the millennia and was observed by the European merchants when they began their overseas journeys. They reported exploitation and injustice similar to that of ancient Egypt. Thus Karl Marx, in a dispatch to the New York *Daily Tribune* (June 25, 1853), castigated British abuses in India, but then added, "I share not the opinion of those who believe in a golden age of Hindostan. . . . We must not forget that these little communities were contaminated by distinctions of caste and by slavery." [16]

It should not be assumed, however, that exploitation under native caste system was similar to exploitation by Western capitalism. There was a difference of qualitative degree between them, as noted in the preceding chapter. "England has broken down the entire framework of Indian society," wrote Karl Marx in the same dispatch in which he castigated India's bonds of caste and slavery. "The loss of his old world, with no gain of a new one, imparts a particular kind of melancholy to the present misery of the Hindoo, and separates Hindostan ruled by Britain, from all its ancient traditions, and from the whole of its past history." [17]

The reason India was cut off "from the whole of its past history" was that it had been integrated into the global market economy, with profound repercussions on all aspects of life. An organically integrated and basically self-sufficient society had been depressed to a dependent Third World status—a subordinate appendage of the metropolitan center. Because of this subordination, India's Minister of Commerce, Mohan Dharia, stated in August 1977 that 200 million of his country's total population of 620 million were either unemployed or underemployed. In the same unhappy predicament were an estimated two thirds of Latin America's work force, as well as 60 million of Africa's total work force of 104 million. Such statistics explain the human cesspools that are to be found today in Calcutta, Djakarta, Cairo, Lagos and Bogotá. And these cesspools reflect the inherent structural condition of Third World countries incorporated into the global market economy as dependent and subordinate components.

Chapter 3

BEGINNINGS OF THE THIRD WORLD IN EASTERN EUROPE

If the adjective "colonial" has any relevance to European conditions at the end of the Middle Ages, the export of cereals [from Eastern Europe] is one, perhaps the only, branch of trade which can conceivably be so classified: not only was it confined to unprocessed agricultural produce, i.e. grain and not malt or beer or flour, but it was largely paid for with manufactured imports; moreover, it was in the hands of outsiders, west European merchants and shippers, and it subjected the fortunes, the economic organization and social structure of eastern economies to the requirements of western markets. There is little doubt that the grain trade, as it developed at the close of the Middle Ages and in the early centuries of the modern era, had an impact on economic conditions and social relations in eastern regions comparable to the impact of modern international commerce on underdeveloped countries exporting primary produce.

M. M. Postan

The Third World commonly is thought of as comprising overseas territories, yet it made its first appearance in Eastern Europe. The economy and social organization of the East European lands were the first to be subordinated and remolded to meet the needs of the Northwest European market. The reason for this subordination and remolding was the unprecedented technological and economic development of Northwest Europe, which generated a new type of mass trade in necessities in place of the traditional peripheral trade in luxuries. The first regions to be integrated into this mass trade system as a dependent periphery were the adjacent Eastern European lands rather than overseas territories.

❧ I. Primacy of Northwest Europe

The regression of Eastern Europe in modern times to the status of a subordinate and underdeveloped area is usually explained in terms of failure by abstention. According to this theory, Northwest Europe took the initiative in expanding overseas and shifting the commercial center of gravity from the Mediterranean to the Atlantic, while the East European lands, because of their inland location, did not participate in these fateful developments. Consequently the economic heartland of Europe, and eventually of the world, this theory holds, shifted to Northwest Europe, while Eastern Europe sank back into centuries of obscurity and stagnation.

In actual fact, the course of events was the precise opposite of the above sequence. Eastern Europe's regression is to be explained not by abstention but by involvement. It is to be explained as the first example of the causal relationship between the economic development of the West and the underdevelopment of its weaker trading partners. This causal relationship had far-reaching repercussions that extended far beyond the confines of the eastern and western regions of Europe.

The shift in early modern times of the principal channels of trade from the Mediterranean to Northwest Europe has been attributed to the great discoveries and the subsequent opening of new trade routes across the Atlantic to the New World, and down the Atlantic to the Cape and east to India. But the commercial center of Europe had moved from the Mediterranean to the Northwest by the late medieval period, before the age of discoveries had begun. The basic reason for this epochal shift was the development in the Baltic Sea of a mass trade in necessities, which by its very nature surpassed in volume, in value, and in socio-economic impact, the traditional trade in luxuries in the Mediterranean and in the rest of the world.

The Mediterranean trade had its origins in South and East Asia, where spices, silks, fine cotton textiles and a few other costly artifacts of Oriental craftsmanship were transported by Muslim traders to ports in the eastern Mediterranean. Thence they were taken by Italian merchants to North Italian cities such as Venice and Genoa and transshipped to other parts of Europe—either by land across the Alps, or by sea through the Straits of Gibraltar. Western Europe paid for these eastern commodities with a few products such as linen, weapons and horses, but mostly gold and silver.

The critical feature of this Mediterranean trade was its luxury character. It satisfied the needs of the rich and powerful—of princes, lords, ecclesiastical dignitaries and merchants. It was outside the mainstream of economic activity, for it did not affect the medieval population or economy as a whole. This traditional Eastern trade, in Postan's words, "did not call for an outlay of labor or other resources on a scale large enough to exert a pressure on economic and social processes in Europe, whether western or eastern." [1]

Fundamentally different was the East-West trade in goods for mass consumption that developed along the length of the Baltic Sea. The Baltic lands in the East supplied Western Europe with two basic commodities. One was lumber, shipped mostly in raw unmilled state for the Western construction and shipbuilding industries, though some was exported in semimanufactured form as boat hulls or as complete ships. The other commodity from the eastern Baltic was grain, which eventually surpassed lumber in value and in socio-economic impact on Eastern Europe.

In return, Western Europe exported to the eastern Baltic mostly textiles. Originally it was high-quality cloth from northern Italy, but this was later replaced by coarser and cheaper cloth made in Flanders. That in turn was displaced by still cheaper "new drapery" turned out by the Dutch and the English. The main sources of the wool for this cloth were Spain and England. It is significant that until 1500 Spanish wool was exported to Italy; in the sixteenth century half went to Italy and half to Flanders, and by the seventeenth century all to Flanders. Likewise, English wool during the fifteenth and most of the sixteenth century went mostly to Flanders. But then England, unlike Spain, began manufacturing cloth for export, so that raw wool exports decreased, while bolts of cloth exported from London jumped from 50,000 in 1500 to 130,000 in 1550.

This East-West Baltic trade was controlled until about 1500 by merchants of the Hanseatic League. After 1500 they were gradually displaced by the Dutch, who had started out as fishermen and exported their North Sea herring (preserved by salting or smoking) to all parts of Europe. From fishing, the Dutch branched out into the carrying trade, building ships and developing facilities for transporting bulky mass commodities. Soon they had become the carriers for all Europe, shipping herring and salt from Biscay, wine from the Mediterranean, cloth from Britain and Flanders, copper and iron from Sweden and cereals, flax, hemp and timber from the Baltic.

Whereas the Italians formerly had controlled the luxury Mediterranean trade and had extended their operations to northern Europe, now the Dutch controlled the mass Baltic trade in necessities, and extended their activities southward. The basic reason for this shift of the economic center of Europe was not external—not overseas discoveries and enterprise. Rather it was internal; industrial and mercantile activities now were concentrated much more in northern than southern Europe.

᭝ II. Eastern Europe Becomes a Third World Region

It was the new mass trade in northern Europe that give birth to the Third World in Eastern Europe. More specifically, the genesis was the displacement of the guild system by the putting-out system in the textile and metal industries of England and Holland in the fourteenth and fifteenth centuries. The guild system, as noted in the previous chapter, liberated these industries from numerous stifling restrictions and thus made possible a substantial lowering of costs and increase in productivity, as well as greater adaptability to market requirements. Local and national markets soon were satiated, so the English and Dutch manufacturers looked to foreign countries to market their surplus output.

Eastern Europe met their needs perfectly because local handicraft production there was poorly developed and could offer little competition to Western textiles and metal products. In addition, Eastern Europe produced certain raw materials that were becoming scarce in the West, so an East-West trade developed quickly and naturally. Poland and Lithuania exported mostly rye, cattle, furs, timber, potash and hemp, while Hungary provided cattle and copper.

During the fourteenth and fifteenth centuries the textile and hardware imports from the West far exceeded these exports in value, so the balance was made up with gold and silver coins. By the mid-sixteenth century the balance of trade reversed sharply, partly because of the current Price Revolution, which generated the steepest rise in the prices of agricultural products. Also the demand for Eastern foodstuffs was growing rapidly in the West, where the urban centers were growing rapidly in population at the same time that arable land was being converted to pasture in order to meet the textile industry's rising demand for wool. The net result was a balance of trade markedly in favor of the Eastern European countries. Between 1565 and 1585 the average annual value of Polish seaborne exports was 1,158,000 thalers, while that of imports was only 400,000 thalers. Likewise in Hungary, the value of exports in 1542 was 323,000 florins, as against imports of only 141,000 florins.

The sixteenth and seventeenth centuries were a critical period for Eastern Europe, as market conditions were favorable then for overall economic development comparable to that which was occurring in the West. The opportunity was not grasped, primarily because the prevailing political forces in the East, in contrast to those of the West, militated against such economic development. In the West, as noted in the previous chapter, the rising monarchs cooperated with the mercantile middle class to their mutual advantage. The monarchs provided order and security as well as financial and naval backing for overseas ventures, while the merchants furnished funds for the royal treasury as well as reliable personnel for the administrative, financial and military services. This marriage of convenience resulted in the development in Western Europe of strong nation-states undergirded by vigorous national economies.

In Eastern Europe the course of politics was precisely the opposite, and consequently so was that of economics. The Eastern monarchs looked not to merchants but rather to Prussian junkers, Polish magnates and other feudal lords for the staffing of their armies and bureaucracies. This automatically meant that the state refrained from intervening in lord-peasant relations, which in turn left the peasants entirely subject to their lords, and therefore depressed to a servile rather than free status. At first the lords did not use their authority to restrict their peasants unduly, either as regards labor services or freedom of movement, because there was no particular incentive to do so. A few days of work per year was all that they required from their peasants, since there was no profitable use that could be made of more labor. But with the golden opportunity presented in the sixteenth and seventeenth centuries for gaining huge profits from the growing trade with the West, the nobles promptly used their power against both merchants and peasants in order to maximize their own profits.

As regards the peasants, the lords first expanded their demesnes, or lands reserved for their exclusive use, by appropriating the commons, and virgin and abandoned lands, and also in various extralegal and illegal ways, the hereditary plots of the defenseless peasants. To obtain the increased labor required for their growing estates, the lords used their dominant influence in the state structure to secure laws limiting peasant freedom of movement. This enabled the lords to compel the captive peasants to provide more and more free labor for raising the profitable crops. In Poland, for example, peasants had been required before 1500 to give only one day to six days of labor service per year. By 1550 this had been raised to three days per week, and by 1600 to six days. In the meantime the peasants also had been completely deprived of the freedom to move. Thus the Eastern European peasants, whose status in the thirteenth century had been improving and had been comparable to that of the Western peasants, now were forced down to serfdom and made completely subject to the will of the lord rather than to the jurisdiction of the state. By 1600 the lord had become the government for the East European serfs. "He was their judge, their police chief, their jailer, their tax collector, and sometimes he chose the clergyman in their church." [2]

Eastern Europe's merchants and cities likewise were subjected to the will and interests of the lords. Prior to the sixteenth century, Polish and Lithuanian towns had been able to hold their own against the feudal nobility, while the merchants had profited handsomely from the export of raw materials. But after the sixteenth century the fortunes of the cities and their merchants declined as precipitously as those of the peasants. At first the Polish nobles had sold their produce to Polish merchants, who transported it to Danzig for export to the West. But the nobles had ancient exemptions from taxation that the merchants did not share, so it was more profitable for the nobles to bypass the merchants and ship their own produce. The nobles, however, did not want to bother with the details of the actual business transactions, so they employed non-Poles (Germans, Dutch, Jews, Armenians) to act as their agents and therefore escaped taxation. These foreign middlemen took the goods to Danzig, where they sold them to other foreigners, mostly Germans, who finally shipped them to the West in Dutch ships.

The nobility did end up with higher profits, but at disastrous cost for the national economy. The power and myopic outlook of the nobles is reflected in a law they passed in 1565 forbidding Polish merchants from going abroad to buy or sell goods. Their objective was to give foreigners full monopoly of Poland's international trade, eliminate native middlemen, and thereby obtain highest prices for their agricultural exports and pay lowest prices for Western manufactured goods. This law was never enforced, but its passage and aims are revealing. The Polish nobility, along with the foreign merchants, wanted free trade and they had their way.

In having their way they doomed Polish cities, along with their merchants and artisans, who were barred from participating in, and gaining from, the favorable commercial conditions of the sixteenth and seventeenth centuries. Western cities and their crafts were growing in size and efficiency, partly because of the markets in the East. But at the same time Eastern cities were declining into sleepy provincial towns, strangled by a nobility that wielded political power to garner profits that benefited only themselves and a few foreigners.

In short, Eastern Europe during the sixteenth and seventeenth centuries had a unique opportunity for rapid and independent economic development, but experienced instead a decline to a subordinate economic relationship with the West. This subordinate status was stabilized and perpetuated during the seventeenth century, when the terms of international trade turned against the producers of raw materials. By this time Eastern Europe had become wholly dependent on Western manufactures as local crafts had atrophied. The importation of these manufactures continued on a substantial scale, so the earlier favorable balance of trade now became chronically adverse.

In this manner Eastern Europe was enveloped by the expanding Western European capitalistic system, and Eastern Europe's economic organization and social structure were distorted to suit the requirements of that system. As Immanuel Wallerstein has noted, "Poland became, in the course of the sixteenth century, an underdeveloped country in the European world economy." [3] The end result was the division of the European continent into a dynamic and industrialized Northwest, and an agrarian and dependent East—a division that was to persist until the mid-twentieth century. [4]

III. Russia Remains Outside the Third World

On the surface Russia appears to have become a Third World region at the same time as the East European countries. The Russian peasants also were subjected to enserfment, and the Russian economy also remained overwhelmingly agricultural. Despite this parallelism, Russia's economy was not subordinated to that of the West, and Russia's society was not restructured to meet the needs of the Western marketplace. Hence Russia did not become a Third World region in early modern times as did Eastern Europe.

The basic reason for the independent development of Russia was the tremendous and constantly expanding area of the country. If Russia were simply another East European state, confined to the territories west of the Urals, and of a size comparable to that of Poland or Hungary, then independent economic development would have been difficult and unlikely.

During the centuries of Mongol rule (1240–1480), when the Moscow Principality was encapsulated within the Mongol Empire and limited to a small space surrounding Moscow, Russia's external economic relations were as dominated by the Hanseatic League as were those of Poland and Lithuania. If the principality had developed later into another East European state, restricted to the lands west of the Urals, then Russia's economy, like those of Eastern Europe, would have fallen successively under Hanseatic, Dutch, German and English control.

But the Moscow Principality expanded instead into a vast Eurasian empire stretching from the Baltic Sea to the Pacific Ocean. Ivan III (1462–1505) extended the frontiers westward to the Baltic and northward to the Arctic Ocean. Ivan IV (1505–84) conquered the Tatar khanates of

Kazan and Astrakhan, thereby acquiring the great Volga basin and reaching the Caspian Sea in the south and the Urals in the east. The way was now open for the great push across the expanses of Siberia to the Pacific. Because of the favorable flat terrain, the network of navigable rivers and the lack of strong resistance by local tribes, the pace of Russian eastward expansion was much faster than the American westward expansion. Cossacks began crossing the Urals about the same time that Sir Walter Raleigh landed on Roanoke Island in 1584. Within half a century, by 1637, the Russians had reached Okhotsk on the Pacific Ocean, covering a distance half as much again as that between the Atlantic and Pacific coasts of the United States. During the same period, English colonists had not yet crossed the Allegheny Mountains a few hundred miles from the Atlantic.

The great trans-Siberian expansion had transformed Russia from an East European state to an empire of continental proportions. The trade that developed among the various parts of that empire enabled it to become not an economic appendage of Western Europe, but a largely self-sufficient economic unit with regional specialization and with consequent interregional trade.

The process is reminiscent of that following the later opening of a United States of similar continental proportions. As settlers poured southward into the Ukraine and eastward into Siberia, agriculture and other activities gradually developed, and what originally had been fortified military outposts became local trading centers, integrated into the national economic life. Just as regional specialization had evolved in the United States, with the Northeast producing manufactures, the South cotton and the West foodstuffs and raw materials, so a comparable specialization evolved now in Russia. Siberia yielded furs, forest products and metals, while the Ukraine produced foodstuffs, and the original center of the empire manufactures along with foodstuffs.

In addition to this internal interregional trade, Russia's territorial expansion had opened trade channels along the Volga to the Caucasus and to several central Asian khanates and Middle Eastern states. Russian merchants soon engaged in brisk commerce with Iran, the Ottoman Empire, the Nagai horde, the Uzbek khanates, and China. They exported furs, weapons, leather goods, metalwares and other manufactured articles (some of Western origin), and imported in return cotton cloth, silk fabrics, jewelry, spices, horses and sheep. Russian merchants engaged in this Eastern trade often accompanied diplomatic missions to Oriental potentates and sometimes they themselves served as the Tsar's emissaries.

This Russian trade with the East was more important than that with the West, though the latter also had been stimulated by territorial expansion, which had opened direct trade routes with the West through ports on the Baltic Sea and through Archangel in the North. Russia imported from the West metalwares, munitions and luxury articles, and exported raw materials such as hemp cordage, flax, pitch, potash, furs, bristles and salted meats. Little grain left the country, as the Tsar's consent was required but usually not forthcoming.

It follows from the above that during these centuries the capitalist West had a minimal impact on Russia's economy. The Western trade was substantially less than the Eastern, so the Western trade could not have the decisive influence on Russia that it did in the East European countries. Also, Western merchants were not allowed to dominate Russia's domestic trade as they did Poland's. In fact, they were specifically forbidden to carry on retail trade or to deal directly with producers, as they had been encouraged to do in Poland. Whereas legislation in Poland had sought to freeze out native merchants, the 1667 Code in Russia, by contrast, decreed, "Any foreigners shall not sell any goods in retail . . . and they shall not visit the fairs or travel with their goods and money into any town or send any salesman." [5]

Despite this protective legislation, the merchant class in Russia never grew as large or as powerful as that in the West. One reason was the excessive competition, for all classes participated in buying and selling goods. Petty retail trade in small stores, booths and on benches was conducted by peasants and artisans who sold their own products along with some that they purchased. Medium-scale merchants traded in salt, furs and grain, and sometimes owned flour mills, distilleries and salt works. In addition, there were a handful of very wealthy entrepreneurs such as the Stroganovs, whose operations extended from Archangel to Moscow to the Volga basin and across the length of Siberia. Even the Tsar participated extensively in commerce, monopolizing in the sixteenth century the trade in commodities such as grain, hemp, rhubarb, raw silk and caviar. In addition to these "forbidden goods," foreign imports were brought first before royal officials or the Tsar himself, who expropriated whatever pleased them at a low price or without any compensation whatsoever. These goods were either used personally by the expropriators or sold at a handsome profit.

It is understandable that the Austrian ambassador, A. von Mayerberg, who came to Russia in 1661 from a world where aristocrats scorned business, reported his surprise that "All the people of quality, and even the ambassadors sent to foreign princes, trade publicly. They buy, they sell, and they exchange without a qualm, thereby making their elevated rank, venerable that it is, subservient to their avarice." [6] Despite this native control of the national economy, it should be noted that very few Russian merchants ventured to the West as they customarily did to the East, and also that virtually no Russian ships were employed in transporting Russian goods to the West.

Serfdom did appear in Russia at about the same time that it did in Eastern Europe, but for very different reasons. In Eastern Europe, as noted above, serfdom was imposed because the rulers depended on the nobility rather than on the middle class, and also because the nobility sought to maximize profits from trade with the West by forcing their peasants into serfdom. In Russia, by contrast, serfdom appeared because of historical conditions and forces peculiar to that country. Market demand was a factor here also, but it was the demand of interregional domestic trade rather than foreign trade, which in any case was oriented more to the East than to the West. Serfdom was imposed by the nobles also because of their mounting debts, which they had contracted at usurious rates with the growth of the market economy and the resulting increased use of money.

A final reason for the emergence of serfdom in Russia was the increasing demands of the state on the time and on the income of the nobles. This was especially true of the gentry (*pomeshchiks*) or holders of land on tenure, as against the lords (*votchinniks*) or holders of hereditary estates. The *pomeshchiks* were tied to the state, being required to staff the administrative and military bureaucracies, the financial agencies and the local government offices. In return for these essential services the state tied the serfs to the *pomeshchiks* so that the latter would be supported sufficiently to meet their obligations to the state.

In 1580 Ivan IV issued his first "forbidden year" decree—the first in which the peasants were forbidden to leave their villages for the freedom of masterless frontier lands. Soon the "forbidden years" became the rule rather than the exception. After 1603 every year was declared "forbidden," and continued to be for $2\frac{1}{2}$ centuries, until the Emancipation Decree of Alexander II. By the seventeenth century, then, the Russian peasants also had succumbed to enserfment, though not because of economic subservience to the West, as was the case in Eastern Europe.

Russia's economic independence was demonstrated by the massive drive for industrialization by Peter the Great (1689–1725). He established foundries, arsenals, shipyards and cloth factories to supply the needs of his military forces. He brought in skilled foreign technicians to operate these enterprises. He encouraged private entrepreneurs with subsidies, loans, exemptions from taxes, protective tariffs and the forced labor of serfs, who were dragooned into mines and factories. Peter left behind him some two hundred large industrial enterprises, including sixty-nine in metallurgy, twenty-three in lumber, seventeen in gunpowder, fifteen in textiles, fourteen in leather, ten in glass, nine in silk, eight in sail-cloth and six in paper.

The industrialization effort was continued after Peter, so that Russia by the end of the eighteenth century had become a major economic power. Her pig-iron production had surpassed that of all other countries by 1785, and the Ural region was one of the greatest industrial centers until the spread of steam-powered machinery in the nineteenth century.

It is understandable that Joseph Stalin had high regard for Peter the Great, viewing his industrialization efforts as comparable to his own Five Year Plans. Both leaders sought to ensure the economic independence of their country vis-à-vis the expanding capitalist West. Stalin correctly sensed the historical significance of Peter's projects: "When Peter the Great, having relations with the developed countries of the west, feverishly built mills and factories for the supply of the army and the strengthening of the country's defense, this was an original attempt to escape from the framework of backwardness." [7]

The "attempt" to which Stalin alludes was successful to a certain degree, as demonstrated at the end of the eighteenth century when Poland, which had remained a weak, underdeveloped Third World country, was partitioned by its neighbors and disappeared completely from the map of Europe. Russia was one of the partitioning powers, so that her frontiers extended from Warsaw to the Pacific Ocean. Peter's industrialization efforts as well as Catherine's diplomatic skills were responsible for this fateful difference in the historical experiences of Russia and Poland.

On the other hand, the industrialization of Russia under Peter was to a certain degree superficial and therefore not enduring. The fact that such a large percentage of the industrial workers were serfs or impressed laborers of one sort or another meant that their pay was minimal and that the domestic market for manufactured goods was correspondingly restricted. Also, technical skills were in short supply, and remained so because only one university in Russia taught technical subjects. Thus W. L. Blackwell concludes, "During the eighteenth century Russia witnessed a superficial type of military industrialization of what remained an agrarian despotism—the society as a whole did not change. There was neither the inner social or intellectual forces to stimulate capitalism and technology, nor did the impulse come from outside." [8]

Russia's industrial development also was seriously handicapped by the lack of coal and iron reserves in close proximity. This did not matter in Peter's time as the rich iron ore of the Urals could be smelted with char-coal made from the local forests. But when these forests dwindled the Russians discovered they had no nearby coal deposits as did the English iron manufacturers. Whereas in 1785 Russia had led the world in iron production, only a few decades later she was to fall far behind in that branch of industry, as well as in others such as textiles, hardware and the application of steam power to transportation and to industrial machinery. In short, with the advent of the Industrial Revolution in the West, Russia's economy found it impossible to keep up, and instead it became subservient to the Western, as will be noted in Chapter 16.

Chapter 4

BEGINNINGS OF THE
THIRD WORLD
IN LATIN AMERICA

Then the Indians had no sickness; they had no aching bones;
they had no burning chest; they had no abdominal pain; they
had no consumption; they had no headache. At that time the
course of humanity was orderly. The foreigners made it otherwise
when they arrived here.

The Book of Chilam Balam of Chumayel
(late seventeenth century)

The profits of a sugar plantation in any one of our West Indian
colonies are generally much greater than those of any other cultivation that is known either in Europe or America.

ADAM SMITH, 1776

The next major region after Eastern Europe to become a part of the
dependent Third World was Latin America. This was in striking contrast
to Anglo America, which soon won both political and economic independence, and eventually became the leader of the developed world. The
divergence of these two basic historical trends in the New World is paradoxical, for Latin America at the outset enjoyed all the advantages of
natural endowment. It was Latin America that yielded unprecedented
quantities of gold and silver bullion, that grew the tropical products
sought after by the northern Europeans, and that possessed the large

native labor force needed for the mines and haciendas. And yet Anglo America forged ahead steadily from the colonial period onward, while Latin America appeared to have been born dependent and underdeveloped, and has remained so to the present day. The origins and evolution of this fateful divergence in the history of the two regions of the New World is the subject of this chapter.

ॐ *I. Conquest*

Hernando Cortes, the conqueror of the Aztec Empire, is buried in a little-known church a few blocks from the main square of Mexico City. An obscure bronze plaque on the wall relates his name, date of birth, date of death, date of burial and nothing else. Cortes has little honor in the nation that he founded. A recent proposal to erect a monument to Cortes on Paseo de la Reforma, the grand boulevard of Mexico City, attracted little popular support. "If they build one," a Mexican worker told an American reporter, "it will be bombed." Another Mexican citizen commented tartly: "No country raises statues to its conqueror." [1]

These sentiments are understandable, despite the interval of over four centuries, because of the brutality of Cortes and of his fellow conquistadors throughout the New World. Columbus himself, when he first landed in the Bahamas, reported that the gentle Arawaks showed "as much lovingness as though they would give their hearts . . . they remained so much our friends that it was a marvel." But this same Columbus soon was writing back to Spain: "From here, in the name of the Blessed Trinity, we can send all the slaves that can be sold. . . . Should your Majesties command it, all the inhabitants could be taken away to Castile, or made slaves on the island . . . for these people are totally unskilled in arms. . . ." [2]

In 1495 Columbus shipped to Spain five hundred "Indians," as he called them, for he was convinced that he was in the East Indies. Only three hundred survived the voyage to Spain, and most of these succumbed within a few years to European diseases against which they had no immunity. The slave trade being impractical because of inescapable genetic laws, Columbus turned to gold as the means for realizing the fortunes he sought for himself and his royal sponsors.

On the large island of Hispaniola (present-day Haiti and Dominican Republic) he required each Indian of fourteen years or over to bring to his forts once every three months one of his hawkbells filled with gold dust. He manufactured copper tokens, and when an Indian brought his or her tribute to the forts, he or she was given a token stamped with the month, to be hung around the neck. With that they were safe for another three months while collecting more gold. Whoever was caught without a token was killed by having his or her hands cut off. Old Spanish prints are available depicting the gruesome spectacle of Indians stumbling away, staring traumatically at their arm stumps pulsing out blood. Thus Hispaniola was a prelude of things to come in Brazil and the Congo, where Portuguese and Belgian entrepreneurs cut off ears and hands when the natives failed to provide the allotted quotas of wild rubber.

The gold quotas in Hispaniola proved impossible of fulfillment. There were no gold fields on the island, and once the Indians had handed over the few gold ornaments they owned, their only hope was to work all day in the streams, washing out minute particles of gold dust. The amounts recovered were quite inadequate, and those Indians who tried to flee to the mountains were hunted down with dogs and killed. The demoralized Arawaks resorted to mass suicide, killing themselves with casava poison. Within two years about half of the island's population, estimated at 125,000 to 500,000, had perished. By 1515 only 10,000 Indians were still alive, and twenty-five years later the entire race had vanished from the earth, apart from a few mestizo descendants fathered by the Spanish conquerors.

The Spaniards were deeply disappointed by their failure to find the coveted gold and spices of the East Indies. Gradually they realized that the Caribbean islands were not the Spice Islands of the East, and that they had stumbled upon a New World that blocked the route to Asia. Thus the first two decades of the sixteenth century became the age of explorers, when numerous navigators probed the entire length of the Americas in search of a passageway to the East. At the same time thousands of adventurers streamed out of the islands in search of the gold strikes that were constantly being rumored.

Finally one of these soldiers of fortune, Hernando Cortes, located the great Aztec Empire in Mexico, about which many reports had long circulated. Landing on the mainland coast in March 1519 with an insignificant force of 600 men, 16 horses, 13 muskets, and a few cannon, he was able to overrun in short order a wealthy empire with a population of tens of millions. Even more audacious was Francisco Pizarro's conquest in 1531 of the highly organized Inca Empire of Peru with a band of 180 men, 27 horses, and 2 cannon.

The spectacular triumphs in Mexico and Peru inspired other conquistadors to march through vast areas of both the American continents in search of more booty. In contrast to the Cortes and Pizarro expeditions, these were not organized military campaigns, with the fighting confined to brief chronological limits. Most Indian societies outside the Aztec and Inca empires lacked the population and organization to offer serious large-scale resistance. So the usual pattern of expansion henceforth was exploratory probing followed by intermittent armed clashes and sporadic colonization wherever the land or mineral resources were sufficiently attractive.

In this manner the Spaniards by the end of the sixteenth century became familiar with the entire coastline of South America from the West Indies south to Tierra del Fuego and north to the Gulf of California. Likewise in North America, Francisco de Coronado and Hernando de Soto led wide-ranging expeditions across the southern part of the United States, from Florida to the Grand Canyon. At the same time French explorers such as Robert La Salle, English explorers such as David Thompson, and American explorers such as Lewis and Clark opened up the northern part of North America, while the Portuguese were taking over the vast Brazilian protuberance of South America in accord with the terms of a papal bull dividing the overseas territories between Spain and Portugal.

It should be noted here that the Spaniards in the Americas, like the British later in India, and like other Europeans in Africa, foisted the cost of conquest upon the conquered. The Spanish Crown met the cost of Columbus' first voyage, and Spanish merchants and nobles flocked to lend support for his larger later expeditions. By 1506 the Spanish colonists had obtained enough gold to finance the conquests of Cuba, Jamaica and Puerto Rico. These large islands in turn financed later expeditions to the mainland, culminating in the fabulous Aztec and Inca windfalls. Thus Spanish activities in the Americas were subsidized by the mother country for little more than a decade. Thereafter American resources were used for building the Spanish American Empire, which by the mid-sixteenth century became sufficiently profitable to support purely Spanish dynastic undertakings in the Old World.

ॐ *II. Conquerors and Conquered*

Why did the American Indians, with their densely populated and highly advanced empires, succumb so easily to a handful of European adventurers? The basic answer is their millennia-long isolation from other branches of the human race, which left them biologically and militarily vulnerable to a fatal degree. Almost all the Indians were descendants of immigrants who crossed the Bering Sea from northeastern Siberia. *Almost* all, because recent research indicates that small numbers of peoples may have reached the Americas centuries before Columbus from West Africa and/or the islands of the South Pacific.

It remains true, however, that the Indians whom the Europeans found in the Americas were descended almost exclusively from the stock that had crossed the Bering Sea, as evidenced by the remarkable uniformity of their blood types. The first crossings probably were made between fifty thousand and one hundred thousand years ago, and they continued intermittently until about three thousand years ago, when the Eskimos arrived and blocked the migration route by settling down on each side of the Bering Strait. The early Indian migrants crossed over to the New World easily because much of the earth's water was frozen, so that a 130-mile-wide land bridge connected northeastern Asia and northwestern North America. With the passing of the Ice Age, the sea level rose and the resulting narrow Bering Strait separated the two land masses. Migrants could still cross over in narrow boats, however, without ever being out of sight of land.

Most of those who crossed to Alaska moved on into the heart of North America through a gap in the ice sheet in the central Yukon plateau. They were impelled to cross forward by the same forces that led them to migrate to America—the search for new hunting grounds and the continual pressure of tribes from the rear. In this manner both the continents were soon peopled by scattered tribes of hunters. Considerable variation exists among these tribes, the earliest arrivals being much less Mongoloid in appearance because they had left Asia before the Mongoloids, as we know them today, had fully evolved. Also, the earliest arrivals spread out and settled in small inbred groups in a variety of climates, which further promoted the evolution of individual physical types. Hence the marked contrast between the flat-faced Northwest Indians with pronounced Mongolian eye fold as against the long-nosed, bronze-skinned Indians of the Southwest United States with comparatively slight eye fold.

The American Indians differed much more in their cultures than in their physiological types. Anthropologists have defined some twenty-two culture areas in the New World—the Great Plains area, the Eastern Woodlands, the Northwest Coast area, and so forth. A simpler classification, on the basis of how food was obtained, involves three categories: hunting, gathering and fishing cultures; intermediate farming cultures; and advanced farming cultures. This scheme is not only simpler but is also meaningful from the viewpoint of Third World history, for it helps to explain the varied responses of the Indians to the European intrusion.

The advanced farming cultures were located in Mesoamerica (central and southern Mexico, Guatemala, and Honduras) and the Andean highland area (Ecuador, Peru, Bolivia and northern Chile). The intermediate farming cultures were generally in the adjacent regions, while the food-gathering cultures were in the more remote regions—the southern part of South America, and the western and northern part of North America.

Maize, which was the basic food for most Indians, was first domesticated about 7000 B.C. in the semidesert valleys of the central highlands of Mexico. Originally it was a weed with ears no larger than a man's thumbnail. The Indians developed it into a plant with rows of seeds on long cobs. So completely did they domesticate maize that it would become extinct if man stopped planting it, for in its domesticated form it cannot disperse its seeds, the kernels. Equally spectacular was the skill of the Indians in utilizing large numbers of poisonous plants, including manioc, known as tapioca after the poison has been removed. Other important plants domesticated by the Indians included squashes, potatoes, tomatoes, bottle gourd, tepary bean, chili peppers, amaranths, avocados, tobacco, cotton and beans, the latter being an important source of protein. So numerous and fruitful are the plants domesticated by the Indians that today they provide almost half of the world's total food supply.

The regions where the Indians developed their most advanced farming cultures were also the regions that supported large empires and sophisticated civilizations. Thus the three major Amerindian civilizations were the Mayan in present-day Yucatan, Guatemala, and Belize, the Aztec in present-day Mexico, and the Inca stretching for three thousand miles from mid-Ecuador to mid-Chile.

The Mayan civilization was outstanding for its extraordinary development of the arts and sciences. Its accomplishments included a unique stone architecture, a sculpture that ranks among the great art of all times, an ideographic writing in which characters or signs were used as conventional symbols for ideas, and a knowledge of the movements of heavenly bodies that demonstrated the Mayans were better astronomers than any in contemporary Europe, and as competent mathematicians. The Aztecs were brusque and warlike compared to the artistic and intellectual Mayas—a contrast reminiscent of that between the Romans and the Greeks in the Old World. The Aztecs paid more attention to the army, training all able-bodied men for war and holding them liable for military service. Their state also was better organized, including a well-developed judiciary, arrangements for the care of the needy, and a capital, Tenochtitlán, with a population of two to three hundred thousand, or several times the size of London about 1500.

The Incas were even more advanced than the Aztecs in their material accomplishments. Their remarkable roads, fortresses, and temples were built of great blocks of stone so perfectly joined that even now, nearly five hundred years later, a knife cannot be inserted between them. An extensive irrigation system surpassed anything developed in the Roman Empire, and irrigated 40 percent more land than agricultural experts are able to do in modern Peru. The National Science Foundation in 1978 financed an expedition by Chicago's Field Museum to unlock the technical secrets that enabled the Indians to grow more food on Peru's desert coast between A.D. 1000 and 1400 than can be grown today. The Incas also organized the only integrated and dynamic state in the Americas—a state geared for indefinite expansion outside and for regimentation and paternalism inside. The instruments of control included state ownership of land, mineral wealth and herds, obligatory adherence to the official Sun religion, careful census compilations for tax and military purposes, deposition of local hereditary chieftains, forced population resettlement for the assimilation of conquered peoples and mass marriages under state auspices. The Inca Empire probably was the most successful totalitarian state the world has ever seen.

Impressive as these achievements were, the fact remains that a handful of Spanish conquistadors easily toppled all three of these civilizations. The explanation is to be found ultimately in the devastating effect of millennia of isolation. Precisely what did this isolation mean when the clash occurred with the arrival of the Spaniards? It meant, first and foremost, that the Indians had no immunity against the disease of the European and African newcomers. This was much more serious than the brutal exploitation by the Europeans, for early observers noted that the first epidemics, which were the most deadly, occurred before excessive exploitation could have exacted its toll. The mortality was so great that in Mexico the Indians found it impossible to bury their dead. "They pulled down the houses over them," reported a Spanish contemporary, "in order to check the stench that rose from the dead bodies, so that their homes became their tombs." [3]

The Indians tried to strike back by kneading infected blood into their masters' bread, but to no effect. The population of Spanish America dropped from an estimated 50 million at the time of the conquest to 4 million in the seventeenth century. Then recovery gradually set in after the Indians with the least resistance had died, and the hardy survivors interbred among themselves and with the European and African immigrants. By the end of the colonial period, in the early nineteenth century, the total population of Spanish America had increased to 17 million, comprising 7.5 million Indians, 3.2 million whites, .75 million blacks, and 5.5 million mixtures of various sorts—white and Indian mestizos, white and black mulattos and black and Indian zambos or coyotes.

The English, needless to say, were as efficient disease carriers as the Spaniards, so that an epidemic swept through New England in 1616–17, clearing the woods, in the words of Cotton Mather, "of those pernicious creatures, to make room for better growth." [4] The Russians, who were the last European immigrants to arrive, had as deadly an impact at the other end of the New World. Thousands of Aleuts, Eskimos and Tlingits were thrust into their graves in Alaska, victims of the same smallpox, measles, typhus and other diseases that the Latins had introduced centuries earlier in the Caribbean basin.

The thousands of years of isolation left the Indians technologically as well as biologically vulnerable. By A.D. 1500 the Amerindians had reached the technological level that Western Europeans had attained in 1500 B.C. and the Middle Easterners in 3500 B.C. Although brilliantly successful in domesticating plants, the Indians never developed their cultivation techniques beyond the bare minimum necessary for feeding populations much smaller than those of the Old World. Their tools were made only of stone, wood or bone. They were incapable of smelting ores, and therefore lacked the swords and firearms of the Spaniards. Initially the Amerindians were terrified by the sound and effects of firearms, as well as by the spectacle of the charging cavalryman, assuming the man and horse to be one fearsome animal.

Isolation also had made the Amerindians psychologically vulnerable, with a religious naïveté that led the Aztec ruler, Montezuma, to greet Cortes as a god, and to pay homage to him and to proffer his throne and possessions. "Our lord . . . you have to come to your city, Mexico. . . . I was in agony . . with my eyes fixed on the Region of the Mystery. And now you have come out of the clouds and mists to sit on your throne again." [5]

Finally, the most populous and highly organized Indian states, the Aztec and Inca empires, proved to be the most fragile because of their excessive centralization. Once Montezuma and Atahualpa had fallen into Spanish hands, their Aztec and Inca empires became bodies without heads. By contrast, the comparatively primitive and loosely organized Indian tribes could retreat before the advancing Spaniards and escape the fatal effects of disease and exploitation. The Chichimecas of northern Mexico and the Araucanians of Chile proved themselves especially formidable adversaries. In response to Spanish military tactics they abandoned their traditional styles of warfare and adopted some of the methods and weapons of their enemies. Both took over the horse, and also learned to use the arquebus and musket, a combination that made them much-feared raiders of Spanish settlements. Yet despite such pockets of resistance, the fact remains that both North and South America fell rapidly under European domination, especially when compared to Africa where the Europeans were confined to the coastal regions until the nineteenth century.

The inherent fragility of the Aztec and Inca empires was accentuated by the dissension that was especially acute at the time of the Spanish arrival. The Incas were badly divided because Atahualpa had just defeated his brother, Huascar, for control of the throne, and had taken brutal revenge on all the clans that had opposed him. He was on his way to a celebration for his victory when Pizarro appeared. Even after he was taken prisoner by the Spaniards, Atahualpa was able to issue binding orders, and one of these was for the execution of his brother.

This was the "crime" for which he was executed in turn by Pizarro. In the case of the Aztecs, they had just conquered various cities that had hitherto been independent and that therefore resented deeply the new imperial rule. Thus they were defeated by a few hundred Spaniards and thousands of Indian allies. The most important of these were the Tlaxcalans, who regarded the war as their struggle for liberation from the Aztecs. The Tlaxcalans could not have foreseen that they were exchanging one imperial rule for another that was to prove substantially worse.

Once the conquest had been completed, the Spaniards were faced with the problem of administration, for it was their territories that were densely populated. Like the British and French in Africa, the Spaniards in the New World were forced to adopt indirect rule because of the shortage of administrative personnel. Being natural respecters of rank, the Spaniards during the period immediately following the conquest readily treated the native ruling class with some deference. It was allowed to retain a few of its traditional privileges, such as receiving tribute and keeping some hereditary lands. In return the native nobles were expected to adapt to Christian and Spanish standards of behavior, while their sons were trained by the friars as a Christian elite and even studied the complexities of Latin.

From the beginning, however, the Indian nobility was subject to a leveling process, being pushed aside by upstart Indians who won the favor of Spanish authorities, and, more commonly, being gradually stripped of their functions and lands by Spanish officials and settlers. At the same time the Indian nobility was decimated, along with the Indian masses, by the epidemics, so that within half a century the Indian upper ranks had been leveled down, apart from a few families that were gradually absorbed into the Spanish aristocracy.

With the Indian population reduced to an undifferentiated mass, a prolonged debate ensued over its inherent character and rights. The champions of the Indians were the clergy, who based their arguments on two Christian propositions: All men are equal before God; and every Christian must assume responsibility for the welfare of his brothers, no matter how alien or lowly they might be.

These premises provoked a controversy regarding the basic character of the Indians as a people. Were they innately capable of living according to the principles of Spanish culture and of the Christian faith? This issue divided the Spaniards into two warring camps: those who regarded the natives as "noble Indians," and those who dismissed them as "dirty dogs." The Dominican friar, Bartolomé de Las Casas, was the most outspoken of the "noble Indian" group. "God created these simple people without evil and without guile. They are most obedient and faithful to their natural lords and to the Christians whom they serve. They are most submissive, patient, peaceful and virtuous. . . . They neither possess nor desire to possess worldly wealth." Quite the opposite were the views of Gonzalo Fernandez de Oviedo, the official historian who considered the Indians "naturally lazy and vicious, melancholic, cowardly, and in general a lying, shiftless people. . . . Their chief desire is to eat, drink, worship heathen idols, and commit bestial obscenities." [6]

This was by no means a debate over abstractions. The stakes were enormous. Should the Indians be exploited for the benefit of the Crown and the settlers, or should the conversion and welfare of the Indians have precedence over material development and profit? The Crown vacillated under the pressure of conflicting theories and interests, but in the end the men on the spot prevailed. When a priest complained to Pizarro about the abuse of the Indians and the failure to win them over to God and the faith, he responded, "I have not come for any such reasons. I have come to take away from them their gold." [7]

These conquistadors and their successors, who numbered about a hundred thousand by 1550, generally had their way. They impressed the Indians to work on the land and in the mines. The Crown, of course, obtained its share of the proceeds in order to defray the expenses of colonial administration, as well as the much greater cost of dynastic and religious wars in Europe.

As for the Church, its efforts were not entirely fruitless. It persuaded the Indians to abandon cannibalism and human sacrifice; to replace the loincloth with trousers; and to accept certain aspects of Christianity that, like the crucifixion with its sacrificial connotations, were easily assimilated into their own modes of thought. More difficulty was encountered when the Christian priests trespassed into the realm of domestic life and morals. Evasion and subterfuge were employed against Spanish attempts to impose Christian concepts of incest or to introduce monogamy and the Christian marriage ceremony. For most Indians Christianity was a veneer concealing an exotic syncretism of the old and new faiths. They dropped the names of native gods but assigned the attributes of these gods to the Virgin Mary and the saints, expecting the images of the Catholic pantheon to cure disease, control the weather and keep them from harm, as they believed their gods had done. Thus the statistics of conversion were spectacular, but their significance proved to be much less so.

The clergy were partly responsible, for they tended to treat the Indians as children to be kept in permanent tutelage. Hence they never took the decisive step of ordaining the Indians as priests and accepting them as their spiritual equals. The clergy were hampered also by their inadequate numbers, by their ignorance of the native languages and by the fact that too many of them exploited the Indians mercilessly. Thus a Spanish official reported to Philip II in 1579 that the Indians prayed on their knees and confessed their sins, but that this was forced compliance and that the Indians were no more Christian than they had been at the time of the conquest. Another official of that period concluded, "The majority of Indians are not Christians." [8]

In conclusion, the conquest meant a definite deterioration of living conditions for the great majority of the Indians of Latin America. It is true that the Aztecs and the Incas had been subjected to forced labor before Columbus, but the work that previously had been done at the behest of the central imperial authorities now had to be done for local settlers whose demands usually were more arbitrary and unpredictable. Equally unfamiliar was the heavy demand for labor in the mines, where conditions were disastrous for both health and morale. Above all, the ceremonial and ritualistic aspects of work, which helped to make it tolerable in the preconquest period, found little or no place in the new order of things. The European concept of labor for wages and of regular hours with enforced leisure on Sundays was entirely alien to Indian traditions. The new system left a gaping spiritual void and induced a demoralization that, together with the trauma of the epidemics, drove the Indians to rampant alcoholism and despair. They wrote many moving accounts of their dreadful plight, such as the following by the Mayas:

> In those days all was good. . . . There was no sin in those days.
> . . . There was no sickness then, no pains in the bones . . . there
> was no small pox, there was no burning in the chest, there was no
> pain in the bowels, there was no wasting away. Then they walked
> with bodies erect.
>
> This was not what the white lords did when they came to our
> land. They taught fear and they withered the flowers. So that their
> flower should live, they maimed and destroyed the flower of others.
>
> Withered is life and dead the heart of the flowers. . . . False
> are their kings, tyrants upon their thrones, miserly with their
> flowers. . . . Marauders by day, offenders by night, murderers of
> the world! . . .
>
> . . . this was the beginning of our poverty, the beginning of tribute, the beginning of begging . . . of looting, of enslavement for
> debt . . . the beginning of constant fighting, the beginning of suffering.[9]

The Aztec cry of despair was equally distressing:

> Broken spears lie in the roads;
> we have torn our hair in our grief.

The houses are roofless now, and their walls
are red with blood. . . .
We have pounded our hands in despair
against the adobe walls
for our inheritance, our city, is lost and dead.[10]

❧ III. Latin America vs. Anglo America

The Spanish and Portuguese in Latin America seemed to possess all
the prerequisites for successful settlement: rich mines, fertile soil and
a docile labor force. In the early colonial period they appeared to be
well on the way to fulfilling this promise. Within a few decades the
Spaniards expanded from a few Caribbean islands to a huge continental
expanse, while the English starved in Virginia, and the French also in
Quebec. The Latin American colonies far surpassed their English and
French counterparts, boasting more people, larger cities, more universities and other cultural institutions and far greater wealth, especially
in the form of the treasure galleons and the profitable plantations that
were the envy of northern Europeans and Anglo Americans. And yet
it was the affluent and precocious Latin America that ended up as a dependent Third World region, while the poorly endowed and inauspicious
Anglo America became the heartland of the developed world.

The explanation for this paradoxical outcome is not that Iberian colonial policies were benighted compared to those of Britain, France or
Holland. All colonial powers during those centuries enforced as strictly
as possible the contemporary mercantilist doctrines that were considered
to be essential for national security and prosperity. According to these
doctrines, the purpose of colonies was to provide a market for the mother
country's manufactures and shipping, and to furnish the needed raw materials and bullion. Under no circumstances were competitive industries
to be tolerated in the colonies, and where they did take root because of
the difficulty of supervising distant overseas possessions, they were to be
ruthlessly destroyed. This was done in Mexico, where the viceroy reported in 1794 the measures taken to end local textile industry:

> . . . with no help of any kind . . . they [local textile crafts] have
> progressed enormously: to such a degree that one is amazed by
> certain types of manufactures, principally cottons and cloth for
> rebozos. . . . In these domains it is very difficult to prohibit the
> manufacture of those things which are made here . . . the only
> way to destroy such local manufactures would be to send the same
> or similar products from Europe, to be sold at lower prices. This
> is what has happened to the great factory and guild which existed

for all sorts of silk textiles, now barely remembered, and much the same fate has befallen the factories manufacturing printed cloth. . . .[11]

Precisely the same mercantilist policies were enforced by the other European colonial powers. The following instructions sent from London to Governor Murray in Quebec in 1763 were in no way different from countless other instructions on this subject dispatched from Madrid and Lisbon:

> . . . it is Our Express Will and Pleasure, that you do not, upon any Pretence whatever, upon pain of Our highest Displeasure, give your Assent to any Law or Laws for setting up any Manufactures and carrying on any Trades, which are hurtful and prejudicial to this Kingdom; and that you do use your utmost Endeavours to discourage, discountenance and restrain any Attempts which may be made to set up such Manufactures, or establish any such Trades.[12]

Since the diametrically opposite course of economic development in Latin America and Anglo America cannot be explained by differing colonial policies, it has been suggested that the answer may be found in the diverse levels of economic development attained by the metropolitan centers at the time of colonization. Retarded mother countries, according to this hypothesis, transmitted their retardation to their colonial offspring.

Certainly the Iberian powers by the end of the fifteenth century had fallen behind northwestern Europe in economic development. In the case of Spain, the dynastic and religious wars of the Hapsburg dynasty left the country exhausted from a full century of squandering natural and human resources. Spain also was held back by archaic feudal institutions and values that denigrated manual work and careers in commerce or industry. Daniel Defoe observed in 1726 that "trade in England makes gentlemen, and has peopled this nation with gentlemen." For the Spanish aristocrats or *hidalgos*, this was sheer anathema. Their views were reflected in the Cortes which, in contrast to the British Parliament, favored sheep farming as against commercial and industrial interests. Thus whereas England had exported raw wool in the Middle Ages, parliamentary legislation sought to discourage the export of wool and encourage the domestic manufacture of cloth. By 1500 London was exporting 50,000 bolts of cloth, and by 1550 about 130,000 bolts. In Spain, by contrast, the powerful *mesta* of sheep raisers prevailed, so that wool exports and cloth imports were encouraged. By the time of the discoveries, Spain had become an importer of northern European manufactures, including textiles and hardware, and an exporter of raw materials such as wool, wine and iron ore. In short, semifeudal Spain had become an economic dependency of capitalistic northwestern Europe. This was equally true of Portugal, which was importing hardwares, textiles, cereals and salt fish and gave in return wine, salt and African gold.

The significance of this dependence of the Iberian states is that they proved incapable of exploiting the worldwide markets opened up by the discoveries of their explorers. Spain and Portugal took the lead in the overseas expeditions, thanks to a fortuitous combination of circumstances —their favorable geographic location, their aggressive crusading tradition, and their adoption of the most advanced ship construction and navigation techniques of the North Atlantic and the Mediterranean. Thus Columbus reached the New World and da Gama sailed into Calicut harbor, thereby opening a new phase in the economic development of Europe and of the entire world.

The pioneering Iberian states, however, were unable to take advantage of the unprecedented new opportunities because of their retarded economic structures. Spanish industry, for example, was undermined by the expulsion of the Jews and the Moors, and by the influx of American bullion, which priced Spanish goods out of the international market. Foreigners consequently won control of the trade between Spain and her colonies, despite the regulations that theoretically assured a monopoly of the imperial trade for Spaniards. But the monopoly could not be enforced because Spanish industry could not meet the needs of the Spanish American colonists. Hence the paradox that the economic windfall from the New World served to buttress rather than demolish Spain's obsolescent society. "Colonial plunder to no small extent," concludes Eugene Genovese, "went into shoring up a decaying *hidalguía*." [13]

As early as 1619 a Spaniard complained that "nine out of ten parts of the Indies trade are carried on by foreigners," while a 1691 French report on this trade analyzed it as being divided as follows: 25 percent French, 21 percent Genoese, 19 percent Dutch, 11 percent Flemings, 11 percent English, 7.6 percent Hamburgers and 3.8 percent Spanish.[14] The accuracy of these figures cannot be checked, but the reality of foreign domination of a supposed Spanish monopoly is borne out by the fact that within a few weeks after the arrival of the silver galleons from America, the metal was scarce again in Seville. The bulk of it was siphoned off to pay for the grain, ironware, textiles, naval stores, paper and banking and shipping services that were needed by peninsular Spain as well as by her colonies. Hence the typical contemporary lament, "All that the Spaniards bring from the Indies after long, prolix and hazardous navigations, and all that they harvest with blood and labour, foreigners carry off to their homelands with ease and comfort." [15]

Portugal suffered even more from her economic retardation. The southern provinces conquered from the Muslims were appropriated by nobles, who imported African slaves to cultivate their large estates. They first arrived in 1441, but eventually as many as ten thousand per year were pouring in—a number that seriously reduced the living standards and purchasing power of the peasants. Thus Portugal lacked a home market and an industry to absorb the wealth accruing from the vast colonial possessions suddenly acquired in Asia and the New World.

During the seventeenth century Portugal lost her East Indian possessions to the superior economic and naval power of the Dutch. This left the Portuguese with a triangular trading system among their country, West Africa and Brazil. Portugal sent hardware, textiles and other manufactures to Africa for slaves, which they shipped to Brazilian plantations to grow sugar, which in turn the Portuguese sold in Europe at lucrative profit. This trade provided an incentive for the development of Portugal's own manufactures, but it did not continue long enough to enable Portuguese industry to take root and become fully independent.

In 1580 Portugal fell under Spanish rule, and remained so until 1640. England took advantage of Portugal's weakness when Portugal regained her independence to dictate the 1654 treaty opening the triangular trade to English merchants. As soon as the triangular trade became quadrangular, its controlling center shifted from Portugal to England because of the latter's super economic and naval power. The subordination of Portugal to England was completed with the 1703 Methuen Treaty by which Portugal reduced duties on textile imports from England in return for reduced duties on Portuguese wine exports to England. This treaty finished off the surviving Portuguese industries and ensured that half to three fourths of the output of the gold fields discovered in Brazil would end up in England. Brazilian gold financed Britain's war against Napoleon, while Portugal became the fourth largest customer for British industries. The cost for Portugal is reflected in the 1763 observation of the British minister in Lisbon: "For the most part the Portuguese in the Brazil trade have been but commissaries for other people." [16]

This subordination of the Iberian economies explains why Latin America was exploited by the northern Europeans rather than the Iberians, but it does not explain why Latin America should have become dependent and exploitable in the first place. It cannot be argued that it was a case of the transmission of dependency from the Iberian Peninsula to Latin America because at the same time English and French colonies in the Caribbean were equally dependent and exploited. In fact, the similarities in the economic evolution of Spanish Puerto Rico and Cuba, of British Trinidad and Jamaica, and of French Martinique and Guadeloupe point to a more basic cause for Latin American underdevelopment than that propounded by the transmission hypothesis.

The significant common feature of the Spanish, French and English Caribbean possessions is that they all started out as white farming communities with diversified economies, and then suddenly changed to sugar-plantation monoculture economies based on African slave labor and completely dependent on their mother countries for their one export and for their sundry imports. Barbados, for example, was first settled by the British in 1627, and by 1640 the population totalled over 30,000 white farmers with their indentured servants and a sprinkling of political prisoners, religious refugees and exiled convicts. The backbone of the settlement consisted of sturdy yeomen who tilled the original grants of small holdings and practiced various handicrafts. The principal products in those early years were tobacco, cotton, indigo, pepper, citrus fruits, cattle, pigs and poultry. This was the same type of self-sufficient farming carried on in mainland Anglo America, or rather northern Anglo America, which differed fundamentally from the cotton-plantation South.

About 1640 Barbados was transformed almost overnight by the introduction of sugar cane. The new crop required large acreage and plentiful cheap labor to be profitable. The independent farmers with their few acres and limited capital could not purchase either the additional land or the slaves. By 1667, some 12,000 of these farmers perforce had emigrated to other British Caribbean islands or to the thirteen American colonies, and by 1786 only 16,167 whites remained. Barbados was transformed into a sugar factory comprising 745 plantations worked by 82,023 imported African slaves. The slaves were brought in simply because the money paid for a white man's labor for ten years would buy a slave for life.

Cuba's evolution under Spanish rule differed in details from that of British Barbados, yet the implications for Latin America's underdevelopment are similar. After occupying Cuba in the second half of the sixteenth century, Spanish officials issued small land grants in order to attract the maximum number of settlers. The policy succeeded, and between the sixteenth and eighteenth centuries the island was populated by farmers and cattlemen who cultivated subsistence plots, raised livestock and occasionally traded hides, salt meat and assorted agricultural products with the Spanish ships that called at Havana once or twice a year, or with the foreign smugglers who showed up sporadically. While the British and French islands were changing into fabulously profitable sugar factories, Cuba continued to grow slowly but steadily along her original lines, shielded by the isolation imposed by Spanish trading restrictions.

In the nineteenth century Cuba gradually followed the pattern of the other islands. One reason was the shortage of sugar created by the black revolt in St. Domingue (later Haiti). Also, new technology was making Cuba's few small sugar plantations obsolete. Hence the appearance in the second half of the nineteenth century of large, efficient sugar mills, or *centrales*, which processed the sugar cane for the grower, or *colono*, in return for a percentage of the final product. In the late nineteenth century the construction of railways made possible the transportation of sugar cane over long distances and precipitated competition among the centrales for the cane supply. In order to ensure dependable cane delivery, the rival centrales either purchased large tracts and had them sharecropped, or else reduced the colono to vassalage by contracts that required him to deliver his entire crop. Thus the original class of independent farmers gradually was squeezed out, especially after the Spanish American War, when the process was accelerated by more railway building, more capital investment and a 20 percent preferential in the United States tariff, which created a vast American market for Cuban sugar.

Cuba now underwent an experience similar to that of Barbados 2½ centuries earlier, with wage labor from Haiti and Jamaica in place of slave labor from Africa, and capital from the United States in place of capital from England. The number of mills declined from 1,190 in 1877 to 207 in 1899 and to 185 in 1927, and most of these were American-owned. The disruptive impact of this transformation on the island society has been analyzed forthrightly by the Cuban historian Ramiro Guerra y Sanchez:

> The latifundium system . . . consolidates thousands of small farms into immense agrarian units; it uproots the farmer from his land; it destroys the rural landowning and independent farming class, backbone of the nation; and finally, it puts an end to national economic independence by converting the society into a mere dependency, a satellite, a workshop, at the service of some foreign power. It . . . is wiping out four centuries of growth in Cuba and is reducing Cuba to an enormous plantation producing sugar for the benefit of foreign consumers.[17]

We may conclude from the above that Latin America's retardation is to be explained not by the transmission of Iberia's retardation, but rather by the nature of the domestic colonial economy—by whether it was a diversified and independent economy capable of development, or a monoculture plantation economy, subordinate to the metropolitan centers, and therefore capable only of economic growth without any possibility of overall economic development. This proposition, based on Caribbean historical experiences, will be applied in the following section to Latin America as a whole.

℘ IV. *Roots of Latin American Underdevelopment*

The fundamental differences between the local conditions and institutions of northern Anglo America and those of Latin America suggest the origins of underdevelopment in the latter region. The Anglo-American economy (that of New England and the middle colonies but not the southern colonies) was from the beginning independent and broad-based, comprising individual proprietors who produced primarily for domestic consumption. They lacked the mines to fill treasure galleons, and they lacked also the labor force as well as the soil and climatic conditions needed for large-scale haciendas and plantations. New England did export furs, but they soon became scarce as settlement expanded and drove the fur-bearing animals away. New England timber was sometimes welcomed by the mother country as a convenient standby in emergency situations, but the cost of transport across the Atlantic made it too expensive to replace the normal supplies from the Baltic lands. Grain and fish were the chief products of Anglo America, but they were not welcomed in markets already well supplied by England's own farmers and seafarers.

Accordingly the Anglo Americans went their own way, developing their resources and seeking markets regardless of imperial restrictions. They shipped their fish, butter, beef and flour to the plantation islands of the West Indies in return for sugar and molasses, which they converted into rum and shipped to Africa, along with fish and grain, for slaves and gold. They also established local industries, such as iron founding, feltmaking and textiles, in direct defiance of London and in competition with English imports. They built and operated an efficient merchant marine, which carried their products not only to the mother country and to other English colonies, but also to foreign colonies and foreign powers in violation of the Navigation Acts. New England and the middle colonies were able to ignore imperial restrictions and develop a relatively independent economy because, in contrast to the southern colonies and to Latin America, they were not shackled by some overwhelmingly profitable enterprise such as sugar plantations, financed and directed by foreign investors for foreign profit.[18]

In Latin America, by contrast, different local conditions produced different products and therefore different relationships with the mother countries. In the first place there was a large native population, estimated to have totaled at the time of the conquest from 3.5 to 7 million in Peru and as high as 25 million in Mexico. This Indian labor force was relatively docile, being accustomed to agricultural work and to accepting orders from the privileged nobles and priests within their own

Inca and Aztec societies. The Spaniards therefore were able, after destroying the native ruling establishment, to compel the Indians to provide the labor force needed for two of the three great mainstays of Latin America's economy, the mines and the haciendas. The third, comprising the coastal plantations, had to depend on imported African slaves because of the sparseness of the Indian populations in the coastal regions.

The institution by which Indian labor was mobilized for mines and haciendas was the *encomienda*, whose origins go back to medieval Spain during the *reconquista* against the Muslims. Christian knights then acquired jurisdiction over Muslim lands and people through the encomienda, which was later introduced in the New World by the conquistadors. The basic objective of this institution is evident in the royal instructions given to Governor Ovando of Española in 1503: "Because of the excessive liberty the Indians have been permitted, they flee from Christians and do not work. Therefore they are to be compelled to work, so that the kingdom and the Spaniards be enriched, and the Indians Christianized." [19]

The terms of an encomienda grant permitted the *encomendero* to exact both commodity tribute and labor service from the Indians he "held." In return he was obliged to render military service in case of Indian uprisings (which were feared but rarely materialized) and to provide for the Christianization of the Indians in his charge. Most encomenderos met the latter obligation by paying the salaries and expenses of resident or visiting clerics. The original encomiendas were granted theoretically for only a few years or for a single lifetime. But the first encomenderos bequeathed their holdings to their widows or children, and the legacies were not challenged. Royal officials, however, feared that hereditary encomiendas might culminate in an independent colonial aristocracy, and made sporadic efforts in the mid-sixteenth century to stop the bequeathing practice. This provoked strong opposition throughout Spanish America and armed rebellion in Peru, so the effort was abandoned. At that time (around 1560–70) the encomiendas numbered about 480 in New Spain and 695 in the viceroyalty of Peru.

Left free to use Indian labor as they wished, the Spaniards concentrated first on obtaining the one American commodity then marketable in Europe—namely, bullion. They acquired this in three stages, the first being the looting during the conquest of the treasures already accumulated by the Indians. The second stage was the use of native labor to extract alluvial gold from the placer deposits that the Indians traditionally had worked. After the mid-sixteenth century the Spaniards opened silver mines that yielded most of the New World bullion, especially after the introduction of the amalgamation technique making possible the use of poorer-grade ores. This process made heavy use of Indian labor with catastrophic results, as described in the following eyewitness account of the annual migration of Indians from the province of Chuquito to the mines of Potosi:

> They all go usually with their wives and children, and having seen them twice I am in a position to say that they amount altogether to more than seven thousand souls. Every Indian of these takes with him eight to ten sheep and a few alpacas to eat; others who are wealthier, take with them thirty to forty sheep, on which they carry their meals of Indian corn and potato flour, their covers for sleeping, mats to guard against the cold, which is sharp, for they always sleep in the open. All this cattle generally exceeds thirty thousand head, and nearly always amounts to about forty thousand. . . . All this wealth in this manner takes the road to Potosi by stages and the distance of about one hundred leagues takes two months, since the cattle cannot travel quicker, nor their children of five and six years whom they take with them. Of all this mankind and common wealth which they take away from Chuquito, no more than two thousand souls ever return, and the remainder, about five thousand, in part, they die, and in part they remain in Potosi. There are others who go to the valleys nearby, and the reason is that when they want to return they have neither cattle nor food for the road.
>
> And for this, and the work, so excessive at that, of six months, four in the mines, working twelve hours a day, going down four hundred and twenty and at times seven hundred feet, down to where night is perpetual, for it is always necessary to work by candlelight, the air thick and ill smelling being enclosed in the entrails of the earth, the going up and down most dangerous, for they come up loaded with their small sack of metal tied up to their backs, taking quite four to five hours, step by step, and if they make the slightest false step they may fall seven hundred feet; and when they arrive at the top out of breath, find as shelter a mineowner who scolds them because they did not come quickly enough or because they did not bring enough load, and for the slightest reason makes them go down again. . . .[20]

Once the mining operations were under way, Indian labor was needed also for the haciendas, which provided the mining communities with pork, mutton, wheat, corn, beans, coarse textiles, horses, mules and burros. These agricultural and ranching haciendas originally were theoretically distinct from the encomiendas, being required to be located at a distance from the Indian communities and not to injure those communities in any way. In practice, however, colonial lawyers found ways to incorporate Indian lands into the haciendas of their clients. This process was stimulated by the catastrophic decline of the Indian population, which fell in Mexico from a possible high of 25 million in 1519 to 6.3 million in 1548, and 1.07 million by 1605. In Peru the depopulation was from a possible maximum of 7 million to 1.8 million by 1580. This demographic disaster undermined the viability of the encomienda, and set the Crown and settlers into sharp conflict for control of such labor and tribute as could still be obtained. By the mid-seventeenth century the hacienda had displaced the encomienda, which meant that the Spaniards were expropriating for their private use most Indian lands, excepting those already set aside for the Church. This shift freed the Indians from their state-imposed obligation for tribute and labor, but on the haciendas they quickly sank into an equally onerous debt peonage. This became a permanent state of servitude with successive advances for food, drink and the sacraments of baptism, marriage and death. Thus the hacienda became the dominant form of land ownership in the interior regions of Spanish America, each embracing many thousands of acres and using Indian peons as herdsmen, laborers and craftsmen. In return the Indians did find a certain security, receiving for their labor assured daily rations, primitive medical treatment and religious consolation.

With the declining output of silver after the mid-seventeenth century, the most dynamic and productive sector of the Latin American economy shifted from the mines and haciendas of the interior to the plantations of the coastlands. In contrast to the haciendas, which tended toward self-sufficiency and normally sold their surplus to neighboring consumers, the plantations were more commerce-oriented, producing for overseas sale some single crop such as sugar, tobacco and cotton, and later rubber, coffee and bananas. The other major difference between haciendas and plantations was in the labor force, consisting mostly of Indians on the haciendas and of imported slaves on the plantations. Sugar cane required much labor for planting, cutting, transporting cane to the mills, purifying the sap in the kettles, refining the heated sugar and finally draining off the sugar brandy. When the Portuguese established the first sugar plantations on the American mainland in Brazil, they found the sparse, seminomadic Indian population quite inadequate as a labor force, so they imported slaves from Africa. With the spread of sugar plantations from Brazil to the Caribbean islands, this process was repeated, with social repercussions already noted. By 1700 the Brazilian sugar economy was in serious crisis because Caribbean sugar could be sold more cheaply in Europe due to lower transportation costs and the protection afforded by the respective metropolitan markets.

Brazilian sugar plantations only began the influx of slaves into the New World. They quickly spread throughout Latin America and to England's southern colonies, as slaves came to be used for working mines, clearing virgin land and cultivating cotton, tobacco, rice and indigo as well as sugar plantations. Eventually slavery extended along the whole length of North and South America, from the St. Lawrence River in the North to the Río de la Plata in the South. P. D. Curtin estimates the following number of slaves imported to the New World between 1451 and 1870, although later studies suggest the number might be 20 percent greater, or a total of nearly 12 million (see Chapter 5, Section II):

Estimated Number of Slaves Imported to the New World, 1451–1870

British North America	399,000
Spanish America	1,552,100
Caribbean Islands (British, French, Dutch, Danish)	3,793,200
Brazil	3,646,800
TOTAL	9,391,100

Source: P. D. Curtin, *The Atlantic Slave Trade* (Madison: University of Wisconsin Press, 1969), p. 268.

V. Underdeveloped Latin American Economy

The mines, haciendas and plantations of Latin America were the envy of northern Europe and Anglo America. Yet it was Latin America that ended up as a dependent Third World region, and the root reason was that the profits from the mines, haciendas and plantations enriched northern Europe and Anglo America far more than they did Latin America. Between the end of the fifteenth century and the middle of the seventeenth century, Spanish America's principal export was bullion, mainly silver. In 1594 it comprised 95.6 percent of all exports, as against 2.8 percent made up of cochineal, 1.2 percent of hides, and 0.3 percent of indigo. This bullion was a bonanza for Spain, since the cost of the forced Indian labor was negligible, and the value of the bullion received was four times that of Spain's exports to her colonies. But so far as Latin America was concerned, mining was an enclave industry with few linkages to the rest of the local economy. The enormous bullion shipments from Latin America contributed very little to the overall economic development of that region. Even Spain, for that matter, benefited little, if at all, for 90 percent of the manufactured goods exported to Latin

America came from the more advanced northern European industries, and the New World bullion accordingly ended up in London or Antwerp rather than Madrid.

During the seventeenth century the output of the mines declined, and the economic significance of the haciendas diminished correspondingly, since their principal market had been the mining communities. The most dynamic and productive sector of the Latin American economy now became the plantations, which produced vast quantities of tropical crops for the European market. The transatlantic trade became for the first time a mass trade comparable to, though much greater than, the original mass trade in northern Europe. It was a three-way or triangle trade, which yielded substantial profits to the European middlemen at all three points of the triangle. The first lap was from some European home port to Africa with a cargo including salt, textiles, firearms, hardware, beads and rum. These were bartered for slaves, who were sold to the New World plantation owners. The final lap was the voyage home with plantation produce such as sugar, molasses, tobacco, rice and cotton.

The historic beneficiaries of this triangle trade were the northern Europeans and also the northern Anglo Americans who, as noted above, participated extensively in all three stages of the exchange. Contemporary observers saw clearly why the Northerners gained more than did the other participants. An anonymous Englishman asserted in 1749, ". . . the extensive employment of our shipping in, to, and from America, the great Brood of Seamen consequent thereon, and the Daily Bread of the most considerable Part of our British Manufactures, are owing primarily to the Labour of Negroes. . . . the natural consequences resulting from it may justly be esteemed an inexhaustible Fund of Wealth and Naval Power to this Nation." [21]

This statement, typical of many in that period, brings out the most critical factor in the emerging global market economy: that of "linkages" or "horizontal economic ties" as against "vertical economic ties." The northern Europeans and the northern Anglo Americans, serving as the middlemen providing varied commodities and services, including manufactures, agricultural produce, fish, shipping, capital and technical expertise, not only amassed most of the profits but also, more significantly, developed broad-based economies with self-generating development capability.[22]

This capability, which explains why one small part of the world today is "developed" while the rest remains the "underdeveloped" Third World, was the direct result of the "linkages" or "horizontal ties" engendered by the multifaceted economic activities of the Northerners. Whereas the West Indies, for example, exported sugar, and only sugar, an eighteenth-century catalogue listed the following commodities they had to import because of their monoculture economy: "woolen, linen, silk, iron, brass, copper, leather, glass, chinaware, clocks, watches, jewels, wrought plate, gold and silver lace, medicines . . . gunpowder . . . brickes, paint, oil, cordage, sugar pots, drips, hoops, candles . . . pipes . . . cards, swords, pistols, walking canes . . . grindstones, paving stones, books, toys, stationery, cutlery, Birmingham and haberdashery wares, all sorts of household goods and furniture; wearing apparel, cabinet ware, chariots, chaises, coppers . . . in short all things necessary for life, and almost the whole consumption . . . is British manufacture." All of these items were imported for the tiny English minority that ruled the islands economically and politically. Entirely different commodities were imported to meet the needs of the slaves. These included "vast quantities of check linen, striped hollands, fustian, blankets for their bedding, long ells and bays for warm clothing, coarse hats, woollen caps, cotton and silk handkerchiefs, knives, razors, buckles, buttons, tobacco pipes, fishing tackle, small glasses, thread, needles, pins and innumerable other articles all of *British* growth or manufacture." [23]

It is not surprising that as late as 1807 a British merchant, C. Bosanquet, was emphasizing the greater benefits derived from trade with the West Indies as against India and China: "The commerce of the West is not only carried on with people amongst whom there are no manufactures, but it is domestic commerce; both ends are British and all the profits accruing, on all the transactions, centre in Great Britain." [24]

If the broad-based, self-generating economy of northern Europe and of the northern colonies is compared with the monoculture plantation economy of Latin America, the reason for the latter's Third World status becomes apparent. Plantation economy by its very nature was dependent and incapable of generating linkages or overall economic development. Only one crop was grown, and this was dictated by price considerations in the metropolitan market rather than by the needs of the local economy or population. In British Guiana, for example, the settlers were expressly forbidden any cultivation other than the profitable sugar cane. They were forced to cut down fruit trees they had planted, and they were not allowed even to fish in the rivers or coastal waters. If these restrictions increased the output of sugar cane, it certainly was at the expense of the settlers' dietary needs and of the general economic development of their colony.

Such imperial restrictions were not so onerous in the northern colonies, where there were no immensely profitable crops such as sugar to motivate close supervision. But in the South, whether in Latin America or the British West Indies or the southern colonies, it was an entirely different matter. Hence the significance of the following conclusion by the English economic historian, W. Cunningham:

The development of the southern colonies [of the present U.S.A.] and the West Indian Islands was promoted by moneyed men in England, who directed the energies of the planters into raising commodities for export. These traders were not especially concerned to foster communities which should be self-sufficing: they preferred that the planters should manage their estates with a view to the requirements of outside markets.[25]

Apart from imperial regulations, plantation economies tended to be inelastic and incapable of adapting in order to make full use of local resources. Heavy capital investments for the growing and processing of some one crop made it difficult to shift or to diversify. A sugar mill, for example, could not be adapted to processing vegetables, nor can ships constructed specifically for the transportation of one product be used for transporting others.

Monoculture also meant unemployment for a good part of each year, as well as inefficient performance during the work seasons. Neither slave labor nor tenant labor was highly productive, since there was little reward incentive to stimulate performance. Finally, monoculture meant inefficient use of natural resources as well as human. Plantation companies usually purchased much more land than they actually used, for a variety of reasons: to assure output flexibility in case of rising demand; to attain continuity of the plantation tracts; to keep out competitors; to speculate against possible future land value increases; and to obtain the political power associated with land ownership in plantation societies. Whatever the reasons, the fact remains that underutilization of human and land resources was contrary to local interests, however much it may have advanced company interests.

These various factors explain why plantation societies were capable of economic growth, or increased output of the particular crop involved, but not of economic development, or overall advance of the local economy until it became independent and self-generating. In the light of historical perspective, the independent variable that decisively affected the fortunes of all the colonies was the availability of human and natural resources that could be exploited by the metropolitan centers. The greater the availability, the greater the exploitation and the greater the economic growth as against economic development. It is not accidental that the most profitable New World colonies of the past are now among the most underdeveloped members of the Third World (West Indies and northeastern Brazil), and that the least profitable colonies have become the leaders of the developed world (Canada and the United States).

Chapter 5

AFRICA A PERIPHERAL AREA

Allowing for the difference between the Moslem and Christian intellectual climates, a citizen of 14th century Timbuktu would have found himself reasonably at home in 14th century Oxford. In the 16th century he still would have found many points in common between the two university cities. By the 19th century the gulf had grown very deep.

THOMAS HODGKIN

In modern times Europeans commonly have associated Africa with savagery, bloodshed and backwardness. This was a rationalization, conscious or subconscious, to justify European enslavement of millions of Africans, European missionary enterprise to Christianize and civilize the barbarous heathen, European partitioning of Africa into dozens of colonies, and the subsequent exploitation of African human and natural resources. The epigraph by a present-day British historian at the head of this chapter points up the absurdity of this "rivers of blood and mountains of skulls" school of thought.

Prior to the appearance of the Portuguese, Africa had generally kept pace with the other continents of the Old World, which partly explains why the Europeans had been kept out of Africa long after they had opened up and colonized North and South America. As late as 1865, when the Civil War was ending in the United States, only the coastal fringe of Africa was known, together with a few isolated sections of the interior. Even by 1900 about a fourth of the interior of Africa still remained unexplored. And yet, as the title of this chapter indicates, Africa ended up as a peripheral and dependent area, subordinated to the interests of the rising capitalist West.

This raises two basic questions that this chapter seeks to answer: Why had Africa's development kept up with that of other continents until the fifteenth century? Why did Africa sink to a subordinate, peripheral status after the appearance of the Europeans?

ᘇ *I. Pre-Portuguese Africa*

Geography contributed to the success of the Africans in keeping the Europeans at arm's length for so long. The hot and humid climate of the low-lying coastal areas, and the accompanying tropical diseases, decimated the Europeans until the advances of tropical medicine in the late nineteenth century. Until then, Europeans entering Africa suffered almost as heavy casualties as American Indians had on their first contact with Europeans. There were the mosquitos, carriers of malaria, yellow fever, blackwater fever and elephantiasis, as well as water-borne plagues, including Guinea threadworm and bilharziasis or schistosomiasis. Lice and fleas also were carriers of infections such as murine plague and relapsing fever. It was the coastal areas, which the Europeans first encountered, that harbored most of these diseases. In 1805 the British African Association sent a Scottish physician, Dr. Mungo Park, to explore the Niger River. Almost all members of the expedition died during an overland trek before even reaching the river. "I am sorry to say," reported Dr. Park, "that of forty-five Europeans who left the Gambia in perfect health, five only at present are alive, viz., three soldiers (one deranged in his mind), Lieutenant Martyn and myself . . . though all the Europeans who are with me should die, and if I could not succeed in the object of my journey [to find the river's outlet] I would at least die on the Niger." [1] Park did die on the Niger, as did his eighteen-year-old son, who set out to find his father.

Africa also is extraordinarily inaccessible. The coastline is unbroken by bays, gulfs, or inland seas, and therefore is even shorter than Europe's, though Africa has thrice the area. The resulting lack of a Mediterranean, Black or Baltic Sea means that Africa's interior is not open to the outside world. This inaccessibility was enhanced by the great Sahara Desert barrier in the North, and by thousand-mile-long sandbars along both the eastern and western coasts. And if these obstacles were overcome, then still another remained—the rapids and waterfalls that blocked navigation of rivers from the coastlands to the salubrious interior plateaus.

An additional factor that discouraged the Europeans from trying to push inland was the lack of readily available sources of wealth in the interior of Africa comparable to the gold and silver of the Americas or the spices of the East Indies. It is true that Africa did yield a valuable commodity for the new market economy in the form of slaves for the New World plantations. But it was not necessary to go inland for the slaves: They were brought to the coast by African slavers who opposed any European penetration simply because it would have deprived them of their profits as middlemen.

The people as well as the geography of Africa contributed to the exclusion of Europeans. First, who were the African people? They were not all of one type, as is often assumed. The contrast between the Pygmies of the Congo and the Masai of Kenya is more marked than that between a Sicilian and a Swede. The origins and diffusion of the numerous African peoples remain in large part a mystery. The classification that, for the present, at least, meets with the fewest objections recognizes four major peoples: (1) Bushmen, who speak the Khoisan language; (2) Pygmies, whose original language is unknown because they adopted those of their later conquerors; (3) Negroes, who speak the Niger-Congo language; and (4) Caucasoids, known also as Capsians, Cushites and Hamites, who speak the Afroasiatic language.[2]

These African peoples enjoyed one fundamental advantage over the American Indians, namely, their greater degree of accessibility, their greater opportunity to interact with the peoples and cultures of Europe and Asia. This interaction, which went on from the beginning of human history, conferred numerous benefits on the Africans. One of the most important was immunity against the European diseases that so devastated the American Indians (see Chapter 4, Section II). In fact, it was the Europeans who were biologically vulnerable in Africa. "It seems," wrote a Portuguese chronicler in the sixteenth century, "that for our sins or for some inscrutable judgment of God, in all the entrances of this great Ethiopia that we navigate along, He has placed a striking angel with a flaming sword of deadly fevers who prevents us from penetrating into the interior to the springs of this garden. . . ."[3]

Prolonged contact with Eurasia also gave the Africans the benefits of technological diffusion, especially of the arts of agriculture and iron metallurgy. Archaeologists disagree over the basic issue of diffusion versus autonomous development—over what was borrowed from abroad and what was originated independently at home. Some believe that agriculture spread from western Asia into the Nile Valley and thence to West Africa, while others hold that West Africa was one of the world's four cradles of agriculture, the others being Southwest Asia, the Middle East and Middle America. West Africa did have certain native drought-resistant cereals that were suitable for domestication, such as the sorghums, the millets and the dry rice called *Oryza glaberrima*.

Likewise some archaeologists believe that iron metallurgy was received from Carthage and from the kingdom of Kush on the Upper Nile, while others maintain that West African communities learned to smelt iron by independent discovery. Alternatively, it is quite possible that both diffusion and autonomous development were involved, depending on whether the particular people concerned were located close to, or distant from, the routes of Eurasian diffusion.

Whatever the cause may have been, there is no question about the receipt of certain plants from the outside, such as wheat and barley from the Middle East, and bananas, Asian yams and cocoa-yams or *taros* from Southeast Asia. The latter group of plants were important because they made possible the extension of agriculture into the humid regions of tropical Africa. Also certain types of cattle, such as the Zebu shorthorn humpbacked cow, came from the outside, providing a supply of protein and a source of power that were denied to American Indians.

The new iron tools and the new domesticated plants enabled the Africans to exploit their natural resources more efficiently, and to increase in numbers correspondingly. Those peoples who used the tools and plants most efficiently had a great advantage over their neighbors and were able to expand at their expense. This explains the rapid spread over most sub-Saharan Africa of a predominantly Negroid linguistic group known as the Bantu. Starting from some still undetermined center, they pushed outward in all directions, assimilating or pushing aside the Pygmies, Hottentots and Bushmen. By the time the Europeans arrived, the Bantu-speaking Negroes were predominant in Africa, whereas a millennium earlier they had shared the continent fairly evenly with the Caucasoids, Bushmen and Pygmies.

The Africans benefited from cultural diffusion as well as technological. A prime example was the impact of the Muslim Arabs, who overran all North Africa in the seventh century A.D. and later extended their influence down the eastern coast as merchants and as colonists. From these coastal bases the Arabs had profound and far-reaching influence on the African peoples. The Arabs used the camel much more than did the Romans, and correspondingly expanded the trans-Saharan trade, which brought salt, cloth and beads to West Africa and took gold, ivory and slaves to the North African coast. Much of the gold eventually ended up in medieval Europe, thereby enabling the Europeans to pay with gold for the spices and silks they imported from Asia. Three principal routes were developed across the Sahara: a western one leading from Morocco to the northern bend of the Niger and to the country west of it; a central route from Tunisia to the region between the Niger and Lake Chad; and an eastern route from Tripoli to the Lake Chad region.

On the eastern coast the Arabs traded with the Africans of the interior for ivory, gold, slaves and later iron ore. This ore was shipped to southern India, made into steel, reshipped to Persia and Asia Minor and worked into the so-called Damascus blades. Among the products imported in return for these African commodities were Chinese and Indian cloth and Chinese porcelain, remains of which can still be found along the entire coast.

These commercial contacts led to Muslim cultural penetration. Islam spread down the coast as far as Zanzibar, and intermittently beyond. From the Mediterranean coast it spread south across the Sahara into the Sudan. Along with religion, the externals of life also were affected, including names, dress, household equipment, architectural styles, festivals and the like. Koranic schools spread literacy, and scholars could pursue higher learning at various Sudanese universities at Fez, Tunis and Cairo.

The adoption of Islam also enhanced the political cohesion of the Sudanic kingdoms. Their rulers traditionally could claim the allegiance only of their own kinship units or clans, and of such other related kinship units as recognized descent from a great founding ancestor. But when the kingdoms were enlarged into great empires this kinship relationship obviously became inadequate as the basis for imperial organization. The more widely an empire was extended, the more alien its emperor appeared to a large proportion of the subjects. Local chiefs could not be depended upon to serve as faithful vassals; they tended instead to lead their own people in resistance to imperial rule. Islam helped to meet this institutional problem by strengthening the imperial administration. Moslem schools and colleges turned out a class of educated men who could organize an effective imperial bureaucracy. These men were not dominated by their kinship alliances; their own interests were tied to imperial authority, and they normally could be counted on to serve that authority loyally. Islam was not a prerequisite, however, to state building, as indicated by the fact that the Ghana Empire had developed and was already beginning to decline before Islam took root. Also the Yoruba and Edo people of West Africa developed state organization even though they were remote from the influences of trans-Saharan trade.

It was this combination of agricultural and metallurgical progress, corresponding growth in economic productivity, flourishing interregional trade and the stimulus from Islam that explain the process of state building that went on in Africa from the eighth century onward. The precise combination that led to state building varied from region to region. Not surprisingly, the most complex political structures appeared in the Sudan, where long-distance trade was most highly developed. Hence the emergence in that region of three great empires: Ghana (700–1200), Mali (1200–1500) and Songhai (1350–1600). The Songhai empire stretched almost fifteen hundred miles from the Atlantic into the interior, and in this expanse the rule of law and a common administrative system were given to many diverse subjects.

In large part because of the marked compartmentalization of the continent, the level of general development varied strikingly from region to region of sub-Saharan Africa. Uniform growth was impossible because of natural obstacles obstructing communication and movement among savannahs, rain forests and deserts. Political units thus included individual village communities recognizing only local chieftains, and the great empires of the Sudan. Economically, the range was as great: from the food gathering of the Bushmen-Hottentot-Pygmies to the interregional and intercontinental trade utilizing currencies consisting of metal coins, gold, brass, salt and cowrie shells.

It was with the highly developed peoples of West Africa that the Portuguese pioneers first established contact. They did so very naturally, because here there was enough population density and economic development to make trading profitable. Thanks to the banana and the yam, there was vigorous economic activity not only in the Sudan zone of West Africa, but also in the forested zone to the south, known as Guinea. The flourishing agriculture supported a relatively dense population and a brisk trade. In these areas the Portuguese were dealing with a people of sophisticated enough background to be able to meet them without fear or wonderment. It is true that the forest dwellers, who had not had direct contact with the Arabs, were astonished by the white skin of the Europeans, by the loud noise of their firearms, and by the fact that these newcomers came from the sea, which was much revered by the coastal peoples. Yet the fact remains that there could be no repetition in Africa of the conquistador victories that dismantled overnight great Amerindian empires.

A Dutch factor on the Gold Coast warned his employers in the year 1700, "There is no small number of men in Europe who believe that the gold mines are in our power; that we . . . have no more to do but to work them by our slaves: though you perfectly know we have no manner of access to these treasures." [4] A British official in 1795 spelled out why "access to these treasures" was denied to Europeans. The blockage stemmed "rather from the jealousy of the inhabitants of the sea coasts, in permitting white men to travel through their country, than from the danger of difficulty attending the penetration." This jealousy he attributed to the middlemen's fear "that the advantages of their trade with Europe should be lessened [and] transferred from them to their neighbors"; or that the inland kingdoms by obtaining arms "would become dangerous rivals." [5]

In retrospect, it is clear that the trans-Saharan trade benefited all parties involved—the Africans to the south, the Arabs to the north and the southern Europeans across the Mediterranean. The same may be said of the East African trade conducted across the Indian Ocean through coastal Arab intermediaries. These long-distance trading operations were particularly important for sub-Sahara Africa because the indigenous agricultural and craft techniques were rudimentary. There was no plow or wheel, and the rather scarce population was able to meet its needs without too much effort from the abundant though not very fertile land. External trade, as distinct from local bartering, was invaluable in stimulating the production and the accumulation of surplus for exchange purposes, and also for promoting political centralization by providing local rulers with weapons, horses, copper and iron bars. During the pre-Portuguese period, Africans participated in long-distance trade as equals, and utilized it to satisfy their own needs. Contemporary Arab accounts attest to the egalitarian nature of the trade and to the autonomy of the African participants.

All this was fundamentally altered with the fateful appearance of the Portuguese on the western coast of Africa in the mid-fifteenth century. This represented another step in the historic shift of Europe's economic center from the Mediterranean Sea to the Atlantic Ocean. The ancient trade route across the Sahara was eventually short-circuited, as was the even more ancient trade route through Egypt and the Red Sea to India and the Spice Islands. A new era in world trade relationships was being ushered in—one in which the autonomy of all the participants no longer was possible. This was the era of Western commercial capitalism, in which Northwest Europe initiated, dominated, and manipulated global trade for its own purposes. The price was paid not only by the serfs of Eastern Europe and by the Indians of the New World, but also by the Italian city-states in the Mediterranean, by the Arabs of the Middle East and by the Africans to the south of the Sahara.

II. The Slave Trade and the Atlantic Economy

The basic reason for the historic economic shift from the Mediterranean to the Atlantic was the technological precociousness of Western European society during the Middle Ages. We have noted the advances in the primary occupation of agriculture, the application of water and wind power to numerous productive purposes and the progress in shipbuilding, navigation and naval ordnance. These technological achievements stimulated corresponding demographic and economic growth. The concurrent proletarianization of the peasantry created a displaced labor force available for trade and the crafts, thereby making possible the emergence of capitalism. This was an inherently expansionist social order that generated mass trade in necessities, and gradually developed an international market economy that enveloped entire continents.

Africa experienced none of this social dynamism that transformed the West. African peasants retained their communal plots and their traditional mode of cultivation. African crafts likewise were not revolutionized by mechanical inventions and new sources of power. This does not mean that there were no "manufactures" in Africa. Taking "manufactures" to mean, literally, "things made by hands," there were many African crafts that turned out an abundance of useful and artistic objects "made by hand."

The famous red "moroccan leather" was actually tanned and dyed by Hausa and Madinga artisans in northern Nigeria and Mali. In the kingdom of the Kongo the early Portuguese found local cloths made from bark and palm fiber that they reported to be as fine as velvet. Cotton cloths made on the Guinea coast were stronger than the Manchester imports. And the superb bronzework of Ife and Benin, produced to glorify chiefs and kings, held their own as artistic creations with the output of any other civilization.

All these objects, however, continued to be made by hand. There were no mechanical inventions comparable to those of Europe, and no nonhuman sources of energy apart from a few regions such as Ethiopia and the Nile Valley. The abundance of land and the communal social organization generated no social pressures or incentives for technological innovation to increase productivity. Also, the prevalence of the tsetse fly in large areas of Africa made survival of draught animals impossible, thereby preventing the use of the wheel for plowing and for transportation. Thus there was nothing comparable to the expansionist commercial capitalism of northwestern Europe. For that reason, it was the Europeans who journeyed to Africa, and not the Africans to Europe. And it was Europeans who utilized African human and natural resources to satisfy their needs, rather than the other way around.

It was in the year 1442, just half a century before Columbus' voyage across the Atlantic, that a young Portuguese captain ventured southward down the Atlantic as far as the southern tip of present-day Morocco. He returned with twelve slaves that he had captured in random raids along the coast. These he presented to Prince Henry, who promptly sent an embassy to the Pope divulging his plans for further raids and even greater conquests. His Holiness welcomed the new crusade and granted "to all of those who shall be engaged in the said war, complete forgiveness of all their sins." [6] The Portuguese responded wholeheartedly to this encouragement, especially when they discovered how lucrative the potential profits were. Thus began the traffic that, at an eventual cost of some fifty million human lives, was to provide the essential labor power for the emerging capitalist world order, and to make the African continent a peripheral, though not an integrated, component of that order.

The original objective of the Portuguese captains in setting sail down the African coast had been to tap the source of gold that had been shipped across the Sahara for centuries. The Portuguese had learned of this ancient trade from Muslim prisoners when they captured Ceuta, opposite Gibraltar, in 1415. Prince Henry therefore sent expeditions southward to divert the flow of gold northward from the old desert route to a new sea route that they would control. But before the Portuguese found any gold they discovered another fount of profit, in African slaves that they captured in raids along the coast. These slaves were in demand as domestic help, and also were needed as field hands in southern Spain and Portugal, which had recently been conquered from the Moors. Labor shortage also was acute in the Atlantic islands, and particularly Madeira, where the settlers were shifting from grain to sugar-cane production, which yielded greater profits but required more workers.

To meet this demand the Portuguese shifted from slave raiding to slave trading with African middlemen. The Portuguese sailed out with cargoes of textiles and horses, and returned with slaves, gold and malaquette pepper. As many as thirty-five hundred slaves were brought in per year, but that proved to be the upper limit. The slave market in Iberia was becoming satiated, and there was no appreciable demand in the rest of Europe. This slave trade thus proved to be essentially similar to, and an integral part of, that which had been conducted in the Mediterranean basin for centuries. It was a trade that always had been of modest proportions and that never had a racial character, as it included European slaves from the Adriatic and Black Sea coasts, Arab slaves from the Middle East as well as Negro slaves from Africa. In the sixteenth century, however, this traditional Mediterranean slave trade underwent a fateful quantitative and racial change when it became a transatlantic trade to meet the almost limitless needs of New World plantations.

The first African slaves arrived in the West Indies at least as early as 1501, only nine years after the initial voyage of Columbus. They had been shipped indirectly through Spain and the Atlantic islands, but by 1518 they were arriving directly from the Guinea coast. With the establishment of sugar plantations, first on the West Indian islands and then on the mainland, the profits from the slave trade soared along with the demand. The Spanish Crown sold *asientos*, or licenses, to buy slaves in Africa and sell them in America. By 1592 a certain Gomes Reynal was paying nearly a million ducats for an asiento authorizing the shipment of 4,250 slaves a year for nine years, or a total of 38,250 slaves. The fabulous profits attracted foreign adventurers such as John Hawkins of Plymouth, who used armed force to break into what was legally a Spanish monopoly. The West African coast became dotted with about forty European forts, which were used for defense against the rival trading nations and for storing slaves while awaiting shipment across the Atlantic. A few of the slaves came from East Africa, but the majority were taken from West Africa along a three-thousand-mile coastline between Senegal and Angola, and from a zone that extended inland several hundred miles, though it seldom included the coastal peoples themselves.

The cargoes for the African trade came from several sources. The East India Company provided cowries, amber, and a variety of cotton goods. Other commodities included Irish linens and tallow, German silesias, Swedish iron, Venetian beads, French brandy, Jamaican rum and Virginia tobacco. From England came worsteds, firearms, gunpowder, copper, brassware and liquor. In 1787, for example, about 36 percent of Liverpool exports to Africa consisted of foreign goods, of which two thirds were East Indian in origin.

Coastal African rulers welcomed the European slavers because of the economic opportunities they provided. The rulers rented land for the construction of the trading posts, which were fortified mainly against attack by other Europeans rather than by African landlords. In fact, the white slavers and their landlords were dependent on each other, and usually cooperated to their mutual benefit. The landlords protected their tenants and acted as middlemen in their trade, from which they excluded inland peoples, who consequently were required to pay commissions to the coastal middlemen. In the conduct of this trade, the Europeans advanced goods to trading agents who were subjects of the landlords. These subjects took the goods inland and returned eventually with slaves or other produce. If any agents defaulted, the landlords paid the debts and reimbursed themselves by selling the defaulters' families or neighbors.

The collaboration of white traders and black rulers prevailed along most of the West African coast. The coastal rulers were as determined and as successful in keeping out European intruders who might challenge their profitable role as middlemen in the slave trade as the Niger bend rulers had been in keeping out foreign intruders who might have threatened their equally profitable position as middlemen in the trans-Saharan trade. South of the equator, however, the Portuguese conquered Angola and indirectly controlled the Kongo Kingdom. Accordingly they themselves were able to go inland and provoke intertribal wars in order to get prisoners who were sold as slaves. About 40 percent of the total number of slaves landed in the New World came from Portuguese Angola and Kongo.

What the total number was that landed in the Americas has been a matter of dispute among historians. Philip Curtin estimated that

9,566,000 slaves were imported during the entire period of nearly four centuries. He concluded that "it is extremely unlikely that the ultimate total number of slaves imported will turn out to be less than 8,000,000 or more than 10,500,000. . . ." [7] Later research by Roger Anstey and J. E. Inikori [8] suggests that the estimate should be increased by about 20 percent, resulting in a total of nearly 12 million slaves. The horrors of the traffic were such that approximately four times as many were captured originally in the African interior as eventually arrived in the Americas. This amounts to a drain of 48 million, nearly all in the prime of their productivity.

The 36 million casualties were sustained in the course of the overland march from the interior to the coast, and then during the dreaded overseas "middle passage" to the New World. Inhuman crowding, stifling heat and poor food resulted in appalling mortality rates during the ocean crossing. Maize and water once every twenty-four hours was the standard diet. If the slaves refused to eat they were lashed and, if that failed, hot irons were used to force them to eat. When epidemics broke out, as they often did under the foul conditions, the sick slaves were drowned in order to prevent infection from spreading. Sometimes the slaves jumped overboard rather than endure the misery. Indeed, this became so common that nets were fixed all around the decks in order to prevent suicides. The following account by a slave of his experiences during the "middle passage" was typical:

> The first object which saluted my eyes when I arrived on the coast was the sea, and a slave ship, which was then riding at anchor, and waiting for its cargo. These filled me with astonishment, which was soon converted into terror, when I was carried on board I was immediately handled and tossed up to see if I was sound, by some of the crew; and I was now persuaded that I had gotten into a world of bad spirits, and that they were going to kill me. Their complexions too, differing so much from ours, their long hair, and the language they spoke (which was very different from any I had ever heard) united to confirm me in this belief. . . .
>
> I became so sick and low that I was not able to eat anything. . .
> I now wished for the last friend, death, to relieve me . . . but soon, to my grief some of the white men offered me eatables; and on my refusing to eat, one of them held me fast by the hands, and laid me across, I think, the windlass, and tied my feet while the other flogged me severely. I have never experienced anything of the kind before. . . .
>
> At last we came in sight of the island of Barbados . . . and we soon anchored . . . off Bridgetown. Many merchants and planters

now came on board. . . . They put us in separate parcels and examined us attentively. They also made us jump, and pointed to the land signifying we were to go there. We thought by this we should be eaten by those ugly men, as they appeared to us; and there was much dread and trembling among us and nothing but bitter cries to be heard all night from these apprehensions. . . .

At last the white people got some old slaves from the land to pacify us. They told us we were not to be eaten, but to work. . . .[9]

Numerous intellectual rationalizations were advanced in support of this trade, but it lasted for over four centuries simply because powerful vested interests refused to give up their profits. These interests included the plantation owners in the Americas, who had far-reaching economic and political influence. The planters in Barbados, for example, held an important bloc of seats in the British Parliament in the eighteenth century. Vested interests in Europe also championed the traffic in slaves, including the traders themselves and various merchants at home who provided the rum and the manufactured goods. A considerable number of distilleries provided the slave ships with rum; the woolen and cotton industries furnished the textiles that were given in exchange for slaves; the metallurgical industry provided chains, locks, bars and guns; and shipyards also were kept busy, since over two hundred English ships alone were engaged in the traffic at the end of the eighteenth century. Finally there were vested interests also in Africa, where the chiefs received as much as £20 or £30 for a single able-bodied slave. One of the chiefs, when told to stop his trade, said, "What! Can a cat stop catching mice? Will not a cat die with a mouse in its mouth? I will die with a slave in my mouth." [10] Indeed, African middlemen organized riots and demonstrations on African soil in protest against the abolitionist movement in Europe!

III. African Response to the Atlantic Slave Trade

The spectacle of Africans agitating for the continuation of the slave trade raises the question of why the African people tolerated this agony and indignity for four centuries. Not only did they tolerate it, but also some of them actively cooperated in making it possible at a time when Europeans lacked the power to carry it on by sheer force of arms alone. One explanation is that slavery flourished in Africa long before the appearance of the Europeans, and that the Africans therefore were accepting something familiar and approvable. This hypothesis is untenable.

Where slavery did exist in pre-European Africa, it varied tremendously from region to region in ways of recruitment, in the status and role of the slaves, and in the manner of manumission. Whatever the variations, there was a fundamental difference between the slavery of the American plantations that engendered the transatlantic slave trade, and the numerous types of slavery prevailing in pre-fifteenth-century Africa. The difference was due to the fact that the slave trade and slave institutions of the Europeans undergirded their intercontinental market economy. With expanding markets for sugar, cotton and tobacco offering the opportunity for boundless profit, slaves inevitably came to be regarded as merely one input into the production process. The sole concern, therefore, was to secure maximum profit regardless of human consequences. By contrast, traditional African slavery had been much less commercial in character because it had functioned in a local or regional milieu rather than in the context of the global market mechanism.

This difference in origins and dynamics was responsible for the corresponding difference in the natures of the old and new forms of slavery. There was, in the first place, a quantitative difference in numbers involved. Traditional slavery needed comparatively few hands because it lacked the commercial incentive to mobilize a huge labor force in order to meet the insatiable demands of the New World plantations and to realize the attendant profits.

Also, there was a qualitative difference in the treatment of slaves. In traditional Africa they were used as laborers, soldiers, traders, domestic workers, concubines and officials. Though definitely inferior in status, they usually were associated with families and had recognized individual rights. Marriage between slaves and free men or women was not prohibited, and by the third generation their descendants were considered equal members of their communities. On the American plantations, by contrast, slaves were viewed and treated as a cost item in the production process. The imperatives of the marketplace, as noted in the preceding chapter, determined the pattern of life on plantations, regardless of whether they were in Latin America or Anglo America. The mere darkness of skin now became presumptive of slave status, and manumission was difficult if not impossible. Whether slaves were worked to death in a few years or whether longevity was taken into account depended simply on which policy yielded more profit, given the prevailing market price of slaves.

We may conclude that the explanation for the centuries of transatlantic slave trade with its tens of millions of hapless victims is to be found in the imperatives of the new global market economy and in the superiority of Western military power as against a discordant agglomeration of coastal kingdoms and chieftancies. As early as 1526 the ruler of the Congo wrote to King John III of Portugal, "we need from [your] Kingdoms no other than priests and people to teach in schools, and no other goods but wine and flour for the holy sacrament . . . *it is our will that in these Kingdoms* [of Congo] *there should not be any trade in slaves nor market for slaves."* [11] The response of the Portuguese was to take half a million slaves out of the Congo during the first century after their arrival, and a full million out of neighboring Angola.

In the 1720s the Baga of present-day Guinea attempted under the leadership of a certain Tomba to organize an alliance against the slave trade, but they were eventually defeated by a coalition of resident English traders, mulattos and slave-trading Africans. In the same period the Dahomey ruler, Agaja Trudo, was more successful, expanding his inland kingdom to the coast precisely in order to drive away the slavers. He looted and burned European forts and slave camps, so that the number of slaves taken from that region dropped sharply during those years. The European traders failed in their efforts to unseat Trudo, but he in turn also failed to develop an alternative economic activity that would provide his people with the European imports that they had become dependent on by this time. By 1750 Trudo found it necessary to resume slave trading in order to obtain these goods, and also the firearms that were essential for survival in the coastal power struggles of the time. Thus Philip Curtin concludes, ". . . the availability of firearms set off a gun-slave cycle in which an African state used the arms to capture more slaves, to buy more arms, and so on—forcing African states to take up slave raiding in self-protection since guns could only be bought with slaves." [12]

This inescapable connection between slaves and guns forced the divided coastal rulers to accept the noxious traffic in their fellow countrymen regardless of their personal predilections. None of them was able individually to challenge this entrenched system, and the African people were not yet ready for the united resistance that alone could have prevailed against the combination of European and native vested interests.

IV. Slave Trade in East Africa

The nature and significance of the Atlantic slave trade becomes clearer if it is contrasted with the concurrent slave trade in East Africa. When da Gama rounded the Cape he found the eastern coast of the continent dotted with harbors filled with shipping and large towns boasting a Swahili written culture of considerable distinction.

This East African civilization was based on two elements: African and Arabic. The African consisted of Iron Age states in the interior, which smelted and forged iron, made iron tools for agriculture, mined copper and gold and built stone palaces and temples, the most famous being the great complex of structures at Zimbabwe. These interior states had contact with the coast from at least the tenth century, by which time Muslim Arab settlers had pushed southward down the coast from Malindi in Kenya to Sofala in Mozambique. The Arabs established several dozen settlements on this long stretch of coastline and on nearby islands such as Pemba and Zanzibar. From these bases they conducted a profitable trade across the Indian Ocean with the cities of the Red Sea, southern Arabia, the Persian Gulf, India, Ceylon, Southeast Asia and even China. The Arabs served as middlemen, exporting ivory, copper, gold and slaves from the interior, in return for Eastern articles such as fine textiles, jewelry and porcelain.

The crucial point is that slaves were only one item in this exchange, and by no means the most important, for the simple reason that there was no overwhelming demand for them in Eastern lands teeming with their own cheap labor. Slaves therefore were a minor factor in this transoceanic trade, as was the case also with the trans-Saharan trade in the pre-Portuguese era. Thus it was possible under these circumstances to realize in East Africa what Basil Davidson has termed "a genuine and fruitful marriage of cultures." [13] The Swahili language, for example, was largely Bantu in construction and vocabulary, but with substantial Arabic elements. This reflected the syncretic civilization that evolved it and that it helped to evolve. And today this firmly rooted language is still spreading and evolving with considerable borrowings from English.

The creative East African integration of cultures gave way to disintegration in the nineteenth century, and for the same reason that it had centuries earlier on the West Coast—namely, the rise of the slave trade to pre-eminent position because of its incorporation into the international market economy, with resulting opportunities for vast increases in volume and profits. For a variety of reasons this incorporation of East Africa did not begin until the 1840s. Prior to that date the Portuguese had ignored their East African colony, because of the silks, spices, gems and textiles of India and Southeast Asia, and the lucrative transit trade with the Far East. Also, their few attempts to ship slaves from East Africa to Brazil proved unproductive because the Cape route was too long and hazardous to compete with the comparatively short transatlantic passage from West Africa. Nor could there have been any significant slave traffic eastward across the Indian Ocean, otherwise the Portuguese would have participated in it, as they had done in the Atlantic slave trade. As late as 1753 there were only 4,399 African slaves in the whole of Portuguese India. The scanty opportunity for profit explains why during these early centuries the Portuguese never maintained more than one hundred civilians and military officials along their two-thousand-mile East African coastline.

By the 1840s these conditions began to change as East Africa gradually became integrated into worldwide trade. Shipments of slaves to the Americas were now beginning to be commercially feasible with the construction of faster ships and with the reduction of slave reserves on the West Coast. Captain Cook, who commanded a British warship on the East African coast in 1836–38, estimated that 15,600 slaves were exported annually to Brazil and Cuba from the two ports of Quelimane and Mozambique. This large-scale trade continued until the 1880s, when Cuba and Brazil decreed the abolition of slavery.

At the same time a profitable new market for East African slaves developed with the establishment of sugar, spice and rice plantations in certain regions along the coast and, more importantly, on the islands of Madagascar, Réunion, Mauritius, Seychelles and Zanzibar. So substantial did their output become that these islands became known as the West Indies of the Pacific. Like the original West Indies they needed large and continuous shipments of slaves to work the plantations, a need that was satisfied mostly by Arab slavers who operated from Zanzibar and from Muscat on the Arabian peninsula. As many as 40,000 slaves a year were shipped to Zanzibar in the 1840s and 1850s, some being retained for the local clove and rice plantations, and the rest re-exported to other islands and to India and Middle Eastern countries. The French island of Réunion was importing 24,000 slaves annually as early as the 1820s, while Madagascar imported 10,000 annually in the 1870s.

Whereas in West Africa north of the equator native slavers retained control of the land phase of the slave trade, in East Africa the Arab slavers conducted the actual rounding up of slaves in the northern part of the interior, while Portuguese adventurers and Portuguese half castes did the same in the southern half. The Arabs, who controlled the larger part of the East African slave trade, developed certain techniques for gaining the confidence and cooperation of the native tribespeople. The individual trader appeared in a village in the guise of a friend, and settled down with his followers. He arranged for a hut to be built more elaborate than the others of the village, and in it he spread ostentatiously a colorful Persian rug, on which he made his daily obsequies toward Mecca. His own dress—long white robe, turban, and curved jeweled dagger in his girdle—won the envy and deference of the natives. The goods he offered for trade—guns, powder, silks and beads—established him as a distinguished representative of the outside world. Most chiefs felt flattered that he had chosen to settle in their particular locality. The Swahili language, the *lingua franca* spreading ever farther inland, facilitated social and commercial exchange.

The chiefs often began to wear the long robe as the mark of a superior man, and Arab prefixes began to be added to native names and even to replace them. Some of the newcomer's goods were exchanged for ivory, and requests then would be made for the greatest prize, firearms and powder. For this the Arabs demanded slaves, and thus slave trading would get under way. Other chiefs soon were bringing in men, women and children for cloth, beads and the coveted arms. Within a few months enough slaves would be accumulated to send a caravan of them to the coast. The proceeds from their sale were used for fresh supplies of trade goods, which were transported inland for another cycle of slave trading. The Arab slaver soon became a dominant figure in his area. The tribe that he chose to support with arms was assured of victory over its neighbors, and in return he received a share of the captives, who became his slaves. Eventually he could operate independently, arming his own bands, which scoured the countryside for slaves without concern for individual chiefs or petty tribes.

Thus did the Arab slavers, and their Portuguese counterparts to the south, devastate large sections of the East African interior. "The Arab system," wrote an observer, "extended to great distances, and octupus-like grasped every small unprotected village community, making the whole country a vast battlefield wherein no one was safe outside the stockades." [14] Likewise Dr. David Livingstone, the famous missionary explorer, described in his *Narrative of an Expedition to the Zambezi and its Tributaries* (1865) the desolation caused by the slavers in the Nyasa region. He met "a long line of manacled men, women and children, with the black drivers armed with muskets, and bedecked with various articles of finery . . . some of them blowing exulting notes out of long tin horns. . . . From what we know and have seen, not one-fifth of the victims of the slave trade ever arrive at their destination and become slaves." [15]

Livingstone remonstrated with the African chiefs about selling their own people. Their responses reflected the same basic dilemma as that which immobilized the West African chiefs. The Arabs and Europeans both used their monopoly of firearms to set tribe against tribe, making the necessary united front impossible of realization. "If so and so gives up selling," replied the chiefs to Livingstone, "so will we. He is the greatest offender in the country. . . . It is the fault of the Arabs who tempt us with fine cloths, powder, and guns. . . . I would like to keep all my people to cultivate but my next neighbor allows his people to kidnap mine. . . . I must have ammunition to defend them." [16] This expressed precisely the so-called "gun-slave cycle" operating throughout Africa. Peoples with access to European slavers acquired guns, which gave them military advantage over the inland peoples, whom they raided for slaves, whom they exchanged for additional guns that further increased their advantage. Thus the Sangu rose to power in south-central Tanzania by getting guns from Arab traders and carrying out slave raids against all the peoples around them. In the same way the Yao expanded deeply into Malawi and Tanzania after 1860.

As damaging as the intertribal warfare was the corruption of some chiefs who distorted traditional legal procedures for their personal aggrandizement. In normal times there were very few crimes punishable by enslavement. Usually it sufficed to pay some sort of compensation to the aggrieved party. But the growing demand for slaves led many chiefs to exploit these customary practices in order to sell their own people as slaves. This was noted by explorer Richard Burton in 1860: "As detrimental to the public interests as the border wars is the intestine confusion caused by the slave trade. It perpetuates the vile belief in Uchawi, or black magic: when captives are in demand, the criminal's relations are sold into slavery. It affords a scope for the tyranny of a chief who, if powerful enough, will enrich himself by vending his subjects in wholesale and retail." [17]

The most recent and careful study of the East African slave trade concludes that at least two million slaves were exported during the nineteenth century to the Americas, to the Indian Ocean islands and to Middle Eastern countries. If Livingstone's estimate of 80 percent attrition is accepted, and bearing in mind that the population of East Africa was generally sparser than that of West Africa, and that the figure is for one century rather than for four, then the drain on East African society in the nineteenth century was comparable to that on the West African. The conclusion of Edward Alpers is unedifying:

> All that Africans received in exchange for ivory and slaves and the other raw materials of the continent were luxury items, inexpensive consumable goods, and Western means of destruction which were always inferior to those which Europeans maintained for their own use. . . . The historical roots of underdevelopment in East Central Africa must be sought in the system of international trade which was established by Arabs by the thirteenth century, seized and extended by the Portuguese in the sixteenth and seventeenth centuries, dominated by Indians in the eighteenth century, and finally commanded by a complex admixture of Indian, Arab and Western capitalisms in the nineteenth century.[18]

❧ V. Aftermath of the African Slave Trade

What was the balance sheet for Africa after four centuries of the slave trade? Edward Reynolds concludes that the "impact was not the same for all areas." Whereas for states like the Kongo and Angola the impact "was wholly destructive," for other states it was the opposite. "Oyo,

Dahomey and Asante which raided or purchased their slaves from the interior were able to transfer the burden and the destructive impact of the slave trade upon other people." [19]

Despite these regional differences, certain generalizations can be made for the continent as a whole. First there was a maleficent congealing effect on African political institutions and practices. Slave trading tended to make authoritarian societies stronger and loosely coordinated ones weaker. Kingdoms or chieftaincies that acted as middlemen organized themselves along more authoritarian lines in order to safeguard their profitable positions. The net effect was to freeze the status quo and obstruct the evolution of new and more effective political institutions and leaders. This was the result of the fact that the slave trade, as noted by Edward Reynolds, was "largely in the hands of the ruling class and the chiefs. It was they who were engaged in a partnership of exploitation with the Europeans: they made wars, sanctioned raids and, by their traditional legal authority, condemned people accused of certain crimes to slavery." [20]

The traffic in slaves also obstructed traditional interregional trade within Africa. The wars and devastation accompanying the seizure of slaves in the interior and their transportation to the coast served to disrupt old trade channels, while the Portuguese imposed their control over long-standing coastal trade routes. In fact, the Portuguese originally were attracted not only by the lure of gold, but also by the opportunity to take over control of the existing local trade networks. On the upper Guinea coast the Portuguese intervened as early as the 1470s in the transfers of raw cotton and indigo dye from one African community to another. Portuguese settlers established a flourishing cotton-growing and cotton-manufacturing industry on the Cape Verde Islands and exported the finished products along the entire coast down to Accra. The Portuguese also took over the trade in salt along the Angolan coast, the trade in high-quality palm cloth between northern and southern Angola, and the trade in cowries in the Congo and its offshore islands. In addition, the Portuguese stopped the old trading by canoe between the Ivory Coast and the Gold Coast by building an intervening fort at Axim. Its function was to sever the old trade route, thereby making the two regions separate economic entities and tied exclusively to Europe. All this was a typical beginning of the classic symptom of present-day Third World dependency and underdevelopedness: the elimination of local horizontal economic ties in favor of vertical economic ties with metropolitan centers.

The substitution of vertical for horizontal economic ties was evident in the crafts as well as in commerce. The Europeans naturally were not interested in promoting local African industries; more often they actively opposed any such development. They were chiefly interested in obtaining slaves during these early centuries, and then with the abolition of the slave trade they sought to encourage the production of raw materials for export but not of manufactures for local consumption. This deliberately fostered dependency pattern was evident as early as 1520, when the Ethiopian Court, impressed by the quality of Portuguese swords, muskets, textiles and books, asked for the technology needed to manufacture such articles. Their request was rejected, as were others that they made periodically to the nineteenth century.

Similar requests and refusals occurred more frequently on the western coast. When Agaja Trudo of Dahomey attempted in the 1720s to check the slave trade, he recognized the need for a substitute economic activity and sent an envoy to England to attract foreign craftsmen. A European visitor to the Dahomey Court in the late 1720s was informed that "if any tailor, carpenter, smith, or any other sort of white man that is free be willing to come here, he will find very good encouragement." [21] No foreigners responded to the invitation, which is scarcely surprising, since craftsmen were strictly forbidden at this time to immigrate with their skills to neighboring European countries or to the American colonies, let alone to remote and unfamiliar African kingdoms. In the mid-eighteenth century, the King of Ashante, Opoku Ware, likewise met with no response when he asked for European technicians to establish factories and distilleries. Similar rebuffs were experienced in the early nineteenth century when the ruler of Calabar in eastern Nigeria sought a sugar refinery, and King Adandozan of Dahomey asked for a firearms factory. African recognition of the significance of technology is reflected in the Dahomey saying, "He who makes the powder wins the war." But Europeans also were aware of the implications of technology transfer, and they acted accordingly.[22]

The slave trade also delayed the emergence of cash-crop agriculture in slave-trading areas, as nothing was allowed to distract energies from the main business of rounding up slaves. Thus the British Board of Trade in 1751 ordered the governor of Cape Castle to stop cotton cultivation among the Fante, and gave the following reason:

> The introduction of culture and industry among the Negroes is contrary to the known established policy of this country, there is no saying where this might stop, and that it might extend to tobacco, sugar and every other commodity which we now take from our colonies; and thereby the Africans, who now support themselves by wars, would become planters and their slaves be employed in the culture of these articles in Africa, which they are employed in Africa.[23]

On the positive side, it can be argued that the diffusion in Africa of food plants domesticated by the Amerindians was an important and beneficial by-product of the slave trade. Maize, peanuts, manioc and other plants did spread rapidly through Africa and became important food staples. The resulting increase in food supply, it is argued, should have supported at least as many people as were lost to the slavers. On the other hand, it should be noted that the slave trade was not essential for the diffusion of these plants. Peanuts and sweet potatoes spread rapidly in far-off China, for example, without the aid of that institution. Furthermore, the following table shows that between 1650 and 1850 the European percentage of the total world population rose from 18.3 to 22.7, an increase of 24 percent, while Africa's proportion during the same period fell from the same 18.3 percent to 8.1 percent, a decrease of 56 percent.

Estimated Population of the World

	1650	*1750*	*1850*	*1900*	*1950*
Millions					
Europe	100	140	266	401	593
United States and Canada	1	1	26	81	168
Latin America	12	11	33	63	163
Oceania	2	2	2	6	13
Africa	100	95	95	120	199
Asia	330	479	749	937	1,379
TOTAL	545	728	1,171	1,608	2,515
Percentages					
Europe	18.3	19.2	22.7	24.9	24.0
United States and Canada	.2	.1	2.3	5.1	6.7
Latin America	2.2	1.5	2.8	3.9	6.5
Oceania	.4	.3	.2	.4	.5
Africa	18.3	13.1	8.1	7.4	7.9
Asia	60.6	65.8	63.9	58.3	55.4
TOTAL	100.0	100.0	100.0	100.0	100.0

Sources: Adapted from A. M. Carr-Saunders, *World Population* (Oxford: Clarendon Press, 1956), p. 42; and *United Nations Demographic Yearbook* (1957), p. 123.

❦ VI. Africa a Peripheral Area

So far as Third World history is concerned, the crucial question is whether the slave trade made Africa an integral component of the international market economy, as Eastern Europe and the Americas had become, or whether Africa remained outside, as Russia had succeeded in doing. On first thought it would appear that the continent of Africa had been effectively integrated. The slave trade had profoundly affected African demography, economics and politics. Also it had provided the basic undergirding for the world capitalist order of the period. It had furnished the labor force for the East African islands and, more important, for the American plantations, thereby making possible the lucrative triangle trade that brought Western Europe, Africa and the Americas together into the basic economic bloc of early modern times. Thus the African slave trade was a more important force in the international market economy of those centuries than the East European trade in foodstuffs and raw materials. An eighteenth-century English economic writer who was well informed on Africa observed, "British trade is a magnificent superstructure of American commerce and naval power on an African foundation." [24]

Yet it does not appear that the African continent as a whole was integrated into the international market economy as Eastern Europe and the Americas had been. In the first place, the largest part of the continent remained unaffected, since the slavers normally operated only several hundred miles inland, and by no means all around the continent. Even the regions that were involved were not basically affected because the slave trade was essentially a "rich" trade that did not impinge on the masses. The goods received in return for the slaves consisted of firearms, textiles, alcoholic beverages and assorted "baubles, bangles and beads." Such commodities reached only the native chiefs and merchants and their retinues. The overwhelming majority of the African people had no connections with the slave trade, either as producers or as consumers, unless, of course, they happened to be one of the minority who were unfortunate enough to be captured and sold. Within Africa itself, the inhabitants had not been reduced to serfdom as had been the East European peasantry, nor had they been exterminated or swept aside, as had happened to the Indians of the Americas.

All this is not to minimize the horrors and devastations of the slave trade, but rather to note that the African lands and peoples remained on the periphery of the international market system because the slave trade was not a mass trade in necessities that impinged on daily lives and occupations. Such an elemental impact had to wait for the nineteenth century, when the Industrial Revolution and the abolition of the slave trade together opened up the continent for exploitation in depth. Until that time, Africa functioned as a peripheral area in the international economy. Africa's position was halfway between the integrated status of Eastern Europe and the Americas on the one extreme, and the independent, external status of Russia and Asia on the other.

Chapter 6

MIDDLE EAST
A PERIPHERAL AREA

He who would behold these times in their greatest glory, could not find a better scene than in Turkey.

T. BLOUNT, 1634
(English traveler)

The Ottoman Empire is one of the richest colonies of France.

CHOISEUL-GOUFFIER, 1788
(French ambassador in Constantinople)

Whereas the continent of Africa in the pre-nineteenth-century period became a peripheral area in relation to the global market economy, the continent of Asia was able to remain entirely outside and unaffected. The great empires of India and China, the kingdoms of Korea and Japan, and the mainland sections of Southeast Asia all were unmindful of, and impervious to, the ubiquitous Westerners.

There was one exception, however, to this general pattern of Asian apartness, and that was the Middle East, comprising the territories located at the juncture of Europe, Asia and Africa. During the pre-nineteenth-century era, most of the Middle East was encompassed within the frontiers of the sprawling Ottoman Empire. At the outset this empire was self-sufficient, self-confident and aggressive, its formidable Janissary Corps being the scourge of Christian Europe, and its impressive administration the envy of Western visitors. But after the late sixteenth century the Ottoman Empire declined precipitously in efficiency and strength.

Superior Western armies overran outlying provinces of the empire, while equally superior Western trading firms—the so-called Levant companies —won considerable economic control over the remaining provinces of the empire. The once-feared Ottoman colossus became a subordinate peripheral area in its political and economic relations with the European world order. The Middle East came to occupy the same halfway position as did Africa—a position between the completely integrated and dependent regions of Eastern Europe and Latin America on the one hand, and the completely external and independent land mass of Asia on the other.

♞ I. *"Furnished with All God's Gifts . . ."*

Sultan Suleiman the Magnificent gave this expression to his imperial powers in an inscription on the citadel of Bender in 1538:

> I am God's slave and sultan of this world. By the grace of God I am head of Muhammad's community. God's might and Muhammad's miracles are my companions. I am Suleiman, in whose name the *hutbe* is read in Mecca and Medina. In Baghdad I am the shah, in Byzantine realms the Caesar, and in Egypt the sultan; who sends his fleets to the seas of Europe, the Maghrib and India. I am the sultan who took the crown and throne of Hungary and granted them to a humble slave. The voivoda Petru raised his head in revolt, but my horse's hoofs ground him into the dust, and I conquered the land of Moldavia.[1]

The objective facts of Suleiman's imperial status matched this grandiloquent rhetoric. His Ottoman Empire encompassed vast territories stretching from Algeria to the Caucasus and from Hungary to the southern tip of the Arabian peninsula. In these lands lived peoples of diverse strains and creeds, totaling approximately fifty million compared to the five million in contemporary England.

Western travelers in the Ottoman Empire in the sixteenth and seventeenth centuries invariably were impressed by the efficiency of its administration, consisting of former Christians who were carefully selected and trained for their government posts. Although nominally "slaves" of the Sultan, they manned the entire imperial bureaucracy, including the office of the grand vizir, which was second only to that of the Sultan. Appointment and advancement depended largely on merit, a striking contrast to prevailing practices in Christian Europe, as the Hapsburg ambassador in Constantinople reported in the mid-sixteenth century.

> In making his appointments the Sultan pays no regard to any pretensions on the score of wealth or rank . . . he considers each case

on its own merits, and examines carefully into the character, ability, and disposition of the man whose promotion is in question. It is by merit that men rise in the service, a system which ensures that posts should only be assigned to the competent. . . . Among the Turks, therefore, honours, high posts, and judgeships are the rewards of great ability and good service. If a man be dishonest, or lazy, or careless, he remains at the bottom of the ladder, an object of contempt. . . . These are not our ideas, with us there is no opening left for merit; birth is the standard for everything; the prestige of birth is the sole key to advancement in the public service.[2]

Contemporary observers of the Ottoman Empire also reported favorably concerning the position of the peasants who comprised the vast majority of the population. Indeed, Balkan Christian peasants under Ottoman rule were better off than Christian peasants across the Danube in Hungarian or German lands. Preference for the Turks was manifested repeatedly during wars when Christian peasants sided with the Turks against their own rulers and nobles, and also when a considerable number of Christian peasants crossed the Danube to the Turkish side of the river, especially after the series of peasant revolts in central Europe in the first half of the sixteenth century.

The basic reason for such opting in favor of Turkish rule was that peasants were better off under the Ottoman land tenure system than that prevailing in Christian countries. When the Turks conquered their empire in the fifteenth and sixteenth centuries, they parceled out the fertile areas as fiefs or *timars*, which they distributed among their most deserving warriors and senior officials. These timar holders, or *spahis*, were strictly controlled from Constantinople, their obligations being carefully defined, as were the rights and privileges of the Christian peasants, or *rayas*. The latter enjoyed hereditary use of their land and could not be evicted unless they failed to till it for three years. Their obligations, consisting of tithes to the spahi, taxes to the state, and limited *corvée* duty, were generally lighter than those borne by the peasantry of Christian Europe. Furthermore, the peasants were protected against extortion by imperial laws or *kanuns*, which specified the taxes and services that could be exacted in each district.

The economic health of the empire at its height also was impressive, thanks to its natural riches and the enlightened policies of the early sultans. Their objective was imperial self-sufficiency, especially because of the economic stranglehold that Venice and Genoa had exercised in the eastern Mediterranean in the declining years of the preceding Byzantine Empire. The sultans took various measures to make Constantinople the center for intercontinental trade among Asia, Europe and Africa. Their measures were largely successful, and both merchants and artisans prospered, especially because they were now operating in a huge empire with correspondingly extensive resources and markets. Cities increased dramatically in size, while foreigners were excluded from operations they formerly had dominated, such as the profitable Black Sea trade.

The empire was largely self-contained, with the fertile plains of Hungary, Romania, Asia Minor and Egypt producing abundant foodstuffs and raw materials, while the skilled artisans of Constantinople, Saloniki, Damascus, Baghdad, Cairo and other ancient cities turned out a multitude of handicraft products. Apart from the considerable transit trade promoted by the empire's strategic position, imports were limited mostly to luxury goods such as European woolens, Indian textiles and spices, Russian furs and Persian silk.

It is scarcely surprising that contemporary Westerners looked upon this ever-expanding Ottoman Empire with awe and fear—"a daily increasing flame, catching hold of whatsoever comes next, still to proceed further." [3] In 1525 the Venetian representative in Constantinople, Piero Bragadin, wrote home: "I know of no State which is happier than this one; it is furnished with all God's gifts. It controls war and peace with all, it is rich in gold, in people, in ships and in obedience; no State can be compared with it. May God long preserve the most just of all Emperors. . . ." [4]

℞ II. "The Old Order and Harmony Departed . . ."

Before the end of the century in which this enthusiastic eulogy was written, the magnificent Ottoman imperial structure was shaken to its foundations and its collapse appeared imminent. Many prophesied that doomsday would fall on the thousandth anniversary of the Hegira, or the Christian year 1622. A contemporary historian, Selaniki, bemoaned that Christian subjects no longer were submissive and that people in the provinces were fleeing to Istanbul because of the tyranny and injustice. With "the old order and harmony departed," warned Selaniki, "catastrophe will surely follow." [5]

Foreign observers were equally pessimistic about the future of the empire. In 1626, 101 years after Bragadin's tribute to Ottoman power and justice, the Dutch vice consul in Aleppo reported to the Court of Directors of the East India Company in Amsterdam, "It has reached such a pitch here that every person does what he likes, especially the powerful, and that is what accounts for the state of the realm. It is not just one pillar that is broken or weakened, but all four pillars of State: religion, justice, politics and finances . . . one must ask oneself whether it can continue thus." [6]

This startling reversal of imperial fortunes was in part the result of internal weaknesses, but more basically it was the impact of expanding Western capitalism, to which the adjacent Ottoman Empire with its relatively static economy was exceptionally vulnerable. One cause for Ottoman vulnerability to Western pressures was the failure of the empire to achieve political integration comparable to that of Western Europe with its nationalism and nation-states. The growth of absolutist monarchies, the appearance of a middle class desiring unity and order, the spread of literacy and the development of new techniques for mass propaganda and indoctrination—all these contributed to the emergence in the West of highly integrated state structures with unprecedented affinity between rulers and ruled. The Ottoman Empire, by contrast, was loosely organized along theocratic lines. Its diverse peoples were recognized on the basis of their religious affiliation (Muslim, Orthodox, Catholic and Jewish) rather than of their ethnic composition (Turks, Arabs, Kurds, Albanians, Armenians, Romanians, Greeks and Slavs).

This primacy of religious affiliation meant that there was no single unifying sense of allegiance within the empire. The average Ottoman subject thought of himself primarily as a member of a guild if he lived in a city, or as a member of a village community if he lived in the countryside. If he had any feeling of broader allegiance it was likely to be directed to the head of his religious community rather than to the person of the Sultan. The Ottoman Empire therefore remained a ramshackle congeries of numerous disparate groups that were to a large degree self-centered and self-sufficient. This looseness of organization weakened the resistance of the empire to foreign aggression, both ideological and political. The absence of a common Ottoman nationalism left an ideological vacuum that was filled by the several Balkan and Arab nationalisms that drew inspiration from the victories of other nationalisms in the West. Furthermore, the European powers were able to annex entire provinces of the Ottoman Empire not only because of superior military strength but also because the populations of those provinces felt no particular attachment to Constantinople. Hence the successive amputations of the trans-Danubian lands, of the entire Balkan Peninsula and of all the provinces in North Africa.

The Ottoman Empire lagged behind the West in scientific progress as well as in political cohesion. By the fifteenth and sixteenth centuries, when the Turks were building their empire, Islam had degenerated to the point where it meant little more than a series of rituals to be performed and a Heaven-sent book to be memorized. Consequently the

Ottoman *medressehs,* or colleges, from the outset emphasized theology, jurisprudence and rhetoric at the expense of astronomy, mathematics and medicine. During the reign of Suleiman the Magnificent (1520–66), when the empire was at its height, there was an almost abnormal interest in literature but very little in the sciences. The Turks knew nothing of the epoch-making achievements of Paracelsus in medicine, Vesalius in anatomy and Copernicus, Kepler and Galileo in astronomy. Their ignorance extended to geography, with often embarrassing consequences. A Russian expedition in 1770 sailed from the Baltic around Europe into the Mediterranean, where it demolished an Ottoman fleet off the coast of Asia Minor. The Turks assumed that a waterway existed between the Baltic and Adriatic seas, and protested strongly to the Venetians for allowing the Russians to sail through and to enter the Mediterranean.

Ottoman retardation in science led inevitably to a corresponding retardation in technology and productivity. The Middle East fell behind, particularly in the development and utilization of nonhuman sources of energy. One example is the more efficient use of horsepower by the invention of a new harness that did not choke the horse when it pulled a load. By resting on the horse's shoulders rather than the neck, the improved harness increased severalfold the amount of available horsepower. This was an early medieval European invention or adaptation that was completely ignored in the Middle East. Likewise windmills and watermills, although known in the Middle East, were never constructed as efficiently or in as large numbers as in the medieval and early modern West. In metallurgy, also, the Middle East fell behind during those centuries, as well as in shipbuilding, naval armaments and the techniques of navigation. The end result of this technological disparity was the shift of the economic center of Europe from the eastern Mediterranean to central and northern Europe.

Scientific and technological backwardness had military repercussions. The core of the Ottoman armed forces was the territorial feudal cavalry, or spahis, who showed up with a number of retainers depending on the size of their fiefs. They were armed with the traditional medieval weapons—bow and arrow, sword and shield—and resisted the use of firearms as unbecoming to their sense of chivalry. The infantry Janissary Corps was developed and expanded in the fifteenth century largely in order to make use of the new firearms, which the feudal cavalry were unwilling to accept. In 1548, for example, Suleiman persuaded two hundred of the regular cavalry to use carbines and pistols, but they were so mocked by their companions and so averse to the new weapons that the experiment failed. Not until the end of the century was the Turkish cavalry generally equipped with small arms, falling far behind the Hapsburg and Russian armies across the frontiers. The lag in artillery was greater, for the Turks had to depend in large part on Western mercenaries for the forging and manning of the guns. Likewise the Ottoman navy lagged in the transition from galleys to sailships, even though an English observer noted in 1607 that one Western warship could defeat ten Turkish galleys. Being a land people with no naval traditions, the Turks depended on Italian naval architects to design their ships, Greek shipyard workers to build them and heterogeneous and usually unreliable Christian crews to man them.

The above weaknesses of the Ottoman Empire were responsible for its military defeats and internal disorders of the seventeenth and eighteenth centuries. Intelligent men were forced to admit that all was not well, and that change of some sort was needed. They specifically advocated the need for reform in a long series of works known collectively as the Nasibat literature. This literature consisted of books of "good counsels for rulers." But the counsels they embodied invariably were based on the assumption that the root of the troubles was the abandonment of old and proven values and institutions. The way out for all these writers was to go back to the glorious days of Suleiman the Magnificent. All were oblivious to the fact that Ottoman decline was relative to the new capabilities and techniques of Western Europe. The basic problem was not internal but external. It was not peculiar to the Ottoman Empire but was to afflict, sooner or later, all non-Western civilizations, including the great and ancient civilizations of Asia.

The problem for them all was not departure from the old ways but adherence to them, at a time when adherence meant fatal weakness as against an expanding Western civilization powered by scientific, technological and political revolutions. This explains why all non-Western civilizations, no matter how venerable and illustrious, experienced stagnation, decline and eventual extinction—the conquest of India in the nineteenth century, the end of the Manchu Dynasty in 1912 and the end of the Ottoman dynasty in 1922. Only the Japanese escaped this fate, because unlike the Nasibat writers and the Chinese literati, they did not look back to the good old days of Suleiman or Confucius. Instead they looked forward, realizing that the West could be resisted only by adopting or adapting at least some of its techniques and institutions.

❧ III. Perils of Proximity

What happened to the Ottoman Empire from the seventeenth century onward was the global norm, and represented the inevitable repercussion of that fateful global exception—the rise and expansion of modern capitalist Western civilization. The only peculiar or distinctive feature of the Ottoman experience was its timing. It was the first of the

Asian civilizations to face the problem of "decline" relative to the West because it was adjacent to the West, and therefore most vulnerable to its expansionism, whether intellectual, political, economic or military. This explains in part why two centuries were to elapse before distant China and Japan were to feel the intrusions and disruptions that the Ottoman Empire did in the seventeenth century.

Most obvious and dramatic was the military intrusion of the West. Hapsburg and Russian armies were on the other side of the Ottoman frontiers, while Venetian, Russian, British and French navies had access to all ports of the Ottoman Empire via the Mediterranean, Adriatic, Aegean, Black and Red seas. Hence the wholesale annexation in the seventeenth and eighteenth centuries of the trans-Danubian provinces by the Hapsburgs and of the Black Sea lands by the Russians, and in the nineteenth century of the North African provinces by the Western powers. Hence also the successive naval defeats inflicted upon the Turks—for example, by a combined Christian fleet at Lepanto (1571), by a Russian fleet at Chesmé (1770) and by a British fleet at Navarino (1827).

Ideological intrusion across Ottoman frontiers was as difficult to block as the military. This was especially so because ethnic groups often sprawled across both sides of the Ottoman frontiers—Romanians, Serbians and Croatians on both the Hapsburg and Turkish sides, and Romanians, Kurds and Armenians on both the Russian and Turkish. Likewise numerous Greeks and Bulgarians established trading communities in Odessa, Naples, Trieste, Venice, Budapest, Vienna and other European cities. Under these circumstances, revolutionary nationalist ideology imbibed in European countries inevitably permeated through the Ottoman Empire, arousing the Christian peoples of the Balkans, and eventually the Muslim Arabs and even the Turks themselves. In a ramshackle multinational empire the various nationalisms functioned like time bombs that demolished successive segments of the Ottoman imperial structure as the diverse ethnic groups became infected by the nationalist virus from abroad. Foreign powers, needless to say, did not hesitate to use these time bombs to further their interests. Napoleon, for example, expressly ordered General Gentili in 1797 to exploit Greek nationalist sentiments in order to facilitate the conquest of the Ionian Islands. "If the inhabitants are inclined to independence, let's foster their tendency, and do not hesitate to speak about Greece, Athens, and Sparta." [7]

Territorial proximity also facilitated Western political pressures on the Ottoman Empire. The classic example of this was the system of commercial arrangements known as the capitulations. After the Turks captured Constantinople in 1453 they signed these commercial treaties with the Christian states in order to stimulate trade. At that time the

Ottoman leaders considered it advantageous to encourage the import of manufactured goods in order to create abundance in the home market and to benefit their treasury with increased revenue. Accordingly import duties were limited to 3 to 5 percent, which made the Ottoman Empire a lucrative market for Western manufactures. The flow of imports did not upset the Ottoman economy unduly at first, as the imported goods were limited to a few items such as woolens, minerals and paper. But as Western industries grew stronger, and as the Ottoman Empire became less capable of resisting foreign pressures, the capitulatory system was grossly distorted and abused in order to impose Western control over Ottoman foreign trade and to destroy Ottoman native industries.

Four features of this trading system were especially onerous for the Ottoman Empire. One was the privilege granted to foreign merchants resident in the empire to be tried in their own consular courts according to the law codes of their own countries. Also, no foreigner could be arrested or held by Turkish police unless an official from his consulate was present. These restrictions persuaded Ottoman officials to ignore most misdemeanors by foreigners in order to avoid confrontations with foreign powers. Some unscrupulous Western merchants took advantage of this situation to carry on shady operations that would not have been tolerated in their home countries.

The capitulatory treaties also exempted foreigners from internal levies or taxes, so that they were able to conduct local business at less expense than could the native citizens themselves. Another inhibiting feature of the capitulations was their 3 to 6 percent limit on import and export duties. This prevented the Ottoman government from setting protective tariffs for native industries, which were progressively decimated as Western industrial techniques improved.

The final abuse of the capitulatory system was its extralegal extension to encompass hundreds of thousands of Ottoman nationals, who thereby enjoyed all the special privileges and benefits of foreigners. This was arranged with a document called a *barat*, which any foreign consul could grant, for a consideration, to any Ottoman citizen, who thereupon acquired all the capitulatory rights of a national of the consul's country. Unscrupulous consuls even sold citizenship papers and passports, usually to Greeks, Jews and Armenians, who conducted most of the empire's domestic trade, since the ruling Turks deemed any business enterprise to be demeaning. In 1808 no less than 180,000 Greeks within the Ottoman Empire were holding Russian barats. Thus the combination of the exploitive capitulatory system and the hundreds of thousands of barat-holding "protected persons" left the Ottoman economy, for all practical purposes, in the control of foreign merchants and consuls and their local protégés. The significance of this foreign control is evident in the fact that one of the main reasons for Japan's unique success in achieving independent economic development was her freedom from any outside economic influence or domination, both before and after the opening of the country in the mid-nineteenth century.

~ *IV. Shifting Trade Routes*

The Ottoman Empire was particularly vulnerable to the West's expanding economy not only because of geographic proximity but also because of the empire's unique dependence on transit trade, which was shifting to new channels in early modern times. The entire Middle East traditionally had profited by serving as the funnel through which flowed the ancient trade between Asia and Europe, both overland across central Asia, and overseas through the Mediterranean, the Red Sea or the Persian Gulf, the Indian Ocean and the Strait of Malacca to the China seas. The exchange of goods provided government revenues in the form of customs duties, and also a source of livelihood for thousands of merchants, clerks, sailors, shipbuilders, camel drivers, stevedores and all the rest who were directly or indirectly connected with the trade.

The dependence on long-range interregional trade was precarious because it could be shut off or deflected by distant political and military upheavals that could not be controlled. Thus the rise of the great Mongol Empire in the thirteenth century greatly enhanced overland trade by providing security across the vast expanse of Eurasian steppes. But conversely, the rapid disintegration of this empire in the fourteenth century blocked the overland routes and damaged the economies of Persia and Asia Minor through which these routes had crossed. The overseas transit trade continued, however, to the profit of Egypt and Syria, since several loadings and unloadings were necessary to traverse those land barriers separating Alexandria from the Red Sea, and the Syrian ports from the Persian Gulf.

This commerce by sea also was imperiled, however, when Vasco da Gama rounded the Cape and sailed into Calicut Harbor, India, on May 22, 1498. The Cape route was longer but cheaper than the old routes through the Middle East. The Cape route avoided the cost of the several loadings and unloadings, of the customs duties at various points along the way, and of the extortions exacted by Bedouin marauders. This combination of high transportation costs, customs dues and extortion had raised the price of spices in Alexandria to more than 2,000 percent above their original cost in India. And there still remained the Italian merchants to levy their far-from-modest charges for transporting the spices from the Levant ports to the consumers in central or northern Europe. It is not surprising, then, to find that in the four years 1502–5, the

Venetians were able to obtain an average of only 1 million English pounds of spices a year at Alexandria, whereas in the last years of the fifteenth century they had averaged 3.5 million pounds. Conversely, Portuguese imports rose from 224,000 pounds in 1501 to an average of 2.3 million pounds in the four years of 1503–6.

The diversion of trade to the new Cape route injured the economies of Syria and Egypt. Sultan Suleiman responded by sending several naval expeditions to the Indian Ocean in an effort to drive out the Portuguese interlopers and restore the trade to the old channels. The Venetians surreptitiously aided in the preparation of these expeditions, since Italian middlemen were hurt as much as Arabs by the shift of commerce from the old Red Sea-Mediterranean route to the new Cape waterway. But Ottoman fleets, even with Venetian support, were no match for the Portuguese, tested on the long voyage around Africa and armed with superior naval artillery.

The failure of Suleiman's expeditions had far-reaching repercussions for the entire Middle East. It marked the beginning of the end of Levantine predominance in world commerce. The stress should be on the word "beginning." The old routes did not dry up overnight. After the first shock of the Portuguese intrusion a gradual recovery occurred. There were even years when the volume of trade through Middle Eastern ports surpassed that which rounded the Cape. In fact, it can be said that throughout the sixteenth century both routes were used, with now the one prevailing and now the other. The survival of the old channels is surprising in view of the natural advantages of the all-water route. For reasons that will be considered in the following chapter, it was not until the more efficient Dutchmen in the seventeenth century had displaced the Portuguese in the Indian Ocean and the East Indies that the balance swung decisively in favor of the Cape route. Once that shift was consolidated, the Middle East became an obscure backwater rather than the center of global trade that it had been before da Gama, and that it was to become again after the opening of the Suez Canal.

V. Levant Companies

As disruptive as the change of trade routes was the appearance of the Levant companies. It was not the Ottoman merchants who organized large joint stock companies for trade with Western Europe, but rather it was the French, English and Dutch who organized their respective Levant companies and exploited the resources of the Ottoman Empire. The first were the French, who negotiated a treaty in 1535 permitting them to reside and trade in the Ottoman Empire without being subject to Ottoman taxation or to the jurisdiction of Ottoman courts. These special privileges, or capitulations, were extended in 1583 to the English and the Dutch. As a result, Western merchants from the sixteenth century onward obtained an increasingly large proportion of the eastern Mediterranean trade formerly monopolized by the Italians.

One reason for the success of the Westerners was the effectiveness of their joint stock companies as instruments for economic mobilization and penetration. By limiting the responsibility of investors and separating the functions of investing and of management, they made possible the mobilization of large amounts of capital for commercial ventures in specific regions such as the Levant or Africa or the East Indies. Ottoman merchants, by contrast, did not organize such companies, preferring to trade as individuals or in private partnership. This was due partly to their conservatism and individualism, and partly to the tendency of Ottoman officials, during the centuries of imperial decline and corruption, to regard any overly rich subject as fair game for extortion and confiscation. In any case the Ottoman merchants, who were almost invariably Armenians, Jews and Greeks, were not organized to compete effectively with the Western companies, which soon got control of most of the large-scale foreign trade, leaving the petty local trade to the Ottoman nationals. And even the local trade was influenced substantially by Western consuls who, as we have seen, issued their barats on a wholesale scale to local merchants, who thereupon came under their jurisdiction.

The commercial predominance of the Levant companies also was based on the technological superiority of their home industries. There was no counterpart in the Middle East (or anywhere else, for that matter) to the rapidly developing Western industries using constantly improved machinery and inanimate power sources. Ottoman industry remained at the handicraft stage in technology and at the guild stage in organization. Ottoman officials supported the traditional guild structure, fearing that innovations would produce disorder and deprive the treasury of revenue. Also, Ottoman administrative and military officials preferred to deal with the old guilds in order to ensure stability in the price and quality of goods. Thus whereas guilds played a minor role in the Western economy by the late seventeenth century, in the Ottoman Empire they continued to dominate both industry and commerce. The native craftsmen and merchants worked and trafficked in little shops built along narrow and crooked streets, and sometimes roofed over, street and all, to form the low, rambling buildings known as bazaars. These were picturesque, but with their rigidly controlled and static methods of production and operation, they were scarcely a match for the rapidly changing and expanding industries and trading firms of the West. The inevitable outcome is depicted in the following observations of an English traveler in Constantinople in 1800:

> Suppose a stranger to arrive from a long journey, in want of clothes for his body; furniture for his lodgings; books or maps for his instruction and amusement; paper, pens, ink, cutlery, shoes, hats; in short those articles which are found in almost every city of the world; he will find few or none of them in Constantinople; except of a quality so inferior as to render them incapable of answering any purpose for which they were intended. The few commodities exposed for sale are either exports from England, unfit for any other market, or, which is worse, German and Dutch imitations of English manufacture. . . . Let a foreigner visit the bazaars . . . he will see nothing but slippers, clumsy boots of bad leather, coarse muslins, pipes, tobacco, coffee, cooks' shops, drugs, flower-roots, second-hand pistols, poignards, and the worst manufactured wares in the world. . . . View the exterior of Constantinople and it seems the most opulent and flourishing city in Europe; examine its interior, and its miseries and deficiencies are so striking that it must be considered the meanest and poorest metropolis of the world.[8]

The impact of the Levant companies was accentuated by the flood of New World bullion, which caused sharp price increases in Western Europe in the mid-sixteenth century. By the 1580s the Ottoman economy also was experiencing inflation—another example of the cost of proximity to the West. The Levant companies were paying for the foodstuffs and raw materials they were obtaining from the Ottoman lands in part with bullion, so that in 1584 it was reported that "one of the main items of trade going to Turkey are Spanish reals sent by the chestful." [9] Other European silver coins also inundated the Ottoman market, causing severe inflation. It is significant that between 1550 and 1600 the price of wheat rose approximately five times in the Ankara region of central Anatolia as against ten times in the Aegean coastal area, where Western merchants bought their cargoes. Similar price trends occurred with other commodities that were being shipped to the West.

The bullion did not remain in the Sultan's domains. Instead, it was exchanged for the spices and the fine fabrics that were brought in across the eastern borders. Thus the Ottoman Empire, like Spain, found itself in an unenviable position in international trade. It had become merely a funnel through which the bullion from the West flowed on to the Middle and Far East. The imperial government was slow to take action, lacking as it did the experience and mercantilist traditions of the West.

When the capital and the army found it increasingly difficult to obtain food supplies, the government in the late sixteenth century banned the export of bullion to the East, and of various materials to the West, including cotton, cotton thread, lead, gunpowder, horses and certain foodstuffs. But Ottoman officials were even more lax in enforcing such restrictions than their Spanish counterparts. So bullion continued to drain out of the Ottoman Empire, as it did out of the Spanish, while Western captains loaded legal or illegal cargoes as easily in the Levant ports as they did in the Spanish colonies. Despite all its efforts, the Ottoman government found it difficult to arrange for adequate supplies for its industries, its armed forces and its urban consumers.

The impact of New World bullion and of Western manufactured goods represented, in the words of a modern Turkish historian, the intrusion of "high pressure Atlantic economy" into the "low tension Ottoman economy." [10] This intrusion set off an uncontrollable chain reaction that disrupted not only the Ottoman economy, but also almost every other branch of Ottoman society.

In the first place, the growing military strength of the European powers blocked further Ottoman expansion into central Europe. Until the mid-seventeenth century, Turkish conquests had provided the imperial treasury with booty and revenue from newly acquired provinces and also had furnished additional fiefs for the feudal cavalry. But by the end of the century the expansion had been checked and the rollback had started, pushing the Ottoman frontiers back to the Danube River by the Treaty of Carlovitz (1699). Furthermore, the Turks had to keep up, however reluctantly, with developing Western military technology. They were forced to adopt new firearms and to organize centralized and permanent armed forces in place of the old self-supporting spahi cavalry. This required heavy expenditures at a time when inflation had impoverished the imperial treasury.

Equally impoverished were the spahi, whose real income from the customary timar dues had declined drastically with the inflation. "It is deemed true," reported a Venetian representative in 1586, "that it is impossible for a soldier, even though he may take up money on the security of his fief for many years into the future, to procure all the equipment he needs for this campaign." [11] The understandable response of the spahi was to evade their obligations to the central government and to usurp the land they had held as fiefs with specified duties and constraints.

The Constantinople government countered this trend by replacing the spahi, who no longer were useful as a military force, with tax farmers. The latter were town notables, or *ayan,* who had political connections and ready cash, and who found tax farming a lucrative investment in a time of inflation. Tax farms (*iltizam*) ultimately became indistinguishable from private property (*mulk*), so that the ayan (or *derebey*, as they were known in some regions) interposed themselves between the government and the peasantry, appropriating much of the revenue they extracted from the peasants as their private income.

The spahis fought back against the expropriators of their fiefs, often with the support of the peasants, who had lost their hereditary rights to their plots when the ayan took over. The end result was a period of anarchy and armed strife, with the spahi and the peasants ranged against the ayan and their government backers. The disorder was so severe and widespread that the early seventeenth century is known as the period of the "Big Escape" (*Buvuk Kacgun*) because of the mass peasant migration to cities. By the eighteenth century the ayan had become the *de facto* rulers of entire provinces. In 1808 they forced the powerless Sultan to give royal recognition to their usurped privileges, which now became legal rights.

The other chief beneficiaries of the Western-induced imperial disintegration were those Ottoman subjects who participated in the growing foreign trade. Despite official restrictions and outright bans, the expanding Western European economy obtained the raw materials it needed from the Ottoman provinces—wheat, maize, cotton, wool, silk, tobacco and dyestuffs. The French, Dutch and English Levant companies handled most of this international trade, but in certain regions such as Syria and the Balkans, native merchants and mariners participated and prospered. Ragusan and Greek merchant fleets grew rapidly, while Greek and Macedonian merchants controlled much of the overland trade up the Danube Valley into central Europe. The Anglo-French wars of the eighteenth and early nineteenth centuries ruined the Western merchants operating in various Ottoman ports. Local merchants promptly took their place, while Greek and Ragusan merchant ships, flying the neutral Ottoman flag, took over the Mediterranean carrying trade with its windfall wartime profits.

While some Ottoman merchants and mariners prospered in this foreign trade, many of the peasants suffered grievously. Just as in Poland and Hungary, the financial gains afforded by the Western markets led to the imposition of serfdom in order to increase productivity, so in certain Ottoman provinces that grew crops needed in the West, the response again was a form of serfdom designed to maximize output. In the plains areas of the Balkan peninsula, for example, the geographic pattern of maize and cotton cultivation corresponded to the geographic pattern of the new *chiflik* institution, which replaced the former timars. Balkan peasants under the timar system had enjoyed hereditary use of their land, while their taxes, tithes and other obligations had been relatively light and strictly regulated by the imperial officials. But when the ayan took over the timars, they responded to the lure of foreign markets by ignoring two features of the timar system that they found most inhibiting. These were the noninheritable nature of the fiefs and the legal limits on the peasants' obligations.

The former fiefs thus were transformed from the early seventeenth century onward into free and heritable property known as chifliks, from which the peasants could be evicted if they did not accept whatever tenancy terms were stipulated. Rents on the chifliks were much higher than on the timars, and after the state tax also was collected, the peasant was left with about one third of his produce. Furthermore, the tenant's freedom of movement was in practice severely restricted, though theoretically he was not tied to the land. His low share of the gross product commonly forced him to borrow from the chiflik owner in order to feed his family and to buy draft animals and tools. So long as he remained in debt he could not leave, and since he rarely could pay off the principal and the high interest, he was in effect bound to the estate. Thus the peasantry who worked on the chifliks were tenants in name but serfs in fact, and they had become serfs for the same basic reason that their counterparts had to the north, in Hungary and Poland.

Trade with the West undermined the status of Ottoman artisans as well as peasants. One reason, as noted above, was the impossibility of protecting traditional crafts because of the capitulatory restrictions on import tariffs. This was especially evident in the cloth industry, where Ottoman producers were caught in a double squeeze. On the one hand, Western merchants purchased Balkan wool in such quantities that the price of wool in the Ottoman Empire was substantially higher than in England. On the other hand, the English Levant company dumped their woolen cloth on the Ottoman market at cut-rate prices because they made their greatest profits importing Ottoman goods (silk, mohair, yarn, wormseeds, currants and aniseeds) into England, where they could set any price, since their charter gave them a monopoly of the Levant trade. Thus a study of the prices at which English cloth was sold at home and in the Ottoman market shows that the prices of English cloth in Istanbul in the 1620s were 20 to 30 percent lower than in London, despite the added cost of shipping.[12] The Ottoman textile industry was decimated by this combination of expensive wool at home and cheap, dumped cloth from England. The capitulatory restrictions precluded any tariff protection even if there had been official will to intervene, and by and large there was not.

In addition, foreign ambassadors and consuls used their considerable influence to hamper the development of local industries that might compete with imports from their respective countries. When, for example, a certain Greek merchant, Sarando Papadopoulo, attempted in the 1760s to establish soap "factories" in Coron and Navarino, he was blocked by the resident French consul, who intervened effectively with the cooperation of local Ottoman officials, thereby ending the possibility of competition for soap imports from Marseilles and Provence. Likewise the French official, Baron Tott, on his return from a special inspection tour of French consulates in the Levant in 1779, advised his government to continue its policy of obstructing any efforts to establish local industries in the Ottoman Empire. This preventive strategy was almost invariably effective because of the venality of Ottoman officials, because of the cooperation of the thousands of barat-holding "protected persons" and also because the embryonic entrepreneurs usually were Greeks, Jews or Armenians, for whom the Turkish authorities usually showed little concern.

ᘐ VI. Ottoman Peripheral Status

Sultan Murad IV's adviser, Koja Beg, submitted in 1640 a memorandum analyzing the crisis of the empire. Again and again he stressed the disintegration of the timar system, which led to the displacement of deserving warriors and officials in favor of mercenaries and usurers. Corruption and venality spread to all branches of public life, and the oppressed populace was driven to banditry. But in his explanation of what precipitated the downward spiral, Koja Beg, like a true conservative, focused on human failings. The sultans since the time of Suleiman had neglected their duties, failing to attend the meetings of their *divans* and listening instead to court rumors and harem intrigues. No grand vizir could feel safe in his office without participating in the machinations and corruption, thereby accelerating the imperial decline. A modern Turkish historian, analyzing the same historical problem, has related the imperial decline to broader global considerations:

> The decline of the established Ottoman social and economic order began as the result of developments entirely outside the area dominated by the Porte, and in particular as a consequence of the establishment in Western Europe of an "Atlantic economy" of tremendous vitality and force. The economic system of the Empire decayed neither through a flaw inherent in its constitution, nor through an organic law, but because of immense historical changes that destroyed its equilibrium, arrested its natural economic evolution, and condemned its institutions to irreparable damage. . . .

> During the second half of the sixteenth century . . . European commerce, sustained by strong commercial organization and encouraged by powerful nation-states, began to be a threat to local

industry. . . . The new European national commerce intended to sell the greatest possible quantity of goods abroad, while restricting imports of any finished products. Thus it provided no market for local Ottoman export industry. The commerce of the Levant changed to a "colonial commerce," turning Turkey into a client for the European industry which was itself to furnish only primary materials, no longer to export finished goods.[13]

Some contemporary observers perceived this subordination of the Ottoman economy and the resulting injury to the empire and its peoples. One of these was C. F. Volney, probably the best-informed and most comprehending European traveler to visit the Middle East before the nineteenth century. After journeying through Egypt and Syria in 1785 he concluded:

Considered relatively to the Turkish empire, it may be averred, that the commerce of the Turks with Europe and India, is more detrimental than advantageous. For the articles exported being all raw unwrought materials, the empire deprives itself of all the advantages to be derived from the labour of its own subjects. On the other hand, the commodities being imported from Europe and India, being articles of pure luxury, only serve to increase the dissipation of the rich and the servants of government, whilst, perhaps, they aggravate the wretched condition of the people, and the class of cultivators.[14]

The French ambassador in Constantinople, Choiseul-Gouffier, expressed the same conclusion when, in 1788, he referred to the Ottoman Empire as "one of the richest colonies of France." [15] The appraisal is essentially correct, yet the Ottoman colony had not yet been fully integrated into the world market economy. This is reflected in the fact that whereas the Ottoman Empire in the late sixteenth century had accounted for half the foreign trade of France, by the 1780s the proportion had dwindled to one twentieth. Likewise for most of the seventeenth century the empire had been responsible for about one tenth of England's foreign trade, but by the 1770s for only 1 percent. These figures indicate that Western economic penetration of the Middle East had remained superficial. The small scale of the operations demonstrated that although specific crafts and the peasants of certain plains areas had been severely affected, the empire as a whole remained only partially integrated.

More specifically, the Mediterranean provinces (Egypt, Syria, western Asia Minor and the Balkans) had been substantially affected by the Levant companies, while the more distant Persian Gulf-Red Sea regions

(Iran, Iraq, the Sudan and the Arabian peninsula) remained largely immune. Thus the Middle East during the pre-nineteenth centuries occupied with respect to the world market economy a position somewhere between that of the completely integrated and subordinate regions of Eastern Europe and Latin America on the one hand, and the completely external and independent land mass of Asia on the other. The integration of the Middle East was to be completed by the private and government loans and the railway and canal building of the nineteenth century, and by the oil discoveries of the twentieth.

Chapter 7

ASIA AN EXTERNAL AREA

. . . strange and costly objects do not interest me. . . . As your Ambassador can see for himself, we possess all things. I set no value on objects strange or ingenious, and have no use for your country's manufactures.

EMPEROR CH'IEN-LUNG to King George III (1793)

Asia in the pre-nineteenth-century period remained an external area in relation to the global market economy. It did not become either an integrated region, as did Eastern Europe and Latin America, or a peripheral area, as did Africa and the Middle East. One reason for the difference was location, the enormous distances separating South Asia and East Asia from Western Europe providing an effective buffer zone during those centuries prior to the telegraph, steamships and transcontinental railways and canals. The significance of this geographic factor becomes apparent if the inaccessibility of remote China and Japan is contrasted with the vulnerability of the adjacent Ottoman Empire to Western military, economic and cultural aggression. Another reason for the separateness of Asia was its high level of economic development, which made its ancient civilizations largely self-sufficient and uninterested in the relatively paltry offerings of Western merchants. Finally, the great land empires of the Moguls in India and of the Ming and Ch'ing dynasties in China were militarily powerful, so that it was out of the question for Western merchants and adventurers to fight their way in, as they did in the Americas, or to impose unequal trade relationships, as they did in Africa and the Middle East. Instead, the Westerners were confined to a few coastal trading stations, which served as encapsulated bases for their trading operations.

It is true that on Asian seas the Europeans enjoyed decisive naval superiority, which enabled them to dominate the newly opened global trade routes. But because of Asian self-sufficiency, Asian products lagged far behind the output of New World plantations in international commerce. Apart from a few coastal regions in India and a few islands in Southeast Asia, the countries and peoples of Asia remained quite unaffected by the expanding West. Until the Industrial Revolution endowed nineteenth-century Europe with irresistible economic and military power, Asia was able to retain its independence and identity as an external area.

ᴥ *I. Asia Before da Gama*

For millennia prior to the appearance of da Gama in the Indian Ocean, its commerce had conformed to the rhythm of the monsoon winds. In the vast oceanic expanses from East Africa to the East Indies, the northeast monsoon blows from about October to March, and the southwest monsoon from May or June to September. Accordingly, the "season" for trade from Gujarat to Aden was from September to May, and from Aden to Malabar it was October to February. Sailing eastward from Gujarat to Malacca, Indians ships would leave from January onward, and return by the end of May. Malacca was the meeting place for traders from the western regions of the Indian Ocean sailing in on monsoon winds, and for traders from the northeast or China seas arriving with the trade winds. The merchants from the northeast were mostly Chinese, while those arriving from the west were mostly Muslims of Arab, Indian, Persian or Turkish ethnic origin. A minority of the Indian Ocean merchants were non-Muslims, namely Hindus or Jains from Gujarat.

Western histories stress the trade in spices that originated in the East Indies and ended up, via Muslim and Italian middlemen, in European households. In terms of total Asian trade, or even in terms of total Asian trade in spices, this commerce with Europe was relatively insignificant. A much larger volume of trade was conducted on many other routes or laps, such as those between the Persian Gulf and India, East Africa and India, the Persian Gulf and East Africa, India and Malacca, Malacca and the East Indies and between Malacca and China.

Commerce along these routes had been conducted for millennia by merchants from the numerous countries or regions of the Middle East, South Asia, Southeast Asia and East Asia. Then came the challenge to this traditional pattern at the end of the fifteenth century with da Gama's historic voyage around the Cape. To appreciate the disruptive impact of the Portuguese intruders, and later of the Dutch and British, it is necessary to understand the manner in which the traditional Asian trade had been conducted. In essence, the Asian merchants, regardless of their ethnic or religious background, enjoyed full autonomy while trading in the various Indian Ocean ports, whether Sofala, Malindi or Mombasa in East Africa, Aden in the Red Sea, Hormuz in the Persian Gulf, Cambaya, Surat, Goa or Calicut in India, Colombo in Ceylon or Malacca in Southeast Asia.

In each of these towns the foreign merchants usually lived in defined districts with fellow merchants from the same place of origin. Normally they selected a leader who respresented them in dealings with the ruler of the particular port. Since most of these ports derived little of economic value from their hinterland, they were dependent on the foreign merchants for their prosperity. Their rulers therefore were careful to avoid any measures that might alienate the merchants and drive them off to other ports. They made every effort to provide favorable conditions for the conduct of trade—namely, reasonable taxes, religious toleration and freedom from arbitrary injustice. Apart from the measures needed to promote such an optimum environment, the local rulers allowed the merchants full autonomy.

In return the merchants paid customs duties, usually about 6 percent ad valorem, plus certain presents, which were assessed by the leader of the group to which the particular merchant belonged. The revenues from the customs duties were the mainstays of most Indian Ocean ports, and to assure the uninterrupted flow of these revenues, the merchants normally were allowed to carry on their operations with security and autonomy. A Persian traveler who visited Calicut in 1442, only half a century before the coming of the Portuguese, reported an ideal laissez-faire regime. "Security and justice are so firmly established that merchants bring thither from maritime countries considerable cargoes, which they unload and unhesitatingly send to the markets and bazaars, without thinking of the necessity of checking the accounts or watching over the goods. . . . Every ship, whatever place it may come from or wheresoever it may be bound, when it puts into this port is treated like other vessels and has no trouble of any kind to put up with." [1]

A final point to note about Asia before da Gama is the fateful withdrawal of the Chinese from the Indian Ocean in the mid-fifteenth century. During the first half of the fifteenth century the Chinese had sent into the Indian Ocean a number of expeditions that were most impressive in size and technological sophistication. The Chinese junks were much larger than the Muslim or West European ships of the time. Yet these remarkable Chinese expeditions were suddenly halted by imperial fiat in 1433. Whatever the immediate reasons for this fateful decision, it reflected the fact that Chinese merchants lacked the political power and social status of their Western counterparts. Chinese merchants and industrialists organized themselves into local guilds headed by chiefs, but these guild chiefs were certified by the government, which held them responsible for the conduct of individual members. Also, the government controlled the production and distribution of basic commodities such as salt and iron, which were necessities for the entire population. Such restraints deprived Chinese merchants of the opportunity for unfettered growth. Whereas Western cities were becoming bases for merchant power and activism, Chinese cities were dominated by the imperial military and bureaucracy. Whereas Western merchants, in partnership with their national monarchs, took the lead in overseas enterprise, the Chinese merchants were powerless to contest the imperial decision to end the remarkable Ming expeditions.

The Chinese withdrawal left a power vacuum in the Indian Ocean, for the individual Muslim traders plying between the various ports were no match for either the departing Chinese supported by the resources of the Celestial Empire, or for the oncoming Portuguese, outfitted and commissioned by the Lisbon royal court. The Portuguese quickly imposed their domination on the great trade area between East Africa and Malacca, and even established a commercial base on the coast of China at Macao. The fact that it was the Portuguese who fought and traded their way to China, rather than the Chinese to Europe, represented a basic turning point in the course of Third World history. It determined which sections of the globe were to comprise the dependent Third World and which were to become the expanding and developed First World.

ᦤ *II. Portugal's Sea Empire*

When Prince Henry the Navigator first sent his captains down the coast of Africa in the early fifteenth century, his objective was not the Spice Islands of the East. Rather his expressed aim was to acquire needed commodities closer to home: the fish in the surrounding seas, the grain and sugar of the Atlantic islands and the gold and slaves of Africa. But as the explorers made their way farther south and established coast ports that tapped the gold and slave trade that formerly had gone northward to the Arabs in North Africa, Portuguese horizons gradually widened to encompass India as well as Africa.

The breakthrough to the Indian Ocean occurred accidentally in 1487, when Bartholomeu Dias, while probing along the coast, was caught by a gale that blew his ships south for thirteen days out of sight of land. When the wind moderated, Dias observed land to the east, and realized that the storm had blown him around the southern tip of the continent. He landed at Mossel Bay on the Indian Ocean, and wished to explore farther, but his weary and frightened men forced him to return. On the homeward passage he first sighted the great cape, and named it the Cape of Storms. It was the Portuguese King Manuel who, upon Dias' return, renamed it the Cape of Good Hope.

Because of political and financial difficulties Manuel did not follow up immediately on Dias' pioneering voyage. But when Columbus sailed westward and claimed to have reached the East Indies, Manuel hastened to secure for Portugal the Cape route to the East. On July 8, 1497, Vasco da Gama sailed from Lisbon with four ships, rounded the Cape and stopped at Malindi in East Africa, where he picked up a famous Arab pilot, Ahmad-Ibn-Madjid, who guided him across the Indian Ocean to Calicut, which he reached at the end of May 1498. In view of the sequel to this voyage, Ibn-Madjid bitterly regretted what he had done, and his memory is still execrated by his coreligionists.

After da Gama's return King Manuel added to his titles the designation, "Lord of the Conquest, Navigation and Commerce of Ethiopia, Arabia, Persia and India." This was not empty rhetoric. Every word was taken quite seriously, and the Portuguese proceeded to take measures to monopolize all commerce along the new Cape route and in the Indian Ocean, where many Asian peoples had traded freely for centuries. Within a few years the Portugese had realized their objective—an extraordinary achievement in view of the tremendous distances involved and the small size and population of Portugal.

One reason for the success of the Portuguese has been noted already—the fortuitous departure of the Chinese half a century earlier, thereby creating a power vacuum in the Indian Ocean that the Portuguese promptly filled. The reason they were able to fill it was the superiority of their naval power. This was due in part to the ability of the Portuguese to execute squadron maneuvers rather than depending on the individual performance of the ships comprising the squadron. More important was the naval artillery and gunnery of the Portuguese. Like other Western Europeans, they were developing efficient new naval artillery that enabled them to use ships as floating batteries rather than as transports for boating parties. The gun, not the foot soldier, was now the main instrument of naval warfare, and the guns were employed against the enemy's ships rather than against his men. The Muslims had no comparable power, their ships not being designed to carry heavy armaments, and their seamen accustomed to fighting near coasts, where they usually had fought off attacks from the sea. Furthermore, Muslim rulers were almost invariably landlubbers, interested not in ships but in mounted warriors ready to gallop into battle. "Wars by sea," declared Sultan Bahadur of Gujarat, "are merchants' affairs, and of no concern to the prestige of kings." [2]

Another reason for the triumph of the Portuguese was their incomparable audacity and aggressiveness, reminiscent in this respect of the handful of Spanish conquistadors destroying the Aztec and Inca empires. Albuquerque likewise considered seriously various preposterous and daring schemes for discomfiting his Muslim enemies, such as diverting the Nile to the Red Sea, and raiding Mecca and holding the Prophet's body for ransom. The following account by a late-sixteenth-century participant describes the dashing élan of the early Portuguese in the East: "André Furtado de Mendonça was the last example of those first captains who founded the State of India—in pride and vanity *fidalgos* [nobles], in greed *vanias* [Gujarati Hindu or Jain merchants], in prodigality nabobs, rough, fanatical, blood-thirsty warriors, heaping up [the bodies of] Muslims and gentiles like wild beasts, but ready for any task or danger, squandering their blood and their lives with the same delight with which they squandered gold and jewels." [3]

Religious fanaticism entered into this ferocious aggressiveness, especially when the Portuguese, with their crusading traditions, encountered their hated old enemies, the Muslims. It was the unfeigned combination of wealth-seeking and religious fervor that made both the Portuguese and the Spaniards so effective in their overseas enterprises. In the South Asian lands of the sixteenth century, Portuguese aggressiveness and calculated brutality effectively cowed the large native populations. Governor D. Jono de Castro de Goa proudly wrote to the King that he had sent on ahead of the main fleet, "D. Manuel de Lima with twenty foists to cover all the gulf and burn and destroy the whole coast, in which he very well showed his diligence and gallantry, because he caused more destruction on the coast than was ever done before, or ever dreamt of, destroying every place from Daman up to Broach, so that there was no memory left of them, and he butchered everyone he captured without showing mercy to a living thing. He burnt twenty large ships and 150 small ones . . . and the town squares were covered with bodies, which caused great astonishment and fear in all Gujarat." [4]

Finally, the Portuguese owed much of their success to the hopeless fragmentation of the Indian Ocean societies they encountered. There was the schism among Muslims between the Sunnites and the Shiites, so that Portugal found an ally in Shiite Persia against Sunnite Turkey. There was also the enmity between Muslims and Hindus, which Portugal exploited to good advantage in India and in Indonesia. The most basic reason for Asian fragmentation and fragility was the social structure of Asian societies at that time. For example, the Sultan of Gujarat, let alone the Mogul Emperor in Delhi, could have expelled the Portuguese easily at any time. They did not do so because they had little interest in, or knowledge of, what was going on in the coastal ports.

Whatever arrangements the native merchants in the ports made with the Portuguese was their affair. The merchants themselves did not want the Sultan to intervene or to war against the Portuguese because the merchants would be caught in the middle and would suffer material losses. Gujarati merchants, like their counterparts elsewhere, were interested primarily in profits, and profits could best be assured by recognizing the naval superiority of the Portuguese, paying the levies they charged and avoiding intervention by inland rulers, which would have led to war and devastation. Consequently, the Portuguese did not have to deal with sultans or emperors, but only with local merchants who could easily be cowed and exploited.

A basic reason, then, for the predominance of the Portuguese throughout the Indian Ocean was that they were dealing with societies in which the operative ties were horizontal rather than vertical. The masses were members of one or more autonomous groups rather than subjects governed by provincial or imperial rulers. These groups were religious orders; assorted crafts; villages with their *panchayats* and *zamindars*; and resident foreign merchants—Portuguese, English, Dutch, Turkish, Armenian and Persian—who lived in their own neighborhoods, selected their own leaders, settled their own disputes and buried their dead in their own cemeteries. Even the Mogul cavalry, which was the main component of the land forces, was recruited by minor leaders, who in turn attached themselves and their followers to a higher chief. Each soldier followed his immediate leader, with little concern for the interests of the whole army. Neither sultan nor emperor could move without at least the tacit consent of their nobles.

In a society organized along such horizontal lines, ties between rulers and ruled inevitably were tenuous. Few contacts existed between the various lower groups and the upper ruling group, comprising the Mogul emperor, the provincial sultan, the nobles, the bureaucrats and the military chiefs. Indian society, like the others in the Indian Ocean basin, was disaggregated, with allegiance felt to some social group rather than to a regional or imperial authority. Hence the ability of the Portuguese to establish bases and collect duties in regions where they easily could have been expelled if there had existed the social cohesion that by this time was the norm in West European national monarchies. The point becomes apparent if it be imagined what the response would have been if an Indian naval force had ravaged the coast of Portugal as Governor Castro's fleet did the coast of Gujarat.

This combination of factors enabled the Portuguese to proceed systematically to impose their domination over the entire Indian Ocean. They justified their actions with the rationalization that the common law making the seas available to all applied only in Europe to Christians, who were governed by the principles of Roman law. Hindus and Muslims, however, were outside the Roman law, as they were outside the law of Jesus Christ. Furthermore, Hindus and Muslims had no claim to right of passage in Asian waters because before the arrival of the Portuguese no one had claimed the sea as hereditary or conquered property. "It is true," argued the official chronicler, João de Barros, "that there does exist a common right to all to navigate the seas and in Europe we recognize the rights which others hold against us; but the right does not extend beyond Europe and therefore the Portuguese as Lords of the Sea are justified in confiscating the goods of all who navigate the seas without their permission." [5] Thus the Indian Ocean was transformed from the *mare librum* that it had been for millennia, into a closed Portuguese preserve. To enforce their claims, the Portuguese resorted to ruthless terrorism, particularly when they encountered the hated Muslims. During one of his later voyages da Gama found some unarmed vessels returning from Mecca. He captured the vessels and, in the words of a fellow Portuguese, "after making the ships empty of goods, prohibited anyone from taking out of it any Moor and then ordered them to set fire to it." [6]

After an initial period of such looting had established their claim to "Lords of the Sea," the Portuguese organized an imperial hierarchy to administer and exploit their monopoly. At the top was the King in Lisbon, assisted by the Casa da India, which supervised the trade with the East. The head of the "State of India" was the viceroy, or governor, resident in Goa and endowed with final authority in both military and civil matters. The greatest of these governors was Alfonso de Albuquerque who, during his term between 1509 and 1515, gained control of the narrow sea passages leading to and from the Indian Ocean.

He seized the islands of Socotra and Hormuz, in which were the keys to the Red Sea and the Persian Gulf, respectively. In India he failed in an attempt to seize Calicut and took instead the city of Goa, located in the middle of the Malabar coast. He made Goa his main naval base and general headquarters, and it remained a Portuguese possession until 1961. Farther to the east he captured Malacca, commanding the strait through which all commerce with the Far East had to pass. Two years later, in 1513, the first Portuguese ship to reach a Chinese port put into Canton. This was the first recorded European visit to China since Marco Polo's day. The Portuguese at first had trouble with the Chinese government because the ruler of Malacca had recognized Chinese suzerainty and had fled to Peking with complaints against the violent and barbarous

Europeans. But in due course the Portuguese secured the right to establish a warehouse and a settlement at Macao, a little downstream from Canton, and from there they carried on their Far Eastern operations.

Each year Portuguese fleets sailed down the African coast, which was dotted with stations for provisioning and refitting the celebrated *naos* or great ships. After rounding the Cape they put in at Mozambique in East Africa, another Portuguese possession. Then they sailed across to India, usually Goa, arriving there toward the end of the year after having left Portugal in February or March. The monsoon winds required that they start back on the return voyage as soon as possible in the new year. From Portugal the expeditions brought men to reinforce the garrisons, money to pay for the return cargoes, and goods such as copper to be sold for the same purpose. The return cargoes consisted of spices, mainly pepper, which were a Crown monopoly, and other goods, especially cotton textiles, owned by private merchants and officials in the East. The royal treasury derived revenues from the monopoly in spices and from the duties on the other commodities.

The early-sixteenth-century expeditions consisted of royal ships, though a large part of the cargoes belonged to private merchants. By the 1540s it was decided that this system tied up too much royal capital in ships and associated expenses, so licenses for these voyages were sold to the highest bidders. Over the years a large number of Portuguese settled permanently in Asia, married local women and served as middlemen and carriers in the inter-Asian trade, which was greater in volume than the trade between Portugal and the East. The Dutch governor-general, van Diemen, later commented: "Most of the Portuguese in India look upon this region as their fatherland, and think no more about Portugal. They drive little or no trade thither, but content themselves with the port-to-port trade of Asia, just as if they were natives thereof and had no other country." [7]

The chief source of revenue for the Portuguese was derived from their *cartaz* or pass system. The cartazes were issued from 1502 onward for a small fee of a few rupees by the competent authority of a Portuguese fort. The functioning of this system was described by a sixteenth-century Muslim author:

> Now it should be known, that after the Franks had established themselves in Cochin and Cannanore, and had settled in those towns, the inhabitants, with all their dependents, became subject to these foreigners, engaged in all the arts of navigation, and in maritime employments, making voyages of trade under the protection of passes from the Franks; every vessel, however small, being provided with a distinct pass, and this with a view to the general

security of all. And upon each of these passes a certain fee was fixed, on the payment of which the pass was delivered to the master of the vessel, when about to proceed on his voyage. Now the Franks, in imposing this toll, caused it to appear that it would prove in its consequences a source of advantage to these people, thus to induce them to submit to it; whilst to enforce its payment if they fell in with any vessel, in which this their letter of marque, or pass, was not to be found, they would invariably make a seizure both of the ship, its crew, and its cargo! [8]

The purpose of this system was not to collect the cartaz fee, which was trivial, but to ensure that the captain paid a 6 percent ad valorem duty on his cargo. The cartaz was required for all Indian Ocean trade, whether done by Christians, Hindus or Muslims, and whether for long-distance trade or local commerce between neighboring ports. During the seventeenth century the duties were increased several times to meet the cost of fighting the intruding Dutch—to 8 percent in 1607, to 9 percent in 1639 and to 10 percent in 1659.

The Portuguese breakthrough into the Indian Ocean at first reduced drastically the flow of spices through the traditional Middle Eastern trade routes (see Chapter 6, Section IV). Within a few years, however, the old channels were competing successfully with the new Cape route. It is estimated that the quantity of spices exported from Alexandria to Europe in about 1560 was as great as in the pre-da Gama years, and that shipments from the Indian Ocean to the Red Sea surpassed in some years Portuguese shipments via the Cape. The continued use of Middle Eastern channels demonstrates that the Portuguese system, which theoretically should have monopolized all trade between Europe and the East, was in fact quite porous. It became increasingly so with the passage of time, until by the seventeenth century the Dutch and British East India companies were able to penetrate the Portuguese preserve and take over control of the Cape route.

Various explanations have been proffered for this dramatic and fateful shift in global economic power. One is that the Portuguese overextended themselves by establishing too many bases, which needed manpower and funds to maintain. Albuquerque was satisfied with control of the exits to the Red Sea (Socotra), the Persian Gulf (Hormuz) and the China Sea (Malacca). But his successors could not resist the temptation to bid for historical recognition by building new forts and having their names carved above the entrances. Thus Portugal ended up with a string of over fifty forts, which seriously drained the limited financial and manpower resources.

Another reason for the decline in Portuguese fortunes was the corruption of the officials, who usually bought their office at auction and therefore had to regain their investment and as much more as possible in the few years of their tenure. Hence the willingness of these officials to allow native ships to slip by into the Red Sea and the Persian Gulf. Also, they forced native merchants to buy merchandise at exorbitant prices—a practice that prompted the merchants to make every effort to evade the Portuguese monopoly.

Equally crippling was the steadily increasing shortage of manpower. Portugal's population of only one million could not meet the drain of men to the Brazilian goldfields and to the Asian expeditions, which suffered high mortality rates due to disease and shipwrecks. The 1571 fleet, for example, reached Goa with only half of the four thousand men who had embarked several months earlier at Lisbon. Portuguese ships accordingly were manned increasingly by half-caste crews that were poorly trained, so that ship losses rose rapidly. During the eighty-three years between da Gama's first voyage (1497) and the union of the Spanish and Portuguese crowns (1580), 93 percent of the ships from Portugal reached India safely, but in the next thirty-two years (1580–1612), only 69 percent reached their destination. These losses were due not only to the sailors' shortcomings but also to the failure of Portugal to keep up with the Dutch and the British in the art of navigation and in the construction of warships. When the northern Europeans appeared in the Indian Ocean, their ships were lighter, better constructed, more maneuverable and more heavily armed.

Finally, the most basic cause for the Portuguese decline probably was the shift of Europe's economic center from the Mediterranean basin to the northern European countries (see Chapter 3, Section I). This shift had vital repercussions in the conduct of trade and war in Asian seas. It enabled the Northerners to show up with superior merchant ships as well as warships, and with cheaper and better manufactured trade goods. The Northerners also enjoyed superior organizations with their large-scale East Indian joint stock companies. These had advantages over the individual Portuguese operators that were comparable to those of the multinational corporations over small local enterprises in today's global economy.

The superior naval power of the Dutch and British companies provided protection against both pirates and the Portuguese, while their superior economic power afforded some protection against market fluctuations. Their financial resources enabled them to influence the market not only in order to maximize their immediate income but also to reduce price fluctuations and thereby allow for long-term planning. When the price of cloves, for example, fell to three florins per pound in the early 1620s, the Dutch company curtailed imports until the price rose to six florins by 1627. When the British took advantage of the high price to increase their imports, the Dutch countered with dumping, which depressed the price down again to almost three florins. Since profit was impossible at that level, the British in turn reduced their imports and the price again went up. Thus the companies learned that a price ceiling as well as a price floor had to be recognized. The overall effect was more economic utilization of resources and hence a fall in spice prices that continued throughout the seventeenth century.

The superior efficiency of the East India companies automatically dried up the old Middle East trade routes. In fact, the Middle East, as the following table demonstrates, now became a prime market for Asian goods that were shipped around the Cape to Northwest Europe and then reshipped to the Middle East, which at one time had prospered by transmitting these same goods to Northwest Europe.

English Re-export of Asian Goods 1626–27

	Pepper (lb.)		Indigo (lb.)		Calico (pieces)	
	1626	1627	1626	1627	1626	1627
Mediterranean	801,347	1,799,693	268,889	145,735	3,709	24,232
Netherlands	62,926	210,603	23,697	37,550	66	6,348
N.W. Germany	145,775	414,214	23,340	8,224	0	927
West France	89,705	37,684	19,055	3,050	2,084	0
Baltic area	11,379	33,476	0	0	0	0
Other areas	7,198	1,945	1,050	3,453	1,295	277
Uncertain dest.	46,207	16,780	4,150	0	0	1,724
IN ALL	1,164,537	2,514,395	340,181	198,012	7,154	33,508

Source: N. Steensgaard, *The Asian Trade Revolution of the Seventeenth Century* (Chicago: University of Chicago Press, 1974), p. 174.

The historic implications of this restructuring of world trade was clearly perceived by a contemporary Turkish observer, Omar Talib:

Now the Europeans have learned to know the whole world; they send their ships everywhere and seize important ports. Formerly the goods of India, Sind and China used to come to Suez, and were distributed by Muslims to all the world. But now these goods are carried on Portuguese, Dutch and English ships to Frangistan [Europe], and are spread all over the world from there. What they do not need themselves they bring to Istanbul and other Islamic lands, and sell it for five times the price, thus earning much money. For this reason gold and silver are becoming scarce in the lands of Islam.[9]

III. East India Companies Oust the Portuguese

The predominance of the East India companies represented the victory of a new form of commercial enterprise. Whereas the Portuguese in Asia operated from the beginning as functionaries of Lisbon, the various East India companies conducted their affairs as independent associations of merchants, exploiting to the full the leverage afforded by the new global leadership of their respective home countries.[10] Although they were established on the basis of government charters, they successfully preserved their independence against governmental intervention. When in October 1600 the Lord Treasurer recommended that a certain gentleman with privateering experience should serve as "principall commaunder" of the British company's first voyage, the company responded bluntly that it had "noe lykin . . . to employ anie gent in eny place of charge or commaundment . . ." and advised "his Lordship . . . to Geave them leave to sort ther business with men of ther owne qualety. . . ."[11]

Such were the circumstances of the penetration of the Dutch and British into Asian seas at the expense of the Portuguese. The process began with Sir Francis Drake's famous voyage around the world (1577–80), which revealed that the Portuguese, so far from being the masters of the East, were defending immensely long trade routes and widely scattered strongholds against a host of enemies. The Portuguese East Indies no longer seemed so invulnerable. And the union of the Spanish and Portuguese crowns in 1580 led the Protestant nations to regard Portugal with the fear and hatred they had formerly reserved for Spain. Portugal now was seen as an enemy in Europe and overseas, and her empire became fair game for the Protestant powers. Then, too, the Netherlands revolt interfered with the distribution of colonial goods in northern Europe because the Dutch no longer were able to pick up cargos in Iberian ports. The English for some time had been obtaining Oriental products in the ports of the Levant, but this trade also was throttled when Spanish and Portuguese men-of-war blocked the passage through the Strait of Gibraltar. Under these pressures, the Dutch and the English decided that since they could no longer obtain their spices in Lisbon and in Alexandria, they would fetch them directly from the Indies.

The first task was to collect reliable data to guide the navigators around the long Cape route. The Portuguese had taken the greatest precautions to keep such information secret. In 1504 King Manuel I issued a decree forbidding the inclusion in maps of any indication of the route beyond the Congo. Earlier maps that divulged such data were collected and destroyed or altered. Despite this censorship, the navigation secrets of the Portuguese gradually leaked out. The most important source of information for the Northerners was the Itinerario, a geographical description of the world published in 1595 by a Dutchman, Jan Huyghen van Linschoten. He had lived in India for seven years as a servant of the Portuguese archbishop of Goa, so that Linschoten was able to include in his book detailed sailing instructions for the Cape route.

Linschoten's work was used the year it was published to guide the first Dutch fleet to the East Indies. The losses were heavy during the 2½-year expedition, only 89 of the original 289 men returning. But the trade was so lucrative that substantial profit remained despite the losses in manpower and equipment. The next expedition was more fortunate and cleared a profit of 400 percent. The Dutch now swarmed into the waters of the East, no less than 5 fleets, comprising 22 ships, sailing in the one year (1598). From the beginning they outmatched the Portuguese. The Dutch were better sailors, and their *fluyt*, or flyboat, was the best merchant ship in the world. Its broad beam, flattened bottom and restricted cabin accommodations gave it maximum hold space and unusual economy of building material. This slow and ugly but cheap and capacious boat was the mainstay of the Dutch merchant marine not only in eastern waters but throughout the world as well. Finally, the Dutch also enjoyed the advantage of being able to offer trade goods that were cheaper and better constructed because their home industries were superior to those of the Iberian states.

An unexpected complication was the tendency of the Indonesian rulers and traders to take advantage of the Dutch-Portuguese competition to raise prices and harbor dues. The Dutch responded in 1602 by amalgamating their various private trading companies into one great national concern, the Dutch East India Company. Under the terms of the charter that the company received from the States-General, it enjoyed a monopoly of trade, so far as the Dutch were concerned, between the Cape and the Strait of Magellan. It was empowered to make war or peace, seize foreign ships, establish colonies, construct forts and coin money. The company utilized these powers to the full in its dealings with the native potentates and in its successful drive against the faltering Portuguese. The British had organized their own East India company two years earlier, in 1600, but they proved to be no match for the Dutch. The subscribed capital of the British company was much smaller, and was, moreover, available only periodically, since the British merchant shareholders financed only individual voyages. After each voyage they distributed both capital and profit and wound up their accounts. Furthermore, the British company received little support from the Stuart kings (understandably, since Britain was still mainly a nation of farmers), while the Dutch had the strong backing of their trade-oriented government. Finally, the British company suffered from the private trade carried on surreptitiously by its own servants—a problem that also plagued the Dutch company, but to a lesser degree.

Despite their advantageous position, the Dutch at first tolerated British competition in the East Indies. They were still fighting for independence from Spain and could not afford to add to their enemies. But when the Dutch concluded the truce of Antwerp with Spain in 1609, the Dutch turned against the British. The outcome of the struggle for monopoly was never in doubt. The Dutch had five times as many ships, and they had built a string of forts that gave them control of the key points in the Indonesian archipelago. Furthermore, the Dutch had the services of a governor-general of genius, Jan Pieterszoon Coen, who did for his country what Albuquerque had done for Portugal. During his term of office (1618–29), Coen drove the Portuguese from the East Indies and made it possible for his successors to expel them from Malacca (1641) and from Ceylon (1658). Coen also harassed the British out of the archipelago, compelling them to retreat to their posts in India. Equally important was Coen's cultivation and development of inter-Asian trade, much greater in volume than the traffic that rounded the Cape to Europe. The Portuguese had participated in this trade, but Coen went much farther, establishing a base on Formosa (Taiwan) and from there controlling the commerce routes to China, Japan and the Indies.

At first the Dutch East India Company consciously sought to avoid acquisition of territorial possessions. Theorists and politicians in Amsterdam attributed the decline of Portuguese power in the East to the dissipation of energy and capital in territorial conquest, and warned the Dutch company against a similar mistake. But in its efforts to establish a trade monopoly, the company was led step by step to the territorial expansion it wished to avoid. Monopoly could be enforced only by a network of fortified posts. The posts required treaties with local rulers, treaties led to alliances, and alliances led to protectorates. By the end of the seventeenth century the Dutch were actually administering only a small area, but numerous states comprising a much greater area had become protectorates. Then during the eighteenth and nineteenth centuries the Dutch annexed these protectorates outright and built up a great territorial empire.

The export of spices to Europe diminished in value after about 1700, but the inter-Asian trade that Coen had developed made up for the shrinkage. Moreover, the Dutch developed a new economic resource at about that time by introducing coffee bushes into the East Indies. In 1711 they harvested a hundred pounds of coffee, and by 1723 they were marketing twelve million pounds. Thus, as Europe acquired a taste for coffee, the Dutch became the principal suppliers of this exotic beverage. Through these various means the Dutch East India Company averaged annual dividends of 18 percent throughout the seventeenth and eighteenth centuries. In the process of collecting these commodities and amassing these profits, the Dutch exploited the native populations in the most brutal fashion. Coen expressed bluntly the prevailing colonialist racism: "May not a man in Europe do what he likes with his cattle? Even so does the master do with his men, for everywhere, these with all that belongs to them are as much the property of the master, as are brute beasts in the Netherlands. The law of this land is the will of the King and he is King who is strongest." [12]

At first the Dutch exploited their "cattle" indirectly, recognizing the local sultans as "regents," who were free to fight among themselves and to oppress their own people so long as they fulfilled certain obligations to the company. These included delivery of set amounts of goods such as rice, sugar, pepper and coffee, provided either as outright tribute or sold at low, fixed prices, and also supplying of labor forces to manufacture salt, cut timber, dredge canals and harbors and construct roads and bridges. This indirect exploitation undermined the position of the regents, who lost popular support, forcing the company at first to prop them up, and eventually to resort to outright annexation. It was only on the East Indian islands that such annexation was feasible. On the Asian mainland the local monarchies and empires were too powerful, but the scattered islands lacked political unity, and furthermore were divided on religious lines between Hindus and Muslims.

Meanwhile, the British East India Company, which was a poor man's version of the united Dutch East India Company, had been forced to retreat from the Spice Islands to India, where it traded mostly in pepper. Payment had to be made mostly with bullion, which made the company unpopular, given the mercantilist doctrines of the times. A way out was found by purchasing Indian cotton textiles, which were sold in Indonesia, where they were in demand. Next the British tried selling Indian textiles in Europe, and found a ready market as these cotton goods were light, bright colored and cheap in comparison with the traditional European woolens. The 5,000 pieces shipped in 1613 became 100,000 by 1620, and 221,500 (or 2.5 million yards) by 1625. By 1700 the British had acquired three chief bases in India—Bombay on the west coast, and Madras and Calcutta on the east—where they conducted a flourishing trade.

In contrast to the Dutch in Indonesia, who dominated and annexed the islands, the British operated in India only on sufferance of the powerful Mogul emperors. When the company came under the guidance of Sir Josiah Child, a gifted and imaginative but arrogant and tempestuous man, he made the mistake of pursuing an aggressive policy in India, even to the point of declaring war on the Mogul Empire. The outcome was disastrous, the company's establishments in Bengal being overrun in a brief campaign. Sir Josiah was forced to sue humbly for peace, to which Emperor Aurangzeb agreed after the British paid a fine and promised "to behave themselves for the future no more in such a shameful manner." In practice they had no choice but to live up to these terms. In 1712, for example, John Russell, governor of Fort William and grandson of Oliver Cromwell, prefaced a petition to the Mogul Emperor with the following obeisance: "The request of the smallest particle of sand, John Russell, President for the English East India Company, with his forehead at command rub'd on the Ground, and reverence due from a Slave . . ." [13] It was not until the end of the eighteenth century that the British were strong enough to take advantage of the disintegration of the Mogul Empire to begin their territorial conquests in India.

With the British, and to a lesser extent the French, active in India, and the Dutch dominating Indonesia, the Portuguese lost the predominance in the East that they had enjoyed during the sixteenth century. The following table shows the extent of their decline during the early decades of the seventeenth century.

Ships Returned to European Countries from Asia, 1590–1630

Date	Portugal	Holland	England
1590	4	0	0
1595	3	0	0
1600	6	8	0
1605	0	8	1
1610	3	1	1
1615	1	5	2
1620	2	6	2
1625	3	4	4
1630	1	9	4

Source: Adapted from Steensgaard, op. cit., p. 170.

IV. Europeans in East Asia

European merchants in China and Japan were fully as subservient as Cromwell's grandson in India, and much more closely restricted. The

Portuguese were the first Westerners to reach China by sea when they sailed into Canton in 1513. They received a cool welcome, as the ruler of Malacca, who recognized Chinese suzerainty, had arrived earlier with reports of the atrocities perpetrated by these barbarous Europeans in the Indian Ocean. By 1557 the Portuguese were able to secure the right to establish a warehouse and a settlement at Macao, a little downstream from Canton. But the conditions were that they should pay rent and accept a Chinese magistrate in residence, as well as Chinese civil and criminal jurisdiction. The Portuguese purchased Chinese silks, wood carvings, porcelain, lacquerware and gold, and in return they sold nutmeg, cloves and mace from the East Indies, sandalwood from Timor, drugs and dyes from Java and cinnamon, pepper and ginger from India. No European goods were involved for the simple reason that there was no market for them in China. The Portuguese were functioning as carriers and middlemen for a purely intra-Asian trade.

The Spaniards followed the Portuguese to China, coming from the Philippines, which they had conquered by 1571 with the capture of the city of Manila. Four years later two Spanish friars journeyed from Manila to China, where they were welcomed because Spanish naval power had suppressed the Chinese pirates who infested the South China Sea with the decline of Ming power. This meeting in China of Portuguese coming from the west and Spaniards from the east epitomized the dynamism of European enterprise during those centuries. Iberian audacity was as manifest in East Asia as in the Americas and the Indian Ocean. In 1584, after the crowns of Spain and Portugal had been united, a Spaniard wrote from Macao, "With five thousand Spaniards, at the most, the conquest of this country [China] might be made, or at least of the maritime provinces." [14]

The Chinese Empire did not prove as vulnerable as the Aztec and the Inca, but the Spaniards did succeed in developing a lucrative trade, especially because Manila became a center for Chinese shipping and for a large resident Chinese population. Junks sailed from the ports of Fukien to Manila laden with Chinese products, which were reshipped from Manila across the Pacific to Mexico, whence some were reshipped once more across the Atlantic to Spain. This trade, which soon attained a large volume, was discouraged by Madrid, as it violated all mercantilist tenets. Spanish colonies were trading with a foreign country rather than with the mother country, and huge quantities of American silver were ending up in China rather than in Spain. Despite official decrees, the silver from American mines continued until the late eighteenth century to cross the Pacific to pay for Asian spices, porcelain and silk and cotton textiles.

After the Portuguese and the Spaniards, the Dutch were the next to appear on China's coast. A Dutch squadron of fifteen ships attempted in 1622 to drive the Portuguese out of Macao. Failing to do so, the Dutch sailed to Taiwan, where they built a fort, which developed a lucrative trade with China, Japan and the Philippines. The Dutch remained on Taiwan from 1624 to 1662, when they were driven out by Cheng Cheng-kung, known to Westerners as Koxinga. He was a partisan of the Ming Dynasty, which was being driven out by the Manchu invaders from the north. Koxinga took refuge on Taiwan, drove out the Dutch and ruled the island, as did his son after him. Not until the latter's death in 1683 did the Manchus finally annex Taiwan to their empire.

Finally, the British East India Company was permitted to establish a factory at Canton in 1685. Business was conducted through the so-called Hong merchants, a monopoly guild of Chinese businessmen invested with the full powers of the Peking government and acting as its agent. The Hong merchants in turn were under the authority of the imperial commissioner of customs, who alone had the right of issuing licenses of trade and who thus controlled the entire commerce through his power over the Hong members. The life of the British at the Canton factory was strictly regulated by the Chinese: No women were allowed into the factory, no British could use sedan chairs, they were not allowed to enter the city or to row on the river for pleasure and they could not communicate directly with the imperial commissioner—only through ·the Hong.

Tea was the main business of the British East India Company in China. Before the end of the eighteenth century tea had become the national beverage in Britain, and it was to pay for the immense quantities imported from China that the company encouraged the sale of opium from India, with complications culminating in the Opium War of 1839–42. Meanwhile the British, like other Europeans, tried to establish diplomatic relations with Peking, sending in 1793 the Macartney mission, which bore a banner with a Chinese inscription identifying him as "Ambassador bearing tribute from the country of England." Although Macartney was treated with the greatest courtesy, the Chinese government refused to make any commercial or diplomatic concessions. The British had to wait until the nineteenth century, when their military technology had so surpassed the Chinese that the British were able to smash their way into the Celestial Kingdom and force the opening of its ports to Western trade.

European merchants who reached Japan found themselves as tightly restricted as they had been in China. The first to appear were a band of Portuguese sailors who were shipwrecked in 1542. It was typical of the Japanese that their local officials were much impressed by the Portuguese firearms and learned how to make guns and gunpowder. Japan at this time was headed technically by an emperor, but the power behind the throne was the *shogun*, who served as commander-in-chief of all military forces and was responsible for the internal and external defense of the realm.

The initial contact with the Portuguese sailors was followed by regular visits by Portuguese traders, who discovered that rich profits could be made in commerce between China and Japan. Because of raids by Japanese pirates, the Ming emperors had banned all trade with Japan. The Portuguese quickly stepped into the void and prospered handsomely, exchanging Chinese gold and silk for Japanese silver and copper. The extent and the profitable nature of this carrying trade are indicated by the meteoric rise of the terminal ports, Macao and Nagasaki. When first visited by the Portuguese in the mid-sixteenth century, they were obscure fishing villages; by the end of the century they had become among the most prosperous ports in Asia.

The Portuguese combined missionary enterprise with their commercial activities. Francis Xavier and other Jesuit fathers landed in 1549 and were allowed to preach among the masses of the people. They were unusually successful, apparently because their revivalist methods of proselytism satisfied the emotional needs of the downtrodden peasantry during this period of endemic civil war. The shogun, Nobunaga, permitted the new faith to prosper, welcoming it as a counterweight to the independent Buddhist communities that were causing him trouble. By 1582, when Hideyoshi succeeded Nobunaga, there were 150,000 converts, mostly in western Japan.

Hideyoshi viewed with concern both the new trade and the new religion. The Portuguese, for example, were demanding the right to administer the city of Nagasaki, and threatened a trade boycott if they were refused. Likewise, the militant activities of the foreign missionaries seemed to the new shogun to be subverting the traditional Japanese society. In 1587 Hideyoshi ordered that all missionaries must leave, but his order was not effectively enforced, because of the fear that it would affect the profitable trade.

With the advent of the Tokugawa shoguns in 1603, Dutch traders, and a few British, were active in Japan alongside the Portuguese. The intense rivalry among these Europeans gave the Japanese a new freedom of action. They could now move against the missionaries without fear of losing the commerce. Furthermore, the Europeans intrigued against each other in their efforts to curry favor and win concessions. The Dutch, for example, reported to the shogun, Ieyasu, Portuguese plots to arm disaffected *daimyo*, or rural lords, and overthrow his rule. Accordingly, Ieyasu decreed in 1614 that all missionaries must leave, and their converts, who by now numbered 300,000, must renounce their faith. This order was ruthlessly enforced. As a control measure, converts were forced to belong to a Buddhist temple, and many were executed on refusing. Missionaries also were martyred, but it often proved difficult to distinguish between commercial and religious activities. The Japanese therefore went a step farther and in 1624 banned all Spaniards, since they had been the most aggressive and defiant. In 1637, all Portuguese also were forced to depart, leaving only the Dutch, who had never shown any interest in propagating Christianity.

Henceforth only the Dutch, besides the Chinese, were allowed to carry on trade, and this under severely restricted conditions on the islet of Deshima in Nagasaki Harbor. Dutch merchants and seamen were not allowed to stay more than a year on the islet. No European women were allowed, and no Japanese women other than prostitutes. Each year the Dutch had to present themselves before the shogun to be allowed to continue trading at Deshima. This isolationist policy was extended in 1636 to Japanese subjects, who were prohibited from going abroad on penalty of death. To reinforce this ban, ship construction was restricted to small vessels for the coastal trade. Thus began over two centuries of seclusion for Japan.

This policy of excluding all foreign influences and freezing the internal status quo was designed to perpetuate the dominance of the Tokugawa shoguns. In practice it proved extraordinarily effective. Japan was reunified and subjected to a centralized political control as thorough and as efficient as in any European state before the French Revolution. But a heavy price was paid for this security and stability. Japan did not experience the transforming and rejuvenating historical movements that Western Europe did during this period. There was no ending of feudalism, no Reformation or Counter-Reformation, no overseas expansion and no Commercial Revolution. For the Japanese, as for the Chinese, the price for two centuries of comforting seclusion was institutional and technological backwardness. This became apparent, more quickly to the Japanese than to the Chinese, when the Europeans forcibly broke into the hermit world of East Asia in the mid-nineteenth century.

ஐ *V. Asia an External Area*

In view of the prominence of spices in medieval trade, it is surprising that when Europeans finally realized their dream of reaching lands in the East directly by sea, the ensuing trade proved to be substantially less than that with the New World. The basic reason was that Asia prior to the nineteenth century had not been integrated into the capitalist world order, and therefore was not a participant in interregional *mass* trade.

American plantations produced commodities for which there was an elastic demand and therefore a mass market. Sugar became an article of

common consumption when it was produced cheaply on large plantations in Brazil and the West Indies, and likewise Virginia's extensive
tobacco plantations made it possible for one ton of tobacco to be sold
in England in 1700 for every pound that had been sold in 1600. The
demand for Asian products, by contrast, was comparatively inelastic and
limited. Spices, for example, were used chiefly for preserving meat, which
was *not* on the daily diet of the masses. This inelastic demand was even
more true of other Asian commodities such as porcelain, silks, jewelry
and wallpaper.

The only exceptions were textiles, coffee and tea. In the case of textiles,
the popularity of Asian imports is evident in words such as "gingham"
from the Malay word meaning "striped," "chintz" from the Hindustani
word for "spotted," "calico" derived from Calicut, and "muslin" from
Mosul. By the beginning of the seventeenth century Asian fabrics were
being imported in such quantities that powerful European textile interests secured embargoes on imports into all Western countries except
Holland. There was less opposition against the importation of coffee and
tea, which were regarded as specifics against corpulence and the vapors.
Coffeehouses throughout Europe served as social centers where workmen
and businessmen could read the daily news. Addison's hope, in founding the *Spectator,* was to bring philosophy "to dwell in clubs, at tea-tables
and in coffee houses." Java was the principal source of coffee, and China
of tea, until Indian tea began to compete in the nineteenth century.

A second reason for the far smaller volume of trade with Asia than
with the New World was the lack of Asian demand for European goods.
Europe was able to pay for African slaves and American plantation
products with its manufactured commodities. But Asians were not interested in these commodities, thereby perpetuating a problem dating
back to classical times, when the Roman Empire was drained of its gold
to pay for Chinese silk and Indian textiles. So it was in the sixteenth,
seventeenth and eighteenth centuries, when Asia remained uninterested
in European goods, while Europe was reluctant to send bullion to pay
for the Asian produce she desired. Western merchants sometimes went
to desperate lengths in their efforts to find a way out of the impasse.
The Amsterdam Company exported to Thailand "thousands of Dutch
engravings to be sold in the market place of Patani. Among the engravings were Madonnas (to be sold to Buddhists and Mohammedans
by order of Calvinist merchants) and biblical scenes; there were, for
classically minded Siamese, prints recording the stories of Livy, and
finally, prints with a more general human appeal, a collection of nudes
and less decent illustrations." [15] The fact is that Europe did not solve
this problem of trade with Asia until Europe developed power machinery
at the end of the eighteenth century. Then the situation was reversed,

for it was Europe that was able to flood Asia with cheap, machinemade textiles. But until that time, East-West trade was hampered by the fact that Asia was willing to receive from Europe bullion and little else. Precious metals comprised over three quarters of the exports of the British East India Company to Asia in 1700, and an even larger percentage of the exports of the Dutch East India Company.

This situation explains why Asia prior to the nineteenth century remained an "external area" in relation to the international market economy. In 1600 the total trade between Asia and Europe amounted to only about ten thousand tons each way, and its annual value was about one million pounds. In 1751 Britain imported three fourths as much from the one island of Jamaica as from the whole of Asia. This separateness of Asia was made crystal clear by the Emperor of China, Ch'ienlung, when he replied as follows to a 1793 message from King George III of Britain requesting the establishment of diplomatic and commercial relations: "Swaying the wide world, I have but one aim in view, namely, to maintain a perfect governance and to fulfill the duties of the States: strange and costly objects do not interest me. . . . As your Ambassador can see for himself, we possess all things. I set no value on objects strange or ingenious, and have no use for your country's manufactures." [16]

The Chinese Emperor's supreme indifference to "strange and costly objects" points up the invulnerability of almost all Asia to the dynamism of Western capitalism. Apart from a few coastal regions of India and some of the East Indian islands, Asia was unaffected by Western expansionism, and the daily lives of its diverse peoples continued along the traditional lines of past millennia. How different was the impact of the West on Eastern Europe, where it was responsible for the enserfment of the peasant masses, and in Africa and the Americas, where it engendered the slave trade, the slave-manned plantations and the ensuing wholesale alteration of the racial composition of the American continents!

Part Two

THIRD WORLD
A GLOBAL SYSTEM:
1770–1870

Under the present system of management, Great Britain derives nothing but loss from the dominion which she assumes over her colonies.

ADAM SMITH (1776)

It would not be worth my while to make [my steam engines] for three counties only, but I find it very well worth my while to make for all the world.

MATTHEW BOULTON (1769)

The Third World emerged when Northwest Europe developed a capitalist economy capable of generating a mass trade in necessities as against the traditional restricted trade in luxuries. This mass trade, as noted in Part One, developed between 1400 and 1800 an intercontinental market economy comprising Eastern Europe as a source of foodstuffs and naval stores; the Americas as the supplier of bullion and of plantation crops such as sugar and tobacco; Africa as the source of slave labor for the plantations; and Northwest Europe as the center of initiative and the provider of capital, shipping and manufactured goods.

Asia was not a part of this economic order because pre-nineteenth-century Europe, though able to dominate Asian seas, was incapable of subjugating Asian lands. The other continents also, for that matter, were still only superficially held by the Europeans. Africa remained the "Dark Continent," unknown as well as unconquered, while the interiors of the two Americas, though not unknown, were nevertheless largely unsettled and unexploited.

Europe's intercontinental capitalist order, prior to the nineteenth century, lacked global coverage because of its inability to encompass the Asian land mass, and it also lacked depth because of the failure to penetrate the overseas continental interiors. The historic role of the Industrial Revolution was to provide Europe with the economic dynamism and military power necessary to overcome these gaps in her global sway. The resulting industrial capitalism was infinitely more powerful and expansionist than the commercial capitalism from which it had emerged. The "Dark Continent" and Asia now were opened up by explorers and merchants. If the symbols of the era of commercial capitalism were the

Royal African Company operating in the ports of West Africa, and the East India companies in the seas of South Asia, so the symbols of the era of industrial capitalism were David Livingstone crisscrossing Africa, and British warships bombarding China's coasts in the name of the divine right of free trade.

Chapter 8

ERA OF INDUSTRIAL CAPITALISM AND WANING COLONIALISM

The whole world is before you. Open new channels for the most productive employment of English capital. Let the English buy bread from every people that has bread to sell cheap. Make England, for all that is produced by steam, the workshop of the world.

EDWARD GIBBON WAKEFIELD (1834)

Matthew Boulton, partner of James Watt in the manufacturing of the first commercially profitable steam engine, declared in 1769 that his venture could be profitable only if he could sell to the entire world. Only twenty-four years later, in 1793, the Emperor of China was to inform George III, "I set no value on objects strange or ingenious, and have no use for your country's manufactures." [1] History soon was to show that Boulton's need for a world market took precedence over the Chinese Emperor's reluctance to be a part of such a market. And inevitably so, for, as Joseph Schumpeter has observed, "Stationary capitalism is impossible." Thus the essence of early nineteenth-century history is that England, as Wakefield urged, became "the workshop of the world."

Britain remained the unchallenged "workshop of the world" during the century between 1770 and 1870. As such, Britain had no incentive to add to her colonial possessions. Rather she followed the dual policy of allowing foreign goods to come freely into her home markets because they offered little competition, and in return forcing weaker powers to open their markets to British manufactures. This was the century, then, when favorable commercial treaties were extracted from Greece (1837), Turkey (1838) and Persia (1836, 1841 and 1857), and when armed force was employed to open China to unfettered trade (Opium War) and to open likewise the lands of the Black Sea region (Crimean War). This was, in short, the century of Industrial Revolution and industrial capitalism at home, and of "free-trade imperialism" rather than colonialism in the Third World.

☙ I. First Industrial Revolution and Industrial Capitalism in the West

In becoming "the workshop of the world," Britain automatically had available the entire world as the market for its manufactured goods. This unprecedented achievement was made possible by the Industrial Revolution and the ensuing industrial capitalism, whose roots were to be found in the preceding centuries of Commercial Revolution and commercial capitalism. One of the prerequisites of the Industrial Revolution was an adequate supply of capital, as indicated by the succession of Scottish inventors and entrepreneurs who found it necessary to move to England to obtain the necessary financial backing for their enterprises. This capital in England originated to a significant degree from earlier overseas activities in the Americas, Africa and India.

Economist Ernest Mandel concludes that "for the period 1760–1780 the profits from India and the West Indies alone *more than doubled* the accumulation of money available for rising industry." [2] Likewise, the historian R. B. Sheridan notes that "the economic growth of Great Britain was chiefly from without inwards, that the Atlantic was the most dynamic trading area, and that, outside the metropolis, the most important element in the growth of this area in the century or more prior to 1776 was the slave plantation, chiefly of the cane-sugar variety in the islands of the Caribbean Sea." [3] Also, it should be noted that the very substantial profits of the slave trade ended up mostly in Britain, since British traders eventually gained control of the bulk of this trade.

Some historians deny a causal relationship between the triangle trade and the Industrial Revolution because of the scarcity of records of West Indian fortunes invested in the new English factories. The reasoning is simplistic, as noted by economic historian C. M. Cipolla:

> European maritime expansion was one of the circumstances that paved the way for the Industrial Revolution. To deny it on the basis that there were no West Indies merchants or West Indies adventurers among the "entrepreneurs" who built factories in Europe is as sensible as to deny any relation between the Scientific

Revolution and the Industrial Revolution on the basis that neither Galileo nor Newton set up a textile mill in Manchester. Interrelationships in human history do not always work so openly and crudely.[4]

Furthermore, recent studies have unearthed ties between the Atlantic trades and British manufactures. The tobacco commerce, for example, was controlled to a considerable degree by Glasgow merchants, but they were hampered by the lack of local industries to provide cargoes bound for the Virginia plantations. Those "tobacco lords," as they were called, accordingly established their own tanneries, printworks, malleable ironworks, bottleworks and soapworks, and also invested in coal mines and linen and cotton textile plants. In 1812, the Merchants House of Glasgow declared that the city was indebted to those who had carried on the American trades not only for "the extension of commerce" but also "for the establishment and for a considerable time, the support of its manufactures, now so highly advantageous to this Kingdom at large." [5]

Finally, Indian economist A. K. Bagchi emphasizes that the capital derived from overseas sources financed not only Britain's Industrial Revolution but also that of continental Northwest Europe. The capital extracted from India alone comprised over 50 percent of the annual British capital exports in the 1820s and the 1860s. This plunder of India was "not carried on under the competitive rules of the game which we have consciously or unconsciously come to associate with the heydey of capitalism in Europe and North America," [6] but rather through monopoly privileges, racial discrimination and outright violence. During the early years immediately after the Napoleonic wars, most of Britain's capital exports were directed across the Channel, helping to create new textile industries in France, Holland, Prussia and Russia.[7]

❧ II. Waning Colonialism in the Third World

The Industrial Revolution contributed in several ways to Western power and expansionism. Most fundamental was its triggering of a chain reaction of continual technological innovations and corresponding increase in economic productivity. Inventions in one industry stimulated balancing inventions in others. The first to be mechanized was the cotton industry, and the new cotton machines created a demand for more plentiful and reliable power than that provided by the traditional waterwheels and horses. This activated successive improvements in the primitive existing steam engines, until James Watt, with the financial backing of Matthew Boulton, evolved his historic successful model. This was to provide power—first in Britain and then throughout the world—for mines, textile mills, iron furnaces, flour mills, locomotives and steamships.

The new cotton machines and steam engines required an increased supply of iron, steel and coal. The need was met by a series of improvements in mining and metallurgy. This combined expansion of the textile, mining and metallurgical industries in turn created a need for improved transportation facilities to move the bulky shipments of coal and ore. Hence the successive booms in the building of canals, new hard-surfaced roads for year-round use, and railroad and steamship lines that spanned oceans and continents.

Technological and economic growth came to be accepted as normal rather than something exceptional and intermittent. Hence the first Industrial Revolution, which got under way about 1770, was followed inexorably by the second Industrial Revolution about 1870, and by the third of our own day.[8]

The new technology's increased productivity together with the advances of medical science generated a sharp increase in Europe's population in the nineteenth century. The resulting population pressure found an outlet in overseas migration. With every decade the tide of population movement increased, reaching a volume by the end of the nineteenth century that was unequaled to that time in human history. In the 1820s a total of 145,000 left Europe, in the 1850s about 2.6 million, and between 1900 and 1910, the crest was reached with 9 million emigrants, or almost 1 million per year. Before 1885 most of the emigrants came from northern and western Europe, and after that date the majority were from southern and eastern Europe.

The Industrial Revolution also provided the new steamships and railways necessary to transport such great masses of people across oceans and continents. When they reached their destinations the emigrants now possessed technological facilities that enabled them to exploit the continental interiors—the steamers plying coastal waters and inland rivers, the canals connecting the riverways, the roads and railways spanning the continents, the telegraph and postal systems for rapid communication, the machines capable of cutting prairie sod and leveling forests and finally the products of medical science for coping with tropical diseases that had decimated earlier emigrants.

The Industrial Revolution also made the European emigrants militarily irresistible by arming them with the repeating rifle and machine gun. The following observation of an Argentinian in 1878 was equally applicable in Africa and Asia: "The military power of the [Indian] barbarians is wholly destroyed, because the Remington has taught them that an army battalion can cross the whole pampa, leaving the land strewn with the bodies of those who dared to oppose it." [9] The Europeans enjoyed a similar military superiority on the world's oceans. When da Gama first appeared in Asian waters his great advantage was the superiority of his ships and artillery. This superiority increased with time because of the rapid development of naval technology. Despite repeated efforts by native rulers to catch up, they fell farther behind with the shift from sails to steampower, and the subsequent chain reaction of explosive shells, thick iron plate, highly maneuverable torpedo boats, oil fuel, the submarine and the dreadnought.

Finally, the Industrial Revolution provided economic incentive for opening up continents and exploiting their natural and human resources. The new factories and machines mass-produced goods that were cheaper and often of better quality than the traditional handicraft products of Asian and African craftsmen. Europe thus overcame the problem encountered by da Gama when he arrived in Calicut with shirts that were more expensive and of lower standard than the local goods. Not only did Europe now produce goods that were marketable, but the European manufacturers also had a powerful compulsion to market them in ever-increasing quantities. Because of heavy financial investments in expensive steam-powered machines and in raw material inventories, the success or failure of business enterprises now depended on a large and steady turnover. The more productive European industry became, the more important that new outlets be found and be kept open. Hence the strong reaction of the pioneer British industrialists against any efforts to foster rival industries abroad, whether in the United States or the German Zollverein or Mohammad Ali's Egypt.

The economic dynamism and military strength engendered by the Industrial Revolution paradoxically decreased interest in empire building. The reason was that Britain had spurted so far ahead of all other countries in industrial development that she had no need for colonies as protected markets for her manufactures, or for any other purpose. By the mid-nineteenth century Britain was producing two thirds of the world's coal, half of the iron and half of the cotton cloth entering trade channels.

Under these circumstances the British understandably came to regard the international division of labor and free exchange of commodities as part of providential dispensation. The apostles of these principles were Adam Smith and David Ricardo, whose underlying concept of laissez-faire was designed to liberate productive forces from the fetters of restrictive state interventionism. They opposed all manifestations of mercantilism, whether they were navigation laws, corn laws or any other tariffs or restraints. All these they viewed as anachronistic hangovers from the preceding centuries of colonial plantations and monopolistic trading practices. Richard Cobden went so far as to claim that free trade acted "on the moral order as the principle of gravitation in the universe —drawing men together, thrusting aside the antagonism of race, and creed, and language, and uniting us in the bond of eternal peace." [10]

The free traders were successful in effecting fundamental policy changes away from mercantilism—changes such as the termination of the trading monopoly of the British East India Company (1813), the banning of the slave trade (1807) and of slavery in British possessions (1833), the lifting of the ban on the export of machinery to foreign countries (1825) and the repeal of the Corn Laws (1846). In securing these basic innovations the free traders envisioned a world in which Britain served as the industrial center into which flowed raw materials and from which came manufactured goods, with no barriers to obstruct the exchange in either direction. An anonymous publicist spelled out in 1832 this global division of labor destined to benefit all mankind:

> It is clearly seen that to our beloved land Great Britain has been assigned the high mission of manufacturing for her sister nations. Our kin beyond the seas shall send to us in our ships their cotton from the Mississippi valley. India shall contribute its jute, Russia its hemp and flax, and ironstone for our factories and workshops, our skilled mechanics and artificers the necessary machinery to weave these materials into fine cloth for the nations; all shall be fashioned by us and made fit for men. Our ships, which reach us laden with raw materials, shall return to all parts of the earth laden. This exchange of raw materials for finished products under the decrees of nature makes each nation the servant of the other and proclaims the brotherhood of man. Peace and goodwill shall reign upon the earth, one nation after another must follow our example and free exchange of commodities shall everywhere prevail. Their ports shall open wide as ours are open for their raw materials.[11]

This vision of a free-trade world involved an absence of political barriers as well as economic. Colonies were regarded as relics of a benighted past, creating expenses and complications for the mother country without yielding in return any increase in trade. During the Corn Law debate of 1846, a Whig declared candidly before the House of Commons that free trade is "the beneficent principle by which foreign nations would become valuable Colonies to us, without imposing on us the responsibility of governing them." [12] Likewise Disraeli in 1853 contemptuously dismissed colonies as "gorgeous and ponderous appendages to swell our ostensible grandeur" without "improving our balance of trade. . . .

After the immense revolution that has been carried into effect, we cannot cling to our rags and tatters of a protective system." [13]

This anticolonialism does not mean that no colonies were acquired by Britain or other European powers during the half century after the Congress of Vienna. Despite the rhetoric of the "Little Englanders," situations did arise making intervention necessary. Sometimes "native" governments were deemed to be hostile to European commercial interests, or were viewed as incapable of maintaining the law and order required for the pursuit of trade, or on other occasions the frontiers of empire were extended to secure a more favorable boundary line. Thus in the second and third quarters of the nineteenth century, Britain fought the Ashanti and Zulu wars in Africa, the Indian Mutiny, the Opium War with China, the Crimean War with Russia, and two wars in Burma as well as bombing Acre and annexing Aden.

More commonly, however, imperial commercial interests were served by measures other than territorial annexation. One outstanding example was the encouragement and overt assistance given by Britain to the revolutions in Spain's New World colonies. As will be noted in the following chapter, this strategy freed from the restrictions of Spanish mercantilism the vast territories between the Rio Grande and the Strait of Magellan. The succession states proved, as expected, an Eldorado for British manufacturers and investors during the following century.

In other parts of the globe, the customary and effective device for promoting commerce was the negotiation of treaties of friendship and free trade. The nature and the impact of these treaties on Third World countries such as the Chinese and Ottoman empires will be analyzed in the following chapters. Commonly the treaties limited to nominal levels, such as 3 to 5 percent, the taxes that could be imposed on imports and exports, and also granted British merchants (and other foreign merchants by the most-favored-nation clause) exemption from a wide range of internal taxes to which native merchants were subject. The net effect of these treaties was to undercut tax-paying native merchants as against their virtually tax-free foreign competitors, and, more important, to expose the traditional native crafts to devastating unrestricted competition with Europe's burgeoning machine-powered industries. Local crafts were badly damaged or wiped out by the ensuing flood of cheap Western imports such as textiles, hardware, arms, glassware and watches.

These were the circumstances behind the waning colonialism of the early nineteenth century. British historians J. Gallagher and R. Robinson have labeled this as "free trade imperialism." They assert that the British government during those decades sought "to establish and maintain British paramountcy by whatever means best suited the circumstances of their diverse regions of interest." The object of paramountcy was the advancement and security of British trade and investments. In support of this goal British governments were prepared, if necessary, to resort to formal annexation, though during these decades this usually was not needed, as the desired paramountcy could be achieved by the more convenient alternative of treaties of friendship and free trade. "The usual summing up," conclude Gallagher and Robinson, "of the policy of the free trade empire as 'trade not rule' should read 'trade with informal control if possible; trade with rule when necessary.'" [14]

Chapter 9

NEOCOLONIALISM
IN LATIN AMERICA

The nail is driven. Spanish America is free, and if we do not mismanage our affairs sadly she is English.

FOREIGN SECRETARY LORD CANNING (1824)

The commerce between the two countries [England and Brazil] is carried on with English capital, on English ships, by English companies. The profits . . . the interest on capital . . . the payments for insurance, the commissions, and the dividends from the business, everything goes into the pockets of Englishmen.

SERGIO TEIXEIRA DE MACEDO,
Brazilian Minister in London (1854)

Half a century after the thirteen North American colonies won their independence, Latin America also became independent, with the exception of a few colonies in the Caribbean basin. But political independence did not end the economic underdevelopedness of the new Latin American countries. Whereas the United States rose rapidly to become the No. 1 industrial power of the world before the end of the nineteenth century, Latin America remained so palpably a member of the Third World that the term "neocolonialism" is used to refer to this continuation of economic dependence after the winning of at least nominal political independence. Thus neocolonialism, which is the status and affliction of most of the Third World today, began in Latin America in the early nineteenth century. Why neocolonialism proved to be the destiny of Latin

America after the successful wars of independence is the subject of this chapter. The question is most relevant for Third World peoples today who, having for the most part won their political independence since World War II, now ask themselves how they can escape the dismal Latin American fate of neocolonialism persisting a century and a half after the formal end of colonialism.

❧ I. Winning of Independent Statehood

In August 1762 the British seized the fortress town of Havana and held it until July of 1763. This was a double shock for the Spaniards and their colonial subjects. It was a military shock, for Havana had been considered an impregnable fortress guarding the route of outgoing treasure galleons. It was equally an economic shock because no more than eleven ships per year had ever sailed into Havana, whereas during the eleven months of English control, over seven hundred merchant ships entered, laden with slaves, with English manufactures and with food-stuffs, timber and hardware from the thirteen colonies to the north.

This dramatic incident pointed up the anomaly of the Spanish imperial mercantile system, keeping cheaper foreign products out of Spanish America, and cheaper Spanish American products out of foreign markets. Yet the fact remains that this colonial system lasted for a full three hundred years. The basic reason for its durability was its permeability. On paper it was rigidly exclusive; in practice it was easily penetrable. The government-appointed House of Trade, established in Seville in 1503 and moved to Cádiz in 1717, enforced commercial regulations that theoretically made colonial trade the monopoly of a self-perpetuating merchant guild. But non-Spanish merchants residing in Seville gained control of the trade by advancing credit to Spanish members of the merchant guild and by bribing them to lend their names to merchandise owned by foreigners. Such corruption permeated colonial trade from top to bottom, involving seamen, stevedores, naval officers, customs officials, merchants and even top bureaucrats and ministers in Madrid. The all-pervasive bribery kept the cumbersome imperial machinery well oiled and functioning until the early nineteenth century.

The corruption not only made the colonial mercantile system viable but also created in the process powerful vested interests opposed to any substantive reform. This was demonstrated when the Spanish Bourbons attempted to neutralize some of the effects of the Treaty of Utrecht imposed by the British in 1713. This had given the British extensive economic privileges, including the *asiento* or monopoly of the slave trade, and the right to send one shipload of general merchandise each year to trade with the Atlantic ports of the Spanish colonies. But the British had grossly violated these privileges, sending many more than the one stipulated ship and also establishing offices and warehouses in various colonial ports, ostensibly to regulate slave imports, but in practice to expand their commercial operations to the point where they controlled much of the Spanish American economy.

During the eighteenth century the Bourbons made various efforts to revamp this system in order to enhance royal prerogatives and reduce British encroachments. They revoked the asiento and other commercial privileges granted to the British; sent out better-trained officials drawn mostly from the officer corps; allowed thirteen Spanish ports to trade with the colonies, thereby ending the monopoly of Cádiz; and permitted intercolonial commerce in colonial products, though not in re-exported European imports.

These measures did have some effect, increasing the productivity and the exports of Spanish factories, and trebling the output of New World mines between 1740 and 1803. This in turn stimulated the haciendas and general commercial operations, as reflected in the increased government revenue from customs duties and sales taxes. But the hope that the reforms would satisfy complainants in Spanish America was not realized. Traditional vested interests within Spain negated many of the reforms. The mercantile oligarchy in Cádiz retained control of 85 percent of the colonial trade, obstructed intercolonial commerce as much as possible and preferred to deal with the more efficient English and French manufacturers than with the less efficient Spanish. It was the typical reaction of citizens of an underdeveloped society who, having adapted to a subordinate relationship with more advanced countries, preferred to continue with the modest returns from such a relationship rather than risk changes that might upset existing arrangements.

Within Spanish America the effect of the economic upswing following the Bourbon reforms was to sharpen the conflict between two opposing camps. On the one side were the interests benefiting from, and favorable to, the existing mercantile system: the mine owners, the export merchants and the imperial bureaucrats. On the other were those who stood to gain by promoting an internal market rather than external dependence: the nascent industrialists, the provincial merchants, the hacienda owners and the Church. The latter was the most important single economic force in the colonies, owning many of the most productive haciendas and providing most of the loans borrowed by landowners, industrialists and small merchants. The more the colonial economy developed and diversified with the passage of time, the greater the disaffection of this group with imperial restraints and exactions. In that sense the Havana episode of 1762–63 was not only a shock to the existing system but also a revelation as to future possibilities.

Another shock and revelation was the revolutionary course of events in England's thirteen colonies to the north. The success of the revolutionaries to the north was contagious, as was also their subversive "philosophy of Philadelphia," as it was known in Latin America. Equally contagious were the doctrines of the Enlightenment, which spread from France across the Pyrenees and also across the Atlantic. Especially appealing, for obvious reasons, was the liberal economic thought of the French physiocrats and of Adam Smith, so that twelve economic societies were founded in Latin America between the 1780s and 1812. Their members were merchants, agrarians and bureaucrats who would soon play key roles in the independence movements and the new governments.

The long years of the French Revolution and the Napoleonic wars, when Spain was preoccupied in Europe and when her colonies were left to shift for themselves, also stimulated revolutionary ideas and forces. Napoleon's domination of Spain and the installation in 1808 of his brother, Joseph, on the Madrid throne were the immediate causes of revolution in Latin America. Both the Spanish Loyalists and the Spanish Americans refused to recognize Joseph and regarded the deposed Ferdinand "the Beloved" as the legitimate ruler. But the question was who should act as regent during Ferdinand's captivity. Spanish loyalists insisted that only they could legally do so, while the *cabildos* (organs of municipal government) in Spanish America insisted that in the absence of the King, sovereignty reverted back to each locality until his return. Implicit in the cabildo argument was the premise that Spanish America had never been a colony of Spain but an association of viceroyalties of the King. It was in this setting that liberals in areas outside the principal imperial centers—Mexico City and Lima—began to make claims for complete independence. By 1809 widespread fighting had broken out between the loyalists and the patriots.

Another push toward a break with Spain came with Napoleon's invasion of Portugal in 1807–8. The Portuguese dynasty and Court fled to Rio de Janeiro with an escort of British warships. The Portuguese ruler then shattered the centuries-old Iberian mercantile system by opening all Brazilian ports to trade with friendly or neutral nations. This had an electrifying effect on Spanish America also, for thousands of English merchants poured into Brazil, whence they infiltrated into the Spanish colonies at many points. Pressure mounted throughout Latin America for putting an end to what was becoming an unviable and frustrating mercantile system.

The British contributed to the pressure, though very discreetly, as they wished for diplomatic reasons to keep Spain's friendship. So they urged the Spanish government to open its colonies to trade, but refused to help the government suppress the colonial rebels in return for commercial concessions. At the same time the British did not permit any other country to help Madrid against the colonists, while the British indirectly aided the rebels through private British merchants and financiers, who provided loans and supplies. Also, the British navy protected the shipment of those supplies, as well as of returning produce and bullion from both the Spanish and Portuguese colonies.

Despite these favorable circumstance the creoles, or native-born whites of Latin America, did not rush to take up arms for independence. The reason is that they had much to lose as well as to gain. This points up a basic difference between the revolutions in Latin America and the thirteen colonies. With the exception of the slaves in the South, the majority of adult males in the thirteen colonies possessed sufficient property to enjoy electoral rights. North American society probably was more free from poverty and class distinctions than any society of the time. In Latin America, by contrast, the majority of the population were a miserable, dispossessed underclass consisting of Indians, African slaves, mestizos and mulattos. Rapid population growth in the late eighteenth century produced rural underemployment and migration to the cities. But very few were able to find productive work, so that German scientist Alexander von Humboldt, who traveled extensively through Latin America at the end of the eighteenth century, found thirty thousand ragged and discontented unemployed in Mexico City alone. He concluded that nowhere had he seen "such tremendous inequality in the distribution of wealth, of culture, of the cultivation of land, and of people," as he had witnessed in Brazil and Spanish America.

The creoles understood quite clearly, despite their grievances against the imperial mercantile system, that they were a part of the colonial establishment and that they dared not arouse the underclass against the prevailing social order. The creoles preferred to remain within the imperial framework if they could extract some concessions to satisfy their main complaints. But instead of concessions the imperial government arrested a number of leading creoles in an effort to smash the opposition movement before it could spread. This intransigence prompted the establishment of revolutionary juntas in various colonies, and finally armed revolt in September 1810 in the Mexican mining town of Guanajuato.

The revolt, led by Miguel Hidalgo, and later by José Maria Morelos, was a radical outburst by rural Indians, mineworkers and the urban unemployed, led by revolutionary middle-class intellectuals. Their demands were profoundly subversive of the status quo, including abolition of slavery, equality for the Indians and mixed races, restoration of land to the Indian communities and a single assembly of representatives of the people.

All this was totally unacceptable to the creoles, who wanted political concessions, not social upheaval. So they allied themselves with the castes (mestizos and mulattos) against the enslaved Africans and the oppressed Indians. This gave the creoles the manpower they needed, for the racial distribution in Spanish America at this time was 3.2 million creoles and 5.5 million castes, as against 7.5 million Indians and 0.75 million Africans. The conservative combination prevailed, and by 1816 the radical first phase of the Latin American revolution had petered out.

The following year began the second phase of revolution supported by the creole oligarchy—the clergy, landholders and middle classes. The military leaders were General Simón Bolívar in northern South America, and General José de San Martín in the southern part of the continent. Bolívar, the "Liberator," virtually created the independent states of Colombia, Venezuela, Panama, Ecuador and Bolivia, the last being named after him. San Martín, after freeing Argentina in 1816, made an historic crossing of the Andes and participated in the liberation of Chile and Peru. The insurrections in South America represented a political and regional movement rather than a social one. Cities such as Buenos Aires, Caracas and Santiago sought to advance their interests against those of Lima. The insurrections did ultimately involve social issues. In order to raise armies, the rebel leaders mobilized indebted peons, slaves and the rural lumpenproletariat. After independence was won, suppression of the social consequences of this mobilization became the first order of business for the new republics.

Meanwhile in Mexico, conservative elements were alarmed by the 1820 revolution in Spain and the establishment of a short-lived republican regime. Rather than risking contamination by a republican Spain, they decided on separation in order to preserve their class prerogatives as well as those of the Church. Under the leadership of a creole officer, Augustin de Iturbide, the independence of Mexico was proclaimed on February 24, 1821. The following year Iturbide persuaded a constituent congress to elect him Emperor, and he was crowned Augustin I on July 25, 1822. The empire failed to sink roots because it was hard to govern people who had experienced a prolonged civil war, and also because Iturbide was regarded even by the conservatives as a military upstart rather than as a true emperor. In 1823 he was forced to abdicate, and the following year a republic was established, with the traditional elite securely in command.

In Brazil it proved possible to win independence without bloodshed. Emperor John VI, who had established a Portuguese government-in-exile in Rio de Janeiro, returned to Lisbon in 1821, leaving his son, Dom Pedro, temporarily in charge in Brazil. Dom Pedro eventually decided against following his father to Lisbon and proclaimed the independence of Brazil. Rather than sending an army against his own son, John accepted the declaration and Brazil became an independent state.

In this way, almost all of Latin America won its independence from European rule. The only exceptions were British, Dutch and French Guiana to the north of Brazil; certain Caribbean islands such as Jamaica, which remained British until winning independence in 1962; the Virgin Islands, which were under Denmark until 1917; and Cuba, which was under Spanish rule until 1898.

The Latin American revolutions brought political independence but not social change. The position of the Indians and of the African slaves, comprising half the total population, remained the same as before. The mestizos and mulattos did improve their lot, spilling over from the haciendas and plantations to fill such occupations in a diversifying economy as weavers, small shopkeepers, itinerant merchants, lower clergy and lesser bureaucrats. Their elevation did not represent a decline in race prejudice but rather the acceptance of the castes as a necessary middle group between the creoles and the Indian-African masses. Members of this group survived only by ruthless pursuit of self-interest, and often were more harsh in the exploitation of their social inferiors than the traditional white elite.

Latin American society was basically unchanged by the wars of independence. It remained a stratified society, which explains in large part why it also remained externally a dependent society. Political independence was followed not by economic independence but by neocolonialism.

❧ II. Neocolonialism After Independence

Lord Canning observed in 1824 that "Spanish America is free, and if we do not mismanage our affairs sadly she is English." Whether this prophecy was to be fulfilled depended on whether the new creole rulers of Spanish America would be willing to accept their traditional economic subservience to Europe or whether they would strive for economic independence as well as political. The fact that the establishments of the various Latin American countries, consciously or unconsciously, willingly or unwillingly, opted for continued economic dependence has molded the course of Latin American history to the present day. The significance of this choice is apparent if it is contrasted with that of the Founding Fathers of the new North American republic who were faced with the same issue after their breakaway from Britain.

The southern plantation interests of the United States favored free trade in order to market their cotton and other plantation products without obstacles in the European markets. Most of the republic's founders, however, insisted that it was essential to attain economic independence in order to safeguard their newly won political independence.

James Madison, for example, asserted that "our own existence requires that, with respect to such articles, at least, as belong to our defence and primary wants we should not be left in a state of unnecessary dependence on external supplies. . . . The champions of 'the let alone policy' forget that theories are the offspring of the closet; exceptions and qualifications the lessons of experience." [1]

The great apostle of protectionism and self-reliance was Alexander Hamilton. In his celebrated *Report on Manufactures* presented to the House of Representatives in 1791 he asserted that an industrial base was essential for the future of the nation:

> Not only the wealth but the independence and security of a country appear to be materially connected with the prosperity of manufactures. Every nation, with a view to those great objects, ought to endeavour to possess within itself, all the essential of national supply. These comprise the means of subsistence, habitation, clothing, and defence. The possession of these is necessary to the perfection of the body politic; to the safety as well as to the welfare of the society. . . . To effect this change, as fast as shall be prudent, merits all the attention and all the zeal of our public councils: it is the next great work to be accomplished. [2]

The need for this "next great work" was demonstrated during the Napoleonic wars, when Britain used her superior naval power to impress American seamen and to seize neutral shipping trading with France. The United States responded with the Embargo Act of December 22, 1807, forbidding American vessels to leave for foreign ports. Both New England shipping interests and southern cotton exporters opposed the Embargo Act, and the American dilemma culminated in the War of 1812. Several years later Jefferson observed that the embargo had been "a trying measure" but that its effect was "to set us all on domestic manufactures." Jefferson was correct. The war did stimulate American industry, and for that reason, Henry Brougham, the parliamentary spokesman for Yorkshire woolen interests, called for dumping on the American market in order "by the glut, to stifle in the cradle those rising manufactures in the United States which the war has forced into existence contrary to the natural course of things." [3]

American policymakers refused to accept dependence on Britain as "the natural course of things." Northern industrial protectionist interests prevailed over southern free traders. The outcome of the Civil War assured continued protectionism and industrial growth in the United States. President Grant noted that earlier mercantilist policies had enabled British industry to develop to the point where it now preferred free trade, and he concluded that American industry likewise needed an initial protectionist period before it could afford free trade:

> For centuries England relied on protection, carried it to extremes, and got good results from it. There is no doubt that it is to this system that that country owes its present power. After two centuries, England has found it desirable to adopt free trade because protection no longer offers advantages. Very well, gentlemen, the knowledge that I have of my country leads me to believe that within two hundred years, when America had gotten all that she can get from protection, she too will adopt free trade.[4]

The validity of President Grant's analysis was borne out by the subsequent economic development of the United States. In 1860 the country was fourth among the industrial nations of the world; by 1894 it was the first. Between 1860 and 1900 the number of industrial establishments increased three times, the number of industrial wage earners four times, the value of manufactured goods seven times, and the amount of capital invested in industry nine times.

Turning to Latin America, we find precisely the opposite course of economic development. The colonial pattern of dependence upon, and exploitation by, the European metropolis was continued into the post-colonial era. One reason was that Latin America had been more dependent on, and controlled by, the Iberian mother countries during the colonial centuries, and this tradition continued after political independence. Another reason was the depressed status of the Indian-African masses, as well as of most of the castes, so that domestic purchasing power was inadequate to support local industry. Lack of capital also was an inhibiting factor, because of the dearth of banking institutions, and the reluctance of the major sources of capital—the Catholic Church and the merchants—to invest in industry. Finally, plantation interests were relatively stronger in Latin America than in the United States, while protectionist industrial interests were correspondingly weaker.

These various factors explain why Lord Canning's expectation was realized. Under Spanish rule the imperial trading system had limited colonials as to the source and nature of their imports and exports, and also had forbidden foreigners from acquiring property or establishing business enterprises in the colonies. During or after the wars of independence these restrictions lapsed. Ships sailed directly from European ports to Latin America, their cargoes varying with the country of origin. Iberia provided mostly wines and food specialties, while France furnished luxury products such as liqueurs, fine textiles, glassware, jewelry and furniture. Britain, by contrast, supplied mass-production goods—

iron and steel equipment, hardware and woolen and cotton textiles—as well as the services of banks, insurance companies, merchant shipping and wholesale firms. Native merchants were left only with the retail trade.

The confrontation between the "conservatives" and the "liberals" through the first century of political independence reflected the clash of two interests. The conservatives, representing primarily the landowners, were interested in developing the internal market, whereas the liberals, whose wealth derived from commerce, sought to integrate Latin America's economy into the world market. Their strategy prevailed for the most part, and they successfully used state power to attain the desired integration with the global market economy through a variety of measures.

In the River Plate region of present-day Argentina, British merchants swarmed in during and after the independence wars. The results were fully reported by British representatives on the scene. On July 2, 1812, a group of British merchants wrote to Foreign Secretary Lord Castlereagh, "The consumption of British manufacturers has of late greatly increased . . . the abundance and consequent low prices of Goods has placed within the reach of the Inhabitants, articles which from their first cheapness they were induced to wear, and which, being now accustomed to, has created new wants." On July 30, 1824, the British consul general reported, "while the [Spanish] colonial System existed, all Manufactures and other European goods sold here at three times their present prices; while the produce of the Country was given in exchange, at a fourth part of what is now paid for it." Likewise the British consul general, Sir Woodbine Parish, reflected in 1852 on his experiences four decades earlier: "The low prices of British goods, especially those suited to the consumption of the masses of the population of these countries, ensured a demand for them from the first opening of the trade. They are now become articles of the first necessity to the lower orders in South America. . . . thus it is that every improvement in our machinery at home which lowers the price of these manufactures, tends to contribute . . . to the comforts of the poorer classes in these remote countries, and to perpetuate our hold over their markets." [5]

These significant reports reveal that the immediate effect of unrestricted trade was beneficial for the local inhabitants. They received foreign manufactured goods of superior quality and lower cost, while they sold their own produce at higher prices. But the end result, as Sir Woodbine pointed out, was "to perpetuate our hold over their markets." The "hold" extended to the markets of all Latin America. Thus Mariano Otero of Guadalajara wrote in 1842, "Trade was merely the passive tool of foreign industry and commerce," and that "cabinets are completely committed to mercantile interests and are profoundly interested in keeping us in a state of wretched backwardness from which foreign commerce derives all the advantages. . . ." The way out, he concluded, was "a general change [in] the material conditions of our society. . . ." [6]

The "general change" that Otero called for was not forthcoming in the nineteenth century. Most policymakers shared the views, not of Otero, but of figures like Tavares Bastos (1839–75), the Brazilian politician who was the spokesman for coffee interests in the Chamber of Deputies. He consistently supported only those foreign loans and those public works that facilitated exports, and he campaigned successfully to open the Amazon River and Brazilian coasting trade to the ships of all nations. Conversely he successfully beat down all efforts to adopt protective tariffs for Brazil. It is scarcely surprising that Brazil ended up a British semicolony, with the British controlling imports and exports, shipping them in British bottoms, insuring them with British firms, providing credit through British banks and using all these facilities to discourage the growth of any native industry that might challenge Britain's stranglehold. A Brazilian cotton magnate recalled in later years "the terrible war of competition to which I was subject at the beginning on the part of foreign merchants in Rio, representatives of English manufacturers, who always tried to smother and demoralize national industry." [7]

⚞ III. Economics of Neocolonialism

In the second half of the nineteenth century Europe's increasing technological and economic power led to a correspondingly increasing control over Latin America's economy. After 1850 Europe was building bigger and faster ships, digging the Suez and Panama canals, constructing transcontinental railways, developing refrigerated transportation systems and exporting the capital needed for these worldwide projects. International trade rose in value from $1.5 billion in the 1820s to $3.5 billion in the 1840s to $40 billion in 1914.

Latin America felt the impact of this new wave of European expansionism as much as any area. Most foreign investments were made during two periods, the first being in the 1820s, and mostly in the territories comprising present-day Argentina. The capital was invested in mining and in land and immigration companies concerned with opening the interior to agricultural development. Also, some government loans were floated for constructing port and sanitary facilities, as well as other public works. By the end of the 1820s all the government loans were defaulted and most of the private investments had failed. A combination of political instability and the failure of the export trade to develop as rapidly as expected was responsible for the fiasco.

After the 1860s large-scale capital investments in Latin America started up again, stimulated by fast steel steamships, effective refrigeration facilities, new mining techniques and other technological advances. Most of the capital went to mines, plantations and privately owned railway and port equipment that transported the raw materials to the coasts for export. By 1914 the value of foreign investments in Latin America had reached $8.5 billion, or one fifth of all worldwide, long-term foreign investments. The source of the capital was as follows: United Kingdom, $3.7 billion; United States, $1.7 billion; France, $1.2 billion; Germany, $0.9 billion; others, $1 billion.

The precise effect of these investments upon Latin America varied according to the nature of the export commodities produced for the world markets. These commodities can be divided into three general categories: temperate agricultural products (wheat, corn, meats, flax and linseed, of Argentina and Uruguay), tropical agricultural products (sugar, tobacco, coffee, cacao and bananas, of Brazil, Colombia, Ecuador, Central America, the Caribbean and parts of Mexico and Venezuela), and mineral products (silver, copper, tin, gold and oil, of Mexico, Chile, Peru, Bolivia and Venezuela).

Temperate agricultural products were not produced in any quantity until the construction of railways opened up the great pampa regions. In 1860 Argentina had only 25 miles of railways, as against 2,800 in 1885 and 21,000 in 1914. The railways completely transformed the economy of the country, which heretofore had consisted of little more than hunting wild cattle, which were slaughtered for their hides—the principal export prior to 1850. The little corn and wheat that was grown during those decades was for purely domestic consumption. But with the railway network, cultivated acreage jumped from 1 million acres in 1870 to 12 million in 1895 to 63 million in 1914. Wheat exports had averaged less than 100,000 tons per year in the 1880s, but in the 1890s they increased to an average of 1 million tons, and by 1914 to 2.5 million tons.

Meat exports jumped along with the grains, thanks to the development of freezing plants (*frigorificos*), which froze meat for overseas markets. Wild cattle were replaced by imported Shorthorns and Herefords, which were crossbred with native stock. Frozen meat exports rose from 25,000 tons in 1900 to 365,000 tons in 1914. Canning factories were built at the same time, and canned meat was exported along with the frozen.

The manpower for this increased productivity was provided by European immigrants, the Indian population being sparse and intractable. In 1889, for example, 260,000 immigrants (mostly Spaniards and Italians) entered Argentina, and by 1912 the number had risen to 380,000. It is true that about 45 percent eventually returned, as against 30 percent in the United States, but whatever the length of their sojourn, they made vital contributions to the Argentinian economy. The migrant laborers were known as *golondrinas* or swallows. They left Italy in October or November, crossing in cheap steerage to Argentina, where they first harvested flax and wheat in the north part of the pampas regions. Then they moved south, usually on foot, harvesting successive crops, until by February they were in the cornfields. By April they had gathered in that crop, and the golondrinas then returned to Italy in time for spring planting in their homeland.

The influx of European labor, capital and technology increased the national wealth of Argentina from $1 billion in 1886 to $15 billion in 1914. Since the population increased only three times during the same period, the per-capita national wealth had risen fivefold in a single generation. But the mass of the people were very far from being five times better off. Rather there was growing disaffection and conflict in the pre-1914 years. One reason was the income disparity—the growing gap between landlord and laborer in the countryside, and between employer and employee in the city. The other reason was the extreme exploitation of the national economy by the foreign investors. "English capital," complained socialist labor leader and politician Juan B. Justo in 1896, "has done what English armies could not do. Today our country is tributary to England . . . the gold that the English capitalists take out of Argentina or carry off in the form of products does us no more good than the Irish get from revenues that the English lords take out of Ireland." [8]

Turning to tropical agricultural exports, they consisted at first mostly of sugar and tobacco, but in the latter part of the nineteenth century both the variety and the quantity of exports increased sharply. Refrigerated shipping made possible huge shipments of bananas from Central America, while rising living standards in the United States and Europe created vast new markets. Coffee exports from Brazil, for example, increased three times between 1875 and 1900, so that by the latter date two thirds of the world coffee production originated in Brazil.

Tropical agricultural exports contributed much less to the overall economic development of the host countries than did the Argentinian exports of grain and meats. One reason was that plantation agriculture, as noted in the preceding chapter, spread from Latin America to Asia in search of cheaper and more abundant labor. World prices for tropical products consequently were low, and the income of Latin American countries was correspondingly depressed. Also, the production and transportation of tropical agricultural products did not require the extensive infrastructure demanded by the grains and meats of Argentina. Little more than railways and ports were needed, so that there was little "spread effect" to stimulate the rest of the economy.

The international corporations that owned most of the plantations producing tropical agricultural products engendered a type of plantation economy that by its very nature precluded overall economic development. The corporations were both horizontal and vertical monopolies— vertical because they controlled not only the production of the particular commodity but also its transportation, processing and marketing, and horizontal because they operated plantations on several continents and therefore expanded or contracted local operations depending on the profit yield for the metropolitan corporation. Thus the few corporations controlling the output of a given agricultural product in any one country operated as self-sufficient enterprises, almost completely independent of the rest of the local economy. There was little "spread effect" or internal money flow from staple production within the host country. The benefits accruing from the global scale of production of tropical agricultural commodities went to the metropolitan corporations rather than to the host countries. The latter consequently were doomed to the usual economic growth without development. (See Chapter 4, Section IV, and Chapter 13, Sections II and III.)

Considering finally the mineral exports of Latin America, they increased tremendously in the late nineteenth century. New industries required much larger supplies of raw materials, and improvements in transportation and in extraction techniques made it possible to meet the increased demand. Copper, for example, was produced in small quantities in colonial times, being used only for kitchen utensils, ships bottoms and ornamentation. Then with the electrical industry, the demand for copper soared in the late nineteenth century. Chile was exporting ten times as much copper in the 1890s as in the 1850s.

But again the host countries received few benefits from the upsurge in mineral exports. The technological know-how and heavy capital investments could be provided only by foreign corporations, so most of the profits went to the Anaconda and Kennecott corporations rather than to Chile or Peru. Also, the corporations employed little labor relative to the value of their total output, so that the local labor force received few benefits, either in money or in technical skills. The mining infrastructure, by its very nature, was highly specialized, and therefore engendered few linkages with the local economy.

Until World War I huge profits were funneled from Mexico, Bolivia, Chile, Peru and other mineral-producing Latin American countries to the metropolitan centers where the corporation headquarters were located. During the twentieth century the host governments began to demand higher royalties and also some local processing of the minerals before they were exported. Yet as late as 1968 the return on American capital invested in Chilean copper was 26 percent, in contrast to an 11.8 percent return on American overall investments in Latin America, and

6.7 percent on investments in Europe. If such was the situation in 1968, it may be imagined what it was in 1898 or 1908.

Whatever the circumstances, Latin America became an important contributor to the world commodity markets during the nineteenth century. By 1913 Latin America was exporting 62.1 percent of the world's coffee, cocoa and tea; 37.6 percent of the sugar; 25.1 percent of the rubber, hides and furs; 17.9 percent of the cereals; 14.2 percent of the fruits and vegetables; and 11.5 percent of livestock products.

Yet all regions of Latin America, regardless of what they exported, had unequal economic relations with the metropolitan centers, and consequently manifested typical symptoms of underdevelopment. One was the prevalence of large estates, whether cattle ranches and wheat farms in Argentina, coffee plantations in Brazil, banana plantations in Central America, or sugar plantations in the Caribbean. Not until 1910 did the first mass uprising occur against such gross inequity. This was the revolution in Mexico where, at the time, over 90 percent of rural households were propertyless.

Another manifestation of underdevelopedness was the production of a single commodity for overseas markets. For the larger Latin American countries this meant a succession of monoculture dependencies. In the case of Brazil it was first sugar cane until the early eighteenth century, then the gold and diamond rushes until about 1830; then coffee, which has remained the key export to the present; and finally rubber tapping, until its collapse in 1914. Chile likewise experienced a succession of dependencies in wheat, nitrates and copper.

A final symptom of underdevelopedness was the prevalence of vertical economic ties with metropolitan centers rather than horizontal economic ties integrating local national economies. Thus Rio de Janeiro, through which were shipped most of Brazil's exports, exported goods in 1848–49 worth 27,329 contos to foreign countries, as against 717 contos' worth to domestic destinations. Likewise roads, railways and ports were all built to expedite trade with overseas countries rather than internal commerce. Latin American ports such as Rio de Janeiro, São Paulo, Montevideo and Asunción were able to communicate more quickly and easily with European capitals than with their own interior provinces. In Brazil, railway lines built with British capital used several different gauges, so that the interchanging of rolling stock remains a problem to the present day. Since the only concern was to transport goods from the hinterland to ports, no attempt was made to link and integrate the various regions of Brazil.

Another illustration of vertical economic ties was the encapsulation of foreign enterprises within local economies. Modern and productive foreign enterprises functioned as isolated enclaves with few spread effects. Thus tin mines in the Bolivian Andes, with blazing lights and high-powered conveyors, contrasted with the immemorial rhythm of traditional life in the surrounding Indian villages. Likewise sugar plantations on the southern side of Puerto Rico, with their sprinkler systems and motorized field machinery, contrasted with the small farms of the hill people barely scraping a meager living from eroded soils.

A 1723 memoir to the viceroy of Mexico complained, "The world's trade flourishes at the expense of the peoples of America and their immense labors, but the riches they draw from the bosom of the fertile earth are not retained." [9] Precisely the same complaint, with equal justification, could have been made at the end of the nineteenth century—or, for that matter, the end of the twentieth.

IV. Culture of Neocolonialism

Latin America after independence had not only a dependent, underdeveloped economic structure, but also a correspondingly dependent, underdeveloped social structure. The two were causally related and mutually reinforcing.

One manifestation of neocolonialism in social relationships was the aping by the local elite of metropolitan values, fashions and products. Hence the conspicuous consumption of metropolitan goods and services, including clothes, drinks, art objects, governesses, tutors and metropolitan schooling for children. The resulting capital drainage reduced substantially the opportunities for local economic development, particularly because the poor people naturally sought to emulate the "great house" living style by spending their meager funds on imported woolen suits, hats, Scotch whiskey and the like.

Equally crippling was a negative attitude toward physical labor as being socially demeaning and fit only for slaves or hired hands. Overseers never stooped to manual labor, and again this attitude was aped by the masses, who resorted to elaborate trickery to minimize their physical work. Such norms were patently inimical to economic development, especially when compared to New England's Protestant ethic. An American traveler in Brazil in 1856 reported that the creoles would "starve rather than become mechanics," so they entrusted most of the crafts to their slaves. "I have seen slaves working as carpenters, masons, pavers, printers, sign and ornamental painters, carriage and cabinet makers, fabricators of military ornaments, lamp-makers, silversmiths, jewelers and lithographers. . . . *All* kinds of trades are carried on by black journeymen and boys." [10] This negative attitude toward physical work persisted after the abolition of slavery in 1888. The government established several agricultural schools by 1914, yet despite recruitment campaigns, enrollment remained small, while droves flocked to the socially prestigious schools of law and medicine.

The rigid pattern of social stratification throughout Latin America also impeded economic development. The landholding aristocracy, descendant mostly from colonial creoles, monopolized the ranks of the legal profession, the upper bureaucracy and other branches of government. Later nineteenth-century European immigrants served as merchants, doctors, engineers and educators. Whatever their profession or status, whites and near-whites looked down on Indians and Africans as biological inferiors who needed guidance and control rather than education and opportunity. This combination of social stratification and racism precluded social mobility and provided little opportunity to the great majority of the population to realize their potentiality. A Frenchman reported in the 1860s that in Brazil "a person's class was immediately ascertainable even in the middle of the forest," while an Englishman in the same decade noted that "Brazilians pay great regard to distinction and rank, and perhaps in no other language are these so precisely determined." [11]

The constricting effect of social stratification was accentuated and reinforced by an educational system that excluded the great majority of children. Whereas in the United States one third of the children in some states attended primary school in 1865, in the province of Buenos Aires, which was the most advanced in Argentina, only one in twenty-five were enrolled in that year. Likewise the percentages of school-age populations attending primary schools in Brazil were 5.2 in 1872, 5.8 in 1889 and 9.1 in 1907. Furthermore, the type of education transmitted was not conducive to national development. It trained only lower-level clerks, since technicians and administrators were imported from Europe, where the decision making was centered. "On the whole," states Jamaican economist George L. Beckford, "the educational system of plantation society is technically backward and contributes to the persistence of underdevelopment." [12] This conclusion is supported by the following statistics on the percentage of undergraduate majors in science or engineering in 1958–59: China and the Soviet Union, 46%; Western Europe, 34%; Africa, 19%; Latin America, 16%.[13]

The low rate of literacy went hand in hand with a correspondingly restricted franchise. During most of the nineteenth century only 2 to 4 percent of Latin American males had the right to vote. In Brazil, for example, 142,000 out of a total population of 15 million were enfranchised in 1881. Until the twentieth century the descendants of the colonial creoles effectively controlled all Latin American societies and political structures.

Beneath the white or near-white ruling elite were the castes which, as noted above, rose to the intermediate ranks following independence. The struggle for survival, or the hope for upward mobility, made them ruthlessly exploitative in dealing with the Indian and African masses. The response of the Indians was to withdraw to their village communities, where they dropped out of national life. Their only contacts with the white man's world were occasional visits by intinerant traders and priests.

The African slaves were worse off, having been uprooted from their ancestral homes and then stripped of their sense of identity by being thrown together under dehumanizing conditions with their varied tribal languages and cultures. The common assumption that slaves were treated more benignly in Latin America than in Anglo America is without foundation. The criteria by which the two races were identified did differ in the two cultures. In the United States it was a genetic distinction, so that any trace of African genes in physical appearance meant automatic relegation to the inferior black status. In Latin America it was more a social distinction, involving manner of speech, dress, education, income and occupation. Yet the end result did not differ significantly between the two societies. In Latin America, as in Anglo America, the "upper class" was overwhelmingly Caucasian in appearance, while the "lower class" comprised "people of color."

One factor determining attitudes to blacks and mulattos was the proportion of whites in the total population. Where the proportion is too small to provide manpower for the intermediary roles of bureaucrat, artisan, clerk, functionary, foreman and so forth, then the mulattos of necessity are allowed to fill the vacuum, and their social status and rights improve correspondingly. But where there are enough whites to staff the intermediary roles, then the distinction between blacks and mulattos is unnecessary, and both suffer full race discrimination. This explains the different race attitudes in the southern United States as against most of Latin America, and also within Latin American states such as northeastern Brazil, with typical Latin American attitudes, as against southeastern Brazil, where the population is overwhelmingly of European origin and where both blacks and mulattos endure the same discrimination as in the United States.[14]

Another factor determining the different race attitudes and policies was the condition of the market available for the export product. If the market offered opportunity for big profits, then the slaves invariably were exploited pitilessly. No concern was shown for their welfare because the high prices made it more profitable to maximize production by driving the slaves to death in a few years and then purchasing a fresh batch from Africa. Travelers invariably reported the savage exploitation in Brazil during the seventeenth-century sugar boom, the early eighteenth-century mining boom and the nineteenth-century coffee boom. But they also reported the relaxed, patriarchal treatment of slaves during the intervening periods of economic decline. The plantation owners during such unpropitious periods had little incentive to increase their output, and tended instead to slow down to self-supporting rather than export-oriented type of operations.

The same causal relationship was reported in the United States between market conditions and treatment of slaves. Hence the easygoing, patriarchal societies of tidewater Maryland and Virginia as against the driving ruthlessness of plantations in the Deep South. David Brion Davis concludes:

> If an exploitive, capitalistic form of servitude was at times common in Brazil and Spanish America, and if North Americans conformed at times to a paternalistic model and openly acknowledged the humanity of their slaves, it may be that differences between slavery in Latin America and the United States were no greater than regional or temporal differences within the countries themselves. And such a conclusion would lead us to suspect that Negro bondage was a single phenomenon, or *Gestalt*, whose variations were less significant than underlying patterns of unity.[15]

Chapter 10

SLAVE TRADE TO LEGITIMATE TRADE IN AFRICA

We hope that by God's blessing on our plans, a large body of such Native Growers of cotton and traders may spring up who may form an intelligent and influential class of society and become founders of a kingdom which shall render incalculable benefits to Africa and hold a position amongst the states of Europe.

> H. VENN, General Secretary of the Church
> Missionary Society (1857)

Pre-nineteenth-century Africa did not become part of the European mercantilist world order. African slave labor had provided the cement that held that world order together, yet Africa as a continent had not been incorporated into it as an integral component. The reasons, as noted in Chapter 5, were that most parts of Africa had not been affected by the slave trade, and even those regions affected had been only superficially so. The masses of the African people had not been involved in either the export or import phases of the trade. All this changed during the nineteenth century, for Europe's Industrial Revolution engendered an industrial capitalism that was incomparably more dynamic and powerful than the preceding commercial capitalism. Europeans now were able to penetrate and exploit continental land masses. In the case of Africa this was done in two stages. The first was the ending of the slave trade, which cleared the way for "legitimate trade" in various African raw materials needed in Europe. The second stage, considered in Chapter 14, was the political partitioning of the continent, which eliminated obstructive native traders and chiefs and made possible direct rule and direct exploitation.

℘ *I. End of Slavery in Africa and the Americas*

The slave trade by its very nature had obstructed the opening up of the interior of the continent. African middlemen had been determined to retain the monopoly of their phase of the slave trade and opposed any European efforts to penetrate into the interior as challenges to their monopoly. European slavers opposed any other type of commerce in Africa because they suspected that it would interfere with their operations. The Europeans also prevented any outsiders from getting in, as they justifiably feared a public outcry if the horrors of their traffic in human beings were made public. It was for this reason that the Portuguese prevented the Papacy from sending any missionaries to Africa unless they were under their direct supervision and control.

The abolitionist movement that first challenged the slave trade was started by a small group of reformers led by William Wilberforce, Thomas Clarkson and Granville Sharp. They established in England in 1787 the Society for the Abolition of the Slave Trade, and in 1823, the Anti-Slavery Society designed to end the institution of slavery as well as the slave trade. These abolitionists believed in freedom of trade, of conscience and of wage contracts. Therefore they opposed slavery as being contrary to the word of God and to individual human dignity, as well as to one's God-given right to dispose of one's labor to best advantage. These arguments won the support of many religious groups, especially Quakers at home and missionaries abroad. The latter viewed the slave trade as an obstacle to the diffusion of Christianity, and therefore favored the substitution in its place of "legitimate trade" in agricultural products. "Christianity, Commerce and Civilization," they maintained, were interconnected and inseparable.

The ultimate success of the abolitionists rested not only on these arguments but also on certain political and economic trends of the times. The 1832 Reform Bill enfranchised the British middle class and in the process eliminated the powerful "West India interest" in the House of Commons. Also, the progress of the Industrial Revolution was making slavery obsolete. The new and rapidly growing technology was creating a demand for overseas markets for manufactured goods rather than for cheap labor on plantations. At the same time, there was growing evidence that free labor on Caribbean plantations was more productive than slave labor, especially because of recurring slave revolts. Finally, the British West Indian interests were losing favor because they no longer could produce sugar as cheaply as the Spanish island of Cuba. They needed subsidies and bounties to remain competitive, but these were strongly opposed by British manufacturing interests, which demanded free trade in order to have unrestricted access to world markets. British consumers also were unhappy about paying more for subsidized West Indian sugar than what they would have paid on the open market.

Much controversy has prevailed as to the relative importance of economic as against religious and humanitarian forces in explaining the triumph of abolitionism. Historian K. Onwuka Dike has properly emphasized that the two factors were complementary and that to focus on either leads to oversimplification.

> . . . it was this mounting economic change which reduced slave interests to manageable proportions and enabled the abolitionists to attack it successfully. On the other hand, had it not been for the spirited and inspired attack of the Christian humanitarians such as Wilberforce and Clarkson, slavery and the slave trade might have lingered on—as indeed other decadent systems did linger on— long after they had outlived their usefulness.[1]

So far as the Africans were concerned, it was the dynamism and the expansionism of the new Industrial Revolution that was as ubiquitous as it was irresistible. "White man now come among us with new face, talk palaver we do not understand, they bring new fashion, great guns, and soldiers in our country." [2]

The combination of political, economic, religious and humanitarian forces led to the 1807 parliamentary bill forbidding the participation of British ships in the slave trade, and the landing of any slaves in British colonies. In 1833 Parliament went farther by abolishing the institution of slavery on British territory, and providing £20 million as compensation for the slaveholders. During the following years British naval units patrolled the coasts of Africa, Brazil and the Caribbean against the slave traders, though without full success until the New World countries themselves abolished slavery as an institution. This was done by Haiti in 1803, by the United States in 1863 and by Brazil and Cuba in 1888.

By the late nineteenth century the slave trade had disappeared in West Africa and the Americas, but it was continued by Arab slavers in eastern and central Africa until World War I. In fact, this Arab slave trading increased in the late nineteenth century because of the growing European demand for the cloves of Zanzibar, the cinnamon of Seychelles and the sugar of Réunion and Mauritius. These plantation islands of the Indian Ocean became an Arab West Indies, so slave trading (either openly or thinly disguised as "contract labor") now flourished on the East African coast as it had earlier in the Caribbean.

ॐ II. Exploration of Africa

The end of slave-trading operations had profound repercussions on Africa. The interior of the "Dark Continent" now was accessible, and a succession of famous explorers quickly dispelled the darkness. To speak of the "discoveries" made by these Europeans is patently ethnocentric, since Africa obviously had already been "discovered" and settled by its own inhabitants. Furthermore, the explorers did not have to hack their way through trackless jungles or deserts. Rather they made use of existing communication systems consisting of well-used intervillage trails, caravan paths and canoe routes. They also utilized the local inhabitants as guides, as guards and as porters. When Henry Morton Stanley set out to find David Livingstone in 1870, Stanley employed a host of African and Arab porters, guides and caravaners. Little wonder that the Scottish missionary, in beholding this motley array, was speechless until Stanley said, "Dr. Livingstone, I presume?" The stereotype of intrepid explorers struggling through virgin territories is almost entirely myth. On the other hand, the Europeans did integrate and publicize the findings of expeditions to various parts of the continent, thereby making the interior of Africa as well known to the outside world as the interiors of the Americas had become two centuries earlier.

The systematic exploration of the continent began with the founding of the African Association in 1788. It was headed by a noted British scientist, Joseph Banks, and its purpose was "to promote the cause of science and humanity, to explore the mysterious geography, to ascertain the resources, and to improve the conditions of that ill-fated continent." [3] The Association's attention was directed first to the problem of the Niger. As yet the river was only a name. Even before the beginning of the European slave trade rumors had circulated about fabulous cities on the banks of a great river called the Niger. No one knew where it rose and where it ended. To solve the mystery the Association in 1795 sent out a Scottish physician, Mungo Park. After enduring blistering heat, sickness, captivity and hunger, he succeeded in reaching the Niger, but illness compelled him to return to the coast instead of following the river to its mouth. In 1805 Park returned at the head of a sizable expedition, but fell victim to fever before achieving his mission. [4]

Many others tried to unlock the mystery of the Niger until finally Richard Lander followed it to its mouth in 1830. In doing so, Lander proved that the so-called Oil Rivers, long known to Europeans as a source of palm oil and slaves, comprised the delta of the Niger. A French explorer, René Caillié, entered West Africa from the far southwest in Muslim disguise. Crossing the Sahara to Tangier, he was the first European of modern times to enter Timbuctu. To his great disappointment, he found that fabled city of golden legend to be only "a mass of ill-looking houses, built of earth." Exploration of West Africa was furthered the most during the 1850s by Dr. Heinrich Barth. This remarkable German visited the most important cities of the western Sudan and then crossed the Sahara and returned to England in 1855. His journey is one of the greatest feats in the history of African travel, and his journals are equally outstanding because of his thorough exposition of the geography, history and ethnology of the lands he visited.

Interest shifted to East Africa after a disastrous trading expedition up the Niger proved that commercial opportunities were scanty there. The big question in East Africa was the source of the Nile. Hostile natives, vast marshes and innumerable rapids had defeated all attempts to follow the river upstream to its headwaters. In 1856 two Englishmen, John Speke and Richard Burton, started inland from the African eastern coast. They discovered Lake Tanganyika, and with Burton ill, Speke pushed on another two hundred miles to discover Lake Victoria. On a second trip (1860–63), Speke saw the White Nile pouring from Lake Victoria at Ripon Falls, and then followed the great river to Khartoum and on through Egypt to the Mediterranean.

Meanwhile, other explorers were opening up south-central Africa, starting out from the Cape Province of South Africa. Head and shoulders above all stands the figure of the great David Livingstone. He had trained himself originally to become a medical missionary in China, but the outbreak of the Opium War diverted him to Africa, where he landed at Capetown and worked his way northward. In 1849 Livingstone crossed the Kalahari River to see what fields for missionary enterprise lay beyond. He discovered Lake Ngami, where he heard that the country ahead was populous and well watered, in contrast to the desert he had just crossed. In 1852 he set forth on the great journey that was to take him first to the Atlantic and then back across the continent to the Indian Ocean, which he reached in 1856. Livingstone then returned to England and delivered at Cambridge University his historic address that stimulated interest in Africa throughout the Western world.

Between 1857 and 1863 Livingstone headed an expedition that explored the Zambezi region, and in 1866 he set forth again to settle various questions concerning the source of the Nile. Disappearing into the African bush, he was unable to send word to the outside world for five years. Finally the New York *Herald* sent Henry M. Stanley, a famous foreign correspondent, to find Livingstone. Stanley did find him in

1871 on Lake Tanganyika in one of the memorable episodes of African exploration. Although Livingstone was weak and emaciated, " a mere ruckle of bones" in his own words, he refused to return home with Stanley. Instead Livingstone continued his explorations until May 1, 1873, when his followers found him dead, in a praying position beside his cot.

These explorers of Africa reacted variously to what they observed. Some tried valiantly, and with some success, to comprehend the strange peoples and cultures they encountered. Barth and Livingstone stand at the head of this group. Others made the effort but were unable to break out of the mold of their own backgrounds and perceptions. Many were simply incapable of any empathy with Africans, who were so patently different from English gentlemen. Finally, all the explorers had traversed a continent in a state of deep crisis. The slave trade had thrown entire regions into disruption and chaos, with neighbors preying upon neighbors. The explorers assumed that "life had always been like this"—an assumption that justified the notion of "trusteeship." Benighted savages, unable to fend for themselves, needed to be taken in hand and shown the way to "civilization." This attitude was reinforced by the racism that was shared to a greater or lesser degree by all explorers of the time. Even the selfless Livingstone, with his strong sense of justice and humanitarianism, could write with certitude: "We come among them [the Africans] as members of a superior race and servants of a Government that desires to elevate the more degraded portions of the human family." [5]

℘ *III. Slave Trade to Legitimate Trade*

In addition to making possible the work of explorers, the abolition of slave trading also cleared the way for trading in other commodities— for "legitimate trade," as it was called by abolitionists. This new trade flourished especially in West Africa, which produced various commodities that were in demand in Europe. These included palm oil, used for soap, lubricants and candles; palm kernels for margarine and cattle food; and ground nuts for cooking oil and soap. Other nineteenth-century exports of West Africa were gum from Senegal; gold from the Gold Coast; and timber, ivory and cotton from the forest zone. In return for these exports, West Africans received cotton and wool textiles, alcoholic spirits, hardware, salt, tobacco, guns and gunpowder.

As in the case of the earlier slave trade, so now with the new legitimate trade, the Africans jealously guarded their role as middlemen. Some withdrew from coastal operations with the abolition of the slave trade and reverted to trans-Saharan exchange. This was the case with

202 / GLOBAL RIFT

the Ashanti state in the middle portion of what is now Ghana. Its leaders reduced trade with the Gold Coast to the bare necessary minimum—mostly guns and gunpowder—and turned to the Hausa caravan traders in the North. The latter brought in cotton cloth, silk and other manufactured goods, which they exchanged for kola—a stimulant that Muslims could use in place of alcohol. Salaga became the center of this trade and it reached a population of forty thousand to fifty thousand by 1874.

Those Africans who continued to trade with the Europeans on the coast were aided by the founding of the African Steamship Company in 1852. The new steam-powered vessels reduced the transportation time between Britain and West Africa from thirty-five to twenty-one days and less. Also the steamships, operating on fixed schedules, were available to all merchants, and enabled native traders to compete with established European companies. By 1857, according to an observer on the Gold Coast, "the old class of large European merchants who greatly monopolized the trade have passed away and the amount of business done formerly by a few, is now in the hands of numerous small traders, chiefly natives." [6]

In the long run the European companies retained their dominant position in the overseas trade because of superior financial resources and useful connections with the European commercial networks. As in the days of slave trading, the European merchants again "trusted" their goods to African middlemen for periods of six months to two years. The latter journeyed inland, traded the goods for interior products and then paid back their European customers the equivalent in palm oil, ivory, timber and other materials. Just as Adam Smith had noted a century earlier that in Africa "it was more difficult [than in the Americas] to displace the natives and to extend the European plantations," so Consul Charles Livingstone wrote in 1872 to the Foreign Office, "The black brokers [middlemen] are strict protectionists, and allow no trade with white or black except what passes through their hands, at their own price: and each tribe on the river or coast, does the same with its next inland neighbor." [7]

Outstanding among the black "strict protectionists" was Jubo Jubogha, founder and king of the state of Opobo, and commonly known as Ja Ja. He controlled the main palm-oil trade routes, and made it clear that all Europeans would have to deal through him. When the British consul pressed him to allow British merchants to operate in the interior, Ja Ja replied, "My first and last words are that the country belongs to me and I do not want white traders . . . there." He added, "Any one who wants to trade . . . with me" would be required to do so at Opobo and nowhere else. The British consul and merchants responded by urging the home government to annex the lands of the obstreperous Ja Ja. "These requests for annexation," commented a Foreign Office official in 1886, "are becoming frequent" and were designed "to break down the middleman system of which Ja Ja is the champion." [8]

The native merchants of West Africa, where most of the trade was conducted, not only retained control over the transactions but also began to demand higher-quality products in exchange. Formerly the Europeans had palmed off beads, used clothing, gaudy cloth and assorted cheap novelties for the African raw materials, which they then sold at home at handsome profit. In 1856 John Tobin, the chief importer of palm oil in the United Kingdom, admitted before a parliamentary committee, "Formerly, it was the custom of white men to fancy that anything was good enough for a black man, and they attempted to impose upon them. [Now] they are as well able to distinguish between genuine articles and fictitious as any person in this country." [9] This testimony has led the historian, Dike, to make the following noteworthy observation:

> It is a matter of reflection that little of permanent value came to West Africa from the 400 years of trade with Europe. In return for the superior labour force, the palm oil, ivory, timber, gold, and other commodities which fed and buttressed the rising industrialism, they received the worst type of trade gin and meretricious articles. When the Old Calabar chiefs demanded capital equipment for sugar manufacture and cotton culture, we have it on Owen's authority [Captain William Owen was a Royal Navy officer who made the standard surveys of African coasts] that the West India interest successfully resisted these "legitimate aspirations."

The new legitimate trade, in contrast to the earlier slave trade, was a mass trade involving the mass of the people. The slave traffic had been monopolized by a few large entrepreneurs, many of whom became rulers or senior officials of the states involved. The new trade in raw materials, by contrast, involved small farmers who could produce the export products with little capital, and using family labor, hired hands and traditional tools. The imports likewise no longer were destined for the local elite, but rather for a mass domestic market generated by a more equal distribution of income than in the days of the slave trade. The mass nature of the new exports and imports is reflected in the sharply increased value of foreign trade. The slave trade at its height at the end of the eighteenth century engendered for West Africa an overseas commerce worth about £4 million a year. By 1850 the value of overseas trade had risen fourfold. Palm oil exports to Britain grew from a thousand tons in 1810 to ten thousand tons in 1830, to twenty thousand tons in 1842, to thirty thousand tons in 1885, and to forty thousand tons in

1855. Likewise British cotton textile exports to West Africa increased thirty times during the three decades from 1816–20 to 1846–50.

The terms of trade during the first half of the nineteenth century were exceptionally favorable for West Africa. The prices fetched by exports rose steadily because of the expanding markets in Europe. By contrast, manufactured imports in 1850 cost only one half to one quarter of what they had cost in 1800, thanks to the ongoing Industrial Revolution and the resulting gains in productivity.

By the mid-nineteenth century, West Africa had made the transition from an economy based on the sale of slaves to one based on the sale of natural produce. African merchants had begun to overshadow the traditional chiefs in wealth and influence. Banks, roads and a uniform currency still were lacking, but the livelihood of people was becoming increasingly dependent on foreign trade as well as domestic. British policymakers were well satisfied with this outcome, and made clear their resolve to focus on trade without territorial entanglements. The Report of the Select Committee of 1865 articulated this resolve unequivocally in opposing "all further extension of territory" and recommending the transfer of administration to the native populations "with a view to our ultimate withdrawal from all." [10]

Within a decade, changing economic conditions in West Africa and changing balance of forces internationally combined to reverse the above policy of anticolonialism. All the Great Powers of Europe plunged into a hectic scramble for African lands, culminating in the virtually total partition of the continent by the end of the century.

Chapter 11

MIDDLE EAST ENTERS
THE THIRD WORLD

At present the greater part of the exports of Turkey consist in
raw material, which it hands over to Europe, and which the latter
returns to Turkey in a manufactured form. . . . Turkey . . .
ought to give up, for the present, all attempts at competing with
Europe for the main objects of manufacture, and to confine herself to bringing forth the natural riches of her soil. . . .

M. A. UBICINI (1856)

Free trade with the capitalist Western countries meant that the less
developed Ottoman economy "went to the wall" and that Ottoman
markets were inevitably captured by large-scale, low-cost Western
goods. Changes of this order were entirely of the essence of Western international trade theory as enunciated by Ricardo. Free-
market forces, acting upon the underdeveloped economy of the
Ottoman Empire had created a situation of compulsory bilateralism with Britain, in particular, which was little removed from
colonial tutelage.

OYA KÖYMEN (1971)

Prior to the nineteenth century the Middle East had been partially incorporated into the global market economy. The capitulatory system, the
influx of New World bullion with its inflationary effect, the activities of
the various Levant companies and the pressures of the adjacent European powers all combined to subordinate certain Middle Eastern regions

to the economy of the expanding capitalist West. This process both broadened and deepened during the course of the nineteenth century, so that the Middle East, like Africa, changed from a peripheral to a fully integrated area vis-à-vis the world capitalist order. The Western powers annexed outright the whole of North Africa, including for all practical purposes the rich province of Egypt, despite the nominal suzerainty of Constantinople. The Ottoman Empire was left only with its Asia Minor heartland and the Arab provinces to the south, these escaping partition only because the European powers could not agree on the division of such strategically located territories.

More important than the military expansionism of the West was its economic dynamism. All the Middle Eastern lands, whether colonies or nominally independent, felt the impact of Europe's Industrial Revolution. Everywhere the flood of cheap machine-made imports increased, facilitated by the new steamships and railways and distance-saving Suez Canal. Western capital also permeated the Middle East, whether in the form of private investments or governmental loans. By the turn of the century, Middle Eastern countries were dominated as much by Western banks as by Western factories. Those parts of the Ottoman Empire that had not been politically annexed as colonies were now economically annexed as semicolonies. The end result for all was the intensified control and exploitation by the West that marked the transition from peripheral to full-fledged status in the Third World.

❧ I. "Turkish Manchester and Leeds"

The changing relationship between the Ottoman Empire and the West was apparent in cultural matters as well as in political and economic matters. In earlier centuries the Moslem Middle Easterners, like the Confucian Chinese, had looked down on Christian Westerners as barbarians beyond the pale. "Do I not know you," broke out the grand vizir to the French ambassador in 1666, "that you are a Giaour [nonbeliever], that you are a hogge, a dogge, a turde eater?" [1] As late as 1756, when the French ambassador announced the alliance between France and Austria that marked a turning point in the diplomatic history of Europe, he was curtly informed that the Ottoman government did not concern itself "about the union of one hog with another." [2]

During the nineteenth century this contempt and arrogance gave way to respect and fear, if not in the villages where most of the population lived, then at least among responsible policymakers who had to cope with the power and aggressiveness of the West. The change in attitude was prompted by the unbroken series of military defeats and territorial losses, as well as by the spread of Western-style educational institutions.

Some were established by the Turks themselves—the School of Medicine (1867), the Imperial Lycée (1868), the University of Constantinople (1869), the School of Law (1870) and the School of Political Science (1878). Catholic and Protestant missionaries also contributed substantially to the spread of new ideas with their schools, their medical work and their outright proselytizing. Graduates of Robert College in Constantinople (1863), of the American University in Beirut (1866) and of the American University in Cairo (1919) provided a large proportion of the political and intellectual leaders of the Middle East during the past century.

The hitherto impregnable Ottoman "iron curtain" was gradually pierced, resulting in the emergence of a reform movement commonly referred to as the *Tanzimat,* as it is called in Turkish. Tanzimat ideology held that modern European society was in many ways superior to the Ottoman, and that imperial survival required adaptation to that society rather than nostalgic hankering for an irretrievable past. More specifically, the basic aim of the Tanzimat reformers was centralization in order to get rid of the *ayan,* or local notables, and their allies who controlled most of the provinces (see Chapter 6, Section V). This goal was gradually achieved, partly by armed force, as in the crushing of the praetorian Janissaries (1826), who had opposed all substantive change, and partly by successive reform decrees that in many ways did not pass the paper stage but that did leave a residue of real progress.

The "men of the Tanzimat" formed a new ruling class of relatively well-educated and well-motivated individuals. They comprised a centralized hierarchy of civil servants in place of the former ayan with their tax farms. Regular salaries from the treasury, together with improved communications by railroads and telegraph, gave the department heads in Constantinople more real power than even the sultans had wielded in the old days. This was not an unmixed blessing, especially because of the lack of popular participation in government, comparable to that which was developing in the West at the time. The fact that the Ottoman Empire continued to be referred to by Westerners as the "sick man of Europe" until its demise after World War I reflects the ultimate failure of the Tanzimat.

Both the political and economic measures of the reform leaders proved futile in the long run. In matters of politics the "men of the Tanzimat" were hampered by their class origins. They were themselves the children of the older Ottoman ruling class, and therefore were unwilling to push reforms to their logical conclusion, which would have imperiled the estates and revenues of parents or relatives. Also, the reform leaders had been educated in European ways, which made them Europeans in dress, in manners and in spirit. This tended to a certain deracination, which led them to scorn or ignore the illiterate village masses. They regarded themselves as Ottoman gentlemen, and they not only wore different clothes and affected different manners, but even spoke a different literary form of Turkish that was far removed from the purer but cruder idiom of the typical Anatolian Turkish peasant. The latter were referred to by the Constantinople gentlemen-officials as Kaba Turk or rough Turk, and Eshek Turk or donkey Turk. This attitude was fully reciprocated, which explains why Sultan Abdul Hamid II was able with virtually no opposition to dismiss the reformers in 1877 and to maintain his autocratic regime until 1909.

In economic matters also, the "men of the Tanzimat" proved equally inadequate. They reflected the traditional Ottoman attitude that economic enterprise was beneath the dignity of Ottoman gentlemen and should be left to their Armenian, Greek or Jewish subjects. Not one of the reform leaders had a clear understanding of economic issues or a genuine interest in them. Even if they had worked out economic guidelines or programs, they would have had little chance of implementing them because of the capitulations and the later conventions, which effectively hamstrung the Ottoman economy (see Chapter 6, Section III).

The classic example of foreign economic domination and exploitation was the 1838 Anglo-Turkish Commercial Convention. Prior to that agreement the Ottoman government had used a variety of restrictions, bans and monopolies in a largely futile effort to curtail exports of raw materials until the needs of the domestic consumers, crafts and armed forces had been met. It became virtually the operating rule that the export of commodities would be banned if their supply decreased to the point of causing inflationary prices or stimulating a black market with prices above the official levels. Also, the government commonly imposed a monopoly on strategic materials such as copper, gold and silver, buying up all supplies to forestall their export by foreigners.

The 1838 Anglo-Turkish agreement effectively removed what little protection these old policies had provided for local consumers and enterprises. It forbade all government monopolies or bans on exports, allowed British merchants to purchase goods anywhere in the empire and exempted them from the numerous taxes to which Ottoman merchants were subject (except for 5 percent duty on imports, 12 percent on exports, and 3 percent on transit). A most-favored-nation clause made these provisions applicable to all foreign merchants, who now were able to carry on trade within the empire on more favorable terms than Ottoman citizens.

Article 6 of this convention provided that "the regulations shall be general throughout the Turkish Empire, whether in Turkey in Europe or Turkey in Asia, in Egypt or other African possessions. . . ." The real target of this article was Mohammad Ali of Egypt, the archrival of the

Ottoman Sultan and the *bête-noir* of the British government. Mohammad Ali had seized power in Egypt at the beginning of the nineteenth century, and then had proceeded to build the first modern army and navy in the Middle East. In support of his modern military establishment he constructed factories and shipyards and arsenals, and to pay for all these undertakings he imposed government monopolies in trade, industry and finance. But for the free-trade England of the mid-nineteenth century, the word "monopoly" was as damning as the word "communism" was to be for the capitalist West in the mid-twentieth century. Accordingly, the antimonopoly article in the 1838 Convention was used against Mohammad Ali's intolerable bid for economic independence, and with the additional prodding of a British expeditionary force, he was finally forced to scrap both his factories and his armed forces.

Meanwhile, the precise opposite was happening within the Ottoman Empire—namely, a little-known but very revealing attempt at industrialization during the 1840s. Mohammad Ali's effort toward modernization was crushed by Britain because of his unacceptable government monopolies in the economic field, and his equally unacceptable political aspirations for control over the Middle Eastern routes to India, which the British viewed as their sacrosanct imperial lifeline. For this reason Mohammad Ali was forced to reduce his army of 130,000 to 18,000, which automatically eliminated the need for most of his factories, and thereby ended the Egyptian drive for political and economic independence.

Toward Sultan Abdul Mejid in Constantinople, however, British policy was altogether different. He was weak and pliant, where Mohammad Ali was strong and aggressive. Foreign Minister Palmerston's strategy, therefore, was to shore up the decrepit Ottoman Empire, and he accordingly supported the expansion and modernization of the Ottoman army. This in turn required supporting industries, so from the early 1840s until the Crimean War, a substantial industrialization program was undertaken by the Turks.

Most of the plants were built in what amounted to an "industrial park" immediately to the west of Constantinople. This included an ironworks with a furnace and two forges, a steam-driven machine shop, a textile factory to spin, weave and print calicoes, other textile plants producing silk and woolen fabrics, and a shipyard equipped to build small steamships. Ottoman industrial independence required a domestic supply of raw materials, so foreign geologists and mining engineers were employed to search for local resources. By 1845 iron ore was being mined from both the Princes Islands in the Sea of Marmora and the adjacent mainland. Limestone also was found west of Constantinople, as well as coal deposits at Eregli. Also a ranch with fifteen thousand Merino sheep was established near Bursa, and a cotton plantation west of Constantinople, where an American expert imported gins and even slaves from the United States. Farther west, near San Stefano, a model farm was developed with new strains of livestock, various experimental crops and thousands of seedling trees. Students were recruited for a new school of advanced agricultural techniques that was located on the premises.

Nearly all the machinery for these enterprises was imported from Europe, along with the foremen and skilled workers. In the streets of Constantinople during these years were to be found foreign draftsmen, fitters, patternmakers, molders, boilermakers, blast furnace keepers, puddlers, bar iron rollers, smiths, burners, millwrights, plate rollers and shipbuilders. Under the supervision of this foreign elite were some five thousand unskilled workers, including Greeks, Armenians, Jews, Bulgarians and Turks. As in Europe during those years, their hours were from dawn to dusk, six days a week.

Some foreign observers were sufficiently impressed by all this activity to speculate about the prospect of "a Turkish Manchester and Leeds, a Turkish Birmingham and Sheffield, all four in one." [3] But within a decade this ambitious program instead had petered out. One reason was the problem of unskilled and undisciplined factory labor, even though thousands of trained handicraft workers had been displaced by the rising tide of European imports. Just as in England and France two or three generations earlier, artisans and peasants disliked intensely the impersonality and regimentation of factory work. Foreign supervisors found efficiency low, absenteeism high, the turnover rate appalling and the number of holidays incredible. The situation became so critical that there were reports of worker intimidation, of factory construction by *corvée* labor and of some workers hobbled in fetters.

The problem, however, was not merely one of restructuring traditional peasant and artisan work attitudes. The foreign personnel compounded the difficulties with their reluctance to train native workers for skilled positions. They understandably had no desire to risk losing their own jobs, for which they were being paid rates at least double those current in Western Europe. Some of the foreigners also complained of "jobbery," or corrupt and incompetent interference on the part of Ottoman officials who indulged in the time-honored practice of milking the Ottoman cow with little concern for the calf. As early as 1848 there were ominous reports of half-completed or idle Ottoman factories and rusting equipment. With the Crimean War in the early 1850s, the Ottoman government for the first time found it necessary to resort to European loans. The first casualty of this financial distress was, not surprisingly, the ailing industrialization program. Thus the vision of a "Turkish Manchester and Leeds" evaporated with little residue left from all the expenditure of capital and energy.

ᛒ *II. Turkey Enters the Third World*

The decisive event in the nineteenth-century Ottoman history was not the spectacular attempt at overnight industrialization, but rather the 1838 Anglo-Turkish Commercial Convention, which effectively ensured the failure of any industrialization program, regardless of any other inhibiting factors. This agreement completed the Western domination over Turkey's economy that had gotten under way centuries earlier. By removing the various obstacles in the way of foreign trade, its total value (exports plus imports) increased dramatically, from £320 million in 1800 to £560 million in 1840, £1.45 billion in 1860, £2.89 billion in 1872 and £8.36 billion in 1913.

This spurt in foreign trade reflected economic growth rather than economic development within the Ottoman Empire. The value of Turkish exports to Britain remained about half the value of British exports to Turkey, a serious and persistent drain that contributed to the need for heavy borrowing and eventual imperial bankruptcy. The principal Turkish exports to Britain were raw materials (dyestuffs, grains, cotton, wool, raw silk and raisins), while British exports were manufactured goods (cotton and woolen goods, iron and steel products, and processed colonial products such as spices, coffee and sugar). Western consuls in various Ottoman cities all reported the decimation of local crafts by the unhindered influx of cheap machine-made European manufactures. For example, in Izmir sixteen of eighteen cloth factories were closed by 1850; in Aleppo half of its original ten thousand looms were shut down by 1858; and in Bursa the four hundred looms of 1820 were reduced to thirty by 1860, and its original one thousand silk workshops to seventy-five by 1868.[4]

The relationship between these shutdowns and the 1838 Commercial Convention was explicitly made in an 1845 French consular report: "Presently, these two large cities [Damascus and Aleppo] consume a greater quantity of these cloths [English and Swiss] than Beirut itself; and of the twelve thousand looms which existed in these two cities, there are but little more than a thousand in Damascus and one thousand five hundred in Aleppo. The 1838 treaty thus wielded a fatal blow to these industries. . . ."[5] As revealing as this report is the fact that during the 1847 political crisis in Syria, foreign trade was temporarily disrupted and some of the abandoned looms were put back in operation. But when the crisis ended and normal trade relations resumed, the shutting down of looms continued apace as before. This episode represented a preview of the twentieth-century Latin American experience, where domestic industries increased rapidly during the foreign-trade disruptions caused by the two world wars and the Great Depression, and then declined once more with the returns to "normalcy."

The subordination of the Ottoman economy to that of Western Europe was almost universally considered at the time as proper and normal. A decade after the French consul had reported the "fatal blow" dealt to Ottoman industries by the 1838 Commercial Convention, French writer M. A. Ubicini was stating forthrightly that this colonization of the Ottoman economy was mutually beneficial!

> Manufacturing industry has greatly declined from what it formerly was in the Ottoman Empire. At present the greater part of the exports of Turkey consist of raw material, which it hands over to Europe, and which the latter returns to Turkey in a manufactured form. . . .

> Turkey should learn two lessons from the past: first that she ought to give up, for the present, all attempts at competing with Europe for the main objects of manufacture, and to confine herself to bringing forth the natural riches of her soil, or to several special branches of native manufacture, destined to give life to her inland trade, such as carpets, shawls, morocco leather, gold embroidery, sadlery, arms, soap, etc. . . . And if she fears becoming impoverished by drawing more from foreign countries than they take in return, I repeat that it is in her power to restore the balance by turning the riches of her soil to account. Cereals alone, without speaking of the other branches of culture, might easily furnish an equivalent to more than 100,000,000 francs per annum. With this sum there would not be much difficulty in paying for many quintals of iron, many barrels of sugar, many ells of cloth, many yards of calico and muslins. . . .[6]

This proposition was considered axiomatic at the time—the proposition that a few Western European countries should become "the industrial workshop of the world," as the current phrase went, and that the peoples of the rest of the world should remain, or rather become, hewers of wood and drawers of water. It is understandable that this tenet should have assumed the proportions of virtually divinely ordained truth in nineteenth-century Britain, which was reaping golden profits from such a lucrative assignment of global tasks. But the fact is that virtually no dissent was heard from within the Ottoman Empire, and the reason is that powerful vested interests had developed in the raw-material export trade, and for these interests the semicolonial economic relationship with the West was both profitable and desirable.

This domestic support for Ottoman economic subservience is evident in the economic development of the province of Iraq in the second half of the nineteenth century. Iraqi exports rose from £147,000 per annum in 1864–71 to £2,960,000 in 1912–13, a twentyfold increase in less than half a century. A major reason for this export boom was the opening of the Suez Canal, which for the first time made it financially feasible for Iraqi products to be sold in Western Europe. The opportunity was seized by an elite group of tribal shaykhs, town notables, bureaucratic officials and military officers. They forced the nomadic tribes to settle down and grow export crops, so that the nomadic element in Iraq's population fell from 35 percent in 1867 to 7 percent in 1930. At the same time the ruling elite acquired former tribal lands at nominal prices and converted them into private estates. As typical Middle Eastern landlords they appropriated a substantial proportion of their tenants' crops, which they sold to merchants for consumption in the cities or for export abroad.

The increase in agricultural productivity did not promote regional economic development because the profits went to the absentee landlords, who soon acquired expensive consumption tastes, especially for foreign luxuries such as alcohol, textiles, clothing and household furnishings. None of the capital extracted from the tenants was used for improving agricultural techniques, let alone for financing industrial enterprises. Instead, Western manufactured goods poured into Iraq, as into the other Ottoman provinces, so that the number of hand-loom weavers in Baghdad declined from 3,500 in 1866 to about 120 in 1934. Thus whereas Iraq before the Suez Canal had exported to her Middle Eastern neighbors simple manufactured goods such as silk articles, boots, shoes and soap, by the end of the century these craft products had given way to foodstuffs and industrial raw materials such as grains, dates, wools, cotton, hides and skins.

Western predominance was evident not only in trade but also in the construction of the Middle East's infrastructure. Foreign enterprise dug the Suez Canal, developed the ports of Beirut, Alexandria and Port Said, built the Syrian, Balkan, Egyptian and Berlin-to-Baghdad railways systems, provided gas, electricity and water for the major Middle Eastern cities and furnished regular steamship services connecting eastern Mediterranean, Red Sea and Persian Gulf ports with the rest of the world.

Ottoman finances also were subject to complete Western control. The Turks contracted their first foreign loan in 1854 during the Crimean War. Being inexperienced in the ways of high finance, they paid little attention to the problem of how they were going to repay this, and several other loans that soon followed. The international bankers not only failed to caution the Turks but also in some instances brought pressure to bear upon them to borrow more at inflated interest rates. By 1875 the Ottoman government had contracted fourteen loans requiring £12 million sterling a year to meet annuities, interest and sinking fund

—a sum amounting to a little more than half the total annual revenues of the empire. Six years later Constantinople, on the brink of bankruptcy, was forced to cede control over certain imperial revenues to an international body consisting of representatives of the foreign creditors. This "Ottoman Public Administration," as it was called, had for all practical purposes a mortgage on the entire imperial economy. By 1911 it had a staff of 8,931 persons, as against 5,472 in the imperial Ministry of Finance. "The Ottoman Empire," observed a resident English merchant in the mid-nineteenth century, "exists for two purposes. First, to act as a dog in the manger, and to prevent any Christian power from possessing a country which she herself in her present state is unable to govern or to protect. And secondly, for the benefit of some fifty or sixty bankers and usurers, and some thirty or forty pashas, who make fortunes out of its spoils." [7] The same point was made more succinctly by a French observer at the end of the nineteenth century: "The Ottoman Empire is the status quo. The status quo is keeping things going and paying coupons." [8]

❧ III. "A Manufacturing Country Egypt Never Can Become . . ."

Egypt stands out in the history of the Third World for its pioneering effort to win political and economic independence from the West and to avoid the semicolonial status of the Ottoman Empire. The moving spirit behind this historic venture was Mohammad Ali, an illiterate Albanian adventurer who took advantage of the chaos following the defeat of Napoleon's Egyptian expedition to make himself the *de facto* ruler of Egypt by 1805. Mohammad Ali had the basic advantage of being the absolute master of his realm. He achieved this by ruthlessly eliminating the Mamluks, a Turco-Circassian military elite that had exploited the province for centuries. But Mohammad Ali was more than a super-powerful Middle Eastern pasha. He was unique in that he began, like many other provincial pashas of his time, by seeking to amass a fortune, but ended by striving to develop his adopted country. He was also unique in realizing at that early date that the key to development was to be found in the West. In this respect he undertook a role in Egypt comparable to that of Peter the Great in Russia. He became the pioneer innovator of the Middle East because, like Peter the Great, he understood that genuine independence required a modern army capable of resisting the West, and that a modern army in turn required a modern industrial establishment to provide the necessary military equipment. Accordingly Mohammad Ali proceeded, with a drive and ability reminiscent of his Russian predecessor, to impose a complete restructuring of Egyptian society.

Egypt's twenty-three thousand villages hitherto had been dominated by tax farmers, who kept the difference between what they collected and what the treasury demanded. Mohammad Ali increased revenues substantially by eliminating these middlemen and requiring the peasants to pay their taxes directly to the government. He further expanded revenues by an extensive irrigation program that increased the land under cultivation as well as the productivity per unit of land. The greatest economic advance was achieved accidentally by a French textile engineer, Louis Alexis Jumel. While working in a Cairo spinning and weaving mill, he noticed in a neighborhood garden a type of cotton plant that produced fiber of greater length and strength than the ordinary Egyptian short-staple cotton in commercial use. Yet it was being ignored by all, except for the neighborhood women, who grew it for their household needs. Jumel grew three bales of this new strain in his own garden and found that its superior qualities fetched two to four times the price of the short-staple variety. Mohammad Ali seized the opportunity by providing the peasants with the new seed and with instructions for proper cultivation, and by building cotton gins and presses in the villages. Jumel cotton, as it came to be called, soon was the No. 1 revenue producer for the government. Mohammad Ali made cotton a state monopoly, which enabled him to pay set low prices to the peasants and charge high prices to the foreign buyers.

The profits accumulated from the export of cotton and other agricultural commodities such as sugar cane and grains enabled Mohammad Ali to import industrial machinery from Europe, along with the necessary technical personnel. By 1830 factories were turning out cotton, woolen, silk and linen textiles, sugar, paper, glass, leather, sulphuric acid, guns and gunpowder. Investments in industrial enterprises amounted to about £12 million by 1838. Some sixty thousand to seventy thousand workers were employed in these factories, comprising 6 to 7 percent of total employment, which is the same percentage of the labor force engaged in "modern" manufacturing in Egypt today.[9] The objective was to replace foreign imports whenever possible with domestic substitutes. In fact, Egypt in the 1830s was exporting a significant quantity of manufactured goods, especially textiles, to neighboring countries.

Since government monopolies dominated industry as well as agriculture, Mohammad Ali had to provide trained personnel in these areas, and also in the rapidly expanding army and navy, which absorbed most of the industrial output. He sent over three hundred students to Europe, where the majority specialized in industrial subjects. Several times as many studied at home in newly opened schools of medicine, engineering, chemistry, agriculture, accountancy and languages.

In short, Mohammad Ali was attempting to impose a program of forced industrialization in order to build a diversified and independent economy. He not only preceded Sultan Abdul Mejid's attempt at a "Turkish Manchester and Leeds," but also he far outdistanced it in scope and achievement. He was more capable and energetic, and disposed of more funds, thanks to the profits from his monopolies in agriculture and foreign trade, as well as his heavy land taxes and forced loans. Having eliminated the old Mamluk ruling class, he was the unquestioned ruler of the country, so that his orders were actually implemented to a degree that was impossible for any sultan working through encrusted layers of imperial bureaucracies and vested interests.

Yet in the end Mohammad Ali failed completely, and his factories did not survive his death in 1849. The reasons were partly domestic—his own failings and those of his subjects—but in a more fundamental sense they were external—the unrelenting opposition of British policymakers, who correctly perceived Mohammad Ali's modernization effort as a direct challenge to their domination and exploitation of the entire Middle East.

The pervasive illiteracy and superstition of the Egyptian population was the first hurdle in the way of Mohammad Ali. Its significance becomes apparent if contrasted with the 50 percent literacy in Japan when that country was opened to the West a decade after Mohammad Ali's death. Even during the centuries of seclusion under the Tokugawas (see Chapter 17, Section I), the Japanese had carefully kept up with current scientific advances in the West, and therefore were intellectually prepared for rapid modernization after the appearance of Commodore Perry. How different it was in Egypt, where the traditional enmity between Islam and Christianity constituted an impenetrable obstacle against cultural interaction. According to an historian, Professor el-Shayyal of the University of Alexandria, "We do not hear of a single Egyptian who had visited Europe in the sixteenth, seventeenth, and eighteenth centuries." [10]

Egypt not only had learned nothing from Europe, and was quite uninterested in doing so, but also, even worse, had forgotten much of what it had known in the past. The library of the famous al-Azhar University, for example, was only a fraction of what it had been in the Middle Ages. As for elementary education, it consisted of learning the orthography of the Arabic language through memorizing the Koran, while the rudiments of arithmetic were taught by the public weigher in the marketplace. The resulting intellectual chasm between Egypt and the West is evident in the following bewilderment of an Arab scholar who visited a laboratory set up by a scientist with Napoleon's expedition to Egypt in 1798:

Among the strangest things I saw in that place was that one of the people in charge took one of the bottles containing distilled waters, and from it poured a little in a test-tube, upon which water he poured a little from another bottle. The two liquids rose, and a coloured cloud ascended therefrom, until it disappeared. The contents of the tube dried up, and became a yellow stone . . . a dry stone which we handled and examined. This he did again using different waters, then produced a blue stone. Repeating the experiment a third time with other waters, he produced a ruby-red stone. Further, he took a pinch of white powder, put it on an anvil and struck it gently with a hammer, then a terrific sound ensued, a sound similar to that of a gun, which gave us a shock. So they laughed at us.[11]

As serious as this unpromising cultural climate in Egypt was Mohammad Ali's own ignorance, despite his keen intelligence and full realization of the need to acquire Western technology. His illiteracy, together with the lack of any enlightened native advisers, meant that he was clear as to his goal, but in the dark as to the precise steps for its realization. This left him vulnerable to faulty advice from foreigners who were either ignorant of Egypt's needs or interested only in their own personal gain. Mohammad Ali's native officials also were responsible for much disruption, partly because they were as corrupt and extortionate as other bureaucrats throughout the Middle East.

In addition to bureaucratic rapacity, Mohammad Ali's drive for modernization bore down brutally at the expense of Egypt's long-suffering masses. Artisans were forced into the new factories, where hours were long and working conditions bad. They responded with theft and sabotage, which became serious problems for the government. More serious was the plight of the peasants. As many as four hundred thousand were rounded up to work four months each year on giant public works, and often they had to bring their own food, water and tools. Peasants also were conscripted to serve for life in the army, where they were poorly paid, miserably fed, and led by Turkish officers who despised them. The peasants resisted in various ways—some by mutilating themselves, others by fleeing to Syria and in some cases by rising in revolt.

Despite these very real and formidable domestic difficulties, it is at least possible that Mohammad Ali would have been partially successful if he had not had to contend also with the implacable hostility of British officialdom, especially of the imperious Foreign Minister, Lord Palmerston. "I hate Mohammad Ali," he declared frankly, "whom I consider as nothing but an ignorant barbarian, who by cunning and boldness and mother-wit, has been successful in rebellion. . . . I look upon his boasted civilization of Egypt as the arrantest humbug; and I believe that he is as great a tyrant and oppressor as ever made a people wretched." [12]

Behind this characteristic explosion were two concerns that preyed on Palmerston, one economic, the other strategic. In 1837 he had sent Sir John Bowring to Egypt to investigate Mohammad Ali's economic policies, about which Palmerston had received many complaints from British merchants and consuls. "A manufacturing country," Bowring reported, "Egypt never can become—or at least for ages; a country giving perpetual cause of anxiety to the European Powers by the restlessness of her Rulers, she cannot be allowed to continue,—but by the peaceful development of her agricultural aptitude she may interest and benefit all." [13]

Palmerston readily accepted this conclusion, conforming as it did to the conventional wisdom of the time concerning the proper and natural role of non-Europeans as suppliers of raw materials and consumers of manufactured goods. But the difficulty was that Mohammad Ali refused to accept this assigned status of economic subservience. Worse still, he was making significant progress with his alternative policy of industrialization and government monopolies in agriculture and foreign trade. The monopolies were anathema during this era, when free access to foreign markets was considered as virtually the divinely ordained right of British merchants and manufacturers. Hence the castigation of Mohammad Ali as a "barbarian," and the concern expressed for his "wretched" subjects. This concern, it might be noted, never again manifested itself once the "barbarian" had been disposed of, though there was at least as much occasion for concern after that achievement as before.

Probably a more important factor behind Palmerston's vituperation was Mohammad Ali's threat to British imperial strategy. During the 1830s several English surveyors and scientists were active in the Middle East, investigating possible ways of expediting the transport of commodities from Europe to India and the Far East. Some favored a canal across the Suez isthmus; others preferred a railway to a canal; and still others urged development of the Euphrates-Persian Gulf route. But whichever of these routes was considered, Mohammad Ali was found to be in the way. With his Westernized land and sea forces he had easily defeated his nominal suzerain, Sultan Mahmud II, and overran Arabia, the Sudan, the island of Crete and the entire Levant coast between Asia Minor and Egypt.

Palmerston's reaction to these conquests was revealingly forthright. Mohammad Ali's "real design," he stated on one occasion, "is to establish an Arabian kingdom, including all the countries in which Arabic is the language. There might be no harm in such a thing in itself; but as it necessarily would imply the dismemberment of Turkey, we could not agree to it. Besides, Turkey is as good an occupier of the road to India as an active Arabian sovereign would be." This was a typical British understatement, for Palmerston obviously much preferred a weak and dependent Ottoman Sultan astride the routes to India, as against that "active Arabian sovereign." Palmerston therefore concluded, "We must try to help the Sultan in organizing his army, navy, and finances; and if he can get those three departments into good order he may still hold his ground." [14]

Sultan Mahmud did receive assistance in rebuilding his armed forces, and in 1839 he attacked the Egyptians in Syria, hoping to regain the provinces he had lost to the upstart in Cairo. But in one fateful week, between June 24 and July 1, 1839, the Turkish army was crushed, the Turkish fleet sailed to Alexandria and surrendered and the old Sultan in Constantinople mercifully died from excessive drinking before news of the disasters had reached him. Palmerston took advantage of the crisis to be rid of the bothersome "barbarian," proclaiming that "Mohammad Ali will just be chucked into the Nile." [15] Palmerston sent warships to transport fresh Turkish troops and Austrian and British marines to Syria. These land forces drove back Mohammad Ali's army, while British warships bombarded coastal towns and military installations at will. With the remnants of his army streaming into Egypt, and with a British squadron anchored before Alexandria, Mohammad Ali was forced to surrender most of his conquered provinces, though in return the new Sultan, Abdul Mejid, recognized him as the hereditary ruler of Egypt.

More significant for Egypt's future were two other conditions imposed on Mohammad Ali. One was the reduction of his army from 130,000 to 18,000 men, which automatically eliminated most of the market for which his new factories had been designed to produce. The other condition was the enforcement within Egypt of the 1838 Anglo-Turkish Commercial Convention. This eliminated Mohammad Ali's state monopolies and allowed foreign traders to buy and sell freely anywhere within the country. Simultaneously deprived of their military market and exposed to the competition of European industries, Egypt's new factories were doomed.

Mohammad Ali's impact on the Middle East of his time was akin to that of a meteorite crashing in from outer space. His efforts between 1820 and 1840 represented an attempt to end Egypt's traditional subsistence economy by developing an export trade and using the proceeds to build up industries and develop a balanced and independent national economy. "The collapse of Mohammad Ali's schemes," concludes an economist, Professor Charles Issawi, "points out one of the major obstacles to economic development in Egypt . . . the lack of political autonomy. Economic development usually requires considerable aid in the form of tariff protection, tax exemptions, rebates on transport rates, cheap power, special credit facilities to certain sectors, educational policies, etc., which only a government enjoying a large measure of political and fiscal independence can provide." [16] But it was precisely "political and fiscal independence" that Palmerston refused to tolerate, for both economic and strategic reasons. With his superior military and economic resources he successfully torpedoed Mohammad Ali's historic bid for independence from the West. Bowring's dictum, "A manufacturing country Egypt never can become," proved to be, not surprisingly, a self-fulfilling prophecy.

IV. Egypt Enters the Third World

With Mohammad Ali's failure to develop an independent diversified economy, the only alternative for Egypt was, in Bowring's words, "the peaceful development of her agricultural aptitude." This development did occur, so that Egypt now became, like Turkey, an economic dependency of Europe. More specifically, Egypt was transformed into an export-oriented monoculture society, relying largely on raw cotton exports to pay for manufactured imports.

One feature of this transformation was the granting of permission to foreigners to acquire any kind of land. They quickly took advantage of the opportunity to obtain much agricultural property through mortgages and other loans. These foreigners were not only Westerners but also assorted Levantine elements (Syrians, Lebanese, Armenians, Jews and Greeks), who first acquired capital by serving as forwarding agents, brokers and intermediaries, and then invested their capital in land. Whether foreign-owned or not, a large proportion of the cultivable land soon passed out of the control of the peasants. Of a total of 914,000 landowners at the end of the nineteenth century, 761,000 had less than 5 *faddans*, the subsistence minimum (a faddan was 4,201 square meters, or just over 1 acre). Two fifths of the land at that time, or 2,243,000 faddans, was owned by 12,000 individuals or firms.

Foreign capital invested in agriculture was paralleled by foreign domination of commerce. The application of the 1838 Anglo-Turkish Commercial Convention to Egypt enabled Western commercial houses in Alexandria to send agents to the villages to buy directly from the peasants. The only competition they encountered was not that of native Egyptians but of Levantine traders. The amount of cotton available for export increased rapidly, especially with the American Civil War, which cut off the chief source for the British cotton industry. In 1861, 500,000 *cantars* of cotton (1 cantar was equal to 99 pounds) were grown on 250,000 faddans of land, but by 1866 the harvest had increased four times and the cultivated area five times. The total cultivated area rose from 4,160,000 faddans in 1862 to 5,283,000 in 1913.

The increased agricultural output necessitated a corresponding expansion of transportation facilities. The first railway was opened in 1853, and by 1913 there were 2,953 kilometers of standard-gauge railways plus 1,376 kilometers of light railways. This transportation network was supplemented by a communications network of 5,200 kilometers of telegraph lines. At the same time the port of Alexandria was repeatedly enlarged and improved, and the new ports of Suez and Port Said were built on the Suez Canal. The opening of the canal itself funneled a vast flow of international traffic through Egypt.

All these developments reflected Egypt's rapid integration into the global market economy. The pace was evident in the growth of foreign trade from £E 2 million in 1798 to £E 5.1 million in 1860, to £E 21.8 million in 1880, and to £E 60 million by 1913. The fundamental consideration, however, is that this impressive economic growth occurred in a dependent Third World context, so that there was no accompanying economic development. All sectors of the Egyptian economy—agriculture, commerce, finance and transportation—were geared to producing cotton and making it available to European industries. The beneficiaries were foreign merchants and financiers, along with the small native elite. The masses remained the illiterate, disease-ridden fellaheen toiling at bare subsistence level on the banks of the Nile, as their ancestors had done before them for millennia.

Under the protection of the capitulatory treaties, European speculators and adventurers were free to operate in Egypt outside the jurisdiction of the native courts and subject only to consular control. Many grew rich by smuggling opium and tobacco, and invariably were protected by the foreign consuls, of whom there were about seventeen. These foreigners, who were completely exempt from taxation, also served as agents in arranging for loans and contracts on extortionist terms. In 1873, for example, the Khedive accepted a loan of face value of £ 32 million, but after the heavy commissions and discounts had been deducted, he received only £9 million, a large part of which was in depreciated treasury notes. The malversations of these "jackals of finance," as they were called, together with the extravagances of the court and the corruption of the officials, left Egypt with debt obligations that by 1877 were absorbing £7,473,000 out of the total national revenues of £9,543,000. After payment of the regular tribute to the Sultan, and dues on the Suez Canal shares that had been sold to England, the government was left with about £1 million for the administrative expenses, or little more than one tenth of the original revenues.

This was the background of the appointment of European "controllers" in 1879 to manage Egypt's finances. Nationalistic Egyptian army officers understandably were outraged by this flagrant foreign exploitation of national resources. They rose in revolt under Ahmed Arabi in 1881 against the Khedive, and were supported by mass rioting in Alexandria in 1882. The British responded by bombarding the city and occupying the entire country. The Foreign Office proclaimed its intention to withdraw the British forces "as soon as the state of the country and the organization of the proper means for the maintenance of the khedivial authority will admit of it." [17] By 1922 the British had repeated this withdrawal promise no less than sixty-six times, yet they still continued the occupation, and continued to do so until finally forced out after three quarters of a century by Gamal Abdel Nasser in 1956.

Egypt's lack of economic development cannot be attributed exclusively to external exploitation and constraints. The native labor force was unskilled and, apart from cotton, Egypt had few raw materials and no fuels. Also there was the formidable cultural obstacle of native disinterest in commercial and industrial enterprise. In Egypt, as in Turkey, this was left almost entirely to Westerners and to Levantines. Wealthy Egyptians were content to buy land, while educated Egyptians mostly entered the rapidly expanding civil service. This left foreigners in control of finance, large-scale commerce and even petty trade and the crafts. Lord Cromer, the British consul-general, noted in his *Annual Report for 1905,* "Bootmending as well as bootmaking, is almost entirely in the hands of Greeks and Armenians. The drapery trade is controlled by Jews, Syrians, and Europeans, the tailoring trade by Jews." Cromer's observations were valid also for the professions, as almost all physicians, pharmacists and engineers were foreigners, as well as a large percentage of the lawyers. Thus it is estimated that by 1914 foreigners owned 15 to 20 percent of Egypt's wealth and absorbed over 20 percent of the national income.

Giving full weight to these internal causes for Egypt's failure to achieve economic development even remotely commensurate with her economic growth, the fact remains that the basic underlying factor was, as Professor Issawi concluded, "the lack of political autonomy." In his *Annual Report for 1891* Lord Cromer stated flatly that "it would be detrimental to both English and Egyptian interests to afford any encouragement to the growth of a protected cotton industry in Egypt." By 1905, however, he was beginning to have misgivings about Egypt's reliance on agricultural exports because of the growing population pressure and rising rents. "Probably the greatest danger which threatens Egypt lies in the fact . . . that the country depends too exclusively on one crop. . . ." [18] Yet Cromer's response to this "greatest danger" was mostly rhetorical speculation about the need to avoid overcropping, to provide better seed and to offer commercial and technical education for the surplus rural population.

Furthermore, when two proposals were made in the 1890s to establish cotton factories in Egypt that would enjoy the advantage of cheap local labor and raw cotton, as well as the modest 8 percent duty on cotton imports, Cromer strongly opposed the projects. He threatened either to end the 8 percent duty or to impose a countervailing excise duty on home-made textiles. Foreign Secretary Kimberley sent a dispatch in June 1895 strongly supporting Cromer, and enclosing a confidential memorandum from the Board of Trade stressing the opposition of Lancashire to the establishment of a "protected" competitor in Cairo. Cromer accordingly levied an 8 percent excise tax on the products of local textile factories. The promoters nevertheless proceeded with their plans and established the two factories. Both ultimately went bankrupt. Although it is disputed to what extent Cromer's opposition was responsible for the failure, "there can be little doubt," concludes an historian who is sympathetic to the official British position, that Cromer's attitude in these cases "could not have failed to discourage entrepreneurs who might have been contemplating the establishment of factory industry of another kind." [19]

In this manner, Egypt became a Third World country during the nineteenth century. Professor Jacques Berque, in his sociological analysis entitled "The Establishment of the Colonial Economy," has described vividly precisely what Third World status meant for Egypt:

According to Herodotus, Egypt was a "gift of the Nile," but for a long time she was nothing more than a mortgaged security in the service of the Public Debt. . . . If we wanted to sketch a schema of the way in which Egypt was set up in that period [late nineteenth century], we would represent it in the following manner: At the base would be the old Egyptian land and the *fallah* barely separated from it. The next layer would be that of the small notables accompanied even at the very level of the village by the small Greek merchant, already responsible for diffusing a few products of faraway Europe—among other things, alcohol, the consumption of which increased every day and which made up one of the most important imports. One degree higher would be the landlords and the intermediaries—the one associated with agriculture and the other with trade. Higher still, in the provincial towns and in the capital cities would be the bank branches, the seat of Barclays, of the Crédit Foncier, of the Crédit Lyonnais, of the Comptoir National d'Escompte, etc., and all that which revolved around them. On top were the central banking power divided between French and British finance, and the budget, bureaucratic Bastille and conscience of the new state; for everything led to the bank by way of cotton. Between the budget and the bank there was, in any case, more than one link, primarily through men, and also through the exchange of courtesies. Towards the top, this level merged with the empire of bondholders, shareholders, important businessmen, the Rothschilds of Vienna, of Paris, of London, and the powerful individuals from everywhere, such as Cassel. In this way, the Egyptian edifice was constructed for two or three generations.[20]

V. Persia Enters the Third World

To the east of the Ottoman Empire was the sprawling Persian Empire, stretching from the Tigris-Euphrates Valley to the borders of India and deep into central Asia. For centuries it had been the great rival of the Ottoman Empire in the Middle East. Especially under the Safavi Dynasty in the sixteenth and seventeenth centuries, Persia was courted by European powers as a counterweight against the sultans at Constantinople. But the power and glory of past ages did not save the Persians from the expansionism of the industrialized West, any more than it did the Turks or the Egyptians. During the nineteenth century the Persian Empire was gradually integrated into the international market economy, though at a slower pace and to a lesser degree than the Ottoman lands. Persia consistently lagged several decades behind in economic development compared to countries such as Syria, Turkey and Egypt.

One reason for the lag was the geography of the Persian Empire. Its huge size (2½ times that of Texas) and its jumble of crisscrossing mountain ranges made central control difficult, particularly because of the absence of any large unifying rivers such as the Nile, the Tigris-Euphrates or the Indus and Ganges. The centrifugal effect of geography was reinforced by the existence of numerous nomadic tribes comprising half the total population in 1800 and a quarter as late as 1914. The nomads were virtually independent of the central government, being largely self-sufficient and getting the few commodities they needed from nearby villages. The Shah had theoretical right to name their chiefs, but almost always he had no alternative to selecting the heads of ruling tribal families.

Local governors also were largely independent so long as they sent in the revenues and made the expected gifts to the Court. The Muslim religious leaders, or *ulema*, also enjoyed substantial independence based on their income from the Muslim community, their ownership of extensive lands, their control of education and religious courts and the respect in which they were held by the population. Under these circumstances the

Qajar Dynasty, which ruled from 1796 to 1925, and which lacked any leader comparable to Egypt's Mohammad Ali, was notoriously feeble and archaic. With both the native ruling class and the domineering foreign powers interested in preventing the central government from becoming too powerful, it is scarcely surprising that the Qajars proved more adept at squandering national resources than providing national leadership.

Another crucial factor explaining Persia's retardation was the location of the country in the heart of the Eurasian land mass, among the Fertile Crescent, Central Asia and India. During the Middle Ages this location was advantageous, as it placed Persia athwart the famous "silk road" running from China to Mesopotamia. But with the shift of world trade to sea routes in the sixteenth century, Persia found itself in an isolated cul-de-sac, eleven thousand miles distant from Western Europe in the pre-Suez era. This isolation was accentuated by the lack of large non-Muslim minorities such as the Greeks, Jews and Armenians, who provided Western contacts for the Ottoman lands. Likewise the number of resident Westerners was infinitesimal (twenty-five Britishers in 1860 and fifty Frenchmen in 1863) compared to the thousands in Egypt, Syria and Turkey.

Finally, Persia was subject to the stultifying effect of Anglo-Russian rivalry. Its effects were much worse than the rivalry of several Great Powers in the Ottoman Empire, which often neutralized each other. In Persia, by contrast, Britain and Russia effectively blocked each other's economic projects, or, even worse, joined forces to divide the entire country into their respective spheres of influence.

Despite these drawbacks, Persia's foreign trade did increase twelve times between 1800 and 1914, even though this was far less than Egypt's fifty-to-sixty-fold increase, and Turkey's fifteen-to-twenty-fold increase. The dramatic rise in foreign trade reflected the gradual envelopment of Persia's economy by world capitalism. One reason for this envelopment was the greater security in the Persian Gulf area thanks to British naval activities against pirates, and in the northern provinces because of Russian forces in that area. Equally important was the lessening of Persia's isolation by the opening of the Suez Canal in 1869, and by the establishment of telegraphic communications between the 1860s and 1880s with various parts of the world as well as with provincial areas within the country and by the starting of steamship services with Russia across the Caspian Sea, with India across the Arabian Sea and later with Western countries. Various projects for railway building, however, were blocked by Anglo-Russian rivalry, so that by 1914 only one six-mile line was in operation, and that ran to a shrine outside Teheran.

Persia's foreign trade was stimulated also by trade treaties imposed by European powers similar to those forced by Britain on the Ottoman Empire in 1838 and on China in 1842. In the case of Persia, Russia took the lead with the Gulistan and Turkmanchai treaties of 1813 and 1828, followed by Britain with the Anglo-Persian Commercial Treaty of 1841 and also by assorted speculators and adventurers who were in search of quick profits and who collaborated with wily courtiers equally eager for self-enrichment regardless of national interests. The major economic concessions included a maximum 5 percent customs duty for imported goods, which was extended to several European countries under the "most-favored-nation clause"; immunity to foreigners from road tolls and internal transit taxes, which were collected, however, from native merchants; a concession to Britain to organize the Imperial Bank of Persia with a monopoly in issuing currency; another concession to Russia to establish the Russo-Persian Bank, which was used as an instrument to assure Russian predominance in the northern provinces; a Caspian fisheries monopoly granted to a Russian businessman; tobacco and oil concessions to British subjects; several loans negotiated under most unfavorable terms; and finally, capitulatory rights were conceded to foreign powers, as had been done earlier by the Ottoman government (see Chapter 6, Section III).

These concessions resulted in a shift in the direction and substance of Persia's foreign trade. Until 1800 it had been mostly with neighboring Turkey, Afghanistan, India and central Asia, and Persian exports included craft products such as textiles. In the first half of the nineteenth century most of the trade was with Britain, through either Turkey or the Persian Gulf. But in the second half of the century Russia's share rose dramatically, thanks to an aggressive program of economic penetration, including road building, port concessions, transport companies, insurance firms, a cigarette factory, warehouse and wholesale establishments, and loans on more favorable terms than those of the rival British Imperial Bank of Persia. By 1914 Persia was importing annually from Russia goods worth 64,060,000 rubles, as against 32,032,000 from Britain, and exporting goods worth 54,371,000 rubles to Russia, as against 10,280,000 to Britain. The following instructions to the new Russian minister to Persia in 1904 reveal that Russia was pursuing the same political and economic objectives in Persia that Britain was in the rest of the Middle East. Just as Britain purposefully sought to keep alive the "sick man of Europe" on the banks of the Bosphorus, so Russia sustained another "sick man" farther to the east.

The main object that has been pursued by us . . . in the course of a long contact with Persia, may be defined in the following manner: To preserve the integrity and inviolability of the Shah's domains, not seeking territorial increases for ourselves and not permitting the dominance of a third power, gradually to subject Persia to our domination without the violation, however, of either the external signs of Persia's independence or her internal structure. In other words, our task is: politically to make Persia obedient and useful; that is sufficiently strong to be a tool in our hands—economically, to preserve for ourselves the major share of the Persian market for free and exclusive exploitation by Russian efforts and capital.[21]

These objectives were successfully realized. Between 1890 and 1913 Russia sent only 2.1 to 3.8 percent of her exports to Persia, and took from her only 3 to 4 percent of her imports, but Persia, by contrast, depended on Russia for 58 to 69 percent of her exports and 38 to 58 percent of her imports. Also, the composition of her exports and imports now were of the usual Third World variety. Whereas textiles formerly comprised one of her chief exports, now they were the chief imports, along with sugar, tea, flour and iron and steel products, while her exports, apart from carpets, were raw materials such as raw cotton, bread cereals, dried fruits and nuts, rice, opium and animal and fish products. In short, Persia had become economically dependent on a Great Power that was itself economically dependent on the more advanced Western states.

Economic subservience had as profound repercussions on Persian society as it had on the Ottoman and Egyptian societies. The pattern was similar in that the chief beneficiaries were the foreign merchants and financiers along with the native ruling class. The latter included the landowners, who extracted from their tenants the maximum produce for the new foreign markets; the moneylenders, who profited from usury in the increasingly monetized society; the large merchants, who engaged in the new trade; and the bureaucrats, courtiers and royal family, who squandered foreign loans even more unproductively than did their counterparts in Constantinople and Cairo.

The pattern was similar also because all these ruling-class gains were made at the expense of the peasant masses. The reports of Western travelers agree that peasant conditions worsened during the course of the nineteenth century. Jean Chardin, a trustworthy observer of seventeenth-century Iran, wrote of the comfortable position of Persian peasants, which he compared favorably with those of the West. As late as 1833 a perceptive Englishman, James Fraser, reported that although the peasants endured "the tyranny of their rulers," nevertheless their houses were "comfortable and neat," they enjoyed a wholesome diet of "good wheaten cakes, some mast or sour milk, and cheese—often fruit makes its appearance, and sometimes a preparation of meat, in soup or pilau." As for clothing, "Their wives and children, as well as themselves, are sufficiently though coarsely clad; and if a guest arrives, there are few who cannot display a numed or felt carpet in a room for his reception." [22] By 1905, however, a Persian traveling through tribal villages noted the absence of cultivation and inquired why the inhabitants did not grow vegetables they could eat themselves, and sell any surplus to travelers. An old man replied,

> What you say is true provided we are left to ourselves. What benefit is there for me that I should spend my life and undertake labour, the fruits of which will be taken possession of entirely by the governor and tax-collector who will prevent me from enjoying them. And, if I undertake this labour once, it will become a hereditary charge on my family. Every year the tax-collector and governors will demand it of me.[23]

Nearly all taxation fell directly or indirectly on the peasantry, with smaller amounts paid by the tribes and by town artisans. The bureaucrats, landlords, upper ulema and wholesale merchants were virtually tax-exempt. As the nineteenth century progressed, the government found it necessary to raise substantially greater revenues. One reason was the disastrous wars with Russia (1828) and Britain (1856), and the subsequent efforts, largely futile, to modernize the armed forces. Another reason was the profligacy of the royal Court, which squandered vast sums at home as well as abroad during periodic visits. Finally, there was the steady inflation throughout the nineteenth century, due partly to the cutting of precious metals in the coinage, but mostly to the fall in the world price of silver, on which Persian coinage was based. By 1914 the exchange value of Persian coinage had fallen to one fifth of its 1800 exchange rate with the pound sterling.

The resulting financial difficulties forced the Teheran government in the second half of the nineteenth century to sell offices regularly to highest bidders. Those who became officeholders through this process naturally raised taxes to gain maximum return on their investment. Higher officials in turn sold lower posts within their jurisdiction, so that ultimately the peasantry were forced to support several levels of extortionist officials.

The peasants were adversely affected also by the growing monetization of society. The government increasingly demanded payment of taxes in cash, while landlords pressed for the growing of crops that could be exported for cash: silk, opium, cotton and tobacco. The peasants' need for credit forced them to moneylenders, and inability to repay meant loss of land. Unpaid debts also tied peasants to landlord properties, since landlord and moneylender often were one and the same. This process was constantly stimulated by the expanding foreign markets for Persian raw materials, which encouraged landlords to expand their holdings by foreclosing on peasants or by buying Crown lands from the hard-pressed government. Merchants and bureaucrats also participated in this acquisition of estates, as they preferred to invest surplus capital in land than in industry—a characteristic common to their counterparts throughout the Third World.

At the same time that the peasants were losing their lands, the urban craftsmen likewise were losing their sources of livelihood because of cheap foreign machine-made imports. Protective tariffs could not be raised because of treaty restrictions, and the scarcity of available capital and of technical skills further discouraged attempts at launching competitive industries. Thus Persian handicrafts, with the notable exception of carpet weaving, were severely damaged, as the well-informed British consul, K. E. Abbott, reported in 1848: "The manufactures of England have in a great measure superseded the use of the Cotton and Silk fabrics of this country, owing to their cheapness, the superiority of the style and execution of the designs, and the greater variety of patterns, which both enabled people to make a more frequent change of dress and to satisfy their taste for novelty of patterns—and even the higher classes have often preferred European chintz to the more expensive silk dresses of their own country." [24]

In conclusion, Persia's peasantry and craftsmen generally suffered from the rapaciousness of their ruling elite and from the penetration of Western and Russian capitalism. Although the various ruling-class elements prospered, they did so, as everywhere in the Third World, in capacities subordinated to foreign interests. "A good deal of trade is done by native merchants," reported Curzon in the 1890s, "but the bulk of mercantile transactions passed through the hands of what may be indisputably described as English firms. . . ." [25] In other words, prosperous Persian merchants functioned as agents of Russian and British commercial firms. This was inevitable, given the predominance of British and Russian banks over the Persian money market; the terms of the commercial treaties that favored foreign interests; and the preference of the local elite to invest in land, leaving industry and large-scale commerce to foreigners. Thus the elevenfold increase in foreign trade during the nineteenth century culminated in the emergence of a dependent bourgeoisie in Persia—the symptomatic characteristic of Third World status.

Chapter 12

INDIA ENTERS
THE THIRD WORLD

The great interest of India was to be agricultural rather than
manufacturing and mechanical.

THOMAS BAZLEY, President of
Manchester Chamber of Commerce, 1862

For 2½ centuries after da Gama, Europeans were effectively excluded
from the Indian subcontinent. Their superior ships and naval artillery
enabled them to gain control of the Indian Ocean, but on land they
were allowed to trade at but a few posts along the coast, where they
were tolerated only on good behavior. The volume of trade during these
early centuries was meager because the West produced little of interest
to Asians, while the exports of Asia were mostly luxuries that few in
the West could afford. Trade with Asia prior to the mid-nineteenth
century was not of the mass variety, as was the trade with the Americas.
England in 1751 imported three fourths as much from the single sugar
island of Jamaica as from the whole of Asia.

This political and economic independence of India rapidly dissolved
during the nineteenth century. Military conquest transformed the Mogul Empire into a British possession. At the same time India was integrated into the international market economy as completely as the
Americas and Africa had been in earlier centuries. Thanks to the Industrial Revolution the West now was able to flood India with cheap
machine-made goods, thereby disrupting the traditional native crafts.
And European consumers who formerly could not afford Indian exports
now imported vast quantities of tea, while their industries absorbed
equally vast quantities of jute, cotton, indigo, hides and oilseeds. Indian

manpower also was exploited, as millions of coolies, under conditions reminiscent of the earlier African slave trade, were set to work in plantations and mines in Southeast Asia, Fiji, East Africa and the Caribbean.

In this manner, India entered the Third World in the nineteenth century. The nature and results of this process of subordination and integration are the subjects of this chapter.

ꙮ *I. Conquest of India*

One background factor explaining the sudden shift in balance of power on the Indian subcontinent was the omnipresent caste system, which focused attention on local affairs rather than national ones. Being born in a particular caste determined one's upbringing in infancy and childhood; the choice of mate in marriage; the work one could legitimately undertake; the appropriate religious ceremonies; the place of residence; and the manner of dressing, eating and most other details of daily living. Caste took care of virtually everything at the village level, so that government above the village was regarded as a superfluous and predatory excrescence generally imposed by outsiders. All this was quite different from China, where the imperial bureaucracy provided society with strong political cohesion. Whereas in China the peasants revolted periodically to replace a "bad" government with a "good" one of the same substance, in India the peasants sought to be rid of government altogether, since their castes performed most of its functions. The amorphous Indian society obviously was more vulnerable to foreign intrusion and manipulation than the highly organized imperial structure of China.

The inherent vulnerability of Indian society greatly increased during the eighteenth century, when the Mogul Dynasty was deteriorating at the same time that the European powers were becoming economically and militarily more aggressive and powerful. Here again there is a striking contrast with China, where the Manchu Ch'ing Dynasty took power in 1644 and maintained effective control until the nineteenth century. The Mogul Dynasty of India preceded the Manchu Dynasty by a century, and reached its height under Emperor Akbar, who followed a policy of religious toleration and light taxation. After his death in 1605 his successors were less capable and less enlightened. This was especially true of Aurangzeb, the last great Mogul Emperor, who came to the throne in 1658. A Muslim fanatic whose religious persecutions alienated his predominantly Hindu subjects, Aurangzeb was forced to wage continual warfare, which in turn led to heavier taxes and to further popular disaffection.

With his death in 1707 the Mogul Empire began to fall apart. There was no settled rule of succession, so that for two years his sons disputed the throne. Between 1712 and 1719 five puppet emperors ruled at Delhi. Under these circumstances the provincial governors began to assert their independence and to establish hereditary local dynasties, such as those of Hyder Ali of Mysore and of the Nizam of Hyderabad. The reins of power slipped away from the Delhi emperors to the provincial potentates and to the Marathas, who represented Hindu nationalism in a vague and incipient sense. The Marathas gained control over a large central area from the western coast to within two hundred miles of Calcutta on the eastern coast. This Maratha Empire, with its capital at Poona, was the only indigenous dynamic political force in India in the mid-eighteenth century.

The Maratha leaders understandably concentrated on taking over the Mogul heritage, but in doing so they overlooked the mortal danger posed by the British merchants in Bombay, Madras and Calcutta. These merchants promptly exploited the endless opportunities for divide and rule presented by the imperial disintegration. They played off Hindus against Muslims, and rival provincial governors against each other and against the Mogul emperors. They were assisted in this strategy by a powerful new Indian capitalist class, which was closely associated with the European merchants and had derived great profits from trade with them.

Prior to the appearance of the Europeans the economy of India had been little affected by foreign trade, which was relatively slight and peripheral. But by the eighteenth century the commodities of trade had shifted from a few luxury items to articles of mass trade such as indigo, mustard seed, hemp, saltpeter, calicoes and muslins. These products of the rich Ganges Valley were funneled down to the ports of Bengal through the agency of the Marwari merchants. With their offices all over North India, the Marwaris soon became millionaires, corresponding to the comprador class of China in the late nineteenth century. Like their Chinese counterparts, the Indian capitalists were dependent upon foreign interests, with whom they collaborated closely, as against the Mogul Dynasty, which they hated as intensely as the compradors did their Manchu Dynasty. India was much more vulnerable than China to Western penetration because the Indian national economy and imperial administration were not as developed and integrated as the Chinese.

The combination of flabby social structure, imperial disintegration and collaborationist native merchants gave the British East India Company the opportunity to dominate the subcontinent where for centuries it had operated only on sufferance. Originally company agents had sailed to India, purchased cargoes and returned home. They soon realized that more profits could be made if they resided for lengthy periods in India, bought goods when prices were the most favorable and stored them till the ships arrived from Britain. This led to the building of permanent warehouses and quarters for the company agents or "factors," the compounds coming to be known as "factories." As anarchy spread in India, fortifications were built around the factories, and Indian guards or *sepoys* were employed to man the fortifications.

With their fortified factories and sepoy troops the British merchants steadily extended their control over the surrounding regions and eventually over the entire country. Typical was the process of establishing the first territorial foothold in Bengal. The local *nawab* or governor was beset by three challenges to his authority: by the Marathas, who were attacking from the West; by domestic enemies led by the fabulously wealthy Marwari merchant, Jagat Seth; and by the East India Company, which was strengthening the fortifications of its Calcutta factory. The nawab ordered the company to stop the construction work, and on refusal, attacked and seized the factory and the city of Calcutta. Robert Clive marched from Madras with relief forces, and the ensuing Battle of Plassey proved to be what Indian historians term "a transaction, not a battle." [1] Jagat Seth had bought the allegiance of the nawab's general, who crossed over to the British side.

For his betrayal the general was made the new nawab of Bengal. In practice he became the helpless puppet of the company, whose greedy officials squeezed every kind of concession from him. The Mogul Emperor now attempted to intervene but his forces were defeated and he was forced to grant to the company the *diwani,* or the right of revenue collection. For a decade the company used this authority to fleece the local population mercilessly. In addition to tax extortion, the company compelled Indian artisans to work for subsistence wages in producing goods that company agents bought at set low prices and then sold for much higher prices. Still another source of plunder was the control of domestic trade by company agents, who refused to pay the substantial internal duties and thus drove out of business the native merchants, who were required to pay.

"To engineer a revolution," state two English historians, "had been revealed as the most paying game in the world. A gold-lust unequalled since the hysteria that took hold of the Spaniards of Cortes' and Pizzaro's age filled the English mind. Bengal in particular was not to know peace again until it had been bled white." [2] Richard Beecher, a servant of the company, wrote to his superiors in London on May 24, 1769, as follows: "It must give pain to an Englishman to have reason to think that since the accession of the Company to the Diwani the condition of the people of this country has been worse than it was before. . . . This fine country, which flourished under the most despotic and arbitrary government, is verging towards ruin." [3]

The British Parliament was moved by such reports of oppression and suffering. It passed various regulatory measures, including Pitt's India Act of 1784, which allowed the company to continue trading but placed political activities under the supervision of a Board of Control in Britain. The Act also stipulated that "schemes of conquest and extension of dominion in India" were "repugnant to the wish, the honour and policy" of the nation.

Despite this official opposition to further aggrandizement, company officials continued to extend their operations. The reason was simply that each new province yielded another flood of riches for the company and its agents. And the London government was seriously handicapped in enforcing its orders because it took a year or more to transmit messages by sailing ship between Britain and India. Thus the company officials eliminated their rivals in India one after the other.

First they defeated the French during the Seven Years' War, which was fought in India as well as in Europe and America. Taking advantage of the superiority of the British navy, Robert Clive moved his forces at will from one part of India to another, and at the same time severed the communications of the French factories with each other and with France. The end came with the surrender in 1761 of the main French base at Pondichéry. By the 1763 Treaty of Paris the French were allowed to retain their factories, but only for trading purposes. They were forbidden to erect fortifications or pursue political ambitions.

The next British advance was made during the American Revolution, when three native rulers took advantage of Britain's preoccupation in the New World to attempt to drive her out of India. The governor-general, Warren Hastings, managed to hold out and eventually to take the offensive. By 1800 only the British and the Marathas were left, and during the following years the British gradually prevailed because of dissension within the Maratha ranks. By 1818 the Maratha capital of Poona had been taken and the British company had become "the paramount power" in India.

After having established themselves in the heart of the subcontinent, the British began pushing northward in search of natural frontiers. To the northeast, in Himalayan Nepal, they defeated the Gurkhas, who henceforth served the British as loyal soldiers outside India as well as within. Likewise to the northwest, the British were able after several campaigns to defeat the proud Sikhs of the Punjab. By the mid-nineteenth century the British had become the rulers of all India, from the Indus to the Brahmaputra and from the Himalayas to Cape Camorin. A few major kingdoms still survived, including Kashmir, Hyderabad, Baroda and Travancore, but they were now isolated from each other and powerless against the might of Britain.

᯲ *II. British Control Techniques*

It has been commonly assumed that, in contrast to China, few peasant revolts occurred in India to challenge British authority. This alleged Indian passivity is usually attributed to the caste system, with its hierarchical divisions among villagers; to the collaborationism of the landlords and the princes, who fared well under British rule; and to the pacifying influence of Gandhi on the peasantry. A British anthropologist, Kathleen Gough, has reviewed this traditional assumption and reached the conclusion that "peasant revolts have in fact been common both during and since the British period, every state of present day India having experienced several over the past two hundred years." [4] Gough unearthed seventy-seven revolts, the smallest of which involved several thousand peasants. About thirty revolts involved several tens of thousands, and about twelve involved several hundreds of thousands.

These uprisings were of several varieties. Some were restorative movements seeking to drive out the British and reinstate earlier ruling families and social relationships. Others were religious or millenarian movements with prophetic leaders who looked forward to a terrestrial state of righteousness and justice. Still others were bandit groups that sought to protect the poor, or served as mercenaries for landlords and princes, or committed terrorist acts with motives of vengeance or justice. Finally there were mass insurrections for the redress of particular grievances, such as that of the Bengal indigo growers in 1866 who rose against gross oppression and exploitation on English plantations.

Despite the frequency and scope of the Indian uprisings, the fact remains that they were not as massive and well organized as those in China. One reason for the difference was the political, linguistic and cultural fragmentation among India's people, so that revolts tended to be uncoordinated and localized. Also, the British government and army were more efficient and better prepared for suppressing uprisings than the Manchu regime in China. These inhibiting factors were evident during the greatest outbreak against British rule, the "mutiny" of 1857–58. It began as an uprising of Hindu and Muslim soldiers against prolonged campaigning, inadequate pay and the greasing of cartridges with cow and pig fat, which was offensive to both Hindus and Muslims. The revolt was backed by conservative elements that were disturbed by Westernization measures such as the building of railways and telegraph lines, the opening of modern schools, the proselytizing of Christian missionaries, the legalization of remarriage by widows and the prohibition of practices such as infanticide and the cremation of widows on the funeral pyres of their husbands. Mass support for the uprising came from millions of impoverished peasants, ruined artisans, exploited plantation and factory workers, and hill tribes people antagonized by tax levies and land seizures.

The rebellion came closer to success than is generally recognized, raging over a five-hundred-thousand-square-mile region for several months. Ultimately it failed because it did not spread throughout the country and was not coordinated. North India was most solidly behind the uprising, but even there most of the princes, wealthy merchants, moneylenders and tax farmers supported the British. The sepoys were divided, half rebelling, a quarter deserting and a quarter obeying their British officers. The rebellion consequently flared up at different times in scattered regions, giving the British respite to recover from the initial surprise and then to overcome the rebel strongholds one by one.

After the fighting was over, restoration of company rule was out of the question, so the government faced the problem of administering India. A variety of control techniques were evolved to buttress British rule and forestall a repetition of the mutiny trauma. The India Act of 1858 and the Indian Councils Act of 1861 defined the nature of the new administration by the Crown. At the head was the Secretary of State for India, who was a member of the cabinet in London. The top official in India was the governor-general, or viceroy, acting as the direct representative of the Crown. The viceroy was assisted by an appointed executive council of five members, none of them Indian till 1909. For legislative purposes six to twelve additional members were appointed to the executive council, and this enlarged body functioned as a legislative council. Its measures, however, were subject to veto by the viceroy and the Secretary of State. Three Indians were appointed to the first legislative council in 1861, and their numbers were gradually increased in later years.

Beneath these top officials was the famous Indian civil service, which collected the revenues, maintained law and order and supervised the judicial system. Almost all its members until 1919 were British graduates of Oxford or Cambridge. The civil service in turn supervised a subordinate provincial service that was exclusively Indian in personnel. A similar two-level system prevailed for the police. The central all-Indian force consisted entirely of Britishers, while the provincial police were recruited from the local populations. The efficiency of British rule is evident in the fact that in 1900 there were a total of 4,000 British civilian administrators in the country compared to 500,000 Indians.

This administrative apparatus was backed by the Indian army, which in 1910 comprised 69,000 Britishers and 130,000 Indians. Some key branches of the armed forces, such as the artillery, were entirely British. The Indian recruits were mostly from what were considered the more "martial" peoples, such as the Sikhs and Pathans of the Northwest and the Gurkhas of Nepal. Also, they tended to be "yeomen peasants" or middle peasants, which the British believed to be more sturdy and reliable. This Indian army consumed a far larger proportion of national revenues than did the military establishments of other countries with much higher per-capita incomes. The following table gives the proportion of Indian military expenditures in early 1920s compared to those of other countries:

Country	Total Revenue	Total Expenditure	Defence Expenditure	4 as. per cent of 3	4 as. per cent of 2
(1)	(2)	(3)	(4)		
(Figures in millions)					
India (rupees)	1332.2	1423.9	919.0	70.7	63.8
U.K. (£)	1426.9	1195.4	642.0	45.0	53.7
Australia (£)	61.78	64.60	31.20	50.0	48.3
Canada (£)	89.38	74.19	17.9	20.0	24.2
S. Africa (£)	29.67	25.69	13.4	45.2	52.2
Spain (pesetas)	1976.66	2550.79	450.36	22.8	17.6
France (francs)	22450.9	24932.0	5027.0	22.4	20.0
Italy (lire)	17603.0	20454.8	3553.77	20.0	17.3
U.S.A. (dollars)	3345.18	3143.41	1201.44	35.9	38.2
Japan (yen)	1319.20	1399.29	646.40	49.0	46.2

Source: K. T. Shah and K. H. Khambata, *Wealth and Taxable Capacity of India* (London and Bombay, 1924), p. 267. Cited by F. Clairmonte, *Economic Liberalism and Underdevelopment* (London: Asia Publishing House, 1960), p. 83.

Not only was the Indian army extravagantly expensive for such a poverty-stricken country, but also it was employed to a considerable degree for non-Indian purposes. Just as the British earlier had used the plunder they obtained from individual Indian states for the conquest of additional states, so now they used this Indian-financed army for territorial aggrandizement outside India. Between 1838 and 1920 the Indian army was used on nineteen occasions for expeditions against neighboring countries such as Afghanistan, Burma, Malay, Siam and Tibet, as well as for extensive campaigning in the Middle East during World War I.

In addition to the bureaucracy and the army, the British used the surviving Indian princes for control purposes, particularly since most of them had opposed the mutiny. Lord Canning, the first viceroy after the mutiny, declared in 1860: "If we could keep up a number of Native States without political power, but as royal instruments, we should exist in India as long as our naval supremacy was maintained." [5] In line with this strategy the British abandoned the former company "doctrine of lapse," whereby a state came under company control if there were no natural heirs. This had been deeply resented, so Queen Victoria officially promised no further annexations of princely states. Even in the case of gross misrule, the British pressed for reform or, in a few cases, deposed the culpable ruler, but never annexed his state. Thus the British purposefully froze a crazy-quilt pattern of some 550 native states, some quite large with tens of millions of subjects, and some too small to appear on a map. The success of this divide-and-rule policy is evident in the following statement of the Maharajah of Mymensingh at a 1938 conference: "If we are to exist as a class, it is our duty to strengthen the hold of the Government." [6]

The divide-and-rule strategy was used also to keep Hindus and Muslims apart. Viceroy Lord Minto introduced this policy by creating a system of separate electorates for Muslims and Hindus. Muslims could be represented only by Muslims, elected only by Muslim voters, and no Muslims could represent a Hindu constituency or vice versa. By this arrangement the two religious communities became separate and conflicting political entities because they were forced to judge all issues from a sectarian perspective. The wife of Lord Minto noted with glee that her husband had by this act ensured for a long time British rule in India. Her elation was quite justified, for separate electorates proved to be the precursor of the two-nation theory that ultimately resulted in the costly and tragic division of the peninsula into two sovereign states.

Another effective instrument for control was the educational system, though in the long run it challenged as well as buttressed British rule. For about half a century after their conquest of India the British made no effort to impose their culture upon the country. They were too busy working out administrative, financial and judicial arrangements. In 1823 a Committee on Public Instruction was appointed, but it split into two factions, the "Anglicists" and the "Orientalists." The latter favored a traditional type of education based on Sanskrit, Arabic and Persian, while the former preferred instruction in the English language and embracing Western science and thought. The deadlock was broken in 1835 by the new committee president, Thomas Babington Macaulay, who prepared a famous "Minute on Education," which concluded, "English is better worth knowing than Sanscrit or Arabic . . . it is impossible for us, with our limited means, to attempt to educate the body of the people. We must at present do our best to form a class who may be interpreters between us and millions whom we govern; a class of persons, Indian in blood and color, but English in taste, in opinions, in morals, and in intellect." [7]

Macaulay's recommendation was adopted and implemented. During the following decades a national system of education was evolved, consisting of universities, training colleges for teachers and vernacular elementary schools for the masses. Between 1885 and 1900 the number of students in colleges and universities rose from 11,000 to 23,000, and those in secondary schools from 429,000 to 633,000. Also, the introduction of the printing press greatly stimulated intellectual life. Sanskrit works became public property rather than the jealously guarded monopoly of Brahmins. And newspapers were published in the various modern Indian languages as well as in English.

These developments affected the intellectual and political climate of India profoundly. English-type education created a new class of Indians familiar with foreign languages and cultures, and committed to liberal and rational ideologies. It also provided for the first time a common language and a common cultural background for the new educated elite in all parts of India. Hitherto they had been separated by linguistic and cultural differences, but these were now overcome by English language, literature and thought. The new all-Indian unity in turn had political repercussions. It stimulated national self-consciousness and eventually a demand for self-government.

The English had introduced their language and culture in India in order to train a class that would help them govern the country. They attained this objective, but in doing so they began the undermining of their authority, for it was this Western-educated class that used European ideology to attack British rule and to organize a nationalist movement that eventually culminated in an independent India.

Indian nationalism was the product not only of English education but also of English economic exploitation (which will be considered in the following sections) and of English racism. The mutiny engendered much of the racism, as the British feared another uprising and therefore advanced racist rationalizations in defense of their rule and repression. Also, more English women went to India after the mutiny, so that "native" wives or mistresses no longer were the acceptable norm. The superiority complex of the British was manifest in all fields—in social life, where Indians were excluded from certain hotels, clubs and parks; and in the army and bureaucracy, where Indians could not rise above certain ranks regardless of their qualifications. Lord Kitchener, commander-in-chief in India, was forthright in justifying this discrimination: "It is this consciousness of the inherent superiority of the European which has won for us India. However well educated and clever a native may be, and however brave he may have proved himself, I believe that no rank we can bestow on him would cause him to be considered an equal of the British officer." [8]

Viceroy Lord Curzon was equally bigoted regarding appointments to the bureaucracy. "The highest ranks of civil employment in India," he wrote to a colleague in 1900, "must be held by Englishmen, for the reason that they possess, partly by heredity, partly by upbringing, and partly by education, the knowledge of the principles of Government, the habits of mind, and the vigour of character, which are essential for the task. . . ." [9] Such blatant and all-pervasive racism contributed decisively to arousing nationalist sentiments among educated Indians who otherwise might have accepted the security and material rewards afforded by British rule. "As a result of this doctrine of prestige and race superiority," concludes an Indian diplomat-historian, K. M. Panikkar, "the Europeans in India, however long they lived there, remained strangers in the country. An unbridgeable chasm existed between them and the people, which was true till the very end of British rule in India." [10]

ᴥ III. India's Traditional Economy

When British officials debated the type of educational system to establish in India, Charles Grant, a director of the East India Company, declared that an English-type education would "also serve the original design with which we visited India . . . the extension of our commerce. . . . Wherever, we may venture to say, our principles and language are introduced, our commerce will follow." [11] His analysis was perceptive and fully justified. The new schools and civil service and military forces did "serve the original design," which was economic penetration, and which had consequences for India that are being felt to the present day. To understand the nature and results of the British impact, it is necessary first to examine the character of the traditional Indian economy.

The village had been the basic unit of the Indian economy for millennia, as it had been in most of the world in the pre-industrial period. Within the village it was not the individual who mattered, but rather the joint family and the caste. This group form of organization was a source of social stability but also of national weakness. Loyalty to the family, to the caste and to the village was the primary consideration, and this prevented the development of national spirit.

The land was regarded as the property of the sovereign, who was entitled to a share of the gross produce or its equivalent. This constituted the land tax, which was the main source of state revenue and the main burden of the cultivator. The share paid to the state varied from period to period from a sixth to a third or even half. Usually the responsibility for making this payment, whether in produce or in money, was collective, resting upon the village as a unit. The peasant had hereditary right to the use of the land so long as he paid his share of the taxes.

Transportation and communication facilities were primitive, so the villages tended to become economically and socially self-sufficient. Each village had its potter, carpenter, blacksmith, clerk, priest, teacher and its astrologer, who indicated the auspicious time for planting, for harvesting, for marriages and other important events. These artisans and professional men served their villages on something akin to a barter basis. They were paid for their services by receiving grain from the cultivating households or by receiving tax-free village land for their own use. These hereditary and traditional divisions of occupation and function were given the stamp of obligation by the caste system. The political structure of the village consisted of an annually elected council of five or more, known to this day as the Panchayat (*pancha* meaning "five"). The Panchayat, which normally consisted of caste leaders and village elders, met periodically to dispense local justice, to collect taxes, to keep in repair the village wells, roads and irrigations systems and to see that the craftsmen and other professionals were provided for.

The village had little contact with the outside world apart from the payment of the land tax and the irregular demand for forced labor. The combination of agriculture and hand industry made each village largely independent of the rest of the country except for a few indispensables like salt and iron. Consequently, the towns that existed in traditional India were not industrial in character. Rather, they were religious centers such as Benares, Puri and Allahabad; political centers such as Poona, Tanjore and Delhi; or commercial centers such as Mirzapur on the trade route from central India to Bengal. On the other hand, India was probably the world's greatest producer of cotton textiles until the invention of machine spinning and weaving in Britain in the late eighteenth century. Four regions in India specialized in producing textiles for export: the Punjab for central Asia and the Middle East; Gujarat for the Middle East; the Coromandel coast for Southeast Asia; and Bengal for Upper India until the early eighteenth century, and thereafter for Europe. The combination of cheap labor, technical skills and locally produced raw materials gave Indian textiles such a great competitive advantage that the East India Company was able to sell them in England at a 100 percent markup on unit cost. Indeed, it was these cheap Indian imports that stimulated English manufacturers actively to seek labor-saving, cost-reducing mechanical devices, thereby contributing to the advent of the Industrial Revolution in England rather than India.

India's traditional economy and society have been frequently romanticized. Group organizations such as the joint family, the caste and the village council did provide the peasants with psychological and economic security. The individual did have recognized duties, rights and status in his native village. If the central government was sufficiently strong to maintain order and avoid excessive taxes, then the peasants did lead a peaceful and contented existence. But as often as not the central government was too weak to keep order, and the villagers were mercilessly fleeced by rapacious tax collectors and by robber bands. This was the case in the seventeenth century when the Mogul Dynasty was crumbling. A Portuguese missionary, Father Sebastian Manrique, who was in India in 1629 and again in 1640–41, noticed that the land tax in Bengal was not only increased repeatedly but also collected four to six months in advance. The cause of this, he said, was the constant change of officials, who were invariably dismissed or transferred after a short term in office. "On this account they always used to collect the revenue in advance, often by force, and when the wretched people have no means of paying, they seize their wives and children, making them into slaves and selling them by auction, if they are heathens" [12] (that is, Hindus rather than Muslims, as were the ruling Moguls).

The Mogul state had been basically parasitic even before its decline. Most of the surplus extracted from the peasantry was used to support the conspicuous consumption of the Court and the aristocracy rather than to promote any long-term economic development. The luxury expenditures of the ruling elites did promote urbanization, commerce and handicrafts. Whether this stimulus was sufficient for an eventual self-generated transition to capitalist industrialization is a question that is often debated but that is virtually unanswerable. In any case, the political takeover by the East India Company eliminated any chance that may have existed for such an independent course of development.

IV. British Impact: Finances and Agriculture

When the East India Company got its first foothold in Bengal, it proceeded, as we noted in Section I, to plunder ruthlessly through tax levies, exploitation of artisans and refusal to pay the internal duties required of local merchants. After the British government took over from the company, the drain continued through procedures that were institutionalized and therefore not so blatant, though just as extortionist. One was the manipulation of public finances for the benefit of the British treasury. An example was the inordinately expensive military establishment, which, as noted above, the Indian taxpayers supported even though it was frequently used for purposes having nothing to do with the defense of India. "Millions of money have been spent," reported a British government commission in 1890, "on increasing the army in India, on armaments and fortifications, to provide for the security of India, not against domestic enemies, or to prevent the incursions of the warlike peoples of adjoining countries, but to maintain the supremacy of British power in the East." [13]

As serious as the misuse of military funds was the systematic debiting of India with what were in reality British expenditures. The "public debt of India" reached substantial proportions through such false debiting. Leland Jenks has summarized the nature and extent of this financial scandal:

> The burdens that it was found convenient to charge to India seem preposterous. The costs of the Mutiny, the price of the transfer of the Company's rights to the Crown, the expenses of simultaneous wars in China and Abyssinia, every governmental item in London that remotely related to India down to the fees of the charwomen in India House and the expenses of ships that sailed but did not participate in hostilities and the cost of Indian regiments for six months' training at home before they sailed—all were charged to the account of the unrepresented ryot [Indian peasant]. The Sultan of Turkey visited London in 1868 in state and his official ball was arranged for at the India Office and the bill charged to India. A lunatic asylum in Ealing, gifts to members of a Zanzibar mission, the consular and diplomatic establishment of Great Britain in China and in Persia, part of the permanent expenses of the Mediterranean fleet and the entire cost of a line of telegraph from England to India had been charged before 1870 to the Indian Treasury. It is small wonder that the Indian revenues swelled from £33 millions to £52 millions a year during the first thirteen years of Crown administration, and that deficits accumulated from 1866 to 1870 amounting to £11½ millions. A Home Debt of £30,000,000 was brought into existence between 1857 and 1860 and steadily added to, while British statesmen achieved reputations for economy and financial skill through the judicious manipulation of the Indian accounts.[14]

For the peasantry who comprised the great majority of India's population, the greatest burdens imposed by British rule were the land-tax systems. Two types were enforced, one being the ryotwari system, which was developed in the Bombay and Madras regions, and later applied in the Northwest and Northeast. This recognized the ryot as the full owner of the plot he tilled, and he was required to pay a heavy annual rent directly to the government. By eliminating the tax farmers, this system increased the revenues reaching the central treasury. On the other hand, the cash levies and the individual rather than communal responsibility for their payment led to the monetization of the rural economy, with dire results for the peasants, as will be noted below.

The second tax system was introduced in the lower Ganges basin in 1793 by the "Permanent Settlement." Hitherto the tax collectors had been state officials charged with securing the state's share of the crops from a number of villages assigned to them. But now these tax collectors were transformed into English-type landlords, or zamindars, so that most of the villagers who formerly had enjoyed hereditary use of the land were reduced to the status of tenants-at-will. The new landlords were expected to collect about £3 million annually from their tenants, of which they passed on to the British authorities ten elevenths, leaving one eleventh for themselves. The "permanent" feature of this arrangement was that the annual sum transmitted by the zamindars was to remain the same indefinitely. But the zamindars, as landlords, were free to raise their rents, which they were able to do frequently because of the growing population pressure. By World War II they were collecting between £12 million and £20 million annually, while continuing to pay the original £3 million to the state.

The motive behind this strange contract was explained in 1829 by viceroy Lord William Bentinck: "If . . . security was wanting against popular tumult or revolution, I should say that the Permanent Settlement, which though a failure in many other respects and in its most important essentials, has this great advantage at least, of having created a vast body of rich landed proprietors deeply interested in the continuance of British Dominion and having complete command over the mass of the people." [15] The validity of this statement was verified exactly a century later, when a zamindar addressing the Bengal Legislative Assembly in 1929 declared, "The British Government will be well advised to beware of agrarian socialism. The Permanent Settlement has proved to be a lasting barrier of the state against Bolshevism." [16]

The British did secure the loyalty of the zamindars, but in the process they effected a revolution in the countryside. The old communal land arrangements gave way to individual ownership, contract law, mortgage, distraint and forced sale. Formerly the land tax had been collected with considerable flexibility. Now the tax was a fixed sum and had to be paid on a set day or the property was put up for tax sale. Furthermore, these strange new laws were enforced by alien officials speaking a foreign language and usually ill acquainted with local problems and practices. Under these circumstances many of the Indian peasants lost their lands or sank hopelessly into debt. Gradually but inexorably the traditional noncommercial and self-sufficient life of the Indian village came to an end.

In order to meet their new financial obligations many of the peasants had to abandon their ancient subsistence economy and turn to the production of commodities that could be sold on the world markets. These commodities were transported to the seaports by a newly built railroad network totaling 4,000 miles by 1870, 7,000 miles by 1880 and 41,000 miles by 1939. The opening of the Suez Canal also facilitated the export of Indian raw materials by reducing the distance traversed by freighters between London and Karachi from 10,800 miles to 6,100 miles. Thus India became one of the world's important sources of raw materials. Wheat poured out of the Punjab, cotton out of Bombay and jute out of Bengal.

The same railroads that carried away the commercial crops brought back cheap, machine-made, industrial products to the villages. These undermined the position of the village artisans, as we shall note in the following section. The net effect was the monetization of the countryside. The peasants soon fell prey to usurers. Being unaccustomed to handling cash, they spent their money when high world prices provided extra income, and then had to borrow at usurious rates during the periodic slumps. The moneylender either took over the land of the bankrupt peasant, leaving him landless, or left the land in the peasant's name but took over most of the crop each year, reducing the peasant to a state of permanent debt serfdom.

The plight of the peasants was worsened by population increase engendered by greater security, health measures and famine relief arrangements made possible by railway transportation. Population rose from 255 million in 1872 to 302 million in 1921. A similar increase in the West in earlier centuries had been absorbed by new urban industries and by immigration to the Americas, Australia and New Zealand. For the displaced Indian peasants, however, there were neither factory jobs at home nor empty land overseas. A possible way out would have been improvement of agricultural techniques in order to raise productivity, as had been done in the West. But India failed to experience not only an Industrial Revolution but also an Agricultural Revolution. Indian landlords and moneylenders, in the context of the prevailing landholding and land-tax systems, could make more profit by rackrenting and usury than by investing in land improvement, fertilizers, irrigation and new seed strains.

The end result for India was that the average population increase per decade between 1901 and 1941 was 6.4 percent, while the average crop-production increase during the same period was 2.3 percent. Population consequently rose nearly three times as much as crop output. Per-capita crop production fell 20 percent during those four decades, and since cash crops were increasing more rapidly than food crops (be-

cause of greater use of irrigation), per-capita *food* crop production fell
32 percent during the same period. The condition of India's peasantry
therefore worsened, as was noted in lectures at Edinburgh in 1879–80
by the outstanding authority William Wilson Hunter:

> After a minute comparison of rural India at present with the facts
> disclosed in the manuscript records, I am compelled to the con-
> clusion that throughout large tracts the struggle for life is harder
> than it was when the country passed into our hands. . . . The sad
> result seems to be, that whether we give over the land to a propri-
> etary class, as in Bengal, or keep it in our hands, as in [the] South-
> ern India [ryotwari system], the struggle for life grows harder to
> large sections of the people.
>
> In provinces where, a hundred years ago, there was plenty of land
> for everyone who wished to till it . . . human beings [are] so
> densely crowded together as to exhaust the soil, and yet fail to
> wring from it enough to eat. Among a people whose sole means of
> subsistence was agriculture . . . a landless proletariate [is] spring-
> ing up, while millions more [are] clinging to their half acre of earth
> apiece, under a burden of rack-rent or usury. . . . More food is
> raised from the land than ever was raised before; but the popula-
> tion has increased at even a more rapid rate than the food sup-
> ply. . . .[17]

The root cause of this mass misery, which has worsened since the days
of Hunter, is *not* the conservatism of the Indian peasant, as is frequently
asserted. Rather it is the nature of British land policy, which for political and financial reasons monetized Indian agriculture without making
it more productive. "In retrospect, the net effect of British rule," conclude Daniel and Alice Thorner, "was to change drastically the social
fabric of Indian agriculture, but to leave virtually unaffected the basic
process of production and the level of technique. The upper strata of
the new agrarian society benefited handsomely. The position of the
cultivators deteriorated. Capital needed for the development of agriculture was siphoned off, and the level of total output tended toward
stagnation." [18]

V. British Impact: Crafts

Britain's official creed in the nineteenth century regarding international economic relations was free trade. Businessmen, politicians and
even poets sang the praises of untrammeled global commerce, which
assuredly would benefit all mankind. British policymakers did not hesi-

tate to resort to force against any foreigners who were so benighted as to erect obstacles against British imports. Lord Palmerston, for example, undercut Mohammad Ali of Egypt when he attempted to develop local industries, and likewise attempted to undermine the Zollverein when it sought to protect Germany's infant industries. But free-trade theory was conveniently forgotten in the case of Indian textile imports when they hurt the English woolen industry. Thomas Bazley, president of the Manchester Chamber of Commerce, declared in 1862, "The great interest of India was to be agricultural rather than manufacturing and mechanical." [19] The Indians, needless to say, were not consulted about their "interest." Rather the British set out purposefully to implement Bazley's dictum. Being India's rulers, there was no problem about having their way, and thus India's industries were destroyed and the country became "agricultural."

The 1814 tariffs levied only 2 percent duty on British woolens and $3\frac{1}{2}$ percent duty on British cotton and silk goods imported into India. Conversely, the duty on Indian raw cotton imported into Britain was nominal, but the duty on Indian cotton textiles was 70 to 80 percent. Thus in the three decades 1814 to 1844 the number of pieces of Indian cotton goods imported into Britain fell from 1.25 million to 63,000, while British cotton imports into India rose from less than 1 million yards to over 53 million yards.

The impact on India's ancient textile crafts was shattering. Robert Clive described the city of Dacca in 1757 as "extensive, populous and rich as the city of London." But Sir Charles Trevelyan testified before a Select Committee in 1840 that "it has fallen from 150,000 to 30,000, and the jungle and malaria are fast encroaching upon the town. . . . Dacca, the Manchester of India, has fallen off from a very flourishing town to a very poor and small town." [20] Likewise the contemporary British colonial historian, M. Martin, testified in 1840 before a Select Committee of the House of Lords that India's textile industry had been destroyed "by reason of the outcry for free trade on the part of England without permitting to India a free trade herself." "This supersession of the native for British manufacture is often quoted as a splendid example of the triumph of British skill. It is a much stronger instance of English tyranny, and how India has been impoverished by the most vexatious system of customs duties imposed for the avowed object of favouring the mother country." [21]

Another example of British government intervention in India's economy directly contrary to free-trade principle was the campaign to increase the supply of Indian raw cotton during the American Civil War. The latter conflict interfered with exports of cotton from the American South to Britain, so the Manchester manufacturers demanded an alternative supply of cotton. They organized the Cotton Supply Association, whose president, John Cheetham, demanded in 1863 that the British government take any necessary measures to stimulate cotton production in India. Cheetham expressed the hope for something better than "the usual stale answer, namely, that it was contrary to the rules of political economy." [22] In other words, Cheetham was unwilling to accept the principle of free trade as a reason for doing nothing.

Secretary of State Sir Charles Wood opposed government intervention to increase the supply of Indian raw cotton. He reminded Manchester's spokesmen that he genuinely believed in the free-trade principle they professed and that he would not tolerate its violation: "My conviction is, that an adequate demand, evidenced by a rise in price, will produce an adequate supply. I have held those political beliefs throughout all my political life with the greatest confidence, and on former occasions they were warmly advocated by gentlemen who belong to what is called the Manchester School, and who declared that the best and kindest thing that could be done for trade and manufactures was to leave them alone, and that bounties and protection were not only hurtful to the community at large, but to the very trade itself which was protected." [23] As long as Sir Charles Wood held office he blocked government intervention to increase the supply of Indian cotton. But when he resigned in 1866 a state-subsidized program was adopted for establishing model cotton farms in India, improving the quality of Indian cotton and facilitating the marketing of the cotton in England.

With the Deccan becoming a cotton bowl, British economists urged the building of railways "which would promote the sale and transmission of the raw products" and compel the Indians "to receive their cotton in a manufactured shape." [24] Again British interests had their way, so that the Indian government ended up guaranteeing the construction costs and interest payments for a costly, ill-conceived, hastily planned and mostly unproductive program for road, railway, canal and port construction. In the words of Daniel Thorner, it was a case of "private enterprise at public risk." [25] As in all colonies and semicolonies, the railways were designed to satisfy metropolitan rather than local needs. Virtually all of the twenty-five thousand miles of railway built in India by 1900 were either for military purposes or for shipping goods to coastal ports, so that interior regions were left largely unconnected with each other.

In most Western countries an important by-product of railway building has been the stimulus afforded to capital-goods industries and technological innovation in engineering. Locomotive factories in England have been called "universities of mechanical engineering." [26] But no such "universities" developed in nineteenth-century India because British firms enjoyed a virtual monopoly in the building of the railways and the supplying of the locomotives. This was so even when German and American firms submitted lower bids and quicker delivery, and when in India itself "the skills necessary for locomotive production were developed from a very early period, and the skills were very widely distributed. . . ." [27]

Discrimination in behalf of British interests was not limited to transportation. Sir Rajendra Nath Mukherjee made a reputation constructing waterworks for Calcutta. But he found that, as T. C. Mookerjee and Company, he could not obtain contracts for building waterworks in the United Provinces, even though his bids were the lowest. He found it necessary "to join forces with Acquin Martin and adopt the name of Martin and Company in order to obtain the contracts." [28] Likewise in the field of shipping, British companies alone obtained government subsidies and mail subventions, and similarly Indian army contracts for boots, blankets and other light equipment went exclusively to British concerns, though the commodities could have been manufactured more cheaply in India.

It does not follow from the above that all Indian crafts were ruined. Some declined, others underwent mutations, while some new ones came into existence using new factory-manufactured machines. Nevertheless, the fact remains that when India won political independence after World War II it was an underdeveloped country, and it has remained so to the present day. The only major centers of industrialization in 1914 were in Calcutta and Bombay, and most of the enterprises were British and of the "enclave" variety, so that there was little spinoff to stimulate the national economy as a whole. Most revealing is the following conclusion by Bipan Chandra:

> . . . in India in 1892 after 100 years of "gestation" only 254,000 persons were involved in modern industrial production under the Factory Acts. This number increased only by 1.1 million by 1931 and by another 1,180,000 by 1951, while population went up from 236 millions in 1891 to 275.5 millions in 1931 and 357 millions in 1951, and labour force from 94 millions to 142 millions between 1891 and 1951. [29]

This conclusion is particularly disappointing because India, in contrast to Latin America, enjoyed favorable terms of trade, which could have been utilized to develop an independent economy. B. M. Bhatia, who has shown that India's terms of trade were favorable except for the years of the First World War and the Great Depression, gives the following reasons for the failure to take advantage of the opportunity:

"Free trade and anti-national fiscal and industrial policy of the Government rather than Eastern love for gold and adverse terms of trade were responsible for keeping India underdeveloped and poor. . . ." [30] Thus the substantial gains from international trade were frittered away in the payment of political and commercial charges to Britain, and in the importation of gold, since there was little local industry in which to invest. After World War I India gained some fiscal autonomy, but with the Great Depression imminent and the terms of trade becoming less favorable, the historic opportunity for India faded away.

VI. India Enters the Third World

The effect of British rule was to integrate the subcontinent into the international market economy. This is reflected in the value of cotton textile imports, which jumped from 50,000 rupees in 1814, to 5.2 million rupees in 1829, to 30 million rupees in 1890, while the value of raw cotton exports rose from 10 million rupees in 1849 to 60 million rupees in 1860, and to 410 million rupees in 1913. Likewise the quantity of other raw-material exports rose as follows:

- *jute*—from 500 tons in 1830, to 35,000 tons in 1857, to 765,000 tons in 1909.
- *wheat*—from negligible quantity in 1870 to 1.3 million tons in 1914.
- *oilseeds*—from negligible quantity in 1840, to 200,000 tons in 1867, to 1.5 million tons in 1913.
- *tea*—from 500,000 pounds in 1854, to 87 million pounds in 1885–89 (average), to 192 million pounds in 1900.
- *hides and skins*—from a value of 6.6 million rupees in 1860, to 74.5 million rupees in 1898, to 160 million rupees in 1913.

India's Foreign Trade in Crores of Rupees

	(10 million rupees)	
	Imports	*Exports*
1841	10	14
1860	23	33
1880	50	74
1900	81	108
1913	191	249

Source: M. Zinkin, *Asia and the West* (London: Chatto & Windus, 1951), pp. 267–71.

* * *

If there is no question as to the fact of India's integration into the global economy, there is a good deal of dispute as to the meaning of this fact. Supporters of British rule emphasize its positive results, such as the maintenance of law and order, the construction of transportation and irrigation systems and the commercialization of agriculture leading to a vast increase of exports and a corresponding increase of imports.

These material achievements are undeniable, but the crucial issue is their economic and social repercussions. How did they affect overall economic development, and also the daily lives of the great mass of the Indian people? Law and order were preserved, but as Bipan Chandra has observed, "It all depends on what the law and order is used for. . . . In fact, law and order is a basic necessity not only for economic growth and welfare, but also for any systematized exploitation." [31] In the case of India the record points much more to exploitation than to growth and welfare. Twenty-five thousand miles of railway were built by 1900, but under terms that were excessively onerous for the Indian treasury, and that engendered little of the spinoff that stimulated the national economies of Russia and the United States. Likewise the new irrigation networks together with the external demand for Indian raw materials made extensive cultivation by large landowners profitable, but this involved an increase in tenant cultivation and tenant rackrenting. Commercialization of agriculture similarly did not lead to superior technology and productivity. Rather it caused more intense exploitation of the peasants, who became victims of the mechanism and fluctuations of the market and of the accompanying landowners, middlemen and moneylenders.

In short, the entire infrastructure created by Britain was purposefully designed to create a dependent colonial economy rather than an independent developed economy. The role of Britain in India was not "creative destruction," as Schumpeter characterized the function of capitalism. Instead it was the preservation of selected precapitalist institutions that favored imperial interests. Barbara Ward recognized this when she stated that Britain failed in India because she did not complete the modernization process, which required "decisive land reform." But "as an alien power," explains Barbara Ward, "Britain could not adopt such a solution in India." [32] The first part of this analysis is correct, but the second is not. We have seen that Britain did not hesitate to intervene vigorously to impose the ryotwari and zamindar land systems and to promote railway building and the production of raw materials needed by home industries. But government intervention was conspicuously lacking when needed for the benefit of the local population rather than of British interests. Examples of such selective nonintervention included the refusal to erect protective tariffs, to introduce progressive taxation and to ban grain exports during periods of famine. The basic problem for India was not Britain's nonintervention or ineffective intervention, but discriminatory intervention.

Part Three

THIRD WORLD A GLOBAL SYSTEM: 1870–1914

Always we are hoping that we need expand no farther; yet ever we are finding that to stop expanding would be to fall behind, and even today the successive improvements and inventions follow each other so rapidly that we see just as much yet to be done as ever. When the manufacturer of steel ceases to grow he begins to decay, so we must keep extending.

ANDREW CARNEGIE (1896)

In the last quarter of the nineteenth century, competitive industrial capitalism gave way to monopoly capitalism, with an accompanying shift in international affairs from free-trade imperialism to global colonialism. The new monopoly capitalism was both broader and deeper in its operations throughout the world. Symbols of the earlier free-trade imperialism had been Livingstone in Africa and the British warships in the China seas. Infinitely more penetrating and disruptive were the symbols of the new era—the Suez and Panama canals linking together the oceans, the several transcontinental railroads spanning Africa, Siberia and North America, the network of cables on oceanbeds and of telegraph and telephone lines on continental land expanses, and great banking houses such as Lloyd's and Barclay's and Rothschild's providing the financial lubrication for the vast superstructure. This dynamism of monopoly capitalism led to the partitioning of Africa in the last two decades of the nineteenth century, and to the integration of China and Russia into the international market economy. The sole exception to this pattern of European global hegemony was, paradoxically, the small island empire of Japan.

Chapter 13

ERA OF MONOPOLY CAPITALISM AND GLOBAL COLONIALISM

In order to save the 40 million inhabitants of the United Kingdom from a bloody civil war, we colonial statesmen must acquire new lands to settle the surplus population, to provide new markets for the goods produced by them in the factories and mines.

CECIL RHODES (1882)

About 1870 the Second Industrial Revolution got under way, characterized by new mass-production techniques and by the systematic application of science to industry. Formerly independent industrial firms such as that of Watt and Boulton were displaced by large cartels with sufficient capital to monopolize industries on a national, and later, on an international scale. At the same time newly industrialized states successfully challenged Britain's primacy as "the workshop of the world." The ensuing rivalries, together with the increasing military and economic power of capitalism in its monopoly phase, led to unprecedented colonial expansion. The free-trade imperialism of the early nineteenth century gave way to pre-emptive territorial imperialism. The entire world was divided into outright colonies, as in the case of Africa, or into semi-colonies, as with the Ottoman and Chinese empires. The greatest land grab in human history ended with the extraordinary spectacle of one Eurasian peninsula dominating the rest of the world!

ᶳ *I. Second Industrial Revolution and Monopoly Capitalism in the West*

During the First Industrial Revolution the pioneer inventions in the textile, mining, metallurgical and transportation industries were the work of talented mechanics rather than scientists. About 1875, however, science began to play a more important role. The laboratories of industrial research, equipped with expensive apparatus and staffed by trained scientists who carried on systematic research on designated problems, supplanted the garrets or workshops of lone inventors.

The impact of science soon was felt by all industries. In metallurgy, for example, a number of processes were developed (Bessemer, Siemens-Martin and Gilchrist-Thomas) that made possible the mass production of high-grade steel from low-grade iron ore. The power industry was revolutionized by the harnessing of electricity and by the invention of the internal-combustion engine which uses chiefly oil and gasoline. Communications also were transformed by the invention of the wireless, or radio. The oil industry developed rapidly as a result of the work of geologists who located oilfields with remarkable accuracy, and of chemists who devised ways to refine crude oil into naphtha, gas, kerosene and both light and heavy lubricating oils. One of the most spectacular examples of the effect of science on industry may be seen in the case of the coal derivatives. In addition to yielding coke and a valuable gas that was used for illumination, coal also gave a liquid, or coal tar. Chemists discovered in this substance a veritable treasure trove, the derivatives including hundreds of dyes and a host of other by-products such as aspirin, wintergreen, saccharin, disinfectants, laxatives, perfumes, photographic chemicals, high explosives and essence of orange blossom.

At the same time, industries were being transformed also by the introduction of mass-production techniques. The United States led in this field, as Germany did in the scientific. Two principal methods of mass production were developed, one being the making of standard interchangeable parts, and the assembling of these parts into the completed unit with a minimum of labor. An American inventor, Eli Whitney, employed this system at the beginning of the nineteenth century in manufacturing muskets. A century later Henry Ford gained fame and fortune by adapting this system to the endless conveyer belt that carried car parts past lines of assembly workmen. The other mass-production system was the manipulation of large masses of material by means of advanced mechanical devices. What this meant in terms of dollars and cents is evident in the justifiable boast of steel magnate Andrew Carnegie:

Two pounds of ironstone mined upon Lake Superior and transported nine hundred miles to Pittsburgh; one pound and one-half of coal mined and manufactured into coke, and transported to Pittsburgh; one half pound of lime, mined and transported to Pittsburgh; a small amount of manganese ore mined in Virginia and brought to Pittsburgh—and these four pounds of materials manufactured into one pound of steel, for which the consumer pays one cent.[1]

This Second Industrial Revolution promoted the shift from competitive to monopoly capitalism. The huge capital investment needed for the new giant plants eliminated most of the small family businesses. The number of American steel companies, for example, fell from 735 in 1880 to 16 in 1950. Likewise new industries, such as the aluminum, chemical and electrical, required heavy capital investment from the beginning, thus making it impossible for the small businessman to participate. Also, the long depression during the last quarter of the nineteenth century forced capitalists to abandon their traditional creed of free competition and to resort to a variety of cartels, mergers, trusts and price-regulating associations in order to moderate slumps in prices and profits. The leading British soap manufacturer, W. H. Lever, summarized this trend in 1903:

> In the old days a manufactory could be an individual concern. Next . . . a partnership. . . . Then it grew beyond the capital available by two or three joining together as a partnership, and limited companies became necessary. . . . Now we have reached a further stage again, when a number of limited companies require to be grouped together in what we call a combine. . . .[2]

These new "combines" or cartels generated superprofits, as will be noted below, and at the same time capital still was flowing in from overseas, and especially from India.[3] Britain therefore was able to continue her investments abroad, though now in the later nineteenth century they were directed primarily not to Europe but to white settlements in North America, Australia and New Zealand. Thus 45 percent of British foreign investments during the period 1865–1914 flowed to North America and Australasia as against 13 percent to Europe and 17 percent to South America, mostly to those countries with substantial European populations. The vast movement of European peoples to "empty" overseas lands was in this manner accompanied by an equally vast movement of European capital to finance their settlement and economic development. "This ability to balance deficits with one part of the world against surpluses with other parts," concludes Bagchi, "enabled Britain to smoothly transfer capital resources from the non-white colonies to the white ones and support industrial growth in the latter."[4]

In the United States net foreign investment accounted for 25 percent of domestic investment between the 1830s and the 1860s inclusive, and over 15 percent during the 1870s. Likewise in Australia, net capital inflow accounted for 35 percent of gross domestic investment between 1868 and 1900, while in Canada the percentage was 26 between 1900 and 1905, and 38 between 1906 and 1910.

Not only were decisive quantities of capital transferred from nonwhite colonies to white, but also the investment in the white colonies were of the noncontrollable portfolio variety, whereas in nonwhite colonies they were closely directed and designed to promote manufactured imports from the lending country and to discourage local industries. In the United States European investors had virtually no control over the funds they committed. In Canada it was not unusual for the British to provide capital that was then spent by Canadian or American management boards to purchase goods in the United States for the actual construction. In Brazil, on the other hand, enterprises usually were conceived by Britons, financed by British investors, constructed by British contractors with imported British capital goods and often sold to the Brazilian government if the projects proved unprofitable. Furthermore, the British lobbied successfully against the industrialization of Brazil until the very end of the nineteenth century.

So far as Britain's position in the global economy was concerned, these investments in Europe and in overseas territories were financially remunerative but also disruptive of her original primacy as "the industrial workshop of the world." We have seen that Germany had led in the application of science to industry, and the United States in the development of mass-production techniques. Thus Britain began to pay the price for her pioneering role in the first Industrial Revolution and for her concentration on foreign investments at the expense of domestic industrial modernization. Her plants became increasingly obsolete as new competitors appeared with more efficient equipment. World industrial production increased seven times between 1860 and 1913, but British production increased only three times, and French four times, as against Germany's seven times and the United States' twelve times. This brought about rapid changes in the order of importance of the leading industrial countries (as indicated in the table on p. 260), changes that have continued to the present day as the dynamics of monopoly capitalism persist unabated.

These developments together were responsible for the shift from waning colonialism to a worldwide scramble for colonies. Disinterest in colonies was natural in the early nineteenth century, when Britain was the pre-eminent economic and military power. But it became increasingly unnatural when several industrial powers were suspicious of each other's

Order of Importance of the Leading Industrial Countries

1860	1870	1880	1900	1980
Great Britain	Great Britain	United States	United States	United States
France	United States	Great Britain	Germany	Japan
United States	France	Germany	Great Britain	Soviet Union
Germany	Germany	France	France	Germany

intentions in what had become a highly competitive world with rising tariff barriers. The British governments felt free to leave their traders and investors to fend for themselves when they had no imperial rivals to fend off. But when competition became severe, they began to consider it necessary to preserve equality of economic opportunity for their nationals by anticipatory annexation of overseas territory or by demarcation of spheres of interest. It is true that the volume of trade between Britain and her "new" empire acquired in the late nineteenth century was small, but that did not necessarily mean insignificant. In the context of the post-1870 British economy, a 3 to 5 percent increase in exports to newly acquired colonies could make the difference between survival and extinction for some industries.

Gunnar Myrdal has described the preferential treatment accorded to the products of metropolitan centers in their colonies as "enforced bilateralism." The reality of the distortion of geographical patterns of trade on the basis of colonial ties is evident in the following table, which compares the share of the United Kingdom and of France in the trade of their own and each other's African dependencies at the end of the colonial period:

The Share of the United Kingdom and France in the Trade of Own and Other's African Dependencies: 1960–62
(in percent)

	Exports to		Imports from	
	U.K.	U.K.	France	France
U.K. dependencies	41.6	1.7	38.9	2.3
French dependencies	1.6	52.7	2.8	60.5

Source: E. Kleiman, "Trade and the Decline of Colonialism," Economic Journal 86 (Sept. 1976): 465. This article provides detailed statistics of trade distortion by country and colony.

The fact that the "bilateralism" reflected in the above statistics was enforced is evident in the decline in the metropolitan share of the trade of these colonies as soon as the political tie was severed. And the longer the period of time since decolonization, the lower the metropolitan share of the colonial trade. "This tends to indicate," concludes Ephraim Kleiman, "that the trade patterns observed in the colonies did not, on the whole, reflect the preferences of their inhabitants. It thus seems justified to regard the bilateralism characterizing colonial trade as being enforced by the colonial power." [5]

Monopoly capitalism also engendered empire building by piling up superprofits that necessitated investment outlets. The cartels set prices at a level that allowed the least efficient member to gain an average rate of profit. This enabled the more efficient companies, which controlled most of the market, to realize exorbitant profits. The same thing happened when companies gained almost full control of a given market. After the formation of U.S. Steel Corporation, steel prices were raised 20 to 30 percent, while the American Can Company, which at the time of its foundation in 1901 controlled 90 percent of the industry's production, promptly raised its prices 60 percent. In the case of Britain, such monopoly profits made possible an increase of average annual investments abroad from only £29 million between 1860 and 1869, to £51 million between 1870 and 1879, and to £68 million between 1880 and 1889.

Any relationship between this capital accumulation under monopoly capitalism and the upsurge in empire building during the same decades of the late nineteenth century is sometimes denied on the ground that the colonies often cost more than the mother countries received in return. But the obvious point is that the costs came out of *public* revenues, whereas the profits went to *private* interests. The latter could, and did, use their political influence in behalf of aggressive colonial policies, regardless of the effect on government exchequers. Colonial empires thus were mechanisms for redistributing wealth *within* the metropolitan centers, rather than the result of national balance-sheet considerations.

Another argument made against economic motives in empire building is that a very small proportion of overseas investments went to the colonies that were being acquired. But "small" did not necessarily mean insignificant, especially since the rate of growth of British investments in the "new" empire was much higher than in the old. Between 1907 and 1913 the increase of British investments in the "new" empire was 51 percent, as against 17.1 percent in India and Ceylon, 16.3 percent in Australia and New Zealand and 21.7 percent in the United States.

Furthermore, it should be remembered that these were decades of *pre-emptive* colonial imperialism. In the competitive atmosphere of the time, imperial officials and agents on the spot frequently emphasized not what would be gained through annexation but what would be lost through annexation by others. What concerned them was not the loss or gain compared to the pre-existing situation but rather the potential loss or gain if a rival were allowed to move in ahead. The pressure of competition, especially during years of depression, falling prices and rising tariffs, led policymakers to think of colonies not only as immediate investment outlets but also as future markets for manufactured goods and sources of raw materials. This was specifically stated by a British author, Sir John Keltie, who wrote in 1895 that not "until Germany came into the field ten years ago" were the complacent British capitalists moved "to look around and look forward." By that time only Africa "remained available," and so "on Africa a rush was made without precedent in the history of the world." [6]

The "rush" on Africa and other continents was also related to the superprofits of monopoly capitalism, which trickled down somewhat to the masses in the home countries. This stimulated new needs for the urban masses, including, soap, margarine, chocolate, cocoa and rubber tires for bicycles. All of these commodities required large-scale imports from tropical regions, which in turn necessitated local infrastructures of harbors, railways, steamers, trucks, warehouses, machinery and telegraph and postal systems. Such infrastructures required order and security to ensure adequate dividends to shareholders. Hence the clamor for annexation if local conflicts disrupted the flow of trade, or if a neighboring colonial power threatened to expand.

The tremendous outflow of capital from Europe in the form of loans and investments often led to *de facto* control over the recipient countries. Foreign rulers did not perceive that the acceptance of treaties of friendship and free trade, and later of financial loans and of economic and military missions, culminated almost inevitably in the loss of economic independence, and frequently of political independence as well. Lord Cromer, Britain's consul-general in Egypt between 1883 and 1907, described how European credit paved the way for European rule, direct or indirect:

> The maximum amount of harm is probably done when an Oriental ruler is for the first time brought in contact with the European system of credit. He thus finds that he can obtain large sums of money with the utmost apparent facility. His personal wishes can thus be easily gratified. He is dazzled by the ingenious and often fallacious schemes for developing his country which European adventurers will not fail to lay before him in the most attractive light. He is too wanting in foresight to appreciate the nature of the future difficulties which he is creating for himself. The temp-

tation to avail himself to the full of the benefits which a reckless use of credit seems to offer to him, are too strong to be resisted. He will rush into the gulf which lies open before him, and inflict an injury on his country from which not only his contemporaries but future generations will suffer.[7]

The current vogue of social Darwinism, with its doctrines of struggle for existence and survival of the fittest, provided a persuasive rationalization for the above expansionist forces. It justified the seizure and exploitation of the largest possible colonial territories not only for profit, but also as an essential means of strengthening the imperial power for the unending future struggles against its rivals. British imperialist Cecil Rhodes had many counterparts in Germany and France when he wrote: "I contend that we are the first race in the world, and that the more of the world we inhabit the better it is for the human race. . . . If there be a God, I think that what he would like me to do is to paint as much of the map of Africa British red as possible. . . ."[8]

Rhodes' expansionism was accepted and justified by European liberals who insisted on self-determination for subject people in Europe, but conveniently abandoned it when it came to the "lesser breeds" overseas. Gladstone thundered against the "Bulgarian horrors" of the bashibazooks and their "bloody Sultan" in Constantinople. Yet the same Gladstone dismissed Arabi's popular uprising in Egypt as the work of a few self-serving army officers, abetted by Egyptian intellectuals representing only themselves. Likewise in India, the British referred contemptuously to the early nationalists as "noisy Bengalee Baboos." Viceroy Dufferin smugly asserted in November 1888, "The chief concern of the Government of India is to protect and foster the interests of the people of India." But he added, ". . . the people of India are not the seven or eight thousand students who have graduated at the Universities, or the Pleaders recruited from their numbers . . . but the voiceless millions whom neither education, nor civilization, nor the influence of European ideas or modern thought, have in the slightest degree transfigured or transformed from what their forefathers were a thousand years ago."[9]

Such rationalizing conveniently justified Europe's global hegemony by assuming that Bulgarians and Macedonians were ready for self-determination, and by asserting that Egyptians and Indians were not.

❧ II. Global Colonialism in the Third World

The net result of the above economic, political and intellectual-psychological factors was the explosion of colonial imperialism in the late nineteenth century. Whereas an average of 83,000 square miles of colonial lands had been acquired each year between 1800 and 1875, the figure jumped to 240,000 square miles for the period between 1875 and 1914. Britain added 4.25 million square miles and 66 million people to her empire during the generation between 1871 and 1900. France added 3.5 million square miles and 26 million people; Russia in Asia added .5 million square miles and 6.5 million people; and Germany added 1 million square miles and 13 million people. Even little Belgium managed to acquire 900,000 square miles and 8.5 million inhabitants. These conquests, added to the existing colonial possessions, produced a fantastic and unprecedented situation in which one small portion of the globe dominated the remainder. The extent of this domination in 1914 is revealed by the following figures:

Overseas Colonial Empires in 1914

Countries having colonies	Number of colonies	Area (square miles)		Population	
		Mother country	Colonies	Mother country	Colonies
U.K.	55	120,953	12,043,806	46,052,741	391,582,528
France	29	207,076	4,110,409	39,602,258	62,350,000
Germany	10	208,830	1,230,989	64,925,993	13,074,950
Belgium	1	11,373	910,000	7,571,387	15,000,000
Portugal	8	35,500	804,440	5,960,056	9,680,000
Netherlands	8	12,761	762,863	6,102,399	37,410,000
Italy	4	110,623	591,250	35,238,997	1,396,176
TOTAL	115	707,116	20,453,757	205,453,831	530,493,654

This table is my compilation, published earlier in my *The World Since 1500* (Englewood Cliffs, N.J.: Prentice-Hall, 1966), p. 236.

The industrialized European powers not only owned outright these vast colonial territories, but they also dominated those economically and militarily weak areas that, for one reason or another, were not actually annexed. Examples are China, the Ottoman Empire and Persia, all of which were nominally independent, but which, in fact, were constantly harried, humiliated and controlled in various direct and indirect ways. Latin America also was an economic appendage of the Great Powers, though in this region military action by Europe was discouraged by the Monroe Doctrine. The latter, however, did not preclude repeated armed intervention by the United States Marine Corps to "restore law and order." The great Russian Empire also was dominated economically to a very large extent by Western Europe, though in this case the military strength of the Tsarist regime was great enough to prevent foreign economic influence from extending into other fields.

Thus we see that Europe's control extended not only over the farflung empires but also over the equally extensive dependent regions. In fact, more European capital was invested in the dependent countries than in the colonies. These investments were safeguarded through various devices and pressures, such as military missions that trained the local armed forces, financial missions that supervised and usually controlled local finances, and extraterritorial and capitulatory arrangements that gave special privileges to Europeans residing or doing business in these areas. If necessary as a last resort, there were always the Marines in the New World and the gunboats in the Old.

This unprecedented primacy of the West over the entire globe meant, conversely, that the Third World now had become a full global system. All of Asia now was encompassed, with the single exception of the small Japanese empire. How fundamentally the global balance had shifted during the course of the nineteenth century may be judged by contrasting the Chinese Emperor's haughty rejection in 1793 of any diplomatic or commercial relations with Britain, with the following reflections of Arminius Vambery a century later as he traveled through central Asia in a railroad coach:

> When, comfortably seated in our well-upholstered railway carriage, we gaze upon the Hyrkanian Steppe, upon the terrible deserts of Karakum and Kisilkum, we can scarcely realize the terrors, the sufferings and the privations, to which travellers formerly were exposed. . . . And great changes similar to those which have taken place in Central Asia may also be noticed in greater or less degree in other parts and regions of the Eastern world: Siberia, West and North China, Mongolia, Manchuria, and Japan, were in the first half of the nineteenth century scarcely known to us, and . . . we now find that the supreme power of the Western world is gradually making itself felt. The walls of seclusion are ruthlessly pulled down, and the resistance caused by the favoured superstitions, prejudices, and the ignorance of the sleepy and apathetic man in the East, is slowly being overcome . . . present-day Europe, in its restless, bustling activity will take good care not to let the East relapse again into its former indolence. We forcibly tear its eyes open; we push, jolt, toss, and shake it, and we compel it to exchange its world-worn, hereditary ideas and customs for our modern views of life; nay, we have even succeeded to some extent in convincing our

Eastern neighbours that our civilization, our faith, our customs, our philosophy, are the only means whereby the well-being, the progress, and the happiness, of the human race can be secured.

For well-nigh 300 years we have been carrying on this struggle with the Eastern world, and persist in our unsolicited interference, following in the wake of ancient Rome, which began the work with marked perseverance, but naturally never met with much success because of the inadequate means at its disposal. . . . We may admire the splendour, the might, and the glory of ancient Rome, we may allow that the glitter of its arms struck terror and alarm into the furthest corners of Asia; but in spite of all that, it would be difficult to admit that the civilizing influence of Rome was ever more than an external varnish, a transitory glamour. Compared with the real earnest work done in our days by Western Powers, the efforts of Rome are as the flickering of an oil-lamp in comparison with the radiance of the sun in its full glory. It may be said without exaggeration that never in the world's history has one continent exercised such influence over another as has the Europe of our days over Asia.[10]

Whether Third World regions were full-fledged colonies or semicolonies made little difference. All had become adjuncts of the European metropolis and all had experienced the attendant repercussions that disrupted profoundly their social orders. Most contemporary Westerners considered this global hegemony of Europe to be a great step forward in the evolution of mankind. "It is commerce which is rapidly rendering war obsolete," wrote John Stuart Mill, "by strengthening and multiplying the personal interests which are in natural opposition to it. And it may be said without exaggeration that the great extent and rapid increase of international trade, in being the principal guarantee of the peace of the world, is the greatest permanent security for uninterrupted progress of the ideas, the institutions, and the character of the human race." [11] Equally enthusiastic are some present-day scholars, such as economist Jacob Viner, who holds that "the nineteenth century international flow of capital, despite its unregulated character and despite the fact that it was motivated almost wholly by considerations of private profits, was one of the many great blessings which cupidity has procured for mankind." [12]

So far as the West was concerned, this euphoria certainly was justified. The West had become the industrial heartland of the world, and its industrial productivity increased spectacularly. Between 1860 and 1913 it rose three times in Britain, four times in France and seven times in Germany. The profits of monopoly capitalism were generous enough to trickle down to the masses to an unprecedented degree. Whether the real wages of the British working class rose or fell during the early years of the Industrial Revolution in the late eighteenth and early nineteenth centuries remains a disputed issue. A definitive answer is difficult because the large-scale urbanization accompanying industrialization altered the structure of worker consumption, as, for example, by the introduction of rent for lodging. But there is no question about the steady rise of real wages in the second half of the nineteenth century. The following figures show that between 1850 and 1913 real wages in Britain and France almost doubled.

Rise in Real Wages, 1850–1913
(1913 = 100)

	Great Britain	*France*
1850	57	59.5
1860	64	63
1870	70	69
1880	81	74.5
1890	90	89.5
1900	100	100

Source: F. Sternberg, *Capitalism and Socialism on Trial* (New York: John Day, 1951), p. 27.

The peoples of the Third World experienced no corresponding improvement in living standards. For them the impact of the West was a wrenching experience, in which everything was turned upside down and inside out. This was inevitable, for all Third World societies, by definition, were integrated into the world market economy, with unavoidable disruptions and distortions of their traditional institutions.

Considering first the political impact of the West, it was at the beginning like a sudden fresh breeze, with its novel doctrines of popular sovereignty emanating from the English, American and French revolutions. These doctrines challenged the millennia-old assumption of a divinely ordained division of humanity into rulers and ruled. Greek revolutionary Theodore Kolokotrones noted this subversive effect of Western ideology on his fellow countrymen in the early nineteenth century when they were under Turkish domination: "The French Revolution and the doings of Napoleon opened the eyes of the world. The nations knew nothing before, and the people thought that kings were gods upon the earth and that they were bound to say that whatever they did was well done.

Through this present change it is more difficult to rule the people." [13]
A century later Jawaharlal Nehru wrote in similar vein of the effect of
the West on his country. "The impact of Western culture on India was
the impact of a dynamic society, of a 'modern' consciousness, on a static
society wedded to medieval habits of thought. . . . The British came to
us on the crest of a wave of new impulse in the world, and represented
mighty historic forces which they themselves hardly realized." [14]

Nehru's perception that the British "hardly realized" the nature of
their influence is significant. The West's revolutionary impact was in fact
automatic and unintended. Consequently, when Westernized native leaders began to act according to the principles of the American Declaration
of Independence and the French Declaration of the Rights of Man and
the Citizen and later of the Communist Manifesto, Western policymakers responded with policies calculated to buttress traditional regimes that
they considered to be indispensable for their imperial interests. Hence
the paradox of the West being almost invariably the implacable enemy
of the Westernizers in the Third World, whether they were Sun Yat-sen
in China, Ghandi and Nehru in India or Kemal Ataturk in the Ottoman Empire. Gunnar Myrdal has concluded justifiably:

> In the world wide colonial power system as it functioned until
> the Second World War, *there was a built-in mechanism that almost
> automatically led the colonial power to ally itself with the privi-
> leged groups.* These groups could be relied upon to share its inter-
> est in "law and order," which mostly implied economic and social
> *status quo.* . . . Often it even happened that new privileges and
> new privileged groups were created by the colonial power in order
> to stabilize its rule over a colony.[15]

The pattern is similar as regards the West's cultural impact on the
Third World. Again the initial effect was one of intoxicating liberation
from the restraints of traditional religions and customs. When the Europeans first appeared on the coasts of Asian empires they were looked
down upon as uncouth barbarians who happened to enjoy a certain superiority in sailing ships and firearms. But with the Scientific and Industrial revolutions, non-Western peoples were forced to come to terms with
the constantly increasing economic and military superiority of the foreigners. Only they had succeeded in mastering the secrets of nature and
exploiting them for the material benefit of mankind.

A Chinese intellectual, Hu Shih, sensed the significance of this Western achievement when in 1926 he visited the city of Harbin in what was
then northern Manchuria. He noted that practically all the vehicles in
the native quarters of the city were rickshaws, or carriages pulled by
"human beasts of burden," whereas in the Russian Concession no rick-

shaws were allowed. In their place were modern tramways and taxicabs. Hu Shih viewed this contrast as symbolizing the fundamental contribution of Western civilization to human progress:

> Let all apologists for the spiritual civilization of the East reflect on this. What spirituality is there in a civilization which tolerates such a terrible form of human slavery as the rickshaw coolie? . . . It is only when one has fully realized what misery and acute suffering the life of rickshaw-pulling entails and what effects it produces on the bodily health of those human beasts of burden—it is only then that one will be truly and religiously moved to bless the Hargreaveses, the Cartwrights, the Watts, the Fultons, the Stephensons, and the Fords who have devised machines to do the work for man and relieve him from much of the brutal suffering to which his Oriental neighbor is still subject. Herein, therefore, lies the real spirituality of the material civilization, of mechanical progress *per se*.[16]

Hu Shih was not alone in this reaction to the triumphant and seemingly irresistible Western civilization. At the same time that he was reflecting on what he had seen in Harbin, the Bengali nationalist leader, Surendranath Banerjea, was reaching a similar conclusion about the initial effect of the British on his country:

> Our forefathers, the first fruits of English education, were violently pro-British. They could see no flaw in the civilization or the culture of the West. They were charmed by its novelty and its strangeness. The enfranchisement of the individual, the substitution of the right of private judgment in the place of traditional authority, the exaltation of duty over custom, all came with a force and suddenness of a revelation to an Oriental people who knew no more binding obligation than the mandate of immemorial usage and of venerable tradition. . . . Everything English was good—even the drinking of brandy was a virtue; everything not English was to be viewed with suspicion. . . .[17]

Hu Shih and Surendranath Banerjea were intellectuals, representing only a tiny minority of the Chinese and Indian populations. Their fascination with Western ideology and technology was not shared by the masses of their fellow countrymen who, being overwhelmingly illiterate, were more familiar with the reality than the theory of Western domination. They recalled their traditional village communities which, before the Western intrusion, had provided land for all their members, had preserved the continuity of interpersonal relationships and had assured a sense of individual worth and of individual status in society. These villages had been vulnerable to war, famine and pestilence, yet they had retained an organic wholeness and had provided a psychological security that disappeared with the coming of the Europeans.

The latter introduced their languages and their cultures, which were adopted by the local elites, who now served as intermediaries between the masses and the foreign powers. The Europeans also imposed their own legal, administrative and security systems in order to meet the needs of the new monetized economies and the more active modern states. All this meant a painful disruption of the familiar communalism of the past. Land now became a mere possession, food a mere commodity of exchange, neighbor a mere common property owner and labor a mere means of survival. Such was the breakup of old institutions and old customs, as described in Chine Achebe, *Things Fall Apart* (traditional Africa), Cheikh Hamidou Kane, *Ambiguous Adventure* (Muslim Africa), Ciro Alegria, *Broad and Alien Is the World* (Peruvian Sierras), and Ning Lao T'ai-t'ai, *A Daughter of Han: The Autobiography of a Chinese Working Woman.*

Considering finally the economic impact of the West on the Third World, the most obvious effect was the unprecedented increase in productivity. The advances of technology and the building of infrastructure facilities made possible for the first time an efficient global division of labor. The international market economy effectively harnessed to Europe's industries the rubber of the Amazon, the tin of Malaya, the jute of India, the copper of Rhodesia and the Congo, the manganese of Russia, the palm oil of West Africa, the wool of Australia, the cotton of Egypt and so forth. This global economic integration increased world industrial production six times between 1860 and 1913, and world trade twelve times between 1851 and 1913.

As noted earlier in this section, the rising productivity doubled the incomes of British and French workers between 1850 and 1913. There was no corresponding increase, however, for Third World workers. At the same time that the global economic pie was increasing in overall size, so was the disparity between the sizes of the wedges available for the Third World as against the West. The precise nature of the West's economic impact varied from region to region. It was more intense on the island of Java than on the subcontinent of India, more pervasive in India as a colony than in China as a semicolony and more controlling in the militarily weak Chinese semicolony than in the militarily strong Russian semicolony. Despite these differences, certain common features are discernible in the economic influence of the West throughout the Third World.

In the realm of industry, the prevailing pattern was the exchange of colonial raw materials and foodstuffs for Western manufactures, which undercut many local crafts. Also, the European powers continued their earlier mercantilist policies of discouraging the development of industries in their colonies that might compete with their own home enterprises. In the case of India, for example, we have seen in Chapter 12 that the flourishing native cotton textile industry was deliberately destroyed by erecting protective tariffs in Britain so long as Indian textiles were cheaper, and then forbidding protective tariffs in India when British textiles became cheaper following the machine revolution.

Turning to agriculture, which involved the great majority of Third World peoples, private-property arrangements displaced the former communal ownership and cultivation of land. Also, in certain regions most of the land was appropriated for use by white settlers or by plantation interests. Where native manpower was needed for white-settler farms or for plantations or mines, this was conscripted directly by forced-labor decrees, or indirectly by levying poll and land taxes that necessitated wage labor for their payment. These measures involved a shift in varying degrees from agricultural production for local needs to production of cash crops or minerals for world markets. The prime example of this shift was the spread of plantations from the Americas to Asia and Africa.

As noted in Chapter 4, plantations originated in the Mediterranean basin, whence they were transplanted to Brazil by the Portuguese for cultivating sugar cane. From Brazil, plantation agriculture spread to the Caribbean islands and North America, so that the Americas remained the center of this type of agriculture until the mid-nineteenth century. Then with the abolition of slavery, New World plantations suffered from a shortage of labor, so they were transplanted once more, this time to Asia, where vast labor reserves were available. Also, improvements in ocean transportation and the opening of the Suez Canal (1869) made it possible to ship plantation produce from South and Southeast Asia to Western Europe—a much longer distance than the short transatlantic passage.

In some regions, such as Java and the Philippines, plantation labor was obtained by dispossessing smallholders and converting them into sharecroppers. In other regions, such as Ceylon, Malaya, Fiji, Hawaii and the West Indies, "coolie" labor was imported from India, China and Japan on the basis of "contracts" providing for long-term indenture and penal sanctions in case of nonfulfillment. For the illiterate coolies, transported far from their native villages, these contracts usually provided little protection against exploitation, either because they were not honored, or because oral promises made by the recruiters were not included in the contract and therefore were not binding. It is revealing that a recent study subtitled *The Export of Indian Labour Overseas 1830–1920* bears the revealing title, *A New System of Slavery*.[18] In this manner more coolie labor was recruited for tropical Asia and the islands of the Caribbean and of the Indian and Pacific oceans than had been slave labor for the Americas during the earlier centuries.

By the early twentieth century, population growth in Asia created land shortages and blocked further expansion of plantations. Accordingly, plantation agriculture was transplanted once more, this time to the relatively empty lands of tropical Africa. There the native population was recruited for work, either by imposing land or poll taxes, or by forced-labor decrees or by contracting for labor from neighboring areas, as in the case of South African and Rhodesian plantations (and mines), which obtained workers from the adjacent Portuguese colonies.

While the plantation system was spreading from the Americas to Asia and Africa, the plantation system's internal structure also was evolving to meet changes in technology and marketing. During the early centuries in the Americas the individual planter was able to operate because land was cheap and the only expense was the purchase of slaves. During the nineteenth century the individual planter gave way to metropolitan corporate enterprises because liquid capital was needed for wages after the abolition of slavery, and because technological advances required heavy capital investments for machinery to process and market the plantation produce.

Driven by the dynamics of the international market economy, the corporate enterprises steadily expanded their operations, both horizontally (by establishing plantations around the world) and vertically (by handling the processing, transporting and marketing of the produce). The growth of horizontal and vertical monopolies involved the metropolitan corporations in building machines, roads, ports, schools, hospitals, ships, storage facilities and worldwide marketing systems that enabled the corporations to branch out to sell new products within their existing structures. This process has continued to the present day, culminating in giant corporations that dominate the economies of the Third World countries in which they operate. The reality of big companies within small countries is evident from the table on page 273.

The rationalization of plantation agriculture increased productivity to the point where prices fell drastically and the terms of trade became increasingly unfavorable for Third World countries. During the 1860s and 1870s the prices of raw materials imported into Great Britain reached their highest point since the Napoleonic wars. But prices began to go down in 1873, and by 1895 the average index of import prices had fallen by 50 percent. With the exception of abnormal periods such as during world wars, the Third World countries have been plagued to the

A Comparison of Company Activity Data and National Aggregates for Selected Plantation Economies, 1967–68
(millions of dollars)

| | Company | | Country | | |
	Annual sales	Net income	National income	Exports Total	Exports Plantation[a]
Firestone	2,131.4	127.0			
Liberia			175.0	85.0	38.0
Booker	198.6	11.5			
Guyana			162.5	108.2	31.8
Tate & Lyle	549.2	27.1			
Jamaica			787.2	219.5	44.9
Trinidad			569.0	466.2	24.2
United Fruit	488.9	53.1			
Panama			634.0	95.2	55.6
Honduras			649.0	181.4	85.4

Source: G. I. Beckford, *Persistent Poverty* (London: Oxford University Press, 1972), p. 131.

[a] Plantation exports refer to exports of the commodity produced in the particular country by the relevant metropolitan enterprise.

present day by unfavorable terms of trade for most of their export products.

The above trends in Third World economies resulted in two common overall features. One was the increasing use of money in all factors of production—land, labor and capital. To a much greater degree than in traditional precapitalist societies, labor now was sold, land was rented and capital was invested. In short, Third World societies had become monetized.

The other common feature was the subordination of local economies to the needs of the European metropolis to a much greater degree than during the preceding mercantilist centuries. The more powerful European industrial capitalism now was able to penetrate and disrupt local economies on a scale far beyond the capacity of the earlier and weaker commercial capitalism.

The most obvious illustration of this unprecedented degree of Western economic intrusion was the emergence of new Third World cities. Their exclusive role was to function as funnels of trade with the West, and in fulfilling this role they completely overshadowed the traditional capital cities. The latter had been usually inland cities serving as administrative and religious centers rather than as economic centers. The few seaports that had existed in earlier times had been scattered, numerous and small, serving only the needs of their immediate surrounding regions. Now all this changed, with the new railways and steamship lines requiring new ports with facilities for handling the huge volume of trade with the West. Hence the rise in India of Bombay, Calcutta, Karachi and Madras, which soon were dispatching 90 percent of the country's foreign trade. Likewise in China the ports of Shanghai, Tientsin, Dairen, Hankow and Hong Kong-Canton were managing a similar percentage of the foreign trade. "The port cities," concludes Rhoads Murphey, "were clearly enough funnels through which primary production and treasure were drained out to the West and manufactured goods were brought in, to the frequent detriment of domestic producers. Increases in commercial crops were usually accompanied by at least relative decreases in food crops, and in several cases (Bengal, Ceylon, Malaya, the Philippines) by rising food deficits and a precariously balanced economy overly dependent on Western prices for two or three primary products as exports." [19]

❧ III. Western Economic Development vs. Third World Economic Growth

All these global economic trends combined to produce the present division of the world into the developed West as against the underdeveloped Third World. But underdevelopment under these circumstances did not mean nondevelopment; rather it meant distorted development—development designed to produce only one or two commodities needed by the Western markets rather than overall development to meet local needs. In short, it was the familiar Third World curse of economic growth without economic development.

The precise nature of this curse becomes apparent if the pattern of Western economic development is compared with that of Third World economic growth. Europe's Industrial Revolution was preceded by an Agricultural Revolution, which forced peasants off the land, promoted more productive agricultural techniques, increased agricultural output 40 percent within forty to sixty years and provided abundant labor for the new industries in the towns. The latter were expanding rapidly because of markets abroad and also markets at home generated by the more productive agriculture, which produced both consumers and capital. Furthermore, over twenty-five million Europeans emigrated during the half century before World War I, creating a drain on labor reserves and making possible trade union organization and the steady growth in real wages noted above.

This pattern of Western economic development was the precise opposite of Third World economic growth. Natives were compelled by various direct and indirect means to work in mines, plantations and settler farms for abnormally low wages, and the resulting profits were not used to finance local industries, as had been the case in Europe, but rather to pay high dividends to Western shareholders and thus further stimulate Western economic development. At the same time population pressure was rapidly mounting in Third World rural areas for several reasons: the rising birth rate due to Western medical science, the impossibility of emigrating abroad because the world's "empty" spaces already had been occupied by Western settlers and the lack of jobs in the cities because the traditional crafts were decimated by Western machine-made imports and modern industries were discouraged by the colonial powers. Hence the growing population pressure in Third World villages, culminating in the unprecedented rural exodus to towns and cities. This exodus, under the prevailing circumstances, has meant urbanization without industrialization. More precisely, it has meant the proliferating shantytowns of Calcutta, Lagos and Mexico City, incapable of providing adequate shelter, water and sewage disposal, let alone jobs.

This contrast between Western economic development and Third World economic growth explains why by 1900 the average per-capita income in the West was about six times greater than that in the Third World. It also explains why by 1913 eight Western countries (Britain, France, Germany, the United States, Italy, Canada, Belgium and Sweden) were producing 80 percent of the world's total industrial output, leaving the Third World populations to function as hewers of wood and drawers

British Exports of Cotton Piece Goods—Percentage of Total

Year	Europe and U.S.A.	Underdeveloped World	Other Countries
1820	60.4	31.8	7.8
1840	29.5	66.7	3.8
1860	19.0	73.3	7.7
1880	9.8	82.0	8.2
1900	7.1	86.3	6.6

Source: E. J. Hobsbawm, *Industry and Empire* (London: George Weidenfeld & Nicolson, 1968), p. 121.

of water. The causal relationship between Western economic development and Third World underdevelopment is evident in the steady rise of
the percentage of India's population dependent on agriculture: from 61
percent in 1891, to 66 in 1901, to 71 in 1911, and to 73 in 1921. And at
the same time Britain was shifting her cotton textile exports from European and American to Third World markets.

This pattern was not limited to Britain and India, as is evident from
the following table:

Country	Year	Share of the Labour Force Engaged in Agriculture
U.S.A.	1929	19.9
Canada	1911	37.2
Australia	1901	25.1
New Zealand	1896	37.0
Argentina	1895	39.6
Chile	1920	38.9
Colombia	1925	68.5
Mexico	1910	64.7
Egypt	1907	71.2

Source: S. Kuznets, *Economic Growth of Nations* (Cambridge, Mass.: Harvard
University Press, 1971), Table 38.

It is relevant to add that in one Western European country where
economic development could be blocked by means similar to those used
in the Third World, they were employed with precisely the same retard-
ing effects. "As early as 1824," writes Professor Arnold Schrier, "under the
pressure of English manufactures, Parliament withdrew the 10 percent
protective tariff on manufactured goods imported into Ireland, a tariff
that had been in effect at the time of the union with Britain in 1800. Deprived of any tariff protection local Irish industries were ultimately
destroyed by the competition of large manufacturing firms in Britain." [20]
Thus Ireland became an "internal" British colony, experiencing the same
"underdevelopment" as "external" colonies in Africa and Asia. The only
difference was that the Irish countryside was depopulated by immigration
to overseas territories where they were accepted, whereas Third World
rural areas were depopulated by immigration that perforce flowed to
local urban centers. Nevertheless, Irish villagers still tell stories about
the "death boats" that crossed the Atlantic with refugees from the potato
blight and the "Great Hunger" of the 1840s, and about the "American

wakes" at which parents said good-bye forever to children who would never be able to afford the return fare.

Other European powers also engendered "internal" colonies, such as Flanders in Belgium, the southern provinces of Italy and the islands of Corsica and Sardinia. It is not surprising that all these underdeveloped "internal" colonies today are demanding the self-determination already gained by the "external" colonies.

Chapter 14

AFRICA ENTERS
THE THIRD WORLD

The partition of Africa was, as we all recognize, due primarily to the economic necessity of increasing the supplies of raw materials and food to meet the needs of the industrialized nations of Europe.

LORD LUGARD

What have these big companies done for the country? Nothing. The concessions were given with the hope that the companies would develop the country. They have exploited it, which is not the same thing as development; they have bled and squeezed it like an orange whose skin is sooner or later discarded.

ANDRÉ GIDE

The transition from the free-trade imperialism of the early nineteenth century to the global colonialism of the latter part of the century was demonstrated most dramatically in the continent of Africa, and particularly by the activities of Henry Morton Stanley. In 1871 Stanley found Livingstone on the banks of Lake Tanganyika in one of the most memorable episodes of African exploration. In 1879 Stanley appeared on the Congo River, but this time he was functioning as an agent for King Leopold of Belgium rather than as an explorer. The age of exploration had given way to the age of African partition. By the First World War the Great Powers of Europe had divided among themselves the entire continent, the only exceptions being the precarious states of Liberia and Ethiopia. With the partition of Africa, the way was clear for the economic penetration of the continent—for the full-scale integration of Africa into the global market economy.

⌾ *I. Partition of Africa*

During the early nineteenth century the trade in slaves gradually was replaced by a flourishing trade in West African natural resources—palm oil, palm kernels, groundnuts, gold, timber, ivory and cotton. The terms of trade were favorable for West Africa until the 1850s, when economic conditions deteriorated sharply. The resulting economic tensions between European companies and native traders combined with changing Great Power diplomatic relationships to precipitate a scramble for African lands and the speedy partitioning of the continent.

After the 1850s, palm-oil prices dropped sharply because of the competition from oil fields opened in the United States in 1860; from groundnuts being imported from India; and from Australian tallow that was being transported profitably to Western Europe after the opening of the Suez Canal in 1869. The effect of this growing competition was accentuated by the shrinking European demand for oils and fats during the Great Depression of the last quarter of the nineteenth century. European firms now received lower prices in Europe for their West African goods and tried to pass on the reductions to the African producers. This started an economic power struggle in which each side indulged in malpractices such as diluting the palm oil and misrepresenting the quality and length of cloth. Demarcation disputes also arose over their respective functions and areas of operation. Some European firms established bases inland to buy commodities more cheaply from the producers by eliminating the African middlemen, and the latter often responded by destroying the company bases. Conversely, some African wholesalers tried to bypass the companies by selling directly in Europe, and they also attempted to keep up prices by withholding supplies.

European firms called on their governments to use force to beat down what they considered to be unreasonable obstructionism by native growers and merchants. Colonial officials often supported this demand for an "active policy," viewing it as a means for advancing their own careers. Furthermore, activism was becoming more feasible and appealing with the vastly increased power made available to Europeans by the Industrial and Scientific revolutions.

Advances in tropical medicine, especially the use of quinine for combating malaria, freed Europeans from the staggering mortality rates they had hitherto suffered. Also, the invention of the Gatling and Maxim machine guns shifted the military balance of power decisively against the Africans. So long as muskets were the standard firearms, a reasonable military balance prevailed between the two sides, especially since the Africans purchased huge numbers of muskets and even some cannon. But with the advent of repeating rifles and machine guns, the Africans were almost as badly outclassed as the Aztecs and the Incas had been by the Spaniards with their muskets. Other technological advances effected during the Industrial Revolution further facilitated penetration of the African continent, including river steamers, railways and telegraphic communications. When the first British steamship appeared in the Niger in 1857, it was foreordained that a decade later the first British consul should be appointed in the interior, at Lokaja.

This increasing power available to Europeans stimulated demand to make use of it to gain certain objectives. One was to lower the cost of goods reaching the coast by eliminating African middlemen and the tolls levied by African states. Another was to build railways into the interior, which it was believed would transform the economy of Africa as it had that of Europe. The most far-reaching objective was outright annexation, which was urged in order to assure law and order, maximize business opportunities and keep out European rivals. To rationalize their demands, the new merchants who wished to penetrate inland (as against those who wanted to safeguard their traditional operations on the coast) began using phrases such as "the regeneration of Africa," "the redemption of the savage" and the "preaching of the Gospel on the Banks of the Niger." But, as Dike observes, "The battle between the two groups was predominantly economic, not ideological." [1] So far as the British government was concerned it was ready to protect them in whatever regions they extended their operations. "Where there is money to be made," wrote a Foreign Office official, William Wylde, in 1876, "our merchants will be certain to intrude themselves, and . . . if they establish a lucrative trade, public opinion in this country practically compels us to protect them." [2]

Outstanding among the annexationists in West Africa was Sir George Goldie. "My dream as a child," this masterful builder once said, "was to colour the map red." He found his opportunity in the Niger Valley, where competing British companies had enabled African leaders such as Ja Ja to preserve their independence. In 1879 these companies under Goldie's direction combined to form the United African Company, which later absorbed French competitors in the upper Niger and was renamed the National African Company. Goldie was quite clear in his mind as to the role of his company in the Niger basin: "With old established markets closing to our manufactures, with India producing cotton fabrics not only for her own use but for export, it would be suicidal to abandon to a rival power the only great remaining undeveloped opening for British goods." [3]

With his customary vigor, Goldie set out to gain mastery over the Niger delta and to present the British government with a *fait accompli*.

He established over 100 trading posts in the interior, and backed them up with some 237 treaties, which his agents concluded by 1886 with African chiefs. These documents invariably ceded to the National African Company "the whole of the territories of the signatories," along with the right to exclude foreigners and to monopolize the trade of the involved territories. To deal with those African leaders who were unwilling to submit, the Company constructed twenty gunboats of shallow draft that were capable of navigating the Niger during the dry as well as the rainy season. Attacks upon company posts were countered by devastating naval bombardments. Thus the Company became the *de facto* government of the Nigerian hinterland before it was claimed by Britain at the 1884–85 Berlin African Conference.

It was not only West Africa that was partitioned between 1880 and 1900. During those same decades other parts of the continent also were annexed, even though they were not generating any large-scale trade of the sort that was causing frictions in West Africa. It is necessary, therefore, to take into account also the background forces engendered by the Industrial Revolution that culminated in the partitioning not only of Africa but also of virtually the entire globe. Entire continents were subjected to either outright colonial status, as in Africa, India and Southeast Asia, or into semicolonial status, as in the Ottoman, Persian and Chinese empires, as well as all of Latin America (details in Chapter 13).

In the case of Africa the partition process was triggered by new intruding powers that annexed choice but unclaimed African regions, thereby precipitating a chain reaction of pre-emptive partitioning by all the Great Powers.[4] King Leopold of Belgium started the partitioning process in Africa by hiring the explorer Henry Stanley to acquire territory in the rich Congo Basin. In 1879–80 Stanley gained title to over nine hundred thousand square miles (over seventy-six times the entire area of Belgium) from local chiefs who could not comprehend the meaning of the scraps of paper they were signing in return for baubles such as cases of gin and rum, and brightly colored coats, caps and handkerchiefs. With their communal landholding traditions, the notion of selling title to tribal lands was as preposterouus to these chiefs as it would be for an American city mayor to sell title to his courthouse or city hall. Yet this was done all over Africa—not only by Stanley for Belgium but also by Count de Brazza for France (north of the Congo), by Dr. Karl Peters for Germany (East Africa) and by other adventurers in the service of other powers.

The race for colonies was under way, so the Berlin African Conference was held in 1884–85 to set down ground rules for future acquisitions of African lands. It was agreed that notice of intent should be given, that claims had to be legitimized by effective occupation and that disputes were to be settled by arbitration. This treaty cleared the way for the greatest land grab in history. In 1879 the only colonies in Africa were those of France in Algeria and Senegal, of Britain along the Gold Coast and at the Cape, and of Portugal in Angola and Mozambique. By 1914 the entire continent had been partitioned, except for Ethiopia and Liberia, as indicated in the following table:

Political Divisions in Africa in 1914

	Square miles
French (Tunisia, Algeria, Morocco, French West Africa, French Congo, French Somaliland, Madagascar)	4,086,950
British (Union of South Africa, Basutoland, Bechuanaland, Nyasaland, Rhodesia, British East Africa, Uganda, Zanzibar, Somaliland, Nigeria, Gold Coast, Sierra Leone, Gambia, Egypt, Anglo-Egyptian Sudan)	3,701,411
German (East Africa, South-West Africa, Cameroon, Togoland)	910,150
Belgian (Congo State)	900,000
Portuguese (Guinea, West Africa, East Africa)	787,500
Italian (Eritrea, Italian Somaliland, Libya)	600,000
Spanish (Río de Oro, Muni River Settlements)	79,800
Independent States (Liberia, Ethiopia)	393,000
TOTAL	11,458,811

This table is my compilation, published earlier in my *The World Since 1500* (Englewood Cliffs, N.J.: Prentice-Hall, 1971), p. 380.

❧ II. African Resistance

The Berlin treaty called for effective occupation of the claimed territories, and in most cases this was achieved with surprisingly small forces. Colonial Kembell overran Sokotra with only twelve hundred men, though it was defended by an army of thirty thousand. The British expedition against Ijebu-Ode consisted of a thousand men, yet it prevailed against native contingents about ten times more numerous. General Dobbs successfully led two thousand troops against a Dahomeyan army of twelve thousand. Furthermore, these victorious "European" forces consisted

1. *Richard Chancellor lands on the White Sea coast in 1553, opening a direct sea route between Russia and Western Europe.*

2. *Indians pouring molten gold down a Spaniard's throat, as other Spaniards are being dismembered and cannibalized.*

3. A sixteenth-century view of the port of Acapulco, the only port in New Spain permitted to trade directly with the East.

4. A Bosch-like depiction of silver mining at Potosi, the richest site in sixteenth-century Peru.

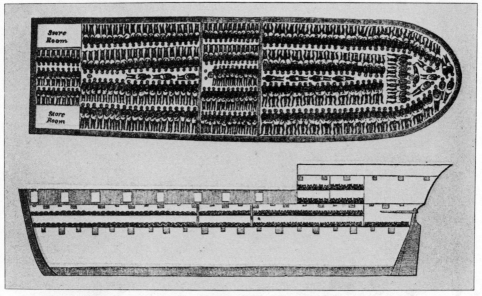

5. *Stowing of slaves in 1786 on the ship* Brookes *of Liverpool.*

6. *Forge in St. Petersburg at the end of the nineteenth century.*

7. *Late-nineteenth-century gold mine in Siberia.*

8. *Baku oil field, opened in the 1870s by the Swedish-Russian industrialist, Alfred Nobel.*

9. St. Petersburg, the "window to the West," constructed by Peter the Great.

10. Cossack horseman of the Caucasus.

11. Suicide in April 1868 by Ethiopian Emperor Theodore, who sought, like Mohammad Ali of Egypt, to modernize his country, but was opposed by Britain. He took his life while the British commander, Sir Robert Napier, saluted.

12. *Western businessmen employing the labor of dispossessed and impoverished Chinese peasants in their rattan factory, about 1875.*

13. *Examination halls in Canton, one of the centers where the government held periodic examinations for students aspiring to enter the bureaucracy.*

14. *Refugees in Shanghai during the last days of the Kuomintang, 1949.*

15. *First Communist soldiers in Peking, 1949.*

16. *British couple at the races, Happy Valley, Hong Kong, 1949.*

17. *Jawaharlal Nehru, with Lord and Lady Mountbatten in 1948.*

mostly of African rank-and-file, trained and led by European officers. French units fighting in Africa were made up largely of Tirailleurs Senegalais, while the British used West Indian troops in most of their African campaigns.

Why were the Europeans able to carve up Africa with so little difficulty? One reason was dissension among the Africans, which prevented them from uniting for common defense. Thus the Europeans were able to pit Africans against Africans, just as they had been able to use Indians against Indians in the Americas. Cortes, for example, had the aid of the Totonacs and the Thaxcalans against the Aztecs, and Pizarro was helped by the Canaris and by "legitimist" Court factions against the Incas. Likewise African leaders cooperated with the Europeans against traditional enemy neighbors whom they shortsightedly considered to be more dangerous. Thus the Ahmadu of Segou fought with the French against Mahmadou Lamine, Tieba of Sikasso with the French against Samori, and Ibadan with the British against Ijebu.

The Europeans also recruited numerous individual natives to serve in their armies. Africans from Senegalese ports put on French army uniforms and fought to establish French rule in the interior. In Mozambique, Africans, mulattos and even Indians fought with the Portuguese to "pacify" large areas of that province. The British made extensive use of what they called "friendlies" in their African campaigns. These were native allies who provided information about local terrain and personalities as well as essential manpower. Many of the recruits were outcasts in their own societies, and therefore were completely dependent on the British officers who clothed, fed, trained, led and paid them. As in India, the British were careful to send the men enlisted in one area to fight natives living in distant areas. Thus they used the West India Regiment to fight against the Bai Bureh in Sierra Leone, the Yoruba recruits to fight against the Ibos, and the Central African Regiment to fight against the Ashantis. For the same divide-and-rule reason the British organized the men in the Northern Nigeria Regiment on the basis of language groups and used them separately as the occasion demanded. They did not leave units too long in one place lest they fraternize with the local inhabitants. The only loyalty tolerated was loyalty to the government through loyalty to the officers. Educated or politically conscious Africans were not recruited for fear that they might corrupt the African rank-and-file.

Another reason for the ease with which the Africans were conquered was their inability to change their battle tactics to cope with a new type of adversary. They persisted in waging frontal, head-on warfare, which left them sitting ducks to the murderous European firepower. Then after being defeated in the field they usually retreated to walled cities, where again they were vulnerable to European artillery. Furthermore, they confined their fighting to daytime because most of them were too superstitious to move about at night. These inhibitions prevented the Africans from waging guerrilla warfare which, with their knowledge of the terrain and their assurance of mass support, might have enabled them to hold out long enough to make conquest prohibitively expensive. On this matter of adaptability, however, it should be noted that the European officers also performed poorly. They had few problems in the grassland regions where conditions approximated those of Salisbury plain and Aldershot, and where the stereotyped maneuvers they had learned proved effective. But they fared badly in thick forests, where their equipment forced them to stick to a few trails, where they were easily ambushed. No effort was made to adapt tactics and equipment to jungle warfare until World War II, when the British learned at high cost in Burma and Malaya that lightness and mobility were essential for survival.

A third reason for the rapid conquest of Africa was the aggressiveness and ruthlessness of ambitious European officers who were eager to prove their mettle and earn promotions. Regardless of the destructiveness and slaughter, they could count on their superiors to support them in the few cases of criticism at home. Lord Lugard, for example, rather obviously rationalized the enormous destruction in Munshi towns and villages in Nigeria during the 1900 expedition:

> I cannot but express my sense of regret at the very great loss of life among these ignorant savages, and the burning of the villages with their food. The Munshis however are a most intractable people, and nothing except extremely severe chastisement of this sort will prevent them from lawless murders and looting of canoes, or induce them to allow the telegraph to be constructed through their country. My own view is that it is far more humane, in the event, to inflict a drastic lesson at first and thoroughly subdue people of this kind than to attempt half measures, which invariably lead to a further outbreak and a greater eventual loss of life.[5]

A different interpretation was offered by the Lagos *Weekly Record* in 1906 when commenting on the inducements (high pay, active service, abundant honors and medals) that Lugard offered in recruiting English officers for service in the West African Frontier Force:

> The influence this hope of fighting and its distinctions exerts in producing military expeditions against the native will never be known for it is only one side of the case which is published and heard; and when a man is intent on doing a thing he is no more at a loss for finding an excuse for his action than he is hampered

in discovering ways and means of effecting his purposes. And most of the plausible stories of the native that adorn official despatches would show up dismally if subjected to the search light of investigation and fact. It is the immunity from such scrutiny that gives inspiration and existence to these fabricated stories against the native, and the only prospect of their ever ceasing with the calamities they involve, is when the game is rendered too dangerous to be indulged in.[6]

A final reason for the relatively easy conquest of Africa was the enormous disparity in military technology. European forces were armed with Gatling and Maxim machine guns, which fired over ten shots per second. The Africans were not able to get any of these guns, nor did they have anything to counter the naval ordnance on river gunboats and coastal warships. The overwhelming advantage enjoyed by the European invaders moved the Lagos *Weekly Record* to comment on the inherent viciousness and immorality of the "pacification expeditions" in the colonial territories:

> . . . a system of warfare carried on at such disparity of arms as to hardly make it war at all, but rather a cowardly, wanton and unrisky raid upon human life. It is the inequality characterising these wars against the native which induces public feeling to revolt at the spectacle of one man armed shooting down another who is unarmed and glorying in his deed; and the feeling of repugnance excited is not without the suspicion that the absence of risk is what largely prompts the undertaking of such wars. But be this as it may, the conviction is irresistible that if the native possessed arms of precision prudence would dictate more caution in determining "the necessity" for such wars which too often is based upon rash misconceptions or wrongful representations and which a little investigation would serve to dispel or correct.[7]

All this does not mean, however, that African resistance to the Europeans was completely nonexistent. Traditional historiography has left this impression because it has interpreted the "scramble for Africa" as a struggle among the European powers alone, with the Africans serving merely as passive pawns. Accordingly, the colonial campaigns have been described through the biographies of European leaders such as Lugard, Dodds, Gallieni and Archinard. Only recently have studies appeared of comparable African leaders such as Samori, Bai Bureh, Lat Dior, Behanzin and Attahiru Ahmadu. In addition to these biographies there have been recent analyses of resistance movements as movements—their origins, composition, dynamics and achievements.

These new works reveal that despite the overall failure of African resistance, it was by no means insignificant. In certain regions it was strong enough to slow up the European forces seriously. This is why the occupation of West Africa took twenty-five years, and why parts of the Ivory Coast, Mali, Niger, eastern and northern Nigeria, and Mauritania were not pacified till the second decade of the twentieth century. The African resistance also was significant in determining the status accorded later within the imperial structures—whether it was that of an outright colony; or an autonomous protectorate; or a completely independent state, such as Ethiopia.

Finally, the resistance leaders whose exploits now are being unearthed and recorded serve today as national heroes for the newly independent states of Africa. An outstanding example is Samori who, by dint of his military genius, his diplomatic skill and his charismatic personality was able to transform the old Konya warrior bands into a new Dyula army, which repeatedly defeated both French and British expeditions before succumbing to overwhelming technological superiority. Samori today is a revered figure in Guinea, as is Bai Bureh in Sierra Leone, Menelik in Ethiopia, Chilembwe in Malawi and Mkwawa in Tanzania.

❦ III. Techniques of Control

The first political act of the new imperial masters was the drawing of the boundaries of the various colonies. Here the prime consideration was the European balance of power rather than the geographic or ethnographic realities in Africa. Thus the Somalis found themselves divided among four sovereignties: French, British, Italian and Ethiopian.

Once the boundaries had been settled, the problem of organizing some administration had to be faced. The main concern of the European governments was that the new colonies should be self-supporting as soon as possible, so they sent out governors with unbelievably small budgets. Sir Harry Johnston undertook to organize the administration of Nyasaland (now Malawi) with his own salary plus £10,000 a year, with which he employed 1 British officer and 75 Indian soldiers. Lord Lugard in Northern Nigeria had an annual budget of a little over £100,000 for a territory of 10 million inhabitants. His staff consisted of 5 European administrative officers and a regiment of the West African Frontier Force comprising 2,000 African soldiers with 120 European officers.

This shortage of manpower forced the colonial officials to resort to various forms of indirect rule by which tribal chiefs were allowed to retain some of their authority. The precise nature of indirect rule depended on the political traditions of the mother country. The French, with their long history of a centralized bureaucracy in Paris, viewed the chiefs as officials or *fonctionnaires* of governmental authority. The British, by contrast, regarded the chiefs as local governmental representatives with legislative functions. The French kept the chiefs on tight leash, depriving them of criminal jurisdiction over their people and also of police authority and police forces. Thus their chiefs were entrusted only with unpopular duties such as collecting taxes, recruiting and supervising forced labor and selecting recruits for military service. With their republican traditions, the French generally viewed the chiefs as necessary evils, to be exploited so long as it suited imperial interests.

The British were more sympathetic to the chiefdom institution, accustomed as they were to the trappings of monarchy. They took care, therefore, to place "legitimate" chiefs on thrones, since they would naturally command popular allegiance. Also, the British interfered as little as possible with the chiefs, and when the British felt it necessary to do so, they operated discreetly behind the scenes. They were under strict orders that the chiefs should appear as independent heads rather than as foreign-controlled instruments.

Whether under British or French aegis, the African chiefs obviously had lost their sovereignty. It was the colonial officers who had the final word in key matters such as raising taxes, promulgating legislation, disposing of land and recruiting of troops. Yet the chiefs paradoxically were often more powerful during the colonial period than before. Formerly they had to negotiate with various groups during the decision-making process, whereas under colonial rule all limitations on their authority from below were eliminated. So long as the chiefs were on good terms with the colonial officers, the chiefs could discredit any critics or challengers of their administrations as malcontents who threatened the imperial order.

Together with the European officials came the Christian missionaries. They had profound effect on African culture because they were the first Europeans who consciously sought to change it. The others affected African culture indirectly and incidentally, as when they forced the natives to leave their ancestral villages to work in cities, mines or European-owned farms. But the missionaries arrived with the avowed purpose of changing the African way of life, and they used three principal instruments to reach their objective: religion, medicine and education.

The primary aim of all missionaries was to win converts to the churches to which they themselves belonged. During the three decades prior to World War I missionary societies of all denominations experienced a boom in recruitment and financial support. In Nigeria alone, for example, were to be found by the end of the nineteenth century representatives of the Church Missionary Society of England, the Wesleyan Methodists, the Scottish Presbyterians, the Southern Baptist Convention and the Catholic Society of African Missions. The response to Christian missionaries in Africa was much greater than in the Middle East or India or China. Pagan Africans not only joined the Christian churches but also served as teachers in the schools and colleges, itinerant evangelists in the villages, full missionaries in the main centers and linguists who reduced the various languages to writing and translated the Bible into them. The converts also actively worked against the slave trade, encouraged the development of legitimate trade and supported British military interventions against native rulers who persisted in the slave traffic.

The only setbacks occurred in areas where Islam already was rooted and conducting a comparable extension of activities from towns to surrounding rural areas. This was the case in Senegal, Guinea, Chad, northern Nigeria, northern Sudan and in the central zone of East Africa. In these areas Islam spread through the quiet missionary work of Muslim traders and preachers. Frequently the trader appeared first, combining proselytism with the sale of his merchandise. Soon after his arrival in a pagan village, he attracted attention by his regularly recurring times of prayer and prostration, during which he appeared to be conversing with some invisible being. Frequently he would marry a native woman, and this often led to the adoption of Islam by members of the woman's family. Soon religious instruction was needed for the children, so schools were established and attended by pagan as well as Muslim children. Some even went on to centers of higher learning and then returned as missionaries among the pagans of their native land.

Their activities were assisted by the easy integration of tribal religious beliefs and customs with Islamic creed and ritual. Allah is identified with Mungu, the creator in the Bantu tribal religion, and the angels and saints that play an important role in Islam in the Middle East are readily identified with the spirits of tribal religion and called by African names. This unique adaptability of Islam to indigenous cultures, together with the popular identification of Christianity with colonialism, explains the success of Islam in more than holding its own against Christianity in Africa.

Missionaries brought not only their religious message but also medical knowledge and facilities that saved the lives of many Africans. This medical work in turn enhanced the appeal of Christianity as against the pagan faiths. In addition to saving lives, Western medicine forced Africans to question their traditional assumptions of what caused illness and death. The white man had the power to make people well even after the traditional petitioning of spirits had not worked. So the old tribal religions no longer could be counted on to meet all emergencies and to provide all the answers. Even though the majority of sub-Saharan Africans clung to their old faiths through the nineteenth century, traditional religion no longer was as effective a cement in holding together the African's whole way of life as it previously had been.

The most effective means for spreading the Christian gospel was the network of village schools in which children of all ages could learn the rudiments of reading, writing and arithmetic, along with the religious instruction leading to baptism and Church membership. These schools were particularly influential, since most colonial governments left education entirely to the missionaries. In addition to academic and religious instruction, some teachers taught their pupils how to build better houses, improve their agricultural methods and observe basic principles of hygiene and sanitation. They also reduced the African languages to writing and so laid the foundations for indigenous African literature.

These schools inevitably undermined traditional African culture as the pupils tended to listen more to their teachers and less to their parents, who now appeared old-fashioned and wrong on many issues. Missionary education encouraged at least a certain degree of individualism, which was contrary to the communal village life. After several years of this type of education, many pupils naturally were reluctant to return to the old village existence. Some found jobs with private business firms or in colonial administration. Others remained in missionary schools to receive further training as catechists and teachers. Foreign missionaries soon occupied only supervisory positions, while most of the teaching and evangelistic posts were filled by Africans. But none of the school systems, whether missionary- or state-operated, serviced more than a tiny proportion of the school-age population. In 1910 there were only about fifteen thousand children in French schools in all French West Africa, or less than 2 percent of the total who were eligible. In 1921 about 9 percent of the school-age population were attending classes in southern Nigeria.

This educated minority gradually became a serious challenge to traditional tribal authorities and also to European officials. They had imbibed in the course of their education certain political concepts such as individual liberty and political freedom, and began to question why these did not apply to Africans as well as to Europeans. This questioning was sharpened by discrimination that they encountered in government and private employment. Regardless of their education, experience and abilities, they could not become more than poorly paid clerks in European firms or minor officials in administration.

As early as 1911 a Nyasaland African wrote this scathing criticism of the hypocrisy of European Christians:

> There is too much failure among all Europeans in Nyasaland. The three combined bodies—Missionaries, Government and Companies

or gainers of money—do form the same rule to look upon the native with mockery eyes. It sometimes startles us to see that the three combined bodies are from Europe, and along with them there is a title Christendom. And to compare and make a comparison between the Master of the title and his servants, it provokes any African away from believing in the Master of the title. If we had power enough to communicate ourselves to Europe, we would advise them not to call themselves Christendom, but Europeandom. Therefore the life of the three combined bodies is altogether too cheaty, too thefty, too mockery. Instead of "Give," they say "Take away from." There is too much breakage of God's pure law as seen in James's Epistle, chapter five, verse four.[8]

This outburst illustrates how Christianity stimulated independent thinking regarding relations with the Europeans. A writer in an Angolan journal noted the political implications of the European churches, and especially of Protestantism; "To tell a person he is able to interpret the Bible freely is to insinuate in him an undue autonomy and turn him into a rebel. . . . A Protestant native is already disposed towards—not to say an active agent in—the revolt against civilized peoples." [9]

Educated African dissenters were regarded patronizingly at first by European officials and native chiefs as young upstarts who represented only themselves. The famous colonial administrator Lord Lugard referred to them contemptuously as "trousered blacks." But because of their education they were able to translate what had been tribal resentment against the Europeans into nationalist resistance. In retrospect they now stand out as pioneer nationalists who were destined to become the political leaders of their peoples after World War I, and especially after World War II.

The African nationalist movement gained recruits not only from discontented school graduates but also from equally discontented peasants. The latter endured social disruption and economic exploitation under colonial rule. The introduction of cash crops led to the alienation of communal lands at the expense of those who immigrated or were forced to immigrate to towns. The increased authority of the chiefs left the villagers vulnerable to merciless exploitation. In northern Nigeria, for example, the feudal Muslim emirs used their considerable patronage to put relatives and friends on the public payroll. Thus they controlled tax collecting, road and bridge building, medical services, police and prisons and so forth. A British official in northern Nigeria wrote in 1924 the following indictment of indirect rule in that colony:

Seventeen years in the Political Service in Nigeria, with personal experience covering the greater part of the Native Administration areas, have satisfied me that . . . the Native Administration op-presses the poor man. . . . Extortion of every sort is rife. Common forms of it are:

(a) Taxes being collected twice over.
(b) People who have been turned out en masse to clean a road, or to build houses, or to do some other sort of work, being either given no pay at all, or a derisory sum, although an adequate amount has been voted and actually paid by the Treasury for distribution to the workers.
(c) Provision, compulsory, by the people of entertainment for the Emir and his followers and his horses, or for his representatives, without any payment being made.
(d) Presents—"dashes"—to the Emir's wives and his relatives and his hangers-on, on demand, and of course with no quid pro quo.
(e) "Loans" to Native Administration personnel, of horses, stock, women, grain, money, etc.[10]

In conclusion, the control techniques of the colonial powers were generally effective, yet they generated tensions that found expression in the African nationalist movement. This consisted of two main elements. One was the urban middle-class elements, which wanted to gain control of the state apparatus and to exploit it for their benefit. The other comprised the peasant masses, who yearned for either the expulsion of the Europeans and their African collaborators, or for elevation to middle-class status through education and cash-earning jobs.

ᴥ *IV. Integration into the World Capitalist Order*

With the ending of the slave trade and the partitioning of the entire continent, the way was clear for achieving the economic goal that hitherto had proven unattainable—namely, the full integration of Africa into the global economy of industrial capitalism. The general effect of this process of integration has been summarized by Immanuel Wallerstein: ". . . the trading operation was now carried on within a single political economy rather than between two political economies."[11]

The emergence of a "single political economy" meant that certain economic features prevailed throughout the continent. One was the curtailment or elimination of African (and Arab) traders as middlemen. Their place was taken by European trading firms, which had the advantages of larger funds of working capital, superior or exclusive credits with European colonial banks and direct access to European commercial networks. Another common economic feature was the development or expansion of commodity exports. Most profitable were the mineral exports from South Africa, the Belgian Congo and Northern Rhodesia, which comprised two thirds of the gross output of all Africa during the colonial period. Agricultural exports also increased rapidly in volume, being grown by native farmers in West Africa and by white settlers in East and southern Africa. A third common feature of Africa's economy under colonialism was the mobilization of native labor, directly through the *corvée*, or indirectly through the hut tax or poll tax. Both rural and urban workers were grossly underpaid for various reasons, including the monopoly of political power enjoyed by colonial authorities, the large labor pool available in the rural areas, the inability of short-term migratory workers to organize and the racist justification of substandard wages for substandard workers.

Despite these common, continentwide economic characteristics, the precise manner in which Africa was integrated into the international market economy depended on local conditions and products. An African economist, Samir Amin, has analyzed three regional patterns of economic integration.[12] These were: first, the West African native farmers, who grew a variety of cash crops for the world market; second, the European concession-owning companies in the Congo Basin, which extracted maximum output from the tribespeople of the forests; and third, the European settlers and mining companies in East and southern Africa, which coerced native labor into working on their farms and mines.

Considering first the realm of the West African peasant producers, both the British and the French encouraged the peasants to grow export crops because this not only met the need for such crops in the home markets but also provided income for the peasants with which they could pay the head tax that was the main financial prop of colonial administrations. The French began by facilitating the growing of groundnuts in Senegal. As they extended their control into the interior they pushed other crops appropriate to local conditions, especially cotton. This in turn led to the construction of railways, which were needed to transport the produce to coastal ports such as Dakar.

The same policy was followed by both the French and the British farther south, from the Guinea coast to Nigeria, where the chief export products were palm oil, cocoa, rubber and forest products, along with gold. Again railways were built from the interior to ports such as Conakry, Abidjan, Lagos and Port Harcourt.

This West African trade in agricultural produce was dominated by a hierarchical trade network comprising European import-export companies, and Lebanese and other minority middlemen. The most powerful by all odds were the European companies, which enjoyed monopolistic advantages. They controlled warehousing, shipping and marketing, and therefore were able to dictate prices to the unorganized small farmers.

Outstanding among these companies were the Compagnie Française d'Afrique Occidentale, Société Commerciale Ouest Africaine and National African Company. These firms enjoyed a double advantage in dealing with the West African farmers. The firms could set low prices on the produce they bought, knowing that the farm families grew a large proportion of what they needed, and that they had to sell in order to obtain cash for the head tax. Conversely, the foreign companies could charge high prices on their imported goods such as tools, clothing and bicycles, because they had no competitors. It is not surprising that these firms were able to pay 25 percent dividend on ordinary shares during poor years, and as high as 90 percent in prosperous years. Shipping companies were equally exploitative, charging 35 shillings per ton for transporting flour from Liverpool to West Africa, as against 7½ shillings for the same distance from Liverpool to New York.

Retail trade was controlled by minority middlemen, mostly Lebanese, Syrians and Greeks in West Africa, as against Indians and Greeks in East Africa, and Arabs in Zanzibar and East African ports. These minorities operated in the villages as well as in the towns, and channeled their profits overseas, as did the large companies. With their industry, frugality and initiative, the minorities pioneered in opening new markets in the interior, but they were also notorious for giving loans at usurious rates, and deceiving the illiterate Africans through the use of false weights and measures.

The West African peasants produced their export crops under a variety of arrangements. In the coastal areas the peasants owned and worked their own plots, though hiring during the busy season migrant workers from neighboring colonies such as Togoland and Upper Volta, which would not produce cash crops and therefore had surplus labor. In the savannah lands from Senegal through northern Nigeria to the Sudan, the production of groundnuts and cotton was organized by the theocratic political power of various Muslim brotherhoods, which levied tribute on village communities and marketed the resulting proceeds on the international market.

Whatever the production arrangements, West African trade boomed during the two decades prior to World War I, as is evident from the table on page 302.

Turning from the realm of the West African peasants to that of the Congo Basin concessionaires, we find a different region of equatorial rain forests. Ecological conditions precluded the population density and the export crops of West Africa, and therefore precluded also an economic basis for collecting the tax and customs revenues that supported the colonial administration and the railway building in West Africa. Accordingly, King Leopold resorted to the granting of concessions, the

Total Trade: Imports and Exports

	British West Africa (£)	French West Africa (£)
1895	4,682,000	3,148,000
1900	7,620,000	5,192,000
1905	10,810,000	6,120,000
1910	20,826,000	11,132,000
1912	25,309,000	10,128,000

Source: M. Crowder, *West Africa Under Colonial Rule* (Evanston, Ill.: Northwestern University Press, 1968), p. 288.

first of which was concluded in 1886 with the Compagnie du Congo pour le Commerce et l'Industrie. The company undertook to build a railway around the lower Congo rapids from Matadi to Leopoldville in return for 1,500 hectares (about 5½ square miles) for every kilometer of railway constructed. Thus over 3,000 square miles were alienated, and as soon as the railway was completed in 1898, similar contracts were signed with two other companies.

In theory, only "wasteland" was involved in these transactions, land actually under cultivation being specifically excluded. But since land without labor was useless, and since there was no supervision of the companies or of their agents, the end result was a horror story of unrestrained exploitation and brutalization rivaling the worst excesses of the earlier slave trade. The most shocking abuses occurred between 1895 and 1905, when the invention of rubber tires for bicycles and for automobiles created a strong demand for rubber. The soaring prices spurred company agents to resort to the most inhuman practices to force the natives to work at wild-rubber extraction.

So brutal were the various methods of forced labor that the population of the Congo declined by one half (from 20 to 10 million) between 1885 and 1908 when it was ruled by Leopold. If the Africans did not bring in the stipulated amount of rubber and ivory they were mutilated or shot. Mutilation meant chopping off a hand or a foot or both. To prove that they were doing their job properly, the bosses of the labor gangs brought to their superiors baskets full of human hands. And because the climate was hot and humid, the hands were sometimes smoked in order to preserve them. A traveler in the Congo Free State recorded his observations as follows: "The inhabitants have disappeared. Their homes have been burned; huge heaps of ashes amid neglected palm-hedges and devastated abandoned fields. Inhuman floggings, murders, plunderings and carryings-off. . . . The people flee into the wild or seek protection in French or Portuguese territory." [13] Such flight frequently brought little relief, for the concession system prevailed also in the adjacent colonies, where the native populations were exploited in a parallel fashion, if not quite as inhumanly.

Considering finally the realm of European settlers and mining companies, this consisted mostly of the high country running from the Kenya highlands southwest to the Cape. The climate was sunny yet cool, because of the high altitude, so the Europeans came to regard it as "white man's country," particularly because it was not as densely settled by native peoples as West Africa.

As in the Congo, the land here also was worthless without labor, so a variety of measures were employed to force the Africans to work for the Europeans at low wages in mines and on farms. These measures included a head tax and a labor tax levied on male adults, who thereby were forced to work in order to obtain the cash for the head tax, or to meet the stipulated number of days of forced labor each year. Another measure was to reserve most of the arable lands for white settlement, thus leaving the Africans landless and forcing them to work on European-owned farms for subsistence wages. These policies solved the labor problem not only for the European landowners but also for the European mineowners, who operated profitable gold and copper mines as well as diamond fields. Later this dispossessed native labor was to be employed in the industries that developed in Kenya, Rhodesia and South Africa.

The German government was most systematic in its efforts to settle its citizens in Africa. Since millions of Germans had for long been immigrating to Latin America and the United States, a concerted effort now was made to use this manpower to build up Germany's overseas colonies. Most of the immigrants settled in Tanganyika and Southwest Africa, though some went to Cameroon and Togoland. Britain was less systematic, leaving it more to the local authorities to determine policies. The Ugandan chiefs were able to obtain special agreements that effectively excluded white settlers, but British immigrants were encouraged and did materialize in Kenya, Nyasaland and Rhodesia.

In Angola and Mozambique, the "scramble for Africa" in the late nineteenth century induced the Lisbon officials to encourage Portuguese immigrants to settle in the interior regions in order to retain control over these huge colonies. The average Portuguese settler, however, differed drastically from his German or British counterparts. During the nineteenth century he tended to resemble a one-man concession company. On his estate he collected taxes and administered summary justice to his African tenants, from among whom he recruited both his laborers and his private police force. These semifeudal arrangements reflected the backwardness of the mother country, an underdeveloped and dependent region of the European continent. Thus in the Zambezi Valley, an area twice the size of Portugal, the number of Portuguese settlers by 1914 totaled only 178. And their contribution to the development of the colony did not go beyond collecting taxes and forcibly recruiting labor for Rhodesian and South African mines, for which they received ten shillings per worker.

In conclusion, colonial rule doubtless increased the productivity of the African lands. The profits, however, were skimmed off and transferred abroad by the European companies, settlers and middlemen. Even more than in Latin America, the new economic linkages were vertical, or with the European metropolitan centers, rather than horizontal, or with neighboring regions or states. This produced the old dilemma of economic growth without development. More copper and iron ore was mined, but none was refined in African smelters. More cotton and peanuts were produced, but none were processed in African mills or factories. When some entrepreneurs in Senegal began to process peanuts into oil, the French government stopped their operations in order to protect olive-oil interests at home. Likewise minority middlemen in other West African colonies who sought to process local products were quickly stopped by imperial fiat.

Supporters of the economic colonialism imposed upon Africa maintain that the white settlers, for example, introduced farming techniques that the natives were incapable of performing. "Rhodesian flue-cured tobacco, for instance, requires a skill in organization and an amount of capital that the ordinary peasant does not possess." [14] The question, however, is whether it is lack of skill and capital, or of incentive and opportunity. Consider the following tribute paid by a British official, Sir Hugh Clifford, to the ingenuity and initiative of West African peasants in the cocoa industry when they had their own land to work, and a market for their produce:

> This man, reputed to be lazy by the superficial globe-trotter or the exponent of the damned nigger school, has carved from the virgin forest an enormous clearing, which he has covered with flourishing cocoa farms. Armed with nothing better than an imported axe and machete, and a native-made hoe, he has cut down the forest giant, cleared the tropical undergrowth, and kept it cleared. With no means of animal transport, no railways and few roads, he has conveyed his produce to the sea, rolling it down in casks for miles and carrying it on his own sturdy cranium. Here is a result to make us pause in our estimate of the negro race. . . . [15]

Far from the European farmers as a group being more efficient and productive than the natives, it is argued by some that the Europeans' farms were viable only because of the extreme preferential treatment they received from the colonial authorities in the form of all the best land they needed at bargain prices; all the labor they needed at similar bargain wages; government subsidies and special privileges in education, health and social services; and protection from African competition by various restrictions imposed on Africans but not on whites. Recent studies of the British planters in Kenya show that they were granted virtually everything they desired, including the "white man's highlands" at nominal prices, preferential rates for their products on the Kenya–Uganda railway, an abundance of labor that was officially described as "probably the cheapest in the world" and exclusive use of the services of government agricultural research bureaus. Yet despite these privileges, the settler farms remained "an inefficient, artificially protected, and, in strict accounting terms, even privately unprofitable use of resources." [16]

At the same time Kenyan African peasants, when given the opportunity, were successful in growing cotton, coffee and maize, demonstrating willingness and ability to learn from expert advice. But this was completely cut off by 1905, and the reason was given candidly in 1906 by a leading official, John Ainsworth: "White people can live here and *will* live here, not . . . as colonists performing manual labor, as in Canada or New Zealand, but as planters, etc., overseeing natives doing the work of development." [17] The difficulty with this strategy was that "overseers" soon became more interested in their leisure and conspicuous display than in maximizing their productivity. And as for the argument concerning the "beneficial example" of European farming for Africans, the fact was that the size of settler land units precluded the transfer of European technology to typically much smaller African plots.

Apart from the relative merits of African and white farmers, the more significant consideration is that colonial rule and integration into the world market economy inflicted the curse of monoculture on many Africans: cocoa on the Gold Coast, palm produced in Dahomey and southeastern Nigeria, cotton in the Sudan, sisal in Tanganyika, cotton in Uganda and peanuts in Senegal and Gambia. As noted in an earlier chapter on Latin America, monoculture meant overspecialization and dependence on food imports in formerly self-sufficient regions. Gambia and Senegal, for example, had grown much rice, but monoculture stopped this and resulted in periodic famines. Likewise Asante, which once had been famous for its yams and other foodstuffs, also suffered periodic famine when it overspecialized in cocoa. The other serious disadvantage of monoculture was its vulnerability to extreme price fluctuations on the world markets, and also to plant diseases, which devastated entire crops and hence entire economies.

As for mining operations, it is maintained by defenders of the European corporations that their capital and technology made available African resources that the natives could not have brought into use. "The foreign investors did not in fact take away from African tribesmen a form of wealth which they had previously enjoyed. . . . The mining companies created a new form of enterprise; they mined ores which communities such as the Lamba and Lala could not have exploited with the technological means available to tribal society." [18] This is quite true, but the issue is the terms under which these mining companies operated, and the end results of their operations. Concrete answer is provided by a British economist whose study itemized the expenditures and profits in 1949 of copper mining companies in Northern Rhodesia.

Expenditures and Output of Mining Industry in Northern Rhodesia
(in thousand pounds)

1. European salaries, wages, bonuses	£ 4,100
2. African wages and bonuses	1,400
3. African rations	600
4. Payments to contractors	1,000
5. Payments to Rhodesia Railways	1,800
6. Income Tax and Customs	3,600
Total expenditure	£12,500
Gross value of output	£36,742

Source: P. Deane, *Colonial Social Accounting* (Cambridge: Cambridge University Press, 1953), p. 37.

These statistics show that of the £36.7 million realized, only £12.5 million were spent in Rhodesia, leaving two thirds of the total to be transferred to foreign shareholders. Moreover, of the £12.5 million spent in Rhodesia, only £2 million reached the Africans working in the mines, as against £4.1 million paid to the Europeans working there, presumably a small minority compared to the number of African miners.

It is true that these miners were paid an average of £41 a year, as against the average of £27 earned by African adult males in Rhodesia. The question is whether this favorable differential justifies mining operations that, if continued under these terms, will eventually exhaust the finite mineral resources of Rhodesia and leave the native population with little more than holes in the ground. Or is it reasonable to expect that, with profits of such extortionist proportions, the companies should contribute to the overall development of their host country by paying royalty rates sufficient to finance schools, roads and health services, by processing the raw material within Rhodesia in order to generate some "spread effect" from their mining operations in the form of new industries and new jobs and by training native workers for more highly skilled work, thereby increasing the "spread effect"? Only such measures could have enabled Rhodesia, as well as other African countries, to break out of the trap of economic growth without economic development, and to put an end to their dependent, underdeveloped, Third World status.

Such measures were totally lacking, as is evident in the fact that after fifty years of European rule, Northern Rhodesia produced only two African graduates with arts degrees, and not a single one with a science degree, not a single African lawyer and not a single African doctor. A 1978 report of the International Labour Office provided the following statistical evidence of how effectively the African majority was denied the benefits of the exploitation of their country's resources, and was permanently relegated to the role of hewers of wood and drawers of water:

• The whites, comprising 5 percent of the total population, received 62 percent of the total wages.

• The whites earned an average of eleven times more than Africans, worked fewer hours and enjoyed more fringe benefits.

• Annual educational expenditures in 1976–77 per African pupil were $45.90, as against $531 per white pupil.

• African trade unions were curbed in the industrial sector, while domestic and plantation workers were subject to the punitive Masters and Servants Act of 1801, which had been abolished in Britain in 1872! [19]

Moreover, the above economic gap between Rhodesian blacks and whites is constantly widening. The November 1977 issue of *The Rhodesian Journal of Economics* disclosed that between 1964 and 1975 average annual salaries for whites in all sectors of the economy increased 103 percent, as against an 89 percent increase for black salaries. "The gap between non-African and African earnings continues to grow, and since 1970 it has been accelerating sharply."

One significant economic contribution of colonial rule was the construction of roads, railways and communication facilities. But virtually all of these ran from the interior to coastal ports in order to serve the needs of the export trade with Europe. Connections among internal regions were, and still are, virtually nonexistent. There is the often-told story of the telephone call from Accra in the British Gold Coast to Abidjan in the neighboring French Ivory Coast. It had to be routed first through London and then through Paris before connection could be

made with Abidjan. This pattern continued later in developing air
transportation systems. Passengers wishing to fly from Niger to neighboring Chad can do so only by flying several hundred miles to Paris and
back. Mail service follows a similar pattern, so that a postal strike in
France paralyzes mail service among former colonies. Such is the legacy
of colonialism in present-day Africa.

Chapter 15

CHINA ENTERS
THE THIRD WORLD

We submitted because we must; we were not a military Power.
But do you suppose our sense of justice was not outraged? Or
later, when every Power in Europe on some pretext or other has
seized and retained some part of our territory, do you suppose
because we cannot resist that we do not feel? . . . It is the nations of Christendom who have come to us to teach by sword
and fire that Right in this world is powerless unless it is supported by Might. O, do not doubt that we shall learn the lesson!
And woe to Europe when we have acquired it!

A HIGH CHINESE OFFICIAL (1906)

The history of nineteenth-century China resembles that of the Ottoman
Empire. Just as the European powers had annexed former Turkish tributary regions such as the trans-Danubian territories, southern Russia,
Egypt and North Africa, so the Great Powers annexed former Chinese
tributary regions such as Indochina, Burma, Korea and the Amur Valley.
In the remaining provinces of the Chinese Empire, Western control was
more direct and extensive than in the remaining provinces of the Ottoman Empire. Whereas European gunboats patrolled China's inland
waterways, the Turks were left in control of their straits. And while the
Europeans did enjoy extraterritorial privileges in the Ottoman Empire,
they never infringed upon Turkish suzerainty to the extent that they did
upon Chinese in the various concessions, and especially in the Shanghai
International Settlement. Nor did Western missionaries ever enjoy such a
free hand in the Ottoman Empire as they did in the Chinese. Generally

speaking, Europe dominated China in the same manner that she dominated Turkey, though the control was more direct and extensive in the case of China. On the other hand, China did escape the outright conquest and direct foreign rule that India suffered. The principal reason for this difference is that by the time China's military weakness had become fully apparent, more than one power was interested in the country, and so none had the freedom of action that Britain had enjoyed and exploited in the early nineteenth century in India.

The humiliations and disasters that China experienced in the latter half of the nineteenth century forced the traditionally self-centered Middle Kingdom to undertake a painful self-searching, reappraisal and reorganization. We will now trace the course of this process, noting how the Chinese slowly and grudgingly tried to follow the Western model, ending eventually as another dependent member of the Third World.

I. Continuity of Chinese Civilization

The Chinese civilization is the oldest in the world. Whereas the classical Roman civilization was ended by the Germanic and Hunnic invasions, and the classical Gupta civilization of India by the Muslim Turkish invasions, China, by contrast, maintained an uninterrupted succession of dynasties that preserved the classical Chinese civilization to the twentieth century.

One reason for this extraordinary and unique achievement is the unparalleled degree of isolation from the other great civilizations of mankind. China possesses nothing comparable to the Mediterranean, which linked together Mesopotamia, Egypt, Greece and Rome, or comparable to the Indian Ocean, which allowed India to interact with the Middle East, Africa and Southeast Asia. Instead, during most of her history, China was effectively cut off on all sides. To the southwest and west are the highest mountain ranges in the world. To the east is the Pacific Ocean, impassable until very recent times. To the north and northwest are deserts and steppe lands that offer considerable protection, which the Chinese reinforced by building their fourteen-hundred-mile Great Wall to keep out the threatening nomads. The significance of this isolation is that it allowed the Chinese to develop their civilization with fewer intrusions from the outside than the peoples of the Middle East or India faced. Consequently, their civilization was both more continuous and also more distinctive—it has more fundamental differences from the other great Eurasian civilizations than they have from one another. These differences are apparent in the type of architecture, the unique religious system and attitudes, the ideographic form of writing, the use of chopsticks, the nonuse of milk and milk products and so forth.

The immense size of China's population has also contributed to the continuity of civilization. From the beginning China has been able to support a large population because of favorable conditions in both the North and the South. In the North a self-sustaining agricultural system developed in the Wei River Basin as early as 5000 B.C. because of the loess soil blown in constantly by winds from the interior. This eliminated the need for long fallow to restore fertility, and therefore made possible much greater population density than could otherwise have been maintained. In the South the monsoon rains came during the warm months of the year, so that two crops per year are possible, in contrast to the Middle East and Europe. Furthermore, rice produces a much larger yield per acre than the wheat or barley grown in most parts of Eurasia.[1]

The census of A.D. 2 showed that Han China had a population of 59.5 million—more than that of the Roman Empire at its height. This population increased rapidly in the Middle Ages because of a veritable agricultural revolution effected by improved tools, organic manure, superior strains of seeds, improved irrigation networks and specialization in crops, which made possible more efficient exploitation of varying resource endowments. "By the thirteenth century," concludes Mark Elvin, "China thus had what was probably the most sophisticated agriculture in the world. . . ."[2] This superior technology, together with the later introduction of New World crops such as peanuts, maize and sweet potatoes, supported a population of over 200 million by 1580 and 410 million by 1850. Such unparalleled manpower resources made it possible for the Chinese to retain their identity regardless of the course of events. They have been conquered and ruled by the Mongols and Manchus, as well as battered and subverted by the West. But in the end the superiority of the Chinese in numbers enabled them until modern times to assimilate or expel the intruders. Never has wholesale transformation been imposed from the outside, as it was in Europe with the Germanic invasions or in the Middle East and in India with the Muslim ones.

Another important factor contributing to the durability of China's civilization is her single written language, going back several millennia to the earliest Shang Dynasty. This written language is of special significance because it is understood by Chinese from all regions, speaking dialects as different from each other as Italian is from French, or Danish from German. The reason it is understandable to all is that it consists of characters representing ideas or objects. These characters are pronounced in different ways in different parts of China, but the meaning of any character is the same no matter how it is pronounced. It is as if a Portuguese, a Swede and an Englishman took the figure 6 and pronounced it in their various tongues; the meaning to each of the three still would be the same. This common written language has been an important force in providing unity and historical continuity to a people speaking numerous mutually incomprehensible dialects.

Related to the common written language was the extraordinary system of public examinations by which for nearly two millennia China staffed her civil service on the basis of merit. At first the examinations were fairly comprehensive, emphasizing the Confucian classics but including also subjects like law, mathematics and political affairs. Gradually, however, they came to concentrate on literary style and Confucian orthodoxy. The net result was a system that theoretically opened offices to all men of talent, but that in practice favored the classes with sufficient wealth to afford the years of study and preparation. This did not mean that a hereditary aristocracy ruled China; rather, it was a hierarchy of the learned, a literocracy, providing China with an efficient and stable administration that won the respect and admiration of Europeans. On the other hand, it was a system that stifled originality and bred conformity. So long as China remained relatively isolated in East Asia, it provided stability and continuity. But with the intrusion of the dynamic West it served instead to prevent effective adaptation, until it was finally abolished in 1905.

Perhaps the most important factor contributing to the cohesiveness of Chinese civilization was the moral code and the literary and intellectual heritage known as Confucianism. Traditional accounts record that Confucius (551–479 B.C.)—his name is the Latinized form of K'ung Fu-tzu or "Master Kung"—was a minor official who failed in his chosen role as a practical politician but had a history-making, though posthumous, success in his incidental occupation as a teacher.

Like most Chinese thinkers, Confucius was concerned primarily with the establishment of a happy and well-organized society. His first principle was "every man in his place"—"Let the ruler be a ruler and the subject a subject; let the father be a father and the son a son." If each individual acted in accordance with his station, then the family would be orderly, and when the family was orderly, the state would be peaceful and all would be harmonious under Heaven. Just as the individual should be subordinate to the family, so the family should be subordinate to the Emperor. But the Emperor in turn should set an example of benevolent brotherhood, and this was to be done by following the ethics of Confucianism rather than a system of law.

One reason for the extraordinary influence of Confucius was that his high ethical principles gave the status quo a stronger foundation than mere hereditary right, and served as a constant stimulus to improve government and social relationships. He gave social justification for the authority and privileges of the triad of landowners, scholars and officials, who comprised the ruling class, or gentry, of China. Usually it was only the landowners who could afford to send their sons to school to study for the public examinations and thus to become officials. Once they were officials they saw to it that the interests of their landlord class were advanced, especially by irrigation works that increased the value of land. As Owen Lattimore observed, behind each imperial project was a powerful minister, and behind each minister a powerful body of landlords.

Finally, the stability of Chinese civilization was enhanced by the absence of an independent middle class that could challenge the hegemony of the ruling gentry. Medieval China had more merchants and wealthier merchants than any European country, but they lacked social status and political power. Chinese merchants at various times suffered restrictions concerning clothing, carrying of weapons, riding in carts and owning land. Their function of transporting commodities from place to place was regarded as nonproductive and parasitic, and they were placed at the bottom of the social scale. Also they lacked power, which was monopolized by the landlord-scholar-official triad backed by the imperial armed forces. Cities were completely dominated by this ruling elite rather than by merchants, as in the West. Furthermore, the ambition of merchants was not to have their sons continue their businesses but rather to take the examinations, enter the bureaucracy, buy land and thus enter the ranks of the gentry.

In addition, government officials kept Chinese merchants in tight rein by controlling their guilds, by regulating and taxing their trading activities and by establishing state monopolies in the production and distribution of numerous commodities that the Court and administration consumed, including arms, textiles, pottery, leather goods, apparel and wine. Government control extended even to the production and distribution of basic commodities such as salt and iron, which were necessities for the entire population. Under these circumstances there was no possibility for Chinese merchants to become lord mayors as in London, or senators as in the German imperial free cities or grand pensioners as in Holland, let alone decisive participants in revolutionary movements such as those in seventeenth-century England or eighteenth-century France.

℘ II. Rebellions Without Revolutions

T. T. Meadows, the well-informed British consul in mid-nineteenth-century China, observed, "Of all the nations that have attained a certain degree of civilization, the Chinese are the least revolutionary and the most rebellious." He was referring to the rise and fall of dynasties that for millennia brought not revolutions but merely changes of ruling families. The above analysis of the reasons for the "continuity of Chinese civilization" explains why China until the twentieth century was a land of "rebellions without revolutions." This phenomenon will become clearer by examining the pattern of the rebellions, from the first stirrings of discontented peasants, to full-fledged rebellions, to the co-opting of the rebel leaders, and finally to the emergence of new dynasties rather than new social orders.

Each new dynasty normally began by ruling the country efficiently and ushering in a period of comparative peace and prosperity. It stimulated intellectual and cultural life, and protected the country by sending military expeditions against the nomads and extending the imperial frontiers. But gradually the dynasty was weakened by the personal degeneration of individual rulers and by Court struggles between gentry cliques and palace eunuchs. This deterioration and factionalism undermined central authority and promoted corruption in the bureaucracy. The corruption, together with the increasing luxuriousness of Court life, meant heavier taxes on the peasantry, who ultimately produced the surplus that supported the entire imperial structure. Taxes tended to increase also because of the costly foreign wars and the emperors' practice of granting tax exemption to many of the gentry and to Buddhist temples and monasteries. And as the government became lax, the irrigation system and other public works essential for agriculture tended to be neglected.

Thus an increasingly impoverished peasantry had to bear the burden of a growing tax load. When to this was added the inevitable crop failures and famines, the explosion point came and revolts broke out against landlords and government tax collectors. In time these local uprisings broadened into general insurrections, which in turn were invitations to the nomads to invade, especially since the imperial armies by this stage were poorly maintained. The combination of internal rebellion and external invasion usually heralded the beginning of a new cycle —the approaching end of the old dynasty and the coming of a new one. The transition to a new dynasty was conveniently rationalized by the concept of the "mandate from Heaven," which each dynasty was believed to possess for a predetermined period, so that a change of dynasty was accepted as marking the end of one divinely ordained mandate and the beginning of another.

Viewing this process from the angle of vision of the peasants, it normally consisted of four stages if it continued through to the final stage of the actual overthrow of a dynasty, which of course very few rebellions achieved. During the first stage a number of peasants, for many possible reasons, would become bandits and rob travelers or rich landlords. During the second stage the band would extend the radius of its operations, thus encroaching on the territories of other bands. The resulting conflict established the dominance of the strongest band, which now was free to extend the range of its activities farther.

During the third stage the band faced the resistance of local land-owners, who called on government troops in the nearest town. If the troops prevailed the band would disintegrate and the cycle would begin anew. But if imperial disintegration were sufficiently advanced, the troops made common cause with the rebels, enabling them to capture the town. During the final stage the band would overrun additional towns and gain control of an extensive region. But this success necessitated cooperation with the scholar-gentry of the region in order to utilize their bureaucratic skills for the administration of the region. Gradually the rebel leaders accepted the mores and institutions of the established order, assuming titles such as general, duke or even emperor in the rare cases of total victory. Thus the rebellion was encapsulated and its leaders co-opted into becoming new pillars of the old society. Successive peasant rebellions were the means by which new ruling elites periodically emerged, thereby reintegrating and consolidating rather than replacing the established social order. This was repeated over many centuries until the intrusion of Western capitalism disrupted traditional society, thereby disrupting also the traditional process of rebellions without revolution.

❧ III. Wars and Unequal Treaties

For over three centuries after the initial appearance of the Portuguese in 1514, the Chinese kept the "long-nosed barbarians" of the West at arm's length. The Chinese restricted commercial relations to a few ports, and refused to establish diplomatic relations on a full and equal basis. They were ignorant of, and uninterested in, the outside world, as Emperor Ch'ien-lung made quite clear in his letter to George III in 1793 (quoted in Chapter 7). During the nineteenth century, however, the Chinese were forced out of their seclusion and complacency by Western powers that had become economically and militarily irresistible with the Industrial Revolution. The hitherto unassailable Celestial Kingdom suffered three humiliating defeats: the first by Britain in 1839–42, the second by Britain and France in 1856–58 and the third by Japan in 1895. The outcome was a chain reaction of intrusion and response that produced a new China and induced repercussions that are still convulsing East Asia and the entire globe.

The first defeat suffered by China at the hands of the Western powers was the so-called Opium War of 1839–42. The origins of this war are significant, as they provide a classic example of "free-trade imperialism" in action. The roots go back to the trade of the British East India Company with India and China. The company imports from China rose from £4,365,847 in 1761–70 to £19,098,326 in 1821–30. Over 90 percent of these import expenditures were for tea, the remainder being mostly for silk and porcelain. The problem for the company was how to pay for these imports. given Britain's reluctance to export bullion, and China's disinterest in Western products. The following table shows how the British solved this problem, and also exposes the seedbed of the Opium War.

British-Indian Imports to China (1761–1833)

Period	British Silver £	%	British Goods £	%	Indian Goods £	%
1761–70	2,493,190	52.3	1,113,951	23.4	1,555,040	24.3
1771–80	750,363	14.0	1,482,967	28.0	3,078,795	58.0
1781–90	3,168,626	24.3	2,865,392	22.0	7,121,936	54.7
1791–99	1,609,743	8.7	6,852,858	37.2	9,961,004	54.1
1801–10	negligible		11,000,000	33.3	22,000,000	66.7
1811–20	"		8,500,000	28.3	21,502,772	71.2
1821–30	"		7,604,126	16.4	38,754,787	83.6
1831–33	"		2,601,289	16.0	13,539,173	84.0

Source: Tan Chung, "The Britain-China-India Trade Triangle (1771–1840)," *Indian Economic and Social History Review* 11 (Dec. 1974): 413.

This table shows that in the eighteenth century the East India Company paid for the Chinese tea that was so popular at home with three commodities: British silver, British goods and Indian goods. After 1800 British silver exports stopped, and the export of British goods continued relatively unchanged, but the export of Indian goods increased about four times between the decade 1791–99 and the decade 1821–30. The reason for this dramatic rise was the Indian opium that European sailors had first introduced in Chinese ports in the seventeenth century. In defense of the burgeoning and highly profitable drug traffic, company spokesmen argued that if Indian opium were not exported to China, then British silver would have to take its place. This justification was not based on fact, as is evident in the table on page 317 showing that British-Indian imports to China, excluding opium and consisting largely of Indian cotton, covered the cost of Chinese imports to Britain.

Not only were company arguments in defense of the drug traffic deceptive, but so were the company clippers, which sailed with chests of opium that were officially designated as "saltpetre" cargoes. And while this was going on, the company Court of Directors declared in 1817, "Were it possible to prevent the use of the drug altogether except for the purpose

British-China Trade Balance (1792–95) (in £)

Year	British Investment in China Goods	British-Indian Imports to China, Excluding Opium	Trade Balance in Favor of Britain
1792	1,522,100	1,461,221	− 60,879
1793	1,279,623	2,013,570	+733,947
1794	1,566,196	1,464,427	−103,669
1795	1,166,280	1,404,761	+238,481
		OVERALL BALANCE	+807,780

Source: Ibid.: 420.

of medicine, we would gladly do it in compassion to mankind." [3] Under these circumstances the annual average number of exported chests, each of which contained between 133⅓ and 149 pounds of opium, rose from 2,043.5 in the period 1795–1800, to 24,355 during the decade 1831–40.

Not only did this drug traffic yield enormous direct profits for the East India Company, but it also increased indirect profits by stimulating Indian purchasing power for British cotton goods. Hence the panic of Manchester industrialists when the Chinese government began to take serious action against opium imports, and the enthusiastic support by those industrialists for the Opium War that followed.

Peking had issued decrees in 1729 and 1799 prohibiting opium imports, but the illegal smuggling (which explains the "saltpetre" camouflage noted above) increased rapidly during the nineteenth century. The effects on Chinese society were devastating: growing addiction and attendant health problems, destitution of the affected families, drain on the imperial finances and corruption of officials who connived with the smugglers.

In 1839 the Chinese Emperor sent to Canton a man of proven integrity and firmness, Lin Tse-hsu, with orders to enforce the prohibition on opium imports. Lin seized twenty thousand chests of opium and destroyed them at a public ceremony. In this era of free-trade imperialism, the British regarded this action as an intolerable infringement on their right to trade freely anywhere in the world. Abstract principles aside, William Jardine, the foremost British opium trader, and founder of the great commercial firm that bears his name, lamented in China at this time, "Not an opium pipe to be seen, not a retail vendor . . . not a single enquiry after the drug." [4] Jardine was able to expound his concern during a long session with the British Foreign Secretary, Lord

Palmerston. It is not surprising that British frigates soon were battling Chinese junks over what London represented to be an issue of freedom of trade.

Full-scale war began in November 1839. The course of hostilities made clear the hopeless inferiority of the Chinese forces. Because of the continued advance of European military technology, the odds were much more uneven than they had been between the conquistadors and the Aztecs. This was illustrated by the Chinese plan to tie firecrackers to the backs of a number of monkeys, which then were to be flung on board the British warships. The theory was that the flames would spread in all directions, and with luck might reach the powder magazines and blow up the ships. Nineteen monkeys actually were delivered to headquarters, but as a Chinese officer admitted, "The fact is that no one ever dared go near enough to the foreign ships to fling them on board, so that the plan was never put into effect." [5] Thus the British were able with a squadron of ships and a few thousand men to seize port after port at will. In 1842 the Peking government capitulated and accepted the Treaty of Nanking, the first of a series of unequal treaties that were to nibble away much of China's sovereignty.

By the Treaty of Nanking China ceded the island of Hong Kong and opened five ports to foreign trade—Canton, Foochow, Ningpo, Amoy and Shanghai. At these ports British consuls could be stationed and British merchants could lease land for residential and business uses. China also agreed to a uniform tariff fixed at 5 percent ad valorem, to be changed only by mutual agreement. This provision deprived China of tariff autonomy and hence of control over her national revenue. Furthermore, a supplementary treaty concluded the following year granted Britain extraterritoriality in criminal cases, and also included a most-favored-nation clause assuring Britain any additional privileges that China might grant other powers in the future.

The Treaty of Nanking did not end the friction between the Chinese and the Europeans. The latter were disappointed because the opening of the treaty did not lead to so great an expansion of trade as they had anticipated. The remedy, they believed, was to secure more concessions. The Chinese, on the other hand, felt that the treaties had granted too many privileges and constantly evaded fulfillment of their treaty obligations. Furthermore, the European merchants and adventurers who now flocked to the treaty ports provoked with their boisterous behavior antiforeign outbursts among the Chinese populace.

With such sentiments prevailing on both sides it is not surprising that hostilities began again in 1856, with France now joining Britain against China. The Western forces proved as irresistible as in the first war, and in June 1858 the Chinese were compelled to sign the Tientsin treaties.

Delays in implementing their provisions led to a renewal of hostilities. The Anglo-French forces now captured the capital and forced China to sign the Peking conventions in 1860. The Tientsin and Peking agreements opened several more ports on the coast and in the interior, redefined and extended extraterritoriality and permitted the establishment of foreign legations in Peking and of Christian missions throughout the country.

The third defeat suffered by China was the most humiliating, for it was at the hands of the small neighboring empire of Japan. We shall see later in Chapter 17 that the Japanese, in contrast to the Chinese, had been able to adapt Western technology to their needs and to build an efficient military establishment. Having accomplished what no other Oriental state had been able to achieve thus far, Japan now pressed certain shadowy claims in Korea. Traditionally, the Koreans had recognized the suzerainty of China, but they also had periodically submitted tribute to Japan. Thus when China sent a small force to Korea in 1894 in response to an appeal for aid in suppressing a revolt, the Japanese also landed a detachment of marines. The two forces clashed, and war was formally declared by China and Japan in August 1894. The Chinese armies again were easily defeated by the modernized Japanese forces. In April 1895, Peking was forced to accept the Treaty of Shimonoseki, which required China to pay an indemnity, recognize the independence of Korea, cede to Japan the island of Formosa, the Pescadores Islands and the Liaotung Peninsula, and open four more ports to foreign commerce. Some of the European powers were not at all pleased with the appearance of a new rival for concessions in China. Accordingly, Russia, France and Germany joined in a demand that the strategic Liaotung Peninsula be returned to China, a demand to which Japan yielded reluctantly.

The great Chinese Empire had been shown up to be completely helpless before a despised neighbor equipped with modern instruments of war. Furthermore, the European powers during the preceding years had been taking advantage of China's weakness and annexing outlying territories that traditionally had recognized Peking's suzerainty. Russia took the Amur Valley, the Maritime Provinces, and for a while occupied the Ili region in central Asia. France seized Indochina, Britain took Burma, and Japan, having established her predominance in Korea by defeating China, proceeded to annex Korea outright in 1910. In addition to these territorial acquisitions, the Western states divided China proper into spheres of influence in which were recognized the political and economic primacy of the respective powers concerned. Thus Yunnan and the area bordering on Indochina became a French sphere, Canton and the Yangtze Valley and the large area in between was a British sphere, Manchuria was Russian, Shantung was German and Fukien was Japanese.

❧ IV. Again Rebellions Without Revolutions

These humiliations and disasters undermined the position of the Ch'ing, or Manchu, Dynasty. Many Chinese held it responsible for the unprecedented national crisis, and it became extremely unpopular, particularly since it was of foreign origin. In the past, such a time of troubles would have been interpreted as indicating that the "mandate from Heaven" had expired, and popular uprisings would have thrown up a new dynasty to replace the Manchu. But this traditional course was blocked by the intervention of the Great Powers.

Several rebellions did break out in the mid-nineteenth century, including the Nien Rebellion (1851–68) in the villages and smaller towns of North China, the Muslim revolts (1855–73) in the Northwest and Southwest, and the Miao minority uprising (1855–72) in the South. All of these lacked ideological consciousness and political organization, being reactions to specific local grievances with no anticipation of a new social order. The great Taiping Rebellion (1850–64) was different in scope and character. It gained control of both banks of the Yangtze, penetrated north almost to Peking, west to Szechuan and south to Kwangtung. In contrast to other peasant rebellions, it was influenced by the West, especially by Christian doctrines, and therefore had numerous social reform objectives. But in China, as elsewhere in the Third World, social reform movements encountered the opposition of powerful Western vested interests that had much to lose if the old order were substantively restructured. Thus the Taiping Rebellion, which at one point seemed likely to prevail, eventually was suppressed, and in part because of strong Western support of the dynasty.

The leader of the Taipings was Hung Hsiu-ch'uan (1814–64), a member of the Hakka linguistic minority in South China, and a frustrated scholar who failed repeatedly in the examinations, which he took in Canton. He was also a mystic who became convinced that he was called upon to become a new messiah—a concept he acquired from the Christianity he learned through contact with Protestant missionaries in Canton. Hung had visions about being the second son of God, a brother of Jesus, and commissioned by God to exterminate the devils of this world. This led to social reform perceptions that were based on early Chinese classics such as the Rituals of Chou (second century B.C.), which represented the utopianism of early Chinese thought. Hung envisaged, and sought to realize, an egalitarian society in which the scholar gentry were abolished and each family received land to work but not to own. Any surplus above the needs of each family was to go to the public granary.

The Taipings also attempted other basic social changes that proved to be prophetic of twentieth-century revolutionary movements and that have made them the favorites of China's present-day Communists. These changes included repudiation of the Manchu Dynasty, banning of opium, tobacco and alcohol, and opposition to ancestor tablets and to Buddhist, Taoist and Confucianist images. Most striking was their stress on equality for women, as reflected in their measures against concubinage, footbinding, polygamy, prostitution and arranged marriages, and their insistence that women have equal access to leadership positions.

Many Westerners at first were pro-Taiping, assuming that Hung's Christian orientation would lead him to establish closer diplomatic and commercial ties with Christian states. A North China *Herald* editorial of January 7, 1854, stated, "We regard him [Hung] as hastening forward, with rapid strides, the real opening of China, and her union with the Western world; and we trust that under his more enlightened sway our merchants will speedily exchange present difficulties and impediments for all the advantages of a free, reciprocal, and unblemished traffic." [6] Westerners also were impressed at the outset by reports of Taiping order and discipline, which they welcomed as conducive to improvement of trade relations. Commodore Perry, who was in Shanghai for two weeks in May 1853, reported that the Taipings were disciplined like the Mormons, and praised the Taipings as "an organized revolutionary army gallantly fighting for a more liberal and enlightened religion and political position." [7]

Gradually this favorable attitude changed, and the basic reason was that European merchants and diplomats decided that their interests would be better served by preserving the Manchu Dynasty and crushing the rebels. Since the expected rapid Taiping victory did not materialize, the protracted civil war was severely reducing the volume of trade. In 1853, for example, the United States exported to China cotton goods worth $2,831,354, but in 1854 and 1855 the exports averaged only $400,000. Also the Peking conventions (1860), signed in the midst of the Taiping Rebellion, opened numerous ports along the coast and in the interior to trade. But since the Taipings controlled much of the interior, they prevented the Europeans from taking full advantage of these new concessions. Finally, the Taiping ban on opium alienated the British, who argued in vain that if there was a demand for the drug, they should be free to satisfy it.

Under these circumstances the North China *Herald* reversed its earlier position. It now denounced the Taipings as "marauding banditti," and stated that "few will care as to what means it may be effected by in order to bring to a speedy conclusion these long-continued disturbances, which are now injuriously affecting the trade." [8] Likewise the British plenipotentiary, Sir John Bowring, who earlier had informed Lord Palmerston, "A manufacturing country Egypt never can become" (see Chapter 11, section III), now wrote to London that it was preferable to support "the existing imperial government, bad, corrupt, and ignorant though it may be." [9] The American commissioner, William B. Reed, similarly reported to Washington, "The Rebellion, to which so great effects were once attributed, is regarded now as a mischievous convulsion that ought to be put an end to. The Imperial Power is to be sustained. . . ." [10]

The Western governments followed this advice by making available maritime customs revenues to the imperial government, and providing it with arms, steamships and technicians. Also, foreign mercenaries entered the imperial service with men and arms furnished by foreign embassies. These mercenaries included an American adventurer, Frederick Townsend Ward, and an officer of the British Royal Engineers, Captain Charles George Gordon, who headed the Ever Victorious Army and came to be known as "Chinese Gordon." In addition, a Franco-Chinese force helped to recapture the key city of Hangchow.

How much of this foreign intervention was responsible for the final defeat of the Taipings is a matter of dispute. It cannot be proven that without Western aid the dynasty would have fallen, but it does seem clear that Western aid did contribute substantially to the dynasty's survival, as did also serious divisions among the Taipings toward the end, and the not surprising refusal of the scholar gentry to collaborate with such threatful rebels.

Whatever the reasons for the eventual defeat of the Taipings, there is no question as to their profound impact on nineteenth-century China. The decade and a half of fighting wreaked immense devastation on the country. Western observers estimated a population loss of 20 to 30 million, but the researches of historian Ho Ping-ti indicate a greater loss in the four lower Yangtze provinces alone. The rebellion also weakened permanently the power of the dynasty, forcing it to accept the development of regional armies led by powerful officials and gentry in the provinces. These new leaders financed their activities by collecting the traditional land taxes and also imposing new levies on commerce. Instead of transmitting these revenues to the imperial treasury, they used them to buy arms from the West and to support their personal armies. Hence a basic shift occurred of military and political power from the imperial government to regional leaders, who did not hesitate to express their views on national issues and to negotiate directly with foreign governments.

The imperial dynasty accordingly was weakened in its relations with foreign governments as well as with its own subjects. The Great Powers henceforth intervened even more extensively in Chinese affairs than they had in the past. They forced the imperial government to dismiss officials that they considered hostile to their interests. They gained control of the collection and administration of maritime customs duties, and excluded Chinese from the higher positions of the customs service with its several thousand employees. The International Settlement of Shanghai extended its boundaries by various illegal means, and the imperial government had no jurisdiction over the Chinese citizens as well as the foreigners residing within its limits. A basic reason for the passivity of the imperial authorities in the face of such foreign aggression was their fear, after the Taiping experience, of another peasant uprising. The Manchu officials preferred to submit to foreigners than to mobilize their own subjects.

Finally, the Taipings left behind them a revolutionary tradition that persisted to modern times. Their slogans such as "land to the tiller" and "down with the Manchu devils," and their demands for equality between men and women and for independence from foreign control influenced profoundly nationalist leaders such as Sun Yat-sen, and even the Communists who followed. This potent Taiping revolutionary tradition perhaps helps to explain the markedly biased and negative treatment of the Taipings by most Western historians to the present day. An American historian, Stephen Uhalley, Jr., has recently noted this "faulty historiographical tradition":

> The impact of the Taiping upheaval was so great and so significant for modern history that serious questions can be raised as to why it has not in fact received more serious, balanced attention over the years. . . . historians have tended to rely heavily on . . . predominantly falsified and otherwise often misleading Taiping documents, Ch'ing intelligence reports, and a voluminous corpus of anti-Taiping propaganda produced by foreigners who supported the Ch'ing cause. . . . An equivalent hypothetical situation would be for most histories of the Indochina War of the 1950's–70's to be written for the next century primarily on the basis of the Saigon government and Pentagon-State Department hand-outs, along with other documents selected by partisans of the policies they represented.

> Yet, just as a vast literature exists which provides a different light on the Indochina War—including the Pentagon Papers and numerous informed, independent reports—so too was there considerable contemporary testimony in the 1850–60's that shed better light on the Taipings. The question is, why was proper use of this evidence not made? . . .

Remember, we're talking about Chinese revolutionaries who tried to be Christian, who tried to be friendly with Westerners, and who had eloquent Western champions, but who for all these efforts were crushed largely with Western connivance—because they threatened the lucrative opium trade, and because the Ch'ing government had already proven itself (in the Peking Convention of 1860) to be promisingly compliant. [11]

The parallel that Uhalley draws between the Taiping Rebellion and the recent Indochina War is borne out by the following account by "Chinese Gordon," who obviously experienced in China the same frustrations that American soldiers did in Indochina, and for the same reasons:

> I am perfectly aware from nearly four years service in this country that both sides are equally rotten. But you must confess that on the Taiping side there is at leas[t] innovation, and a disregard for many of the frivolous and idolatrous customs of the Manchus. While my eyes are fully open to the defects of the Taiping character, from a close observation of three months, I find many promising traits never yet displayed by the Imperialists. The Rebel Mandarins are without exception brave and gallant men and could you see Chung Wang, who is now here, you would immediately say that such a man deserved to succeed. Between him and the Footai, or Prince Kung, or any other Manchoo officer there is no comparison.

> It is simply impossible to seize the cunning, cruel cowards [the Taipings,] in the labyrinthine lanes of the Delta. All around they have spies on our movements, and know, as well as we do what these are, so they are comparatively safe in continuing their incendiary tactics within a few hundred yards of our column; then off they escape through ditches and across fields, where it is impossible to get at them. This the rascals are perfectly aware of, especially if pursued by foreign soldiers, encumbered with their heavy equipment. Hunting grasshoppers in a hay-field with foxhounds would be a more sensible occupation than sending soldiers about a country intersected by a network of creeks, in the expectancy of catching swift-footed and slippery-skinned Taipings.[12]

✌ V. Integration into the Capitalist World Order

The unequal treaties provided the legal basis for Western economic penetration of China, which proceeded apace after the suppression of the Taipings. The treaties provided for the opening of about ninety "treaty ports" in which Western businessmen operated, through extraterritoriality, under Western laws of contract and personal liability, administered by Western consular courts. In these ports Westerners could hold property on ninety-nine-year leases, which enabled them to establish factories, banks and trading firms. Also, there were spheres of influence where foreigners built railways, acquired mining concessions and stationed their own police forces, so that they effectively controlled entire regions such as Manchuria (Russian), Shantung (German) and Fukien (Japanese).

The maritime customs and post office were technically Chinese institutions, but were administered by foreigners, who occupied all the top posts. The entire proceeds from customs went directly to service the foreign debts. The latter consisted mostly of the indemnities imposed on China after the three wars and the Boxer uprising (1900), when foreign legations in Peking were besieged by outraged Chinese until rescued by an international expeditionary force. To pay the £30 million indemnity following the defeat by Japan, the Chinese were forced to make loans that cost them £100 million to repay. Likewise the $333 million Boxer indemnity required annual installment payments that absorbed almost all of the imperial government's income.

Finally, Western companies exploited Chinese labor not only in textile mills, mines and dockwork, but also in the nefarious "pig trade," which resembled the earlier African slave trade (see Chapter 5, Section II). Despite the objections of the imperial government, Chinese laborers from 1847 onward were shipped illegally to overseas mines, plantations and construction projects such as railways. Because of the abolition of slavery, this traffic in coolie labor, from India and Japan as well as China, grew until it surpassed even the earlier slave trade in numbers involved. Chinese contractors received a capitation fee for every person brought to the shipping depots.

Theoretically this was voluntary indentured labor (though the voluntarism was a myth when illiterate coolies accepted meaningless written contracts), but abduction and kidnapping were not uncommon. From the depots the coolies were transported overseas on ships known as "floating hells," with mortality rates sometimes reminiscent of those of the earlier slave ships. When Chinese authorities tried to regulate this traffic, the contractors moved their operations to Macao, whence in a single year 5,207 laborers were shipped to Cuba, and 8,417 to Peru. San Francisco alone received 108,471 laborers before 1863, most of whom were assigned to mine operators or railway builders. Others were shipped to the West Indies, Hawaii, Sumatra and Malaya. In all these places the "pig trade," as it came to be called, provided the basis for today's flourishing overseas Chinese colonies.

These various Western intrusions into China's economy inevitably had extensive repercussions. The most obvious was the rapid increase in the value of trade between China and the West. Between 1868 and 1913 Chinese imports increased nine-fold, and exports nearly seven-fold. China's crafts, however, were not disrupted as much as might have been expected, given the 5 percent limit set by the unequal treaties on tariff imports. This restriction did hamper the imperial government in obtaining revenue and protecting infant industries. But China's highly developed producing and marketing system proved remarkably resistant, so that Western machine-made products did not take over completely, as happened in Argentina, Egypt, Indonesia, India and most other parts of the Third World. For example, native weavers were able to hold their own by using foreign and domestic factory yarn. The relative imperviousness of China's economy to Western capitalism was demonstrated by the fact that China's exports in 1900 amounted to only $.30 per capita, as against $1.20 in India, and $3.70 in the rest of the Third World.[13] As late as 1933, the share of handicrafts in total manufacturing in terms of net product was still 72 percent on the average, and the share of textiles was about 63 percent.[14]

Equally revealing was the trivial nature of the major Chinese exports: pig bristles, eggs, sausage casings, tung oil, antimony, silk, tea, wool, hides, straw braid and fireworks. Such exports, Rhoads Murphey concludes, "could not by any assessment be regarded as more than a tiny proportion of traditional production." Thus the treaty ports did not restructure the national economy of China as basically and pervasively as they did the economics of India and Southeast Asia. "The perspective of contemporary China has revealed the treaty ports as tiny and isolated islands in an alien Chinese sea which all along resisted, and then rejected them."[15]

Nevertheless, most of the symptoms of underdevelopment and dependence were manifest in nineteenth-century China's economy. Native cotton spinning was ruined, as well as most iron and steel production. Standard Oil's kerosene replaced vegetable oil in the "lamps of China." French companies had obtained mining concessions in Yunnan, Kwangsi and Kwantung, Russian and Japanese companies in Manchuria, German companies in Shantung and British in Honan and Shansi. By 1920 foreigners controlled 99 percent of the iron ore and pig iron produced by modern methods, 76 percent of the coal, 93 percent of the railways, 83 percent of steam tonnage cleared through maritime customs and 73 percent of steam tonnage on the Yangtze. What modern industries existed were of the consumer variety (textiles, food processing, cigarettes), and almost all these industries, as well as the railways, were located near the coast. The focus was on satisfying the economic needs of the West rather than the overall economic development of China. For example, the Russian-built Chinese Eastern Railway running through Manchuria to Port Arthur was constructed with the wide Russian gauge in order to link with the trans-Siberian and to obstruct linkage with China's railways. China's average annual outpayment in 1902–13 was U.S. $31.8 million, and in 1914–30 was U.S. $72.3 million. For the period 1902–30, the inflow-outflow ratio was .57. Likewise foreign insurance companies refused to insure Chinese ships, leaving them little chance of competing with foreign ships. A final indication of the depressing effect of foreign capitalism on China's economy is the fact that the most prosperous period for China's industry (as for Latin America's) was during World War I and immediately thereafter, when Western industry was preoccupied with war production and with reconstruction.

Nineteenth-century China was subject to Western cultural as well as economic imperialism. This was evident in the activities of the Christian missionaries, who were free to go anywhere in the country, and who operated in about half of China's *hsien* or counties. They worked hard to convert the local populations, and in the process they had some cultural impact. As in other parts of the Third World they had a positive influence with their schools and hospitals. Yet they were generally disliked because they were associated with the military defeats inflicted by the West and with the unequal tactics that stipulated admission of the missionaries. Most Chinese, therefore, were contemptuous of the "rice Christians," as they derisively called the comparatively few converts to Christianity. On one occasion a city mob, driving away a missionary, cried out after him. "You burned our palace, you killed our Emperor, you sell poison to our people, and now you come professing to teach us virtue." [16]

Not only were the missionaries unwelcome and aggravating to most Chinese, but so was the openly contemptuous attitude of many Westerners. In the seventeenth and eighteenth centuries Europeans held the Chinese civilization in high esteem because of its Confucian morals, its examination system for government service, its respect for learning rather than for military prowess and its exquisite handicrafts. By the nineteenth century the esteem had turned to disdain because of the weakness of the Chinese on the battlefield, together with their reluctance to accept Western manufactured goods and Western Christianity. The following poem published in the British humor magazine *Punch* during the Taiping Rebellion reflected this European contempt, which must have been particularly painful for as proud a people as the Chinese with their own traditions of past glory:

With their little pig-eyes and their large pig-tails,
And their diet of rats, dogs, slugs, and snails,

All seems to be game in the frying-pan
Of that nasty feeder, JOHN CHINAMAN.
Sing lie-tea, my sly JOHN CHINAMAN,
No fightee, my coward JOHN CHINAMAN:
JOHN BULL *has a chance—let him, if he can,*
Somewhat open the eyes of JOHN CHINAMAN.[17]

American journalist Edgar Snow found the same superiority feelings among Europeans when he visited Shanghai after World War I: "Western businessmen who lived in Shanghai when I arrived in 1928, acted as if the Settlement were real and would last forever. In their euphoria they felt that they were the continent and the four hundred million Chinese beyond were a kind of suburb put there by God for trading purposes." [18]

VI. Imperial Disintegration

The dependent and underdeveloped economy of China had the distinctive quality of economic growth without development—growth in the volume of raw materials exported and of manufactured goods imported, but no integrated national economic development. Instead of economic unity there was economic disunity, which added to the fragility of the empire. What little industrialization carried on by the Chinese themselves was the work of provincial gentry and officials who usurped much of the imperial power during the Taiping Rebellion and who in the following decades undertook industrial and commercial projects that enhanced their own wealth and power. Because of their social origins they lacked technical experience in the management of modern industry, and they viewed their enterprises as secondary to traditional landholding. Despite their involvement with Western capitalism they remained gentry first and entrepreneurs second.

The other Chinese elements involved in economic development were the compradors, who also were beyond imperial control and challenged the imperial order. The compradors (derived from the Portuguese *compra*—to buy) were Chinese managers of foreign firms in China, serving as middlemen between the firms and the local communities. They supervised the Chinese staff, supplied market intelligence, assumed responsibility for native bank orders and served as interpreters with their "pidgin" English, a mixture of Chinese, Malay, English and Portuguese. During a poisoning incident, for example, an English merchant asked, "Comprador, what's all this row?" The comprador replied, "My no savey. Talkee that blead got spilum. My savey this house blead all light." ["I don't know. They say the bread is spoiled. I only know the bread we have in this house is all right."] [10]

The compradors were quite different from the provincial gentry, who conducted business enterprises within a Confucian context that subordinated them to the surrounding agriculture. The compradors, by contrast, operated in treaty ports, were not bound by Confucian values, and were safe from the depradations of imperial officials. They were the first Chinese merchants in history who were able to amass great wealth and influence without being subjected to the "squeeze" or extortion of state officials. Whereas in the Confucian hierarchy prevailing in China they were, as merchants, at the bottom of the social ladder, in the treaty ports they enjoyed high status as indispensable and wealthy middlemen. In contrast to the gentry businessmen, the compradors did not send their sons to take the Confucian-based examinations and enter the civil service. Rather they sent them to missionary schools within China and to universities abroad, with the aim of training them to expand the family business rather than joining the bureaucracy.

The compradors commonly were denounced by Chinese nationalists as virtual traitors who served as the tools of foreigners and who became wealthy at the expense of their own countrymen. This was partly true because the compradors did facilitate the foreign economic intrusion into China. On the other hand, the compradors were the most effective business rivals of the foreigners, as they charged very heavy commissions and opened their own rival business concerns. Also, some compradors took a leading role in reform, and even revolutionary, movements directed against the imperial establishment. From their personal experiences some soon realized that both the dynasty and the foreign firms were inimical to Chinese national interests, and therefore supported in various ways and to varying degrees certain organizations dedicated to substantive change of the status quo. Accordingly the compradors as a class were divided between staunch nationalist champions and equally committed collaborators with the foreigners.

Imperial disintegration was hastened not only by the roles of the provincial gentry and the compradors, but also by the increasing misery of the peasant masses during the nineteenth century. One reason was the population increase, from roughly 430 million in 1850 to 600 million in 1950. Also, there was the imperial disintegration, leading to ineffective flood control and water management, inability to construct new works, and excessive levies by the provincial warlords. The increasing Western intrusion promoted the commercialization of agriculture, involving the production of commodities of high market value such as tea, opium, silk and tobacco. The end result of these various trends was growing disparity in land ownership and therefore mounting land hunger. It is estimated that by 1932 about 40 to 50 percent of all peasant families did not own enough land to meet their family needs. It should be added, however, that conditions varied greatly from region to region, and that most peasants did own some land, even though it might be inadequate to meet their needs.

The industrial workers also were a beleaguered class in late nineteenth-century China, being subject to all the abuses and exploitation characteristic of the early stages of industrialization. By 1919 they numbered 1.5 million, of which three fourths worked in transport or light industry, especially textiles. Three fifths of this labor force worked in Chinese plants, and the remainder in Western-owned plants. Almost all were to be found in a few large cities in the eastern provinces; three hundred thousand in Shanghai and fifty thousand in Hong Kong. Because of their concentration in cities and their direct experience with the pressures generated by the new Western-induced industrial order, the workers were among the most volatile elements in Chinese society. Usually they were the most ready to support the students who were the pioneers of resistance and revolution.

With the ending of the Confucian-based examination system in 1905, traditional scholarship lost prestige and students turned increasingly to Western knowledge and Western educational institutions. Whereas only nine Chinese students were studying in Japan in 1896, ten years later there were fifteen thousand. A total of over one hundred thousand studied abroad in various countries between 1872 and 1949. Although these students, of necessity, were mostly from well-to-do families, they were the most turbulent element in Chinese society. Influenced by new ideas and values, and fully aware of the degree of Western exploitation and humiliation of their country, they took the lead in organizing protests and resistance. In 1905 they led an anti-American boycott in Canton because of the ill treatment of Chinese immigrants in the United States, and in 1908 the students organized an even more extensive boycott against Japanese goods. In 1915, Ch'en Tu-hsiu, professor at Peking University and later founder of the Chinese Communist Party, gave voice to student sentiments in his *Call to Youth*:

> *Be independent, not servile!*
> *Be progressive, not conservative!*
> *Be aggressive, not retiring!*
> *Be cosmopolitan, not isolationist!*
> *Be utilitarian, not formalistic!*
> *Be scientific, not imaginative!* [20]

These slogans represented a very different outlook from that of the "self-strengthening" movement, which had been the initial response to the Western challenge. The phrase "self-strengthening" was itself from the Confucian classics, and was used in the 1860s to mean the preservation of Chinese civilization by grafting on protective Western technology. In the words of one of the reformers of this period, "China should acquire the West's superiority in arms and machinery, but retain China's superiority in Confucian virtue." [21] This "self-strengthening" movement was doomed to failure because the basic assumption on which it rested was fallacious. Westernization could not be a halfway process; it was all or nothing. Westernization in tools led inevitably to Westernization in ideas and institutions. So Western science could not be used to preserve a Confucian civilization; rather it was bound to undermine that civilization.

A shift in the perception of China's needs was evident in occasional demands for popular participation in government. Hitherto the Western concepts of democracy and nationalism had been conspicuously absent. Instead, the emphasis had been on the family, and, so far as a broader allegiance was concerned, it took the form of "culturalism" rather than nationalism. By culturalism is meant identification with the native cultural tradition, which was viewed simply as the alternative to foreign barbarism. China's ruling scholar bureaucracy was steeped in this tradition, and many of its members still avowed that it was "better to see the nation die than its way of life change." [22] But against the standpatism of this traditional culturalism the reform leaders now affirmed revolutionary Western concepts. "What does nationalism mean?" asked one of these reformers. "It is that in all places people of the same race, the same language, the same religion, and the same customs, regard each other as brothers and work for independence and self-government, and organize a more perfect government to work for the public welfare and to oppose the infringement of other races. . . . If we wish to promote nationalism in China, there is no other means of doing it except through the renovation of the people." [23]

The new reform spokesmen in China seemed to have a chance in the summer of 1898, when they persuaded the young Emperor, Kuang-hsü, to break away from the influence of the Empress dowager, Tz'u-hsi, and to issue a series of reform decrees known collectively as the Hundred Days Reform. But the Empress dowager, with the support of the military, deposed the Emperor and rescinded the reform decrees. The reaction that followed led to the Boxer uprising and to the siege of foreign legations in Peking. Within a few months international armies relieved the legations and forced China to grant further commercial concessions and to pay more indemnities.

The fiascos of the Hundred Days Reform and of the Boxer Rebellion dramatically demonstrated the futility of trying to change China from above. The alternative was revolution from below, and by this date there were elements in Chinese society prepared for revolutionary remedies. At the same time, support for the dynasty had largely evaporated, as was proven in 1911, when it collapsed from internal weakness rather than being overthrown by revolutionary power. And since the dynasty had been propped up by the West, its downfall represented the beginning of the end of Western domination over China.

Chapter 16

RUSSIA ENTERS
THE THIRD WORLD

German and French money is rolling to Petersburgh to feed a
regime that would long ago have breathed its last without this
life-giving juice. Russian czarism is today no longer the product
of Russian conditions; its root lies in the capitalist conditions
of Western Europe.

ROSA LUXEMBURG, *The Crisis of Social Democracy* (1916)

Russia, like China, had not been enveloped into the world market
economy prior to the nineteenth century (see Chapter 3, Section III).
Thanks to her continental proportions, Russia enjoyed a diversity of
resources and markets that enabled her to develop independently and
to avoid the subordination to the West's economy that befell East European states such as Hungary and Poland-Lithuania. Then under the
whiplash of Peter the Great, Russia experienced during the eighteenth
century her first great economic leap forward—a leap that was a prototype
of the later Soviet Five Year Plans and that made Russia a substantial
industrial power. But the foundation was fragile, being weakened by
dependence on forced labor and by lack of adequate technology and
transportation facilities. Consequently Russia was left behind when the
Industrial Revolution got under way in England in the late eighteenth
century.

The resulting economic backwardness was painfully manifest during
the Crimean War, when Western steamships outmaneuvered Russian
sailships, and Western artillery and rifles outshot Russian cannon and
muskets. The Crimean debacle, however, provided the shock needed to

induce institutional reforms that contributed to successive later phases of Russia's economic growth. And yet, only six decades later, the guns of World War I were to sound the death knell of Russian capitalism, just as those of the Crimean War had heralded its birth. This chapter analyzes the reasons why Russia assumed the historic role of leading the first great breakaway from the West-dominated world order—a breakaway that was to be followed by others during the following decades.

ᘓ *I. Slavophils vs. Westerners*

Russia failed to take a leading role in the Industrial Revolution at its beginning in part because of geographic handicaps. Peter the Great had found it necessary to go one thousand miles from Moscow to the Urals to find adequate iron ore resources. These were smelted with charcoal during the eighteenth century, but when the forests began giving out, the Russians discovered that they could not turn to coal and coke, as the English had long been doing. The nearest coal deposits were at the distant Donets coal basin in the Ukraine, with which there were no river or canal connections. Thus whereas the British, by smelting their iron ore with coke, increased their iron production thirty times during the first half of the nineteenth century, the Russians were unable even to double their output in the same period.

Geography was not alone in cramping Russia's economic development. There was also the incubus of serfdom, which bound the peasants to the land, thereby blocking the supply of labor for industry, and also limiting the domestic market, since the purchasing power of the serfs was so limited. The flowering of industrial capitalism in the West was based on the separation of the agricultural worker—whether slave, serf or yeoman peasant—from the land that was simultaneously the means of his livelihood and the source of his economic backwardness. The dispossession of the peasants usually had followed in the wake of technological improvements in agriculture that made it possible to feed large groups of people no longer engaged in farming. In fact, such technological innovation in the West had created a class of unemployed peasants who were forced to earn their living by selling their labor power to entrepreneurs endowed with capital and ready to undertake commodity production in search for profits.

This pattern of capitalist economic development was impossible so long as the majority of the Tsar's subjects were bound to the soil as serfs. Some Russian manufacturers did produce for the state, especially military materials, while others turned out luxury products for members of the ruling class of landowners and bureaucrats. But this did not make up for the lack of a mass home market, which had provided the main stimulus for Western industrial growth.

The continued existence of serfdom together with the lack of any representative institutions in the autocratic Tsarist regime divided Russian thinkers into two groups, the Westerners and the Slavophils. The Westerners deplored the differences between feudal, agrarian and autocratic Russia, and the industrialized societies of the West, with their representative political institutions. They interpreted these differences as products of Russia's slower rate of development. Accordingly, their hero was Peter the Great, and they urged that other rulers match Peter's heroic efforts to goad Russia to catch up with the West.

The Slavophils, on the other hand, rejected the Westerners' basic assumption of the unity of human civilization. They maintained that every state embodies and expresses the peculiar national spirit of its people, and that if an attempt is made to model one state after another, the inevitable result will be contradiction and discord. They held the differences between Russia and the West to be fundamental and inherent, reflecting profound dissimilarities in national spirit rather than degrees of advance. Especially after the great Russian victory over Napoleon in 1812, the Slavophils were convinced of the superiority of their institutions over those of the West. "In contrast to Russian strength, unity and harmony," wrote one of those Slavophils, "there is nothing but quarrel, division, and weakness, against which our greatness stands out still more—as light against shadow." [1]

China's resistance against the intrusion of Western capitalism was ended by the Opium War of 1839–42; Russia's resistance was ended a decade later, by the Crimean War of 1854–56. Russia's defeat in the Crimea was a severe shock for the Slavophils. They had confidently predicted that the superiority of Russia's autocratic institutions would lead to a victory comparable to that of 1812 over Napoleon. Instead Russia was defeated on her own soil, and the defeat exposed the corruption and backwardness of the old regime. Russia's soldiers had fought as gallantly in 1855 as in 1812. But the odds were hopelessly against them. They had rifles that shot only a third as far as those of the Western armies. They had only sailing ships to use against the steamships of the British and the French. The Russians had no medical or commissariat services that were worthy of the name. And the lack of railways in the Crimean Peninsula forced them to haul military supplies in carts, and to march on foot for hundreds of miles before reaching the front. In short, the war was lost because, as the Westerners had warned, "Europe has been steadily advancing on the road of progress while we have been standing still."

II. Second Phase of Russia's Economic Growth, 1856–91

The Crimean defeat was a shattering blow for the Tsarist regime, which was forced to accept changes that opened up Russia to Western capitalism and brought the country into the world market economy. The first change was the emancipation of the serfs, who had been intensely restless even before the war. In fact, over five hundred peasant disturbances had broken out during the three decades of Nicholas I's reign, between 1825 and 1855. With the disaster in the Crimea, the mounting pressure of the serfs became irresistible and the new Tsar, Alexander II, accepted emancipation as the only alternative to revolution.

Alexander's decision was encouraged also by many nobles, especially in the South, where the land was more fertile and productive. They favored emancipation in order to take advantage of the growing demand for grain in a Europe that was becoming increasingly industrialized and urbanized. They discovered that they could not produce a substantial surplus for exports so long as all the land was divided among the serfs, who grew only enough for their own needs, and a little extra for the noble proprietors. So the more forward-looking nobles were all in favor of freeing the serfs from the bonds that hitherto had bound them to their plots. In this way the nobles planned to consolidate the small plots, introduce efficient, large-scale agricultural techniques and employ as day laborers only those former serfs whose labor they actually needed, instead of being required to support the whole of a rapidly growing serf population. In other words, the progressive-minded Russian nobles in the South favored emancipation for the same reason that the English gentry had supported and effected the enclosures during the preceding three centuries.

These circumstances combined to make possible the Emancipation Decree issued on March 3, 1861. By its terms all serfs were given their personal freedom, a measure that involved about fifty million of the sixty million inhabitants of European Russia. The landlords kept those portions of their estates that had been farmed for them by their former serfs, and that now were worked by hired labor, as often as not by that of the ex-serfs. The communal open fields were divided among the former serfs, whether those of the landowners or the state (and they were roughly equal in number). The landlords were paid for their communal fields by the state in treasury bonds. The peasants in turn were to refund the treasury by installments, known as redemption payments, which were spread over a period of forty-nine years. The land was not given directly to the individual peasants, but rather to their village communes, or *mirs*, which distributed it among the village members according to the size of the peasant family. To assure equality of treatment the land was redistributed by the mirs every ten or twelve years. The members of the commune were held jointly responsible for the redemption payments.

Under serfdom the peasants said: "We are yours, but the land is ours." Now they no longer belonged to their masters, but the land still was not fully theirs. Many peasants greeted with derisive laughter the provision for forty-nine years, or "two generations," of redemption payments. So many peasants were convinced that the "real emancipation" had been falsified by landowners and officials that Tsar Alexander told a delegation of peasants in August 1861: "There will be no emancipation except the one I have granted you. Obey the law and the statutes! Work and toil! Be obedient to the authorities and to noble landowners!" [2]

These orders did not go down well. Acts of insubordination were reported in 1861 on 1,176 estates, but government troops were ready and the disturbances were quelled. By 1865 peace and order had been restored, at least for the time being. Yet the peasant grievances were real, and became more acute with the passage of time. In the first place the peasants theoretically received the fields they had previously worked, but because of arrangements made in favor of the landlords as to pasture, meadow and woodland, the holdings and subsistence rights of the peasants were seriously diminished. Also, the state had bought out the landlords at rates on the average much higher than the market prices of land, so that the redemption annuities were correspondingly high. Moreover the peasants were required to pay a salt tax and a poll tax in addition to the redemption installments, and the communes were collectively responsible for all.

Finally, it should be noted that the prereform allotments had been intended to provide employment for only half of the serfs' time, the other half to be spent in work on the lands reserved for their masters. Thus the peasants after emancipation were seriously underemployed, even if they were hired as wage laborers by their former masters, because wage labor was more efficiently utilized, and therefore less was needed. This underemployment pressure in the countryside increased steadily because of the high birth rate. Hence the recurring famines, that of 1891–92 being on a scale comparable to the worst Indian famines of 1876–78 and 1899–1900. The government responded by abolishing the salt tax in 1880, the poll tax in 1886 and by periodically reducing or deferring the redemption dues. And yet peasant indebtedness still continued to mount, and with it peasant unrest and violence, until finally the great 1905 peasant revolt forced another round of institutional reforms comparable to that after the Crimean War.

So far as the overall economic development of Russia was concerned, the emancipation of the serfs did give a considerable boost to the development of capitalist enterprise. The formerly landbound serfs were now available for industrial work, particularly because in 1861 about one fourth of them had insufficient land to support themselves, and by 1913 the proportion had doubled to one half. Also, the redemption dues and other financial obligations forced the peasants to produce more in order to obtain the needed cash. Furthermore, foreign markets were opening up for Russian raw materials and foodstuffs with the growing industrialization of Western Europe. The repeal of the Corn Laws in 1846 led to rapid growth of Russian grain exports to Britain. Railways were built connecting the rich Ukrainian interior with Black Sea ports, so that the annual average export of wheat, rye, barley and oats increased from 69 million *poods* (1 pood = 36 pounds) in 1856–60, to 120 million in 1866–70, and to 257 million in 1876–80.

As significant as the Emancipation Decree and the growth of agricultural exports were various government measures that stimulated industry. One was the construction of railways, of which Russia in 1855 had only 1,000 *versts* (1 verst = 0.66 mile). By 1881 this had increased to 21,000 versts, and by 1895 to 33,000 versts. This was a considerable achievement, which aided various industries during the construction process, as well as providing transportation facilities that strengthened the entire economy.

Equally helpful for Russia's industrialization was the adoption of a high protective tariff in 1822 (even though its main objective was to raise revenue) and the encouragement given to foreign capital and technology. Swedish-Russian industrialist Alfred Nobel began the Baku oil industry in the late 1870s, and by 1900 Russia was the largest oil producer in the world. A Welshman, John James Hughes, exploited the iron ore of Krivoi Rog and the coal of the Donets Basin, thus laying the basis for the Ukrainian steel industry. In his honor, the town of Yuzhovka was named after him. Likewise a German-English entrepreneur, Ludwig Knoop, established large cotton textile mills, importing machines and yarn from Britain. Western and native firms also developed machine-building industry in the Moscow and St. Petersburg areas.

Defining a "factory" as an enterprise employing at least 16 workers, Russia had 2,500 to 3,000 such factories in 1866; 4,500 in 1879; 6,000 in 1890; and 9,000 in 1903. Likewise the urban population of Russia rose from 6.6 percent in 1811, to 10 percent in 1863, to 15.3 percent in 1913.

This industrial expansion, together with the new railway network, made possible regional economic specialization: export-oriented agriculture in the Ukraine, oil industry in the Caspian region, mining and metallurgy in the southern Ukraine and textile plants in Moscow, St. Petersburg and Poland, which received one third of their raw cotton from the central Asian provinces.

In this manner the institutional and policy changes following the Crimean War quickened the Russian economy and impelled it into the international capitalist world order. The growing dependence of Russian agriculture on Western markets and of Russian industry on Western capital and technology signified the extension of the Third World to include the great Eurasian land mass between the Baltic Sea and the Pacific Ocean. One symptom of this envelopment of the Russian economy was its vulnerability to the periodic world economic crises. Soviet economist S. Strumilin has analyzed the effects of this vulnerability during the decades following the Crimean War. After complaining that his fellow Soviet scholars had failed to note the impact of world economic crises on nineteenth-century Russia, he concluded:

> It is now possible to say with certainty that none of the international cyclical crises up to 1907 failed to influence Russian industries to some extent. There is nothing surprising in this. No matter what stage of industrial development a country had reached, once drawn into the orbit of world trade it was unable to escape the pervasive and elemental impact of world crises. . . . Statistics of foreign trade show that in each world crisis, accompanied as it was by a lowering of prices and effective demand, there was a decline in Russia's total external trade. I have estimated that the extent of this decline during the six crises following the emancipation of the serfs in 1861, that is from 1867 to 1908, amounted to not less than 2,000 million roubles, of which the drop in exports alone was more than 1,112 million roubles. Falling prices for the products of Russian agriculture, such as grain, butter, eggs, flax and hides, were responsible for much of this large decline in export values. Clearly such a decrease in rural earnings, effectively sacrificing many millions of Russian workers to the Moloch of world capitalism, would not be without consequence for Russia's internal market. In a world depression, the peasants were unable to sell a significant part of their marketable produce and what they could sell fetched miserably low prices. As a result, the Russian village reduced its demand for domestic industrial products such as textiles, sugar, kerosene and metal manufactures. If we remember also the direct dependence of many of Russia's industries on imported

goods (machinery, raw cotton, paints, chemicals, etc.), then the impact of a world slump on Russia's industry can be clearly appreciated.[3]

₴ III. Third Phase of Russia's Economic Growth, 1892–1914

The great famine of 1891–92 signaled the end of the economic advance initiated by the Crimean War. The pause proved short-lived, for in 1892 Sergei Witte was appointed Minister of Finance, a post he held till 1903, and which he used to steer the Russian economy to new heights. Witte was vigorous, honest and efficient, a rare combination among Tsarist officials. He was a man of wide vision who was concerned about the economic backwardness of Russia as against the West, and who read widely to find a way out for his country. In the process he came upon Friedrich List's *National System of Political Economy* (1841), which influenced him profoundly, as List was the prophet of the underdeveloped countries of the time. List's program called for the development of national industry, which, he maintained, would reduce dependence on foreign markets, strengthen agriculture, stabilize currency and civilize the country as a whole by promoting punctuality and stimulating international exchange of ideas.

Witte adapted List's ideas to Russian conditions by promoting railway construction on a huge scale—an undertaking that was facilitated by the 1891 Franco-Russian alliance, which stimulated an abundant flow of French capital to Russia. Witte's program did have a powerful catalytic effect, initiating what might be termed the third phase of Russia's economic growth. This continued, with a brief interlude during the disastrous Russo-Japanese War and the ensuing 1905 Russian Revolution, until the outbreak of the First World War.

Russia's railway mileage increased 42 percent between 1892 and 1902, thereby completing the basic pattern of the national railway network. Grain-producing areas were linked to ports and to grain-consuming areas, strategic north–south arteries were completed and new lines were built into central Asia to service the cotton-producing regions and to counter the British in India. The railway boom did stimulate other industries, so that during Witte's tenure coal output doubled, pig iron production in the Ukraine increased five times and the output of metal working industries rose 175 percent between 1887 and 1897. The overall industrial production of Russia doubled during Witte's eleven years in office—a remarkable achievement by any criterion.

The years between 1900 and 1909 were a period of stagnation, due to the international recession, which was prolonged in Russia because of the war with Japan and the 1905 Revolution, which nearly toppled the Tsarist autocracy. If proof were needed of Russia's integration into the global capitalist system, it was demonstrated by the political and financial assistance rushed by the Western powers to preserve the Tsarist regime with which they now had important commercial, financial and diplomatic ties (see Chapter 18, Section IV).

By 1909 the period of stagnation ended and a new boom got under way, which continued to the outbreak of the First World War. The economic growth of these years differed from that of the Witte era because it was based more on consumer demand than stimulation by government policies and investments. The consumer demand was fostered by various concessions that the government was forced to make during the revolutionary crisis. It ended the redemption payments in 1905, just as it earlier had abolished the salt and poll taxes. It encouraged peasant migration across the Urals, so that western Siberia by 1914 had become an important dairy region with flourishing peasant marketing cooperatives. The government also subsidized the Peasant Land Bank generously, enabling it to purchase over 4 million *dessiatines* (1 dessiatine = 2.7 acres) of land for redistribution between 1906 and 1915, compared to 1 million in the preceding decade. Finally Peter Stolypin, who emerged as the strong man of the Tsarist regime after the 1905 Revolution, introduced land reforms in 1906 and 1910 that allowed voluntary disbandment of mirs, and abolition of joint landholding and joint responsibility for tax payments. This was Stolypin's "wager on the strong"—his strategy being to create a class of prosperous peasants who would provide a political base for Tsarism in the countryside.

The above measures, together with the continued influx of Western capital, enabled Russian industry to more than double the value of its output between 1900 and 1913. The annual rate of industrial growth, which had been 8.03 percent between 1890 and 1899, and which had fallen to 1.45 percent between 1900 and 1906, now climbed to 6.25 percent between 1907 and 1913.

IV. *"Weakest Link in the Imperialist Chain"*

Despite the rapid industrialization of Russia during the six decades following the Crimean War, the fact remains that the period ended with an elemental upheaval that destroyed both the Tsarist dynasty and the Tsarist regime. The basic reason is that in the process of industrialization Russia had become a part of the Third World, and, like other Third World countries, had experienced economic growth without economic development. We have seen that this form of industrialization everywhere involved foreign control of the key sectors of the national economy, and the enrichment of foreign investors and the small local elites at the expense of the masses of the native populations.

This pattern was especially evident in Latin America where, as in Russia, political independence went hand in hand with economic dependence. Yet this combination persisted in Latin America for a full century before World War I, with no social eruptions comparable to the 1917 Russian Revolution in magnitude and in depth. The question arises, therefore, why Russia proved to be the first country to extricate itself from the Third World, rather than China or India or some Middle Eastern or African or Latin American country. Why did Russia, during the great testing time of the First World War, prove to be, in Lenin's words, the "weakest link in the imperialist chain"?

First there is the indubitable fact of foreign domination of the Russian economy. Foreign investors by 1914 owned 40 percent of the railway mileage, 40 percent of the engineering plants, 42 percent of the banking stock, 50 percent of the chemical industry, 50 percent of the coal and oil output, 60 percent of the copper and iron ore output and 80 percent of the coke output. Of a total of £500 million invested in Russian industry in 1917, just over one third comprised foreign investments. Also, foreigners held almost 50 percent of the Russian national debt of 8,811 million rubles in 1914, making Russia Europe's largest debtor.

Second, the middle class that developed in Russia with the industrialization of the country soon became discontented with the Tsarist autocracy because the middle class could not assume a political role commensurate with its economic power. The political organization reflecting the views of this group was the Constitutional Democratic party, commonly known under the abbreviated title of Cadets. The program of this party, founded in 1905, resembled that of the English Liberals: a constitutional monarchy balanced by a parliamentary body similar to Britain's House of Commons. The Cadets included many of Russia's outstanding intellectuals and businessmen. When the Tsar was forced to accept an elected assembly (Duma) following the 1905 Revolution, the Cadets played a leading role in its deliberations because of their articulateness and their knowledge of parliamentary procedures. And yet the Cadets never won a mass following comparable to that of the Social Democrats or the Socialist Revolutionaries. One reason was that the middle class was relatively small in Russia, thanks to the retarded development of commerce and industry. The middle class was further weakened because so much of the national economy was controlled by foreign interests. And the Cadets were peculiarly vulnerable to the pressures of the Tsarist autocracy, because, with their middle-class background, they were less willing to meet force with force. A contemporary English observer analyzed the weakness of their position as follows: "The Cadets, who deserved their reputation of being the best organized party in the Empire, had not a firm hold on the nation, because they were not of it, they could not place themselves at its angle of vision, were incapable of appreciating its world-philosophy, were not rooted in the people. Hence they did not enlist the peasant and the workingman in their party and stood only for themselves." [4]

More dissatisfied and more violent than the middle class were the peasant masses. A basic reason was that the industrialization of the country was conducted largely at their expense. In addition to the redemption dues, the salt and poll taxes and a variety of local levies, they had to pay inflated prices for manufactured goods because of the high tariffs protecting native industry, and at the same time they had to sell their produce at deflated prices because the revenues from cheap agricultural exports paid for costs of industrialization. A guiding principle was expressed in the 1880s when the Finance Minister, I. A. Vyshnegradskii, declared, "We must export though we may die."

The periodic famines attested to the grim reality of this maxim. Brutal measures were used to force the peasants to pay their taxes in full and to sell their harvest when prices were at a seasonable low, even if little was left for the lean spring months. Freight rates were lowered for grain exports, and bonuses were paid to sugar exporters, so that sugar was dumped on the London market at a third of the domestic price, while Russian peasants drank their tea unsweetened. The effects of these measures were accentuated by the growing land hunger as the population increased, so that half the peasant population had insufficient land by the First World War. The problem was not so much the inadequacy of the holdings as the primitiveness of agricultural techniques, which resulted in far lower yields per unit of land than in Western Europe, even taking into account the severity of the Russian climate. The Tsarist government unfortunately failed to tackle this problem effectively with experimental stations and agricultural experts.

The extent and the intensity of peasant discontent became apparent with the increasing frequency of violent peasant outbreaks against landlords and unpopular government officials. This peasant disaffection found political expression in the Socialist Revolutionary party, which was organized in 1898. Since no political parties were allowed in Russia prior to the 1905 Revolution, the Socialist Revolutionaries had to operate as an illegal underground group. The main plank of their platform was the distribution of state and noble lands among the peasantry. In two important respects the Socialist Revolutionaries differed from the various types of Marxist socialists. In the first place, they regarded the peasantry rather than the urban proletariat as the main revolutionary force in Russia. In the second place, they advocated and practiced individual acts of terrorism, rather than relying on mass organization and pressure. Within the Socialist Revolutionary party was the highly secret Fighting Organization, which directed the terroristic activities. Its success may be gauged from its long list of illustrious victims, including governors of provinces, ministers of state and even the Tsar's uncle, Grand Duke Sergei.[5] After each successful operation, the Fighting Organization issued a statement explaining and glorifying the deed. After the assassination of the Minister of Interior, D. S. Sipiagin, it proclaimed: "The crack of the bullet is the only possible means of talking with our ministers, until they learn to understand human speech and listen to the voice of the country. We do not need to explain why Sipiagin was executed. His crimes were too notorious, his life was too generally cursed and his death too generally greeted." [6]

As dissatisfied and violent as the peasants were the workers in factories and mines. The beginnings of industrialization in Russia, as elsewhere in Europe, involved gross exploitation of labor: sixteen-hour working days, low wages, child labor and abominable working and living conditions. According to a report on working-class housing in Moscow in 1895: "These places can only be compared, without exaggeration, to places where cattle are kept. Even in summer, when the doors and windows are open, the air is stifling; along the walls and on the sleeping benches traces of mould are to be seen. The floor is invisible because it is covered with dirt." [7]

A common grievance was the custom of paying workers only three or four times a year, or even only twice—on Easter and Christmas. This practice left the determination of wages largely to the discretion of the factory administration. Another grievance was the imposition of fines for infractions of a wide range of factory rules. In the John Hughes ironworks in the Ukraine, fines as high as three months' wages were not unusual. Trade unions were until 1906 subject to criminal law, while strikes were punishable by arrest and imprisonment up to three months. Money wages in most industries rose between the 1860s and the 1890s, but real wages declined by as much as 20 to 30 percent. The reason was the displacement of cottage craft articles by cheap machine-made products, which swelled the ranks of unemployed men and women seeking jobs in factories. Since industry did not expand rapidly enough to absorb the available manpower, wages were correspondingly depressed, with the exception of a few highly skilled occupations. Furthermore, most industrial workers were peasants who maintained contact with their native villages, where their families often continued to live. This enabled employers to pay substantially lower wages than if their workers were maintaining family establishments near their place of employment.

Despite the repressive labor laws and the abundance of available workers, strikes nevertheless did break out spontaneously against particularly oppressive conditions. These disturbances, together with the pressure of a public opinion increasingly conscious of worker exploitation, led the government to adopt minimal labor regulations. A law of June 1, 1882, prohibited the employment of children under twelve years of age, limited to eight hours the working day of those aged twelve to fifteen, prohibited juveniles from working on Sundays or holidays and required their employment to be so arranged as to allow school attendance. Another law, of June 3, 1885, prohibited night work in textile mills for women and young persons under seventeen. A year later, the government required that wages be paid at least once a month, prohibited payments in kind and prohibited the charging of interest on advances made to workers. The enforcement of all these regulations was entrusted to factory inspectors, but their numbers were inadequate, and their zeal depended on the varying predilections of the government ministers.

Under these circumstances the Russian workers, like those of central and Western Europe, came under the influence of Marxist doctrines. Thus a Social Democratic party was organized in 1898 as similar socialist parties had been established elsewhere in Europe. And like the other socialist parties, that of Russia split into revisionist and orthodox factions, or, as they were called in this instance, the Mensheviks and the Bolsheviks.

The split occurred during the second party congress held in London in 1903. The issues concerned party membership and party discipline. Nicolai Lenin, the leader of the orthodox faction, maintained that because of the repressive Tsarist autocracy, the Social Democratic party had to operate very differently from other socialist parties. Membership should be open not to any sympathizer who paid his dues, but only to a small group of full-time professional revolutionaries. And this select membership was to function according to the principle of "democratic centralism." Any major issue facing the party was to be discussed freely by the members until a decision was reached democratically by a vote. But then the "centralism" part of the principle became operative. Every party member, regardless of his personal inclinations, was required on pain of expulsion to support undeviatingly what was now the "party line."

Only with such rigid discipline, Lenin maintained, could Russian socialists carry on effectively their underground operations. Lenin won the support of most of the delegates to the 1903 congress, so that his followers henceforth were known as Bolsheviks, after the Russian word for "majority," and his opponents as Mensheviks, or "minority." It should be noted, however, that the Bolsheviks remained a small group until the outbreak of the 1905 Revolution, in which they played a leading role with their worker soviets or councils. With the suppression of the Revolution, the number of strikes declined to a low point of 200 in

1910, involving 47,000 workers. But by 1912 the respective figures were 2,000 and 725,000, and between January and July 1914, 4,000 and 1,449,000.

The militancy of Russian labor, despite repressive government policies and actions, was due to two basic factors. One was the exceedingly low level of wages. In 1913 the average monthly wage in all industries was 22 rubles, ranging from 16 to 17 rubles in the textile industry to 33 to 34 in the metals industry. Studies of workers' budgets reveal that practically their entire income was spent on necessities—shelter, food and clothing. An average of only half a ruble per month was left for "recreation and cultural needs," which included postage, streetcar fares and visits to public bathhouses.

The other chief reason for labor militancy was the unusually high concentration of workers in large factories, which facilitated collective organization and action. Since modern machine industry arrived late in Russia, it started at an advanced, large-scale level. In 1866, of the workers employed in factories with more than 100 workers, over 27 percent worked in factories with 1,000 or more workers; in 1879 the percentage was 40, and by 1890 it was 46. In the same year, the average number of people employed per establishment in Russian factories or mines having 1,000 or more employees each was larger than the average for Germany in 1895 by more than 600 workers. This combination of abnormally low wages and high concentration of workers in large factories and mines contributed to the militancy of labor in both the 1905 Revolution and the 1917 Revolution.

Whereas the 1905 Revolution ultimately was contained, that of 1917 destroyed the Tsarist regime. The reason for the difference between 1905 and 1917 was the First World War. Just as the later Chinese Revolution of 1948 was greatly facilitated by World War II, so the Russian Revolution of 1917 was by World War I. The hammer blows of the German and Austro-Hungarian armies in 1914 and 1915 exposed the structural backwardness and weakness of Russia compared to the Western European societies. In February 1900 Sergei Witte had warned the Tsar of the dangers ahead if Russia failed to catch up to the other Great Powers:

> International competition does not wait. If we do not take energetic and decisive measures so that in the course of the next decades our industry will be able to satisfy the needs of Russia and of the Asiatic countries which are—or should be—under our influence, then the rapidly growing foreign industries will break through our tariff barriers and establish themselves in our fatherland and in the Asiatic countries mentioned above and drive their roots into the

depths of our economy. . . . Our economic backwardness may lead to political and cultural backwardness as well.[8]

Despite the advances made at the turn of the century, Russia was unable to overcome the comparative "economic backwardness" that Witte had warned against. On the eve of World War I, per-capita income in 1913 gold rubles was for the United States 682.2, Britain 446.6, France 354.7, Germany 300.1, Italy 209.9, Russia 101.4, Bulgaria and Romania 97.2. In other words, Russia was virtually as underdeveloped as Bulgaria and Romania, or one sixth as wealthy as the United States, and one third as wealthy as Germany. Put in other terms, the per-capita output of Russia was:

- in electric power: one fifth of Germany and one seventeeth of the United States
- in pig iron and steel: one eighth of Germany and one eleventh of the United States
- in coal: one fifteenth of Germany and one twenty-sixth of the United States

Some have argued that given the rapid industrialization of Russia during the decades prior to World War I, the country ultimately could have caught up and attained modernization if the war had not intervened. But the fact is that Russia's rate of economic growth, even at its highest level, was not equal to that of the Western countries. The per-capita pig iron production of Russia was one eighth that of the United States in 1900, but only one eleventh by 1913. Likewise in 1900 it was one sixth that of Germany's pig iron production, and by 1913 only one eighth. The more Russia tried to catch up, the more she fell behind.

One reason for this relative economic failure was that Russia, like all Third World countries, did not exploit her natural and human resources on an integrated national basis. Prior to the nineteenth century, as noted in Chapter 3, Section III, Russia had been able to preserve her economic independence by trading more with her eastern provinces and eastern neighbors than with the West. During the nineteenth century the massive economic intrusion of the West led to the distorted economic development typical of dependent Third World societies. Russia's economy was skewed westward by the needs of Western markets, the investments of Western entrepreneurs and the dictates of Western alliances. Industrialization was limited largely to European Russia, so that by 1913 only 4.7 percent of total industrial output came from the Urals, 2.4 percent from Siberia, and 1.8 percent from Turkestan, as against 50 percent from the central provinces and 20 percent from the Ukraine. This imbalance was promoted by railway rates that facilitated raw cotton exports from central Asia to textile mills in European Russia. Conversely, railway rates were raised for Siberian grain exports in order to protect the landowners of the central provinces.[9]

Equally serious were the cultural obstacles in the way of Russia's development. Industrialization was opposed not only by peasants, who bore most of the burden, but also by the landed aristocrats, who instinctively wished to preserve their traditional agrarian institutions and loathed the rising capitalists, whether native or foreign. It was for this reason that Witte became a political liability for the Tsar and was dismissed in August 1903. Hence E. H. Carr's dismissal as "an unhistorical fantasy" the fashionable thesis that "Russia had already begun to industrialize herself before 1914, and that all that the revolution did was to continue —and perhaps temporarily to delay—the process." Carr concludes instead, "The hostility of the landowning interests which brought about Witte's downfall would have been fatal to any far-reaching development of industry. This could have occurred only at the expense of their way of life and of the quasifeudal society which they represented; it was only after their overthrow by the revolution that the modernization of the Russian economy could be undertaken."[10]

Chapter 17

THE JAPANESE EXCEPTION

Japanese policy should, I think, be that of keeping Americans and Europeans as much as possible at arm's length. . . . you should take every precaution to give as little foothold as possible to foreigners. . . . Apparently you are proposing . . . to open the whole Empire to foreigners and foreign capital. I regret this as a fatal policy. If you wish to see what is likely to happen, study the history of India.

HERBERT SPENCER to Baron Kaneko Kentario (1892)

When Commodore Matthew Perry cast anchor at Edo Bay on July 8, 1853, the Japanese island empire seemed to have slight chance of escaping the fate of Third World status that had befallen other non-Western countries. After more than two centuries of self-imposed isolation, Japan lagged as far behind Europe in industrial and military technology as had the Ottoman, Mogul and Manchu empires. Furthermore, Japan lacked the abundant natural resources of those empires, so that she seemed doomed by insuperable material as well as technological obstacles in the way of economic development and national independence. Yet the Japanese proved to be the only people who succeeded in entering the world market in the nineteenth century on equal terms. They alone benefited from this association, and became strong and independent, rather than exploited and subordinate. The only other countries that had been able to achieve such a breakthrough were the overseas extensions of Europe—countries such as the United States and the British dominions, which enjoyed the unique advantages of open lands for settlement and ethnic bonds with the mother country. All the other overseas regions inhabited by non-Western indigenous populations had fallen under the direct or indirect domination of the European powers. Only the Japanese escaped subjugation, and the reasons for this fateful exception are of obvious significance for the entire Third World, both in the nineteenth century and today.

✎ I. Japan in Seclusion

Historians have proffered several factors in explanation of the unique Japanese response to the intrusion of the West. One is the remoteness of the Japanese islands from the industrialized countries of the West. This gave the Japanese a greater opportunity to work out their own economic destiny in accord with their own traditions. If their homeland had been situated in close proximity to the industrialized West, they would have felt the Western impact in the fifteenth century, as did Eastern Europe, or in the sixteenth century, as did the Americas. The Japanese would have exchanged their coal, raw silk, marine products and other raw materials for Western manufactured goods, and thus declined to a dependent Third World status at an early date. Instead, the extreme remoteness of the Japanese islands in the northwestern Pacific, together with the strict seclusion policy of its Tokugawa leaders, left the Japanese unaffected until the second half of the nineteenth century. And when the Westerners finally did show up, they did not bring as much pressure to bear as on other parts of the Third World, precisely because of the remoteness and comparative poverty of Japan.

In addition, the physical compactness of the Japanese islands facilitated both the forging of national unity and the spread of new values and new learning. It also made the country vulnerable to, and aware of, foreign pressures when they finally reached that remote corner of the world. Perry's ships sailed within sight of the capital, Edo, and within a few weeks all of Japan knew of this disturbing event. The significance of this compactness and accessibility is apparent if contrasted with the opposite conditions prevailing in China. The vast and densely populated interior provinces of the Chinese Empire were for long inaccessible and impervious to Western influences, and served as reservoirs of traditional attitudes and forces that blocked adaptation to the intruding West.

Japan also enjoyed an exceptionally high degree of cultural homogeneity. Its people were unusually well educated and accustomed to following the leadership of their ruling elite. Thanks to the centuries of isolation from the outside world there were no local merchants or lords who, as in India, had developed closer ties with Western merchants than with their own rulers.

Another factor that facilitated Japan's successful adaptation to the

West was her long tradition of borrowing from the great Chinese cultural world. This made similar borrowing from the Western world less jarring and painful. Japan had taken selected aspects of Chinese culture with the slogan "Japanese spirit and Chinese knowledge." Now Japan borrowed what she wished from the West with the slogan "Eastern morale and Western arts." Even during their centuries of seclusion the Japanese leaders had gone out of their way to keep informed of developments in Europe. They had allowed the Dutch to continue trading at the Deshima islet primarily so they could question them concerning the outside world. Japanese appreciation of Western technological attainments is evident in the following eulogy of England written by a Japanese scholar about the same time that the Emperor of China was scornfully informing King George III that China had no use for anything from the barbarian West:

> When it comes to grand edifices, no country in the world can compare with England. There is no country comparable to England in the manufacture of very fine things. Among the articles which have been imported into Japan by the Dutch, there have been none more precious than the watches. Some of them are so exquisite that hairs are split to make them. London is considered to produce the finest such workmanship in the world. Next comes Paris, in France, and then Amsterdam in Holland. In these three capitals live people virtually without a peer in the world, who are the handsomest of men. . . . Why is it that the people of these three cities, who are human beings like everyone else, have attained such excellence? [1]

The Japanese also were the beneficiaries of sheer good luck. During the 1850s and 1860s the European powers happened to be so preoccupied elsewhere that they never were able to concentrate on securing control over a cluster of poor and distant islands in the northwestern Pacific. China offered a much more lucrative prize to the Europeans after the Opium War forced that country to open its doors in the 1840s, while the Crimean War of 1854–56 and the Indian Mutiny of 1857–59 preoccupied the most powerful and aggressive of the Westerners. In this respect the Japanese were infinitely more fortunate than the Africans, who were quickly conquered in the last two decades of the nineteenth century by European powers that happened to be free from major distractions during those decades, and therefore able to focus on the partitioning of an entire continent.

The most important single factor explaining Japan's uniquely successful entrance on the world stage was, paradoxically, the instability of her society after centuries of seclusion. The aim of the Tokugawa leaders had been to keep Japan isolated and unchanging in order to perpetuate their regime. But in spite of, or because of, their efforts, certain developments did occur that gradually altered the balance of forces in the country and undermined the status quo.

The power of the long succession of Tokugawa shoguns, dating back to 1603, was based on their numerous estates scattered strategically throughout the country and comprising one fifth to one fourth of the total national territory. Top government posts were filled by members of the Tokugawa family or personal retainers. As part of their effort to prevent any change that might undermine their rule, the Tokugawa perpetuated a rigid, hereditary class structure. At the top was the Emperor, the powerless sovereign, and the shogun, the *de facto* ruler. The shogun sustained the fiction that he ruled because of the power delegated to him by the Emperor, but in fact the shogun exploited the imperial spiritual authority, while maintaining the Emperor in powerless isolation in his court at Kyoto. The headquarters of Shogun administration was first at Edo, where the feudal lords, or *daimyo*, were required to reside at regular intervals, and to leave both their wives and heirs as hostages when they returned to their lands.

After the shogun came the aristocracy, comprising about 6 percent of the total population. This included the Court nobles, who had social priority but no power or property, and were therefore dependent on the shoguns for support. Much more important were the daimyo, of whom there were 266 immediately before the 1868 Restoration. With the support of their numerous samurai retainers, the daimyo were ensconced in their castles, whence they dominated their *han* or fiefs, and collected revenue in the form of rice from the surrounding peasantry.

Below the aristocrats on the social ladder were the farmers, including landless tenants as well as landholders with plots ranging from $1\frac{1}{4}$ acres to as many as 85 acres. Whatever their holdings, they had no political power, and they were forced to surrender a large portion of their produce to pay the rents and taxes that supported the aristocracy and the Court. Peasant uprisings steadily increased during the Tokugawa era, thereby contributing to the social tensions that culminated in the Meiji Restoration.

The last two classes recognized by the Tokugawa were, in order of rank, the artisans and the merchants. The long peace enforced by the Tokugawa allowed these townspeople to grow enormously in wealth and numbers. The national population jumped from 18 million in 1600 to 26 million in 1725. Cities grew disproportionately, Edo approaching the million mark by 1700. The population spurt increased the demand for commodities and encouraged merchants and rich peasants to invest surplus capital in new forms of production, including the domestic, or putting-out system. They provided materials and equipment for peasants and craftsmen, and marketed the finished products.

The rising production led to wide-scale exchange of goods, which in turn stimulated the development of a money economy. Rice brokers and money exchangers became the most important merchants, disposing of the surplus produce of the feudal aristocracy and providing credit on high interest. Many of the daimyo, and sometimes the shogun himself, became indebted to these merchant-financiers. One reason was the heavy expense of maintaining at Edo the large establishments required by the shogun's hostage system. Also, the aristocrats acquired a taste for luxuries and competed with each other in ostentatious living. By the eve of Restoration, over 90 percent of the national wealth had fallen into the hands of the entrepreneurs. The anomaly of political power remaining a monopoly of the shoguns and aristocrats, while economic power was being appropriated by the merchant-financiers, became a source of social tension.

One reason the tension did not build up to revolution by the subordinate bourgeoisie, as had happened in Britain and France, was that the Japanese merchants had not been allowed to conduct overseas trade, and therefore had no source of overseas strength. They were dependent completely on the domestic economic structure, which functioned in an aristocracy-dominated political context. Edo was the largest city in the world by the late eighteenth century, but it was controlled completely by shoguns, daimyo and samurai. The merchants, despite their economic power, had no legal protection from debt cancellation, forced levies or outright confiscation. Consequently the Japanese bourgeoisie never acquired the strength and self-confidence to attempt to overthrow the old order. Instead they improved their position within it, and in this they were eminently successful. They bought their way into the aristocracy by intermarriage or adoption, and by the eighteenth and early nineteenth centuries they dominated not only the economy but also the art and literature of Japan.

Nevertheless, the social fabric remained strained by the antagonistic polarization of economic and political power. Another source of social tension was the deteriorating position of the armed samurai, who became superfluous anachronisms during the centuries of Tokugawa peace. The mass of the peasants also were suffering severely because of the increasing levies imposed by the hard-pressed aristocrats, and because the price of rice failed to keep pace with the rising prices of other goods. Many peasants migrated to the cities, but not all were able to find employment, for the growth of the national economy was not keeping pace with the growth of population. Hence the rising incidence of peasant revolts in the later Tokugawa years.

Japanese society was in a state of transition by the nineteenth century. It was experiencing profound economic and social change, which generated corresponding political tensions. It might well have disrupted and reverted to a state of feudal anarchy, which had beset Japan in earlier centuries. But this outcome was averted when Admiral Perry forced Japan to end her isolation and participate in the global market economy. One reason the Japanese proved so ready to reorganize their society in order to cope with the intruding West was precisely that many of them were all too aware that their society needed reorganizing. This realization, together with their long tradition of borrowing from foreigners, made the Japanese infinitely more capable of adapting for survival than the self-centered and self-satisfied Chinese. The contrast between these two peoples was described at the time in the following remarkable passage by a British official, Lord Elgin:

> One result of the difference between the habits and the mode of feeling of the Chinese and the Japanese is undoubtedly this, that as the Chinese are steadily retrograding and will in all probability continue to do so until the Empire falls to pieces, the Japanese, if not actually in a state of progressive advancement, are in a condition to profit by the flood of light that is about to be poured into them and to take advantage of these improvements and inventions which the Chinese regard with contemptuous scorn, but which the Japanese will in all probability, when they come to know us better, be both able and anxious to adopt.[2]

ᛅ II. Western Intervention and Meiji Restoration

Foreign pressure upon Japan had been mounting since the early nineteenth century because of the increasing commercial activity in northern Pacific waters. Ships engaged in whaling and fur trading needed Japanese ports to obtain provisions and to make repairs, but they were denied all access. Instead, the Japanese normally killed or maltreated foreign seamen shipwrecked on their shores. Toward the middle of the century the introduction of the steamship aggravated the situation by creating a need for coaling stations. Finally the United States government decided to take the initiative and to force the issue. On July 8, 1853, Commodore Matthew Perry cast anchor in Edo Bay and delivered a letter from President Millard Fillmore asking for trading privileges, coaling stations and protection for shipwrecked Americans. Within a week Perry sailed away after warning that he would be back for an answer the following spring. When he returned in February 1854, he made it clear that the alternative was a treaty or war. The Japanese yielded and on March 31 signed the Treaty of Kanagawa. Its terms opened the ports of Shimoda and Hakodate for the repair and provisioning of American ships, provided for proper treatment and repatriation of shipwrecked Americans, permitted the appointment of consular representatives if either nation considered it necessary and promised most-favored-nation treatment for the United States.

In accordance with the provisions of this treaty, the United States sent Townsend Harris, an unusually able man, as its first consul to Japan. With his extraordinary tact and patience, Harris gradually won the confidence of the Japanese and secured the Commercial Treaty of 1858. This opened four more ports to trade, provided for mutual diplomatic representation, gave to Americans both civil and criminal extraterritoriality, prohibited the opium trade and gave freedom of religion to foreigners. Before the end of 1858 Japan had found it necessary to sign similar pacts with Holland, Russia, Britain and France.

This series of treaties did not attract much attention in the Western world. But for Japan they represented the great divide of her history. Almost three centuries of seclusion had come to an end, and the impact of Western capitalism was immediate and traumatic. Foreign traders bought much of the large amount of gold that had been accumulated in Japan under the Tokugawa at less than half the going world rate. Also, imports poured into the country, so that whereas in 1863 only 34 percent of total trade consisted of imports, by 1867 the figure had become 61 percent, and by 1870 it was 71 percent. Cheap English textiles flooded local markets, destroying domestic industry. The decline of cottage industry narrowed the tax base while the flight of specie from the country created monetary chaos. The government debased the coinage, inflation soared and the price of rice fluctuated violently.

This economic disruption created a difficult dilemma for the Tokugawa shogunate. On the one hand the populace became increasingly antiforeign and critical of the new treaties, while on the other the Western powers demanded strict implementation of all treaty provisions. The popular unrest was exploited by the anti-Tokugawa clans, especially the Satsuma, Choshu, Hizen and Tosa, often referred to as the Satcho-Hito group. Between 1858 and 1865, attacks were made upon Europeans and their employers with the slogans "Revere the Emperor! Expel the barbarians!" The foreign powers retaliated by bombarding ports and coastal defenses. This action impressed the clan leaders, who now dropped their antiforeignism and decided that priority had to be given to obtaining Western armaments.

Their decision points up the contrast between the Japanese and the Chinese ruling elites. The latter, consisting of literati, were ignorant and contemptuous of Western military technology, whereas the Japanese clan leaders, because of their martial background and interests, were very sensitive and responsive to the spectacle of foreign warships shelling their homeland with impunity. Thus whereas the literati allowed their country to drift into a hopeless and disastrous war with the despised Western barbarians, the Japanese leaders instead set out to learn from the barbarians in order better to resist them.

With the death in 1866 of both the Emperor and the Tokugawa shogun, the way was cleared for the wholesale reorganization known as the Meiji Restoration. By January 1868 the Tokugawa troops were driven out of Kyoto, the imperial capital, and Edo was proclaimed the national capital and renamed Tokyo ("eastern capital"). The Tokugawa were shorn of their power and fiefs, and their place was taken by the Satcho-Hito clans, which henceforth controlled the government in the name of the new Meiji Emperor. It was young samurai in the service of these clans who now provided the extraordinary leadership that made possible the "Japanese exception."

‿ III. Revolution from Above: Political

The basic political achievement of the samurai was the construction of a new state apparatus capable of coping with both the foreign threat and domestic political tensions. This represented a purposeful and carefully executed revolution from above. The class composition of the new ruling elite at the head of the remodeled state structure was the same as that of the old, even though the actual personnel were quite different. The conservative objective of preserving the social status quo while effecting a technological revolution was reflected in the choice of Prussia as a political model. When Ito Hirobumi, the Choshu official who masterminded the new political system, went on an extended tour of Europe to study the constitutional alternatives, he wrote back in August 1882 that he was rejecting "the works of the extreme liberal radicals of England, America and France," and turning to the teachings of Prussian scholars. "I believe I have rendered an important service to my country [and contributed to] the great objective of strengthening the foundation of the imperial sovereignty. . . ." [3]

The new Meiji state took over twenty years to build from the overthrow of the Tokugawa in 1867–68 to the adoption of the Constitution in 1889. The early years were devoted to consolidating the new regime and removing the obstacles in the way of revolution from above. First it was necessary to crush the peasant insurrections, which had contributed significantly to the defeat of the shogunate. In a few regions, such as the Oki Islands, these revolts had resulted in the establishment of local self-government institutions. All these were now suppressed, sometimes with the assistance of former Tokugawa officials. The introduction of conscription in 1873 hastened the end of peasant resistance and ensured the future of the new regime.

Having eliminated the threat of revolution from below, the Tokyo officials next faced the threat of feudal counterrevolution by the daimyo and samurai. The daimyo were co-opted by a combination of show of force and generous financial compensation in return for the surrender of their fiefs. Former feudal territorial magnates deriving income from their peasants now became financial magnates investing their new monetary wealth in banking, industrial and mercantile enterprises. Thus the old feudal landed interests and the emerging new entrepreneurial oligarchy were fused into a homogeneous elite that was to rule the country henceforth with little opposition.

The numerous samurai were co-opted along with their overlords. The government passed a law in December 1871 allowing the samurai to engage in occupations other than their traditional military careers, and then provided them with employment opportunities in administration and in business. In the central government bureaucracy, samurai totaled 78.3 percent of all officeholders in the years immediately after 1868. In local government, over 70 percent of all positions were filled by former samurai between 1872 and 1877. The urban police forces consisted almost exclusively of ex-samurai, as did about three fourths of administrators and teachers in the new national school system. Likewise in business the government between 1876 and 1882 provided funds for nearly 200 samurai enterprises in shipbuilding, construction, cement works, fertilizer concerns, saltworks and artisan projects.

With the class foundations of the new state well secured, the Tokyo officials proceeded to organize a bureaucratic machine that controlled firmly all key areas of power before the adoption of the Constitution in 1889 and the election of the first Diet in 1890. At the head of the new system was the imperial institution, which Hirobumi had viewed as the lynchpin of state ideology and bureaucratic authority; hence the support accorded to Shinto as the state cult, which exalted the Emperor as the descendant of the sun goddess, and the personification of national unity and patriotism.

The educational system also was organized to serve the same political objective. The first Minister of Education, Mori Arinori, was selected by Hirobumi because Arinori also favored German theories and practices in his field. Arinori developed a two-layer educational system, with the lower part providing compulsory mass education, which was permeated with the spirit of self-subordination to the state. The top part, by contrast, trained the future ruling elite in an atmosphere of critical rationalism. The two layers were linked by the normal, or teacher-training school, where students were subjected to nationalistic and militaristic indoctrination, including six hours of military drill per week. When the Educational Rescript was issued in 1890, it exhorted all students to "offer yourselves courageously to the State; and thus guard and maintain the prosperity of Our Imperial Throne, coeval with heaven and earth." [4]

In accordance with the objective of placing all centers of power beyond the reach of the elected Diet, the armed forces were given veto power over the appointment of the military ministers of a cabinet. Even though a government could muster majority support in the Diet, it could be, and as early as 1891 was, hamstrung by the refusal of the armed forces to approve the military ministers. As regards technical organization, the old feudal levies were replaced by a modern military establishment based on conscription. A German military mission aided in the buildup of the army, and a British mission in that of the navy.

After these precautionary measures, the oligarchs considered it safe to introduce parliamentary trappings. The Constitution of 1889 promised the citizens freedom from arbitrary arrest, protection of property rights and freedom of religion, speech and association. But in each instance the government reserved the authority to curb these rights when it deemed it necessary. Furthermore the lower House, based on a minute franchise, did not control the cabinet; the House of Peers was not elected and could not be dissolved; the Emperor chose the Premier on the advice of the extraconstitutional *genro*, or elder statesmen; the bureaucracy was beyond the control of governments; and the armed forces held veto power over all cabinets. In general, the Constitution provided Japan with a democratic façade while preserving oligarchic rule and Emperor worship. The first article provided, "The Empire of Japan shall be reigned over and governed by a line of Emperors unbroken for ages eternal," and the third article stipulated, "The Emperor is sacred and inviolable."

With the adoption of the Constitution in 1889, as well as of modern legal codes in the preceding decade, the Japanese were in a position to press for the abolition of the unequal treaties. They could fairly argue that Japan now had taken her place in the comity of civilized nations and that there was no longer any need for extraterritoriality and for the other infringements on their sovereignty. After prolonged diplomatic efforts they were able in 1894 to persuade Britain and the United States to terminate extraterritoriality and consular jurisdiction in five years. In the same year the Japanese won their unexpected and spectacular victory over the Chinese Empire. Henceforth there could be no more question of treating Japan as an inferior country, and the other powers soon followed Britain and the United States in yielding their special privileges. By 1899 Japan had gained legal jurisdiction over all foreigners on her soil, and in doing so, she became the first Asian nation to break the chains of Western control.

❦ IV. Revolution from Above: Economic

The new Japanese state proved capable not only of ending foreign restraints but also of modernizing the economy and increasing national productivity. Given the conservative political context in which the economic reorganization occurred, the resulting surplus was allocated primarily for the benefit of the armed forces and the ruling elite. The purchasing power of the peasants and workers was severely restricted, government social services were kept to a minimal level and light industry necessarily produced for foreign markets, while heavy industry was geared almost exclusively to meeting the needs of the military.

The capital for the economic modernization was obtained largely from agriculture. A substantial increase in agricultural yield was attained at relatively low cost by introducing better seed strains, improving land use and expanding irrigation and drainage. Between 1878 and 1892 the area under cultivation increased by 7 percent, the yield by 21 percent and the population by 15 percent. The resulting agricultural surplus was siphoned off by taxes, which furnished the capital for industrialization. Between 1871 and 1875 land taxes comprised 85 to 93.2 percent of total government tax revenues, and did not drop below 50 percent of the total until 1896. In fact, taxation was so heavy that considerably more than the surplus was extracted, and farm income dropped sharply. Between 1883 and 1890 some 368,000 peasant proprietors lost their holdings for failure to pay taxes.

Despite these wholesale expropriations, there was no mass exodus to the cities, as occurred in Britain with the enclosures. One reason was that the new landowners were in a position to extract such high rents from the peasants that it was more profitable to allow them to remain as tenants than to drive them off the land. Another reason was the rapid expansion of the textile industry, which was located largely in rural areas, and employed labor from the villages, mostly female. The women customarily were sold off to labor bosses and forced to send most of their wages back to their families.

The textile industry was profitable and for long provided most of Japan's exports. But heavy industry also was needed to support the new army and navy. By granting subsidies or purchasing stock, the government established, directly or indirectly, financial institutions, commodity exchanges, shipping companies, railways and telegraph lines. With this infrastructure provided, the government turned to heavy industries such as mining, steel and shipbuilding, which were needed by the military.

Most of the enterprises established in this manner were eventually sold to various favored private interests at extremely low prices. In this manner a few wealthy families, collectively known as the Zaibatsu, gained a stranglehold on the national economy that has persisted to the present.

Most significant for Third World history is the fact that Japanese industrialization was achieved independently, with little foreign investment. This fundamental difference between the development of Japan and other non-Western countries was due partly to the centuries of Tokugawa seclusion, during which no Japanese trading group could develop the common Third World pattern of importing luxury items and cheap consumer goods. This left the Tokyo government free to take control of foreign trade easily, and to see to it that imports were limited to such prerequisites for economic development as raw materials and capital goods for industry. Also, the Japanese government from the early seventies foresightedly discouraged foreign investments within the country, and bought back the few foreign-owned enterprises already operating. These included the Takashima Coal Mine (British and Dutch capital), the American Pacific Steamship Company and the British-French-owned postal services.

By the early 1880s Japan had rid itself of all foreign investments. This elimination of foreign capital was facilitated by the heavy war indemnities paid by China to Japan after the Sino-Japanese War (369 million yen) and after the Boxer Rebellion (38 million yen). The end result of these favorable financial circumstances—the negligible foreign investments, the inflow rather than outflow of indemnity payments and the negotiation of foreign loans with smaller charges than those obtained by the Chinese—resulted in a considerable net inflow of foreign capital into Japan, in contrast to the considerable net outflow from China.[5]

In addition to these advantageous conditions, the most important factor behind the rapid capital accumulation in Japan was the success of employers, backed by the entire state apparatus, in keeping wages severely depressed. The paucity of public social services left employees at the mercy of employers. The high proportion of female labor in textile and other light industries also served to keep wages low. Another factor operating in this direction was the familistic ethic that permeated mass education. The entire nation was viewed as one family, in which subjects owed loyalty to the Emperor, and workers likewise to their employers.

In return the employers offered a paternalistic "life employment system," but this was not as benevolent and generous as appeared on the surface. If a worker moved to another firm, he automatically was paid the lowest wage rate regardless of his skill—an effective device for checking labor mobility. Also, permanent job security usually was not achieved until between the ages of forty and forty-five. A survey of the huge Yawata Iron and Steel Works revealed that 70 percent of its twenty-one thousand workers were "temporary," even though some of them had been with the company for fifteen years.

The general relationship between employer and worker was depicted as one of "benevolence," under which the employer "gave" the employee his means for livelihood. Wages often were paid only once every three or six months, and then in "tickets" that could be used only in company stores. Companies also deducted money from wages as forced savings, which were not refunded if the worker left the company or was dismissed. The introduction of the electric light in the 1870s and 1880s did not help working conditions but rather lengthened the working day. Girl employees at reeling plants in the 1890s were working fifteen to sixteen hours daily. When the first Factory Act finally was passed in 1911, it allowed employers fifteen years' grace to carry out their provisions, and even then the wording was hedged around with numerous proemployer qualifications. Until 1933 mining companies, which were responsible for the worst abuses, allowed women and boys under sixteen only two days' rest a month.[6]

Whatever the means and the social cost, Japan alone, of all non-Western countries, achieved independent economic development in the nineteenth century. This is not to say that Japan became a great industrial power. Nearly all the industrial raw materials were lacking, so Japan developed mainly light industry, while the great majority of the population remained in agriculture. In 1900 less than half a million people were employed in the country's 7,171 industrial enterprises, of which only 2,388 were using mechanical power. The major industrial advances were made during the Russo-Japanese War and the First World War. The number of factory employees rose to 854,000 by 1914 and to 1,817,000 by 1919, while the number of factories equipped with motors increased 3.6 times between 1905 and 1918.

V. Japanese Imperialism

Japanese industrialization was stimulated by war but was also responsible for war. Depressed wages meant a correspondingly depressed domestic market, which compelled Japanese policymakers to search for markets abroad. The almost complete lack of industrial raw materials in the homeland also led the Japanese to expand on the mainland. Furthermore, the familial ideology of loyalty to the Emperor lent itself to foreign expansion by equating loyalty to the Emperor with patriotism and united national effort to make Japan a great power. Businessmen, for example, exhorted one another to greater effort "in the competition of foreign trade, which is peacetime war." [7] Finally, there was the example of the Western powers engaged in the late nineteenth century in unprecedented land grabbing all over the globe. The practical-minded leaders of Japan drew the obvious conclusion that each people must grab for themselves and that nothing would be left to the weak and the timid. A civilian bureaucrat expressed this viewpoint as follows: "This is like riding in a third-class train; at first there is adequate space but as more passengers enter there is no place for them to sit. If while rubbing shoulders and supporting yourself with your arms you lose your place you can't recover the same position. . . . The logic of necessity requires the people to plant both feet firmly and expand their elbows into any opening that may occur for, unless this is done, others will close the opening." [8]

Although the United States had "opened" Japan, it was Russia that for decades had been pressing down from the north. By the Aigun and Peking treaties of 1858 and 1860, respectively, Russia had obtained from China all the land north of the Amur River and the Pacific Coast territories south to the Korean border, including the magnificent harbor of Vladivostok. Next the Russians had occupied Manchuria in 1859, northern Sakhalin in 1870 and in the 1890s had built the Trans-Siberian Railway. To counter the Russian advance the Japanese turned first to Korea, where China had vague suzerainty rights. As noted in Chapter 15, Section III, the Sino-Japanese War (1894–95) and the Shimonoseki Treaty (1895) enabled Japan to acquire Formosa, the Pescadores and the Liaotung Peninsula, as well as a huge war indemnity of 360 million yen. Since Japan had spent 200 million yen on the war, she was able to use the surplus to convert from the silver to the gold standard, which facilitated the floating of foreign loans.

Japan was not allowed to keep the strategic Liaotung Peninsula, being compelled by the Russian-German-French triplice to return it to China. Worse still, from Japan's viewpoint, the European powers now took advantage of China's demonstrated weakness to acquire strategic footholds on the mainland opposite Japan. Britain took the "New Territories" in 1899, Germany got control of the Shantung Peninsula and France of Yunnan Province. Russia obtained a twenty-five-year lease of the Liaotung Peninsula in 1898, and two years later occupied the entire province of Manchuria during the Boxer Rebellion. At the same time the Korean King was resisting Japanese efforts to gain control of his country, going so far as to replace his Japanese advisers with Russians, and to grant a timber-cutting concession to a Russian company.

These Russian advances engendered warm debates among the ruling group in Tokyo. Some favored trying to reach an accord with Russia that would be based on a division of the spoils. Others preferred an alliance with Great Britain as the country with which Japan most nearly had common cause. With such an alliance to back her up, Japan would then be able to stand up to Russian expansionism.

Feelers were sent out to both the British and the Russian capitals, and it was soon evident that London was as receptive as St. Petersburg was intractable. The old policy of splendid isolation had by this time lost its splendor for the British. Confronted by a rising Germany and an aggressive Russia, they welcomed an ally in the Far East that could serve as a check on Russia. On January 30, 1902, the Anglo-Japanese alliance was signed, providing for the independence of China and Korea, and recognizing Britain's special interests in central China and Japan's special interests in Korea. If either Japan or Britain became involved in war with a third power, the other party would remain neutral, but if another power intervened, then the other party was bound to aid its ally. Since Russia and France had been allied for the past eight years, the Anglo-Japanese alliance obviously was designed to keep France from aiding Russia in the event of war.

Japan was now in a position to force the issue with Russia. In mid-1903 Japan offered to recognize Russia's primacy in Manchuria if Russia would reciprocate concerning Japan's position in Korea. The negotiations dragged on, with the overconfident Russians temporizing and evading. The Japanese concluded, with good reason, that the Russians were not negotiating in good faith, and severed diplomatic relations on February 6, 1904. Two days later, without an ultimatum or declaration of war, the Japanese attacked the Russian base at Port Arthur on the Liaotung Peninsula.

In the campaigns that followed, the Japanese David consistently defeated the Russian Goliath. The single-track Trans-Siberian Railway proved quite inadequate to meet the supply needs of Russian armies fighting several thousand miles distant from their industrial centers in European Russia. In the first stage of the war, the Japanese surrounded Port Arthur and, after a siege of 148 days, captured the fortress on December 19, 1904. The second stage consisted of a series of battles on the plains of Manchuria. The Japanese were victorious here also, driving the Russians north of Mukden. These campaigns, however, were not decisive, because the Russian armies remained intact, and were reinforced and strengthened as communications improved. But on the sea the Japanese won an overwhelming triumph that led to the beginning of peace negotiations. With incredible shortsightedness the Russians dispatched their hastily refitted Baltic fleet to sail down the entire length of Europe and Africa, around the Cape of Good Hope and then across the Indian Ocean and north along the East Asia coast to Japan—a distance equivalent to more than two thirds the circumference of the globe. On May 27, 1905, the Russian fleet finally arrived at Tsushima Strait between Japan and Korea. At once it was attacked by a Japanese fleet superior in both numbers and efficiency. Within a few hours virtually all the Russian units had been sunk or captured, while the Japanese lost merely a few destroyers.

With this debacle the Russians were ready to discuss peace, especially since the war was very unpopular at home and the 1905 Revolution had started. The Japanese also wanted peace negotiations because, although they had won the victories, their still-meager resources had been strained by the burden of the war. On September 5, 1905, the Treaty of Portsmouth was signed, by which Russia acknowledged Japan's "paramount political, military and economic interests" in Korea, surrendered all preferential or exclusive concessions in Manchuria and ceded to Japan the southern half of Sakhalin Island and the lease of the Liaotung Peninsula.

The stunning defeat of Russia established Japan as a major world power and altered the balance of forces in the Far East. More significant is the fact that an Asian state had defeated a European state, and a great empire at that. A thrill of hope ran through the nonwhite races of the globe. The Russo-Japanese War was the prelude to the great awakening of the non-European peoples that today is convulsing the entire globe.

VI. Significance of the Japanese Exception

During the half century after the Meiji Restoration, Japan entered the world market economy. This is evident in the dramatic increase between 1868 and 1908 of Japanese exports from 15.5 million yen to 378.2 million yen, and of Japanese imports from 10.7 million yen to 595.7 million yen. Such increase in foreign trade after incorporation in the world market economy was not unique with Japan. But what *was* unique was the nature of the incorporation—the fact that after the first few years of initial shock and disruption, Japan was able to proceed systematically to abolish the unequal treaties and to conduct her foreign trade with the view to promoting independent economic development. If Japan had followed the customary route to Third World status, she would have exported a few raw materials such as coal, tea, marine products and raw silk, and received in return luxury items for her upper class and cheap consumer goods for her masses. This would have led to economic growth but not to economic development. It would have meant a permanent state of dependence and of consequent exploitation.

The historic significance of Japan's achievement is pointed up by the warning given in 1892 by Herbert Spencer to his friend Baron Kaneko Kentario, then ambassador to the United States:

Respecting the further question you ask, let me, in the first place, answer generally that Japanese policy should, I think, be that of keeping Americans and Europeans as much as possible at arm's length. In presence of more powerful races your position is one of chronic danger, and you should take every precaution to give as little foothold as possible to foreigners. It seems to me the only forms of intercourse which you may with advantage permit are those which are indispensable for the exchange of commodities—importation and exportation of physical and mental products. No further privileges should be allowed to people of other races than is absolutely needful for the achievement of these ends. Apparently you are proposing by revision of the treaty with the powers of Europe and America to open the whole Empire to foreigners and foreign capital. I regret this as a fatal policy. If you wish to see what is likely to happen, study the history of India.[9]

The validity of Spencer's advice soon was borne out by history. Japan did keep the Westerners "at arm's length," and the end result was an economic independence that contrasted dramatically with India's typical Third World plight, as Spencer had foreseen. In 1913 almost two thirds of Japan's imports consisted of raw materials (49 percent) and half-finished goods (17 percent), while imports of finished goods amounted to only 17 percent of the total. Thus Japan's industries were capable even before World War I of processing the major part of the goods she imported. Indian imports of raw materials and half-finished goods, on the other hand, amounted to less than 6 percent of the total in 1913, while finished goods accounted for no less than 80 percent of the total. Likewise as regards exports, half-finished goods in Japan amounted to 52 percent of the total in 1913, finished goods 29 percent while raw materials represented only 8 percent of the total. India's exports, by contrast, comprised in the same year nearly 50 percent raw materials and only 23 percent of finished goods. The same pattern is discernible if the per-capita industrial production of Japan and India are compared. During the period 1896–1900 per-capita industrial production in Japan was less than four times bigger than in India ($5.70 vs. $1.50), but in 1936–38 Japan's production was more than thirteen times greater ($65 vs. $4.90).

The gap between India and Japan has persisted and widened because of the failure of India, both after the winning of political independence as well as before, to achieve "arm's length" relationship with the developed nations. Japan, on the other hand, due to the combination of factors noted above—fortuitous circumstances, cultural traditions, preceding centuries of isolation, exceptionally capable leadership, social tensions that invited drastic though not radical reorganization, and opportunities for imperialist expansion that stimulated economic development—was able to follow Spencer's advice to give "as little foothold as possible to foreigners." This was the basic reason why Japan was able to achieve what so many other non-Western countries had desired in the nineteenth century but failed to achieve.

The mere listing of the factors that made possible the "Japanese exception" underscores why the Japanese model is irrelevant to Third World countries today. They have experienced not centuries of isolation, but periods of colonial rule and neocolonial exploitation. They obviously have no opportunities for imperialist expansion. And the task of developing their own industries for their own national needs is infinitely more difficult in the present era when technology has become enormously more complex and expensive, when Western trade unionists fiercely oppose cheap manufactured imports and when the opposition of multinational corporations backed by trilateral commissions and Bilderberg groups is incalculably greater than anything encountered by the Japanese a century ago.

Chapter 18

BEGINNINGS OF THIRD WORLD RESISTANCE—TO 1914

The old century is very nearly out, and leaves the world in a pretty pass. . . . The whole white race is revelling openly in violence, as though it had never pretended to be Christian. God's equal curse on them all! So ends the famous nineteenth century into which we were so proud to have been born.

W. C. Blunt, December 22, 1900
(English diplomat and writer)

. . . All powers, all profits are in the hands of the masters with the blue eyes, the red barbarians. And we, the yellow race, are subjected by force to demoralization, to complete degradation. . . . This is the reason why we have formed an organization. . . . At the present time there are about six hundred students from Indochina in Japan. Our only aim is to prepare the population for the future. . . . Have you created any organization for this purpose in your region?

Appeal of Annamite student (December 1905)

The nineteenth century was the era of worldwide Western hegemony. Viewed from another angle of vision, it was the era when the Third World had become a global system. By the end of the century this division of the globe into rulers and ruled, into exploiters and exploited, appeared to be an unassailable and eternal arrangement. Many Third World peoples were convinced that this was the case. In India they addressed their European masters as "sahib," in the Middle East as "effendi," in Africa as "bwana," and in Latin America as "patron." Under these circumstances it is scarcely surprising that Europeans assumed the innate superiority of their civilization and of their "race." Apart from a few mavericks such as W. C. Blunt, they were convinced that their worldwide empires were the harbingers of civilization, with beneficial results for all mankind.

Western businessmen at the turn of the century looked forward with quiet confidence to new fields to conquer. Cecil Rhodes was only the most exuberant when, ahead of his time, he dreamed of conquests in outer space: "The world is nearly parcelled out, and what there is left of it is being divided up, conquered, and colonized. To think of these stars that you see overhead at night, these vast worlds which we can never reach. I would annex the planets if I could; I often think of that. It makes me sad to see them so clear and yet so far." [1] An academician, Professor W. R. Shepherd, more realistically voiced the generally shared views of the business community when he declared in 1915:

> In the world today there are just two great fallow areas that apparently call for exploitation. Whether the people who inhabit them are altogether pleased at the thought of being exploited for the benefit of the foreigner is quite another matter. I am afraid that, in questions of business, it isn't always possible to consult the wishes of those who are actually on the soil. The world at large has progressed to its present material position mainly through the utilization of regions held by people who were unable of themselves to develop their resources. . . . The two areas to which I refer are South America and China. In . . . respect of possessing immense natural resources which have not been developed in any commensurate degree, they are quite alike.[2]

In addition to South America and China, two other "great fallow areas" attracted contemporary businessmen: Russia and Africa. Over and over again these four regions—South America, China, Russia and Africa—were held forth as promising regions for future trade and investment.

Contrary to these confident expectations, the "fallow" regions became the centers of great upheavals that convulsed the entire globe. The revolutionary process was well under way before the First World War. It began as far back as the eighteenth century with the black slave up-risings in the Americas, where overseas exploitation began the earliest and was the most brutal. As Western imperialism extended its control over Eurasia, resistance movements became correspondingly widespread, emerging in South and East Asia, the Middle East and Africa.

These early upheavals were not truly revolutionary movements. Their leaders did not seek to restructure class relationships or to subvert the global market economy. Rather they were either conservative traditionalists hankering to return to "the good old days," or else conformist Westernizers trying to resist the West by imitating it. This is not to say that before 1914 the resistance to Western domination was negligible. In fact it was much more widespread and resolute than is generally realized. But it did not represent a revolutionary challenge to the prevailing world capitalist order. Such a challenge had to wait for World War I with its accompanying Russian Revolution, and World II with its accompanying Chinese Revolution.

I. Black Resistance in the Americas

Armed resistance by black slaves against white masters in the New World occurred in the plantation regions. As noted above (Chapter 9, Section IV) the degree of exploitation varied according to the extent of the market available for the export product. If the market was expanding, then both Latin American and Anglo-American landowners permitted nothing to stand in the way of maximizing production and profits. John Newton, the master of a slave vessel, was told by a planter in Antigua in 1751 that it was cheaper to work slaves to death: "by little relaxation, hard fare and hard usage to wear them out before they became useless, and unable to do service; and then to buy new ones, to fill up their places." [3]

Such ruthless exploitation spawned many slave uprisings. Their frequency varied greatly from region to region, depending on the degree to which the objective conditions offered promise for success. Revolts therefore were more likely in areas such as the West Indies, where the slaves were a large majority, than in regions such as the Old South, where they were a minority in all but a few localities. Revolts also were more likely in the Caribbean, where the plantations averaged one hundred to two hundred slaves, than in the United States, where they averaged only twenty. Conversely, uprisings were less frequent where the ruling white elite was united, as in the Old South, than in the West Indies, where it was divided by local issues as well as by wars among the slaveholding powers.

In addition to the frequency of revolts, there was a difference also in their objectives. The earlier ones were directed not against slavery as a system but against particularly severe injustices within that system. This was true also of wars waged by maroons or runaway slaves, who sought to withdraw from slave society by resurrecting archaic African social orders in inaccessible regions. By the end of the eighteenth century, rebel slaves were turning against slavery as a social system. The outstanding example was the great Toussaint L'Ouverture of Saint Domingue, who headed the first successful slave revolt in history and created an independent black state. Toussaint's achievement was due partly to his extraordinary talents, but also to what Eugene Genovese defines as "the conjuncture of ideal preconditions for slave revolt." [4]

One of these favorable "preconditions" was the complex class conflict within Saint Domingue, which Toussaint ably exploited. The bureaucrats from Paris were opposed by the *colons* or white planters, who wanted more self-government and relief from trade restrictions. The colons, in turn, were resented by the free people of color (Negroes and mulattoes) who could conduct any business, such as the buying and selling of property, including slaves. Profiting from this opportunity, the free coloreds had prospered, owning one third of the landed property of the island by 1789. They were dissatisfied, however, because they were socially excluded by the colons, and also denied access to all official posts, to some professions and to the ranks of the nobility. The demand of the free colored for equal rights was resisted most vehemently by the poor whites, whose only asset was their privileged racial status in an overwhelmingly black island. Finally, the great majority of the population consisted of black slaves who wanted freedom, but who were opposed by the local colons and poor whites, as well as by vested interests in France dependent on the sugar trade.

The outbreak of the French Revolution brought these conflicts to a head. Despite the efforts of the abolitionist *Société des Amis des Noirs*, the National Assembly refused to sacrifice commercial prosperity to principle and voted for continuing both the slave trade and slavery. But in Saint Domingue the slaves and the free coloreds, inspired by the revolutionary rhetoric in Paris, took up arms to implement the principles of liberty, equality and fraternity. A black slave, Toussaint L'Ouverture, quickly rose by virtue of his intelligence and organizational abilities to the leadership of the insurrection. French troops arrived in Saint Domingue at the same time that news reached the island that the monarchy had been replaced by a republic. The white planters split into warring monarchical and republican factions. The Spaniards, on their part of the island, seized the opportunity to offer the slaves an alliance against the French. Toussaint accepted the offer and won control of the northern regions. Fearing that they would lose everything, the colons stopped fighting among themselves and offered the island to the British. The latter promptly sent an army, so that the French government was confronted with an alliance of the Spaniards and the slaves, and one between the colons and the British.

By this time the radical Robespierre had risen to power in Paris and had decreed in February 1794 the abolition of slavery in all French colonies. Toussaint responded by joining the French against both the Spaniards and the British. His black soldiers went into battle dressed in the colors of the republic and singing the "Marseillaise." By May 1800 Toussaint was the master of the entire island. But the new French leader, Napoleon Bonaparte, refused to accept the *de facto* independence of Saint Domingue. He sent an army to recover the rebellious colony, but Toussaint fought it to a standstill. The French signed an armistice with full amnesty for all blacks and no change in the new status of the former slaves. Toussaint trusted the French guarantee and laid down his arms. His faith proved his undoing. He was taken prisoner and sent to France, where on April 7, 1803, he died in an Alpine prison.

With the "first of the blacks" out of the way, Napoleon sent additional expeditionary forces to solidify his control over the island and to rebuild France's colonial empire. Under new leaders, the Saint Domingue blacks resisted desperately. Battle casualties and yellow fever decimated the French army. In November 1803 the few French survivors sailed for home. After thirteen years' struggle, Saint Domingue belonged to the blacks. On New Year's Day 1804, they renamed their part of the island Haiti, after the Carib term for mountain.

The only successful slave revolt in history had repercussions far beyond the Caribbean. It strengthened enormously the antislavery movement in England. It inflicted one hundred thousand casualties on the British, decisively weakening them in their war against revolutionary France. A British military historian, Sir John Fortescue, has observed that the secret of Britain's failure to crush the French Revolution "may be said to lie in the fatal words, Saint Domingue." [5] These words also spelled the end of Napoleon's dream of an American empire, forcing him to sell Louisiana, which doubled the area of the United States. And in the latter country, the slaveholders feared the spread of the revolutionary Saint Domingue example, an apprehension that contributed substantially to their decision to close the African slave trade.

Eloquent testimony to the significance of revolutionary Haiti was the hostility that it induced in the other American republic—the United States. It would appear that a new independent nation in the New World would have been welcomed in Washington. But Haiti was a republic with a difference. It was a black republic of former slaves surrounded by slave societies. The very existence of Haiti constituted a threat to those societies. Although Britain recognized Haiti in 1825, and France likewise in 1838, the United States refused to follow suit. The reason, as Thomas Pinckney of South Carolina stated bluntly, was fear that recognition of Haiti would incite subversive notions among the slaves in the United States. Thus Washington not only withheld recognition, but also tried to starve the new sister republic. On February

28, 1806, President Jefferson signed a bill prohibiting all trade with Haiti. The parallel with the later American embargo against Cuba is obvious. The first embargo sought to destroy the threatening example of a free black republic; the second to subvert the equally threatening example of a socialist republic.

❧ II. Conservative Reactions in Asia

As Western capitalism penetrated Asia, it stimulated protective reactions. These tended to be of a conservative nature, reflecting the powerful influence of millennia-old civilizations. Hence the tendency to try to "go back to the good old days," which never remotely approached the romanticized ideal. There were many cases during the nineteenth century of this conservative escapism, classic examples being the Indian Mutiny in 1857–58, the Boxer Rebellion in 1900, and the Korean resistance of 1906–10.

The Indian Mutiny, as noted in Chapter 12, Section II, was started by discontented *sepoys* and supported by conservative elements that were disturbed by British modernization measures. The Boxer Rebellion was very similar, being an uprising of Chinese antiforeign secret societies encouraged behind the scenes by reactionary Court officials and provincial governors. Preceding the Boxer Rebellion was the humiliating defeat of China by Japan in 1895. This disaster enabled Chinese reformers to gain the ear of the young Emperor Kuang-hsü, and to launch in 1898 a series of reform decrees known collectively as the Hundred Days' Reform. The Empress dowager was adamantly opposed, and with the backing of the conservative bureaucracy she deposed the Emperor and rescinded all the reform decrees. The collapse of the reform program encouraged the conservatives to channel social and political discontent against foreigners. Antiforeign secret societies, incited by Court circles and provincial governors, organized local militias to combat Western influences. Chief among these societies was the I Ho T'uan or Righteous Harmony Fists, popularly termed Boxers.

The Boxers began to attack foreigners and their Chinese Christian converts, especially in North China, where they killed a considerable number. European naval detachments were landed at Tientsin, whereupon the Boxers declared war on all foreigners and besieged the foreign legations in Peking. Within two months the international forces relieved the legations, and the imperial Court fled from the capital. Once more China was forced to sign an "unequal treaty," including further commercial concessions and heavy financial indemnities. The Boxer Rebellion, like all other escapist conservative reactions to Western intrusion, had failed ignominiously.

Equally futile, and for the same basic reason, was the Korean resistance to Japanese aggression. Korea, like China and Japan, initially reacted to the West by a seclusion policy so rigid that Korea came to be known as the Hermit Kingdom. But the Koreans, lacking both the resources of the Chinese and the modernization capabilities of the Japanese, were doomed to subjection. The pressures came from Russia, which had occupied the neighboring Chinese province of Manchuria during the Boxer disturbances, and from Japan, which planned to occupy Korea as a countermeasure against Russian expansionism and as a first step in a program of continental conquest.

In July 1903 the Japanese proposed to the Russians that they recognize Japan's "preponderant interests" in Korea, and in return Japan would recognize Russia's "special interests in railway enterprises in Manchuria." Russia's refusal of this offer led to the Russo-Japanese War of 1904 and the Portsmouth Treaty of 1905, which, *inter alia*, recognized Japan's "paramount political, military and economic interests" in Korea. The Japanese quickly exploited this gain by appointing Ito Hirobumi in February 1906 as resident-general in Korea, with power to control both the internal affairs and international relations of the country. He began by abolishing all foreign diplomatic agencies, so that the British, American, Chinese, German, French and Belgian ministers left Seoul in March 1906. Korea had, in fact, become a part of Japan. The readiness of the Great Powers to accept Japanese predominance is not as surprising as it might seem. President Theodore Roosevelt had made a bargain with the Japanese as early as July 1905 by which he supported a Japanese protectorate in Korea in return for Japanese acceptance of American control over the Philippines. This arrangement was reaffirmed by the Root-Takahira Agreement of November 30, 1908, which approved the maintenance of "the existing status quo" in Asia and pledged respect for each other's territorial possessions.

The Koreans did not accept Japanese rule passively. In June 1907 the Korean Emperor sent a secret envoy to the Meeting for International Peace at The Hague in Holland. The envoy disclosed the sufferings of the Koreans under the Japanese and pleaded for international pressure against the Japanese occupation. Despite the idealistic rationale of the conference, no international support materialized for the Koreans. Instead the Japanese used the incident as a pretext to disband the Korean army and to force the Korean Emperor to abdicate. Finally in August 1910 the Japanese formally annexed Korea. Not until August 1945 was Korea to exist again as a nation.

Some Koreans believed that the only practical course under the circumstances was to accept Japanese authority without resistance. They organized the Ilchinhoe Society, which gained over one million members, and which entrusted the future of the Korean nation to the benevolence of the Japanese Emperor. The society attracted the support of ambitious political figures who hoped to win the favors of the Japanese, and also of many peasants who were politically inert and who therefore accepted obedience as prudent behavior.

Many Koreans, however, were unhappy over the Japanese domination of their country and expressed their opposition through three main groups. The least effective consisted of former officials who refused to humble themselves before the Japanese and who wanted Korea restored to independence under its Yi Dynasty. Somewhat more effective were Western-educated intellectuals who had founded in the 1890s the Independence Club. It popularized ideas of liberty, civil rights and independence from foreign economic and political control. The intellectuals published periodicals and newspapers espousing these concepts, and continued to do so under Japanese rule for as long as they were allowed. After the Japanese clamped down on these hostile publications, similar ones were put out by the Koreans in Vladivostok, Hawaii and the United States.

The most serious opposition came from the soldiers of the Korean army, which the Japanese had disbanded. The unemployed soldiers refused to submit to the Japanese, either for patriotic reasons or because resistance offered the only means for livelihood, since support was provided by Korean sympathizers. The soldiers organized the Righteous Army, which operated in mountain areas and also in the villages, where the insurgents disguised themselves as peasants. They attacked in bands of one hundred to one thousand, and retreated to the mountains after each operation. The Japanese retaliated by burning entire villages suspected of harboring rebels but the indiscriminate repression swelled the ranks of the resistance. According to the Japanese statistics in the table on page 375, the number of engagements and of insurgents involved reached substantial proportions by 1908.

The rapid decline of the Korean resistance after 1908 is to be explained by its failure to develop beyond the concept of restoring traditional rule by the Emperor and the literati class. It is not surprising that so many peasants joined the collaborationist Ilchinhoe Society. Only the intellectuals of the Independence Club had a broader vision, but there was no contact between them and the soldiers fighting in the mountains. Revolutionary doctrine and organization were lacking, and therefore prolonged struggle against the Japanese was impossible. In Korea, as in India and China, conservative reaction proved inherently incapable of mobilizing the mass resistance necessary to counter imperialist aggression, whether of the Western or the Japanese variety.

Collisions Between Japanese Forces and Korean Insurgents, 1907–11

Period	Times	Number of Insurgents
1907 (Aug.–Dec.)	323	44,116
1908	1,451	69,832
1909	898	25,763
1910	147	1,891
1911 (Jan.–June)	33	216
TOTAL	2,852	141,815

Source: Headquarters, Japanese Garrison Army in Korea, *Bōta tōbatsushi* [Record of Subjugation of Insurgents] (Seoul, 1913), Appendix, table 2. Cited by Chong-Sik Lee, *The Politics of Korean Nationalism* (Berkeley: University of California Press, 1963), p. 81.

III. Resistance in Cuba and the Philippines

Two other notable failures of Third World resistance movements at the turn of the century occurred in Cuba and the Philippines. The reason was not conservative traditionalism, for Cuba and the Philippines were spared the incubus of ancient and glorious pasts that hobbled India, China and Korea. Rather the failure in these cases stemmed from the hopeless odds facing Cuban and Filipino nationalists when they tried to resist both Spanish and American imperialism.

The ensuing hostilities are commonly referred to as the Spanish-American War. This designation is historically inaccurate and misleading. It obscures the remarkable national liberation struggles of the Cuban and Filipino peoples. There were actually two separate wars in Cuba and the Philippines, and each of these wars went through two phases because of American interventionism. Thus the original Spanish-Cuban War became the Spanish-Cuban-American War, and likewise the Spanish-Philippine War became the Spanish-Philippine-American War. The background and course of the hostilities make clear the need for this renaming.

In the case of the Philippines, Spain always had difficulty in pacifying the archipelago during the more than three centuries of its rule. Almost annual revolts broke out against *corvée* labor, commercial monopolies, excessive land rent, landgrabbing and imposition of the Catholic faith. These revolts, however, invariably failed because the fragmented, insular nature of the country and the separate regional ethnic and religious groupings prevented a coordinated national struggle. In the late nineteenth century the rise of a native moneyed class, consisting mainly of

Chinese-native (or Indio) mestizo elements, engendered a liberal reformist movement striving for political and economic concessions from Spain. This Propaganda Movement, as it came to be called, was not revolutionary. Its adherents sought a more favorable status within the Spanish colonial structure.

The failure of the Propagandists against entrenched Spanish authority led to the formation in 1892 of a secret society, the Katipunan. After some indecision it recognized the futility of the earlier reformist efforts and took a revolutionary course. The concurrent revolutionary struggle in Cuba hampered Spanish repression efforts, so that by 1896 some thirty thousand Katipunan fighters were in the field. The founder of Katipunan was an artisan, Andres Bonifacio, but in March 1897 he was replaced by a landowner, Emilio Aguinaldo. By November 1897 the basis for a Philippine Republic was laid with the adoption of a Provisional Constitution. This prompted the Spanish authorities to open negotiations, during which wealthy Filipinos who had opposed the revolution persuaded Aguinaldo to accept a compromise settlement. The Spaniards promised to consider the Katipunan demands in exchange for the surrender of the rebel army, and Aguinaldo went to exile in Hong Kong after having been paid four hundred thousand pesos.

This arrangement did not end the fighting, for the Spaniards did not follow up with reforms, while militant Katipunan leaders refused to lay down their arms until independence had been won. So successful were the revolutionaries that they soon won full control of the islands, with the exception of the capital city of Manila, where the Spaniards were surrounded. On December 14, 1897, the American consul in Manila reported: ". . . there is no peace . . . battles are practically daily occurrences, ambulances bring in many wounded, and hospitals are full. Prisoners are brought here and shot without trial. . . . The Crown forces have not been able to dislodge a rebel army within 10 miles of Manila." [6] Equally revealing is the analysis made on May 14, 1898, by the German Secretary of State, Bernhard von Bulow: "It may be quite true that the Spanish regime in its present form cannot be maintained in the Philippines. The question is whether the archipelago will be taken over by a single power or under foreign protection. . . . Should the Americans or the English try it, they may have some unpleasant surprises, such as the French experienced in Mexico or the Italians in Eritrea." [7]

Von Bulow's premonitions were soon borne out. The Americans experienced many "unpleasant surprises" after Commodore George Dewey steamed into Manila Bay in May 1898. He had arranged for Aguinaldo to be brought back from Hong Kong to lead the Filipinos against the Spaniards. At the same time the Secretary of the Navy, John D. Long, wired Dewey not to have "political alliances with the insurgents . . . that would incur liability to maintain their cause in the future." Likewise President McKinley issued orders to General Wesley Merritt, in command of the land forces, to maintain "law and order" and to ensure that "the powers of the military occupant are absolute and supreme and immediately operate upon the political conditions of the inhabitants." [8] These were instructions to an army of occupation rather than of liberation.

The Filipino leaders correctly appraised American motives because their efforts to obtain assurances for postwar independence were invariably evaded. Nevertheless, they decided to cooperate with the Americans in order to obtain arms. At the same time Aguinaldo issued a Declaration of Independence (June 12, 1898) stating, "in the name and by the authority of the inhabitants of all these Philippine Islands, that they are and have a right to be free and independent. . . ." On June 23 a revolutionary government was established with Aguinaldo as President and with local as well as national administrative institutions. On August 1 a convention of 190 municipal presidents from 16 provinces ratified the Declaration of Independence. When the first American troops arrived on June 30 a national government, supported by the overwhelming majority of the population, was administering the Philippine Republic with the sole exception of the city of Manila. Indeed, the commanders of the newly arrived American troops had to request the Filipino army officers to evacuate some of their siege trenches surrounding Manila so that Americans could participate in the battle for the city! Thus the stage was set for the "unpleasant surprises" that were to transform the original Spanish-Philippine War into the Spanish-Philippine-American War.

Meanwhile, a similar confrontation between local nationalists and American interventionists was developing in Cuba. The island had emerged as the world's greatest producer of sugar following the destruction of the sugar economy of Saint Domingue (Haiti). The increase in sugar output involved a corresponding increase in the Negro population, so that by 1842 the official census reported a population of 448,291 whites, 152,838 free coloreds, and 436,495 Negro slaves. The whites in turn were divided into Creoles, who were born in the New World, and Peninsulares, who were born in Spain. The Creoles were mostly landowners and professional people, while the Peninsulares controlled commerce and administration. Because of the advantages they derived from Spanish rule, the Peninsulares supported the connection with Madrid, whereas the Creoles resented the restrictions on their political aspirations and on the marketing of their products. Independence movements were retarded by this split among the whites, as well as by the fear of a slave insurrection. The more the number of blacks increased, the more the whites accepted

Spanish military power as an indispensable protective shield.

In the 1860s Creole toleration of Spanish rule waned with the failure of a reform commission to produce any results, and with the imposition in 1867 of a new tax ranging from 6 to 12 percent on real estate, incomes, and all types of business. Coming on top of the traditionally heavy customs duties, and at a time of economic depression, the new tax brought to a head the long-standing grievances. This was especially true in Oriente, the eastern section of the island, where the smaller planters felt the burden of Spanish rule more sharply. It was in Oriente that the first War for Independence broke out, in October 1868. Although it raged for ten years, it finally failed for a variety of reasons, including dissension between black and white rebels, petty jealousies among their leaders, a chronic shortage of arms and supplies, and the refusal of the wealthy planters of the western section (Occidente) to lend their support.

The 1878 Treaty of Zanjon ending the revolt proved to be only a truce. Some revolutionaries fought on, and they gained new recruits with the abolition of slavery in Cuba in 1880. The tie with Madrid, which hitherto had been regarded as a necessary protection against slaves, now was no longer necessary. Many Cubans became attracted to the advantages of independence, especially the free trade with the rich American market only a few miles distant.

The outstanding leader of the revolutionary movement leading to the second War for Independence was José Martí, "the Apostle." A writer, poet and brilliant political organizer, he had been jailed during the first War for Independence. In 1880 he escaped to New York, and thereafter devoted himself to rousing Cuban emigrés to revolutionary action. On January 5, 1892, he organized the Cuban Revolutionary Party and recruited the two outstanding leaders of the first war, Máximo Gómez and Antonio Maceo. In April 1895, after careful preparations for a coordinated uprising, Martí landed in Cuba. From the beginning he made it clear that he wanted no outside aid, and especially none from Americans. He deeply suspected them because of their repeated official and unofficial statements that Cuba was destined for the same fate as Texas and California. "Once the United States is in Cuba," asked Martí, "who will get her out? . . . The Cuban war has broken out in time to prevent . . . the annexation of Cuba to the United States." [9]

The uprising began tragically, for Martí was killed on May 19 in his first encounter with the Spaniards. Gómez carried on as the military commander, with Maceo as his chief lieutenant. Madrid sent out General Martínez Campos, the victor of the first war, with forces that eventually totaled 240,000 regulars and 60,000 irregulars. The rebels, by contrast, never numbered more than 54,000, and were always short of arms and supplies. Yet they more than held their own, for Gómez and Maceo were masters of guerrilla tactics, with ten years of experience from the first war. They enjoyed the support of the peasants, who supplied them with food and with information on enemy fortifications and movements. The basic guerrilla strategy was the scorched earth—the burning of sugar cane crops and the destruction of buildings, machinery and transportation facilities. The objective was to end the profits from sugar and to bleed the Spanish treasury with military expenditures until the financial strain forced Madrid to give up Cuba.

The strategy proved successful. In an epochal campaign through Occidente to the western coast, Maceo in 90 days fought 27 battles and captured 22 towns from an enemy overwhelmingly superior in numbers and equipment. In January 1896 the Spanish government replaced General Campos with General Valeriano Weyler, who promptly issued his notorious reconcentration order. This required all rural inhabitants within 8 days to move with their cattle into fortified areas occupied by troops. Provisions for their support were hopelessly inadequate, so that the American consul in Havana estimated that half of the 400,000 *reconcentrados* perished from disease or starvation. Increased repression of an activized peasantry stimulated increased resistance.

The reconcentration policy left Weyler in control of only a few large cities. The rebels had such mastery of the countryside that in the summer of 1897 they were able to hold elections for a General Assembly. Meanwhile, the attrition strategy was taking its toll, with sugar production falling from 1,054,000 long tons in 1894 to 220,000 in 1896. By this time heavy fighting had broken out also in the Philippines. The drain of two wars so distant from the homeland proved too much for Spain's slender resources. A new Liberal Party government recalled Weyler and offered autonomy to the Cuban revolutionaries. General Gómez scornfully rejected it as "the final insult which comes to profane the decency and honor of the Cuban people." On March 1, 1898, the United States Department of State assessed the Cuban situation as follows: ". . . the Cubans continue to dominate the Eastern half of the island, and its columns are operating in the Western provinces without the Spaniards being able to stop them. [The autonomy proposal is] an utter and complete failure."

This appraisal indicates the fallacy of the common assumption that American intervention made Cuba's liberation possible. Rather it was the collapse of the autonomy plan and the reports of an imminent victory that prompted President McKinley to intervene before the victory materialized and made Cuba independent of the United States as well as of Spain. The United States ambassador in Madrid, Stewart L. Woodford, proposed the purchase of Cuba to the Queen Regent and Prime Minister Praxedes Sagasta, but the offer was rejected. With a financial settlement precluded, President McKinley prepared for intervention. Just as the Spanish-Philippine War had become the Spanish-Philippine-American War, so now the Spanish-Cuban War became the Spanish-Cuban-American War.

American intervention was facilitated by the fact that the United States had become by 1894 the first industrial power of the world. Its value of manufactured exports rose from $130.3 million in 1888 to $308 million in 1898. The manufacturers of products such as armaments, textiles, hardware and railway equipment now were quite interested in the accessibility of foreign markets, and therefore concerned about the great wave of imperialist landgrabbing in the late nineteenth century. Following the 1895 defeat of China by Japan, for example, Russia, Germany, Britain and France all acquired new bases and spheres of influence in the Far East. Three years later Senator Albert J. Beveridge delivered the classic statement of the imperialist ideology of his times:

> American factories are making more than the American people can use; American soil is producing more than they can consume. Fate has written our policy for us; the trade of the world must and shall be ours. And we will get it as our mother [England] has told us how. We will establish trading posts throughout the world as distributing points for American products. We will soon cover the ocean with our merchant marine. We will build a navy to the measure of our greatness. Great colonies governing themselves, flying our flag, and trading with us, will grow about our posts of trade. Our institutions will follow our flag on the wings of commerce. And American law, American order, American civilization, and the American flag will plant themselves on shores hitherto bloody and benighted, but by those agencies of God henceforth to be made beautiful and bright. . . . The Philippines are logically our first target.[10]

Fortunately for Beveridge and others of similar persuasion, the outbreak of insurrections against Spanish rule in Cuba and the Philippines provided them with an ideal opportunity to satisfy their aspirations. This was especially true of General Weyler's reconcentration strategy in Cuba, which created sentiment for American intervention in circles that were usually anti-imperialist, such as trade unions, churches and universities. This sentiment was inflamed by the "yellow press" of William R. Hearst (New York *Journal*) and Joseph Pulitzer (New York *World*). Weyler was described to American readers as a "butcher," "wolf," "mad dog" and "human hyena." For such readers the sinking of the battleship *Maine* in Havana Harbor underscored the guilt of Spain and the need to intervene. Although no proof was found of the responsibility for the explosion, the slogan of the Hearst press became, "Remember the *Maine*, to hell with Spain." Intervention now was demanded to avenge national honor as well as to rescue the long-suffering Cuban people.

Many American business leaders, especially in the East, opposed intervention in the early months of 1898 because they feared it would endanger currency stability and interrupt trade. But by mid-March such business giants as John Jacob Astor, William Rockefeller and J. P. Morgan declared themselves in favor of an aggressive policy in order to end quickly the unsettling state of suspense. With the support of most of the business community as well as of an inflamed public opinion, President McKinley delivered his war message to Congress on April 11, 1898. He requested authority "to take measures to secure a full and final termination of hostilities between the Government of Spain and the people of Cuba." But he explicitly rejected recognition "of the so-called government of Cuba" because in case of such recognition "our conduct would be subjected to the approval or disapproval of that government." McKinley made it clear that the United States alone was to determine the future of Cuba.

After the declaration of war, Cuban troops, according to Admiral William Samson, were of "great assistance" in the capture of Guantánamo. There also attacked Spanish units in the interior, so that American forces were able to land in Santiago without encountering a single Spaniard. Yet no Cuban was allowed to participate in the negotiations leading to the surrender of Santiago, and none was permitted to enter the city bearing arms. The final insult was an American order that Spanish civil authorities should remain in charge of all municipal offices. In Santiago, as in Manila, the exclusion of the revolutionaries was justified on the grounds that they might have indulged in an orgy of looting and reprisals against the Spaniards. A large number of Santiago citizens signed a petition to President McKinley protesting the exclusion of Cuban troops and the retention of Spanish laws and officials. No reply was received, since it was the President himself who had stipulated this line of conduct.

The same exclusion of Cubans from Cuban affairs was enforced when their General Calixto García ordered elections for mayors and councilmen in all cities and towns liberated by Cuban forces. On orders from President McKinley, American General William Shafter forbade such elections: "A dual government can't exist here; we have to have full sway of the Cubans." García later undermined the Cuban cause by accepting three million dollars to pay off the revolutionary forces, though many opposed such a settlement. With the subsequent dissolution of Martí's Cuban Revolutionary Party and of its local clubs, the resistance to American rule was effectively subverted.

Meanwhile, American policy in the Philippines had been identical to that in Cuba: There was no recognition of the existing Philippine Republic in order to have full control after the expulsion of the Spaniards. At the time of the capitulation of Manila, the Filipinos held seven miles of the siege lines and the Americans the remaining three-fourths mile. Yet the Filipinos were excluded from the surrender negotiations, and the terms agreed upon by Spain and the United States provided for the transfer of the city from the one power to the other, with no consideration of the wishes of its inhabitants. With the strategic capital city under its control, the United States now proceeded to build up its military power for the future confrontation with the nationalist forces.

In the light of these developments in Cuba and the Philippines, the terms of the Treaty of Paris (Dec. 18, 1898) were to be expected. In the negotiation of the terms the United States proposed the exclusion of the Cuban and Filipino representatives who had arrived in Paris. Spain took pleasure in exacting revenge on her former subjects by agreeing. In fact, the bankrupt and defeated Spaniards had no choice but to accept all the American demands. Thus they ceded Puerto Rico and the Philippines to the United States. Regarding Cuba, Spain was willing to accept independence or an American protectorate or annexation to the United States, but preferred the latter. The reason was that annexation would have relieved Spain of a Cuban debt of over four hundred million dollars.

The United States decided against annexation, partly because of the financial liability but also because it was feared that annexation would jeopardize ratification of the treaty by the Senate. The final arrangement provided that Spain should relinquish all claims to Cuba and that the United States should occupy the island and assume responsibility for protection of life and property during the occupation. The apprehension concerning ratification proved justified, for the treaty received only one more vote than the required two-thirds majority when it passed the Senate on February 6, 1899.

The United States encountered little serious opposition in consolidating its occupation of Cuba. The earlier disbandment of the guerrilla army and of the Cuban Revolutionary Party had emasculated the nationalists. Furthermore, General Leonard Wood, in command of the occupation forces, won some popular support by eradicating yellow fever, reforming the jail system, reorganizing municipal government, expanding educational programs and building roads, harbors, sewers and streets. Encouraged by the American occupation and by the construction of infrastructure facilities, United States investors quickly moved in. By the end of the occupation in 1902 they had gained control of 80 percent of mineral exports and 90 percent of cigar exports. They also bought up much agricultural land at bargain prices because the farmers had been ruined by the war devastation, and because General Wood refused to extend government assistance to small cultivators. The general further encouraged foreign investors by ruthlessly suppressing all efforts by Cuban labor to organize for higher wages and shorter working hours.

American domination of Cuba was institutionalized by the passage in 1901 of the Platt Amendment, authorizing United States military intervention under almost any circumstances, virtual United States control of Cuban diplomatic and fiscal matters and establishment of a major naval base at Guantánamo. A Cuban Constitutional Convention was persuaded to accept the amendment with the argument that acceptance was better than indefinite occupation, and with the bait of a reciprocity tariff on sugar and tobacco.

The inauguration on May 20, 1902, of Estrada Palma as the first President marked the birth of the Republic of Cuba. The United States had succeeded in imposing political and economic subservience behind a façade of independence.

Imperialist forces clamored that the Cuban model of neocolonialism should be reproduced in the Philippines. But it did not prove to be so easy in those islands, because the nationalists there still had weapons in hand. Fighting between Americans and Filipinos had started on February 4, 1899. The duration and character of the ensuing campaigns bring to mind the Vietnam War, of which it was a veritable dress rehearsal. At the outset the overwhelming superiority of American firepower and the willingness of the Filipinos to wage positional warfare made it a "quail shoot," as it was called by the American soldiers. The Filipinos soon learned to resort to hit-and-run tactics, in which they had the advantage because of their knowledge of the terrain and the support they enjoyed among the people. General Arthur MacArthur, father of Douglas, World War II U. S. Army commander in the Pacific, admitted that originally he had assumed "that Aguinaldo's troops represented only a fraction," but that he was "reluctantly compelled" to abandon this assumption because the "unique system of warfare" adopted by the Filipinos "depended upon almost complete unity of action of the entire native population." [11]

By April 1899 General William Shafter, who already had fought against guerrillas in Cuba, gave an ominous portent of the future conduct of the war: "It may be necessary to kill half the Filipinos in order that the remaining half of the population may be advanced to a higher plane of life than their present semi-barbarous state affords." [12]

The more the Americans pursued the guerrillas, the more the fighting spread to other islands, where the Americans encountered the same harassment and public hostility. The exasperated American soldiers resorted to the usual tactics of a regular army floundering in such a quagmire. They burned villages, killed noncombatants, tortured peasants to extract information, and indulged in unrestrained racism against "bar-barians," "savages," "niggers," and "goo-goos."

The spreading warfare was embarrassing for President McKinley, who faced an election in November 1900, so he sent a federal judge, William Howard Taft, to Manila with instructions to establish a "civilian" gov-ernment by September 1, 1900. The obvious purpose was to persuade American voters that all was progressing smoothly in the Philippines. Taft pieced together a government consisting of mestizo landlords and merchants who were attracted by the promise of preference for their agricultural exports in the rich United States market. Having created puppets, it now was argued that those who "loyally sided with the Americans" must be protected against the *ladrones* or bandits. The Democratic presidential candidate, William Jennings Bryan, tried to make colonialism a major issue in the campaign but the public did not respond. The heavy press censorship; the timely establishment of a civilian government; and the lack of television coverage, which played so vital a role during the Vietnam War, all combined to prevent serious debate over what was going on in the Philippines.

McKinley won an easy victory, and with the election hurdle overcome, the "pacification" of the Philippines was pursued relentlessly. In the notorious Samar campaign, General Jacob Smith ordered his men to kill "everything over ten," and to turn Samar into a "howling wilderness," so that "even the birds could not live there." The general henceforth was known as "Howlin' Jake Smith." Peasants were forced into detention camps similar to Weyler's reconcentrados in Cuba. As American com-manders rediscovered several decades later in Vietnam, there was no alternative to the Samar or to the My Lai massacres when the orders were to subjugate a politicized peasantry.

In April 1901 Aguinaldo finally was captured. The Americans assumed the war was practically over, especially after they persuaded him to sign an oath of allegiance and a proclamation calling on his comrades to give up the struggle. President Theodore Roosevelt proclaimed the war to be over on July 4, 1902, amid playing bands and soldiers marching in parade. Still, many Filipinos refused to give up after 3½ years of re-sistance against desperate odds. In March 1903 guerrilla attacks reached the point where detention camps were filled with more peasants than ever before.

New resistance leaders emerged from the rank and file, mostly of lower-class origin, in contrast to the middle-class background of the earlier leaders. Fighting raged on, and news of Japanese victories over the Russians boosted Filipino morale. Cheap color prints of little brown men slaying big white men filtered into the most remote corners of the Philippines. Not until 1906 did most of the Filipino leaders surrender.

Even then, sporadic resistance continued to flare up, especially in Muslim Mindanao, where skirmishes were reported as late as 1916.

After so much bloodshed and suffering, the people of the Philippines did not succeed in their bid for independence. In the light of later resistance movements the reasons for failure are clear. Being pioneer Third World insurrectionists, they understandably lacked revolutionary theory regarding the nature of imperialism, the class factor in their own resistance, and the strategy of guerrilla warfare. Also, there were no socialist states or international revolutionary organizations at that time, so that the Filipinos received no outside aid, in contrast to the worldwide official and private aid given to the Vietnamese. Finally, the American Anti-Imperialist League did oppose the Philippine War, but for reasons noted above, it did not approach the effectiveness of the antiwar movement that contributed significantly to the retirement of President Lyndon Johnson.

At the time of the signing of the Treaty of Paris, a Wall Street banker, Senator Chauncey M. Depew, looked forward to the future with confidence. "The American people now produce $2,000,000,000 worth more than they can consume, and we have met the emergency and by the providence of God, by the statesmanship of William McKinley, and the valor of Roosevelt and his associates, we have our markets in Cuba, in Puerto Rico, in the Philippines, and we stand in the presence of 800,000,000 people, with the Pacific an American lake. . . . The world is ours. . . ." [13]

The euphoria was justified, at least for the foreseeable future. The neocolonialism institutionalized by the Platt Amendment worked so well in Cuba that the Jones Bill was passed in 1916 "to establish a qualified independent government for the Philippines and to fix the date when such qualified independence shall become absolute and complete." Independence was granted in 1946, but before and after that date neocolonialism functioned as effectively for American imperialism in the twentieth century as free-trade imperialism had for British imperialism in the nineteenth century.

✎ IV. Japanese Victory and Russian Revolution

The greatest impetus to Third World resistance in the early nineteenth century was provided by the inflammatory combination of Japanese victory over the Russian Empire, and the resulting Russian Revolution of 1905. The fateful chain reaction began when the Japanese proposed to the Russians in July 1903 mutual recognition of their respective interests in Korea and Manchuria. The Russian Finance Minister, Count Witte, favored acceptance because he was interested in economic penetration rather than political expansion with its dangers of war. But he was opposed by Russian adventurers with timber concessions in Korea, and by Russian military circles that wanted a base on Korea's coast. Also, certain Russian politicians, concerned by mounting domestic disturbances, favored a "little victorious war" to divert attention from internal problems. There was no doubt in their minds, or in those of the military, that Russia would win a war with Japan. In fact, they referred contemptuously to the Japanese as *makaki*, or "little monkeys," and they seriously debated whether one Russian soldier was worth one and a half, or two, Japanese soldiers.

This group of adventurers, militarists, and politicians had their way, so the Japanese offer was rejected. Tokyo responded promptly, being emboldened by an alliance with Britain that had been signed on January 30, 1902. The Japanese therefore attacked the Russian fleet at Port Arthur on February 8, 1904, without a formal declaration of war. As noted in Chapter 17, Section V, Japan surprised the world by defeating the great Russian Empire. The military debacle forced the Tsarist government to discuss peace, especially since the war was very unpopular at home and the 1905 Revolution had started. By the Treaty of Portsmouth (Sept. 5, 1905) Russia acknowledged Japan's "paramount political, military and economic interests" in Korea, surrendered all preferential or exclusive concessions in Manchuria and ceded to Japan the southern half of Sakhalin Island and the lease of the Liaotung Peninsula.

While the Russo-Japanese War was being fought in the Far East, revolution was spreading behind the lines within Russia. The basic cause is to be found in the chronic dissatisfaction of the peasants, the urban workers and the middle class. (See Chapter 16, Section IV.) This dissatisfaction was aggravated by the war with Japan, especially after the "little victorious war" became a humiliating defeat inflicted by a small Asian state. Finally, the "Bloody Sunday" of January 22, 1905, provided the spark that set off the first Russian Revolution.

On that fateful Sunday a crowd of several thousand unarmed men, women and children, headed by a priest, Father Georgi Gapon, marched peacefully toward the Winter Palace in St. Petersburg. Gapon was a concerned cleric who sought to alleviate the misery of the urban poor by peaceful reforms that he considered essential for the future of both the Crown and the Church. "I must state frankly," warned Gapon, "that if the Church does not identify itself with the people, the pastor soon will remain without a flock." [14]

In line with this reformist strategy, the St. Petersburg demonstration that Gapon headed was virtually a religious procession, with the marchers bearing ikons and chanting Church hymns. Their petition respectfully requested reforms such as a representative assembly, free education, an eight-hour working day and better working conditions. Had the Tsar or his representative received the petition and promised to give it careful consideration, the crowd almost certainly would have dispersed peacefully. Instead, the Tsar's uncle inexplicably ordered the Imperial Guard to fire. Between ninety-six and one thousand were killed, and two hundred to two thousand wounded, the discrepancy in the figures being due to the fact that some witnesses reported only the Sunday casualties, whereas the disturbances continued in the capital for another two days.

"Let's take vengeance on him [the Tsar] and on his entire family," exhorted Gapon on the evening of Bloody Sunday. "Vengeance on all his ministers and on all the exploiters of Russian soil. Go, pillage the imperial palaces." [15] Thus a reform-minded priest ironically sparked the great Revolution of 1905. Gapon was swept aside and forgotten amid the tumultuous events that came close to overthrowing the Tsarist autocracy. The elemental upheaval passed through two stages before the imperial government was able to reassert its authority.

The first, between January and October 1905, was the rising wave of revolution. All classes and interests came out against the autocracy: the subject nationalities demanded autonomy; the sailors of the Black Sea fleet mutinied and seized their ships; students everywhere walked out of their classrooms; peasants pillaged manor houses and seized estates; and workers staged strikes in the cities. In order to coordinate their activities, the workers began to elect councils, or soviets. The spontaneous soviet movement spread from workers to peasants in the countryside and to soldiers in the army. Before the 1905 Revolution was over, worker soviets had been elected in forty locations, soldier soviets in five, and combined worker-soldier soviets in two.

The world was witnessing the extraordinary spectacle of an entire nation on strike. Count Witte informed the Tsar that he must choose between two alternatives—a new constitutional regime, or a dictatorship to crush all opposition by force. When the military advised Tsar Nicholas that the armed forces could not be counted on to enforce repressive measures, he reluctantly accepted the constitutional course. So he issued the October Manifesto (October 30, 1905), which promised freedom of speech, press and assembly, and also granted Russia a constitution and an elective national assembly, or Duma.

During the second stage of the revolution, between October 1905 and January 1906, the uprising continued at high pitch, but the opposition no longer was united. The moderates, consisting of middle-class elements, accepted the October Manifesto, while the radicals, including the Social Democrats and the Social Revolutionaries, demanded that a constituent assembly rather than the Tsar's ministers prepare the new constitution. The radicals tried to have their way by organizing more strikes and disturbances, but the government now was strong enough to crack down. The ending of the war with Japan on September 5, 1905, had freed many troops, who were sent home to restore order. Equally important was a huge loan of 2.5 billion francs that Witte obtained on April 12, 1906, from French, English and Belgian banks.

The loan had been strongly opposed by liberal and radical circles in the West and by the opposition within Russia, which warned that the loan was illegal and would be repudiated at the first opportunity. But Witte got his way by bribing the Paris press to keep silent and by warning Western governments that revolution was a danger to them as well as to the Tsar. France provided most of the loan funds because it stood to lose a military ally as well as more billions of francs advanced earlier by private French investors as well as by the government. In a letter of April 15 the Tsar praised Witte for the loan, which represented "for the Government a great moral triumph and a pledge of Russia's undisturbed and peaceful development in the future." [16]

The commendation was amply justified. The lifting of financial pressures enabled the Tsarist government to crush a strike that had paralyzed Moscow between December 22, 1905, and January 1, 1906. With the end of the strike, and with sufficient funds for the Tsar's ministers to defy the forthcoming elective Dumas, the danger of revolution had passed.

Before 1906 *Almanach de Gotha*, the yearbook of European royalty, had classified Russia as an absolute monarchy; after 1906 the classification was changed to constitutional monarchy ruled by an autocrat. This reflected accurately the ambiguous outcome of the Revolution. Russia had a constitutional regime with its elective Duma, but the so-called Fundamental Laws issued on May 6, 1906, proclaimed the Tsar as autocrat, with full control over the executive, the armed forces and foreign policy. Workers were granted the right to organize and to strike, though in a peaceful manner. Peasants were relieved of the redemption payments and were allowed to buy and sell land allotments in the communes. The purpose of this innovation was to encourage the growth of a class of rich peasants who would serve as supporters of the Tsarist regime in the countryside. It was expected that within twenty years this desirable rural metamorphosis would have occurred, and the Tsar's position thereafter would be substantially strengthened. The two decades of grace, however, did not materialize, so that the end result proved to be not revivified Tsarism but the Bolshevik Revolution.

Although the effect of the 1905 Revolution within Russia was equivocal, it had a deep influence on much of the Third World, as did also the Russo-Japanese War. The latter demonstrated the possibility of overthrowing Western imperialism, whereas the Russian 1905 Revolution indicated that domestic autocracy could be challenged and a constitutional regime established. Since most Third World countries were saddled with both foreign imperialism and native despotism, the impact of the Japanese victory combined with revolution in Russia was profound and lasting.

Considering first the triumph of a small Asian kingdom over a giant European power, it understandably sent a tremor of hope and excitement throughout the colonial world. A British diplomat in Constantinople reported to his government at the time: "The success of Japan over Russia the traditional enemy of the Turk made every fibre of the latter's body tingle." [17] At the other end of Asia, Sun Yat-sen declared, "We regarded the Russian defeat by Japan as the defeat of the West by the East. We regarded the Japanese victory as our own victory." [18] Likewise Ba Maw, the Prime Minister of Burma during World War II, records in his memoirs the electrifying effect of Japan's success on his generation. He and his schoolmates all wanted to be the Japanese in their war games, and the British fostered this enthusiasm by distributing pro-Japanese pictures. Jawaharlal Nehru recalled similar experiences as a schoolboy in India: "Japanese victories stirred up my enthusiasm. . . . Nationalistic ideas filled my mind. I mused of Indian freedom. . . . I dreamed of brave deeds of how, sword in hand, I would fight for India and help in freeing her." [19]

Equally inflammatory for Third World peoples was the spectacle of the mighty Tsar almost toppled by the spontaneous uprising of the Russian masses. The effect was heightened by the common frontiers shared by the Russian Empire with several Asian countries, and by the ethnic groups that overlapped on both sides of those frontiers, with resulting interaction back and forth. Furthermore, considerable numbers of Persians, Chinese and Turks resided or studied or worked in Russia, where they picked up ideas from revolutionary student and worker organizations. Finally, the twenty million Muslim minority in the Russia of 1905 was generally disaffected. It participated in the 1905 Revolution and held three Muslim Congresses between 1905 and 1907 in order to promote Islamic culture and religion. This political and cultural ferment among Russia's Muslims had far-reaching repercussions on fellow Muslims beyond Russia's frontiers, especially in Persia and Turkey. A Britisher who was in Persia at the time sensed an undercurrent of aroused emotions and expectations in all the colonial lands. In a letter of August 1906 he wrote:

> It seems to me that a change must be coming over the East. The victory of Japan has, it would appear, had a remarkable influence all over the East. Even here in Persia it has not been without effect. . . . Moreover, the Russian Revolution has had a most astounding

effect here. Events in Russia have been watched with great attention, and a new spirit would seem to have come over the people. They are tired of their rulers, and, taking example of Russia, have come to think that it is possible to have another and better form of government . . . it almost seems that the East is stirring in its sleep. In China there is a marked movement against the foreigners, and a tendency towards the ideal of "China for the Chinese." In Persia, owing to its proximity to Russia, the awakening would appear to take the form of a movement towards democratic reform. In Egypt and North Africa it is signalized by a remarkable increase in fanaticism, coupled with the spread of the Pan-Islamic movement. The simultaneousness of these symptoms of unrest is too remarkable to be attributed solely to coincidence. Who knows? Perhaps the East is really awakening from its secular slumber, and we are about to witness the rising of these patient millions against the exploitation of an unscrupulous West.[20]

V. "The Strangling of Persia"

Persia was more affected by the 1905 Russian Revolution than any other country. One reason was the large number of long-standing contacts between Russians and Persians. A considerable number of Persian students were enrolled in Russian universities, where some of them inevitably were affected by radical student groups. Also, the centuries-old economic ties between the two countries involved numerous transactions between Russian and Persian merchants. Most important was the large number of Persian workers employed in the oil fields of Baku and Grozny, and also in the factories of Tiflis, Erivan, Vladikavkaz, Novorossiisk, Derbent and Temir-Khan-Shuro. According to official Russian statistics, sixty-two thousand workers crossed over from Persia in 1905 alone, apart from additional thousands who slipped across without passports in the manner of Mexican laborers crossing into the United States. By 1910 the number of Persian workers entering Russia reached almost two hundred thousand each year.

The other main reason for the great impact of the Russian Revolution was the extraordinary degree of corruption and obscurantism under the rule of Persia's Qajar Dynasty and ruling elite. Their ignorance and avarice had left the country open to foreign economic exploitation, as noted in Chapter 11, Section V. In April 1902, for example, Shah Mozaffar ed-Din borrowed 10 million rubles from Russia, on top of another 22.5 million borrowed in 1900. He then proceeded to spend such huge sums during a tour of Europe in the summer of 1902 that the treasury again was empty and negotiations were started in 1903 for still another loan.

In the same year, it should be noted, the Shah ordered a large lump sum and a pension of £3,000 a year to be paid to his favorite astrologer, the reason being that His Majesty had dreamed that the astrologer had saved him from drowning. His grand vizier, who was responsible for securing the funds for such largesse, lost his temper and said that he had enough difficulty raising money for the Shah's tours and toys without also paying for his dreams. This candor cost the grand vizier his office, which was filled by a certain Eyn od-Dowleh, a cruel and ignorant bigot. He had shocked even the hardened commander of the Persian Cossack Brigade by ordering a criminal to be "shod, like a horse, with horseshoes, nails having been driven into his bare heels, into his flesh." [21]

The resulting anarchy and demoralization in Persia made its people especially responsive to revolutionary events across the frontier in Russia. In December 1905, only two months after the Tsar's October Manifesto, a general strike was waged in Teheran in protest against rising sugar prices and against the unpopular grand vizier, Eyn od-Dowleh. The Shah promised reforms, which he made no effort to fulfill. A second strike, in July 1906, forced the Shah to dismiss the grand vizier, but the crowds then demanded a constitution. With the *ulema* (religious leaders) and some units of the armed forces supporting the demonstrators, the Shah followed the example of the Tsar, agreeing on August 5 to grant a constitution. Following the elections, the assembly, or Majlis, was convened by the Shah on October 7. Because of the restricted franchise the Majlis membership consisted of aristocrats, landlords, wealthy merchants, ulema and a few skilled artisans.

This legislative activity was accompanied by direct action at the grass-roots level. *Anjomans* were organized, corresponding to the soviets of the Russian revolutionaries. They were local units elected independently of the Shah's government, and including not only Muslims but also Zoroastrians, Christians and Jews. They spread rapidly, especially in North Persia, where they became a state within a state. As central authority crumbled during the revolution, the anjomans assumed responsibility for preserving order and controlling the price and distribution of bread. By mid-1907 the anjoman movement had become national in scope, with 40 units in Teheran, this number increasing to 180 by June 1908. Whereas the Russian soviets were exclusively radical (Social Revolutionaries, Mensheviks and Bolsheviks), the Persian anjomans were of all political persuasions, and usually led by liberal landowners, merchants and especially the clergy, who still were the best-educated section of the population apart from the bureaucrats.

In May 1907 the British ambassador, Sir Cecil Spring-Rice, described the growth of the anjomans in a dispatch to London:

> In every town there is an independent Assembly, which acts without consulting the Governor or the Central Assembly at Tehran. One after another, unpopular Governors have been expelled, and the Central Government and the Tehran Assembly have found themselves powerless to resist. The danger of universal disorganization seems a real one. A spirit of resistance to oppression and even to all authority is spreading throughout the country. . . . The sentiment of independence in the widest sense, of nationality, of the right to resist oppression and to manage their own affairs is rapidly growing among the people.[22]

Nikolai Hartwig, the Russian ambassador in Teheran who was as violently opposed to revolution in Persia as in his own country, voiced his concern about the anjomans in a dispatch of April 24, 1908. He noted their "all-embracing power" and added that "recently they have begun to give orders to the representatives of the Government, as if to their own agents, giving them instructions and interfering directly in all the affairs of every department." [23]

Meanwhile, the Majlis had been meeting in Teheran and had prepared a rather liberal constitution, which the Shah signed on January 1, 1907. Unfortunately, he died a week later, an untoward event that marked the beginning of the stormy second phase of the Persian Revolution. Confrontation followed confrontation, culminating in Russian occupation and "the strangling of Persia," as it was put by W. Morgan Shuster, the American financial adviser who led the resistance against the usual combination of domestic and foreign vested interests.

The new ruler, Mohammad Ali, was a thorough reactionary who opposed all the reforms proposed by the Majlis, and who was determined to be rid of both the assembly and the constitution. He was strongly backed by Hartwig who, by training and temperament, was firmly committed to the principle of absolute imperial authority. But the Shah and the Russian ambassador had to cope with an aroused populace. For the first time in the modern period, Persia was being shaken by a reform movement with genuine mass following. This movement was strongly nationalistic and anti-Western because of the humiliation and exploitation suffered at the hands of foreigners.[24]

Despite the merits of their cause, the nationalists were weakened by dissension within the Majlis and the anjomans. Personal political ambitions were involved, as well as basic differences of opinion between senior and junior members of the clergy. There was also conflict over the jurisdiction and authority of the Majlis as against the anjomans.

As the latter spread across the country they tended to treat the Majlis as another anjoman—the greatest of the anjomans, of course, but an anjoman nevertheless. This weakened the prestige of the Majlis, which had to cope also with the court and the bureaucracy in the ongoing struggle for power.

Even more serious for the nationalist cause than the internal discord was the external threat posed by the signing of the Anglo-Russian Entente in August 1907. The preamble made the customary bow to the "integrity and independence of Persia," but the text designated northern and central Persia as a Russian sphere of influence, southeastern Persia as a British sphere and the intervening territory as a neutral buffer zone. The nationalists understandably reacted with bitter disillusionment and anger. They had been assured earlier by London that the rumors of an entente were "without foundation," and that even if the end of the Russo-Japanese War made possible an improvement in Anglo-Russian relations, "the Persian Government might rest assured that we had no intention of in any way encroaching upon the integrity and independence of Persia." [25] The deceit shocked the Persians, who always expected the worst from an autocratic Russian government engaged in crushing its own revolution. But from the mother of parliaments they naïvely assumed support for their democratic aspirations, especially since British envoys had ceaselessly lectured them on probity and honor.

The British ambassador in Teheran, Sir Cecil Spring Rice, shared the feelings of the nationalists. He wrote bluntly to his superior, Foreign Secretary Sir Edward Grey, that "we are regarded as having betrayed the Persian people," and he added with undiplomatic tartness, "there is at least a prima facie case for those who are ready to criticise you for all you do either in cooperation with an autocratic power or in opposition to the liberties of smaller nations." Finally Sir Cecil warned that Russia might exploit the Entente to pursue her old designs in Persia under a new guise. "It will be more serious from the point of view of public opinion if the old policy is still carried on under the new Convention." [26]

The ambassador's premonition proved prophetic. Despite the treaty's preamble, Hartwig continued his efforts to subvert the constitution and the Majlis. Foreign Minister Izvolski insisted on caution because he needed Britain's support to realize his Balkan objectives. Overt intervention in Persian affairs was out of the question, but covert intervention was authorized so long as it remained covert. This left plenty of leeway for Hartwig, who could count on the cooperation of Colonel Vladimir Liakhov, commander of the only efficient military unit in Persia, the Cossack Brigade.

Hartwig and Liakhov advised the Shah to "abolish the Constitution, disperse the Majlis." The Shah eagerly accepted advice that accorded with his own views, so on June 22, 1908, he appointed Liakhov governor of Teheran. The Russian promptly proclaimed martial law, surrounded the Majlis building with his Cossack Brigade, and blasted the building with artillery fire, killing several hundred occupants. The crisis center now shifted to Tabriz where, after the dispersal of the Majlis on June 23, 1908, the nationalists repudiated the Shah as the legitimate ruler of the country. The Persian soviets or anjomans now took over and appealed to the revolutionaries of the Russian Caucasus for support against the Shah's advancing forces. Hundreds of Georgian, Armenian and Azerbaijanian revolutionaries reached the city before it was surrounded and cut off from the rest of the country.

The Shah's army of six thousand men consisted mostly of undisciplined, bloodthirsty nomads, attracted by the prospect of capturing and looting the prosperous city of Tabriz. Food supplies ran short, and the Russians feared that the considerable number of their compatriots caught in the city would suffer from famine or the sword. This danger paradoxically forced the Russians to send troops to break the blockade, thereby saving the nationalists as well as their fellow countrymen. Meanwhile, Bakhtiari tribesmen and nationalist warriors known as *fedayeen* ("those who sacrifice themselves") captured Teheran on July 13, forcing the Shah to flee to the Russian legation. On July 16, 1909, Mohammad Ali was deposed, and his fat, twelve-year-old son, Ahmad Mirza, was proclaimed Shah.

The nationalists were triumphant but also financially bankrupt, while the northern part of their country was occupied by Russian troops. Repeated appeals for loans and for the withdrawal of the troops elicited only rationalizations justifying inactivity. Despite the ouster of their pliant tool, Mohammad Ali, the Russians were becoming more aggressive in Persia because of the changing international situation. Izvolski had been ousted as Foreign Minister, and influential forces in Russia were seeking to repudiate his entente with England in favor of an agreement with Germany. The strongly anti-German British Foreign Secretary, Sir Edward Grey, was willing to accede to the most high-handed Russian actions in Persia for the sake of preserving the 1907 Entente. This was especially true during the Franco-German Moroccan Crisis of 1911, when Britain strongly backed France against Germany. The Russians rightly assumed that Britain would not dare to confront both Germany and Russia at the same time, so they cavalierly proceeded to force Mohammad Ali on the hapless Persian people.

Mohammad Ali was in exile in Odessa where, contrary to international law and to a specific agreement reached with the nationalist Persian government, Moscow allowed him to send money and agents to incite the Turcomen tribesmen against Teheran. Then Mohammad Ali was permitted to leave Odessa for Vienna, where he purchased arms and ammunition. From Vienna he journeyed to the Russian port of Petrovsk on the Caspian Sea, and thence he crossed to the Persian coast near Astarabad on July 17, 1911. Earlier in the month the Russian minister in Teheran had predicted at a large dinner party that the Persian government would cease to exist within a few weeks.

It now appeared that this prediction was justified. Turcomen tribesmen rallied behind Mohammad Ali, along with the Russian consular and military officials stationed in Persia. The Teheran government was demoralized, having already lost control of many regions because of financial shortages and the intrigues of Mohammad Ali and his Russian backers. The day was saved by W. Morgan Shuster, an American who had been hired by the Majlis, over Russian objections, to reorganize national finances. As treasurer-general, Shuster had carried out his duties energetically and fearlessly, thereby winning the enmity of the Russians, who made every effort to secure his dismissal. During this 1911 emergency Shuster assumed leadership in organizing and supplying combat units to stop the advancing cavalry forces of Mohammad Ali. On September 5, 1911, the Shah's cavalry was defeated, and the nationalist government gained still another respite.

It proved to be short-lived. The Russians were more determined than ever to get rid of the Majlis and the troublesome Shuster, while the British, apart from halfhearted protestations, offered no opposition to the grossest violations of Persia's sovereignty. When the Teheran government proposed to hire a number of Swedish officers to train its army and restore security in the country, St. Petersburg reacted negatively. The Tsar's reaction was revealing: "Since it is harmful to Russia, it is therefore impermissible. We are the masters in the North of Persia." [27]

The Russians likewise opposed certain actions and appointments that Shuster had made with his usual unconcern for diplomatic niceties. On November 11, 1911, the Russian ambassador delivered a forty-eight-hour ultimatum to the government, demanding an apology for the acts and cancellation of the appointments. The Teheran cabinet responded by resigning, whereupon the ambassador ordered the Russian troops in North Persia to advance southward. On December 20, 1911, the Majlis was surrounded and forced to accept the ultimatum. On December 24 the Majlis disbanded and Shuster was fired. A few days later he left for the United States. The new British ambassador, Sir George Barclay, who had faithfully carried out Sir Edward Grey's policy of undermining Shuster, now pondered the consequences: "It is enough to make the angels weep to see all Shuster's machinery fall into incapable hands. . . . I *really* liked that man." [28]

With the dispersal of the Majlis and the departure of Shuster, Persia virtually ceased to exist as a state. A reign of terror was unleashed, which reached the point of Russian consuls actually arresting Persian nationalists and shipping them to Baku. "While admitting that this measure is not foreseen by the existing juridical norms," wrote Consul Nekrasov of Rasht, "I deem it my duty to call the attention of the Imperial Legation to the fact that existing circumstances utterly preclude the application of such norms intended for normal international relations." [29] In official Russian circles the following jingle was popular at this time: "Persia is not a foreign country just as a hen is not really a bird."

The combination of external pressures and internal weaknesses was responsible for the failure of the Persian nationalists to establish an independent constitutional regime. The Russians were the most aggressive, but Sir Edward Grey also conceded that the "integrity and independence" of Persia did not exist. The fact is that both Britain and Russia were typical of the Great Powers during these decades in their refusal to treat non-Western governments as independent political entities. The fate of Persia differed only in detail from that of other semicolonies such as China, the Ottoman Empire, Afghanistan or Ethiopia.

Foreign intervention both aggravated and was stimulated by domestic fragility and vulnerability. The numerous tribes were still largely independent of any government in Teheran, especially as they obtained modern breech-loading rifles at the turn of the century. By 1910 nearly every tribesman had arms equal to those of the national army. As for the clergy, they still enjoyed wide popular support, and they played an important role in the turbulent events of those years. But in the final analysis they had no answers to the basic problems facing Iran as it was being catapulted willy-nilly into the modern world. The clergy were effective in mobilizing public opinion for achieving immediate political objectives or redressing specific grievances. But they had no perception of the long-range consequences of their actions and no comprehensive strategy to guide their periodic interventions in political affairs.

The nationalists-constitutionalists in the Majlis and the anjomans were weakened by ideological differences comparable to those that had crippled the anti-Tsarist elements in Russia. On the one hand were the Western-educated middle-class merchants and intellectuals who demanded separation of religious and temporal powers, compulsory military service, land distribution and secular public education. They were known as "Social Democrats," to be distinguished from the "Social Moderates," who comprised most of the clergy, landlords and military, and who wished simply to curb the excesses of the Shah. In Teheran itself, three elements competed for power: the Shah and his Court, the factions in the Majlis, and the bureaucrats in the ministries. All three of these groups, however, became increasingly isolated in Teheran during the turbulence of these years. Peasants refused to pay taxes, road concessionaires were unable to collect tolls, smugglers defied customs collectors, and merchants raised prices at will.

Shuster was fully justified in writing *The Strangling of Persia* after being forced by the Russians to give up his post and depart. But the strangling of that country, as of others in the Third World, was the work not only of foreign hangmen, but also of witting and unwitting domestic collaborators who made necks vulnerable to the noose.

❧ VI. Young Turk Revolution

After the Russian and Persian revolutions, the next great upheaval occurred in the Ottoman Empire with the Young Turk revolt of 1908. The Turks, unlike the Russians and Persians, had a constitutional tradition, the so-called Midhat Constitution having been adopted in 1876. But it was a short-lived experiment, as Sultan Abdul Hamid adjourned the first parliament elected in March 1877, and none met again until the 1908 Revolution. Whereas Russian and Persian reformers struggled for the adoption of a constitution, the Turkish reformers sought the restoration of the Midhat Constitution.

In doing so the Turks and other Ottoman subjects had to contend with the all-pervasive Hamidian repressive system. Multitudes of spies operated in the bureaucracy, army, schools and even in families. A rigid press censorship isolated the population from Western influences, so that the words "republic," "constitution," "liberty," "equality" and "tyranny" were banned. The works of Voltaire, Tolstoi and Byron were prohibited, while Shakespeare's *Hamlet* was banned from the stage so that audiences would not witness the murder of a king.

The repression drove dissidents abroad where, after the manner of Russian exiles, they waged journalistic warfare against the autocracy at home. Not only Turks, but also revolutionary leaders of the subject peoples sought refuge in foreign capitals, especially Paris. All these exiles—Turks, Arabs, Greeks, Armenians, Albanians, Kurds and Jews—held a congress in Paris in February 1902, with the aim of organizing a common front against the autocracy. But they soon realized that they agreed on nothing except that they all disliked the Sultan. One group wanted Turkish predominance and centralized rule, while another favored a decentralized empire with full autonomy for the non-Turkish minorities.

While the exiles were quarreling in Paris, militant revolutionaries were organizing at home. The 1905 Russian Revolution gave considerable encouragement to the opposition in Turkey. Abdul Hamid quickly sensed the dangerous implications of the Revolution for his autocracy.

When congratulated by one of his officers on the defeat of Turkey's traditional enemy, Russia, by Japan in 1905, he replied that the defeat of the Tsar was a defeat for autocracy everywhere. Abdul Hamid was especially concerned by the mutiny of the crew of the warship *Potemkin* of the Russian Black Sea fleet. Fearful lest the Russian mutiny produce similar disaffection in his own armed services, Abdul Hamid began strengthening the defenses of the Straits in case the *Potemkin* mutineers attempted to steam through. The Tsar paradoxically called on the Sultan to intercept the *Potemkin* in case it did enter the Straits. The Sultan was spared such embroilment because the crew of the *Potemkin* sought refuge in Romania, where they sank their ship by opening the seacocks.

Nevertheless, Abdul Hamid was not able to insulate his empire completely against the virus from Russia. Many peasants in eastern Anatolia traditionally had gone back and forth across the Russian frontier in search of work. When Abdul Hamid stopped these migrations to prevent a repetition of what was happening in Persia, he aroused much disaffection among the peasants deprived of their means of livelihood. Also, Muslim refugees from the Russian Caucasus, Crimea and central Asia had for years been migrating to the Ottoman Empire, where many had been welcomed into the armed services because of their strong anti-Russian sentiments. But with the 1905 Russian Revolution they suddenly found themselves viewed with suspicion, a reversal that induced some to join the Turkish revolutionaries.

The latter in the meantime had been organizing secretly in the Military Medical School, the Military Academy, the Veterinary School, the School of Administration, the Naval Academy and the Artillery and Engineering School. It was in these modern professional schools that the Young Turks, as the dissidents were collectively called, laid the foundations for their underground revolutionary movement. In 1908 they were forced to action earlier than they had planned because the Sultan's spies were penetrating their ranks, and also because the Great Powers were openly considering intervention in Macedonia. To forestall both threats, the Young Turk leaders decided to strike first in the Macedonian city of Saloniki, which was the center of their movement.

The flag of revolt was first raised on July 3, 1908, by two Young Turk officers who took to the hills of Macedonia with arms, ammunition and two hundred followers. The insurrection spread rapidly in the army's III Corps, so an ultimatum was telegraphed to the Sultan, threatening a march on Constantinople unless the 1876 Constitution was restored within twenty-four hours. The State Council advised Abdul Hamid to accept the ultimatum, while the religious leader, the Sheik-ul-Islam, refused to issue a *fetva* authorizing suppression of the rebels. The Sultan had little choice but to yield, so on July 24 he proclaimed the restoration of the Constitution.

News of the capitulation was greeted with wild rejoicing. The long reign of repression was at an end. Christians and Muslims embraced one another in the streets. The Young Turk leader, Enver Pasha, exclaimed: "There are no longer Bulgars, Greeks, Rumans, Jews, Mussulmans. We are all brothers beneath the same blue sky. We are all equal, we glory in being Ottoman." [30] This euphoric atmosphere did not last long. The issues that had divided the exiles in Paris now had to be faced as urgent issues of policy rather than differences in theory. Three political groupings began to emerge at this point.

The dominant one corresponded to the faction in Paris that had favored Turkish predominance and centralized rule. They were organized as the Committee of Union and Progress (CUP), and had been responsible for the underground network that had toppled Abdul Hamid. When they surfaced after their coup, it was discovered that they were quite different from the mid-nineteenth-century reformers who had come from the old Ottoman ruling elite. The Young Turks of the CUP, by contrast, were much younger and had emerged from the ranks of the petty bourgeoisie. They were lawyers, journalists, college lecturers, low-level bureaucrats and junior army officers.

Although they had full power in their hands after the Sultan's abdication, the Young Turks did not actually take over the top government posts until 1913. One reason was the opposition of the Ottoman bureaucracy and of the ulema to what were considered to be young upstarts. The other reason was that they themselves accepted the popular view that they did not possess the skills and the experience necessary for running an empire. Lacking confidence in themselves, they began by ruling indirectly through their control of the armed forces and of the majority they had won in the parliament elected in 1908.

The second political group that existed at this time was the Liberal Union, headed by Prince Sabaheddin. Its basic principle was that only through local autonomy and full development of communal life could the empire retain the support of its peoples. There is no way of knowing whether this proposition was sound because it was never put into practice. The Liberal Unionists never had a chance to take office. Many Turks suspected them because of the support they received from the minorities. More important was the military power that the Young Turks commanded and that Sabaheddin and his followers lacked completely. Finally they lost whatever chance they may have had when they made the mistake of supporting an abortive bid for power by the third political group.

This was the conservative League of Mohammad, which professed to support the constitution but which also demanded strict enforcement of the Sheri, or Sacred Islamic Law. The league opposed the Young Turks, claiming that their leaders were Jews, freethinkers or Westernized Turks who did not observe the precepts of the Koran. This argument was effective with the devout Muslim population, as was demonstrated on April 12, 1909, when a counterrevolution in Constantinople suddenly left the capital in the hands of the conservative Muslim forces. The Young Turks quickly sent an army from their stronghold in Macedonia and retook Constantinople after only a few hours' fighting. They forced Abdul Hamid to abdicate, though he probably had not been involved in the counterrevolution, and installed in his place the compliant Mohammad V.

The Young Turks now were the unchallenged masters of the empire, and they remained in control through the First World War. Two stages are discernible in the evolution of their thinking and policies: the reformist stage from 1908 to 1913, and the revolutionary stage from 1913 to 1918. During the reformist period the Young Turks were naïve in their handling of both domestic and foreign problems.

In domestic affairs they believed that the end of absolutism and the restoration of the constitution would ensure competent government and the cooperation of the minorities. Government, however, remained as ineffective as ever, for the simple reason that the old Ottoman bureaucracy had been allowed to remain in charge. As for the minorities, the Young Turks allowed them to participate freely in the 1908 elections, so that the parliament reflected reasonably accurately the ethnic composition of the empire: 147 Turks, 60 Arabs, 27 Albanians, 26 Greeks, 14 Armenians, 10 Slavs and 4 Jews. But the assumption that fair representation would guarantee minority loyalty proved unfounded. Perhaps a century earlier this would have been the case, but by the twentieth century the virus of nationalism was too widespread.

In the early days of the revolution many Greeks in Asia Minor had unfurled the blue-and-white flag of the Hellenic Kingdom rather than the star and crescent of their own empire. Other nationalities reacted in the same way, considering themselves to be first Slavs or Albanians or Arabs, and only secondly Ottomans. Furthermore, this minority secessionism was promoted, albeit erratically, by the Great Powers. Russia incited the Balkan Slavs, and France and England the Greeks, Armenians and Arabs. Thus instead of a unified Ottoman Empire, the Young Turks had to cope with the onslaught of the Balkan states in the Balkan Wars of 1912–13, at the end of which they lost nearly all their Balkan lands.

In their relations with the Great Powers the Young Turks were equally naïve and unsuccessful. They accepted uncritically the free-trade doctrines of the period. Cavit Bey, the future Minister of Finance, wrote in 1909:

> . . . in my opinion, we must accept foreigners in such enterprises for the sake of establishing a skill, that of management and rationalization, which we lack so badly. As to important public works, these can be done only with foreign capital. . . . All countries in a state of opening themselves to civilization will inevitably stumble and fall in their new path if they seek to advance by their own forces. . . . All new countries have been able to advance only with the help of foreign capital.[31]

In line with this thinking the Young Turks believed that the Great Powers would abrogate the stifling capitulations, since it would be to their mutual benefit to do so. The Young Turks were especially anxious to be rid of the capitulations because under their aegis a comprador class of Greek, Armenian and Jewish merchants, together with the Western companies, had gained control of the national economy. (See Chapter 6, Section III.) Accordingly, the Turkish reformers adopted modern civil and commercial laws, assuming that this would clear the way for ending the capitulations. Their touching faith in "civilization" and "foreign capital" was soon dispelled. Despite repeated requests the Great Powers refused to cancel the capitulations, refused any increase in customs duties, refused any loans to the new Turkish government and refused any tax levies on foreign merchants comparable to those collected from the locals.

These disillusioning experiences at home and abroad forced the Young Turks into their second phase, that of revolutionary nationalism, which culminated fatally in their joining the Central Powers in 1914. In the political field this phase involved several sharp changes. The Law of Associations prohibited the formation of political associations based on ethnic communities, and after the proclamation of this law, all ethnic organizations were banned. The 1912 general election, in contrast to that of 1908, was known as the "big-stick election." Young Turk pressure and manipulation reduced Greek representation from 26 to 15, and Albanian from 27 to 18, while the number of Turkish representatives increased from 147 to 157, and of Arabs from 60 to 68.

The Young Turks cracked down on the old Ottoman establishment as well as on the minorities. They created a new provincial and local administration, a new national police force and a new system of secular primary and secondary schools. They also extended educational opportunities for girls, preparatory to their entry into the professions and public life. Along the same lines they reduced the role of the ulema in the judicial and state machinery, and undermined their economic independence by transferring the administration of their foundations and endowments to a government ministry. Finally, the Young Turks developed the expansionist ideology of pan-Turkism. This was a reaction to the humiliating defeats suffered in Libya and the Balkans, and involved not only the expulsion of Western imperialism in the Ottoman Empire but also the liberation of central Asian Turkish peoples from Russian rule, and of other Muslims in North Africa and India from Western colonialism. This pan-Turkism was essentially an escapist doctrine, as impossible of implementation as the earlier Ottomanism.

Regarding economic matters, the Young Turks during this second phase turned against both the foreign powers and the minority comprador elements associated with them. The latter functioned as the representatives within the Ottoman Empire of European manufacturers, and also directed the flow of raw materials from the empire to Europe. Turkish popular sentiment against the Greek minority was especially inflamed with the loss to Greece of Crete in 1908, of Mytelene and Chios in 1909, and of Epirus, Thessaly, Macedonia and western Thrace in 1913. The influx of Turkish refugees from these lost territories further excited nationalistic passions.

The Turks retaliated by organizing an economic boycott against Greek merchants, while paramilitary bands recruited from the refugees and local Turks harassed the long-established Greek communities of Asia Minor. The popular objective was the "nationalization of infidel Izmir," and so ruthlessly was this pursued that approximately 130,000 Greeks were forced to emigrate in 1914. This displacement of both Turks and Greeks continued through World War I, finally totaling some 400,000 Turks and 1.3 million Greeks. At the same time the Armenians also were bearing the brunt of Turkish nationalist fury. Since many of the Armenians were located in the inaccessible interior provinces of the empire, they suffered persecution reaching genocidal proportions.

Meanwhile, the Young Turks had also attacked the economic privileges of the Great Powers. The Young Turks made final efforts in 1913 and 1914 to negotiate the end of the capitulations but again they were turned down. Their response was to accept on August 2, 1914, a secret treaty of alliance that Germany offered on the equal terms that the other powers had refused. By November of the same year the Turks were embroiled in the war that was to prove their undoing.[32]

In conclusion, the Young Turks had two advantages in waging their struggle that were denied to the Persian nationalists. One was the lesser power of the ulema in the Ottoman Empire, so that after suppressing the League of Mohammad in 1909, the Young Turks were free to proceed with relatively little opposition. The other advantage was that several Great Powers contended for influence in Constantinople, enabling the

Young Turks to play off one against the other, in contrast to the overwhelming Anglo-Russian Entente in Persia.

Nevertheless, the final result of the Young Turk Revolution was the disappearance of the Ottoman Empire. This probably was inevitable sooner or later, as suggested by the simultaneous extinction of another multinational empire—that of the Hapsburgs. The process might not have been so devastating, however, if the Young Turks had carried their revolution one stage further. As it was, they did cast off quickly their original illusions concerning free trade and Western civilization, and they did learn that economic independence was the prerequisite for meaningful political independence. Accordingly they turned against the capitulatory regime and sought to create a national bourgeoisie to replace the minority compradors.

In the process, however, the Young Turks allied themselves with the feudal landowners of eastern and central Anatolia. In 1913, large landowners who made up only 5 percent of the farm families of the Ottoman Empire owned 60 percent of the arable land. Peasants with medium or small holdings comprised 87 percent of farm families, leaving only 8 percent of farm families as completely landless.[33] But the great majority of the 87 percent who had medium or small holdings did not have enough to support their families, and therefore had to work part-time on the estates of the large landowners. For the Young Turks, the alliance with these landowners was a marriage of convenience that made it possible to obtain the peasant recruits needed to wage the successive wars against Italy, the Balkan states and the Western allies. But the end result was that the vast rural mass of the Ottoman Empire was left in its immemorial squalor and isolation.

This failure to mobilize national human resources explains in part the escapism into pan-Turkism, and the dependence on one imperial power to fight against the others. The end result was imperial disintegration and the wasting of Turkish armies in Poland, Russia and Romania, as well as on several Middle Eastern fronts. Not until Mustafa Kemal Pasha were the peasant masses mobilized effectively for a desperate struggle for national liberation.

VII. Chinese Revolution

China's 1911 Revolution, according to nationalist mythology, was the work of Sun Yat-sen and his dedicated republican revolutionaries. In actual fact, Sun played a relatively minor role in both the outbreak and the outcome of the Revolution. The dynasty fell primarily because of the erosion of its legitimacy; this erosion began early in the nineteenth century with the defeats sustained in the Opium War and in the later aggressions by Western powers and by Japan. By 1911 the erosion process was so far advanced that only a slight push by Sun's republicans sufficed to end Manchu rule. But the end result of the revolution was determined not by the republicans, who proved militarily powerless, but by the two elements that did hold power: the leaders of the armed forces and the gentry in the provinces.

The undermining of the Manchu regime was essentially the result of Western capitalist intrusion. Its manifestations, as noted in Chapter 15, Section IV, were landless peasants, exploited industrial workers, comprador merchants in the treaty ports, increasingly powerful gentry in the provinces and rebellious students questioning Confucian philosophy as well as Manchu rule. In the years immediately preceding the 1911 Revolution the dynasty was further weakened by the Japanese defeat of Russia and by the ensuing Russian Revolution. The Japanese victory over the Tsarist Empire made all the more unbearable the weakness and failures of China. The Russian Revolution pointed up the possibility of overthrowing an obsolete and ineffective regime at home.

China, like Persia, had long-standing ties with Russia, and was correspondingly affected by the 1905 Revolution. The Russians had occupied Manchuria, as they had North Persia, and the Russo-Japanese War had been fought on Chinese soil. Chinese workers joined the Russians in the 1906–7 strikes on the Chinese Eastern Railway during the Russian Revolution. In January 1907 Chinese and Russian workers again united to wage a "political" strike to commemorate the second anniversary of Bloody Sunday. Soviet sources claim that thirty-five hundred Bolshevik Party members were active in Manchuria at that time, and General Linevitch described Harbin in 1905 as "a city resembling a nest of various types of revolutionaries and agitators." [34]

The Manchu Dynasty did try to save itself with belated reforms, but its efforts only worsened the situation. Modernization under the circumstances stimulated Chinese nationalism, and heightened popular antipathy to the foreign Manchus. One example of this boomerang effect was in the field of education. In 1906 the old examination system based on the Confucian classics was abolished, and in its place were established new schools under a new Ministry of Education. Tokyo was the favorite center for Chinese students seeking a foreign-university education. From eighteen in 1898, they increased to two hundred in 1899, to one thousand in 1903, to thirteen hundred in 1904 and to thirteen thousand in 1906, when the old examination system ended. But a Tokyo education inevitably meant radicalization, for the students were exposed to the literary realism of Dickens and Balzac, to the Social Darwinism of Herbert Spencer, to the classical economics of Adam Smith and to the political theories of Montesquieu and J. S. Mill. After such an intellectual experience, the Manchu regime seemed hopelessly archaic, and the students became revolutionaries.

The same undermining of the dynasty occurred with the modernizing of the armed services. During the Taiping Rebellion personal armies were organized in the provinces by local leaders. These armies consisted of professional fighting men rather than the usual part-time farmer-soldiers, and their loyalty was to the provincial establishments rather than the central government. The latter did commission an imperial official, Yuan Shih-k'ai, to train a modern army with German instructors. He succeeded in organizing the most disciplined and best-equipped force in China. It came to be known as the Peiyang Army, but again it was used to advance Yuan's career rather than to buttress the Manchu regime.

Equally frustrating was the attempt at constitutional reform. Many Chinese were impressed by the victory of the Japanese constitutional monarchy over the Tsarist autocracy, and by the subsequent trend toward constitutionalism in Russia. In 1908 the Empress dowager announced that constitutional government would be introduced gradually during the following nine years. The first stage was the election of advisory provincial assemblies, but the local gentry in these assemblies quickly assumed legislative functions. Under threat of mass resignations they forced the provincial governors to accept and implement their recommendations. Thus the constitutional reform did not secure gentry support for the dynasty, but rather created provincial centers of rival gentry power.

The reality of this rival power was manifested during the struggle for control of China's expanding railway network. Provincial gentry had invested heavily in the construction of local railway lines, but the central government understandably sought to create a centralized network. When it announced the nationalization of all local lines in 1911, a "railway protection" movement spread across the country. It championed the interests of the provincial ruling elites and became strongly antidynastic in rhetoric and actions. By the turn of the century the balance of power in China was passing from Peking to the provincial gentry. They controlled the armed forces and the business enterprises, and also were sending most of the students abroad to acquire the new learning necessary for exercising their authority.

This precarious position of the dynasty explains why it was toppled so easily in 1911. The leader of the republicans was China's first professional revolutionary, Dr. Sun Yat-sen (1866–1925). Compared to the reform leaders who had hitherto been prominent, Sun was a strange and anomalous figure. He was not one of the upper-class literati; in fact, his training was as much Western as Chinese, and his knowledge of the traditional classics was far from secure. He was born in the Canton Delta, which had been subject to foreign influence longer than any other area in China. At the age of thirteen he joined his brother in Honolulu, where Sun remained five years and completed a high school course in a Church of England boarding school. Then he went to Queen's College in Hong Kong, and after graduation he enrolled in Hong Kong Medical College and received his medical degree in 1892.

Sun had acquired an excellent scientific education, which he could have used to acquire wealth and status. But China's defeat by Japan in 1895 convinced him that the government of his country was rotten to the core and that nothing short of a revolution would provide the remedy. So he embarked on the career of a revolutionary and organized anti-Manchu societies among overseas Chinese in Europe, America and Southeast Asia. In Tokyo, with its largest concentration of Chinese students, he founded in 1905 the T'ungmenghui or United League. Its amorphousness is reminiscent of the Young Turk groups that flourished at the time in Paris. The T'ungmenghui included factions with diverse views ranging from anarchism to Buddhism. The only common bond was opposition to the Manchu Dynasty, as opposition to Sultan Abdul Hamid was for the Young Turks.

The Manchus were blamed for all of China's problems, and it was naïvely assumed that their replacement by a republic somehow would solve these problems. Like the Young Turks, Sun's republican followers had a naïve faith in the efficacy of constitutionalism and other Western institutions as cure-alls for their national ailments. And like the Young Turks, the Chinese students came mostly from well-to-do families and were ignorant of the plight of the peasantry, which comprised the overwhelming majority of the total population. The students talked vaguely of social reform and equality, but had no serious plans or even intentions for meaningful social restructuring. Given this lack of roots in Chinese reality, it is understandable that several uprisings they organized within China all failed miserably.

In 1911 the dynasty finally was overthrown by accident, and one in which Sun was not involved. On October 10, 1911, an accidental explosion in an underground bomb factory in Wuhan attracted police, who found the membership list of the local revolutionary group. When the authorities began making arrests, the conspirators decided to revolt immediately. They forced a well-known colonel, Li Yuan-hung, to serve as their leader, and proclamations of revolution went out to the rest of the country under his name.

The accidental rebels succeeded spectacularly because of two lucky breaks. One was the flight of the local governor and military commander, which gave the insurrectionists precious time to mobilize support. The other was the use of Colonel Li, who was not a republican revolutionary, and whose name attracted conservative elements that otherwise would have remained aloof. This was particularly true of the provincial gentry who, seeing the Revolution still extant after a week, and led by the respectable Colonel Li, responded by declaring their independence from Peking. One province followed another, until virtually all had seceded from the central government. The Manchus relied on Yuan and his Peiyang Army to crush the rebels, but the ever-realistic and opportunistic Yuan instead opened negotiations with them. When they offered him the presidency of the new republic, he accepted, and in March 1912 Yuan was inaugurated President in place of the Manchu Dynasty, which had ruled for over $2\frac{1}{2}$ centuries.

In view of the origins and nature of the Chinese Revolution, its dismal aftermath is not surprising. It was a revolution in which the peasant mass was inert and ignored. Sun's republicans were delighted with their unexpected success, but success revealed their impotence and shallowness. The political parties they organized after the Revolution had neither contact with the masses nor the backing of any military force. Once the long-awaited republican panacea had been attained, they did not know precisely what to do next. So they squandered their energies in personal jealousies and factional squabbling. By contrast, the gentry and the military who controlled the provinces set out single-mindedly to maintain their control. The Shansi gentry stated flatly that so long as "local autonomy" was respected, "members of the [provincial] government are quite indifferent as to who occupies the Throne . . . as this will have little connection, under the new proposed form of government, with their local affairs." [35]

Given this predilection, the provincial gentry naturally supported the conservative Yuan as against the republican Sun. The Great Powers also supported Yuan for the same reason that in Russia they had supported the Tsar, and in Persia the Shah. In November and December 1911 the American minister to China sent repeated messages to the Secretary of State stressing Yuan's need for money and urging that the department support a loan to him.

With this backing of the Great Powers, as well as of the military and the bureaucracy within China, Yuan quickly pushed the republicans aside. When the National Assembly was elected in April 1913, the majority of seats was held by Sun's Kuomintang or National People's Party rather than by Yuan's Chinputang or Progressive Party. This did not deter Yuan, who turned to the Great Powers for a loan of £25 million. The Kuomintang leaders warned the Great Powers that the Constitution required parliamentary approval of loans, and since such approval would never be given for this loan, it would not be legally binding. The Great Powers nevertheless granted the loan to their protégé on April 26,

1913, though on terms that netted China only £21 million of the £25 million, and yet was required to repay principal and 5 percent interest until 1960 for a total of £67,893,597. Yuan used the loan to consolidate his position. His measures included bribery, political assassinations, illegal intimidation of the National Assembly and transference of provincial governors. Finally he disbanded the Kuomintang majority party, suspended the National Assembly and ruled as the virtual dictator of the country.

Many Chinese had accepted Yuan in order to forestall further Great Power aggression, but they found themselves saddled with both Yuan and continued aggression. In order to secure Russian recognition of his government, Yuan agreed to autonomy for Outer Mongolia, which meant Russian domination. Likewise for the sake of British recognition he granted autonomy to Tibet, which came under British domination. Much worse were Japan's Twenty-one Demands made in January 1915, when the other Great Powers were embroiled in the First World War. No Western state supported Yuan, though the British minister, Sir John Jordan, stated that "Japan's action toward China is worse than that of Germany in the case of Belgium." In May 1915 Yuan was forced to accept most of the Twenty-one Demands, including acceptance of Japan's dominant position in Shantung, South Manchuria, eastern Inner Mongolia and the Han-Yeh-P'ing industrial base in central China. Though never ratified by the Chinese National Assembly, Japan used these agreements with Yuan as the basis for later continental expansion.

The final aftermath of the 1911 Revolution was Yuan's announcement that he would assume the title of Emperor on January 1, 1916, in response to a popular demand that he had carefully orchestrated. But the opposition proved unexpectedly strong and widespread, including armed resistance in Yunnan. The pragmatic politician had misjudged, and was forced in March 1916 to abandon his imperial plans. Humiliated and embittered, Yuan died in June of the same year. After his death the army commanders who had served under him divided the country among themselves. Ignoring the nominal government in Peking, they pillaged the countryside mercilessly. The warlord era, which lasted to 1926, was one of the worst periods in the long history of China.

The latest research underscores the complexity of the Chinese Revolution and the dangers of generalizations as to its failure, particularly because of many regional differences in that vast country. "In many areas in which the Revolution is studied," concludes a review of recent literature, "the configuration of participating elite groups seems different. In Canton, gentry and merchants seem to be in separate camps. In Shanghai, the two seem well merged, although in that most commercialized of Chinese cities, the role of the bourgeoisie in the alliance seems stronger than in any other place. In the interior, the urban gentry were unquestionably the senior partners in the merchant-gentry alliance which emerged. In the North, as one moves further from China's great commercial centers, the domination of officials and gentry seems even more pronounced." [36]

Although relations between merchants and gentry varied from region to region, it is safe to generalize that in the country as a whole the merchants were too few in number to play a leading role when the Revolution came. The revolutionaries also proved quite unprepared when the Revolution unexpectedly materialized in 1911. Many of them were uncompromisingly radical in their writings while they were abroad, but proved to be quite willing to compromise their principles on returning to China. Also, they lacked the military power of the Young Turks to impose their will on enemies, whether foreign or domestic. Like the Young Turks they cherished illusions about the universal applicability and efficacy of Western institutions. They tried to set up in China carbon copies of what they had observed abroad, without taking into account the needs of the great peasant mass. They had much less contact with, and understanding of, this peasant mass than the Taipings before them or the Communists after them. What they established had no meaning for the Chinese people and crumbled quickly before the realities of Chinese politics and foreign pressures.

∿ VIII. Mexican Revolution

In Mexico, as in the rest of Spanish America, the war of independence in the early nineteenth century resulted in political change but not social change. The ties with Spain were severed but domestic social relationships remained unchanged. In the first stage of the war for independence, a village priest, José Morelos, proclaimed social revolutionary objectives, including an end to discrimination against Indians and castas, and restoration of land to Indian communities. The Church, the landowners and the army united against this threat to their privileges, crushed the rebellion and executed Morelos in 1815. When Mexico finally did win independence from Spain in 1821, the traditional elites were firmly in control, and remained in control for the rest of the century.

The history of Mexico during that century was basically similar to that of other Latin American countries—the same exploitation by the latifundium, the same succession of military coups and the same graft and extortionate foreign loans culminating in financial bankruptcy. In its first fifty years as an independent nation, Mexico had over thirty presidents; more than fifty governments; and one man, Santa Anna, served as President nine times. Mexico had the additional drawback of proximity to the United States, which led to the loss in 1848 of over half the national territories—Texas, New Mexico and California. The country was further weakened by recurring Indian rebellions along the northern frontier. In 1861 a joint British, French and Spanish expeditionary force landed in Mexico to collect overdue debts. The British and Spaniards later withdrew, but Louis Napoleon attempted to create a French client state under Emperor Maximilian. The Mexicans resisted under Benito Juárez and forced the French to withdraw, leaving the hapless Maximilian to face a firing squad in 1867.

The struggle against French intervention meshed with a domestic conflict between liberals and conservatives. The latter had been weakened by mismanagement of the war with the United States, so the liberals were able to push through in 1855 the Reforma legislation designed to make Mexico a secular and progressive state. It abolished the special courts of the Church and the military, assigned Indian lands as individual properties to their current tenants, confiscated Church lands, suppressed monastic orders and instituted civil marriage. The conservatives tried to stop the reforms by taking up arms and fighting with the French against Juárez. With the defeat of Maximilian and his Mexican allies, the liberals were free to proceed with the building of a new society based not on the traditional privileged corporations but on freedom of the individual.

Just as the war of independence had ended Spanish rule but failed to realize Morelos' egalitarianism, so the reforms ended traditional corporation restraints but imposed new forms of servitude. Freedom for the landowner meant opportunity to acquire still more lands to add to his existing estates. Freedom for the Indian meant liberation from community restraints and the right to sell his land and join the ranks of the landless unemployed. The fetters of tradition had given way to social anarchy; and the end result was to be the great Revolution of 1910.

The social implications of the new order based on individual freedom became uncomfortably clear during the dictatorship of General Porfirio Díaz, who succeeded Juárez in 1876. For more than a quarter century Díaz subjected Mexico to his iron rule in the name of liberty, progress and order. Liberty was for the private entrepreneur; progress meant rapid industrial and commercial growth; and order was imposed by a judicious combination of rewards and repression, or *pan y palo* (bread and club).

For most Mexicans the outstanding change under Díaz was the passing of immense tracts of land into private hands. First there were about 40,000 ecclesiastical properties worth about $100 million that were transferred from the Church to private holders. Then there were about 2 million acres of former Indian communal lands that were sold or forfeited for overdue debts to haciendas and land companies. Also, the government sold public lands to development companies, and allowed companies to survey and divide land, of which they retained one third as compensation for their services. Finally, peasants who did not have clear titles to their lands were considered to be squatters and were dispossessed.

The original dream of a nation of small farmers ended in the complete victory of the hacienda owners. By 1910, 11,000 of these *hacendados* owned 57 percent of the land, while 96.6 percent of rural families were landless. Some proprietors owned from 2 to 15 haciendas each. One proprietor who owned 15 was Luis Terrazas of Chihuahua, whose estates totaled 2 million hectares, and who owned 500,000 head of cattle and 250,000 sheep. The growth of the latifundium did not generate a corresponding growth in overall agricultural production. Cotton output increased to meet the needs of the Mexican textile industry, and likewise industrial export crops increased, including coffee, chick-peas, vanilla and sisal. Cattle also were raised in ever larger numbers for the international market. But food crops for domestic consumption declined. Per-capita production of maize fell from 282 kilograms in 1877 to 154 in 1894 and to 144 in 1907. The resulting scarcity of maize led to an increase in the price of this staple food, but wages remained stationary. Similar decline in per-capita production occurred with other staples such as beans and chile.

The difficulty was that a small number of haciendas responded to the market opportunities and increased substantially their output of export commodities. But the great majority were content to repeat the nineteenth-century phrase *hacienda no es negocio* (a hacienda is not a matter of business).[37] Hence production of export raw materials increased 6.5 percent annually between 1877 and 1907, but production of foodstuffs for home consumption fell at an annual rate of .5 percent. This trend caused many contemporary observers to warn that the Mexican campesino was being starved to death. In fact, the mortality rate rose from 31 to 33.2 per thousand between 1895 and 1910, and infant mortality likewise increased.

Another basic feature of the Mexican economy under Díaz was the influx of foreign capital to the point where it surpassed Mexican investment. Foreign investors, mostly Americans, concentrated first on railroads and the mining of precious ores. Then after 1900 they turned to oil, copper, tin, lead, rubber, coffee and sisal. The statistics of economic growth were impressive. Railroad mileage rose from 400 in 1876 to 12,000 in 1910. The value of foreign trade during the same period soared from 89.5 million pesos to 502 million pesos. Exports of precious metals, which comprised 79 percent of the value of all exports in 1877–78, declined to 63 percent in 1890–91, to 58 percent in 1900–1 and to 46 percent in 1910–11. Output of industrial metals increased 5 times between 1891 and 1910. The industrial work force, however, did not increase as rapidly as industrial output. Between 1895 and 1910 the number of workers rose only .6 percent annually, as against an annual growth in industrial production of 3.6 percent.

The industrial workers put in 12 to 14 hours a day, and were often paid in chits redeemable only at company stores, where prices were high and quality was low. Bosses arbitrarily levied fines as punishment, and deducted from paychecks for Church dues and religious festivals. Another source of grievance was the higher pay of American workers, who monopolized the skilled jobs. This sparked the strike at Cananea against American copper mogul William C. Greene. But the local governor, Rafael Izabal, used Mexican federal troops and American Rangers from Arizona to crush the strike with a loss of 6 American lives and 30 Mexican lives. Nevertheless, strikes increased in frequency, totaling 250 between 1881 and 1911, including 75 in textiles, 60 in railways and 35 in tobacco. Yet workers were better off than the peasants. Textile workers in Cananea earned only 2 pesos daily, but villagers plowed land with oxen for 50 or 60 centavos a day.

The intellectuals who rationalized this economic strategy of the Porfiriato were known as the *cientificos*. They justified the wealth and privileges of Mexico's oligarchy on racist grounds. Dismissing the Indians as genetically inferior, they viewed Mexico's future as dependent on white leadership, both national and international. They held up the United States and the industrialized European countries as models for Mexico, and considered foreign capital and even foreign settlers to be essential for future development. These views, however, were not universally accepted. Rogelio Fernández Guell, author and director of the National Library, wrote of his fear that Mexico "had been transformed into an enormous market to which people of all nationalities flocked to make their fortunes, converting it into a land of adventurers, without country, religion or family, whose god was gold." [38] The validity of this assessment is indicated by the close correlation between the location of heavy American investments and the degree of support for the Revolution.

Mexico under Díaz was integrated much more thoroughly into the international market economy by the early twentieth century than had been the case in the early nineteenth century, when exports had consisted mostly of precious metals. The process of integration followed the usual Third World pattern of economic growth without economic development. Hence the exploitation of peasants on large estates, the distortion of agriculture for export purposes, the dislocation of millions of villagers who were unable to find employment in the cities, the foreign control of industries and natural resources and the dependence on foreign capital and foreign markets. This outcome of a quarter century of the Porfirian regime was the breeding ground of the 1910 Revolution.

The spark that set off the Revolution was the 1907 world depression, which ended fourteen years of prosperity. Mexican exports to the principal market in the United States dropped sharply, including minerals, fruits and vegetables from Sonora, cattle from Chihuahua, cotton and guayule from Coahuila and sisal from Yucatán. Land values fell correspondingly, causing the failure of banks that had overextended themselves in loans to hacendados or large landowners. The sudden drying up of credit hurt badly the merchants, miners, ranchers and planters, all of whom held the cientificos to blame.

By this time Díaz was in his seventies and becoming increasingly rigid and intolerant. He surrounded himself with old cronies, who constituted a corrupt gerontocracy controlling the administration, judiciary and army. Moving into the resulting vacuum was a young northern landowner, Francisco Madero. He represented the progressive hacendados who wanted to go into business but felt blocked by the foreign domination of the economy. A member of one of the wealthiest families in the country, Madero was anything but a social revolutionary. What the Mexican people needed most urgently, so far as he was concerned, were personal freedoms and "liberty of thought." He doubtless surprised the textile workers of Orizaba when he informed them that he did not want to "incite passions" or "to raise wages or to reduce the hours of toil," because "that is not what you want; you want liberty . . . for liberty will give you bread." In his Plan de San Luis Potosi he opposed wholesale land redistribution because of his expressed commitment to the "principle of private property." It is "one thing to create small property by dint of hard work and another to redistribute large landholdings, something I have never thought of doing or offered in any of my speeches or programs." [39]

Madero's timid reformism attracted to him liberal businessmen and landowners who feared disruptive revolution and therefore were ready to accept mild reforms and to replace the aged dictator with a more flexible leader. When Madero challenged Díaz and campaigned openly for the presidency, Madero attracted enthusiastic, large crowds throughout the country. Díaz responded by jailing Madero, and on election day the official count accorded him exactly 196 votes nationwide. Madero was then released on bail, whereupon he fled to Texas, where he issued his Plan de San Luis Potosi, calling for a revolt against Díaz, free elections and legal review of land grabbing.

Uprising erupted throughout the country, and the surprised oligarchy vacillated in coping with the crisis. The insurrection gathered momentum, so that in 1911 the rebels were able to take the city of Juárez. The oligarchy agreed to exile Díaz and to hold a new election for Madero to win, on the implicit condition that they continue to control national affairs from behind the scenes. This arrangement was carried out, and after Madero's electoral victory, he was inaugurated as President in November 1911.

The oligarchy now discovered to its dismay that their traditional manipulation no longer was feasible. As old restraints weakened, workers waged strikes in the cities, and peasants broke out in armed rebellion in several southern states. The alarming disintegration of the social order prompted certain plutocrats and generals to execute a coup in February 1913. Madero resigned as President and after an interlude of confusion, General Victoriano Huerta seized power. Lacking popular support, he established a dictatorship to beat down the opposition. But the greater the repression, the greater the resistance. Revolutionary forces won control of most of the country, and Huerta fled to Europe in July 1914. By August the oligarchy had lost control of the country. Its principal members fled abroad and the Porfirian old order lay in ruins. Fortunately for the revolutionaries, foreign intervention was impeded by the outbreak of the First World War, so responsibility for evolving a new order was left to the Mexicans themselves.

During the following decade of bloody civil war, three principal groups emerged. In the South were the agrarian revolutionaries led by Emiliano Zapata. With a granduncle who had fought under Morelos in the War of Independence, and with a grandfather and father who had served with Díaz against the French, Zapata was a colorful revolutionary figure. His tight trousers, big spurs, short vest, big gold-braided hat, dashing white charger and egalitarian impulses all made him the natural representative of the hopes of the inarticulate masses. To the present day Zapata symbolizes the spirit of revolution in Mexico. He began by leading his region in resisting the hacienda owners who were encroaching on the community lands. In November 1911 he issued his Plan de Ayala, in which he announced that "the lands, woods and waters which have been usurped by haciendos, Cientificos, or caciques, through tyranny and venal justice, will be restored immediately to the pueblos or citizens. . . . They shall maintain such possession at all costs through force of arms." [40]

The strength of the Zapatistas was their broad base in the villages, to which they returned after their campaigns. This, however, was also their weakness, for their village background limited their perspective and prevented them from functioning effectively as a national force. They wanted only to obtain land, and were not interested in other issues. They were reluctant to fight beyond their own regions, and had little contact with city workers, let alone foreign interests and foreign powers.

In the North was Francisco (Pancho) Villa, once a bandit and then a rebel chief with a Robin Hood reputation of taking from the hacendados and giving to the poor. This attracted wide support in his native Chihuahua, where seventeen individuals owned two fifths of the state. By 1914 Villa had forty thousand followers, mostly cowboys, ranchers, miners and smugglers. These Villistas, like the Zapatistas, were incapable of organizing an effective national movement. They were not interested in social issues, so they did not divide the haciendas they seized, as did the peasants in the South. Instead they handed the properties over to the "state," on the condition that the income from them be used to feed widows and orphans after the war. In practice, many estates were taken over by Villa's generals, who became a new landed group.

The third revolutionary group consisted of the Constitutionalists. They were a coalition of two factions: the liberals, led by Venustiana Carranza; and the radicals, led by Álvaro Obregón. Carranza was a former Díaz politico who wanted to restore law and order with as few social changes as possible. Obregón favored nationalist legislation and agrarian reforms that would curb American economic penetration, break the power of the great landed families and provide greater opportunities for urban labor and the middle class. At first both Obregón and Villa were generals under the civilian leader, Carranza. Then Villa and Carranza quarreled, and the latter joined forces with Obregón to destroy Villa. Of necessity, Villa looked to Zapata for an ally, but effective cooperation was not possible, given the localism of the Southerner and the primitiveness of the Northerner.

The limitations of the two men were strikingly manifested when they occupied Mexico City but did not know what to do with their valuable prize. They made no moves to dismantle the old administrative apparatus or to deal with the controlling economic interests, both foreign and domestic. Instead they vacillated, and finally they abandoned the capital and returned to their respective strongholds. Villa's comment on departing revealed why the Mexican Revolution ended as it did—why, in fact, it was not a revolution at all: "This ranch is too big for us, it's better back home. . . ." [41]

The Constitutionalists were more sophisticated and knowledgeable about both national and international affairs. Lacking the popular following of Zapata and Villa, the Constitutionalists paid more attention to social reform despite their natural conservatism. When they won Yucatán with its sisal plantations, the Constitutionalists impressed both workers and peasants by abolishing debt peonage, aiding trade unions and passing labor legislation.

With the support of the city workers, the Constitutionalists were

416 / GLOBAL RIFT

able to destroy the two uncoordinated enemy forces in turn. Obregón first attacked Villa, who persisted in his wild cavalry charges even when Obregón's forces were in trenches and armed with machine guns. By October 1915 Villa's División del Norte had been smashed and Obregón was the master of northern Mexico. Meanwhile, Zapata, in his home base at Morelos, was implementing his Plan de Ayala by expropriating haciendas without compensation. The terrified hacendados abandoned their alcohol and sugar mills along with their lands, so the Zapatistas took over these rural industries and used the profits to pay for military expenses and to support war widows. This was a primitive form of "socialism," evolved extemporaneously to meet the exigencies of the moment and quite inadequate for coping with the problems facing the Zapatistas and their Mexican Revolution as a whole. The degree of inadequacy is reflected in the single-minded campaign that Zapata waged against the hacendados, while at the same time welcoming "with pleasure the manufacturer, the merchant, the mine-owner, the businessman, all the active and enterprising elements, which open new paths for industry and provide work to great groups of workers. . . ." [42] Zapata failed to realize that the most dangerous enemies of the Revolution were not the reactionary hacendados he was attacking but the "enterprising elements" he was courting.

Despite his fatally flawed strategy, Zapata did command the fervent support of the Morelos peasantry. Repeated attacks by a thirty-thousand-man Constitutionalist army were repulsed with the aid of the entire population, which served as informers and food suppliers as well as combatants. Despite their successes the Zapatistas remained isolated, and the Constitutionalists, who could not tolerate the glaring contrast between radical Morelos and the rest of the country, kept up the pressure with continual assaults. The struggle degenerated into a war of extermination. Villages were systematically burned, fruit trees cut down, crops destroyed and women and children herded into camps. In the process about one third of the population of Morelos was killed. By 1919 all the cities and haciendas had been reoccupied by the Constitutionalists, and the lands restored to the old landowners. The remaining Zapatistas were forced to take refuge in the mountains. Toward the end, Zapata saw more clearly the identity and nature of the enemy. In an open letter addressed to Carranza in March 1919 he stated:

> Since you first had the idea of rebelling, . . . since you first conceived the project of making yourself Chief and director of the misnamed "constitutionalist" cause, you . . . have tried to convert the revolution into a movement for your own gain and that of your little group of friends . . . who helped you to get on top and are

now helping you to enjoy the spoils of war: riches, honors, business banquets, luxurious fiestas, Bacchanalian pleasures, orgies of satiation, of ambition, of power and of blood.

It has never crossed your mind that the Revolution was for the benefit of the masses, for that great legion of the oppressed which you aroused with your preachings. . . .

In the agrarian reform [you have betrayed your trust]; haciendas have been given or rented to [your] favorite generals; the old landlords have been replaced in not a few cases by modern landholders dressed in charro costumes, military hats, and with pistols in their belts; the people have been mocked in their hopes.[43]

Less than a month after writing this letter Zapata was dead, the victim of an ambush laid by a Colonel Jesus Guajardo, who had posed as a deserter and who was rewarded for his deed with a medal, fifty thousand pesos in gold and a generalship. With the hated and dangerous Zapata out of the way, Carranza proved too rigidly conservative to accept even the simulation of reform that was needed after such a national ordeal. Before the 1920 elections Carranza was ousted by the tough and canny Obregón. With his presidency the Revolution may be considered to have run its course. Obregón consolidated the power of the central government and institutionalized what gains the Revolution had achieved.

The cost had been appalling. Well over one million were killed, or one out of every fifteen persons in the country. Material destruction was severe, especially of railways, which were systematically wrecked by losing forces in order to impede the movement of enemy units. Also, the output of mines fell by 40 percent between 1910 and 1920, while manufacturing declined by 9 percent.

But there were a few compensating gains. Labor rights were codified and a national labor organization, the Regional Confederation of Mexican Workers (CROM), was created in 1918. From the beginning to the present day this has served as an instrument for establishing government control over the increasingly active trade-union movement. More attention was paid to education under the guidance of a nationalist philosopher, José Vasconcelos. Between 1921 and 1931, expenditures for schools rose from 4 percent to nearly 13 percent of the national budget. In foreign affairs, Obregón recognized the Soviet Union in 1924, the first Latin American government to do so. Most significant was the failure to alter the old property structure inherited from Díaz. Only .6 percent of the land area was distributed during Obregón's administration. Agrarian leaders who pushed for land redistribution were assassinated by landowners or government agents, and referred to as *bandidos.* Obregón's successor, Plutarco Elías Calles, organized in 1929 the National Revolutionary Party, which has ruled the country to the present. Starting out as a coalition of politicians and generals who cooperated for sheer survival, it gradually developed into a flexible political instrument representing groups with sufficient organization and resources to warrant consideration in government councils.

Obregón's administration can scarcely be called a failure, since it achieved what virtually all the revolutionaries wanted. This was not to abolish private property but rather to end the traditional system of privilege, which prevented the full development of free enterprise and competition. The Villistas and Zapatistas were antihacienda, not anticapitalist. Their movement resembled more the traditional peasant jacqueries of medieval and early modern times than it did the twentieth-century revolutions in Russia, China, Cuba, Southeast Asia, Portuguese Africa and other Third World regions. For this reason the customary term "Mexican Revolution" is essentially a misnomer. More accurate would be "the Great Mexican Rebellion," which, in fact, is the title selected by an historian, Ramon Ruiz, for his study of Mexico between 1905 and 1924.

There is no question that it was "great" in numbers and in degree of violence. The extent of capitalist penetration and exploitation of the country, the resulting social disruption and suffering and the absence of foreign intervention because of World War I all explain the great scope, duration and violence of the rebellion. There was also no lack of class hatred, as evident in the following exchange between Zapata and Villa when they met on December 4, 1914, to conclude an alliance:

> ZAPATA: All the fellows have already told you: I always said so, I always told them, that Carranza is a son of a bitch.
>
> VILLA: [He and his crowd] are men who have slept on downy pillows. How are they going to be friends of people who have spent their whole lives in pure suffering?
>
> ZAPATA: The other way around, they have been used to being the scourge of the people. . . .
>
> VILLA: The [politicians] will soon see that it's people who give the orders and that the people are going to see who are their friends. . . .
>
> ZAPATA: Those son-of-a-bitch politicians, as soon as they see a little chance to get in, then quick they want to make their way, and they take off to brown-nose the next big shot on the rise, like a son of a bitch. That's why I've busted all those sons of bitches. I can't stand them. . . . They're all a bunch of bastards. . . . I'd just like to run into them some other time.[44]

Class hatred and violence, no matter how extensive, do not constitute revolution. This is evident in the following two accounts: the first a description of the indecision and ambivalence of the Zapatistas when they captured Mexico City, and the second a statement by Lenin on October 25, 1917 announcing the triumph of the Bolshevik Revolution and the plans for a socialist Russia and a socialist world:

ZAPATISTAS:
They filtered quietly, almost embarrassedly, into the capital. Uncertain of their role there, they did not sack or plunder but like lost children wandered through the streets knocking on doors and asking for food. One night they heard a great clanging and clattering in the street—a fire engine and its crew. To them the strange apparatus looked like enemy artillery, and they shot at it, killing twelve firemen. Zapata himself was no calmer. . . . [He] holed up in a grimy, gloomy little hotel. . . . He was invited to ceremonies in his honor at the National Palace, but would not attend. Reporters interviewed him, but he hardly muttered sentences. And when the Villistas moved into the northern suburbs to join forces with him on November 28, he took off back to Morelos.[45]

LENIN:
We shall win the confidence of the peasants by a single decree abolishing the property of the landowners. The peasants will understand that the salvation of the peasantry lies only in union with the workers. . . . We have the mass strength of organization which will conquer all and lead the proletarian world revolution.
Hail the world-wide socialist revolution.[46]

This difference between the Zapatistas and the Bolsheviks is the difference between, on the one hand, traditional peasant rebels striking out against immediate oppressors, with little understanding of the institutional origins of their exploitation and little vision of a truly alternative society, and on the other hand, modern revolutionaries with a comprehensive theory of social institutions and dynamics, and a strategy for destroying the past and building the future within the framework of that theory.

IX. African Resistance

In Africa there were numerous cases of resistance against European intrusion and European rule. All were futile, however, for various reasons, including the lack of continental or regional unity against European aggression, the partitioning of the continent into a large number of separate colonies, the resulting lack of coordination when resistance began and the superior military technology enjoyed by the Europeans. Also noteworthy is the diversity in the origins and motivations of African resistance movements. Some were religious in nature, such as the Islamic Mahdiya, which ruled the Sudan in the 1880s and 1890s, and the recurring Nyabingi possession cult, which immobilized colonial administration in British Uganda and German Ruanda between 1908 and 1928. Other resistance movements erupted when it became clear that the Europeans were pushing on from commercial coexistence to permanent political domination. This was the case with Abushiri, who successfully defied the Germans in the coastal area of Tanganyika between 1888 and 1891, and also with Samori Touré, who fought with remarkable success against the French in West Africa between 1870 and 1887. A final type of resistance was waged by Africans seeking to halt the encroachments of European settlers who drove them from their lands and then exploited their labor. Chief Moorosi of British Basutoland withstood an eight-month siege in 1879 in his mountain fortress before he was killed and his people scattered, and likewise the 1906 Zulu Rebellion in Natal was provoked by the harsh imposition of a poll tax on a people already overburdened and impoverished by a British settler regime.

The one outstanding exception to this pattern of futile resistance was the Ethiopian Emperor Menelik's victory over the Italians at Adowa in 1896. Unlike confrontations elsewhere between Europeans and Africans, the Adowa battle in the Tigre highlands was a positional engagement between large massed armies. Thanks to the incompetence of General Baratieri and to the misleading information supplied by his African spies, the Italians were defeated in what has been called "the most incredible and absurd battle that has ever taken place in modern history." [47] The European capitals reacted with surprise and alarm at this eruption of "African savagery" even though it was the reaction to blatant Italian aggression. Typical was the following expression in Paris of European solidarity against barbarism: "No one here—I have not to take notice of this or that scatterbrained person, or a few habitually malevolent minds—wishes for the success of the Abyssinians at the price of the discomfort of a civilized nation, from which it is possible to differ in aims and opinions without being supposed to cherish any ill will when that nation is face to face with a brave but barbarous foe." [48]

Adowa has been described as having the same effect on Africans as Japan's defeat of Russia had on Asians.[49] Yet the traditional isolation of Ethiopia from the rest of Africa, together with the partitioning of the continent into numerous segregated colonies, precluded any mobilization of black Africa to exploit the unique victory. Instead Adowa served only to strengthen an existing political symbolism based on Ethiopia. This symbolism was rooted in part on biblical authority, especially the oft-quoted Sixty-eighth Psalm: "He hath scattered the peoples that delight in war. Princes shall come out of Egypt; Ethiopia shall haste to stretch out her hands unto God." These revolutionary words for long had been a message of hope and a voicing of African aspirations. The writings of pan-Africanists such as Edward Wilmot Blyden, W. E. B. Dubois, Marcus Garvey and J. A. Rogers were replete with references to Ethiopia's legacy.

The term "Ethiopianism" also was used for the Ethiopian Church movement comprising numerous secessionist and independent native churches in southern Africa in the 1890s. Europeans viewed this as a pan-African conspiracy masquerading under the guise of religion. Their suspicion was partly justified, as the pervasive racism in southern Africa drove separatist churches to become the media for antiwhite forces.

This political symbolism of Ethiopia was enhanced by the Adowa victory. The triumph over the Italians was viewed as a symptom of African valor and resistance. It also stimulated pride in African values and traditions. Nationalists such as the Sierra Leonan Reverend Orishatuke Faduma challenged the prevailing assumption that in order to civilize and Christianize the African, "he must be foreignized." At the Congress on Africa held in Atlanta in 1896, he deplored the tendency of "native" converts to abandon their indigenous names, dress and food. The Gold Coast nationalist leader, Casely Hayford, editorialized in his newspaper in 1924: "Today when we speak of our prospects we speak of the prospects of the entire Ethiopian race. By the Ethiopian race we mean the sons and daughters of Africa scattered throughout the world." [50]

The term "Ethiopian" was used at the turn of the century to describe the various organizations formed at home and abroad by African nationalists. In 1905 West African and West Indian students in Liverpool formed the "Ethiopian Progressive Association" with the aim of forging a bond among all members of "the Ethiopian race at home and abroad." In the United States, Marcus Garvey, a Jamaica-born African leader, popularized such slogans as "Africa for the Africans" and "Ethiopia Awake." His anthem, "Ethiopia, Thou Land of Our Fathers," created a feeling of international solidarity among the scattered peoples of African descent.

In addition to Adowa, there was one other case of successful resistance to the European powers, namely that of the Boers in South Africa. They had been planted on the Cape of Good Hope in 1562 by the Dutch East India Company to provide fuel, water and fresh provisions for the ships en route to the East. The Boers were a hard-bitten, intractable lot who wanted only to be left alone to pasture their herds on vast interior tracts, and to rule over their families and native slaves like patriarchs of old. When the British took over the colony in 1814 and began to interfere with the treatment of slaves, the Boers trekked northward beyond the Orange River and some pushed on beyond the Vaal. The British continued to claim jurisdiction over them, resulting in continual friction between the two white peoples. In 1854 the problem seemed to be solved by the Bloemfontein Convention, by which the British accepted the Orange River as their northern frontier and recognized the independence of the Boer republics of the Orange Free State and the Transvaal. But the discovery of diamonds and gold north of the Orange River, and the subsequent influx of miners from all over the world, made the Bloemfontein Convention obsolete.

Mining interests led by the legendary Cecil Rhodes pressured the British government to annex the rich mineral territories. Wealth for Rhodes was not an end in itself; it was the means to a greater goal—the aggrandizement of the British Empire. "That's my dream—all English," he would say when he was a mere youth at Kimberley, waving his hand comprehensively northward toward the great interior of Africa. As premier of Cape Colony, Rhodes worked for the realization of his dream, but the London governments vacillated. In 1895 he decided to force the issue by financing a revolution against Paul Kruger, President of the Transvaal, and organizing a raid into the Transvaal led by Rhodes' friend Dr. L. S. Jameson. Both the revolution and the raid failed, and Rhodes was forced to resign as premier. But these incidents further embittered British-Boer relations until finally, in 1899, full-scale war broke out.

The Boers resorted to guerrilla tactics, which prolonged the war for three years and compelled the British to mobilize three hundred thousand troops against the sixty thousand to seventy-five thousand Boers. The course of the war was revealing of the pervasive racism in the relations of Europeans with Africans as against their relations with each other. During the sieges of Kimberley, Ladysmith and Mafeking, the British inhabitants were provided rations, but not the Africans, Coloreds and Asians, who consequently died in droves from starvation and disease. The non-Europeans, it was argued, were free to leave, so it was wasteful to give them food. Unfortunately, there was no place for them to go, except to the Boers, who did not want them. One Britisher wrote of the pathetic plight of the victims: "I saw them fall down on the veldt and lie where they had fallen, too weak to go on their way. The sufferers were mostly little boys—mere infants ranging in age from four or five upwards." Another observer wrote in his diary: "It is really pitiful to see. . . . Last month one died in the Civil Commissioner's yard. It was a miserable scene to be surrounded by about 50 hungry beings, agitating the engagement of your pity and see one of them succumb to his agonies and fall backwards with a dead thud." [51]

The British did use (and feed) a few Africans during the war in various capacities: to drive oxen that pulled naval guns, to guard the blockhouses that were built to hamper the guerrillas, and to serve as scouts in locating the Boer *laagers* or camps. John E. Dyer, an American doctor with the Boers, wrote indignantly to the British commander against the arming of blacks: "You have committed an enormous act, the wickedness of which is certain, and the end of which no man can foresee. . . . It has hitherto been a cardinal in South African ethics, both English and Dutch, to view with horror the idea of arming black against white, and I would ask you . . . to disarm your blacks and thereby act the part of a white man in a white man's war." [52]

When the peace negotiations began on February 28, 1901, Boer General Louis Botha objected vigorously to the arming of blacks, and expressed fear that they would be enfranchised after the war. The British commander-in-chief, Lord Kitchener, assured Botha that "it is not the intention of His Majesty's Government to give such a franchise before representative government is granted to these colonies, and if then given it will be so limited as to secure the just predominance of the white race." [53] The blacks, not being aware of this exchange, believed that with British victory they would no longer be treated as second-class subjects. Nothing of the sort happened, so that their plight was little improved by the war. The *Times History* put the matter succinctly: [54]

> The natives had in many instances become insolent, owing to unduly high wages and to the familiarity with which the soldiers had treated them. They expected the Boers to be treated as a conquered race, to whom they would no longer stand in a dependent relation. But they soon discovered that the British conquest, though it might give the black man greater security against oppression and more clearly defined rights, involved no essential alteration in the superior status of the white man, be he Briton or Boer.

After the peace treaty (1902), both the Transvaal and the Orange Free State were granted constitutions, and in 1909 they were united with Cape Colony and Natal to form the self-governing Dominion of South Africa. The large African majority continued to be politically disfranchised and economically exploited, as it remains to the present day. The Boers, who had been defeated in battle, became the political masters of South Africa after the 1924 elections. And today they are the practitioners and beneficiaries of the thinly disguised system of racial subjugation and exploitation known as apartheid.

✤ X. *Nature of Pre-1914 Movements*

The pre-1914 revolutions and resistance movements were in response to the worldwide expansionism of the imperialist powers at the turn of the century. Those were the years when the Panama Canal "was stolen fair and square" and the Berlin-to-Baghdad Railway opened the Middle East to German economic penetration; when all of Africa was partitioned and additional concessions extracted from China; and when the United States formally entered the imperialist ranks by seizing Cuba, Puerto Rico and the Philippines.

As noted above, all efforts to stop these imperialist aggressions proved unsuccessful. The only exception was Japan, which, for reasons analyzed in Chapter 17, was able to acquire and develop Western economic and military technology and to join the club of imperialist powers. All other Third World peoples proved incapable of resisting the imperialist onslaught, for reasons that were partly external and partly internal.

The external reason was the lack during this early period of any international mutual support organization among Third World peoples. About the only exception was the aid given by a few hundred revolutionaries from the Russian Caucasus who crossed over to fight beside the Persian constitutionalists in Tabriz. By contrast, the imperialist powers aided each other repeatedly all over the globe. The European governments supported the Tsar with a timely loan; Britain and Russia between them "strangled" the Persian constitutionalists; the United States and Spain cooperated against the Cuban and Filipino nationalists; the Western powers collectively opposed change in China by supporting first the Manchu Dynasty and then Yuan Shih-k'ai; and in Africa the isolated resistance movements were crushed one by one, while the British and the Boers agreed that whatever their differences, the African majority was to remain subservient to them both.

The internal reason for the failure of the pre-1914 resistance movements was the inadequacy of their theory and practice. We noted above the great variety of political, economic and cultural influences that motivated the opponents of imperialist aggression. In very general terms they can be divided into two categories: the conservative traditionalists and the conformist Westernizers. The former were doomed from the outset by virtue of their escapist hankering for a romanticized and irretrievable past. The conformist Westernizers, by contrast, accepted in varying degrees political and economic relations with the capitalist world order. They soon discovered, however, the discrepancy between Western rhetoric and Western practice. The Young Turks learned this when they attempted to get rid of constricting capitulations, and the Chinese republicans likewise when they tried to modify the unequal treaties. The Persians soon were stripped of their illusions when they appealed to democratic England and the United States to support their constitution, and so were the Cubans and Filipinos when they requested "the Powers of the civilized world" to recognize their popularly supported revolutionary governments. Whether or not the conformist Westernizers resorted finally to armed resistance, they were ultimately all forced into a subordinate and exploited Third World status.

Even if the conformist Westernizers had been more realistic in their appraisal of the imperialist powers, it is doubtful that the conformist Westernizers would have been more successful because of the unfavorable objective conditions in their home countries, which made their efforts historically premature. In China, the merchants and the student revolutionaries were too few in numbers as well as too inexperienced and irresolute. In the Middle East the Young Turks were dependent on the feudal landowners of eastern and central Anatolia, who limited their freedom of action; while the Persian constitutionalists were even more restricted by the power of the tribes, the clergy and the traditional vested interests, as well as by their own illusions and dissensions. Where the masses were activized by foreign invasion, as in the case of the Philippines, the popular uprising was fatally weakened by elitist leadership that was ready to compromise and collaborate. Even in the massive 1905 Russian Revolution and 1910 Mexican Revolution, most workers and peasants were interested in land, jobs and wages much more than they were in structural reorganization.

There was an alternative to the ineffectual conservative traditionalists and conformist Westernizers, namely, the dissident Westernizers. Rather than accepting Western capitalism with its international market economy, they envisaged a new socialist world order. Rather than following Adam Smith and John Stuart Mill, they turned to Karl Marx and the assorted Marxists who followed him. In the pre-1914 period, however, the dissident Westernizers were too few in number to exert any influence. Furthermore, Marxist theoreticians did not concern themselves seriously with colonial questions during these early years.

Marx himself had assumed that socialism would come first in industrialized Europe and worried that the new socialist Europe would find itself surrounded by a capitalist periphery. Later Marxists such as Edward Bernstein accepted imperialism as an unavoidable stage during which the West would enjoy the advantage of having access to needed raw materials. As for the inhabitants of the colonies, Bernstein propounded the view that imperialism conferred upon them the blessings of

Western civilization. "The colonies are there, they must be taken care of, and I consider that a certain tutelage of the civilized peoples over the uncivilized peoples is a necessity." [55]

Lenin, with his roots in Eurasian Russia, viewed imperialism from a different angle of vision. He welcomed the Japanese victory over Russia, and the ensuing revolutions in Persia and Turkey. "The politically-conscious European worker," he wrote in 1908, "already has Asian comrades, and their number will grow, not daily but hourly. . . ." [56] Lenin carried this line of thought a step forward in 1913 with an article entitled "Backward Europe and Advanced Asia":

> One could hardly quote a more striking example of this rotten-ness of the entire European bourgeoisie than the support it gives to reaction in Asia in aid of the selfish interests of financiers and capitalist swindlers.
>
> Throughout Asia a mighty democratic movement is growing, spreading and gaining in strength. . . . Hundreds of millions of people are awakening into life, light and freedom. . . .
> And what of "advanced" Europe? She is plundering China and helping the enemies of democracy, the enemies of China's free-dom! . . .
> But the whole of young Asia, that is to say the hundreds of millions of working people in Asia, has a trusty ally in the prole-tariat of all the civilized countries. No force in the world can pre-vent its victory, which will liberate both the peoples of Europe and the peoples of Asia.[57]

Although Lenin was more attuned to Third World problems and potentialities than most of his fellow Marxists, he was relatively isolated and powerless during the pre-1914 years. The Tsar had survived the 1905 Revolution and was cracking down on those dissenters who refused to accept his eviscerated Constitution. Lenin found himself in the minority even among Russian Marxists, let alone those of Western Europe. Consequently dissident Westernizers in the Third World had to wait until World War I enabled Lenin to establish the first socialist state and the Communist International. With these developments the dissident Westernizers became a force in the Third World, though they had to wait for World War II before conditions were ripe for actual seizure of power beyond the borders of the U.S.S.R.

If revolution is defined as the seizure of the state mechanism and of political authority in order to effect radical restructuring of social in-stitutions and class relationships, then the so-called Chinese and Young Turk and Mexican revolutions were all rebellions rather than revolutions. The fact is that revolution in the true sense of the term did not appear anywhere until the First World War had disrupted the world capitalist order and made possible the breaking of "the weakest link in the imperialist chain." It is appropriate that this was Lenin's phrase, for it was Lenin also who emphasized repeatedly that without theory there can be no revolution.

The fundamental difference between rebellion and revolution is the reason why this Chapter 18, dealing with the period to 1914, is entitled "Beginnings of Third World Resistance," whereas Chapter 20, on the period 1914–39, is entitled "First Global Revolutionary Wave."

Part Four

THIRD WORLD STRUGGLE FOR INDEPENDENCE: TWENTIETH CENTURY

At the particular time when these discoveries were made, the superiority of force happened to be so great on the side of the Europeans, that they were enabled to commit with impunity every sort of injustice in those remote countries. Hereafter, perhaps, the natives of those countries may grow stronger, or those of Europe may grow weaker, and the inhabitants of all the different quarters of the world may arrive at that equality of courage and force which, by inspiring mutual fear, can alone overawe the injustice of independent nations into some sort of respect for the rights of one another.

ADAM SMITH (1776)

What escapes most observers is that we are not living through a small mutation, but a total rupture, a trauma that breaks with 500 years of history.

GOMES FEREIRA, Bishop of Oporto (1975)

An Indian historian-diplomat, K. M. Panikkar, has referred to the centuries following Vasco da Gama's arrival at Calicut in 1498 as the "da Gama epoch" of world history. The defining feature of this epoch, states Panikkar, was "the dominance of [Western] maritime power over the land masses of Asia," [1] and, it might be added, over the land masses of the entire non-Western world. It is singularly appropriate that almost five centuries after da Gama's exploit, a fellow Portuguese, Bishop Fereira of Oporto, should have perceived the end of the "da Gama epoch" amid the shambles of Portugal's African empire and Portugal's domestic dictatorship. Not only had Western control of overseas land masses been shattered, but also revolution in Portugal's colonies had engendered revolution in Portugal itself, terminating Europe's oldest dictatorship.

The distinctive characteristic of the Third World in the nineteenth century had been its global range. The only overseas regions that escaped subordination and exploitation were the white-settled British dominions, the United States and the Japanese Empire—the sole non-Western land that achieved industrialization and thereby retained economic and political independence. The distinctive feature of the Third World in the twentieth century, by contrast, was its progressive dismantling. Contrary to Marxist doctrine, the underdeveloped Third World proved to be the center of global revolutionary initiative. The metropolitan centers sought to halt the imperial disintegration with a comprehensive counterrevolutionary strategy—political, economic and cultural (see Chapter 19). Nevertheless, the colonial establishments steadily crumbled, three stages being discernible in the erosion process.

The first, to 1914, which was analyzed in the preceding chapter, was a gestation phase during which uncoordinated resistance but not revolutionary movements began their struggles against the encroachment of Western capitalism. The second stage, from 1914 to 1939, witnessed the first global revolutionary wave, sparked by the 1917 Russian Revolution (see Chapter 20). Despite Bolshevik expectations, the Revolution did not spread beyond Russia, so the interwar years in the Third World were marked by nationalist rather than social revolutionary movements (see Chapter 21). The third stage, since 1939, was heralded by the 1949 Chinese Revolution (see Chapter 22). Although the Chinese Marxists, in contrast to the early Bolsheviks, did not assume worldwide revolution, nevertheless it was during the post-World War II decades that the centuries-old European empires disintegrated. Some former colonies won full independence through social revolution. Others gained political freedom but still suffered foreign economic control and therefore a neo-colonialism similar to that prevailing in Latin America since the early nineteenth century (see Chapter 23).

The future of the Third World depends on the nature, strength and interaction of global revolutionary and counterrevolutionary forces. The outcome will decide whether the current national liberation movements represent a stage in the socialist transformation of the world or in the global development of capitalism (see Chapter 24). The Bishop of Oporto has rightly noted that the current struggle that "breaks with 500 years of history" is a "trauma." It will indubitably overshadow the course of world history during the forthcoming decades.

Chapter 19

ERA OF DEFENSIVE MONOPOLY CAPITALISM, REVOLUTION AND NEOCOLONIALISM

Current inventions comprise the biggest technological revolution men have ever known, far more intimate in the tone of our daily lives, and of course far quicker, either than the agricultural transformation in neolithic times or the early industrial revolution. . . .

C. P. SNOW (1966)

Whereas mechanics were primarily responsible for the First Industrial Revolution, and industrial scientists for the Second Industrial Revolution, it was the military that sparked the Third Industrial Revolution of the late twentieth century.

Throughout history, preparation for war has stimulated technology. The ancient Greeks were notoriously uninterested in practical application of their scientific speculations, yet they did produce giant crossbows, flamethrowers and catapults. During the Middle Ages, gunpowder was put to military use with the rapid development of muzzle-loading smooth-bore cannons and flintlock muskets. In early modern times, Napoleon awarded a prize to a Paris confectioner for developing a process for canning foodstuffs to supply France's revolutionary armies. Likewise during World War I, the military adapted recent inventions to develop new weapons such as warplanes, tanks and poison gasses. But during World War II a qualitative change occurred. Military technology became the senior partner. Industry henceforth depended on spinoffs from the military rather than vice versa. The result was the Third Industrial Revolution, which has affected both the center and the periphery more rapidly and more profoundly than did the two earlier Industrial Revolutions.

❧ I. Third Industrial Revolution and Defensive Monopoly Capitalism in the West

The impact of World War II technology on industry was exceptionally direct and overt. The explosion on the desert floor of New Mexico on July 16, 1945, signaled the harnessing of the power of the atom and the beginning of the Atomic Age. Meanwhile Londoners, bombarded with V-2s, were witnessing the birth of rocket flights, which were to lead to the Space Age. And the anti-aircraft batteries on the British coast were being fitted with predictors which, as computers with feedback, were the precursors of the electronic marvels of the Cybernetics Age. These three wartime developments—atomic power, cybernetics and the rocketry leading to space exploration—comprise the foundation for the new "high technology" of the Third Industrial Revolution.

The harnessing of nuclear power is reminiscent of the harnessing of fire. When humans learned to use fire about half a million years ago, they applied it in ways that were familiar, such as to secure heat on sunless days, and light on moonless nights. Only very gradually did they learn of other possibilities for fire, such as cooking foods, smelting metals, firing pottery and driving steam engines. Likewise nuclear energy is being adapted from its original military purpose for use in nuclear power stations, nuclear power ships, biomedical research and medical diagnosis and therapy.

The second main element in contemporary high technology was introduced on October 4, 1957, when Sputnik I was shot into orbit around the earth. This advent of the Space Age may be compared to the venture of the first amphibians from water to land over three hundred million years ago. Humans likewise are now venturing from planet earth, which gave birth to them. But whereas fish needed millennia to develop feetlike lower fins and lungs that functioned without gills, humans use machinery to survive in their new environment and thus can dispense with protracted physiological evolution. Hence the current plans for a space shuttle, automated pharmaceutical space factories producing vaccines and pure tissue cultures for enzymes, automated space factories creating near-perfect crystals for use in electronic circuits, giant solar collectors beaming energy from the sun to earth stations via microwave, and space colonies serving as launching pads for new exploration missions into deep space.

Scientists such as American physicist Gerald K. O'Neill and Soviet astrophysicist Iosif S. Shklovsky foresee the eventual construction in outer space of a vast "artificial biosphere" capable of supporting ten billion people, or more than twice the earth's present population. Indeed, they view space colonization as inevitable because of mounting population and environmental pressures on earth. Expansion into space, they assume, will unfold as naturally and inexorably as did the discovery and colonization of overseas lands after da Gama and Columbus.

The third major component of today's technological revolution is cybernetics, the label given to the combination of computers and automation. Computers consist of devices that perform with unprecedented speed routine or complex logical and decision-making tasks, replacing or improving on human capacities for performing these functions. Automation involves the use of highly automatic machinery or processes, which largely eliminate human labor or detailed human control. This general field of electronics has advanced rapidly in recent years with the development of microconductors that shrink machines. Microconductors—commonly silicon chips—can be made to conduct electric current or to block it. This makes them ideal components of computers, which work by alternately blocking and passing electric current. By putting more electric circuits on the silicon chips, they have been converted into computers-on-chips, known as microprocessors. These have become all-pervasive in modern technology, being used in the operation of power stations, business offices, supermarket checkout stands, textile mills, telephone switching systems and factory production lines. Fiat justifiably boasts in a television commercial that its cars are "designed by computers, silenced by lasers and hand-built by robots to the strain of Figaro's aria."

Turning from industry to agriculture, the impact of the Third Industrial Revolution has been equally far-reaching. Just as the United States was the pioneer in the development of microelectronics, so it was with capital-intensive agribusiness technology. And again the Second World War was the great catalytic agent. Before the war, American farms were small-scale family affairs operating without the use of migratory workers, huge machines and numerous chemical fertilizers, insecticides and herbicides. The effect of the war was to increase tremendously the demand and prices for farm products. Within a few years American agriculture changed in character from an agglomeration of family units to an economy dominated by agribusiness corporations.

The transformation was made possible by two favorable circumstances. One was the availability during the 1950s and 1960s of extremely cheap oil for operating the increasingly complex machinery and manufacturing the mounting list of chemicals. The other was the generous federal support of agribusiness in the form of direct government subsidies, preferential tax treatment and billion-dollar research programs designed specifically to aid agribusiness rather than family farming.

Agribusiness's ultimate justification for its predominance is superior productivity. One oft-quoted statistic is that 1 American farmer now feeds 48 other persons. The farm population has declined from 30.1 percent of the total U.S. population in 1920 to 4.8 percent in 1970. Yet these figures are misleading, for they reflect high manpower efficiency but ignore equally high energy consumption and wastefulness. In the case of corn, for example, new hybrid seeds are responsible for 20 to 40 percent of the increased yield per acre. The remainder is due to increased energy input, including fuel for new machines, and petroleum-based fertilizers, insecticides and herbicides. The net result is that the equivalent of 80 gallons of gasoline is expended to produce an acre of corn. This energy-production ratio makes the Western high-energy agriculture system one of the least efficient in history. Asian wet rice cultivation yields 5 to 50 food calories for each calorie of energy invested. The Western system requires 5 to 10 calories to obtain 1 food calorie. Also noteworthy is a U.S. Department of Agriculture study concluding that the "fully mechanized one-man farm . . . is generally a technically efficient farm" and that the incentive for large farms "is not to reduce costs per unit of production, but to increase the volume of business, output, and total income." [1]

Despite these considerations, the number of small American family farms continues to shrink. From a peak of 6.8 million units in the mid-1930s, they fell to 2.8 million in 1980 and to an estimated 1 million in 1985. Six percent of today's farms are producing over 50 percent of the total agricultural output. Most of these large farms are not directly owned and operated by the corporations. A Tenneco spokesman observed: "Agriculture is a high risk business and typically shows little if any profit, especially for large corporations." [2] Although there are some spectacular corporate farming ventures, such as Boeing's potato-growing enterprise in the Pacific Northwest, the dominant trend is toward contract farming. Companies sign up farmers and tell them what to do. Whereas in 1970 about 22 percent of the entire U.S. food supply was produced under contract, by 1980 it reached 50 percent, and by 1985 it is expected to be 85 percent. The crucial issue in the current agribusiness food system is not who owns the farm but who owns the farmer. And the farmer is owned not only by individual contracts, but also by corporate monopolies in key links of the food chain, including fuel, equipment, fertilizers, animal feed, food processing and marketing.

The above "food system," which has little to do with pre-World War II "agriculture," has uprooted most family farmers and disrupted America's rural social structure. A large proportion of the Department of

Agriculture budget paradoxically goes to feeding inner-city poor who were uprooted from their farms in part by the department's research programs in behalf of agribusiness technology rather than family-farm technology. The remaining communities in the American countryside have been impoverished socially as well as economically by the exodus to the cities. A 1974 study analyzed two communities in California's Central Valley. One was dominated by large corporate holdings and the other was a community of small farms. The latter enjoyed a higher living standard, more parks, more stores with more retail trade, superior physical facilities such as streets and sidewalks, twice the number of organizations for civic improvement and social recreation, and two newspapers (whereas the other community had one newspaper). In short, the quality of life was better in the small-farm community.

The Third Industrial Revolution has affected daily life more deeply and more speedily than any of the preceding technological revolutions. Its impact has not been confined to the industrialized countries, where silicon chips and agribusiness technology originated. Almost simultaneously the rest of the globe has been affected, and with even more disruptive repercussions, including the uprooting of hundreds of millions of peasants, urbanization without industrialization, environmental degradation and widening income gap between rich and poor nations and between rich and poor citizens within Third World societies. The result is that the Third World has become the center of global revolutionary activity in the twentieth century. The great paradox of our time is that the very technological precociousness and dynamism of monopoly capitalism has forced it back on the defensive. In place of the aggressive colonial expansionism of the late nineteenth century, monopoly capitalism today has formally surrendered its overseas empires, and now is striving to retain indirect control through the strategy of neocolonialism and diverse counterrevolutionary activities, both overt and covert.

☙ II. Marx Turned Upside Down

The Third Industrial Revolution did not get under way until World War II, whereas the Third World revolutionary movement (as against the earlier resistance movements) began during the First World War. The explanation for the earlier revolutionary upsurge is to be found in the combination of circumstances that upset Karl Marx's prognosis that the industrialized West would initiate global revolution. Marx, like all socialist theoreticians of the nineteenth century, believed in the existence of a law tending toward international equalization of levels of economic development. Because wages in the industrialized countries were kept down to the low level needed for the physiological subsistence and biological reproduction of the working class, domestic markets were accordingly very limited. Profits therefore tended to decline, and capital investment at home became correspondingly unprofitable. Hence the automatic flow of capital and technology from developed to under-developed regions, which offered a higher rate of profit in the early stages of their development. Marx therefore anticipated that revolution would come first in the declining centers of original industrialization in Europe. Indeed Marx feared the possibility of a future socialist Europe being surrounded and threatened by an outer world that remained capitalist! On October 8, 1858, he wrote to Engels: "The difficult question for us is this: on the Continent [of Europe] the revolution is imminent and will immediately assume a socialist character. Is it not bound to be crushed in this little corner, considering that in a far greater territory the movement of bourgeois society is still in the ascendant?" [3]

Along the same lines, Rosa Luxemburg pointed out that the surplus capital of northern Italian cities financed the development of Holland in the sixteenth and seventeenth centuries, and that Dutch capital in turn contributed to the industrialization of England in the eighteenth century. Likewise Lenin wrote in his *Imperialism: The Highest Stage of Capitalism* (1917): "The export of capital influences and greatly accelerates the development of capitalism in those countries to which it is exported. While, therefore, the export of capital may tend to arrest development in the capital-exporting countries, it can only do so by expanding and deepening the further development of capitalism throughout the world." Thus Lenin, like Marx, foresaw the Western developed states exporting their capital and technology to rising new centers, with the result that socialist revolution would occur first in the older and declining industrialized center.

Shortly before his death Lenin realized that his original assumption of revolution at the center was no longer justified. In his last article, dictated in February 1923, he asked, ". . . shall we be able to hold on [in the Soviet Union] with our small-scale and very small-scale peasant production, with our country in its present dilapidated state until Western European capitalist countries complete their development towards socialism?" His answer was in the negative, "But they are not completing this development as we previously expected they would. They are completing it not through a steady 'maturing' of socialism, but through the exploitation of some states by others through the exploitation of the first of the states to be defeated in the imperialist war combined with the exploitation of the whole of the East." And then, with characteristic perceptiveness, Lenin concluded:

Ultimately, the outcome of the struggle will be settled by the fact that Russia, India, China, etc., constitute the vast majority of the world's population. And it is this majority of the population which, during the past few years, has been drawn into the struggle for emancipation with extraordinary rapidity; in this respect there cannot be the slightest doubt concerning the final outcome of the world struggle. In this sense, the complete victory of socialism is absolutely assured.[4]

The history of the Third World during the twentieth century is a tribute to this flash of premonitory insight. Two factors stand out as being primarily responsible for the fateful switch from the anticipated revolutions in the center to the actual revolutions in the periphery. One was the increased power of workers in the Western industrialized countries after they had won the rights to vote in elections and to organize in trade unions. This enabled French and English workers, for example, nearly to double their real incomes during the second half of the nineteenth century. With wages no longer limited to biological reproduction levels, the domestic markets of the metropolitan centers expanded tremendously, while the workers naturally became more interested thereafter in ballots than in bullets.

This trend was sustained by the increasingly important role assumed by the Western states that introduced comprehensive welfare systems. Under these circumstances the Social Democratic parties before World War II, and even the Communist parties after World War II, abandoned their original vision of a new and qualitatively different society. Instead they adopted the reformist strategy of improving the position of labor within the framework of the existing social order. In doing so they accepted the division of the world into an exploiting center and an exploited periphery, a division that made possible the relative affluence of the center's labor force.

This leads to the second factor behind the revolutionary course of the Third World—namely, the deterioration of incomes and living standards at a time when they were rising in the center. The two contrasting trends were interrelated. Monopoly capital was able to pay higher wages at home because of the possibility of greater exploitation and increasing profits in the periphery. Hence the shift about 1873 in the terms of international trade against the Third World producers of raw materials and in favor of the metropolitan producers of manufactured goods. The application of Western capital and technology greatly increased the productivity of overseas plantations and mines, but the lack of political and trade union rights, together with the rapidly mounting population pressure and unemployment, deprived Third World workers of the substantial improvement in living standards enjoyed by their metropolitan counterparts. Instead Third World workers were caught in a price scissors of stagnant wages and rising cost of manufactured imports; with the rise of monopolies in the center, the prices of manufactured goods rose rapidly, since they were no longer determined by competition.

The following statistics indicate the degree of deterioration in trade relations experienced by Third World countries. Between 1800 and 1880 Britain's terms of trade steadily worsened, falling from index 245 in 1801–3, to 118 in 1843–46, to 110 in 1848–56 and to 100 in 1880. Thus Britain by 1880 had to export $2\frac{1}{2}$ times as much in manufactured goods as had been necessary in 1800 to receive the same amount of raw materials from the Third World. After 1880 the trend reversed, as the index for Third World exporters of raw materials fell from 163 in 1896–1900, to 120 in 1926–30, and to 100 in 1938. Third World countries could buy, with the same quantity of primary product exports, less than 60 percent of the manufactured goods they would have received in 1880. A United Nations study, *Relative Prices of Exports and Imports of Under-Developed Countries,* concluded that between 1876 and 1948 the terms of trade deteriorated between 35 and 50 percent at the expense of the countries exporting raw materials.

III. Multinational Corporations in the Third World

This chronic imbalance between developed and underdeveloped countries has been accentuated since World War II by the Third Industrial Revolution and the role of the multinational corporations (MNCs). This is evident in the manner in which the MNCs have extended the new high technology in agriculture and industry from the First World to the Third World.

In the case of agriculture, we have seen above (see Section I) that during and after World War II, American agriculture shifted from self-reliant family farms to a high-technology, energy-intensive food system in which agribusiness corporations dominated all links of the production chain—from seeds, fertilizers, pesticides and machinery to food processing and marketing. After World War II, this new food-production system spread rapidly overseas, replacing traditional family agriculture as it already had done in the United States. The supporters of agribusiness agriculture asserted that only in this way could the global race between food production and popualtion growth be won.

The overseas extension of the American agricultural system is commonly known as the Green Revolution. In the course of the exportation of the Green Revolution the interests of Third World peasants have been disregarded as completely as have the interests of American family farmers. In Mexico, for example, 97.7 percent of the land planted in corn and the overwhelming percentage of wheat lands were nonirrigated. A Mexican research group, the Institute for Agricultural Investigation, started a program to improve corn and wheat seeds for the small nonirrigated farms, but their efforts were superseded by those of Rockefeller Foundation scientists, who concentrated on increasing yields through genetic changes that require irrigation and fertilizer. The resulting new "miracle" strains enabled Mexico to become self-sufficient in wheat, but the beneficiaries were the wealthy landowners, who could afford the fertilizers and irrigation. The mass of the Mexican peasants have experienced increased unemployment or underemployment with the growing mechanization of the large estates.

Nevertheless, the Rockefeller Foundation was delighted with its "successful" Mexican test project. It established the International Center for Improvement of Maize and Wheat, with eight regional research organizations. This arrangement has benefited American corporations by opening up new global markets for their machines and chemicals at a time when the United States market is saturated and when concern about environmental abuse is mounting. In the Philippines, for example, the Esso Standard Fertilizer and Agricultural Company staffed and ran 400 agroservice stores in the early 1960s. The Philippine government supplied credit to farmers for purchases of seeds, fertilizers and chemicals and also introduced a sales force of government agents. The profitability of the Esso venture into agricultural development was guaranteed by government assurances of subsidies to farmers who desired to purchase the Esso products.

But in the Philippines, as in India and Pakistan—these three countries forming the vanguard of the Green Revolution—the final results have been disappointing. The basic problem is the same one that arose in Mexico: Seventy to 90 percent of the farmers of these countries have no irrigation and little money to purchase fertilizers. India's Minister of Agriculture, Mohan Ram, summarized the situation in 1969:

> The beneficiaries of the Green Revolution are the privileged minority of medium and large scale farmers. . . . Three to four percent of the biggest farmers exert all the political power, wield their influence, make all the decisions in collaboration with the State administration and take all the resources and the technical knowledge of government experts for themselves, while the poor receive very little. . . . The economic and political position of the rich peasantry has been strengthened and consolidated. . . . Large landowners are attempting to get rid—if necessary by force—of their

sharecroppers and former tenant farmers, with the objective of exploiting the land themselves or with the help of agricultural laborers.[5]

The overall effect of the Green Revolution has been to create conditions in the countryside precisely the opposite of the general prosperity and tranquillity that was anticipated. It has caused land reform, which is the prerequisite for any substantive and lasting improvement, to be shunted aside as a goal and forgotten. It is inducing the few farmers who can afford the new agricultural technology to introduce labor-saving mechanization. This mechanization in turn forces the already underemployed rural lower classes to flee to the slums in the cities, where they find themselves as superfluous as they had been in the countryside. This new urban lower class is now becoming the majority of the populations of the Third World cities. The net effect is to accentuate economic inequality and social tensions, leading some observers to predict that the Green Revolution will prove to be the prelude to Red Revolution.

Equally disruptive has been the impact of the Food for Peace program on Third World agriculture. Close to $30 billion worth of food was distributed by this program to over 130 countries between 1954 and 1980. Most Americans assume that this aid represents a humanitarian enterprise in support of needy peoples. In fact, the 1954 Agricultural Trade and Development Act (Public Law 480) was designed specifically to "improve the foreign relations of the United States" and to "promote the economic stability of American agriculture and the national welfare." Not until 1961 was the law's statement of purpose amended to include the goal of combating world hunger.

The need to buttress "the stability of American agriculture" was so urgent after the Korean War that the president of the American Farm Bureau warned that the accumulating food surpluses "will wreck our economy unless we can find sufficient markets to sustain the volume of production." [6] So successful was P.L. 480 in finding the needed markets that during the first twelve years of the program, one fourth of all U.S. agricultural exports were financed by the law's easy credit terms. But the flood of U.S. food lowered food prices in the recipient countries to the point where local farmers were unable to compete. The net result was the undermining of local food production and increased reliance on U.S. food imports. This pattern was reinforced by trade associations representing the U.S. food industry, which encouraged local populations to adopt American-style eating habits, using P.L. 480 local currencies to promote their campaigns. Hence the growing shift from fish to hamburgers, from rice to bread and from local to American soft drinks.

The success of P.L. 480 not only expanded U.S. markets at the expense of Third World self-sufficiency in food but also realized the law's other objective—to "improve the foreign relations of the United States." Senator Hubert Humphrey, one of the earliest champions of the Food for Peace program, explicitly recognized and lauded this achievement before a Senate committee (1957):

> I have heard . . . that people may become dependent on us for food. I know that was not supposed to be good news. To me, that was good news, because before people can do anything they have got to eat. And if you are looking for a way to get people to lean on you and to be dependent on you, in terms of their cooperation with you, it seems to me that food dependence would be terrific.[7]

Precisely the same viewpoint was expressed by Reagan's Secretary of Agriculture, John Block, during his confirmation hearings (1980): "Food is a weapon but the way to use that is to tie countries to us. That way they'll be far more reluctant to upset us." [8] Because of adverse publicity, Block several days later changed his terminology, if not his views, by terming food "a tool for peace."

This is not to say that Third World agriculture has not become more productive as a result of the new seeds and fertilizers and machines. But the beneficiaries of the increased productivity are *not* the peasants, who in fact now find themselves worse off than before. Production of export crops has risen dramatically, but subsistence crops have stagnated or declined. In Latin America, per-capita output of export crops increased 27 percent between 1964 and 1974, while in the same period per-capita output of subsistence crops declined 10 percent. This pattern goes back to the nineteenth century, when the colonialists promoted crops that could be exported for profit rather than crops needed by the local population. In the French colony of Vietnam, 40 percent of the arable land between 1860 and 1931 was diverted to export crops such as coffee, tea, rubber and export rice. The result was a 40 percent decline in food availability for the Vietnamese. The recent spread of agribusiness operations throughout the Third World has correspondingly spread the anomaly of increased agricultural productivity accompanied by increased malnutrition. In 1978 the UN Food and Agricultural Organization reported a sharp rise in the world's number of chronically undernourished, to a total of 450 million people. In the same year the U.S. Department of Agriculture reported that global per-capita food production was 27 percent higher than in the early 1960s and that in the 49 countries with the lowest per-capita income, the per-capita food increase had been 40 percent.

Mexico provides a typical example of the effect of the global diffusion of American agribusiness technology. Wealthy farmers in Mexico use the same production techniques as their counterparts in the United States. The wealthy farmers in Mexico plant the same hybrid seeds, buy the same machinery, fertilizers and pesticides from the same companies, borrow capital from the same banks and sell to the same corporations. Their vegetable exports now supply 60 percent of the U.S. market. But the number of landless Mexican peasants has increased from 1.5 million in 1950 to 5 million in 1980. While Americans consume Mexican strawberries and winter vegetables, uprooted Mexican peasants cross over into the United States as legal or illegal immigrants in search of work. At the other end of the world, the same pattern is manifest in India. Between 1956 and 1978 food production in that country rose 100 percent, while population grew 50 percent. Yet during the same period, per-capita grain consumption decreased, leaving over 315 million people below the poverty line—that is, with household incomes less than $8.00 a month in the countryside and $9.00 a month in cities.

The combination of more hunger amid more food explains the unprecedented migration into Third World cities. Djakarta's population rose from 1.7 million in 1950 to 5.5 million in 1975. Nairobi in 1900 was a village of 2,000. By 1980 it had grown to 1 million, and further growth to 4 million is expected by 2000. Mexico City was almost unmanageable in 1980 with a population of 14 million, yet an increase of another 14 million is expected during the next two decades. Since this urbanization is not accompanied by corresponding industrialization, the newcomers to the cities are forced into the kind of employment that saves them from outright starvation but that contributes nothing to the national economy. They resort to street vending, petty hawking, shoe shining, errand running, pushing a cart or pedaling a rickshaw.

The lack of adequate industrialization points up the fact that the Third Industrial Revolution has distorted Third World industrial as well as agricultural development. As noted in Chapter 13, overseas industrialization was actively discouraged during the colonial era. The rationalization for this policy was that continued export of raw materials would expand the export-oriented economies of the Third World, which in turn would increase per-capita income, generate funds for education and social services and eventually develop advanced modern societies in the periphery similar to those of the center.

The Great Depression and the Second World War forced a reappraisal of this traditional assumption. The Depression deflated catastrophically the price level of raw materials, making it impossible for Third World countries to import manufactured goods because of exchange shortages. The predicament worsened during World War II, when consumer manufactures no longer were available from Great Powers totally engaged in military production. Third World governments consequently were forced to supplement their exporting of raw materials with import-substitution industrialization. This was done by such measures as protective tariffs against manufactured imports, cheap credit for domestic industries, government construction of necessary industrial infrastructure and government participation in industrialization through development institutes and corporations.

The economic boom engendered by reconstruction following World War II and by the demands of the Korean War encouraged the belief that import-substituting industrialization was a viable long-term economic strategy. Latin America, which pioneered in this strategy, appeared for a few years to be on the way to developing industries that would process local raw materials, reduce dependence on foreign capital and foreign manufactured goods and thus attain at long last the economic independence needed to supplement the political independence won in the early nineteenth century.

About 1955 this hope began to evaporate. The industries that grew behind protective tariff walls proved inefficient, and required the importation of capital-intensive machinery, which worsened exchange problems and increased unemployment. Most basic was the inadequate domestic market for local industries. So long as the overdue land reforms were avoided, so long income distribution remained grossly inequitable and local purchasing power remained correspondingly deficient. The new industries consequently were forced to concentrate on producing luxury and semiluxury goods, such as refrigerators, dishwashers, washing machines and television sets for the local elite, which formerly had imported them from abroad. But only limited quantities of such goods could be sold at home, because they were far beyond the reach of the masses of the local population. Nor could such goods be exported, since they were usually produced more efficiently and more cheaply in the developed countries. Thus import-substituting industrialization soon reached a dead end, with Third World countries still plagued by the usual symptoms of underdevelopment: continued economic dependency, massive structural unemployment and runaway migration from the countryside to the cities, with the resulting scourge of urbanization without industrialization.

The failed strategy of import-substituting industrialization was followed by a new economic strategy offered by the MNCs. Several factors made possible the extraordinarily rapid growth of the MNCs after World War II. One was steady technological advance in the center, which has been the prerequisite for every surge of overseas expansion, from the days of the conquistadors to those of the jet-propelled corporate executives. The centrally directed global operations of today's MNCs are possible because of certain technological innovations of the Third

Industrial Revolution, including containerized shipping, satellite communications and computerized cash-management systems. Also, the division and subdivision of the production process has been carried to the point where the fragmented operations require little skill and can be learned in a very short time. Another factor facilitating the growth of MNCs was the existence of the tariff barriers designed to protect the import-substitution industries. When the corporations found that tariffs were obstructing the export of their products to Third World countries, they simply installed their plants behind the tariff walls and produced directly for local markets and also for external markets, which they were able to penetrate because of their low labor costs and efficient operations. Finally, the MNCs were assisted in their growth by Third World governments eager to attract foreign capital and industry in order to relieve their unemployment and exchange difficulties. Thus the MNCs received very generous concessions, including cheap or free sites; infrastructure facilities; preferential tax treatment; unrestricted repatriation of profits; and closely restricted, poorly paid labor supply. All this makes possible the "export platforms" where MNCs use cheap local labor to process imported materials and components into sophisticated industrial products that are sold at high profit in the markets of developed countries.

It is not surprising that since 1950, MNCs have grown at an average rate of 10 percent a year, as against 4 percent for noninternational corporations. The median MNC now produces 22 products in 11 different countries. In 1980, a business organization, the Conference Board, ranked the world's 100 largest economic units. The top ones, as might be expected, were countries such as the United States, the Soviet Union, Japan, West Germany, France and China, in that order. But 39 of the 100 turned out to be not countries but MNCs. The largest company, Exxon, has sales larger than the output of all countries except for the top 15. Only three socialist countries (U.S.S.R., China and Poland) surpass Exxon, and only two in the Third World (Brazil and India).

The proliferating MNCs have been effusively praised by Western spokesmen such as Dr. Daniel Moynihan, who stated in 1975 when he was United States representative to the United Nations that "the multinational corporation, combining modern management with liberal trade policies, is arguably the most creative international institution of the 20th century." [9] Moynihan's statement is akin to that of nineteenth-century spokesmen of the Manchester school of economics who insisted that global free trade was beneficial for everybody concerned. All the while, nevertheless, India's textile industry deliberately was being ruined, the peasants of Java and India were being compelled to grow jute and cotton and indigo rather than the foodstuffs they needed to avert recurring famines, and China was punished by force of arms for daring, in defiance of the sacred principle of freedom of trade, to prohibit the importation of British opium from India.

So it is today. Regardless of the proclamations of nineteenth-century Manchesterites and twentieth-century Moynihans, equality of treatment is equitable only among equals. Consequently the touted "liberal trade policies" were beneficial for Manchester but not for India, and today they are beneficial for the MNCs but not for Third World countries.

It has been argued, for example, that the MNCs provide jobs in countries where they are desperately needed, but the nature of these jobs is not usually examined. Numerous American corporations have set up plants in Hong Kong, where 60 percent of the labor force works seven days a week. Part of that labor force are 34,000 children of age 14 or younger, half of whom work 10 hours or more per day. The largest number of American plants abroad are located in Mexico, where the original attraction was a minimum hourly wage of 50 cents for adult males. But when union pressure raised the wage to $1.13, the companies began moving to Haiti, where the minimum wage is $1.30 for a full day's work.

Such low pay perhaps could be justified if these jobs provided a means for the transmission of technological skills needed for local development. But not much skill is required to assemble electronic equipment, toys, clothes or sports goods. And the skills that workers may acquire are for the most part irrelevant to local needs. Thus, if a foreign plant is closed in pursuit of still lower wages elsewhere, its employees are left stranded without applicable skills. More serious is the fact that when a MNC signs a contract with a Third World government for the transfer of technology, the fees are usually exorbitant. Mexico, for example, is paying technology royalties amounting to no less than 15.9 percent of the value of its exports! In addition, 80 percent of the contracts, according to a UN study, prohibit the use of the technology for producing exports. The multinationals' wish to restrict competition is understandable, but the effect, nevertheless, is to prevent Third World countries from earning foreign exchange through exports. Furthermore, the transferred technology is usually of the capital-intensive, labor-saving variety, which further aggravates the already serious problems of capital shortage and chronic unemployment that plague underdeveloped countries.

It has also been argued that multinationals provide the capital necessary for the industrialization of the Third World. In fact the precise opposite is the case; more capital flows from underdeveloped to developed areas than the other way around. A 1970 UN study revealed that between 1957 and 1965, American-based multinationals financed 83 percent of their Latin American investments locally, either from reinvested earnings or from Latin American savings. In addition, the global operations of the MNCs enable them to buy and sell to their own subsidiaries, and hence to export Third World commodities at bargain rates and to price their imports at inflated levels. The end result is a net flow of capital each year from the poor to the rich countries, a trend accelerated by the mounting debt load of the poor countries. This debt load has skyrocketed from $19 billion in 1960, to $64 billion in 1970 and to $376 billion in 1979. In the process of meeting the charges on these debts the underdeveloped countries are now paying the developed countries more than they receive in the form of aid.

MNCs have proven no more successful than import-substituting industrialization in coping with the problems of the underdeveloped countries. Rather than ending the economic subordination of the Third World to the First World, the MNCs have intensified the subordination. The reason is that in the past, most capital was exported from the center to the periphery to finance locally organized enterprises producing raw materials needed by the center. Today, however, MNCs establish and operate their own plants within Third World countries, thereby gaining a degree of control over the economies of those countries that would have been unattainable in the earlier period of portfolio investments. Whereas before World War I, three fourths of all foreign investments in the Third World were of the portfolio variety and only one fourth were direct and controlling investments, the ratio at present is exactly reversed. Thus the head of West Germany's largest commercial bank describes the vulnerability of underdeveloped states to his financial power:

> A prime necessity . . . is the improvement of the investment climate in the developing countries themselves, as well as an improvement in the whole attitude towards business activity. . . . In the longer term the necessary investment climate will be created by sheer force of circumstance, because automatically investment capital will flow to those countries providing the necessary conditions—and there are already a number of them. The others will undoubtedly learn the lesson and follow suit in their own interest.[10]

Such confidence that sovereign nations will "learn the lesson and follow suit" suggests that nominally independent countries are in reality "company countries," reminiscent of comparable "company towns" in the United States, such as Bethlehem, Pennsylvania (Bethlehem Steel), Bisbee, Arizona (Phelps-Dodge Copper) and Butte, Montana (Anaconda Copper).

The second reason why the MNCs offer no way out for Third World countries is that the MNCs intensify the degree of exploitation as well as of subordination. Indeed, the purpose of the latter is to ensure the former, as is clearly implied in the above statement by the West German banker. The degree of exploitation is reflected in the rate of foreign dividends of MNCs, which invariably is substantially higher than the rate of their domestic earnings. This was spelled out in revealing detail in a letter sent to the New York Times (Jan. 12, 1977), by C. Fred Bergsten, Assistant Secretary for Internal Affairs of the U.S. Department of the Treasury:

> . . . the rate of return in 1976 on U.S. investments in the developing countries was 25 percent—more than twice the rate of return on our direct investments in the developed countries. . . . In 1976 earnings on our direct investments in developing countries totaled $7 billion compared to investment outflows of only $2.8 billion. These investments expand the output of critical raw materials needed by our economy. They increase our exports by stimulating demand in the host countries for U.S. goods, technology and managerial skills. U.S. sales in the non-oil developing countries now total about 25 percent of total U.S. exports creating hundreds of thousands of jobs in this country.

The significance of Bergsten's testimony is increased by the fact that the high profits currently extracted from the Third World are being reinvested mostly in developed countries. Thus we are witnessing today a repetition of the nineteenth-century pattern when Britain invested equally generous dividends from India in the United States and the dominions (see Chapter 13, Section I). Gerard Chaliand has noted this recurring pattern of taking from the poor to give to the rich:

> While receiving nearly half of U.S. foreign investments in 1965, Western Europe contributed only little more than a fifth of the repatriated profits the rest of the world turned over to the United States. Latin America took in $1.1 billion between 1965 and 1968 and paid out $5.4 billion in profits, for an overall loss of $4.3 billion, while for Europe, the figures add up to a gain of $800 million. In short, it is as though the poor countries, through the intermediary of the United States, had been financing part of the development of Western Europe and the United States itself.[11]

Third World countries are being drained not only of their raw materials and capital but also of their scientific labor power. A United Nations study discloses that during the decade 1961–71, over 53,000 scientists (including engineers and doctors) immigrated to the United States from the Third World. Of the net addition to the number of scientists employed in the United States during 1965–70, more than 20 percent came from abroad. The study also notes that in 1970 the immigrant scientists added $3.7 billion to the U.S. national income, in contrast to the $3.1 billion of American official development assistance to the Third World in the same year.[12]

All this means a continual widening of the gap between rich countries and poor. The share of the underdeveloped countries in world income has fallen from 65 percent in 1850 to 22 percent in 1960. In his valedictory address as president of the World Bank (Sept. 30, 1980), Robert S. McNamara foresaw a continuation of this past pattern. Over the next five years the underdeveloped countries are likely to show an average annual growth of 1.8 percent, compared with 2.7 percent during the past decade, and 3.1 percent in the 1960s. The 1980 *Annual Report* of the World Bank concludes that "the rich and poor nations alike form a world community and . . . this community will be hard-pressed to survive future decades filled with shocks and turbulences without social upheaval." [13]

Social upheaval indeed is the prognosis indicated by the above analysis of the historical forces operating in today's Third World. And upheaval is likely to erupt more frequently and to be more radical than it has in the past.

IV. Revolutionary Movements in the Third World

The continually widening gap between the First World and the Third World has not resulted in automatic outbreak of worldwide revolution, but the gap has created for the first time the potentiality of revolution on a global scale. However, the step from revolutionary potential to revolutionary act is extraordinarily difficult and seldom negotiated.

Many obstacles inhibit the leap from disaffection to open armed revolution. Some are economic, such as the independence of peasant productive units; the tyranny of the peasants' work routine, which is broken only at grave peril for the peasant's family; and the temptation to withdraw from conflict back into independent subsistence production. Also, there are strong social factors working against recourse to revolution. The village is the center of continuity and security, in which each peasant has an acknowledged place in the order of things. Ties of family, Church and community are strong, while the life of the guerrilla is notoriously arduous and precarious. Finally, there are the powerful psychological inhibitions induced by millennia of subjugation and obedience. Peasants traditionally have been excluded from the decision-making process in the wider world, so that they lack the knowledge and confidence to articulate their aspirations and to act upon them.

For these reasons, revolutions have occurred mostly during difficult transition periods when old social systems are dissolving and new ones have not yet crystallized. One such period in the past was the early medieval era, when the process of enserfment provoked scattered revolutions in the Holy Roman Empire during the ninth and tenth centuries. The next was in late medieval times, when European peasants rose against the monetization of what by then had become the established feudal order (see Chapter 2, Section I). Today, with the penetratration of capitalism into the countrysides of the entire globe, peasants everywhere are being dispossessed and forced into increasingly unlivable urban centers in the greatest mass migration of all time.

Even the wholesale uprooting of tens of millions of peasant families has not resulted in worldwide revolutionary outbreaks. It required two world wars to provide the sparks needed to ignite the revolutionary potential. The world wars weakened the colonial powers while stimulating the nationalist aspirations and social visions of the subject colonial peoples.

Yet even the disruption and chaos of world wars cannot by themselves engender basic social revolutions as distinct from nationalist takeovers. Social restructuring requires the vision of an alternative new order sufficiently impelling to induce the guerrilla fighter to jeopardize himself and his family. Such vision, however, does not originate with peasants, who necessarily comprise the great majority of Third World guerrilla forces. Peasants furnish the manpower but others must provide the ideology and the leadership. The course of twentieth-century revolutions, therefore, has been determined largely by which of the following three ideologies succeeded in attracting peasant support: the ideologies of religious revivalism, of reform or of revolution.

Religious revivalism is related to the "conservative reaction" of the pre-twentieth-century period, noted in Chapter 18, Section II. But today a movement formerly associated with archaic dynastic and landed interests now is attracting a mass following in certain regions and is expressing not only traditional tenets but also progressive and even revolutionary doctrines. Religious revivalism is a reaction to the failures and crises of both reformist and revolutionary regimes. The internal and external pressures besetting these regimes have induced their citizens to seek refuge in religion as the only absolute in a sea of uncertainties. An Egyptian journalist, Mohammed Heikel, has stated that "religion has become an idiom for political expression . . . faith has become a citadel where encircled nationalisms have fortified themselves for a last-ditch stand in the battle for their future, not their past."[14]

Religious revivalism is not restricted today to the Third World. Whenever people in any society, developed or underdeveloped, sense a loss of control and of direction, their reaction frequently is to seek historical identity and unity through religion. Since religion thus becomes "an idiom for political expression," it is used for both conservative and revolutionary purposes. In the United States, a 1976 Gallup Poll revealed that nearly fifty million adult Americans, more than one third of those old enough to vote, have experienced "born again" religious conversions. These evangelicals are of all political persuasions. Some support radical causes and practice alternative life-styles in extended families and communes. The radical Wesleyans—Nazarenes, Free and Wesleyan Methodists, the Salvation Army and the Church of God Reformation Movement—are motivated by John Wesley's determination to apply the ethic of "perfect love" to social evils such as poverty. Increasingly articulate are the fundamentalists, who take "profamily" positions on issues such as abortion, homosexuality and prayer in the schools. They also tend to equate biblical doctrine with rugged capitalism, unlimited material accumulation and military preparedness to combat "atheistic communism."

Such conflicting trends in American revivalism have their counterparts in the Third World. In the Middle East, for example, Islam is harnessed by the most disparate political groups to attain their political objectives. Libya's Colonel Qaddafi, referred to by both Egypt's Sadat and Iran's ex-Shah as "crazy," is striving to transform his country into a *jamahiriya* or "state of the masses." In his *Green Book* he has set forth principles reminiscent of Mao's Cultural Revolution. Neon signs everywhere flash slogans such as "Partners, not wage earners," "Revolution forever" and "No democracy without people's committees." Colonel Qaddafi has chosen for himself the role of "revolutionary instigator," dedicated to awakening Libya and the entire world to the need for a new social order in which "the masses take command of their destiny and their wealth." [15]

The Koran's principles of justice and social equality are stressed also in other radical Moslem countries such as Algeria and South Yemen, as well as in the Moro and Polisario national liberation struggles in the Philippines and the Sahara, respectively. At the other end of the political spectrum are reactionary Islamic regimes such as those in Pakistan and Saudi Arabia. In the latter country, Koranic precepts dominate all institutions and practices to a degree that even many Moslems feel straitjacketed. But because the standards are so absolute, the dangers of falling from grace are that much greater. Hence the furious reaction of the Saudi government against a British television documentary drama, *Death of a Princess*, with its allusions to corruption and illicit sex in the royal family. Hence also the panic of the Saudi regime when Moslem militants seized the Grand Mosque in Mecca (Nov.

1979), demanding the overthrow of the dynasty, which they accused of using religion to mask its corruption and degeneracy.

The conflicting interpretation and utilization of Islam is especially striking in Iran. The leftist Islamic guerrillas, the Mujahidin, issued the following statement in 1973 when they were an underground resistance group fighting against the Shah:

> Marxism and Islam are not identical. Nevertheless, Islam is definitely closer to Marxism than to Pahlevism. Who is closer to Islam: the Vietnamese who fight against American imperialism or the Shah who helps Zionism? . . . The Shah is terrified of revolutionary Islam. This is why he keeps on shouting a Muslim cannot be a revolutionary. In his mind a man is either a Muslim or a revolutionary; he cannot be both. But in the real world, the exact opposite is true. A Muslim is either a revolutionary or not a true Muslim.[16]

It is not happenstance that precisely the same point is made in the Latin American "theology of liberation"—a Christian must be a revolutionary or he is not a Christian (see Chapter 23, Section IID). And just as the Shah persecuted the Mujahidin, so the Stroessners and the Pinochets hound radical priests who interpret Jesus as a revolutionary leader and try to follow his example.

Turning from religious revivalism to reform, we find a movement motivated essentially by nationalism and supported primarily by Westernized merchants, teachers, clerks, officials and military officers. Although their rhetoric is often revolutionary, their objectives are strictly reformist. They carefully avoid basic social change and therefore reject the essence of Marxism, which is class struggle. They pay compensation for expropriated land and encourage the development of a new rural middle class, which becomes one of the pillars of the new social order. The main changes occur in the cities, where the wealth of the bourgeoisie is evident in its new industrial and commercial activities and in its investments in rural properties.

Early examples of such national bourgeois regimes are the Chinese republicans who overthrew the Manchu Dynasty; the Young Turks who dethroned Sultan Abdul Hamid; the Constitutionalists who beat back the radical Zapatistas and Villistas in the Mexican revolution; the Wafd Party, which extracted concessions from the British in Egypt; and the Congress Party, which did likewise in India. Post-World War II examples of reformist regimes are Egypt under Nasser, Guinea under Sekou Touré, Mali under Modibo Keita, Ghana under Kwame Nkrumah,

Indonesia under Sukarno, Peru under General Velasco and Algeria under Ben Bella and Boumedienne.

The third ideology, that of revolution or socialism, emerged as a practical alternative in the Third World with the 1917 Bolshevik Revolution. It was not accidental that this revolution occurred in a country where an impoverished peasantry had been sufficiently radicalized by an exploitive Tsarist regime and by a disastrous war to follow the socialist leadership of Lenin rather than the bourgeois leadership of Kerensky. Likewise it was not accidental that the Bolshevik Revolution failed to spread to Germany, where the peasants were relatively prosperous and therefore supported the reformist Social Democrats rather than the revolutionary Spartacists. With the failure of social revolution in Central and Western Europe, the colonial powers were able to forestall revolutionary movements in the Third World during the interwar years.

The Second World War, however, let loose a new wave of social revolution, beginning in China and spreading to Southeast Asia, Cuba and Portuguese Africa. In addition, Communist regimes were established in Eastern Europe, some gaining power by their own efforts, as in the case of Yugoslavia and Albania, but most being installed by the advancing Soviet armies.

Such were the circumstances in which, contrary to Marx's expectation, the great revolutions of the twentieth century have occurred, and are occurring, in Third World countries. A noteworthy feature of these colonial revolutions is the speed with which they have become sophisticated and effective. A considerable number of the earliest insurrections predated the First World War, as noted in the preceding chapter. These pioneer uprisings or resistance movements in the Philippines, Mexico, Persia, Cuba, Korea, Africa and other regions had no historical precedents on which they could draw for guidance. They lacked revolutionary theory regarding the nature of imperialism and the need for protracted guerrilla warfare. Nor could they depend on support from international revolutionary organizations or sympathetic peace societies and social reform groups.

Today Third World revolutionaries no longer need operate in isolation and ignorance. The Vietnamese during their decades of struggle against French, Japanese and American interventionists received worldwide backing, both official and unofficial. More important, they evolved a successful operational strategy through trial and error, and through the study of other revolutionary movements. "On the way to socialism and communism," declared a prominent Vietnamese leader, "no country is always right. Each sometimes makes mistakes and must correct them. Nothing is stable—there must be changes, because it is a new path, and we must learn from others' experience as well as from our own, from our work, and from reality. We must always be correcting ourselves. The road from socialism to communism is a rough and uneven way. It isn't all plain sailing." [17]

The writings of Mao, Ho, Cabral and Guevera now are studied throughout the Third World, and their teachings adapted to local conditions. Revolutionary leaders have gained immeasurably in self-confidence and independence during the few decades since World War II. The first resistance organization to challenge Western counterrevolution after the war was the National Liberation Front (EAM) of Greece. The EAM had massive popular support because of its leadership in the struggle against the Axis occupation. But the Communist leaders of the EAM were so accustomed to following the Kremlin line that they allowed Stalin's British allies to land troops in Greece, who were then used to smash the EAM forces. Stalin meanwhile kept diplomatically silent, in accord with his bargain with Churchill for the division of the Balkan Peninsula into Soviet and British spheres of influence.

By contrast, Third World revolutionaries today accept aid but no dictation from Moscow and Peking. Mao at one time had urged Third World leaders to persist on their revolutionary course regardless of Moscow's foreign policy. His advice now is being followed in the Third World, and at the expense not only of Moscow, but also of Peking and any other capital with "hegemonistic" aspirations. President Samora Machel of Mozambique typifies this independence and self-confidence:

> We made mistakes and saw how to correct them. We had successes and saw how to improve on them. In doing this, we evolved a theory out of our practice; and then we found that this theory of ours, evolving out of our practice, had already acquired a theorization under different circumstances, elsewhere, in different times and places. This theory and theorization is Marxism-Leninism. . . . Marxism-Leninism is not something we chose out of a book. . . . It was in the process of struggle that we synthesized the lessons of each experience, forging our ideology, constructing the theoretical instruments of our struggle. . . .[18]

Revolutionary movements have made substantial gains during this century, albeit with much tacking back and forth. Since 1917 a variety of noncapitalist regimes have been established in the Soviet Union, China, North Korea, Indochina, Cuba, Portugal's African ex-colonies, South Yemen, Ethiopia and Somalia. These comprise about 28 percent of the world's land area and one third of the world's population. This pattern is likely to persist, so that the last two decades of the twentieth century probably will witness a revolutionary wave comparable to that during the two decades after World War II. But whereas the earlier revolutions were predominantly nationalistic, those of the future, because of the demonstrated unviability of neocolonialism, will be predominantly social revolutionary, and of both the secular and religious variety.

℣ V. Counterrevolutionary Strategies of the First World

Western powers from the beginning have opposed, directly or indirectly, Third World revolutionary movements. In the nineteenth century they bolstered the Manchu Dynasty in China, the princes and landlords of India, the tribal chiefs of Africa and the shahs and sultans of the Middle East against their respective enemies, who were usually nationalists and/or constitutionalists. Hence the paradox of the West being the enemy of Third World Westernizers. This pattern prevailed also in the twentieth century, with the Western powers supporting Chiang Kai-shek, Syngman Rhee, Thieu, Marcos, Shah Reza and Mobutu against revolutionary leaders of the stature of Mao, Ho, Cabral, Machel and Castro. The prevailing pattern was recognized by Mao after firsthand experience:

> From the time of China's defeat in the Opium War of 1840, Chinese progressives went through untold hardships in their quest for truth from Western countries . . . every effort was made to learn from the West. In my youth, I, too engaged in such studies. They represented the culture of Western bourgeois democracy, including social theories and natural sciences of that period, and they were called the "new learning" in contrast to Chinese feudal culture, which was called "old learning."
>
> Imperialist aggression shattered the fond dreams of the Chinese about learning from the West. It was very odd—why were the teachers always committing aggression against their pupil? [19]

The persistent counterrevolutionary strategy was not the result of miscalculation or perverse obscurantism on the part of Western policymakers. Its unbroken continuity through the centuries suggests more fundamental institutional roots. The dynamics of industrial capitalism in the early nineteenth century engendered the free-trade imperialism that precipitated the Opium War, obstructed the Taiping rebels and sabotaged Mohammad Ali's efforts to develop an economically independent Egypt. Likewise the monopoly capitalism of the late nineteenth century generated the pre-emptive colonial imperialism that divided up most of the Third World into possessions of a few European powers.

Monopoly capitalism persists to the present day, but now it must cope with nationalist and social revolutionary movements convulsing the peripheral lands. Direct colonial rule has become either militarily impractical or financially prohibitive. Hence the wholesale decolonization and shift from colonialism to neocolonialism. If colonialism is a system of direct domination by the application of superior power, then neocolonialism is a system of indirect domination that cedes political independence in order to preserve economic dependence and exploitation.

Colonialism depended on metropolitan administrators, civilian and military, who bolstered and utilized the most obscurantist segments of indigenous society, including semifeudal and tribal personages. Neocolonialism, by contrast, turns to the bourgeois elements, formerly the most vocal opponents of colonialism during its waning years, but now serving as its principal allies. Amilcar Cabral perceptively defined the essential aim of neocolonialism as being "to create a false bourgeoisie to put a brake on the revolution, and to enlarge the possibilities of the petit bourgeoisie as a neutralizer of the revolution." [20] Gunnar Myrdal has similarly defined the origins and nature of neocolonialism:

> In the worldwide colonial power system as it functioned until the Second World War, *there was a built-in mechanism that almost automatically led the colonial power to ally itself with the privileged groups.* Those groups could be relied upon to share its interest in "law and order," which mostly implied economic and social *status quo.*
>
> To support its reign, the colonial power would thus generally feel an interest in upholding or even strengthening the inegalitarian social and economic structure in a colony. . . . Often it even happened that new privileges and new privileged groups were created by the colonial power in order to stabilize its rule over a colony.
>
> There is no doubt that a similar mechanism has been operating after the liquidation of colonialism and that, now as before, it also has its counterpart in relation to those underdeveloped countries that were politically independent, primarily in Latin America. *This is the* main justification for the use of the term *"neo-colonialism."* [21]

It follows from the above that the neocolonial system of indirect control is feasible only if the newly independent regimes are purely nationalist in character and objectives. But if they are social revolutionary and seek to restructure institutions and relationships with the metropolitan center, then neocolonialism obviously becomes impossible. Revolutionaries striving for economic as well as political independence by promoting horizontal rather than vertical economic linkages inevitably will clash with a neocolonial system designed to preserve dependency.

This explains why the granting of political independence to dozens of colonies after the Second World War was far from indiscriminate. It was readily extended to *nationalist* leaders or parties, except in a few regions such as Algeria, Kenya and Rhodesia, where white settlements existed. By contrast, independence was implacably denied wherever there was the danger of a social revolutionary regime. In such cases the response was armed repression or covert "destabilization" or any other tactic necessary to deny power to the revolutionaries, or to oust them from power. The difference in reaction was not a matter of chance or personal caprice. Rather it was dictated by the requirements of monopoly capitalism, which are basically the same in the present decades of multinational corporations as they were in the past decades of international cartels.

Monopoly capitalism today is plagued and driven by the same inequitable distribution of income and wealth as it was in the nineteenth century. This leads to a consumer demand inadequate to absorb the output of existing productive facilities, much less to provide profitable investment opportunities for surplus capital. Domestic efforts to resolve this dilemma in the United States included the government measures to impose stabilization and integration during the Progressive era and the New Deal, and the heavy military spending in the post-World War II years. Neither of these policies worked, as evidenced by the high unemployment persisting until the outbreak of World War II, and by the stagflation prevailing today. Hence the growing importance of the Third World as a source of raw materials, as a market for surplus capital and more recently as a haven for runaway industries seeking cheap labor. These roles can be fulfilled, however, only if the Third World remains an integral part of the world market economy. To ensure that it does remain is the *raison d'être* of the West's counterrevolutionary strategy today, as it has been in the past.

During the nineteenth century Britain was the leading imperialist power and therefore the leading counterrevolutionary force throughout the world, whether directed against the Taiping rebellion or the Indian mutiny or the periodic insurrections in Africa. After World War I the United States gradually replaced Britain, especially in the Western Hemisphere. And after World War II the United States became the unchallenged leader of the capitalist world. In contrast to other belligerents, the United States emerged from the war with her territory unscathed, her industries expanded and her technology unrivaled. In 1948 the GNP of the United States was almost three times that of Britain, France, West Germany and Italy combined ($260 billion as against $88 billion). Equally important was the fact that the American economy did not experience a postwar depression, as some had feared. Pent-up consumer demands at home, together with the needs of American-financed reconstruction and rehabilitation abroad, assured the prosperity of the Truman years. Then after a relative slowdown during the two Eisenhower terms, there was another sustained spurt beginning with Kennedy. This was facilitated by the steady increase in military expenditures, which in turn provided backing for an aggressive foreign policy. Henry Luce very plausibly looked forward to the future with confidence, and hailed the advent of the "American century."

As soon as the Second World War began, American policymakers began thinking in terms of an "American century" and of the strategy necessary for its realization. The Council on Foreign Relations, which has played a key role in the formulation and execution of American foreign policy, presented a memorandum on July 24, 1941, to the President and Secretary of State outlining the council's views on "American policy, its function in the present war, and its possible role in the postwar period." It began by emphasizing that the "economy of the United States is geared to the export of certain manufactured and agricultural products, and the import of numerous raw materials and foodstuffs." Continuation of this exchange was considered essential if the American economy were to avoid "possible stresses making for its own disintegration, such as unwieldy export surpluses or severe shortages of consumer goods."

The memorandum defined a "Grand Area" that the American economy needed "to survive without major readjustments." This consisted of virtually the entire world outside German-dominated Europe, namely, the Western Hemisphere, the United Kingdom, the remainder of the British Commonwealth and Empire, the Dutch East Indies, China and Japan. Failure to defend militarily and to economically integrate the "Grand Area" would seriously strain the American economy by cutting off vital imports and restricting the export of American agricultural and manufactured surpluses. For the immediate future, therefore, the objective of American foreign policy should be to contain the German and Japanese danger to the "Grand Area." After the war, "much would have to be done toward reshaping the world, particularly Europe." The memorandum therefore listed topics for further study, and these included the creation of international financial institutions to stabilize currencies, and of international banking institutions to facilitate investment in, and development of, backward areas.[22]

The Roosevelt administration, in close touch with the Council, accepted these guidelines, as did succeeding administrations. This is evident in American wartimes measures to assist Britain and contain Japan, and also in postwar economic and political policies, such as the establishment of the International Monetary Fund and the World Bank, the waging of the Cold War against the Soviet Union and the mobilizing of counterrevolutionary movements in the Third World. All of these policies were designed to maintain control over the "Grand Area" and thereby enable American capitalism to continue without basic restructuring.

For two decades after World War II the United States effectively controlled its "Grand Area." But by the late 1960s the "American century" obviously was coming to an early end in the face of the Vietnam debacle, the growing economic challenge by the hitherto dependent states of Western Europe and Japan, the novel and intractable domestic problem of stagflation and the recurring explosions in the volatile Third World. The ensuing "Great Debate" over how the United States should cope with the chaotic new world engendered three main schools of thought. One is Kissinger's *Realpolitik* or balance-of-power approach, stressing military strength; global stability; and unilateral moves, which on some occasions embarrassed America's allies (as the opening to China did Japan) and on other occasions put the United States in a go-it-alone position (as it did in Vietnam). The second school is that of the Trilateralists, who seek unity among the United States, Japan and the West European countries in order to present a common front against the Soviet bloc and radical Third World regimes. Finally, there is the right-wing school, articulated by Reagan administration spokesmen, which holds that the United States is yielding ground to an imperialistic and increasingly strong Soviet Union, and which therefore favors all-out military preparedness and unyielding confrontation against any Soviet aggression or Third World revolution—the two being considered interactive and inseparable.

The above three schools differ sharply on specific issues such as SALT, détente, the Panama Canal and military preparedness. But these are differences regarding the tactics necessary to attain basic strategic objectives concerning which all parties agree: free access to Third World raw materials and markets, preservation of the existing Western global predominance, and perforce, preservation also of the prevailing inequities in the global distribution of wealth and power. This overarching conservative goal is apparent in all phases of United States foreign policy—political, economic and cultural—which will be analyzed successively in the following sections.

A.
Political Strategy of Counterrevolution

The initial step in the political strategy of counterrevolution has been noted above—namely, the selective granting of independence to leaders or movements that were nationalist rather than social revolutionary. Hence the relatively peaceful winning of independence in India, Ceylon, Burma and most of the British and French colonies in Africa. In all these cases colonialism was followed by neocolonialism. The skin color of the ruling elites took on a darker hue, but there was no basic restructuring of local institutions or of economic relationships with the metropolis. How comfortable, harmonious and superficial was the transition to independence under those circumstances is evident in the following account of social life in the Indian mountain resort of Darjeeling, persisting in the year 1977 virtually unchanged from the days of the British Raj:

As the baking heat of summer creeps across the broad, flat Ganges River valley, pushing the temperature toward 120 degrees, Indians by the thousands are heading for the hills, as they do every year at this time.

Darjeeling, which the British celebrated as the queen of the hill stations, is gloriously back in season. "Of course it's not like the old days, when the crowd was really gay and glittering," said the Maharajah of Burdwan, who has spent most of his 71 summers at the mountain resort 300 miles north of Calcutta. "But one still comes back and enjoys it". . . .

Now the tourists at places like this are Indian not British, but little else seems to have changed. The summer people, as they are called, still delight in the chance to wear their scratchy tweeds and ascots as they stroll with their walking sticks along Darjeeling's mall, which is like a beachfront boardwalk except that the view is of some of the world's highest mountains. . . .

They stay in guest houses that have gingerbread gables and names like the Windamere Snuggery, the Evergreen and Summer Boon, and, in the manner of summer tourists escaping to Michigan or Maine, they take great pleasure in reading in the Calcutta newspapers how hot it is back home. . . .

Members sit on the veranda behind the rickety green railing and sip strong Darjeeling tea brewed from the leaves that grow on the steeply terraced slopes all around here.

But Marigold Wisden, an English woman who runs the place, says it's not the same as the old days, when the young bachelor members, most of them tea planters, would dress up in long white stockings and silver-buckled slippers for the annual Knight-Errants Ball. Now, in the dining rooms of some of the hotels, the highest form of night life is a stately fox trot, performed by rich Calcutta businessmen and their wives, who appear in diamonds and gold-flecked saris.

"It's a bit of the old India, you know," said a Bombay housewife who was there for drinks the other night.

"That's one thing we love about Darjeeling—it reminds us of the past." [23]

This account of Darjeeling social life makes clear why Western governments adopted one policy toward Third World nationalists and quite another to Third World revolutionaries. Armed repression and years of bloody struggle were the fates of colonies that aspired to economic as well as political independence. On the other hand, the experiences of former colonies that chose or were forced to follow the path of neocolonialism did not prove altogether unruffled and nonviolent. Frequently it turned out that the storms were merely delayed. The reason was that nationalist leaders faced an insoluble predicament. They were expected to defer to the interests of foreign governments and investors, as well as of their own local elites, but in doing so they reduced the chances of implementing their promises for economic development and higher living standards.

This contradiction is the root cause for the chronic instability of Third World governments, and for the prevailing pattern of military elites replacing the civilian elites that assumed office on the granting of independence. Most Third World countries have experienced a circulation of elites, beginning with the colonial administrators of the pre-independence period, and followed by nationalist political leaders and then by military bureaucrats. All three of these elites generally shared similar ideological predilections, having been trained under colonial auspices or influences.

The varied constraints, internalized as well as imposed, under which these elites functioned made it difficult for them to cope with the basic problems facing all Third World countries in the postindependence period. Hence the increasing frequency of insurrections, and the prognosis of the 1980 World Bank Report that the increase will persist in the 1980s. Faced with this dilemma, Western policymakers have resorted to the second tactic in their political strategy of counterrevolution, namely, a variety of repressive measures, including overt and armed intervention, covert "destabilization" and bolstering of conservative "subimperialist" powers to serve as junior partners in maintaining the status quo in strategic regions.

American armed intervention has been employed to a degree that is little appreciated. A report entitled "Instances of Use of U.S. Armed Forces Abroad, 1798–1945" was prepared at the request of Senator Everett McKinley Dirksen and published in the *Congressional Record* (June 23, 1969). It lists nearly 160 occasions when American forces were used abroad, and an overwhelming majority of these were in Third World countries. Between 1900 and 1925, for example, U.S. troops intervened in China and Honduras 7 times each, Panama 6 times, the Dominican Republic 4 times, Colombia, Mexico and Cuba 3 times each, Guatemala, Haiti, Korea, Nicaragua and Turkey 2 times each, and once each in Morocco, the Philippines and Syria. Of the longer interventions, American soldiers occupied Haiti from 1915 to 1934 "to maintain order during a period of chronic and threatened insurrection," and Cuba from 1917 to 1933 "to protect American interests during an insurrection and subsequent unsettled conditions." [24]

Following World War II the pace of American interventionism increased to cope with the rise in the frequency of insurrections. In 1976 the Brookings Institution issued a 700-page report commissioned by the Defense Department listing 215 occasions when U.S. armed forces were used abroad for political purposes between January 1, 1946, and October 31, 1975. These ranged from the dispatch of the battleship U.S.S. *Missouri* to transport the remains of the Turkish ambassador from Washington to Istanbul in 1946—at a time when the Soviet Union was demanding bases in Turkey—to the Vietnam War.

Although the degree to which armed forces have been used abroad for political purposes is staggering, it should be noted that some of the most grandiose efforts at armed intervention have failed disastrously. Outstanding examples of such failures are the Allied expeditionary forces sent against the Bolshevik revolution, the American support of Chiang Kai-shek against the Chinese communists, and the French and American interventions in Vietnam.

After the disastrous experience in Vietnam, the United States downplayed counterinsurgency in Third World countries and turned its attention to the revitalization of NATO. But only six years after Vietnam, Secretary of State Alexander Haig said that "international terrorism"—the Administration's euphemism for Third World revolution—"will take the place of human rights in our concern."

This was not mere rhetoric. A string of military bases were constructed or expanded in the Middle East, from the Egyptian port of Las Banas to the Indian Ocean island of Diego Garcia. A $982 million military aid program was made available in March 1981 to provide arms and training to right-wing dictatorships facing indigenous guerrilla movements—in Turkey, Morocco, Oman, Persian Gulf and Southwest Asian countries etc. Also Rapid Deployment Forces were rapidly expanded, providing the United States for the first time since Vietnam with the power to intervene throughout the world. Most prominent in early 1981 were the few dozen U.S. military trainers sent to El Salvador, but few Americans were aware that Pentagon plans provided that by September 1981 the United

States will have three hundred twenty-three Security Assistance teams totaling 1,677 personnel in fifty-three countries.

More effective than overt armed intervention against radical regimes and insurrections has been covert "destabilization." The extent to which it has been used is being realized belatedly with piecemeal revelations by ex-CIA agents such as Philip Agee (*Inside the Company: A CIA Diary*), Victor Marchetti (*The CIA and the Cult of Intelligence*), John Stockwell (*In Search of Enemies: A CIA Story*), Wilbur Eveland (*Ropes of Sand*), and Kermit Roosevelt (*Countercoup: The Struggle for the Control of Iran*); with United States Senate reports such as *Alleged Assassination Plots Involving Foreign Leaders* (1975) and *Covert Action in Chile 1963–1973* (1975); and the detailed studies by Michael T. Klare, *Supplying Repression: U.S. Support for Authoritarian Regimes Abroad,* and by Noam Chomsky and Edward Herman, *The Political Economy of Human Rights* (1979, 2 volumes).

The magnitude of covert operations is evident in Marchetti's estimate that 11,000 of the CIA's 16,500 personnel, and $550 million of its yearly budget of $750 million were earmarked for "Clandestine Services." Through these "Services," the CIA was involved to a greater or lesser degree in the assassination of foreign leaders such as Diem, Lumumba, Trujillo and Schneider, as well as in repeated futile attempts to assassinate Castro. The official name for the CIA unit involved in assassination attempts against foreign leaders was "Health Alteration Committee." The CIA also was involved in varying degrees in the overthrow of governments headed by Mossadeq in Iran, Arbenz in Guatemala, Allende in Chile, Sukarno in Indonesia and Goulart in Brazil. An American political scientist, Hans Morgenthau, concluded in 1974:

> With unfailing consistency, we have since the end of the Second World War intervened on behalf of conservative and fascist repression against revolution and radical reform. In an age when societies are in a revolutionary or prerevolutionary stage, we have become the foremost counterrevolutionary status quo power on earth. Such a policy can only lead to moral and political disaster.[25]

In addition the CIA, according to the *Wall Street Journal* (March 1, 1977), "knew about and probably encouraged" payoffs by American corporations to foreign political figures. Some of the millions of dollars surreptitiously distributed by the corporations "was intended to buy intelligence information for the U.S. government or to reward pro-American politicians." The CIA has also used American missionaries to gather information. In a letter to Senator Mark Hatfield, William E. Colby, the CIA director, offered the following explanation, which was not warmly received by Church leaders in the United States: "Such relationships [between the missionaries and the CIA] are purely voluntary and in no way reflect upon the integrity or the mission of the clergy involved." [26]

The CIA used American labor unions as well as American corporations and missionaries to further its covert operations abroad. Cooperation between government and unions goes back in the United States to World War I, when Samuel Gompers and William Green of the American Federation of Labor worked closely with President Wilson, and likewise to World War II, when William Green and Philip Murray (CIO) cooperated with President Roosevelt. After World War II, however, American labor for the first time became heavily involved in *clandestine* operations financed by government agencies. These operations began modestly toward the end of World War II with the establishment under AFL auspices of the Free Trade Union Committee (FTUC) to assist trade unions operating underground in Europe and Japan. Jay Lovestone, the executive secretary of FTUC, was a former leader of the American Communist Party who, after being expelled for revisionism, became militantly anti-communist, along with his close collaborator, Irving Brown. Lovestone and Brown soon were receiving $2 million a year from the CIA, and Thomas Braden, CIA officer in charge of anti-Communist fronts between 1950 and 1954, has explained why such funds were provided:

> Lovestone and his assistant, Irving Brown . . . needed to pay off strongarm squads in Mediterranean ports so that American supplies could be unloaded against the opposition communist dock workers. . . . With funds from Dubinsky's union [International Ladies' Garment Workers' Union] they organized the Force Ouvrière, a non-communist union. When they ran out of money they appealed to the CIA. Thus began the secret subsidy of free trade unions. . . . Without that subsidy postwar history might have gone very differently.[27]

In addition to splitting radical trade unions in France, Germany, Italy, Greece and other European countries, CIA funds were funneled through the Agency for International Development for similar operations in the Third World. Special organizations were established for this purpose, including the African-American Labor Center (1966), the Asian-American Free Labor Institute (1968) and the American Institute for Free Labor Development (1962), the latter focusing on Latin America. The operations of the first two bodies are still largely unknown, but recent disclosures concerning the third—the AIFLD—suggest a common pattern of creating and utilizing "free" (that is, anti-Communist) labor bodies in order to further the economic interests of American corporations and the counterrevolutionary objectives of the American government.

One of the several corporate executives on the AIFLD board of directors was J. Peter Grace, head of the corporation bearing his name, which has heavy investments in Latin America. Grace defined the purpose of AIFLD as being to preach "cooperation between labor and management and an end to the class struggle. . . ." Beyond that, he urged unionists "to help increase their company's business . . . prevent Communist infiltration, and where it already exists to get rid of it." [28]

These injunctions were zealously implemented by AIFLD representatives throughout Latin America. In Guatemala they supported Colonel Carlos Castillo's "liberation army," which toppled the Arbenz government and which was praised by George Meany for overthrowing a "Communist-controlled regime." In the Dominican Republic, AIFLD subsidized the establishment of a small union, CONATRAL, which was the only labor body that called for military action against the Bosch government and that supported President Johnson's armed intervention. In Guiana, AIFLD financed political strikes and lockouts that ultimately ousted Cheddi Jagan, who twice had been elected President.

In Chile, CIA director William Colby admitted spending "at least $8 million" (worth more than $40 million on the black market) to destabilize the Allende government. AIFLD had trained 8,837 Chileans in seminars in Chile and in a special school at Front Royal, Virginia, where their numbers suddenly increased in 1972–73. These trainees were prominent in distributing the $8 million to subsidize strikes by miners, truckers, shopkeepers and taxidrivers that crippled the Allende regime and paved the way for the coup. In February 1973 a U.S. intelligence chief, Colonel Gerald Sills, told Chilean General Pinochet that the general was "on a sinking ship" and asked him "When are you going to act?" Pinochet replied, "Not until our legs get wet. . . . the armed forces cannot move against Allende until the people get out into the streets to beg us to act." [29] The role of AIFLD was to use CIA funds to get the people "out into the streets." Pinochet then was free to scuttle the "sinking ship."

Likewise in Brazil, an AIFLD director, William Doherty, bragged of his role in the overthrow of the Goulart government and the advent of the military dictatorship still in power. "What happened in Brazil," declared Doherty shortly after the coup, "did not just happen—it was planned—and planned months in advance. Many of the trade union leaders—some of whom were actually trained in our institute—were involved in the revolution, and in the overthrow of the Goulart regime." [30] A few years after the coup it was disclosed that one of the Brazilian labor leaders trained by AIFLD conducted anti-Communist seminars for telegraph workers. After every class he quietly warned key workers of coming trouble and urged them to keep communications going no matter what happened. When the military staged the coup in April 1964, "The Communists . . . called a general strike, with emphasis upon communications workers. But to their dismay, the wires kept humming, and the army was able to coordinate troop movements. . . ." [31]

Such covert destabilizing of radical regimes is supplemented by overt stabilizing of reactionary regimes, particularly those in strategic regions of the Third World. The upsurge of colonial revolution after World War II was countered by the intervention of Western ground armies—French in Southeast Asia and Algeria, American in Vietnam and Latin America and Portuguese in Africa. This strategy boomeranged because of mounting opposition in the home countries as well as resistance in the colonies. Western political and military leaders therefore have been evolving a more viable counterrevolutionary course.

A variety of techniques currently are being tested throughout the Third World. In addition to economic measures, which will be analyzed in the following section, there is the training and arming of the police forces and of the military establishments of favored regimes. In reaction to Castro's revolution, President Kennedy established in 1962 the Office of Public Safety (OPS) in the Agency for International Development to expand the training and arming of foreign police agencies. An International Police Academy based in Washington, D.C., trained ten thousand police from seventy-seven countries with courses such as "Domestic Intelligence," "Building Strategic Hamlets" and "Bombs I, II and III." After their return home the police were provided with the tools needed for their newly acquired expertise, including armored cars, rifles, machine guns, explosive devices, gas grenades and torture instruments such as thumbscrews, shackles, leg irons and truncheons. Under Secretary of State U. Alexis Johnson supported OPS activities during his congressional testimony in 1971: "Effective policing is like 'preventive medicine.' The police can deal with threats to internal order in their formative states. Should they not be prepared to do this, 'major surgery' [military intervention] would be needed to redress these threats." Following Vietnam and Chile, the activities of OPS became embarrassing and it was abolished in 1974 by Congress. The ban proved meaningless, as numerous loopholes existed through which the pipelines of repression could be fueled. One was the International Narcotics Control Program, which funneled $142 million to foreign police forces in the first four years after the abolition of OPS. And even such Latin American countries as Nicaragua and Uruguay, which were excluded from any military aid because of serious human rights violations, were able to continue purchasing arms and torture instruments from private American manufacturers. Also noteworthy is the training given to over one million policemen by American "public safety advisers" stationed in forty countries.

Selected foreign military establishments as well as police forces have received American arms and expertise. President Carter criticized during his first presidential campaign "our nation's role as the world's leading arms salesman" and pledged to "increase the emphasis on peace and reduce the commerce in weapons." Yet foreign military sales rose sharply during his administration. Despite his "human rights" rhetoric, most of the arms went to countries with the worst records on this issue: Argentina, Brazil, Chile, Indonesia, Ethiopia, Iran, Thailand, Uruguay, South Korea and the Philippines.

Closely related to arms sales is the training of foreign military officers. Between 1973 and 1977 a total of 12,723 officers from the above ten countries attended American military schools. Most received training in conventional military topics, but a substantial number took courses in counterinsurgency operations, military-intelligence interrogation, security management and other such subjects that relate to internal policing rather than external defense. Outstanding in this activity has been the School of the Americas operated by the U.S. Army in the Panama Canal Zone. More than thirty-three thousand Latin American military officers were trained there between 1949 and 1976. Charles E. Maw, Under Secretary of State for Security Assistance, testifying before the House International Relations Committee (Mar. 23, 1976), explained the objective of such training: "The facts of life are that in many countries of the world the military are the conservative forces helping maintain stability in their countries." The validity of this justification is manifested by a framed letter hanging on a wall of the School of the Americas. It is dated November 6, 1973, and signed by Chilean dictator General Augusto Pinochet, who expresses his personal thanks and that of the Chilean army for the work of the school. Two months earlier, in September 1973, Pinochet had overthrown the constitutional government of Salvador Allende.

More significant than the School of the Americas and the many other similar establishments is the Inter-American Defense College (IADC) at Fort Lesley J. McNair on the Potomac River. Established in 1962 with the help of a $1 million grant from Washington, it functions as a veritable graduate school for juntas. By 1976 it had graduated 497 students from 18 Latin American countries, who went on to become prominent members of the military dictatorships now in power. IADC courses deal with subjects such as the world situation, the inter-American system, continental security, industrial and financial management, agriculture, energy and communications. The stated objective of this curriculum is "to develop techniques for the collective planning at the highest international level in order to achieve greater unity in matters of doctrine relating to the security of the continent." [32]

Retired Admiral Gene La Rocque, who was director of IADC from 1969 to 1972, explains: "The college is training people to more efficiently manage a government, without any encouragement for them to take over." But La Rocque, now the head of the Center for Defense Information, a project of the Fund for Peace in Washington, sees disturbing implications in such training.

> It's unhealthy to build up a cadre of military governors all over the world and this is what we do to some extent. We've contributed to keeping the military in power by increasing the efficiency of individuals. . . . there is no question that they become more competent administrators.
>
> But my worry transcends this. I worry about strengthening military forces in general. In Latin America, the more efficient the military are . . . the more powerful *our* military are. . . .
>
> Now this wasn't too much of a problem in the past because the military dictatorships, historically speaking, were short-lived. They would step in to restore order, and then not too much later return the government to civilians. We opted for that over communism. But the new development is that the military is staying in power. We ought to draw a lesson from what is happening in Latin America.
>
> There is a growing military there—and here. [33]

Finally, if all the above counterrevolutionary measures fail, there remains a last-resort measure: selective granting of asylum to refugees, and selective implementation of the human rights campaign. Americans pride themselves on their nation's humanitarian traditions, symbolized by the Statue of Liberty. But it has long been clear that some of the "tired and poor" are welcome and others are not, depending on Washington's relations with the country being fled. If those who seek asylum are fleeing a country labeled unfriendly (usually socialist), they are immediately accepted, since the government is defined as oppressive. But if it belongs to the friendly category, asylum is usually denied, as oppression in such cases is ignored or depreciated.

Example: Approximately 800,000 Eastern Europeans were accepted after World War II as they were fleeing from Communist regimes. But in 1938, when American policymakers were careful not to antagonize Hitler, only 19,500 out of a total of 139,000 German Jews and trade unionists who applied for entry into the United States were granted admission. That figure was 10,000 below the quota set for German immigrants. And when a bill was introduced in Congress in 1939 to admit 20,000 German Jewish children over the next two years, it died in committee.

Example: About 725,000 refugees from Castro's Cuba have been granted asylum in the United States, as well as 250,000 Southeast Asians from the Communist Indochinese countries. But Haitian "boat people" were systematically turned back by the Immigration and Naturalization Service on the ground that they were economic rather than political refugees. The official American position was rejected by Florida's Senator Richard Stone, Florida's Governor Bob Graham, and the Congressional Black Caucus. The latter charged racism, as well as Washington partiality for dictator Jean Claude Duvalier as against the Communist Castro. With the approach of the 1980 elections, Washington reversed its position and admitted Haitians on the same terms as Cubans.

Example: In contrast to the 725,000 refugees admitted from Cuba, less than 1,000 Chilean refugees have been admitted since the fall of President Allende. As explained by a Washington "source," "given the U.S. interest in the overthrow of the Allende government, it is obvious that it is not going to fling its doors open to the same people it helped unseat." [34]

Example: Temporary refuge was given to citizens from Nicaragua after the fall of the Somoza dictatorship, but refugees from El Salvador were sent back home, despite the estimate of the Latin American expert, Professor Blase Bonpane, that "somewhere between 5 and 10 percent of those who are returned are executed." A proposal to grant unofficial temporary refuge to Salvadorans was rejected because, according to a former State Department official, "it might suggest that the United States, which had been pushing for a political settlement of the Salvadoran conflict, did not have faith in the ability of the Salvadorans to resolve their own problems." [35]

The United States is not alone in its global counterrevolutionary activities, though it plays the leading role, as befits its primacy in the Western world. France has been especially active, particularly in Africa, where its former colonies remain at least as closely bound to Paris, economically and culturally, as before World War II. Militarily, France is in a stronger position in Africa than any other Western power. From the Indian Ocean islands of Réunion, the Comorros and the Malagasy Republic to newly independent Djibouti in the Horn, through Cameroon, Gabon, Niger and Chad in central Africa, to the Ivory Coast, Senegal and Mauritania in western Africa, more than twenty thousand French troops are permanently stationed to counter revolutionary activities anywhere in Africa. These troops have been used to bolster pliant regimes in Cameroon (1959–64), Senegal (1959–60), the Ivory Coast (1963) and

Gabon (1964–66). France also has not hesitated to use her power to "preserve order" outside her own sphere, as demonstrated by her unsuccessful effort to defeat the MPLA in Angola, and by her successful interventions in Zaïre to bolster the corrupt and tottering Mobutu regime. Hence the observation of an unnamed American diplomat, quoted in the *International Herald Tribune* (Aug. 2, 1977): "France now is our best ally outside Europe."

B.
Economic Strategy of Counterrevolution

General Smedley Butler testified how in the early twentieth century he operated with his Marines as a "racketeer for capitalism on three continents." Now, in the late twentieth century, bankers with their briefcases have replaced Marines with their machine guns. Indeed, it has been observed that more Third World governments have been overthrown by the International Monetary Fund than ever have been by the Marine Corps.

The financial vulnerability of the less-developed countries (LDCs) stems from their chronic shortage of foreign exchange. The shortage plagues virtually all Third World countries, with the exception only of the fortunate few endowed with oil resources. This difficulty is the end result of chronically unfavorable terms of trade, large-scale profit remittances by the multinational corporations and rapidly growing debt loads whose servicing is absorbing as much as 40 percent of the foreign earnings of some LDCs.

Western officials and bankers have been willing, and even eager, to provide loans on a lavish scale for reasons that were set forth by Secretary of State William Rogers before the House Foreign Affairs Committee during its 1973 foreign aid hearings:

> With 6 percent of the world's population, the United States consumes nearly 40 percent of the world's annual output of raw materials and energy. Increasingly, we depend on the developing countries for those supplies.
>
> On the other side of the trade ledger, the developing countries are becoming increasingly important as markets for U.S. goods. In 1970, they accounted for 30 percent of all U.S. exports. The investments of U.S. corporations in the developing countries presently total some $30 billion, and are growing at about 10 percent a year. Fifty percent of our foreign investment income comes from the developing countries.
>
> The developing assistance program contains direct benefits for

the United States. *Eighty percent of the funds* are spent in this country, creating additional jobs and income for Americans. Undoubtedly, in each one of your districts there are farms, factories or universities that directly benefit from this program.

For all of these economic, political and moral reasons, a sustained U.S. response to the challenge of underdevelopment is as much in our interest as it is in that of the developing nations.[36]

Foreign aid was not only popular with donors for the above reasons, but also with the recipients, who welcomed it as an alternative to tax increases and to structural reforms. Thus the foreign debts of LDCs totaled $54.9 billion by the end of 1970. This indebtedness increased even more rapidly during the following years because of the 1973–74 stagflation, which devastated the nonoil-exporting LDCs by reducing sales and price levels of their raw-material exports, and raising the cost of their oil and manufactured imports. The trade deficits of nonoil-exporting LDCs rose from $12 billion in 1973, to $34 billion in 1974 and to $41 billion in 1975. But the stagflation, which created cash shortages for LDCs, also created cash gluts for Western banks, which therefore provided still more credit to LDCs. Net lending by U.S.-based banks to LDCs rose from $882 million in 1971, to $2.131 billion in 1973, to $6.648 billion in 1974 and to $6.878 billion in 1975.

An even more important source of loans than American banks was the "Eurocurrency market," which supplied "Eurodollars." These Eurodollars originated in the large U.S. payments deficits of the 1960s, which were financed in large part by foreigners' willingness to hold the dollars they were paid for their exports to the United States. As the supply of Eurodollars increased, their holders turned to LDCs and loaned billions at rates far above what could be obtained in their own countries. Publicized Eurocurrency credits to LDCs rose from $1.475 billion in 1971, to $4.080 billion in 1972, to $9.116 billion in 1973, to $9.605 billion in 1974 and to $11.530 billion in 1975. Since such credits need not be publicized, it has been estimated that actual Eurocurrency credits are double the above figures.

Total LDC debts to national governments, international agencies and private banks had jumped to $400 billion by the end of 1980.[37] Roughly half these debts were owed to private banks, and about two thirds of these private loans were from American banks. The profits that the banks made on these loans were so high that W. B. Wriston, chairman of the Board of Directors of Citibank, is fond of saying, "Around here, it's Jakarta that pays the check." [38] At the same time, however, a European banker stationed in Jakarta looked around at the modern new air-conditioned buildings and bustling streets and said, "Obviously they are making money, but every banker in this town can also produce figures that point to disaster. When will it come? Who knows?" [39]

The servicing of the mountainous debts is becoming impossible for the debtor countries, which are obtaining extensions on repayments. A typical example was Peru, which, by the end of 1977, owed $700 million on $5 billion foreign debts, but had only about $33 million in foreign reserves. For the first time private banks as well as the International Monetary Foundation insisted on continuous monitoring of Peru's economic policies as the condition for rescheduling debt repayments. They demanded that Peru implement a drastic stabilization plan. It included wage freezes, removal of price controls, reduction of imports, limits on government spending and borrowing, measures to encourage foreign investments, and curtailment of expenditures of health, education, housing and other social needs.

This plan, which is typical of many now being imposed on LDCs in financial straits, makes no contribution toward an independent and diversified economy, which is the basic need of all these countries. Rather it affords only temporary relief from immediate exchange difficulties. And the cost is reinforcement of the dependence on traditional exports and on foreign markets and capital, which were the root causes of the instability in the first place. In the case of Peru, the unions responded with a strike that crippled all cities, while five bishops publicly denounced "the fact that a privileged minority is throwing the weight of the economic crisis on the shoulders of the popular sectors." [40]

In response to charges that they were making harsh demands on the Peruvian government, American bankers denied responsibility for any pressures:

> We did not lay down the conditions. The Peruvians needed to borrow more money. We told them we could not make the loan while we were not confident of their ability to repay. They came to us with an austerity program they said they would impose. We indicated we did not think it would be sufficient and they came back with other proposals. We did not tell them what to do. The Peruvians recognized they had to show us they were taking their debt problems seriously.[41]

The sophistry of the bankers is not surprising, given the fact that their presence in the Third World was dictated by considerations of profit rather than of popular welfare. But the World Bank also has played a similar role on crucial occasions. In his *Annual Report* of September 25, 1972, Robert McNamara, president of the World Bank, pointed to the "massive poverty within the developing world" as the crucial problem of our age. He identified the "two overriding reasons" for this poverty:

"The affluent nations are not moving effectively enough to assist the indigent nations; and the indigent nations are not moving effectively enough to assist the poorest 40 percent of their own populations." He carried his analysis further by noting: "The problems of poverty are rooted deeply in the institutional frameworks, particularly in the distribution of economic and political power within the system. . . . It is governments that have the responsibility of essential domestic reform, and there is no way they can escape that responsibility. . . . It will manifestly require immense resolve and courage. The task of political leadership in the wealthy world is to match that resolve and courage with a greater commitment between their own affluent nations and the grossly disadvantaged developing nations."

McNamara, in effect, was calling on Third World elites and on the affluent nations to cooperate in dismantling a system from which they both profit. His logic was irrefutable but also irrelevant, given the framework within which the World Bank operates. Hence the persistent discrepancy between McNamara's rhetoric and policies. This was most evident in the bank's role in undermining the Allende regime in Chile and in supporting the succeeding junta.

President Allende was violently opposed by American government and business executives before and after his election. "I don't see why we need to sit by and watch a country go Communist due to the irresponsibility of its own people," declared Secretary of State Henry Kissinger. President Nixon was equally ruthless: "Not a nut or bolt shall reach Chile. We must make the economy scream." The table on page 475 [42] shows how McNamara cooperated in keeping out the nuts and bolts, and this despite the fact that Allende was one of the very few Third World leaders who implemented the reform that McNamara himself had urged.

Noteworthy in these statistics is the increase in U.S. military aid during the Allende years, the only category to be so favored. This proved to be a shrewd and typical investment by Washington, which paid dividends when the favored Chilean officers overthrew Allende and established a regime that McNamara promptly decided was worthy of immediate support. This was a bit too much for Representative Henry S. Reuss, chairman of the International Economic Subcommittee and one of the most economically knowledgeable members of Congress. On March 19, 1976, he sent an eight-page letter to McNamara challenging the resumption of World Bank aid to Chile as soon as Allende had been ousted:

> . . . the economic situation in Chile now is far worse than at any time under Allende, and almost incomparably worse than at the time the Bank originally suspended credits to Chile in 1971. . . .

U.S. Govt. & International Bank Aid to Chile

All figures in millions of dollars

	1968–70 (Frei)	1971–73 (Allende)	1974–76 (Junta)
Military aid	20	33	18
A.I.D.	111	3	41
Food for Peace, I	25	0	107
Food for Peace, II	20	15	16
Housing Investment Guarantees	0	0	55
Export-Import loans and guarantees	42	5	79
Commodity Credit Corp loans	0	3	50
Debt rescheduling	0	0	297
World Bank	42	0	66
Inter-American Development Bank	94	19	168

IADB figures are for calendar years, all others are for fiscal years ending June 30. All figures except World Bank and IADB refer to U.S. government aid only.

Source: Dollars & Sense, December 1976, p. 12.

The economic data . . . lend no support to the idea that Chile is more credit-worthy now than it was under its last democratic institution. Quite the reverse.

One is left with the unhappy conclusion that the Bank succumbed to political pressure to shore up an inhuman right-wing dictatorship tottering on the edge of bankruptcy. That 9 of the Bank's 20 directors, representing 41 percent of the Bank's voting stock and virtually every country in Western Europe—Britain, France, Germany, Belgium, Holland, Austria, Luxembourg, Israel, Cyprus, Denmark, Norway, Sweden, Finland, Iceland—plus Rumania, Yugoslavia and many nations of the Middle East, either voted no or abstained on this loan suggests that others are as disturbed as I.[43]

In conclusion, this section, on economic strategy of counterrevolution, brings to mind the observation of Cambridge University economist Joan Robinson that the objective of Western economic aid to the Third World is to perpetuate the institutions that made the aid necessary in the first place. The fluctuations in World Bank aid to Chile bear out this proposition, as does also the $283 million spent between 1961 and 1971 by the Agency for International Development in supporting Third World police forces. This expenditure was funded by the agency under the heading of "development assistance." When the rationale of this funding was questioned during appropriation hearings, the Acting Assistant Secretary of State for Latin America John Hugh Crimmins responded: "These [security] programs are essentially developmental in nature—addressing the problems of modernizing a key public sector institution, the police." [44]

C.
Cultural Strategy of Counterrevolution

Imperialism involves cultural domination as well as the political and economic domination noted above. Cultural imperialism is not peculiar to modern times. During the Roman Empire, provincial cities were Roman enclaves disseminating Roman language, religion, architecture and civic culture among Syrians, Egyptians, North Africans, Gauls, Britons and other subject peoples. With the fall of Rome, imperial culture was replaced by numerous local cultures. Because of the requirements of dynasties and merchants, and the assimilative powers of printing presses and school systems, local cultures gradually were consolidated into a small number of national cultures—the French, Spanish, Italian, English and so forth.

When the nation-states expanded overseas, the resulting imperialism manifested itself in the cultural realm from the beginning. European explorers and conquerors everywhere stated explicitly that they were interested in converting the heathen as well as divesting them of their gold, their lands and any other valuables. During the following centuries two types of cultural imperialism evolved. First was the official variety, designed to facilitate and sustain imperial authority during the era of colonial empires. Then with decolonization and neocolonialism, an unofficial cultural imperialism emerged, associated with the global operations of the multinational corporations (MNCs) and particularly of the American-dominated communications industry.

Examples of official cultural imperialism abound through the centuries in all parts of the Third World. In Africa, for example, schoolchildren in French colonies read textbooks beginning with the words, "Our ancestors, the Gauls." British traders on the Gold Coast in the nineteenth century observed that many Africans believed that "the school was a very good thing for the white men but not for the black." A mulatto trader explained the reason for the skepticism regarding English-type education:

All the young men leaving schools become traders as they see that all the Europeans are Merchants; I believe not one boy that can read or write has yet become a Canoeman or a planter of corn; the whole of these instructed young men are following one occupation, that of trading and hawking goods about the country. . . . It is a very great pity that something has not been done to induce some to become Carpenters and Bricklayers.[45]

Likewise in India, Babington Macaulay declared his intention in 1835 to form "a class of persons, Indian in blood and color, but English in taste, in opinions, in morals, and in intellect." Such a class of persons was indeed created, as acknowledged emphatically by Jawaharlal Nehru:

> We developed the mentality of a good country-house servant. Sometimes we were treated to a rare honor—we were given a cup of tea in the drawing room. The height of our ambition was to become respectable and to be promoted individually to the upper regions. Greater than the victory of arms or diplomacy was this psychological triumph of the British in India.[46]

The dynamic center of the second or unofficial form of cultural imperialism is the United States, and the reason is the unprecedented expansion since World War II of American foreign trade and foreign investments. Between 1955 and 1975 U.S. exports quintupled in value to $107 billion a year, while the book value of U.S. investments abroad jumped between 1953 and 1973 from $16.3 billion to $107.3 billion. This massive global spread encompassed the Third World with profound cultural repercussions. The establishment of industrial enterprises within Third World countries engendered greater cultural intrusion than in the old days of portfolio investments or of direct involvement primarily in encapsulated extractive industries isolated from their surrounding societies. An Indian scientist, A. K. N. Reddy, has noted that technology transfer has profound cultural implications, for technology "is like genetic material":

> It carries the code of the society in which it was born and sustained, and tries to reproduce that society . . . its structure, its social values. The adoption of a capital-intensive, luxury oriented western culture in India has thus created a dual society—metropolitan centres of western oriented affluence amidst vast expanses of rural poverty, mass unemployment, large migrations to cities and wide income disparities.[47]

The foreign affiliates of the MNCs do, in fact, reproduce their parent societies in the host countries. They determine what is manufactured, and they stimulate consumer demand to absorb the output through familiar advertising campaigns. Thus the rise of global corporations and global banks led inevitably to the globalization of Madison Avenue operations. In 1954 the top thirty U.S. advertising agencies derived a little over 5 percent of their total revenues from overseas operations. By 1972 the percentage had increased nearly sevenfold, so that one third of their $7 billion total revenues came from abroad. In 1974 Colgate-Palmolive spent 57 percent of its total advertising budget outside the United States, Procter & Gamble and American Home Products spent 30 percent each, General Motors 27 percent, Ford Motor Company and General Foods 26 percent each and Bristol-Myers 24 percent. In 1975 the ten largest U.S. advertising agencies reported that foreign accounts represented the following proportion of their total business: McCann-Erickson 70 percent, Ted Bates & Company and Ogilvy & Mather International 54 percent each, J. Walter Thompson 52 percent, Young & Rubicam International 40 percent, Leo Burnett Company 36 percent, Foote, Cone & Belding 31 percent, BBDO and D'Arcy, MacManus and Masius 30 percent each and Grey Advertising 28 percent.

The social impact of the allocation of such vast sums in Third World countries may be judged from the fact that in Brazil the advertising expenditures by American manufacturing affiliates comprise more than one third of public expenditures on all forms of education. The upper- and middle-income groups in Brazil traditionally have responded to such advertising, but the working classes also have recently entered consumer society. Since real wages of Brazilian workers have been declining in recent years, the purchase of radios, television sets, refrigerators and even cars has been made at the cost of heavy indebtedness and diet deficiency. A study of nutrition in Latin America by the Food and Agriculture Organization of the United Nations concluded that "availability of calories per capita, availability of proteins, and availability of animal proteins remain below international norms in a good many countries. . . . there may be a nutritional loss as regards home-produced vegetables, etc., while family expenditures are diverted in part to bottled beverages and packaged foods of relatively low nutritional content." [48]

Apart from its effect on nutrition standards, Madison Avenue has profoundly affected value systems in Third World societies, where high illiteracy rates leave the information field wide open to American radio and TV networks. Columbia Broadcasting System distributed its programs to 100 countries. Its news-film service, according to its 1968 report, was received by satellite "in 95 percent of the free world's households." *Hawaii Five-O* was dubbed in 6 languages and sold in 47 countries, while *Bonanza* was seen in 60 countries with an estimated weekly audience of 350 million. The pattern is the same in other communications media. CBS, for example, sold 100 million records abroad in 1970. *Reader's Digest* is published in 101 countries with a total circulation of 11.5

million outside the United States. And for the millions of semiliterates who find *Reader's Digest* too difficult, there are foreign editions of *Superman, Batman* and *Terry and the Pirates.*

Richard Barnet and Ronald Muller, authors of *Global Reach: The Power of the Multinational Corporations*, reach the following sobering conclusion concerning the impact of the MNCs on the minds of the majority of the human race living in the Third World:

> The role which the Ministry of Propaganda plays in shaping values, tastes, and attitudes in what the U.S. Government likes to call "closed societies" global corporations are playing in many parts of the "free world." Through TV, movie-house commercials, comic books, and magazine ads, foreign corporations unquestionably exert more continuing influence on the minds of the bottom half of the Mexican people, to take one example, than either the Mexican Government or the Mexican educational system. A small fraction of the Mexican population goes to school beyond the third grade. The officially admitted illiteracy rate is more than 27 percent. Contact with school is for the vast majority of the population fleeting, but exposure to TV and the transistor radio is lifelong. . . .
>
> Nor can government propaganda match the power of advertising. On some of the main thoroughfares of Mexico City, government slogans exhorting the population to cleanliness compete for attention with huge billboards advertising beer, cosmetics, smart clothes, and other symbols of the good life. These billboards, prepared with the latest techniques of modern advertising, offer Technicolor fantasies of luxury, love, and power that no message from the Department of Health, however uplifting, is likely to disturb.[49]

All this amounts to intellectual imperialism, or colonization of minds, even though these phrases are not well received in Western government and business circles. Yet consider the implications and repercussions of the situation of MNCs exerting greater influence on the minds of citizens than do their own governments and schools. One result is a subtle racism leading to self-denigration by Third World peoples. Billboards, magazines and TV screens invariably depict blond, blue-eyed men and women as the creators and practitioners of the good life. Such "white is beautiful" advertising inevitably reinforces feelings of inferiority, which are the essence of colonial mentality. Frantz Fanon has described the alienation and inferiority complex that colonialism imprinted on French West Indians:

> The colonized is elevated above his jungle status in proportion to his adoption of the mother country's cultural standards. He be-

comes white as he renounces his blackness, his jungle. . . . Out of the blackest part of my soul, across the zebra striping of my mind, surges this desire to be suddenly *white*. I wish to be acknowledged not as *black* but as *white*.[50]

Another result of the globalization of Madison Avenue is rampant consumerism. Whereas churches in the past pacified the poor with the promise of a rosy afterlife, advertising agencies today offer material blandishments in this life. Traditional values are abandoned, and self-esteem becomes dependent on material possessions. A United Nations survey of the Caracas slums revealed twenty-four inch color television sets in two-room, tin-and-cardboard shacks with dirt floors and with no running water or bathroom facilities. When the inhabitants were queried as to why they purchased such expensive sets when smaller black-and-white models would serve as well, they replied that the more expensive sets were better because they were preferred by the wealthy white Venezuelans. Their responses are reminiscent of slave plantations in which the "great house" of the owner or overseer set the fashion for costly woolen suits and hats and for Scotch whiskey. A Jamaican economist, George Beckford, describes how such consumption patterns persist to the present day: "The dresses, suits, and hats that are worn by poor people in plantation villages on a Sunday afternoon belie their low levels of living. Any visitor to the scene not knowing the situation would be impressed by the obvious signs of opulence." [51]

Consumerism also inhibits social change by creating ego involvements that uphold the status quo. Governments desirous of tackling basic social and economic problems find it difficult to mobilize public support for reducing the supply of familiar consumer goods in favor of low-cost housing, mass education, health facilities and long-range economic development.

". . . we must recognize," concludes a study prepared for the Congressional Research Service, "that the international flow of mass communication is imbalanced and the United States is the major source of origination. This phenomenon, coupled with other vast and varied U.S. international involvements, gives credence to the notion that a world culture imprinted 'made in America' exists today." [52] The "made in America" world culture resulting from the "imbalanced" flow of mass information is being increasingly challenged by Third World countries. The reasons are obvious and compelling. The "imbalance" represents a direct and serious threat to both national culture and national economic development. To cope with this threat, international conferences have have been held in Algiers (1973), Quito and Lima (1975), San José, New Delhi, Colombo and Nairobi (1976), Florence (1977), Paris (1978), Kuala

Lumpur (1979) and Belgrade (1980). The general position of most Third World governments at these conferences is that "a new international information order" is the prerequisite for "a new international economic order."

Increasingly there is heard the phrase "information sovereignty," connoting that nations have the inherent right to use as they see fit any information about their citizens and their country. Another new phrase is "developmental journalism," which, in the words of an Indian journalist, Narinder Aggarwala, stresses "development-oriented news" rather than the usual fare of "wars, disasters, famine, riots and political and military intrigues," which make "better copy" in the Western press. Aggarwala holds that "the increasing Third World demand for development-oriented news" has been "erroneously equated" with "government-controlled news and information handouts." He adds: "Developmental journalism, a relatively new genre of reporting in the Third World, is not much different from what usually appears in Western newspapers in community or general news sections. But an international counterpart of community news is missing from Western media files." [53]

A concrete example of Aggarwala's complaint was presented in the April 1977 issue of the *Unesco Courier*, devoted to "A World Debate on Information." The former Dutch Guiana became the independent Surinam on November 25, 1975. Yet between November 24 and 27, this event occupied only 3 percent of the space devoted to foreign news by sixteen leading daily newspapers in thirteen Latin American countries. This 3 percent came entirely from international news agencies of the industrialized countries. And this despite the fact that Surinam is larger than England in area, and is the world's third biggest producer of bauxite. During those same four days, 70 percent of the foreign news published by those sixteen newspapers concerned industrialized countries, and four fifths of this news originated in the same news agencies.

The understandable conclusion drawn from such habitual treatment was that "the developing countries find it hard to accept a situation in which they are mere 'consumers' of a 'product' (information) over whose manufacture and distribution they have no control. . . . For its part, Unesco intends no longer to confine itself to speaking generally about 'freedom of expression' and 'freedom of information,' but also to talk in terms of 'access to and participation in communication' and a 'balanced flow of information.' " [54]

One measure designed to gain "access" and "participation" was the establishment of a collective news agency, Pool, to which contribute the news services of forty nonaligned countries. Coordinated by the Yugoslav news agency, Tanjug, Pool is described by its director, Pero Ivacic, "not as a challenge to or competition with existing news reporting systems," but as a supplement "to fill the previously existing vacuum in the international information system." [55]

Such assurances are received with skepticism in official American circles. Leonard R. Sussman, former journalist with United Press and executive director of Freedom House, concludes, ". . . the choice is only between a government-run system and a system independent of government. There are no other real alternatives, no halfway houses. . . . A free but badly performing press serves its peoples far better than an efficient, government-controlled press." [56]

This stark differentiation between a "free" private press and a "government-run system" is questioned by Abbas Sykes, Tanzania's ambassador to France. "Your press is independent within the U.S., but abroad it represents national interests along with the State Department and the multinationals." Sykes and other Third World officials note the U.S. Senate disclosure that large sums were paid by the CIA to the Chilean press to oppose Allende, and also the House Committee disclosure that "at least 29 percent of CIA's covert actions over the years were for media and propaganda projects."

In addition to "free flow" versus "balanced flow," there is the increasingly urgent problem of "uncontrolled flow" of transnational border data and remote sensing data. The latter are compiled from airborne platforms, and yield comprehensive inventory of the physical features of any nation (oil deposits, mineral concentrations, soil types, crop conditions, etc.) regardless of the state's willingness to have its economic-geographic profile known. Transnational border data concerning finance, insurance, manufacturing, trade, transport and education circulate *inside* transnational corporate business structures but *across* national boundaries. Despite the crucial importance of these data, the vast bulk are private and beyond public scrutiny or knowledge. The resulting threat to sovereign states has been emphasized in the "Clyne Report" of a Canadian committee appointed to investigate the implications of telecommunications for Canadian sovereignty. The Report urged the Ottawa government to "alert the people of Canada to the perilous position of their collective sovereignty that has resulted from the new technologies of telecommunications and informatics, [and also] to establish a rational structure for telecommunications in Canada as a defense against the further loss of sovereignty in all its economic, social, cultural, and political aspects." [57]

Perhaps the most revealing commentary on the international information system is unwittingly provided by the following New York *Times* dispatch (Aug. 1, 1980), from post-Somoza Nicaragua. The account of the indigenous cultural upsurge since the revolution presents a meaningful alternative to the culture of imperialism currently enveloping the Third World.

Last year's revolution has brought a surge of cultural activity, with ordinary Nicaraguans for the first time encouraged to express themselves artistically, in painting, dancing, singing, writing and handicrafts.

"Now there is a burst of energy and enthusiasm," one folk singer said. "There is some good work and some awful work, but the main point is that people are no longer scared of culture."

The downfall of the Somoza regime is the main theme of the new poetry, murals and theater, but the Government is also trying to rescue Nicaragua's own cultural traditions, long smothered by imported music, movies and television soap operas.

"Culture must be taken to the people so they can produce art as well as consume it," said the Rev. Ernesto Cardenal, the Minister of Culture and a well-known poet. "We want to transmit the revolutionary message, but the cultural activity is spontaneous. We don't insist that art be political. The artist should have total freedom to create." . . .

Coinciding with the current adult literacy campaign, a program was organized to give slum children the opportunity to dance and paint; many of them recorded scenes from last year's insurrection. Indian artisans are being supported in their handicrafts and primitive painting. Some talented stone sculptors have been discovered.

Perhaps the most successful experiment to date, though, has involved the poetry workshops. Since the Nicaraguan poet Rubén Darío gained fame in the Spanish-speaking world early this century, poetry has been the preferred literary form of Nicaraguan intellectuals. But most families, neighborhoods and villages also have "their" poet. . . .

The aspiring bards are given a set of "rules"—adapted, amazingly, from guidance once prepared by Ezra Pound—on how to write poems. They include the suggestions that verses should not rhyme, that poets should be as specific as possible in their descriptions and that, at all costs, they should avoid such clichés as "cruel tyrant." And, in practice, while the revolution is often mentioned, it usually serves as a context for personal, natural or sentimental experiences.

Chapter 20

FIRST GLOBAL REVOLUTIONARY WAVE, 1914–39: INITIATIVE OF THE 1917 RUSSIAN REVOLUTION

The failure to strangle Bolshevism at its birth and to bring Russia, then prostrate, by one means or another, into the general democratic system, lies heavy upon us today.

WINSTON CHURCHILL, April 1, 1949

The Russian Revolution was the first great revolution in history to be deliberately planned and made. . . . It would be wrong to minimize or condone the sufferings and the horrors inflicted on large sections of the Russian people in the process of transformation. This was a historical tragedy, which has not yet been outlived, or lived down. But it would be idle to deny that the sum of human well-being and human opportunity in Russia today is immeasurably greater than it was fifty years ago. It is this achievement which has most impressed the rest of the world, and has inspired in industrially undeveloped countries the ambition to imitate it.

E. H. CARR (1969)

In the autumn of 1914, as one European country after another was being dragged into the holocaust of World War I, the British Foreign Secretary, Earl Grey, remarked, "The lamps are going out all over Europe." His comment indeed was justified, and to a much greater degree than he could have foreseen at the time. The war brought down in ruins the Europe with which Earl Grey was familiar. It destroyed the centuries-old Hapsburg, Hohenzollern, Romanoff and Ottoman dynasties, and, more significant, it made possible the Bolshevik Revolution—an elementary convulsion that heralded the dawn of a new era. The upheaval occurred in Russia, a peripheral region that was politically and militarily a European Great Power, but that economically was a dependent Third World country. The latter quality, as we shall see, explains in large part why the Revolution began in Russia and why, once it got under way, it managed to survive.

On the evening of November 7, 1917, Lenin announced the triumph of the Revolution and forecast its spread throughout the globe. "We have the mass strength of organization which will conquer all and lead the proletariat to world revolution. . . . Hail the world-wide socialist revolution." [1] If Lenin's expectation had been realized, the Third World theoretically would have suddenly disappeared, for Lenin had made it clear that world proletarian revolution involved self-determination for all peoples and an end to their exploitation. But at the same time that Lenin spoke, another world leader, President Woodrow Wilson of the United States, was propounding an entirely different world order for the future. This was the world order of liberal capitalist internationalism, opposed to both Bolshevik revolution on the left and traditional European imperialism on the right. This position at the center of the global ideological spectrum suited American interests for the same reason that free-trade imperialism suited British interests in the mid-nineteenth century. The dominant capitalist power of each era naturally favors the elimination of all barriers to global markets as well as the elimination of all revolutionary threats to the prevailing world market economy.

Although Wilson was to suffer political defeat at home, nevertheless it was his vision that largely prevailed during the interwar years. Lenin's "world-wide socialist revolution" failed to materialize. On the other hand, the homeland of revolution did manage to survive and to develop into the world's second Great Power, the Union of Soviet Socialist Republics. In the light of historical perspective, 1917 marks the beginning of a global civil war that has persisted to the present day, and that has accelerated in tempo since World War II.

✌ *I. Revolution in Russia*

The epoch-making Russian Revolution, whose significance largely escaped contemporary observers outside Russia and the revolutionary labor movement, is now generally acknowledged to be the most important consequence of the First World War. Its repercussions still are being felt, as evident in Winston Churchill's expression of regret more than three decades later that the interventionist forces, which he had masterminded, failed to "strangle Bolshevism at its birth." Why were a handful of Bolsheviks able to overthrow the entrenched Tsarist regime and, more implausible, to repulse the prolonged efforts at strangulation by Churchill and his powerful allies in the United States and continental Europe?

The war between Russia and Germany was popular with the Russian people, who were convinced that it was a war of defense against the aggression of their traditional Teutonic enemies. The only exception to this national rally behind the Tsar came from the Bolsheviks, whose leader, Lenin, branded the war as an imperialist struggle over markets and colonies. There was no reason why workers should sacrifice themselves in such a conflict, so Lenin tirelessly repeated his slogan "Turn the imperialist war into a class war!" But this sole discordant note was insignificant, as the Bolsheviks were only a tiny faction within Russia, and their outstanding leaders, including Lenin and Trotsky, were abroad when the war began.

The Russians not only were united against the Germans but they also were confident that they would win the war in short order. But instead of quick victory they sustained disastrous defeats. Two Russian armies that penetrated into East Prussia in 1914 were thrown back with heavy losses. In the following year came the great rout, when a combined German-Austrian offensive cracked open the Russian front and overran the most densely populated and highly industrialized provinces of the empire. The Tsarist regime never recovered from these disasters; within two years it had been relegated, in Trotsky's contemptuous phrase, to "the dustbin of history."

The roots of the debacle were many and varied, reaching far beyond the defeats at the front (see Chapter 16, Section IV). Fundamental was the endemic disaffection of Russian workers and peasants, who constituted a revolutionary potential lacking in the more affluent and stable societies of central and Western Europe. The peasants were land hungry because of incomplete agrarian reform, and had expressed their frustration in widespread uprisings. The original spokesmen for the peasants had been the Social Revolutionaries, but when they shrank back from a radical solution in 1917, the Bolsheviks quickly exploited the revolutionary temper in the countryside. Their propaganda was particularly successful because of the appalling war casualties. By February 1917 they totaled eight million killed, wounded or missing, and it was the peasants who bore the brunt of this dreadful bloodletting.

Workers in factories and mines were equally discontented, being denied elementary rights which had been won by Western workers in the nineteenth century. The Tsar's October Manifesto of 1905 had promised freedom of assembly and association, but this was essentially rescinded by the ensuing legislation. Trade unions could not be organized without official authorization, which was frequently and arbitrarily refused. Also, central organizations comprising of several trade unions were completely banned. Such restrictions, together with the customary intervention of Russian officialdom on the side of employers, had the effect of transforming labor disputes into political struggles. Tensions were greatly exacerbated by the war and the ensuing inflation and food and fuel shortages amid provocative display of wealth by speculators and profiteers. The far higher level of labor unrest in Russia before and during the war is evident in the following two tables:

Percentage of Strikers in Relation to the Number of Factory Workers

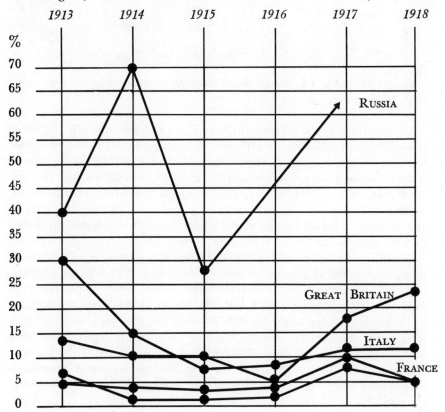

Source: M. Ferro, *The Great War 1914–1918* (London: Routledge & Kegan Paul, 1969), p. 179.

Movement of Strikes

	1913	1914	1915	1916	1917	1918
Russia	2,404*	3,534	928	1,410	1,938	
	887,096	1,337,458	539,528	1,086,384		
Great Britain	1,459	972	672	532	730	1,165
	664,000	447,000	448,000	276,000	872,000	1,116,000
France	1,073	690	98	314	697	499
	220,000	162,000	9,000	41,000	294,000	176,000
Germany	2,127	1,115	137	240	561	531
	266,000	61,000	14,000	129,000	667,000	392,000
Italy	810	782	539	516	443	303
	385,000	173,000	132,000	121,000	164,000	158,000

* The first figure indicates the number of strikes, the second the number of strikers.

Source: M. Ferro, *The Great War 1914–1918* (London: Routledge & Kegan Paul, 1969), p. 178.

As important as the disaffection of workers and peasants was the weakness of Russian industry. The Tsarist regime simply lacked the economic strength to wage modern warfare against first-class industrial powers. Russian soldiers did not receive needed arms and munitions, and in some cases even shoes and blankets. This economic weakness became much worse with the loss of the industrialized provinces of the empire in 1915, and with the Turkish closing of the straits through which the Allies had shipped supplies to southern Russia.

Contributing factors to Russia's defeat were incompetent military leadership and political dissension on the home front. The Duma and the imperial bureaucracy were constantly feuding over their respective jurisdictions and prerogatives. Both of them, in turn, clashed with the military in assigning responsibility for the shortage of war supplies and, ultimately, for the defeats at the front. This discord might have been minimized and controlled if there had been strong leadership at the top. Unfortunately, Tsar Nicholas was a well-meaning but weak and vacillating ruler with limited intelligence and imagination. His crowning error was his decision in August 1915, in the midst of disaster at the front, to dismiss his uncle, Grand Duke Nicholas, as commander-in-chief, and to assume personal command of military operations. Tsar Nicholas was even less qualified to do so than his uncle, and proved to be a nuisance at General Headquarters. Yet he had a mystical belief that his self-sacrifice might save the situation. "Perhaps a sin offering is needed to save Russia. I shall be the victim. God's will be done." Ultimately he was indeed the victim, for henceforth he was held personally responsible for military defeats. Thus the final outcome was the destruction of his family, the ending of the Tsarist regime and the advent of the Bolsheviks.

Two revolutions occurred in Russia in 1917: The first, in March, ended Tsarism and created a Provisional Government, while the second, in November, toppled the Provisional Government and substituted Soviet rule. The first revolution was an unplanned affair that took everyone by surprise. Strikes and riots broke out in Petrograd on March 8 because of the desperate shortage of food and fuel arising from inadequate transportation facilities. The authorities ordered the army to restore order, but instead the soldiers mutinied and fraternized with the demonstrators. The Tsar, always distrustful of the Duma, suspected it of complicity and ordered its dissolution on March 11. The Duma leaders refused to comply with the order, and the Tsar discovered that he no longer could enforce obedience. This realization of powerlessness was to all intents and purposes the revolution itself. Suddenly it became apparent that the Tsarist government was a government in name only. Tsar Nicholas abdicated on March 15 in favor of his brother, Michael. When Michael in turn gave up the throne the following day, Russia no longer had a functioning government.

Duma representatives acted quickly to prevent radical elements from taking over. On March 12 they organized a Provisional Government to administer the country until a Constituent Assembly could be elected. The head of the new government was the liberal Prince Georgi Lvov, and it included the Cadet leader, Professor Paul Miliukov, as Minister for Foreign Affairs, and Alexander Kerensky, the only socialist, as Minister of Justice. This was a bourgeois liberal cabinet, which introduced typical liberal bourgeois reforms. These included freedom of speech, press and assembly; amnesty for political and religious offenses; legal equality for all citizens without religious or racial discrimination; and labor reforms for workers, including the eight-hour day.

Despite these progressive measures the Provisional Government never sank roots in the country. The basic reason was that it refused to accept the two things that most Russians wanted: land and peace. Prince Lvov and his ministers insisted that such fundamental issues as land distribution and withdrawal from the war must wait until the election of a Constituent Assembly that would be truly representative of the people. The argument was rational but politically suicidal. The war-weary and land-hungry masses increasingly deserted the Provisional Government and turned to the soviets, with their slogans for immediate peace and immediate distribution of land.

The origin of the soviets goes back to the 1905 Revolution, when the workers elected councils, or soviets, to coordinate their struggle against Tsarism (see Chapter 18, Section IV). Although suppressed at that time, the soviets had proven their value as organs for agitation and direct action. Consequently they reappeared with the crisis precipitated by the First World War. Because of their grass-roots origins they gave voice to popular yearnings, and spread rapidly throughout the country. Village soviets incited seizures of nobles' estates; city soviets organized the unceasing riots and demonstrations in the streets; while soldiers' soviets gradually usurped the authority of the officers to the point where they gained control of weapons and countersigned orders before they could be executed. In short, a *de facto* soviet authority was steadily displacing the *de jure* authority of the Provisional Government.

At the same time that soviet power was spreading throughout the country, the soviets themselves were becoming more radical. At the beginning the delegates elected to the soviets were predominantly Socialist Revolutionaries and Mensheviks. The Bolsheviks remained relatively insignificant until the return of Lenin from abroad in April 1917. Immediately he issued his famous "April Theses" demanding peace, land to the peasants and all power to the soviets. At the time, these demands seemed preposterous and irresponsible, even to many Bolsheviks. Most delegates to the soviets were Marxists, and as such they regarded the March Revolution as a bourgeois uprising, and believed that a second, or socialist, revolution was out of the question until Russia had completed its capitalist economic development. Consequently they believed that the Provisional Government should be allowed to remain in office, though constantly prodded for desired reforms.

Lenin was almost alone in challenging this strategy and calling for the second socialist revolution at once. Time, however, was on his side, for the longer the war continued, the more the popular disaffection increased, and the more reasonable his "April Theses" appeared. By July 1917, when Kerensky formed a new government, public opinion had swung so far to the left that the cabinet consisted mostly of Socialist Revolutionaries and Mensheviks. Gone were the days when the Cadets were regarded as the radicals of Russian politics. Now Kerensky was cooperating with the Mensheviks and the Socialist Revolutionaries in order to withstand Lenin and his Bolsheviks.

Kerensky declared that his main objective was to "save the revolution from the extremists." He failed, however, to attract mass support because of his insistence on continuing the war, and he failed also to win over the military men who regarded him as a weak, loudmouthed politician. A certain General Lavr Kornilov staged an army revolt against Kerensky, but its effect was precisely the opposite from that which was intended.

It was the soviets that took the lead in organizing resistance against Kornilov and ultimately defeating him. Kerensky found himself dependent on the soviets, which in turn were falling under the domination of the Bolsheviks. By October 1917 both the Moscow and Petrograd soviets had a majority of Bolshevik members. Lenin now decided that the time had come for the second, or socialist, stage of the revolution. To his skeptical followers he responded that 240,000 Bolshevik party members could govern Russia in the interest of the poor against the rich as easily as 130,000 landlords previously had governed in the interest of the rich against the poor.

After threatening to resign, Lenin persuaded the Central Committee of his party to vote for revolution. The date was set for November 7. The actual revolution was anticlimactic. Bolshevik forces seized the key buildings, bridges and railway stations of Petrograd with almost no resistance. Casualties totaled one Red soldier and five Red sailors. Kerensky managed to escape and fled to exile abroad. The Provisional Government had not been overthrown. It had collapsed as helplessly and ignominiously as the Tsarist regime had in March, and for the same basic reason: It had lost the support of the Russian people.

II. "Socialism in One Country"

Lenin was in deadly earnest when he proclaimed immediately after the revolution that it was the prelude to "world-wide socialist revolution." Like all his comrades, Lenin took it for granted that either the Bolshevik Revolution would spread to Germany and beyond, or else it would be snuffed out by the imperialist powers. "If the people of Europe do not arise and crush imperialism," declared Trotsky at this time, "we shall be crushed—that is beyond doubt. Either the Russian Revolution will raise the whirlwind of struggle in the west, or the capitalists of all countries will stifle our struggle." [2]

At first it appeared that Lenin's forecast of world revolution would be realized. The Kaiser was forced to abdicate on November 9, 1918, following a mutiny in the navy and the spread of insurrections from the Baltic ports into the interior of Germany. Workers' and Soldiers' Councils, similar to the Russian soviets, appeared in all the major cities, including Berlin. News of the German uprising convinced Lenin that world revolution was imminent. "The international revolution," he wrote "has come so close in *one week* that it has to be reckoned with as an event of the *next few days*." But Lenin also noted an ominous cloud darkening this bright horizon. "Europe's greatest misfortune and danger is that it has *no* revolutionary party." [3] And without a revolutionary party, Lenin emphasized, revolution would be impossible.

To remove this peril to the revolutionary cause, Lenin organized in March 1919 the Communist International, which he described as the "world party of revolution." In closing the First Congress of the Comintern, Lenin spoke of the future with confidence. "The victory of the proletarian revolution on a world scale is assured. . . . The comrades present in this hall saw the founding of the first Soviet republic; now they see the founding of the Third, Communist International, and they will all see the founding of the World Federative Republic of Soviets." [4]

At the same time, however, another wartime leader was making diametrically opposite plans for the future course of world history. President Woodrow Wilson of the United States, like Chairman Nikolai Lenin of the Council of People's Commissars, began with an eye to consolidating his home base. Just as Lenin considered world revolution the prerequisite for the survival of the Bolshevik Revolution, so Wilson viewed the preservation of the international market economy as the prerequisite for the preservation of American capitalism. On the eve of his first presidential campaign, Wilson told the Virginia General Assembly that "we are making more manufactured goods than we can consume ourselves . . . and now, if we are not going to stifle economically, we have got to find our way out into the great international exchanges of the world." Furthermore, Wilson was confident that superior technological efficiency guaranteed American success in international competition, and that given equal chance, "the skill of American workmen would dominate the markets of all the globe." [5]

Also, just as Lenin assumed that world revolution would be mutually beneficial for the peoples of Russia and the whole world, so Wilson assumed that open world markets would be mutually beneficial for the peoples of the United States and the entire globe. The American national purpose, according to Wilson, was one of seeking "to enrich the commerce of our own states and of the world with the products of our mines, our farms, and our factories, with the creations of our thought and the fruits of our character." This messianic vision of an America with a combined moral and material mission for humanity is evident in the following speech by Wilson to a salesmanship congress in Detroit:

> This, then, my friends, is the simple message that I bring you. Light your eyes to the horizons of business . . . let your thoughts and your imaginations run abroad throughout the whole world, and with the inspiration of the thought that you are Americans and are meant to carry liberty and justice and the principles of humanity wherever you go, go out and sell goods that will make the world more comfortable and more happy, and convert them to the principles of America.[6]

Wilson was fully aware of the fact that the First World War was making the United States the No. 1 military and economic power. "We have become not the debtors but the creditors of the world," he told an audience the day before the 1916 presidential election. "We can determine to a large extent who is to be financed and who is not to be financed . . . we are in the great drift of humanity which is to determine the politics of every country in the world." [7] Wilson hoped to use this power in the manner of the nineteenth-century British free-trade imperialists. With this end in mind he sent Colonel House on repeated missions to convince Europe's leaders that it would be mutually advantageous to create a new political and economic world system in which traditional exclusive imperialism would be replaced by open seas, free markets and cooperative financial expansion into underdeveloped regions. Colonel House described this new world order to a British audience:

> My plan is that if England, the United States, Germany and France will come to an understanding concerning investments by their citizens in underdeveloped countries, much good and profit will come to their citizens as well as to the countries needing development. Stability would be brought about, investments would become safe, and low rates of interest might be established.[8]

It should not be assumed that Wilson entertained any notion of restructuring the inequitable relationships existing between the developed and underdeveloped segments of the globe. In the words of Secretary of State Robert Lansing, Wilson was "more and more impressed that 'white civilization' and its domination over the world rested largely on our ability to keep this country intact as we would have to build up the nations ravaged by the war." [9]

The mandate system that Wilson incorporated into the peace settlement is a classic example of his paternalistic, pro-status-quo vision of the future. It was a system that denied to non-European colonial subjects the right to self-determination that was freely granted to Europe's minorities—a continuation of what European liberals had been practicing in the nineteenth century (see Chapter 13, Section 1).The colonial subjects were declared "not yet able to stand by themselves under the strenuous conditions of the modern world." Therefore the "tutelage of such peoples" was entrusted to the "advanced nations," which would decide when their wards were sufficiently mature to be entrusted with the responsibilities of freedom.

It is apparent that this Wilsonian vision of a liberal capitalist world order was quite different from, and incompatible with, Lenin's expectations for a "World Federative Republic of Soviets." By the time of the

Second Comintern Congress (1920) it was apparent that the world revolution that Lenin had expected within the "next few days" had been badly derailed. A soviet republic in Hungary and a workers' republic in Bavaria both had been crushed, while the German revolution had ended with the bourgeois Weimar Republic. At the Third Comintern Congress in the summer of 1921 it was reluctantly conceded that the "final struggle" would have to be postponed.

The glaring discrepancy between the euphoric predictions of the First Congress and the cold realities of the Third Congress was due partly to countermeasures by Wilson but primarily to miscalculation by Lenin. Wilson wanted to purge Germany of the Kaiser and the militaristic autocracy he represented, but at the same time he was aware of the danger from the left. The latter was considered by Secretary of State Lansing to be a greater peril than the former. "There are two great evils at work in the world today, Absolutism, the power of which is waning, and Bolshevism, the power of which is increasing. We have seen the hideous consequences of Bolshevik rule in Russia, and we know that the doctrine is spreading westward. The possibility of proletariat despotism over Central Europe is terrible to contemplate." [10]

Wilson agreed with this diagnosis, and by November 1918 he was actively supporting the moderate elements in Germany against the Spartacists, who were the German counterparts of the Bolsheviks. In language reminiscent of President Harry Truman and Secretary of State George Marshall after World War II, Lansing described the anti-Bolshevik strategy being pursued in Germany. "To make Germany capable of resisting anarchism and the hideous despotism of the Red Terror, Germany must be allowed to purchase food; and to earn that food industrial conditions must be restored by a treaty of peace. It is not out of pity for the German people that this must be done and done without delay, but because we, the victors in this war, will be the chief sufferers if it is not done." [11]

In line with this strategy, the relief director, Herbert Hoover, effectively used food as an anti-Communist weapon in central and Eastern Europe, and clashed with the French, who wanted to maintain the wartime blockade of Germany. "The governing classes," wrote Colonel House in exasperation, "are the last to see the hand-writing on the wall. They do not seem to understand that while today quiet and comparative contentment reigns, tomorrow, through mob psychology, the whole situation may change." [12]

In his customary manner of rationalizing the simultaneous pursuit of moral and material objectives, Wilson noted the advantage of getting rid of surplus American farm produce while at the same time advancing what he termed "the high mission of the American people to find a remedy against starvation and absolute anarchy." Again in language reminiscent of the post-World War II Marshall Plan, the Commission to Negotiate Peace sent the following telegram to Washington in January 1919:

> It would be well to impress upon Congress that there is in the United States at present a considerable stock of surplus food especially wheat and pork which was accumulated principally for supplying the Allies and which would have been required by them had the war continued but which must now be disposed of in order to relieve storage and financial facilities in the United States. . . . While it is most important for us to dispose of this surplus in order to avoid difficulties in the United States, it is most fortunate that we have this surplus which is necessary to save human lives and stem the tide of Bolshevism in Europe.[13]

Wilson strengthened the anti-Bolshevik elements in Germany by providing food and by moderating the extreme French demands on issues such as reparations and frontiers. But a more important factor in determining the final outcome in Germany was the objective power balance in that country, which was altogether different from that which Lenin imagined on the basis of his experience in Russia. Lenin's basic miscalculation was his assumption that the progressive and uninterrupted radicalization that occurred in Russia between March and November 1917 would be repeated everywhere else: ". . . the general course of the proletarian revolution is the same throughout the world. First the spontaneous formation of Soviets, then their spread and development, and then the appearance of the practical problems: Soviets, or National Assembly, or Constituent Assembly, or the bourgeois parliamentary system; utter confusion among the leaders, and finally—the proletarian revolution." [14]

Lenin's belief in a common revolutionary pattern for all countries was patently unjustified. We have seen that Bolshevik Revolution proved to be the end result in Russia because of an exceptional combination of factors. These included the prewar disaffection of workers and peasants; the weakness of Russian industry and therefore of the Russian middle class; the catastrophic military defeats, which left the Russian army broken and mutinous; and the resulting popular clamor for immediate peace, which only the Bolsheviks promised to satisfy.

In Germany, by contrast, the workers and peasants had been relatively prosperous and contented in the prewar years. Consequently the German Social Democratic Party, although the strongest labor party in Europe in 1914, was basically conservative and committed to social reform rather than to revolution. Likewise the German peasants had not fared badly during the war years, so that the Bolshevik slogan "Land to the Peasants," which had been so effective in Russia, had little influence in Germany. Also, the war had already ended at the time of the German revolution, and therefore the demand for peace, which had been the most helpful for the Bolsheviks, was irrelevant to the Germans. Finally, the German army was far from being as demoralized and mutinous as the Russian army of 1917, so that the opponents of revolution in Germany were able to call upon reliable military forces when the showdown came. Hence the defeat of the Spartacists and the establishment of the Weimar Republic, which lasted only a decade and a half until demolished by Hitler.

With the discrediting of Lenin's assumption of imminent world revolution, the critical issue became the validity of his related assumption that the revolution in Russia could not survive in isolation. On March 3, 1918, Lenin had signed the draconian Brest-Litovsk Treaty with the Central Powers in the hope that he would gain time to cope with domestic problems. Instead he was forced to fight on for three more years against counterrevolution and foreign intervention.

The counterrevolution was in part the work of members of the propertied classes—army officers, government officials, landowners and businessmen—who for obvious reasons wished to be rid of the Bolsheviks. Equally ardent in their counterrevolutionary activities, however, were the various elements of the non-Bolshevik left, of whom the Socialist Revolutionaries were by far the most numerous. They agreed with the Bolsheviks on the need for social revolution, but they bitterly resented the Bolshevik monopolization of the revolution. They regarded the Bolshevik coup of November 7, 1917, as a gross betrayal, particularly because the Constituent Assembly elected on November 25, 1917, included only 175 Bolsheviks as against 370 Socialist Revolutionaries and 159 other assorted representatives. But the Bolsheviks had the power and they promptly dispersed the Constituent Assembly. Lenin's justification was blunt and to the point: "The Bolsheviks talked of the bourgeois-democratic revolution in 1905. But now when the Soviets are in power . . . there can be no question of a bourgeois-democratic revolution." [15] The non-Bolshevik left responded by organizing underground opposition, while the rightist elements led armed forces in open revolt.

Wilson characteristically opposed both the Bolsheviks and the Russian rightists, who were supported by the other Allies. He considered the liberals of the Provisional Government to represent the "true Russia," and hoped for a reconciliation of all Russian factions into a liberal synthesis. After the Bolsheviks eliminated the Constituent Assembly, Wilson realized that the Bolsheviks could not be co-opted and that they were serious about revolution throughout the world, including the United States.

Wilson therefore participated in the Allied armed intervention in Russia, though with restraint and ambivalence, because he correctly foresaw that excessive foreign interference in domestic Russian affairs would backfire in favor of the Bolsheviks.

The combination of external intervention and internal counterrevolution made possible the establishment of a string of anti-Bolshevik governments all along the borders of Russia—in the northern Archangel-Murmansk region, the Baltic provinces, the Ukraine, the Don territories, Transcaucasia and Siberia. These governments were provided by the Western powers with funds and war materials, as well as with military advisers and small detachments of troops on certain fronts. The beleaguered Bolsheviks at one point were fighting for survival on two dozen fronts. At first they suffered one reverse after another, simply because the old Russian army had disintegrated and there was nothing to take its place. By the end of 1918 the Russian Socialist Federal Soviet Republic had been reduced to the frontiers of medieval Muscovy before the conquests of Ivan the Terrible.

Few people believed that the Bolsheviks could survive, but survive they did. A common pattern is evident in the campaigns. Usually the White Russian generals took the initiative with sudden attacks from their bases on the periphery of the country. They gained easy victories at the beginning and came within reach of full victory. But as the Commissar for Defense, Leon Trotsky, built up a new Red Army, the White Russian forces were stopped and gradually pushed back, until finally routed. By the end of 1919 General Denikin had been driven back to the Crimea, General Yudenich to the Baltic and Admiral Kolchak over the Urals and into Siberia, where he was captured and shot. By early 1920 it appeared that the war was over, but another full year of fighting lay ahead because of generous French support to the Poles attacking from the west and to General Wrangel advancing from the Crimea. Again the invaders won early successes, but by the end of the year the Poles had been driven back to their frontier, while Wrangel's army was forced to flee from the Crimea in French warships. In the same year British and American troops also were evacuated from Vladivostok, leaving only Japanese contingents in eastern Siberia. They stayed on, hoping to retain control through a puppet regime, but local resistance and American diplomatic pressure finally persuaded them to leave in 1922.

Lenin's Communist Party at last was in control of the entire country. Several factors explain this surprising outcome, including disunity and vacillation among the interventionist powers, conflicting ambitions and policies of the White Russian leaders, cohesion and discipline of the Communist Party and brilliant leadership by Trotsky as Commissar of

War. Most important, however, was the success of the Bolsheviks in winning the support of the peasant masses. It was not a case of ideology but rather of self-interest, as Lenin had foreseen from the very beginning. On November 7, 1917, he explained before the Petrograd soviet the strategy necessary to retain the power they had just seized. "A single decree putting an end to landed proprietorship will win us the confidence of the peasants. The peasants will understand that the salvation of the peasantry lies only in an alliance with the workers." [16]

Lenin's analysis proved prophetic. The majority of peasants, especially the poor peasants, supported the Red Army simply because they wanted to keep the land they had seized from the landlords, the state and the Church. The vast amount of this land is evident in the fact that the landlord estates alone had comprised 40 percent of all cultivable land in Russia in 1916. The peasants were fully aware that the Red Army had made it possible for them to satisfy their land hunger, and also that landlords were prominent in the White Russian forces. So the worker-peasant alliance that Lenin had foreseen did materialize. This alliance, more than any other factor, enabled the Bolsheviks to prevail against seemingly impossible odds. And conversely, the breakup of that alliance after the fighting ceased has been a root cause for many of the basic problems that have plagued Soviet society to the present day.

With the defeat of revolution in Europe and the victory of revolution in Russia, the Bolsheviks had to revise their strategy, which had been based on the assumption that the fate of revolution in the two regions was interdependent and inseparable. At the Fourth Comintern Congress (1922), the last in which Lenin participated, the traditional dogma still persisted. "The proletarian revolution can never triumph completely within a single country, rather it must triumph internationally, as world revolution." [17] Stalin went along with this view, stating in May of the same year: "For the final victory of socialism, for the organization of socialist production, the efforts of one country, particularly of a peasant country like Russia, are insufficient; for that the efforts of the proletarians of several advanced countries are required." [18]

By 1924 Stalin began to change his position in the course of his feud with Trotsky for leadership of the party. By the time of the Sixth Comintern Congress (1928), which was dominated by Stalin, the theory of socialism in one country had become official Comintern doctrine. "Unevenness of economic and political development is an absolute law of capitalism, and is even more marked in the imperialist epoch. Hence the international proletarian revolution cannot be conceived as a single act taking place everywhere simultaneously. The victory of socialism is therefore possible at first only in a few capitalist countries, or even in one." [19]

With the acceptance of the feasibility of socialism in one country, the crucial question was the type of society that would emerge in what was now the isolated socialist fatherland. Three fateful trends stand out, which were to have profound repercussions on the Third World. One was the "deproletarianization" of the Communist Party and of the Soviet regime. Second was the succession of Five Year Plans, which industrialized the Soviet Union rapidly and therefore appeared to provide a model for underdeveloped countries. Finally, there was the transformation of the Comintern from the General Headquarters of world revolution to the pliant tool of a Soviet foreign policy that usually sought to dampen rather than foment world revolution. These developments are the subjects of the following three sections.

III. "A Bourgeois and Tsarist Hotch-potch"

When the Bolsheviks set out to build "socialism in one country," they knew there was no model they could follow. Marxist literature was of little use, since it was concerned almost exclusively with how to seize power rather than with what to do once this had been accomplished. The traditional definition of a socialist society—one in which the state owns the means of production—was no guide for the actual materialization of the society. Lenin himself admitted, "We knew when we took power into our hands, that there were no ready forms of concrete reorganization of the capitalist system into a socialist one. . . . I do not know of any socialist who has dealt with these problems. . . . we must go by experiments." [20]

Lenin was able to conduct the "experiments" in building socialism for only a few years before his death in 1924. Shortly before his final illness he reflected ruefully on the Soviet society that was emerging, and concluded that it was socialist more in appearance than in substance. It was nothing, he said, but the machine "which . . . we took over from Tsarism and slightly anointed with Soviet oil." And he added that "the apparatus we call ours is, in fact, still alien to us; it is a bourgeois and Tsarist hotch-potch. . . ." [21]

If a resurrected Lenin were to look about in the Soviet Union today, he would see little to warrant a different conclusion. A Soviet journalist pinpointed the key issue when he commented to his Western colleagues in 1971 that Russia's basic problem was not the shortage of consumer goods, which the Western correspondents were stressing in their reports, but rather the *meshchantsvo* or bourgeoisification of Soviet society.[22] By this he meant the growth of bourgeois values, the emphasis on self-advancement and self-gratification to the exclusion of social considerations, and the connotation of the word "they," used by the average

Soviet citizen to refer to Party and state leaders as though they were strangers from another planet. All this represents the complete antithesis of the new socialist society envisaged by Marx in the mid-nineteenth century and by the Bolsheviks in 1917.

In the light of retrospect, certain features of Russian society and of the Bolshevik Party stand out as contributing factors to this shattering of dreams. One was the numerical weakness of the Bolsheviks, who numbered only about twenty-four thousand in January 1917, and by November barely exceeded one hundred thousand. Furthermore, they were almost exclusively an urban group, with few contacts among the great peasant majority of Russia's population. Their November revolution was virtually a coup, involving merely the overthrow of Kerensky's moribund authority in the cities of Moscow and Petrograd. There was none of the protracted guerrilla warfare and the gradual evolution by trial and error, of peasant-based administration of liberated provinces that occurred during and after World War II in countries such as China, Vietnam, Yugoslavia and Albania. Instead, the urban-based Bolsheviks were largely ignorant, and even distrustful, of the peasant masses of their country.

This inherent weakness was accentuated by the appalling manpower losses sustained during the civil war and intervention. Bolsheviks were in the forefront of the fighting and suffered disproportionate casualties. White Russian army officers systematically weeded out Communist Party members among their prisoners and executed them out of hand. Many workers, both Communist and non-Communist, returned to their native villages because of unemployment and food shortages in the cities. By 1922 the number of employed workers had shrunk to less than half the prewar figure—4.6 million, as against 11 million in 1913.

This attrition reduced working-class representation in party, state and trade union ranks. The vacuum was filled by bourgeois men and women who were eager to conceal their class origin. Lenin was aware of this disturbing influx and urged a purging of the "lordly ones" by accepting as workers only those who had worked at least ten years in large industrial enterprises. But the shortage of manpower was too pressing and nothing was done. Hence the infiltration of bourgeois personnel and principles throughout the economy, the Party and the state.

In industry the tempo of nationalization was much faster than planned because of the flight of many owners. Worker control was established, but this resulted in anarchical activity by thousands of local factory committees. Each of these claimed its particular factory as an independent unit of production, the collective property of its workers. Each operated autonomously, deciding what should be produced, where it should be sold and at what price. Attempts to coordinate factory operations with military and civilian needs were rejected by the workers as "confiscation" of the power they had wrested from the original capitalist owners. The Bolsheviks finally resorted to establishing one-man management in the factories. By the end of 1920 between 80 and 90 percent of the factories were operating on this basis. The "one man," however, frequently was a bourgeois engineer or technician who alone possessed the needed skills. The social and political implications of this policy were reflected in the results of a poll taken in the summer of 1922 among officials possessing an engineer's diploma. Only 9 percent of the "old" officials and 13 percent of the "new" ones declared themselves favorably inclined to the Soviet regime for which they were working.

A similar trend was occurring at this time in the *sovkhozy* or state farms. At the Seventh Congress of Soviets in December 1919 the sovkhozy were accused of attracting expert managers by paying them high salaries and providing them with the stately homes of the former landlords. The latter, indeed, frequently contrived to return to their homes in the guise of "managers of state farms." A delegate to the Seventh Congress charged that the state farms "have been turned into instruments of counter-revolutionary agitation against the Soviet power." [23]

In the educational system it was not necessary for bourgeois teachers to find a way to recover their positions, because they remained in control from top to bottom. Despite the Bolshevik Revolution, primary education continued to be dominated by the Union of Primary School Teachers, led by Mensheviks and Social Revolutionaries. In secondary schools and universities the teachers were mostly associated with the Cadet Party. Despite a few attempts at innovation, the Soviet educational system during the 1920s did not differ substantively from the Tsarist prototype. Lower-class students continued to find it hard to enter a university and even harder to graduate. The few who managed to do so almost inevitably assimilated the bourgeois ideology of their teachers.

The Communist Party itself did not escape bourgeois infiltration. In 1919 only 11 percent of its members were working in factories, the remainder having been drained off to fill army, state and Party positions. Lenin pointed out the danger of this "deproletarianization" of the Party. The Eighth Party Congress (1919) required all members engaged in full-time administration work to return to factory jobs for at least one month in every four. The pressures of the civil war, however, were too urgent, so the Congress directive was ignored and eventually forgotten. Since these Communist administrators were working alongside many former Tsarist officials, they were affected to a greater or lesser extent by bourgeois ideology and attitudes. Thus the deproletarianization of the Party led to a process of what was termed "bureaucratization" or "bourgeoisification." This was the meshchantsvo referred to by the Soviet journalist in the 1970s, but which had its roots half a century earlier.

These developments in the early years of the Soviet regime amounted to the elimination of the old private bourgeoisie in favor of an emerging new state bourgeoisie. One symptom of this transition was increasing income differentiation. Factory managers and engineers expected and received relatively high salaries for their services. A decree of February 21, 1919, authorized a minimum wage of six hundred rubles a month and a maximum salary of three thousand rubles. "Very highly qualified" administrative and technical staff could be paid salaries exceeding three thousand rubles. This income was much greater than what had been considered acceptable in the period immediately after November 1917.

In addition to the widening income differentiation, there was emerging during these years a new style of Party functioning—a shift from the original proletarian discipline to a new bureaucratic discipline. Lenin defined proletarian discipline in terms almost identical to those used by Mao to describe what he called the "mass line." Proletarian discipline, according to Lenin, was the "ability to link up, maintain the closest contact, and—if you wish—merge, in certain measure, with the broadest masses of the working people—primarily with the proletariat, *but also with the nonproletarian masses* of working people." The Party's role was to convince them of the correctness of this line by reference to "their own experience." Under these conditions, Lenin added, proletarian discipline could be achieved, but "without these conditions, all attempts to establish discipline inevitably fall flat and end up in phrasemongering and clowning." [24]

These "conditions" that Lenin set forth as prerequisites for proletarian discipline became conspicuously absent in Soviet society. In one of his last works, Lenin concluded: "We have bureaucrats in our Party institutions as well as in the Soviet institutions." [25] By this he meant that Party and state officials were becoming independent of the rank-and-file. They were turning into "functionaries," "members of the apparatus" or, as they were already beginning to be called, *apparatchiki*. A famous Red Army commander, Marshal Budenny, was keenly aware of "forms of coercion" and "bureaucratic methods" against which his peasant recruits were complaining:

> There are too many punitive measures, and too few attempts to activize the peasants themselves. This type of coercion must be stamped out as soon as possible, for it is bureaucracy at its worst, a show of violence and power directed at the peasants who, more often than not, cannot even understand what is wanted of them. . . . The population itself (in the villages) including batraks [agricultural wage laborers], bednyaks [poor peasants] and serednyaks

[middle peasants], live quite apart. . . . Nothing is done to make contact with them in their work, to provide guidance in the field of socialist construction.[26]

Lenin tried to cope with this bureaucratism by driving the bureaucrats out of the Party. Power and success had swollen membership from 24,000 in 1917, to 612,000 in March 1920 and to 732,000 in March 1921. Then Lenin launched a purge to get rid of "non-Communist elements" and "proletarianize" the Party. By January 1923 membership had dropped to less than 500,000. But it was not necessarily the "non-Communist elements" that had been expelled. The purge had been conducted by the entrenched apparatchiki, who used the opportunity to get rid of members who were critical of their bureaucratic style of work or to silence them through fear of getting purged.

Lenin expressed doubt that the Communists were "directing" and suggested that they were "being directed." It was at this point, shortly before his death, that he described the Soviet regime as "a bourgeois and Tsarist hotch-potch." Lenin then proposed a course of action strikingly reminiscent of the Cultural Revolution, which Mao launched decades later to cope with a similar dilemma. "It is the task of the Soviet government to completely destroy the old machinery of the state as it was destroyed in October, and to transfer power to the Soviets." [27]

What might Lenin have achieved had he lived for a quarter century after the Russian Revolution, as Mao lived after the Chinese? What if Lenin had been able to direct the building of the new society? Would a Russian Cultural Revolution have toppled the apparatchiki and transferred "power to the Soviets"? This is one of the great "ifs" of history that cannot be answered. There is only the knowledge that with Lenin gone, the way was clear for the master apparatchik to assemble and manipulate the massive bureaucratic apparatus that constitutes the U.S.S.R. to the present day.

୬ *IV. Five Year Plans*

The *de facto* alliance between workers and peasants that had saved the Bolshevik Revolution began to unravel when defeat of the White Russian armies ended the danger of landlord return. In fact, friction between peasants and Bolsheviks had developed even before the fighting was over, and thereafter it increased steadily to crisis proportions.

The basic reason, as Lenin noted, was that a "proletarian revolution" had occurred in the cities, in contrast to the "bourgeois revolution" in the countryside. This meant that the Bolsheviks, as Marxists, wanted to create a social order in which peasants were transformed into workers and assimilated into the proletariat, whereas the peasants, as non-Marxists, wished to remain peasants and to preserve traditional rural social relationships except for the transfer of land into their hands.

At stake was not only ideology but also urgent bread-and-butter issues. At first the Bolsheviks had little opportunity for social experimentation because the military struggle for survival took precedence over everything else. The "war communism" that prevailed between 1917 and 1921 evolved out of the desperate measures taken to supply the beleaguered Red Army with needed materials and manpower. Land, banks, foreign trade and heavy industry were all nationalized. Also, surplus agricultural produce was forcibly requisitioned in order to feed soldiers and city dwellers. The original plan was to compensate the peasants with manufactured goods, but this proved impossible because almost all factories were producing for the front.

By the end of the civil war and intervention, the peasants were up in arms against the confiscation of their produce without compensation. As one of them put it: "The land belongs to us; the bread to you; the water to us; the fish to you; the forest to us: the timber to you." [28] At the same time the economy of the country was paralyzed, partly because of the years of warfare, but also because of a peasant strike. In response to confiscation without compensation, the peasants restricted production to little more than their own needs, especially since the rampant inflation made it easy for them to pay their taxes. Grain production declined from an average of 72.5 million metric tons between 1909 and 1913 to under 30 million in 1919. Industrial output fell even more catastrophically, to 10 percent of prewar levels. The crowning disaster was the widespread drought of 1920 and 1921, which contributed to a famine in which millions died of starvation. Even the Kronstadt sailors, hitherto the staunchest supporter of the Bolsheviks, now revolted with the slogan "The Soviets without the Bolsheviks."

The practical-minded Lenin realized that concessions were unavoidable—hence the adoption in 1921 of the New Economic Policy (NEP), which allowed a partial restoration of capitalism, especially in agriculture and trade. Peasants were permitted to sell their produce on the open market after paying to the state a tax in kind that consisted of about 12 percent of their output. Private individuals were allowed to operate small stores and factories. Both the peasants and the new businessmen (or Nepmen, as they were called) could employ labor and retain what profits they made from their operations. Lenin, however, saw to it that the state kept control of title to the land and what he termed "the commanding heights" (banking, foreign trade, heavy industry and transportation). So far as Lenin was concerned, the NEP did not mean the end of socialism in Russia; rather it was a temporary retreat, "one step backward in order to take two steps forward."

The great question in the following years was how these "two steps forward" should be made. The NEP did give the people a breathing spell, and it did allow the economy to recover from the utter prostration of 1921. By 1926, industrial and agricultural production had reached pre-1914 levels. But recovery did not solve the problem of long-range economic strategy. Rather it led to impasse, for the peasants were holding back on the supplies of foodstuffs and raw materials for the cities. They were eating more, being freed of onerous rent payments to landlords and they were feeding more grain to their livestock. Also, their productivity was reduced by lack of tools and implements, while the scarcity of consumer goods depressed their incentive to sell what surplus was available.

In 1926 the state received only 428 million poods of grain as against the 500 million needed to maintain reserves at a safe level. The following year the flow of supplies from the countryside was even less. By January 1928 the situation was reaching crisis proportions. Uzbekistan should have received 3.8 million poods of grain that month, but actually got only 40 percent of that amount. The Abidzhan region reported that by March 15, 1928, it had received only 277,000 of the scheduled 1,301,-000 poods of grain. Faced with this emergency, the Party leadership found itself isolated and bewildered because of its bureaucratization during the preceding years. "The regime failed to learn during the years of NEP," states historian M. Lewin, "how best to reach an understanding with the peasants, how to consolidate its position in the countryside, how to build up a powerful non-State co-operative movement, or to devise efficient collective structures. Thus, the regime wasted time, and failed to give sufficient attention to the preparation of effective instruments of government which, before long, were to be sorely needed. When the difficulties materialized, the Soviet regime . . . was to a great extent regarded in the villages as an alien force. . . ." [29]

The natural response of a beleaguered bureaucracy in such extremity was to view the peasantry as an enemy who must be brought under state control and forced to deliver whatever the state required. The leader who emerged to devise and execute this strategy of force was Joseph Stalin, "the master-builder of bureaucratic structures." [30] While the "Old Bolsheviks" clung to their egalitarian ideals, Stalin saw clearly that the only real power in the country was the Party, and that the basis of its power was its discipline and its bureaucratic apparatus, for which he himself was largely responsible. Stalin had made himself, as general secretary, the supreme apparatchik in what was becoming a party of apparatchiki. By a process of substitution, as Trotsky put it, the Party substituted itself for the working class, the Stalinist faction for the Party, and its general secretary for society at large.

After prolonged debate among several Party factions, Stalin decided in favor of a succession of Five Year Plans prepared by the State Planning Commission (Gosplan), and involving forced collectivization of land and accelerated tempo of industrialization. Most controversial and tempestuous was the land decision, which was based on two assumptions that seemed self-evident to the Party bureaucrats. One was the economic assumption that the small peasant holdings had reached the limits of their productivity and that it was therefore necessary to shift over to large-scale operations utilizing tractors and other modern machines. The political assumption was that the *kulaks* or wealthy peasants were implacable enemies of the Soviet regime and largely responsible for the withholding of food supplies. Their destruction therefore was considered essential to end the danger of counterrevolution and the restoration of capitalism. Thus the wholesale collectivization of land was designed to solve simultaneously the economic problem of inadequate and undependable food deliveries, and the political problem of incipient counterrevolution.

A French Marxist scholar, Charles Bettelheim, has challenged both these assumptions,[31] which hitherto have generally been accepted outside the Soviet Union as well as within. Regarding the kulaks, their threat apparently was exaggerated, since they comprised in 1926–27 only 3.1 percent of the total peasant population, as against 67.5 percent in the case of the middle peasants and 29.4 percent for the poor. The kulaks did market a disproportionately larger percentage of farm produce, yet it still was only 11.8 percent of the total. It does not follow that the kulaks were an insignificant force in the countryside, but neither can they be considered to have been primarily responsible for the economic crisis of the mid-1920s. The Commissioner for Trade, A. Mikoyan, recognized this in 1928: "The real bulk of the grain surplus was owned by the *serednyaks* [middle peasants] who were often in no hurry to sell, if the appropriate quantities of consumers' goods which they needed to buy were not available, or if they were not pressed by the need to discharge debts owing to the State or to the co-operative movement." [32]

Likewise the low productivity of peasant holdings appears to have been due not so much to their small size as to the lack of simple necessities such as tools, seeds and horses. This explains why a significant proportion of peasant holdings was not being cultivated even though there was much underemployment and unemployment in the countryside. In 1928, 5.5 million peasant households had available only a primitive wooden plow, "at least as old as the Pharaohs." A quarter of the farms had no horse, so it was not unusual to see "a wretched wooden *sokha* [plow], dating from the Flood . . . often dragged along by a miserable yoke of lean oxen, or by the farmer, or even his wife. . . ." [33]

The drive to establish *kolkhozes,* or collective farms, got under way in the summer of 1929. Between July and October, membership doubled, but it consisted largely of poor peasants who had little to contribute. The new kolkhozes consequently lacked resources, and faced the prospect of stagnation or bankruptcy. Without the participation of the middle peasants, who comprised over two thirds of the peasant population, the kolkhoz program would collapse, and with it would collapse also the ambitious plans for industrialization. Thus the fate of the entire Five Year Plan was at stake.

Stalin's response was to use all the repressive power of the Party and state to force the middle peasants into the kolkhozes. Membership shot up dramatically in 1929. In the Central Black Earth Region only 8.3 percent of households were collectivized in October 1929, but by the end of January 50 percent had joined, and by March 1 no less than 81.8 percent. In the country as a whole, about 60 percent had been dragooned into joining. The cost, however, was catastrophic. Many peasants, to use their words, were determined to enter the kolkhozes "naked as the falcon." They destroyed their equipment and slaughtered their livestock. Their fury was reaching the explosion point. Stalin drew back, and in his article "Dizzy with Success," published in *Pravda* on March 2, 1930, he chastised his comrades for their overzealousness (though they were only following his orders) and granted the peasants the option of withdrawal.

Within a few weeks 9 million households left the kolkhozes, the percentage of collectivization dropping from 59.3 to 23. Nevertheless, nearly a quarter of the households remained, and after a short lull the collectivization drive was resumed in 1931. By 1938 almost all peasant holdings had been amalgamated into 242,400 kolkhozes and 4,000 *sovkhozes* or state farms. The ferocity of the struggle was admitted by Stalin when Churchill asked him in 1942, in the midst of the Second World War: "Tell me, have the stresses of this war been as bad to you personally as carrying through the policy of the Collective Farms?" Stalin replied, "Oh no, the Collective Farm policy was a terrible struggle. . . . It was fearful. Four years it lasted." [34]

Indeed it was "fearful," with hundreds of thousands of peasant families uprooted and shipped off to prisons or Siberian labor camps. Even after the collectivization had been completed, many more years were to pass before Soviet agriculture recovered from the mass slaughter of livestock. Most important was the final and definitive ending of the alliance between the Bolsheviks and the peasants, a rupture that always had been feared by Bolshevik leaders as a calamity to be avoided at all costs.

The repercussions of the breakup of the alliance dating back to civil war days were far-reaching and momentous. One was the passive resistance of the peasants, who henceforth dragged their feet, regarding the kolkhozes as something alien that had been imposed upon them. Hence the contrast between their high productivity in their own small plots where they worked hard and sold the produce in the open market for their personal profit, and their consistently low productivity in the collective fields, where the produce was sold at low, government-set rates. Even in 1953, when Stalin died, food output per Russian was less than in 1913. Nor have Stalin's successors been more successful, as evidenced by the continued heavy purchases of foreign grain despite substantially increased capital investments in agriculture.

The second result of the Bolshevik-peasant split was that the resulting low productivity of agriculture did not leave enough surplus to sustain the projected fast pace of industrialization. Consequently the factory workers also were squeezed in order to secure the capital necessary for the successive Five Year Plans. The Soviet government withdrew about 40 percent of the national income each year for reinvestment, in contrast to about 20 percent in the United States. The low rate of pay, together with the scarcity of consumer goods and the lack of meaningful worker participation in the decision-making process in factories, made Soviet workers almost as alienated as Soviet peasants. Trade unions were transformed into instruments for serving state purposes rather than protecting worker interest. "They pretend they are paying us," declared a Soviet worker in 1975, "so we pretend we are working." [35] After more than half a century under the Soviet system, Russian workers today are repeating the nineteenth-century syndicalist slogan, "Poor work for poor pay."

The result is pervasive lack of initiative and creativity in the Soviet economic system. The slogan during the early plans was "Overtake and surpass America," and this seemed at the time to be a realizable goal. The rate of industrial growth, however, has steadily slowed down, from about 6 percent in the 1950s to 5 percent in the 1960s and to under 4 percent in the 1970s. The Soviet Union also is falling behind the capitalist world in the science and technology that undergird modern industry. Just as the Soviet authorities find it necessary to purchase foreign grains to make up for their lagging agriculture, so also are they purchasing foreign technology and borrowing foreign capital to bolster their sclerotic industries.

The alienation of both workers and peasants left the Communist Party with only the rising bureaucrats as its social base. Thus the third result of the breakup of the Party-peasant alliance has been the formation of the Party-state bureaucrat alliance. This amounts to a new exploitive ruling class that does not own property but that does possess political power to allocate goods and services. The end result is similar, though by no means identical, to that under capitalism. The circulation of surplus value that normally occurs in a capitalist economy has simply been replaced by the organized redistribution of surplus value directed by, and for the benefit of, the technobureaucrats of Party, state and industry.

The emergence of this new ruling elite explains why the Soviet state has not "withered away." According to Marxist theory, the state as an instrument of class repression should have gradually disappeared in Russia after the abolition of capitalism with its exploiting and exploited classes. The coercive organs of the Soviet state, however, have proliferated rather than disappeared. Stalin's explanation was that the hostile capitalist world surrounding the Soviet Union necessitated the retention of the restraining state organs in order to protect the country against foreign spies, saboteurs and assassins. But after more than six decades of Soviet rule, why cannot the responsibility for countering this foreign threat be shifted to the masses, who should be at least as ready to resist foreign intrigues and intervention as they were after November 1917? Why is it that, to the contrary, the enormous state apparatus is constantly expanding rather than shrinking? The answer seems to be that domestic contradictions are more pressing than foreign pressures. The apparatchiki, by definition, must preserve their apparatus if they are to retain their power and privileges.

V. Russian Revolution and the Third World

Soviet society today scarcely embodies the socialism envisaged by Marx in the mid-nineteenth century or by the "old Bolsheviks" in the early twentieth. Yet it is a success if viewed from the perspective of its bureaucratic elite, for it has become a major economic and military power in the contemporary world. The kolkhozes obviously have not tapped the creative resources of the Soviet peasantry, but they have enabled the state to collect enough surplus product to support the industrialization program, and they also have provided the means for political control over the countryside. Likewise in industry the Soviet authorities continuously have denounced malingering, alcoholism and theft of state property, yet by the end of the first Five Year Plan in 1932 Russia had leaped ahead from the fifth to the second industrial power of the world. This spectacular advance was due in part to the decline of productivity in the West during the Depression years, but it was due also to the unprecedented mobilization of human and natural resources made possible by the plans. The latter also provided a national program and goal, which in the early years stimulated genuine mass enthusiasm and support.

The Soviet share of total global industrial output rose from 1.5 percent in 1921 to 10 percent in 1939 to 20 percent today. Soviet economists claim a twenty-one fold increase in per-capita national income between 1928 and 1966. A Western computation using different weights and base years shows an increase of only $3\frac{1}{2}$ times. "Even accepting the Western estimate," concludes an American economist, "it should be emphasized that this increase was achieved over a period of only 37 years, interrupted by years of devastating warfare while, in comparison, per-capita output of goods and services in the United States was 4 times as large in 1968 as in 1890 (a period of 78 years), and per-capita disposable income 3 times as high in 1968 as in 1899." [36]

In social terms, the Five Year Plans transformed Russia from a primitive to a modern society. In education, literacy rose from 28.4 percent in 1897, to 56.6 percent in 1926, to 87.4 percent in 1939 and to 98.5 percent in 1959. In medical care, between 1913 and 1961, the number of physicians increased from 23,200 to 425,700, life expectancy rose from 32 to 70 years and infant mortality declined from 273 to 32 per thousand. Likewise in social services, Soviet citizens now enjoy free medical care, old-age pensions, sickness and disability benefits, maternity leaves, paid vacations and children's aid.

A Soviet economist, Professor Alexander Birman, wrote on the fiftieth anniversary of the establishment of the U.S.S.R. State Planning Committee: ". . . mankind ought to mark this date, just as it would the first round-the-world trip or Copernicus's discovery, as a historical event, signifying man's attainment of a basically new stage in human development." [37] If Lenin were alive today it is doubtful that he would subscribe to Professor Birman's ecstatic appraisal, for the flaws he deplored in the early 1920s are now institutionalized in Soviet society. Yet even after making all the reservations that need to be made, the fact remains that the Russian Revolution and the Five Year Plans have affected fundamentally the course of contemporary history. They made possible, for example, the decisive Soviet contribution to the defeat of Nazi Germany. And for the Third World, the Soviet system represents the first breakaway from the international market economy and the first viable alternative model to traditional Western capitalism.

The Soviet model involved certain development strategies that are commonplace today but that were stunningly bold and innovative in the interwar years. One was social revolution as the prerequisite for the wholesale political and social restructuring needed to mobilize human and natural resources. A second feature of the Soviet model was the cutting of established economic ties with metropolitan centers so that local resources might be utilized to satisfy local rather than imperial needs. Finally, the Soviet model entailed successive nationwide campaigns to develop human capital through education, technical training and public health services.

Soviet achievements were particularly influential in the Third World because the U.S.S.R. is a great Asian as well as European state. Its frontiers stretch from Korea, past Mongolia, Sinkiang, Afghanistan and Iran to Turkey. In almost all these regions, kindred people exist on both sides of the frontier, thus facilitating interaction and comparison of conditions. In most cases, the Soviet Union has fared well by comparison, thanks to the revivifying effect of the Five Year Plans on its eastern regions. The other side of the long frontier has had few counterparts to the substantial material advances made in the Soviet central Asian republics: the 185-mile Ferghana irrigation canal, the 900-mile Turksib Railway, the new textile fertilizer and farm-machinery plants as well as the impressive advances in mass education and public health.

Soviet policies in central Asia did not meet with unanimous approval. Thousands of Kazaks fled into Chinese Sinkiang to escape the repression of the early days of the plans. Also, many central Asians opposed the growing Russification of their republics—a result of deliberate government policy and large-scale Slavic migration into the new industrial centers. But this internal disaffection did not affect substantially the attraction that the Soviet model held for many who lived in colonial and semicolonial territories. The reason is apparent in the statistics in the table on page 512.

The impact of those statistics on Third World people is evident in the following passage from the autobiography of Jawaharlal Nehru:

> While the rest of the world was in the grip of the depression and going backward in some ways, in the Soviet country a great new world was being built up before our eyes. Russia, following the great Lenin, looked into the future and thought only of what was to be, while other countries lay numbed under the dead hand of the past and spent their energy in preserving the useless relics of a bygone age. In particular, I was impressed by the reports of the great progress made by the backward regions of Central Asia under the Soviet regime. In the balance, therefore, I was all in favor of Russia, and the presence and example of the Soviets was a bright and heartening phenomenon in a dark and dismal world.[38]

Nehru's enthusiastic appraisal of the Soviet Union was written in the mid-1930s, when the contrast between the burgeoning Five Year Plans and the devastating capitalist Great Depression was stark and overwhelming. Few Third World leaders today would be so fervent in their appraisal of Soviet society, nor is that society any longer the sole alternative to Western capitalism. Nevertheless, it is noteworthy that when

Nonmonetary Indicators of Economic Development for Soviet Central Asia and Selected Underdeveloped Countries: Before and After Soviet Development

Country	Percent of adults literate	Percent of population in cities over 20,000	Percent of population in secondary and higher education	Electricity generation, kwh per capita	Physicians per 100,000
Soviet Central Asia					
"before" (1926–28)	16	9.3	.16	4	17.4
"after" (1960–62)	87	27.8	5.46	820	139.1
Colombia (1960–62)	62	22.4	1.88	259	41.3
India (1960–62)	24	11.9	2.34	51	17.4
Turkey (1960–62)	30	14.5	2.00	99	34.4
Iran (1960–62)	15	15	1.53	44	25.4

Source: C. K. Wilber, *The Soviet Model and Underdeveloped Countries* (Chapel Hill: University of North Carolina Press, 1969), pp. 148ff.

the 1978–79 Iranian revolution swept the Shah into exile, there were no discernible reverberations among the six million inhabitants of the Soviet Republic of Azerbaijan, who share a common history, religion and language with the five million Azerbaijanis in neighboring northwestern Iran. The reason is that Soviet Azerbaijan is a completely different world, in which most of the issues convulsing Iran are simply irrelevant. The few remaining mullahs lack the influence of their counterparts in Iran. Equally important, the above statistics regarding relative economic development in Iran and Soviet central Asia suggest that the Soviet Five Year Plans have resolved many of the socioeconomic grievances behind the extraordinary mass uprising against the Shah. Thus whereas the 1905 Russian Revolution contributed to the 1906 Constitutional Revolution against the Qajar Dynasty, by contrast the 1978–79 revolution against the Pahlavi dynasty incited no challenge to Soviet rule in the Azerbaijan Republic.

Chapter 21

FIRST GLOBAL REVOLUTIONARY WAVE, 1914–39: GLOBAL MANIFESTATIONS OF REVOLUTION

This war is an end and also a beginning. Never again will darker people of the world occupy just the place they had before. Out of this place will rise, soon or late, an independent China, a self-governing India, an Egypt with representative institutions, an Africa for the Africans, and not merely for business exploitation. Out of this war will rise, too, an American negro with the right to vote and the right to work and the right to live without insult.

W. E. B. Du Bois, 1918

The more I think of the President's declaration as to the right of "self-determination," the more convinced I am of the danger of putting such ideas into the minds of certain races. It is bound to be the basis of impossible demands on the Peace Congress, and create trouble in many lands. What effect will it have on the Irish, the Indians, the Egyptians, and the nationalities among the Boers? Will it not breed discontent, disorder and rebellion? Will not the Mohammedans of Syria and Palestine and possibly Morocco and Tripoli rely on it? How can it be harmonized with Zionism, to which the president is practically committed? The phrase is simply loaded with dynamite.

Secretary of State Robert Lansing, 1918

The European powers were weakened during the bloodletting of World War I, yet they managed to retain their empires intact during the postwar years. One reason was that, apart from China, the Third World revolutionary movements were primarily nationalist in character. Their leaders were of bourgeois background: merchants and lawyers as in India, military officers as in Turkey and Iran, or teachers and clerks as in Africa. All these elements had one thing in common. They wanted independence but they rejected class struggle and basic social change. Their parties and their programs were nationalistic rather than social revolutionary. Third World movements during the interwar decades also were affected by Great Power policies, particularly by the fact that Soviet commitment to the cause of world revolution proved less resolute than Western commitment to the preservation of colonial empires. Thus the political frontiers of the Third World in 1939 were very similar to those a quarter century earlier, in 1914. If anything, the empires were larger in 1939, for they included former Ottoman provinces under the guise of mandates.

🎜 I. Dynamics of Third World Politics

The prestige of the colonial powers was damaged during the First World War by the spectacle of European Christians slaughtering each other in defense of God and country. No longer were they regarded by Asians and Africans as almost divinely ordained rulers. Equally disruptive of European authority was the participation in the war of colonial and semicolonial manpower. India alone provided 800,000 soldiers and 414,000 laborers for service on the Western Front and in Mesopotamia. Nearly 200,000 Chinese and large numbers of Indochinese served in labor battalions behind the lines, while 175,000 Africans in French uniforms fought in northern France.

Those who returned home after such experiences were not likely to be as deferential to European overlords as before. A French administrator observed that "the 175,000 soldiers enrolled during the years 1914–1918 dug the grave of the old Africa in the trenches of France and Flanders." [1] A French governor-general of Indochina wrote in 1926: "The war which covered Europe with blood has . . . awakened in lands far distant from us a feeling of independence. . . . All has changed in the past few years. Both men and ideas and Asia herself are being transformed." [2] The degree of the transformation is evident in the following acid observation by Ho Chi Minh when France used African troops in the occupation of the Ruhr in 1923: "Imperialism has now reached a degree of almost scientific perfection. It uses white proletarians to conquer the proletarians of the colonies. Then it hurls the proletarians of one colony against those of another. Finally, it relies on the proletarians of the colonies to rule white proletarians. . . . Only recently, French soldiers in the Ruhr were surrounded by native soldiers, and native light infantry were sent against German strikers." [3]

Revolutionary ideas in the colonies were also spread by propaganda associated with the conduct of the war. It is true that Wilson's Fourteen Points had referred only to the "interest" rather than to the desires of the colonial peoples. But this was an overfine distinction in a time of war, and the revolutionary phrase "self-determination of peoples" left its imprint on the colonial world as well as upon Europe. Equally influential were the ideologies of socialism and communism. Before World War I, Asian intellectuals had been inspired by Western liberalism and nationalism. They had quoted Voltaire, Mazzini and John Stuart Mill. But their sons now were likely to quote Marx, Lenin or Harold Laski. Dr. Sun Yat-sen, on July 25, 1919, gave evidence of this shift when he declared: "If the people of China wish to be free . . . its only ally and brother in the struggle for national freedom are the Russian workers and peasants of the Red Army." [4]

Dr. Sun's dream of an alliance between the Soviet Red Army and colonial revolutionaries never materialized. One reason was the unfavorable local conditions and balance of forces. These varied tremendously from one part of the Third World to another. Geographic location, for example, exerted appreciable influence. China's proximity to Bolshevik Russia contributed to the rapid diffusion of Communist ideology in that country during the 1920s, whereas the revolutionaries in Mexico a few years earlier were little influenced by communism because of their relative isolation. If Bolshevik Russia rather than the capitalist United States had been Mexico's neighbor, then the nature and course of the Mexican Revolution would have been significantly different. Also, there was much diversity in levels of economic development among and within Third World regions—difference such as those between Egypt and Yemen in the Islamic World, between Chad and the Ivory Coast in black Africa and between Mexico and Haiti in Latin America.

By far the most important domestic factor determining the course of events in the Third World between the two world wars was the bourgeois leadership in the anticolonial struggle. None of the local Communist Parties attracted popular support or exerted influence comparable to that of the Chinese Communist Party. Most colonies and semicolonies remained quiescent or generated nationalist movements that modified political arrangements but left intact the dependency relationships with metropolitan centers.

Finally, the colonial empires survived because the counterrevolutionary activities of the imperialist powers were more single-minded and effective than the revolutionary efforts of the Soviet Union. Wilson's Fourteen Points specifically spelled out how the aspirations of the various European minorities were to be satisfied, but as for the overseas colonies, Point Five declared that "the interest of the populations concerned must have equal weight with the equitable claims of the government whose title is to be determined." The significant point here is the reference to the "interest" rather than the "wishes" of the colonial peoples. Needless to say, it was the Europeans themselves who decided what the "interest" was, and the outcome was a modified form of imperial rule known as the mandate system.

Article 22 of the League of Nations Covenant referred to the inhabitants of the colonies taken from the Central Powers as "people not yet able to stand by themselves under the strenuous conditions of the modern world." The article accordingly provided that "the tutelage of such people should be entrusted to advanced nations who, by reason of their resources, their experience, or their geographical position can best undertake this responsibility . . . and that this tutelage should be exercised by them as Mandatories on behalf of the League."

The mandates article divided the foreign and overseas territories of Germany and the Ottoman Empire into Class A, B and C mandates. The category varied according to the level of development of the territory concerned. On this basis the former Ottoman possessions were put in Class A, and the German colonies in B and C. Of the Ottoman territories, Mesopotamia and Palestine were allotted to Britain as the mandatory power, and Syria and Lebanon to France. Of the German colonies, the greater part of Tanganyika went to Britain and the remainder to Belgium; Togoland and the Cameroons were divided between Britain and France; South-West Africa was allotted to the Union of South Africa; and Germany's Pacific islands north of the equator went to Japan, and those south of the equator to Australia and New Zealand.

The mandatory powers assumed specific obligations toward the inhabitants of the mandated territories. For fulfillment of these obligations they were accountable to the Permanent Mandates Commission, and were required to report annually to the Council of the League of Nations. The obligations of the mandatory powers varied according to the type of mandate. In the case of Class A, the mandates article looked forward specifically to the granting of independence as soon as feasible. The duty of the mandatory power was merely "the rendering of administrative advice and assistance . . . until such time as they [the people of the mandated territory] are able to stand alone. The wishes of these communities must be a principal consideration in the selection of the Mandatory." But for Class B and Class C mandates, there was no reference to eventual independence. The obligation rather was to provide administration in accord with the interest of the inhabitants.

It is significant that neither the Permanent Mandates Commission nor the League itself had authority to coerce a recalcitrant mandatory power. It is also significant that the provision for "tutelage" under mandatory powers was not extended to the colonies of the victorious Allies, whose inhabitants in many cases were at a similar level of underdevelopment as those of the colonies that were mandated. Likewise little attention was paid in the allotting of mandates to the expressed desires and aspirations of the peoples involved. Even in the case of Class B mandates in Africa, there was acute dissatisfaction with the arrangements made. The dissatisfaction was much more assertive and violent in Arab provinces of the Ottoman Empire. The Syrians and Lebanese, for example, did not want mandated status, and were particularly opposed to France as their mandatory power. But their wishes were completely ignored, while at the same time the much less advanced peoples of the Arabian peninsula were spared foreign tutelage because their desert lands were assumed to be of no economic value. Had there been any inkling of the vast oil riches under those desert sands, the local inhabitants assuredly would have been judged as "not yet able to stand by themselves," and would have been assigned foreign rulers, as were the Syrians, Lebanese, Palestinians and Iraqis.

Allied statesmen were quite candid privately, if not publicly, about the selective applicability of the self-determination principle. The British Foreign Secretary, A. J. Balfour, warned in December 1918 that self-determination should not be applied "pedantically where it is really inapplicable, namely, to wholly barbarous, undeveloped, and unorganized black tribes, whether they be in the Pacific or Africa. . . . you cannot transfer formulas more or less applicable to the populations of Europe to different races." [5] This attitude is not surprising in a spokesman for British imperial interests, but precisely the same restrictive interpretation was expressed in the same month by the American Secretary of State, Robert Lansing, who rejected blanket application of self-determination as political "dynamite." (The text of Lansing's statement is in the prologue to this chapter.)

Since self-determination was denied to Third World peoples on grounds of principle, it follows that social revolution was deemed even more intolerable. To ensure that it would not have to be tolerated, the Western powers supported the most conservative Third World elements, whether it was Chiang Kai-shek as against the Communists, the Ottoman dynasty as against Kemal, or African chieftains as against local nationalist leaders. In the few cases where the Western powers did not have their way, the

result was that a feudal or conservative regime was replaced by a bourgeois nationalist rather than a socialist regime. Western policymakers
were able to reach acceptable compromises with the Kemals and Rezas
and Gandhis and Batistas of the Third World.

In contrast to the unrelenting counterrevolutionary policies of the
colonial powers, the Bolsheviks were ambivalent despite their inflammatory rhetoric. They organized the Communist International in March
1919 to serve as "the general headquarters of world revolution." The
manifesto of the First Congress of the Comintern stated that "the purpose
of Wilson's program, on the most favorable interpretation, is merely to
change the label of colonial slavery. . . ." and concluded that "liberation of the colonies is thinkable only in connexion with the liberation
of the working class in the metropolitan countries." [6] In the same month
of March 1919 Nikolai Bukharin stated candidly before the Eighth Congress of the Russian Communist Party that world revolution would assist
the beleaguered Soviet state as well as the colonial subjects:

> If we propound the solution of the right of self-determination for
> the colonies, the Hottentots, the Negroes, the Indians, etc., we lose
> nothing by it. On the contrary, we gain; for the national gain as a
> whole will damage foreign imperialism. . . . The most outright
> national movement, for example, that of the Hindus, is only water
> for our mill, since it contributes to the destruction of English im-
> perialism." [7]

Thus the international proletarian struggle for world revolution and
the Soviet struggle for national survival were from the beginning in-
extricably interwoven. With the passage of time Soviet state interest
prevailed over international proletarian considerations in the formulation
of the Comintern policies. The emphasis shifted from promoting world
revolution to exploiting capitalist rivalries in order to forestall anti-
Soviet coalitions. An early indication of this shift was manifested in the
Soviet reaction to developments in Turkey. On September 13, 1919, the
Peoples' Commissar for Foreign Affairs, George Chicherin, broadcast an
appeal from "the workers' and peasants' government of Soviet Russia" to
"the workers and peasants of Turkey" to stretch out a brotherly hand in
order to expel the European robbers by simultaneous and combined
force. . . . [8]

At about this time the Turkish military leader, Mustafa Kemal, was
renouncing his allegiance to the subservient Ottoman Dynasty in Constantinople and beginning to organize a resistance movement against
the victorious Western powers. Kemal was a nationalist rather than a
socialist, and Chicherin's appeal to "the workers and peasants of Turkey"
doubtless grated on his ears. "As to the Bolshevists," he declared late in

1919, "there is no room whatever in our country for this doctrine, our religion and customs as well as our social organization being entirely unfavorable to its implantation." [9] Nevertheless, Kemal desperately needed help, and on April 26, 1920, he sent a note to the Soviet government expressing his "desire to enter into regular relations with it to take part in the struggle against foreign imperialism which threatens both countries." [10] Chicherin responded positively, and in March 1921 a Soviet-Turkish treaty of friendship and aid was signed. Despite the formidable economic and military problems confronting the Bolsheviks at that time, they supplied Kemal with ten million gold rubles and considerable quantities of arms.

This aid contributed substantially to Kemal's successful resistance against the Allied powers and the Greek army that had invaded Asia Minor. But while soliciting and accepting Soviet assistance, Kemal was mercilessly destroying the fledgling Turkish Communist Party, which had been formed in 1920. It was led by Mustafa Subhi and consisted of three elements: prisoners of war in Russia who had been won over to communism during their confinement, Istanbul members who had been influenced during the Allied occupation after World War I, and a local group that had emerged within Anatolia. At one point Subhi won the support of partisan units known as the Green Army, which were fighting primarily for agrarian reform. The Communists together with the Green Army posed a serious challenge to Kemal. The latter, however, outmaneuvered his opponents politically and defeated them militarily in January 1921. Subhi and fourteen of his companions then were herded on a boat in Trabzon on the Black Sea, strangled and their bodies thrown overboard. Other Communist leaders were put on trial for "high treason," and the decimated Turkish Communist Party never again was a force in Turkish politics.

Should the Soviet government help a nationalist movement that on the one hand was successfully resisting the imperialist powers, but on the other was murdering Communists and repressing agrarian reforms? The answer was affirmative, as indicated by the signing of the treaty with Kemal only weeks after the massacre of the Turkish Communists. The Soviet leaders obviously gave priority to an alliance that enhanced the security of their southern borders and of their Caucasus oilfields. Likewise the Third Comintern Congress ignored the fate of the Turkish comrades for fear of precipitating a break with Kemal. The Congress adopted a resolution protesting repressive measures being taken against German Communists, but it made no protest whatsoever about the murders at Trabzon.

Equally revealing was the trade agreement the Russians signed on March 16, 1921, with Britain. This included a provision stipulating that "each party refrains from hostile action or undertakings against the other and from conducting outside of its own borders any official propaganda, direct or indirect . . . and more particularly that the Russian Soviet Government refrains from any attempt by military or diplomatic or any other form of action or propaganda to encourage any of the peoples of Asia in any form of hostile action against British interest or the British Empire, especially in India and in the independent state of Afghanistan." [11]

This subordination of world revolution to Soviet state interest occurred in Lenin's time. It became more pronounced after Stalin's rise to power and his acceptance of the principle of "socialism in one country." Everything thereafter was deemed secondary to the security and interest of that "one country." This subjection of the Comintern to the status of a tool of Soviet foreign policy was based on two implicit assumptions. One was that the interests of the Soviet state and of the world revolutionary movement were identical. The other was that the "building of socialism in the U.S.S.R." would proceed at such a rapid tempo that Soviet society soon would surpass world capitalism, which still was considered to be in a terminal state. Despite the far-reaching implications of these two assumptions, any questioning of their validity was rejected out of hand as intolerable sacrilege. Whatever doubts may have been harbored by individual members or national Communist Parties had no chance for serious consideration. The Comintern was a highly centralized organization with all the reins of power held firmly by the leaders of the parent Communist Party of the Soviet Union (CPSU).

The controlling Comintern organ was its Executive Committee, whose directives had immediate "force of law" for all national parties. It could expel individual members or entire factions, even against the will of a majority of the local membership. The headquarters of the Executive Committee was in Moscow, so that its members were dependent upon, and manipulated by, the CPSU. Expel the reformist wing of your party, Lenin told the Italian delegates to the Third Comintern Congress, and the majority of workers will support us. This strategy did work in Russia under the unique conditions prevailing there during and after World War I, but in the rest of the world it led to the isolation of the Communist Parties during the interwar years. Comintern membership, apart from the CPSU, declined steadily, from 887,745 in 1921, to 648,090 in 1924, to 445,300 in 1928 and to 328,716 in 1931 or little more than one third of what it had been a decade earlier.[12]

Trotsky scathingly denounced this "dumb monolithism," this "destructive unanimity." [13] But in the light of retrospect it was the inevitable manifestation abroad of the prevailing bureaucratism at home. "Monolithism" within the Soviet Union could scarcely be expected to tolerate multilithism among dependent foreign parties. How "destructive" this "monolithism" was became apparent first in China, the one Third World country where social revolution was feasible, in contrast to the nationalist revolutionary movements prevailing everywhere else. Yet the Chinese revolution was sacrificed on the altar of self-interest, as interpreted by Comintern leadership.

℃ II. Comintern and the Chinese Revolution

Intellectuals in China had embraced Marxism to a degree unequaled in the rest of the Third World. With the overthrow of the Manchu Dynasty (see Chapter 18, VII), they no longer had a scapegoat that could be held responsible for the dreary succession of national calamities. They were forced to reappraise traditional Chinese culture, and almost unanimously they concluded that it was inadequate and irrelevant for the modern world. But rather than turning to Western capitalist society, as was the pattern in most of the Third World, the Chinese instead embraced Marxist dogmas from neighboring socialist Russia.

One reason was that the Soviet model seemed to offer a method for more effective party organization, a technique for seizing and holding power and a strategy for rapid industrialization and general modernization. Another reason for the appeal of Marxism was that it provided a new scapegoat for China's humiliating backwardness—Western imperialism, which had assaulted and exploited China, and forced the country to a dependent, semicolonial status. Also, Marxism offered to the faithful a discipline, a purpose to life, an optimism and self-confidence because of the inevitable downfall of Western imperialism, and a feeling of brotherhood with fellow comrades throughout China and the entire world.

Chinese leaders turned to Marxism not only because of its intrinsic appeal but also because of their disillusioning experiences with the imperialist powers, including Japan. The Chinese government declared its neutrality at the beginning of World War I, but this did not protect it from renewed foreign aggression. Japan declared war on Germany, landed troops at the German concession in Shantung and proceeded to occupy the entire province. The Japanese followed this up by presenting secretly to President Yuan Shih-k'ai on January 18, 1915, their infamous Twenty-one Demands, which would have given them general control over the Chinese government through a system of advisers, and specific control over the police, arms purchases and arsenals. Yuan leaked these demands to the foreign press with the hope of stimulating assistance from some power. None came to his aid, even though the British minister in Peking, Sir John Jordan, expressed the opinion that "Japan's action toward China is worse than that of Germany in the case of Belgium." [14]

The Twenty-one Demands aroused intense nationalist indignation, which escalated to open resistance at the end of the war. China entered the war in August 1917 in order to forestall Japanese annexationist designs on Shantung. But Japan already had reached secret agreements with Britain, France and Italy recognizing Japan's claims to German rights in Shantung. Furthermore, Japan forced the Peking government in 1918 to sign a secret note confirming these claims. Consequently the Chinese delegation to the Paris Peace conference discovered that President Wilson's doctrine of self-determination did not apply to the Far East. Student-led demonstrations broke out on May 4, 1918, in protest against Japanese aggression and against the Peking government's secret sellout. "China's territory may be conquered," declared the student manifesto, "but it cannot be given away. The Chinese people may be massacred, but they will not surrender. Our country is about to be annihilated. Up, brethren!" [15]

The warlord Peking government cracked down on the demonstrating students, imprisoning over one thousand. But girl students now joined the boys in the streets, while merchants sympathetically closed their shops and workers went on strike. A truly national movement had erupted, forcing the cabinet to resign and its successor to refuse to sign the Versailles peace treaty with Germany. This May 4 Movement, as it came to be called, proved to be a major turning point in modern Chinese history. Chinese Communist historians view 1919 as a more significant date than 1911, when the Manchus were ousted. The events on May 4 triggered an intellectual revolution that was best expressed by Professor Ch'en Tu-hsiu of Peking University, later founder of the Chinese Communist Party. In the following lines he challenged the foundations of Confucian society:

> We really don't know which if any of our traditional institutions can be adapted for survival in the modern world. I would rather see the destruction of our "national essence" than the final extinction of our race because it is unable to adapt. The Babylonians are no more; what good does their civilization do them today? In the words of a Chinese proverb, "Where there is no scalp, what can the hair adhere to?" The world is constantly moving forward, and it will not wait for us. [16]

During the twenty years between the May 4 events and the Second World War, the Chinese intelligentsia moved steadily leftward toward Marxism. The most frequently translated foreign authors were, in descending order, Marx, Engels, Lenin and Bukharin. According to a survey made in several Christian universities a few months before World War II, Chinese students increasingly were specializing in social sciences, preferring Marxist textbooks, becoming indifferent to religion and looking forward to fundamental social change as the only solution to national problems. The liberal Hu Shih, who remained loyal to Western ideologies, observed bitterly: "Now that the slaves of Confucius and Chu Hsi [a twelfth-century neo-Confucian philosopher] are declining in number, the slaves of Marx and Kropotkin are taking their place." [17]

The Chinese Communist Party (CCP) was founded in Shanghai in 1921 by twelve men, one of the most obscure being a delegate from Hunan Province, Mao Tse-tung. The son of a well-to-do peasant, Mao was a provincial who read his first paper at the age of eighteen and who graduated from an unprestigious normal school at the age of twenty-five. This modest background spared Mao the blinkers of a traditional Confucian education or of a Western university education. The resulting freedom from the fetters of venerated dogmas proved to be Mao's distinguishing characteristic and chief source of strength, enabling him to use Marxism as a useful tool rather than anesthetizing dogma. His unique and most significant achievement was to Sinicize Marxism, so that it became relevant to Chinese reality. "Marxism-Leninism has no beauty; no mystical value," he reminded Party intellectuals, "it is simply very useful." And he added for the benefit of "those who regard Marxism-Leninism as a religious dogma," "Your dogma is less useful than excrement. We see that dog excrement can fertilize the fields and man's can feed the dog. And dogmas? They can't fertilize the fields, nor can they feed a dog. Of what use are they?" [18]

Despite Mao's talents, he and the Communist Party were unknown and insignificant in the early 1920s. Sun Yat-sen therefore appealed to the Western powers for aid against the warlords, but received no response. Sun then turned to a Soviet agent, Adolph Joffe, and on January 26, 1923, the two men reached a comprehensive agreement. Joffe conceded that "the Soviet system cannot actually be introduced in China," the objective conditions being unsuitable. Russia instead would help China "to achieve national unification and attain full national independence." To implement this strategy the Russians sent their able Mikhail Borodin to Moscow, where he became Sun's right-hand man and made three basic contributions to Sun's Kuomintang Party (KMT).

The first contribution was the organization of an efficient modern army, which was to be the instrument for defeating the warlords, uniting China and resisting the imperialist powers. This was done by opening in June 1924 the Whampoa Military Academy, headed by Chiang Kai-shek, who had received military training in the Soviet Union. By 1925 there were about a thousand Russian military representatives in China, as well as Russian arms for equiping the Whampoa cadets. Thus was organized the modern KMT "party army," which provided the military power needed to attain Sun's lifelong ambition, the unification of China.

The second contribution of the Russians was the establishment in 1924 of the Farmers' Training Institute, which operated between 1924 and 1926. It trained rural leaders, who returned to their villages and organized the local peasantry. It proved very effective, as most of its recruits came from areas near large cities and along main transportation routes. Their preparatory work among the peasants cleared the way for the spectacularly successful Northern Expedition of the KMT armies in 1926–27.

The final contribution of the Russians was the development of KMT party organization. Sun had evolved a party ideology that he entitled the Three Principles of the People. These were nationalism or self-determination, democracy or people's rights, and livelihood principle or economic betterment of the people. It was a typically confused and eclectic collection of ideas that specifically denied the basic Marxist thesis of class struggle. More important than Sun's ideology was the new party organization based on the communist principle of democratic centralism. The KMT was restructured with numerous local cells, which elected delegates to congresses at the county and provincial levels, each of which in turn elected an executive committee. The national party congress chose a central executive committee, which was able through this pyramidal structure to control the entire party, after the fashion of the CPSU.

The Russians actually made a fourth contribution to Sun and his KMT by delivering to them the CCP as a virtually hostage body. In line with the established policy of subordinating the interest of the national Communist Parties to those of the Soviet state, the Comintern in August 1922 imposed on the CCP a policy unprecedented in the history of the world Communist movement. It required CCP members to join the KMT as individuals and to accept KMT discipline, while preserving their own Party organization. Sun favored this arrangement, as he had noted how effective the Communists were in organizing workers and peasants, and he had no doubt that he could control them since they still were few in numbers.

The Comintern on its part calculated that strengthening Sun was the best means for checking imperialism in East Asia and thereby advancing Soviet interests. It rationalized that this policy did not harm the revolutionary cause in China because it assumed that only a bourgeois nationalist revolution was feasible at this stage, and that social revolution must wait until after the bourgeois phase had run its course. The First Congress of the CCP (July 1921) had taken a contrary position in a resolution declaring that it should "stand up on behalf of the proletariat, and should allow no relationship with the other parties or groups." [19] Likewise Mao had expressed his opposition to the strategy of giving up on social revolution through a preliminary bourgeois phase. "How can we bear this?" he asked indignantly. "It would mean that for a whole century two thirds of humanity would continue to be mercilessly exploited by imperialist powers!" [20] The Chinese objections, however, were overruled by the Comintern, and the singular KMT-CCP alliance was consummated.

The fragility of the alliance was exposed in 1925, when Communist-organized unions in Shanghai waged strikes that were supported by Chinese industrialists, who were suffering from competition by foreign imports. When British-officered police on May 30 killed thirteen demonstrators, there followed a nationwide outburst of demonstrations, boycotts and strikes. This "May 30 movement" stimulated a boost in CCP membership from one thousand in the spring of 1925, to thirty thousand by July 1926 and to fifty-eight thousand by the spring of 1927. The CCP obviously was gaining mass support in the cities, and at the same time was rapidly organizing the peasants in the countryside.

The Communist gains created tensions within the KMT among three factions: the conservatives led by General Chiang and his Whampoa army officers, who were mostly of upper class origin; the Communists who had been dragooned into individual membership; and between them, a vacillating group comprising the KMT left wing. The tensions escalated to open rupture with the victories of the KMT armies during the Northern Expedition.

Six armies under Chiang began in July 1926 the drive northward from Canton to smash the warlords and unify China. Aided by Communist propaganda among the peasants, the Nationalists advanced rapidly, dispersing or absorbing numerous warlord forces. They reached the Yangtze before the end of the year, and the following spring they resumed their offensive into central China with continued success. But the closer the KMT forces came to full victory, the sharper became the internal contradictions. The Communists were caught between the pressure of the growing mass revolutionary movement in both cities and countryside, and their commitment to submit to KMT discipline. Many wanted to recover their freedom of action by leaving the KMT, but Stalin opposed this categorically when it was suggested at a meeting of the Comintern Executive Committee, November–December 1926.

Stalin's decision, which perforce was obeyed by the Chinese Communists, was for them a virtual death sentence. There was not only one Chinese revolution, but two: the one headed by Chiang being bourgeois, and the other by Communists being socialist. Chiang had behind him the landlords, merchants and bankers as well as the army officers, but the Communists had formidable mass support, having mobilized during the 1926 campaign 1.2 million workers and 800,000 peasants—and this at a time when they were under Comintern orders to go slow and to prevent proletarian uprisings in the cities and jacqueries in the countryside. The two sides therefore were not unevenly matched. But Stalin's directive left Chiang free to act with no fear of reaction by his opponents.

This was dramatically demonstrated when Communist-led workers in Shanghai staged a general strike on March 21, 1927, and on the next day won full control of the city. In line with Comintern policy to maintain the "anti-imperialist alliance" with the KMT, the Communist leaders used their influence to disarm the workers and to allow Chiang and his troops to enter the city on March 26. Chiang did not allow the "anti-imperialist alliance" to hamper his freedom of action. Perceiving the obvious threat of the burgeoning mass movement, he prepared to destroy it, while his intended victims of necessity waited passively. With military support from the staunchly anti-Communist Kwangsi Army, financial support from Shanghai bankers and at the very least the moral support of the foreign powers, Chiang sprang his counterrevolutionary coup in Shanghai in the early morning hours of April 12, 1927. Tens of thousands of workers and peasants were massacred over the next few months in a reign of terror that extended far beyond Shanghai.

The Chinese Communists took years to recover from this crushing blow, and never did recover in the cities. The roots of the debacle are to be found in the internal and external isolation of the CPSU, which manipulated the Comintern in accord with what it deemed to be the security interests of the Soviet state. And these interests, in the perspective of the Kremlin bureaucrats, required cooperation with Chiang in order to avoid the danger to Russia of imperialist intervention if the Chinese Communists won power. This perspective and this policy continued virtually unchanged until the Chinese revolution, which Stalin continued to fear and to oppose, was finally achieved after World War II by new Chinese Communist leaders who no longer viewed Marxism-Leninism as "religious dogma," and no longer heeded Comintern dictates.

It does not follow from the above that if the CCP leadership had shown more independence from Moscow it would have been able in the 1920s to transform China from a warlord state to a socialist state. But it does follow that a chance for transformation did exist (though how much remains a matter of dispute), and that this chance was effectively forfeited by Stalin's global strategy and by the refusal of the CCP to resist this strategy.

᭪ III. Gandhi Deradicalizes India

India remained the classic example of the results of imperialism in the interwar period as it had been in the nineteenth century. In certain respects India enjoyed more favorable conditions for economic development than most colonial countries. Her continental size offered a vast potential domestic market and a considerable diversity of natural resources. Also, British rule had provided the country with a substantial infrastructure of railways, ports, irrigation works and communication facilities. And British educational policy evolved institutions that trained a considerable number of indigenous professionals and administrators to assume subordinate roles to imperial governance.

Despite these advantages, India experienced during the quarter century between the two world wars the same stagnation as the rest of the Third World. The percentage of the total population employed in industry fell from 5.5 in 1911, to 4.9 in 1921 and to 4.3 in 1931. Conversely, the percentage of the population engaged in agriculture rose from 61 in 1891, to 73 in 1921 and to 65.6 in 1931, which was still a higher ratio than four decades earlier. India's foreign trade reflected the general economic stagnation. Imports rose from 1.833 billion rupees in 1913 to 2.408 billion in 1929, and during the same period exports increased from 2.442 billion rupees to 3.108 billion. But prices had risen about 50 percent between 1913 and 1929, so the actual volume of trade had declined.

The basic reason for this paralysis was the same in India as in other colonies—namely, the lack of the social restructuring necessary for releasing the productive potentialities of human and natural resources. The forces and conditions that hobbled Indian society in the nineteenth century continued to do so in the twentieth. There was the same rackrenting, which drained the countryside of capital and left agricul-

All-India Estimates of Food Crop, Commercial Crop and Total Crop Production, 1893-94 to 1945-46

	Index of average annual crop output			Non-food to food crop
Years	Food	Commercial	Total	output ratio
1893–94 to 1895–96	100	100	100	.22
1896–97 to 1905–06	96	105	98	.24
1906–07 to 1915–16	99	126	104	.28
1916–17 to 1925–26	98	142	106	.32
1926–27 to 1935–36	94	171	108	.41
1936–37 to 1945–46	93	185	110	.44

Source: F. Clairmonte, *Economic Liberalism and Underdevelopment* (London: Asia Publishing House, 1960), p. 106.

ture underdeveloped; the same stress on cash crops for export, resulting in declining production of food crops.

Per-capita food-grain consumption declined from 24 ounces per day in 1880 to 14 ounces in 1936–38.[21] "I conclude that poverty in India," states Professor Thomas Weisskopf, "was at least as widespread at independence [1947] as it was a century earlier, and that since independence it has been alleviated at best very marginally."[22] Royal commissions were appointed after the periodic famines to "enquire" into the "causes" of these catastrophes. The commission following the 1877–78 famine with 9 million victims pointed to "the unfortunate circumstance that agriculture forms almost the sole occupation of the masses of the people," and recommended "the introduction of a diversification of occupation, through which the surplus population may be drawn from agricultural pursuits and led to find the means of subsistence in manufactures. . . ."[23] Both the analysis and the recommendation were repeated with unfailing regularity during the following decades, but with no ascertainable influence on government policy. The 1935–36 India budget, for example, allocated 500 million rupees for military services and 203 million rupees for the administration of justice, jails and police, as against 27 million rupees for agriculture and 9 million rupees for industry.

Despite the suffocating stagnation and inertia, India did not experience during those decades anything comparable to the upheavals that were convulsing China. The explanation for the passivity cannot be attributed to British repression, actual or potential, since in 1914 a mere 4,000 British administrators and 69,000 British soldiers were in charge of 300 million Indians. Rather the reason for continued British rule is to be found in the class structure and class relations within India.

In the countryside there was a traditional elite of native princes and absentee-landlord-*cum*-moneylenders. They owed their wealth and power entirely to the British, with whom they cooperated in maintaining order in rural areas. Below this small and parasitic ruling class were many intermediate layers of cultivators, a few owning substantial holdings but the great majority having plots barely sufficient to support one family. At the bottom of the agrarian class structure, comprising roughly a fourth of the rural population, were the landless agricultural laborers, who often were bound by serflike restrictions because of debt obligations.

Similar class stratification existed in urban centers, with a handful of immensely wealthy Indian capitalists at the top. They had developed slowly during the nineteenth century and then gained rapidly in wealth and power during the two world wars. Below them was an elite of professionals and administrators who gradually came into their own with the progressive "Indianization" of public administration. Next in the economic scale were a rather small class of organized industrial workers, and a larger number of white-collar workers in government services. Finally, the great majority of urban workers consisted of an independent petty bourgeoisie self-employed in services or household industry, and of a lumpenproletariat that was either unemployed, or underemployed in hawking, begging, porterage or any other available odd jobs.

Within this class structure appeared in 1885 the Indian National Congress, organized by a small, moderate group of Indian and British professionals. Its basic objective was to secure reforms that would improve the position of the Indian upper class within the British imperial framework. Until 1930, the Congress Party consisted merely of a few lawyers and merchants in each town. Mohandas Gandhi was largely responsible for transforming this isolated and ineffectual group into a movement with mass following in both rural areas and urban centers. But the crucial point is that this movement always was controlled by the Indian bourgeoisie to further its class interests.

One reason for the successful constriction and manipulation of the Congress Party was the lack of viable alternatives, especially because the Moscow-controlled Communist Party vacillated and had little following. Another reason was the astute British strategy, which skillfully employed a combination of repression and conciliation, while at the same time playing off Hindus against Muslims. Most important was the role of the Indian capitalists, who shrewdly cooperated with the charismatic Congress leaders, Gandhi and Jawaharlal Nehru. This was a natural and successful *de facto* alliance, as all parties concerned were interested in attaining political independence and forestalling social revolution.

The Indian capitalists, such as the houses of the Tatas, the Birlas, the Dalmia Jains, the Singhanias, the Modis and others equally illustrious, wanted political independence in order to attain certain economic goals. These included tariff protection, Indianization of banking, heavy industries and coastal shipping, comprehensive state aid for the development of the national economy and the appointment of Indians to administrative posts where critical economic decisions were made. These objectives motivated the capitalists to support the Congress Party, but they used their influence to avoid prolonged confrontations that might lead to mass activization and radicalization. G. D. Birla, for example, referred to direct political action by the masses as "disorder." Likewise the official history of the Congress Party by one of its Gandhian leaders, described in the following revealing language the activities of the *Kisan sabhas* or peasant leagues:

There were the hordes of *Kisans* organizing themselves into huge

parades marching hundreds of miles along the villages and trying
to build up a party, a power and a force more or less arrayed
against the Congress. . . . The flag they chose to favor was the
Soviet flag of red colour with the hammer and sickle. This flag
came more and more into vogue as the flag of the *Kisans* and the
Communists, and even loud and repeated exhortations of Jawaharlal Nehru would not keep it to its place or proportions. Almost
everywhere there were conflicts between Congressmen and *Kisans*
over the question of the height and prominence of the flag, and the
virtual attempt of the latter to displace the Tricolour flag symbolized the contest between Socialism and Gandhism. Really it was
less of Socialism and perhaps more of Communism that was gradually permeating the atmosphere. . . .[24]

Because of their fear of "disorder" and of "Communism," the Indian
capitalists supported the Congress right wing against the left. More
specifically, they backed up Gandhi, who was the key figure in channeling the Congress Party on a course that was not social revolutionary.
The genius of Gandhi was that he realized that a Congress Party consisting of only a few lawyers and merchants could never successfully
challenge British rule. He saw clearly that the masses had to be mobilized. Despite his training in London as a lawyer, he had remained
profoundly Indian, so that he was able to communicate with villagers
and win their support. Best known were his campaigns for *satyagraha*
or nonviolent passive resistance, and for *hartal* or boycott of British
goods and the wearing of homespun cloth in place of imported machine-
made goods. The combination of satyagraha and hartal, Gandhi taught,
would make possible the realization of *swaraj*, or home rule.

Gandhi also identified himself with virtually all the progressive movements of the time, but he then used this prestige to deradicalize each
of these movements. Thus he helped organize a labor union in Ahmeda-
bad but he stressed class harmony and refused to allow the union to
participate in all-India union federations. He rallied the peasants in
the villages, but his organizational structure was from the top down, in
contrast to the Chinese Communists, who organized from the bottom up
with a poor peasant base. Gandhian activists, however, were usually
drawn from the Brahman and merchant castes, and from rich peasants,
all of whom were naturally opposed to social revolution at the village
or national level. Gandhi also led no-tax campaigns against the British
government, but he refused to allow these to turn into no-rent campaigns against Indian landlords, and he also opposed the formation of
peasant leagues. When political movements got out of control, Gandhi
took strong stands against "disorder." During the 1924 "quit India"

campaign, a full-scale insurrection developed in some districts, with telephone lines cut, trains robbed, government buildings burned and a "parallel government" established in challenge to the status quo. Gandhi, who had been jailed, was shocked by the violence, and began a twenty-one-day fast in protest to British charges that he was responsible for the outbreak.

Gandhi did speak up for the abolition of untouchability but at the same time championed the essentials of an idealized caste system and opposed most independent activities by Untouchables. Gandhi also championed the oppressed Indian women and opposed their traditional fetters, including child marriage, discrimination against widows, *sati* and *purdah*. But he chose Sita, the monogamous, chaste, self-sacrificing spouse of Rama, as his ideal woman. According to the Sita-Rama model, the wife's relationship to her husband was to be one of worship, self-sacrifice and spiritualization of the so-called animal instincts, above all the sexual drives.

Nehru, by contrast, had socialist leanings of the Fabian variety, and was a firm believer in science, technology and secularism. Consequently he differed from Gandhi on certain specific matters, but he followed him on the central issue of reformism as against revolution. The two men were an effective combination, with Gandhi appealing particularly to the peasantry, and Nehru to the urban elements and to the left wing of the Congress Party.

In conclusion, Gandhi's historic role in India was to make national revolution against the British establishment possible, and social revolution against the native establishment impossible. After the winning of independence in 1947, Nehru's role (and also Indira Gandhi's, for that matter) was essentially similar—to block social revolution and to facilitate social reform, which under the circumstances was to prove largely illusory.

᭰ IV. *Middle East Mandates*

Political developments in the Middle East during the interwar years differed from those in India, whereas economic developments were basically similar. Before World War I the Middle East constituted the independent Ottoman Empire, so that with the defeat and partitioning of the empire, new political arrangements had to be worked out. Economically, however, the succession states of the Middle East remained as much a part of the Third World as the Ottoman Empire had been, so they also remained subordinate to, and exploited by, the Western imperialist powers.

Considering first the new political arrangements, the entire Ottoman

Empire, including its Anatolian heartland, appeared at one point to be destined to become dependencies of the victorious Allied powers. Virtually the whole region was divided into spheres of influence by a series of four secret treaties among Britain, France, Russia and Italy (Constantinople Treaty, Mar.–Apr. 1915; Treaty of London, Apr. 26, 1915; Sykes-Picot Agreement, Apr. 26, 1916; Saint-Jean-de-Maurienne Treaty, Apr. 1917). These treaties provided for the amputation of not only the Arab provinces but also of most of Anatolia, leaving to the Turks only twenty thousand square miles in the northern section of their homeland.

The provisions of these secret treaties directly conflicted with certain agreements that Britain was concluding at the same time with Arab representatives. As soon as Turkey joined the Central Powers in November 1914, the British opened negotiations with the leading dignitary among the Arabs—Emir Hussein of the Hashimite family, keeper of the holy places and prince of Mecca. Protracted correspondence between Hussein and Sir Henry McMahon, British high commissioner in Egypt, between July 1915 and March 1916 resulted in a military alliance and an ambiguous political understanding that was to plague the Middle East for decades. In return for an Arab revolt against the Turks, the British recognized the independence of the Arab provinces of the Ottoman Empire, which included all of the empire south of Asia Minor. McMahon made the reservation, however, that the agreement could not infringe upon unspecified French interests in Syria. Hussein replied that he would not consent to any Arab land becoming the possession of any power, meaning France. This disputed point remained unclarified with unfortunate results a few years later.

While the British Foreign Office was dealing with Hussein, the India Office was negotiating with Ibn-Saud, Sultan of the Nejd, whose territories were nearer the Persian Gulf. On December 26, 1915, an agreement was reached by which the India Office recognized Ibn-Saud's independence in return for his benevolent neutrality during the war. That a different British government agency was involved did not alter the fact that contradictory commitments had been made to Ibn-Saud and to Hussein.

More ominous for the future was another conflicting commitment, this one being the Balfour Declaration (Nov. 2, 1917), affirming that the British government favored the establishment in Palestine of a "national home for the Jewish people . . . it being clearly understood that nothing shall be done which may prejudice the civil and religious rights of existing non-Jewish communities in Palestine . . ." (details in following section). It is evident that this Balfour Declaration conflicted with McMahon's commitment to Hussein, as well as with the secret treaties among the Allies for the partitioning of the Ottoman Empire.

This bundle of contradictions led to conflicts that persist to the present day. With the United States withdrawing into isolation, and Russia convulsed by revolution and civil war, Britain and France were primarily responsible for the Sèvres Treaty (Aug. 10, 1920) imposed upon the defeated Turks. France obtained Syria and Lebanon as mandates, and Britain likewise secured Mesopotamia and Palestine, in addition to a protectorate over Egypt. Italy acquired the Dodecanese Islands, while Greece obtained several Aegean islands, eastern Thrace, and the right to administer the Smyrna region for five years, after which its final disposition was to be determined by a plebiscite.

These provisions, so contrary to the promises made to the Arabs and to the professed Allied principle of self-determination, aroused a wave of armed resistance throughout the Middle East. Most successful were the Turks who, under the leadership of Kemal Ataturk, waged a successful national liberation struggle and forced a revision of the Sèvres Treaty. It was superseded after protracted negotiations by the Lausanne Treaty of July 24, 1923, by which Turkey recovered eastern Thrace and some of the Aegean islands. Also, Turkey was to pay no reparations, and the capitulations were abolished in return for a promise of judicial reform. The Straits remained demilitarized, and open to ships of all nations in time of peace or war if Turkey remained neutral. If Turkey was at war, enemy ships, but not neutrals, might be excluded. Finally, a separate agreement provided for the compulsory exchange of the Greek minority in Constantinople for the Turkish minority in western Thrace and Macedonia.

While the Turks were successfully scrapping the Sèvres Treaty, the Arabs were stubbornly resisting the mandatory powers to which they had been assigned. Arab nationalism had been inflamed by the high-handed parceling out of Arab lands in violation of the Hussein-McMahon Agreement. Allied propaganda concerning self-determination also had stimulated Arab sentiment for national independence. The successful operations of Arab military units further aroused national consciousness and pride. Arab soldiers had fought side by side with British in a campaign that liberated Damascus, Aleppo and other historic Arab centers. Equally significant was the widespread suffering and outright starvation caused by the disruption of trade during the war. It is estimated that at least 300,000 people died of hunger or diseases due to malnutrition. Finally, there was the all-important religious consideration, especially for the *fellahin* in the villages. In the 1950s an Egyptian sociologist concluded after firsthand research, that "for the villager, the world is classified into believers and nonbelievers on the basis of the Moslem faith," and that "they are hardly aware of concepts like race or class" [25] This religionbound outlook undoubtedly was even more pronounced in the immediate post-World War I years. This is borne out by the fact that Arab nationalist leaders in the cities often were surprised by the degree of support they received from the peasantry, with whom they had little contact. The inference is that the village uprisings were spontaneous movements motivated by religious feelings against the infidel foreign rulers.

This combination of factors generated the postwar Arab struggle for independence. A common pattern is discernible in the evolution of the struggle. First there were explosions of defiance and armed revolt, as in Egypt in 1918–19, in Iraq in 1920 and in Syria-Lebanon in 1925–26. Then Britain and France gradually restored order and reasserted their authority. Finally they granted varying degrees of autonomy, which did not entirely satisfy the nationalists, but which did preserve an uneasy peace until World War II.

In Iraq, where the British had enthroned as King the third son of Hussein, Prince Feisal, a compromise settlement was reached in 1930. Britain agreed to terminate the mandate and to support Iraq's application for admission to the League of Nations. In return, Iraq agreed that Britain should maintain three air bases in the country, and also should have full use of rivers, railways and ports in time of war. In Egypt the British in 1936 negotiated with the nationalists of the Wafd Party a twenty-year alliance treaty. This provided that Britain should end her military occupation of the country and arrange for Egypt's admission to the League of Nations. In return, Egypt agreed to stand by Britain in time of war, to accept a British garrison along the Suez Canal and to continue the joint British-Egyptian administration of the Sudan.

In Syria and Lebanon, the French proved less flexible than the British and therefore less successful. Nationalist outbreaks occurred periodically, the most serious being in 1925, when the French were forced to shell Damascus in order to retain control. Finally in 1936 the French government negotiated treaties with Syria and Lebanon modeled after the Anglo-Iraqi treaty of 1930. Neither of these treaties, however, was ratified by the French Chamber of Deputies, so that the conflict remained unresolved when World War II began.

The end result throughout the Arab world was a *de facto* alliance between the mandatory powers and the local ruling elites that could be counted on to respect imperial interests because they were utterly dependent on imperial support. This basic power relationship will be illustrated with the case of Iraq, though any of the other Arab countries could be substituted, as the dependency institutions were basically similar.

In selecting Feisal as King, a Foreign Office official was quite candid about the motive behind the choice: "What is wanted is a king who will be content to reign but not govern. . . ." [26] Equally forthright was the official statement that "What we want . . . is some administration with Arab institutions which we can safely leave while pulling the strings ourselves; something that won't cost very much . . . but under which our economic and political interests will be secure." [27]

This was precisely the sort of administration that was developed during the years of the mandate. It was in no sense popular or broadly representative. It was based on a small group of tribal sheikhs and landlords, whose power and wealth were greatly enhanced during the British occupation. On those occasions when the authority of this elite was seriously challenged, the Royal Air Force was available to bomb the malcontents into submission. "If the writ of King Feisal runs effectively throughout his kingdom," reported L. S. Amery, Secretary of State for the Colonies, "it is entirely due to British aeroplanes. If the aeroplanes were removed tomorrow, the whole structure would inevitably fall to pieces." [28] Three parties did compete for seats in the parliament, and cabinets did rise and fall, but the commotion signified nothing more than shifting alliances among the cliques within the ruling establishment. Not one of these cliques challenged the status quo based domestically on the ascendancy of the new landowners and bureaucrats, and externally on the client-state relationship of Iraq with Britain. The following conclusion of British historian Peter Sluglett, summarizes the political implications of mandatory rule not only in Iraq but also throughout the Middle East:

> In any balance sheet for the Mandate, the Iraqi people outside the small circle of government . . . were the losers. The Government was not carried on for their benefit, but for the benefit of the Sunni urban political class within a framework created and supported by the British authorities. . . . When it was clear that British interests would no longer be at risk, and when the necessary mechanism to protect them had been perfected, it was time to withdraw. . . . the terms of the 1930 Treaty . . . enabled Britain to make her formal departure. . . . It is profitless to blame the British Mandatory authorities for failing to ensure that the Iraq Government concerned itself with the wider interests of the nation, or made efforts to reconcile rather than to exacerbate the tensions within the state: to do so would be to misunderstand the nature of imperialism.[29]

Turning from the political to the economic interwar development of the Middle East, its salient characteristic was continued dependency. This was inevitable, given the political ossification noted above, which eliminated any possibility of social restructuring anywhere in the Middle East. Peasant exploitation continued as before, and that in turn precluded the mass purchasing power necessary for independent economic development as against dependent economic growth. This intrinsic physiognomy of Third World societies will be illustrated with analyses of economic developments and institutions in independent Persia, in semi-independent Egypt and in the mandate of Iraq.

In Persia, the dominant figure between the two world wars was Reza Khan, a colonel in the Persian Cossack Brigade organized by the Russians before World War I. When that war began, the Shah proclaimed his country's neutrality, but he lacked the power to enforce his decision. The northern provinces were overrun by Russian and Turkish troops, and the southern by British. The authority of the Shah scarcely extended beyond the environs of his capital. The anarchy continued after the war, creating a political vacuum that Reza promptly filled. In February 1921 he led a coup against the civilian government and thereafter rose rapidly to the posts of commander-in-chief, Minister of War and Prime Minister. On December 15, 1925, he dethroned the Shah and founded his Pahlavi Dynasty, which survived with timely Western assistance to the revolution of 1978–79.

Reza had a naïve faith in the superiority and transferability of Western institutions. He set out to Westernize almost every aspect of private and public life. His operating procedure was to work from the top down—a strategy that resulted in much waste and many failures. One example was the construction of a modern hospital supplied with the latest equipment and staffed with doctors trained in Vienna and New York. It failed to function properly because of a shortage of trained nurses and orderlies and the lack of understanding of the elementary rules of sanitation among the patients. A preventive-medicine and public-health program in the villages would have contributed infinitely more to raising national health standards.

Reza had little time for theories; he was an impatient man of action, reminiscent of Peter the Great of Russia. Reza encouraged light industry in order to decrease imports and reliance on the West. A considerable number of factories were built, including textile mills, cement plants, sugar refineries, cigarette factories, distilleries and breweries. Yet despite high protective tariffs, almost all operated at a loss. There was no coordinated plan, and individual projects were not conceived in the light of the overall economic needs of the nation. This failing was most evident in the planning and construction of the trans-Iranian railroad between the Persian Gulf and the Caspian Sea. Ignoring the advice of experts, Reza laid out his own route. It was spectacular, if not economically practical, requiring over 4,700 bridges and 224 tunnels in the course of its 870 miles. This line bypassed all major cities except Teheran and Ahwaz, and did not reach any neighboring country, whether Iraq, Turkey, Russia, Afghanistan or India!

Reza did use his modernized army to establish his authority over the oil-producing province of Khuzestan. But he failed completely in his efforts to secure better terms from the Anglo-Persian Oil Company, which had been operating the oil fields since 1909. The British Admiralty had become the controlling partner in the company in May 1914, and thereafter the British navy obtained oil at very low rates, or conceivably free of any charge, since the company books were closed to all outsiders! In November 1933 Reza canceled the original contract with the company and ordered negotiations for better terms. With characteristic impatience he soon took over the conduct of the negotiations and quickly signed a new agreement. It reduced the area of the concession to 100,000 square miles, but the company's geologists knew where the oil reserves were probably located, and those regions were included in the concession area. Also, the royalty rate was rearranged in order to guarantee Iran a fixed income. This was good during depression years, but in prosperous times Iran received only 20 percent of the dividends distributed to ordinary stockholders. In addition, the company gained substantially by being exempt from paying taxes and by extending the duration of the concession to 60 years from 1933. All in all, the government lost heavily and the company remained unintegrated into the national economy.

Most revealing is the following conclusion from a biography by D. N. Wilber, which throughout seeks to present the Shah in the most favorable light:

> Wealth was concentrated at Tehran, largely in the hands of contractors, merchants, and individuals associated with the monopolies. Industrialization failed to benefit the growing class of industrial workers. Wages remained low, and a rudimentary labor law of 1932 did little to protect workers from exploitation. The lack of a comprehensive, impartially enforced system of taxation of income widened the gap between the haves and the have-nots.
>
> The condition of the peasants on the land did not improve during the period. Indeed, it has been asserted that they were further impoverished by taxes on necessities of life and by the failure of the regime to curb their exploitation by the feudal landlords. Riza Shah did attack the landlords as individuals through the purchase of desirable property, but he carried out no campaign against the bases of feudalism.

Finally the effects of the worldwide depression of the 1930's . . . struck the structure of state capitalism with devastating force. Riza Shah at last was forced to say [in 1939]: "I am dissatisfied with the way things are presently going, which is not good at all." [30]

If such was the plight of independent Persia, it is not surprising that dependent Egypt and Iraq also failed to cope with the deep-rooted problem of underdevelopment. In the case of Egypt, that country was transformed after Mohammad Ali's downfall into an export-oriented monoculture society, relying mostly on raw cotton exports to pay for manufactured imports (see Chapter 11, Section IV). After World War I this economic system became increasingly unviable because of the deteriorating terms of trade and the rapidly growing population, which could not be supported by agriculture alone.

Index of Egypt's Price Terms of Trade, 1913 = 100

Years	Terms of trade	Years	Terms of trade	Years	Terms of trade
1885–89	82.5	1910–14	96.6	1935–39	50.4
1890–94	63.3	1915–19	61.6	1940–44	29.2
1895–99	58.5	1920–24	86.5	1945–49	46.8
1900–04	74.8	1925–29	92.1	1950–54	66.6
1905–09	83.4	1930–34	55.6	1955–59	56.2

Source: S. Radwan, *Capital Formation in Egyptian Industry & Agriculture 1882–1967* (London: Ithaca Press, 1974), p. 243.

In response to these difficulties, Egypt launched an industrialization campaign, especially after 1930, when fiscal autonomy was gained from Britain. Some progress was made, with the active support of Bank Misr, founded in 1920 with Egyptian capital. The nationalist Wafd Party urged its followers to place their funds in this bank, whose deposits accordingly grew from £E201,000 in 1920, to £E3,190,000 in 1925 and to £E7,250,000 in 1929. The bank financed native enterprises in building materials, fisheries, air and maritime transport, insurance, tourism, mining and pharmaceuticals. World War II also stimulated Egyptian industries to meet the greatly expanded military and civilian demands. By the end of the war Egyptian industry was supplying 86 percent of domestic needs for consumer goods, and accounting for 8.4 percent of total employment.

Despite this progress, Egypt still was far from economic independence during the post-World War II decades. Agriculture continued to provide

Egypt: Growth of Population, 1800–1960

Year	Population	Percentage increase during decade
1800	2.4–3 million	—
1836	3–3.5 million	—
1871	5,250,000	—
1882	6,804,000	—
1897	9,715,000	—
1907	11,287,000	16.2
1917	12,751,000	13.0
1927	14,218,000	11.5
1937	15,933,000	12.1
1947	18,947,000	18.9
1960	26,080,000	36.8*

* Increase over 13 years.

Source: C. Issawi, *Economic History of the Middle East 1800–1914* (Chicago: University of Chicago Press, 1966), p. 373.

employment for 70 percent of the population and to generate 30 percent of the national income and 90 percent of exports. The Egyptian economy consequently still was vulnerable to world price fluctuations and to unfavorable terms of trade, as evident in the above table. Industry did not develop beyond the easy import-substitution stage, which yielded high monopoly profits behind tariff walls. The crucial additional advance to intermediate and capital-goods industries had not been achieved. Thus per-capita GNP fell 20 percent between 1913 and 1939, and production per worker in agriculture declined one third during the same period.

In Iraq the economic pattern was basically similar, though the intervention of Britain as the mandatory power was more marked. The socioeconomic changes effected in Egypt after the downfall of Mohammad Ali were now introduced in Iraq with much more speed and disruption. They began in 1916 when the British occupation forces issued the Tribal Disputes Regulation. This sought to create security in the areas in which British troops were stationed, and therefore tribal sheikhs who were considered to be friendly were recognized as paramount sheikhs. They were given absolute judicial authority over their tribes, they served as accredited agents of the central administration and they were empowered to function as judges and juries in civil and criminal cases.

Since the central government was dependent on these local leaders, no effort was made to collect land taxes from them, even though they were

rapidly taking over as their private properties the lands that traditionally had been held and used by all tribal members. Land taxes consequently fell from 42 percent of the national income in 1911 to 14 percent
in 1933. The difference was made up by slowly increasing oil revenues
and by excise and customs taxes that were regressive in nature. After
the British mandate ended, the new absolute powers of the landlords
were institutionalized by legislation. For example, in 1933 the Law
Governing the Rights and Duties of Cultivators held peasants responsible on negligence grounds for almost any crop failure, regardless of
whether the real cause was flood, drought, insects or any other natural
source. This increased the indebtedness of peasants, who were reduced
to virtual serfdom because they could never rid themselves of debts. If
they tried to leave the land, the owner was entitled to call on government troops to have them brought back. Even so, increasing numbers
of peasants escaped to the slums of Baghdad, which soon were swamped
with an unemployed or underemployed lumpenproletariat.

"During this time," concludes Peter Sluglett, "a society of generally
free tribesmen became transformed into one of groups of near-serfs
bound to the soil, in which traditional leaders and 'new' landowners
gained unprecedented legal and economic powers over their peasantry." [31-32]

V. Palestine Triangle

Palestine differed from the rest of the Arab world because there was no
evolution toward independence or autonomy for the local Arab population. Rather the history of Palestine was marked by persistent impasse
and crises, which have continued to the present day. The reason for
this difference was the intrusion of a third element—the Zionists—between the Palestinian Arabs and the British mandatory power. Since
the Zionists were better organized and more effective than the Arabs,
the Zionists generally prevailed before World War II as well as after.
Even though they were a decided minority of the total population, they
successfully blocked the Arab demands for representative government
and for a halt to Jewish immigration. Hence a growing Arab resistance
developed against both the Jews and the British, resulting in a triangular
struggle that convulsed Palestine until the establishment of the state of
Israel in 1948.

The Zionism that was responsible for most of the Jewish immigration
is a complex movement comprising at least three major elements: theopolitics, colonialism and binationalism.

The theopolitics is based on the Bible (the Old Testament), from
which is derived the basic belief that the Jews are a separate and exclu-

sive people chosen by their God to recover the land of Canaan (Palestine) as patrimony from their ancestors, the ancient Israelites. Their historic duty and destiny is to occupy and settle this land, and to pass it on to their descendants forever. David Ben-Gurion referred to the Bible as the Jewish people's "sacro-sanct title-deed to Palestine." Zionist colonization of Palestine accordingly supersedes the rights of current inhabitants. "The rights to Palestine," declared Ben-Gurion, "do not . . . belong to the existing settlers, whether they be Jews or Arabs. The crux is the Right of Return of Jewry dispersed." [33] Menachem Begin was in accord with this tradition when he steadfastly referred to the West Bank by the biblical names Samaria and Judea, and claimed it as a part of Israel by historic right. After a stormy meeting with President Carter in Washington in March 1978, Begin returned to declare before the Knesset, "The settlement of Jews in Eretz Israel [the biblical land of Israel] is absolute and in accord with international law." [34]

Zionism also involved colonialism, or to be more specific it involved a nationalism that because of the historical circumstances of its appearance, manifested itself as colonialism. Reacting to the discrimination, persecution and economic hardships experienced in Europe, the Zionists propagated the idea of a Jewish homeland in Palestine that would provide security and sustenance. But Palestine already was inhabited by a stable Arab population that numbered about five hundred thousand in the mid-nineteenth century, and over six hundred thousand in 1914, and that had resided there since the seventh century A.D., or well over a millennium. This fact automatically made Zionism different from the contemporary nationalist movements in Eastern Europe, Asia and Africa. Whereas the latter sought to get rid of foreign domination, the Zionists in opting for settlement in Palestine necessarily were forced to act as colonizers driving out a long-established indigenous population. Only the binationalists resolved this predicament, but they remained an ineffectual minority.

The colonialist component of Zionism was articulated from the very beginning by pioneers such as Moses Hess (1812–75) and Theodor Herzl (1860–1904). Living during the golden age of European imperialism, they naturally sought Great Power support and protection by depicting a Jewish Palestine as a strategic link in overseas colonial enterprise. "After the work on the Suez Canal is completed," declared Hess, "the interests of world commerce will undoubtedly demand the establishment of depots and settlements along the road to India and China, settlements of such a character as will transform the neglected and archaic states of the countries lying along this road into legal and cultivated states." This necessary transformation of backward societies he perceived as the historic contribution of the Jewish people, and he called on them to seize the opportunity: "A great calling is reserved for you: to be a living channel of communication to the primitive people of Asia . . . open the roads that lead to India and China—those unknown regions which must ultimately be thrown open to civilization." [35]

Herzl was more specific and assiduous in promoting the proposition that the Zionists and the imperialist powers had common overseas in- terests. "If His Majesty the Sultan were to give us Palestine," he argued in his classic *The Jewish State* (1896), "we could in return undertake the complete management of the finances in Turkey. We should there form a part of a wall of defense for Europe in Asia, an outpost of civilization against barbarism. We should as a neutral state remain in contact with all Europe, which would have to guarantee our existence." [36]

On being elected president of the World Zionist Organization by the First Zionist Congress at Basle in August 1897, Herzl decided that the German Kaiser was "the most suitable person" to serve as patron and guarantor of a "publicly recognized, legally secured homeland in Pales- tine." Herzl met with the Kaiser during the latter's visit to Constantino- ple in October 1898, and accompanied the royal party on a pilgrimage to Palestine. It soon became apparent, however, that the Kaiser lacked the will or the power to support actively the Zionist cause, so Herzl turned to Great Britain. He wrote to Lord Rothschild, "you may claim high credit from your government if you strengthen British influences in the Near East by a substantial colonization of our people at the strategic point where Egyptian and Indo-Persian interests converge." [37]

Herzl also communicated with the Colonial Secretary, Joseph Cham- berlain, and discussed various regions for possible Jewish settlement. "He liked the Zionist idea," Herzl reported. "If I could show him a spot among the British possessions which was not yet inhabited by white settlers, then we could talk." [38] So Herzl did talk about several localities, including Uganda, Cyprus and the Sinai. In addition he corresponded with Italians regarding Tripoli, with Portuguese con- cerning Mozambique, and with Belgians about the Congo. Herzl viewed the prospect of Jewish settlers outside Palestine as a *nachtasyl*, or tempo- rary refuge, in which the beleaguered Jews could find immediate relief as well as training for the ultimate return to the Holy Land. "I do not believe that for the sake of a beautiful dream or a legitimate flag we ought to withhold relief from the unfortunate." [39]

Chaim Weizmann, who became the most prominent Zionist in England after Herzl's death, used precisely the same arguments in behalf of a Jewish homeland. In July 1921 he wrote to Winston Churchill, then British Colonial Secretary, that

the existence of a Jewish Palestine leaves you absolutely free to

follow whatever policy may be most convenient to you, and enables
you, if you wished, to evacuate Egypt altogether and to concentrate on the Canal Zone with your army based on Palestine. . . .
All one has seen and heard of the Arab movements leads one to
believe that it *is* anti-European. The Palestine Zionist policy, far
from being waste, becomes a necessary insurance that we quote to
you at a lower rate than anyone else could dream of.[40]

For Herzl, Weizmann and their successors, Zionism was essentially a
belated colonizing movement in search of a patron. As such, it paid rich
dividends, for Great Britain as patron led to the Balfour Declaration
and the Palestine mandate, while the United States as patron assured
the establishment and the viability of the independent state of Israel.
Yet the fact remains that Zionism was a *belated* colonialism, and this
birthmark has plagued it from its origins to the present day. Implicit
in the strategy and attitude of this predominant Zionist element was
the assumption that the existing Arab inhabitants of Palestine could be
ignored. This reflected the prevailing European axiom that overseas
territories, regardless of indigenous populations, were empty and available for pre-emption.

Hence the constant Zionist refrain that Jewish people would serve as
propagators of civilization among barbarians at the same time that they
were fullfilling their historic destiny of recovering the ancestral home.
Hence also the observation by a Zionist leader in Palestine, Aharon
Cohen, that "one of the chief surprises awaiting [the early Jewish immi-
grants] to Palestine was the fact that it was populated. They had been
under the impression that it was empty and uninhabited, and that if
there were any local residents, they were so primitive that they could be
ignored. However, on arrival they found Arabs, some of whom were
shrewd, intelligent townsmen who controlled most of the country's
commerce and trade, but the majority of whom were farmers who were
spread out over the whole of the country." [41]

If the Jews had appeared in Palestine half a century earlier, they
might have achieved their "return" with relatively little opposition. In
fact, the Ottoman government in 1857 had issued a settlement decree
offering immigrants free land, religious freedom and exemption from
taxes and military service for six years in the European provinces and
for twelve years in the Asian. Ottoman representatives abroad were
swamped with inquiries from prospective immigrants all over Europe
and even from the United States. But Jewish applicants were conspicuous by their absence. A Turkish historian, K. H. Karpat, explains: "Tsar
Alexander II's promised reforms which, it seemed, would lead to better
days for minorities and especially for Jews, and the desire of many

prosperous Jewish merchants of Russia to be assimilated into the Russian culture are possibly some of the reasons which prevented Jewish mass emigration to Palestine in the 1850s and 1860s." [42]

By the turn of the century, when *pogroms* and economic pressures were forcing Europe's Jews to think of a Palestinian homeland, conditions in the Middle East had completely changed. By that time the Ottoman authorities had no desire to foster another disaffected minority group, and therefore would accept Jewish immigration in any province *except* Palestine. More important, the virus of nationalism had spread among the Arabs during the intervening decades, so that a belated Jewish colonialism had to cope with a simultaneous Arab national awakening. Contrary to popular belief, the few Jewish immigrants before World War I were not welcomed or accepted by local Arabs. "The Turks and Arabs," writes N. Mandel, quickly "took active cognizance of the Jews who came to Palestine motivated by nationalist ideals from 1882 onwards, and . . . by 1914 the 'Zionist question' had become a ramified issue of some importance in Ottoman politics." [43]

Arab hostility increased proportionately during the following decades with the rise in the volume of Jewish immigration. Thus the Zionists, despite their spectacular and repeated victories, still are rejected not only by the displaced Palestinian Arabs, but also by most of the surrounding Arab states and by the Third World in general, which remains allergic to anything smacking of colonialism. In January 1978 Israel's former Foreign Minister, Abba Eban, wrote that there was "a sense of something choked and strangled" in Israeli life, for all its exuberance. "The claustrophobic sense of exclusion from any affirmative human contact with the neighboring world has worked on Israeli morale and emotion more deeply than we have ever wanted to confess." [44]

The inherent flaw in Zionist strategy was to regard Palestine as an "empty" land, and the Palestinian Arabs as a nonexistent people—an assumption that has been, and is being, expressed repeatedly by leaders of various political parties. This flaw was perceived from the beginning by the third element in the Zionist movement in addition to the theo-politicians and the colonizers, namely, the binationalists. The latter were a disparate group—though mostly leftist—that shared in common the conviction that the Jewish and Arab national liberation movements were compatible and complementary, and could be realized harmoniously. They all looked forward to a free Palestinian commonwealth encompassing both the Jewish and Arab peoples.

The binationalists have been generally ignored because they failed, and history is written by victors rather than losers. Nevertheless, the binationalists included in their ranks an impressive array of philosophers, politicians and labor leaders. The scope of their following and thinking has been set forth in Aharon Cohen's magisterial study *Israel and the Arab World*, which was welcomed by a distinguished philosopher, the late Martin Buber, as "an extremely important scientific work." [45] Buber himself was typical of a group of well known thinkers who steadfastly expressed binationalist views. One of the earliest was a spiritual leader, Ahad Ha'am (1856–1927), who visited Palestine in 1891 and who wrote a famous article, "Truth from the Land of Israel," published in June 1891. He noted that "we are accustomed to believing that the Arabs are all wild beasts of the desert, a people akin to jackasses," and he warned that "this is a great mistake. . . ." Sensing the dangers of the future he added, "should a time come when the life of our Jewish brethren in Palestine develops so far that they push out the inhabitants of the country on a small or on a large scale, then the latter would not yield their places." [46] In the same year, 1891, he wrote of the importance of preserving neighborly relations with the Arabs and gave a warning that unfortunately was generally ignored:

> We could certainly learn from our past and present history how . . . cautious we have to be in our behavior toward a non-Jewish people among whom we are coming to live once more, to treat these people with love and respect and—it goes without saying— with justice and respect for the law. And what are our brethren in Palestine doing? The exact opposite! They were slaves in the land of their exile and suddenly they found themselves in the midst of unlimited freedom. . . . This sudden change has produced in them a tendency to despotism, which always happens when "a slave becomes a king." They treat the Arabs with hostility and cruelty, trespassing on their territory unjustly, beating them shamefully without any valid reason and then boasting about it. No one is calling a halt to this contemptible and dangerous trend. Our brethren were right when they said that the Arabs only respect those who display courage and bravery; but this only applies when the Arab feels his adversary is in the right, not when he has good reason to believe that his acts are oppressive and unjust. But when this is the case, the Arab may keep silent and exercise restraint for a long period, but in his heart he will cherish animosity and harbor vengeance.[47]

Likewise Martin Buber in March 1919, when postwar political arrangements were being debated, wrote of the harmonious role open to Jews "since they are at once of the East and of the West. . . . We must hereby emphasize that we will refrain from any foreign policy—except for the paths and activities necessary for instituting a permanent and friendly accord with the Arab in all areas of life, to achieve a compre-

hensive fraternal creation." [48] At the Twelfth Zionist Congress in Karls-
bad in September 1921, Buber insisted on serious consideration of the
"Arab problem." He affirmed that "a solid nucleus of the Jewish people
has determined to return to its ancient homeland and to build a new
life in it based on independent work." But he added,

> Our settlement, whose sole purpose is the rescue of our people and
> its rejuvenation, neither aims at capitalistic exploitation of terri-
> tory, nor serves any imperialistic ends. . . . a profound and con-
> stant solidarity of real interests will develop between us and Arab
> working people, and overcome all opposition that may result from
> fleeting complications. Recognizing this tie, the members of the
> two people will come to respect each other, and each will seek the
> other's good in private and public life.[49]

Buber's brand of Zionist ideology was expounded also by his brilliant
disciple, Chaim Arlosoroff. "An Arab movement really exists," he warned,
"and no matter what sort it is, it will be calamitous if we negate its
importance or rely on bayonets, British or Jewish. Such support is valid
for an hour, but not for decades. . . . only one course is open to us:
the peaceful one—and only one policy: a policy of mutual understanding." [50] Similar conciliatory views were held by Dr. J. L. Magnes, a
rabbi who was secretary of the Zionist Organization of America between
1905 and 1908. He visited Palestine in 1907 and 1912, and settled there
in 1922, devoting his efforts to the establishment of Hebrew University,
over which he presided until his death. Throughout his life he was
prominent in calling for Arab-Jewish cooperation and in working for
that cause.

Another group that supported the policy of Arab-Israeli accord were
the Sephardic Jewish intellectuals from Eastern countries. Their outlook
was quite different from that of Eastern European Zionists. The Sephardic
Jews had deep roots in the Arab cultural world and could have served
as intermediaries between the Jewish and Arab national movements.
"Men like Professor A. S. Yehuda, David Yellen, Rabbi Nahum of Egypt,
and several leading Sephardic Jews in Palestine," writes Aharon Cohen,
"could have contributed a great deal to the creation of a relationship of
understanding and cooperation between the two peoples, but were not
given the opportunity to do so. The upshot was that they resigned in an
atmosphere of bitterness, and some of them even became confirmed opponents of anything connected with Zionist leadership and its policy." [51]

The most numerous champions of binationalism were in left Zionist
groups such as the Socialist League, the Young Guard and especially
the dominant MAPAI or Jewish Workers Party, and its associated Hista-

drut or General Federation of Jewish Workers in Palestine. The latter two organizations, which were by far the most influential, were social democratic, reformist and above all, Zionist and nationalist. Consequently there was a chronic discrepancy between their rhetoric and their actions. They all espoused socialism and the brotherhood of man, especially of Jews and Arabs, but at the same time they steadfastly demanded unlimited Jewish immigration and full freedom of Jewish settlement. The Palestinian Arabs refused to accept terms that ultimately would make them a minority in their own country. The resulting Arab-Jewish conflict forced the left Zionists to abandon in practice the binationalist principles they supported in theory.

A typical example of this left Zionist ambivalence is to be found in David Ben-Gurion, leader of MAPAI and later the first Prime Minister of Israel. His pronouncements in behalf of Jewish-Arab partnership were unceasing. In 1925 he declared: "The Arab community in Palestine is an organic, inseparable part of Palestine. . . . Zionism has not come to inherit its place or rise on its ruins . . . the thing is simply not possible." Two years later he added: "In my view of morality, we have no right to discriminate against a single Arab child, even if thereby we attain everything we desire." Likewise in 1930 Ben-Gurion declared, "The regime in Palestine must at all times assure both the Jews and the Arabs the possibility of unhampered development and full national independence, so as to rule out any domination by Arabs of Jews, or by Jews of Arabs." In 1931 he expressed the same views before the Seventeenth Zionist Congress: "We declare before world opinion, before the workers' movement and before the Arab world, that we shall not . . . accept the idea of a Jewish state, which would eventually mean Jewish domination of Arabs in Palestine." [52]

Very different, however, was Ben-Gurion's reaction in 1941 when confronted with a specific proposal by Adil Jabr, a highly educated Arab member of the Jerusalem Municipal Council, for a binational Palestine based on full equity for the two peoples. "Before he had had a chance to even glance at the Jabr proposal," reported a Zionist official, "he pushed it aside in unrestrained anger and said: 'I don't want to deal with this document at all, it's an abomination.' " [53]

This incident was only one of many in which Zionist leaders consistently through the years professed binationalism in principle but rejected or evaded it in practice. Whatever chance there might have been of transforming rhetoric into reality was undercut by the fairly consistent British policy of pitting Jew against Arab in order to perpetuate British control by the traditional imperial tactic of divide and rule. Also, the Nazi barbarities of the 1930s strengthened the position of Zionists who opposed any limits on immigration and settlement. Nevertheless, at *the decision-making level,* Zionist negativism regarding binationalism was steadfast.

Josef Gorni, in his careful study "Zionist Socialism and the Arab Question," notes that the most important socialist party of the Palestinian Jewish community was *Ahdut ha-Avodah* (Unity of Labor). From its ranks were to come later presidents and prime ministers of the independent state of Israel. This body from the early 1920s, when the Jews comprised less than 10 percent of the total population of Palestine, "claimed that the Jews enjoyed national rights over Palestine as against the residential rights of the Arab population." Gorni concludes that ". . . the uncompromising demand for the establishment of a Jewish majority . . . to a large degree foiled hopes of Arab-Jewish agreement." [54]

Aharon Cohen documents numerous cases, during all periods, of Zionist rejections of specific Arab proposals for a binational state, and concludes: "Thus the principle of non-domination remained little more than a pious wish. It was not given concrete expression in the form of political proposals capable of serving as a basis for Jewish-Arab negotiations." He attributes this failure to implement the Zionist binational rhetoric to "the sharp conflict within the various Zionist parties between those favoring parity and those opposing it. . . . In these circumstances, no responsible Zionist body could do more than offer the vague slogan of 'non-domination.' " [55]

Chief Justice Gad Frumkin later acknowledged candidly the reason and results of Zionist official policy during the mandate period:

> A person viewing that period in retrospect will no doubt find that Shertok [later Moshe Sharett, Prime Minister 1953–55] and his colleagues maintained their position wisely and with foresight. The state of Israel and our numerical preponderance in it proved the rightness of their stand. An accord with the Arabs would have postponed the end; we would not have achieved what we did in the war of independence with arms and Divine guidance.[56]

Turning from the dynamics of Zionism to its historical evolution, it should be noted that although binationalism seems quaint and quixotic today, it was Zionism that appeared to be so at the outset. Its founder, Theodor Herzl, published in 1896 his book *The Jewish State,* which attracted wide attention throughout Europe and prepared the ground for the First World Zionist Congress in Basle in 1897. The Congress founded the World Zionist Organization, designed to "create for the Jewish people a home in Palestine secured by public law." Zionism did not win at the outset the general support of world Jewry. The religious

Jews already residing in Palestine mostly opposed political Zionism, holding that God will bring Israel back to Zion in His own time, and that it was impious to anticipate His decree. West European Jews also were lukewarm, being relatively satisfied with their status in their respective countries and not being willing to immigrate to Palestine or otherwise support the "homeland" concept. Zionism consequently attracted only the persecuted Jews of Eastern Europe, along with a few West European Jews such as Dr. Chaim Weizmann, who viewed assimilation as "gradual decay and disruption under emancipation." Even among the East European Jews, only a minority supported Zionism. The remainder either were inactive, or immigrated to America, or entered national revolutionary movements along with non-Jews of similar political persuasion or joined the Bund (General Jewish Workers Union of Lithuania, Poland and Russia), which also was revolutionary but whose membership was exclusively Jewish. This relative isolation of the Zionists prompted Dr. Weizmann to make the following revealing assessment concerning the Balfour Declaration in favor of a Jewish homeland in Palestine:

> The Balfour Declaration of 1917 was built on air, and a foundation had to be laid for it through years of exacting work; every day and every hour of these last ten years, when opening the newspapers, I thought: Whence will the next blow come? I trembled lest the British Government would call me and ask: "Tell us, what is this Zionist Organization? Where are they, your Zionists?" For these people think in terms different from ours. The Jews, they knew, were against us.[57]

Despite Dr. Weizmann's apprehension, the issuance of the Balfour Declaration (see the preceding section) represented a crucial victory for Zionism. It did not provide for the creation of a Jewish state. The term "national home" was ambivalent, and Dr. Weizmann candidly declared, "it would mean exactly what we would make it mean—neither more nor less."[58] Zionist efforts during the following years were directed toward ensuring that the Balfour Declaration meant what they wanted it to mean.

President Woodrow Wilson posed a threat by insisting on self-determination in the Near Eastern settlement, and sending the King-Crane Commission to ascertain the views of the local populations. The commission reported that in Palestine only the Zionist Jews, about one tenth of the total population, favored the establishment of a Jewish national home, and the remaining 90 percent of Palestine's population were utterly opposed. "To subject a people so minded," concluded the King-Crane report, "to unlimited Jewish immigration, and to steady financial and social pressure to surrender the land, would be a gross violation of

. . . the people's rights, though it kept within the forms of the law."
The authors of the report expressed "a deep sense of sympathy for the
Jewish cause" but recommended that "only a greatly reduced Zionist program be attempted . . . and that the project for making Palestine
distinctly a Jewish commonwealth should be given up." [59]

Equally threatening was Article 22 of the League of Nations Covenant,
which referred specifically to "certain communities formerly belonging to
the Turkish Empire," and stipulated that, "The wishes of these communities must be a principal consideration in the selection of the Mandatory." [60] The communities, however, were completely ignored, thanks to
Wilson's incapacitation by illness, and to the vested interests of Britain
and France embodied in their secret wartime treaties for dividing up
the Ottoman Empire between themselves. Thus Palestine was allotted to
Britain as a mandate, with the understanding that the Balfour Declaration would provide the framework of administration. Accordingly the
London government appointed a British Jew, Sir Herbert Samuel, as
the first high commissioner in Palestine, and Zionist leaders Norman
Bentwich and Albert Hyamson as attorney general and director of immigration, respectively.

The quarter century of British mandatory rule was a critical period
when the foundations of the future Israeli society and state were laid.
Although the Arabs were a large majority throughout this period, they
were consistently outmaneuvered, so that the Zionists were in a much
stronger position at the end of the mandate than they had been at the
beginning. A basic reason for this was the lack of a common Arab strategy
and course of action. This reflected the atomization of Arab society
during the centuries of Ottoman rule. Political alliances and activities
were determined not by programs or ideologies but by the interests of a
few landed families, each of which had its followers among district
clans and village heads. Vertical lines of allegiance were the distinctive
feature of this traditional clientage type of political system.

The Arabs were divided by class differences as well as political differences. The dominant socioeconomic group was a small urban elite
consisting of large landowners, religious dignitaries, professionals and
merchants. This oligarchy paid scant attention to the urban working
class of artisans and unskilled laborers, and to the peasants and agricultural laborers, who comprised 80 percent of the Arab population. The
latter were exploited as mercilessly by the landowners as their counterparts were in the rest of the Arab world. The ruling families—the Khaladis,
Nashashibis, Husseinis and others—loaned money to the peasants at
usurious rates. Indebtedness led to foreclosures, and the new owners,
being quite oblivious to the idea of Palestinian nationalism, readily sold
their large land parcels to the Zionists. In this way the Jewish National

Fund acquired in one transaction in 1920 the entire Jezrel Valley with over twenty Arab villages. The fatal weakness of the Palestinian peasants in the 1920s and 1930s was that they were an illiterate and unorganized mass, lacking the large, well-educated and self-confident middle class that now exists in the West Bank.

Finally, the Palestinians were seriously weakened by their relative isolation from the rest of the Arab world during the mandatory period. The splintering of the Arab bloc in the Middle East contrasted with its relative unity under the Turks. Prior to 1914 the Arabs had formed various organizations against Ottoman rule, organizations that were open to all Arabs regardless of their geographic origins. This early unitary Arab nationalism gave way to provincialism when the British and French fostered in each of their Middle Eastern mandates local dependent elites of tribal sheikhs and landlords. In the preceding section we noted how this strategy was implemented in Iraq, transforming a nationalistic, turbulent, pan-Arabist country into a quiescent client state of Great Britain, slumbering in dull provincialism like neighboring Syria under the French. Handpicked puppet dynasties also played their role in this pacifying process, so that the Feisal who was made King of Iraq was also the Feisal who concluded an agreement with Dr. Weizmann in 1919 stipulating that "in the establishment of the constitution and administration of Palestine, all such measures shall be adopted as will afford the fullest guarantees for carrying into effect the British Government's Declaration of November 1917 [the Balfour Declaration] . . . provided the Arabs obtain their independence as demanded in my memorandum dated 4 January 1919 to the Foreign Office of the Government of Great Britain. . . ." In other words, Palestine was to be sacrificed in return for fulfillment of Hashimite dynastic interests in the rest of the region. The client elites and dynasties of the Arab world not only refrained from supporting the Palestinian nationalists but also, as we shall see, actively undercut them when they resorted to armed resistance.

The Jews also had their differences as to long-term strategy and short-term tactics. There were what might be described as "spiritual Zionists" such as Ahad Ha'am, Martin Buber and Dr. J. L. Magnes, who supported binationalism in practice as well as in theory. There were also the more official Zionists such as Dr. Chaim Weizmann, David Ben-Gurion and Moshe Sharett, who exploited the rhetoric of Jewish-Arab cooperation but at the same time insisted on unlimited Jewish immigration and settlement, which effectively negated their professions. Finally there were the revisionists, led by Vladimir Jabotinsky (one of his disciples being Menachem Begin), who correctly insisted that "never before in history have the native inhabitants of a country agreed of their own free will that their land should be colonized by foreigners." [61] Jabotinsky consequently concluded that a Jewish Legion was essential to satisfy Jewish needs, which he defined as a large independent state extending over both sides of the Jordan River.

Although the Jews were divided among themselves, they presented a common front against the Arabs and skillfully took advantage of the differences among them. They made tactical alliances with the Muslim Arab majority, states N. Caplan, thereby "discreetly fostering the latter's suspicions of the powerful Christian Arab minority. The Jews also promoted friendly relations with minority non-Muslim sects such as the Samaritans, Druzes and Circassians. Finally they fostered the Arab countryside notables' resentment against the Arab townsfolk." [62]

Most important was the organization by the Jews of various institutions for coordinating their work and maximizing their effectiveness. Outstanding was the Jewish National Fund (JNF), established at the Fifth Zionist Congress in 1901. Its objective was defined as being "the attainment of a Jewish majority." In working toward this objective it was assisted by the fact that great tracts of land had been appropriated in the late nineteenth century by indigenous town merchants and tax farmers. In Palestine, as in other Ottoman provinces, these entrepreneurs had taken advantage of the 1858 Ottoman Land Code introducing private property and land registration. By various legal and extralegal machinations they acquired the lands traditionally tilled in communal fashion by the villagers. The resulting new class of absentee landlords eagerly accepted the high prices offered by JNF, whose holdings rose from 12,400 dunams in 1907 (1 dunam = .2471 acre), to 16,000 in 1914, to 197,000 in 1927 and to 370,000 in 1936. The British government sought to restrict Jewish land purchases in its 1939 White Paper, but without success. JNF holdings continued to grow, reaching 473,000 dunams by September 1939, and 835,000 by September 1946.

Title to this JNF land was held in perpetuity as "the inalienable property of the Jewish people." It could not be leased for more than two consecutive forty-nine-year periods, and the lessee had to be Jewish. Accordingly the Jewish land acquisition engendered corresponding Jewish immigration and settlement. The Jewish population of Palestine rose from about 60,000 in 1914 to 83,794 in 1922, when the British took the first modern census, and to 174,000 in 1931, at the time of their second census.

The influx of Jewish money and skilled Jewish immigrants improved substantially the living standards of the Palestinian Arabs. Whereas a wage of 5 piasters a day was considered high in most of the Arab world, in Palestine an unskilled Arab worker earned 15 to 20 piasters, and a skilled worker two or three times that amount. Wages of Arab farm workers also rose sharply, reaching 14 to 16 piasters during the busy season in citrus groves. The indirect benefits enjoyed by the Arabs were equally impressive. The Palestinian Arabs did not pay the British mandatory government more taxes than they had paid to the Ottoman government, nor more than were paid by Arabs in neighboring countries. But thanks to the tax revenues from Jewish settlers, the health and education services available to Palestinian Arabs were unique in the Middle East, as indicated by the following figures representing 1936 government expenditures in mils per capita (1 mil = 0.001 English pound):

	Egypt	Iraq	Trans-Jordan	Syria and Lebanon	Palestinian Arabs
Health	153	108	42	23	156
Education	283	217	73 (1935)	96	259

Source: A. Cohen, Israel and the Arab World (New York: Funk & Wagnalls, 1970): p. 227.

The resulting improvement in Palestinian health standards is reflected in the increase of births over deaths per thousand of population between 1917 and 1937. In Egypt this amounted to 11; in Syria and Lebanon, 14; in Trans-Jordan, 9; in Iraq, 9; and in Palestine (during the 1920 to 1941 period), 25!

These substantial advances accruing from Jewish human and material resources did not induce Jewish-Arab amity in Palestine, just as the fact that African workers in South Africa earn considerably higher wages than workers in black Africa has not endeared the Afrikaners to the Africans. This is not to suggest that the position of Arabs in Palestine or Israel is identical to that of Africans in apartheid South Africa. Yet the fact remains that Arab displacement and anti-Arab discrimination did exist in Palestine and does exist today in Israel. One example is MAPAI's effort to make the Jewish community as independent as possible by means of a threefold campaign: "conquest of the land" (establishing maximum Jewish ownership and cultivation of Palestinian land); "conquest of labor" (forcing Jewish employers to hire only Jewish workers rather than the cheaper Arab labor); and "produce of the land" (boycotting cheaper Arab-made goods in order to stimulate Jewish agriculture and industry).

These discriminatory policies were in sharp contradiction to MAPAI's professed socialist principle of class solidarity, but they were justified by asserting the uniqueness of the Jewish situation. Nevertheless, David Hacohen, a longtime MAPAI leader, could not help voicing misgivings over this blatant and continuing conflict between principle and practice:

I remember being one of the first of our comrades [of Ahdut ha-Avodah] to go to London after the First World War. . . . There I became a socialist. . . . When I joined the socialist students— English, Irish, Jewish, Indian, African—we found out that we were all under English domination or rule. And even here, in these intimate surroundings, I had to fight my friends on the issue of Jewish socialism, to defend the fact that I would not accept Arabs in my trade union, the Histradut; to defend preaching to housewives that they not buy at Arab stores; to defend the fact that we stood guard at orchards to prevent Arab workers from getting jobs there. . . . To pour kerosene on Arab tomatoes; to attack Jewish housewives in the markets and smash the Arab eggs they had bought; to praise to the skies the Keren Kayemet [Jewish National Fund] that sent Hankin to Beirut to buy land from the absentee effendi [landlords] and to throw the fellahin [peasants] off the land—to buy dozens of dunams from an Arab is permitted, but to sell, God forbid, one Jewish dunam to an Arab is prohibited; to take Rothschild, the incarnation of capitalism, as a socialist and to name him the "benefactor"—to do all that was not easy. And despite the fact that we did it—maybe we had no choice—I wasn't happy about it.[63]

The repercussions of this all-embracing discrimination against the Arabs were noted by Sir John Hope Simpson in his official report on the background to the 1929 disturbances:

. . . the result of the purchase of land in Palestine by the Jewish National Fund has been that land has been extra-territorialised. It ceases to be land from which the Arab can gain any advantage now or in the future. Not only can he never hope to lease or to cultivate it, but by the stringent provisions of the lease of the Jewish National Fund, he is deprived for ever from employment on that land. The land is in mort-main and inalienable. It is for this reason that Arabs discount the professions of friendship and good will on the part of the Zionist in view of the policy which the Zionist Organization deliberately adopted.[64]

In retrospect, the rise of Hitler and the ensuing barbarities against European Jewry constitute the great divide of modern Palestinian history. Despite the efforts of the Zionist Organization, Jewish immigration had tapered off by the late 1920s to a net flow of only a few thousand each year, and might have remained at that modest level had normal conditions prevailed. But in 1932 began the stream of refugees fleeing from Nazi persecution. Between 1932 and 1936 about 174,000 Jews arrived in

Palestine. This doubled the Jewish population of the country, since there had been only 174,000 at the time of the 1931 census.

The repercussions of this demographic revolution were devastating. The horrors of the Holocaust led most Jews to forego even lip service to the principle of binationalism. It was at this time that Ben-Gurion rejected as "an abomination" an Arab proposal for a Palestine based on full equality for the two peoples. A similar hardening occurred among Arabs, who pointed out that there was no reason why they should lose their country because of Western anti-Semitism. "Anti-Semitism is a deplorable Western disease. . . . We aren't anti-Semites; we are also Semites. Yet this Western problem is being smoothed out at our expense. Is that your idea of right?" [65] This bitterness and alarm culminated in the Arab strike and armed revolt of 1936.

The British authorities responded by increasing their army of occupation to 20,000 and resorting to mass arrests, collective fines, forced opening of businesses closed during the strike and demolition of villages and city neighborhoods suspected of harboring guerrillas. The resistance continued, and the neighboring Arab rulers—Abdullah of Trans-Jordan, Ghazi of Iraq and Ibn Saud of Saudi Arabia—became concerned by the mass militancy, which threatened to infect their own subjects. On October 8, 1936, they appealed "To our Sons the Arabs of Palestine. . . . to resort to quietness in order to prevent bloodshed, confident in the good intentions of our ally, the British Government, which has declared its desire to administer justice. Rest assured that we shall continue our efforts for the purpose of assisting you." [66]

On October 11 the six-month-old strike was ended and the British sent out the Peel Commission to investigate the Palestine problem and make recommendations. Its 1937 report was starkly simple: Britain's obligations to the Jews could not be fulfilled in the face of implacable Arab opposition, and it therefore proposed not the self-government that the Arabs were demanding, but rather the partition of Palestine into an Arab state and a Jewish state. The Arabs rejected partition, fearing that even if the borders of the proposed Jewish state were strictly circumscribed, it would be difficult to prevent their extension in the future.

Guerrilla activities broke out again in September 1937, and by mid-1938 the rebels controlled 80 percent of the countryside, where they levied taxes and administered justice. Britain unleashed the Royal Air Force in addition to the 20,000-man occupation force. Also 14,500 Jewish settlers were armed and organized into "night squads," while others were employed in building a barbed-wire fence in northern Palestine to keep out Arab volunteers from Syria and Lebanon. By 1939 Arab resistance was worn down and British authority re-established. Human and property losses had been heavy and the Arab cause had suffered a serious set-back, with 5,000 Arabs killed, as against 463 Jews and 101 British. The Jewish position in Palestine had been correspondingly strengthened, setting the stage for the climactic events of 1948, when the Zionists finally were able, in Dr. Weizmann's words, to make the Balfour Declaration mean what they wanted it to mean.

❧ VI. Tropical Africa

Tropical Africa was dominated and exploited by the Western powers during World War I and the interwar years to an even greater degree than the Middle East. African raw materials sustained the Allied war economies, while African manpower was tapped for labor and combat purposes. Over 180,000 West Africans served in French armies during the war against Germans in Europe and also against Germans in Togo-land and the Cameroons. Likewise the British used African recruits, along with Sikhs and Punjabis, in their East African campaigns. Conversely, the Germans at the beginning of the war had in Tanganyika a regular force of 216 Europeans and 2,540 African *askiri*. Comparable proportions of African and European combatants were to be found in the British West African and East African regiments.

These war contributions, together with the Wilsonian self-determination rhetoric, encouraged politically conscious Africans to look forward to a new postwar order. But the imperial structures were not dismantled; rather they were consolidated and extended with the aid of the mandate fig leaf, as was done at the same time in the Middle East. Whereas the Arab lands were divided as Class A mandates, Germany's African colonies were distributed as Class B and Class C mandates. Britain took most of former German East Africa as Tanganyika Territory, while Belgium took the remainder as Ruanda-Urundi. South Africa acquired former German South-West Africa, and France and Britain each took parts of the Cameroons and Togoland.

After legitimizing their control of the entire African continent, the victorious Allies proceeded to implement their authority through local chieftains, who were the counterparts of the sheikhs of the Middle East. Whether it was the indirect rule of the British, or the direct rule of the French, Belgians and Portuguese, actual authority was wielded by the metropolitan governments. They paid the salaries of the chiefs and as-signed colonial administrators to advise them in their duties, which were usually unpopular assignments such as collecting taxes and recruiting laborers and soldiers. The European administrators naturally favored the chiefs against the small group of young Africans who had received a Western education. The latter were said to lack the respect of their own people, though in fact it was the support of the colonial officials that more often was missing. "No important decisions were made by Africans," conclude two staunch supporters of imperial rule, Roland Oliver and Anthony Atmore, "and in a sense there were fewer Africans of importance in this period than there had been in the period before 1914, when a few of the old leaders still survived from the pre-colonial period." [67]

All the colonial powers used their unchallenged authority between the two wars to attain essentially the same strategic objectives, though there were certain differences in their tactical procedures. One objective was set forth by Earl Grey as early as 1852: "The surest test for the soundness of measures for the improvement of an uncivilized people is that they should be self-supporting." [68] In line with this dictum, all the European governments saw to it that their colonial subjects paid for the institutions that kept them in subjection, including the bureaucracy, judiciary, police and armed forces.

A second common objective of the European powers was to promote export-oriented colonial economies that would provide needed raw materials and absorb manufactured commodities. British officials, for example, assumed that it was the duty of the colonies to import British manufactures, even when they were more expensive than the Japanese. In June 1920 the British government "invited" the colonies to grant preferences to goods of empire origin, and by 1922 twenty-six governments had done so, though not entirely of their own free will. This "imperial preference" proved a godsend to the hard-pressed British industries during the Depression years. Sir Philip Cunliffe-Lister of the Colonial Office spelled this out in Commons on April 22, 1932:

> I am not sure that it is realised enough what a standby that Colonial Trade has been in the difficult past years. . . . In 1924 only 6.8% of our export trade was done with the Colonial Empire. In 1931 that proportion had risen to over 10%, and that at a time when values were crashing in the Colonies and their purchasing power had been enormously diminished. That shows the value of that trade, and it emphasises . . . how very wide and valuable were the preferences which had for years past been given by those Colonies to this country. Since this House took its decision [on imperial preference] in February new preferences have been given. . . . The result is that nearly every colony which has a tariff on manufactures and which is free to do so is at the moment giving a substantial preference to this country.[69]

Although the benefits of imperial preference for the mother country were freely acknowledged, it was maintained that it was equally beneficial for the colonies because they were naturally predestined to serve simply as raw-material producers. According to W. G. Ormsby-Gore, Under Secretary of State for Colonies, on April 13, 1929:

> I do not think there are many industrial developments, either immediately taking place or likely to take place in the vast bulk of our Colonial Empire. Looking to the future, practically nowhere is there any coal or iron to be found within the Colonial Empire, and you are dealing with peoples and with financial conditions which are not likely to lend themselves to factory production. The whole emphasis is likely to be upon forest, animal and agricultural development.[70]

This rationalization, so reminiscent of John Bowring's pronouncement a century earlier that "A manufacturing country Egypt never can become. . . ." (see Chapter 11, Section III), was accepted in British Labour Party circles, which were haunted by the scourge of unemployment. Thus a Labour MP, Margaret Bondfield, provided her own rationalization for aborting colonial industries by idealizing the traditional African way of life as against the social griefs of industrialization. "We want to prevent these colonies," she declared before Commons, "having to go through the dreary process of the ordinary industrial countries, of a period of economic slavery, a period of sweated conditions of labour, a period which has the terrible effect of blighting whole generations of people." [71]

In addition to imperial legislation, European officials resorted to direct measures within the colonies to ensure maximum benefits for the ailing metropolitan economies. One was the levying of taxes—on land, cattle, houses, and the people themselves—as a means to compel reluctant Africans to become cash-crop farmers or to labor in mines and plantations. This goad was unnecessary in regions such as West Africa, where long contact with Europe had stimulated a popular demand for imported manufactures. But in most parts of Africa, persistent prodding was required, as acknowledged candidly by a Kenya white settler, Colonel Grogan. "We have stolen his [kikuyu] land. Now we must steal his limbs. Compulsory labor is the corollary of our occupation of the country." [72]

Where taxation failed to engender the needed work force, colonial officials resorted to outright forced labor. A given number of payless work days per year were exacted for the construction of "public works" such as castles for governors, bungalows for officials, barracks for troops and roads, railways and ports for exporting the cash crops. The extent of the exploitation of African manpower is indicated by Governor-General Delavignette's report that French West Africa on the eve of World War II provided annually 175 million francs in poll tax and cattle tax, 21 million days of forced labor and 12,000 soldiers. This accounting was far from complete. To the official levies were added a host of other impositions, including "customary" payments collected by the chiefs, "presents" to superiors at processing plants, sales of compulsory crops below cost price, repayment at extortionate interest rates of seasonal debts and commodities "requisitioned" for the entertainment of administrators, chiefs on tour and their hangers-on.

From the viewpoint of the imperial powers, the above administrative techniques proved eminently successful. They effected the much-desired economic integration of colonies and mother countries, as indicated by the trade statistics in the table on page 560.

Equally impressive advances were made in building infrastructure facilities needed for the increasing trade. Railway lines were constructed from interior regions to new coastal ports. Dedicated missionaries founded schools and provided elementary health services. New steel machetes made easier the work of cleaning the bush. The Royal Botanical Gardens at Kew developed improved strains for coffee, cocoa, kola, maize, oil palm, citrus and other fruits, which benefited local diets as well as export products. Likewise the Southern Protectorate of Nigeria introduced new crops, some of which proved successful, including mangoes, tobacco, cocoa, kapok, cinnamon, rafia and kola. The epitome of this "modernization" process was the proliferation of new urban centers. Accra swelled from 40,000 in 1921 to 138,000 in 1948, Abidjan from 5,000 in 1921 to 45,000 in 1945 and Nairobi from 14,000 in 1906 to 250,000 by 1962.

These achievements support the conclusion of historians Peter Duignan and L. H. Gann that "the brief span . . . between the onset of late-Victorian imperialism and decolonization in Africa was in fact marked by astonishing progress in many fields. . . ."[73] But such an assessment, whether of Africa then or of Africa today, must be followed by the query: "Progress for what purpose and for whose benefit?" There are many well-publicized cases of Third World countries that have experienced impressive rates of growth that have been accompanied, however, by such mass repression, exploitation and actual decline in real living standards that the end result has been social turmoil and finally revolution. It is essential, therefore, to look beneath the surface and analyze what the "astonishing progress" involved in terms of human lives and societal health. When this is done, it soon becomes apparent that the cost of the roads, railways, ports, cities and burgeoning foreign trade was serious social dislocation and mass suffering. Nor will it do to counter that the original Industrial Revolution in Europe exacted a similar toll, because in Europe there was the reward of eventual self-generating growth and developed industrial societies with broadly diffused benefits. In the colonies, by contrast, the reward was continued economic dependence and underdevelopment, with all the attendant social dislocation

Growth of Foreign Trade in Selected Parts of Africa
(In pounds sterling)

Gold Coast	1913	1938–39
Imports	4,952,494	10,626,284
Exports	5,427,106	16,235,288
Nigeria	1913	1938
Imports	7,201,819	11,567,104
Exports	7,352,377	14,390,700
Kenya	1913–14	1938
Imports	2,147,937	8,004,690
Exports	1,482,876	8,504,650
Tanganyika	1913	1939
Imports	2,667,925	3,039,673
Exports	1,777,552	4,585,658
Northern Rhodesia	1919	1939
Imports	434,354	4,521,082
Exports	454,366	10,220,182
Southern Rhodesia	1910	1939
Imports	2,786,321	9,054,359
Exports	3,199,956	10,168,152

(In francs)

French Equatorial Africa	1913	1936
Imports	21,182,000	178,419,950
Exports	36,865,000	161,761,251
French West Africa	1912	1936
Imports	134,781,892	968,112,000
Exports	118,567,231	978,431,000
Belgian Congo	1912	1938
Imports	61,864,000	1,022,639,930
Exports	83,465,000	1,897,153,811

Source: L. H. Gann and P. Duignan, eds., *Colonialism in Africa 1870–1960;*
Vol. 2, The History and Politics of Colonialism 1914–1960 (Cambridge: Cambridge University Press, 1970), pp. 15, 16.

and misery that remains the fate of the majority of the human race trapped in the Third World.

Forced labor, for example, theoretically was limited to a specified number of days per year, but in practice it was often seriously abused. Many lives were sacrificed in constructing the railway in the British colony of Sierra Leone at the end of the nineteenth century. Likewise the French in the early twentieth century rounded up some ten thousand workers annually for building the Brazzaville to Pointe-Noire Railway, and at least a fourth of this labor force perished each year from starvation and disease. Even in the case of paid laborers hired by the Gold Coast Transport Department, the records for the year 1900 reflect appalling conditions:

> . . . with constant walking for a twelve month averaging 400 miles a month, the work this year having been rather harder than usual, a large number of carriers have been incapacitated from sore feet, the metalling of new roads making matters worse. In one gang . . . the majority had their soles completely worn through, to say nothing of cracks. The experiment was then tried of tarring the carriers' feet. Coal tar is most suitable. It fills the cracks and is good antiseptic, besides affording some protection if applied thick. The results have proved quite good and many carriers are now able to keep to the road who would otherwise have to lie up.[74]

The comment of A. G. Hopkins regarding the above episode is noteworthy. "On the occasions when high wages were paid in West Africa, labour was usually forthcoming. . . . The justification for forced labour and coercive taxes was entirely bogus; Africans did not need educating in the ways of the modern money economy, and even assuming they did, there were better ways of setting about it." [75]

Abuse of forced labor was sufficiently widespread in the British territories (where conditions usually were least bad) to call forth in 1923 a "Native Authority Ordinance" regulating the use of compulsory labor. The same objective was behind a "Forced Labor Convention" signed in 1930 by all the colonial powers. It proved difficult, however, to enforce the provisions of these regulatory measures in the distant colonies, even when the officials were sincerely desirous of doing so. And all too frequently they were not so inclined. French administrators, for example, evaded the regulations by recruiting able-bodied males as soldiers and then using them as unpaid laborers.

As serious an affliction as forced labor was the migratory labor to mines and plantations engendered by the need to pay the assorted taxes imposed for this purpose. The migrants were adult males who left their wives and children behind in the villages or reserves. They usually took employment for limited periods—between six months and two years. Most repeated the labor stints several times, so that their lives consisted of alternating terms of outside employment and of residence at home. This revolving system of employment made difficult the acquisition of skills and the organization of trade unions, so wages remained extremely depressed. Furthermore, the frequent absence of a large proportion of the men had disastrous social repercussions for the home communities. "The whole fabric of the old order of society is undermined," noted a 1935 Nyasaland (Malawi) official report, "when 30 to 60 percent of the able-bodied men are absent at one time . . . the family-community is threatened with complete dissolution." [76]

It is not surprising under these circumstances that African workers, white collar as well as blue, were among the most poorly paid in the world. An American shipping company, Farrell lines, was paying stevedores in African ports in 1965 one-sixth as much as it was paying stevedores handling the same cargoes in American ports. Nigerian coal miners at Enugu were paid on the eve of World War II as much for a six-day week as Scottish and German miners were being paid in one hour. In Northern Rhodesian mines, European truck drivers received thirty pounds per month as against seven shillings paid to African drivers doing the same work. The famous gold mines of South Africa actually have very deep and very low-grade ore. If they were located in the United States they would not be worked and would be of interest only to students of geology. Yet they have been for long the No. 1 gold producers of the capitalist world, a pre-eminence made possible by the plentiful supply of ludicrously cheap labor from the surrounding African states as well as from South Africa.

In Southern Rhodesia in 1949, Africans employed in municipal areas were paid a minimum wage of 35 to 75 shillings a month, as against white workers (working 8 hours a day to the 10 to 14 hours of the Africans) who received a minimum wage of 20 shillings a day plus free quarters and other benefits. Such discriminatory wage scales persisted long after the Second World War. This was fortuitously revealed in April 1978 when Rhodesia's Ian Smith government, fighting for survival, appointed Byron R. Hove, a London-trained black attorney, as joint Justice Minister. Hove promptly made several speeches on the need for "adjustments" to give blacks fairer treatment and more representation in the police and judiciary. To support his charges of discrimination, he revealed previously unavailable statistics showing that twelve thousand white civil servants earned fifty-eight million dollars a year, while twenty-seven thousand black civil servants earned twelve million dollars. The figures also showed that one in twenty whites was a civil servant as against one in two hundred blacks.[77]

As serious as the exploitation of human resources was the misuse of natural resources to meet the needs of foreign markets rather than of local populations. French officials, for example, assumed that Senegal could best produce the groundnut cash crop, and directed agronomic research and infrastructures toward that end. In fact the country was well suited for livestock rearing and for labor-intensive diversified cultivation of rice, sugar cane, fruits, early vegetables and oil palm. If the capital spent in behalf of the one crop had been allocated for the comprehensive development of Senegal's natural resources, the Senegalese would have been much better off during the colonial era and after.

Another form of misuse of natural resources was the neglect, and in some cases the suppression of industrialization possibilities. In East Africa, for example, it was economically feasible to manufacture simple articles of mass consumption such as cotton textiles, shoes and matches, and also to process local raw materials such as yarn and bale twine into semi-manufactures. Such first steps toward industrialization were opposed at the 1935 Governors' Conference, which considered a proposal to establish a blanket factory in Uganda. The governor of that colony opposed the project on the ground that "if industrial undertakings were started in East Africa a certain loss of revenue through the falling off of customs duties might accrue to Uganda." [78] The governor of Tanganyika took the same position, and justified it by quoting from a dispatch from the Secretary of State (Dec. 4, 1935) stating ". . . that it was undesirable to accelerate the industrialization of East Africa which must, for many years to come, remain a country of primary produce." [79]

The influence of European manufacturers against colonial competition was felt also in French West Africa. A groundnut crushing industry in Senegal had to wait until World War I, when it became imperative to economize on scarce shipping space. The industry then took root and continued to prosper during the postwar years, though it was opposed by Marseilles processing firms, which secured a limit on oil exports from West Africa to France. The quota prevailed until World War II, when the national emergency again freed colonial industry from metropolitan constraints. Groundnut crushing quickly spread from Senegal to the Sudan, Upper Volta and Niger. Exports of groundnut oil rose from six thousand tons before World War II to thirty-one thousand by 1945. Other enterprises also appeared with the lifting of restraints during the war emergency, including cement plants, cigarette factories, sawmills, cotton gins, fish canneries and sugar mills.

Finally, the African colonies had to cope with monopolistic or oligopolistic domination by the European trading companies. After the conquest of the continent, native traders no longer could function as middlemen between the coastal ports and the interior. Foreign trading firms merged into large-scale corporations enjoying important advantages over the African competition. They commanded superior or exclusive credits to European colonial banks, and they had direct access to overseas commercial networks. Also, they could afford to establish branches in the interior and to ride out the sudden fluctuations in overseas trade. In addition, they benefited from economies of scale, and bought manufactured goods more cheaply than their rivals. Finally, the large firms could count on support from government officials, who preferred to deal with a few established expatriate companies. Consequently, African and Arab traders had been mostly displaced by the end of World War I.

The predominance of the foreign trading companies was not conducive to colonial economic development. A large proportion of trading profits and expatriate salaries was transferred abroad rather than invested in Africa. Also, little effort was made to train Africans in modern business management; instead they were consigned permanently to minor posts requiring little skill. Most serious was the natural tendency of the companies to take advantage of their commanding position to overcharge on the manufactured goods they sold, and to underpay on the raw materials they bought. The latter practice was encouraged by the knowledge that the African peasant producers could keep alive because they grew their own food staples.

The widening gap (especially during the Depression years) between prices paid for exports and prices charged for imports constituted what economists refer to as "deteriorating terms of trade." More specifically, African raw-material producers could buy in 1939 only 60 percent of the manufactured goods they had obtained in 1870–80 with the same quantity of their produce. No objective economic law made this "unequal exchange" inevitable. Rather it was the end result of the political supremacy of the Europeans, who used their power to compel native peasant producers, plantation laborers and mine workers to accept subsistence or below-subsistence remuneration.

Imperial preference worsened the situation, as it prevented Africans from buying cheaper Japanese consumer goods. Nor did African producers benefit from various funds and marketing boards that were established to stabilize prices and incomes. This is scarcely surprising in view of the fact that John Cadbury (of the Cadbury Chocolate manufacturing family) showed up on the Cocoa Board of the Ministry of Food, and former employees of Unilever likewise appeared in key posts in the Oils and Fats Division of the Ministry of Food. "The main beneficiaries of the statutory monopolies," concludes A. G. Hopkins, "were the large expatriate firms. Official patronage confirmed and extended the private 'pooling' arrangements which they had operated previously. These firms not only supported state intervention; they even helped to plan it."[80]

Despite the profiteering and inequities, relations between rulers and ruled were generally relaxed during the 1920s. The general prosperity of the capitalist world and the flourishing state of international trade meant that the global economic pie was growing, even though it was being cut into grossly unequal slices. During the prolonged Great Depression of the 1930s, however, the pie shrank, whereupon it was cut into even more unequal slices. The deteriorating terms of trade made more sharp and visible the conflicting interests that hitherto had been somewhat obscured. The resulting tensions caused African farmers, traders and wage earners to demonstrate their dissatisfaction with the prevailing international market economy and with the foreign administrators and businessmen who presided over it.

The leaders of the opposition movement were known in the French colonies as the *évolué*, in the Belgian as the *immatriculé*, in the Portuguese as the *assimilado* and in the British as the "new men." They were the graduates of European or European-type schools who had studied law, medicine, engineering, accounting or public administration. The types of careers they chose after graduation are indicated in the following table:

Estimated Number of Africans Engaged in Elite
Occupations in Ghana, 1940s

Occupation	Total Number
Civil servants	3,295
Lawyers	114
Doctors	38
Dentists	7
Journalists and newspaper owners	32
Surveyors and engineers	210
Merchants	1,443
Teachers	3,123
Clergymen	435
Bank tellers	61
Bookkeepers	103
Druggists	231
Cocoa brokers and buyers	1,313

Source: M. Kilson, "The Emergent Elites of Black Africa, 1900 to 1960," in Gann and Duignan, op. cit., Vol. 2, p. 354.

The number and influence of these elites varied from colony to colony, being stronger in British and French West Africa than in British East

Africa or Belgian and Portuguese Africa. Thus the first African lawyer did not appear in Kenya until 1956, whereas there were no fewer than sixty practicing in Ghana by the early 1920s. Yet whatever the colony, all these elites had one feature in common: their concern with civil liberties rather than national liberation. Most had no experience with the independent Africa of preconquest times. Being trained along European lines, they equated Europe with civilization, and Africa with barbarism. "People can say what they want," declared Samuel Chimponde in 1925, "but to the African mind, to imitate Europeans is civilization." [81] Chimponde was then the president of the Tanganyika African Civil Servants Association.

The status of the new African elite obviously rested not on their class origins in traditional Africa, but rather on possession of Western education and skills. They felt more at home in the new alien order than in the old traditional one. But they were not accepted as equals by the Europeans with whom they associated. The "new men" were bourgeois nationalists, driven by slights in their social relationships and by discrimination in their professional careers. Accordingly they demanded equal rights in politics, equal opportunity in economic affairs, mass schooling in education, recognition of African traditions and achievements in cultural matters and Africanization of personnel in all fields.

In short, the rising African elites were preoccupied with their relations with Europeans, but gave little thought to their relations with their untutored fellow countrymen, who comprised the overwhelming majority throughout Africa. Thus a Nigerian leader, Obafemi Awolowo, declared, "The educated minority . . . are the people who are qualified by natural rights to lead their fellow nationals into higher political development." [82] Another Nigerian leader, Nnamdi Azikiwe, stated that ". . . in view of the status quo, any change would be in the form of a sacrifice by the ruling elite. . . ." [83]

Such leaders did finally realize that mobilization of mass support was necessary, but they directed it against the injustices of European rule rather than the fact of that rule. As bourgeois nationalists they never questioned Africa's subordination to, and exploitation by, the global market economy. They wanted concessions that would enhance their social status and their economic interests. Their basic demand was for reform rather than independence. "To speak of independence," declared Félix Houphouet-Boigny, "is to reason with the head on the ground and the feet in the air; it is not to reason at all. It is to advance a false problem." [84] Despite this view, Houphouet-Boigny later became President of the independent state of Ivory Coast, because of the force of "winds of change" that he had not foreseen. Given his bourgeois nationalist outlook, it is not surprising that little changed in the independent state over which he presided, other than the skin color of the ruling elite. Indeed, the volume of French investments and the number of French technicians and businessmen increased rather than decreased after the winning of independence. And despite the burgeoning foreign trade and GNP, Senegal's subordinate economic relationship to the French metropolis remained unchanged.

The same can be said of the neighboring British colony of Ghana, as well as of Kenya on the eastern coast. This pattern of bourgeois nationalist leadership followed by postindependence neocolonialism was broken only in the Portuguese colonies, where independence was won after prolonged armed struggle. During that struggle the masses were activized, social issues were discussed at the grass-roots level and the basic consensus was reached that political independence without economic independence was a cruel deception for a people accepting the onerous sacrifices of a national liberation struggle.

Finally, given the nature of the above colonial experiences, it is understandable that the numerous colonies that won political freedom during the 1950s and 1960s began their independent existence as underdeveloped societies. The symptoms of underdevelopment were omnipresent. There was marked disparity in the development of regions within a given colony, so that the per-capita income in 1960 in northern Ghana was 38 pounds, as against 165 pounds in southern Ghana. There was also the rural-urban dichotomy, which remains the trademark of Third World societies to the present day. The dichotomy was between, on the one hand, the poverty-stricken countryside, which the peasants were beginning to leave in what became the greatest mass migration in history, and on the other hand, the cities, consisting of affluent centers comprising administrative structures, business buildings and white-occupied villas, but surrounded by dreary expanses of warrenlike shantytowns where the African populations lived.

Another symptom of underdevelopedness at the end of the colonial period was the high rate of unemployment produced by the distinctive Third World combination of urbanization without industrialization. In relatively prosperous Ghana, unemployment approached 20 percent of the male urban force in 1960. Closely related was the lack of home-based, self-generated economic development because the foreign domination of colonial economies led to the transfer abroad of the capital needed for development. The transfer took the form of "visible" export of capital from commercial profits and administrative salaries, plus the "invisible" export inherent in "unequal exchange" or "unfavorable terms of trade."

A final manifestation of the underdevelopedness of African states when they began their independent political existence was their retarded and irrelevant educational systems. In French West Africa, 2.2 percent of the school-age population was in schoolrooms in 1937, and in the Gold Coast 9 percent were enrolled in 1930, and 13 percent in 1940. These colonies were far in advance of Portuguese Angola and Mozambique, where less than 1 percent of the population had seen the inside of a school, no matter how rudimentary. Furthermore, the curricula in all the colonies were designed to provide the primitive literacy and arithmetic needed by hewers of wood and drawers of water. It was, in short, an educational system calculated to preserve a dependent colonial status quo.

A miniscule African elite did manage to acquire higher education in the colonies or in Europe, and some of its members did play an important role in the struggle for African rights. But they were the exceptions, for most of the privileged elite were content to accept the values and authority of their masters, along with the accompanying privileges and comforts. It is not accidental that Leopold Senghor, the philosopher-poet-statesman who was educated in Paris and became President of Senegal, opted for preserving the traditionally close ties with France, whereas Sekou Touré, a self-made man, was alone in leading Guinea toward immediate and complete independence. Another African head of state, Julius Nyerere of Tanzania, has noted that his country inherited a system of education that was "both inadequate and inappropriate." It was inadequate because not enough were educated to fill government posts, and inappropriate because it emphasized "subservient attitudes" and "white collar skills," and encouraged "the individualistic instincts of mankind, instead of his cooperative instincts." [85]

Nyerere's appraisal fits in with the judgment of a British historian, Basil Davidson, about the overall significance of the colonial period of African history. Colonial rule did carry through the necessary dismantling of traditional African society which was imprisoned in "the Iron Age limits of the past." But dismantling was not followed by reconstruction. "Nothing could be less true" concludes Davidson, than the colonialist argument that "we have at least prepared these peoples for their own emancipation." To the contrary, states Davidson, with the end of colonial rule, "everything of basic social meaning remained to be begun or built afresh." [86]

VII. South African Exception

The southern tip of Africa alone was able to pursue an independent course of development. The local settler regime was free to exploit ruthlessly the native human resources and the rich natural resources, thereby building a strong industrialized economy and gaining complete political independence. As noted earlier (Chapter 18, Section IX), both the British and Afrikaner combatants in the Boer War agreed that, whatever the outcome, the black majority should remain subservient. Consequently no provisions protecting the status of the African majority were included in the Vereeniging Treaty (1902) ending the war, which meant the same black subservience in the future as in the past. This subservience continued in the Union of South Africa, which was established in 1909 and which was recognized as a self-governing dominion of the British Empire.

The first governments in the new dominion were formed by two ex-Boer generals, Louis Botha and Jan Smuts. Their pro-English orientation and support for Britain in World War I aroused Afrikaner nationalism, which rallied around another ex-Boer general, J. B. M. Herzog. He organized the opposition Nationalist Party, which at first appeared to have little chance of success, since the Boers were a minority within the white minority of South Africa. But the fateful 1922 strike of white miners led to an alliance between labor and the Boer Nationalists that has dominated South African politics to the present day.

Until the discovery of diamonds at Kimberley in 1871, and of gold in southern Transvaal in 1886, South Africa's economy had been inconsequential. The only noteworthy export had been wool, and the potentiality of this trade had been exhausted before the diamond discovery because of the limited grazing lands. With the diamond- and gold-mining operations, the economy of South Africa was transformed, especially after the discovery of large adjacent coal deposits. The deep subterranean mining of diamonds and gold engendered considerable local technology, while the coal production stimulated chemical industries. South African mining consequently was not encapsulated and isolated from the surrounding economy, as was the case with copper mining in the Congo and Rhodesia, and with tin mining in Bolivia and Malaya. Instead there were linkages that promoted comprehensive economic development rather than the hobbled economic growth characteristic of the Third World.

Equally important was the abundance of cheap, regimented labor, which enabled South African mining to yield extraordinarily high profits. These also contributed to the rapid development of the national economy. Black workers and their families lived on reserves, so the mines employed migrant labor. Able-bodied males were hired for short periods, and lived in bachelor compounds that were closed to the public, allegedly for security reasons. Since the workers' families stayed on the reserves and grew their own food, the mining companies could set wages at sub-reproductive levels. The short-term labor contracts prevented the black laborers from organizing unions or acquiring skills, which in any case were adamantly opposed by the white miners.

South African manufacturing industries and farms also needed cheap black labor, but the demand did not raise wages because the mining companies imported laborers from surrounding countries such as Portuguese Mozambique and British Nyasaland (Malawi). The end result was a grotesquely underpaid black labor force, and an equally overpaid white labor force. A 1914 economic commission reported that white miners' wages were 40 percent higher than in the United States and 225 percent higher than in any European country. Likewise in factories, the average annual wage paid in 1915–16 was £171 for whites, £32 for Africans, £48 for coloreds and £26 for Asians. This gross disparity persisted after World War II, as evident in the following table based on data supplied by the South African Department of Statistics in 1971:

Racial Composition of Labor and Wages in Major South African Industries

	Mining and Quarrying	Manufacture	Construction
Whites No:	61,782	279,700	60,800
Average wage per month	£195.82	£170.81	£178.10
Africans No:	592,819	644,000	270,000
Average wage per month	£9.48	£29.16	£28.03
Coloreds No:	6,352	201,300	47,200
Average wage per month	£41.90	£41.16	£61.74
Asians No:	578	76,500	5,300
Average wage per month	£51.46	£43.58	£79.92

Source: B. Turok and K. Maxey, "Southern Africa: White Power in Crisis," in P. C. W. Gutkind and I. Wallerstein, eds., The Political Economy of Contemporary Africa (Beverly Hills, Calif.: Sage Publications, 1976), p. 243.

The first white miners were British, and then followed Eastern Europeans, and finally Afrikaners. Whatever their origin, they all closed ranks against the black miners to retain their monopoly of high-paying skilled jobs. Both white labor and white capital in South Africa had a common interest in keeping the blacks disfranchised, unorganized and exploitable. Consequently discriminatory legislation was passed long before the Afrikaners gained political control in 1924. A Mines and Work Act of 1911 reserved skilled mining jobs for Europeans. Two years later the Natives' Land Act limited the land available to Africans to little more than one tenth of the total South African land mass, and at the same time directed the eviction of nearly one million African squatters from white farms. In 1923 the Native Urban Areas Act authorized municipal authorities to control the number and location of Africans living in cities.

The white capital-labor front against the blacks was broken when the mining companies attempted to use Africans in more skilled jobs in order to reduce their wage costs. The white miners resisted with armed force and with this paradoxical slogan: "Workers of the world unite and fight for a white South Africa." The companies, backed by government military units, defeated the white miners, but they had lost the war while winning the battle. Henceforth South African labor allied itself with the Afrikaner Nationalist Party, enabling it to win the 1924 elections. This proved a critical turning point in South African history. The domination by mining capital over the state apparatus was now permanently broken, and the white monopoly of skilled mining jobs was henceforth assured. South Africa has been ruled since the 1924 elections by the coalition of Afrikaner nationalism and unionized white labor.

Both elements of this coalition feared that the mineral resources were nonrenewable assets that were being drained for the benefit of capital. Therefore they pressed successfully for economic diversification by industrialization through import substitution. The largest corporation, Anglo-American, transformed itself from a mining enterprise to a conglomerate engaged in diverse activities such as fruit farming, real estate, brick- and tilemaking, ranching, breakfast foods, fertilizers, chemicals and cold storage. The government also supported economic diversification by establishing state corporations such as ISKOR, which developed a steel industry based on the extensive iron ore and coal deposits. Foreign capital also was invested in South Africa, attracted by the high profits made possible by cheap labor.

In addition, agriculture was revolutionized, especially after 1945. South Africa's distinctive climate, water distribution, pests and diseases required the development of an indigenous agricultural science. The application of this science generated linkages to the agricultural and chemical industries. Thus a highly productive, capital-intensive agriculture was evolved, comparable to that of the United States but enjoying a crucial advantage over its American counterpart. Whereas important sectors of United States agriculture are dependent on migratory labor, often of Latin American origin, South African agriculture has available a black labor supply that is much cheaper and more coercible. South African agribusiness therefore enjoys cost advantages over other high-technology, capital-intensive agricultural competitors in world markets.

It was under these circumstances that South Africa achieved an independent, comprehensive and self-generating economic development, in direct contrast to the foreign-dominated, lopsided and encapsulated economic growth typical of Third World countries. The basis of this achievement was the apartheid system—the political subjugation and economic exploitation of the black majority for the benefit not only of foreign interests, but primarily of the local privileged white minority. The latter constituted a substantial domestic market for durable goods, thereby solving the dilemma of underdeveloped countries such as Mexico and India, which have been hobbled by lack of domestic purchasing power. The extreme income disparity presented in the above table represents what has been termed "polarized accumulation." [87] Apart from moral issues and unavoidable future political confrontations, the economic strategy of polarized accumulation has enabled South Africa to become the great exception of the African continent.

Since the 1924 election, Afrikaner political hegemony has been steadily consolidated. During the Great Depression, Herzog and Smuts combined to organize the United Party and to direct a coalition government from 1933 onward. This compromise arrangement was strongly opposed by the *Broederbond*, a deeply nationalistic, quasisecret society founded after World War I and committed to the concept of apartheid. In theory this rested on the proposition that the races of the world develop best when physically separated from one another, and that each race therefore should go its own way on its own territory. In practice, apartheid involved the exclusion of all nonwhites from any share in South African political life, and the relegation of blacks to eight separate areas or Bantustans (preserves for the "Bantu," as the Africans have been called). This program is not economically viable, since the South African economy cannot dispense with black labor, and the Bantustans cannot begin to support the vast black majority. Nor is apartheid politically viable, since the great majority of Africans refuse to be isolated into separate tribal entities and demand a fair share of, and a meaningful role in, the united South Africa of which they are an integral part. Whether the product of cynical self-serving or of religious fanaticism or both, the fact remains that apartheid utilizes the fig leaf of ostensible self-government to freeze the black majority into permanent political, economic and social subservience.

On the basis of these apartheid principles the *Broederbond* opposed the United Party and supported a new Nationalist Party led by a former Dutch Reform Church minister, Dr. D. F. Malan. In the 1948 election, Smuts and his United Party were defeated by the Nationalists, who campaigned for the implementation of apartheid. Malan's victory was narrow, but it began a period of Nationalist Party domination backed by steadily increasing support from all segments of the European population. Malan retired in 1954, and was succeeded first by J. G. Strijdom, then by Dr. Hendrik Verwoerd, and on the latter's assassination, by John Vorster, who had spent the World War II years in jail because of his pro-Nazi proclivity. In September 1978 Dr. Vorster resigned because of financial scandals, and was succeeded by Pieter Botha.

In the early years of South Africa, Cecil Rhodes had set forth certain guiding principles, which amounted to the present-day system of apartheid:

> I will lay down my policy on the Native question. . . . either you will receive them on an equal footing as citizens or call them a subject race. . . . I have made up my mind that there must be class (race) legislation. . . . The Native is to be treated as a child and denied the franchise. We must adopt the system of despotism. . . . These are my politics and these are the politics of South Africa.[88]

Rhodes' "system of despotism" was fully realized, though he could not have foreseen that the descendants of the defeated Boers were to emerge as the masters of the system, and the British as junior partners. In the November 1977 election the Nationalist Party won its greatest victory ever, with the largest opposition party getting only 17 out of 165 seats in the national legislature.

VIII. Latin American Neocolonialism

After World War II, when the relationship of colonies with European powers was being widely debated, there was general agreement among Africans that Latin American neocolonialism was a model to be avoided at all costs. "Before us," declared the conservative Félix Houphouet-Boigny, "there was the emancipation of the countries of South America. These states belonged to Spain and Portugal. For a hundred years these states, called independent, have been scarcely that, because economically they depend on the great North America. We do not want that in our territories of Black Africa." [89]

This observation points up the fact that the neocolonial status of Latin America in the nineteenth century (see Chapter 9) persisted into the twentieth. This does not mean that no changes occurred within Latin America during those decades. Significant new developments affected both internal institutions and external relationships, but all these took place within the context of neocolonialism.

The first cluster of significant changes was engendered by the First World War. The Latin American countries had no common policy toward the belligerents. Mexico, Venezuela and Chile were generally pro-German, whereas Argentinians inclined toward the Allies, especially Italy, while Brazilians sympathized with France, which they regarded as the heart of Latin civilization. With the entry of the United States into the war most of the Latin American states followed suit, although none were directly involved apart from a few naval skirmishes in their waters.

Despite its military aloofness, Latin America decidedly felt the impact of the war, particularly in economic matters. The steady stream of European immigrants and European capital suddenly dried up. Exports to Europe dropped temporarily because of the shortage of shipping space, but they recovered quickly in response to the urgent Allied demand for food and raw materials. On the other hand, imports of European manufactures dropped sharply and did not recover as European industry concentrated on meeting war needs. This stimulated some import-substitution industrialization, especially in the ABC states (Argentina, Brazil and Chile). The chief beneficiaries were textile plants producing for the home market and canneries preserving local food supplies.

Another effect of the First World War was a great increase, both absolute and relative, in American exports to Latin America. This trend continued, and even developed further after the war, despite strenuous efforts by British and French firms in the 1920s to recover their lost ground. Capital followed trade, so that American investments in Latin America doubled between 1914 and 1929, reaching a total of $3.462 billion. This figure made the United States No. 1 investor in that region, ending Britain's primacy, which had prevailed throughout the nineteenth century.

During the 1920s Latin America by and large was peaceful and prosperous. There were a few exceptions, such as Chile's nitrate industry, which was undercut when the Germans during the war invented synthetic nitrate for manufacturing nitroglycerine. After the war the use of synthetic nitrate became general, so that the Chilean share of world nitrate production fell from about 70 percent at the turn of the century to 35 percent in 1924 and to 11 percent in 1931. Chile's experience, however, was exceptional. In Brazil, by contrast, cotton growing and cattle raising ended the former excessive dependence on coffee exports. The biggest boom in the 1920s, however, occurred in the republics of the northern Andes—Peru, Colombia, Ecuador, and above all, Venezuela —where immense oil fields were discovered. Exporting of oil began in 1918, and by 1930 Venezuela was producing over 10 percent of the world's supply.

The second cluster of significant changes in Latin America was induced by the Great Depression, which dramatically demonstrated the vulnerability of the region's monocultural economies. Not only did the volume of world trade fall drastically, but also the prices of raw materials declined more than did the prices of manufactured goods. Thus

Latin America was battered by the economic hurricane to a greater degree than the industrialized countries. The extent of the damage is evident in the following table depicting the effect on foreign trade:

Latin America: Evolution of External Trade

	Quantum of Exports	Terms of Trade	Capacity to Import
1930–34	−8.8	−24.3	−31.3
1935–39	−2.4	−10.8	−12.9

Source: C. Furtado, *Economic Development of Latin America* (Cambridge: Cambridge University Press, 1970), p. 40.

Although Latin America as a whole was hard hit by the Depression, the precise impact varied from country to country depending on the nature of the export commodities. Countries such as Argentina, exporting temperate-zone food products (wheat, corn, meat) were less affected because demand for these products is relatively inelastic, while their supply is elastic, as crops can be reduced from one year to the next. By contrast, countries such as Brazil, exporting tropical goods (rubber, coffee, bananas) were severely affected, as the demand in this case is more elastic, while the supply of the perennial crops is inelastic. Also, tropical goods tended to be replaced to a greater degree by synthetic products such as synthetic rubber and fibers. Latin American countries suffered further by attempting to maintain prices by reducing the volume of exports such as coffee and cocoa, while African competitors took advantage of the opportunity to increase their exports. Finally, the hardest-hit countries were the mineral exporters, affected by extreme decline of both the prices and volume of their exports. Hence the disparity in the impact of the Depression, as reflected in the first table on page 576.

Foreign investments as well as foreign trade shrank during the Depression years. The value of American investments in Latin America declined from $3.462 billion in 1929 to $2.803 billion in 1936 and to $2.696 billion in 1940.

These negative developments of the 1930s did have one positive effect: The decline in the export of raw materials and the resulting shortage of funds to purchase manufactured goods from abroad forced a certain degree of import-substitution industrialization. This is evident in the tables on page 576 depicting the decline of imports and the increase of industrial output in relation to Gross Domestic Product.

External Trade Indicators for Selected Latin American Countries
(% variation from annual average for 1925–29)

	Quantum of Exports	Terms of Trade	Capacity to Import	Quantum of Imports
Argentina				
1930–34	−8	−20	−27	−32
1935–39	−11	0	−11	−23
Brazil				
1930–34	+10	−40	−35	−48
1935–39	+52	−55	−32	−27
Chile				
1930–34	−33	−38	−58	−60
1935–39	−2	−41	−42	−50
Mexico				
1930–34	−25	−43	−55	−45
1935–39	−11	−36	−39	−26

Source: C. Furtado, op. cit., p. 41.

Evolution of Import Coefficient in Selected Countries
(imports as % of GDP)

	Argentina	Mexico	Brazil	Chile	Colombia
1929	17.8	14.2	11.3	31.2	18.0
1937	13.0	8.5	6.9	13.8	12.9
1947	11.7	10.6	8.7	12.6	13.8
1957	5.9	8.2	6.1	10.1	8.9

Evolution of Industrialisation Coefficient in Selected Countries
(industrial output as % of GDP)

	Argentina	Mexico	Brazil	Chile	Colombia
1929	22.8	14.2	11.7	7.9	6.2
1937	25.6	16.7	13.1	11.3	7.5
1947	31.1	19.8	17.3	17.3	11.5
1957	32.4	21.7	23.1	19.7	16.2

Source: C. Furtado, op. cit., p. 86.

The significance of the above statistics is apparent. A Brazilian economist, Celso Furtado, reaches this conclusion:

> The fact that industrialization in those countries was intensified during the depression of the external sector is a clear indication that the process could have started sooner if these countries had had the benefit of appropriate policies. In other words, advance beyond the first stage of industrialization required economic measures designed to change the structure of the industrial nucleus, and in default of such measures the industrial sectors found themselves in a relatively depressed situation.[90]

The economic ravages of the Depression inevitably had far-reaching social and political repercussions. Bad business helped to make bad governments intolerable. Between 1930 and 1931, eleven of Latin America's twenty republics experienced political upheavals and irregular changes of government. By the mid-1930s only five Latin American states had civilian-controlled governments. New populist leaders emerged, who tried to mobilize the disaffected masses against the domestic and foreign establishments. Outstanding were Getulio Vargas (1930–45), Juan Perón (1946–55) and Lázaro Cárdenas (1934–40). All three sought to attract popular support through social reforms and economic rationalism. All three also were careful that the masses did not get out of control. Much was done for them, but very little by them.

Vargas provided Brazil for fifteen years with a moderate personalist dictatorship. In 1937 he arbitrarily altered the constitution and established the Estado Novo or New State. This was a "corporative" institution, reminiscent of fascist Italy, though the genial Vargas was no Mussolini. He used the expanded powers of government to establish institutes for regulating the production and marketing of basic commodities such as coffee, sugar, cotton and rubber. Also, he furthered agricultural diversification and industrial development, of which the Volta Redonda Steel plant was the core.

Perón was elected President of Argentina in 1946, and proceeded to implement a Five Year Plan for the development of industry, transportation, public works and education. Like other Latin American leaders he was an economic nationalist and expropriated telephones (1946) and railways (1948). Also, he extended the franchise to women and adopted progressive labor legislation, including social insurance and increased participation of workers in the ownership and direction of corporations. These measures won Perón the enthusiastic support of the ragged masses (*descamisados*). Under the cloudy ideology of *justicialismo* Peronismo represented a variety of extreme nationalism based on the twin pillars of labor and the army.

Cárdenas was the revered folk hero of the Mexican peasants after the waning of the great revolution and of its ideals. Obregón's successor, Plutarco Calles, who either as President or as the power behind the presidency dominated Mexican politics from 1924 to 1934, publicly declared in 1929 that land reform had gone far enough. During the early thirties redistribution had virtually ceased. But with the election of Cárdenas to the presidency in 1934, land policy was completely reversed. During his six years in office, forty-seven million acres were distributed among more than one million peasant families, compared to twenty million acres granted to three quarters of a million in the preceding twenty years of "revolutionary" governments.

Cárdenas no longer confined expropriation to owners who had acquired land by illegal means, who farmed inefficiently or who had given political offense. Most landowners with a sizable area of arable land were dispossessed of all but a small tract. Cárdenas also favored the grant of *ejidos* or communal lands to villages, rather than of plots in permanent ownership to individuals who tended to grow only enough for immediate subsistence. He therefore passed laws that collectivized the formerly individual ejidos so that they could operate more efficiently, gave ejidos preference for water and irrigated lands and created state institutions such as the Ejido Credit Bank to assist the peasants.

Cárdenas also won enthusiastic support for his nationalization of foreign railroads and oil companies. Millions rallied behind him; Catholics prayed, workers gave their paychecks, women offered wedding rings, farmers sent in poultry and pigs while army units paraded in exuberant celebrations. To hold the support of the aroused populace, Cárdenas organized the workers into the Confederation of Mexican Workers or CTM (1936) and the peasants into the National Country Confederation or CNC (1938). Both bodies were organized from above, run from above and carefully kept apart to forestall independent grass-roots initiative. Cárdenas took advantage of the national exhilaration to restructure the shaky National Revolutionary Party (PNR) into the Party of the Mexican Revolution (PRM). This was a vast umbrella organization encompassing the CTM, CNC, the civil service and the army.

Despite these sweeping reforms, Mexican society ended up as exploitative and inequitable as the others in Latin America. One percent of the gainfully employed population received 66 percent of the national income. It is estimated that after World War II, about one third of the population had benefited from the national development, leaving two thirds excluded from its benefits. Mexico also continued to suffer from the distinctive Third World characteristics of economic dependency and high unemployment.

The basic reason for Mexico's plight was that Cárdenas, like Vargas

18. *Iron smelting in "backyard furnace" during China's Great Leap Forward, 1958.*

19. *Volunteers building the Ming Tombs Dam in five months and ten days during the Great Leap Forward, 1958.*

20. *Moro National Liberation Front guerrillas, Cotabato province, Mindanao, Philippines.*

21. *The "finger lickin'" colonel in Kuala Lumpur, Malaysia.*

22. When Robert Goizueta, Coca-Cola's chairman, opened his company's first bottling plant on the China mainland since 1949, he said: "April 15, 1981, may be one of the most important days in the history of our company, and in more ways than one, in the history of the world."

23. Sign of U.S. electronics industry in Indonesia.

24. *National Liberation Front command post at Dien Bien Phu, with Ho Chi Minh in center and Vo Nguyen Giap at right.*

25. *Police Special Forces with arrested students outside Thammasart University, Bangkok, October 6, 1976.*

26. *Massage parlor in Thailand catering to Americans.*

27. *Symbol of the old order in* **Mexico**: *peasants harnessed to factories.*

28. *During the Mexican Revolution entire families swarmed over the haciendas, breaking open safes, burning deeds and taking over the land.*

29. *Interior of home of migrant worker, Gavino López Hernández, in Nuevo Porvenir, Durango, Mexico (1980).*

30. Breakfast buffet at the Hotel Fiesta, Tortuga, Acapulco, 1981.

31. Residents of hills above Acapulco, being forcefully relocated to make room for more hotels and tourist facilities.

and Perón, was a populist who effected reforms *for* the people, but opposed initiative *by* them. This left them vulnerable to the shifting winds of the notoriously volatile Latin American political scene. When a populist leader with social concern was followed, as usually happened, by a corrupt and self-seeking politician or general, there was no built-in or institutionalized opposition to resist the retrogression. Thus retrogression did prevail after Vargas and Perón and Cárdenas.

Taking Mexico as an example, the three Presidents who followed Cárdenas—Ávila Camacho, Miguel Alemán and Ruíz Cortínez—adopted a policy of undoing the agrarian reforms and breaking up the collective ejidos. Economic developments in the United States provided strong incentive for this policy. After Cárdenas' departure in 1940, American industry geared up to produce for Allied war needs, and looked to Mexico for cheap raw materials and agricultural products such as cotton, sugar and vegetables. To take advantage of the vast new markets across the border, the new Mexican administrations abandoned the ejido system and instead invested state funds (including massive American loans) to stimulate large-scale, privately owned agricultural enterprises.

This export-oriented agricultural policy involved slowing land distribution and hobbling government institutions such as the Ejido Credit Bank, which had made the ejidos viable. The new policy also entailed the financing of costly irrigation and transportation systems, which made possible the irrigation of 1.7 million acres of formerly unproductive land. The newly irrigated lands ended up in the possession of capitalist entrepreneurs rather than landless *campesinos*.

Agricultural productivity increased but the social repercussions were disastrous. By 1957 60 percent of Mexican agricultural output was destined for export, with only 2 percent of the farms accounting for 70 percent of the value in sales. Capital-intensive operations yielded high profits for a handful of large-scale growers and their American partners. The peasants who owned some land barely managed to survive, while the increasing number of landless crossed the border to work as farm laborers. Some 800,000 contracted themselves in the United States during World War II under the *bracero* program. The flood of legal and illegal braceros swelled after the war as an increasing proportion of campesinos failed to find work in their country.

Thus the peonage exploitation of past decades gave way to capitalist wage exploitation between the two world wars. The international ramifications are reflected in the rise of American investments from 60 percent of total foreign investments in Mexico in 1938 to 80 percent in 1957. Likewise the United States accounted for 65 percent of Mexican imports in 1935, and for 73 percent by 1957. This persistence of vertical rather than horizontal linkages in Mexico's economic structure made independent, self-generating growth impossible. Capital was drained out of the country in the form of corporate profits, and a domestic market adequate for full-scale industrialization was unattainable with two thirds of the population impoverished and excluded from the national economic life. In 1978 an American AID official estimated that between 15 and 20 percent of the total adult population of Mexico was living "illegally" in the United States, and that about 20 percent of Mexico's population was dependent on wages earned in the United States!

Under these circumstances it is understandable that Latin America, after more than a century of "independent" existence, should be regarded as an antimodel by Africans appraising their future. For a few years during World War II and the Korean War, we shall see that Latin America received an artificial economic stimulus. But recession followed this war-induced prosperity, and in order to control the increasingly disaffected masses, the outright military dictatorships of Pinochet, Videla and Geisel took the place of the populist regimes of Perón, Vargas and Cárdenas.

Chapter 22

SECOND GLOBAL REVOLUTIONARY WAVE, 1939– : INITIATIVE OF THE 1949 CHINESE REVOLUTION

Politically, economically and emotionally, my life has been transformed. For that I will always be grateful to the party and to Chairman Mao. . . . I was essentially a slave, not a human being, before liberation, working 16 or 17 hours a day, with never enough rest or enough money or enough food. Now I have security and enough to take care of my family. We don't have to worry about the future. . . . Whenever I try to educate them [my children] so they can share my happiness in how far China has come, they listen to me, but I'm not sure they understand. Sometimes they just say, "Oh, Papa, we've heard your stories before."

CHANG PING-KUEI, candy salesman at the Peking
No. 1 Department Store (Sept. 31, 1979, thirtieth
anniversary of the People's Republic of China)

Mao, together with Marx and Lenin, stands out as one of the great revolutionary leaders of modern times. Marx's basic contribution was his analysis of the workings of capitalist society. Lenin evolved and implemented the strategy for overthrowing capitalism, but he did not live to cope with the subsequent problem of creating a new socialist society. His successors did create the powerful Soviet state, but this was not synonymous with attaining socialism, if by socialism is meant not only cooperative or state ownership of the means of production and distribution, but also self-management in the workplace and in political and cultural life. Mao continued the work of his illustrious predecessors by beginning, though far from completing, the task of evolving socialist institutions and practices. He did so by creatively Sinifying Marxism and by challenging the hitherto sacrosanct Soviet model.

In leading the 1949 Chinese Revolution, Mao defied Stalin, who was backing Chiang Kai-shek in accord with his overall strategy of seeking a global settlement with the United States. Equally significant was Mao's break with the Russians in launching his Cultural Revolution, with the aim of creating a full-fledged socialist society—participatory rather than bureaucratic, egalitarian rather than elitist. Mao also perceived that his Cultural Revolution was a mere beginning rather than an end. Post-revolutionary societies, he came to realize, engendered their own contradictions, which, depending on the fortunes of class struggles, progress toward socialism or regress under the domination of a new exploiting class based not on private ownership of the means of production but on control of a repressive state apparatus. Mao therefore issued a warning, which appears to be prophetic in the light of developments since his death: "The Great Proletarian Cultural Revolution presently going on is only the first of its kind. In the future such revolutions will necessarily take place at several occasions. . . . All Party members, and the population at large, must refrain from thinking that all will be smooth after one, two, three, or four Cultural Revolutions." [1]

‍ I. Revolution in China

The weakness and misery of China during the interwar years offered little inkling of the profound social upheaval and restructuring that were to follow. As noted earlier (Chapter 21, Section II), China during those years suffered from the ravages of three concurrent wars. One was the recurring struggle between Chiang Kai-shek ensconced in Nanking and the warlords entrenched in certain provinces. The second was the civil war between the Kuomintang led by Chiang and the Communist Party led by Mao. The third was the war against the Japanese, who invaded Manchuria in 1931 and thence fanned out through North China.

The outbreak of World War II in Europe and the involvement of the United States after Pearl Harbor made China a member of the great coalition against the Axis powers. Chiang's hard-pressed government now was eligible for military and economic aid. But delivering that aid was fabulously expensive, as it involved flying supplies over the "hump" of the Himalayas between India and China. Furthermore, the aid that did reach Chiang in his wartime capital of Chungking was not used effectively for carrying on the war against Japan.

One reason for Chiang's ineffectiveness was beyond his control, because it was engendered by the Japanese invasion of the eastern coast as well as of the northern provinces. This deprived Chiang of the support of the relatively enlightened class of big businessmen, which was largely eliminated, and left him dependent on the shortsighted and self-centered landlords of the interior. The Chungking government became increasingly reactionary and corrupt, leaving the peasant masses vulnerable to unbridled extortion and inflation. Using an index of 1 for 1937 prices, by August 1945 they had soared in Chungking to 1,795, and by December 1947 to 83,796. The American commander in China, General Joseph W. Stilwell, used strong words in the privacy of his diary to describe the Chiang regime. "Corruption, neglect, chaos, economy, taxes, words and deeds. Hoarding, black market, trading with the enemy." [2] Stilwell's successor, General Albert Wedemeyer, spelled out the meaning of these words in a remarkable memorandum he sent to Chiang regarding the condition of the conscript Chinese army:

> Conscription comes to the Chinese peasant like famine or flood, only more regularly—every year twice—and claims more victims. . . . The conscription officers make their money in collaboration with the officials and through their press gangs. They extort big sums of money from conscripts which have been turned over to them by the officials and replace them with captives. Private dealers in conscripts have organized a trade. They are buying able-bodied men from starved families who need rice more urgently than sons, or, they buy them from the Hsienchangs [county magistrates] who have a surplus. . . .
>
> Having been segregated and herded together the conscripts are driven to the training camps. They are marched from Shensi to Szechuan and from Szechuan to Yun[n]an. Over endless roads they walk. . . . Many of those who run away run off during the first few days. Later they are too weak to run away. Those who are caught are cruelly beaten. . . .
>
> As they march along they turn into skeletons; they develop signs of beriberi, their legs swell and their bellies protrude, their arms and thighs get thin. . . . If somebody dies his body is left behind. His name on the list is carried along. As long as his death is not reported he continues to be a source of income, increased by the fact that he has ceased to consume. His rice and his pay become a long-lasting token of memory in the pocket of his commanding officer. His family will have to forget him.[3]

The second reason for Chiang's ineffective use of American aid was his basic strategy of giving priority to the war against the Communists rather than to the war against the Japanese. Chiang believed, and with much justification from his viewpoint: "The Japanese are a disease of the skin. The Communists are a disease of the heart." A highly reliable French intelligence source quoted him as saying in 1944: "For me the big problem is not Japan but the unification of my country. I am sure that you Americans are going to beat the Japanese some day, with or without the help of the troops I am holding back for use against the Communists in the Northwest. On the other hand, if I let Mao Tse-tung push his propaganda across all of Free China, we run the risk—and so do you Americans—of winning for nothing." [4]

Chiang had pursued his anti-Communist strategy for many years prior to the Second World War. When Mao established his rural soviets in Kiangsi in the late 1920s, Chiang launched a series of campaigns against what he called "bandits." Eventually he succeeded in driving them out of Kiangsi and, during the legendary Long March, pursued them for six thousand miles westward across southern China, and then northward to the province of Shensi. There Mao found a small and isolated Communist base, which he transformed into his headquarters, centered in Yenan. In that small, drab provincial town, Mao developed a revolutionary strategy and trained revolutionary cadres that in fifteen years were to make him the master of the entire mainland. The body of revolutionary doctrine and practice known as Maoism came to represent a profound challenge to both the Western and Soviet worlds, as well as an increasingly influential model for the Third World.

Several factors explain this fateful outcome, including geographic environment, cultural traditions and the leadership of Mao. The vast area and population of China provided a base sufficiently broad for maneuvering and for fresh starts after the initial Communist failures in the cities and in the southern countryside. Also, the decades of wracking civil war followed by brutal Japanese invasion produced a degree of mass misery and social unraveling that constituted a favorable milieu for Communist insurgency. By contrast, in India, where the nationalists were handed independence without a revolutionary interlude, a native ruling class moved comfortably into the place of the foreign raj with little turmoil or social dislocation.

The traditional Chinese concern for social morality also provided a cultural environment favorable to communism. Confucianism was a system of ethic rather than a metaphysic. The Confucian ideal was a state of social justice, insofar as this was feasible within the bureaucrat-landlord framework. The emphasis of Confucianism was on duties rather than rights, so that the child was brought up to define "self" in terms of relationships with other people—in terms of filial piety, brotherly deference and service to superiors, who in turn had reciprocal obligations. Thus the omnipresent Communist slogans of "Fight self" and "Serve the people" do not sound as unreal and Boy Scoutish to Chinese ears as they do to Western ears. Such slogans are quite congenial with the old peasant saying, "We may be poor people but we know right from wrong."

Finally, there is the crucial factor of Mao's role as leader of the revolution. There can be little doubt that Mao's historical significance for the twentieth-century world is comparable to that of Lenin. Future historians may well judge Mao's impact to have been greater, for Lenin died in 1924, when Soviet institutions and practices were still in the formative stage, whereas Mao engineered and directed not only the 1949 Political Revolution, which established the People's Republic of China, but also the 1966 Cultural Revolution, which determined the character and course of the People's Republic at least until his death in 1976.

Behind Mao's success was his profound faith in, and empathy for, the peasant masses of his country. In contrast to the Russian Bolsheviks, who were mostly urban intellectuals, Mao began life as a peasant. He did not read a newspaper until age eighteen, when he moved to the capital of his native province of Hunan. When he graduated from a normal school he was twenty-five years old, and not until two years later did he begin to learn about Marxism. This belated start proved a boon when Mao began his career as a revolutionary. Not being steeped in Marxist doctrines from childhood, as were most of the Bolshevik intellectuals, Mao was able to challenge, and, when necessary, to discard the most sacrosanct of Marxist dogma.

From the outset Mao was a shrewd observer of social realities. Not only was he born a peasant but also he lived and fought with the peasants for most of his life. In the course of this long grass-roots experience he came to realize keenly the need to make Marxism Chinese—to adapt it to the conditions and needs of China's hitherto ignored millions.

> There is no such thing as abstract Marxism, but only concrete Marxism. What we call concrete Marxism is Marxism that has taken on a national form, that is, Marxism applied to the concrete struggle in the concrete conditions prevailing in China. . . . If a Chinese Communist who is part of the great Chinese people, bound to his people by his very flesh and blood, talks of Marxism apart from Chinese peculiarities, this Marxism is merely an empty abstraction. The Sinification of Marxism . . . becomes a problem that must be understood and solved by the whole Party without delay.[5]

Throughout his career Mao was faithful to his principle of the "Sinification of Marxism." The three main examples of this are to be found in Kiangsi, where he shifted from the city proletariat to the peasants as the basis for revolution, and proceeded to organize rural soviets; in Yenan, where he shifted emphasis from social revolution to national resistance against the Japanese, and at the same time developed the "Yenan way" for mobilizing the masses into an invincible force; and in Peking, where he launched the Cultural Revolution so that Communist China would develop into a modern state on the basis of the egalitarian Yenan way rather than the elitist Russian way.

The roots of the Kiangsi shift are to be found in Mao's classic *Report of an Investigation into the Peasant Movement in Hunan*, published in March 1927, or before the Kuomintang-Communist split. The occasion was a widespread, spontaneous peasant revolution in Hunan, which Mao was instructed by his Party in investigate. He spent five weeks with the peasants, and then wrote what has become a classic of world revolutionary literature. Vibrant with passion and disdainful, if not unaware—of Lenin's dictum that "only the revolutionary proletariat can carry out the program of the poor peasants," Mao concluded from his firsthand observations that the "revolutionary vanguard" could only be the poor peasants:

> Within a short time, hundreds of millions of peasants will rise in Central, South, and North China, with the fury of a hurricane; no power, however strong, can restrain them. They will break all the shackles that bind them and rush towards the road of liberation. *All imperialists, warlords, corrupt officials, and bad gentry will meet their doom at the hands of the peasants.* All revolutionary parties and comrades will be judged by them. *Are we to get in front of them and lead them or criticize them behind their backs or fight them from the opposite camp?* Among these three alternatives every Chinese can choose freely, but the current situation demands a quick decision. . . .
>
> If you are a person of firm revolutionary ideology and visit the countryside, you will experience a satisfaction never felt before; tens of thousands of slaves—the peasants—are overthrowing their man-eating enemy. . . . All revolutionary comrades should realize that the national revolution requires a tremendous change in the villages. The Revolution of 1911 did not achieve such a change, and therefore it failed; now there is such a change, and it is one of the major factors in the accomplishment of the revolution. Every revolutionary comrade should support this movement; otherwise he is against the revolution. . . .[6]

With his characteristic sensitivity to objective reality, Mao had found a new proletariat for the Chinese revolution. True revolutionaries, he warned, must place themselves at the head of the peasants and lead them on to revolution, rather than lagging in the rear and applying the brakes. In a word, revolution in China could mean only agrarian revolution—a thesis that Mao steadfastly observed throughout his career.

Following the decimation of the urban Communist organizations by Chiang's coup in April 1927, Mao led a band of followers to the rugged mountainous region on the Hunan-Kiangsi border. There he was joined by a small group headed by the Communist military officer, Chu Teh. During the following years Mao and Chu developed political and military concepts and policies that clashed directly with those of the national party and the Comintern. Their basic tenets were:

• Hit-and-run guerrilla tactics were necessary to counter the superior manpower and resources of the Kuomintang.

• The prerequisite for successful guerrilla warfare was peasant support, which required rigid discipline and good behavior by the troops.

• The peasants were interested primarily in obtaining land, and their support therefore could not be retained unless the guerrillas helped them to revolt and to seize and redistribute the land.

• The revolutionary peasants could be protected against Kuomintang and landlord retaliation only by establishing a free territory or territorial base, which would also provide revenues and materials for the guerrillas, as well as a core from which the guerrillas could expand into surrounding territories.

On the basis of this strategy, Mao and Chu during the late 1920s organized their armed force and established political control over the liberated regions, or soviets. In November 1931 representatives from the various soviets met in Juichin, Kiangsi, and proclaimed the establishment of the Chinese Soviet Republic. Using the phraseology of the earlier Russian model, the new entity was described as a "democratic dictatorship of the proletariat and peasantry." The "proletariat," however, was conspicuous by its absence in this primitive rural area, the closest approximation being village artisans, handicraftsmen and farm hands. Legislation therefore was geared to satisfying peasant needs. Decrees provided for confiscation without compensation of lands belonging to "feudal barons and landlords, the *t'u-hao* [village bosses] and the gentry," as well as to "religious institutions or to temples." The expressed objective of this land redistribution was to "demolish the feudal order of society, destroy the power of the KMT, and build up the workers' and peasants' Soviet regime." [7]

The soviets were indeed a "disease of the heart," as Chiang Kai-shek put it, especially as the Chinese Soviet Republic grew to encompass some nine million people. Late in 1930 Chiang launched an "annihilation campaign," which failed to realize its objective as several more such campaigns proved necessary in the following years. The fifth, in late 1933, followed the directions of Chiang's German advisers. The central soviet area was tightly blockaded by a circle of fortifications, and the noose was drawn by building constricting circles of fortifications. The crisis was heightened by the intervention of the national Communist Party, which sent representatives to assume leadership of the defense. They lacked Chu Teh's mastery of guerrilla tactics, so that Chiang seemed about to attain his objective of "annihilating" the Communists.

Faced with this prospect, Mao decided to abandon the Kiangsi base. In the fall of 1934, the Red Army and all the Party's administrative personnel—totaling perhaps a hundred thousand—broke through the surrounding Kuomintang fortifications and began their historic Long March. The six thousand miles to Shensi in the Northwest were covered in one year and three days, averaging sixteen miles a day. With Kuomintang and hostile local forces in pursuit, the Red Army fought minor skirmishes every day, and major battles on at least fifteen days. About five thousand, at the most, survived the ordeal, along with several thousand more who joined along the route. Mao henceforth was their undisputed leader, rather than the urban-based functionaries backed by the Comintern.

Looking back on the fate of the Kiangsi soviet, Mao decided that its ultimate failure was due to lack of a sufficiently broad base among the local population. He decided to rectify this error by adopting a "New Democracy" program based on a broad anti-Japanese united front, and by evolving what came to be called the Yenan Way—a strategy for mobilizing the peasants behind the Communist Party and its People's Liberation Army. The slogans that were popularized stressed patriotism and self-sacrifice for nation rather than for class: "Everything subordinate to the war"; "Let those who have money give money, those who have guns give guns, and those who have knowledge give knowledge." [8]

A dramatic manifestation of the new United Front policy was the intercession of the Communists to secure the release of Chiang Kai-shek, who had been captured at Sian in December 1936 by the Manchurian warlord, Chang Hsüeh-liang. Chiang had flown to Sian to organize a more vigorous campaign against the Communists, but the Manchurians, whose homeland had been occupied by the Japanese for years, were more receptive to the United Front logic of Chinese fighting against the Japanese rather than against each other. Accordingly Chang arrested Chiang, whereupon Communist representatives arrived and unexpectedly urged his release. Apparently the Communists were motivated by the desire to prove the sincerity of their offer to end the civil war in order to fight Japan, and also by the fear that pro-Japanese elements would seize power in Nanking after Chiang and create even more disunity in the country. In any case, Chiang was set free, and in 1937 the Kuomintang and the Communist Party reached a United Front agreement in which the Communists agreed to accept Sun Yat-sen's *Three Principles*, give up armed rebellion and antilandlordism and place the Red Army under the National Government as the Eighth Route Army.

The Japanese decided to strike before Chinese national unification advanced any farther. In July 1937 they attacked near Peiping; the Chinese resisted and the Sino-Japanese war had begun. Faced with the technological superiority of the Japanese invaders, and being incapable of organizing Communist-type guerrilla resistance, Chiang Kai-shek decided to trade space for time. His armies retreated, while more than six hundred coastal factories were dismantled and moved to the interior. The Japanese were left in control of the northern and eastern provinces, where they installed a puppet government under a former Kuomintang leader, Wang Ching-wei.

Meanwhile, the Communist forces had been spreading rapidly from Yenan across the Yellow River into Shansi Province, and thence across the North China plains to the coastal Shantung Province. In 1937, by agreement with the Nationalists, the Communists created the New Fourth Army in the Lower Yangtze Basin, using remnants left over from the Kiangsi soviets. By 1945 the Communists were active in an area of over 250,000 square miles, and Party membership had risen from 40,000 in 1937 to 1.2 million in 1945. The Red Army had grown correspondingly, the estimates ranging from 45,000 to 90,000 in 1937 and from 500,000 to 900,000 in 1945. In addition to these Red Army regulars, the Communists had organized a People's Militia of over 2 million men. Also noteworthy were the large numbers of young men and women —students, journalists, artists and professionals of all types—who made the long trek to Yenan, which they viewed as the heart of Chinese resistance against the invaders.

An American scholar, Chalmers Johnson, has attributed the Communist success to the strength of Chinese nationalism. World War II and the Japanese invasion aroused mass nationalist feelings, which the Communists exploited by presenting themselves as patriotic leaders of the resistance against Japan. Communism, concludes Johnson, was falsely presented to the peasants as a "species of nationalist movement," and it was as such that it was able to win final victory.[9]

This analysis is true as far as it goes, but it does not go far enough. The Communists did win support as patriots, but they also won it as social revolutionaries, and the second appeal was at least as essential as the first. A French scholar, Lucien Bianco, makes this point by stating that the Kuomintang lost the civil war because "War puts every belligerent power to the test and shows up outmoded regimes for what they are." Mass support for the Communists, states Bianco, "lies less in the anti-Japanese activities of the party's cadres and the Red Army's officers and men than in their unprecedented conduct and responsiveness to the people's needs":

> The high and mighty district magistrate before whom one prostrated oneself gave way to a "delegate" who brought his camp bed with him and could hardly be distinguished from the local villagers. Above all, the way the Eighth Route Army behaved toward the peasants contradicted their entire previous experience of the military. What strange soldiers they were; who paid for what they bought, cleaned up the rooms they stayed in, mingled socially with the villagers, and were not above lending a hand in the fields!
>
> Why did the Communists succeed in winning over the peasant masses? Because in addition to being authentic patriots they were genuine revolutionaries, men who understood the needs of the people, knew what changes had to be made, and set about making them.[10]

The Communists "understood the needs of the people" and how to satisfy them because of the Yenan Way—the second outstanding example of Mao's Sinification of Marxism. This was not merely a way of fighting but also a way of life, a vision of man and society, and an approach to development based on mass participation and egalitarian values.

The roots of the Yenan Way go back at least to the Kiangsi soviets, but its accelerated evolution occurred as a response to the twofold crisis confronting the Communists in 1942. One was external—the simultaneous onslaught on the Communist base areas by a Japanese offensive and a Kuomintang blockade. Japanese intelligence estimated that during that year the population of the base areas shrank from forty-four million to twenty-five million and the Eighth Route Army from four hundred thousand to three hundred thousand men. The second aspect of the crisis was internal—the failure of land redistribution to change traditional patterns of life and work in the isolated villages. Tenancy had been largely eliminated but the peasants now concentrated on their individual plots, so that agricultural techniques remained primitive and productivity low.

Mao's Sinification of his Party is apparent in the two measures taken to meet the crisis: a thorough program for cadre self-criticism and retraining, and several campaigns to stimulate mass participation by the peasants and to maximize the bonds between cadres and peasants. The self-criticism and retraining was needed because the Party membership had increased some twenty-five times within three years after the outbreak of the war with Japan in 1937. Hundreds of thousands of members now underwent nine months of study, criticism and self-criticism. This included exhaustive discussion of twenty-two writings, of which between six and thirteen had been written by Mao, and only six were of Russian origin. During this process the cadres were re-educated, institutions were critically appraised and new leaders were accepted who had demonstrated their ability in the group sessions, where rank was ignored.

This rectification movement was followed by the campaigns to mobilize the peasants and to reduce the gap between them and the cadres. The depth and scope of these campaigns is indicated by the following expressed objectives, which were largely realized:

• Reduce and curb bureaucracy in the government, Party and army, and encourage lower-level leadership and popular participation.

• Assign cadres to the villages to teach and also work with, and learn from, the peasants, and thereby to bridge the gap between city and country, and between mental and manual labor.

• Organize cooperatives to expand peasant concern from the family to the mutual-aid group and to the village, and thereby to restructure village economic patterns and facilitate sustained development.

• Open throughout the Communist territories day schools, night schools, winter schools and literary groups, all under local control, and designed to reach all segments of the population in order to spread literacy, teach fundamentals of health and hygiene, and propagate the concept of "serve the people."

The distinguishing characteristic of this Yenan Way was its emphasis on mass participation, its reliance on the creativity of the Chinese people and especially the peasants and its conviction that they could and would rid themselves of their age-old shackles of ignorance, poverty and exploitation. "The basic method of leadership," declared Mao on June 1, 1943, "is to sum up the views of the masses. Take the results back to the masses so that the masses can give them their firm support and so work out sound ideas for leading the work on hand." [11] This "mass line" concept, which undergirded the later Cultural Revolution as well as the Yenan Way, represented the basic insight derived by Mao and his followers from their long guerrilla experience. Leadership depended primarily on responsiveness to popular needs and aspirations, which could be ascertained only by constant contact with the peasants in the villages. In this way the energies and creativity of the masses could be released and harnessed for armed resistance, for economic development and for social transformation. Mao's triumphant entry into Peking in 1949 was made possible by the successful implementation of this "mass line."

It was also facilitated by the moderating of the original Communist policy of confiscating and redistributing landlord holdings. For the sake of the United Front, the Communists during the war required merely a reduction of rent and interest charges. But if landlords fled to Japanese-controlled cities or in any way cooperated with the Japanese, the Communists confiscated their property and divided it among the poor peasants.

If the Yenan Way is contrasted with what the Japanese and the Kuomintang had to offer to the peasants, then the reason for the Communist victory becomes clear. The Japanese army operated on the basis of its "three-all" policy—"burn all, kill all, loot all." It is understandable that millions of peasants decided that they were more likely to survive if they joined the Communist guerrilla detachments. The Kuomintang, with its pervasive corruption and runaway inflation, did not present a persuasive alternative to the Japanese. Official incompetence, grain hoarding and speculation so aggravated the 1942–43 famine that an estimated two million peasants died from starvation. When the Japanese invaded Honan in 1944 they met no resistance from the peasants. Instead the peasants in some cases attacked, disarmed and even killed Kuomintang soldiers.

World War II ended suddenly in August 1945. The Chinese had been fighting since 1937, in contrast to the Europeans, who were not involved until 1939, and the Americans, not involved until 1941. During those eight years of grueling warfare the Chinese had inflicted one quarter of the total casualties sustained by the Japanese on all fronts. But the devastation of human and natural resources endured by the Chinese was on a scale comparable to that sustained by the Russians. Yet the Chinese were now faced with four more years of civil war, for the defeat of Japan precipitated the long-building confrontation between the Kuomintang and the Communist Party.

The Kuomintang was by far the stronger force, at least on paper. It enjoyed a four to one superiority in number of troops, and a much greater superiority in arms and equipment. Furthermore, the Kuomintang was recognized internationally as the ruling body in China, and Chiang Kai-shek had won considerable prestige as the leader of the national resistance against Japan. On the day Japan surrendered (August 14, 1945), the Russians signed a treaty of friendship and alliance with Chiang's government. The most important provision was the Russian commitment to give moral and material aid only to the Nanking regime, and to hand over to it immediately all territories liberated by Soviet armies. On the same day, General Douglas MacArthur, supreme commander for the Allied powers, designated Chiang the sole authority empowered to accept the surrender of the Japanese in China.

Mao Tse-tung, however, had made clear his refusal to accept Mac-Arthur's directive. On August 10 Generalissimo Chiang Kai-shek had sent the following order to his nominal subordinate, General Chu Teh, commander-in-chief of the Eighth Route Army: "Remain in your positions and do not accept the surrender of any unit whatsoever of the Japanese army." But on the same day, Chu Teh had issued a precisely contradictory order to his forces: "Disarm all Japanese and puppet troops immediately, seize and take over cities and communication lines previously held by the Japanese or their Chinese lackeys." [12] On August 13 Mao supported Chu by announcing that he, Mao, considered the generalissimo's order entirely political and self-serving, and that the sacrifices and achievements of the Communist forces in the field had earned them the right to confront the enemy at the surrender table.

The issue was much more than legalistic quibbling. About 12.5 million Japanese troops and 1.7 million Japanese civilians were stationed in northern and eastern China. They were besieged by Communist forces rather than by the Kuomintang, which had retreated to southern and southwestern China. Thus if the Japanese surrendered to the surrounding Communists, the latter would become overnight the masters of the most developed and populous regions of the country.

Such a Communization of China was quite unacceptable to Washington. The basic objective of United States policy was to restore the prewar status quo in China, and then gradually to reform the country in order to make China a profitable field for American enterprise. This aim was in line with the overall strategy of building up an American-dominated "grand area" of global proportions (see Chapter 19, Section V). Thus banker Edwin A. Locke, Jr., who was President Truman's personal representative in China for economic affairs, stated at this time: "We want a China with close economic, political and psychological . . . ties with the U.S." He foresaw reasonable American investments that would industrialize such a China "on a thoroughly practical and realistic basis," thereby creating over a fifty-year period "a large permanent and growing market for U.S. goods. . . ." [13]

President Truman acted promptly to forestall the imminent takeover by the Chinese Communists. He ordered Japanese troops in China to "maintain order" until the arrival of American or Kuomintang forces. And to discourage the Japanese from surrendering to the Communists, he notified the Tokyo government that its troops would be guaranteed return to their homeland only if they surrendered to Kuomintang or American units. To back up this policy, the Americans in September and October 1945 airlifted Nationalist troops to key cities and communication points in northern and eastern China. At the same time, fifty thousand United States Marines from Okinawa occupied ports and airfields in Tsingtao, Tientsin and Peking.

Washington announced that the mission of the Marines was to repatriate the Japanese and to prevent civil war. But as Admiral David E. Barbey later pointed out, ". . . the Marines were in no hurry to have the Japanese withdraw, for they were useful allies. They protected the bigger cities and guarded the bridges and rail lines from Communist-led guerrillas." [14] Likewise a Marine lieutenant complained to a reporter that his men were asking him why they were stationed in North China. "As an officer I am supposed to tell them, but you can't tell a man that he's here to disarm Japanese when he's guarding the same railroad with Japanese." [15]

President Truman's measures were successful at the outset. Within three months after the war ended, the Nationalist government was in control of the chief cities and communication centers in the key coastal area from Canton to Peking. But the danger of civil war still remained, and Truman made every effort to forestall it because of the popular pressure "to bring the boys home," and the fear of becoming involved in another war in Asia.

On Christmas Eve of 1945 General George Marshall arrived in China to try to fend off the impending civil war. His mission ended in complete failure because the differences were irreconcilable. The Communists refused to submit their armies and territories to government control unless they were admitted into a coalition government in which they could genuinely participate in the decision-making process. Chiang Kai-shek promised political liberalization in the future but insisted that the Communists first disband their armies—a condition that the Communists rejected as tantamount to suicide. In the background were more fundamental, nonnegotiable differences. One side was bent on seizing power, the other on retaining it; one was determined to bring about social revolution, the other on thwarting it. By November 1946 the negotiations had collapsed and Chou En-lai left Chungking for Yenan for the last time.

The ensuing civil war began, as expected, with sweeping victories by the Nationalist armies. Within months they had taken Manchuria and North China, including the Communist capital of Yenan. But everywhere the Nationalists' control was limited to cities, which frequently were so surrounded by Communist guerrillas that they had to be supplied by airlifts. The government forces soon were overextended and vulnerable to the Communists, who had spread through the villages and isolated the cities. By late 1947 the Communists were strong enough to shift from guerrilla operations to positional warfare. First they overran

Manchuria and then proceeded to carve up the Kuomintang forces in North China. With remarkable speed the Communists continued southward to the Yangtze, and in April 1949 crossed that formidable barrier with little opposition. Plagued by low morale in the ranks and by dissension and corruption at the top, the Kuomintang armies disintegrated before the Red offensives. Nanking fell in April, Shanghai in May and Canton in October. Chiang Kai-shek fled to Taiwan with some two million troops and civilians. In Peking, Mao proclaimed the founding of the People's Republic of China on October 1, 1949. "The Chinese people have stood up," he declared before cheering multitudes in Tien An Men Square.

The crucial question now was whether the Yenan Way could be applied on a national as well as a local scale, and in a society in the process of industrialization as well as in a primitive rural community. Would the egalitarian socialism of Yenan give way to the meritocratic but bureaucratic socialism of the Soviet Union? The search for an answer to this question was to generate profound differences among the Communist Party leadership during Mao's lifetime, and even more after his death.

❦ *II. Yenan Way or Soviet Way?*

The first order of business after the Revolution was land reform, for the basic Communist commitment to the peasants had been "land to the tiller." In fact, when the People's Republic was established in 1949, land redistribution already had been carried out in one fifth of the country's villages. This was extended to the remaining four fifths by the Agrarian Reform Law of 1950, which distributed among landless and poor peasants the properties of landlords (4 percent of the rural population, who owned 30 percent of the cultivated land), and also the lands controlled by various religious and educational institutions. But rich peasants, comprising 6 percent of the rural population and responsible for nearly half of agricultural output, were allowed to keep the lands they cultivated themselves or with hired labor, as well as land they rented to tenants equal to the acreage they cultivated themselves and with hired help. This measure represented a social but not an economic revolution. Traditional agricultural technology remained unchanged, so that increase in grain food production barely kept up with population growth. Land reform had not lightened the age-old burden of rural poverty; rather it distributed it more equitably. Party leaders realized that land reform had to be supplemented with modernization of agricultural techniques and with development of industry.

To achieve these economic advances, Mao turned to the Soviet Union. He had no alternative, as repeated overtures to Washington were ignored. In the 1950 Sino-Soviet Treaty of Assistance, Mao agreed to recognize the independence of Mongolia, and to accept continued joint Sino-Soviet administration of Manchuria and joint use of Port Arthur and of the Changchung Railway. In return for these substantial concessions, he got credits of $300 million, a commitment of aid for the industrialization of China, and an arrangement for Russian and East European ships to transport cargoes to Chinese ports, thereby breaking the Nationalist blockade and the American embargo.

China benefited enormously from this pact with the Soviet Union. It was not so much the Russian financial aid, for that amounted to only 3 percent of total Chinese state investment in the first Five Year Plan. More significant was the contribution of Soviet technology and Soviet experience in centralized economic planning. Over twelve thousand Russian and East European engineers and technicians went to China in the 1950s, while over six thousand Chinese students attended Russian universities and some seven thousand Chinese workers gained experience in Soviet factories. Some two hundred complete industrial plants were shipped to China, and detailed blueprints were provided for many more factories and construction projects. As a result, the Five Year Plans proved as successful in boosting production in China as in the Soviet homeland. GNP growth in China between 1950 and 1966 was almost 6 percent per annum, or roughly equal to that of the Soviet Union between 1928–38 and 1950–66.

Despite this progress, Mao became progressively disenchanted and apprehensive about the extreme dependence on the Soviet Union. One reason was political—the efforts of the Russians to make China a satellite similar to those in Eastern Europe. This was especially true in Manchuria, where most Soviet aid was concentrated. The local governor, Kao Kang, was so close to the Russians that he was purged in 1954 on the charge that he was seeking to establish an "independent kingdom." Likewise in 1958, when Chiang Kai-shek assembled two hundred thousand troops on Quemoy Island, a stone's throw from the Chinese mainland, Nikita Khrushchev demanded, in return for Russian aid, that Soviet naval and air bases be established at the principal Chinese ports. Mao responded that he would take to the hills and begin a new resistance movement before accepting such a demand.

Mao also had misgivings about the basic assumptions of the Five Year Plans, though originally he had embraced them enthusiastically. But now he questioned the rationality of slighting agriculture and the peasants, who comprised over 80 percent of the total population, and he was dubious about capital-intensive technology amid capital scarcity and labor surplus. Perhaps most disturbing to Mao was the incompatibility of Soviet development strategy with the fundamental principles of the

Yenan Way. In place of the "mass line," with its emphasis on grass-roots creativity and participation, Mao perceived an emerging bureaucracy effecting a peaceful transition from socialism to capitalism in China, as he believed had already occurred in the Soviet Union and Eastern Europe. Learning from their "negative example," Mao was reinforced in his conviction that political and economic revolution does not suffice without a simultaneous revolution in men's minds—without a new morality placing public interest before private. Hence the repeated efforts during these years to create the "new man."

One manifestation of Mao's growing independence was his reversal of Soviet rural strategy in pressing for collectivization before mechanization. The 1950 land reform had transformed China into a land of peasant owner-cultivators but had failed to increase productivity. Also, the Five Year Plans were financing urban industrialization at the expense of the rural economy. Poor peasants were being forced to sell out and flock to the cities, causing serious urban unemployment and underemployment— the all-pervasive curse of Third World countries. The Communist leaders were concerned about an emerging *kulak* class in the countryside, which would restore and consolidate rural class differentiation if collectivization were delayed for decades until industrialization was sufficiently advanced. Mao therefore launched in 1952 a three-stage program for transforming individual peasant proprietorship to collective farming.

Starting with mutual-aid teams in which the members helped each other in the working of their still individual family farms, the second stage involved "lower" producer cooperatives in which land was farmed cooperatively but families retained private ownership of the land and divided the proceeds according to the amount of labor and property contributed. The final stage consisted of "higher" cooperative farms in which private land ownership was excluded and members were paid on the basis of the socialist principle of "to each according to his labor."

The transition from one stage to another was much faster than anticipated. By 1955 about 65 percent of peasant households were in mutual aid teams, with another 15 percent in "lower" cooperatives. Then came a big spurt, so that by the summer of 1956 there were 100 million households (90 percent of the total peasant population) in 485,000 higher cooperatives, and by the 1957 spring planting the remainder of the population had joined. In comparison with Soviet collectivization, the transformation of the Chinese villages was remarkably peaceful. One reason was that in Russia, two thirds of the rural population consisted of "middle class" peasants who aspired to kulak status and therefore resisted collectivization. In China, by contrast, two thirds of the peasants were, in Mao's words, "badly off," and therefore receptive to radical institutional change. Also, the Chinese Communist Party, in contrast to the Russian, consisted mostly of peasants who were able to organize a genuine mass movement from below. Unlike Stalin, Mao had neither the inclination nor the need to impose a violent "revolution from above."

The other major manifestation of Mao's rejection of the Soviet model was his launching in 1958 of the Great Leap Forward. This is commonly identified with communes and backyard production, but it involved a good deal more. It was an unprecedented campaign to indoctrinate the entire population with "correct" ideology. The rallying cry was for everyone to be "red and expert," with the aim of narrowing the gap between the masses and the political-technical elites. The rationale was that it was feasible to have a simultaneous technological revolution and social revolution, and that the latter was the prerequisite for the former. In asserting that "proletarianization must precede mechanization," Mao rejected the Stalinist orthodoxy that industrialization combined with state ownership of the means of production ensured the eventual development of a Communist society.

In industry, the Great Leap Forward was a campaign to replace material incentives such as piece rates for workers and bonuses for managers, with nonmaterial incentives such as emulation drives and honorary titles. Another innovation in industry was "the policy of walking on two legs" —namely, developing a dual industrial economy integrating modern capital-intensive plants with local labor-intensive units. The latter included small rural hydroelectric stations built with local labor and raw materials, and backyard steel furnaces, again using local labor and ore and fuel resources.

In agriculture the Great Leap Forward involved the combining of the existing cooperatives, which had evolved from earlier mutual-aid teams, into twenty-six thousand communes. The rationale for these large units was to make efficient use of the hitherto underemployed rural labor for land reclamation, water conservation and afforestation—all essential for increased agricultural productivity. The communes also contributed to the making of the "new man" by transforming isolated peasant communities into an interdependent complex of communes capable not only of stimulating agriculture and industry, but also of organizing welfare, educational, cultural and health services, as well as communal laundries and grain mills, which freed women for work in field and factory.

The Great Leap Forward is generally considered to have been a failure. The backyard furnaces were inefficient and produced steel of inferior quality. The amount of labor siphoned off to urban and commune industries upset the rural economy. Also, some communes experimented unsuccessfully with full communism by basing income on need rather than on work. These difficulties were aggravated by the "three bitter years" of natural disasters (1960–62) and by the withdrawal of Soviet support in 1960. The Russians viewed as impractical romanticism Mao's reliance on revolutionary mass zeal rather than on the technical and administrative competence of managers, engineers and bureaucrats. Yet the Great Leap Forward was not entirely negative in its results. There was some positive residue, including important technological experience for millions of peasants, the success of a considerable number of new local industries (small shale-oil plants and small chemical works producing acid, soda, fertilizer and insecticides) and the completion of huge public works on such an incredible scale that in a single year, October 1957 to September 1958, the mobilized peasantry removed fifty-eight billion cubic meters of stone and earth, equal to three hundred Panama Canals. Noteworthy is the firsthand observation of David and Nancy Milton that "it was the firm view of the peasants that without this new form of extensive farming [the communes] they could never have dealt with the exigencies of the natural disasters." [16]

Nevertheless, the period 1960–65 was one of retreat from the Great Leap Forward. Communes were decentralized in organization and reduced in size, so that their total number rose from twenty-six thousand in 1958 to seventy-eight thousand in 1966. Also, the peasants were encouraged to cultivate private plots and to sell the produce in open markets. Material incentives were restored in industry, and by August 1961, Foreign Minister Ch'en Yi was stating that not everyone could be "red and expert" and that China desperately needed experts who should not be criticized for devoting less time to politics. Mao found it necessary to relinquish his post as Chairman of the People's Republic to Liu Shao-ch'i. "I was most dissatisfied with that decision," Mao observed later, "but there was nothing I could do about it. . . . At that time most people disagreed with me. They said my views were out of date . . . it appeared probable that revisionism would triumph, and that we would lose." [17]

By 1965 China seemed to have returned in most respects to the Soviet road of development, based on bureaucratic elitism and marked income differentiation. A. Doak Barnett, writing on the eve of the Cultural Revolution, observed:

> One of the most significant trends in recent years has been the seemingly irresistible growth of complex bureaucratic patterns of social stratification even within the ranks of the Party cadres in Communist China. The Party has tried in many ways to resist these trends—for example, by promoting physical labor by cadres, sending personnel to work in rural areas, and taking such drastic steps as abolishing ranks within the army—but as the egalitarian heritage of active revolutionary struggle has tended to recede into the background, deep-rooted authoritarian and bureaucratic predispositions,

especially the tendency to differentiate people by rank, have re-asserted themselves.[18]

If Mao had died at this point, as Lenin had died at an even earlier stage of Soviet evolution, the crucial question of Yenan Way or Soviet Way would have been settled then in favor of the latter. But Mao lived on, and he refused to give up the egalitarian wartime vision and to accept social regression as the price of economic growth. He set out to reverse the revisionism personified by Khrushchev in Russia and by Liu Shao-ch'i at home. This required a decade-long struggle of two stages: the first an external struggle to break loose from the control exerted by the Soviet Union, and the second an internal struggle to break the power of the Chinese advocates of the Soviet model of modernization.

III. Great Proletarian Cultural Revolution

Mao's break with the Soviet Union was precipitated in June 1959 when Khrushchev suddenly abrogated the nuclear-sharing agreement made with China two years earlier. The underlying reason for this move was Khrushchev's desire for détente with the United States as well as an alliance with China. But Washington, by maintaining its hard-line pressure on China, forced Khrushchev to choose between détente and alliance. Khrushchev opted for détente, one reason being that the death of Secretary of State John Foster Dulles and the accession of Christian Herter to that post had increased the possibility for meaningful détente. Also, Khrushchev viewed the Chinese as unorthodox and unreliable allies who were given to "wild pseudorevolutionary" experiments and who could scarcely be trusted with nuclear weapons, especially if the price would be the détente with America. Hence the series of Soviet decisions reflecting the choice of détente over alliance, including the refusal to support China in her border dispute with India, the withdrawal of ten thousand Soviet technicians from China and the decision to sign the nuclear-test-ban treaty (1963) over China's objections.

The Soviet pursuit of détente was behind the great polemical exchange between Russia and China in 1963–64. To use the terminology of Mao's own Marxism-Leninism, he was beginning by 1964 to view the Soviet Union in terms of an antagonistic rather than merely a nonantagonistic contradiction. This was to lead in a few years to official Chinese doctrines equating Soviet "social imperialism" with American "imperialism," and eventually to categorizing "social imperialism" as the ascendant force and therefore as enemy No. 1.

With the external enemy pinpointed and pilloried, Mao turned against the domestic champions of revisionism. Since they were entrenched in the Party and state apparatuses, Mao took a step that was unprecedented for a head of state. With the backing of the People's Liberation Army (PLA) headed by Lin Piao, Mao waged revolution by calling on the students organized in the Red Guards "to struggle against and crush those persons in authority who are taking the capitalist road." These "capitalist roaders," as they were called, were accused of elitism in their attitude to workers and of using their positions to protect and extend their privileges. "Taking the capitalist road" thus meant obstructing socialism in the superstructure, which eventually would lead to destruction of the socialist base.

In late 1966, millions of Red Guards rampaged through city streets and rural areas, carrying portraits of Mao and waving copies of his "little red book." They "arrested" officials and forced them to confess their "crimes" at public rallies. They branded Liu Shao-chi'h as the "leading capitalist roader," and Teng Hsiao-p'ing as the "second leading capitalist roader." By the end of 1966 the Red Guards had performed their assigned role of undermining the Party and state establishment. But Peking now discovered that the young revolutionaries could not be reined in at will. PLA efforts to restore order provoked a violent reaction against all authority. In the major industrial city of Wuhan, the factionalism between two rival mass organizations reached the point of armed confrontation and raised the specter of civil war.

Most threatening for Peking was the establishment on February 5, 1967, of the Shanghai People's Commune. Modeled after the 1871 Paris Commune, its worker members demanded direct participatory self-rule with no intermediaries, whether state or Party organs. This was too much for Mao, who now turned against the forces he had unleashed. When the Shanghai revolutionaries demanded the abolition of all "heads," Mao responded: "This is extreme anarchism, it is most reactionary. . . . In reality there will still always be heads." To eliminate the danger of "extreme anarchism," Mao ordered the replacement of the communes that had appeared in Shanghai and a few other cities, with "revolutionary committees" based on what was called the "triple alliance" of mass revolutionary organizations, pro-Maoist Party cadres and the PLA—with the last possessing the military power and therefore being the dominant partner. Mao then used the PLA to restore order on campuses, and he sent the students off to the countryside to be "re-educated by the peasants." In the light of later charges against the radical "Gang of Four" associated with Mao, it is noteworthy that as late as 1967 it was anything but radical in its dealings with the Shanghai People's Commune.

The disbandment of the Shanghai People's Commune and of the Red Guards did not signify that the Cultural Revolution had been all in vain. A hurricane of such elemental proportions inevitably had some lasting consequences. In view of the concerted campaign after Mao's death to denigrate the significance of the Cultural Revolution, it is noteworthy that Mao assessed it as an historical event comparable to the preceding liberation of the country from the Japanese and the Kuomintang. In his later years he defined two great objectives to which he had dedicated his life: "Driving Japanese imperialism out of China and overthrowing Chiang Kai-shek, on the one hand, and, on the other, carrying through the Great Proletarian Cultural Revolution." [19]

So far as daily life was concerned, the influence of the Cultural Revolution was felt mostly in the countryside. Despite the fact that the Revolution was primarily an urban movement, the big winners were the peasants. They benefited from the elimination of the former cadre corruption in workpoint allocation for collective labor. Most important for the peasants was the massive revival of programs for rural industrialization. Local labor and raw materials were used to supply local markets with tools, simple machinery, insecticides, fertilizers and consumer goods. By the early 1970s, 60 percent of China's chemical fertilizer and 40 percent of the cement output were supplied by rural factories, while one third of all hydroelectric power was generated by small local stations. In the southern provinces so many small, peasant-operated coal mines were opened that the traditional dependence on coal from the urban North had almost ended. On the outskirts of Peking the Red Star Commune had a powdered-milk factory, flour mill, soybean oil mill and seed oil mill—all of which processed local products—as well as small workshops to which nearby urban factories farmed out the manufacture of parts, such as sewing-machine fixtures, small cables and wire, light switches and lamp holders.

These new rural enterprises lessened the chronic village underemployment, transformed many peasants into full- or part-time industrial workers, increased substantially the purchasing power of rural inhabitants and generated new capital for further investments in both rural industry and agriculture. All this represented an alternative to the pervasive Third World pattern of urbanization without industrialization. The Cultural Revolution offered a strategy for achieving the precise opposite—industrialization without urbanization.

A final benefit derived by the peasants from the Cultural Revolution was a substantial increase in locally controlled medical and educational services. Small communes were provided with at least one clinic with simple equipment and a few doctors and nurses prepared to treat the most common rural ailments—diarrhea, flu and bronchitis—and to perform relatively simple operations such as appendectomies. Large communes boasted several clinics, a well-equipped hospital, and two or three dozen doctors who performed all but the most complicated operations, which they referred to the regional hospital. In addition to treating their patients, doctors also trained the "barefoot doctors" to provide basic medical care. And if the number of patients dwindled, as happened in certain seasons, then the doctors left their clinics and joined the peasants working in the fields.

Educational facilities also varied, depending on the size of the commune, from a few elementary and secondary schools to an establishment including an agricultural school and an experimental and research station working to improve seed and livestock strains. During the Cultural Revolution the admissions criteria and curricula in middle schools and universities were changed to enhance opportunities for rural youth. Several years of productive work in agriculture or industry, together with letters of recommendation from fellow workers, became prerequisites for admission to universities, and students were expected to return to work in their home areas after graduation. In short, the Cultural Revolution promoted what foreign observers have termed "a policy of positive discrimination," which is comparable to the "affirmative action" introduced in the United States on behalf of underprivileged minorities.

As significant as the impact of the Cultural Revolution on the Chinese countryside was its contribution to revolutionary theory and practice. During these years, Mao elaborated the proposition that every revolution engenders its own contradictions, so that after overthrowing the old ruling classes, it is then necessary to recognize and confront a "new bourgeoisie" inevitably emerging from the revolution itself. The process of economic development, asserted Mao, requires the training of large numbers of administrative and technological experts who can, as they did in the Soviet Union, become a new ruling elite.

Stalin also had sought to prevent a privileged stratum from entrenching itself in the Party and state hierarchy, but his methods were periodic purges and reshuffling of the elite. Having failed to organize a mass base as a counterbalance to the elite, and to infuse the schools and all society with a socialist morality, his death left a vacuum that was quickly filled by his entrenched enemies. Mao's historic contribution in waging the Cultural Revolution was that he was the first Marxist head of state to unleash a new type of class war—a war against the growing "new class" acquiring hereditary privilege in socialist society. By the end of the Cultural Revolution the bureaucracy of the central government had shrunk from sixty-thousand to ten-thousand, and there was a corresponding reduction of the managerial ranks in factories and communes.

In addition to attacking the "capitalist roaders," Mao encouraged the development of a variety of what might be termed "counterinstitutions" to forestall the reappearance of revisionism and to promote egalitarianism and mass participation.

• *Example:* an egalitarian educational system that after the Cultural Revolution stressed community control and the combining of study with physical labor from the elementary grades through the university.

• *Example:* political indoctrination designed to inculcate the qualities of the "new Maoist man," involving literally the entire population in regular study and discussion of Marxism-Leninism-Maoism and of current affairs.

• *Example:* mass representation and participation in the Revolutionary Committees, which were elected by the members of all institutions, whether factories, communes, hospitals, schools, hotels, army units, etc.

• *Example:* criticism and self-criticism sessions on a nationwide scale, allowing each person to seek the understanding and help of others in recognizing and changing feelings, attitudes and actions that serve "self" instead of the people.

• *Example: hsia fang* or going down principle, providing that those at the top of any institution must spend at least two months per year working at the bottom, so that factory managers worked on production lines, university professors cleaned dormitory rooms, surgeons scrubbed operating rooms, and hotel managers worked in kitchens.

• *Example:* May 7 schools or farms, where cadres such as teachers, state administrators and Party functionaries did physical labor periodically for three-to-six-month periods.

These counterinstitutions appear to have had some effect, as indicated by the list compiled by Barry Richman of terms commonly used to describe the characteristics of the Chinese people before the revolution and today. Typical words used before 1949 were ". . . suspicion, nepotism, despotism, favoritism, corruption, the dominance of conservative ruling elites, avoidance of responsibility, venality, face-saving at any cost, sloth, a lust for money, emphasis on family loyalty. . . ." Current visitors to China, on the other hand, describe their impressions with adjectives such as ". . . hard-working, dedicated, self-sacrificing, nationalistic, proud, pragmatic, flexible, well-disciplined, clear, resourceful, energetic, entrepreneurial, inventive, productive, well-motivated, honest, puritanical, sincere, cooperative with each other, thifty, frugal, respectful of the virtues and dignity of labor. . . ." [20]

The above adjectives may seem unrealistic in view of the negative post-Mao interpretations of Maoism, both within China and without. But current Chinese criticisms of the Maoist era are in accord with the tradition of each new dynasty or regime rewriting the history of its predecessor. Thus David and Nancy Milton observed with surprise the disparagement of post-1949 achievements by the supporters of the Cultural Revolution:

Many of the remarkable achievements which, in 1964, had been credited to the Chinese Revolution were now attributed solely to the Cultural Revolution. We were startled to hear from various individuals that they had never been self-critical, had never done manual labor, had never been aware of the peasants, had never thought of serving the people before the awakening experience of the Cultural Revolution. Perhaps they were a breed of person whom we had never encountered before the Cultural Revolution, for we had previously met no one to whom these ideas would have come as revelations.[21]

The Hua-Teng team followed this traditional pattern in belittling the achievements of the preceding Maoist era. The "Gang of Four" now is held responsible for virtually all current problems and failures, and the years of the Cultural Revolution are commonly stigmatized as "ten lost years."

Equally derogatory are most Western estimates of Maoism, and understandably so. The anti-intellectualism of the Cultural Revolution offended Western academic circles, while the striving for egalitarianism and self-reliance threatened Western economic interests. Thus *Time* magazine welcomed Teng Hsiao-p'ing as its "Man of the Year," while most Western scholars, according to Maurice Meisner, "have viewed with relative favor the periods in the history of the People's Republic that have seen the growth of modern-style bureaucratic structures (such as the early and mid-1950s and the early 1960s) and have condemned as abnormal and aberrant such Maoist-inspired eras as the Great Leap and the Cultural Revolution for having violated the dictates of 'bureaucratic professionalism' and 'instrumental rationality.' "[22]

One of the most serious charges levied against the Cultural Revolution is that it damaged the national economy because it overemphasized moral incentives at the expense of material. This accusation is groundless for two basic reasons. One is that Maoist economic strategy and institutions were carefully designed to link personal advancement and community welfare. In his analysis entitled "Maoism and Motivation," economist Carl Riskin notes:

> . . . funds for the establishment and expansion of schools, hospitals, clinics, old age homes, cultural and recreational facilities, increasingly are coming from the incomes of the local units which they will serve. . . . By permitting the teams and brigades to keep enough of their net income to take responsibility for such undertakings, rather than siphoning off this income in the form of taxes or price differentials to be reallocated centrally, the state provides the collective material incentives to spur socialism locally. . . .

The evolving system seems to permit increasing equality of distribution to coexist with the retention of material incentives.[23]

The second reason for discounting the Hua-Teng charge of economic deterioration is that it simply did not occur. The National Foreign Assessment Center of the Central Intelligence Agency issued statistics in 1977 concerning China's economic growth that reflected not the alleged regression, but rather substantial economic progress. In 1978 the CIA issued another analysis of China's economy, and again concluded that the record was one of "impressive, but uneven, economic growth":

> China's GNP by 1975 was some 2.7 times that of 1957, the final year of the First Five-Year Plan. With population growing at an annual average rate of over 2 percent, this works out to per capita GNP growth of just over 3 percent yearly. An overwhelming share of this growth has come from industry, where output has expanded at an average annual rate of about 4 percent. In contrast, as one would expect of a sector employing traditional, centuries-old production technologies on relatively fixed land area, agriculture has grown much more slowly—2 percent annually, or approximately the same rate as population growth.[24]

More significant than these statistics is the fact that they were attained without the dehumanizing extremes of wealth for the few and poverty for the many. No one can say of Maoist China what the President of Brazil said of his own country: "Brazil is doing well but Brazilians are not." There was no parallel in China to the report of Brazil's Finance Minister that "for 1960 the poorest 40 percent [of the population earned] 11.2 percent of the total income and in 1970 hardly 9 percent." [25]

◆ IV. After Mao

When Mao died on September 9, 1976, he was as keenly aware of the fragility of his achievements as Lenin had been of his a half century earlier. Mao expressed this awareness when President Nixon visited him in Peking in February 1972 and said, "The Chairman's writings moved a nation and have changed the world." Mao replied, "I have not been able to change it. I have only been able to change a few places in the vicinity of Peking." [26] Likewise, just as Lenin had referred caustically to his Soviet creation as "a bourgeois and Tsarist hotch-potch," so Mao on the eve of his death not only insisted on the need for repeated Cultural Revolutions but also declared, "You are making the socialist revolution, and yet you don't know where the bourgeoisie is. It is right in the Communist Party—those in power taking the capitalist road. The capitalist roaders are still on the capitalist road." [27]

Mao's apprehension was fully vindicated by developments after his death. The memorial address was delivered by Hua Kuo-feng, who had been appointed earlier in the year as acting Premier, bypassing the higher-ranking Teng Hsiao-p'ing, who was denounced at the time by Mao as a person who "knows nothing of Marxism-Leninism," who "represents the bourgeoisie" and "who can't be counted on." Hua praised the Cultural Revolution, which had "smashed the schemes of Liu Shao-chi, and Teng Hsiao-p'ing for restoration." But on October 6, less than a month after Mao's death, Hua executed his *coup d'état* by arresting the so-called "Gang of Four," consisting of Mao's wife, Chiang Ch'ing, the press czar, Yao Wen-yuan and two Shanghai leaders, Wang Hung-wen and Chang Ch'un-ch'iao. Just as Lin Piao had been deposed as an "ultra-leftist" by the Maoists, so the latter were deposed as "revisionists masquerading as ultraleftists." On October 8 the Central Committee under dubious circumstances designated Premier Hua as its chairman and as commander-in-chief of the army. More startling was the rehabilitation of Teng, who by July 1977 had been appointed vice premier, vice chairman of the Party and assistant chief of staff of the army.

Within less than a year, the same Teng who had been dismissed by Mao as an "unrepentant capitalist roader" had become the power behind Hua and the *de facto* successor of Mao. One reason for this dramatic reversal was the restrictive anti-intellectualism of the group around Mao. Populism was carried to sectarian and xenophobic extremes, so that the development of science and the arts was seriously disrupted by excessive controls over publications, performances and contacts with the outside world. Such coercion naturally alienated the majority of intellectuals, who readily supported the campaign against the Gang of Four.

A more basic reason for the political turnabout in China was the contradiction between Mao's theory and practice regarding mass self-determination. Mao heartily agreed with Lenin when the latter insisted that the Soviets should be organs of government *by* the people rather than *for* the people. This crucial principle was enunciated during the Cultural Revolution in the Communist Party's "Sixteen Points" (Aug. 8, 1966): "The only method is for the masses to liberate themselves, and any method of doing things on their behalf must not be used." (Point 4) The following year (Jan. 9, 1967) a new series of guidelines stipulated: "Of all the ways for the revolutionary masses to take their destiny into their own hands, in the final analysis the only way is to take power! Those who have power have everything; those who are without power have nothing. . . . We, the worker, peasant, and soldier masses, are the indisputable masters of the new world." [28]

But when the Shanghai People's Commune attempted to put the above theory into practice, Mao reversed himself, insisting that the Party was indispensable: "If everything were changed into the Commune, then what about the Party? Where would we place the Party? . . . There must be a party somehow. There must be a nucleus, no matter what we call it." [29] Mao also insisted that Party cadres should be re-educated rather than expelled: "Cadres who have made errors should be treated correctly and should not be overthrown indiscriminately . . . unless they persist in their errors and refuse to correct them after repeated education." [30]

In actuality it was the Party that was deradicalized rather than its cadres re-educated. Most of the old provincial Party leaders, unconverted and unrepentant, were reappointed to high offices, though in provinces other than those they had governed in 1966, so as to avoid embarrassment. Likewise the old Communist Youth League replaced the Red Guards, and a trade union federation replaced the workers' congresses. By August 26, 1971, the *People's Daily* was proclaiming: "Now the new Party committees have been established at all levels, the Party's unified leadership must be efficiently reinforced." The paper stressed the necessity for "absolute submission of state and army to the Party." The "absolute submission" was exacted, but the price was the repudiation of the essence of the Cultural Revolution. The "revolutionary masses" obviously had not "liberated themselves." They had not emerged as the "indisputable masters of the new world."

Meanwhile, as dramatic a reversal was occurring in Chinese foreign policy as in its domestic policy. In 1967 Mao had declared China "the political, military and technical center of world revolution." But he abandoned this global revolutionary vision with the Soviet invasion of Czechoslovakia (August 1968) and with the proclamation of the "Brezhnev doctrine" of "limited sovereignty" for socialist countries. For Peking, the threat was serious, with over one million Russian troops on the Sino-Soviet border, and with the Kremlin threatening a "pre-emptive" attack on Chinese nuclear installations. To counter the menace from the North, Mao and Chou En-lai ended what support they had given to world revolution and sought a tactical accord with the United States. The end result was Henry Kissinger's visit to Peking in July 1971, and Richard Nixon's in February 1972.

The chief opponent of this reversal of domestic and foreign policies was Lin Piao, who had become identified with the radical elements in the Cultural Revolution. At one time Mao's official heir apparent, Lin now refused to support the rapprochement with the United States and the deradicalization of the Party. But the combination of Mao and Chou was too much for Lin. Between the Kissinger and Nixon visits he disappeared from public view, and in July 1972 it was announced that he had plotted to assassinate Mao and had perished in a plane crash in Mongolia while fleeing to the Soviet Union.

With the removal of Lin Piao, two rival groups jockeyed for position during Mao's last days. One, led by those later branded as the Gang of Four, was closer to Mao and sought to use his prestige to preserve the radical vestiges of the Cultural Revolution. The second group, comprising Party leaders, veterans of the Long March and close associates of Chou, favored modernization with the reconstituted Party in absolute command. The former group dominated the national media, the leading universities and cultural affairs, but the latter controlled the levers of power in the army, the Party, the national economy and the provinces. It was the latter group, therefore, that was able to seize power soon after Mao's death.

The new regime under Hua Kuo-feng and Teng Hsiao-p'ing set out to implement Chou's earlier call for a national mobilization to make China a great world power by the end of the century. This was to be achieved through the "four modernizations"—in agriculture, in industry, in national defense and in science and technology. Modernization per se can only be welcomed, as it involves increased productivity and correspondingly higher living standards. But the crucial question is the social context and results of modernization. The answer to that question is evident in Hua's "Report on the Work of the Government," delivered on the opening day of the Second Session of the Fifth People's Congress (June 18, 1979). The report included the following dictums:

• No fundamental conflict of interests exists among workers, peasants and intellectuals.
• Class enemies consist of criminals, enemy agents, and remnants of the "Gang of Four" and of the landlord class.
• Class struggle no longer is the "principal contradiction" in Chinese society, so the "central task" is to support "socialist modernization." In promoting socialist modernization, "the ultimate aim is to realize the great Communist ideal of 'from each according to his ability, to each according to his needs.' " [31]

Hua underscored the primacy of productivity above all other considerations in a speech to the National Finance and Trade Conference (July 7, 1978):

> . . . many aspects of our superstructure and relations of production are still not perfect. . . . We should have the courage to face up to and expose those things in our concrete policies, rules and regulations, working methods and ideological concepts that are not

in harmony with the goal of the four modernizations, and have the gumption to transform, firmly and in appropriate manner, those aspects of the superstructure and the relations of production that are not in harmony with the productive forces.[32]

The significance of the above political tenets is obvious. In contrast to Mao, who warned of a new ruling class emerging from privileged cadres and intellectuals, Hua sees danger only in "bad" elements and in social remnants from the past. In contrast to Mao, who insisted on the simultaneous transformation of the superstructure (ownership and work relations) along with the forces of production (technology and labor skills), Hua refers vaguely to "ultimate aims" that cannot begin to be realized until productivity and modernization reach some appropriate level. Finally, with class struggle relegated to a minor contradiction, almost any labor-management relations can be justified so long as productivity is increased, and demands for worker decision-making power can be dismissed as "ultraleft." All of this obviously could prove to be precursory to a new ruling elite of managers, technicians and Party-state cadres.

These and other statements by Hua did not save him from the "pragmatists" who distrusted him because of his ambiguous role under Mao, and who suspected that Hua still had not "emancipated" himself from the "pernicious influence of the ultraleftists." Hua therefore was forced to surrender his premiership in September 1980 to Teng's close associate, Chao Tse-yang. A few months later a public trial was held of ten formerly prominent Communist Party leaders and generals, including Mao's widow, Chiang Ch'ing. They were found guilty on numerous counts and given sentences ranging from 16 years to life imprisonment and, in Chiang's case, a suspended death sentence.

Meanwhile Teng was implementing his philosophy which he had succinctly summarized in the 1950s when he declared that it made no difference whether a cat was white or black so long as it caught mice. In Marxist ideological terms, Teng was stressing the primacy of productive forces as against the Maoist strategy of simultaneous development of the forces and relations of production. Manifestations of the basic conflict between the Teng and Maoist programs were manifest as the modernization drive got under way: emphasis on scholastic achievement rather than on combining mental work with manual; "one-person management" in factories and universities as against collective administration by revolutionary committees; encouragement rather than discouragement of private family plots and rural fairs; regional agricultural specialization as against regional self-sufficiency; mass importation of industrial plants and technologies as against self-reliance; and more dependence on free market economics than on administrative plans and controls.

By early 1981 Teng's pragmatic approach to modernization was in trouble. Billions of dollars worth of contracts with foreign corporations were cancelled, and commitments for oil exports were drastically reduced. An inflation rate of 15 percent to 18 percent during 1980 was widely resented and protested. Some 20 million were unemployed in the cities, and the housing shortage was more intractable than the unemployment. A confidential memorandum circulated among senior officials in late 1980 assessed the situation in the cities as "very bad," and warned of "very serious consequences" if action were not taken. In December 1980 the Peking leadership, after prolonged debate, announced a retreat from free market economics and reimposition of a large measure of central planning. The purpose of the planning was to stimulate agriculture and light industry in order to raise living standards.

These economic difficulties and policy disputes have engendered varied reactions amongst the populace. One is a recrudescence of Maoism, as noted by an American scholar, A. Doak Barnett: "There is almost certainly some strong opposition from many different kinds of people including those who opposed Teng in earlier years, those who now see their power and positions endangered and those who are genuinely and strongly committed to Maoist egalitarianism. For all those who oppose current trends, Mao's legacy and name provide a potential rallying point." [33]

A small human rights movement also has emerged in China, encouraged by the early Hua-Teng support for the right to put up wall posters and to speak out freely. Wei Ching-sheng, the leading underground newspaper editor, placed a poster on Peking's "Democracy Wall" demanding "China's fifth modernization"—democracy and self-rule. Without this freedom, Wei argued, the Communist Party never would be able to mobilize popular support for its much-touted "four modernizations" in agriculture, industry, science and defense. Wei was making precisely the same point that Andrei Sakharov has in the Soviet Union in explaining why Russia's economy and technology have been falling farther behind those of the West. Wei has been treated more harshly than Sakharov, being sentenced to fifteen years in prison for agitating "to overthrow the dictatorship of the proletariat," and "violating the vital interests of the state." [34] The short-lived underground press has disappeared, and posters are no longer allowed on "Democracy Wall," now popularly known as "Bureaucracy Wall."

At least as significant as the opposition of the pro-Maoists and of the dissidents is the growing alienation and cynicism. When asked recently what they believed in, nearly as many students at Shanghai's Fudan

University replied, "nothing at all," as did those who answered "communism." And at Peking University, a sociologist concluded after a similar survey, "nihilism is reaching dangerous levels." [35] The malaise is not limited to university campuses. A Shanghai newspaper printed in early 1980 a candid account of what it called "China's crisis of confidence." It reported that many citizens believe that "Marxism-Leninism no longer works," that "political lessons are not well received" in schools, and that in offices and factories, political study classes are "just occasions for killing time." [36]

Under these circumstances it remains an open question whether the pragmatists in Peking will be able to evolve the viable economic and social policies essential for a new national consensus.

❧ V. China's Revolution and the Third World

Until 1917 the only societal model available to the Third World was that of Western capitalism. After the Bolshevik Revolution and the Five Year Plans, Soviet society offered a second choice, and one that was especially impressive during the Great Depression and the Second World War. With the Chinese Revolution and the ensuing Great Proletarian Cultural Revolution, a third option was available, which was markedly different from the first two.

The Chinese often refer to "learning by negative example," a process that naturally emphasizes the weaknesses of Soviet society. But in stressing the "negative example," the Chinese are implicitly recognizing the great advantage they have enjoyed in appearing after the Bolshevik Revolution. One is reminded of Isaac Newton's observation that he had been able to see as far as he did because he had stood on the shoulders of giants. This analogy is valid for the Chinese Revolution in relation to the Russian. An analysis of the disadvantages under which the Bolsheviks labored because of their pioneering role during World War I points up the advantages accruing to the Chinese in following after the Bolsheviks during World War II.

The first difficulty the Bolsheviks faced was the lack of precedent. They had little socialist theory and no practice to guide them in their task of destroying the old Tsarist regime and creating a new socialist society. A second drawback for the Bolsheviks was that they were narrowly based urban intellectuals, in contrast to the Chinese Communists, who had lived and fought with the peasants for two decades before seizing power. Also, the Bolsheviks had to fight a civil war and a foreign intervention immediately after assuming power, and were left with a devastated and war-weary country after the cessation of hostilities. The Chinese Communists also had to fight a protracted civil war, but they won it before rather than after gaining national control. Consequently they began the rebuilding process on a positive note of victory and popular acclaim.

When the reconstruction process began, the Bolsheviks were seriously handicapped by the decimation of their cadres, which forced them to depend, as Lenin complained, on "hundreds of thousands of old officials whom we got from the Tsar and from bourgeois society and who, partly deliberately and partly unwittingly, work against us." [37] (See Chapter 20, Section III.) The Chinese Communists, by contrast, could draw upon a large pool of experienced and dedicated cadres trained during the years of administering liberated provinces with tens of millions of inhabitants. Equally important, the Chinese benefited enormously from the economic and military support afforded by the Soviet Union. The Bolsheviks, by contrast, had to fight alone, and justifiably saw themselves as an isolated and beleaguered socialist island in a surrounding capitalist ocean. Finally, the Bolsheviks had the grave misfortune of losing Lenin soon after the civil war ended, whereas Mao survived for another quarter century to lead the Cultural Revolution as well as the overthrow of the Kuomintang regime.

The above historical factors, together with the unique traditions and conditions prevailing in China, resulted in the evolution of the People's Republic of China, which was as different from the Soviet Union as it was from the United States. The society that finally took shape during the decade between the Cultural Revolution and the death of Mao had certain distinctive and significant characteristics. In the realm of economics it stressed agriculture and the peasants, it was based on decentralization and local self-sufficiency and it achieved a considerable degree of industrialization without urbanization. In politics, Mao's "mass line" emphasized interaction between top and bottom, and fostered this interaction with a variety of "counterinstitutions." Likewise the educational system was designed to combat the "private ownership of knowledge," while in the People's Liberation Army, politics came first and technological factors second.

These distinctive Maoist values and institutions, which crystallized between the mid-1960s and mid-1970s, attracted considerable attention and following in Third World countries seeking to attain economic development and facing obstacles similar to those prevailing in China. Since Mao's death, however, the Chinese model has lost some of its appeal. Doubts naturally have risen with the constant allusions to the "lost decade," and with the not-too-subtle references to a "Gang of Five" that includes the former "Great Helmsman" himself. Peking's image also has been tarnished by the shift from a global revolutionary foreign policy to one that places the struggle against "Soviet imperialism" above everything else. The resulting strategy of "my enemy's enemy is my friend" has led Peking to support the Pakistan military regime during the Bengali revolt, the Bandaranaike government of Ceylon during the 1971 uprising, the Pinochet dictatorship in Chile, the Mobutu regime in Zaïre and the UNITA faction in Angola, which was also backed by South Africa. Peking also censured Washington for not preventing the fall of the Shah of Iran. Such a course has made a mockery of China's proclaimed principle of "proletarian internationalism."

Yet whatever policies Peking might have followed, the fact remains that the Maoist societal model by its very nature can appeal to only a handful of Third World countries. Mao himself stated that guerrilla warfare was essential not only for revolution but also for the later carrying out of socialist economic development. In other words, social revolution is the prerequisite for establishing a Maoist-type socialist order. Without a preceding revolution the local and foreign vested interests entrenched in Third World countries would block such key elements in Maoist strategy as land redistribution, establishment of communes, rural industrialization, mass education and health care, and worker participation in the decision-making process. Thus the Marxist-socialist countries that have been, or might be, receptive to the Maoist model comprise a very small portion of the Third World. This small stage could, of course, expand suddenly and substantially, as indicated by recent developments in the former Portuguese African colonies.

In conclusion, the chief factor determining the future impact of China on the Third World will be the nature of events within China itself. If the next generation is able to devise new institutions for continuing the revolution under new conditions, then China inevitably will exert great influence beyond its borders. But that influence, in any case, can be only that of a precedent rather than a blueprint. In the present age, with its global self-determination impulse, each society will set its own course in line with its own particular needs, historical experiences and cultural traditions. The future influence of the Chinese consequently will depend on the extent to which they succeed in resolving contradictions that remain unresolved in both the First World and the Second World as well as in the Third World—contradictions such as moral versus material incentives, hierarchical bureaucracy versus mass participation, city versus country, and physical labor versus mental labor. Increased GNP by itself cannot cope with these contradictions, as has been amply demonstrated by the United States and the Soviet Union, as well as by Third World countries from Brazil to Iran to Indonesia.

Chapter 23

SECOND GLOBAL REVOLUTIONARY WAVE, 1939– : GLOBAL MANIFESTATIONS OF REVOLUTION

After nearly 120 years of British rule, the vast majority of Asiatics were not sufficiently interested in this rule to take any steps to ensure its continuance. And if it is true that the government had no share in the life of the people, it is equally true that the few thousand British residents who made their living out of the country—practically none of whom looked upon Malaya as being their home—were completely out of touch with the people. . . . British rule and culture and the small British community formed no more than a thin and brittle veneer.

LONDON *Times,* February 18, 1942

The Chinese Communists, unlike the Russian Communists, did not cherish chiliastic expectations of worldwide revolution as the aftermath of their own Revolution. Mao and his comrades had developed their movement in an insular national setting, isolated physically and intellectually from international revolutionary currents. Yet the upheavals in the Third World were much greater in breadth and depth after the Second World War than after the first. Within two decades after 1945, nationalist and social revolutionary insurrections had dismantled the great European empires that had appeared so impregnable and enduring only a few years earlier. The extent of the global transformation is reflected in the composition of the United Nations, which consisted of 51 member countries when organized in 1945. By 1981 its membership reached a total of 156 countries. The 105 new members consist largely of the Third World states that have emerged from the ruins of shattered empires.

Consideration of all the manifestations of this epochal upheaval is clearly not feasible. It will be more manageable and meaningful to group the new postwar regimes into three categories, even though this arrangement unavoidably will exclude certain geographic regions and historical events. However, the will to exclude is the prerequisite for an historical study encompassing over half a millennium and most of the globe. The three categories that will be analyzed in this chapter are nationalist, social revolutionary and white settler regimes. These will be considered in turn after a preliminary section on the dynamics of the postwar revolutionary wave.

I. Dynamics of Third World Politics

The origins of decolonization are to be found in the awakening and activization of colonial subjects to the point where the amount of force necessary to preserve imperial ties became prohibitively expensive and unacceptable. Several factors explain the dramatic leap of hundreds of millions of Third World peoples onto the stage of world history. One was the gradual maturation of nationalist movements between the two world wars. They had gained in popular following, and were headed by more knowledgeable and sophisticated leaders. Those who directed the successful struggles for independence were not unreconstructed Malayan sultans or Nigerian chiefs or Indian princes, but rather men who had studied in Western universities, who had participated in the operation of Western institutions and who were also familiar with the Soviet alternative to the Western societal model—men like Gandhi, Nehru, Sukarno, Nkrumah, Nyerere and Nasser.

The worldwide colonial awakening was further stimulated during World War II with the service of millions of colonials in both Allied and Japanese armies and labor battalions. Many Africans fought under the British, French and Italian flags, while over two million Indians volunteered for the British forces, and an additional thirty-five thousand to forty thousand Indian prisoners captured in Hong Kong, Singapore and Burma signed up for the Japanese-sponsored Indian National Army. More tens of thousands of Indonesians, Burmese and Malayans volunteered for Japanese-trained armies in their respective countries. When all these men returned home at the end of the war, they inevitably regarded in a new light the local colonial officials and native leaders. They were more likely to insist on the implementation of the wartime Allied propaganda regarding freedom and self-determination.

Equally important was the unprecedented weakening of the foremost colonial powers during the Second World War. France, Holland and Belgium were overrun and occupied, while Britain was debilitated economically and militarily. At the same time, anti-imperialist sentiment was spreading within the imperial countries themselves. Gone were the days when white men in the colonies confidently asserted, "We are here because we are superior." Now their presence was questioned, not only by their subjects but also by their own fellow countrymen. Mussolini's attack on Ethiopia in 1935 was widely regarded in Western Europe as a deplorable throwback, while the Anglo-French assault on the Suez in 1956 aroused vehement popular opposition in both Britain and France. The end of the West's global hegemony was due as much to the lack of will to rule as it was to lack of strength.

Finally, the colonial revolution was stimulated by the unprecedented material and political destructiveness of the Second World War. It quickly became a truly global struggle, with German armies operating from Norway to North Africa to the Volga, and Japanese forces from the Aleutians to Hawaii to Burma. On most of these far-flung fronts resistance organizations were active, whereas during World War I they were relatively unknown. Precisely because the Germans and the Japanese conquered such vast territories so rapidly, resistance movements spontaneously erupted in most of the occupied lands. They began with individual acts of protest—defacing enemy posters, scrawling slogans on walls, flying forbidden flags and listening to proscribed radio programs. Gradually individual actions became collective resistance movements involved in building up stores of arms, operating clandestine presses, supplying intelligence to the Allies and committing minor sabotage acts. In the final stage of their development, resistance organizations disrupted railroads, staged strikes in mines and factories, assassinated leading occupationists and their quisling collaborators and staged open insurrection and guerrilla warfare.

Communists frequently assumed leadership of these resistance movements because of their prewar experience with clandestine operations. They had underground organizations to fall back upon and they knew how to obtain arms and how to generate mass organizations for mobilizing workers, peasants, students, housewives, war veterans and other segments of the subject populations. It is not surprising, then, that membership in Communist Parties (beyond Soviet frontiers) increased enormously during the war years—from less than a million in 1939 to fourteen million by the end of 1945. As in the exhilarating days following November 1917, once again there was euphoric optimism about the prospects for worldwide revolution.

All these factors promoting revolution were counterbalanced by equally powerful counterrevolutionary pressures. The leaders of the European imperial nations made clear their determination to hold onto their colonies after the war. Winston Churchill made his oft-quoted pronouncement in 1942 that he had "not become the King's First Minister in order to preside over the liquidation of the British Empire." Likewise the Brazzaville Conference held in 1944 under the auspices of the Free French government declared: "The attainment of self-government in the colonies even in the most distant future must be excluded." [1]

More significant than the counterrevolutionary role of the European powers was that of the United States. It is not generally realized that the United States emerged from World War II not only as the No. 1 global power, but also as the only power with a plan for a new world order. Stalin was interested primarily in carving out security zones that would safeguard Russia against future invasions, while Churchill's main concern was to preserve the British Empire. Only the United States had the power and the vision necessary for a global strategy, and the Council on Foreign Relations formulated that strategy with its concept of an America-dominated "Grand Area" (details in Chapter 19, Section V). The basic objective was to revive the prewar capitalist order, but in a modified form that would make it more viable and that would open European colonial possessions to American corporations. Just as Great Britain, the dominant nineteenth-century economic power, favored "free-trade imperialism" in order to have access to world markets, so the United States, the dominant twentieth-century economic power, favored, for the same reason, anticolonial imperialism. The British were quite aware of this, Anthony Eden being typical in noting in his memoirs: "[Roosevelt] hoped that former colonial territories, once free of their masters would become politically and economically dependent upon the United States, and had no fear that other powers might fill that role." [2]

Counterrevolution was the strategy not only of the United States and the West European powers but also, paradoxically, of the Soviet Union. Whereas Lenin had actively fomented world revolution through the Communist International, Stalin abandoned this course in order to reach agreements for spheres of influence with his Western allies. His foreign policy was based on two main strategic rules: to subordinate the Comintern to the interests of the Soviet state, and to exploit contradictions between imperialist powers in order to insure generous and secure Soviet spheres of influence. This meant acceptance of the capitalist status quo in Western Europe, establishment of Soviet-type societies in Eastern Europe and avoidance of confrontations in the Third World.

The above guidelines explain Stalin's numerous wartime negotiations and arrangements with the Western powers:

• *Example:* the Stalin-Eden negotiations (Dec. 1941) in which Eden rejected Stalin's proposal that Britain recognize the Soviet "areas of influence" as defined in the 1939 Stalin-Hitler Pact, and in return Britain would be free to establish bases in northern France, Belgium, Denmark, Norway and the Netherlands.

• *Example:* the Molotov-de Gaulle negotiations (May 1942) in which Molotov agreed to persuade the French Resistance and the French colonies to recognize de Gaulle's authority, in return for de Gaulle's support for the opening of a second front.

• *Example:* Stalin's dissolution of the Comintern (June 10, 1943), designed to clear the way for the Big Three (the United States, the Soviet Union and the United Kingdom) to agree on the structure of the postwar world without the distractive threat of world revolution.

• *Example:* the Stalin-Churchill agreement in Moscow (Oct. 1944) defining the exact percentages of British and Russian postwar influence in each Balkan state.

• *Example:* Moscow's pressure on foreign Communist Party leaders to accept the spheres-of-influence agreements among the Big Three—pressure that was accepted by most of those leaders, the few holdouts including Tito, Mao and Ho.

In light of the above wheeling and dealing, British historian A. J. P. Taylor concluded that it was Stalin "rather than the Americans who preserved western Europe for capitalist democracy." [3] Likewise an American historian, Gabriel Kolko, reaches this judgment in his analysis of the diplomacy of the Second World War:

> . . . during the critical period of 1944–1947 the Russians gave the Western European social system a reprieve during which to consolidate its power. The Russians wanted a respite from the war to obtain their own breathing spell, and if this required stability for their former allies, the Russians were willing to provide it if at all possible. Succinctly, the Russians were as committed to revolution as the West was to democracy, and they both opposed a radical transformation of Western Europe and its long-range consequences threatening instability for the entire face of the globe. Without such a Soviet policy . . . no one can predict with confidence what the social outcome of the war in Western Europe might have been in the hands of local, self-guiding left parties.[4]

Stalin was not successful in arranging a spheres-of-influence settlement. The end result was the Cold War, to which Stalin responded by establishing the Communist Information Bureau (Cominform) in September 1947. This was a defensive move, as evident in Andrei Zhdanov's report to the initial conference of the organization. Zhdanov ignored the ongoing civil wars in China, Greece and Vietnam, despite the fact that the United States was involved directly or indirectly in all three. The reason for the slight is apparent in a speech made a few days earlier by Andrei Vyshinsky in the United Nations. He declared that "in the present situation any new war turns *without fail* into a world war." Consequently he viewed Third World uprisings as a threat to the "fundamental task," which he defined as the "building of Communism in the U.S.S.R." [5] It followed from his postulate that Third World insurrections were to be avoided because of the danger of a confrontation between the Soviet Union and the West. Hence the persistent efforts of the U.S.S.R. and its subservient Communist Parties, as well as of the Western powers, to forestall revolutionary eruptions in the Third World.

When thousands of nationalists were massacred in the Constantin district of Algeria in May 1945, the Communist ministers of the Paris government continued to hold their posts, while the French Communist Party leader, Maurice Thorez was satisfied to issue a statement deploring "the painful events of last month" and recommending improvement of the food supply and dismissal of the responsible officials.[6] When a French expeditionary force bombarded Damascus in the same month, Thorez again deplored the action and supported Arab right to self-determination, but then added gratuitously that "the right to divorce does not mean the obligation to divorce." [7] In Vietnam a French army in effect re-established the colonial regime in the South of the country, while a French fleet shelled Haiphong with heavy civilian casualties on November 23, 1946. During the ensuing colonial war, a Communist was Minister of Defense for four months (Jan.–Apr. 1947), and the Communist ministers in the cabinet voted military credits for the war in order to maintain "ministerial solidarity." The Communist Party leader, Jacques Duclos, insisted that such "solidarity" was essential because the four-power conference (among the U.S.S.R., the U.S.A., Britain and France) was about to begin in Moscow, and "our Foreign Minister will be defending the cause of France.[8] The cause of Vietnam, therefore, would have to wait.

While the Moscow conference was in session, French troops suppressed an insurrection in Madagascar as brutally as they had the uprising in Constantin. Again the Communists restricted themselves to formal protests because "ministerial solidarity" was needed to plead "the cause of

France" at Moscow. And so the cause of Madagascar, like the cause of Vietnam, had to wait.

The same Communist strategy was followed in India, where Gandhi declared forthrightly: "India cannot regard herself as involved in a war said to be for democratic freedoms, when she herself is deprived of freedom." The Indian Communist Party, by contrast, followed the Kremlin line of national unity against the Axis, and therefore supported the colonial administration. The British responded by arresting Gandhi and suppressing the Congress Party, while at the same time legalizing the Communist Party, which had been proscribed since 1934.

Most significant was Soviet policy in China, where Stalin, during World War II and after, consistently supported Chiang Kai-shek and opposed Mao's revolutionary strategy (See Chapter 21, Section II). In February 1948 Stalin admitted to a Yugoslav Communist, Edvard Kardelj, and to a Bulgarian Communist, Georgi Dimitrov, that he had erred in China:

> . . . after the war we invited the Chinese comrades to come to Moscow and we discussed the situation in China. We told them bluntly that we considered the development of the uprising in China had no prospects, that the Chinese comrades should seek a *modus vivendi* with Chiang Kai-shek, and that they should join the Chiang Kai-shek government and dissolve their army. The Chinese comrades agreed here in Moscow with the views of the Soviet comrades, but went back to China and acted quite otherwise. They mustered their forces, organized their armies and now, as we see, they are beating Chiang Kai-shek's army. Now, in the case of China, we admit we were wrong.[9]

The fact that Stalin proved wrong and Mao right was of inestimable significance for the entire Third World. Mao had successfully challenged the fundamental assumption of Soviet foreign policy, that the interests of the Soviet Union and of Third World peoples were identical. In April 1946 Mao presented to the leading cadres of his party an analysis of the international situation that was unprecedented in Communist circles at that time. He recognized the possibility that the United States and the Soviet Union might reach a settlement, but he added that this does not require that the peoples of the different countries of the capitalist world should therefore make compromises in their own countries. "The aim of reactionary forces," he warned, "is resolutely to destroy all democratic forces," so that the latter had the alternative of waging revolutionary armed struggle or perishing.[10]

Events since 1946 have proven the validity of Mao's judgment. The

Second World War, in contrast to the First World War, was followed by successive revolutions, which persist to the present. These revolutions have not been uniform in character or centrally directed. Their diversity reflects the great variety of local conditions and balance of forces that spawned the insurrections. Three main types of revolutions are discernible, and the imperial powers have reacted to the three in quite different ways.

In the first, the native leaders were primarily nationalists who wanted to end foreign rule but not to change social institutions or class relationships. They did not seek to challenge fundamentally the local or foreign vested interests, whether they were traditional landholdings, plantations, commercial firms, banks, railways, mines or government debt arrangements. Such nationalist leaders or movements were more likely to be entrusted with political power because it was understood implicitly that they would not use that power to effect social or economic change. The colonies thus gained political independence but were not free of imperialism; rather they became dependent neocolonial states.

The second type of independence movement was that in which the native leaders and movements were social revolutionary as well as nationalist, and therefore planned for a new social as well as political order. This led to confrontations with both local and foreign vested interests, which usually joined forces to resist social revolution to the bitter end. This hard-line position, it should be noted, was taken not only by the established imperial powers but also by the United States. Thus Britain was willing to grant independence to an India led by the Congress Party and the Muslim League, whereas France and the United States fought against the Communist Ho Chi Minh in Indochina for three full decades. Likewise in the Americas, the British readily granted independence to the nationalist-minded Federal Labor Party in the West Indies, but refused it to leftist Cheddi Jagan in Guyana, even after he had won majority support in parliamentary elections. The British, it should be added, were strongly supported, if not prompted, by the United States, which was unalterably opposed to a socialist regime on its front doorstep —an article of faith that was amply demonstrated also against Castro in Cuba.

The third type of revolution in the colonies was that conducted against local European settlers. In most cases the settlers eventually were forced to give way, as in Algeria, Kenya and the Portuguese African colonies. The exceptions are in South Africa and Israel, where white settler regimes have been able to take root because of certain inherent sources of strength.

The world that has emerged after decolonization is different from that envisaged by Marx and Engels when they wrote in the *Communist Mani-*

festo that "working men have no country." Far from a world dividing along class lines, it is state frontiers that are decisive and meaningful. The evolving world system is dominated not by class interests but by nationalist considerations, which are being pursued resolutely by all states, regardless of political coloration. This means an absence of a unified world revolutionary movement and strategy, but it does not mean a cessation of revolutionary activities on a national scale. Rather these activities persist to the present, and have engendered the three types of Third World states—nationalist, social revolutionary and white settler—which will be examined in the sections that follow.

⁊ *II. Nationalist Regimes*

The dependent colonial states almost invariably have had turbulent postindependence histories. Beset by economic difficulties, they were unable to satisfy the exaggerated expectations of their newly aroused publics. The combination of economic pressures (lack of capital, high unemployment, social inequities and vulnerability to world market fluctuations and to foreign-owned firms) and mass unrest forced most of these regimes to turn from neocolonialism to state capitalism. This was usually effected by coups led by members of the civil or military bureaucracies. Lacking an independent socioeconomic base, they depended primarily on control of the armed forces and the state machinery, and therefore ended up usually with a military dictatorship or a one-party state.

The state capitalist regimes were inherently ambivalent, as reflected in their zigzag tactics. On the one hand they decreed land reforms, nationalized foreign-owned enterprises, established state industries, welcomed aid from the Soviet Union as well as the Western powers and generally sought to attain economic as well as political independence. On the other hand the state capitalist regimes rejected Marxist class-struggle ideology and substituted nationalistic forms of "socialism" that rationalized the muzzling of labor to enhance national capital accumulation. Thus state capitalism was weakened by inherent contradictions. It sought to combat foreign capitalism but at the same time it repressed and exploited its own workers and peasants. Of necessity it resorted to demagogic ideological appeals (Arab and African "socialism") that were intrinsically hollow and ineffective.

Ultimately the state capitalist regimes were overwhelmed by debt overloads, trade deficits, development failures and limited access in Western markets for their industrial and agricultural exports. Hence the ultimate reforging of foreign economic bonds by financial and industrial multinational corporations, and by Western-dominated international agencies such as the World Bank and the International Monetary Fund. This general pattern of neocolonialism to state capitalism to renewed dependence and subordination to the world capitalist order is evident, with many local variations, in the following regional surveys.

A.
India

By far the most important victory of the nationalist variety was won in India. That subcontinent, with its vast human and material resources, had from the beginning been the keystone of the British Empire and the epitome of European imperial authority. One reason for the relatively conservative nationalist character of the independence movement in India was that for more than a century British rule had prepared that colony for self-rule. Also, the dominant Congress Party, under the leadership of Gandhi was committed to peaceful and gradual reform. The fact that Gandhi selected Nehru rather than Subhas Chandra Bose as his successor was in itself revealing. Nehru, with his scattered allegiances to Fabian Socialism, Gandhian nonviolence, Western humanism and Vedanta precepts, was more inclined to a "moderate" course than the strong-minded and militantly socialistic Bose. The latter, although elected president of the Congress Party twice, finally left its ranks altogether because of frustration with the unrelenting opposition of the conservative leadership. During World War II Bose fled from India to Berlin, and then to Tokyo, where he organized the Indian National Army to fight against Britain.

A final factor contributing to the nationalist outcome in India was that that colony did not undergo a Japanese invasion and occupation. Thus it did not generate an armed resistance movement, which probably would have catapulted to the forefront social revolutionary leaders at least as radical as Bose, as happened in China and Indochina with the emergence of Mao and Ho. Instead, uninterrupted British rule made it possible for the relatively conservative Gandhi and Nehru to take over power after the war with minimum violence and social disruption.

Despite these circumstances favoring smooth relations between the British authorities and the Indian nationalists, the outbreak of World War II precipitated a political confrontation. When Britain declared war on Germany on September 3, 1939, the viceroy in Delhi, the Marquis of Linlithgow, proclaimed on the same day that India was at war. Although this was a constitutionally correct procedure, Nehru protested bitterly against the high-handedness. "One man, and he a foreigner and a representative of a hated system, could plunge four hundred millions of human beings into war, without the slightest reference to them. . . . In the dominions the decision was taken by popular representatives after full debate. . . . Not so in India, and it hurt." [11] Congress Party protestations were curtly rejected by London until the national emergency created by the fall of France and the beginning of the Battle of Britain. The viceroy then announced that basic changes were not feasible during the war, but that afterward India would be granted dominion status. The Congress Party promptly rejected this offer, and the deadlock continued.

Japan's precipitous conquest of Southeast Asia in early 1942 fundamentally changed the Indian situation. With Japanese armies poised on Bengal's borders, India was transformed from a reluctant ally in a quiet byway to one positioned directly in the path of the rapidly advancing enemy. Churchill responded by sending to India on March 22 a cabinet member, Sir Stafford Cripps. Again major change was excluded for the duration of the war, but as soon as it was over, India could become fully autonomous, with the right to secede from the Commonwealth. The Congress Party turned down Cripps' offer, the basic reason being the refusal of the British government to accept the Indian people as equal and essential partners in the war effort.

When the Congress Party demanded the Defense Ministry, London reluctantly agreed, but then limited the Minister's authority to trivial matters such as public relations, demobilization, canteens, stationery, printing and reception of foreign missions. Nehru had worked out a plan for raising an army of five million men, to be armed by expanding India's existing factories that were producing rifles, hand grenades and explosives. The scheme was to prepare a mass guerrilla army that would be available in case the professional military failed in India, as they had in Southeast Asia. But British official policy remained unchanged. India was to be defended by a professional army surrounded by a population that was passively neutral at best and actively hostile at worst.

The Congress Party responded with its "quit India" resolution (Aug. 7, 1942), demanding immediate freedom, "both for the sake of India and for the success of the cause of the UN." [12] The Congress Party threatened, if its demand was not met, to wage "a mass struggle on nonviolent lines." The British government struck back hard with wholesale repression. Over 60,000 people were arrested, including all the Congress Party leaders; 14,000 were detained without trial, 940 were killed; and 1,630 were injured in clashes with the police and military. British repression provoked open insurrection in some districts, with telephone lines cut, trains robbed, government buildings burned and a "parallel government" established to challenge the status quo. The British held the Congress Party leaders responsible for the violence, but the fact is that Gandhi with his nonviolence convictions was shocked by the outbreak and condemned it.

This proved a critical turning point; foreign and domestic developments now unfolded that defined India's history for decades to come. Abroad the Germans reached the Volga and were only thirty miles from Alexandria, while the Japanese had overrun Burma. The gigantic German and Japanese pincers were separated only by India, which was seething with disaffection, and by the Middle East Muslim countries, which sided more with the Axis than with the Allies. If the Germans and Japanese had pushed on into these countries, they would have set fire to smoldering tinder. They might well have closed in the Eurasian land mass with incalculable repercussions.

The near catastrophe for the West was averted only because Hitler chose to squander his divisions on the Russian plains, and because the Japanese, despite their threats and feints, never really planned to invade India. There was no need for Nehru's five-million-man guerrilla force, so India, unlike China and the Southeast Asian countries, did not develop any resistance forces or fight any war of liberation. This turn of events was fortunate for Nehru and the rest of the Congress Party leaders. Japanese occupation and a prolonged resistance struggle probably would have ended with Bose, or others even more radical, pushing them off the historical stage, as happened to Chiang Kai-shek in China and to Emperor Bao Dai in Vietnam.

Domestically also the balance of power was being decisively altered by the growing power of the Muslim League at the expense of the hobbled Congress Party. The Muslim League's leader, Muhammad Ali Jinnah, was a Bombay lawyer of impeccable Western dress and taste. He was willing to cooperate with the Congress Party on a coalition basis, but the Congress Party would have nothing to do with the Muslim League; it would admit only Muslims who came in as individuals. Jinnah turned to the Muslim masses with the cry, "Islam is in danger." He exaggerated slights and discriminations by the Congress Party as he campaigned tirelessly for an independent Pakistan. "Muslim India cannot accept any constitution which must necessarily result in a Hindu majority government. . . . Mussulmans are a nation according to any definition of a nation, and they must have their homelands, their territory, and their state." [13]

The domestic situation in India was being transformed also by the huge military mobilization and by the substantial industrial expansion. The Indian Army increased during the war from 175,000 to 2 million men, the Indian Navy also grew markedly and the Indian Air Force was established. These units fought with distinction against the Japanese in Malaya and Burma, and against the Germans and Italians in North Africa, Ethiopia, Syria and Iraq. At the same time India became the supply center for the Allied armies operating in the Middle East. Industries grew rapidly, especially steel, cement and aluminum, as well as small enterprises producing blankets, uniforms and light arms.

The enlarged military forces meant new experiences and skills for millions, as well as an upsurge of national pride because of their notable achievements. Likewise the industrial expansion provided many openings for Indians as technicians and administrators. Many thousands attained responsibility, status and know-how. When the war ended, India had enough of its own officers to take over the armed forces, and enough executives and technicians to operate the commercial and industrial enterprises. All this added up to an enhanced awareness of nationality and a growth of national confidence. By the end of the war India had already become independent in spirit, though this was tempered by a pervasive suspicion that the British somehow would manage to preserve their rule despite their public commitments.

With the surrender of Germany in May 1945, a triangle conflict burst out into the open among the British, the Congress Party and the Muslim League. London's government under the redoubtable Conservative Party leader, Winston Churchill, believed that at least one more year of war against Japan lay ahead. It assumed that during that year Britain would be able to negotiate with the Indian nationalists from a position of strength, as many British and other Allied troops still were stationed in India. This presumption was shattered by two totally unexpected developments in 1945. The first was Churchill's electoral defeat in July by the Labour Party, which for decades had championed self-government for India. The second was the sudden surrender of Japan in August following the atomic bombing of Hiroshima and Nagasaki. Almost overnight the political situation in India had been transformed, and Britain's freedom to maneuver had disappeared.

With the Germans and Japanese defeated, and with Churchill removed from office, it was clear that the British public was in no mood for continued warfare in India in order to preserve the imperial tie. British and Allied forces in India were rapidly reduced at the same time that tensions were building up between the Congress Party and the Muslim League. From being a referee with power to make and enforce decisions, Britain now found itself to be a go-between trying to reconcile two independent and belligerent parties.

The precarious position of the British in India was spotlighted by two dramatic events involving the armed forces. The first was the public furore aroused by the announcement of the commander-in-chief, Sir Claude Auchinleck, that the officers of Bose's Indian National Army would be put on trial for seeking to overthrow His Imperial Majesty's Government of India. The uproar of protest throughout India was such that a trial obviously would involve unacceptable political risks, so the whole matter was quietly dropped. The other episode was an extraordinary mutiny of the sailors of the Royal Indian Navy in 1946. The rebels won control of seventy-four ships and twenty shore establishments, and the movement began to spread to the Air Force and the streets of Bombay, where workers poured out in support of the mutineers.

The slogan of the mutineers was "Long Live Revolution!" and they renamed the Royal Indian Navy, which they now controlled, the Indian National Navy. But no leadership was forthcoming from any national party or leader. The Communist Party was following the Kremlin line of national unity, while the Congress Party joined the British in identifying the mutiny as an "economic" rather than a "political" affair. The sailors, quite unjustifiably, were assumed to be concerned only with grievances such as the quality of food, and the conditions of service. The Congress Party leaders urged them to surrender, with the assurance that they would support them in their complaints. The testimony of one of the leaders of the mutiny is as poignant as it is revealing:

> To be sure, we were innocents in the political jungle. But our very naïveté exposed the hollowness of certain public postures . . . the politicians of India at that point of time were already smiling to the radiance of coming power. And to those in power, service indiscipline is a nightmare. . . . Where the RIN mutiny was concerned, the rulers and the leaders of the ruled were no longer adversaries, but allies. . . . How, in retrospect, one wishes for the knowledge that they were already committed mentally to the continuation of the very order they were non-violently resisting! The pity of it! The pity, pity of it! [14]

The two warning flashes of the canceled trials and the naval mutiny made clear to the British the urgent need for a quick political settlement to facilitate their own disengagement.

The basic question still remained whether the Congress Party represented virtually all India, as it claimed, or whether the Muslim League was a serious contender that had to be involved in any political arrangement. The elections held in the spring of 1946 answered this conclusively. The Congress Party dominated the Hindu part of India, but the Muslim League to an equal degree dominated the Muslim part, winning 74 percent of all Muslim votes cast. London sent another Cripps mission to work out a constitutional arrangement acceptable to both sides. When negotiations broke down on May 12, 1946, the mission published its own plan. This sought to retain Indian unity while placating the Muslims by granting them regional autonomy. Negotiations dragged on amid charges and countercharges until Jinnah broke away and declared August 16 "Direct Action Day" to hasten the creation of an independent Pakistan. In Calcutta this triggered riots that lasted four days and became known as the "Great Calcutta Killing." In Behar the Hindus retaliated by massacring Muslims. It was the beginning of a civil war in its most fanatical religious form.

A Constituent Assembly elected in July 1946 was immobilized by the same deadlock between the Congress Party and the Muslim League. On January 22, 1947, the Assembly adopted a resolution by Nehru creating an independent all-India republic, but the Muslim League refused to cooperate. Incapable of either commanding or persuading, the Attlee government announced on February 20, 1947, that it would withdraw from India not later than June 1948, and appointed Lord Mountbatten as viceroy to supervise arrangements before withdrawal. Mountbatten quickly realized that an independent Pakistan was inevitable, and after consultations in London and India he proposed a plan on June 2 that both sides accepted. It provided for the establishment of an independent Pakistan comprising northwestern India and eastern Bengal. Communally mixed provinces such as Punjab, North West Frontier Province, Sind, Baluchistan and part of Assam were to decide by vote as to their allegiance, either as integral or partitioned units. Princely states were released from their allegiance to the Crown and strongly urged to join either India or Pakistan.

In July 1947 the British Parliament passed the Indian Independence Act, and on August 15 both Pakistan and the Union of India became free nations in the British Commonwealth. Since Hindus and Muslims were not neatly divided in separate regions, the establishment of India and Pakistan was accompanied by wholesale massacres and migrations. By mid-1948 nearly thirteen million refugees had moved to new homes, and almost one million had been killed in the process. The assimilation of the princes also was a prolonged and complicated operation, since they numbered over five hundred, and their territories comprised one fourth of the total area of undivided India, and one fifth of its total population.

The decision of the British to relinquish control over their prized Indian colony affords a classic example of the selective granting of independence by the Western imperial powers. What if the Japanese had invaded India and provoked a national resistance struggle under a leader such as the militant S. C. Bose or someone even more to the left? Churchill then would have received more support in opposing the granting of independence, and General Wavell likewise in proposing a plan for military intervention and control. According to Maurice and Taya Zinkin, "Britain could . . . have held on for ten years at least if it had taken the determined action Lord Wavell recommended." [15] The British did take "determined action" in cooperation with the French and the Japanese against Ho's Viet Minh. It is safe to assume that they would have

been equally determined had they been confronted with an Indian counterpart of the Viet Minh.

The British were spared the painful predicament of having to choose
between armed suppression and social revolution in India. Since the
Japanese stopped at the frontier, Britain was confronted instead by the
relatively conservative Congress Party led by men such as Gandhi, Nehru
and V. B. Patel, and by the more conservative Muslim League under
Jinnah. The Zinkins state correctly: "No bases were asked for [by the
British in 1947]. No alliance was suggested. No protection was obtained
for British investments." Nor was any protection needed. "No British
investment was confiscated," add the Zinkins. "No British investor has
been prevented from remitting his profits." [16]

The nature of the newly independent India was reflected in Nehru's
speech to the Constitutional Assembly in April 1948: "After all that has
happened in the course of the last seven or eight months, one has to be
very careful of the steps one takes so as not to injure the existing structure too much. There has been destruction and injury enough, and certainly I confess to this House that I am not brave and gallant enough to
go about destroying any more." [17]

In line with this "don't rock the boat" sentiment, Nehru appointed
the conservative V. B. Patel to the crucial Home Ministry. Patel retained
almost intact the British administrative system with its colonial philosophy and biases, and he also used all necessary police and military force
to crush the Communist movement in the Telangana region in the
South. Since Nehru was uninterested in administrative details, Patel was
able by the time he died in December 1950 to leave an unmistakably
conservative imprint on independent India. Gunnar Myrdal has characterized that imprint as "the Indian political pattern of bold radicalism
in principle but extreme conservatism in practice. . . ." [18]

Typical of India's rhetorical boldness are the goals set forth in the
1950 Constitution and in the successive Five Year Plans: "an adequate
means of livelihood" for all citizens, control of the material resources so
"as best to subserve the common good," guarantee not only of civil rights
but also of the "right to work, to education and to public assistance . . .
in cases of undeserved want" and an end to dependence on foreign aid
by 1965–66.

None of these goals has been even remotely approached; indeed, the
objectives are generally farther from realization now than at the time of
independence. The failure is not due to lack of foreign aid. India has
received between 1947 and 1977 a total of $28 billion in foreign aid—
more than any other Third World country. Nor is the failure due to
want of trying, for India has enacted as much progressive legislation designed to aid the underprivileged as any developing country. Yet there

are more underprivileged today than at the time of independence.

The root cause for this predicament is that independence ended British rule but left intact existing institutions and power relationships. Myron Weiner's study of the Congress Party in the mid-1960s disclosed that its leadership and active members came from "the small merchant community, the professionals, and the 5 percent of the land-owning population with more than thirty acres of land." [19] This small ruling elite naturally was interested in preserving the status quo, and to a large degree succeeded in doing so.

The resulting ossification is especially evident in the countryside, where 80 percent of the population lives. Immediately after independence, the central government did curb the powers of some of the most parasitic elements at the top of traditional rural society, and also passed land-reform legislation that redistributed some of the properties of the largest absentee landowners. But land redistribution was for the most part blocked by local landowners in league with local officials.

Disappointed with the lagging pace of agricultural reform and productivity, the central government in the 1950s tried to increase production by technological innovations—greater use of fertilizers, pesticides, improved seeds and irrigation. But this "Green Revolution" further polarized the rural classes, as only the wealthy afforded the new technology and had access to technical advice and marketing facilities. Thus the percentage of the rural population depressed to below the minimum living standard increased from 38 in 1960–61 to 54 in 1968–69.

Growing popular unrest against perceived inequities moved the central government to revive land reform in the late 1960s and early 1970s, but with no more success than before. The 1972 Review of Land Reform by the planning commissions concluded that "programmes of land reform adopted since Independence have failed to bring about the required changes in the agrarian structure. . . . The lack of political will is mainly responsible for [this]. . . . the bureaucracy is, by and large, a part of the powerful anti-land reform bloc." [20]

The discrepancy between legislative reforms and social reality is manifest also in the efforts to improve the lot of the Dalits, or ex-untouchables. Numbering 100 million to 120 million out of a total population of 650 million, they have been granted quotas that give them a specified percentage of seats in schools and of jobs in government offices. But, as in the case of affirmative-action programs in the United States, there has been strong opposition, especially from Hindus of the lower castes, who fear that gains by the Dalits will be at their expense—a not unreasonable assumption in a time of increasing unemployment and economic insecurity. In the countryside, Dalits who have fought for higher wages or a bit of land have been driven from their homes, beaten and even murdered. They are also abused even for using the same village well as do the caste Hindus, who fear religious "pollution" by the Dalits. "Caste is everything," said a merchant in Patna, whose vegetable stall was trampled during a demonstration. "They say we are doing away with caste in modern India. But here, in Patna at least, it is still everything." [21]

Equally revealing is the fate of the provision in the 1950 Constitution providing for the organization of village *panchayats* (traditional councils of five members) with "such powers and authority as may be necessary to enable them to function as units of self-government." But local self-government falls under the authority of state governments, which are reluctant to share power with village bodies. Thus although the number of village panchayats between 1950 and 1955 rose by 34,600 to only 117,600 (out of a total of 500,000 villages in India), an investigation by a central government commission in 1957 disclosed that none of the panchayats made "more than negligible" contribution to local administration and development." [22]

The only exception to this pattern of local stagnation has been in West Bengal, where a Marxist state government was elected in June 1977 on a pledge to shift the balance of power in favor of the rural poor. The following year, for the first time in two decades, 25 million West Bengalis elected local as well as regional panchayats. The village bodies are being entrusted with health and education services, and are encouraged to start small local industries. They have been given authority to levy taxes to finance their programs, and the state government is establishing training camps with technical personnel to alleviate the lack of local administrative experience and accounting skills. "It's no fake," a political analyst said. "The transfer of power is real, and seems to be working." Yet little hope is held for the spread of this successful panchayat revival to other states. "There are states which delegate some power to their panchayats, but nothing like the West Bengal experiment," observed a central government official. "It's a combination of a strong, cadre-based political party operating in a politically progressive state which has made it succeed there. That combination is rare." [23]

The discrepancy between radical rhetoric and social reality is as manifest in the nonagricultural sectors of India's economy as in the agricultural. Political leaders and economic planners originally were outspokenly hostile to a purely capitalist strategy of economic growth. Instead they favored central planning to restrict large private corporations and to support small private enterprises and traditional handicrafts. Prospects appeared promising at the outset, for India began her independent political existence with significant economic assets. A substantial industrial structure was inherited from the British era. The various industries had grown enormously during the war, rather than suffering devastation, as in the case of China. Also, India in 1948 enjoyed foreign-exchange reserves totaling £1.2 billion, derived from unrequited wartime exports to Britain.

Indian planners wrongly assumed that their projected Five Year Plans could be financed from the reserve holdings, supplemented by modest amounts of foreign aid. Their first plan, in fact, was a great success, with national income rising 18.4 percent rather than the projected 11–12 percent. The second Five Year Plan therefore called for public expenditures double those for the first, as well as greater emphasis on industrialization and on expansion of the public sector. At the same time the government lavishly granted import licenses, while harvests were less bountiful than during the first plan. Before the officials had realized the seriousness of their miscalculation, the foreign-exchange reserve was virtually wiped out. Delhi applied for credit to the World Bank, which responded that it considered the plan overambitious and unrealistic. This meant simply that it was unwilling to finance the type of public-sector heavy-industry projects that were at the heart of Indian economic strategy. "We are great believers in the private sector . . ." declared the vice president of the World Bank, Burke Knapp, "we do everything we can for the climate to be created in which private enterprise can make the maximum contribution to the development of the country." [24]

When credits finally were disbursed, the price was the distortion of the plan in the direction of industries that foreign companies were willing to finance. These companies naturally expected a return on their investments, so that remittance of dividends to foreign corporate headquarters rose rapidly during the early 1960s. By 1964 India's economy again was in crisis, and a World Bank mission called for the devaluation of the rupee and abolition of many of the controls over foreign trade.

During the next two years India was overwhelmed by droughts, war with Pakistan and the death of Nehru and of his successor, L. B. Shastri. The new Prime Minister, Indira Gandhi, was forced to accept more devaluation of the rupee and freer importation of a wide range of materials. But the expected boost to exports did not materialize. Instead India by now was heavily in debt, and so bound by restrictions and commitments that the original program for self-reliant and egalitarian economic development was hopelessly lost.

A further crippling factor from the beginning was the absence of effective agrarian reform, which deprived industries of an adequate domestic market. Textile plants, for example, could not sell adequate quantities of coarse cloth to the rural poor, and therefore were forced to switch to finer cotton or synthetic goods, which had limited domestic and foreign markets. Thus the annual growth rate of industrial production declined steadily: 7.4 percent in 1951–56, 6.8 percent in 1956–61, 8.9 percent in

1961–65, 3.3 percent in 1965–70 and 2.8 percent in 1970–74. Whereas per-capita annual income had increased modestly during the first three plans (1.8, 2.9 and 2.3 percent, respectively), the rate slumped to 0.3 percent for the whole decade from 1960–65 to 1973–74. Furthermore, the distribution of this income was becoming increasingly inequitable, so that the living standard of the urban and rural poor was actually declining.[25]

In 1974 the general economic crisis was aggravated, though *not* caused, by the steep rise in the cost of wheat and oil imports. "The country today is in the throes of a crisis much worse than any that has plagued it since Independence," wrote an Indian economist, Arun Shourie. "The economy has ceased to progress. Per-capita income is probably lower than it was a decade ago. Prices are rising about 30 percent a year. . . . Today, one institution after another is crumbling away in India." [26]

The crumbling was reflected in scattered armed outbreaks in the countryside and unceasing strikes and demonstrations in the cities. On July 26, 1975, Prime Minister Indira Gandhi declared a state of emergency on the pretext of a threat to her government by the right opposition, which had been trying to remove her from office on the legal grounds of having violated the election laws. Between 175,000 and 200,000 persons were detained without trial, but rightist leaders were mostly released, while those of the left remained imprisoned. "Oh, it's just wonderful," said a member of the Oberoi family soon after the imposition of emergency rule. "We used to have terrible problems with the unions. Now when they give us any trouble the Government just puts them in jail." [27] Strikes decreased dramatically and profits rose correspondingly. Bombay's *Economic and Political Weekly* of December 20, 1975, summarized the new economic climate under this title: "Corporate Sector: Never Had It So Good." It reported "serious shortfalls in every industrial sector," and an overall industrial performance that was "the poorest of all Plans so far." Yet "despite such poor performance . . . profit margins and profitability ratios have since equalled and even surpassed the highest levels achieved in the past."

Foreign corporations as well as Indian corporations prospered under the emergency, thanks to favorable government concessions. World Bank President Robert McNamara, during a week-long visit in India in November 1976, candidly emphasized the causal relationship between the government's concessions and the increasing volume of foreign aid:

> The reason for the turn in the country's [foreign] aid fortunes has to be sought in the changes in the government's economic policies. Industrial licensing has been diluted through a series of relaxations and exemptions, the restrictions on large houses have been rendered virtually inoperative, import policy has been relaxed, a variety of

generous subsidies and concessions have been extended to exports, foreign companies are being encouraged to expand . . . personal income tax and indirect taxes have been cut and there is confident expectation of a cut in the rates of corporation taxation in the next budget. In other words, major advances have been made in the direction of an open, free market, private enterprise economy. The World Bank has never made a secret of the fact that these are the policies it favors. Private businessmen, whether American or British, have sought to conceal their preferences even less.[28]

The combination of soaring profits, low productivity and underutilization of plant capacity meant high unemployment and increasing polarization. The Minister of Commerce, Mohan Daria, declared in a speech in London on August 30, 1977, that two hundred million people in India were unemployed. The defeat of Indira Gandhi in the March 1977 elections and the advent of a Janata Party government under Morarji Desai solved nothing, as reflected in Desai's brief tenure in office. By 1979 strikes were as frequent as before the declaration of the emergency in 1975. Not only workers and peasants, but even some police forces were defying the government, while white-collar workers for the first time were organizing in considerable numbers.

In the January 1980 elections, Indira Gandhi staged a dramatic comeback, winning two thirds of the parliamentary seats, though only 42 percent of the popular vote. She won because she appeared as a "can do" leader, in contrast to the factional bickering and aimless drifting of the Desai government. In practice, Indira Gandhi was able to do little more than her predecessor. The country was torn by chronic problems and turmoil—by Hindu-Muslim riots in Hyderabad, riots in Assam over Bengali-speaking outsiders, growing liberation movements demanding independence in the Northeast, endemic inflation approaching 30 percent annually and above all, the pervasive and proliferating poverty. By September 1980 Indira Gandhi once again had to resort to repression to control the mounting tumult. She issued an ordinance authorizing national and state governments to detain any person for up to twelve months without trial if necessary to maintain public order, supplies or essential services. She justified her action on the ground of "communal disharmony, caste conflicts, social tension, atrocities against minorities and other weaker sections of the society and increasing tendencies on the part of various interested parties to engineer agitation on different issues." [29]

All these troubles were very real, and yet only symptoms. The root problem was the fact that between 1956 and 1978 India's food production had risen 100 percent, her population had grown 50 percent but at the same time the number of malnourished Indian citizens had increased rather than decreased. The country was self-sufficient in grains, yet the per-capita grain consumption of the already malnourished population was dropping. In 1980 over 315 million of India's 650 million people lived below the poverty line, which is put at a household income of $8.00 a month in the countryside and $9.00 a month in the cities. The government boasts that in 1950 the country's chief exports were jute, cotton and tea, whereas in 1980 the single most important export product was engineered machinery. Yet Indian industry in 1978 created 750,000 new jobs, while the number of new entrants into the job market totaled 2.5 million. Industry cannot do more because lack of domestic purchasing power limits it to producing for the small percentage of native rich and for limited foreign markets. It cannot even start producing for the limitless needs of India's destitute in both rural and urban areas.

Raj Thapar, editor of *Seminar*, India's most prestigious intellectual magazine, has defined the basic problem in almost the exact words used by Raúl Prebisch concerning Latin America (see Chapter 24, Section III): "At first we all assumed that growth in and of itself would bring all the other blessings—employment, social justice and greater national welfare. Now we know that this is simply not true." [30] The reason it is not true is that economic growth without social restructuring has led in India, and most other Third World countries, to greater economic inequity and corresponding social polarization and political instability. Writing in 1970, Gunnar Myrdal foresaw little likelihood for the needed restructuring because of the "lack of organized pressure from below." [31] A decade later, the political scientist, Francis Frankel, was describing the emergence of precisely such "pressure from below."

> Since independence in 1947 political mobilization in India has followed a vertical pattern. The dominant castes and the landowning families controlled the "vote banks" of the poor within their jurisdiction, delivering them to a Congress Party that was dominated by a Westernized urban and intellectual elite. Now this has broken down. The various castes and classes are pursuing their own interests as they define them. There has been a greatly accelerated politicization of the backward, poorer classes, who are challenging the domination of their particular oppressive elites.[32]

India has reached a turning point in her development as an independent country. For decades the Congress Party has served as an "umbrella party," to use the phrase of Dr. Sun Gupta. As such it effectively preserved the status quo with progressive rhetoric and paper reforms. Now the umbrella is being rejected, as various clusters of differentiated groups break away "with their own leaders and ambitions." [33-35] Unless

Indira Gandi is able and willing to revolutionize her party—a most implausible eventuality—the past era of the Congress umbrella will give way to a new era of fragmentation and confrontation. Indeed, the transition already is well under way.

B.
Middle East

The post-World War II evolution of the Middle East was generally similar to that of India. With the exception of Palestine-Israel, which will be considered in a later section, newly independent Middle Eastern states resembled India in that they underwent more of a change in constitutional status than in social structure.

In 1939 the Middle East was dominated by Britain and France, either directly through the mandates, or indirectly through dependent and subservient local dynasties and elites (see Chapter 21, Section IV). During the war years the Middle East, like India, did not experience invasion or occupation. The Germans and Italians did not advance far beyond the Libyan-Egyptian border, just as the Japanese did not beyond the Indian-Burmese frontier. Also, there was much ambivalence in the Middle East, as in India, about supporting the Allied powers or the Axis. The Arabs resented Anglo-French domination as much as the Indians did British rule. Referring to the unhappy experiences of the interwar years, an Arab scholar observed that "there was nothing to choose between the oppression exercised in the name of democracy, and that exercised in the name of Fascism." [36]

These considerations explain the April 1941 uprising in Iraq, which was more anti-British than pro-German. Since the loudly promised German aid did not materialize, British and Trans-Jordanian troops crushed the revolt and occupied the country. Likewise in Egypt, King Farouk refused to appoint a pro-Allied Premier until British armored units surrounded his palace and threatened to depose him unless he complied. Farouk submitted, and Cairo became the secure base for the Allied Middle East Supply Center. Over half a million British, American, Indian, New Zealand, Australian, South African, Polish, Greek, Czechoslovak and Yugoslav soldiers passed through Egypt en route to various battlefronts.

In Iran, also, the Allies imposed their will when Reza Shah rejected Soviet and British requests to use his country as a supply route after the Nazi invasion of the Soviet Union. British and Russian troops invaded Iran in August 1941, the Russians occupying the five northern provinces, and the British the remainder of the country. Reza Shah was replaced with his twenty-year-old son, and in January 1942 Iran, Britain and

Russia signed a treaty granting the Allies transit rights, but also stipulating that Allied troops be withdrawn six months after the defeat of the Axis.

Although the nationalists had been unable to satisfy their aspirations during the war, the new postwar balance of power offered them an opportunity that they promptly exploited. Britain and France were much weaker in 1945 than they had been in 1939, and the resulting power vacuum in the Middle East was soon filled by the United States and the Soviet Union. The Arabs took advantage of the Anglo-French weakness and the American-Russian rivalry to play off one side against the other. They were further aided by their control over vast oil reserves, which quickly became indispensable to Western industry. Thus the Arabs were able to win concessions in quick order, and to cast off the centuries-old Anglo-French domination.

On March 22, 1945, eight Middle Eastern states combined to form the Arab League. Each member remained sovereign, and the Arab League decisions were not binding, yet Arab nationalism now did have for the first time a common instrument for use against the Western powers and the Zionists in Palestine. The Arab League won its first victory against the French in Syria and Lebanon. These two states had been administered by Vichy officials until June 1941, when they were driven out by British and Free French forces. General de Gaulle proved no different from other French leaders in his determination to retain control over all colonial possessions. This provoked strikes and demonstrations, and De Gaulle retaliated with an expeditionary force, which bombed Damascus in May 1945. The Arab League promptly demanded the evacuation of all French forces, and was supported by Churchill, who was anxious to avoid a confrontation with Arab nationalists while the war was still in progress. Under British pressure the French withdrew their troops and in July 1945 they accepted the end of their rule in the Middle East. With the departure of the British in 1946 Syria and Lebanon finally were completely free.

Although Arab nationalism had triumphed against the French, it suffered humiliating defeat in 1948 at the hands of the Israelis. The Palestine debacle discredited the old regimes in the Middle East, contributing to the overthrow of Egypt's King Farouk. His place soon was taken by the charismatic Gamal Abdel Nasser, who became immensely popular throughout the Arab world as the apostle of "Arab socialism" and Arab unity.

Nasser's first victory was the negotiation of an agreement (Oct. 19, 1954) by which the British withdrew their troops from the Canal Zone and left their installations to the Egyptians. Nasser's greatest triumph occurred when a combined British-French-Israeli attack on the Suez miscarried. The roots of the aggression went back to the unresolved Arab-Israeli conflict, and to the intrusion of the Cold War into the Middle East. The United States had sponsored the Baghdad Pact signed on November 1, 1955, by Britain, Turkey, Iraq and Pakistan. The American aim was to implement its strategy of uniting the "northern tier" of Middle Eastern countries to form a barrier against any Soviet push southward. The theory was that this would divert Iraq's attention northward against Russia, thereby isolating the aggressive Nasser and encouraging him to turn toward Africa rather than toward Israel and the Middle East.

The strategy boomeranged, as Nasser and the Soviets retaliated by concluding an arms pact that exchanged Egyptian cotton for Soviet war materials. This deal gave the Soviet Union a toehold in the Middle East that it had never had before. The next unpleasant surprise for the West was Nasser's nationalization of the Suez Canal (July 26, 1956) in retaliation against Secretary of State John Foster Dulles' sudden retraction of a provisional offer to finance the building of the High Dam at Aswan. This led the British Conservative Party government to think of armed action against Nasser, especially since it held many of the shares of the nationalized Suez Canal Company. The French, too, had been thinking along these lines because of Nasser's propaganda and material aid to the Algerian rebels. At the same time Israel had been planning a preventive war against Egypt to stop the unceasing border raids. Hence the decision for a combined operation, with the Israelis attacking through the Sinai peninsula and the British and French along the Canal Zone.

The Israelis swiftly cut through the Sinai, but the unprepared British and French did not begin actual landings until a week later, on November 5, 1956. The delay proved fatal, with overwhelming criticism mounting on all sides. The Soviet Union sent a virtual ultimatum, while the United States, which had received no word of the planned attack, also reacted strongly in opposition. The UN passed with a large majority a resolution demanding the withdrawal of all foreign troops from Egypt. The aggressors were forced to yield, and by the end of December the last of the Anglo-French units had returned home. Far from overthrowing Nasser, the Suez War had left him the master of the Canal, and had made him the hero of the entire Arab world.

The Arab nationalist fervor contributed to the joining of Egypt and Syria in the United Arab Republic in February 1958. Anti-Western elements were further strengthened with the overthrow in July 1958 of the British-backed Hashimite monarchy in Iraq. A few months later the last British units left their Iraqi air bases and the new republican government denounced the Baghdad Pact and terminated some thirty years of alliance with Britain. At about this time an American correspondent in

Egypt reported an incident that symbolized the new spirit sweeping the Arab world:

> On a height overlooking the site of the future High Dam at Aswan, in the Nile Valley of southern Egypt, this correspondent asked a ragged laborer to pose for a picture with his arm outstretched, pointing to the site.
>
> He posed and the writer held out a coin for baksheesh. Baksheesh —a tip—has been for so long so much a part of daily life in Egypt that old timers begin the day by acquiring a pocketful of coins.
>
> But the laborer at Aswan turned on his heel when offered baksheesh and he was restored to good humor only by a hearty handshake and profuse thanks. The guide explained that Mahmoud knew what he was pointing at and its meaning, and was insulted to be offered a tip for such a gesture. . . . many Egyptians feel, for the first time in their lives, a sense of national dignity, a sense that nationally they are doing something and going somewhere.[37]

The feeling of "going somewhere" was indeed widespread among the Arabs in the late 1950s and early 1960s. There was strong nationalist backing for the often-proclaimed goal of "Arab unity," as well as much talk about "Arab socialism." After every confrontation with the West, Nasser moved steadily to the left with wholesale nationalizing of domestic and foreign enterprises. In doing so, he won acclaim and support throughout the Arab world as the new Saladdin who was defeating the Western imperialist powers. The decade after 1956 was the radical decade in the Middle East. The Western-backed monarchs of Iran and the Arabian peninsula were on the defensive against Nasser. In addition to forming the United Arab Republic with Syria, Nasser in 1965 sent troops to support republican rebels in Yemen, thus challenging the Saudi dynasty in its own backyard.

Then came the terrible thunderbolt—the humiliating Six Day War of June 1967. At the end of those disastrous six days, Israeli soldiers stood along the Suez Canal in the South, the Jordan River in the East and the Syrian heights overlooking Lake Galilee in the Northeast. They had captured nine Egyptian generals, over three hundred officers, thousands of rank-and-file prisoners and mountains of new Russian-made military equipment.

The progressive Arab forces represented by Nasser never recovered from that calamity. Since 1967 rightist elements have prevailed in the Arab world and Soviet influence has given way before American. An additional shove to the right was provided by the 1973 Arab-Israeli War, during which the oil states enforced an embargo against most Western countries and raised their oil prices from two to six dollars per barrel.

The unprecedented increase in oil revenues gave the conservative bloc—Iran, Saudi Arabia and the Gulf sheikhdoms—powerful economic and political leverage throughout the Middle East. This was especially true in the crucial state of Egypt, where Nasser had died in 1970 and had been succeeded by the relatively conservative Anwar Sadat. The Saudis supported Sadat when he turned against the Soviet Union and toward improved relations with the United States.

In their relations with Israel, however, the Arabs were frustrated by their failure to recover the territories they had lost in 1967. Neither UN resolutions, nor economic boycotts against Israel nor guerrilla attacks along Israel's frontiers succeeded in getting the Israelis to evacuate the occupied territories. The basic reason for the failure was that the much-touted "Arab unity" and "Arab socialism" were much more impressive in rhetoric than in reality.

Arab spokesmen since World War II have stressed the unity of "one Arab nation," but in practice they have acted as different nations with conflicting interests. The only common bonds are those of language and religion, but these have not sufficed to unite them, any more than they have the Roman Catholic, Spanish-speaking peoples of the Americas. More powerful than common language and religion have been the numerous centrifugal forces. One of these is the great variety of governmental institutions—monarchies, theocracies, republics, military dictatorships and the assorted small sheikhdoms of the Persian Gulf. Also there are vast differences in cultural backgrounds and in attitude to the modern world, so that countries like Lebanon and Egypt probably have more in common with Italy and Greece than with Saudi Arabia and Yemen. Then there are rivalries between dynasties such as the Hashimites and the Saudis; between national leaders such as Sadat and Qadaffi; between religious groups such as those between and within the Muslim and Christian faiths; and among ideologies such as the varieties of "socialisms" espoused by the Nasserites, the Baathists and the splintered Communist Parties and Palestinian revolutionaries. Also, profound economic differences separate the haves from the have-nots among and within Arab countries. Saudi Arabia, Kuwait and Iraq do not respond to proposals that their oil resources be used for more comprehensive regional economic development. Likewise the *nouveaux riches* of Cairo, Baghdad and Damascus show little concern for the rural landless and the urban unemployed, other than opening foreign bank accounts lest existing social constraints break down in the future.

Arab socialism has proven as illusory as Arab unity. One reason was the weakness of the Arab Communist Parties. There was no counterpart in the Middle East to Mao in China or Ho in Vietnam. The reason is that the local Communist Parties followed the Kremlin line, which led to a dead end because the Soviet Union wanted only to draw the Middle East out of the American sphere of influence. It had no intention of supporting or fomenting social revolution, for that would endanger the overall Soviet objective of coexistence with the West. Thus local Communist Parties followed the Kremlin line and failed to provide leadership and to win any mass following, even though the revolutionary potential in a country such as Egypt was equal to that in China and Vietnam. Hence the field was left clear for Nasser and his "Arab socialism."

Nasser had no coherent social theory or political program when he and his fellow officers seized power in 1952. He was of petty bourgeois origins, his father being a postal employee, as Sadat's was a small farmer. Like most of the free officers who overthrew Farouk, Nasser's intellectual outlook was that of the radical wing of Islamic fundamentalism. He found that the import substitution industrialization of the interwar years had yielded very modest results. To achieve a more rapid rate of industrialization he replaced the old ruling elite with technocratic personnel consisting of military officers, economists and engineers.

The first measures of the Nasser regime included abolition of the monarchy, dissolution of all existing political parties and organizations, and land redistribution designed to increase the number of small landowners and to redirect capital investment to industry. To facilitate industrialization, Nasser established a new Industrial Bank and a Permanent Council for National Production. But Egypt's bourgeoisie was not so easily weaned away from its traditional preference for fast dealing and quick profit-taking, so that 70 percent of new investments went into the building industry—mostly apartments for the middle and upper classes.

After his Suez victory Nasser was emboldened to try more radical economic measures. These included nationalization of foreign and Egyptian banks, heavy industries, insurance firms and transportation and land companies. Also, economic planning got under way with the first Ten Year Plan for 1960–70. These economic measures ended foreign domination of Egypt's economy and enabled the state to determine the goals, methods and tempo of national economic development. The stress now was on large-scale industrialization, prospecting for new sources of energy, desert land recovery and construction of the Aswan High Dam.

Nasser also introduced political innovations as drastic as the economic ones. He banned all political parties along with the monarchy, and on May 21, 1963, he presented to the National Congress of Popular Forces his Charter of National Action. This proclaimed that "socialism is the way to social freedom" and that "scientific socialism is the suitable style for finding the right method leading to progress." Furthermore, it appeared during the early 1960s that the road to "progress" indeed had been found. The average rate of GDP growth between 1959–60 and 1964–65, was 5–6 percent, or about 3 percent per capita.

In the end Nasser's "Arab socialism" proved abortive. One reason was the population explosion precipitated by a rapidly declining death rate and a much slower declining birth rate—a widespread trend in the Third World at the time. Another reason was the drain of military expenditures because of the Arab-Israeli conflict, capped by the military disaster of 1967. But the basic reason was that Nasser's "Arab socialism" was simply an Egyptian version of the state capitalism of India and other Third World countries. As such, it was inherently incapable of mobilizing national human and material resources for independent and equitable economic development.

The land reforms of 1952 and 1961 resulted merely in the substitution of one class of notables by another. The aristocratic landowners of the past gave way to a new class of rich and middle peasants who obtained credit, machinery and chemical fertilizers, thereby becoming efficient capitalist farmers. But the great majority of peasants who were landless or who owned less than 5 feddans (1 feddan = 1.04 acres) "were no better off in 1970 than they had been when they rejoiced at the overthrow of the old regime in 1952. . . . Land reform struck at the power basis of the royal family, the landed aristocracy, and very large landlords, but not that of the rich peasants and village notables." [38]

Another weakness in Nasser's "Arab socialism" was that it encouraged the consumption pattern of a welfare state type of economy. Imports comprised an excessively large percentage of consumer goods such as TV sets and household appliances, which weakened the capital goods sector essential for independent, self-sustaining economic development. Thus manufacturing created new jobs for only 18 percent of the increase in the labor force between 1937 and 1960, and only 16 percent of the increase between 1960 and 1970.[39] While the industrial sector was lagging, the state bureaucracy was overexpanding. Between 1962 and 1966, the number of bureaucrats increased by 61 percent, and their incomes by 215 percent. Meanwhile, the number of blue-collar workers was actually declining.

Nasser's "Arab socialism" proved incapable of resolving the contradictions between rich and poor peasants, and between urban workers and the new bourgeois class of contractors, distributors, import-export traders and state-military bureaucrats. The resulting tensions prompted Nasser not only to eliminate the political parties but also to jail over two thousand Communists. This effectively liquidated the left, but the rightist bourgeoisie and the landowners retained their economic power and gradually reorganized politically as a class. They did not lose all their

capital nor all their land, and they found new outlets for capital investment in real estate and construction. Also they retained much of their
influence in the countryside, and they made alliances with sectors of the
army, the bureaucrats and the technocrats. Thus Nasser found himself
with a vacuum on the left and with growing pressure groups on the right.

Nasser was able to resist the resulting steady pull to the right in
Egyptian politics. But he resisted only as an individual and never as the
representative of an organized left-wing force. His "socialism" was socialism by presidential decree, implemented by the army and police.
There was no initiative or participation at the grass-roots level. The
failure to buttress Arab socialism with socialists explains why, after
Nasser's death in 1970, Sadat was able to reverse course with so little
opposition. The peasants were unorganized; the workers lacked a consciousness that could affect national politics; the old leftists were broken
or co-opted: the Nasserist left was as ineffective as were the Peronists after
Perón: the middle class was interested primarily in consumerism; and
the military had been bought off with generous privileges. This left only
the students, who staged demonstrations and organized "committees for
the defense of democracy." But the response was weak, and the students
were neutralized by economic pressure and military force.

Sadat was free to proceed with his new strategy which, in the economic
realm, was based on the notion of "triangular investment" linking
American technology, Arab capital and Egyptian labor. Most importantly,
this involved the principle of *infatah* or open door, which meant the economic de-Nasserization of Egypt. Economic planning and nationalization
of enterprises were given up in order to attract foreign capital. In February 1974, "free zones" exempt from taxes and duties were established
along the Suez Canal. Corporations investing elsewhere in Egypt were
granted five-to-eight-year exemption from taxes, and investment banks
were freed from currency controls. In June 1974 an investment law opened
industry, metallurgy, banking and insurance (all previously nationalized)
to foreign investments. Speaking before the New York Economic Club in
November 1975, Sadat spoke about the need for a "blood transfusion" for
the Egyptian economy, mentioning the sum of "over $3 billion."

Despite Sadat's enticements, very few Western corporations took advantage of the "open door." They were discouraged by the inefficiency of
the cumbersome Egyptian bureaucracy and by the archaic communications and transportation infrastructure. Also the Egyptian bourgeoisie,
while welcoming the "open door" policy, nevertheless saw foreign capital
as a threat to its domestic interests and insisted that joint ventures be
formulated on its own terms. The end result of Sadat's innovations was
a worsening of Egypt's economic position. The elimination of central
planning led to an increase of imports from $3.94 billion in 1973 to $5.7

billion in 1976, with luxury items being prominent in the upsurge. An estimated 25 percent of the work force of 9 million remained unemployed or underemployed.

By 1976 Egypt was on the brink of bankruptcy, incapable of repaying short-term loans that were due. A consortium comprising the World Bank, the International Monetary Fund and the governments of the United States and Saudi Arabia provided the necessary aid. The price was the devaluation of the Egyptian pound and the abolition of subsidies for basic necessities. The latter injunction immediately drove up the price of propane gas 46 percent, flour 63 percent, meat 26 percent and rice 16 percent. For a population already living at bare subsistence level, this was intolerable. A virtual insurrection broke out in January 1977 in cities throughout the country. Sadat backed down by restoring the subsidies, a retreat that the foreign financial interests accepted because the fall of Sadat would have brought down the whole house of cards.

The devaluation of the pound, however, was enforced because its disruptive impact on the economy was not recognized by the aroused populace. The cost of imported goods, on which Egyptian industry and agriculture are structurally dependent, rose commensurately with the deflation. At the same time the cost of labor was increasing because of the inflation and the competition of an Arab market open to Egyptian workers. Small manufacturing firms went bankrupt, leaving the dismissed workers the choice of joining the underemployed in peripheral occupations or emigrating. Egypt, like Mexico, has some 20 percent of its labor force working in foreign countries. The remittances help to counter the unfavorable trade balance, but also contribute to the unwholesome change in the value system toward consumerism.

The quality of life in Cairo retains its nightmarish quality, with whole families sharing one small room, with refuse from overloaded sewers flooding the streets, and with passengers hanging off the back and sides of packed buses in order to get to work. The resentment against this misery is aggravated by the proliferation of black marketeers, speculators, smugglers and assorted entrepreneurs under the aegis of infatah. A legislator charged, during a parliamentary debate in December 1975, that Egypt then had five hundred millionaires compared with four before King Farouk's ouster in 1952. Nightclubs, discotheques, liquor stores, expensive limousines and other symbols of the enormity of social inequity were the special targets of the demonstrators during the January 1977 riots.

If conditions in the cities are appalling, those in the countryside are even worse. Life expectancy still is less than forty years. The illiteracy rate is 70 percent, higher than it was ten years ago. An estimated 60 to 70 percent of the rural population suffers from debilitating bilharzia.

Agricultural productivity is increasing 2 percent a year, or less than the rate of population increase. In 1975 agricultural imports for the first time exceeded in value the total agricultural exports. A study of contemporary rural Egypt foresees sharpening class contradictions and conflicts between the poor and landless peasants on the one hand, and the rich peasantry on the other.

Sadat has resorted to three tactics to cope with this ominous social disintegration. One is political; he has proclaimed the end of Nasser's "totalitarianism," and pledged a Bill of Rights that will mark "the start of a new life in Egypt." In his 1977 May Day speech he identified Nasserism with "detention camps, custodianship and sequestration, a one-opinion, one-party system." As a contrast, he virtually created in November 1976 three political parties: the center Arab Socialist Party, the left National Progressive Grouping Party and the right Socialist Liberal Party. The strongest force on the right, however, is the Muslim Brotherhood and its underground paramilitary bodies. In practice Sadat has favored the center, tolerated the right and repressed the left. During the January 1977 riots he overlooked the leading role of the Muslim Brotherhood, but arrested prominent members of the National Progressives as well as trade unionists and Communists. He repeated this selective repression in 1979 against opponents of his peace missions to Jerusalem and to Camp David.

Sadat's second tactic is to make Egypt the successor of Iran as the gendarme of the Persian Gulf and of adjacent African territories. By ensuring the smooth flow of oil to the West, Sadat hopes to attract massive financial assistance for Egypt's faltering economy. Hence the dispatch of eight thousand Egyptian troops to Oman to replace the departing Iranians who had been sustaining the reactionary Sultan Kaboos against rebel guerrillas. Hence also the Egyptian contingent sent to Zaïre to support the corrupt President Mobutu during the 1977 uprising in Shaba Province. Replacements for Egypt's old and deteriorating Soviet-made arsenal have been provided by China, ever ready to support any enemy of her Soviet enemy.

Sadat's chief tactic for survival is his dramatic peace initiative, culminating in the September 1978 Camp David accords. He has presented peace to the Egyptian public as the solution to current problems and the key to future prosperity. The immediate response has been gratifying for the hard-pressed Sadat. Internationally it has earned him the Nobel Prize for Peace, and at home public support has been whipped up by the government press, which portrays the Palestinians as greedy ingrates who would fight to the last drop of Egyptian blood. On his return from Jerusalem, Sadat was greeted by enthusiastic crowds bearing signs such as "Egypt first, Egypt second, Egypt last."

Yet two basic questions remain unresolved. The first is whether Camp David is in fact the prelude to peace. An affirmative answer seems quixotic, with the West Bank Arabs on the one hand demanding an independent Palestinian state, and on the other the Begin government acting as though the peace treaty gave it *carte blanche* to settle and permanently subjugate the West Bank.

Even more cheerless is the second question, whether a durable Middle East peace would presage the "golden age" that Sadat is promising. In 1978 Sadat proclaimed that 1980 would be "the year of prosperity." The United States has made every effort to help realize the prosperity. Between 1975 and 1980 the United States allocated $5.3 billion in civilian assistance to Egypt—the most ambitious aid project since the Marshall Plan. On a per-capita basis, Egyptians are receiving more aid in real dollars than West Europeans did after World War II. The aid is pouring into the country faster than it can be absorbed, so that in July 1980, only half of the $100 million monthly disbursement was actually spent.

The bonanza has stimulated a boom in luxury consumer goods and apartments, but these do not help the great majority of Egyptians.[40] The lavish American aid is papering over the cracks for the moment, but it cannot continue indefinitely. As soon as it slackens, then Sadat or his successor will have to face up to the persisting institutional impasse: to the dependent and exploitative relationship between the workers and the new "parasitic bourgeoisie" in Cairo, between the poor peasants and the new *kulaks* in the countryside and between the debt-ridden Egyptian state and its controlling creditors in the Western capitals. This was sensed by a government clerk who, in quiet despair, told an American correspondent: "You know, my children will be as poor as I." [41]

It might be argued that Egypt is not typical of the Middle East because of its heavy load of built-in problems—the lack of extensive oil deposits or other natural riches; the limitations on agriculture because of the surrounding desert; and the population explosion, creating an adverse and constantly worsening land-population ratio. In contrast to these handicaps, Iran is a Middle Eastern country that is blessed with oil revenues adequate for any economic program, with abundant other natural resources and with a favorable land-population ratio. Nevertheless, Iran was beset with social and economic difficulties of such magnitude that the Shah was overthrown in 1977 despite his superbly equipped army of 450,000 men.

The revolution was as surprising as it was elemental, for the Shah had been portrayed in the West as a benevolent and popular reformer who was distributing land to the poor, performing "economic miracles" with Iran's oil revenues and creating a better life for his thirty-six million subjects. The Shah himself was not averse to gilding the lily, boasting that Iran would be the world's fifth greatest military power by 1980, that it would equal Western Germany's per-capita income by 1986 and that it would then become a "great civilization" superior to all past and present societies because he would have eradicated "the concept of class and class conflict." President Carter contributed to this fantasy with this toast to the Shah during a 1978 New Year's Eve party in Teheran: "Iran under the great leadership of the Shah is an island of stability in one of the most troubled areas of the world. This is a great tribute to you, your Majesty, and to your leadership and to the respect, admiration and love which your people give to you." [42]

A year later, on January 16, 1979, the self-styled "King of Kings" and "Shadow of God" was forced to flee his capital and seek exile abroad, where he died the following year. To understand the reason for this unexpected dénouement, it is necessary to note that the Shah was essentially a Western creation. Once before he had been forced into exile, in 1953, when he tried to oppose a popular Prime Minister, Dr. Mohammad Mossadeq, who had nationalized the oilfields at the expense of Anglo-Iranian Oil Company. A State Department intelligence report prepared in January 1953 by the outgoing Truman administration concluded that Mossadeq's nationalization measure had "almost universal Iranian support." It also pictured Mossadeq as strongly anti-Communist, and noted that the Communist Tudeh Party was at odds with Mossadeq, and deemed his overthrow a "high priority." [43]

Despite this report, Secretary of State John Foster Dulles and CIA Director Allen Dulles convinced President Eisenhower that Mossadeq was a Soviet stooge who had to be ousted to safeguard Western interests. The "destabilizing" assignment was given to Kermit Roosevelt, grandson of Theodore Roosevelt and CIA bureau chief in the Middle East. Roosevelt arrived incognito in Iran in August 1953 and proceeded to plot the coup with General Fazollah Zahedi. Assured of American support, the Shah willingly dismissed Mossadeq and appointed Zahedi in his place. The Shah then fled abroad until General Zahedi entered Teheran with his armed forces. On August 22, Allen Dulles personally escorted the Shah back to his capital.

Once safe on his throne, the Shah first organized a highly centralized government apparatus. With the aid of oil revenues and American expertise, he modernized the police, bureaucracy, armed forces and the notorious SAVAK security apparatus. By 1970 he was ready to begin the transformation of Iran into a subimperialist power, or a "regional influential," to use Washington terminology. Between 1972 and 1976 the Shah purchased $10.4 billion of American arms, and there were another $12.1 billion in the pipeline when the Shah fell in 1979.

Iran thus became the ideal state for implementing the Nixon Doctrine, which called for local clients with massive U.S. military aid and training to do the fighting necessary for preserving the status quo in strategic Third World regions. The Shah had the money to pay for the most modern weapons systems, which fascinated him, and also the will to use them to suppress radical regional movements—as he did in Oman against the Dhofar uprising, in Pakistan against Baluchistan dissidents and in Somalia against Ethiopia. Since Saudi Arabia did not have the manpower for such an active regional role, Washington viewed Iran, together with Israel, as the guardians of the Middle East status quo. The later Egyptian-Israeli accord reached at Camp David was essentially an arrangement for extending and strengthening this pro-status quo framework.

Despite this imposing façade, the Shah's imperial edifice was inherently fragile and flawed. It had become increasingly dependent on oil, which represented 19.5 percent of GDP in 1972–73 and 49.7 percent in 1977–78. In the latter year it accounted for 77 percent of government revenue and 87 percent of foreign-exchange earnings. But the oil industry was encapsulated within the national economy, with few "backward linkages" or "forward linkages." It employed a tiny labor force, it acquired its technology from abroad and most of the output was exported. Furthermore, the oil reserves are finite, so that production will begin declining in the 1990s, with a corresponding decline in revenues.

The basic problem facing Iran was to develop its agriculture and industry in the remaining time so as to become independent of oil. In both areas, however, the country faced disaster despite the grandiose plans and the vast expenditures. The land-reform program, which got under way in 1972, proved as abortive as the Egyptian, so far as the welfare of the peasant class as a whole was concerned. "Land reform has not improved the socio-economic status of the peasantry," concludes a 1974 study. "It has affected a large proportion of the peasants adversely. . . . instead of creating an independent peasantry and a more autonomous urban bourgeoisie, the reform has led to the further consolidation of the traditional socio-economic power of the state over all social classes." [44]

Land was distributed to about half the landless, but there was no follow-up with technological help. Agricultural productivity stagnated, causing the Shah to turn to foreign agribusiness corporations. Their capital-intensive operations displaced peasants, so that since 1973 about 8 percent of the rural population was driven to the cities each year, where the lack of jobs turned them into bitter critics of the regime. Nor did the agribusiness operations increase productivity sufficiently to meet the soaring demand for foodstuffs stimulated by the oil revenues, by the high population growth and by the presence of increasing numbers of well-paid foreigners. Despite all the government efforts, agricultural production rose 2 to 2.5 percent annually, as against population growth of 3 percent. Between 10 and 20 percent of the petrodollars were used to pay for food imports, creating a dangerously anomalous situation. Whereas agriculture has been exploited in most countries to subsidize industrialization, in Iran it was oil that was used to pay for the agricultural deficit. "Looking back," said a former cabinet minister who supported the Shah, "if we should have done one thing differently, it should have been to strike a balance between urban industry and agriculture. We distributed land but we did not do enough to keep people in the countryside. It would have made this country more stable." [45]

The prospect for industry was equally bleak. The Shah's megalomania in military matters led him to invest more in foreign armaments than in domestic industry. The service sector of the economy was so bloated that in 1974 it accounted for 39.4 percent of GDP in contrast to only 16.1 percent from industry. The cumbersome bureaucracy was not geared to promoting rapid economic development, so that both Iranian and foreign entrepreneurs spent much time and money coping with regulations and bribing their way through bottlenecks. The industries that were established were mostly of the import-substitution variety, and they usually assembled imported parts rather than manufactured components. Also, the high protective tariffs promoted inefficiency, so that a Chevrolet in 1976 took 45 hours to assemble in Iran as against 25 hours in Germany. Furthermore, whatever was manufactured—whether cars or steel or household appliances—was likely to be consumed at home because of the purchasing power generated by petrodollars. Thus nonoil exports declined from 22 percent of imports in 1959, to 19 percent in 1973 and to 5 percent in 1975. Equally disturbing was the fact that in 1974–75, 72 percent of nonoil exports came from the traditional sector (for example, Persian rugs) as against 28 percent from the new industrial sector.

This economic fiasco inevitably had negative social repercussions. The population remained 60 percent illiterate, and of the 325,000 students who went abroad to study during the decade 1969 to 1978, only 22,000 returned. Personal income taxes were low and usually evaded. The Finance Minister revealed in 1975 that only 9,362 of the 20,000 registered companies filed tax returns. Of these, 43 percent declared losses, so that less than a quarter of the companies paid any taxes. Also, the gap between rural and urban living standards was widening, which swelled the influx into urban slums. A 1973 study by the International Labor Organization (ILO) of income distribution in Iran concluded that while 10 percent of the population at the apex of the incomes scale accounted for 40 percent of total private consumption, the 30 percent of the population at the bottom of the incomes scale accounted for only 10 percent of private consumption.[46] A 1975 Hudson Institute report concluded: "Iran, in the final decade of this century, could prove to be no more than a half-completed industrial edifice, with the trappings of power and international influence and none of the substance." [47]

Such was the background of the prolonged revolutionary crisis that began on November 25, 1977, when five thousand university students clashed with police. This triggered cycles of rioting, which reached a peak in September 1978, when huge demonstrations and much bloodshed led the Shah to declare martial law and to appoint a military government headed by chief of staff General Azhari. By this time workers were joining what had started as a predominantly middle-class movement, and their strikes paralyzed the urban economy. Also, the entire movement gained unity and leadership with Ayatollah Khomeini's move from Iraq to Paris, where he had far greater access to the world media and thereby to Iran. By December 1978 the opposition forces had mobilized such overwhelming mass support that the military government was rendered helpless.

The Shah then appointed as Prime Minister the French-educated Shahpur Bakhtiar, who offered a peaceful transition to a democratic regime. He dissolved the hated SAVAK and promised to yield power to a government elected under proper constitutional procedures. With the support of Washington, which realized that the Shah was doomed, Bakhtiar persuaded the monarch to leave the country on January 16, 1979. But the hopes for a peaceful solution were doomed because Bakhtiar was identified with the Shah, who had appointed him. Strikes and demonstrations continued, while Khomeini refused to meet with envoys sent by Bakhtiar. Instead the Ayatollah returned to Teheran on February 1, and nominated Mehdi Bazargan as the head of a new provisional government. The intolerable anomaly of two rival governments came to a head on February 9 when junior officers and technicians at the Dosh Tappeh air base near Teheran clashed with their senior officers and with the "Immortals" section of the Imperial Guard. The fighting precipitated a general uprising in Teheran, which smashed the pro-Shah sections of the military and forced Bakhtiar to resign and flee. During the following days similar clashes occurred in the provincial towns, and everywhere the revolutionaries seized large stores of military equipment from the military bases they overran. In place of the American-backed Pahlavi dynasty, the Ayatollah now was the *de facto* ruler of Iran.

This extraordinary revolution is as significant as it was unexpected. It was remarkably broad-based and sustained, with some twenty thousand demonstrators sacrificing their lives during the resistance, which persisted for more than a year. Also, it was an urban revolution, in contrast to all the other post-World War II peasant insurrections in the Third World—in China, Southeast Asia, Portuguese Africa and Algeria. Finally, it was the first successful revolution in a subimperialist state. The victory of the revolutionaries, despite unlimited American support for the Shah, has obvious implications for other states primed to play a similar "regional influential" role—states such as Brazil in Latin America, Saudi Arabia in the Middle East and Indonesia in Southeast Asia.

The revolution ended the Pahlavi chapter of Iran's history, but also began a new chapter that is likely to prove as turbulent. When Khomeini insists that the revolution was "Islamic," he is using that term to obscure the actual multiclass composition of the revolution, and to deny the legitimacy of demands by various oppressed groups for social as well as political change. The fact is that a combination of forces carried out the revolution, including urban workers, intellectuals, middle class professionals, students and the petty bourgeoisie. Of these, the professionals and the students were fighting long before any *mollahs* appeared in the streets. And the most effective force in overthrowing the Shah consisted of the workers who went on strike in the factories and in the oilfields. The military, as a last resort, could have mowed down the demonstrators in the streets, but they knew they could not force the workers to show up at the factory gates and at the oil installations.

Islam, like other religions, is used by both progressive and reactionary forces to justify their respective interests and activities. In the present chaotic era of transition, Islam is being drawn into the pervasive conflict between capitalism and socialism. Currently it is associated in Morocco, Turkey, Pakistan and Indonesia with ruling-class attempts to preserve their local interests and their links with the global capitalist order. Conversely, Islamic egalitarian principles are being stressed to justify social restructuring in Algeria, South Yemen, Libya and in liberation movements such as the Polisario Front in Western Sahara, the Palestine Liberation Organization in the Middle East and the Moro National Front in the Philippines.

In the case of Iran, postrevolutionary power was firmly held by the secret Islamic Revolutionary Committee established by Khomeini, and by local Revolutionary Committees of mollahs and their associates in the provincial towns. Their political instrument was the Islamic Republican Party (IRP), led by the astute Ayatollah Mohammad Beheshti. The IRP won the spring 1980 parliamentary elections, thereby isolating Abolhassan Bani-Sadr, who had been elected President in February 1980. Bani-Sadr tried to appoint a Premier loyal to himself, but the IRP overrode him and installed Mohammad Ali Rajai as Premier (Sept. 1980) with a cabinet of hard-line Islamic militants.

The main opposition to the IRP comes from three groups. On the left the chief organizations are the fedayeen, a militant Marxist body of about two thousand members; the moujahedeen, an Islamic Marxist group that mixes leftist doctrines and Moslem traditions; and Tudeh, a pro-Moscow Communist Party founded in 1942. The demands of these leftist groups include industrialization free from foreign domination, jobs for the unemployed, land reform for the peasants, democratic rights for the national minorities and equality for women. The chief centrist organization is the National Democratic Front headed by a grandson of Dr. Mossadeq. Composed largely of liberal political figures and intellectuals, the National Democratic Front stresses civil liberties and opposes Islamic rule as a new dictatorship replacing that of the Shah.

Both the left and the center are anathema to Khomeini and the IRP. Khomeini's conception of Islam is such that it determines a person's actions from birth to death, even in the most minute details of life. Hence secular democracy is for him meaningless and intolerable. "Our enemy is not only Mohammad Reza Pahlavi. Our enemy is anyone whose direction is separate from Islam. Anyone who uses the words 'democratic' or 'republic.'" [48] The fundamentalists also attacked the leftist organizations, imprisoning their leaders, censoring their newspapers, taking over control of worker and peasant councils and neighborhood committees and organizing the Pasdarans or Revolutionary Guards. These number thirty thousand, are personally loyal to Khomeini and are assuming the security responsibilities formerly entrusted to the regular armed forces.

In addition to the center and left, Khomeini and the IRP must contend with national minorities (Kurds, Baluchis, Turkomans, Azerbaijani and Arabs) who comprise 60 percent of the total population; with religious minorities such as Christians, Jews, Zoroastrians and Bahai; and also with modern-minded women who face discrimination in several spheres. The confrontation of so many disparate elements is responsible for the domestic turmoil in Iran following the departure of the Shah. From many quarters is heard this complaint: "The dictatorship of the crown has been replaced by the dictatorship of the turban."

Domestic conflicts are exacerbated by the intrusion of foreign influences. So fundamental an upheaval as the Iranian Revolution inevitably has become enmeshed with Great Power rivalries and Persian Gulf balance-of-power politics. It is now known that while the Iranian Revolution was under way, American General Robert E. Huyser, who had been sent to Teheran by President Carter, was urging a military coup to abort the revolution. On January 23, 1979, a week after the Shah had fled, Huyser sent a report to his superior, General Alexander M. Haig,

Jr., then the NATO commander. Headed "top secret" and "eyes only for Gen. Haig from Gen. Huyser," the report first described Huyser's efforts to shore up the Bakhtiar government. "If that fails, then my guidance to them is we must go to a straight military takeover." On February 10, 1979, only two days before the revolution, the State Department called Ambassador William Sullivan in Teheran to inquire if it was feasible to launch a military coup. A U.S. Navy tanker was ordered to stand off the coast of Iran to supply fuel to the military if a coup materialized. But by this time it was too late. Huyser had warned in his report about what would happen if Khomeini returned to Iran: "I believe there would be a big upheaval. Then things would go to hell in a handbasket." [49] Khomeini had returned on February 1, and within a fortnight Huyser was proven a prophet.

The seizure of the personnel of the American embassy in Teheran in November 1979 brought into the open the clash between Washington and revolutionary Iran. President Carter responded by freezing all Iranian assets in American banks, orchestrating trade sanctions against Iran and finally sending an ill-fated rescue mission in April 1980. Within Iran, the hostage issue became a political football. Bani-Sadr favored a speedy settlement in order to normalize foreign relations and to revive the disrupted national economy. The IRP, by contrast, supported the student militants' demand that the hostages be tried for espionage, thereby exploiting the prevailing anti-imperialist sentiment.

The Islamic fundamentalists had their way, so that Iran was left diplomatically isolated and economically weakened. This led directly to the Iraqi invasion of Iran on September 22, 1980. Iraq's President Saddam Hussein was aspiring for the political and military hegemony over the Persian Gulf region formerly exercised by the Shah. Seeing Iran isolated and unhinged, Hussein assumed that a short war would topple the Khomeini regime. His invasion was welcomed and discreetly supported by other Arab leaders, who preferred to see the conservative Bakhtiar installed in place of the firebrand Ayatollah. With all its contradictions, revolutionary Iran was greatly feared by its neighbors, especially because of Khomeini's incessant calls for the Islamic masses to rise against their corrupt and impious rulers.

With the assistance of American diplomacy, the American hostages were released after 444 days of captivity, on the date when the Carter administration in Washington gave way to the Reagan. The chief Iranian negotiator, Behzad Nabavi, boasted that Iran "has managed to rub the nose of the bigger superpower into the dust." In fact, Teheran dropped most of its original demands, including the Shah's fortune, which was left in legal limbo, and the frozen assets abroad, a large portion of which were intercepted by foreign banks to recoup their loans.

Second Global Revolutionary Wave, 1939– /

The ending of the protracted hostage issue paradoxically threatened Iran's revolution by further sharpening the conflict between Premier Rajai and the IRP on one side, and the followers of President Bani-Sadr on the other. The IRP has the upper hand in the streets, enjoys easier access to Khomeini, and is supported by many leftist groups. The Tudeh Party and the majority of the moujahedeen and fedayeen favor the IRP as against Bani-Sadr, viewing the latter as close to bourgeois elements linked to the West and opposed to the continuation of the revolution. Bani-Sadr is backed by the educated urban population, the merchants of the bazaar, and possibly by the armed forces, whose leadership he has carefully cultivated. To add to the complications, the several minorities remain unreconciled to the Persians who still reject the demands for regional autonomy.

The future of Iran after the settlement of the hostage issue is obscure and perilous. Basic political conflicts remain unresolved, the economy is in a shambles, and foreign pressures will persist, both from the ongoing war with Iraq as well as from the Great Powers. But the experience of General Huyser demonstrates that the Iran of Khomeini is very different from that of Mossadeq. Mass activization made it impossible for General Huyser to repeat Kermit Roosevelt's successful intrusion into Iran's internal affairs. This historic fact will leave an indelible imprint on Iran and the entire Middle East, regardless of the final outcome of the revolution that unseated the "King of Kings."

In contrast to poverty-stricken Egypt and strife-ridden Iran, prospects appear rosy for Gulf oil states such as Saudi Arabia, Kuwait and the United Arab Emirates. On the surface these oil states seem to be in an enviable position, with abundant revenues flowing in and with sparse populations to support. Thus Kuwait is regularly credited with the highest per-capita GNP in the world. But the precious oil reserves are being misused with even less foresight than in Iran. And the consequences will prove far more disastrous because Iran at least has other resources to fall back upon after the oil is gone. The oil states, however, have little more than sand, so their now bloated populations, grown accustomed to foreign luxuries, will find it impossible to support themselves by reverting to the traditional pasturing, fishing, pearling and trading.

The ruling elites in the desert states spend their lives squandering money at home and abroad. Their inclination for expensive prestige projects has been quickened by foreign businessmen eager to turn a fast petrodollar. Dubai built more than seventy shipping berths at the port of Jebal Ali, which provides that postage-stamp state with a larger port capacity than New York City. The two neighboring ministates of Dubai and Sharjah both have built modern international airports capable of handling jumbo jets. The two airports are closer together than Washington's Dulles and National airports, and Dubai's airport is actually closer to Sharjah than to Dubai. Saudi Arabia has built a new international airport outside Jeddah to handle the annual pilgrimage traffic to Mecca. The cost was seven billion dollars, or ten times that of America's most expensive airport, at Dallas-Fort Worth.

The citizens of the desert oil states are "employed" in sundry government "services." In practice, these people are paid to do virtually nothing. A UN survey found that a Kuwaiti civil servant works an average of seventeen minutes per day. Most of the meaningful and productive work is performed by the immigrant labor recruits from Egypt, Iraq, Palestine, Pakistan and other neighboring countries. These foreign workers usually have no political or trade union rights and receive a fraction of the wages that are paid to local citizens for the same jobs. Thus the citizens are being subjected to a process of deproductivization, which may be satisfying as long as the oil resources last. But when this great regional heritage is expended, it will mean disaster not only for the citizens of the states involved, but also for the entire region.

Maurice Guernier, a leading French economist, spelled out for *An-Nahar: Arab Report and MEMO* what he considers to be the Arab world's "last chance":

> . . . the prerequisite for the survival of the Arab world is that its oil wealth must be seen as the wealth of all Arabs. . . . The only solution for the Arab world is for oil revenues to be invested in the Arab world, for the Arab world.
>
> It is the region with the fewest resources in water and in cultivable land. And it is a region whose population is inevitably going to increase by the year 2000 from 135 to 270 million. Yet even today it is incapable of feeding its people . . . 20 years from now it will no longer have any oil. How is it going to buy food? . . .
>
> I cannot understand the suggestion that there is not enough capacity for investment. Today, 100 million Arabs are living in sub-human conditions. There is much to do. . . . If there is insufficient capacity, it is because the Arab world has not drawn up its development plan. . . .
>
> Saudi Arabia must take part in an overall development plan. . . . There may be mines to be opened [in Saudi Arabia] . . . but that doesn't alter the fact that it is not a country that can be developed. It is not a viable country. . . . Saudi Arabia believes it can survive in the coming years with revolt at its doors. Revolt in Iraq, Syria, in Egypt. I do not think it does. . . .[50]

Some Arabs are aware of the growing crisis. The Arab Authority for Agricultural Investment and Development (AAAID) has warned that unless there is planning and investment on a regional scale for increased agricultural production, the Arab countries' food consumption by the year 2000 will be triple their production capability. Oil revenues will be insufficient to pay for a food deficit of such magnitude. AAAID proposes the development of an Arab "wheat belt" extending from Iraq and Syria in the east to Algeria and Morocco in the west. Training of agronomists and efficient exploitation of arable land could reduce Arab food imports by 70 percent within twenty years.[51]

AAAID thus far has been ignored and treated as a stepchild by the oil-producing states. Thus Guernier concludes, "I am more worried about the future of the Arab world than I am about India. And God knows, India is catastrophic enough. But at least it rains in India, at least there is land and you can grow whatever you wish." [52]

C.
Tropical Africa

Just as the first postwar decade witnessed the liberation of Asia, so the second witnessed the liberation of Africa. Nationalist movements had gotten under way during the interwar years (see Chapter 21, Section VI), but in restrospect they were "archaic and prehistoric." They consisted of "followers grouped around an influential protector." [53] These "followers" comprised a small professional elite with no ties to the great rural mass. Their influence was limited to a few towns such as Dakar, Accra, Lagos and Khartoum-Omdurman. They were interested primarily in improving their position within the colonial framework; hence their demand for the Africanization of the bureaucracy, the judiciary and the elected local legislatures. It seemed quite natural and justified that a senior British colonial official should state at a 1939 conference that "at any rate in Africa we can be sure that we have unlimited time in which to work." [54]

Such comfortable conviction was shattered by the Second World War. Many Africans served overseas, no less than 120,000 in Burma alone. During their campaigning in Burma, and while stationed in their bases in India and Ceylon, the Africans noted that the British received higher pay and more privileges, even when they were of the same rank. The Africans also were affected by contact with Asian activists who were more advanced in their political theories and organization. The Indian Congress Party had a direct influence on Kwame Nkrumah and his Convention People's Party (CPP), which was based on the Gandhian principle of absolute nonviolence. CPP members out of prison sported P.G. (Prison Graduate) caps, which were the Gandhi caps with the letters P.G. affixed. Nkrumah also borrowed from Gandhi the concept of a mass-based party for winning political concessions, and became known as the "Gandhi of Ghana." [55] The influence of Asia increased tremendously with the winning of independence by several Asian colonies. Africans naturally asked why they too should not be rid of the bonds of colonialism.

Most important was the great wartime economic expansion because of the urgent demand for African raw materials. British West African producers more than doubled the value of their exports between 1938 and 1946. Likewise the value of Congo exports increased fourteen times between 1939 and 1953, while government revenues rose four times. The general economic upsurge led to a boom in the building of schools, construction of roads and the improvement of housing, sanitation and medical services. These innovations, together with the impact of the returning veterans, combined to shake up and awaken tropical Africa. Native cash farmers were making more money than ever before. African workmen were moving up the ladder to semiskilled and even into a few skilled industrial jobs. More Africans were getting positions as government clerks, court interpreters, head messengers and agricultural demonstrators. City populations soared to an unprecedented degree, so that between 1931 and 1960 these typical African cities increased as follows (in thousands): Dakar, 54 to 383; Abidjan, 10.2 to 180; Accra, 60.7 to 325.9; Leopoldville, 30.2 to 389.5; and Nairobi, 29.8 to 250.8.

The resulting social disruption engendered a new breed of political leaders, impatient and aggressive, like Kwame Nkrumah, Nnamdi Azikiwe, Jomo Kenyatta, Sekou Touré, Leopold Senghor and Félix Houphouet-Boigny. Unlike the Casley-Hayfords and Blaise Diagnes of the interwar years, the new leaders organized mass parties involving the lower middle class and the peasants. These parties were better organized and more disciplined than the earlier associations, and their members made good use of the improved roads to penetrate into remote villages in private cars, party vans and even bicycles. The new nationalist leaders also operated internationally, meeting at the Fifth Pan-African Congress in London in 1945 to challenge the colonial powers to honor the Atlantic Charter and grant self-government. Churchill responded that the Atlantic Charter applied only to victims of Axis aggression, while the French declared at Brazzaville in 1944 that the introduction, "even in a far-off future, of self-government in the colonies is out of the question."

This intransigence appeared natural at the time, but it was soon reversed in the face of the nationalist triumphs in Indochina and Algeria. The significance of these stunning events for the colonial world as a whole was noted by Frantz Fanon:

> A colonized people is not alone. In spite of all that colonialism can do, its frontiers remain open to new ideas and echoes from the world

outside. . . . The great victory of the Vietnamese people at Dien
Bien Phu is no longer strictly speaking, a Vietnamese victory. Since
July, 1954, the question which the colonial peoples have asked
themselves has been, "What must be done to bring about another
Dien Bien Phu? How can we manage it?" Not a single colonized
individual could ever again doubt how best to use the forces at
their disposal, how to organize them, and when to bring them into
action. This encompassing violence does not work upon the
colonized people only; it modifies the attitude of the colonialists
who become aware of manifold Dien Bien Phus. This is why a
veritable panic takes hold of the colonialist governments in turn.
Their purpose is to capture the vanguard, to turn the movement
of liberation toward the right, and to disarm the people: quick,
quick, let's decolonize. Decolonize the Congo before it turns into
another Algeria. Vote the constitutional framework for all Africa,
create the French Communauté, renovate that same Communauté,
but for God's sake, let's decolonize quick. . . .[56]

Decolonization did take place quickly. The British took the lead in the
Gold Coast, where Nkrumah's Convention People's Party won an overwhelming majority in the 1951 election. Nkrumah was in prison on Election Day, but the British governor, sensing the trends of events, released
him and gave him and his colleagues top administrative posts. After this
apprenticeship in self-government, the Gold Coast became in 1957 the
independent state of Ghana. With the colonial dam broken at one point,
it was impossible to hold back the flood. Nigeria, the most populous
country in Africa with its 35 million people, became independent in
1960, and was followed by the other British West African colonies, Sierra
Leone and Gambia, in 1961 and 1963, respectively.

The Paris governments were as conciliatory south of the Sahara as
they were stubborn to the north. In 1956 France enacted a "framework
law" that granted representative institutions to its twelve West African
territories and to the island of Madagascar. Two years later the new De
Gaulle regime, brought into power by the crisis in Algeria, decided to
avoid a similar ordeal in tropical Africa. The sub-Saharan colonies were
given the option of voting either for full independence or for autonomy
as separate republics in the French "Community" that was to replace
the empire. At first this strategy appeared to be successful; in the ensuing
referendum, all the territories except Guinea, which was under the influence of the trade union leader, Sekou Touré, voted for autonomy. The
arrangement, however, proved transitory. In 1959, Senegal and the
French Sudan asked for full independence within the French Community
as the Federation of Mali. When this was granted, four other territories—

the Ivory Coast, Niger, Dahomey and Upper Volta—went a step farther
and secured independence outside the French Community. By the end
of 1960, all the former colonies of both French West Africa and French
Equatorial Africa had won their independence, and all but one had become members of the United Nations.

Because of the paternalism of Brussels and the intervention of the
superpowers, the Belgian Congo underwent prolonged fighting before
winning independence, as will be noted below. Likewise in East Africa,
the presence of a white settler community necessitated the Mau Mau rebellion to force the British Colonial Office to accept the independent
state of Kenya in 1963. The neighboring states of Uganda and Tanganyika
(later, with Zanzibar, Tanzania) made the transition to statehood without
turmoil. The net result was the emergence of thirty-two independent
African countries during the decade after Ghana's debut in 1957. The
few colonies that remained in the continent stood out painfully as obsolete hangovers from the past.

The onrush of decolonization did not signify that independent status
was granted gratuitously or indiscriminately. At least three factors determined the time and place for conferring independent statehood. One was
the economic and military power of the mother country. Britain and
France had sufficient strength and confidence to be willing to concede
independence with reasonable expectation that they would be able to
defend their interests in their ex-colonies against encroachment by other
Great Powers. In most cases their calculation proved correct, and they
continued to dominate the economies of the new African states and to
provide many of the technicians, administrators and educators. By contrast the Portuguese, lacking the economic and military resources of the
British and French, refused to surrender political control over their
colonies, as they justifiably feared European, American and Japanese
interlopers. Thus it was Portugal's weakness that forced her to resist
decolonization and to continue fighting against African liberation movements long after Britain and France had bowed out. This paradox was
explicitly recognized by the Portuguese Overseas Minister, Adriano
Moreira: "We know that only political power is a defense against the
economic and financial invasion of our territories by . . . former colonial
powers." [57] Not only did Portuguese officials recognize this power consideration but so did their colonial subjects. In Guinea-Bissau, Amilcar
Cabral, the leading African theorist and practitioner of revolution, observed in 1965:

> Portuguese colonialism in our time is characterized fundamentally
> by a very simple fact: Portuguese colonialism, or if you prefer, the
> Portuguese economic infrastructure, cannot afford the luxury of neo-

colonialism. In view of this, we can understand the whole attitude, the whole stubbornness of Portuguese colonialism toward our people. If Portugal had an advanced economic development, if Portugal could be classed as a developed country, we certainly would not be at war with Portugal.[58]

The second factor determining the time and place of decolonization was the role of the superpowers—the United States and the Soviet Union. Neither one had appreciable influence in Africa before World War II, but the weakening of the colonial powers during the war gave Russia and America an opportunity that both promptly exploited. Russia was the weaker of the two, because of its inferior economic and military resources and because it lacked the contacts within Africa and with the colonial powers that the United States enjoyed. But the Soviet Union was able partly to make up for this weakness by supporting African governments and liberation movements more freely than the United States, which had to take into account the interests of its Western allies and of its corporations. Thus the Soviet Union at various times and with varying results gave overt or covert aid and/or arms to Nasser's Egypt, Nkrumah's Ghana, Touré's Guinea, Barre's Somalia, Selassie's Ethiopia and the revolutionary movements in the Portuguese colonies. America's postwar role in Africa vacillated between determination to buttress the status quo against Soviet intrusion, and desire to break into the lucrative economic preserves of Britain, France, Belgium and Portugal. The mineral-rich Belgian Congo affords the classic example of superpower intervention in African affairs—first in 1959–61 and then again in 1978. A more recent example is that of the Central African Empire, where Jean Bokassa was installed in office in 1965 by the French, and then unceremoniously ousted by them in 1979 when his unpredictable barbarities became embarrassing.

The third and probably most important factor determining the course of decolonization was the political complexion of the organizations and leaders agitating for independence. In postwar Africa as throughout the Third World in all centuries, independent status was conceded selectively, depending on the prospective degree of social change. If the expectation was for merely political change, independence was usually conceded rather than resorting to extreme repressive measures. But if there was any likelihood of social restructuring that threatened metropolitan and local vested interests, then all possible measures were used to keep the social revolutionaries out of power. In such cases the usual outcome was the gradual co-option of the revolutionary leaders who, lured by the prospect of wealth and office, changed their political coloration and became the supporters (and beneficiaries) of the status quo.

A typical example of such co-option is the case of Félix Houphouet-Boigny of the Ivory Coast. During and immediately after World War II he militantly opposed French rule and the local French planters. In 1946 he publicly praised "the precious help given to the Overseas Territories by the Communists in their struggle against the common enemy, imperialist and colonialist reaction. . . ."[59] By 1950 Houphouet-Boigny had completely reversed his position. He severed his ties with the Communists, cooperated closely with Paris and opposed independence when it became an option in 1958. After the course of events brought independence to the Ivory Coast along with the other French sub-Saharan colonies, Houphouet-Boigny became President, and to the present day preserves as close economic and cultural ties with France as in colonial times.

Very different was the experience of Kwame Nkrumah of Gold Coast Colony. After being released from prison in 1951, he declared flatly: "I am a friend of Britain. . . . I want for the Gold Coast Dominion status within the British Commonwealth. I am no Communist and never have been. . . ."[60] This statement encouraged the British to grant independence to the Gold Coast and to accept Nkrumah as its President. But when economic setbacks caused Nkrumah to switch to socialist economic policies, Western attitudes and policies toward him changed completely. According to an ex-CIA agent, John Stockwell, Washington was involved in the 1966 army coup that deposed Nkrumah: "The Accra [CIA] station was encouraged by headquarters to maintain contacts with dissidents of the Ghanian army. . . . So close was the station's involvement that it was able to coordinate the recovery of some classified Soviet military equipment . . . as the coup took place . . . inside CIA headquarters the Accra station was given full, if unofficial credit for the eventual coup."[61]

The above factors behind Africa's decolonization were responsible for three types of postliberation regimes: nationalist, social revolutionary and white settler. Considering first the nationalist regimes (the other two categories being analyzed in later sections), they varied considerably in their institutions and policies. For the sake of convenience they may be divided into two types: the conservative neocolonial and the reformist state capitalist.

A basic feature of the neocolonial society was its emphasis on production for foreign markets as the prerequisite for getting started on the road to economic growth. This led to the encouragement of cash crops at the expense of traditional food production. Cash crops were stimulated by the allotment of the best arable lands, by supporting road and railway systems, by government-sponsored irrigation schemes and by a wide range of scientific inputs, including fertilizers, pesticides and high-yield seeds. In addition to emphasizing cash-crop production, the conservative regimes strove to attract foreign capital by creating a hospitable investment climate through such measures as tax holidays, protective tariffs and free repatriation of profits.

This economic strategy underlay the first African national economic plans, usually prepared by Western experts. As the decade of the sixties unfolded, it became clear that the multiplier effects expected from cash-crop exports and from foreign investments were not materializing. Prices for raw-material exports declined, while the cost of manufactured imports rose. Food production for domestic markets lagged, causing increasing food costs for urban dwellers, as well as large-scale food imports, which upset the trade balance. Displaced peasants streamed into cities, where jobs were lacking because the foreign-financed industrialization was capital-intensive and geared to producing only luxury or semiluxury items for a limited middle-class market. The tragedy of uprooted African peasants crowded into urban shanty towns was heightened by the fact that peasant farmers, given a modicum of opportunity, can better the large plantations not only in terms of output per unit of land, but more important, in terms of cost per unit produced. In Kenya, for example, peasant families who took over the farms of former European settlers made impressive gains, in some cases nearly doubling the level of output.[62]

Under these circumstances the typical African conservative regime ended up with a dual economy, comprising an encapsulated export-producing enclave surrounded by a traditional, underdeveloped agrarian sector. As illustrated in the following diagram, the enclave is sustained by a cheap labor supply from the underdeveloped sector and by an array of government-provided incentives. The multinational corporations, which control imports and exports as well as plantations and mines, realize high returns on their investments because of their domination of world markets through their global marketing structures. The result is the siphoning of surplus value out of African countries to such a degree that, as indicated in the table on page 672, U.S. corporations between 1965 and 1975 extracted a net total of $2,998 billion out of Africa, or 25 percent more than they invested there.

The classic example of a neocolonial state is the Congo, now known as Zaïre. When Belgium granted the colony independence in June 1960, Patrice Lumumba emerged as the only Congolese leader with any pretense of more than a regional following. His unwillingness to accept manipulation made him unacceptable to Brussels and, more important, to Washington. Just as the nationalistic Mossadeq was eliminated in Iran on suspicion of being a Soviet stooge, so the nationalistic Lumumba was condemned in telegraphic instructions from CIA Director Allen Dulles (Aug. 26, 1960): "IN HIGH QUARTERS HERE IT IS THE CLEAR-CUT CONCLUSION THAT IF LUMUMBA CONTINUES TO

HOLD HIGH OFFICE, THE INEVITABLE RESULT WILL AT
LEAST BE CHAOS AND AT WORST PAVE THE WAY TO COM-
MUNIST TAKEOVER OF THE CONGO. . . . HIS REMOVAL
MUST BE AN URGENT AND PRIME OBJECTIVE. . . . THIS
SHOULD BE A HIGH PRIORITY OF OUR COVERT AC-
TION. . . ." [63]

Surplus Value Extracted Directly from African Countries, Excluding South Africa, from 1965 to 1975, by U.S.-Based Transnational Corporations

Year	Direct New U.S. investments in Africa, excluding South Africa ($ millions)	U.S. transnational corporations' extraction of surplus value (I) ($ millions)	Amount by which surplus value extracted exceeds new direct investments ($ millions)
1965	$171	−$249	−$ 78
1966	83	−270	−187
1967	135	−284	−149
1968	374	−207	(167)
1969	246	−616	−370
1970	387	−610	−223
1971	255	−481	−262
1972	138	−410	−272
1973	−625	−466	−466 (2)
1974	−143	−799	−799 (2)
1975	164	−356	−192
TOTAL, 1965–1975			$2,998

Source: A. Seidman, "Post World War II Imperialism in Africa," *Journal of Southern African Affairs* II (Oct. 1977): 409.

Notes: (1) It is difficult to obtain an accurate estimate of surplus value directly extracted for several reasons. This is intended to provide only an indication of the order of magnitude. It is underestimated, since it is based on official reports to the U.S. Government by transnational corporations of their interest, dividends, branch earnings. It does not include managerial and licensing fees or compensation for government purchases of shares of ownership, which, in recent years, have become increasingly important forms of direct extraction of surplus value.

(2) In 1973 and 1974, there was a *decline* in total investment, or a disinvestment. If this was *added* to the reported surplus values shipped out the totals would be much higher in those years, $1,091 million and $942 million, respectively.

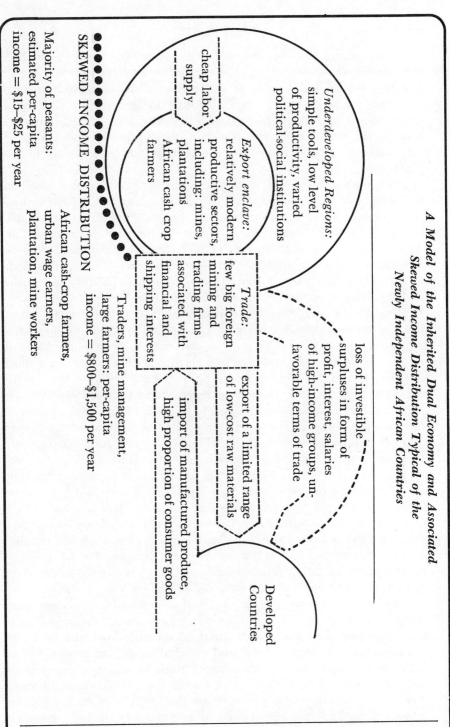

A Model of the Inherited Dual Economy and Associated Skewed Income Distribution Typical of the Newly Independent African Countries

Source: A. Seidman, *Planning for Development in Sub-Saharan Africa* (New York: Praeger, 1974), p. 13.

Without going into the long and sordid record (set forth in the 1975 U.S. Senate report on *Alleged Assassination Plots Involving Foreign Leaders*), Dulles' orders were in fact carried out. Lumumba was murdered on January 21, 1961, and according to Stockwell, a CIA agent drove about in Lubumbashi (then Elizabethville) "with Lumumba's body in the trunk of his car, trying to decide what to do with it." [64] Lumumba was then succeeded by his CIA-supported chief of staff, Joseph Mobutu.

American investments in Zaïre thereupon increased sharply, totalling by 1977 $1 billion in mining, construction and oil, as well as $500 million in U.S. bank loans. According to information by a State Department official in 1976, "the United States viewed the position of Zaïre within Africa as roughly similar to that of Brazil in South America"—that is, mineral-rich, strategically located and pro-Western. The official added: "There was a thrust within the State Department to bolster Zaïre in the hope it could extend its hegemony throughout the continent." [65]

The difficulty with this American strategy was that, as usual, it was based solely on geopolitical considerations and ignored the condition and aspirations of the people actually involved. In this case, the Mobutu regime was notoriously inefficient and corrupt, with a quarter to a third of the national GNP being siphoned off by the ruling clique. The resulting mass suffering and disaffection became evident when on May 13, 1978, a force of twenty-five hundred to thirty-five hundred guerrillas of the National Front for the Liberation of the Congo attacked the copper mining town of Kolwezi. With the aid of urban and rural sympathizers they captured the city and its mines in two days. Since this was the post-Vietnam era, the Carter administration limited overt support to Mobutu to $17.5 million of "nonlethal" military aid. But covertly the administration encouraged and financed other countries—Western and Third World—to intervene with armed force. U.S. Air Force planes transported Belgian soldiers from Brussels to Zaïre, while French planes airlifted French Legionnaires and Moroccan troops. French and Belgian military advisers directed all intelligence and logistical operations, while West Germany and China provided food and medicines.

Mobutu continues to revel in his eleven palaces and to cruise on Zaïre River accompanied by four of France's master chefs; his subjects continue to subsist on manioc, with one third suffering from deficiencies in both protein and caloric intake; and the vital cobalt and copper, not to mention debt-repayment installments, continue to flow to Western countries. Economist Albert Ndele, governor of the Central Bank of Zaïre from 1961 to 1970, warns the West of the fragility of their creation: "There is unbelievable poverty and misery in my country. A recent report says there is 70 percent infant mortality in Kinshasa. Even the medicines given by charity are sold to the people—by Mobutu's family. The road system is a shambles. The sanitary situation is as bad. The same is true of education. If you think that Mobutu is the man for the West, you had better think again." [66] Also noteworthy is the observation of a European-educated Zaïrian doctor: "The West likes to say this conduct is very African, very compatible with our tradition of chieftains. That, of course, is nonsense. Mobutu is not in the least a product of our African heritage. He is nothing more than a product of Western capitalism." [67]

President Julius Nyerere, in a lecture to the foreign envoys in his capital, also has expressed his views on current Western activities in Zaïre:

> We must reject the principle that external powers have the right to maintain in power African governments that are universally recognized to be corrupt, or incompetent, or a bunch of murderers, when their peoples try to make a change. Africa cannot have its present governments frozen into position for all time by neocolonialism, or because there are cold-war or ideological conflicts between the big powers. The peoples of an individual African country have as much right to change their corrupt government in the last half of the 20th century as, in the past, the British, French and Russian peoples had to overthrow their own rotten regimes. Are African peoples to be denied that same right? [68]

Africa affords examples of more successful neocolonial states than Zaïre, outstanding being Kenya and the Ivory Coast. In the latter country, Houphouet-Boigny has staunchly espoused the economic institutions and policies inherited from colonial times. "I have nothing to do with this false policy of nationalization. Our policy is to attract foreign capital, not nationalize business. We want our foreign friends to make a profit, and if they do, pay us a reasonable part." This economic strategy has yielded an average annual per-capita income of $300, an 8 percent annual growth of GNP and a favorable trade balance from the export of coffee, cocoa, timber, bananas, pineapples and other agricultural products.

But this represents economic growth rather than balanced national economic development. It is economic growth that has led to French control of 40 percent of total investment capital in the country, with another 25 percent shared by Britain, the United States and Japan. The remaining 35 percent is owned by 40,000 French citizens resident in the country, several hundred Lebanese and 3 percent of the Ivorians. Thus the impressive economic statistics have involved little "trickling down" of the benefits of growth. The infant mortality rate is 138 per 1,000 births (as against 28 in Cuba), life expectancy is 35 years and the illiteracy rate is 60 percent. Natural resources are being abused as recklessly as the human. According to forestry experts, Ivory Coast forest stock "has sustained a level of destruction that cannot last for more than three or four more years." [69] The Ivory Coast often is referred to as "the only African country that works." But it should be asked: For what purpose does it work, and for whose benefit?

The above pattern prevails also in Kenya, where President Jomo Kenyatta, like Houphouet-Boigny, adopted strongly pro-Western business-oriented policies. The first billboard outside the Nairobi airport reads: "General Motors Kenya Limited—With Full Confidence in the Economic Future of Kenya." The confidence is warranted, for Kenya offers a well-developed infrastructure network, a stable investment climate and the right of foreign corporations to remit all their profits. Nairobi, like Abidjan of the Ivory Coast, is a modern capital city of banks, business buildings, luxury hotels, well-stocked restaurants and fashionable nightclubs. But only a few blocks away from these symbols of affluence begin the sprawling ghettos, with hungry people living in shacks without running water. Crime, especially robbery, is booming in Nairobi, as is prostitution. Nor are conditions better in the countryside, where over 80 percent of the country's 13 million people live. A 1977 United Nations survey, undertaken with the cooperation of the Kenyan government, disclosed that 72 percent of household heads never attended school, one third of the children suffer from malnutrition, less than 2 percent of the households have electricity and half the women trudge at least three times each day between their villages and the springs, with large, heavy urns on their backs. An American who worked in Kenya in the 1960s and 1970s has analyzed why both the animal and human populations of that country are starving. His account is noteworthy, as it graphically describes the food-crop-to-cash-crop trend that is devastating Third World countries in Asia and Latin America as well as in Africa:

> Pity the poor beasts: The last of the world's great herds are dying. East Africa's primitive savannah country is shrinking as the land comes under the farmers' ploughs. Thus are the herds vanishing, pushed from their natural grounds. Within the forseeable future, the glory of the primeval migrations across Africa's plains will be gone forever. . . .
>
> A ride through Kenya's rich farm country quickly reveals that much of Africa's best agricultural land is not used to feed people. Nor is it used for the starving wildlife. Instead, this wonderful soil supports export crops. Thousands of acres grow coffee trees—for coffee to be consumed in Germany, England and America. Drive north of Nairobi and you find an endless vista of pineapples—fruit to be loaded onto jetliners and shipped fresh to Europe. Head west-

ward into the Rift Valley and you find ranches and farms used for cattle raising and for growing wheat. While these last two efforts produce food which is consumed within Kenya, the consumers are not farmers vying with the wildebeest for a precious resource but the people who live in the burgeoning cities. The irony is that these new city dwellers only a few years back were farmers capable of feeding themselves. . . .

The real problem in Kenya is that land is used for cash crops instead of for foodstuffs. Kenya has enough productive farmland to feed all of its people without destroying the habitat of the wild animals. There is no necessity for choosing between the life of a human and that of a gazelle. If a more balanced economic and agricultural system can be created, both humans and beasts will survive on the African plains.[70]

On the other hand, Kenya boasts one of the largest black middle classes in Africa. Although the national economy is dominated by Europeans, and to a lesser extent by Arabs and Indians, nevertheless the black elite is prosperous. It profits from its share of the economy, and especially from its control of the state apparatus, which is a lucrative source of sub-rosa income. Bribes are essential to acquire anything, whether it be a driver's license, a construction contract or a peddler's permit. Some have protested against this well-oiled system, but with little success. Josia Kariuki, a popular member of parliament, attacked the blatant social inequity, dismissing the existing Kenya as a country of ten millionaires and ten million beggars. In March 1975 he was shot in the streets of Nairobi. A parliamentary investigation implicated police officials and top Kenyatta aides.

Despite these anomalies, the fact remains that the growing black middle class in countries such as Kenya and the Ivory Coast provides a measure of stability that is lacking in a society such as that of Zaïre, where only a handful have access to the trough. If enough blacks derive benefit from the status quo, then the vast dispossessed majority cherish the hope of upward mobility and refrain from militant mass action. This is why former Secretary of State Kissinger and State Department specialists proposed a "Kenya model" for an independent black-ruled Rhodesia, before this option evaporated with Robert Mugabe's electoral victory.

The experiences of the neocolonial states suggest that domestic institutions and international economic relationships inherited from the colonial era cannot overcome the underdevelopment that has persisted since independence. These institutions and relationships were designed to satisfy foreign rather than local interests, and have continued to do so to the present day. Consequently economic dependence and exploitation continue despite the winning of political independence. Underdevelopment can be overcome only by restructuring the inherited institutions and altering the existing relations with the international market economy.

This leads to the reformist state-capitalist type of postcolonial African regimes. Their leaders recognize the need for change, but do not set out to eliminate institutions and create new ones. Rather they seek to reform existing institutions in order to cope with immediate problems. This is the distinctive feature of Nkrumah's Ghana, Touré's Guinea, Keita's Mali, Obote's Uganda and Nyerere's Tanzania.

In the political realm the reformist regimes do not set out to revamp the inherited state structure and class relationships. Rather they replace big landowners with rich peasants, and monopoly or comprador businesses with small industrialists, professionals and civil servants. Striking though these changes may be on the surface, they do not end exploitation of the mass of workers and peasants. In the villages the large landowners are gone, but the peasants, comprising the great majority of Africa's population, continue to be victimized by merchants, usurers and kulaks. Overall, a new ruling elite emerges, which staffs the state bureaucracy, administers the nationalized industries, runs the village cooperatives and directs the military establishment. Class differentiation and exploitation have not been eliminated; rather they have assumed new forms.

This pattern is evident even in Tanzania, where President Julius Nyerere issued his Arusha Declaration on January 29, 1967, to combat "an economic and social elite whose prime concern was profit for themselves and their families, and not the needs of the majority for better basic living standards." [71] Through the medium of the Tanganyika African National Union (TANU), Nyerere sought to replace capitalist forms of growth with alternative practices based on self-reliance, democratic participation and eventual socialism. Traditional mutual aid or *ujamaa* was to be expressed in new forms of cooperative village organization. Yet despite Nyerere's ardent support, the desired self-reliance and mass participation were subverted by bureaucratic intervention from above, while the ujamaa villages were exploited by relatively rich peasants.[72] The following revealing explanation is given by an inside source, Abdul Rahman Babu, formerly Tanzania's Minister of the Economy:

> One reason is that we lacked trained cadre. In Mozambique, where they went through a protracted armed struggle for independence, they developed a good team of disciplined cadre. In Tanzania we did not have that experience. Independence came and immediately we had to run the government and the economy. There was no proper training for cadre, certainly no opportunity to test them first. In spite of our official policy, some of these cadre forced

peasants to move into the communal villages. People didn't know why they were there. Our official policy advocated voluntariness, mobilization and education. In implementation, things took a different course.[73]

Translated into terms of human lives, the post-World War II experience of most African states has been an unmitigated disaster. In 1976 Africa, with 7.5 percent of the world's population, subsisted with only 1.2 percent of the world's GNP. Per-capita GNP is $277 for Africa, $315 for Asia and $1,050 for Latin America. Africa's illiteracy rate is 74 percent, as against 47 percent in Asia and 24 percent in Latin America. Life expectancy for Africans is less than 40 years, 1 of every 4 has insufficient food, 1 of every 2 cannot find a job, 7 percent of Africa's population takes 40 percent of the income and the resulting inequities in life-styles are eroding the traditional communal spirit of African society. "There is increasing evidence," concludes one observer, "that injustices meted out by blacks to their racial brethren may in some instances make white rule look rather benevolent." [74] This judgment is corroborated by the testimony of the dispossessed blacks. "Sometimes the black bosses are worse than the whites," states a black servant in Nairobi. "They hate us poor very much." [75]

Such economic and social disruption inevitably has political repercussions. The job market has failed to keep pace with the burgeoning supply of diplomaholders, creating the serious problem of the "unemployed school leaver." This in turn has led to a resurgence of tribalism, as the unemployed graduates organize on ethnic lines to compete in a situation of increasing scarcity. National leaders perforce use ethnic groups as the basis of their support, leading to unstable conditions and political fragmentation. Since the indigenous middle class generally lacks an independent economic base, political office has become the principal means for personal gain. By extending control over the economy, the new rulers are able to manipulate the national surplus. "African socialism" has become a smoke screen for corruption and self-aggrandizement. The resulting mass disaffection invites intervention of the military, which by 1980 ruled twenty African countries. These circumstances explain the startling warning by Edden Kodjo, secretary-general of the Organization of African Unity (OAU), at its meeting in Lagos in April 1980:

Africa is passing through such terrible times that the question is now survival. The future remains unclear. We are being cheerful to say that should things continue as they are, only eight or nine African countries out of the 50 OAU members could still survive a few years from now.[76]

D.
Latin America

In 1971 an Argentine economist, Raúl Prebisch, called for "a new type of development in Latin America," adding that "this new type of development cannot be based solely on import substitution." [77] This was a significant statement, as more than two decades earlier, Prebisch had been the first to advocate the import-substitution economic strategy in his famous work *The Economic Development of Latin America and Its Principal Problems (1949)*. Furthermore, Prebisch had been able to implement his theories on an international scale, as the head of the Economic Commission for Latin America, as the driving force behind the Central American Common Market and the Latin American Free Trade Area and as the secretary-general of the UN Commission on Trade and Development. Consequently import substitution was widely adopted through such measures as protective tariffs, exchange controls, preferences for the importation of raw materials and intermediate goods, provision of cheap credit for domestic industries, government furnishing of industrial infrastructure, and government participation in industry through development institutes and corporations.

Despite this generous government support, import substitution did not prove successful in stimulating comprehensive economic development and ending Latin America's traditional economic dependence. The protective tariffs and other government supports spawned inefficient industries, which produced luxury or semiluxury consumer goods for a limited middle-class market. These industries were incapable of advancing from the easy consumer-goods stage to the difficult capital-goods stage of economic development. Hence the continued importing of capital and intermediate goods, which created an adverse balance of trade and perpetuated financial dependence. Latin America's share of total world exports fell from 7.1 percent in 1960 to 5.5 percent in 1968. The commodities exported continued to be largely primary products, so that in 1968, oil and iron comprised 95 percent of Venezuela's products, coffee and bananas 85 percent of Guatemala's, wool and meat 77 percent of Uruguay's, copper and nitrates 77 percent of Chile's, bananas and coffee 75 percent of Ecuador's, coffee and oil 70 percent of Colombia's and tin and silver 59 percent of Bolivia's.

The failure of the import-substitution strategy cleared the way for the multinational corporations, which installed their plants behind the existing tariff walls in Third World countries (see Chapter 19, Section VB). Whereas foreign capital in Latin America originally had been concentrated in the mining and agricultural sectors, now it flowed increasingly into manufacturing. And whereas foreign capital formerly had been encapsulated in enclaves, now it was substantially integrated into the Latin American economies, with correspondingly greater influence on those economies. The shift away from the import substitution of the immediate post-World War II period did not solve Latin America's economic problems. A Chilean economist, Oswaldo Sunkel, concluded in 1972 that Latin America was "in the midst of a profound structural crisis; future growth will have to find new dynamic forces. A new development strategy is therefore called for." [78]

The manifestations of the "structural crisis" to which Sunkel alluded are numerous and well known. One is the inadequate rate of economic growth. Only two South American countries—Bolivia and Brazil—attained the Alliance for Progress target of raising per-capita income by 2.5 percent annually during the 1960s. Argentina's average annual growth rate in per-capita productivity was only 1.9 percent, and Venezuela's 1.3 percent, while Uruguay's suffered a net loss of −0.6 percent. Inadequate economic expansion has meant increasing unemployment, both urban and rural. Between 1950 and 1960, urban population grew 5.6 percent annually, but industrial employment only 2.1 percent. City dwellers were plagued with unemployment and underemployment, the latter taking the form of redundant services—shoeshining, car washing and parking, street hawking of flowers, cigarettes, shoelaces, "art" objects and so forth.

The same situation prevails in agriculture, where grossly inequitable land distribution remains the rule, as indicated in the following table:

Estimated Percentage Distribution of Land Holdings in Latin America, 18 Countries, 1960–65

Size of farms in hectares	Percentage of farms	Percentage of total land area
0–20	75.6	6.6
20–100	16.8	9.5
100–1000	6.6	24.1
over 1000	1.0	59.8
TOTAL	100	100

Source: E. R. Wolf and E. C. Hansen, *The Human Condition in Latin America* (London: Oxford University Press, 1972), p. 148.

The large estates, which encompass most of the arable land, are not farmed efficiently. A 1975 World Bank analysis of the comparative performance of large and small farms in Argentina, Brazil, Chile, Colombia, Ecuador and Guatemala found that the small farms were three to four-teen times more productive per acre than the large farms. Furthermore, much of the large estate acreage is allowed to stand idle. A 1960 study of Colombia showed that while farmers owning up to 13 acres farmed two thirds of their land, the largest farmers, who own 70 percent of the arable land, cultivate only 6 percent of their holdings. In Latin America as a whole, it is estimated that only 270 million of the 2.2 billion acres of arable land are worked full-time. This obsolete landholding system together with the extremely high rate of population growth has resulted in declining per-capita agricultural output. If an index number of 100 is assigned for each country's per-capita agricultural production in the period 1961–65, the index for 1971 was only 98 in the case of Argentina, 92 in Colombia, 96 in Ecuador, 84 in Uruguay and 80 in Peru.[79]

As serious as the low agricultural productivity is the shift to growing cash crops for foreign markets rather than food crops for domestic con-sumers. In Colombia, for example, a hectare planted to carnations yields 1 million pesos a year, as against 12,500 pesos yielded by wheat or corn. So the best Colombian land is used to grow carnations, and also asparagus and strawberries, which are airlifted to foreign markets, while increasing amounts of scarce foreign exchange are used to import foodstuffs that formerly had been grown at home. Theoretically, more food can be im-ported with the high return from the luxury crops, but the profits from those crops go to the multinational corporations. Thus the formerly self-sufficient peasant finds himself forced to eke out a living on the remaining marginal land, or to scramble for the few available jobs in the cities, where he must feed his family with expensive imported foodstuffs. Under these circumstances Latin America, like other Third World re-gions, is suffering from massive peasant exodus to the cities. In 1950 Latin America's urban population was 40 percent of the total; by 1970 it had risen to 56 percent urban. With the peasants comprising a rapidly decreasing proportion of the total population, governments feel less ur-gency about carrying out agrarian reforms.

Another manifestation of "structural crisis" in Latin America's econ-omy is inequitable income distribution, which is greater than in India. The 5 percent at the top receive over 30 percent of total regional income, while the lower 50 percent receive 13.4 percent. Thus Carlos Martínez, regional director of the UN Children's Fund, disclosed in 1979 that hunger afflicts 40 percent of Latin American children, 60 million of whom live in homes with incomes below the poverty line.

Increasingly important has been the role of the multinational cor-porations, which have exacerbated the "structural crisis" of Latin Amer-ica's economy. American corporations obtain 83 percent of the capital they invest in Latin America from either reinvested earnings or from Latin American investors. The multinationals also obtain extremely favorable concessions from the hard-pressed host governments, including free sites, freedom from taxation for a given period and unrestricted repatriation of profits. Because of their monopoly of vertical operations, the multinationals are able to underprice exports from the host country and overprice imports. Also, they employ complex accounting methods to reduce the taxes they pay to both their host and their home countries. The multinationals can and do move their plants from country to country within Latin America and throughout the world, to take advantage of the cheapest available labor supply. The American electronics industry, for example, established its first plant in Mexico in 1961, attracted by daily wage rates that were less than hour rates in the United States. By 1977 there were 193 American electronic plants in Mexico, but workers were organizing trade unions and their wages were rising rapidly. So the plants are being moved to other Latin American countries such as Haiti, where the minimum daily wage is little more than the hourly wage in Mexico, and where union problems "simply do not exist."

The above practices generate considerable nationalist and anti-American feelings. For this reason some multinationals are abandoning direct ownership of factories in favor of management and service contracts by which a firm undertakes to perform specific functions. Thus an American company cannot be nationalized because it does not own property. Yet it continues to control local economies by signing contracts to sell raw materials on the international market, and to set up and manage large plants.

The end result is that multinationals earn disproportionately high returns from their investments in Latin America and other Third World regions. The vice president of an American bank confided: "I should not really tell you this, but while we earn around 13 to 14 percent in our U.S. operations, we can easily count on a 33 percent rate of return on our business conducted in Latin America." [80] This explains why, between 1966 and 1974, foreign profits returning to the United States exceeded foreign investments leaving the United States by $3 billion each year. It also explains the adverse balance of payments that Latin American countries must contend with each year.

Adverse balance of payments leads inevitably to foreign loans and chronic indebtedness—another symptom of Latin America's "structural crisis." Foreign banks eagerly provided more loans to the debt-ridden Latin American governments because higher profits could be made abroad than at home. How precarious the debt situation became was detailed by an American Aid official, Abelardo L. Valdez, in a speech before the Center of Inter-American Relations in April 1978. In 1977, for "every new dollar made available in the year for Latin America through international and U.S. banks, Latin America's net take was seven cents." This situation still prevails, and the reason is that the international development banks and the U.S. government are receiving from the Latin American countries almost as much in loan repayment as they are providing in new lending. In some cases the U.S. receives more than it lends, as in 1977, when it got back $150 million more than it provided Latin America in new AID and Export-Import Bank loans. Valdez noted that this is the case also with the international development banks. According to the UN Commission for Latin America, the region's external debt ballooned from $10 billion in 1965 to $150 billion in 1980.[81]

Overindebtedness raises the specter of a wave of defaults, which would jeopardize the very existence of the lending institutions. At this point the International Monetary Fund plays a crucial stabilizing role in Latin America, as throughout the Third World, by imposing strict disciplinary measures on debtor countries seeking new loans. None is granted unless the debtor governments reduce their balance of payments deficits, state expenditures, credit expansion and real wages. These measures are designed to stabilize national finances and to divert more of the scarce hard-currency export earnings to servicing foreign debts.

For Latin American populations already reduced for the most part to bare subsistence levels, austerity measures trigger violent resistance, as demonstrated by widespread rioting in numerous countries, including Peru, Colombia, Ecuador, Jamaica and Mexico. Such popular upheavals lead to repressive measures, so that IMF-dictated austerity and repressive Latin American regimes often are causally related. They not only are related, but once the dictatorial regimes are established, they usually receive prompt support from the international lending agencies and private banks because they are able to impose by force the necessary financial restraints needed to service debts. For this reason the 1976 coup in Argentina was called the "coup for foreign credit." Three weeks before the coup, the Economy Minister ordered drastic austerity measures in order to obtain needed foreign credit. He froze wages and at the same time raised prices on necessities by over 100 percent. A general strike put an end to this plan, and IMF thereupon denied the credit that had been requested. The same credit, however, was granted within a few days after the 1976 coup.

Such manipulations are sufficiently common and well known to engender widespread anti-U.S. sentiment in Latin America. Gunnar Myrdal views this as paralleling "what has happened in Vietnam and is now happening in Southern Africa, though in Latin America there is practically *no anti-Western and certainly no anti-white feeling*. It is more simply and exclusively anti-American." [82]

The all-pervasive anti-Americanism concerned Washington policy-makers. Arthur Schlesinger of the Kennedy administration wrote of the worrisome paradox that the poorly financed Communists "were reaching the people who mattered for the future—the students, the intellectuals, the labor leaders and the nationalist militants—while our billions were bringing us into contact only with governments of doubtful good faith and questionable life expectancy." [83] American apprehension became acute with Castro's revolution in 1959 and the Bay of Pigs fiasco in 1961. Hence the launching of the Alliance for Progress with the double objective of brightening the tarnished image of the United States and forestalling any further Castroite revolutions in Latin America. Proclaimed at Punta del Este, Uruguay, on August 17, 1961, the Alliance for Progress committed the nations of the Americas to a $100 billion, ten-year program of tax and land reform, designed to achieve an annual per-capita growth rate of 2.5 percent, more equitable distribution of income, trade diversification, increased agricultural productivity, elimination of adult illiteracy, low-cost housing and improved tax collection.

The Alliance for Progress never had a chance because of its inherent contradictions. Its fundamental, though unstated, objective was to safeguard American investments in Latin America, but the proposed reform measures threatened those investments. Trade diversification clashed with the interests of the American multinationals, and meaningful agrarian reform was a mortal danger to Latin America's ruling elites, which traditionally had been Washington's chief allies. The contradiction was reflected in the juxtaposition of Kennedy's idealistic reform rhetoric and his counterinsurgency schools teaching Latin American officers the latest techniques for suppressing any peasants who might attempt to transform the Kennedy rhetoric into reality. It was not accidental that sixteen military coups occurred in Latin America within eight years after the promulgation of the Alliance for Progress.

From the outset the Alliance for Progress was opposed by the native oligarchies and the multinationals, both of which were interested in preserving the status quo and maximizing opportunities for private investment. The oligarchies blocked land reform and welcomed counterinsurgency measures. The multinationals endorsed the building of roads, utilities and other works providing an infrastructure supportive of American investments. At the same time the multinationals secured Washington legislation requiring harsh punitive measures against countries that nationalized American properties (the Hickenlooper Amendment) and tying aid eligibility to restrictive investment guarantees.

With President Kennedy's assassination the contradictions of the Alliance for Progress were resolved by dropping the reform aspirations and returning to the old policy of unrestrained government aid in support of private investments. Governor Nelson Rockefeller articulated this policy following his 1969 mission to Latin America for President Nixon. Rockefeller acknowledged the "current anti-U.S. trend" and even foresaw a "time when the United States would be politically and morally isolated from part or much of the Western Hemisphere." Rockefeller then assumed that this anti-Americanism was "mistaken" and recommended as a solution that "the United States should provide maximum encouragement for private investment throughout the hemisphere." This recommendation was followed, so that American investments in Latin America rose from $3 billion in 1946 to $9 billion in 1970. Nelson's brother, David Rockefeller of Chase Manhattan, applauded the increased opportunities for private capital:

> In my view, a primary reason for this relatively good performance [increased investment] is a change in the policy which prevailed in the early years of the Alliance, placing too much emphasis on rapid and revolutionary social change and on strictly government-to-government assistance. This approach, while it took account of the fact that there is genuine and urgent need to do away with social inequities, did not encourage the conditions which are essential to stimulating private investment and economic growth. Revolutionary change which shakes the confidence in the fair treatment of private property is incompatible with rapid economic expansion. Now that the vital role of private enterprise is being recognized in a number of Latin American nations, we see the development of a more favorable business climate.[84]

The "favorable business climate" that won David Rockefeller's approval was the result of certain specific American policies. One was a shift in the objective of U.S. military aid to Latin America. In the 1950s the aid was designed to strengthen hemispheric defenses against external attack. After the Castro Revolution a group of Washington strategists led by Walt Rostow and Maxwell Taylor argued that the main threat was internal insurrection rather than external aggression. President Kennedy accepted this proposition, which henceforth influenced profoundly United States policies. American dollars, arms and expertise were provided to Latin American police forces and military establishments for the purpose of crushing domestic revolution. The School of the Americas based in the Panama Canal Zone has graduated nearly forty thousand Latin American military students since its foundation in 1946. Among its alumni are many officers who became the military dictators of their countries: Generals Augusto Pinochet of Chile, Hugo Banzer Suárez of Bolivia, Omar Torrijos Herrera of Panama, Juan Alberto Melgar Castro of Honduras, Carlos Humberto Romero of El Salvador and Romeo Lucas Garcia of Guatemala.

The meaning of this counterinsurgency strategy was presented in dramatic form in the Costa-Gavras movie *State of Siege*. The 1978 report of Amnesty International reported that some thirty thousand people in Latin America had disappeared during the preceding ten years after being seized by official security forces or by associated rightist terror groups such as the "Death Squad" of Brazil, the "White Hand" of Guatemala, the "White Brigade" in Mexico and the "Band" of the Dominican Republic. While many of the "disappeared" persons are activists, the majority are workers and peasants who are whisked off from work or home by secret police or vigilante groups. Those who are killed outright become additions to the lists of the "disappeared." Others are tortured and then released, to spread the desired fear and demoralization. Thus the Latin American Bishops' Conference held in Pueblo, Mexico, in February 1979 listed as an undesirable ideology the concept of "national security." This is used, according to the bishops, "to impose a guardianship on the people by an aristocracy of political or military powers." [85] Likewise the October 1979 conference of the Organization of American States proclaimed that "the practice of disappearances is an affront to the conscience of the hemisphere," noted that "in certain countries torture apparently is an ordinary practice" and recommended "an inter-American treaty defining torture as an international crime." [86]

David Rockefeller's "favorable business climate" was attained also through covert and overt interventions by successive American administrations. Outstanding among the covert operations were the overthrow of President Jacob Arbenz in Guatemala (1954), of João Goulart in Brazil (1964) and of President Salvador Allende in Chile (1973). The best documented of these subversions is that in Guatemala, thanks to over a thousand pages of telegrams, memo papers and research studies obtained in June 1978 by Stephen Schlesinger under the Freedom of Information Act. Schlesinger found that Arbenz' overthrow "was conceived of and run at the highest levels of the American Government in closest cahoots with the United Fruit Company and under the overall direction of Secretary of State John Foster Dulles, backed by President Eisenhower." [87]

Arbenz was stubborn, prickly and visionary, but definitely a reformist socialist rather than a revolutionary Communist. But Arbenz, like Allende, committed the unpardonable sin of infringing on American corporate interests. Arbenz expropriated in 1953 some 200,000 acres of unused land belonging to United Fruit. This company controlled all of Guatemala's banana exports, ran 580 of the country's 732 miles of railroad, held a monopoly of its telephone and telegraph facilities, owned its largest electric plant and administered one of the most important ports on the Caribbean coast. In addition it employed numerous publicists in Washington, and had close ties with the top officials of the Eisenhower administration, including Secretary of State John Foster Dulles, whose law firm represented United Fruit; Assistant Secretary of State John Moors Cabot, who was a large U.F. shareholder; U.S. Ambassador to the United Nations Henry Cabot Lodge, who was on U.F.'s board of directors; and former CIA Director Walter Bedell Smith, who became president of U.F. after the ouster of Arbenz. Allende also made himself unacceptable to Washington policymakers by making it clear immediately after his election in September 1970 that he intended to practice as well as preach socialism. In quick order he nationalized large U.S.-owned copper mines, numerous industrial enterprises and over two thirds of the banks.

Washington's reaction to the developments in Guatemala was to mobilize all its resources to overthrow the offending government. No thought was given to American obligations by virtue of membership in the United Nations, whose principles expressly exclude interference in the internal affairs of other nations or unilateral military intervention anywhere. The hatchet man for the Guatemala job was John Peurifoy, a self-proclaimed tough guy from South Carolina who carried a pistol in his belt, and who already had proven his toughness by making and unmaking governments in Athens.[88] Appointed ambassador to Guatemala on December 23, 1953, he promptly exploited the arrival of a shipment of Czech arms, which Arbenz had bought since American weapons no longer were available. Washington leaked the arms story to the press and then shipped cargoes of arms to nearby Nicaragua. That compliant Somoza fiefdom became the base for the impending *putsch* that was to be led by a handpicked Guatemalan exile, Castillo Armas—"a prototypal banana republic military officer."[89]

On June 18, 1954, Castillo's motley troops crossed the border into Guatemala from Honduras, while several F-47s manned by American mercenary pilots bombed Guatemala at will. CIA planes parachuted Russian arms on Guatemalan locations to lend credence to Washington's charge that the Soviet Union was establishing a beachhead in Latin America. Commando raids led by CIA operatives cut railroad lines and bombed some trains and ships. Lacking the means to resist this coordinated assault, Arbenz abandoned his office and fled the country.

Meanwhile, the Soviet delegate to the UN Security Council had denounced the border crossing from Honduras as a U.S. plot, and asked that UN peacekeeping units be sent to Guatemala. Both Britain and

France accepted the Soviet proposal to the indignation of U.S. Ambassador Lodge. He called in the English and French envoys for the sort of dressing down that the United States was able to administer to any Western ally in the midfifties. As Lodge wired to Dulles:

> I now had an important statement to make to them, and I had asked them to come to my office so that I could do so in person. I said that this statement was not (repeat not) in any sense of the word a threat because of course they represented strong independent governments that would do whatever they wanted, but that I was instructed by the President to say to them that if Great Britain and France felt that they must take an independent line backing the present government of Guatemala, we would feel free to take an equally independent line concerning such matters as Egypt and North Africa in which we had hitherto tried to exercise the greatest forebearance so as not (repeat not) to embarrass Great Britain and France. My announcement was received with great solemnity.[90]

The chastised British and French obediently dropped the Soviet proposal, and the UN Council adopted instead a meaningless resolution calling for an end to any action likely to cause bloodshed. By this time the debate had become academic, as Arbenz had been overthrown and Castillo ensconced in the presidency. Washington had gotten its way, but at heavy cost for the United States. "In the minds of Latin Americans," concludes Schlesinger, "it tore FDR's 'Good Neighbor Policy' to tatters and unequivocally reinstated the 'right' of U.S. intervention throughout the hemisphere. Within the ranks of U.S. intelligence, it fostered a swaggering band of covert CIA agents fully convinced that they could crush any 'leftist' government or guerrilla war below the border—an attitude that led to American schemes to oust Castro in Cuba, eradicate 'revolutionaries' in the Dominican Republic in 1965, and kick Allende out of Chile." [91]

The end result of the interplay of the above domestic and external forces in Latin America has been a variety of regimes reminiscent of those in Africa. The majority are conservative and for the most part have become military dictatorships; a few are reformist and striving against mounting odds for peaceful change; and only one, which will be considered in a later section, is social revolutionary.

By far the most important of the conservative countries is Brazil, which is larger than the continental United States (excluding Alaska) and has a population of 114 million people as of January 1979. It dominates the rest of Latin America with its vast natural resources and its economic and military power. The turning point in recent Brazilian history was the overthrow in 1964 of the elected Goulart government and the establishment of a military dictatorship headed by a succession of generals: Castelo Branco, Artur da Costa e Silva, Emilio Garrastazu Medici, Ernesto Giesel and João Batista Figueiredo. Recently declassified documents reveal that the United States ambassador to Brazil, Lincoln Gordon, was in contact in August 1962, at the latest, with Carlos Lacerda and other plotters against Goulart. Lincoln encouraged a coalition of the military and the landlords with promises of arms, and the insurrection operation, "Brother Sam," was set in motion. Two American aircraft carriers with supporting boats, helicopters and Marines were dispatched to the Brazilian coast "to establish U.S. presence in this area when so directed and carry out such additional tasks as may be assigned." The armada was designed to aid and encourage the rebels, but it was preferred that it remain secret for fear of arousing popular sympathy for Goulart. Since the coup succeeded without overt U.S. intervention, operation "Brother Sam" remained a secret for over a decade.[92]

From the vantage point of the Montevideo station, a CIA operative, Philip Agee, noted in his diary on April 1, 1964:

> Our campaign against him [Goulart] took much the same lines as the ones against communist infiltration in the Velasco and Arosemena governments two and three years ago in Ecuador. According to Holman [chief of the Montevideo station] the Rio station and its larger bases were financing the mass urban demonstrations against the Goulart government, proving the old themes of God, country, family and liberty to be effective as ever. Goulart's fall is without doubt largely due to the careful planning and consistent propaganda campaigns dating at least back to the 1962 election operation.[93]

As in the rest of Latin America, the dictatorship was welcomed by Washington with all-out support. Philip Agee wrote in his diary on April 5 and 18, 1964: "It's clear that the Rio station is going all out to support the military government. . . . The decision was made, apparently by President Johnson himself, that an all-out effort must be made not only to prevent a counter-coup and insurgency in the short run in Brazil but also to build up their security forces as fast and as effectively as possible in the long run. Never again can Brazil be permitted to slide off to the left where the Communists and others become a threat to take things over or at least become a strong influence on them." [94]

In line with this top-level decision, the CIA organized Brazil's security agencies, AID trained over 100,000 Brazilian policemen and one fourth of all U.S. military assistance to Latin America between 1964 and 1971 went to Brazil. Also, financial aid by the United States government and by international lending agencies, which had been exceptionally parsimonious during the Goulart years, now blossomed forth in a pattern that was to be repeated in Argentina, Chile and other countries where favored military dictatorships replaced constitutional regimes. Thus total amount of aid to Brazil from the World Bank, the International Finance Corporation, the Inter-American Development Bank and the UN Development Program amounted to only $27.6 million in 1962, to $23.1 million in 1963 and to $25.9 million in 1964. But the total jumped to $159.9 million in 1965, to $242.0 million in 1967, to $377.4 million in 1970 and to $681.9 million in 1972. Beyond this official government support, heavy private American investments were made in Brazil's industries and natural resources, as well as substantial loans by U.S. banks.[95] Brazil's foreign debt by the end of 1978 totaled $40 billion, and yet, according to a Brazilian banker, "There is not a single (foreign) country with a reasonably large banking community that is not in here trying to market loans." [96] Thus the 1978 annual report of New York's Citicorp showed that 20 percent of all its profits came from Brazil, more than those generated in the United States.

The grand strategy of the five generals ruling Brazil since 1964 was evolved in Brazil's Higher College of War. This institution has been providing instruction since 1949 in techniques of regional planning, infrastructure building and theories of economic development. By the 1960s the Higher College had evolved what is termed the National Security Doctrine, which combines geopolitics and strategy to form "geostrategy." This doctrine is based on the principle that Brazil and the United States should share hegemony in the Western Hemisphere, with Brazil controlling the South Atlantic.

The economic policies of the Brazilian generals were the precise opposite of those that had been followed by President Goulart. Under the pressure of mass unrest during the recession years 1962–67, Goulart had adopted a radical populist program. It included agrarian reform, income redistribution, reliance on domestic capital, restriction of foreign investments, massive state intervention in the national economy and pursuit of new markets in Latin America, Africa and the socialist countries. To implement this program, Goulart sought political support from rural and urban workers and from the lower middle class. Under the influence of the Cuban Revolution, Goulart's movement took on socialist overtones, which provoked the military to oust him in 1964.

Once in power the generals reversed Goulart's program. Instead of trying to stimulate mass purchasing power, they set out to depress wages in order to increase profits, attract foreign capital and expand into markets abroad. Income was redistributed upward rather than downward. After a period of consumption restriction and economic growth, it was expected that the resulting benefits would trickle down in the form of more jobs with rising wages. Thus the military dictatorship gradually would attract popular support, acquire a broader political base and thereby safely negotiate the transition to full industrialization and self-generating growth.

For several years it appeared that the generals had hit upon a successful strategy. A boom got under way in 1968 and lasted until 1974. During those years multinational capital poured into Brazil. "Where compatible with the higher interest of the nation," declared President Geisel in 1976, "foreign business enterprises, including those of a transnational nature, will find a place in the industrial model adopted by Brazil. The government recognizes their important role as vehicles for the channeling of foreign financial resources, for transforming technology and instilling management skills in the country's business community, as well as for broadening and diversifying the scope of exports." [97] This enticing rhetoric was backed up by generous concessions to the multinationals, including state subsidies, tax exemptions and virtual outlawing of unions.

The Brazilian economy responded dramatically, with GNP growth rate averaging 10 percent a year. At the same time, inflation fell to 17 percent in 1972 and perhaps as low as 12 percent in 1973. Exports jumped from $1.4 billion in 1964 to $8.2 billion in 1975—a sixfold increase in eleven years. The "Brazilian miracle" was hailed in conservative circles throughout the world as the long-sought capitalist alternative to Marxist models for the industrialization of Third World countries.

In 1974 the "miracle" began to peter out. The blame was put on OPEC for quadrupling the cost of oil imports and causing an adverse balance of trade of $3.5 billion in 1975, after several years of favorable balance. The roots of economic distress, however, went far deeper than OPEC. More basic was the inadequacy of the domestic market because of the deliberate policy of keeping wage increases artificially below the growing rate of labor productivity. This was responsible for the rapid increase in production of expensive consumer goods such as TV sets, refrigerators and especially cars. But the production of mass-consumption goods such as clothing and shoes rose by only 1 percent between 1969 and 1972. After seven years of such skewed economic growth, the entire economy became unbalanced. By 1974 the restricted middle-class market for costly commodities had become saturated, so the annual GNP growth rate fell from 10 percent to 4 percent in 1975, and it failed to pick up thereafter. At the same time inflation climbed to 30 percent in 1975, to 40 percent in 1976 and to 109 percent in 1980.

An equally basic factor behind the economic slowdown was the role of the multinational corporations and the foreign banks. By 1978 Brazil's $40 billion debt was absorbing 40 percent of the nation's annual export earnings, about double the percentage considered safe and manageable. Also, the multinationals had gained control of 40 percent of the liquid assets of the main industrial and mining enterprises, and were retaining 55 percent of the profits of those enterprises. The profits were transferred to the home countries of the multinationals, thus aggravating Brazil's financial problem. In 1980, exports increased by 24 percent, but imports by 50 percent. Efforts to redress the balance met with resistance in the developed countries, suffering from recession and goaded by labor protests against cheap foreign imports. This is especially true of Brazil's chief customer, the United States, where Assistant Treasury Secretary C. Fred Bergsten warned the Brazilian-American Chamber of Commerce (May 15, 1978) that unless Brazil abandoned subsidies to its exporters, the United States would retaliate. Export incentives to Brazilian manufacturers, he noted, "run directly afoul of countervailing duty statutes in the United States," and if continued, would "jeopardize the openness of the entire trading system." [98]

By 1980 Brazil was saddled with a debt of over $55 billion—the largest in the Third World. The cost of amortization during the following five years totals $35 billion. President Figueiredo has despairingly concluded that his country "has nothing left over for development." [99] Thus even the colossus of Latin America, despite massive foreign aid, or rather because of it, remains bound by the shackles of dependency.

The military dictatorship faces a developing crisis in the 1980s. Local businessmen are protesting against "denationalization"—an expression commonly used throughout Latin America to connote economic domination by foreign multinationals. Workers also are becoming militant against a system of exploitation and repression that has benefited only the top 5 percent of the population along with the foreign corporations. Hence the rash of strikes in the spring of 1978 beginning in the automobile plants and spreading to electrical firms, tire and heavy-equipment manufacturers and metal shops.

The unrest and agitation of workers is paralleled by that of students. They have organized demonstrations throughout the country demanding restoration of the democratic freedoms destroyed by military rule in 1964. When Rosalynn Carter visited Brazil in the summer of 1977, she was presented with a letter of student grievances:

We want to emphasize that what is happening at the University of Brasilia [where a strike by sixteen thousand students was in progress] is not an isolated incident, but a symptom of the oppression that we as students have lived with nearly all our lives. The regime that has governed our country since 1964 may have guaranteed a certain degree of stability that may be beneficial to American interests, but this has been done at the cost of freedom of expression, freedom of the press and freedom of assembly.[100]

More serious for Brazil's military rulers than the student unrest is the growing opposition of the Roman Catholic Church. A statement by the National Conference of Bishops issued in November 1976 excoriated the regime for allowing policemen to go unpunished for tortures and murders, for tolerating inequitable distribution of land, for failing to protect the dwindling Indian population and for "the ideology of national security, which is placed above personal security." [101] More detailed was the declaration signed on May 6, 1973, by three archbishops and ten bishops of the northeastern region. In this thirty-page document the ecclesiastics detail the country's unemployment, hunger, illiteracy and high infant mortality, and brand Brazil's "so-called economic miracle as merely a means to make the rich richer and the poor poorer." They attribute the growing income inequity directly to the subordination of Brazil's human and material resources to the global market economy:

The social and economic structure in Brazil are built on oppression and injustice that evolve from a situation of a capitalism dependent on the great international centers of power. . . .

Malnutrition, infant mortality, prostitution, illiteracy, unemployment, cultural and political discrimination, growing imbalance between rich and poor and many other consequences characterize the institutional violations in Brazil.

The need of repression to guarantee the functioning and security of an associated capitalist system shows itself ever more imperious, revealing itself inexorable in closing legislative constitutional institutions and rural and urban workers' unions, depleting student leadership, imposing censorship and measures of persecution of workers, peasants and intellectuals, harassing priests and militant clergy, and assuming the most varied forms of imprisonment, tortures, mutilations and assassinations.

Finally, the ecclesiastical leaders warn that "the Church no longer is able to remain inert, waiting passively for the hour of changes. . . . The suppressed masses of workers, peasants and numerous unemployed have taken note of what is going on and are progressively assuming a new liberating conscience." [102]

To cope with the popular disaffection, the generals have resorted to "viable democracy"—a new political strategy designed to appease popular unrest and to institutionalize counterrevolution in Brazil and throughout Latin America. The press prints what it wants, opposition parties operate openly, labor unions wage strikes and in 1982 all state governors and every member of the Congress are scheduled to be elected by popular vote. But all this is window dressing, since there are no plans for the election of the all-powerful President. Loss of the state governorships would mean little because state governments have no real strength. Likewise, Congress remains dominated by the President, who also controls the federal budget, as well as the operating funds of state and city governments. Government spokesmen readily concede that the purpose of the concessions is to defuse the opposition rather than to create a representative political system. "Nothing is being institutionalized," states a Brazilian history professor. "There is nothing to prevent the generals from simply announcing an end to the process, without Congress or the people having any say at all." [103]

Meanwhile, Washington continues to support Brazil's military regime. Henry Kissinger in February 1976 negotiated a special relationship with Brazil, involving "a mechanism of regular consultation between the two countries at the ministerial level." [104] Secretary of State Cyrus Vance reaffirmed this special relationship in behalf of the Carter administration. On the other hand, the Brazilian generals resented Carter's human rights campaign, and flouted U.S. leadership repeatedly; voting with the Arabs in the UN to condemn Zionism as a form of racism; signing a $4 billion nuclear power deal with West Germany, which may give Brazil's military nuclear capability; recognizing the MPLA in Angola; and selling arms to various Third World countries.

Washington and Brasilia obviously have an overriding common interest in preserving the status quo throughout Latin America against revolutionary forces. On the other hand, Brasilia has aspirations to advance from subimperial to coimperial status in the Western Hemisphere. The future of the dictatorial regime will be determined by the outcome of its contradictory relationships with the United States and, more important, with its own people.

Turning from conservative to reformist Latin American states, Peru attracted worldwide attention in the early 1970s as the land of generals who were trying to find a third way—*ni comunismo, ni capitalismo.* Before the attempted restructuring from above by the military, Peru had been largely unaffected by the world market system. Foreign capital was prominent only in the copper mines and in coastal export agriculture.

Half the population was engaged in subsistence agriculture in the sierra highlands under semifeudal conditions. One percent of the property owners controlled 80 percent of the arable land, with some of the largest haciendas in the world—some over one million acres in extent. Haciendas were sold with so many head of Indians, and the Indians themselves identified their place of origin not as a village but by the name of the estate owner, "to whom we belong." Peru's political system was equally archaic. The American Revolutionary Popular Alliance (APRA), organized in 1924 by Victor Raúl Haya de la Torre, had originally been a progressive political movement, but by the 1970s its founder was an obese old man talking irrelevantly about Inca social theories. Likewise, Fernando Belaúnde's Acción Popular Party had made its peace with the establishment and had become an instrument for nepotism and corruption.

This anachronistic status quo in Peru, as in other Latin American countries, had been propped up by the traditional tripod comprising the Roman Catholic Church, the armed forces and the landed aristocracy. The Church had become deeply split by the theology of liberation, but this was true in most Latin American countries. What was novel and alarming in Peru was that the armed forces stopped functioning as the "watchdog of the oligarchy" when they seized power from a civilian government in 1968. The radical rhetoric of the new military rulers was not taken seriously at first, since it was standard procedure for all putschists to start off by proclaiming their commitment to the "people's welfare." But General Juan Velasco Alvarado and his followers were disturbingly different in that they meant what they said.

They were different in part because the color of the Peruvian officer corps had been changing gradually from aristocratic white to Indian brown as the upper classes forsook the armed forces for more lucrative careers in business. Then came the 1962–65 peasant uprising, which forced the young officers to ask themselves why the peasants had fought so ferociously, and why they should be suppressing people of the same stock as their own families. Their questioning was directed toward the left by radical social scientists teaching at CAEM (Centro de Altos Estudios Militares). The ideology the officers imbibed at CAEM was that of a "third way" between capitalism and communism. Consequently, when these graduates seized power in 1968 they set out to make Peruvian society more independent and more equitable through three basic innovations.

One was an agrarian reform program by which the large estates were not broken up into small *minifundia* but rather converted into cooperatives. The land now was owned by the workers rather than by absentee landlords, and the state provided funds for education, technical guidance and new strains of livestock and grains. The effect of the reform, however, was to create new sets of "haves" and "have-nots." The "haves" now were the workers who had been employed full time on the estates before the expropriation, and who alone were eligible to be members of the new cooperatives. This left out the seasonal laborers and the neighboring peasant villagers, who comprised 85 to 90 percent of the campesinos. They derived no benefits from the rural reform, and therefore moved in great migration waves out of the Andean highlands. Some went eastward to the jungles of the Amazon Basin, while others went westward to the coastal cities, where they lived as a chronically unemployed or underemployed lumpenproletariat.

The second innovation of the Peruvian military was to invest foreign capital in mining and industry, and in the construction of infrastructure. Worker participation and profit-sharing also were introduced as key features of the "third way," corresponding to the cooperatives in the countryside. A certain number of new jobs were created, though not enough to employ the 130,000 new workers showing up each year, much less to absorb those already unemployed, who comprised 30 percent of the labor force. Even of the employed workers, the majority did not qualify for profit-sharing and management participation because they were temporary help.

The third innovation of General Velasco was the nationalization of key foreign enterprises, including those of Gulf, Exxon, ITT, W. R. Grace, Anaconda and Chase Manhattan. The government was not opposed to foreign capital in principle, but wanted to change its nature and thrust to sustain national development plans. Closely related to nationalization was extensive state investment and intervention in order to promote an independent and self-sufficient economy. "Producto Peruano" appeared on many goods as a result of the output of large public corporations such as Mineroperu in minerals, Siderperu in steel, Pesceperu in fish and Petroperu in oil.

As this ambitious program unfolded, two fatal flaws became apparent. One was that the beneficiaries of the reforms comprised a small percentage of the total population—a minority of the workers and peasants along with a few industrialists. And even the few who did benefit were often alienated by the militaristic "top-down" methods—by the fact that this was a "revolution from above" with little meaningful input from below. The generals were aware of the problem and, typically, they created an organization to cope with it. This was the National System of Support for Social Mobilization (SINAMOS), the initials of which spell "Without Masters" in Spanish. SINAMOS' sixty-five hundred employees were to mobilize financial and technical support for peasant, labor and youth groups, as well as for cooperatives and community action programs. The general objective was to cut through the red tape that enveloped the new enterprises and to form a bridge "between the bottom and the top." But the pamphlets that instructed SINAMOS' agents to encourage the Indians to think for themselves consistently were illustrated with pictures showing the agents lecturing and the Indians listening. The generals' training unwittingly led them to treat the country as an enormous barrack.

The second defect of the Peruvian experiment was that the drive for economic independence was based on a greatly increased financial dependence. The compensation for nationalized estates and foreign enterprises, and the construction of new schools and infrastructure facilities all required much capital, as did large purchases of armaments from abroad. The U.S. government and the multinational agencies it controlled could not be tapped because of the nationalization of American properties. Peru therefore borrowed from private banks $147 million in 1972 and $734 million in 1973, by which year Peru had become the third largest borrower among Third World countries, with a debt of $3 billion.

Neither the borrowers nor the lenders were concerned because of the high price of copper exports and the promising oil strikes in the Amazon Basin. Their optimism appeared justified at first. Between 1969 and 1973 GNP increased by 5.5 percent a year, real wages rose 6.6 percent annually, inflation was held to an average of 7.2 percent and the trade balance remained positive. But 1974–75 revealed the inherent vulnerability of Third World countries like Peru, dependent on the export of a few raw materials whose prices are notoriously erratic. In quick succession the price of copper plummeted, the anchovy schools off the Peruvian coast mysteriously disappeared and the oilfields, to which a billion-dollar pipeline had been built, yielded a fraction of what had been expected. The trade balance became negative, unemployment increased and the growth rate faltered.

The economic crisis precipitated a coup in which the radical Velasco was displaced by the conservative General Francisco Morales Bermúdez. Leftist military officers were forced to resign, orthodox economic policies were introduced, striking labor and peasant leaders were imprisoned without trial and the revolution was renamed "humanist" rather than "socialist." The usual cycle of Third World debtor nations was now repeated: more loans, more austerity measures, more unemployment, higher prices, increased resistance and correspondingly increased repression.

By 1979 Peru's economy had recovered substantially, thanks to the austerity measures, and also to the rising price of copper, the increase in the oil flow and the return of the anchovies. A cartoon in a Lima newspaper showed a doctor helping a patient—symbolizing the Peruvian economy—arise from a sickbed. "Your recuperation is unbelievable," the doctor is saying.[105]

So far as Peru's foreign creditors were concerned, the recovery doubtless was "unbelievable." For the people of Peru, however, it was a somewhat different story. Over half the workforce is unemployed or underemployed. Fifty percent of Peru's children were malnourished in 1972; by 1979 the percentage had risen to 65. Researchers report a steady decline in IQ scores of children in Lima's poorer districts, and doctors report a sharp increase in TB—a nutrition-sensitive disease. A health team visiting a village of five thousand people in northern Peru found that 80 percent of the households had at least one active case of TB. A Lima magazine, *Oiga,* has given this account of the desperate search for food by the city's poor:

> In Lima's markets, hundreds of children, known as "fruit birds," must beat out stray dogs in search of spoiled fruit. Mothers, their small children slung on their backs, engage in a Kafkaesque struggle against buzzards for the refuse in areas where fish and other animals are eviscerated. The pelicans that used to fill the markets in search of refuse have been eaten by hungry families.[106]

In Peru, as in all Latin America, and indeed throughout the Third World, assessment of the economic health of any nation depends on the angle of vision—on whether it is viewed from above by the local and foreign elites who profit from the "austerity" measures, or from below by those in urban ghettos and wretched villages who pay every day with their dignity, their health and their lives.

It might be argued that Peru is not a fair example of the reformist model in Latin America, being one of the more underdeveloped countries and with a large Indian population that is exceptionally depressed. Yet the prospects appear equally dismal in Venezuela, with oil revenues amounting to $10 billion in 1975. Like the Peruvian generals, President Carlos Pérez depended on reform from above when he launched a $52 billion Five Year Plan on his accession to office in 1973. The aim was to attain economic independence and income distribution by launching major development programs and by nationalizing foreign-owned mines and oilfields. Theoretically the benefits were to trickle down to the poor, but in a hierarchically organized society the benefits inevitably were sucked upward into well-lined private pockets. As a Venezuelan agronomist has pointed out, "You cannot put a poorly educated bureaucrat out in the countryside and say, 'OK, here's the money you want, go organize the peasants' cooperative.' The illiterate peasants don't know what the government official is talking about and the bureaucrat, who can't tell one strain of grain from another, doesn't know what he is talking about either, yet the government in Caracas keeps pouring in the money. And then they wonder why food production has declined." [107]

The decline has been so marked that Venezuela, with rich agricultural resources, now can meet only half its food needs. After having been a sugar and meat exporter, it now imports both commodities. The economy has been increasingly dependent on oil revenues, with predictably disastrous results that already are becoming evident. In 1978 Venezuela faced the biggest balance of payments deficit in its history with foreign earnings totalling $8.85 billion (95 percent from oil) but imports rising to $11.89 billion, leaving a deficit of over $3 billion. By 1979 the external debt was estimated at $12.2 billion and debt service payments had risen from $767 million in 1974 to over $2 billion in 1979.

The combination of trade deficits, increasing foreign debts, rising inflation, shrinking oil revenues, and declining productivity of the non-oil sectors of the economy, is an indicator that Latin America's "brightest star" is setting. This is the conclusion of Juan Pablo Pérez Alfonso, the Venezuelan oil executive who was a prime mover behind the creation of OPEC: "I have seen what a big illusion I had in thinking that any money we would bring into Venezuela from oil, however we would invest it, would reproduce itself for the benefit of the country. I now see all too clearly that the result has been just the opposite, that the income from oil has actually hurt the country." [108] It has not hurt the new crop of oil millionaires who spend their weekends on private yachts or in Miami, but it has indeed hurt the overwhelming majority who have received no benefits from the encapsulated, capital-intensive oil industry but who instead have been ravaged by the inflation induced by the deluge of petrodollars.

A 1981 report by a team of Israeli economists reveals that almost 45 percent of Venezuelan children under 11 suffer from some type of malnutrition, and that more than 50 percent of workers do not earn enough to provide their families with a minimum nutritional standard. Even if they did, the report states, working class families do not know what nutritional food is, so that 70 percent of these families suffer from malnutrition.[109] "What has happened to oil money?" asks Sister Aura Delia González, a Roman Catholic nun who works among the slum dwellers of Caracas. "We have seen nothing good from the petrodollars—only the rise in price of milk and meats, more delinquency, shortages of schools and hospitals." [110]

Similar questions about petrodollars will be asked in Mexico, where vast new oilfields are being tapped. Despite the increased royalties, the trade deficit in 1978 was $2.1 billion, a 50 percent increase over 1977. The oil industry employs only 125,000 workers, in a country where half of the 17 million workforce is unemployed or underemployed. Current industrial plans prepared by President López Portillo call for using oil revenues to develop capital-intensive industries, such as petrochemicals, which also provide few jobs. Likewise in agriculture, the emphasis is on capital-intensive, export-oriented agribusiness operations which, together with the soaring birth rate, will continue to generate wholesale exodus from rural areas.

The prospect is for continued mass migrations to overcrowded Mexican cities, and to the United States, where one fourth of Mexico's working population now labors. Thus the two wealthy oil-producing Latin American countries seem destined to remain the two with the most inequitable income distribution—Venezuela being No. 1, and Mexico No. 2. A decade hence, Portillo's successors may look back and conclude, like Juan Pablo Pérez in Venezuela, that "the income from the oil has actually hurt the country." If that happens, the United States may well be confronted in Latin America with a repetition of what happened in Iran, as some State Department officials already are speculating.

Some Mexicans also are speculating along these lines. They note the billions of petrodollars are accompanied by rising unemployment and inflation, by growing dependence on oil exports and food imports. During the 1970s the acreage of corn dropped an annual average of 4.8 percent, so that by 1980 one third of the corn consumed was imported from the United States. The same was true of other staples such as beans and sugar. The establishment of government-controlled stores in the countryside did not help much because of the high cost of basic items. *Coplamar,* the government agency that administers the stores, estimates that over 60 percent of the population consumes little if any animal protein, and are reducing their consumption of corn. Thus a Mexican economist has observed: "It's called the oil syndrome. We saw it at work in Venezuela and Iran. We were determined to avoid it. Now here it is." [111]

Finally, in considering the prospects for the future of Latin America, it is worth recalling Castro's answer when he was asked during an interview why he was so active in Africa. "Because Africa," he responded, "is the weakest link in the imperialist chain." His reply is understandable in the light of his setbacks in trying to break the Latin American link of the imperialist chain. In contrast to Africa, the conservative forces buttressing the status quo in Latin America are impressively strong.

In the first place, neocolonialism is solidly entrenched in Latin America, its roots going back for a century and a half, in contrast to only a few decades in Africa. Consequently there are powerful bourgeois elements ranged against any revolutionary change and ready to cooperate with metropolitan centers to block such change. Chile is an obvious illustration of this peripheral-metropolitan axis in action, though other examples can be found in the past and others will materialize in the future. This means that the primary enemy for Latin American guerrillas is domestic, which makes difficult the broad antiforeign coalitions that made possible the successful revolutions in other parts of the Third World— the coalitions against the Japanese in China, against the French and Americans in Indochina and against the Portuguese in Africa.

Latin American guerrillas also have been handicapped by their foco strategy, articulated by Regis Debray in his *Revolution in the Revolution.* This strategy departs from classic Marxist doctrine by emphasizing the role of a "mobile strategic force"—a highly dedicated band of insurrectionists who would catalyze the countryside by exemplary military operations. Foco theory obviously represents the antithesis of the traditional Communist doctrine for the long-range agitation, education and organization followed by Mao, Ho and Cabral. In practice, however, the orthodox Communist Parties of Latin America rejected foco strategy, so that the guerrillas found themselves in the untenable position of being isolated from leftist forces as well as from the bourgeoisie. Foco theory has never worked, not even in Cuba. It is true that the guerrillas defeated some Batista forces, but the most damaging blows were delivered by urban residents who rioted, sabotaged and generally made the dictator's position untenable.

Revolutionary potential in Latin America is further reduced by the fact that the native Indian population is infinitely weaker than the native population in Africa. The Spaniards and Portuguese either displaced the Indians altogether, or else left them in a dependent and powerless position, subordinate to a large mestizo intermediate class as well as to the dominant whites. Throughout Africa, by contrast, the Europeans remained isolated and insignificant minorities, with the exception of South Africa, and even there the isolated and minority position of the Afrikaners is becoming increasingly manifest and threatened. In Latin America, the situation is reversed, with the whites and their mestizo allies comprising the solidly entrenched majority, and the Indians relegated to the position of encapsulated minorities outside the mainstream. Furthermore, foco strategy does not allow for the necessary long-range organizational work among the American Indians that the Vietnamese Communists, for example, conducted among their minorities. Hence the failure of Ché Guevara to rally the Bolivian Indians, with whom he did not have even linguistic contact, let alone organizational bonds.

Finally, the imperialist link in Latin America is immeasurably strengthened by the proximity of the United States. Philip Agee's account of his activities as a CIA operative in Montevideo reveals the degree to which Washington has access to all segments of Latin American society—not only policemen and generals, but also politicians, businessmen, labor leaders, journalists, churchmen, academicians and professional people. The aid that revolutionary African organizations such as ZANU, ZAPU and SWAPO received from neighboring states could not possibly be duplicated in Latin America. Instead, Latin American states cooperated with each other and/or the United States to launch the Bay of Pigs invasion, to overthrow Arbenz and Allende, to track down Ché Guevara and to harass and assassinate exiles scattered in Latin American capitals and even in Washington, D.C.

On the other hand, the strength of the status quo forces in Latin America and elsewhere should not be exaggerated. Iran under the Shah appeared to be, and was believed by Washington to be, a solid pillar supporting the prevailing Middle Eastern order. Yet that pillar crumbled before the verbal onslaught of a disaffected cleric in France directing his followers within Iran. Likewise, no Western government foresaw the successful revolutions in Portugal's African colonies, or the speed with which revolutionary movements currently are spreading through southern Africa. There is no reason for assuming that Latin America will prove permanently immune to corresponding dismantling of seemingly invulnerable regimes. Repression is rampant at present, and appears to be irresistible. Yet the fact remains that repression sooner or later breeds resistance. And in Latin America the resistance has been far more widespread than is generally realized.

E. J. Hobsbawm has noted that "there is a tradition of endemic peasant rebellion in certain Mexican areas and in a large part of the region of dense Indian settlement in the Andes, notably Peru." In the 1960s alone, Peronist guerrillas were active in Argentina, armed peasants' and miners' militias in Bolivia, "zones of armed self-defense" in various parts of Colombia as well as guerrilla outbreaks in Venezuela and Guatemala. Hobsbawm reaches this conclusion concerning Latin American revolutionary prospects:

> What is at issue is not the existence of revolutionary social forces on this continent, but the exact form in which they find practical expression, their means of success or that of the alternative policies designed to dissipate them or to satisfy the needs which gave rise to them. . . .
>
> Revolution in Latin America is likely to be a combined operation, either in a situation of internal political crisis within the established regime or, more rarely, of such permanent institutional instability that such a crisis can be precipitated. It is likely to combine social forces—peasants, workers, the marginal urban poor, students, sec-

tors of the middle strata—institutional and political forces, e.g. dissidents in the armed forces and the church, geographical forces, e.g. regional interests in what are normally very divided and heterogeneous republics, etc. Unfortunately the most effective cement of such combinations, the struggle against the foreigner, or more especially the foreign ruler, is rarely applicable except in the small central American states, where the U.S.A. is in the habit of intervening directly—but with potentially overwhelming forces—and perhaps, alas, by local nationalisms directed against Latin American neighbours. Latin America has been economically colonial, but its republics have been politically sovereign states for a very long time. [112]

Hobsbawm's analysis is borne out by the 1979 revolution in Nicaragua, which unseated the long-established Somoza Dynasty, and by the subsequent revolutionary rumblings in the rest of Latin America. The current generation of guerrilla revolutionaries has learned from the failures of the past. They are attracting peasants and workers into their ranks, and also spending years with the Indians, learning their languages and sharing their lives and problems. For the first time the Indians are being mobilized and activized, a fact of prime importance in Guatemala, where they comprise half of the total population, and in southern Mexico, where they are a sizable minority.

In addition to this endemic revolutionary ferment, it should be noted that the military dictatorships, despite their repression and all the overt and covert support they receive from the metropolitan centers, have failed to attract anything resembling mass support. In contrast to the European fascist movements, the Latin American dictatorships lack charismatic leadership, lack a totalitarian ideology and lack a supportive mass following outside of limited bourgeois circles. Even within these circles there is significant disaffection. Capitalists supported the establishment of military dictatorships in order to protect their property. They did not foresee the increased expenditures on armaments, the soaring national indebtedness, the continuing inflation and the growing control over Latin American economies by state enterprises and by foreign multinationals. Brazil, which began with a Milton Friedman economic model, now has nationalized more industries than did Allende's government in Chile. Orlando Saez, a spokesman for Chile's national bourgeoisie and an implacable foe of Allende, has complained against the economic policies of Pinochet's junta: ". . . it is truly incredible that it should have been this government that would terminate the national firms which produce capital goods." [113]

The military dictatorships also are encountering growing opposition from a former dependable ally—the Roman Catholic Church. Just as Islam is embedded in the local cultures of the Middle East, so Catholicism is a basic component of Latin America's political and social fabric, with 90 percent of the people being baptized Catholics. The new social awareness of the Catholic Church was expressed in the 1968 Latin American Bishops' Conference (CELAM) in Medellin, Colombia. The "root causes" of Latin American poverty were diagnosed in terms that sounded more Marxist than papal. The bishops denounced the "depreciation of the terms of exchange," which makes the "value of [Latin American] raw materials . . . increasingly less in relation to the cost of manufactured products." They noted the "rapid flight of economic and human capital" from their countries. They urged an end to the international credit system that subjects Third World economies to the "international imperialism of money." Above all, the bishops formally approved of the growing numbers of clergy working among the people for land redistribution and other basic economic reforms.

Encouraged by official commendation, priests and nuns became increasingly politicized. They helped organize farm workers' unions and day-care programs, and worked to free political prisoners and to find the "disappeared." They established some one hundred thousand "base communities throughout Latin America to involve the poor in "Christian activities" aimed at improving their lives. A few even left the Church and joined the guerrillas in armed resistance. These activities provoked retaliation by the authorities. According to Vatican sources, over a thousand priests, nuns and lay preachers were imprisoned, tortured or murdered during the 1970s. Nevertheless, the religious leaders persisted, so that Nicaragua's revolution was openly supported by the seven bishops of the country. "All of us are affected by the extremes of revolutionary insurrection," said the bishops. "Nevertheless, it is not possible to deny the moral and judicial legitimacy of such insurrection in the case of a prolonged tyranny that destroys fundamental human rights and endangers the common good of the nation." Father Miguel D'Escoto, a Maryknoll missionary and now Nicaragua's Foreign Minister, described the cooperation of his Church with the Sandinist revolutionaries:

In the beginning, the Sandinist Front of National Liberation was Marxist and anticlerical, perhaps because a process of Christianization had not yet begun in the Nicaraguan Catholic Church, and it was identified with the interests of the privileged class. But with our evangelical radicalization, placing ourselves on the side of the poor and oppressed and not betraying Christ so much, the Front opened itself to Christians because they believed the Church an important factor in the struggle for liberation and because they realized they were wrong in believing that only a Marxist could be a revolutionary. Thus the Front acquired maturity and it became authentically Sandinist.[114]

The independence of the Catholic Church is but one sign of a new balance of forces in Latin America with which the United States must contend. There is also the growing assertiveness of the large states, the increasing competition of European and Japanese business rivals and the perennial threat of revolutionary outbreaks. The new situation calls for a reappraisal of American policy, which was undertaken by the Commission on United States-Latin American Relations, chaired by Sol Linowitz, former ambassador to the OAS and a senior partner of the Coudert Brothers law firm. The commission, sponsored by the Center for Inter-American Relations, issued a report in December 1976 entitled "The United States and Latin America." Its recommendations included settlement of the Panama Canal issue, support for basic human rights, normalization of relations with Cuba, reduction of arms transfers and nuclear proliferation, and financial assistance and liberation of trade policies with an eye toward the objectives of the developing nations.

Some of these recommendations were implemented, including those regarding the Panama Canal and human rights. Also when Dominican generals prepared to nullify the election of a progressive president, Carter's administration, in sharp contrast to Lyndon Johnson's, cooperated with the governments of Venezuela, Colombia and Panama to forestall the imminent coup. On the other side of the ledger, however, the Latin American policy of Carter, as well as of other presidents, was constrained by a basic consideration articulated by President Kennedy in August 1961 when seeking a safe successor to the murdered Dominican dictator, Rafael Trujillo: "There are only three possibilities   in descending order of preference: a decent democratic regime, a continuation of the Trujillo regime or a Castro regime. We ought to aim at the first, but we really can't renounce the second until we are sure we can avoid the third." [115]

Carter's acceptance of this guiding rule explains his maneuvering up to the last minute to prevent the Sandinistas from taking power—by proposing an OAS peacekeeping force, and by pressuring for the preservation of the National Guard and for the inclusion of Somoza associates in the new government. It also explains why, after suspending economic aid to El Salvador because of suspected involvement of Salvadoran security forces in the deaths of three American nuns and a Catholic lay worker,

Carter resumed both forms of aid in January 1981.

Carter's successor in the White House was not plagued by indecision, being convinced that the Soviet Union is responsible for "all the unrest that is going on." Immediately after his inauguration, President Reagan escalated the military and economic aid to El Salvador, sent military instructors to train the junta forces, and issued a White Paper designed to justify those measures. The basic objective appeared to be to obliterate the "Vietnam syndrome," which both Carter and Reagan repeatedly deplored. The world was to be convinced that Vietnam was an exception, and that the United States had both the power and the will to crush social revolution in the Third World.

Certain factors favor the United States in El Salvador as against Vietnam. El Salvador is smaller in area and in population. Its fragile Democratic Revolutionary Front does not begin to match Ho Chi Minh's National Liberation Front in discipline, cohesion and revolutionary experience. Also the Reagan administration appears ready to send promptly anywhere in the Third World its growing Rapid Deployment Forces in order to wipe out guerrillas while they are still weak. On the other hand, both west European and Latin American governments have expressed publicly or privately their opposition to American military intervention in Central America. And in marked contrast to the general support of U.S. intervention in Vietnam by American religious communities, they have from the very beginning generated substantial opposition to intervention in El Salvador.

More crucial is the question whether the "unrest" in El Salvador is made in Havana and Moscow. This proposition, generally assumed by Reagan administration officials, is widely challenged not only in Latin America and Western Europe but also within the United States. Three experts at the University of North Carolina (F. G. Gil, E. A. Balyora and L. Schoultz) prepared for the State Department in December 1980 a report entitled *Democracy in Latin America: Prospects and Implications.* Concerning El Salvador, they note that the "unrest" predates not only Castro but even the 1917 Russian Revolution. It goes back to the late nineteenth century when a coffee-based oligarchy began the dispossession of the peasantry, of which 65 percent is left completely landless today. After analyzing the domination of the country during the intervening decades by the landed families and the military, the report concludes that the Washington-supported junta represents not a reformist center but "the extreme right [which] has become a state within the state." Washington policy therefore is appraised as "a diplomatic mistake and a misreading of Salvadoran history that is not going to help the democratic cause in Latin America and elsewhere."

Likewise Murat Williams, a career foreign officer for twenty-five years, and ambassador to El Salvador from 1961 to 1964, has explicitly challenged current U.S. policy in that country.

> The "evidence" offered by our government [to justify aid to the Salvadoran junta] stressed the flow of arms from Cuba and the Soviet Union. This has a touch of irony, since U.S. arms have been flowing in El Salvador for more than three decades. It [the junta] is neither centrist, nor Christian, nor democratic, nor reform-minded. . . . Those who want the "security equipment" to maintain the status quo are raising again the specter of Cuban subversion. If there is such subversion, it will come not for lack of weapons but for lack of social progress.
>
> Our military-assistance programs will not pacify the country any more than they have pacified other countries where we have sent "counterinsurgency" teams. Peace will come only when El Salvador works out its own destiny and solves its problems of extreme wealth in the midst of extreme poverty.[116]

The same viewpoint is presented in a 30-page unsigned paper that circulated in Washington in November 1980. Although not a "dissent channel" document in a technical bureaucratic sense, it was prepared by "current and former officials" of the State Department, National Security Council and C.I.A. The paper states that Salvadoran troops being trained in Panama for counterinsurgency warfare represent the "largest training program ever sponsored by the United States for any Latin American country in a single year." The report also cites "the stockpiling of arms in the Canal Zone, the upgrading of detailed contingency plans for . . . deployment of military forces in El Salvador and Guatemala," and other "preparatory steps to intervene militarily." If such intervention materializes, the paper argues that it would prove futile, and could widen into a regional war "from Colombia to the Mexican border." The United States, Guatemala and Honduras would be aiding the El Salvador junta, against Nicaragua and Cuba, with Panama and Costa Rica destabilized, and with Mexico and Venezuela alienated from the United States.

Resolution of the dilemma, according to the paper, requires acceptance of the fact that popular opinion in El Salvador supports not the *junta* but the *frente*, or Democratic Revolutionary Front, a coalition of anti-government groups. The frente therefore should be recognized by the United States as "a legitimate and representative force in Salvadorian politics." This would be the crucial first step towards negotiations that might culminate in a Zimbabwe-type peaceful settlement rather than a Vietnam-type bloodletting.[117-122]

❦ *III. Social Revolutionary Regimes*

Between the two world wars the Soviet Union had been the only "socialist island in a capitalist sea." Then the Second World War opened the dikes for another revolutionary breakthrough, and a considerable number of new Communist regimes originated during the wartime and postwar upheavals. They were of two distinct varieties, one comprising the Eastern European Communist states installed in office by Soviet military power. With the exception of Yugoslavia and to a certain degree Romania, these states have followed the Russian model and have remained largely dependent on the Red Army.

In addition to these Communist regimes imposed from the outside World War II engendered in the Third World a second type of Communist state. These were based on indigenous peasant revolutions rather than on the Soviet armed forces. The peasant revolutions were directed either against Axis occupation, as in Asia, or against Western colonial rule, as in Africa. In both cases the new revolutionary regimes were quite different from the housebroken variety installed in the East European capitals by the Red Army. Some of these regimes from the beginning were led by indigenous Communist Parties, which continued to rule after liberation, as happened in China and Vietnam. Other regimes emerged from radical nationalist movements, which in some cases were opposed by small urban-based Communist Parties. But after liberation a new synthesis was evolved, with the minority Communist Parties aligning themselves with the guerrillas, while the latter gradually became virtually ruling Communist Parties. This process occurred in Cuba and South Yemen, and has been accompanied by close relations with the Soviet Union. The same process, in a less clear-cut fashion, has transpired in Portugal's ex-African colonies, though they have been able, because of more favorable geopolitical circumstances, to avoid the extreme dependence on the Soviet Union that Cuba and South Yemen have found inescapable.

Whatever their origins, the social revolutionary states in the Third World labor under extreme common advantages and disadvantages. Whereas the conservative nationalist states, as noted above, have suffered from continued economic subservience after liberation, the social revolutionary states, by definition, have from their beginnings aimed for both social restructuring and economic independence. In addition to clarity regarding objectives, the radical regimes also have enjoyed the basic advantage of leaders and masses activized and trained in the course of armed struggle. Thus Tanzania, which won independence peacefully, "lacked trained cadre," as noted by Abdul Rahman Babu (see Section

II C of this chapter). Contrariwise, Mozambique's President Samora Machel has regretted that the armed struggle in his country was ended suddenly in 1974 by the revolution in Portugal. Continued warfare would have mobilized the population of the southern part of the country as well as the northern. "Armed struggle," declared Machel, "is a wonderful university." [123] Likewise, Mozambique's Minister of Economic Planning has observed:

> At the basis of all our economic and social plans is discipline. The development of this unity stems from the singular liberation struggle waged by the Frelimo guerrillas for 11 years against a force of 70,000 Portuguese. . . . Frelimo was able to fuse disparate nationalist elements within a single command and evolve an ideology and program that went beyond mere independence.[124]

Precisely the same point has been made in the other ex-Portuguese colony of Angola. A New York Times correspondent, Michael Kaufman, noted that in the capital, Luanda, "it was apparent that a revolutionary enthusiasm and neighborhood cohesion had taken hold." Tinito, a twenty-nine-year-old former law student who had spent seven years in a Portuguese prison camp, explained to him the roots of the mass mobilization:

> We think that this kind of organization is our own revolutionary adaptation and comes from our special experience. It is an irony that if we were given independence in 1961 like other African countries we would not have had a chance to develop our consciousness and nationalism through struggle. We might have been a neocolonial country but now we have achieved real unity.[125]

The new social revolutionary states, however, have also suffered from serious handicaps that have made their histories turbulent and even tragic. One is the unremitting hostility of the West, as manifested in the American invasion and then embargo of Cuba, the American invasion and then nonrecognition of Vietnam, and the South African raids against Angola and Mozambique. Almost as burdensome is the Soviet-Chinese feud, compelling radical movements and radical states to choose between Moscow and Peking. The ferocious in-fighting amongst India's splintered leftist factions derives in part from the Soviet-Chinese enmity. The Vietnamese and the Cambodians also have both borne the heavy burden of this cross, as will be noted below. "The Chinese love reactionaries," commented Prince Norodom Sihanouk ruefully. "Look at the way they have no time for the Eurocommunists and the splinter Communist parties. They are too busy courting the American reactionaries, the British reactionaries, the German reactionaries and the Japanese reactionaries.

Why can't they learn to love a Cambodian reactionary like me?" [126] The answer, of course, is the *haute politique* of the Great Powers, Communist as well as capitalist.

The greatest obstacle confronting the social revolutionary states of the Third World is their poverty. This has served, paradoxically, as a protective shield at the outset, providing freedom to strike out in new directions. Retardation involves isolation from the global market economy, lowering the vulnerability to external economic and political pressures and increasing the freedom to innovate and restructure. The 1917 Bolshevik Revolution survived the catastrophic years of civil war and intervention because four fifths of the population lived on farms, and the remaining fifth had retained life-sustaining contacts with their village relatives. Likewise during the Chinese Revolution, hundreds of millions of peasants ultimately prevailed, regardless of who controlled the cities and communication routes. In Vietnam, backwardness tempered by mass activism prevailed over computers, firepower and electronic gadgetry. And in Portugal's African colonies, it was their unparalleled primitiveness that enabled subsistence-level peasants to wage revolutionary struggles unequaled in the more advanced but also more vulnerable regions of Africa and Latin America. The obvious contrast is with the comparatively developed Chilean society, where the subversion of democratic socialism was facilitated by dependence on foreign markets, on foreign banks, and on foreign armament industries.

If extreme retardation can help in winning political independence, it is a crushing millstone in the postliberation struggle for economic independence. It forces disruptive choices between consumption and development, and the resulting complications are compounded by the sabotage of departing colonists and by subsequent trade embargoes and financial boycotts. The legacy of underdevelopment also necessitates abandonment of original plans for nonalignment in foreign affairs. Sheer survival dictated Cuba's dependence on the Soviet Union, and Cambodia's on China—and when the latter proved inadequate, the consequences were a national tragedy.

The above combination of external pressures and internal constraints explains the turbulence of the postliberation histories of social revolutionary states, as evidenced in the following analysis of three of these states: Vietnam, Mozambique and Cuba.

A.
Vietnam

After India had gained independence, Nehru stated before the Constituent Assembly in April 1948 that care should be taken "not to injure the existing structure too much," and then he added, "I am not brave and gallant enough to go about destroying any more." [127] By contrast, after the U.S. withdrawal from Indochina, the Fourth Congress of the Vietnam Communist Party quoted President Ho Chi Minh as saying: "In order to build socialism we must, above all, have socialist people, animated by socialist patriotism and proletarian internationalism." The tasks defined for these new people included the following: "Stimulate the socialist construction of the country; build the material and technical base for socialism; ensure that our country passes from small-scale to large-scale socialist construction." [128]

This basic difference in goals and strategies explains in large part the corresponding difference in the histories of India and Vietnam since 1945. The British government sent Lord Mountbatten to arrange the transfer of power to safe and predictable leaders such as Gandhi, Nehru and Jinnah. But in Vietnam the leader of the anti-Japanese national resistance was the Communist Ho Chi Minh. Hence the dispatch of British troops to help the French regain control of their colony. Hence also the statements of successive American Presidents branding Vietnamese communism as a mortal danger not only to the United States but also to all of Western civilization.

Eisenhower declared, ". . . we are supporting the Vietnamese and the French in their conduct of that war; because, as we see it, it is a case of independent and free nations operating against the encroachment of communism." Johnson informed one of the Senate's more serious students of foreign affairs that "if we don't stop the Reds in South Vietnam, tomorrow they will be in Hawaii and next week they will be in San Francisco." Nixon was apocalyptic in warning, ". . . . victory for the Vietcong. . . . would mean ultimately the destruction of freedom of speech *for all men for all time* not only in Asia but in the United States as well." [129]

These fervid affirmations are paradoxical in view of the fact that Indochina was the colony that President Franklin D. Roosevelt felt most strongly should not be subjected again to French rule. "France has had the country for nearly one hundred years," he explained to Lord Halifax, "and the people are worse off than they were at the beginning." [130] But Roosevelt was opposed by elements in his State Department as well as by the British and the French. By March 15, 1945, he conceded reluctantly: "If we can get the proper pledge from France to assume for herself the obligations of a trustee, then I would agree to France retaining these colonies with the proviso that independence was the ultimate goal." [131] Thus Roosevelt in effect accepted postwar control of Indochina by France.

After Truman assumed the presidency, the United States moved quickly toward full support for the colonial interests of her Western allies. One reason was the American commitment in the Truman Doctrine (March 12, 1947) "to support free peoples who are resisting attempted subjugation by armed minorities or by outside pressures." Another reason was the establishment of the People's Republic of China, which was viewed by American policymakers as a major calamity. Also the Korean War, according to William P. Bundy, reflected "a recognition that a defense line in Asia, stated in terms of an island perimeter, did not adequately define our vital interests, that those interests could be affected by action on the mainland in Asia." [132] This represented an important shift from MacArthur's statement in 1949 that "our line of defense runs through the chain of islands fringing the coast of Asia"—a chain that he defined as running from the Philippines to Okinawa, Japan and the Aleutian Islands.[133] Finally there was the growing East-West confrontation evident in the formation of the two military blocs, NATO and the Warsaw Pact.

Under these circumstances American policymakers moved rapidly toward full backing for the French in Indochina, and in doing so they assumed the same success that they already had enjoyed in Greece and South Korea. Thus began the American involvement that was to drag on for a quarter century with appalling cost to all concerned. The following analysis will focus on (1) how the Vietnamese organized a successful resistance against both France and the United States; (2) how the Vietnamese succeeded militarily but were then betrayed three times after signing the Agreement with France (Mar. 1945), the Geneva Accords (July 1945) and the Paris Agreements (Jan. 1973); (3) how the Vietnamese were betrayed not only by their antagonists, the French and Americans, but also by their allies, the Russians and the Chinese; and (4) how the final success of the Vietnamese in expelling the Americans was soured by the continuing clash in Southeast Asia of Soviet, Chinese and American policies, and by their own effort to impose Indochinese unity as an essential barrier to foreign interventionism.

One reason for the success of the Vietnamese resistance was the exceptionally exploitative and repressive nature of imperial rule under the French. They adopted the common imperial policy of divide and rule, exacerbating regional differences and setting one group of Vietnamese against another. In order to increase rice and rubber exports they introduced the plantation system, leaving most peasants with no land or insufficient land. Exports did increase, to the profit of French merchants, but the per-capita consumption of rice by the peasants actually declined. Elementary education was available for 2 percent of the population, and secondary education for .5 percent. The native graduates of the one so-called university encountered such discrimination in employment opportunities and salary differential that many ended up in any of a score of prisons.

The earliest resistance was led by the old mandarin elite in the late nineteenth century. Then the French-educated intellectuals of middle-class origin took over, but they lacked contact with the mass of peasants and workers. A Communist writer, Nguyen Khac Vien, is not unfair in describing these intellectuals as "totally incapable of organizing a strike, working for years on end in mines or on plantations, waging guerrilla warfare for decades, or plodding through the mud of rice paddies." By contrast he notes: "The first directive issued by the Communist Party in Vietnam shortly after its founding ordered its political activists to work in the mines, become rickshaw pullers and to live and work among the peasants—to build a base of support among the people." [134]

The life of Ho Chi Minh, the revered Communist resistance leader, illustrates this point of contrasting class backgrounds and attitudes. A schoolboy rebel at fifteen, a youthful revolutionary at Hue, a merchant seaman, an assistant chef in London, a gardener at Sainte-Adresse, a photographic retoucher in Paris and a member of the Communist Parties of France, the Soviet Union and China, he was imprisoned at various times by the French, British and Chinese. These experiences, combined with theoretical study, led him, in his words, to understand that "only Socialism-Communism can liberate the oppressed nations and the working people of the world from slavery." [135] Like Mao, Ho viewed Marxism not as an abstract philosophy but as a useful tool. And even though he served as a Comintern agent, he did not hesitate to denounce Maurice Thorez for his "most remarkable opinion" that French rule should be restored in Indochina after World War II.

During the war, Ho formed a united-front organization, the League for the Independence of Vietnam (Viet Minh for short). With the Japanese preoccupied elsewhere, the Viet Minh were able to overrun French garrisons in rural outposts. Securing arms from American airdrops and French supply depots, they won control by the summer of 1945 over large sections of five northern provinces. When the war ended, Viet Minh troops marched into Hanoi, where Ho proclaimed on September 2, 1945, the establishment of the Democratic Republic of Vietnam. The new regime quickly divided among the landless peasants the holdings of the French and of their collaborators. Also, it opened new schools, decreed the eight-hour working day in cities, lowered taxes, nationalized public utilities (which hitherto had been exclusively foreign-owned), helped workers to set up their own unions and released thousands of incarcerated political prisoners.

On March 6, 1946, Ho signed an agreement with the French that recognized the Democratic Republic of Vietnam as "a free state with its own government, parliament, army and finances, forming a part of the Indochinese Federation and the French Union." In exchange, Ho agreed to the return of fifteen thousand French troops. "I am not happy about it," Ho remarked at the signing, "for basically it is you who have won. But I understand that you cannot have everything in one day." [136]

Ho's apprehension proved justified, for now began the first of the three betrayals of the Viet Minh. It had been arranged that the Japanese were to surrender to the Chinese Nationalists in the North, and to the British in the South. Their task supposedly was the "roundup and disarming of the Japanese, and the recovery of Allied Prisoners of War and Internees." [137] In actuality the Chinese in the North concentrated on pillaging, while the British went to great lengths to enable the French to return to power. They rearmed French troops interned in the Saigon area, and looked the other way as these troops seized control of the capital. In the countryside the British, with Indian and Japanese soldiers, fought against the Viet Minh until the French arrived to take over. Then the French made demands on Ho amounting virtually to surrender. When Ho refused, the French fleet on November 23, 1946, bombarded the Vietnamese sections of Haiphong, killing six thousand civilians. Less than a month later the Viet Minh cut off the water and electricity supply for Hanoi and launched an attack. Lacking sufficient arms, they failed to capture the city, so the Viet Minh soldiers slipped away with their leaders into the countryside.

The war for Indochina had begun! The Communist Paris paper, *L'Humanité,* followed the current Kremlin antirevolutionary line in asking its readers: "Are we, after having lost Syria and Lebanon yesterday, to lose Indochina tomorrow, North Africa the day after?" [138] Ho's answer was succinct and prophetic. "Today it is a case of the grasshopper pitted against the elephant, but tomorrow the elephant will have its guts ripped out." [139]

The Viet Minh waged a people's war, basically similar to that of the Yenan Communists, though evolved locally by trial and error. The emphasis again was on mass activation and mobilization in order to satisfy immediate peasant needs as well as to wage resistance. This involved more land redistribution, new schools, mass literacy campaigns, public health facilities, road building and village industries.[140] The spirit of the Vietnamese resistance was grudgingly admired by a hawkish journalist, Joseph Alsop, who traveled through the Viet Minh areas of the Mekong Delta in the winter of 1954:

> I would like to be able to report—I had hoped to be able to report —that on that long, slow canal trip to Vinh Binh, I saw all the signs of misery and oppression that have made my visits to East Germany

like nightmare journeys to 1984. But it was not so. . . . At first it was difficult to conceive a Communist government's genuinely "serving the people." I could hardly imagine a Communist government that was also a popular government and almost a democratic government. But this is just the sort of government the palmhut state actually was while the struggle with the French continued. The Vietminh could not possibly have carried on the resistance for one year, let alone nine years, without the people's strong, united support.[141]

The French responded in the traditional manner by establishing control over urban centers and communication routes, and then seeking to "pacify" the countryside. But the villagers were so well organized and prepared that the French found themselves isolated in their strongpoints —like the Japanese and the Nationalists in China. By 1950 French garrisons were being overrun in northern Vietnam. At the same time Americans were fighting in Korea, so Washington viewed the two wars as the result of an international Communist conspiracy to conquer all Asia. The United States therefore increased its financial subsidy to France from $150 million in 1950 to $1 billion in 1954. Despite this massive American intervention the Viet Minh continued to gain ground. By the spring of 1954 it controlled three fourths of the whole country. Its troops now were well armed with American weapons seized from the French or provided by the Chinese Communists from the huge stores left behind by the fleeing Nationalists.

The crisis came in April 1954, when twelve French divisions were trapped in the village of Dien Bien Phu. In the ensuing battle the Viet Minh methodically "ripped out" the guts of the French "elephant." General Henri Navarre had selected Dien Bien Phu as a strongpoint because it controlled Viet Minh supply routes to Laos and China. But he overlooked the fact that the surrounding roads were vulnerable to enemy attack as well as to adverse weather. Instead of building up a base for hunting down the enemy, the French found themselves surrounded by Viet Minh troops who had man- and pony-handled through "impassable" jungle two hundred heavy guns as well as multiple-tube rocket launchers.

The French command had to parachute in a minimum of two hundred tons of supplies a day, and even then the French soldiers in the valley had to crawl in the open, under fire, to collect the cannisters. The Viet Minh, by contrast, were provisioned by thousands of men, women and children who walked along jungle trails at night with their loads on poles, small oil lamps furnishing the pinpoints of light that enabled them to follow each other in unending human chains. Rice comprised the bulk of the supplies. Only one tenth of each carrier's burden could reach its destination; the remaining nine tenths went to feed the carriers on their long march.

Primitive though it was, the Viet Minh supply system prevailed over the French. Viet Minh artillery poured down fire from the surrounding heights, decimating the besieged garrison and reducing the exposed French gunsites to rubble. The Paris government appealed to Washington for direct armed intervention. Secretary of State John Foster Dulles suggested the use of nuclear weapons, and Vice President Richard Nixon supported him because "The United States as a leader of the Free World cannot afford further retreat in Asia." [142] But Churchill was flatly opposed. Congress feared domestic and international complications, and the French public had become sick of the war. On May 7 close to ten thousand French soldiers surrendered, another two thousand lay dead on the valley floor and only seventy-three managed to escape.

After this stunning victory the Viet Minh experienced its second great betrayal at the ensuing Geneva peace conference. The French were interested primarily in finding the least disastrous path to diplomatic extrication. The Americans, however, made every effort behind the scenes to dissuade their allies from any compromise. Vyacheslav Molotov and Chou En-lai also participated, and both aggressively sought to further their respective national interests, which conflicted with those of the Viet Minh. The chief objective of Soviet diplomacy at this time was to foil the ratification by France of the European Defense Community. There is no documentary evidence that Molotov made a deal with Premier Mendès-France for a favorable Indochinese settlement in return for French rejection of EDC. But such deals are arranged more by gestures and moves than by written accords. And as a Pentagon historian had noted:

> It was certainly in Soviet interests to pressure the Viet Minh for concessions to the French, since removal of the French command from Indochina would restore French force levels on the Continent and thereby probably offset their need for an EDC. Soviet interests thus dictated the sacrifice of Viet Minh goals if necessary to prevent German remilitarization.[143]

The Pentagon historian adds that the Soviet position at the Geneva conference "dovetailed with what seems to have been the Chinese outlook." [144] Just as the Russians were preoccupied with European affairs, so the Chinese were with the security of their southern borders. Chou En-lai therefore urged at the conference the neutralization of Indochina, including the prohibition of foreign bases and the withdrawal of foreign troops. To secure this objective, Chou suggested to Anthony

Eden and Mendès-France that Viet Minh forces be withdrawn from Laos and Cambodia, that Vietnam be partitioned and that some links might be preserved between Vietnam and the French Union. These proposals were scarcely in the interest of the Viet Minh, which protested strongly against them. Chou then traveled to the Chinese-Vietnamese border, where he met personally with Ho. After the meeting, Chou informed the French that the results were "very good" and "would be helpful to France." [145]

The Pentagon historian naturally concluded that ". . . the Chinese were negotiating for their own security, not for Viet Minh territorial advantage. . . . The Chinese were clearly out to get from the conference what they could. . . ." [146] The French representative at Geneva, Jean Chauvel, likewise concluded, ". . . both Russians and Chinese give Viet Minh fairly free hand to see how far they can go but that when they find Viet Minh demands have gone beyond limit which French can be expected to accept, they intervene. . . ." [147] Chauvel therefore was hopeful that ". . . Chinese-Russian moderating influence will now be brought to bear on Viet Minh." [148]

With such a line-up at the conference, it is not surprising that the victors of the war emerged the losers of the peace. The final agreement reached in July 1954 provided for the temporary partition of Vietnam at the Seventeenth Parallel into two zones for the regroupment of the two sides' military forces pending the holding of *national* elections in July 1956. Civil administration was to be in the hands of the Viet Minh in the North and the French in the South. The Viet Minh were to be free to participate fully in the political activities in the South prior to the elections. To ensure the neutralization of the country, both zones were forbidden to make military alliances with other nations, or to receive troops and military equipment from outside. An international Control Commission (ICC), consisting of members from Canada, India and Poland, was formed to supervise the execution of the agreement.

The Vietnamese presumably were induced to accept this arrangement partly by the pressures from all sides but also by the commitments for neutralization and for elections. These commitments, however, were violated from the beginning by the United States. If Hanoi was bitter about the outcome of the conference, Washington was even more so. According to Assistant Secretary for Far Eastern Affairs Walter S. Robertson: "It would be an understatement to say that we do not like the terms of the cease-fire agreement just concluded." [149] Likewise the Pentagon historian notes that the Geneva settlement was viewed by Washington as a "disaster," and that this attitude entailed ". . . a progressively deepening U.S. involvement in the snarl of violence and intrigue within Vietnam, and therefore a direct role in the ultimate breakdown of the Geneva settlement." [150]

One of the few voices of sanity in Washington at this time was that of General Matthew B. Ridgway, former commander in Korea, and Army chief of staff in 1954. A few months after the Geneva conference he prepared a secret memorandum for the Secretary of Defense in which he pointed out the weakness of the prevailing American policy of opposing and provoking China. Instead he advocated a new strategy designed ". . . to split Communist China from the Soviet Block. . . . In fact, I would regard the destruction of such a military power (as China) as inimical to the long-range interests of the U.S. It would result in the creation of a power vacuum in which but one nation could move, namely Soviet Russia. . . ." Ridgway concluded from this premise: "The statesmanlike approach would seem to be to bring Red China to a realization that its long-range benefits derive from friendliness with America, not with U.S.S.R., which casts acquisitive eyes on its territory and resources. . . ." [151]

The Chinese needed no persuading about the "benefits" of "friendliness with America," since they were sending messages to Washington even before they seized power urging precisely what Ridgway now was recommending. But the anti-Communist obsession of these Cold War years so dominated American policymakers that Ridgway's memorandum was ignored. Decades of disaster were needed before Ridgway's proposal for an opening to Peking was finally taken up by Nixon and Kissinger, and developed further by Carter and Brzezinski.

Eisenhower rejected the extreme military measures favored by Dulles, Nixon and Admiral Radford. A compromise course was selected, which General Gavin described as follows: "We would not attack North Vietnam, but we would support a South Vietnamese government that we hoped would provide a stable, independent government that was representative of the people." [152] This was a flagrant violation of the neutralization provisions of the Geneva agreement, yet this policy was pursued by the United States until its failure necessitated armed aggression in the North as well as in the South.

In preparation for increased intervention in Vietnam, John Foster Dulles organized only a month after Geneva the Southeast Treaty Organization (SEATO). Its members were the United States, Britain, France, Australia, New Zealand and only three Asian countries—Pakistan, Thailand and the Philippines. SEATO extended unilateral protection to Cambodia, Laos and the "free territory under the jurisdiction of the State of Vietnam"—a euphemism for the southern zone, and therefore another violation of Geneva. Indeed, Dulles informed a New York

Times correspondent, Cyrus Sulzberger, that SEATO's principal purpose was to "provide our President legal authority to intervene in Indochina." [153] At the same time, General J. Lawton Collins announced that the United States would spend $2 billion in support of an American military mission that "will soon take care of instructing the Vietnam Army in accordance with special American methods which have proved effective in Korea, Greece and Turkey, and other parts of the world. . . ." [154]

In addition to this military intervention, it was necessary to find a political figure who would play the same role in Vietnam that Syngman Rhee did in Korea, and Ramon Magsaysay did in the Philippines. Dulles was impressed by Colonel Edward Lansdale's success in directing the suppression of the Huks in the Philippines, and sent him to Vietnam just as Dien Bien Phu was falling. Lansdale decided that Ngo Dinh Diem was the man for the job. A mandarin mystic and a Catholic, Diem had served in the French civil service in the 1930s, had refused to work for the Japanese and chose exile in the United States in 1950. He lived in Maryknoll seminaries in New Jersey and New York, and became known as a militant anti-Communist. He attracted the attention and support of influential Americans such as Cardinal Spellman and Senators Mike Mansfield and John F. Kennedy. It was on American urging, therefore, that the French appointed Diem as Premier in the southern zone. Diem immediately set to work to save Vietnam from the Communist "world plan."

He had three principal sources of support, of which the most important was unstinted American aid. This included $250 million a year plus military equipment, military advisers, CIA agents to train his police, Michigan State University professors to provide a respectable front for these activities, and public-relations men to build up his image in the United States.

The second source of support came from the Catholics who were a minority in predominately Buddhist Vietnam. The Catholics were strongly reinforced, however, by the influx of 880,000 refugees from the North in 1954–55. This exodus has been cited as proof of Communist tyranny in the North, but this ignores the very active role of the CIA and of local parish priests. They spread rumors among Catholic peasants that the Communists would repress all religious activities, that their priests would be put on trial and that the Americans would drop atom bombs on their villages. The resulting mass flight, according to French scholar Bernard Fall, "was admittedly the result of an extremely intensive, well-conducted, and, in terms of its objective, very successful American psychological warfare operation." [155] The refugees were totally dependent upon, and loyal to, Diem, who appointed them to key posts in Saigon as well as to provincial offices.

The third group that supported Diem were the large landowners of the Mekong Delta. This small but influential group was a creation of the French plantation system. Since the Viet Minh had distributed much of their land among the peasants, they were delighted when Diem restored rents that had been abolished, and re-established estates that had been broken up.

Diem's agrarian policy was hardly popular in the countryside. Assured of American backing, Diem resorted to wholesale repression. He abolished elected councils that had ruled South Vietnam's 2,560 villages, replacing them with officials appointed by his provincial governors. He also introduced "agrovilles" (renamed after repeated failures of "strategic hamlets" and "new life hamlets"), which were built by forced labor and surrounded by barbed-wire fences and spiked moats. Their purpose was to counter the revolutionary strategy of guerrillas operating freely like "fish in the sea," by draining out the sea—that is, by forcing the peasants into the relocation centers and thereby depriving the guerrillas of their mass support. By 1963 no less than eight million villagers were crowded into what, as American officials conceded, amounted to "concentration camps." [156]

In order to remain in office despite an obviously hostile population, President Diem refused to hold the elections provided for in the Geneva agreement. His rationalization was that free elections were not possible in North Vietnam, and therefore could not be held on a nationwide scale. His real motive is evident in President Eisenhower's statement in his memoirs, *Mandate for Change*: "I have never talked or corresponded with a person knowledgeable in Indochinese affairs who did not agree that had elections been held as of the time of the fighting, possibly 80 percent of the population would have voted for the Communist Ho Chi Minh as their leader. . . ." [157]

North Vietnam protested the repression and the refusal to hold elections. Although no satisfaction was received, Ho decided against renewed warfare. Apparently confident that a separate state in the South could not take root, he assumed that a new government eventually would appear that would be willing to reunite with the North. The ex-Viet Minh cadres in the South, however, could not afford to take such a long-range view. Hounded by Diem's police, they felt betrayed by the Geneva conference and abandoned by their northern comrades. So in December 1960 they organized the National Liberation Front of South Vietnam (NLF), and called for a nationwide uprising against the Saigon regime.

The NLF quickly won widespread support, and for the same basic reason that the Viet Minh had earlier when fighting against the French. In contrast to Diem's police and soldiers, the NLF guerrillas were polite, spoke the peasants' language, shared their poverty, opened schools and health centers and redistributed the land or reduced the rents. According to an American administrative adviser, the NLF by late 1961 controlled in varying degrees 80 percent of the countryside. Even the South Vietnamese army was demoralized by Diem's insistence on personal loyalty in military appointments. Americans at home began to learn of the popular disaffection with the Buddhist riots and self-immolations that began in May 1963.

This disintegration of the regime was the background for the assassination of Diem and his brother during a coup by Vietnamese generals on November 2, 1963. A United States Senate Committee investigating the circumstances of the assassination concluded that "the United States government offered encouragement for the coup, but neither desired nor was involved in the assassinations. Rather Diem's assassination appears to have been a spontaneous act by Vietnamese generals, engendered by anger at Diem for refusing to resign or put himself in the custody of the leaders of the coup." [158]

After Diem's downfall the United States placed its trust and support in the South Vietnamese military establishment. President Lyndon B. Johnson pledged an increased war effort, and used the Tonkin Gulf incident of August 2, 1964, to obtain a joint resolution from Congress authorizing "all necessary measures to repel an armed attack against the forces of the United States and to prevent further aggression." Subsequent studies of this incident [159] indicate that evidence of the alleged attack on the U.S. Navy destroyer *Maddox* is inconclusive, and that the Johnson administration exploited a crisis atmosphere, created by its own covert war measures against North Vietnam, to secure authority from Congress to make war in Southeast Asia whenever and wherever it saw fit.

Johnson used the authority to bomb North as well as South Vietnam, with the aim of coercing Hanoi to stop sending troops southward and to recognize South Vietnam as a separate state. The accelerating American involvement in the war reached the point where the bombing surpassed World War II and Korean levels, and over half a million American troops were committed to the land war. It was assumed that the accelerating escalation of the war would inevitably overwhelm the Vietnamese. "Every quantitative measure shows we're winning the war," declared Robert McNamara, Secretary of Defense, in 1962. Johnson's adviser Walt Rostow confidently predicted in 1965: "The Vietcong are going to collapse within weeks. Not months, but weeks." And General Westmoreland announced in 1968: "The enemy has been defeated at every turn."

These illusions were shattered by the enemy Tet offensive launched on January 30, 1968, against all major cities in South Vietnam, as well as against thirty-six provincial capitals and sixty-four district headquarters. The United States struck back with mass bombardments of the occupied cities to drive the NLF out. In one of the memorable comments of the war, an American army adviser to the South Vietnamese, surveying the ruins of Ben Tre in the Mekong Delta, said, "We had to destroy it in order to save it." [160]

American public support for the war plummeted, and Senator Eugene McCarthy, running as an antiwar candidate, won 40 percent of the vote in the March 1968 New Hampshire presidential primary of the Democratic Party. Three weeks later Johnson stopped the bombing beyond the Twentieth Parallel in North Vietnam and announced that he would not run for re-election.

Richard Nixon won the November 1968 presidential election with the promise of a plan to end the war. This proved to be withdrawal of American land forces, which was unavoidable because of the state of public opinion, plus continued support of the Thieu regime in Saigon. The new strategy was "Vietnamization" of the war. This involved more money, arms and noncombative military personnel, together with supportive bombing that surpassed the scale of that under Johnson. Still the war dragged on, so Nixon resorted to armed "incursions" into Cambodia (Apr.–June 1970) and Laos (Feb.–Mar. 1971). On February 8, 1971, the United States launched its last major offensive in South Vietnam. The operation was the first real test of the South Vietnam army fighting alone—without advisers but with American air support—and it was a disaster for the South. Finally, faced with growing demonstrations at home and with no prospect for a military solution, Nixon turned to Peking— to the strategy that had been proposed by General Ridgway in 1954.

The United States now exploited the contradictions between China and Russia to use both to pressure Hanoi to sign a peace treaty that it otherwise would have rejected. The differences between Moscow and Peking were greater than those between either capital and Washington. The Chinese were just as anxious now as they were during the Geneva conference to see the United States withdraw from Indochina so that they would have more options in confronting the Soviet Union. The latter, in turn, had chronic economic and technological problems, including a serious agricultural crisis. Kissinger shrewdly exploited the Soviet difficulties by dangling the carrot of increased trade and technological aid. The situation was basically similar to that which prevailed during the Geneva Conference, and Kissinger therefore was able to negotiate the third betrayal of the Vietnam resistance in the form of the Paris Agreements of January 1973.

During the course of the protracted negotiations, while Moscow and Peking applied "persuasion and pressure" on Hanoi, Washington enjoyed a free hand in blockading and bombing North Vietnam. Neither the Soviet Union nor China did anything more about this American aggression than to issue *pro forma* protests. I. F. Stone, with characteristic perceptiveness and candor, wrote at the time that "the chief running dogs of imperialism now seem to be Brezhnev and Chou En-lai. This is how it must look from Hanoi." [161] In fact, this is how it did look to Hanoi, and it was so stated at the time in the Hanoi Communist Party paper, *Nan Dan*, though in necessarily more diplomatic language:

> The imperialists pursue a policy of détente with some big countries to have a free hand . . . to bully the small countries and stamp out the national liberation movement. . . . With regard to socialist countries . . . to care for its immediate and narrow interests while shrinking from its lofty international duties, not only is detrimental to revolutionary movement in the world but will also bring unfathomable harm to itself in the end.[162]

Hanoi's criticism was later vindicated by Henry Kissinger's candid statement in his memoirs that "Peking's priority was not the war on its southern border but its relationship with us. Three months later [after Nixon's trip to Peking] Moscow revealed the same priorities, more crudely. Moscow and Peking, for all their hatred of each other, or perhaps because of it, were agreed on this point: North Vietnam would not be permitted to override their greater geopolitical preoccupations." [163]

These circumstances explain why the 1973 Paris Agreements resembled the 1954 Geneva Agreements, especially in the vagueness of the political provisions, which again were made only to be broken. Negotiating under pressure, Hanoi dropped its long-standing demands for the "disbanding at once" of the Saigon regime and for the immediate resignation of President Thieu. The Paris Agreements consisted essentially of two parts. The first was that the United States would stop its bombing and mining in exchange for the release of American POWs held by Hanoi. The second was a bargain for a cease-fire in South Vietnam in exchange for a process of political competition and accommodation designed to settle peacefully the struggle for control of South Vietnam. Accordingly the Paris Agreements included articles that reaffirmed that Vietnam is one country and that the division along the Seventeenth Parallel is a temporary line of demarcation; asserted the "independence, sovereignty, unity, and territorial integrity of Vietnam" as recognized by the 1954 Geneva Agreements; pledged that the United States would not continue its military involvement or intervene in the internal affairs of South Vietnam; provided for freedom of movement between the military zones and for release of political prisoners and for the establishment of a national council of reconciliation; and finally guaranteed the right of the provisional government to join in the preparation for and the administration of internationally supervised elections.

It was these provisions for a peaceful political process that were ignored as soon as the POWs had been returned to the United States. Thus the Paris Agreements represented still another betrayal of the Vietnamese people, as had the earlier Geneva Agreements. The basis for betrayal was the transfer of huge quantities of American arms to the Thieu government before and immediately after the Geneva Agreements, and also Nixon's written assurances to Thieu (on Nov. 14, 1972, and Jan. 5, 1973) that the United States would "take swift and severe retaliatory action" if North Vietnam violated the agreements.

Fortified with this backing, Thieu took aggressive measures that violated the Paris Agreements and led inevitably to North Vietnamese retaliation. He made it a crime to publish the text of the Paris Agreements in South Vietnam, prohibited movement between the zones, reclassified political prisoners as common criminals to keep them in jail, effectively banned all political parties but his own, prevented establishment of a national council of reconciliation and at the moment the cease-fire was to come into effect he launched aggressive military operations. Admiral Thomas Moorer reported in February 1974 that Thieu's forces had "increased their control overall from 76 percent to 82 percent during the past year." Equally significant was his report that North Vietnamese policy was "to concentrate on political action . . . and not go forward with large-scale military activity. They have openly published this track, and they have been following it." [164] Likewise Maynard Parker wrote in *Foreign Affairs* (Jan. 1975) that "the Communists . . . were unprepared for—and staggered by—the aggressiveness of the government's operation. . . . What is extraordinarily important in this military picture is, of course, the degree of restraint shown by the North Vietnamese forces."

When finally in early 1975 the North Vietnamese and the Provisional Revolutionary Government of the South retaliated with an offensive, they were in no sense responsible for the breakdown of the Paris Agreements. To charge them with responsibility is to require them unilaterally to renounce force in the face of Saigon's armed aggression and political repression. Yet Kissinger held North Vietnam responsible for violating the Paris Agreements, and on that basis declared that they were "dead"— a position that conveniently absolved the United States of its pledge in Article 21 to "contribute to healing the wounds of war and of postwar reconstruction of the Democratic Republic of Vietnam and throughout Indochina."

The North Vietnamese were surprised by the rapid and complete victory of their forces. It was not their military power that was decisive, but rather the dry rot of the Saigon regime. After a series of setbacks, President Thieu ordered a retreat from the central highlands. The retreat turned into a rout that developed its own momentum, so that the North Vietnamese could not keep up with the fleeing enemy. Frequently they did not arrive in villages and towns until a day or two after the Saigon soldiers and officials had run off. It is charged in some quarters that the Thieu regime fell because Washington did not provide it with as much aid as was received by Hanoi from China and the Soviet Union. According to the Senate Foreign Relations Committee, basing its sources on the "U.S. intelligence community," the combined Chinese-Soviet military aid to North Vietnam was $300 million in 1973 and $400 million in 1974. American military aid to South Vietnam amounted to $2.2 billion for fiscal year 1973, $937 million for fiscal year 1974 and $700 million for fiscal year 1975. And this does not include the vast stores transferred to Saigon around the time of the Paris signing.

During the last days of the Thieu regime, President Gerald Ford proved as myopic as his predecessors in the White House. In an attempt to gain congressional approval for more aid to Saigon, he declared on April 3, 1975: "At the moment I do not anticipate the fall of Vietnam. . . . There's an opportunity to salvage the situation by giving the South Vietnamese an opportunity to fight for their freedom." By the end of the same month Ambassador Graham Martin was fleeing Saigon with the American flag tucked under his arm, and the Provisional Revolutionary Government of the South was announcing, "Saigon is liberated."

The cost for the United States of being forced to accept in 1975 what it had rejected in 1954 was the longest war in American history, 56,717 American deaths, over 300,000 wounded and an expenditure of well over $100 billion. For South Vietnam the cost was over 180,000 killed, and for North Vietnam and the National Liberation Front in the South it was over 925,000 killed. The material destruction and the ecological deterioration throughout Indochina from the years of bombing and chemical warfare are immeasurable and unspeakable.

The basic purpose of United States policy in Vietnam was to demonstrate that social revolution in the Third World is not feasible because it can and will be crushed by American military power. The historic significance of Vietnam is that this American objective was defeated, thereby proving that a numerically small people, living in a comparatively small country, if fully mobilized and adequately led, are capable of winning and defending their independence. This basic point was made at the time of Saigon's fall in an editorial of Japan's influential *Asahi Shimbun*: "The war in Vietnam has been in every way a war of national emancipation. The age in which any great power can suppress indefinitely the rise of nationalism has come to an end." [165]

The second lesson that Vietnam offers to the Third World is that ideological ties have little bearing on Great Power decision-making. The "lofty international duties" to which Hanoi plaintively referred are honored only if they conform with national interests. If they do not, then they are ignored and policies antithetical to the "duties" are unhesitatingly followed. This was amply demonstrated by the policies of China and the Soviet Union during the struggle for Indochina's independence. It was also demonstrated after independence, contributing substantially to the ensuing wars among the Communist states (Vietnam, Cambodia and China), although the historic rivalries among these states also were important factors.

With the American withdrawal from Indochina in 1973, Peking feared Soviet intrusion into the resulting power vacuum, and therefore urged Washington to maintain forces in the region, and also cultivated the conservative ASEAN (Association of South East Asian Nations). This was in accord with the three-stage evolution of China's view of the Soviet Union, culminating in the "three worlds theory." China under Mao had first regarded the Soviet Union as a revisionist superpower along with the United States, then as a more dangerous superpower than the United States and finally as the proper target of a global alliance of the three worlds, including the United States and China, as well as the developed countries of the Second World and the underdeveloped countries of the Third World.

This three-stage evolution of China's anti-Soviet policy triggered a corresponding three-stage evolution of Vietnam's anti-Chinese policy. Hanoi originally regarded the United States as the primary threat to its security and interests. Then Hanoi put the United States and China on an equal footing as enemies of Vietnam, regarding both as "international imperialists and reactionaries." Finally Hanoi concluded that the main threat was from China, and that rapprochement with the United States was justified to counter that main threat.

The deterioration of relations between China and Vietnam was induced partly by China's urging the United States to remain in Southeast Asia. Hanoi viewed this as an encirclement threat, and as an attempt by Peking to force Vietnam into China's orbit. This suspicion was strengthened by the economic and military aid that China was giving to Cambodia, and also by Washington's trade embargo against Vietnam and opposition to Vietnam's entry into the United Nations.

The failure to normalize relations between Washington and Hanoi was due to miscalculations on both sides. First Hanoi rejected two American offers in 1977 for normalization, demanding U.S. aid for reconstruction as part of the agreement. With Brzezinski's trip to Peking in May 1978, Washington shifted to normalization of relations with China before a SALT II agreement. Meanwhile Hanoi's relations with China and Cambodia had deteriorated to the point where Hanoi indirectly informed Washington in July 1978 that it was ready to drop its precondition for normalization. But Washington by this time had decided on an agreement with China, to be followed by an agreement with Vietnam "within four to six weeks." The Vietnamese leaders then decided that Chinese hostility and American unpredictability necessitated invasion of Cambodia and a treaty with the Soviet Union as deterrents against Chinese attack. Hence the November 1978 Soviet-Vietnamese Treaty of Friendship and Cooperation, and in the following month the Vietnamese invasion of Cambodia and the installation in Phnom Penh of a puppet regime.

The Vietnamese invasion of Cambodia and the later Chinese invasion of Vietnam were aggressive actions whose roots go back to centuries-old historic rivalries as well as to current Great Power manipulations. Long before the appearance of the Soviet Union, and even of Karl Marx, successive Chinese dynasties had tried to subjugate Vietnam, and likewise the Vietnamese had encroached on Cambodian lands. When the Indochinese Communist Party was organized in 1930, the Vietnamese were the dominant element, and they assumed an "Indochinese Federation" of Vietnam, Laos and Cambodia after the expulsion of the French colonialists. During World War II, three separate parties were organized in order to give the Cambodian and Laotian resistance fighters more credibility as authentic anti-French nationalists. But at the same time the Vietnamese explicitly foresaw "long-term cooperation after the resistance . . . in order to help one another on the road to people's democracy."

This vision of Indochinese unity was marred by the ultranationalistic Pol Pot faction (Khmer Rouge), which won control of Cambodia by overthrowing the American-supported Lon Nol regime. The Khmer Rouge were highly suspicious of the Vietnamese, charging them with betraying Cambodian interests in negotiating with Kissinger a cease-fire that left the United States free to continue bombing Cambodia. The Khmer Rouge also had plans for their postwar society that were quite different from those of the Vietnamese. The latter favored a practical balancing of self-reliance with diversified economic and diplomatic relations with foreign powers to obtain maximum assistance for reconstruction. The Khmer Rouge, by contrast, emphasized self-reliance to a much greater degree, setting out to create a tough, disciplined and self-sufficient society that would be able to resist anticipated pressures from neighboring Vietnam, as well as from the Great Powers.

The forced pace of agricultural construction on a vast scale, together with the rejection of foreign aid, bore heavily on Cambodia's peasantry and to an appalling degree on the urban dwellers and intellectuals. At the same time the Pol Pot regime, backed by China, was uncompromising on frontier issues with Vietnam, and in April 1977 launched major attacks on Vietnamese border regions. This was the background of Vietnam's invasion, thinly disguised as a spontaneous insurrection by the Cambodian people against Pol Pot.

Peking responded by openly threatening to "teach a lesson" to the Vietnamese. In addition to the Vietnam-Soviet Treaty and Vietnam's occupation of Cambodia, Peking was reacting to the wholesale expulsion of ethnic Chinese from Vietnam. Those who fled from southern Vietnam included many Chinese merchants who did not fit into the new socialist society and resisted official pressures to work in the rural resettlement zones. Indeed, they were equally dissatisfied when they reached the Chinese state farms in Yunnan Province. "These people," declared the Chinese director of refugee resettlement, "want to do private business, but obviously this cannot be done in China. They do not like farm work, so they just stay home and live off what we give them." [166]

Peking's invasion preparations were sufficiently conspicuous so that the CIA, according to Representative Les Aspin, made a "prescient forecast" of the Chinese attack well before it occurred.[167] The warning apparently did not stir Washington sufficiently to pressure Teng against military action when he visited the United States in January 1979. In the ensuing four-week war, China acknowledged twenty thousand casualties, and claimed to have inflicted fifty thousand on Vietnam. American correspondents in the field described the human cost of "teaching a lesson." They reported bridges blown up, roads mined and destroyed, hospitals demolished, concrete electric power poles dynamited, villages lying in ruins and mass graves being uncovered. The Vietnamese government decided to leave many of these ruins untouched, to serve as a reminder of Chinese aggression. But at the same time foreign correspondents were reporting wholesale looting by the Vietnamese in Cambodia. "Convincing proof of plunder can be found in the antique shops of the Ho Chi Minh City and Hanoi. The theft and export of Cambodian art treasures must be widespread, judging from what can be found in Vietnamese shops." [168]

Meanwhile, Peking and Hanoi were conducting futile peace negotiations, and Peking was threatening to "teach a second lesson." Peking also continued to support the scattered Khmer Rouge remnants with the aim of making Cambodia Vietnam's Vietnam. Indeed, Teng has said candidly that his policy is "to force the Vietnamese to stay in Cambodia because they will suffer more and more."

Vietnam's continuing ordeal is attributed by its leaders to a combination of objective and subjective factors. The objective are the weather—a devastating series of typhoons, floods and droughts—and foreign complications leading to the invasion of Cambodia and the war with China. The subjective factors are acknowledged in the Communist Party newspaper, *Nan Dan*, as including economic mismanagement and corruption of Party and state officials, who "have become degenerate and deviant, taking advantage of their positions to misappropriate state property, take bribes, oppress the masses and enter into collusion with dishonest people to carry out illegal business." [169] Whatever the combination of factors, the plight of Vietnam's people was described as follows in August 1979 by the country's most renowned physician, Dr. Ton That Tung:

> The Vietnamese people do not have enough to eat. You see it on people's faces. They are pale, anemic and skinny. A whole generation will bear the stigmata all their lives. I see the effects on my people who work here [in the hospital]. After two operations my surgeons are tired. . . . Infants and younger children are particularly affected by the chronic food shortage. . . . The average birth weight has dropped below earlier norms, and nursing mothers are producing insufficient milk. [170]

B.
Mozambique

When President Samora Machel delivered his address on the occasion of the birth of the Republic of Mozambique on June 25, 1975, he declared forthrightly:

> The colonial State, an instrument of domination and exploitation by a foreign bourgeoisie and imperialism, has already been partially destroyed by the struggle. It must be replaced by a people's State, forged through an alliance of workers and peasants . . . a state which wipes out exploitation and releases the creative initiative of the masses and the productive forces. . . . We need to be aware that the apparatus we are now inheriting is, in its nature, composition and structure, a profoundly retrograde and reactionary structure which has to be completely revolutionized in order to put it at the service of the masses. [171]

It is not accidental that revolutionary regimes have not emerged in the former British and French colonies that were granted independence through peaceful constitutional procedures. Such peaceful transition tends to preserve colonial institutions, as occurred in India, Malaya and Ceylon, as well as in Kenya, Nigeria and the Ivory Coast. Revolutionary regimes took root in former colonies where independence was won through armed struggle, in the course of which the colonial structures and comprador elements were displaced by new institutions and mass organizations. In Asia, this happened in China during the course of prolonged warfare against the Kuomintang and the Japanese, and in Indochina during the armed resistance against the French and the Americans. Likewise in Africa, revolutionary regimes emerged in the two areas that experienced the most violence. One is the Horn of Africa, where the ossified Ethiopian Empire engendered revolutionary outbreaks within Ethiopia and also secessionist struggles in Eritrea and Somalia. The second revolutionary center is in the ex-Portuguese colonies, where the lack of a reform option forced the nationalists to a revolutionary course.

Focussing on the Portuguese colonies, the overthrow of the Portuguese republic in 1926 and the establishment of Salazar's Estado Novo in 1932 effectively foreclosed any possibility of peaceful colonial evolution. "We will not sell;" declared Salazar, "we will not cede; we will not surrender; we will not quit one fragment of our sovereignty. . . . Our constitutional laws forbid it, and even if they did not, our national conscience would do so." [172] In 1950 Lisbon declared its colonies to be "overseas provinces," and therefore refused to report to the UN Trusteeship Council. The Portuguese representative at the UN stated: ". . . my country does not practice any type whatever of colonialism. . . . We are a multiracial nation . . . our land and our people are dispersed over several continents . . . but we comprise only one unit . . . one country with the same strong national feeling." [173]

The fatal weakness of this rationalizing was precisely the absence of "strong national feeling," at least of the Portuguese variety, on the part of the native populations in Angola, Mozambique and Guinea-Bissau. Theoretically all colonial subjects could acquire full Portuguese citizenship through "assimilation." This involved speaking fluent Portuguese, finishing military service, earning sufficient income to support a family, adopting the European way of life and giving up tribal rights. So few natives were able to meet these requirements that in the 1950 census 0.74 percent of the native population was listed as *assimilados* in Angola, 0.44 percent in Mozambique and 0.29 in Guinea-Bissau. Virtually all Africans were denied citizenship rights and were excluded from any political participation.

This left the Africans defenseless against exploitation, which was more open and brutal in the Portuguese colonies than in any others. Portugal's Constitution provided that each territory "should serve the Portuguese national economy and [be] integrated into the world economy." [174] The role of the African peasants therefore was to grow cash crops—coffee, cotton, sisal, copra—and consume Portuguese manufactured goods, many based on raw materials from the colonies. Machel relates that his own political education began "Not from the writing in the book. Not from reading Marx and Engels. But from seeing my father forced to grow cotton for the Portuguese and going with him to the market where he was forced to sell it at a low price—much lower than the white Portuguese growers." [175] Most onerous was the forced labor that comprised the basis of the economies of the Portuguese colonies to a much greater degree than in other colonies. No less than six different types of forced labor were inflicted on the Africans:

1. Correctional labor. This was a legal penalty imposed for infringement of the criminal or labor codes, or for failure to pay the head tax.

2. Obligatory labor. This was exacted by the government for public works when voluntary labor was insufficient.

3. Contract labor. Any African who could not prove that he had been employed for at least six months of the previous year was liable to compulsory labor for state or private employers. Wages varied according to area and employer, but never rose above token levels.

4. Voluntary labor. Voluntary workers contracted directly with their employers instead of being recruited through officials. The threat of contract labor forced workers into voluntary labor under virtually identical conditions, except for the advantage that voluntary labor was done in the region where the worker lived.

5. Forced cultivation. Africans were given seeds by companies holding monopoly concessions, assigned acreage quotas by the government and forced to cultivate the assigned crop on their land and to sell it to the companies at prices well below market levels. The land forcibly converted to cash crops was subtracted from the subsistence economy, resulting in frequent famines in fertile regions.

6. Migrant labor. The 1909 Mozambique-Transvaal Convention renewed in 1928, 1934, 1936 and 1940, provided for a maximum of 100,000 Mozambique Africans to be supplied each year for work in the Transvaal gold mines. The Portuguese government received 18s for each recruit, along with other compensations. So desperate were conditions in Mozambique that the Africans willingly signed up for mine work, and many crossed over illegally to the Rand, as Mexicans do to the United States.

In January 1947 Henrique Galvão, one of the senior officials in the colonial administration, reported to the Portuguese National Assembly on conditions in the African empire:

Entire regions are being depopulated, and only old people, sick people, women and children are now to be found there. . . . It is clandestine emigration which, ever more rapidly, drains away the peoples of Guinea, Mozambique and Angola. . . . The most accurate description of this impoverishment is given us by the catastrophic fall in the birthrate, the incredible level of infant mortality, the growing number of sick and infirm, as well as the mortality figures due to various causes, the most important being the conditions of work and the recruitment of labourers. . . .

The idea that the native is simply a beast of burden still prevails; the indifference for the physical and moral health of their labourers is evident. . . . In some respects the situation is more grave than that created by pure slavery. Under slavery the bought man, acquired as a head of cattle, was regarded as an asset by his master. He was interested in keeping him healthy and strong and agile in the same way as he would look after his horse or his bull. Today, the native is not bought—he is simply rented from the Government, though he may have the status of a free man. His master could hardly care less if he falls ill or dies as long as he goes on working while he lives. . . . When he becomes unable to work or when he dies the master can always ask to be supplied with another labourer. . . . Only the dead are really exempt from forced labour.[176]

These inhuman conditions confronted the miniscule group of assimilados with a stark choice. They could accept permanently their privileged status, which meant denying their ethnicity and closing their eyes to the plight of their fellow countrymen. Or they could resort to the only other alternative left to them by the Portuguese—armed revolution. The African students in Lisbon who pondered this alternative opted for revolution. But the problem was—how to make revolution? European Marxism, with its dependence on the urban proletariat, was obviously irrelevant for the most backward colonies of Africa, where proletarians were virtually nonexistent. The Lisbon students decided they had no choice but to return home and "re-Africanize" themselves. Revolutionary strategy could be evolved only by trial-and-error experimentation based on careful analysis of the prevailing objective conditions. In contrast to the Latin American revolutionaries, who depended on the military foco as the hearth of insurrection, the African leaders spent years living with the peasants, learning as well as teaching.[177] The same emphasis on close rapport with the masses is evident in the following oft-quoted passage from the great Guinea-Bissau revolutionary, Amilcar Cabral:

. . . keep always in mind that the people are not fighting for ideas, for the things in anyone's head. They are fighting . . . for material benefits, to live better and in peace, to see their lives go forward, to guarantee the future of their children. National liberation, war on colonialism, building of peace and progress—independence—all that will remain meaningless for the people unless it brings a real improvement in conditions of life.[178]

In line with this approach, the revolutions that broke out in Angola (1961), Guinea-Bissau (1963) and Mozambique (1964) were all preceded by two to three years of preparation. The insurgents received little help from the Organization of African Unity, which lacked both funds and military competence. Algeria and Egypt provided a little equipment and training, but the significant aid came from the Communist world. The Sino-Soviet feud worked in favor of the revolutionary movements as the two Communist powers vied for revolutionary leadership in Africa. Mozambique's Frelimo benefited mostly from Chinese help, Angola's MPLA from Russian and Cuban, and Guinea-Bissau's PAIGC from Russian, Cuban and North Vietnamese. The Western powers, and especially the United States, provided Portugal the financial and military aid that enabled that poverty-stricken country to fight three protracted colonial wars. One reason for Washington's generosity was the strategic Azores air base, which was an essential refueling station for U.S. Air Force operations in the Middle East. Thus Frelimo's leader, Eduardo Mondlane, reached the following conclusion in 1969, which since then has been borne out by the exposés of ex-CIA agents Victor Marchetti and John Stockwell:

Western diplomacy pays lip service to multi-racialism and democracy, while governments quietly continue to act against both. Britain reaffirms her alliance with Portugal; she stops selling arms to South Africa, but makes no attempt to reduce other types of trade. . . . France steps in to replace Britain as arms supplier to South Africa and sends oil to Rhodesia, while De Gaulle proclaims himself the champion of the Third World. The United States sends arms to Portugal; West Germany helps her to manufacture her own arms; the United States, France and West Germany all have bases on Portuguese territory; all these countries have large enterprises which are investing vigorously in South Africa, in Portugal, in Mozambique and Angola. Clearly whatever diplomats may say, the weight of the Western alliance is being thrown behind white dictatorship, against the liberation movements.[179]

The odds against the revolutionaries were discouraging. In Guinea-

Bissau it was about 6,000 guerrillas against 40,000 Portuguese troops; in Mozambique 10,000 against 70,000; and in Angola 5,000 (3,000 in MPLA plus 2,000 in UNITA and FNLA) against 50,000. The revolutionary leaders expected the fighting to continue through the 1970s, when suddenly it ended with the revolution of April 25, 1974, in Portugal. The Portuguese revolution is of extraordinary historical significance as it represents a case of colonies molding events in the mother country!

The three simultaneous colonial wars had forced the Lisbon dictatorship to devote 40 percent of its budget to military expenditures and to draft one of every four men of military age into the armed services. The protracted campaigning not only strained the meager resources of Portugal but also won some of the officers over to the revolutionary ideology of the guerrillas they were fighting. Long conversations with their prisoners led them to realize, as they put it, that "those who benefited from the war were the same financial groups that exploited the people in the metropolis and, comfortably installed in Lisbon or Oporto or abroad, by means of a venal government obliged the Portuguese people to fight in Africa in defense of their immense profits." Thus the colonial experience led to a reappraisal of what was going on at home. "What we saw was that Portugal was itself part of the Third World. Lisbon and Oporto were an illusion, the country within was underdeveloped with an illiterate and exploited peasantry." [180] Thus revolution in the colonies led directly to revolution in the mother country. Whatever the outcome of the Portuguese revolution, it is as significant as it is novel that Admiral Antonio Rosa Coutinho should lecture a group of businessmen that "the Armed Forces Movement considers itself a liberation movement like those in Africa, and seeks not only formal independence but total liberation of the people." [181]

The revolutionary policies and institutions of the newly independent former Portuguese colonies followed naturally from the revolutionary policies and institutions evolved during the struggle for liberation. The struggle was based on the mobilization and activization of the peasantry. "The people are to the guerrillas like water is to fish," declared a Frelimo military command bulletin. ". . . without the support of the people, the guerrillas cannot survive." [182] To earn the support of the peasants, the guerrillas held weekly meetings with them in the liberated territories. For the first time the peasants had an opportunity to make their voices heard, and soon they were actively participating in the discussions. They elected their own community leaders, in whom they had confidence, to replace the chiefs who had collaborated with the Portuguese and appropriated the community wealth. The new leaders, both men and women, organized collective production, presided over public meetings and helped organize people's militias. The latter blurred the distinction between the Frelimo guerrillas and the peasants, thereby creating the "sea" for the "fish" to swim in.

This mass awakening and activization not only made possible the winning of the liberation struggle but also provided the basis for the postliberation state building. Focusing on Mozambique, the mass mobilization was continued during the independence period, when the guiding principle was *poder popular* or people's power. "The basic principle," concluded Basil Davidson after five weeks of travel and discussion in Mozambique, May–June 1979, "is that every community should organise itself to analyse its own problems and possibilities, find appropriate solutions and policies, and act to bring these solutions and policies into force. . . . The point is that 'they' are not doing things for 'us'; 'they' are only helping 'us' to do things for ourselves." [183]

One of the means for implementing poder popular was the use of *grupos dinamizadorea* or dynamizing groups. These groups, which were elected by popular assemblies in villages, city neighborhoods and factories, had three basic functions: to "raise the political consciousness of the working masses," to increase production through collective work and to mobilize people to cope with the social problems of their communities. Professor Allen Isaacman of the University of Minnesota has described how these dynamizing groups operate:

At *reuniões* [weekly meetings] I attended throughout the country, the participants examined such diverse questions as the divisive effects of tribalism, the need to forge an alliance between workers and peasants, the problems of national reconstruction, the necessity for vigilance, and the value of collective actions. In addition, members of the dynamizing group explained important government directives and newly-initiated national programs.

Beyond these national issues serious consideration was given to problems of political mobilization within the community or work place. Participants often engaged in rather blunt criticism and self-criticism. Individuals were chided for refusing to participate in co-operative activities, not doing their share of work, alcoholism, profiteering, and exploiting their wives—all of which undercut efforts to transform the society. After hearing the charges the accused had the opportunity to respond and to indicate what actions he would take to remedy the situation.

Throughout these meetings I was particularly impressed by the large voluntary turnouts and the active participation of the members in the debates. Time and again individuals, silent for so many years, refused to give up the floor until they had made their point and underscored it repeatedly. While such presentations necessarily extended the meetings (which to a foreigner often seemed tedious and non-defined), they provided a unique opportunity for direct participation and instilled a new level of public awareness. Reflecting on this somewhat cumbersome process of grassroots political education, Marcelino dos Santos noted that "it created a new sense of confidence in the oppressed masses and it helped convince them that they had the capacity to transform Mozambique." He concluded our discussion by reminding me that "This is the very essence of people's power." [184]

In addition to the dynamizing groups, the other principal organization for social change in Mozambique is Frelimo, which reorganized itself in February 1977 into a "Marxist-Leninist Party." The reason for the transformation is that Frelimo's original liberation goal was attained with the winning of independence, and the new task of creating a socialist society required a nationwide "vanguard party" to provide leadership. The mode of recruiting for the new Frelimo Party is revealing. Many more new members are needed for the formidable task of social restructuring, so candidates are invited to fill forms requesting membership. The qualifications of the candidates are then discussed by their colleagues —whether in a village, a factory, a cooperative, an office or a military unit. These fellow workers know the strengths and weakness of the candidate, which they debate publicly and exhaustively. The same procedure is followed in elections for local, provincial and general assemblies; candidates again have to undergo the scrutiny of voters in public meetings. But the difference between general elections and party recruiting is that in the first the voters select the candidates they prefer, whereas in the second it is the provincial party committees that decide which candidates will be accepted as Party members, though their decisions are based primarily on the opinions expressed at the public meetings.

The most urgent task facing the state and the Party after liberation was the economic development of a wretchedly underdeveloped country. Independent Mozambique was born with a retarded industrial structure. Its agriculture was geared for exports and incapable of meeting domestic needs. The overall economy was dependent internally on a white-settler technical and managerial class, and externally on white-settler Rhodesia and South Africa. Furthermore, this precarious economy was devastated by several setbacks at the time of liberation, including the massive exodus of the Europeans, the serious droughts in the North and floods in the South, the government's principled but costly closing of the border with Rhodesia, the damage inflicted by numerous Rhodesian attacks in the border areas and the expense of feeding some 40,000 refugees from Rhodesia.

Frelimo first set out to restructure the countryside by organizing communal villages. This was opposed by the chiefs and the relatively prosperous African farmers. The dynamizing groups launched an educational campaign to explain the benefits of cooperative agriculture, as had already been demonstrated during the war years in the liberated zones. As of March 1978 the government reported approximately 1,500 communal villages with an estimated population of 1.5 million out of a total population of 9.8 million. Despite many individual variations, all communal villages are based on three principles: collective participation in all decision-making processes, collective labor and proportional distribution of profits, and basic social services such as schools and health facilities. More specifically, all adult members of a communal village help to build roads, dig wells, clear fields and construct all the homes, as well as the school and infirmary. After these basic tasks are completed, the members divide into agricultural brigades of twenty to thirty men and women, each with a specified task. The brigades hold regular meetings to discuss ways of increasing production, and to hold criticism and self-criticism sessions. The usual work week is $5\frac{1}{2}$ days, leaving Saturday afternoons and Sundays for relaxation, festivities and for cultivating the small individual plots to which each family is entitled.

In addition to the communal villages, the government has used 2,000 abandoned estates to establish a network of state farms. Here also the workers are divided into brigades and hold frequent meetings to increase their productivity. Each brigade selects a representative to sit on a council that oversees the general farm operations. The council, as the representative of the employees, meets with a state-appointed production commission to set production goals for the next year, and to establish salary rates which, unlike those in the communal villages, vary from one job category to another. Whether in communal villages or state farms, Mozambican peasants appear to be moved, according to a French journalist, by "a spirit of self-reliance and initiative; instead of waiting for their problems to be solved by some distant central authority, they are aware of their own capabilities and take it upon themselves to improve their daily life slowly but surely, with the means at their disposal." [185]

Reorganizing the industrial sector has proven to be more difficult because of the wholesale destruction of machinery by the departing Portuguese, the illegal transfers of hard currency and the exodus of skilled labor. There is also a problem with the African workers, who frequently react to the ending of colonialism by refusing to work with whites or obey factory supervisors, and who demand huge wage increases and sometimes wage short strikes. The government responded with reforms by which the workers of each factory elect a production council to supervise daily operations. The chief concerns of the council have been to improve worker skills, assure a steady flow of raw materials, upgrade working conditions, set objective criteria for promotions and establish social services such as literacy classes, nurseries, comfortable rest areas and medical facilities. The government expected that by 1980 industrial output would reach the level of the end of the colonial period.

Finally, Frelimo has emphasized from the beginning the importance of improving the quality of life of all Mozambicans. During the first year it established universal free education, nationalized health care, relocated thousands of families from shantytowns to previously segregated modern city dwellings and organized a network of people's shops to provide basic commodities at fair prices. Special emphasis is placed on schools, which are viewed, in President Machel's words, as "the forger of new men, the forger of scientific ideas, the forger of a new society . . . the students must be workers who are prepared to serve the people." [186] The curriculum no longer extols the exploits of Henry the Navigator and the civilizing mission of the Catholic Church. Students learn about their national identity, their cultural heritage and the long struggle of the Mozambican people against colonialism. They also learn, however, about the reactionary elements in traditional society, including the role of African merchants in the slave trade, the collaboration of African chiefs with the colonial authorities and the exploitation of women through polygamy and bride price. Both teachers and students are required to work part of each school week in the fields. At the university level, all students, faculty and staff spend the month of July in the rural areas building latrines, planting crops, disseminating health information and helping the literacy campaign. The *jornais do povo* or people's press has been designed specially for the newly literate population. Consisting of large billboards, messages in simple Portuguese reinforced with numerous pictures describe the latest news events and explain government programs.

The significance of the revolutionary regimes of Africa is twofold. First, they have demonstrated how to wage and win a war for liberation, and second, they are pioneering in the evolution of new socialist institutions and practices to replace the colonial. The outcome of the ongoing social experimentation is by no means certain. A study of postliberation developments in Guinea-Bissau depicts their "socialist orientation" but concludes that "there is no guarantee that it will survive." [187] Likewise Raimundo Voloi, president of a successful Mozambican production cooperative, replied to an American's query about future prospects with the observation: "Walking from colonialism to the future is a long, long walk." [188]

It is indeed a long walk, and one that is beset with formidable obstacles. Externally there is the ongoing struggle with the white-settler bastion of South Africa, and also pressures from the Western powers as well as from the feuding Russians and Chinese. Internally there is serious dissension over basic policies, so that actual armed strife has erupted over the issue of reverse racism. Also there is inherent resistance against radical social change, taking such forms as elitism, tribalism, sexism and bureaucratism. The magnitude of these was emphasized by Machel at an all-minister conference in February 1980:

> We have not broken with the colonial methods of work. We live in our offices, inundated with piles of paper, do not know our own secretaries, do not visit hospitals, schools, farms, etc., do not listen to popular opinion, knowing reality only through memorandums and dispatches. We lose direction and focus only on small, daily, routine problems. . . . We don't punish saboteurs, we coexist with them and even pay their salaries. Courtesy, serving the public with delicacy, with good presentation are not integrated into the behavior of the workers of the state apparatus. . . .[189]

Despite these handicaps and uncertainties, significant progress is being reported. Michael Kaufman of the New York *Times,* during a three-thousand-mile tour of Mozambique, found "a sense of discipline without actually turning the country into an armed camp. . . . a widespread confidence that rests on national mobilization and self-sacrifice, and that is exceptional in the experiences of independent black Africa." Kaufman quoted President Machel as stating that "the thing history will remember us for is not defeating colonialism but learning how to use the armed struggle as a mechanism for changing the mentality of the people." Likewise a young Mozambican told Kaufman: "It is 60 years that we have been waiting for the new man to be born in Moscow. It is a long pregnancy and perhaps a miscarriage, but maybe in Cuba, in Vietnam or here, he will still come." [190]

There is no assurance that Mozambique's pregnancy will prove more fruitful than Moscow's, but if it does, the repercussions will be profound for the rest of black Africa, and indeed for white Africa as well. Finally, it should be noted that other African regions are in various stages of pregnancy (Angola, Guinea-Bissau and the Horn countries) and that others will follow later. Most important, each country will go its own way, as indicated in the following significant report by New York *Times* columnist Anthony Lewis following a conversation with the Zimbabwe Prime Minister, Robert Mugabe: "Having lived in Mozambique these last years, he does not like the ideological rigidity and economic troubles he has seen here, and does not want to make the same mistakes. His repeated talk of 'realities' and what was 'feasible' matched what some Westerners who know him will say of Robert Mugabe." [191]

C.
Cuba

Fidel Castro's significance does not derive from the success of his guerrilla movement. Insurrections have been endemic in Latin American history, and some, such as those led by Zapata and Villa, controlled extensive territories for several years. Castro's guerrilla campaign was insignificant in scope and duration compared to many others in Latin America. But Castro has two unique and immensely significant achievements to his credit. First, he was able not only to seize power in 1959, but also to remain in power and to organize a regime that now is considered entrenched and irreversible. Second, Castro effected a basic social revolution that also is irreversible, and that has profound implications for all Latin America, and even for the entire Third World, especially Africa.

One reason for Castro's success was that his eventual espousal of communism was quite unexpected, and therefore he was not opposed as resolutely by domestic and foreign vested interests as he otherwise would have been. Before his revolution, Castro definitely was not a Marxist of any variety. One of his earliest associates, Haydée Santamaria, testified that "all of the groups [about Castro] limited themselves to Martí. . . . We wouldn't be telling the truth if we said that they were studying Marxism." [192] Likewise Fidel's brother Raúl told New York *Times* correspondent Herbert Matthews: "Fidel never wanted to join any party because he didn't want to be restricted or be under any orders or discipline. He never could stand for any kind of formalism. This is a trait of his that he has never abandoned." [193] It was a trait that contributed decisively to Castro's initial victory, for it disarmed potential opponents within Cuba and without. Certainly it is infinitely more difficult now for other Latin American revolutionaries to emulate Castro's seizure of power by force of arms. In reaction to his sweeping social revolution and his alliance with the Soviet Union, the United States has mobilized much more effective antirevolutionary forces throughout Latin America than had existed before 1959.

Another reason for Castro's success was the exceptionally favorable situation in Cuba for a revolutionary movement. The 1902 Platt Amendment (see Chapter 18, Section III) had made Cuba "a United States protectorate." [194] Between 1906 and 1927 American private investments in Cuba increased in sugar from $30 million to $60 million, in railroads and shipping from $25 million to $120 million, and in utilities from $17.5 million to $115 million. Leland Jenks, writing in 1928, concluded: "American capital . . . has been making of Cuba a sugar estate run by chartered accountants and bond salesmen. It has raised seriously the question whether a country can long endure on the basis of one-crop latifundia managed by absentee proprietors. . . .[195]

The Platt Amendment facilitated American political as well as economic control. "The United States government regularly interfered in the internal affairs of the [Cuban] republic,"[196] usually in support of conservative elements that were favorably disposed to American interests. Leland Jenks' perceptive conclusion is relevant not only for the Cuba of his time but also for the entire Third World today:

> Cuba is in much the same position economically as a great part of the lower South [of the United States] producing a single crop, under contracts involving a permanent debtor-creditor relationship at prices beyond the control of the struggling planter. . . . The efforts of Cuba to reconcile nationality with the persistent penetration and domination of alien enterprise and capital, throw into high relief the major problem in the present phase of world history. They focus attention upon the latent conflict of the institutions of business with those of politics, which may be as momentous in its consequences as the conflict between the papacy and the state at the outset of modern times.[197]

The Platt Amendment was repealed in 1934, but this merely meant that American representatives obtained the desired political decisions through bribery rather than through force. Sugar remained the king, which meant endemic underemployment for the island's inhabitants. The sugar harvest took only four to five months, so that the rest of the year was known as the *tiempo muerto*, or dead time, when over 20 percent of the workers were unemployed. Even during harvesttime unemployment rates did not fall below 10 percent. Cities could not absorb the surplus labor, as their industries were confined to processing local raw materials and servicing tourists. Imports of capital goods actually increased from 52.6 percent in 1949 to 60.9 percent in 1958. Thus an English economist, Dudley Seers, concluded about the time of Castro's revolution: "Cuba in the 35 years from 1923 to 1958 showed little progress. The stagnation was more serious and lasted longer than in any other Latin American economy—excepting perhaps the economies of one or two very small and poor nations such as Bolivia and Haiti. . . . The existing state of affairs—in which people were short of food and work but land lay idle and factories not built—could not continue."[198]

The structure of Cuban society was as fragile in 1958 as its economic underpinnings. There was no independent middle class or national bourgeoisie. American corporate interests prevailed to such a degree that no protective tariffs shielded Cuban industries until 1927. Labor unions were controlled by the government and were responsive to politicians rather than to their members. The intelligentsia was a bitter and disaffected minority, with little opportunity to influence state policy. The Catholic Church was virtually nonexistent in rural areas, with only 725 priests ministering to a population of 6 million, or 1 priest for every 8,276 people. The quality as well as the numbers of the priesthood was low, with many of the members being ecclesiastical offenders from mainland churches. Thus the Church in Cuba lacked the power to mobilize public support in behalf of its own interests or of the existing social order. Finally, the main political parties were discredited organizations, interested primarily in the spoils of office. Fulgencio Batista's regime particularly lacked legitimacy, being born of a military coup and based on fraudulent elections, constitutional abuses and naked repression.

Such was the situation in Cuba when a young lawyer, Fidel Castro—bold, astute and charismatic—made his bid for power in the *caudillo* tradition going back to the days of Antonio Maceo and José Martí. After an abortive attack in July 1953 on the Moncada Barracks in Santiago de Cuba, Castro was amnestied and took refuge in Mexico. In December 1956 he tried again, landing in Oriente Province and reaching the mountains where he began his guerrilla campaign. The odds were his band of twelve men, each with a rifle and ten cartridges, against Batista's army of thirty thousand equipped with machine guns, cannons, tanks and planes. The seemingly hopeless disparity was neutralized in Cuba in basically the same way that it had been in China and Southeast Asia. The guerrillas paid for everything they took. When they got materials to construct a field hospital in the Sierra Maestra, they provided medical care for the *campesinos* as well as for their wounded. Within two years they had set up thirty rebel army schools for campesino adults and children. Most important was agrarian reform, which actually got under way in the Sierra during the fighting, and was proclaimed for the whole country on October 10, 1958, before the definitive Agrarian Reform Law of May 17, 1959. The impact of these measures was greatly magnified when Radio Rebelde began broadcasting on February 24, 1958, "from the Territory of Free Cuba in the Sierra Maestra."

In this manner the original handful of middle-class revolutionaries were first provided with food by the campesinos, and then strengthened with peasant recruits. The newcomers were given a quick course in guerrilla warfare, and then they put their learning to practice with raids on Batista arms depots. On May 5, 1958, Batista launched an offensive with twelve thousand men to crush the rebels once and for all. Within three months the offensive had fizzled out, with 10 percent of the original force having deserted or been captured, killed or wounded. The rebels now descended from the mountains to the plains, where they were aided by underground saboteurs. With city after city falling to the guerrillas, Batista boarded a plane that took him to exile on New Year's Eve 1958.

The agrarian reform assured Castro of peasant support, but it soured his relations with Washington. Also, some middle-class members of his government began to drop away when they realized that Castro was a social revolutionary as well as a caudillo. His critics have argued that Fidel promised one kind of revolution and made another, and have used this postulate to justify the Bay of Pigs invasion. But Castro was quite consistent in wanting social revolution to make Cuba independent of the United States. He did not know beforehand how the social revolution was to be attained, and therefore had to resort to trial-and-error experimentation. His ideas changed as he tried various policies with varied results. His ideas and policies are changing to the present day, the only constant being his goal of national independence and social justice. "Had he compromised on his social revolution," concludes Matthews, "had he come to terms with the United States; had he maintained the corporate-capitalistic-congressional prerevolutionary Cuban system—then indeed, he would have 'betrayed the revolution.' " [199]

An outstanding example of Castro's experimentation was his all-out drive to harvest 10 million tons of sugar in 1976. In a famous speech Castro admitted its disastrous failure. He conceded that output had fallen short by 1.5 million tons, that the concentration on sugar had reduced the supplies of rice, milk, fertilizers, shoes, clothes and bread, and also had disrupted foreign trade and transportation. In short, it was a catastrophic economic defeat. Many were demoralized, worker absenteeism rose and the government had to take steps to penalize those who did not show up for work. The Castro regime recognized the need for new policies, recognizing that moral incentives and mobilization were not enough and that the speed and scope of social change had to be adapted to objective conditions. Cuba's leaders now paid more attention to the experience of the Soviet Union and other socialist countries. They depended less on voluntary labor; they combined material incentives with moral; and they eased the rate of savings to allow more spending on consumer goods. They also accepted Comecon membership, which provided price stability for Cuban exports and assured supplies of oil, machinery and consumer goods at subsidized prices. Integration into Comecon, however, also meant continued dependence on the Soviet bloc and, in some cases, goods of quality inferior to those of the capitalist countries.

More specifically, Cuban economic strategy has deliberately starved Havana in order to redress the traditional imbalance between the capital and the provinces. Havana looks seedy and run-down, with few consumer goods in the shops, dilapidated cars on the streets and buildings in need of repairs and paint. Conversely, however, Havana is the only Latin American capital that is not surrounded by a ring of slums and misery. The schools, hospitals, roads, dams, experimental farms and factories that are sprouting in the rural areas have effectively forestalled the influx of poverty-stricken peasants who are overrunning virtually all other Third World capitals.

Another distinctive feature of Cuba's economy since 1970 has been its rapid diversification. Labor is being released from the sugar industry by mechanization; the output of noncane agricultural products (cereals, tubers, vegetables and fruits) is increasing rapidly; the fishing industry has ships operating in the Atlantic from Newfoundland to South Africa, and in the Pacific off Peru; while new dairy farms are making Cubans for the first time an ice-cream-eating and a milk-drinking people. The construction industry has boomed with the islandwide building of roads, schools, housing, dams, reservoirs and irrigation and drainage systems. Unemployment is virtually nonexistent, with all men employed, and about 35 percent of the women—a percentage that is increasing yearly with the expansion of child-care facilities and services. Consumer goods have become much more plentiful during the decade following 1970, although citizens still complain of high prices, low-quality goods and red tape.

Cuba's most serious economic weakness is the continued dependence on sugar for most of the export earning—a precarious basis for a national economy in view of the wild fluctuations in the world price of sugar. Yet solid progress is being made, and recent economic ties with Europe and Japan, along with support from the Soviet bloc, enable Cuba to resist the U.S. embargo indefinitely, although it does retard the rate of economic growth. Cuba still finds it necessary to export many commodities that are in short supply at home. "We have to create an export mentality," explained Castro in December 1978. "If we have a new cement factory, we have to export more cement. If we have a new textile factory, we don't consume more textiles, we export them." [200]

Cuba's economic achievements are basic but not paramount or exclusive. "No greater mistake can be made about the Cuban Revolution," concludes Herbert Matthews, "than to judge it in economic or material terms. Fidel Castro . . . is giving them a great deal they never had, such as honesty in government, excellent educational, medical and social services for every citizen, and almost full employment." [201] The results of the "excellent" social services are apparent to the most casual traveler in Cuba. Children everywhere are obviously well nourished. They wear shoes that protect them from hookworm and other infections. They attend school rather than loiter on streets and beg for pennies. A government literacy drive raised the adult literacy rate by late 1961 to 96.1 percent—the highest in Latin America and among the highest in the world.

Outstanding are the ESBECs or High Schools in the Countryside (Escuelas Secundarias Básicas en el Campo). These are new rural boarding schools, one hundred of which existed in 1974, and another one hundred of which were built each year until 1980, when they were able to enroll almost all the secondary students in the country.

These ESBECs are expensive. In addition to the initial outlay for the school buildings, the students receive free transportation to and from their homes. One estimate puts the yearly cost to the government at $750 per student per year—a substantial sum for an underdeveloped country. That is one reason why physical work is combined with study from elementary school through university. Castro has stated that unless students work hard to defray the cost of their education, the alternative must be the prerevolutionary system of education for a small elite.

Farmlands are set aside for cultivation by students at all levels. Half the students and teachers work on the ESBEC land in the morning, while the other half attend classes. In the afternoons they exchange positions. By the 1980s, it is expected, the productive work of the students and teachers will make the ESBECs self-supporting. This work-study program also has an ideological objective—to raise a generation with strong communal feelings and free of the traditional Latin aversion to and disdain for manual labor.

The aim is manifest at Havana University, where in 1972 nearly sixteen thousand students combined work with study, while another fourteen thousand workers registered for courses and continued with their regular jobs. The ultimate goal is to transform the university into a vast complex of schools, factories, hospitals and mines, where the distinction between workers and students will gradually disappear. "A university," Castro insists, "cannot form a man better than a factory can." [202]

In health care as in education the aim is to combine mental and physical work and to minimize the traditional inequalities between rural and urban areas. Medical students work in fields and factories along with other students, and when they begin practice they must serve for three years in rural health centers. After the revolution, half of Cuba's six thousand doctors emigrated. A crash government program more than made up for this loss, so that nine thousand doctors are now in practice, with another thousand being added each year. Ten percent of these doctors serve in more than a dozen developing countries, including Jamaica, Guyana, Algeria, Congo, Vietnam, Guinea, Tanzania, Angola, Somalia, Mozambique and South Yemen.

The emphasis of Cuban medicine is on prevention through regular checkups, mass immunization, hygiene education, dietary information and maternal care. These services, along with hospitalization when necessary, are provided free of charge through a comprehensive network that includes provincial health and hospital centers, and polyclinics at the local level. The results are most impressive—polio was wiped out in 1963, malaria in 1968 and diphtheria in 1967, and infant mortality had dropped by 1974 to 27.4 per 1,000 live births, as against 4-to-10 times higher rates in other Latin American countries.

Dr. Daniel Joli, the World Health Organization's representative in Cuba, concluded in 1980: "There is no question that Cuba has the best health statistics in Latin America. Cuba is poor but its health organization is that of a very much developed country." [203] At the same time that infant mortality rates have been declining, so has the island's birth rate. The number of live births per 1,000 population has fallen from 26.1 in 1957 to 15.3 in 1978. Again this is in marked contrast to the rest of Latin America, which has a higher birth rate than either Asia or Africa. According to gynecologist Dr. Celestino Alvarez Lejonchere, responsible for infant protection and women's equality, the birth rate has dropped because of the rising educational level and the increasing number of women who work full-time.

As notable as the changes in education and health care are those relating to the status of women. The labor force in 1953 consisted of 17.2 percent women, but by 1975 this had increased to 28 percent. Women comprise 46 percent of the student body in medical schools, half the enrollment in natural sciences, 42 percent in economics and the usual large majority in elementary and secondary school teaching. The novel family code adopted in 1975 stipulates sex equality not only in the workplace and the courts, as might be expected in a revolutionary society, but also within the family. "Both parties must care for the family they have created and each must cooperate with the other in education, upbringing and guidance of the children. . . . Both parties have the right to practice their profession or skill and it is their duty to help each other . . . to study or improve their knowledge." (Articles 26, 28.)

The powerful Federation of Cuban Women sees to it that these provisions do not become mere rhetoric. With a membership of 2 million, and headed by the redoubtable Vilma Espín, wife of Raúl Castro and mother of four children, the federation is one of the most influential of the mass organizations. Its campaigns, since its organization in 1960, have included a struggle against female illiteracy, training domestic workers for productive jobs, establishing a nationwide network of nursery schools, providing abortion operations on demand and eradicating prostitution. Despite these efforts, Cuba's Latin tradition of male superiority is still very much alive. Women are conspicuously distant from the levers of real political power. Addressing the second congress of the Federation of Cuban Women (Nov. 29, 1974), Castro conceded that "there are still objective and subjective factors that discriminate against women. . . . many habits remain from the times when women were property within society. . . . Women and men have to become seriously and profoundly aware of the problem. They have to wage the battle together." Little progress has been made toward winning this "battle," judging from a report presented to the Second Congress of the Cuban Communist Party (1980): "We cannot feel satisfied with the results that have been achieved in the promotion of women to high-ranking levels of government." [204] This admission was decidedly an understatement, given the fact that at the time of the Second Congress, Vilma Espín was the only woman among the 100 members of the Central Committee of the Communist Party.

The realm of sex relations is not the only one in which there is a considerable gap between official rhetoric and social reality. Dominguez notes that despite recurring drives against bureaucratism, a government elite is enjoying privileges reminiscent of Djilas' "new class":

> Privileges accrue to bureaucrats, technicians, foreign advisers, and the formerly rich. Their income can be spent in luxurious restaurants, to which they are admitted without having to wait in frequently long lines. Restaurants for bureaucrats serve better and unrationed food. The privileged, even in the 1960's, were given preference in the purchase of cars. Vacation resorts are more accessible to them; their housing is better, and they seem to be less affected by the housing shortage. They can go abroad, serve on diplomatic missions, be invited to diplomatic receptions. . . . In 1970 Castro bitterly denounced those party members benefiting from "privilege, and even from corruption" and demanded their expulsion.[205]

Dominguez, however, also provides a table on crime rates (see p. 749), which suggests a degree of social health that is becoming rare in developed countries as well as underdeveloped.

In the field of politics the guideline is mass activization and participation. Castro has defined this in terms reminiscent of Mao's mass line. "Without the masses socialism loses the battle; it becomes bureaucratic. . . . We don't believe in a group of super-intelligent people directing the passive masses. That isn't a revolution. . . . In a collectivist society, battles are won only with the broadest participation of the masses in the solution of their problems." [206] The medium for achieving the desired mass participation is an array of mass organiza-

Crime Rates, 1959–68 (per 100,000 population)

Year	All Crimes	All Crimes Against Property	Homicide and Murder
1959	2,905	543.1	38.2
1960	2,855	482.7	36.7
1961	2,440	461.6	37.2
1962	2,304	489.4	35.0
1963	2,415	232.6	13.7
1964	2,033	133.2	8.0
1965	1,529	272.2	8.4
1966	1,638	317.0	7.6
1967	1,270	335.2	6.8
1968	1,179	341.4	6.1

Source: J. I. Dominguez, *Cuba: Order and Revolution* (Cambridge, Mass.: Harvard University Press, 1978), p. 507.

tions such as the Committees for the Defense of the Revolution, Central Organization of Trade Unions, Federation of Cuban Women, National Association of Small Farmers, Federation of Secondary Education Students and Union of Pioneers of Cuba.

The Committees for the Defense of the Revolution, for example, were organized in 1960 when the revolution was seriously threatened by counterrevolutionaries at home and by militant exiles abroad. Their principal function was to combat subversion, and there is still a certain amount of such activity. But with the revolution now well consolidated, the CDRs have assumed numerous other functions, serving as a kind of ombudsman or intermediary between the people and the bureaucracy. The CDRs organize the parents of children, act as truant officers, arrange for vaccination programs, collect and recycle waste materials and prepare contingency plans for natural disasters such as hurricanes. Membership in the CDRs increased from 1,119,835 in 1962 to 4,800,000 in 1976, or over 80 percent of the total adult population.

The Cuban army also is in effect a mass social organization, consisting of what have been defined as "civic soldiers." [207] To blunt criticism that the armed forces are an excessive burden, the Cuban military has undertaken social and economic tasks to a greater degree than their counterparts in any other country, including China. Indeed, the army more than the Party provided the basis for mass mobilization after Castro took over. In 1970 the army cut 29 percent of the sugar-cane harvest, and in the process they built roads, railroad tracks and temporary housing. The Cuban military also has purchased planes suitable for aerial crop spraying, and has transferred 250 pilots to that agricultural task. When troops went to Angola, their order from Castro was that they "must be workers and soldiers at the same time." Elsewhere Cuban "civic soldiers" have built roads and airports in Guinea, hospitals in Peru and schools in Tanzania, at the same time that they served as military trainers and advisers.

The most recent political trend has been the growing popular participation in both the workplace and administration, under the slogan of poder popular or people's power. The administration of many economic enterprises has been transferred to municipal assemblies whose members must be nominated in open neighborhood assemblies, run against at least one other candidate and elected by a majority of the votes cast in direct, secret elections. In office, the delegates must hold weekly office hours in the districts they represent, justify their conduct before bimonthly local "accountability assemblies" and be subject to recall. An American observer has found poder popular to be a reality in practice:

> . . . an evening spent observing a local delegate's office hours confirmed what I had been told in conversation: that Cubans view this local representation as their democratic right and insist that *their* delegate solve *their* problems. If anything, one delegate confessed, the difficulty was that his constituents expect too much of *poder popular*. He could not solve their job, housing or marital problems, he explained, although he could often direct them to the appropriate agency and perhaps telephone ahead to ease their path. At first glance, local democracy seems to be taking root in Cuba.[208]

Less clear is the degree of democratic reality in the provincial assemblies and the National Assembly which are elected by the municipal assemblies rather than by direct vote. The provincial assemblies are entrusted with the administration of the economic plan, while the National Assembly, on paper at least, has authority to pass legislation, supervise the work of state ministries and agencies, and pass on ministerial appointments, economic plans and government budgets. The new Constitution, ratified by a national plebiscite in 1976, resembles those of other socialist countries with its impressive list of guaranteed political, economic and social rights. Cuban spokesmen assert that their distinctive heritage and revolutionary experience in mass participation will make their guaranteed constitutional rights more meaningful than they have proven elsewhere. Time will test the validity of their assumption that Soviet structural forms and local conditions and aspirations will culminate in a unique Cuban synthesis.

The significance of revolutionary Cuba is that President Kennedy launched the Alliance for Progress in August 1961 in order to stimulate economic development and mass well-being in Latin America, and thereby to provide an alternative to Castroism. But Cuba today is the only Latin American country where these populist aspirations of the Alliance for Progress have been realized. Cuba's success, paradoxically, has reversed the continental drift envisioned by the Kennedy strategy. Instead of a reformed and prosperous Latin America turning its back on Cuba, it is Cuba that is providing an increasingly alluring alternative to the contradictions and tensions of Latin American neocolonialism. This ironic dénouement of the Alliance for Progress was noted by Senator Edward Kennedy in an April 1970 speech in which he evaluated a decade of his brother's initiative:

> And so today it is a personal tragedy that I can repeat nearly the same somber facts about Latin America that President Kennedy cited in 1960 and that Robert Kennedy cited in 1966. The Alliance for Progress has been a human failure. More than 30 percent of the population still die before their 40th birthday. Poverty, malnutrition and disease continue to deny strength and incentive to the majority of the people. . . .
>
> The Alliance has been an economic failure. Even our hopes for economic development are far from realization. The rate of economic growth per capita has averaged 1.8 percent for the decade, lower than it was . . . in the years when there was no Alliance. . . .
>
> The Alliance has been a social failure. Land remains in the hands of a minute percentage of the population. In some countries less than 10 percent of the people own 90 percent of the land. One-third of the rural labor force is unemployed. . . . And we know that the cities have not yet demonstrated the capacity to absorb their present labor force.
>
> The Alliance has been a political failure. It was intended to write a new page of political history in Latin America, to end the depressing chapter of family dictatorships and military coups. Instead, 13 constitutional governments have been overthrown in nine years. . . .
>
> And the spirit of the Alliance has failed here at home. Despite our strong traditions of democracy, the U.S. continues to support regimes in Latin America that deny basic human rights. . . .[209]

Senator Kennedy's appraisal is not unique. Following a visit to Cuba in July 1974, Pat Holt, staff director of the U.S. Senate Foreign Relations Committee, reported that under Castro the island had become "a Socialist showcase in the Western Hemisphere." Likewise an American historian, Kalman H. Silvert, has stressed the positive historical implications of revolutionary Cuba:

> An aspect of the Cuban experience that has been little understood in the United States is that socially and politically the little island is the Iberian cultural world's first almost-modern state . . . the Cuban government seems to have been the first to evoke as well as impose forcefully a kind of natural coherence throughout its society. Latin American interest in Cuba thus goes far beyond an understandable pride in "one of our boys making it" in standing up to the United States and surviving. . . . It is taken for granted in Latin America . . . that Cuba has broken out of traditional Latin American molds into the early stages of modern nationhood.[210]

The impact of modern revolutionary Cuba extends far beyond Latin America, as manifested in the presence of numerous Cuban doctors, teachers, technicians, military advisers and soldiers throughout the Third World, and especially in Africa. Conversely, two thousand Mozambican and Angolan children, and one thousand Ethiopian children are studying and working in the huge boarding school on the Isle of Pines, along with twenty thousand Cuban children. In explaining this Cuban activism abroad, C. L. Sulzberger of the New York *Times* concluded that "Castro, a latecomer to communism, today puts ideological considerations above immediate state interests, and that this has been the motivation behind a long series of Cuban military interventions around the earth: not only Angola but Algeria, Syria, Congo, Guinea, Guinea-Bissau, Somalia, South Yemen and even Oman, to say nothing, in the 1960s, of Zaïre, the Dominican Republic, Venezuela, Panama and Bolivia." [211]

Sulzberger's analysis is borne out by a report prepared by the State Department's bureau of intelligence and research (April 13, 1976) and published by columnist Jack Anderson in the Washington *Post* (Oct. 12, 1979). The report concluded that while Castro has aligned himself with many Soviet policies he "remains something of a maverick who still conceives of himself as a leader of the Third World." Looking at over twelve years of Cuban involvement in Africa, the report finds that "the extent to which the Soviet Union can direct and/or restrict Cuban activities in Africa is a moot question. Soviet policy probably determines the outer boundaries of Cuban options, in the sense that Cuba would not undertake an initiative directly opposed by the Soviet Union, and any large-scale Cuban military operations require Soviet logistical and financial support. . . ." The report pictures Castro as a sort of gun-toting missionary. "In opposing Western 'economic imperialism,' the remaining vestiges of European colonialism, and white minority regimes of South Africa and Rhodesia, Castro brings to his mission an almost messianic zeal," the report states, adding that "Castro seems less concerned with the strict Marxist orthodoxy of a movement he helps than with its potential or actual ability to oppose the forces of 'capitalist imperialism.' "

The repeated alarm expressed by Washington over the number of Cuban troops in Africa is considered inconsistent in many African, and for that matter, American circles. Professor Gerald Bender notes that there are over two thousand French nationals working in French-speaking Africa as advisers and technicians, as well as over ten thousand French soldiers and sixteen hundred French officers actively serving in African armies. If the National Security Council estimated the number of French in Africa on the basis of the same categories that it applies to Cubans, then, according to Bender, "the French presence would turn out to be considerably larger than Cuba's." Many Africans also observe, states Bender, that Cuba has no economic stake in Africa, in contrast to French corporations, which control over 50 percent of the modern economic sectors of Senegal, Gabon, Cameroon and the Ivory Coast. "Thus, criticizing the Cubans while condoning and even assisting the French," concludes Bender, "may not only strain American credibility in Africa but leave our fledgling African policy vulnerable to the charge that the Carter administration is primarily interested in assisting French neocolonialism." [212]

Bender's conjecture is supported by the statement made before the OAU Assembly in Khartoum (July 1978) by the head of the largest sub-Saharan African state, General Olusegun Obasanjo of Nigeria:

> We are aware, Mr. Chairman, of the West's concern at what they consider to be Soviet and Cuban intervention in Africa. Our own assessment is that, considering the peculiarities of our social systems, no African country is about to embrace communism wholesale any more than we are willing to embrace capitalism. To the extent that any African country can be considered by the West to have "gone communist," it was a direct result of the failure of Western policies.
>
> The fact of the matter is that Africa was colonised by Western powers and not the Soviets. In the struggle for independence and freedom, the only source of effective support was the Eastern Bloc countries. The Soviets were therefore invited into Africa for a purpose and that purpose was to liberate the countries to which they were invited, from centuries of cruelty, degradation, oppression and exploitation. Unless we wish an undesirable situation to remain in Africa—and recent maneuvers in Europe and America strengthen our suspicion in this respect—we should not be over concerned by the presence of those we invited to fight for specific causes and no more.

The Cubans are, of course, much of a new comer to Africa. Their presence has the same background as the Soviets. In every case where Cuba's intervention was established, they intervened as a consequence of failure of Western policies and on behalf of legitimate African interests. We have no right to condemn the Cubans nor the countries which felt they needed Cuban assistance to consolidate their sovereignty or territorial integrity.

In conclusion, how does the above analysis square with the mass exodus from Cuba to the United States in the summer of 1980? Does it not substantiate the view of the Castro regime as a "totalitarian dictatorship" repressing a "captive people" ever ready to take the first available "freedom flight"? The exodus, in fact, is quite revealing of both the strengths and weaknesses of the Cuban Revolution. A survey by the U.S. Immigration and Naturalization Service (INS) of the first 15,000 emigrés who arrived in April and May disclosed that only 15 percent were black or mulattos, though they comprise 30 to 40 percent of Cuba's total population. Also, only 15 to 20 percent of the emigrés were from the countryside, as against the 35 percent of Cuba's population that is rural. These figures support the contention that it is the nonwhite and rural segments of Cuban society that have made the greatest gains. Also revealing was the contrast between the Cuban and Haitian boat people who landed simultaneously on the Florida coast. The Haitians were generally uneducated, undernourished and unemployed. They left their homeland because their basic needs were not being met. The Cubans were educated, healthy and employed. They left their homes because of monotonous diet, inadequate housing and limited supplies of clothing and other consumer goods. For them, the revolution had failed to satisfy their aspirations for an American middle-class living standard.

The 1980 Cuban exodus was sparked more by the lure of consumerism than by the failure of communism. American life-style has been promoted by the Voice of America on Havana's radios, projected on Cuban television screens by Miami's Spanish-language channels and extolled throughout Cuba by growing numbers of foreign tourists, especially Cuban Americans. During 1979 over 100,000 of these emigrants had returned to their former homes, many bearing evidence of their success and affluence. The message was clear and often proved persuasive. The fact that it did so is significant, for it reveals that after two decades of revolution, personal comforts and advancement remained for many more important than collective welfare and goals.

This was a bitter pill for Castro, and he reacted with a twofold policy: more stress on material incentives, and correction of bureaucratic abuses and high living. Raúl Castro bitterly attacked Cuban officials for "using and abusing the prerogatives that go with their post and the resources of their enterprise to solve problems of their own and of their friends." [213] Likewise Fidel acknowledged that "we have problems of labor discipline." He attributed this to basing "all production efforts on moral incentives while ignoring the material ones. It seemed as if enthusiasm could solve everything, but it's not enough." [214] Accordingly a new salary policy, effective July 1, 1980, substantially increased minimum earnings for Cuban workers and provided direct monetary bonuses for individuals and facilities that exceeded their quotas. The conclusion of Peter Winn of Yale University seems a reasonable summary of the current state and prospect of the Cuban revolution:

> The current situation is more than a mere embarrassment, but it is something less than a crisis of Cuban socialism. At a time of economic difficulty, the departure of a large number of alienated Cubans who will produce as little as possible, consume as much as they can and spread their discontent far and wide may be less traumatic internally than internationally.
>
> Most important, the current crisis presents Cuba's leaders with the chance to correct their course and remedy the deficiencies it has revealed. In the past, the strength of Fidel Castro and *compañeros* has not rested in their ability to avoid errors—they have made more than their share—but rather in their capacity to learn from their mistakes and reshape the revolution in the light of these lessons of experience. That capacity is as relevant in 1980 as it was in 1970, when the disastrous campaign for a ten-million-ton sugar harvest presented them with a far more serious crisis of Cuban socialism than they face today. If they can confront the current crisis with the same critical and innovative spirit, then the loss of even several hundred thousand Cubans may be more than compensated by the gains of the strengthened revolution that the emigrés leave behind.[215]

IV. White Settler Regimes

The third type of states that emerged after World War II, in addition to the nationalist and social revolutionary, were the white settler regimes. The most outstanding of these are South Africa and Israel.

In Africa, several white settler regimes originally were scattered throughout the continent: Algeria, Kenya, Angola, Rhodesia, South-West Africa and South Africa. Most of these settler states were overwhelmed by what Harold Macmillan defined as "the wind of change blowing through Africa." In Algeria the nationalists prevailed after years of savage warfare during which the French Republic itself almost succumbed. In Kenya the British were too few in numbers to maintain a viable settler state, so the

London government, after crushing the Mau Mau revolt, accepted a Kenyatta government under which British interests have thrived. Angola's Portuguese colonists increased rapidly after World War II, reaching a total of four hundred thousand. But the authoritarian Lisbon government refused self-rule to its own emigrants as well as to the African majority, so that when revolution swept Lisbon, the Angola settlers were too unprepared and untrained to strike out on their own. Thus the only settler regimes that survived were in southern Africa, comprising the powerful white bastion of South Africa, and the dependent satellites in Rhodesia (Zimbabwe) and South-West Africa (Namibia).

Israel is not commonly thought of as a settler state, but the fact is that the Israelis themselves view their mission to be one of settlement—of returning to Zion. We have seen (see Chapter 21, Section V) that the Zionists from the beginning consciously assumed the role of colonizers, making effective use of European imperialist power and ideology. At the end of the nineteenth century, Theodor Herzl offered a "wall of defense for Europe in Asia" if Britain allowed "substantial colonization of our people at the strategic point where Egyptian and Indo-Persian interests converge." Half a century later Moshe Dayan, then chief of staff of Israel's defense forces, explicitly acknowledged the success and the implications of the "substantial colonization" that had been effected in the interim. In the course of a funeral oration he delivered in 1953 for a young Israeli pioneer killed by Arab marauders, Dayan declared:

> Let us not today fling accusations at the murderers. Who are we that we should argue against their hatred? For eight years now they sit in their refugee camps in Gaza, and before their very eyes, we turn into our homestead the land and the villages in which they and their forefathers have lived. We are a generation of settlers, and without the steel helmet and the cannon we cannot plant a tree and build a home. Let us not shrink back when we see the hatred fermenting and filling the lives of hundreds of thousands of Arabs, who sit all around us. Let us not avert our gaze, so that our hand shall not slip. This is the fate of our generation, the choice of our life—to be prepared and armed, strong and tough—or otherwise, the sword will slip from our fist, and our life will be snuffed out.[216]

South Africa and Israel are by no means identical settler societies, as will be noted later. Yet they do have certain characteristics in common, which explain why they alone have survived and flourished to the present day. Both these settler societies have a sufficiently large ruling ethnic population to provide a solid foundation, the Jews comprising a substantial majority in Israel (85 percent), and the Europeans a sizable minority in South Africa (18 percent). Both the Jews and the Afrikaners base their claims on biblical injunction, the Jews regarding their acquisition of Palestine as the reclaiming of their Promised Land, and the Afrikaners considering it their divine mission to civilize the inferior blacks. South Africa has developed by far the most advanced economy of the African continent, and Israel has done likewise in the Middle East. Both countries have built up military establishments commensurate with their economic strength and therefore dominate their respective regions militarily as well as economically. Finally, both South Africa and Israel have received crucial economic and diplomatic support from the Western powers, which has enabled them to overcome crises in their development and to attain their present hegemony.

The basic reasons for Western support of Israel and South Africa are geopolitical and economic. In the case of Israel the stakes are obvious: the strategic importance of the Middle East at the junction of three continents, and the economic paramountcy of the Middle Eastern oilfields. The overthrow of the Shah of Iran in 1979 doubtless increased the significance and value of Israel in the calculations of Western policymakers. Likewise South Africa is a country of major economic and geopolitical importance for the Western powers. It possesses extraordinarily rich natural resources that are crucial for the West, it has attracted Western investors to the tune of some $25 billion and it serves as a strong subimperialist power protecting the interests of Western capital throughout sub-Saharan Africa.

Despite their intrinsic strength and their powerful external support, South Africa and Israel (*in its expanded post-1967 dominance*) remain settler states in an era that relegates them to the status of anachronisms. This central point has been made recently by General Yehoshafat Harkabi, former chief of Israeli intelligence and now a specialist in Middle Eastern studies at Hebrew University. General Harkabi, who once was a hard-liner regarding the Palestinians, wrote to Prime Minister Begin in 1978, resigning as an intelligence adviser. When Begin failed to reply, Harkabi sent a long letter of explanation to *Ma'ariv*, leading organ of the Israeli establishment. His letter included the following passage, which explains why both Israel and South Africa, despite their overwhelming military power, remain beleaguered fortresses and the focal points of chronic internal tensions and recurring international crises:

> I do not believe that it is possible to prevent the establishment, sooner or later, of Arab rule in Judea and Samaria. Every period is characterized by a number of hegemonic ideas or norms. The central norm of our period is self-determination for recognized communities. The attempt to obstruct the self-determination of such a community is an anachronism that cannot last for long.[217]

A.
South Africa

When South African Pieter Botha was elected to his office in 1978 (see Chapter 21, Section VII), he was widely known as a "carpetchewer." His ruthlessness as Defense Minister in earlier administrations had won him the nickname of Piet "Wapen"—the Afrikaans word for weapon. But instead of the expected hard-nosed conservatism, Botha has pushed various reforms through Parliament and has opened discussion on further changes. The government now permits some blacks to stay with security in urban areas, to join legal trade unions and to take skilled jobs in mines and industries. On the social front, blacks are permitted to participate in some sports with whites and to mix with whites in some theaters, restaurants, hotels and parks. To top it off, Botha and his ministers made the unprecedented gesture of touring the Bantustans and visiting the black city of Soweto.

Botha now is considered to be one of the *verligte* or enlightened Afrikaners. This has caused a split in his National Party, with a small but vocal group of right-wingers breaking off to form the Hertzige (Purist) National Party. Also, the labor unions are unalterably opposed to black competition for the highly paid skilled jobs. Despite the furore, David Willers of the South African Institute of International Affairs has noted that the recent changes amount to "merely rearranging the deck chairs on the *Titanic*. There's an amelioration of social and work place apartheid, but they don't address themselves to the fundamental issues of political power." [218]

This analysis is fully justified. Botha is pragmatic rather than enlightened. He realistically distinguishes between petty apartheid or discrimination, and grand apartheid or dispossession, and is discarding the former in order to preserve the latter. In preserving grand apartheid, Botha is pursuing the long-term strategy of "separate development" through Bantustans. This ensures that the whites, comprising 18 percent of the total population, will alone have citizenship rights and ownership in perpetuity of 87 percent of the land, including the best agricultural areas and virtually all industries. The rationale of grand apartheid is that South Africa is a multinational rather than a multiracial society. Each African language group is regarded as having an ethnic identity, and therefore entitled to its own homeland or Bantustan. If this hocus-pocus be accepted, then it follows that there is no black majority in South Africa. Rather there is a congeries of "nations"—the 5-million-member Zulu nation, the 4.8-million-member Xhosa nation, the 4.3-million-member white nation and so forth.

The apostles of apartheid originally planned to force the members of each of these nations into their respective homelands. But industrialization and the resulting need for black labor made the cities predominantly black as early as 1940, and the black majority has steadily increased ever since. Indeed, 60 percent of all Africans live in "white" South Africa rather than in their Bantustans. This inconvenient disparity between theory and reality is resolved by allowing Africans to commute between their Bantustans and "white" South Africa as visiting workers. The volume of commuting on buses increased from 34 million trips in 1973 to 110 million trips in 1976.

According to plans, the number of Bantustans will increase within five years from the present three to the final ten. When that process is completed, there will be no more black South Africans—only citizens of the various Bantustan countries, where they will enjoy full citizenship rights, including "one man, one vote." This privilege, of course, will be confined to *within* the Bantustans. In 1968 the then Prime Minister, John Vorster, told Parliament: "The fact of the matter is this: We need them, because they work for us . . . but the fact that they work for us can never . . . entitle them to claim political rights. Not now, nor in the future. . . . Under no circumstances can we grant them those political rights in our territory, neither now or ever." [219] Botha was just as adamant in November 1979 when he bitterly scolded a group of coloreds (mixed-race persons) after failing to win their support. "One man, one vote is out in this country. That is, never." [220]

Under this arrangement the Africans are entitled to 13 percent of the most unproductive land of South Africa, even though they comprise 75 percent of the total population. In effect, this amounts to a system of labor reservations camouflaged as Bantustans. To make this gross exploitation viable, every effort is being made to create a black bourgeoisie based on the Bantustan bureaucracies under the leadership of tribal chiefs. Such a bourgeoisie is now emerging, but it is minute and discredited. The inescapable fact remains that the black masses lack sufficient land to grow their own food, and lack sufficient jobs in the neighboring "white" regions. Thirty percent of the total black working force is unemployed. Per-capita GNP in the Bantustans is lower than in all but ten African states, and infant mortality in "independent" Transkei is 287 per thousand (12 per thousand for white South Africans), which is higher than in most Third World countries. These statistics demolish South Africa's long-standing claim that its Africans are economically better off than those in the rest of the continent.

Botha made innovations in South African foreign as well as domestic policy. Just as the foundation of his domestic policy is grand apartheid, so the foundation of his foreign policy is "internal settlement," which originally was to be imposed on Zimbabwe and Namibia. In the case of Zimbabwe, it took the form of the March 1978 Salisbury Agreement negotiated by Ian Smith with selected black leaders led by Bishop Abel Muzorewa. The terms created the illusion of majority rule: a constitution that left the whites (4 percent of the population) in control of the police, the military, the courts and the civil service; staged elections that were flawed by any Western standards but that suggested self-determination; the dismantling of petty segregation; and finally, an appeal to the Western powers for lifting the trade embargo. The Carter administration correctly appraised the Muzorewa government as a façade for continuing control by Rhodesia's white minority. Washington's opposition persuaded Prime Minister Margaret Thatcher to hold the 1979 Lancaster House Conference, where an agreement was reached with the Patriotic Front leaders for a new constitution and for elections in March 1980 to lead to independence.

In a victory that stunned Western observers and white Rhodesians alike, Robert Mugabe's Zimbabwe African National Union (ZANU) won fifty-seven seats in the hundred-member Parliament, and the other main guerrilla leader, Joshua Nkomo, won an additional twenty seats. Of the remaining twenty-three seats, three went to the heavily subsidized Muzorewa, and the other twenty had been reserved by the Lancaster House Agreement for the whites. These returns were especially jarring for Botha, who had declared shortly before the election that South Africa aspired to be the "foster mother" of a "constellation of states," including Zimbabwe and Namibia. Now South Africa's outlawed African National Congress (ANC) announced, "The victory in Zimbabwe marks the beginning of the end for South Africa."

The ANC was not merely indulging in empty rhetoric. The Zimbabwe election galvanized it into a militancy very different from its conservative past. Founded in 1912, the ANC for forty years had waged a restrained petitioning and lobbying campaign for black rights. Then it passed rapidly through successive phases of nonviolent civil disobedience and sabotage against nonhuman targets, until it decided in the 1960s that only all-out armed struggle would free the black majority of South Africa. Early guerrilla efforts had failed miserably, but the revolutions in Angola and Mozambique together with the electoral victory in Zimbabwe gave ANC convenient bases for training recruits and staging operations. Thousands of young people fled abroad where they got arms and training, and organized the ANC guerrilla army, Umkonto we Sizwe (The Spear of the Nation).

ANC arms come mostly from the Soviet Union and Eastern Europe. There is no alternative source, since the Western powers choose to arm South Africa, as earlier they did the Portuguese colonial regimes. With these arms, ANC is seeking to establish *not* black rule but what it terms a "nonracial" South Africa. Its membership includes a few whites, and more are welcome. The tempo of armed struggle is accelerating with attacks on police stations, banks and oil refineries. After such operations the guerrillas now are able to escape into the surrounding populace, indicating a degree of organized mass support that is new and significant.

Anti-apartheid activities no longer are confined to the armed militants. A broad groundswell is emerging in various guises and levels. Eminent Church leaders, black and white, are deliberately breaking the apartheid laws and being hustled off in police vans. Large numbers of previously quiescent mixed-race students reject the apartheid schools, declaring themselves "black" in solidarity with Africans. Urban black workers also are becoming increasingly militant, with strikes by municipal workers in Johannesburg, by Cape Town meat factory workers, by construction workers in the secret oil-to-gas SASOL plants, by assorted workers in Durban and Port Elizabeth and by the employees in Ford, General Motors, Volkswagen and Goodyear plants.

Urban black militancy will continue because of rising unemployment and wage discrimination. One of every four blacks is unemployed, and according to a recent study by Aart Roukens de Lange of the University of Witwatersrand, the proportion will be four of every ten by the year 2000. At the same time, the gap between the wages paid to whites and to Africans is increasing. *Business Week* of October 24, 1977, reports: "Whites in the mines average $1,027 per month compared with $124 for blacks, a gap of $903 against 1974's gap of $722." Likewise South Africa's Department of Statistics for June 1980 shows blacks earning an average of 79 percent less than whites in mining, manufacturing, construction, electricity, transport and communications. Conditions are worse in the Bantustans where half the black population lives and works, or from where they migrate regularly as contract workers to the 87 percent of the country designated as the "white area." The hunger, overcrowding and disease are worse in these Bantustans than in rural Zimbabwe, which provided such fertile ground for the Patriotic Front guerrillas.

This combination of external and internal developments is responsible for South Africa sliding into what the liberal *Rand Daily Mail* has called "a state of revolutionary war." Judging from the past record, however, Botha can count on Western support to cope with the gathering storm. The fact is that South Africa's natural resources (gold, chrome, platinum, coal, diamonds, copper and uranium) are vital for the Western world. According to *Fortune* (Aug. 14, 1978): "From the American viewpoint, South Africa is to strategic materials what Saudi Arabia is to oil." Also, American banks held in 1978 about $2.27 billion of the total of $7.8 billion of South African foreign debts, and the rate of U.S. bank lending is rising. Furthermore, there are the $25 billion invested by Western corporations in South Africa. The reason why these investments also are increasing sharply is that in 1974, American investors received 19.1 percent in South Africa as against an average of 11 percent for all their foreign investments.

These substantial and lucrative Western interests explain the sub-rosa but *de facto* alliance between South Africa and the West. During every crisis that has beset the apartheid regime, Western governments and corporations have provided economic, military and diplomatic aid. The Sharpeville Massacre of March 1960, during which 69 demonstrators against the pass law were killed, was followed by severe political repression dictated by the then Police Minister, John Vorster. The resulting worldwide protests hurt South Africa's economy, but the continuation of apartheid was ensured by a timely $40 million loan arranged by a consortium of U.S. banks. The next major crisis was the 1976 Soweto uprising, during which officials listed 231 dead and 1,200 wounded. This reduced investments by industrial corporations, but American banks showed no such restraint. Also, the International Monetary Fund, with strong U.S. banking, loaned South Africa $464 million, which paid for Pretoria's sharply increased military spending during that period.

As important as Western financial aid has been the military aid that enabled South Africa to build a powerful modern army to use against its own blacks and against the African states to the north. When the UN voted an arms embargo in 1963 against South Africa, that country had an army of only 13,000 equipped with old British and American weapons. By 1978 South Africa had an army of 55,000 regulars and 130,000 reserves, equipped with 362 combat planes, 91 helicopters, 170 tanks and 1,600 armed cars. This buildup was achieved through various measures, one being the purchase of patents from Western firms to manufacture weapons from small arms to the Cactus-Crotale surface-to-air missile. Another arrangement is the production in South Africa of sophisticated arms under French, Italian, American and British licenses. South Africa also has been able to purchase abroad "nonmilitary" items such as computers, light aircraft and transport planes, which are then used for military purposes. South Africa's well-known nuclear capability likewise is the end result of direct and indirect technological input from Europe, Israel and the United States. A flash of light over the South Atlantic on September 22, 1979, was detected by satellite observation, and is generally believed to have marked South Africa's entry into the nuclear club.

Finally, South Africa has received Western diplomatic support, albeit camouflaged for domestic political reasons. Washington's procolonial orientation was clearly set forth in the "tar baby" report of 1969—National Security Staff Memorandum 39. This interdepartmental policy review commissioned by White House adviser Henry Kissinger questioned the "depth and permanence of black resolve" and dismissed insurgent movements as "not realistic or supportable." In early 1970 President Nixon adopted Option 2 of the NSSM 39 report, which called for the following "general posture" to be adopted:

> We would maintain public opposition to racial repression but relax political isolation and economic restrictions on the white states. We would begin by modest indications of this relaxation, broadening the scope of our relations and contacts gradually and to some degree in response to tangible—albeit small and gradual—moderation of white policies. Without openly taking a position undermining the United Kingdom and the UN on Rhodesia, we would be more flexible in our attitude toward the Smith regime. We would take present Portuguese policies as suggesting further changes in the Portuguese territories. . . .

In line with this strategy, Washington relaxed sanctions against Rhodesia, evaded the arms embargo against South Africa and supported Portugal in its colonial wars. By contrast, the liberation movements were branded as terrorist organizations and as pawns of the Soviet Union. Then came the Portuguese revolution of April 1974, which exposed the fallacious assumptions and unviability of this Nixon-Kissinger strategy. Washington's response was to try to do to Agostinho Neto and his MPLA (Popular Movement for the Liberation of Angola) what it had done years earlier to Patrice Lumumba in the Congo. An exposé of the American attempt to roll back the revolution in Angola has been published by the CIA agent in charge of the operation. John Stockwell's *In Search of Enemies* [221] reveals that the initial intervention in Angola by an outside power, and each subsequent escalation, was made by the United States and not by the Soviet Union or Cuba. Also, the Cuban troops were sent to Angola in response to an MPLA appeal after a South African attack on October 23, 1975, and the Soviet Union was informed of the Cuban decision after it was made rather than before. Kissinger decided to support the pro-Western FNLA (National Front for the Liberation of Angola) and UNITA (National Union for the Total Independence of Angola) because, as Stockwell was informed, Kissinger "saw the Angolan conflict solely in terms of global politics and was determined that the Soviets should not be permitted to make a move in any remote part of the world without being confronted militarily by the United States." [222]

Assistant Secretary of State Nathaniel Davis resigned in August 1975 because Kissinger rejected his recommendation for a multinational peaceful settlement in Angola. Support to FNLA and UNITA, Davis warned, would fail because "Neither Savimbi [of UNITA] nor Roberto [of FNLA] are good fighters. It's the wrong game and the players we've got are losers." [223] Within sixteen months a disillusioned Stockwell arrived at the same conclusion and left the CIA. In an open letter published in the Washington *Post* (Apr. 10, 1977) he presented his reasons:

> After Vietnam I received the assignment of Chief, Angola Task Force. This was despite the fact that I and many other officers in the CIA and State Department thought the intervention irresponsible and ill-conceived, both in terms of the advancement of United States interests, and the moral question of contributing substantially to the escalation of an already bloody civil war, when there was no possibility that we would make a full commitment and ensure the victory of our allies.
>
> From a chess player point of view the intervention was a blunder. In July 1975, the MPLA was clearly winning, already controlling 12 of the 15 provinces, and was thought by several responsible American officials and senators to be the best qualified to run Angola; nor was it hostile to the United States. The CIA committed $31 million to opposing the MPLA victory, but six months later the MPLA had nevertheless decisively won, and 15,000 Cuban regular army troops were entrenched in Angola with the full sympathy of much of the Third World, and the support of several influential African chiefs of state who previously had been critical of any extracontinental intervention in African affairs.
>
> At the same time the United States was solidly discredited, having been exposed for covert military intervention in African affairs, having allied itself with South Africa, and having lost.[224]

In reaction to this fiasco the Senate passed in 1976 the Clark Amendment prohibiting covert American military aid to antigovernment forces in Angola. But both Brzezinski and CIA officials lobbied in favor of renewed aid to Savimbi's UNITA. Powerful elements in and out of Congress supported such aid. The Carter administration responded by refusing to establish diplomatic relations with Angola, leaving the United States the only major Western power in that stance. During the 1980 presidential campaign, Ronald Reagan declared that he saw "nothing wrong" with "providing weapons" to those in Angola "who are fighting the Cubans." Meanwhile, South Africa was actively assisting UNITA as a means of destabilizing the Angola government and thus indirectly curbing the SWAPO guerrillas in Namibia. Thus it is possible that under the new Reagan administration the United States again will become involved in a covert war in Angola, and in a *de facto* alliance with South Africa.

The implication of such a course is evident in the following statement by President Shehu Shagari of Nigeria, which is the second most important supplier of oil for the United States: "Nigeria will not only continue to provide money and other support to guerrillas fighting for the liberation of Namibia, but will also assist freedom fighters in South Africa itself. We will contribute our quota, materially and morally. This fight we regard as our own, and not just of the oppressed people of South Africa." [225]

In October 1979 a Pacific Radio reporter asked President Nyerere of Tanzania: "How will you be viewing the [U.S.] elections of 1980?" His response is worth noting as a measure for judging future policies and events:

> The moral stature which was put forward by President Jimmy Carter made life very easy for us because here is a person you can sit down and talk to and he will understand what you are talking to him about and, if we say, "We are not fighting for communism in Southern Africa," he will understand that we are not fighting for communism. If I differ with him he will not think that I have horns. So, it can make personal relations easier.
>
> I'm not sure it makes all that much difference in policies. Policies are the policies of the power structure of the U.S. . . . If the U.S. is disappointing the Third World, the problem cannot be Carter. The problem is the system. The U.S. is capitalist. It is imperialist. It's a superpower. Hegemonic.
>
> I don't know whether one is being fair or not, but I say a good President makes life easier for us. Because you can sit down: you can discuss. But the problems of Tanzania will remain the same. The problem of the Third World will remain the same. Why? Not because of the person who is in the White House, but because of the power structure of the U.S. And this will continue, elections or no elections.[226]

B.
Israel

One of the early Zionist slogans was, "A land without people for a people without land." It was a compelling slogan, but it was wrong. Its utter disregard for indigenous populations was the quintessence of the settler mental process. But the twentieth century was not the sixteenth. The Palestinian Arabs were not American Indians or Siberian Yakuts. The Jewish immigrants to Palestine could not do what the Spaniards had done in the New World or the Russians in Siberia. Arab national consciousness had been stimulated by Western imperialist aggressions in the nineteenth century, by the traumatic experiences and broken promises of World War I and by the propaganda and victories of the Axis powers during the 1930s (see Chapter 21, Section V).

As World War II approached, the British government sought to neutralize the pro-German elements in the Arab world. In May 1939 it issued a White Paper that declared that Palestine would not become a Jewish state against the will of its inhabitants, and limited future immigration of Jews so that they would never exceed one third of the total population. The Jewish community was outraged, but when war broke out three months later, it had no choice but to support Britain against Hitlerite Germany. A total of twenty-six thousand Palestinian Jews (including four thousand women) volunteered and served on scattered fronts all over the world, including the Middle East, North Africa, Ethiopia, India, Australia, England and continental Europe. They received training in medical services, workshops, signal corps, artillery, air force, navy, parachutists, commando units and women's auxiliary corps. In playing their part in the war against the Nazis the Jews gained valuable experience and training for their own forthcoming struggle in Palestine.

World War II not only gave the Jews the opportunity to acquire military skills, but also impelled them toward militant nationalism in reaction to the horrors of the Holocaust and the refusal of Christian states to open their doors to Jewish refugees. The new aggressiveness was reflected in the Biltmore Program, adopted in New York in 1942. The demand was for a "Jewish Commonwealth," [227] which was a camouflage phrase for a Jewish state that should have its own army fighting under its own flag. Immigration was to be unrestricted and under the control of the Jewish Agency.

In view of later developments it should be noted that socialist-minded binationalists continued to favor a common front with the Arabs in order to resist the common enemy of both peoples—imperialism. But David Ben-Gurion dominated the Biltmore conference with his passionate oratory. "Either Zionism provides a radical and speedy satisfaction of the consuming need of thousands of uprooted Jews and, through mass immigration and settlement, lays the sure foundations of a free, self-governing Jewish Palestine, or it is meaningless." [228] Moshe Smilansky, a veteran immigrant of the 1890s, spoke for the small nonconforming minority when he complained, "Since the Biltmore days, freedom of thought and speech have been banned. Scribes have turned into 'shofars' [horns] trumpeting the slogans dictated from above. Anyone who dares to have an opinion of his own is considered a traitor. Writers of any independence have been forced to remain dumb." [229]

With the end of the war the Jews assumed that they would be rewarded for their loyal services, especially after the electoral victory of the "friendly" British Labor Party in July 1945. Their hopes were quickly dashed, as the Laborites sought to balance Jewish demands against Arab pressures and their own imperial interests. The Zionists responded with a two-pronged strategy that may be summarized as the "diplomacy Zionism" personified by the venerable Dr. Chaim Weizmann, and the "gun Zionism" by Menachem Begin.

"Gun Zionism," a phrase originated by an Israeli deputy, Uri Avneri, had its roots in Jabotinsky's revisionism noted earlier. Although dismissed by mainstream Jewish leadership as "the lunatic fringe of Zionism," Jabotinsky and his underground Irgun armed force enjoyed considerable following because of their dashing exploits and, more importantly, because events proved them right more often than wrong. With prophetic accuracy they insisted that the Jewish people never would achieve national independence unless they were prepared to fight for it.

After Jabotinsky's death in 1939, the Irgun was headed by Menachem Begin. He was no gunman or revolutionary poet or romantic legendary figure. Diminutive in build, far from handsome, and fastidious in dress and manner, he resembled more a small-town lawyer or teacher than a commanding revolutionary leader. Yet his courage and determination, his flair for underground activities and his grasp of strategic options made him the undisputed head of Irgun in its later phase as Jabotinsky had been in its earlier days. In his calculations, Begin simply ignored the Arabs as inconsequential. "Of course the Arabs have rights, but our rights are far more important, our needs override theirs." [230] Begin regarded the British as enemy No. 1, and was convinced that they could be driven out of Palestine by armed force. "History and our observation persuaded us that if we could succeed in destroying the government's prestige in Eretz Israel [land of Israel] the removal of its rule would follow automatically. Thenceforward we gave no peace to this weak spot. Throughout all the years of our uprising, we hit the British Government's prestige, deliberately, tirelessly, unceasingly." [231]

Begin implemented this strategy with stunning success despite the seemingly hopeless odds. The revolt began in 1944 with only six hundred Irgunists and less than one hundred weapons. Yet day after day, Begin's "Hebrew fighters," as they were termed by the British press, blew up bridges, mined roads, derailed trains, sank patrol boats, attacked barracks and installations and plundered armories and pay vans. Most spectacular was the blowing up of the King David Hotel, housing British military and civilian headquarters. More than eighty-eight people—mostly British, Arabs and Jews—perished in the rubble. British authorities responded with the usual security measures: barbed wire, barricades, sandbags, guards and curfews. The Palestine mandate was transformed into a prison, yet the revolt raged on. Finally, on February 14, 1947, the British government announced to the world that it saw no prospect of resolving this conflict and that it had decided "to refer the whole problem to the United Nations." [232]

"Gun Zionism" had prevailed in Palestine. Now it was up to "diplomacy Zionism" to seal the victory in the United Nations. Weizmann and Ben-Gurion were the leaders of the new phase of the struggle. Their main resource was the Jewish community in the United States, to which President Truman was politcally responsive. "I am sorry, gentlemen," Truman said to American ambassadors in the Arab world, "but I have to answer to hundreds of thousands who are anxious for the success of Zionism; I do not have hundreds of thousands of Arabs among my constituents." [233] The chief immediate concern of "diplomacy Zionism" was to open Palestine and only Palestine, to the rising flood of Jewish refugees. An American lawyer, Morris Ernst, who had been appointed by President Roosevelt to persuade as many countries as possible to accept refugees, was surprised by the hostile reaction of the Zionist organization. "I was amazed and even felt insulted when active Jewish leaders decried, sneered and then attacked me as if I were a traitor. At one dinner party I was openly accused of furthering this plan for freer immigration in order to undermine political Zionism." [234]

The UN became a cockpit in which member nations strove to secure acceptance of their respective solutions for the Palestine dilemma. In the end the issue was decided by the fact that the Soviet Union as well as the United States lobbied in favor of partitioning Palestine. The unexpected stance of the Soviets apparently stemmed from their underestimation of the potential strength of Arab nationalism, and their overestimation of the advantages they would derive from the existence of an independent Jewish state.

The steps leading to the fateful UN resolution for partitioning Palestine are well known. In August 1945, President Truman proposed that one hundred thousand Jews be allowed to enter the mandate. In April 1946, an Anglo-American investigating committee reported in favor of the President's proposal. The Arab League responded by warning that it was unalterably opposed to such an influx, and that it was prepared, if necessary, to use force to stop it. The United Nations then sent a fact-finding commission to Palestine, and the General Assembly, after receiving the commission's report, voted on November 29, 1947, in favor of partitioning the mandate. On May 14 of the following year the Jews invoked the partition resolution and proclaimed the establishment of a Jewish state to be called Israel. On the same day, President Truman extended recognition to the new state. The following day the

Arabs carried out their long-standing threat and sent their armies across the Israeli border.

As it turned out, the Arab attack proved a godsend for the new Jewish state. Of the ten thousand square miles of Palestine, the UN had allotted fifty-seven hundred square miles to the Jews, and the remaining forty-three hundred square miles to the Arabs. Thus the proposed Jewish state would have begun with a population comprising almost as many Arabs as Jews—a particularly dismal prospect in view of the much higher birth rate prevailing among the Arabs. The Jews never had to face up to this embarrassing predicament because the Arab invasion made possible what the Zionists termed the "cleansing" of their homeland, as well as its expansion substantially beyond the UN frontiers.

The 1948 war between Israel and the Arab League states (Egypt, Jordan, Syria, Iraq and Lebanon) appeared to be a David vs. Goliath contest. In actuality it was the Arabs who proved to be by far the weaker. The Palestinian Arabs had been crushed by the British in the 1930s, so that in 1948 they could muster only some irregular bands and local defense units, which were poorly armed and trained and which lacked logistical support. The war therefore was primarily one between the Zionist and Arab League forces. Although estimates differ, the two sides appear to have been roughly equal in numbers, but with contrasting strengths and weaknesses.

The Israelis were better trained, better led, and above all, united and highly motivated. The longer the war continued the stronger they became, with additional arms and volunteers being steadily supplied by the efficient Zionist network operating in Europe and the United States. By the end of the war, some sixty thousand Jewish soldiers were facing about forty thousand Arabs. The latter were better equipped at the outset, possessing a modest number of tanks and Spitfires. They also enjoyed the advantage of operating in areas where the native populations usually were friendly and cooperative. Yet despite these advantages the invading Arab armies proved to be as hollow and decadent as the governments they represented.

Musa Alami, a distinguished Palestinian, went on a tour of the Arab capitals to learn what kind of help his people could expect from their Arab brethren. Everywhere he was given extravagant assurances. Confidants of Ibn Saud informed Musa Alami that "once we get the green light from the British we can easily throw out the Jews. . . ." In Iraq he was told that all that was needed was "a few brooms" to drive the Jews into the sea. The secretary-general of the Arab League stated confidently: "If the Arabs do not win the war against the Jews . . . you may hang all their leaders and statesmen." Most confident was the Syrian President, who assured Musa Alami that ". . . our Army and its equipment are of the highest order and well able to deal with a few Jews, and I can tell you in confidence that we even have an atomic bomb." Seeing Musa's expression of incredulity, the President added, "Yes, it was made locally; we fortunately found a very clever fellow, a tinsmith. . . ." [235]

In addition to this empty bombast, Musa found that the leaders of the Arab states were feuding rivals rather than partners in a joint enterprise to aid the Palestinians. "Their announced aim was the salvation of Palestine," concluded Musa, "and they said that afterward its destiny should be left to its people. This was said with the tongue only. In their hearts all wished it for themselves; and most of them were hurrying to prevent their neighbors from being predominant, even though nothing remained except the offal and bones." [236] Musa's conclusions were borne out by the double-crossing among the Arab forces after the fighting began. The Egyptians, for example, fearing King Abdullah's ambition to take over Palestine, deliberately took action to undercut Trans-Jordanian effectiveness by seizing military supplies destined for Trans-Jordan. Furthermore, the commanders of the Arab armies proved to be for the most part incompetent political adventurers rather than trained military leaders. Their operations were improvised rather than planned. Their most successful actions were fortuitous, and their few gains were never properly exploited. Many of the rank-and-file also were interested more in personal gain than in the Palestinian cause. "The Arab and foreign volunteers who came to Haifa to fight for an Arab victory," wrote Elias Kussa, a Haifa Arab leader, "were a great disappointment to its residents. They behaved arrogantly, treated the local population with contempt, and indulged in acts of robbery and plunder. All complaints to the 'public committee' in Damascus that had sent these volunteers were in vain." Other Arab sources relate cases of violence, looting and raping committed by the Arab "rescuers" against the Palestinian Arabs. According to Muhammad Nimr Al-Khatib, the Jaffa Arabs feared the "Rescue Army" more than it feared the Jews, and were not unhappy when their "rescuers" were chased away by the victorious Jews.[237]

Under these circumstances the Jewish victory in the 1948 war was not a "miracle"; rather a Jewish defeat would have been a veritable miracle. When the war was over, the Zionists were in control of 77 percent of the country rather than the 57 percent allotted to them by the UN. Furthermore, 900,000 of the 1.3 million Arabs in the battle zones had fled, leaving the Jews a strong majority in their newly enlarged state.

Dr. Weizmann referred to this transformation as "a miraculous clearing of the land." But this "clearing" was no more of a miracle than the military victory had been. The causes for the mass flight of Arabs out of their cities and villages is a controversial issue. Arabs charge that Zionist terrorism was the primary catalyst, while Jews claim that the refugees fled on orders from their own leaders in order to clear the ground for a later Arab assault. The prime factor, however, was the collapse of Arab morale with the departure of British administrators, the successive Jewish victories, the disappearance of Arab leaders and the breakdown of all functions of government. The Zionist leadership exploited the Arab demoralization with devastating success. In some regions where a tradition of Arab-Jewish cooperation existed, the Jews urged the Arabs to remain. But overall the Zionist carried out their Plan Dalet, whose aim was "control of the area given to us by the UN in addition to areas occupied by us which was outside these borders," and also to "cleanse" such areas of their Arab inhabitants.[238] Execution of this plan involved "a sophisticated combination of physical and psychological *blitz,* mounted by official Haganah and dissident Irgun forces alike, which finally drove the Palestinians out." [239] The physical blitz consisted of armed attacks, of which the most notorious was the massacre of the inhabitants of the Arab village of Deir Yassin. The psychological blitz included rumormongering and alarmist broadcasts in Arabic from clandestine Zionist radio stations and loudspeakers mounted on armored cars. Menachem Begin, then leader of the underground Irgun, has testified to the coordinated Jewish operations that drove the Arabs out of the territories assigned by the UN to the new Jewish state:

> In the month preceding the end of the Mandate, the Jewish Agency decided to undertake a difficult mission as a prelude to taking over the Arab cities before the evacuation of British forces and the dispersal of their Arab population. The Jewish Agency came to an agreement with us that we should execute these arrangements while they would repudiate everything we did and pretend that we were dissident elements, as they used to do when we fought the British. So we struck hard and put terror into the hearts of the Arabs. Thus we accomplished the expulsion of the Arab population from the areas assigned to the Jewish state.[240]

Former Prime Minister Yitzhak Rabin also describes in his memoirs how he participated in operations that forced Arabs to flee from Lydda and Ramle, both near Tel Aviv. The relevant passage was deleted by a censorship committee headed by Begin's Minister of Justice.[241]

The Arab armies crossed over into Palestine when the British mandate ended in mid-May 1948. After a month of fighting the defeated Arab states agreed to a truce that the UN undertook to monitor. The truce, which lasted just one month, was used by both sides to bolster the fighting capacities of their forces. The Israelis were more effective, so that they emerged at the end of the truce far stronger than they had been before. The Arab governments, however, had led their peoples to expect an early victory, so they now found it necessary to refuse to extend the truce. When fighting broke out again on July 8 the Israeli armies advanced on all fronts and greatly enlarged the area they controlled. Finally Israel signed separate armistice agreements with the various Arab states between February and July 1949.

The 1948 war was fought within a framework of global politics that is noteworthy. This was the period of the beginning of the Cold War—the civil war in Greece, the consolidation of Soviet hegemony in Eastern Europe and the triumph of Mao in China. In Israel the left Zionists were strongly anti-imperialist after the war with Britain and the support given by the Soviet Union. Accordingly they opposed the armistice and favored continuing the "war against Britain's Arab puppets" until all of Palestine had been liberated. Then they planned either to establish a binational state or to hand over certain regions to the Palestinians. The left Zionists were outmaneuvered by Ben-Gurion, who worked with Jordan's Abdullah to end the war and then brought the new Israeli state into the Western camp.

The 1948 war transformed the former Palestine mandate into the state of Israel, the Egyptian-administered Gaza Strip, and the Jordanian West Bank. This political transformation in turn transformed the original Arab-Israeli communal conflict within Palestine into an interstate conflict between Israel and the three adjacent Arab states. The Palestinian Arabs now were subordinated to the status of either subjects within Israel or refugees outside of Israel. They became a secondary factor in the Arab-Israeli conflict, being viewed as a "problem" rather than as a principal in the struggle. The Palestinians themselves generally accepted this subordinate position. Thoroughly demoralized by the unexpected outcome of the war and by the uprooting from their ancestral homes, they tended to look to the surrounding states for salvation from their desperate plight. This was the distinctive feature of the period after 1949 and until 1967.

Palestinian dependence on the surrounding Arab world proved totally unjustified. The 1948 disaster had left the Arabs demoralized and divided. The Muslim Brothers reacted by urging a return to the rules of Islam. Secular Arab nationalists disagreed but had no common organization or ideology. Some supported the Ba'ath Socialist Party, which in turn was divided into feuding Syrian and Iraqi components. Others backed Egypt's charismatic Nasser with his plans for Arab unity and "Arab socialism." Still others joined the amorphous Arab Nationalist Movement, of which one part led by Dr. George Habash drifted from nationalism to Marxism. Finally all these factions distrusted the established Arab governments and dynasties, regarding them as corrupt, inefficient and unreliable.

The governments and dynasties, in turn, resorted to anti-Israel bombast in order to detract popular attention from the obvious need for domestic reform that their military defeat had revealed. Syria's Prime Minister declared: "Syria, Iraq and Egypt must agree among themselves upon a united plan that will enable them to bring about the annihilation of Israel." Radio Baghdad informed its listeners: "The Arabs will never cease to regard Israel as a hostile country. The Jews are our enemies irrespective of the degree of appeasement they display. . . . We do not pause for a single moment in our preparations for the day of vengeance." King Saud went so far as to proclaim: "The Arab nations must be prepared to sacrifice up to 10 million out of their 50 million human beings if necessary, in order to wipe out Israel. . . . It must be uprooted like a cancer." [242]

These threats, empty though they were, undercut those Jewish elements who still maintained that victorious Israel should take the initiative for promoting "peace and cooperation between the two peoples." [243] Their reasoning could make no headway under the prevailing circumstances, so that it was Ben-Gurion, then in a hard-line phase of his checkered career, who prevailed during these years. The end result was a constant state of confrontation between Israel and the Arab states, with each side contributing to the self-perpetuating cycle of aggressive measures.

Arab measures included a boycott and a land and sea blockade against Israel. Administrative headquarters for the blockade was established in Damascus, with branches in other Arab states. The Suez Canal was closed to Israeli ships, and "blacklists" of vessels that called at Israeli ports were drawn up to prevent the servicing of such ships at Arab ports. Holders of passports bearing Israeli visas were refused entry into the Arab states. Petroleum companies operating in Arab countries were warned not to supply oil to Israel. All these measures did not cripple the Israeli economy but they did inflict a considerable financial burden on the new state. It is estimated that Israel lost $40 million to $50 million annually in higher shipping costs, oil prices and shipping rates. In addition, there were the substantial though incalculable losses due to potential foreign trade and investments that were not realized because of Arab economic pressure.

The Arab economic boycott of Israel was supplemented by a political boycott, so that Arabs refused to participate in regional organizations or sports events or political conferences in which Israel was represented. Thus because of the Arab threat to boycott the Bandung Conference of

Asian and African states (Apr. 1955), Israel was not invited to attend despite the principles of equality and universal representation upon which the conference was convened. More serious was the campaign of Arab raids designed to make life unbearable in the Israeli border settlements. *Fedayeen* units were organized for this purpose, with recruits coming mostly from the refugee camps. Backed by petrodollars from the oil states, the fedayeen engaged in acts of espionage, robbery, sabotage and murder.

These combined Arab aggressions were constant irritants for the Israelis, but never a serious threat. The Israeli military organized efficient countermeasures and scored a far higher kill rate than that of the Arabs. Also, the Israeli government evolved various policies that effectively restrained the Arab minority within the country. The great majority of Arabs were subject to a military government based on the Defense Regulations introduced by the British in 1945. At that time, Dr. Yaacov Shapira, future Israeli Minister of Justice, denounced the Defense Regulations as "unparalleled in any civilized country," not even "in Nazi Germany." [244] Yet these laws were enforced with greater severity by Israel against its Arab population. The Israeli military was empowered to uproot whole communities at will, impose a curfew within the bounds of military government, seize land and destroy or requisition property, enter and search anyplace and imprison any individual without trial or confine him to his home.

The other principal means for Israeli control was land acquisition. This was effected by expropriation of the properties of those who had fled during the 1948 war, and thereafter by special legislation such as the Emergency Regulations—Cultivation of Waste Lands (1948), Emergency Land Requisition Law (1949), Absentees' Property Law (1950), Land Acquisition Law—Validation of Acts and Compensations (1953), Prescription Law (1958) and the selective application of the Defense Regulations (1945). By means of these judicial devices as well as by taking advantage of the mass Arab flight, about two thirds of the lands cultivated prior to 1948 by Arab villages that came under Israeli sovereignty after the 1948 war were confiscated for cultivation or other use by the Jews. This still left Arab villages in pre-1948 Israel with 22.6 percent of the cultivated area of field crops, but the government allocated this Arab-held 22.6 percent only 1.98 percent of the national agricultural water consumption.

Deprived of financial and technical assistance as well as irrigation water, many Arab farmers left to work in towns at menial and dirty jobs. Not until 1959 did the trade union federation (Histadrut) admit Arab workers into its ranks. On July 1, 1967, the number of Arabs admitted comprised only 4.5 percent of Histadrut's total membership. Because of the Defense Regulations, Arabs from the occupied territories working in Israeli cities cannot live there. "Most Arab workers," concludes Aharon Cohen, "are discriminated against insofar as wages and social benefits are concerned. They lose much time and money in long journeys to work. Often they wander from job to job and from place to place . . . without a proper social life, and cut off from home for long periods. Employment opportunities for the Arab worker are not what they should be, especially for young men and women." [245]

In matters of health, the condition of the Israeli Arabs improved substantially. Infant mortality fell from 96 per thousand live births in 1947 to 31 in 1978 (Jews had 14.2). Immunization against infantile paralysis encompassed Arab children as well as Jewish, and the Ministry of Health established health stations, community centers and mother-and-infant clinics in some Arab villages. Despite this progress, Aharon Cohen notes that "as in other realms, the achievements in improving the health of the Arab population do not keep up with those of the state as a whole, and as time passes, the gap becomes more obvious and more painful. Even in June 1966 almost half of the Arab villages did not have a doctor and were almost entirely without medical services." [246]

In the field of education, the Arab primary school population in 1975 in pre-1967 Israel comprised 21.4 percent of the total primary school population (a proportion that corresponded to the 15 percent Arab share of the total population because of the large Arab families), but the percentage in secondary schools dropped to 10 percent and in universities to 2.23 percent. The imbalance is partly the result of deliberate Israeli policy, as indicated in the following statement of Uri Lubrani, former adviser on Arab affairs to the Prime Minister: "If there were no pupils the situation would be better and more stable. If the Arabs remained hewers of wood it might be easier for us to control them. But there are certain things that are beyond our control. This is unavoidable. All we can do is to put our advice on record and suggest how the problems are to be dealt with." [247]

This desire for "hewers of wood" finds expression in numerous discriminatory practices in education. Candidates for admission to Hebrew University, regardless of the level of their matriculation grades, are required to take intelligence tests that are notoriously ethnocentric and therefore difficult for Arab students. Also, certain subjects are out of bounds for Arab students, including aeronautical engineering and advanced electronics at the Technion. Those Arab students who overcome these obstacles and obtain university training find that they are ineligible for jobs in almost all industries based on advanced technology because they are classified as security establishments. Other industries require completion of compulsory military service, which indirectly but effectively eliminates Arab applicants. Such obstacles force many Arab graduates to emigrate, thereby leaving behind the preferred "hewers of wood."

The prevailing view among Jews is that the position of Arabs in Israel is better than in the past, and better also than that of their brethren in Arab countries. "This sort of thinking," states Aharon Cohen, "actually avoids the essence of the problem. It cannot be assumed that, were it not for the state of Israel, the Arabs within her borders would have remained static in terms of general development, public services, etc., over the past twenty years, the development in neighboring countries bear witness to this." More importantly, Cohen also notes that the Palestinian Arabs, "constantly hearing talk of democracy, civic equality, and so on, and seeing all this being increasingly realized in the Jewish sector—judges its own situation, not in comparison with that of its brethren in this or that Arab state, but in comparison with that of its Jewish neighbors in the same state." [248] In short, to contrast the position of the Palestinian Arabs with that of Arabs in surrounding countries is as irrelevant and unpersuasive as contrasting the position of South African blacks with that of blacks in surrounding countries, or the position of American blacks with that of African blacks.

Regardless of their material well-being, absolutely or relatively, the fact remains that the Palestinian Arabs have not become reconciled to Israeli rule. Indeed, the opposite has happened, especially after the second Arab catastrophe—the Six Day War of 1967. This demonstrated the hopeless ineffectiveness of the Arab states against modern Israel. After the first catastrophe of 1948 the Palestinian Arabs, left fragmented and leaderless, naturally looked to the Arab states for salvation. After the second catastrophe they realized that salvation could come only through their own efforts. And now there was some basis for their own efforts because there was no Arab flight in 1967 comparable to that of 1948. The Arabs of the newly occupied territories remained strong in numbers and in organization. Whereas the victorious Israeli leaders expected that their sweeping 1967 conquests would give them a generation of peace, instead they now perceived a triumphant Zionism generating a Zionism in reverse.

The reverse Zionism took the form of the Palestine Liberation Organization (PLO) and its bands of fedayeen or "men who sacrifice themselves." These men, organized in the Fatah and other groups, took Zionist Israel as their model. "Our people, the people of the Catastrophe, know by instinct that Israel will not disappear by a natural disaster, not by persuasion, not by the decision of Arab international bodies, or vain and sterile politics. . . . Israel says, 'I am here by the sword.' We must complete the saying—'and only by the sword shall Israel be driven out.' " [249]

The PLO leadership under Yasir Arafat decided after 1967 on a bold new strategy. Hitherto the fedayeen had confined themselves to hit-and-run raids across the armistice lines. Now Arafat and his lieutenants crossed the Jordan River with the aim of organizing a self-sustaining guerrilla movement among the one million Palestinian Arabs who had fallen under direct Israeli rule. In accordance with Mao Tse-tung's famous dictum, the fedayeen now theoretically would become fish within a revolutionary sea in which they could swim freely. Hiding in the rabbit warren comprising the Nablus Kasbah, Arafat recruited personnel, fashioned an underground organization, decided on tactics and planned operations. Young men, trained in Syria, crossed over with arms and explosives to join in the struggle.

Despite the selfless sacrifices of the fedayeen and the financial and logistical support received from the outside, the PLO record proved to be spotty, with at least as many failures as successes. Their armed resistance did restore Palestinian pride and self-confidence, especially after the Karameh Battle in which a Fatah band decided to dig in and fight. It inflicted heavy casualties on an Israeli force of fifteen thousand men and numerous tanks, which crossed the Jordan River at dawn on March 21, 1968. Although half the guerrillas were wiped out, refugee camps throughout the Arab world "celebrated the resurrection of the Palestinian people." Huge funerals were held for the "martyrs," and volunteers flocked into Fatah recruitment centers. No longer were the Palestinians regarded merely as passive victims subsisting in refugee camps on UN rations. In addition the PLO scored diplomatic victories in 1974 at the Arab summit conference at Rabat, where it was recognized as the representative of the Palestinian people, and at the UN General Assembly, where Arafat spoke amid ceremonies normally reserved for heads of state. The following year the UN General Assembly branded Zionism "a form of racism and racial discrimination." Israel also was expelled from UNESCO in protest against its Judaization of Arab Jerusalem, while the PLO was admitted as an observer to such UN bodies as the International Labor Organization and the International Atomic Energy Agency.

PLO failures, however, were at least as weighty as the successes. PLO claims of victories and of inflicted casualties were grossly exaggerated, so that the Israelis justifiably scoffed at "Oriental fantasy." Also, the increasing effectiveness of Israeli defenses led the Fatah bands to resort to indiscriminate terrorism involving civilians. This practice was extended by rival guerrilla groups into "foreign operations" such as the hijacking of airliners and the killing of Israeli athletes at the Munich Olympic games. Such activities did attract worldwide attention but they reflected Palestinian weakness rather than strength. They were far removed from the real battlefield, and their net effect probably was negative.

The PLO was also plagued by dissension as some Arab governments spawned guerrilla organizations of their own. In addition, there was Dr. George Habash's Popular Front for the Liberation of Palestine, which was Marxist-oriented and to the left of most of the PLO on the ideological spectrum. Most serious was the constant threat of backstabbing by Arab governments when PLO activities were considered to be antithetical to national interests. Palestinians still refer bitterly to "Black September" when in September 1970 King Hussein ordered his Bedouin troops to drive the PLO bands out of Jordan. Moshe Dayan justifiably observed that Hussein "killed more Palestinians in eleven days than Israel could kill in twenty years." [250] The PLO suffered a similar setback in 1976 when President Assad of Syria sent his troops against the Palestinian bands in Lebanon. The net result was that the hoped-for war of national liberation failed to materialize. The surrounding sea did not prove sufficiently revolutionary for the PLO fish, so Arafat soon was forced to abandon his campaign in the West Bank and to recross the Jordan River.

If 1967 engendered a reverse Zionism among the Palestinians, it also stimulated a more aggressive and self-confident Zionism among the Jews. Prior to the war Israel had been wracked by economic difficulties and self-doubt, according to Israeli economist Aharon Dovrat, but all that changed after the military victories and the territorial expansion:

> This country was suffering a genuine depression before the Six Day War. People were depressed psychologically, and many were looking for opportunity elsewhere. There was a standing joke in 1966: "Would the last person to leave Lydda Airport please turn out the light."
>
> The war snapped the country out of that mood. Suddenly there were opportunities everywhere. We had a million new consumers in the occupied territories and a new source of labor. Since then everything has been on the upswing: Government spending, immigration, foreign investment.[251]

The reference to the "new consumers" and "new source of labor" in the occupied territories is significant. Between 1968 and the end of 1974 the number of Palestinians from the occupied lands who worked in Israel grew from 12,000 to 78,000, or 49.8 percent of the total labor force of the West Bank and the Gaza Strip. They took the most menial and poorly paid jobs, so that a report of the Bank of Israel found a 50 percent gap in the 1972 average wage of the Israeli salaried worker as against that of the Arabs from the territories. The gap is even wider because the Palestinian workers are not eligible for various insurance funds normally available to Israeli workers. Palestinian workers also are forbidden from sleeping overnight in Israel without special permit. This regulation is often violated with the connivance of employers, so the workers usually sleep under makeshift arrangements near their place of work—in factory basements, in cellars of buildings under construction, in kitchens of restaurants, in yards of farms and in orchards. The wages paid to these migratory workers are substantially higher than what they would receive at home.

The percentage of unemployed in the West Bank has fallen from 20 in 1967 to 0.5 in 1979. Arab villagers now enjoy consumer goods that formerly had been far beyond their means. But their labor is being used to develop Israel rather than their own localities, which are so drained of workers that local enterprises are closing down. Former small entrepreneurs in the occupied territories are becoming wage hands, further expanding the proletarian Palestinian working class. By 1973 the West Bank and the Gaza Strip were obtaining no less than 90 percent of their total imports from Israel, while Israel obtained only 2 percent of its imports from the occupied territories. Thus the occupied territories were the second largest market for Israeli goods, surpassed only by the United States and exceeding Britain.

This relationship between occupiers and occupied adds up to a "classic pattern of colonial economic dominance and exploitation," as noted by the UN Special Committee in 1972.[252] The same point is made by Mohammed Milhem, mayor of Halhoul on the West Bank:

> It is certainly true that people often have more money now than they ever dreamed of. But this is individual money linked to the Israeli economy which the government is trying each day to increasingly drag us into. We are becoming a satellite.
>
> Yes, the standard of living has gone up dramatically, the shops are full but in the long run, we will lose out because no base is being created for an economy of our own.[253]

If the occupied territories are tied to Israel's economy, the reverse also is true. The dependence of Israeli industry on the labor and the markets of the occupied territories creates a formidable obstacle to the termination of the occupation, apart from any security considerations.

The same colonial type of dependency relationship prevails in agriculture, large numbers of Palestinians working in Israeli orchards, while oranges in Gaza orchards remain unpicked for lack of workers. The impact of this cheap labor supply on Israeli society has caused considerable concern, as indicated by the following widely publicized letter written to Moshe Dayan by a mother living in a *moshav* (a communal settlement similar to a kibbutz). The mother explained that after the 1967 war her husband, a farmer, became a labor contractor providing Arab workers for Israeli agriculture. "Today we have five workers," she wrote. "We've gotten to the point where we don't lift a finger on the farm. My son refuses even to mow the lawn—'Mohammad will mow it'—much less irrigate the fields or do other such dirty work."

The woman added that her husband and most men on the moshav had built small huts on the edge of the settlement to accommodate their Arab workers despite the regulation that the Arabs must return to their villages in the occupied territories each night. "The Arabs sleep in a grove a few meters from our house," she wrote, "and our life-style has become that of the effendis," or Arab feudal landowners.

Arguing that the country has been "flooded" with these workers, the woman urged Moshe Dayan to bar them from entering Israel. "If the situation is this appalling after five years, what will happen in another ten or more? Each passing year will make the problem worse and turn the contractors, who today are getting rich with slight pangs of conscience, into pressure groups that will block all change tomorrow." [254]

The woman's fear that changing the profitable status quo in the occupied territories would become increasingly difficult has proven justified. When Israel went to war in June 1967, Moshe Dayan, Minister of Defense, read the following order of the day: "Soldiers of Israel, we have no goals of conquest. Our single purpose is to put to naught the Arab armies' attempt to conquer our land, to break the blockade by which they shut us in, and to thrust back the aggression that threatens us." [255] By January 1970 Dayan's objectives had changed to the point where he wrote in the *Publications of the Israeli Ministry of Defense:*

> For twenty years, from the War of Liberation to the Six Day War we had the feeling we were living at the summit, breathing pure air. We had fought to reach the summit; we were content with what we had achieved . . . but in our heart of hearts, deep down, we were not really happy and content. We made ourselves accept Eilat as our southern frontier, a State of Israel which from Qalqilia to the sea was less than fifteen kilometers broad. Old Jerusalem stood outside its frontiers—this was Israel. In our daily life we made our own private peace with all this. The source of the great disturbance we feel today lies in our understanding of the fact that we were wrong. We have to acknowledge this. We thought we had reached the summit, but it became clear to us that we were still on the way up the mountain. The summit is higher up.[256]

Later in the same year Dayan elaborated on what he meant by the "summit" being "higher up":

This is what used to be called "Jew after Jew," *Aliyah* (wave of immigration) after *Aliyah*, or "acre by acre," "goat by goat." It meant expansion, more Jews, more villages, more settlement. Twenty years ago we were 600,000; today we are near three million. There should be no Jew who says "that's enough," no one who says "we are nearing the end of the road". . . . It is the same with the land. There are no complaints against my generation that we did not begin the process . . . but there will be complaints against you [Dayan is addressing the Kibbutz Youth Federation on the Golan Heights] if you come and say: "up to here." Your duty is not to stop; it is to keep your sword unsheathed, to have faith, to keep the flag flying. You must not call a halt—heaven forbid—and say "that's all; up to here, up to Degania, to Mufallasim, to Nahal Oz!" For that is not all.[257]

The Labor Party-dominated governments of Golda Meir and Yitzhak Rabin acted in accordance with this expansionist ideology. They rejected the idea of a separate Palestinian state in the West Bank and planted between 1967 and 1977 a total of 90 settlements in that region at a cost of about $350 million. In addition, much land in the Jerusalem area and on the West Bank has been purchased openly or secretly by private Israeli citizens, by non-Israeli Jews and by the Land Administration and Jewish National Fund. One estimate is that by mid-1977 Israeli land ownership on the West Bank, aided by government assistance, totaled 160,000 hectares or one third of the region's total surface.

Further evidence of the intention of the "moderate" Labor Party governments to retain the occupied territories is to be found in the incentives they offered to Israeli firms to establish plants in those lands. In 1972 the government gave loans of up to 50 percent of the necessary working capital, lent loans at up to 9 percent interest and with the borrowers being required to provide only 20 percent of the total capital needed for any enterprise. The government also provided grants of up to a third of the investment in machinery and equipment, and up to 20 percent of the investment in building and site development, in addition to generous depreciation allowances and exemption from income tax for five years.[258]

Despite these aggressive government policies in the occupied territories, Menachem Begin won the 1977 elections partly by claiming Judea and Samaria (the West Bank) as historically and immutably Jewish, and calling for mass immigration to make them Jewish in fact as well as in dogma. Immediately after his electoral victory Begin was asked what his plans were for the occupied territories. "What occupied territories?" he replied. "If you mean Judea, Samaria, and the Gaza Strip, they are liberated territories, part of the land of Israel." [259] That Begin meant what he said is evident in his hard-line policies following the March 1979 peace treaty with Egypt. The treaty provided that the West Bank and Gaza be given "full autonomy," and that "the Israeli military government and its civilian administration will be withdrawn."

Begin's interpretation of "full autonomy" was so circumscribed that it constituted an obvious subterfuge. The military government would be "withdrawn," but only to strategic points within the territories, from where it would continue to exercise its authority. Likewise "full autonomy" was to apply to people, not to land, so Israel would continue to acquire more land, control the vital water resources, and retain security in the hands of its own military. Begin further declared that Israel would never permit the establishment of a Palestinian state in the West Bank and Gaza, and that after a five-year transition period, Israel would insist on claiming sovereignty over the two regions.

At the same time Israel followed an aggressive settlement policy in the occupied territories. In June 1979, Agriculture Minister Ariel Sharon candidly explained his government's policy. "In another year, settlement activity might be impossible. So we must act now—to settle vigorously, quickly. First of all to establish facts of foothold, and then to beautify the settlements, plan them, expand them." [260] This policy has been vigorously implemented. When Begin took office in 1977 there were 32 Israeli settlements on the West Bank with 3,200 inhabitants. By the end of 1980 there were 69 settlements, with 17,400 settlers. Four more settlements were in the planning stage, and the operating program called for 100,000 Jews on the West Bank by 1984.

Mattiyahu Drobles, head of the settlement division of the Zionist organization, presented this strategy in the Foreword to his 1977 master plan for settlement projects: [261] Settlement throughout the entire land of Israel is for security and by right. A strip of settlements at strategic sites enhances both internal and external security alike, as well as making concrete . . . our right to Eretz Israel (the land of Israel). . . . the disposition of the settlements must be carried out not only around the settlements of the minorities, but also in between them."

By "minorities" Drobles meant the local Arab population, which in 1980 numbered 750,000 compared with the 17,400 Jewish settlers. This is the settler mentality par excellence. So long as it prevails, so long as current policies are pursued, so long Israel will remain a settler society. An Israeli civil libertarian, Shulamit Aloni, writes about an emerging "Apartheid Israeli-style." [262] Such a label may seem farfetched, but it is so only in degree—not in essence. Israel's leaders obviously did not set out to create an apartheid state. But they did work purposefully and zealously to create a settler state, and the one does lead to the other, as pioneer Zionists warned many decades ago. Yitshak Epstein, who immi-

grated to Palestine in 1886 and worked as a farmer and a teacher, wrote
an article entitled "A Hidden Question":

> Among the grave questions linked with the concept of our people's
> renaissance on its own soil there is one question *which is more
> weighty than all the others put together.* This is the question of our
> relations with the Arabs. Our own national aspirations depend
> upon the correct solution to this question. It has not been elimi-
> nated. It has simply been forgotten by the Zionists. . . .
>
> This people [Palestinian Arabs] forms only a small part of a
> great nation, which holds all the territory surrounding our country:
> Syria, Iraq, Arabia and Egypt. . . . We should not trust the ashes
> which cover the embers: one spark may rekindle the fire and bring
> about a conflagration which will not be extinguished. . . .
>
> I am not suggesting for a moment that we should humble our-
> selves and give in to the local inhabitants. But we shall commit a
> grave sin against our people and our future if we throw away so
> lightly our principal weapons: righteousness and sincerity. . . .
> Our purpose is not to Judaize the Arabs, but to prepare them for
> a fuller life . . . so that in the course of time they can become
> faithful allies of ours, true friends and brothers.[263]

This binationalist strain in Zionism has persisted to the present, as
noted above, but it never prevailed. Instead the goal of a Jewish homeland took precedence over the means, as evident in the speeches and policies of the dominant Zionist leaders. Herzl's associate Max Nordau explained that at the 1897 Basle Zionist Conference he used the term
"National Home" as "a circumlocution that would express all we meant,
but would say it in a way so as to avoid provoking the Turkish rulers of
the coveted land. I suggested *'Heimstätte.'* . . . It was equivocal, but we
all understood what it meant. To us it signified *'Judenstaat'* then and it
signifies the same now." [264] When the Balfour Declaration was issued,
Dr. Chaim Weizmann hurried to Palestine to assure the Arabs: "It is not
our aim to get hold of the supreme power and administration in Palestine, nor to deprive any native of his possession." [265] But only two years
later Dr. Weizmann told a London audience: "I trust to God that a
Jewish state will come about; but it will come about not through political declarations, but by the sweat and blood of the Jewish people. . . .
we can pour in a considerable number of immigrants, and finally establish such a society in Palestine that Palestine shall be as Jewish as England is English, or America is American." [266]

Today we are witnessing the unextinguishable "conflagration" foreseen
at the beginning of the century by Epstein. And the reason is self-evident.
Palestine can be made as Jewish as England is English only by dispos-

sessing the native Arabs; only by creating a settler state. But settler regimes, by their very origin and nature, involve unceasing struggle with the natives being displaced and also, under certain circumstances, with the metropolitan country, leading to secession from the metropolis. The histories of both South Africa and Israel inevitably have been dominated by this twofold struggle. Both won independence after armed struggle against British rule—open colonial rule in the case of South Africa and camouflaged mandate rule in the case of Israel. Then both sides coped with the problem of keeping their native populations in subordinate status, and perforce resorted to comparable, though not identical, measures.

First, both countries took official and unofficial measures to drive the natives off their lands and to transform the former peasants into agricultural laborers and industrial workers. Both countries also found it necessary to adopt various security measures, including travel controls, residence regulations, curfew restrictions, destruction of houses, administrative detentions and so forth. As a last resort both states resorted to torture, wholesale and blatant in South Africa, marginal and discreet in Israel, yet prevalent enough to warrant investigations and critical reports by institutions such as the London *Sunday Times*, the Swiss League for Human Rights, Amnesty International and the International Red Cross.

Israel and South Africa also have become increasingly close in their economic and diplomatic relations. Their economies supplement each other, so Israel provides military equipment and advanced technology in return for South African raw materials such as coal, diamonds and uranium. There are also other less material ties between the two countries, both having a common biblical heritage and both sharing the beleaguered mentality of settler societies, as noted by C. L. Sulzberger of the New York *Times*:

> The Afrikaner sees Israel as another small nation, surrounded by enemies, where the Bible and a revived language are vital factors. As Jannie Kruger, former editor of *Die Transvaler* wrote: "The Afrikaners . . . are par excellence the nation of the Book." The fundamentalist Boers trekked northward with gun in one hand and Bible in the other. . . .
>
> Prime Minister Vorster even goes so far as to say Israel is now faced with an apartheid problem—how to handle its Arab inhabitants. Neither nation wants to place its future entirely in the hands of a surrounding majority and would prefer to fight.
>
> Both South Africa and Israel are in a sense intruded states. They were built by pioneers originating abroad and settling in partially inhabited areas. . . . Vorster says, "We view Israel's position and

problems with understanding and sympathy. Like us they have to deal with terrorist infiltrators across the border; and like us they have enemies bent on their destruction." [267]

The parallel between Israel and South Africa is real and inherent, yet there remains a vast difference between the two societies. South Africa appears to be frozen into its settler mold for the foreseeable future. The European colonists from the beginning assumed that the land was theirs to expropriate, and its inhabitants theirs to exploit. This assumption remains the foundation of the apartheid system to the present day, and is enthusiastically supported by the great majority of whites. Even the cosmetic reforms of Botha, designed as they are to preserve the fundamentals of the system, have aroused passionate opposition. "He is making his reforms within the framework," complained one of his associates, "yet even so, see what trouble he's getting into." [268]

In Israel, by contrast, exclusivist Zionism has been challenged from the very beginnings of the movement and of the state. It is revealing that Israeli critics of Israel report no major obstacles in voicing their opinions in their homeland, though they are subject to harassment by Jewish American organizations when speaking in the United States. Major General (Ret.) Matityahu Peled stated in June 1978 when he was a visiting professor at Harvard University that, despite his vocal opposition to official Israeli policy, "The Ministry of Justice . . . would never impute any dishonest or treacherous motives to what we are doing. Although I did come to realize that within the American Jewish community there is a greater tendency to view any deviation from the official line in these terms. I have felt this personally on several occasions, but as yet this hasn't crossed the ocean to Israel." [269] Likewise Professor Israel Shahak of Hebrew University testified before a U.S. Senate subcommittee on October 19, 1977:

> . . . for the last $2\frac{1}{2}$ years or more there has been no difficulty whatsoever in the State of Israel. The difficulties from the United States continue. . . . If I am sponsored by a church group, then usually all the Jewish organizations in a given city are putting pressure on this church group to revoke my sponsorship even at the last moment. Also anonymous literature is circulated against me. It is full of lies. There are no dates and addresses given. . . . Those people who I have identified are coming from special organizations . . . employed in harassing me . . . B'nai B'rith and the so-called Anti-Defamation League.[270]

The leeway allowed to Israeli dissenters in Israel has been fully utilized. A distinguished philosopher, Martin Buber, advocated a "dialogue" and rapprochement between Jewish and Arab nationalists. An historian, Michael Brecher of Hebrew University, accuses Begin of "negotiating in bad faith" on the Palestinian problem. Yael Lotan, former editor of *Ariel*, a magazine on Israeli art and culture sponsored by Israel's Foreign Ministry, has challenged official policy bluntly:

> . . . *nothing* is worse than the continued occupation of the West Bank and the Gaza Strip. No mystagogical formulations will ever make it an acceptable status for the inhabitants. Their repression is undoing us all, and the Zionist dream is fast turning into a nightmare. We must therefore resolve to get out—not negotiate or haggle but simply *get out of there.* . . . An independent Palestine is the only chance Israel has of surviving the twentieth century.[271]

Israeli dissidents act as well as talk. On September 9, 1978, one hundred thousand Israelis marched in the largest political demonstration of the nation's history. They demanded that Begin show flexibility at the Camp David talks. Their banners proclaimed: "Peace is better than the Greater Land of Israel." They marched again after Camp David to protest Begin's obduracy regarding Palestinian autonomy. When Israeli colonization on the West Bank was pushed aggressively, thirty thousand supporters of "Peace Now" demonstrated in Tel Aviv. Their placards bore messages such as "Give Peace a Chance." These mass protests were sufficient to move Ariel Sharon to complain that Israel's television network and newspapers had persuaded "quite a few good and loyal" citizens to "side with the country's enemies."[272]

The pro-peace movement within Israel is paralleled by a corresponding procompromise trend within the Palestine Liberation Organization. The crushing 1967 defeat of the Arab armies by Israel had enabled the PLO to assume the leadership of the Arab national struggle at the expense of the discredited Arab governments and their Arab League. Conversely, the credible showing of the Arab armies in the October 1973 war restored the prestige of the governments and the Arab League. This trend was furthered by the astronomic rise of oil prices, which correspondingly increased the resources and influence of the conservative oil-rich states. The changing balance of power in the Arab world explains the setbacks sustained by the PLO in "Black September" in Jordan in 1970, and in Lebanon in 1972 and 1973. The 1979 Camp David accords were another blow for the PLO, so that Brzezinski dismissed it with his taunt, "Bye, bye, PLO."

But far from disappearing, the PLO has survived and flourished by adapting to the changing circumstances. Its policies are not frozen, having been changed repeatedly by the Palestine National Council. In 1974 this organization officially adopted the Transitional Program, which advo-

cated that the PLO assume sovereignty over *any portion* of Palestine subsequently liberated. Abu Iyad, deputy chief of the PLO, has interpreted
this to mean that "there will be no more subversive Palestinian activities
the day we have a state to run and above all to safeguard." [273] This position was reiterated by Farouk Kaddoumi, director of the political department of the PLO during a meeting in Damascus in January 1979
with a delegation of Americans, including Alan Solomonow, director of
the Middle East Peace Project. Kaddoumi said: "As soon as we have a
state, we shall recognize Israel's secure borders and Israel's right to live
in peace." He added that some gesture by Israel would produce a significant shift within the PLO, enabling the moderates to speak up more
candidly.

Precisely the same point in reverse was made at the time by "Peace
Now" elements in Israel. The resulting deadlock was well summarized
in a New York *Times* editorial: "Because the PLO's leaders look upon
acknowledgment of Israel's right to exist as their one diplomatic trump
card, they will not play it—if at all—except in exchange for some sort
of counterrecognition from Israel. And no such recognition is remotely
likely, given Israeli Prime Minister Begin's evident conviction that the
PLO can never be more than a terrorist body committed to Israel's
destruction." [274]

Despite this deadlock, hope for conversion from settler-state institutions
and practices is much brighter in Israel than in South Africa. Yet even in
Israel there remains a wide chasm between the hope and its realization.
Powerful theopolitical and economic interests within Israel will fight to
the last ditch against any withdrawal from the occupied lands with their
biblical associations and their lucrative markets and labor reserves.
Equally powerful foreign interests also are determined to preserve that
status quo. "We are trying to get a [Middle East] settlement in such a
way," Henry Kissinger said as national security adviser, "that the moderate regimes are strengthened and not the radical regimes." [275]

The reason for the preference for "moderate regimes" is that the geopolitical and economic importance of the Middle East for the West is
greater than even that of South Africa. Hence the steadfast effort
by Washington to buttress Israel, to favor the conservative oil states
and to isolate the PLO. The Camp David accords represent the cul-
mination of this policy, being intended to play the same role in the
Middle East as the internal settlements in southern Africa—that is, to accept cosmetic changes in order to preserve the essence of white domination in the one case, and of Israeli domination in the other. But Israeli
domination appears as unviable in the long run as does white domination
in southern Africa. It involves perennial Israeli occupation, which is unacceptable to all Arab states, including the conservative ones with oil,

as well as the radical regimes. The alternative, preferred by Washington and the Israeli Labor Party, is a Jordanian solution, dividing the West Bank between Israel and the Hashimite King. But many Palestinians are ambivalent about such a course. Furthermore, it was the Labor Party under Golda Meir and Yitzhak Rabin that planted dozens of settlements in the occupied lands, annexed East Jerusalem and ringed it with Jewish suburbs.

A final obstacle in the way of changing the settler-state institutions and practices of Israel is the legacy of two thousand years of persecution, with the resulting obsession summarized by the slogan "Never Again!" The obsession is not alleviated by the fact that in 1980 Israel was recognized by only 50 states, as against 115 that recognized the PLO. Furthermore, a November 1979 poll revealed that for the first time nearly half of the American public favored negotiations between the United States and the PLO. Hence the insistence by many Israelis that retention of the post-1967 frontiers is the prerequisite for ensuring national security in a hostile world.

The assumption is questioned, however, not only by the "Peace Now" movement, but also by leading figures in the intellectual, political and military establishment of Israel. A noted Israeli historian, Jacob Talman, wrote shortly before his death in June 1980 that "the attempt to rule a million Arabs against their will may make our beautiful dreams of national and spiritual renewal seem ridiculous." Continued control or annexation of the occupied territories he regarded as a threat rather than a safeguard for Israel. "In the modern era," he wrote in the Israeli newspaper *Haaretz*, "it is not territories of a country that pass down in heritage, but the consciousness and the will of the people who live in them. The true danger to Israel's existence lies in the continuation of the Sisyphean effort to subjugate the Palestinians. He is blind who does not see that we are threatened by a racial war." [276]

Likewise General Peled contends that expanded frontiers do not mean more security—that this assumption is a case of "dogmatic hibernation." He notes that before 1967 an Israeli frontier force of only a few thousand men sufficed, and the defense budget then equaled only 12 percent of GNP. After the acquisition of the presumably more defensible 1967 frontiers, several divisions of tens of thousands of soldiers were needed, and the defense budget skyrocketed to 36 percent of GNP. The explanation for the paradox is that it is much more expensive to maintain defense forces stationed across the Sinai Desert rather than concentrated on the eastern edge, as had been the case before 1967. Peled also maintains that the Golan area now occupied by Israel is far too small to be of any strategic significance. Finally, Jordan maintained before 1967 two divisions in the West Bank, which caused Israel no undue concern. Peled therefore concludes that a Palestinian state with an army of less than two divisions, a demilitarized Golan Heights restored to Syria and a demilitarized Sinai restored to Egypt would leave Israel with at least as great a degree of security, and at a much lower cost. If the new Palestinian state were to use its armed forces against Israel in any way, "this would mean war in which the newly gained Palestinian state would be lost forever." [277]

David Ben-Gurion reached a similar conclusion at the end of his distinguished career:

> First, never forget that *historically* this country belongs to two races—the Arabs of Palestine and the Jews of the world—each of whom, first the Jews and then the Arabs, have controlled it for some 1,300 years apiece.
>
> Second, remember the Arabs drastically outbreed us, and that to insure survival a Jewish state must at all times maintain within her own borders an unassailable Jewish majority.
>
> Third, the logic of all this is that to get peace, we must return in principle to the pre-1967 borders. We simply haven't the available Jews to populate all biblical Palestine. So when I consider the future of Israel, I only consider the country before the Six Day War. We should return all gains except East Jerusalem and the Golan. And on these we must negotiate. . . . Peace is more important than real estate. With proper irrigation we now have quite enough land here in the Negev to care for all the Jews in the world— if they come. And they certainly will not all come.
>
> As for security, militarily defensible borders, while desirable, cannot by themselves guarantee our future. Some sections of our people still have not learned this lesson. *Real* peace with our Arab neighbors, mutual respect and even affection; perhaps an Arab Israeli alliance; in any case a settlement they will not reluctantly agree to live with, but will enthusiastically welcome from their hearts as essential for our common future—that is our only *true* security. Then together we could turn the Middle East into a second garden of Eden and one of the great creative centers of the earth.[278]

The observations of Peled and Ben-Gurion are carried to their logical conclusion by Nathan Yalin-Mor, commander between 1946 and 1948 of the Stern group, an underground Jewish liberation organization:

> . . . when I hear Prime Minister Begin using the terms "murderous organization" and "Nazi organization" in regard to the PLO, I recall the history of the Irgun. . . . Begin became Irgun commander in 1944. It may be convenient for him to forget the organization's history before that date. But it exists, written in the blood

of innocent Arabs, in an undiscriminating war. [After detailing examples of Irgun attacks in which "innocent Arabs" were killed,
Yalin-Mor states:] It is possible to call the Palestinian organizations
saboteur or terrorist organizations, and at the same time to ignore
the fact that we were called terrorists by almost all of the mass
media. We *were* terrorists, and I am not ashamed to admit it. Our
forces were very weak compared to the forces of the conqueror and
we would have been wiped out in a frontal confrontation. The only
path left to us was terror, a constant terrorizing of the rulers, until
they were convinced they could never totally eliminate the fighters
among our people until we got what we desired: freedom.

It is not this or that label that prevents me from extending my
hand to a representative of the PLO. What bothers me is its final
goal, as it is expressed in the Palestinian Covenant, in which there is
no room for a free and sovereign life for my people in their state.
The changing of the covenant will be a sign that the PLO under-
stands there is no way out of the conflict other than the recognition
of the right of coexistence of the two nations in sovereign independent states, one beside the other, until the federative stage is
reached.

If the PLO arrives at this understanding, there will be no more
value to the pronouncements by different Israeli Prime Ministers
that "we will never sit with the PLO at the conference table, we will
meet them only on the battlefield." Battles, of all types, require victims. The job of a good statesman is not to mourn for the victims
and to defame the "criminal organization" that produces these victims, but rather to create a situation in which there will be no more
victims, no more bloodshed. And the sooner the better.[279]

Yalin-Mor's statement puts the issue squarely. Can the Israelis—
messianic, militarily superior, backed from abroad and tormented by
history—draw back from their present colonialist position? And can the
PLO relinquish its "diplomatic trump card" of withholding recognition
of Israel's right to exist? Can both sides face the question of whether
colonialism and trump cards alike have become not sources of strength
but of mutual destruction?

Chapter 24

A COMMON VISION

—✦————————————————————————————✦—

I see Teheran today and I could be seeing Mexico in 1915.
We had Pancho Villa, Zapata, Lagos Chazaro. It was chaos and
it took years to settle down, but something was being born. . . .

If there is one thing that is happening around the world, it is
the determination of peoples not simply to accept the two versions
of inevitable progress—that of Western capitalism or Soviet socialism—but to find ways of combining the power of technology
with the energy of their own traditions.

CARLOS FUENTES (1980)

The Agricultural Revolution some ten thousand years ago began the
displacement of food gatherers by peasants, who thereafter comprised
the overwhelming majority of the human race. Today the peasants in
turn are being displaced by the dynamic capitalist technology engendered
by the Third Industrial Revolution. If current trends continue for several
decades, the world's peasantry will follow the food gatherers into historical oblivion. This is the root cause for the ongoing revolutionary
impulse convulsing the Third World and, indirectly, the rest of the globe.
Premier Chou En-lai, in his report to the Tenth National Congress of the
Chinese Communist Party (August 24, 1973), fittingly described the
worldwide ferment as "great disorder under Heaven." This disorder is
the most important force in global affairs at present and for the foreseeable future.

ଏ *I. "Great Disorder under Heaven"*

One factor behind the "disorder" characterizing the late twentieth
century is economic—the widening gap between rich nations and poor,

and also between rich and poor citizens within Third World countries. The technology of the Third Industrial Revolution is uprooting peasants everywhere and forcing them into shantytowns (see Chapter 19, Sections I–III). The curse of urbanization without adequate industrialization is transforming former peasants into a surplus and expendable underclass. Forty percent of the Third World's total labor force of 1.2 billion is currently unemployed. Of the nearly 2 billion people that will be added to the world's population during the next two decades, 90 percent will be born in underdeveloped countries. During those two decades the number of job seekers will double. There is little chance that there will be enough new jobs to accommodate the young people who wish to enter the work force.

The new permanently unemployed are manifestly less willing to accept their lot in life than were their parents. The psychological factors behind current global disorders are as important as the economic factors. The histories of past civilizations are punctuated by peasant uprisings, but these were normally restorationist. Peasants usually did not challenge the existing social orders. They rose to their defense. In the late Middle Ages, European peasants took up arms to preserve the traditional feudal social order, which was then being undermined by the emerging capitalist economy. In the Russian empire the peasants regarded the Tsar almost to the end as the Little Father who, had he only known, would never have tolerated the injustices inflicted by rapacious officials and landlords. The pre-capitalist era, in the words of Dostoyevsky's "Grand Inquisitor," was one of "miracle, mystery and authority," when "the universal and everlasting craving of humanity" was "to find someone to worship."

Traditional acceptance of the status quo has been undermined by capitalism's quantum leap from Europe to the countrysides of the Third World. Land is being transformed into a commodity, bought and sold and used in response to market forces rather than to the needs of local peasant communities. The resulting commercialization, pauperization and urbanization is devastatingly disruptive. But the process of disruption is also shattering the psychological shackles of "miracle, mystery and authority"—the shackles of age-old acceptance of poverty and exploitation as the divinely ordained fate of humans. The blind peasant outbursts of the past are giving way to purposeful peasant revolutions seeking to overthrow rather than reform existing social orders.

The shedding of constraints is manifest also among the intellectuals leading current revolutions. As late as the mid-1940s the Communist leaders of the Greek National Liberation Front (EAM) resistance movement handed over control of their country to Churchill because they could not bring themselves to challenge the authority of the father figure in the Kremlin. And when the Yugoslav Communists did finally dare to do so in 1948 their entire leadership, including Tito himself, suffered serious psychosomatic ailments. Today, by contrast, revolutionary leaders everywhere state openly that foreign aid from almost any quarter is welcome, but that no obligations or allegiances are thereby incurred.

This simultaneous radicalizing and maturing of Third World masses and leaders explains why the 1980s were heralded by successful revolutions in Iran, Zimbabwe and Nicaragua, and why revolutions continue to blaze in Afghanistan, Eritrea, Western Sahara, Namibia, East Timor, San Salvador and the Philippines. In Iran, the CIA's Kermit Roosevelt was able in 1953 to overthrow the Mossadeq government with the aid of a satchel of dollar bills and a handful of Iranian army officers. But when General Robert Huyser tried in 1979 to forestall Khomeini's triumph by promoting a "straight military takeover," it was the politicized populace rather than the Shah's army that effected the "takeover."

II. Global Confrontations

The distinguished political scientist Hans Morgenthau observed that the basic issue facing American foreign policy is not how to *preserve*, but how to *create*, stability in the face of revolution. The dilemma of creating rather than preserving is confronting not only the United States government but all governments, whether in the developed First and Second Worlds, or in the underdeveloped Third World. Thus far, creativity has been conspicuous everywhere by its absence.

Considering first the various Third World governments, they comprise in very general terms two varieties: conservative nationalist and social revolutionary. Both types have failed to a greater or lesser degree in responding creatively to Third World revolution. In the case of the conservative regimes, some have received substantial economic and military backing from the United States in return for serving as supportive "regional sub-imperialisms" against local insurrections. But the revolution in Iran, and the chronic turmoil in Saudi Arabia, Indonesia, Brazil and the Philippines, all raise serious questions as to whether propped-up regional powers can stem the flood of Third World revolution.

The inherent economic vulnerability of these conservative regimes becomes evident if their position is compared to that of England in the early days of the Industrial Revolution. With medieval guilds atrophied, and trade unions not yet legalized, industrialists exploited their workers mercilessly. Hence the agitation of the Luddites and the Chartists, and the Peterloo massacres of 1819, and the revolt of the agricultural workers in 1830. But by the mid-nineteenth century real wages were rising, so that the last case of real starvation in the West European countryside was in 1846–47. The stock breeder Robert Bakewell could seriously assert that he was raising sheep for the masses as well as for the gentlemen's tables, and Matthew Boulton likewise declared of his brass-button works, "We think it of far more consequence to supply the people than the nobility only." [1]

Thus the "trickle down," which is so talked about in the Third World today but which so rarely materializes, did actually occur and did benefit the British working class after the mid-nineteenth century. But this was possible because British industry enjoyed the unique advantage of a monopoly of world markets. The Lancashire cotton industry was able to "take off" because of the combined African and American markets to which it had access. By 1814, Britain was exporting 14 percent more cotton cloth than was being used at home, and by 1850 the differential had increased to 24 percent, even though domestic consumption had risen sharply.

Today, however, no such world market is available to Third World countries seeking to industrialize. Instead, both workers and employees in industrialized countries campaign strenuously against imports—whether textiles, steel, shoes or clothing—that jeopardize their jobs and their profits. Free trade is fine so long as there's plenty of trade for everyone. But with the current prospect for prolonged and worldwide economic crisis, the growing demand is for "fair trade"—the most recent euphemism for protectionism.

Equally serious for Third World countries is the inelasticity of their own domestic markets. Native industries not only have problems of access to foreign markets but also are fettered by inadequate purchasing power at home. Underpaid industrial workers and displaced peasants experience little of the "trickle down" presumed by economic theorists. Instead there is "trickle up" to local elites and "trickle out" to multinational corporations. Hence the chronic conflict between labor organizations on the one hand, and on the other the governments trying to impose austerity measures demanded by private banks and by international lending agencies such as the World Bank and the International Monetary Fund. Brazil's working-class hero, the metalworker Luis Inacio da Silva, popularly known as "Lula," was sentenced to three and a half years in jail for leading an "illegal" strike, and faced another thirty years' imprisonment for allegedly inciting "class violence." The report of an observer for the United Automobile Workers union at Da Silva's trial is revealing of how conservative Third World regimes seek to "preserve" rather than "create" stability. "It's incredible to me that in comparing Brazil and Poland, a Communist country, there seems to be more freedom there than here. Walesa is freer than Lula. There the government agreed to hold a dialogue with him, here not. That is a basic and astonishing difference." [2]

If the conservative Third World states are beset by inherent contradictions, the same holds true for the social revolutionary societies. Although
they are explicitly or implicitly Marxist in their orientation, their post-
revolutionary development has frequently taken non-Marxist, and even
anti-Marxist forms. They have not eliminated classes, nor are they likely
to do so in the foreseeable future. They have not dismantled the state,
which instead is becoming more controlling and omnipotent. In economic affairs they have failed to become independent of the global
capitalist order and to develop the desired self-reliant economies. Instead, the precise opposite has happened.

At one time it appeared that China, with its vast human and natural
resources, and led by the iconoclastic Mao, might attain the desired
economic independence. But after Mao's death, Chinese policies shifted
rapidly and radically. "Chinese revisionism knows no bounds," declared
a Japanese businessman observing the Chinese scramble for capitalist
technology, credits and cooperative production deals. Symbolic of the
new revisionism was the changing of the name of the Peking street on
which the Soviet Embassy is located. During the height of the Cultural
Revolution it was given a new name: Antirevisionism Street. In 1980
its original name was restored. The Chinese Communist Party implicitly
acknowledged the turnabout in late 1979 when it circulated a document
among its leading cadres informing them that the Soviet Party no longer
should be considered revisionist.

Some Third World Marxist leaders are aware of the dilemmas they
face and have discussed them publicly. President Samora Machel was
asked how Mozambique proposed to deal with the "serious abuses of
power by party members" that have occurred in some socialist countries.
Machel replied that during the course of the independence struggle, his
party had developed and institutionalized certain procedures for exposing
and punishing those who misused their authority. Free use of these
procedures is protected and encouraged, so that party and state leaders
have been publicly censured for improper conduct and removed from
office. "In these circumstances," concluded Machel, "we can safely say
that the eventual abuses of power that arise will be rapidly detected and
punished." [3]

Even if Machel's optimism proves justified, it should be noted that he
has addressed himself only to the political aspects of the Marxist crisis.
There still remains an equally serious economic dilemma. President
Machel, in a major policy speech in August 1979, expressed confidence
that Mozambique could attain economic development without subordination and exploitation. He acknowledged need for capital and technology,
but offered labor and natural resources in return. He invited "cooperation with private firms from other countries," but insisted that Mozam-

bique would "refuse to participate in the international division of labor in a subordinate position, paying more and more to buy finished products and selling our labor power for less and less." [4]

Machel's objective is laudable, but the strategy for attaining the objective still eludes revolutionary regimes. This is evident in the writings of two West Indian economists, George Beckford and Clive Thomas. Both seek a self-reliant model of development, as does President Machel. Beckford proposes distributing five to twenty-five acres to peasant families because such families have proven more innovative and productive than large landholders. But Thomas calls for collectivization as the prerequisite for introducing advanced agricultural technology. Collectivization, however, runs the risk of peasant resistance, while land distribution may block technological advance. Thus the basic problem of how to attain autonomous economic development remains unresolved, both in theory and in practice.

The governments of the developed First and Second Worlds have not been more creative in coping with global revolution than have the governments of the Third World. Whereas Washington has generally tried to forestall or suppress revolutions, Moscow has sought to exploit them in behalf of its national interests. Both strategies have been conspicuously unsuccessful, and have wreaked untold damage and suffering on Third World peoples. Most fanciful have been successive American policymakers, from Henry Kissinger, who saw no reason for standing by and watching a country go Communist because of "the irresponsibility of its own people," [5] to President Reagan, who asserts that "the Soviet Union underlies all the unrest that is going on" and that if it were not for Kremlin machinations, "there wouldn't be any hot spots in the world." [6] It follows from these propositions that current Third World insurrections are neither indigenous nor legitimate, and therefore they are now branded and outlawed as "international terrorism."

The self-evident fact is that if a geologic cataclysm were to remove the Soviet Union from the face of the globe, the deplored "hot spots" and "international terrorism" would persist undiminished. This truism is the basic reason for the setbacks experienced by the United States in its efforts to preserve an untenable status quo in the Third World. These setbacks—ranging from Vietnam to Iran to southern Africa and to the current difficulties in Central America—are paralleled by corresponding Soviet losses throughout the Third World. A study by the Washington-based Center for Defense Information concludes that the Soviet Union enjoyed influence in 9 percent of the world's nations in 1945, then peaked at 14 percent in the late 1950s, and declined to 12 percent (or 19 of the world's 155 countries) in 1980.[7] Major countries in which the Soviet Union made heavy financial and military investments and then was expelled include Iraq, Egypt, Indonesia and China. The latter country enjoys the distinction of having been "lost" twice, once by each of the superpowers. It may be presumed that other countries soon will share the distinction. Despite Peking's dire warnings about "hegemonism," the fact is that the Third World has for years been beyond the control of both Washington and Moscow.

III. "Concessions or Structural Changes"?

Mahbub ul Haq, director of policy and planning at the International Bank for Reconstruction and Development, observes that the underdeveloped countries have not made up their minds as to what they are really seeking, "short-term concessions" or "long-term structural changes." [8] Behind this question of alternatives is the inescapable predicament of capital accumulation faced by underdeveloped countries. Wassily Leontief, in his United Nations report *The Future of the World Economy*, estimates that these countries must save between 30 and 40 percent of their national incomes to achieve self-reliant development. Leontief also notes that to attain such a level of savings it will be necessary to adopt "significant social and institutional changes," including "more equitable income distribution." [9]

This analysis points up the inherent contradiction within all schemes for a course of Third World development that is evolutionary and also independent. Savings of the magnitude necessary for self-reliant development are inconceivable in societies in which the surplus extracted from peasants in the form of rent and interest is squandered by landowners on luxury consumption. Consequently the mobilization of economic resources requires, as Leontief suggests, social restructuring at the expense of local elites and their associates in metropolitan centers. In practice this has meant nationalistic social revolutionary regimes that adopt development policies hostile to local and foreign vested interests. This in turn leads to retaliation by the threatened vested interests, and to stoppage of "investment resources coming from abroad," which Leontief viewed as a necessary supplement to "internal sources."

The inherent contradiction in this situation confronts Third World elites with a painful dilemma. On the one hand, the status quo on which their wealth and rank are based has proven patently unviable, as proven by the failure of the two development decades. On the other hand, like all elites throughout history, they are unwilling to surrender their privileges and sources of income in response to moral appeals. Hence their current strategy of opposing radical social changes by seeking concessions through a New International Economic Order (NIEO).

Champions of NIEO seek to extract concessions from the developed countries in order to cope with three of the most urgent Third World problems. First, they seek to improve the deteriorating terms of trade by linking raw-material prices to the prices of the manufactured exports of the developed countries. Secondly, they want to curb the great price instability of their major exports by securing a massive international fund to operate a system of "buffer stocks." When prices of raw materials begin to fall, the fund would be used to buy sufficient quantities of the raw materials to maintain their prices. Finally, the NIEO reformers propose to cope with Third World overindebtedness by canceling part of the outstanding debt and rescheduling or lengthening the payback period for the rest.

Innumerable international conferences have been held to discuss these proposed reforms. In 1975 it appeared that the reform route was succeeding. OPEC had demonstrated the power of raw-material-producing countries acting in concert, and the commodity boom had sent the price of everything, from copper to soybeans, soaring upward. But the unpredictability of the raw-materials market soon manifested itself again as prices plummeted with the piling up of surpluses. Third World export earnings shrank at the same time that the cost of their imports was pushed upward by the inflation in the industrialized countries. First World leaders were unwilling to come to the rescue, as was made clear by Kissinger's blunt speech at the fourth United Nations Conference on Trade and Development (UNCTAD) in Nairobi (May 5, 1976): "The United States better than almost any nation could survive a period of economic warfare. We can resist confrontation and rhetorical attacks if other nations choose that path. And we can ignore unrealistic demands and preemptory [sic] demands." [10] Other First World leaders were equally uncooperative, though not so abrasive, at the 1979 UNCTAD conference in Manila, and at the 1980 conference of the UN Industrial Development Organization in New Delhi.

Meanwhile, reformers within the developed countries were active with plans for institutionalized assistance to the Third World. Barbara Ward proposed "a genuine system of international taxation" as a "fundamental expression of mutual obligation at the planetary level." Just as the progressive income tax has been a prerequisite in the evolution of modern nations, so it must be for "our small planet." Barbara Ward concluded: "Automatic transfers must come, or we shall live in an order of privilege and patronage. Such orders, as we know from history, simply do not last." [11] Likewise, Nobel laureate economist Jan Tinbergen of the Netherlands headed a team that prepared for the Club of Rome a report entitled *RIO: Reshaping the International Order*.[12] It noted the widening gap between rich and poor countries, and made various recommendations, including an "international solidarity tax" of 0.07 percent of the GNP of the rich countries. Tinbergen also recommended that multinational corporations should pay taxes into an international development fund.

Such proposed aid from the First World to the Third has failed to cope substantively with the problem of global economic inequity. In the first place, the amount of aid provided has proven inadequate. Frequently UN resolutions have called on the developed countries to increase the amount of their aid to 1 percent of their GNP, but very few have reached that figure, except for the newly rich oil-producing countries that have contributed an average of 2 percent of their GNPs. By contrast, the leading industrialized states were giving in 1980 less than 0.25 percent of their GNPs.

More important than the inadequacy of funds is the misallocation of what funds are available, because of faulty procedural principles. The Institute for Food and Development Policy has analyzed in various publications [13] how the aid projects of national and international agencies are essentially exercises in economics divorced from the political, social and cultural factors responsible for the poverty in the first place. In response to quantified poverty, outside experts prepare policy papers and allocate external resources designed to stimulate production of export crops. Taken for granted is the assumption that, in the words of a 1975 World Bank policy paper, "avoiding opposition from powerful and influential sections of the rural community is essential if the Bank's program is not to be subverted from within." This approach was underscored by World Bank President Robert McNamara when he stipulated that the bank's agricultural program "will put primary emphasis not on the redistribution of income and wealth—as necessary as they might be in many of our member countries—but rather on increasing the productivity of the poor thereby providing for a more equitable sharing of the benefits of growth." [14]

Despite the wishful thinking at the end of this statement, it boils down to depending on the efficacy of the "trickle down," which practical experience and theoretical studies have shown to result today in "trickle up." Joseph Collins and Frances Moore Lappé, of the Institute for Food and Development Policy, have concluded about the World Bank (and other aid agencies) that "intervening with funds for profit-generating investments, while opting to keep intact the social structures that generate poverty, only strengthens the grip of the elites. The result is that the poor are further impoverished—despite the bank's claim that it is helping the poor escape poverty." [15] Likewise President Carter's Commission on World Hunger recommended in March 1980 that the United States should increase its foreign aid and urge Third World elites to help "their poor." This means a continuation of policies that already have failed in the past. They have failed because the root cause of the poverty of Third World peasants is their powerlessness—their lack of power to alter the social structures responsible for their poverty. By buttressing these social structures directly (as in Chile and Guatemala) and indirectly (through national and international aid organizations), the United States has perpetuated rather than alleviated the "world hunger" investigated by the presidential commission.[16]

A final reason for the failure of aid programs to narrow the gap between rich nations and poor is that the allocation of aid has been determined less by the needs of the recipients and more by the political objectives of the contributors. This is contrary to official theory which, as early as the 1943 United Nations Relief and Rehabilitation Administration (UNRRA), stipulated that "no discrimination was to be made in distribution [of aid] for racial, religious or political reasons.[17] In practice, the monarchists in Greece and the Kuomintang in China were favored, while India was overlooked during the 1946–47 famine because that country was not viewed by Secretary of State Acheson as an anti-Communist front zone. Likewise under the Marshall Plan, vast quantities of grain were supplied on credit to France and Italy to keep those countries from going Communist. Marshall himself stated at the time: "Food is a vital factor in our foreign policy." This strategy has persisted to the present day, as noted above in Chapter 19, Section Vb. Thus foreign aid may be defined as the giving of tactical handouts to buttress a preferred status quo. Secretary of State Dean Rusk gave essentially this definition in testimony before Congress in March 1964, when he stated that the foreign aid program from its beginning in the 1940s was "planned and administered to serve the vital interests of the United States. . . . Our security would be in great jeopardy without the aid program." [18]

Cambridge University economist Joan Robinson summed it all up when she observed: "The aim of aid is to perpetuate the system that makes aid necessary." [19]

The above realities of life in the Third World today have led historian Geoffrey Barraclough to conclude: "The one thing that is clear at the moment . . . is that the liberal world economy as it existed for a quarter of a century after 1945 is on the way out." [20] It follows that the original question of "concessions" or structural changes" has been at least partially answered. Concessions do not work, for the simple reason that they are not forthcoming to any meaningful degree from the dominant vested interests in both the First World and the Third World. And understandably so, since the wealth and power of those interests depend on the preservation of the existing world order.

If "concessions" are not viable means for attaining the desired New

International Economic Order, then the question is whether "structural changes" offer a practical alternative. Can they solve the basic problem posed by Leontief—the need for the Third World countries to save 30 to 40 percent of their national incomes to achieve self-reliant development? Given the wretched poverty of the typical Third World village, it seems self-evident that capital accumulation on such a scale is out of the question. Yet that is not so, and the reason is that capital is something more than money in the bank. The grossly underutilized land and labor that is typical of most Third World villages represents potential capital. If the potentiality is realized, as was done most spectacularly in China after 1949, then there can be sudden and substantial accumulation of capital.

"Structural changes," however, are the prerequisite for bringing together land and labor, and transforming their potentiality into capital. In China, according to the researches of John Lossing Buck in the 1930s, rural idleness due to seasonal variations in work averaged 1.7 months per able-bodied man, or 14 percent of the year. Buck also found 9 percent of the arable land uncultivated because of tenure terms and social practices such as grave sites and boundaries between parcels. In addition, a large percentage of actual production was siphoned off and wasted on unproductive luxury expenditures by various parasitic elements. The siphoning off took the form of rent to landlords, interest to usurers, excessive payments to tax collectors, and extortion payoffs to bandits and warlords.[21]

After 1949 the Communists established communes not merely for ideological reasons, but also because they provided an institutional mechanism for realizing to a greater degree the potential of the land and labor resources, and for ending the millennia-old diversion of extracted surplus into nonproductive channels. The size of the communes made possible large, communal year-round projects, thus converting hitherto surplus manpower into capital in the form of wells, hydroelectric works, irrigation systems, reclaimed land and rural factories. Also, the greater availability of water, electricity and grain mills released women from time-consuming traditional chores for work on communal lands. The Tachai brigade was held up as the agricultural model for all China, precisely because a barren area in Shensi Province was made fruitful by a group of peasants who depended on their own collective efforts rather than on assistance from the outside. The end result was that the area of land cultivated in China in 1956 was 9.3 percent greater than the amount in 1933 (1.677 billion mou as against 1.533 billion mou) or almost equal to Buck's estimate of land underutilization in the 1930s. Also, Peter Schran has calculated that between 1952 and 1956 the total average number of workdays spent annually in agriculture increased by 40 percent, and production increased by 35 percent. Thus the net savings ratio in China rose from 1–2 percent in 1949 to 20 percent in 1953.[22]

Another example of capital accumulation and self-reliance in seemingly poverty-stricken villages is provided by the observations of anthropologist Kathleen Gough in southeastern India and in the Red River region of Vietnam.[23] In the Indian region of Thanjavur, three fourths of the land is owned by absentee landlords who extract half to three fourths of agricultural output for personal consumption and for investment outside of agriculture. In the Vietnamese region of Thai Binh, the land is cooperatively owned and worked, and 45 percent of the harvests and a good portion of the livestock products and craft goods are bought by the national distribution system. The money received, plus the remaining 55 percent of the crops, is divided among the villagers. Seventy percent goes for wages and running expenses, 20 percent is spent on engineering projects, machinery and fertilizer, and 10 percent on social welfare, including housing and medical care. Thus the value of what is produced is plowed back into village developments rather than diverted to personal luxury consumption and outside investment.

The contrasting use of human resources in the two regions is as striking as the contrasting use of land resources. In Thanjavur, 60 percent of the villagers are unemployed for at least half the year, and only 11 percent of the women are active in the labor force. In Thai Binh every able-bodied adult works a 40-hour week in the cooperative, in addition to maintaining a small family garden where extra vegetables, pigs and poultry are grown for home use or for market. If not needed in the communal fields, the peasants work in craft shops making mattresses, towels, carpets, mosquito nets, ceramics, tiles, ropes, furniture or clothing for local use or for sale to the government. Thanjavur's handicrafts, by contrast, have declined in the face of manufactured goods brought in from the outside. This accentuates the already serious underemployment, compelling marginal peasant families to give up and to join the urban unemployed.

Equally significant is the differential in technological efficiency between the two regions. A typical Thai Binh village uses 12 irrigation pumpsets to irrigate 300 acres, whereas a corresponding village in Thanjavur needs 18 pumpsets for 175 acres, or 50 percent more pumpsets for 42 percent less land. The explanation is that privately owned pumps in Thanjavur are located to irrigate only individual plots, so that Indian agronomists, according to Gough, found it difficult to move an embarkment or a channel "even one foot" because of need to obtain permission from several owners.

In Thai Binh *all* peasants collect every scrap of animal and human refuse for fertilizer. Also, they use bomb craters for fish breeding and for growing algae for fertilizer. Trees are planted to provide fuel, shelter for crops and green manure. The Thai Binh villages thus produce enough organic manure for 70 percent of their total fertilizer needs, whereas in Thanjavur costly chemical products have almost replaced organic manure, with certain deleterious side effects on crops, fish and animals. Similar technological differential is evident in stock raising, fish breeding and the manufacture and use of agricultural machinery such as rice mills, tractors, threshing machines and produce trucks. All these, according to Gough, "are more often locally made and are lighter, smaller, cheaper and more plentiful in Thai Binh than Thanjavur." [24]

The above analysis suggests that the prerequisite for independent economic development is not the availability of foreign capital and foreign technology. Otherwise, countries such as Nigeria, Iran, Indonesia and Venezuela, with their large earnings in petrodollars, should by now have become shining showcases. Rather, the prerequisite is "structural changes," or social restructuring designed to promote mass participation without which independent economic development is impossible. Mass participation in turn requires social equity, even though this proposition has been questioned in economic literature. It has often been assumed that inequitable income distribution is needed to support a wealthy minority that will invest its surplus and thereby stimulate economic growth. But the fact is that such a minority is more likely to spend capital for luxury consumption or for real estate and commercial ventures in the national capital or in foreign countries. Contrariwise, where small farmers are accorded equal access to irrigation, improved seeds, fertilizer, credit and technical guidance, they usually surpass the large farmers. In such circumstances they also save and invest at impressive rates when financial institutions are designed to meet their needs.

Experience has shown that mass participation and initiative must be genuine to yield results. A common failing has been that the alleged self-reliance is actually management from above. People then feel that they are working for the government—that they are clients rather than the motive force. Such manipulation from above has been at the root of the problem plaguing agriculture in countries as diverse as Sri Lanka, Tanzania and the Soviet Union.

Where self-reliance and mass involvement are genuine, then the way is clear to adopt the basic strategy of disengagement or decentralization or "Food First," to use the slogan popularized by the Institute for Food and Development Policy (IFDP). Food First means that the aim of agriculture in any given country should be not to maximize production of some export crop but to maximize production that will meet the nutritional needs of the local population. IFDP asserts: "There is no country in the world in which people could not feed themselves from their own resources." Whether or not they do so depends not on the numbers of people or the acres of land, but on who controls the land, and on what that land is used to produce.

Food First does not mean isolation but rather a set of priorities. Only after food production has been diversified and after people are feeding themselves is it possible for food exports to play a positive role. After basic needs are met—and this is the absolute prerequisite—then trade can become a means for further satisfying local needs rather than a means for meeting foreign demand at the expense of local needs. Food First is a strategy to ensure that trade does not become—as it is today in most of the Third World—a desperate hinge on which survival hangs, but rather that it is used as a way to widen choices after local basic needs have been met.

Concrete illustration of this basic point is offered by the contrasting cases of Cuba and the Dominican Republic. In Cuba, after the overthrow of the Batista regime by Castro, the revulsion against sugar monoculture was so strong that sugar production at first was cut back in favor of food crops. In 1969 the National Agrarian Reform Institute adopted a more balanced and practical policy, which stressed mechanization of sugar operations in order to free manpower for diversified agriculture and industry. Cuba today still remains the world's largest exporter of sugar, but at the same time nonsugar agricultural production increased by 38 percent between 1971 and 1975. In 1971 sugar harvesting was only 1 percent mechanized: by 1975 it was 25.8 percent mechanized. During the same period poultry output trebled, vegetable production doubled, fruit supplies rose by 60 percent, and the output of the fishing industry increased six times between 1959 and 1974. Per-capita food consumption rose 20 percent during the period 1971–75, while at the same time 40 percent of all cropland continues to grow sugar, which earns foreign exchange for needed imports. And the improved nutrition, together with a vigorous public health program, has raised the physical well-being of the Cuban people to a level far above that in any other Latin American country.

In the Dominican Republic, government policy has been the precise opposite, and so have been the social repercussions. In 1965 President Lyndon Johnson sent 22,000 U.S. Marines to prevent Juan Bosch from returning to the presidency and to ensure a reliably pro-American conservative regime. Joaquín Balaguer, who became President instead of Bosch, adopted tax and labor policies favorable to foreign corporations. Gulf + Western, originally an automotive-parts business in the U.S. Midwest, responded to the Dominican lure and bought in 1967 the South Puerto Rican Sugar Company. G + W rapidly extended its holdings and also signed up landowners to grow sugar for its mills. It now owns 9 percent of the country's land and has an interest in approximately

90 other island enterprises, including cattle ranches, luxury tourist hotels, vegetable and fruit production for export, and financial companies. These enterprises have enhanced G + W profits and holdings, if not the welfare of the Dominicans. The former one-line midwestern company now is a conglomerate that has expanded into movies (Paramount Pictures), candy (Schraffts), cigars (El Producto and Muriel), books (Simon & Schuster), sports (Madison Square Garden) and beauty queens (Miss Universe Pageant).

Meanwhile wages in the Dominican Republic are lower than in 1967, despite the intervening inflation. Thirty percent of Dominican workers are unemployed, three fourths of the population suffer from malnutrition, and infant mortality is over 30 percent, as against less than 3 percent in Cuba. A Consumer's Union study of Robert Ledogar concludes: "To the undernourished small farmers, subsistence farmers and landless laborers—who together comprise about 75 percent of the rural population—the endless vista of canefields looks like a great green plague slowly destroying their land." [25] The Minister of Finance, Bolívar Báez Ortiz, has defined another result of subordination to the international market economy. "In 1975 our sugar sales brought $550 million, and our oil purchases cost $50 million. In 1979 our sugar sales brought $225 million, and oil purchases cost $325 million." [26]

Such is the end result of food production to enhance corporate profit rather than to meet local needs. The alternative is first to achieve self-sufficiency in the basic staples of life. Then, and only then, will it be possible for Third World states to participate in world trade on terms that are equitable and mutually beneficial.

The proposition that social reconstruction is the first order of business for today's underdeveloped societies was emphasized in a recent statement by the distinguished Argentine economist Raúl Prebisch. Following World War II he won international recognition for publications in which he set forth his import-substitution strategy. This consisted of a variety of state measures designed to stimulate local industries to produce the manufactured goods hitherto imported. The strategy was widely adopted, and often it did increase local industrial productivity. Yet in a 1979 interview Prebisch acknowledged that the problem was primarily sociopolitical rather than economic. "We thought that an acceleration of the rate of growth would solve all problems. . . . This was our great mistake." Prebisch noted countries with thirty years of high GNP growth, but with 40 percent of their populations receiving no benefits. The reason, he explained, is that "we are resisting changes in the social structure," so that the beneficiary of economic growth is the "privileged consumption society." All development plans, he concluded, are bound to fail without "a complete social transformation." [27]

❧ IV. A Common Vision

The key Third World problem today is how to realize the basic "social transformation" called for by Prebisch. In essence it requires readjustment of power relationships, and the readjustment, if it is to be effective, must be across the board. It must be implemented not only within Third World countries but also in the relations between developed and underdeveloped countries. And this, in turn, requires that the readjustment be extended to power relationships within the developed countries of the First and Second Worlds.

Considering first the internal structures of Third World countries, India provides a revealing case because of the juxtaposition of economic growth and social misery, even under the auspices of successive reform-minded administrations (see Chapter 23, Section IIa). The anomaly has been analyzed in *Foreign Affairs* (January 1973) by Arun Shourie, economist at the International Bank for Reconstruction and Development and consultant for the Indian Planning Commission. He notes that much reform legislation and many welfare programs have been adopted by successive Indian governments, and yet poverty continues to grow. His explanation is crucial:

> The expectation has been that the pattern of land ownership and operation can be transformed by passing laws in national and state capitals, by relying on itinerant officers to implement them and by making the reforms justiciable. In brief, the expectation has been that outsiders—the distant legislator, the itinerant officer, the scholarly judge—can transform the most important feature of village life, the ownership and operation of land. But how are such men to monitor every lease, to examine the precise relationship between each sharecropper and his landlord, to ascertain the extent to which each landlord actually tills his own land? And how is a lowly tenant —who must continue to live in the village long after the officer has driven off; whose lease, in all probability, is an oral one; who is, most likely, illiterate, weak and indebted to his landlord—to gather written evidence, muster witnesses and accuse his landlord in an open court that passes all the western norms of justiciability?
>
> In a milieu of this kind—in which the poor are desperately poor, in which they are dispersed and unorganized—almost everything a government does ultimately ends up benefiting the rich and powerful more than the poor and the weak.

With the poor powerless and the wealthy powerful, Shourie demonstrates how government credit agencies end up giving credit to landlords, traders and moneylenders, how canals dug to provide water for all actually provide it only for the large and the strong, and how state trading corporations, designed to replace intermediary traders, in practice operate through these very traders. Thus Shourie, like Prebisch, concludes that the problem basically is political: ". . . the poor will not obtain a proportionate share in the benefits of growth until the character of growth is radically altered . . . this alteration can only be brought about as part of a major political transformation. . . ." Such a transformation, Shourie adds, would require Indira Gandhi to reverse her past course:

> . . . to transform her party into a party of the masses—a party that mobilizes the dispossessed so that they may acquire the self-confidence to assert their rights and the capacity to police the reforms, a party whose members work with the masses in constructive programs, a party that is no longer dependent on money raked in from the rich, a party whose dedication to the interests of the masses is proven by the life-styles and the social practice of its members. . . . the political leadership . . . must give up its present life-style—its insistence on living in luxury houses, on traveling in air-conditioned comfort, on receiving imported cars, telephone services, electricity and other amenities at rates far lower than are charged the people they are meant to represent and serve.

Such a transformation has not occurred, which explains India's current social and political ferment. This is the prevailing pattern in the Third World, with the resulting unrest taking many forms—from the electoral turmoil in India to armed insurrection in Central America, and many gradations in between.

Turning to power relationships between developed and underdeveloped countries, restructuring is as essential here in the global arena as within an Indian village. As noted in the preceding section, the need is for autonomous economic development involving a certain degree of withdrawal—a putting of distance between developing national economies and the global market economy. But economic autonomy has been opposed, both in the past and present, by those whose interests are imperiled. When Mohammad Ali in the early nineteenth century tried to make Egypt economically and militarily independent, Lord Palmerston fulminated against that "ignorant barbarian" and vowed to "chuck" him into the Nile—a threat that he figuratively fulfilled. Likewise, when President Allende introduced reforms in Chile that impinged on American corporate interests, President Nixon ordered: "Chile must be saved. . . . $100 million available, and more if necessary . . . make the economy scream. . . ." [28] The retribution of an American President proved to be more swift and lethal than that of a British Prime Minister.

The experiences of the Egypts and Chiles of the Third World demonstrate that Prebisch's call for a "complete social transformation" is as needed in the First and Second Worlds as it is in the Third, and not merely for the latter's sake. Meaningful self-determination is denied today to citizens of developed countries as well as underdeveloped ones. Manifestations of this fact are visible everywhere for those who have eyes to see.

• Rank-and-file Polish Communist Party activists demanded in April 1981 sweeping changes in their Party's structure, and removal of Politburo members whom they blamed for the nation's problems. "We need really popular leaders," declared one of the activists. "This is a 'we-them' society with the people and the Solidarity union classified as 'we' and the government and party as 'them.' The party must join the 'we' group." [29]

• Vladimir Klebanov, a forty-five-year-old former Ukrainian coalmine foreman, announced in Moscow in January 1978 the birth of the "Trade Union for the Defense of Workers"—the first independent trade union in Soviet history. Klebanov voiced numerous worker grievances, including violations of safety regulations in factories, firings without cause, low pay and corrupt supervisors. "We can't do anything about injustices individually," declared Klebanov, "we have to work together." [30] The union members were not able to "work together" for long. In February 1978 the leading members were arrested by police and put under psychiatric detention in their hometowns.

• The New York *Times* of January 3, 1980, carried a poignant report from the Bolivian mining town of Milluni, describing how the combination of silicosis, accidents and poor living conditions allow few of the local citizens to grow old. When twenty-five-year-old José Acho was asked whether he knew that current projections on the life-span of miners left him with only seven more years, he replied simply: "Yes, but I have to work." One month earlier, on December 3, 1979, the New York *Times* carried a similar dispatch from Gouverneur in northern New York State, where local miners are contracting "white lung disease" from digging out asbestoslike talc. Although their parents and friends are suffocating from the disease, the region's young men still report for work. Unemployment in the area is 14 percent, and "there is nowhere else to go."

• Standard operating procedure for multinational corporations in the Third World is continually to move plants to take advantage of the lowest available wage rates. Hence the successive shifts from Mexico to Haiti, from Hong Kong to Malaysia and from Singapore to Indonesia. Similar transplanting of factories without regard for the effect on local communities occurs in the United States. Executives usually explain that the closed plants have ceased to be profitable. But a Cornell University study disclosed that many profitable plants are closed because they do not meet targets of return specified by conglomerate officials. Chicopee Manufacturing Company of central Massachusetts yielded a 12 percent rate of return on its apparel products. But the parent firm, the pharmaceutical Johnson & Johnson Company, would not accept anything below 16 percent, and therefore shut down Chicopee. Uniroyal closed its eighty-seven-year-old inner-tube factory in Indianapolis in 1978 for the same reason. A Wall Street analyst gave the following explanation: "You have one very large entity looking at a very small entity, but the small entity being very large to those people that work there. I think it's a truism that many companies have grown too big to look at the small market." [31]

• The pesticide industry has been growing explosively, now producing 4 billion pounds yearly, or one pound for every person on earth. The United States leads in this industry, and 20 percent of its output goes to Third World countries. At least one quarter of these American exports are of pesticides that are heavily restricted, or have never been registered for use in the United States. The effect is lethal in the Third World, where lack of regulations, illiteracy and repressive working conditions can turn even a "safe" pesticide into a time bomb. Since Third World agribusiness increasingly is producing for export to the United States, an estimated 10 percent of imported food consumed by Americans is contaminated. Nor is it a case of pesticides increasing food supplies for Third World poor, as the pesticides are used mostly on the profitable export crops. The most detailed study of this worldwide problem, by David Weir and Mark Schapiro, reaches a conclusion of significance for both the developed and underdeveloped countries:

> The differences in our material standards of living too often obscure our similarities—a common powerlessness in facing the increasing concentration of private power in the hands of a relatively few global companies. The reality of global corporate power, here reflected in the pesticide trade, forces us to seek solutions involving new ways of working with Third World people for a worldwide redistribution of economic power. We must begin to see Third World people not as a burden or a threat but as allies.[32]

The above statement points up the inescapable and crucial conclusion disclosed by Third World history: that the problem we face is not only the underdevelopment of the Third World, but also the overdevelopment or maldevelopment of the First World, and that the two are interrelated and interactive. The characteristics of underdeveloped societies are well known, but there is less awareness of the parallel existence of overdeveloped societies. Their pathological symptoms have been masked by what Kenneth Boulding has termed "cowboy economics." [33] The leaders of the overdeveloped societies have assumed that their natural resource base is a limitless frontier that can be exploited indefinitely to support ever-rising living standards.

The basic problem today is that the frontier is contracting rather than expanding, as indicated by the persistent "stagflation." Limitless expansion has been fettered by resource depletion, by environment degradation and by increasing Third World resistance that is debilitating rather than sustaining metropolitan centers. At one time, colonies could be counted on to provide cheap raw materials, protected markets and investment preserves. Now there are the ex-colonies, requiring economic aid and even military intervention, which can prove to be financially and politically disastrous, as France and the United States discovered in Indochina, and which may well be repeated in fragile regions such as the Middle East and southern Africa.

The worldwide crisis was the subject of a symposium organized under UN auspices by the International Foundation for Development Alternatives and held in Holland in July 1979. The symposium agreed that a new development strategy is needed, and that it must encompass the maldeveloped First World as well as the underdeveloped Third World. The maldevelopment of the First World was defined as "waste of resources, degradation of the environment, institutionalized consumerism, total dependence on external sources of life support, growing unemployment and recession, persistence of substantial pockets of poverty and a deep crisis of values and cultural identity." The symposium characterized these symptoms as rooted in societal organization and requiring "structural remedies."

> There is a crisis in the North, which is no less basic than that in the South. Therefore the new development strategy should be a global strategy which is addressed to the South, the North and the institutions and processes that relate the two. The strategy should encompass what is basically wrong with the North, as with the South, as well as the relationship between the maldevelopment in the North and the inadequate, unjust and unbalanced development patterns in the South—phenomena which incidentally provide the context for the universal revolt of the younger generation and its alienation, cutting across both North and South. The new development strategy must relate itself to this large global context of structural and cultural change.[34]

More specifically, the symposium defined the components of a new common vision for the restructuring of both North and South. "Without decentralization and participation of large sections of the people and of suppressed and exploited regions of the world, it is not going to be possible to restructure the socio-economic order; this is basically a political task."

What are the prospects for acceptance and implementation of this common vision based on decentralization and mass participation? First it should be noted that the two precepts ring true historically. The "modern" societies of each historical period have been those that led the way in raising the level of mass involvement to a new plateau. Such quantum jumps constituted the modernity of these pioneering societies, providing them with qualitatively superior social cohesion and dynamism, and thereby enabling them in every case to prevail over all other contemporary societies and to stamp their imprint on their times.

Such a quantum leap into "modernity" explains Alexander the Great's triumphal procession from the Aegean to the Punjab, toppling over kingdoms and empires despite their enormous superiority in manpower. It explains also the Spanish Conquistadors' conquest of the Aztec and Inca empires, and later the conquest of the Mogul Indian Empire by a handful of British merchants. In both cases, the European soldiers and merchants were able against overwhelming odds both to conquer and to hold and administer vast territories—and more because of social than technological superiority.

Likewise today, the "modern" societies that will leave their imprint on our era will be those that most effectively satisfy the current participatory impulse. Few will be so bold as to attempt to identify those societies. We live in an era in which John Kenneth Galbraith asks, "Why in the world do we need economists in these [stagflation] circumstances?" [35] and in which Paul Sweezy, the dean of American Marxists, writes of the "Crisis in Marxian theory." [36] Even in less turbulent times, the foresight of both politicians and academicians has been conspicuous by its absence. How many anticipated such historic turning points of the past half century as the Great Depression, the Hitler-Stalin Pact, the post-World War II dismantling of empires, the Soviet-Yugoslav and Soviet-Chinese schisms and the current stagflation in the capitalist world and stagnation in the socialist?

Yet if past patterns do not yield crystal balls, they can serve as signposts indicating the contours and general characteristics of what lies ahead. The "creativity" that Hans Morgenthau called for in the face of revolution can be attained only through global restructuring on the basis of the two principles of decentralization and mass participation set forth by the UN symposium in Holland. A world order based on those principles will represent a shift in the direction of the decentralized world of the pre-da Gama era. During the millennia prior to 1500, human communities had existed in regional isolation. The Australian aborigines and the American Indians were completely unknown to the rest of humankind, the Africans were almost as unknown except for those in a few coastal areas and even the peoples of Eurasia had only tenuous and sporadic contact with each other. Obviously a return to such regional isolation is out of the question. But quite likely, as well as desirable, is a shift from today's highly integrated world to one of regional autonomy. In contrast to the isolation of early times, and to the inequitable integration of unequals today, regional autonomy would involve the voluntary participation of autonomous components, on equal terms and for mutual benefit. The prerequisite for such a global restructuring is a comparable restructuring of national units. Their economies would be oriented toward internal rather than external markets. Adequate internal markets would necessitate increased incomes for the masses, and these being at present predominantly peasants, agrarian structures necessarily would be transformed.

Multinational corporations would be less prominent in such a decentralized world than they are today. But that could prove a blessing, for who is it who gains when Massachusetts imports 85 percent of its food, a tenth of it from California 3,000 miles away. As recently as 1900, over 50 percent of the food eaten in the United States was grown within 50 miles of where it was consumed, and today, 80 percent of the vegetables consumed in each Chinese city are grown within 6 miles of that urban area. Conventional wisdom would have it that these statistics reflect the underdevelopment of the United States in 1900 and of China today. But for a country plagued by soaring energy costs, it surely is a case of *over*-development that the average chicken today travels 1,200 miles to reach the table of the American consumer.

Looking beyond national borders, who is it who gains when American farms produce huge grain crops for export to Third World countries, whose peasants no longer can grow their own food and instead work to satisfy foreign cashew-nut munchers and pet-food purchasers? This topsy-turvy world food scene is now the scourge of a large part of the human race and warrants more attention.

In the early 1970s the U.S. government was faced with surplus food supplies and mounting trade deficits, especially after the OPEC oil crisis. It was decided to stimulate food exports to balance the trade deficits. The strategy seemed unquestionable, but it proved definitely not so in its repercussions. The drive for increased agricultural output led to a corresponding increase in cultivated acreage, much of it including land highly susceptible to erosion. In Iowa, according to the Institute for Food and Development Policy, farmers are losing two bushels of topsoil for every bushel of corn they harvest—a rate of loss that will deplete all the topsoil of that fertile state in less than a century. Likewise, groundwater levels are dropping so rapidly that existing irrigation systems in many states will become useless within a few years. At the same time, agribusiness corporations are squeezing out moderate-sized farms, which are at least as efficient food producers but which are penalized by government policies.

Repercussions in the Third World have been equally harmful. Subsidized imports of American grains undercut local production of traditional foodstuffs. The best soils are taken over for capital-intensive agribusiness operations devoted to cash crops for Western markets. Displaced peasants end up in nearby cities or in foreign countries. Mexico is typical, with its simultaneous export of winter fruits and vegetables for American consumers and surplus labor for American fields and factories.

Since U.S. oil imports and the resulting trade deficits are important factors in these global dysfunctions, a simple way out is suggested by two studies completed in 1981 of the American energy situation. The first was conducted for the U.S. Department of Energy by the Solar Research Institute in Golden, Colorado. The study concluded that heavy investments to promote energy efficiency and the use of renewable resources could reduce American energy consumption 25 percent by the end of the century, and thus eliminate the need for any oil imports. The second study, by the Energy Productivity Center of the Carnegie Mellon University in Pittsburgh, reached the same conclusion. Energy conservation measures could reduce expenditures for foreign oil from about $80 billion in 1980 to an average of $15 billion annually in the 1990s to zero expenditures after the year 2000.[37]

Despite the findings of these two reports, the Department of Energy announced in March 1981 that it was preparing legislation to eliminate or drastically curtail all programs to encourage energy conservation and to develop renewable fuel sources and other alternatives to oil. The list of federal programs affected by the proposed legislation includes: solar energy research and development, wind energy and ocean thermal development, research on electric vehicles and methane-fueled transport, residential energy efficiency, energy conservation for commercial buildings, consumer education on energy conservation, small-scale hydroelectric projects and energy audits by public utilities.

If the proposed Energy Department legislation is passed and implemented, the consequences are self-evident: continued unprecedented profits for the multinational oil companies currently supplying U.S. oil needs; continued unprecedented profits for the five multinational grain corporations now controlling 80 percent of the world's grain trade; and continued U.S. dependence on foreign oil, especially from the Persian Gulf region.

Little imagination is needed to extend this scenario further. The Persian Gulf states are notoriously fragile. This was demonstrated in November 1979, when Mecca's Grand Mosque was seized by a local Islamic fundamentalist group that rejected the Saudi dynasty for having betrayed Islam "in the pursuit of worldly things." A Saudi ambassador with more than twenty years in the diplomatic service observed that the uprising was long overdue, that "there is a spreading feeling of unrest and impatience with the uneven injustice," that "the people in Mecca were asking for a change in the ruling system," and that "this movement is much bigger than its leadership suggests." [38] The ambassador's views were shared by the CIA. In January 1980 a CIA analyst called in two reporters from *Newsweek* and the Washington *Star* to confirm that the agency had warned the Carter administration that the survival of the Saudi regime "could not be assured beyond the next two years." [39]

Should the CIA warning prove justified, Washington doubtless would use its naval units in surrounding waters and bases, and dispatch its Rapid Deployment Forces now being strengthened for precisely such contingencies. But half the workers in the Saudi oilfields are Shiites who have staged repeated violent demonstrations in support of Ayatollah Khomeini. Two army officers who worked in the White House, Major Daniel W. Christman and Major Wesley K. Clark, concluded in a study entitled "Foreign Energy Sources and Military Power," that "U.S. military forces will be ineffective in coercing petroleum-producing states to respond to America's wishes." [40] Instead, the outcome could be the disruption of oil operations in the Persian Gulf, with repercussions far surpassing those of Vietnam, and affecting Western Europe and Japan as well as the United States.

The end result of this far-from-fanciful scenario is, at best, an economic catastrophe comparable to that of the 1930s and, at worst, a confrontation with the Soviet Union and a new Sarajevo whose casualties would be infinitely greater than those of the Romanoff, Hapsburg, Hohenzollern and Ottoman empires. If this be considered unduly alarmist, consider the following exchange between Senator Claiborne Pell and Secretary Alexander Haig during the latter's confirmation hearings. "Have you believed, at any time since the inception of the hostage crisis in Iran, that the use of tactical nuclear weapons might be a viable option?" Haig replied: "Well, I think the very act of definitizing an answer to this question undercuts the fundamental deterrent upon which our peace and security rest today. And I'm not going to indulge in it." [41] Haig's answer raises another question: whether the Vietnam tactic of "destroy the village in order to save it" has been extended into global strategy.

The world of the late twentieth century can ill afford superpower *realpolitik* that ends up as crackpot realism. The need is to recognize and to address the interdependent problems of overdevelopment as well as underdevelopment. And this requires a common vision relevant to the unprecedented peril and unprecedented promise now confronting all humanity.

Notes

A Note from the Author

1. Cited by D. Moberg, "Labor's Strategies for the Future," *In These Times* (Jan. 30–Feb. 5, 1980), p. 2.
2. Los Angeles *Times* (Oct. 19, 1980).
3. Ibid. (Sept. 25, 1980).
4. New York *Times* (July 13, 1978).
5. Cited in column by William Raspberry, in Los Angeles *Times* (Jan. 4, 1977).
6. K. B. Clark, *Dark Ghetto* (New York: Harper & Row, 1965), p. 28.
7. Los Angeles *Times* (Nov. 27, 1974).
8. Cited by Washington *Spectator* (Sept. 1, 1980).

Part One

Chapter 1

1. G. Chaliand, *Revolution in the Third World* (New York: Viking Press, 1977), p. 12. Emphasis in original.
2. W. L. Langer, *Diplomacy of Imperialism, 1890–1902*, 2nd ed. (New York: Alfred A. Knopf, 1935), p. 67.
3. H. S. Maine, *Village-Communities in the East and West* (New York: Henry Holt, 1880), pp. 237, 238.
4. J. Schumpeter, *The Theory of Economic Development* (Cambridge, Mass.: Harvard University Press, 1949), p. 63.
5. G. Myrdal, *Rich Lands and Poor* (New York: Harper & Brothers, 1957), p. 26.
6. New York *Times* (January 10, 1981).

Chapter 2

1. Cited by C. M. Cipolla, *Before the Industrial Revolution* (New York: W. W. Norton, 1976), p. 209.
2. E. Hobsbawm, "From Feudalism to Capitalism" in R. Hilton, ed., *The Transition from Feudalism to Capitalism* (London: NLB, 1976), p. 162.
3. R. H. Bautier, *The Economic Development of Medieval Europe* (New York: Harcourt Brace Jovanovich, 1971), p. 228.
4. Cited by H. Pfeffermann, *Die Zusammenarbeit der Renaissancepäpste mit den Türken* (Winterthur, Switzerland, 1946), p. 14.
5. Cited in *Encyclopaedia of Islam*, Vol. III, p. 1187.
6. Cited by J. Needham, *Science and Civilization in China*, Vol. 4, Pt. III: *Civil Engineering and Nautics* (New York: Cambridge University Press, 1971), p. 533.
7. Ibid., p. 534.
8. A. Smith, *The Wealth of Nations* (New York: Everyman's Library, 1910), Vol. I, pp. 393–94; Vol. II, pp. 121–22.
9. Ibid., Vol. I, p. 394; Vol. II, pp. 121–22.
10. B. Spencer, *Native Tribes of the Northern Territory of Australia* (New York: Macmillan, 1914), p. 36.
11. Lewis Morgan, *Houses and House-Life of the American Aborigines* (New York, 1881), p. 45.
12. Cited by C. S. Coon, *A Reader in General Anthropology* (New York: Henry Holt, 1940), pp. 65, 77, 78.
13. F. Boas, "Racial Purity," *Asia* XL (May 1940):231.
14. New York *Times* (Jan. 22, 1980, and Oct. 18, 1980).
15. V. Gordon Childe, *Man Makes Himself* (New York: Mentor Books, 1951), p. 149.
16. S. Avineri, ed., *Karl Marx on Colonialism and Modernization* (Garden City, N.Y.: Anchor Books, 1969), pp. 89, 94.
17. Ibid., p. 90.

Chapter 3

1. M. M. Postan, *Eastern and Western Europe in the Middle Ages* (New York: Harcourt Brace Jovanovich, 1970), p. 127.
2. J. Blum, "The Rise of Serfdom in Eastern Europe," *American Historical Review* LXII (July 1957):826.
3. I. Wallerstein, "Three Paths of National Development in Sixteenth-century Europe," *Studies in Comparative International Development* VII (Summer 1972):98.
4. S. P. Pach, "Favourable and Unfavourable Conditions for Capitalist Growth: The Shift of International Trade Routes in the 15th to 17th Centuries," *Fourth International Conference of Economic History* (1968), p. 68.

5. P. I. Lyashchenko, *History of the National Economy of Russia to the 1917 Revolution* (New York: Macmillan, 1949), p. 227.
6. Cited by J. Blum, *Lord and Peasant in Russia* (Princeton, N.J.: Princeton University Press, 1961), p. 129.
7. Cited by L. J. Olivea, *Russia in the Era of Peter the Great* (Englewood Cliffs, N.J.: Prentice-Hall, 1969), p. 115.
8. W. L. Blackwell, *Beginnings of Russian Industrialization* (Princeton, N.J.: Princeton University Press, 1968), pp. 37–38.

Chapter 4

1. Los Angeles *Times* (Oct. 31, 1974).
2. H. Konig, *Columbus: His Enterprise* (New York: Monthly Review Press, 1976), p. 53.
3. Cited by A. W. Crosby, Jr., *The Columbian Exchange: Biological and Cultural Consequences of 1492* (Westport, Conn.: Greenwood, 1972), p. 57.
4. Cited ibid., p. 41.
5. M. Leon-Portilla, ed., *The Broken Spears: The Aztec Account of the Conquest of Mexico* (Boston: Beacon Press, 1969), p. 64.
6. Cited by L. Hanke, *The Spanish Struggle for Justice in the Conquest of America* (Philadelphia: University of Pennsylvania Press, 1949), pp. 1–13.
7. Cited ibid., p. 8.
8. Cited by N. Wachtel, *The Vision of the Vanquished* (New York: Barnes & Noble, 1977), p. 154.
9. Ibid., pp. 31, 32.
10. *The Broken Spears*, pp. 137–38.
11. Cited by A. G. Frank, *Lumpenbourgeoisie, Lumpendevelopment* (New York: Monthly Review Press, 1972), p. 24.
12. Instructions to Governor Murray (Dec. 7, 1763), in W. P. M. Kennedy, ed., *Statutes, Treaties and Documents of the Canadian Constitution 1713–1929* (London: Oxford University Press, 1930), pp. 421–22.
13. E. D. Genovese, *The World the Slaveholders Made* (New York: Pantheon Books, 1969), pp. 57, 58.
14. Cited by J. C. Vives, "The Decline of Spain in the Seventeenth Century," in C. M. Cipolla, ed., *The Economic Decline of Empires* (New York: Methuen, 1970), p. 144.
15. Cited in *New Cambridge Modern History* (Cambridge: Cambridge University Press, 1957), Vol. I, p. 454.
16. Cited by S. Sideri, *Trade and Power: Informal Colonialism in Anglo-Portuguese Relations* (Rotterdam: Rotterdam University Press, 1970), p. 21.
17. *Sugar and Society in the Caribbean: An Economic History of Cuban Agriculture* (New Haven, Conn.: Yale University Press, 1964), p. 86.
18. David Macpherson, *Annals of Commerce* (London, 1805), Vol. III, p. 568.

19. Cited by R. Davis, *The Rise of the Atlantic Economies* (London: George Weidenfeld & Nicolson, 1973), p. 43.

20. Cited by Salvador de Madariaga, *The Rise of the Spanish American Empire* (New York: Macmillan, 1947), pp. 90–91.

21. Cited in *The Cambridge History of the British Empire* (Cambridge: Cambridge University Press, 1960), Vol. I, p. 437.

22. R. B. Sheridan, *Sugar and Slavery: An Economic History of the British West Indies, 1623–1775* (Baltimore, Md.: Johns Hopkins University Press, 1974), p. 475.

23. Cited by J. B. Williams, *British Commercial Policy and Trade Expansion 1750–1850* (London: Oxford University Press, 1972), pp. 9–10.

24. Ibid., p. 7.

25. W. Cunningham, *The Growth of English Industry and Commerce* (Cambridge: Cambridge University Press, 1925), p. 342.

Chapter 5

1. Cited by J. H. Plumb, "The Niger Quest," *History Today* II (Apr. 1952):247.

2. P. Bohannan, *Africa and Africans* (New York: Natural History Press, 1964), pp. 67, 68.

3. Cited by C. M. Cipolla, *European Culture and Overseas Expansion* (Harmondsworth, Middlesex: Pelican Books, 1970), p. 105.

4. Cited by B. Davidson, *The African Slave Trade* (Boston: Little, Brown, 1961), p. 10.

5. Cited by K. O. Dike, *Trade and Politics in the Niger Delta 1830–1885* (New York: Oxford University Press, 1956), p. 7.

6. Cited by Davidson, op. cit., p. 10.

7. P. D. Curtin, *The Atlantic Slave Trade: A Census* (Madison: University of Wisconsin Press, 1969), p. 87.

8. R. Anstey, *The Atlantic Slave Trade and British Abolition, 1760–1810* (London: Macmillan, 1975); J. E. Inikori, "Measuring the Atlantic Slave Trade: An Assessment of Curtin and Anstey," *Journal of African History* XVII (1976):197–223; "Discussion: Measuring the Atlantic Slave Trade," *Journal of African History* XVII (1976):595–627; and E. Reynolds, *Stand the Storm: African Slavery and the Slave Trade* (London: Oxford University Press, forthcoming), Ch. XII. This chapter estimates that over a period of thirteen centuries, the trans-Saharan and East African slave traders bled Africa to the tune of another 14 million persons.

9. *The Life of Olaudah Equano, or Gustavus Vassa, Written by Himself* (Boston: Beacon Press, 1969), pp. 27–32.

10. Cited by H. Russell, *Human Cargoes* (London: Longman, 1948), p. 36.

11. Cited by Davidson, op. cit., pp. 147, 148. Emphasis in the original.

12. P. D. Curtin, "The Slave Trade and the Atlantic: Intercontinental Perspectives," in N. Huggins et al., eds., *Key Issues in the Afro-*

American Experience (New York: Harcourt Brace Jovanovich, 1971), Vol. I, p. 89.

13. Davidson, op. cit., p. 172.
14. Cited by R. M. Beachey, *The Slave Trade of Eastern Africa* (London: Rex Collings, 1976), p. 186.
15. Ibid., p. 95.
16. Cited by T. Jeal, *Livingstone* (London: William Heinemann, 1977), p. 304.
17. Cited by E. A. Alpers, *The East African Slave Trade* [Historical Association of Tanzania Paper, No. 3] (Nairobi: East African Publishing House, 1967), p. 19.
18. E. A. Alpers, *Ivory and Slaves: Changing Patterns of International Trade in East Central Africa to the Later Nineteenth Century* (Berkeley: University of California Press, 1975), pp. 266, 267.
19. Reynolds, op. cit.
20. E. Reynolds, *Trade and Economic Change on the Gold Coast 1807–1874* (London: Longman, 1974), p. 13.
21. Cited by W. Rodney, *How Europe Underdeveloped Africa* (Washington, D.C.: Howard University Press, 1974), p. 107.
22. Ibid., p. 108.
23. Cited by A. Adu Boahen, *Topics in West African History* (London: Longman, 1966), p. 113.
24. M. Postlethwayt, *The African Trade* (1745), cited by Rodney, op. cit., p. 75.

Chapter 6

1. Cited by H. Inalcik, *The Ottoman Empire: The Classical Age 1300–1600* (New York: Praeger, 1973), p. 41.
2. C. T. Forster and F. H. B. Daniell, eds., *The Life and Letters of Ogier Ghiselin de Busbecq* (London, 1881), pp. 221–22.
3. Cited by Mehmed Pasha, *Ottoman Statecraft: The Book of Counsel for Vezirs and Governors*, ed. and tr. by W. L. Wright (Princeton, N.J.: Princeton University Press, 1935), p. 21.
4. Cited by N. Steensgaard, *The Asian Trade Revolution of the Seventeenth Century* (Chicago: University of Chicago Press, 1974), p. 75.
5. Cited by Inalcik, op. cit., p. 46.
6. Cited by Steensgaard, loc. cit.
7. Cited by E. Kuran, "The Impact of Nationalism on the Turkish Elite in the Nineteenth Century," in W. R. Polk and R. L. Chambers, eds., *Beginnings of Modernization in the Middle East* (Chicago: University of Chicago Press, 1968), p. 109.
8. E. D. Clarke, *Travels in Various Countries of Europe, Asia and Africa* (Cambridge, England, 1810), Vol. I, pp. 689–91.
9. Cited by Inalcik, op. cit., p. 49.
10. O. L. Barkan, "The Price Revolution of the Sixteenth Century: A

Turning Point in the Economic History of the Near East," *International Journal of Middle East Studies* VI (1975):7.
11. Cited by Steensgaard, op. cit., p. 79.
12. B. Braude, "International Competition and Domestic Cloth in the Ottoman Empire, 1500–1650: A Study in Underdevelopment," *Review* II (Winter 1979):442–51.
13. Barkan, op. cit., pp. 5, 7.
14. C. F. Volney, *Travels Through Syria and Egypt* (London, 1787), Vol. II, p. 431.
15. Cited by *Encyclopaedia of Islam*, Vol. III, p. 1187.

Chapter 7

1. Cited by G. B. Sansom, *The Western World and Japan* (New York: Alfred A. Knopf, 1950), p. 91.
2. Cited by M. N. Pearson, *Merchants and Rulers in Gujarat* (Berkeley: University of California Press, 1976), p. 91.
3. Cited ibid., p. 31, fn. 3.
4. Cited by Pearson, op. cit., p. 96.
5. Cited by K. M. Panikkar, *Asia and Western Dominance* (New York: John Day, 1953), p. 42.
6. Ibid.
7. Cited by J. B. Harrison, "Europe and Asia," *The New Cambridge Modern History* (Cambridge: Cambridge University Press, 1970), Vol. IV, p. 646.
8. Cited by Pearson, op. cit., p. 40.
9. Cited ibid., p. 173.
10. Ibid., pp. 7, 10.
11. Cited ibid., p. 115.
12. Cited by Panikkar, op. cit., p. 111.
13. Cited by R. Pearson, *Eastern Interlude: A Social History of the European Community in Calcutta* (Calcutta: Thacker, 1954), p. 64.
14. Cited by G. F. Hudson, *Europe & China* (Boston: Beacon Press, 1961), p. 234.
15. B. H. M. Vlekke, *Nusantara: A History of the East Indian Archipelago* (Cambridge, Mass.: Harvard University Press, 1943), p. 198.
16. Cited by F. Whyte, *China and Foreign Powers* (London: Oxford University Press, 1927), p. 38.

Part Two

Chapter 8

1. Cited by F. Whyte, *China and Foreign Powers* (London: Oxford University Press, 1927), p. 38.
2. E. Mandel, *Marxist Economic Theory* (London: Merlin Press, 1962), Vol. II, p. 445.
3. R. B. Sheridan, *Sugar and Slavery: An Economic History of the Brit-*

ish West Indies, 1623–1775 (Baltimore: Johns Hopkins University Press, 1974), p. 475.

4. C. M. Cipolla, *European Culture and Overseas Expansion* (Harmondsworth, Middlesex: Penguin Books, 1970), p. 108.

5. Cited by T. M. Devine, *The Tobacco Lords* (Edinburgh: John Donald, 1975), p. 34.

6. A. K. Bagchi, "Some International Foundations of Capitalist Growth and Underdevelopment," *Economic and Political Weekly* (Aug. 1972): 1561.

7. L. H. Jenks, *The Migration of British Capital to 1875*, cited by Bagchi, ibid.: 1563.

8. W. Lippmann, *Preface to Morals* (New York: Macmillan, 1929), p. 235.

9. Cited by S. Zavala, "The Frontiers of Hispanic America," in *The Frontier in Perspective*, ed. W. D. Wyman and C. B. Kroeber (Madison: University of Wisconsin Press, 1957), p. 40.

10. Cited by B. Porter, *The Lion's Share: A Short History of British Imperialism 1850–1970* (London: Longman, 1975), p. 6.

11. Cited by L. C. A. Knowles, *The Industrial and Commercial Revolution in Britain During the Nineteenth Century* (London: Routledge & Kegan Paul, 1921), p. 128.

12. Cited by B. Semmel, *The Rise of Free Trade Imperialism* (Cambridge: Cambridge University Press, 1970), p. 8.

13. Hansard, Third Series, CXXIV, 1036 (Mar. 3, 1853). Cited by F. Clairmonte, *Economic Liberalism and Underdevelopment* (London: Asia Publishing House, 1960), p. 21.

14. J. Gallagher and R. Robinson, "The Imperialism of Free Trade," *Economic History Review* VI (1953):1–15.

Chapter 9

1. Cited by F. Clairmonte, *Economic Liberalism and Underdevelopment* (London: Asia Publishing House, 1960), p. 27.

2. Ibid., p. 26.

3. Ibid., p. 31.

4. Cited by A. G. Frank, *Lumpenbourgeoisie, Lumpendevelopment* (New York: Monthly Review Press, 1972), p. 59.

5. Cited by H. S. Ferns, *Britain and Argentina in the Nineteenth Century* (Oxford: Clarendon Press, 1960), pp. 79–80.

6. Cited by Frank, op. cit., p. 57.

7. R. Graham, *Britain and the Onset of Modernization in Brazil 1850–1914* (Cambridge: Cambridge University Press, 1968), p. 68.

8. Cited by S. J. Stein and B. H. Stein, *The Colonial Heritage of Latin America* (London: Oxford University Press, 1970), p. 151.

9. Ibid., p. 86.

10. Cited by Graham, op. cit., p. 16.

11. Ibid., p. 16.

12. G. L. Beckford, *Persistent Poverty* (London: Oxford University Press, 1972), p. 208.
13. B. R. Wolf and E. C. Hansen, *The Human Condition in Latin America* (London: Oxford University Press, 1972), p. 198.
14. C. Degler, *Neither White nor Black* (New York: Macmillan, 1971).
15. D. B. Davis, *The Problem of Slavery in Western Culture* (Ithaca, N.Y.: Cornell University Press, 1966), p. 229.

Chapter 10

1. K. Onwuka Dike, *Trade and Politics in the Niger Delta 1830–1885* (Oxford: Clarendon Press, 1956), p. 12.
2. J. Corry, *Observations upon the Windward Coast* (London, 1807), p. 127, cited ibid., p. 15.
3. Cited by T. W. Wallbank, *Contemporary Africa* (Princeton, N.J.: D. Van Nostrand, 1956), p. 25.
4. J. H. Plumb, "The Niger Quest," *History Today* II (Apr. 1952):247.
5. *The Zambesi Doctors: David Livingstone's Letters to John Kirk, 1858–1872*, ed. R. Foskett (Edinburgh: Edinburgh University Press, 1964), p. 45.
6. Cited by E. Reynolds, *Trade and Economic Change on the Gold Coast, 1807–1874* (London: Longman, 1974), p. 119.
7. Cited by Dike, op. cit., p. 103.
8. Ibid., pp. 215, 216.
9. Ibid., pp. 113, 114.
10. Cited by Reynolds, op. cit., p. 167.

Chapter 11

1. Cited by A. C. Wood, *A History of the Levant Company* (London: Oxford University Press, 1935), p. 230.
2. Cited by W. Eton, *A Survey of the Turkish Empire . . .* (London, 1809), p. 109.
3. Cited by E. C. Clark, "The Ottoman Industrial Revolution," *International Journal of Middle East Studies* V (1974):68.
4. O. Köymen, "The Advent and Consequences of Free Trade in the Ottoman Empire," *Études balkaniques* 2 (1971):53.
5. Cited by D. Chevallier, "Western Development and Eastern Crisis in the Mid-Nineteenth Century: Syria Confronted with the European Economy," in W. R. Polk and R. L. Chambers, eds., *Beginnings of Modernization in the Middle East* (Chicago: University of Chicago Press, 1968), p. 218.
6. M. A. Ubicini, *Letters on Turkey* (London, 1856), Vol. II, pp. 339–44.
7. N. W. Senior, *A Journal Kept in Turkey and Greece* (London, 1859), p. 84.
8. C. Loiseau, *Le Balkan slave et la crise autrichienne* (Paris, 1888), pp. 275–76.

9. R. Mabro and S. Radwan, *The Industrialization of Egypt 1939–1973* (Oxford: Clarendon Press, 1976), p. 16.

10. Cited by G. el-Din el-Shayyal, "Historiography in Egypt in the Nineteenth Century," in B. Lewis and P. M. Holt, eds., *Historians of the Middle East* (London: Oxford University Press, 1962), p. 410.

11. Cited by A. Abdel-Meguid, "The Impact of Western Culture and Civilization on the Arab World," *Islamic Quarterly* II (December 1955):289.

12. Cited by H. Temperly, *England and the Near East: The Crimea* (London: Longman, 1936), p. 89.

13. Cited by J. B. Williams, *British Commercial Policy and Trade Expansion 1750–1850* (London: Oxford University Press, 1972), p. 300.

14. H. L. Bulwer, *The Life of . . . Viscount Palmerston* (London, 1870), Vol. II, p. 145.

15. Cited by W. L. Langer, *Political and Social Upheaval 1832–1852* (New York: Harper & Row, 1969), p. 303.

16. C. Issawi, ed., *The Economic History of the Middle East 1800–1914* (Chicago: University of Chicago Press, 1966), p. 363.

17. Cited by W. L. Langer, *European Alliances and Alignments 1871–1890* (New York: Alfred A. Knopf, 1956), p. 281.

18. Cited by E. R. J. Owen, "The Attitudes of British Officials to the Development of the Egyptian Economy, 1882–1922," in Cook, op. cit., p. 490.

19. E. R. J. Owen, "Lord Cromer and the Development of Egyptian Industry 1883–1907," *Middle Eastern Studies* II (Apr. 1966):293.

20. J. Berque, "The Establishment of the Colonial Economy," in Polk and Chambers, op. cit., pp. 223, 242–43.

21. Cited by M. L. Entner, *Russo-Persian Commercial Relations, 1828–1914* (Gainesville: University of Florida Press, 1965), pp. 41–42.

22. Cited by N. R. Keddie, "Historical Obstacles to Agrarian Change in Iran," *Claremont Asian Studies* 8 (Sept. 1960):4.

23. Cited by A. K. S. Lambton, *Landlord and Peasant in Persia* (London: Oxford University Press, 1953), p. 162.

24. Cited by C. Issawi, ed., *The Economic History of Iran, 1800–1914* (Chicago: University of Chicago Press, 1971), p. 258.

25. G. N. Curzon, *Persia and the Persian Question* (London: Longman, 1892), Vol. II, p. 41.

Chapter 12

1. K. M. Panikkar, *Asia and Western Dominance* (New York: John Day, 1954), p. 100.

2. E. J. Thompson and G. T. Garratt, *Rise and Fulfillment of British Rule in India* (New York: Macmillan, 1934), pp. 91–92.

3. Cited by Panikkar, op. cit., p. 101.

4. K. Gough, "Indian Peasant Uprisings," *Bulletin of Concerned Asian Scholars* (July–Sept. 1976):3.

5. Cited by K. Goshal, *The People of India* (New York: Sheridan, 1944), p. 129.
6. Cited by F. Clairmonte, *Economic Liberalism and Underdevelopment*, op. cit., p. 116.
7. Cited by W. T. de Bary et al., *Sources of Indian Tradition* (New York: Columbia University Press, 1958), p. 601.
8. Cited by Panikkar, op. cit., p. 150.
9. Cited by J. McLane, "The Drain of Wealth and Indian Nationalism," *Contributions to Indian Economic History* (Calcutta, 1963) II:38.
10. Panikkar, op. cit., p. 153.
11. Cited by R. Mukherjee, *The Rise and Fall of the East India Company*, new ed. (New York: Monthly Review Press, 1974), p. 421.
12. Cited by L. S. S. O'Malley, ed., *Modern India and the West* (London: Oxford University Press, 1941), p. 14.
13. Cited by McLane, op. cit.:32.
14. L. Jenks, *The Migration of British Capital to 1875* (London: Thomas Nelson, 1938), pp. 223–24.
15. Cited by A. B. Keith, *Speeches & Documents on Indian Policy 1750–1921* (London: Oxford University Press, 1922), Vol. I, p. 209.
16. Cited by Clairmonte, op. cit., p. 116.
17. Cited by D. Thorner and A. Thorner, *Land and Labour in India* (London: Asia Publishing House, 1962), p. 110.
18. Ibid., p. 111.
19. Cited by P. Harnetty, *Imperialism and Free Trade: Lancashire and India in the Mid-Nineteenth Century* (Vancouver: University of British Columbia Press, 1972), p. 6.
20. Cited by Clairmonte, op. cit., p. 86.
21. Cited ibid., pp. 86, 90.
22. Cited by Harnetty, op. cit., p. 125.
23. Cited ibid., p. 51.
24. Cited by T. Raychaudhuri, "Some Recent Writings on the Economic History of British India," *Contributions to Indian Economic History* (Calcutta, 1960) I:147.
25. D. Thorner, *Investment in Empire* (Philadelphia: University of Pennsylvania Press, 1950), Ch. 7.
26. Cited by A. K. Bagchi, "Foreign Capital in India," in K. Gough and H. P. Sharma, eds., *Imperialism and Revolution in South Asia* (New York: Monthly Review Press, 1973), p. 49.
27. F. Lehmann, "Great Britain and the Supply of Railway Locomotives of India: A Case Study of 'Economic Imperialism,'" *Indian Economic and Social History Review* II (Oct. 1965):299.
28. A. K. Bagchi, "European and Indian Entrepreneurship in India 1900–1930," in E. Leach and S. N. Mukherjee, eds., *Elites in South Asia* (Cambridge: Cambridge University Press, 1970), p. 227.
29. B. Chandra, "Reinterpretations of Nineteenth Century Indian Economic History," *Indian Economic and Social History Review* V (Mar. 1968):61–62.

30. B. M. Bhatia, "Terms of Trade and Economic Development: A Case Study of India—1861–1939," *Indian Economic Journal* XVI (Apr.– June 1949):433.
31. Chandra, op. cit.:46.
32. B. Ward, *India and the West* (New York: W. W. Norton, 1961), p. 129.

Part Three

Chapter 13

1. Cited by L. Huberman, *We, the People*, rev. ed. (New York: Harper & Brothers, 1947), p. 218.
2. Cited by E. Mandel, *Marxist Economic Theory* (London: Merlin Press, 1962), Vol. II, p. 399.
3. S. B. Saul, *Studies in British Overseas Trade* (Liverpool: Liverpool University Press, 1960).
4. A. K. Bagchi, "Some International Foundations of Capitalist Growth and Underdevelopment," *Economic and Political Weekly* (Aug. 1972): 1565.
5. E. Kleiman, "Trade and the Decline of Colonialism," *Economic Journal* 86 (Sept. 1976):478.
6. Cited by O. C. Cox, *Capitalism as a System* (New York: Monthly Review Press, 1964), p. 173.
7. Lord Cromer, *Modern Egypt* (London: Macmillan, 1908), Vol. I, 58–59.
8. Cited by Huberman, op. cit., p. 263.
9. Cited by A. Seal, *The Emergence of Indian Nationalism* (Cambridge: Cambridge University Press, 1968), pp. 198–99.
10. A. Vambery, *Western Culture in Eastern Lands* (London: John Murray, 1906), pp. 1–14.
11. Cited by F. Clairmonte, *Economic Liberalism and Underdevelopment* (London: Asia Publishing House, 1960), p. 161.
12. Cited ibid., p. 140.
13. T. Kolokotrones and E. M. Edmonds, *Kolokotrones: Klepht and Warrior* (London, 1892), pp. 127–28.
14. J. Nehru, *The Discovery of India* (New York: John Day, 1946), p. 290, and *Toward Freedom: The Autobiography of Jawaharlal Nehru* (Boston: Beacon Press, 1958), p. 285.
15. G. Myrdal, *The Challenge of World Poverty* (London: Allen Lane, 1970), p. 72. Emphasis in original.
16. H. Shih, "The Civilizations of the East and the West," in *Whither Mankind*, ed. C. A. Beard (London: Longmans, 1928), pp. 28–29.
17. Cited by L. S. S. O'Malley, *Modern India and the West* (London: Oxford University Press, 1941), p. 766.
18. By Hugh Tinker (London: Oxford University Press, 1974).
19. R. Murphey, "Traditionalism and Colonialism: Changing Urban

Roles in Asia," *Journal of Asian Studies* (Nov. 1969):84.
20. A. Schrier, *Ireland and the American Emigration 1850–1900* (Minneapolis: University of Minnesota Press, 1958), p. 13.

Chapter 14

1. K. Onwuka Dike, *Trade and Politics in the Niger Delta 1830–1885* (Oxford: Clarendon Press, 1956), p. 171.
2. Cited ibid., p. 205.
3. Ibid., p. 211.
4. I. Wallerstein, "The Colonial Era in Africa: Changes in the Social Structure," in L. H. Gann and P. Duignan, eds., *Colonialism in Africa 1870–1960; Vol. 2, The History and Politics of Colonialism 1914–1960* (Cambridge: Cambridge University Press, 1970), pp. 403, 404.
5. Cited by S. C. Ukpabi, "British Colonial Wars in West Africa: Image and Reality," *Civilisations* XX (1970):396.
6. Ibid.:383.
7. Ibid., pp. 383, 384.
8. Cited by R. Oliver and A. Atmore, *Africa Since 1800* (Cambridge: Cambridge University Press, 1967), p. 158.
9. Cited by T. Hodgkin, *Nationalism in Colonial Africa* (New York: New York University Press, 1957), p. 98.
10. J. F. J. Fitzpatrick, "Nigeria's Curse—The Native Administration," *The National Review* LXXXIV (1924):623.
11. Wallerstein, op. cit., p. 405.
12. S. Amin, "Underdevelopment and Dependence in Black Africa," *Journal of Modern African Studies* X (1972):503–24.
13. Cited by L. Bauer, *Leopold the Unloved* (Boston: Little, Brown, 1935), p. 264.
14. L. H. Gann and P. Duignan, *White Settlers in Tropical Africa* (Harmondsworth, Middlesex: Penguin Books, 1962), p. 117.
15. Cited by Crowder, op. cit., p. 349.
16. R. D. Wolff, *The Economics of Colonialism: Britain and Kenya, 1870–1930* (New Haven, Conn.: Yale University Press, 1974), p. 146.
17. Cited ibid., p. 54.
18. L. H. Gann and P. Duignan, *The Burden of Empire* (New York: Praeger, 1967), p. 236.
19. *International Labour Office, Labour Conditions and Discrimination in Southern Rhodesia (Zimbabwe)* (Geneva, 1978).

Chapter 15

1. Ping-ti Ho, "The Chinese Civilization: A Search for the Roots of Its Longevity," *Journal of Asian Studies* XXXV (Aug. 1976):549.
2. M. Elvin, *The Pattern of the Chinese Past* (Stanford, Calif.: Stanford University Press, 1973), p. 129.
3. Cited by Tan Chung, "The Britain-China-India Trade Triangle

(1771–1840)," *Indian Economic and Social History Review* 11 (Dec. 1974):421.

4. Ibid.:425.
5. Cited by A. Waley, *The Opium War Through Chinese Eyes* (London: George Allen & Unwin, 1958), p. 170.
6. Cited by Yuan Chung Teng, "American-China Trade, American-Chinese Relations and the Taiping Rebellion, 1853–1858," *Journal of Asian History* III (1969):100.
7. Cited ibid.:101.
8. Cited by S. Y. Teng, *The Taiping Rebellion and the Western Powers* (London: Oxford University Press, 1971), p. 214.
9. Ibid., p. 230.
10. Ibid., p. 116.
11. S. Uhalley, Jr., "The Significance of Jen Yu-wen's Magnum Opus on the Taipings," *Journal of Asian Studies* XXXIII (Aug. 1974):679; and "Correspondence: Stephen Uhalley, Jr., and Westerners in China: A Commentary," *Journal of Asian Studies* XXXIV (May 1975):870.
12. Cited by J. Spence, *To Change China: Western Advisers in China 1620–1960* (Boston: Little, Brown, 1969), pp. 87, 92.
13. P. Bairoch, *The Economic Development of the Third World Since 1900* (Berkeley: University of California Press, 1975), p. 109.
14. F. V. Moulder, *Japan, China, and the Modern World Economy: Toward a Reinterpretation of East Asian Development ca. 1600 to ca. 1918* (Cambridge: Cambridge University Press, 1977), p. 107.
15. R. Murphey, *The Outsiders: The Western Experience in India and China* (Ann Arbor: University of Michigan Press, 1977), pp. 225–27.
16. Cited by K. M. Panikkar, *Asia and Western Dominance* (New York: John Day, 1954), p. 434.
17. Cited by Spence, op. cit., p. 78.
18. E. Snow, *Journey to the Beginning* (London: Victor Gollancz, 1960), p. 5.
19. Cited by Hao Yen-p'ing, *The Comprador in Nineteenth-Century China: Bridge Between East and West* (Cambridge, Mass.: Harvard University Press, 1970), p. 182.
20. Cited by E. R. Wolf, *Peasant Wars of the Twentieth Century* (New York: Harper & Row, 1969), p. 138.
21. Cited by E. Swisher, "Chinese Intellectuals and the Western Impact, 1838–1900," *Comparative Studies in Society and History* I (Oct. 1958): 35.
22. Cited by J. R. Levenson, *Confucian China and Its Modern Fate* (Berkeley: University of California Press, 1958), p. 105.
23. Cited by J. K. Fairbank, "China's Response to the West: Problems and Suggestions," *Journal of World History* III (1956):403.

Chapter 16

1. Cited by H. Kohn, *The Mind of Modern Russia* (New Brunswick, N.J.: Rutgers University Press, 1955), p. 64.

2. Cited by M. T. Florinsky, *Russia: A History and an Interpretation* (New York: Macmillan, 1958), Vol. II, p. 922.
3. S. Strumilin, "Industrial Crises in Russia 1847–1867," in *Essays in European History 1789–1914*, ed. F. Crouzet, W. H. Chaloner and W. M. Stern (London: Edward Arnold, 1969), pp. 157–58.
4. E. J. Dillon, cited in M. Hindus, *The Russian Peasant and the Revolution* (New York: Holt, 1920), p. 214.
5. G. T. Robinson, *Rural Russia Under the Old Regime* (New York: Macmillan, 1932), p. 64.
6. Cited by J. Mavor, *An Economic History of Russia* (New York: E. P. Dutton, 1925), Vol. II, p. 49.
7. Cited ibid., p. 402.
8. Cited by T. H. Von Laue, *Why Lenin? Why Stalin?* (Philadelphia: J. B. Lippincott, 1964), pp. 53–54.
9. S. S. Balzak et al., eds., *Economic Geography of the USSR* (New York: Macmillan, 1961), pp. 130–31.
10. E. H. Carr, *1917: Before and After* (New York: Macmillan, 1969), p. 168.

Chapter 17

1. Cited by C. R. Boxer, "Sakoku, or the Closed Country, 1640–1854," *History Today* VII (Feb. 1957):85.
2. Cited by K. M. Panikkar, *Asia and Western Dominance* (New York: John Day, 1953), p. 133.
3. Cited by J. Halliday, *A Political History of Japanese Capitalism* (New York: Pantheon, 1975), p. 37.
4. *The Japan Year Book, 1937–1940* (Tokyo: Foreign Affairs Association of Japan, 1939), p. 633.
5. Hou Chi-ming, *Foreign Investment and Economic Development in China, 1840–1937.* (Cambridge, Mass.: Harvard University Press, 1965), p. 101.
6. Halliday, op. cit., p. 62.
7. Ibid., p. 111.
8. Cited by R. F. Hackett, "Nishi Aurane—A Tokugawa—Meiji Bureaucrat," *Journal of Asian Studies* XVII (Feb. 1959):224.
9. D. Duncan, *Life and Letters of Herbert Spencer* (London: Williams and Norgate, 1911), p. 319.

Chapter 18

1. W. T. Stead, *The Last Will and Testament of Cecil John Rhodes* (London: Review of Reviews Office, 1902), p. 190.
2. Cited by O. C. Cox, *Capitalism as a System* (New York: Monthly Review Press, 1964), p. 174.

3. Cited by P. S. Foner, *History of Black Americans* (Westport, Conn.: Greenwood Press, 1975), p. 140.
4. E. Genovese, *From Rebellion to Revolution* (Baton Rouge: Louisiana State University Press, 1979), p. 87.
5. Cited by Foner, op. cit., p. 436.
6. Cited by P. S. Foner, *The Spanish-Cuban-American War and the Birth of American Imperialism 1895–1902* (New York: Monthly Review Press, 1972), Vol. I, p. 125.
7. Cited by W. J. Pomeroy, *American Neo-Colonialism* (New York: International Publishers, 1970), p. 42.
8. Ibid., p. 44.
9. Cited by Foner, op. cit., Vol. I, pp. xxx, xxxiv.
10. Cited by W. J. Pomeroy, op. cit., pp. 28, 33, 34.
11. Cited by L. Francisco, "The First Vietnam: The Philippine-American War of 1899," *Bulletin of Concerned Asian Scholars* V (Dec. 1973):5.
12. Ibid.:4.
13. Foner, op. cit., Vol. II, p. 672.
14. Cited by I. Spector, *The First Russian Revolution* (Englewood Cliffs, N.J.: Prentice-Hall, 1962), p. 8.
15. Cited ibid., p. 1.
16. Cited by H. D. Mehlinger and J. M. Thompson, *Count Witte and the Tsarist Government in the 1905 Revolution* (Bloomington: Indiana University Press, 1972), p. 237.
17. G. H. Fitzmaurice to Mr. Tyrell (Aug. 25, 1908), in G. P. Gooch and H. Temperley, eds., *British Documents on the Origins of the War 1898–1914*, Vol. X, No. 210 (London: H.M.S.O., 1936), p. 268.
18. Cited by Spector, op. cit., p. 81.
19. *Toward Freedom: The Autobiography of Jawaharlal Nehru* (Boston: Beacon Press, 1958), pp. 29, 30.
20. E. G. Browne, *The Persian Revolution of 1905–1909* (Cambridge: Cambridge University Press, 1910), pp. 120, 122, 123.
21. Cited by F. Kazemzadeh, *Russia and Britain in Persia, 1864–1914: A Study in Imperialism* (New Haven, Conn.: Yale University Press, 1968), p. 457.
22. Cited by A. K. S. Lambton, "Persian Political Societies 1906–11," *St. Anthony's Papers*, No. 16, *Middle Eastern Affairs*, No. 3 (Carbondale: Southern Illinois University Press, n.d.), p. 54.
23. Cited by I. Spector, *The First Russian Revolution: Its Impact on Asia* (Englewood Cliffs, N.J.: Prentice-Hall, 1962), p. 46.
24. Browne, op. cit., pp. xix–xx.
25. Cited by Kazemzadeh, op. cit., pp. 497, 498.
26. Ibid., pp. 500, 501.
27. Ibid., p. 613.
28. Ibid., p. 645.
29. Ibid.
30. Cited by H. Temperley, "British Policy Towards Parliamentary Rule

and Constitutionalism in Turkey (1830–1914)," *Cambridge Historical Journal* IV (1932):186.

31. Cited by D. Ergil, "A Reassessment: The Young Turks, Their Politics and Anti-colonial Struggle," *Balkan Studies* XVI (2) (1975):54.
32. Ibid., p. 69.
33. D. Ergil and R. I. Rhodes, "Western Capitalism and the Disintegration of the Ottoman Empire," *Economy and History* XVIII (1975):49.
34. Cited by Spector, op. cit., p. 78.
35. Cited by J. E. Sheridan, *China in Disintegration: The Republican Era in Chinese History, 1912–1949* (New York: The Free Press, 1975), p. 44.
36. J. W. Esherick, "1911: A Review," *Modern China* II (Apr. 1976): 169–70.
37. Cited by R. D. Hansen, *The Politics of Mexican Development* (Baltimore, Md.: Johns Hopkins University Press, 1971), p. 24.
38. Cited by R. E. Ruiz, *The Great Rebellion: Mexico 1905–1924* (New York: W. W. Norton, 1980), p. 109.
39. Cited ibid., p. 147.
40. Cited by E. R. Wolf, *Peasant Wars of the Twentieth Century* (New York: Harper & Row, 1969), p. 31.
41. Cited by P. Russell, *Mexico in Transition* (Austin, Texas: Colorado River Press, 1977), p. 30.
42. Ibid., p. 33.
43. Ibid., p. 38.
44. J. Womack, Jr., "The Mexican Revolution, 1910–1940: Genesis of a Modern State," in F. B. Pike, ed., *Latin American History: Select Problems* (New York: Harcourt, Brace & World, 1969), pp. 312, 313.
45. J. Womack, Jr., *Zapata and the Mexican Revolution* (New York: Alfred A. Knopf, 1968), p. 219.
46. Cited by E. H. Carr, *The Bolshevik Revolution 1917–1923* (New York: Macmillan, 1951), Vol. I, pp. 106, 107.
47. Cited by S. Rubenson, "Adowa 1896: The Resounding Protest," in R. L. Rothberg and A. A. Mazrui, eds., *Protest and Power in Black Africa* (London: Oxford University Press, 1970), p. 121.
48. Ibid., p. 128.
49. S. K. B. Asante, *Pan-African Protest: West Africa and the Italo-Ethiopian Crisis, 1934–1941* (London: Longman, 1977), p. 11.
50. Cited ibid., p. 14.
51. Cited by B. Farwell, *The Great Anglo-Boer War* (New York: Harper & Row, 1976), pp. 281, 282.
52. Ibid., p. 282.
53. Ibid., p. 395.
54. Ibid., p. 449.
55. Cited by H. C. d'Encausse and S. R. Schram, *Marxism and Asia* (London: Allen Lane, Penguin Books, 1969), p. 130.
56. Ibid., p. 136.
57. Ibid., pp. 138–39.

Part Four (introductory section)

1. K. M. Pannikkar, *Asia and Western Dominance* (New York: John Day, 1954), p. 12.

Chapter 19

1. W. R. Bailey, *The One-Man Farm* (Washington, D.C.: U.S. Department of Agriculture Economic Research Service, 1973), pp. v, 3.
2. Cited by R. Burbach and P. Flynn, *Agribusiness in the Americas* (New York: Monthly Review Press, 1980), p. 31.
3. S. Avineri, ed., *Karl Marx on Colonization and Modernization* (New York: Anchor Books, 1969), p. 464.
4. Cited by H. Carrère d'Encausse and S. R. Schram, *Marxism and Asia* (London: Allen Lane, Penguin Books, 1969), pp. 198–99.
5. M. Ram, "Les contradictions de la Révolution Verte en Inde," *Le Monde Diplomatique* (Oct. 1974).
6. Cited by R. Freund, "Food for Peace or for Selfishness?" Los Angeles *Times* (Dec. 3, 1979).
7. Cited by Burbach and Flynn, op. cit., p. 67.
8. Washington *Post* (Dec. 24, 1980).
9. *Commentary* (Mar. 1975).
10. Cited by H. Stephenson, *The Coming Clash: The Impact of the International Corporation on the Nation State* (London: George Weidenfeld & Nicolson, 1972), p. 12.
11. G. Chaliand, *Revolution in the Third World* (New York: Viking Press, 1977), pp. 11, 12.
12. UN Conference on Trade and Development, *The Reverse Transfer of Technology: Economic Effects of the Outflow of Trained Personnel from Developing Countries* (New York, 1975) (TD/B/AC. 11/25/Rev. 1).
13. *World Bank: Annual Report, 1980* (Washington, D.C., 1980), p. 24.
14. New York *Times* (Feb. 4, 1980).
15. Ibid. (Aug. 22, 1980).
16. E. Abrahamian, "The Guerrilla Movement in Iran, 1963–1977," *MERIP Reports* (86) (Mar.–Apr. 1980):11.
17. Hoang Tung, member of the Central Committee of the Workers' Party of Vietnam and editor of the daily newspaper *Nhan Dan*, cited by K. Gough, "A Hanoi Interview," *Monthly Review* (May 1977), p. 27.
18. Cited by B. Davidson, "The Revolution of People's Power," *Monthly Review* (July–Aug. 1980), pp. 77, 78.
19. Cited by D. Milton and N. D. Milton, *The Wind Will Not Subside: Years in Revolutionary China—1964–1969* (New York: Pantheon Books, 1976), p. 23.
20. Cited by J. Woddis, *Introduction to Neo-Colonialism* (New York: International Publishers, 1967), p. 83.

21. G. Myrdal, *The Challenge of World Poverty* (New York: Pantheon Books, 1970), pp. 72–73. Emphasis in original.
22. L. H. Shoup and W. Minter, *The Council on Foreign Relations and U.S. Foreign Policy* (New York: Monthly Review Press, 1977), pp. 135–40.
23. New York *Times* (May 30, 1977).
24. Cited by M. T. Klare, *War Without End* (New York: Vintage Books, 1972), p. 24.
25. Cited in New York *Times* (July 21, 1980).
26. Ibid. (Jan. 29, 1976).
27. T. W. Braden, "I'm Glad the CIA Is Immoral," *Saturday Evening Post* (May 20, 1967), pp. 10–12.
28. Cited by S. Lens, "Partners: Labor and the CIA," *Progressive* (Feb. 1975), pp. 35–39.
29. Cited ibid.
30. Panel discussion, Mutual Broadcasting System (July 12, 1964). Cited by R. Dockery, *Survey of the Alliance for Progress: Labor Policies and Programs*, Subcommittee on American Republics Affairs, Senate Committee on Foreign Relations (July 15, 1968), p. 14.
31. E. Methvin, "Labor's New Weapon for Democracy," *Reader's Digest* (Oct. 1966), pp. 21–22.
32. Cited by J. Stein, "Grad School for Juntas," *Nation* (May 21, 1977), p. 622.
33. Ibid., p. 623.
34. Los Angeles *Times* (Feb. 22, 1976).
35. New York *Times* (Mar. 2, 1981).
36. Cited by *American Report* (Apr. 29, 1974).
37. These statistics, from the *1980 World Bank Report*, p. 21, include the following regions under "LDC": Subsaharan Africa, North Africa and Middle East, East Asia and Pacific, South Asia, Latin America and the Caribbean. Also New York *Times*, March 23, 1981.
38. S. Rose, "Why They Call It a Fat City," *Fortune* (Mar. 1975).
39. Los Angeles *Times* (Nov. 27, 1977).
40. New York *Times* (July 28, 1977).
41. Los Angeles *Times* (Oct. 3, 1977).
42. *Dollars & Sense* (Dec. 1976), p. 12.
43. Text supplied by office of Representative Henry S. Reuss.
44. Cited by W. Wipfler, "Latin America: U.S. Colony," *Christianity and Crisis* (Apr. 3, 1972), p. 70.
45. Cited by E. Reynolds, *Trade and Economic Change on the Gold Coast, 1807–1874* (London: Longman, 1974), pp. 87, 88.
46. J. Nehru, *Toward Freedom* (Boston: Beacon Press, 1958), p. 264.
47. A. K. N. Reddy, "Is Indian Science Truly Indian?" *Science Today* (Jan. 1974), p. 13, cited by E. G. Vallianatos, *Fear in the Countryside* (Cambridge, Mass.: Ballinger, 1976), p. 100.
48. Cited by V. Di Giorgi, "The Pseudosovereign," *Ceres* IX (Sept.–Oct. 1976):25.

49. R. J. Barnet and R. E. Muller, *Global Reach: The Power of the Multinational Corporations* (New York: Simon & Schuster, 1974), pp. 172, 173.

50. F. Fanon, *Black Skins, White Masks* (New York: Grove Press, 1967), pp. 18, 63.

51. G. L. Beckford, *Persistent Poverty* (London: Oxford University Press, 1972), p. 205.

52. *The Role and Control of International Communications and Information: Report to the Subcommittee on International Operations of the Committee on Foreign Relations, U.S. Senate* (Washington, D.C.: U.S. Government Printing Office, June 1977), p. 34.

53. Cited by L. R. Sussman, *Mass News Media and the Third World Challenge*. Center for Strategic and International Studies, the Washington Papers, Vol. V (Beverly Hills, Calif.: Sage, 1977), p. 13.

54. M. Makagiansar, "UNESCO and World Problems of Communication," *Unesco Courier* (Apr. 1977), pp. 6, 10.

55. P. Ivacic, "The Non-Aligned Countries Pool Their News," *Unesco Courier* (Apr. 1977), p. 20.

56. Sussman, op. cit., p. 72.

57. Cited by H. Schiller, "Whose New International Economic and Information Order?" paper presented to an International Conference "Alternative Development Strategies and the Future of Asia" (Oct. 15–21, 1979), New Delhi.

Chapter 20

1. Cited by E. H. Carr, *The Bolshevik Revolution 1917–1923* (New York: Macmillan, 1951), Vol. I, p. 107.

2. Cited by E. H. Carr, *The Bolshevik Revolution 1917–1923* (New York: Macmillan, 1953), Vol. III, pp. 17, 18.

3. F. Claudin, *The Communist Movement* (New York: Monthly Review Press, 1975), p. 53.

4. Ibid., pp. 55–56.

5. Cited by N. G. Levin, Jr., *Woodrow Wilson and World Politics* (London: Oxford University Press, 1968), p. 14.

6. Ibid., p. 18.

7. Ibid., p. 22.

8. Ibid., p. 24.

9. Ibid., p. 25.

10. Ibid., pp. 133–34.

11. Ibid., p. 138.

12. Ibid., p. 140.

13. Ibid., p. 148.

14. Cited by Claudin, op. cit., p. 57.

15. Cited by Carr, op. cit., Vol. I, p. 122.

16. Cited by C. Bettelheim, *Class Struggles in the USSR: First Period 1917–1923* (New York: Monthly Review Press, 1976), p. 85.

17. Cited by Claudin, op. cit., p. 71.
18. Ibid.
19. Ibid., p. 75.
20. Cited by S. Webb and B. Webb, *Soviet Communism: A New Civilization* (London: Victor Gollancz, 1973), Vol. II, p. 605.
21. Cited by Bettelheim, op. cit., p. 331.
22. New York *Times* (Aug. 6, 1971).
23. Cited by Bettelheim, op. cit., p. 167.
24. Ibid., p. 192.
25. Ibid., p. 313.
26. Cited by M. Lewin, *Russian Peasants and Soviet Power* (New York: W. W. Norton, 1968), pp. 35–36.
27. Cited by Bettelheim, op. cit., pp. 331, 525.
28. Cited J. Maynard, *Russia in Flux* (New York: Macmillan, 1949), p. 218.
29. Lewin, op. cit., p. 517.
30. Ibid.
31. C. Bettelheim, *Class Struggles in the U.S.S.R. Second Period 1923–1930* (New York: Monthly Review Press, 1978).
32. Cited by Lewin, op. cit., p. 221.
33. Ibid., p. 29.
34. W. S. Churchill, *The Second World War: The Hinge of Fate* (London: Cassell, 1951), p. 447.
35. Los Angeles *Times* (Nov. 8, 1975).
36. Harry G. Shaffer, "Economic Performance Under the Plan: The Soviet Union and East Europe," paper presented at McMaster Conference on Current Problems of Socialist Economics (Oct. 23–24, 1970), p. 21 (mimeographed).
37. New York *Times* (Mar. 10, 1971).
38. *Toward Freedom: The Autobiography of Jawaharlal Nehru* (Boston: Beacon Press, 1958), pp. 228, 229.

Chapter 21

1. R. Delavignette, *Freedom and Authority in French West Africa* (London: Oxford University Press, 1950), p. 149.
2. Cited by K. M. Panikkar, *Asia and Western Dominance* (New York: John Day, 1953), p. 262.
3. B. B. Fall, ed., *Ho Chi Minh on Revolution: Selected Writings, 1920–1926* (New York: Praeger, 1967), pp. 31, 60, 61.
4. Cited by Panikkar, op. cit., p. 364.
5. Cited by W. R. Louis, "Great Britain and the African Peace Settlement of 1919," *American Historical Review* LXXI (Apr. 1966):880.
6. Cited by E. H. Carr, *The Bolshevik Revolution 1917–1923* (New York: Macmillan, 1953), Vol. III, p. 235.
7. Ibid., Vol. III, pp. 235–36.
8. Ibid., Vol. III, p. 245.

9. Cited by G. S. Harris, *The Origins of Communism in Turkey* (Stanford, Calif.: Hoover Institution Press, 1967), p. 3.

10. Cited by Carr, op. cit., Vol. III, p. 248.

11. F. Claudin, *The Communist Movement* (New York: Monthly Review Press, 1975), p. 109.

12. E. H. Carr, *Socialism in One Country 1924–1926* (New York: Macmillan, 1964), ch. 43.

13. Cited by Claudin, op. cit., pp. 120–21.

14. Cited by J. K. Fairbank, E. O. Reischauer and A. M. Craig, *East Asia: The Modern Transformation* (Boston: Houghton Mifflin, 1965), p. 649.

15. Cited by E. R. Wolf, *Peasant Wars of the Twentieth Century* (New York: Harper & Row, 1969), p. 138.

16. Cited by L. Bianco, *Origins of the Chinese Revolution, 1915–1929* (Stanford, Calif.: Stanford University Press, 1971), p. 42.

17. Ibid., p. 49.

18. Ibid., p. 79.

19. H. C. d'Encausse and S. R. Schram, *Marxism and Asia* (London: Allen Lane, Penguin Books, 1969), p. 51.

20. Ibid.

21. M. Zinkin, *Asia and the West* (London: Chatto & Windus, 1951), p. 88.

22. T. E. Weisskopf, "The Persistence of Poverty in India: A Political Economic Analysis," *Bulletin of Concerned Asian Scholars* (Jan.–Mar. 1977):28.

23. Cited by F. Clairmonte, *Economic Liberalism and Underdevelopment* (London: Asia Publishing House, 1960), pp. 107–8.

24. Cited by G. Omvedt, "Gandhi and the Pacification of the Indian National Revolution," *Bulletin of Concerned Asian Scholars* (July 1973):6.

25. H. Ammar, *Growing Up in an Egyptian Village* (London: Routledge, 1954), pp. 72–73.

26. Cited by P. Sluglett, *Britain in Iraq 1914–1932* (London: Ithaca Press, 1976), p. 31.

27. Ibid., p. 37.

28. Ibid., p. 290.

29. Ibid., pp. 297–98.

30. D. N. Wilber, *Riza Shah Pahlavi: The Resurrection and Reconstruction of Iran* (Jericho, N.Y.: Exposition Press, 1975), pp. 196, 266.

31–32. Sluglett, op. cit., p. 231.

33. D. Ben-Gurion, *The Rebirth and Destiny of Israel* (New York: Philosophical Library, 1954), p. 38.

34. Los Angeles *Times* (Mar. 30, 1978).

35. Cited by S. Halbrook, "The Philosophy of Zionism: A Materialist Interpretation," in I. Abu-Lughod and B. Abu-Laban, eds., *Settler Regimes in Africa and the Arab World* (Wilmette, Illinois: Medina University Press International, 1974), p. 22.

36. Ibid.
37. M. Lowenthal, ed., *The Diaries of Theodor Herzl* (London: Victor Gollancz, 1958), p. 371.
38. Ibid., p. 375.
39. Cited by B. Halpern, *The Idea of the Jewish State* (Cambridge, Mass.: Harvard University Press, 1961), p. 154.
40. Cited by M. S. Agwani, "The Palestine Conflict in Asian Perspective," in I. Abu-Lughod, ed., *The Transformation of Palestine* (Evanston, Ill.: Northwestern University Press, 1971), pp. 445–46.
41. A. Cohen, *Israel and the Arab World* (New York: Funk & Wagnalls, 1970), p. 46.
42. K. H. Karpat, "Ottoman Immigration Policies and Settlement in Palestine," in Abu-Lughod and Abu-Laban, op. cit., p. 63.
43. N. Mandel, "Turks, Arabs and Jewish Immigration into Palestine, 1882–1914," in St. Antony's Papers, No. 17, *Middle Eastern Affairs*, No. 4 (London: Oxford University Press, 1965), p. 78.
44. Cited by Anthony Lewis in New York *Times* (Apr. 3, 1978).
45. Cohen, op. cit., p. xi.
46. Cited ibid., p. 50.
47. Ibid., pp. 60–61.
48. Ibid., pp. 240–41.
49. Ibid., pp. 241–42.
50. Ibid., pp. 243–44.
51. Ibid., p. 245.
52. Ibid., pp. 248, 260, 291.
53. Ibid., pp. 285–86.
54. J. Gorni, "Zionist Socialism and the Arab Question," *Middle Eastern Studies* XIII (Jan. 1977):53, 68.
55. Cohen, op. cit., pp. 256–57, 263.
56. Ibid., pp. 273–74.
57. Cited by W. T. Mallison, Jr., "The Balfour Declaration: An Appraisal in International Law," in Abu-Lughod, op. cit., pp. 85–86.
58. Ibid., p. 86.
59. J. C. Hurewitz, *Diplomacy in the Near and Middle East* (Princeton, N.J.: D. Van Nostrand, 1956), Vol. II, pp. 70–71.
60. Ibid., p. 62.
61. Cited by Cohen, op. cit., p. 221.
62. N. Caplan, "Arab Jewish Contacts in Palestine after the First World War," *Journal of Contemporary History* 12 (1977):662.
63. Cited by Z. Lockman, "The Left in Israel: Zionism vs. Socialism," *MERIP Reports*, No. 49, p. 5.
64. Cited by J. Ruedy, "Dynamics of Land Alienation," in Abu-Lughod, op. cit., p. 130.
65. Cited by W. R. Polk, "What the Arabs Think," *Headline Series*, No. 96, p. 38.
66. Cited by B. Kalkas, "The Revolt of 1936: A Chronicle of Events," in Abu-Lughod, op. cit., p. 271.

67. R. Oliver and A. Atmore, *Africa Since 1800* (Cambridge: Cambridge University Press, 1967), p. 168.
68. Cited by A. G. Hopkins, *An Economic History of West Africa* (New York: Columbia University Press, 1973), p. 190.
69. Cited by E. A. Brett, *Colonialism and Underdevelopment in East Africa* (New York: NOK Publishers, 1973), p. 150.
70. Cited ibid., p. 75.
71. Cited ibid., p. 76.
72. Cited by W. Rodney, *How Europe Underdeveloped Africa* (Washington, D.C.: Howard University Press, 1974), p. 165.
73. L. H. Gann and P. Duignan, eds., *Colonialism in Africa 1870–1960. Vol. 4, The Economics of Colonialism* (Cambridge: Cambridge University Press, 1975), p. 689.
74. Cited by Hopkins, op. cit., pp. 230, 231.
75. Ibid., p. 231.
76. Cited by B. Davidson, *African History* (New York: Macmillan, 1968), pp. 257, 258.
77. New York *Times* (Apr. 29, 1978).
78. Cited by Brett, op. cit., p. 274.
79. Ibid.
80. Hopkins, op. cit., p. 266.
81. Cited by Chinweizu, *The West and the Rest of Us* (New York: Vintage Books, 1975), p. 86.
82. Ibid., p. 95.
83. Ibid., p. 96.
84. Ibid., p. 97.
85. J. K. Nyerere, *Freedom and Socialism* (London: Oxford University Press, 1968), pp. 269–70.
86. Davidson, op. cit., pp. 269–70, 274.
87. P. Ehrensaft, "Polarized Accumulation and the Theory of Economic Dependence," in P. C. W. Gutkind and I. Wallerstein, eds., *The Political Economy of Contemporary Africa* (Beverly Hills, Calif.: Sage Publications, 1976), pp. 58–89.
88. Cited by Chinweizu, op. cit., p. 70.
89. Cited by I. Wallerstein, *The Road to Independence* (La Haye: Mouton, 1964), p. 36.
90. C. Furtado, *Economic Development of Latin America* (Cambridge: Cambridge University Press, 1970), p. 92.

Chapter 22

1. Cited by M. Meisner, *Mao's China: A History of the People's Republic* (New York: The Free Press, 1977), p. 361.
2. J. W. Stilwell, *The Stilwell Papers* (New York: Sloane, 1948), p. 316.
3. C. F. Romanus and R. Sunderland, *United States in World War II. China-Burma-India Theatre: Time Runs Out in the CBI* (Washington, D.C.: Department of the Army, 1959), pp. 369–71.

4. Cited by G. Kolko, *The Politics of War* (New York: Random House, 1968), p. 205.
5. Cited by M. Selden, *The Yenan Way in Revolutionary China* (Cambridge, Mass.: Harvard University Press, 1971), pp. 191–92.
6. C. Brandt, B. Schwartz and J. K. Fairbank, eds., *A Documentary History of Chinese Communism* (New York: Atheneum, 1967), pp. 80–85. Emphasis in the originals.
7. Ibid., pp. 224–25.
8. Cited by Selden, op. cit., pp. 123, 125.
9. C. A. Johnson, *Peasant Nationalism and Communist Power: The Emergence of Revolutionary China, 1937–1945* (Stanford, Calif.: Stanford University Press, 1961).
10. L. Bianco, *Origins of the Chinese Revolution 1915–1949* (Stanford, Calif.: Stanford University Press, 1971), pp. 158–59.
11. Cited by Selden, op. cit., p. 274.
12. Cited by Bianco, op. cit., p. 168.
13. Cited by G. Kolko, *The Politics of War* (New York: Random House, 1968), p. 616.
14. Cited by D. Wilson, "Leathernecks in North China, 1945," *Bulletin of Concerned Asian Scholars* IV (Summer 1972):34.
15. Ibid.:36.
16. D. Milton and N. Milton, *The Wind Will Not Subside: Years in Revolutionary China, 1964–1969* (New York: Pantheon Books, 1976), p. 19.
17. Cited by Milton and Milton, op. cit., p. 36, and K. Mehnert, *China Returns* (New York: E. P. Dutton, 1972), p. 173.
18. A. Doak Barnett, *Cadres, Bureaucracy and Political Power in Communist China* (New York: Columbia University Press, 1967), p. 433.
19. Cited by C. Bettelheim, "The Great Leap Forward," *Monthly Review* XXX (July–Aug. 1978):65, 66.
20. B. Richman, *Industrial Society in Communist China* (New York: Random House, 1969), pp. 224, 225.
21. Milton and Milton, op. cit., p. 357.
22. Meisner, op. cit., p. 258.
23. C. Riskin, "Maoism and Motivation: Work Incentives in China," *Bulletin of Concerned Asian Scholars* (July 1973):17, 19.
24. Central Intelligence Agency: National Foreign Assessment Center, *China Economic Indicators: A Reference Aid* (Washington, D.C., Oct. 1977, ER 77-10508); and Central Intelligence Agency: National Foreign Assessment Center, *China: In Pursuit of Economic Modernization: A Research Paper* (Washington, D.C.: Dec. 1978, ER 78-10680), p. 1.
25. Cited by R. O'Mara, "Brazil: The Booming Despotism," *Nation* (Apr. 27, 1974), p. 519.
26. H. Kissinger, *The White House Years* (Boston: Little, Brown, 1979), p. 1063.
27. Cited in *Peking Review* (June 25, 1976).

28. *Peking Review* (Jan. 26, 1967).
29. Cited by Milton and Milton, op. cit., p. 198.
30. Ibid., p. 202.
31. *Beijing Review* (June 22, 1979).
32. *Peking Review* (July 28, 1978).
33. Los Angeles *Times* (Feb. 8, 1979).
34. Ibid. (Oct. 17, 1979).
35. Ibid. (Nov. 23, 1980).
36. Ibid. (May 15, 1980).
37. Cited by J. G. Gurley, *China's Economy and the Maoist Strategy* (New York: Monthly Review Press, 1976), p. 204.

Chapter 23

1. Cited by H. Luethy, *France Against Herself* (New York: World, 1955), p. 218.
2. A. Eden, *Memoirs: The Reckoning* (Boston: Houghton Mifflin, 1965), p. 593.
3. A. J. P. Taylor, *The Second World War* (London: Hamish Hamilton, 1975), p. 205.
4. G. Kolko, *The Politics of War: The World and United States Foreign Policy, 1943–1945* (New York: Random House, 1968), p. 455.
5. Cited by F. Claudin, *The Communist Movement* (New York: Monthly Review Press, 1975), Vol. II, p. 470.
6. Ibid., p. 337.
7. Ibid., p. 338.
8. Ibid.
9. Cited by V. Dedijer, *Tito Speaks* (New York: Simon & Schuster, 1953), p. 331.
10. Cited by Claudin, op. cit., p. 432.
11. J. Nehru, *The Discovery of India* (New York: John Day, 1946), p. 432.
12. Ibid., p. 299.
13. Jamil-ud-Ahmad, ed., *Some Recent Speeches . . . of Mr. Jinnah* (Lahore: Ashraf, 1943), Vol. I, p. 180.
14. B. C. Dutt, *Mutiny of the Innocents* (Bombay: Sindhu, 1971), pp. 135, 202.
15. M. Zinkin and T. Zinkin, *Britain and India* (Baltimore, Md.: Johns Hopkins University Press, 1964), p. 98.
16. Ibid., p. 99.
17. Cited by G. Myrdal, *Asian Drama: An Inquiry into the Poverty of Nations* (New York: Pantheon Books, 1968), Vol. I, p. 275.
18. Ibid., p. 261.
19. M. Weiner, *Party Building in a New Nation* (Chicago: University of Chicago Press, 1967), p. 300.
20. Cited by D. Hiro, *Inside India Today* (London: Routledge, 1976), pp. 98, 99.

21. New York *Times* (Apr. 10, 1978).
22. Cited by Hiro, op. cit., p. 49.
23. Los Angeles *Times* (Sept. 15, 1979).
24. Cited by C. Payer, *The Debt Trap* (New York: Monthly Review Press, 1974), p. 171.
25. A. G. Frank, "Unequal Accumulation: Intermediate, Semi-Peripheral, and Sub-Imperialist Economies," *Review* II (Winter 1979):313, 314.
26. Cited ibid.:316.
27. Ibid.:319.
28. Ibid.:329.
29. Los Angeles *Times* (Sept. 23, 1980).
30. New York *Times* (Sept. 12, 1980).
31. G. Myrdal, *The Challenge of World Poverty* (London: Allen Lane, 1970), pp. 424, 431, 486.
32. New York *Times* (Dec. 20, 1979).
33–35. Ibid.
36. A. H. Hourani, *Syria and Lebanon* (London: Royal Institute of International Affairs, 1946), pp. 230, 231.
37. New York *Times* (Dec. 29, 1959).
38. M. Abdel-Fadil, *Development, Income Distribution and Social Change in Rural Egypt 1952–1970* (Cambridge: Cambridge University Press, 1975), pp. 49, 121.
39. R. Mabro and S. Radwan, *The Industrialization of Egypt 1939–1973* (Oxford: Clarendon Press, 1976), p. 239.
40. New York *Times* (July 28, 1980).
41. Ibid. (July 21, 1977).
42. Cited by E. Ahmad, "The Iranian Revolution: A Landmark for the Future," *Race & Class* XXI (Summer 1979):3.
43. Los Angeles *Times* (Mar. 29, 1979). Details in K. Roosevelt, *Counter-coup: The Struggle for the Control of Iran* (New York: McGraw-Hill, 1979).
44. M. A. Katouzian, "Land Reform in Iran: A Case Study in the Political Economy of Social Engineering," *Journal of Peasant Studies* (Jan. 1974):220.
45. New York *Times* (Nov. 16, 1978).
46. *Employment and Income Policies for Iran* (Geneva: ILO, 1973).
47. Cited by F. Halliday, "Iran: The Economic Contradictions," *MERIP Reports,* No. 69 (July–Aug. 1978), p. 17.
48. New York *Times* (May 25, 1979).
49. New York *Times* (Apr. 20 and June 3, 1980); and M. Ledeen and W. Lewis, "Carter and the Fall of the Shah," *The Washington Quarterly* (Spring 1980), pp. 3–40.
50. *An-Nahar: Arab Report and MEMO,* Vol. 2, No. 2 (Apr. 17, 1978).
51. Los Angeles *Times* (Nov. 26, 1978).
52. *An-Nahar: Arab Report and MEMO,* op. cit., p. 15.

53. T. Hodgkin, *Nationalism in Colonial Africa* (New York: New York University Press, 1957), p. 140.
54. Cited by M. Perham, *The Colonial Reckoning: The End of Imperial Rule in Africa in Light of the British Experience* (New York: Alfred A. Knopf, 1962), p. 114.
55. K. Nkrumah, *I Speak of Freedom* (New York: Praeger, 1961), p. 19.
56. F. Fanon, *The Wretched of the Earth* (New York: Grove Press, 1968), p. 70.
57. Cited by M. Harris, "Portugal's Contribution to the Underdevelopment of Africa and Brazil" in R. H. Chilcote, ed., *Protest and Resistance in Angola and Brazil* (Berkeley: University of California Press, 1972), p. 222.
58. Cited by B. Davidson, "African Peasants and Revolution," *Journal of Peasant Studies* 1 (3) (Apr. 1974):288.
59. Cited by B. Davidson, "Outlook for Africa," *The Socialist Register, 1966*, ed. R. Miliband and J. Saville (New York: Monthly Review Press, 1967), pp. 207, 208.
60. Cited by B. Fitch and M. Oppenheimer, "Ghana: End of an Illusion," *Monthly Review* (July–Aug. 1966), pp. 36, 37.
61. J. Stockwell, *In Search of Enemies: A CIA Story* (New York: W. W. Norton, 1978), pp. 160, 201.
62. M. F. Lofchie, "Political and Economic Origins of African Hunger," *Journal of Modern African Studies* 13 (4) (1975):562. See also H. Ruthenberg, *African Agricultural Production Development Policy in Kenya, 1952–1965* (Berlin: Springer, 1966).
63. *Alleged Assassination Plots Involving Foreign Leaders: An Interim Report of the Select Committee to Study Governmental Operations with Respect to Intelligence Activities,* U.S. Senate, 94th Cong., 1st sess. (Washington, D.C.: U.S. Government Printing Office, 1975), p. 15.
64. Stockwell, op. cit., p. 105.
65. New York *Times* (Jan. 4, 1976).
66. *International Bulletin* (June 19, 1978), p. 3.
67. Los Angeles *Times* (Mar. 4, 1979).
68. Text of Nyerere's speech (June 8, 1978) in *Nation* (July 8–15, 1978).
69. Los Angeles *Times* (Oct. 24, 1979).
70. A. Dobrin, "The Vanishing Herds," *Food Monitor* (May–June 1978), p. 23.
71. Cited by B. Davidson, *Let Freedom Come: Africa in Modern History* (Boston: Little, Brown, 1978), p. 330.
72. Ibid., pp. 331, 332.
73. *Internews* (June 18, 1979).
74. P. Kiven Tunteng, "External Influences and Subimperialism in Francophone West Africa," in P. C. W. Gutkind and I. Wallerstein, *The Political Economy of Contemporary Africa* (Beverly Hills, Calif.: Sage Publications, 1976), p. 212.

75. *International Bulletin* (Aug. 29, 1977), p. 3.
76. Cited by Obi Bini, "OAU Holds Conference," *Guardian* (May 28, 1980), p. 15.
77. Cited by R. L. Ayres, "Development Policy and the Possibility of a 'Livable' Future for Latin America," *American Political Science Review* 59 (June 1975):507.
78. Ibid.
79. World Bank, *The Assault on World Poverty* (Baltimore, Md.: Johns Hopkins University Press, 1975), p. 215; F. M. Lappé and J. Collins, *Food First: Beyond the Myth of Scarcity* (Boston: Houghton Mifflin, 1977), passim: and U.S. Agency for International Development, *Summary Economic and Social Indicators, 18 Latin American Countries: 1960–71* (Washington, D.C.: AID, 1972), p. 44.
80. R. J. Barnet and R. E. Muller, *Global Reach* (New York: Simon & Schuster, 1974), p. 154.
81. New York *Times* (May 18, 1981).
82. G. Myrdal, *The Challenge of World Poverty* (London: Allen Lane, Penguin Books, 1970), p. 469.
83. A. Schlesinger, *A Thousand Days* (Boston: Houghton Mifflin, 1965), p. 792.
84. D. Rockefeller, "What Private Enterprise Means to Latin America," *Foreign Affairs*, Vol. 44 (Apr. 1966), p. 408.
85. New York *Times* (Feb. 12, 1979).
86. Los Angeles *Times* (Oct. 27, 1979).
87. S. Schlesinger, "How Dulles Worked the Coup d'État," *Nation* (Oct. 28, 1978), p. 425.
88. A. Papandreou, *Democracy at Gunpoint: The Greek Front* (Garden City, N.Y.: Doubleday, 1970), pp. 85–93.
89. Schlesinger, op. cit., p. 441.
90. Ibid., p. 443.
91. Ibid., p. 439.
92. G. Kolko, "A Major Documents Collection," *Journal of Contemporary Asia* VIII (1978):545, 546, and J. K. Black, *United States Penetration of Brazil* (Philadelphia: University of Pennsylvania Press, 1977), pp. xi, xii, 253–61.
93. P. Agee, *Inside the Company: CIA Diary* (London: Allen Lane, 1975), p. 362.
94. Ibid., pp. 363–65.
95. Detailed statistics in Black, op. cit., pp. 263–66.
96. Los Angeles *Times* (Nov. 8, 1978).
97. New York *Times* (Jan. 24, 1976).
98. Los Angeles *Times* (May 15, 1978).
99. New York *Times* (Sept. 16, 1980).
100. Ibid. (June 13, 1977).
101. Ibid. (Nov. 20, 1977).
102. Ibid. (May 19, 1973).
103. Los Angeles *Times* (Nov. 27, 1980).

104. Ibid. (Feb. 20 and 22, 1976).
105. Ibid. (Oct. 9, 1979).
106. Ibid. (Oct. 18, 1979).
107. Cited by P. Lernoux, "On the Petroleum Merry-Go-Round," *Nation* (Feb. 15, 1975), p. 166.
108. Los Angeles *Times* (Feb. 20, 1979).
109. Ibid. (Feb. 22, 1981).
110. New York *Times* (May 20, 1975).
111. Ibid. (Aug. 22, 1980).
112. E. J. Hobsbawm, "Guerrillas in Latin America," *Socialist Register* (1970), pp. 51, 53, 59–60.
113. Cited by A. Boron, "New Forms of Capitalist State in Latin America," *Race and Class* XX (Winter 1979):274.
114. Cited by P. Lernoux, "The Church Revolutionary in Latin America," *Nation* (May 24, 1980), p. 623.
115. P. Gleijeses, "Carter's 'New Policy' in Nicaragua is Neither Moral nor New," *In These Times* (Nov. 8–14, 1978), p. 17.
116. New York *Times* (Apr. 17, 1980; Los Angeles *Times*, Mar. 11, 15, 1981).
117–122. Los Angeles *Times* (Nov. 28, 1980).
123. New York *Times* (Nov. 12, 1977).
124. Ibid.
125. Ibid. (Jan. 31, 1976).
126. Los Angeles *Times* (Oct. 28, 1979).
127. Cited by Myrdal, *Asian Drama*, Vol. I, p. 275.
128. *Guardian* (Feb. 2, 1977).
129. A collection of such statements is given in the chapter "Justification of the War—Public Statements" in *The Pentagon Papers: The Senator Gravel Edition* (Boston: Beacon Press, 1970), Vol. I, pp. 584–629. Hereafter referred to as *Pentagon Papers*.
130. Cited by R. J. Barnet, *Intervention and Revolution: The United States in the Third World* (Cleveland, O.: World, 1968), p. 182.
131. Cited by W. LaFeber, "Roosevelt, Churchill, and Indochina: 1942–45," *American Historical Review* (Dec. 1975):1293.
132. *Pentagon Papers*, Vol. III, p. 726.
133. Cited by A. S. Whiting, *China Crosses the Yalu: The Decision to Enter the Korean War* (Stanford, Calif.: Stanford University Press, 1968), p. 39.
134. Nguyen Khac Vien, "The Vietnamese Experience and the Third World," *Bulletin of Concerned Asian Scholars* VI (Sept.–Oct. 1974): 10.
135. Cited by C. Fenn, *Ho Chi Minh* (New York: Charles Scribner's Sons, 1973), p. 41.
136. Cited by Barnet, op. cit., p. 184.
137. *The Indochina Story by the Committee of Concerned Asian Scholars* (New York: Bantam Books, 1970), p. 13. Hereafter referred to as *Indochina Story*.

138. Cited by Barnet, op. cit., p. 185.
139. Cited in *Indochina Story*, op. cit., p. 14.
140. Ibid., p. 16.
141. Ibid., p. 17.
142. Ibid., p. 19.
143. *Pentagon Papers*, Vol. I, p. 168.
144. Ibid.
145. *United States-Vietnam Relations, 1945–1967: Study Prepared by the Department of Defense*, 12 books (Washington, D.C.: U.S. Government Printing Office, 1971), Book 9, pp. 582, 589, 590, 622.
146. *Pentagon Papers*, Vol. I, pp. 154, 157.
147. Ibid., p. 549.
148. Ibid.
149. Cited by *Indochina Story*, op. cit., p. 21.
150. *Pentagon Papers*, Vol. I, p. 283.
151. *United States-Vietnam Relations*, op. cit., Book 10, pp. 712, 713.
152. Cited by *Indochina Story*, op. cit., p. 24.
153. Ibid.
154. Ibid., p. 25.
155. Ibid., pp. 30, 31.
156. New York *Times*, international ed. (Dec. 3, 1969); cited ibid., p. 33.
157. Cited by *Indochina Story*, op. cit., p. 26.
158. *Alleged Assassination Plots Involving Foreign Leaders: An Interim Report of the Select Committee to Study Governmental Operations. . . .* United States Senate, 94th Cong., 1st sess (Washington, D.C.: U.S. Government Printing Office, Nov. 20, 1975), p. 217.
159. "The Gulf of Tonkin: The 1964 Incidents," *Hearing Before the Committee on Foreign Relations, United States Senate, 90th Cong., 2nd sess* (Washington, D.C.: U.S. Government Printing Office, 1968); A. Austin and E. G. Windchy, *Tonkin Gulf* (Garden City, N.Y.: Doubleday, 1971).
160. New York *Times* (May 1, 1975).
161. I. F. Stone, "Why Nixon Won His Moscow Gamble," *New York Review* (June 15, 1972).
162. Cited by M. Thee, "The Indochina Wars: Great Power Involvement —Escalation and Disengagement," *Journal of Peace Research* XIII (2) (1976), p. 125.
163. H. Kissinger, *The White House Years* (Boston: Little, Brown & Co., 1979), p. 1087. See also pp. 1090, 1091, 1144.
164. *Vietnam 1976: A Report by Senator George McGovern to the Committee on Foreign Relations, United States Senate*, 94th Cong. 2nd Sess. (Washington, D.C.: U.S. Government Printing Office, Mar. 1976), p. 10.
165. Cited by New York *Times* (May 2, 1975).
166. New York *Times* (Sept. 11, 1979).
167. Ibid. (Mar. 26, 1979).
168. Los Angeles *Times* (Oct. 24, 1979).

169. New York *Times* (Nov. 19, 1980).
170. Ibid. (Aug. 20, 1979).
171. *Southern Africa* VIII (Oct. 1975):8.
172. Cited by B. Davidson, "In the Portuguese Context," in C. Allen and R. W. Johnson, eds., *African Perspectives* (Cambridge: Cambridge University Press, 1970), pp. 331, 332.
173. Cited by R. von Albertini, *Decolonization: The Administration and Future of the Colonies 1919–1960* (Garden City, N.Y.: Doubleday, 1970), p. 517.
174. Cited by A. Isaacman, *A Luta Continua: Creating a New Society in Mozambique* [Southern Africa Pamphlets No. 1] (State University of New York at Binghamton, Fernand Braudel Center, 1978), p. 10.
175. Cited ibid., p. 10.
176. Cited by J. Duffy, *Portugal in Africa* (London: Penguin Books, 1963), p. 15.
177. B. Davidson, "African Peasants and Revolution," *Journal of Peasant Studies* I (Apr. 1974), 280, 281.
178. Cited by Davidson, "In the Portuguese Context," op. cit., p. 344.
179. E. Mondlane, *The Struggle for Mozambique* (London: Penguin Books, 1969), p. 209; V. Marchetti and J. D. Marks, *The CIA and the Cult of Intelligence* (New York: Alfred A. Knopf, 1974), pp. 143–45; Stockwell, op. cit., pp. 47–53.
180. K. Maxwell, "The Hidden Revolution in Portugal," *New York Review of Books* (Apr. 17, 1975), pp. 31, 32.
181. New York *Times* (June 30, 1975).
182. Cited by Isaacman, op. cit., p. 17.
183. B. Davidson, "The Revolution of People's Power: Notes on Mozambique," *Race and Class* XXI (Autumn 1979):135, 136.
184. Isaacman, op. cit., p. 38.
185. *Le Monde* (Sept. 5, 1976); cited ibid., p. 54.
186. Cited by Isaacman, op. cit., p. 72.
187. L. Rudebeck, "Development and Class Struggle in Guinea-Bissau," *Monthly Review* (Jan. 1979), p. 30.
188. Cited by A. Beccar-Verela and F. M. Lappé, "Mozambique: Nourishing a New Nation," *Food Monitor* (Nov.–Dec. 1978), p. 13.
189. Cited by P. Epstein and A. Epstein, "Mozambique Reorganizes," *Southern Africa* (June 1980), p. 16.
190. New York *Times* (Nov. 12, 14, 1977).
191. Ibid. (Feb. 10, 1979).
192. New York *Times* (Oct. 4, 1974).
193. H. L. Matthews, *Revolution in Cuba* (New York: Scribner's Sons, 1975), p. 47.
194. J. I. Dominguez, *Cuba: Order and Revolution* (Cambridge, Mass.: Harvard University Press, 1978), p. 13.
195. L. H. Jenks, *Our Cuban Colony* (New York: Vanguard Press, 1928), p. 302.
196. Dominguez, op. cit., p. 18.

197. Jenks, op. cit., p. 312.
198. Cited by Matthews, op. cit., pp. 34, 35.
199. Matthews, op. cit., p. 146.
200. Los Angeles *Times* (Apr. 22, 1979).
201. New York *Times* (Dec. 14, 1972).
202. Matthews, op. cit., p. 345.
203. Los Angeles *Times* (June 16, 1980).
204. New York *Times* (Dec. 19, 1980).
205. Dominguez, op. cit., pp. 232, 233.
206. *Guardian* (June 15, 1977).
207. Dominguez, op. cit., Ch. 9.
208. P. Winn, "Evolution in the Revolution," *Nation* (Apr. 29, 1978), p. 496.
209. Speech by Senator Edward Kennedy delivered at the annual Mansfield Lecture, University of Montana (Apr. 17, 1970).
210. K. H. Silvert, "A Hemispheric Perspective," in J. Plank, ed., *Cuba and the United States* (Washington, D.C.: Brookings Institution, 1967), p. 120.
211. New York *Times* (Feb. 25, 1976).
212. Ibid. (June 5, 1978).
213. Cited by P. Winn, "Is the Cuban Revolution in Trouble?" *Nation* (June 7, 1980), p. 685.
214. Washington *Star* (Feb. 10, 1980).
215. Winn, "Is the Cuban Revolution in Trouble?" loc. cit.
216. Cited by D. Hirst, *The Gun and the Olive Branch* (London: Faber & Faber, 1977), p. 172.
217. Cited by M. Viorst, "A Dialogue After Darkness," *Nation* (Sept. 30, 1978), p. 289.
218. *Wall Street Journal* (July 27, 1979).
219. Cited by L. Phillips, "No Easy Walk to Freedom,'" *Working Papers* (Mar.–Apr. 1979), p. 30.
220. Los Angeles *Times* (Nov. 11, 1979).
221. New York: W. W. Norton, 1978; another important source is the Cuban-authorized account by García Marquez, written for the Mexican weekly *Proceso* and excerpted in the Washington *Post* (Jan. 10–12, 1976).
222. Stockwell, op. cit., p. 43. William Colby gave the same reason for supporting the Angola intervention, in his *Honorable Men* (New York: Simon & Schuster, 1978), pp. 339, 340.
223. Seymour Hersh, New York *Times* (Dec. 14, 1975).
224. Stockwell, op. cit., pp. 271, 272.
225. New York *Times* (Sept. 25, 1980).
226. *Guardian* (Oct. 31, 1979).
227. Text in J. C. Hurewitz, *Diplomacy in the Near and Middle East* (Princeton, N.J.: D. Van Nostrand, 1956), Vol. II, pp. 234, 235.
228. D. Ben-Gurion, *Rebirth and Destiny of Israel* (New York: Philosophical Library, 1954), p. 663.

229. Cited by Hirst, op. cit., p. 112. Details of the activities of Arab as well as Jewish binationalists are given in A. Cohen, *Israel and the Arab World* (Funk & Wagnalls, 1970), pp. 289–308.
230. Cited by J. B. Bell, *Terror out of Zion* (New York: St. Martin's Press, 1977), p. 107.
231. M. Begin, *The Revolt* (Los Angeles: Nash, 1972), p. 52.
232. Cited by B. Halpern, *The Idea of the Jewish State* (Cambridge, Mass.: Harvard University Press, 1961), p. 360.
233. Cited by Hirst, op. cit., p. 114.
234. Ibid., pp. 114, 115.
235. Cited ibid., p. 135.
236. M. Alami, "The Lesson of Palestine," *Middle East Journal* (Oct. 1949):385.
237. Cohen, op. cit., pp. 457–59.
238. Cited by Hirst, op. cit., pp. 138, 139.
239. Ibid., p. 140.
240. *Al-Hayat* (Beirut) (Dec. 20, 1948); cited by Alami, op. cit., pp. 381, 382.
241. New York *Times* (Feb. 19, 1980).
242. Cited by Cohen, op. cit., pp. 477, 478.
243. Ibid., pp. 490, 491.
244. Cited by Hirst, op. cit., p. 185.
245. Cohen, op. cit., p. 500.
246. Ibid., p. 503.
247. Cited by A. A. Elrazik, R. Amin and U. Davis, "Problems of Palestinians in Israel," *Journal of Palestine Studies* VII (Spring 1978):48.
248. Cohen, op. cit., p. 504.
249. Cited by Hirst, op. cit., p. 274.
250. Cited by P. Duff, ed., *War or Peace in the Middle East?* (Nottingham: Spokesman, 1978), p. 17.
251. New York *Times* (Sept. 4, 1973).
252. *UN Special Committee Report*, Doc. A/8828 (1972), para. 77, p. 38.
253. Los Angeles *Times* (Nov. 2, 1979).
254. New York *Times* (Apr. 12, 1973).
255. Cited by Cohen, op. cit., p. 538.
256. Cited by Hirst, op. cit., pp. 220, 221.
257. Ibid., p. 221.
258. *The Colonization of the West Bank Territories by Israel: Hearings before the Subcommittee on Immigration and Naturalization of the Subcommittee on the Judiciary*, United States Senate, 95th Cong., 1st sess. (Oct. 17, 18, 1977) (Washington, D.C.: U.S. Government Printing Office, 1978).
259. *Time* (May 30, 1977).
260. New York *Times* (June 16, 1979).
261. Los Angeles *Times* (Nov. 24, 1980).
262. Hirst, op. cit., p. 245.
263. Cited by Cohen, op. cit., pp. 67, 69; emphasis in original.

264. D. Ingrams, ed., *Palestine Papers 1917–1922* (London: John Murray, 1972), p. 5.
265. Ibid., p. 30.
266. Cited by Hirst, op. cit., p. 40.
267. New York *Times* (Apr. 28, 1971).
268. Los Angeles *Times* (Oct. 14, 1979).
269. J. Judis, "General Peled on Israel and the PLO," *In These Times* (June 14–20, 1978), p. 2.
270. *The Colonization of the West Bank Territories by Israel*, op. cit., pp. 8, 9.
271. Y. Lotan, in "Symposium" in *Nation* (Nov. 3, 1979), p. 426.
272. New York *Times* (June 16, 1979).
273. M. Garbus, "The Politics of the PLO," *Nation* (Nov. 3, 1979), p. 429.
274. New York *Times* (Sept. 2, 1977).
275. Cited by E. Ahmad, "Whose Third World?" in New York *Times*, op-ed page (Mar. 28, 1979).
276. New York *Times* (June 18, 1980).
277. New York *Times* (Dec. 16, 1977).
278. Ibid. (Feb. 8, 1975).
279. Los Angeles *Times* (Nov. 25, 1979).

Chapter 24

1. Cited by C. Hill, *Reformation to Industrial Revolution* (London: George Weidenfeld & Nicolson, 1967), p. 202.
2. New York *Times* (Apr. 3, 1981).
3. *Southern Africa* (July–Aug. 1979), p. 4.
4. Ibid. (Nov.–Dec. 1979), p. 18.
5. New York *Times* (Sept. 26, 1974).
6. Ibid. (July 17, 1980).
7. "Soviet Geopolitical Momentum: Myth or Menace—Trends of Soviet Influence Around the World from 1945 to 1980," *The Defense Monitor* (Jan. 1980).
8. Cited by G. Barraclough, "Waiting for the New Order," *New York Review* (Oct. 26, 1978), p. 51.
9. W. Leontief et al., *The Future of the World Economy: A United Nations Study* (London: Oxford University Press, 1977), p. 11.
10. Speech by the Secretary of State (May 6, 1976), Nairobi, Kenya (Department of State, Bureau of Public Affairs), p. 2.
11. Los Angeles *Times* (Dec. 30, 1977).
12. New York: E. P. Dutton, 1976.
13. F. M. Lappé and J. Collins, *Food First* (Boston: Houghton Mifflin, 1977), and *The Aid Debate* (San Francisco: Institute for Food and Development Policy, Working Paper No. 1, Jan. 1979).
14. Cited in *The Aid Debate*, ibid., p. 23.
15. Los Angeles *Times* (Sept. 24, 1978).

16. *Overcoming World Hunger: The Challenge Ahead. Report of the Presidential Commission on World Hunger* (Washington, D.C.: U.S. Government Printing Office, Mar. 1980).
17. Cited in *The Aid Debate*, op. cit., p. 11.
18. *Hearings of Committee on Foreign Affairs, House of Representatives,* 88th Cong., 2nd sess. (Mar. 23, 1964), p. 19.
19. Cited by A. Foster-Carter, "Neo-Marxist Approaches to Development and Underdevelopment," *Journal of Contemporary Asia* III (1973):20.
20. G. Barraclough, "The Struggle for the Third World," *New York Review* (Nov. 9, 1978), p. 56.
21. J. L. Buck, *Land Utilization in China* (Shanghai, 1937).
22. C. Riskin, "Surplus and Stagnation in Modern China," in D. H. Perkins, ed., *China's Modern Economy in Historical Perspective* (Stanford, Calif.: Stanford University Press, 1975), pp. 49–84; J. Gurley, "Rural Development in China," in E. D. Edwards, *Employment in Developing Nations* (New York: Columbia University Press, 1974), p. 385.
23. K. Gough, "The Green Revolution in South India and North Vietnam," *Monthly Review* (Jan. 1978), pp. 10–21; K. Gough, *Ten Times More Beautiful* (New York: Monthly Review Press, 1978).
24. Gough, "The Green Revolution . . . ," ibid., p. 17.
25. Cited by Lappé and Collins, op. cit., p. 377.
26. New York *Times* (Aug. 25, 1979).
27. R. Prebisch, "North-South Dialogue," *Third World Quarterly* II (Jan. 1980):15–18.
28. J. Palacios, *Chile: An Attempt at Historic Compromise* (Chicago: Banner Press, 1979), p. 150.
29. Los Angeles *Times* (Apr. 16, 1981).
30. Ibid. (Jan. 27, 1978).
31. *Wall Street Journal* (Mar. 22, 1978).
32. D. Weir and M. Schapiro, "The Circle of Poison," *Nation* (Nov. 15, 1980), p. 516. Full details in their book, *Circle of Poison: Pesticides and People in a Hungry World* (San Francisco: Institute for Food and Development Policy, 1981).
33. K. Boulding, *Beyond Economics* (Ann Arbor: University of Michigan Press, 1968).
34. The symposium was held at the initiative of the director-general for development and international economic co-operation, and its proceedings published as UN General Assembly Document A/34/467 (Sept. 18, 1979). Republished in *Alternatives*, V (1979–80):397–426.
35. New York *Times* (May 7, 1979).
36. P. M. Sweezy, *Post-Revolutionary Society* (New York: Monthly Review Press, 1980), Ch. 9.
37. Summary of the two studies in New York *Times* (Mar. 27, 1981, and Apr. 6, 1981).

38. New York *Times* (Feb. 25, 1980).
39. Washington *Post* (July 22, 1980), cited by J. Stork, "Saudi Arabia and the U.S." *MERIP Reports* No. 91 (Oct. 1980), p. 29.
40. Cited by R. J. Barnet, *The Lean Years* (New York: Simon and Schuster, 1980), p. 227.
41. New York *Times* (Jan. 10, 1981).

Bibliography

Chapter 2

Amin, Samir. *Unequal Development: An Essay on the Social Formations of Peripheral Capitalism.* New York: Monthly Review Press, 1976.

Dobb, M. *Studies in the Development of Capitalism.* New York: International Publishers, 1947.

Frank, A. G. *World Accumulation, 1492–1789.* New York: Monthly Review Press, 1978.

———. *Dependent Accumulation and Underdevelopment.* New York: Monthly Review Press, 1979.

Hilton, R., ed. *The Transition from Feudalism to Capitalism.* London: NLB, 1976.

Mandel, E. *Marxist Economic Theory,* 2 vols. London: Merlin Press, 1962.

Myrdal, G. *Rich Lands and Poor.* New York: Harper & Brothers, 1957.

Rhodes, R. I., ed. *Imperialism and Underdevelopment: A Reader.* New York: Monthly Review Press, 1970.

Ribeiro, D. *The Civilizational Process.* New York: Harper & Row Torchbook, 1968.

Stavrianos, L. S. *World History,* 3rd ed. Englewood Cliffs, N.J.: Prentice-Hall, 1982.

Wallerstein, I. *The Modern World System: Capitalist Agriculture and the Origins of the European World Economy in the Sixteenth Century.* New York: Academic Press, 1974.

Chapter 3

Blum, J. "The Rise of Serfdom in Eastern Europe," *American Historical Review* LXII (July 1957): 807–36.

————. *Lord and Peasant in Russia from the Ninth to the Nineteenth Century.* Princeton, N.J.: Princeton University Press, 1961.

Kirchner, W. *Commercial Relations Between Russia and Europe 1400 to 1800.* Bloomington: Indiana University Press, 1966.

Lyashchenko, P. I., *History of the National Economy of Russia to the 1917 Revolution.* New York: Macmillan, 1949.

Malowist, M. "Poland, Russia and Western Trade in the 15th and 16th Centuries," *Past & Present* 13 (1958):26–41.

Pach, S. P. The Shifting of International Trade Routes in the 15th–17th Centuries," *Acta Historica* XIV (1968):287–319.

————. "Diminishing Share of East-Central Europe in the 17th Century International Trade," *Acta Historica* XVI (1970):289–305.

Postan, M. M. et al. *Eastern and Western Europe in the Middle Ages.* New York: Harcourt Brace Jovanovich, 1970, Ch. IV.

Rich, E. E. and Wilson, C. H., eds. *Cambridge Economic History, Vol. IV: The Economy of Expanding Europe in the Sixteenth and Seventeenth Centuries.* Cambridge: Cambridge University Press, 1967.

Wallerstein, I. *The Modern World System: Capitalist Agriculture and the Origins of the European World Economy in the Sixteenth Century.* New York: Academic Press, 1974.

Chapter 4

Beckford, G. L. *Persistent Poverty: Underdevelopment in Plantation Economies of the Third World.* London: Oxford University Press, 1972.

Chiappelli, F., ed. *First Images of America: The Impact of the New World on the Old,* 2 vols. Berkeley: University of California Press, 1976.

Crosby, A. W., Jr. *The Columbian Exchange: Biological and Cultural Consequences of 1492.* Westport, Conn.: Greenwood, 1972.

Farb, P. *Man's Rise to Civilization as Shown by the Indians of North America. . . .* New York: E. P. Dutton, 1968.

Frank, A. G. *Lumpenbourgeoisie, Lumpendevelopment; Dependence, Class, and Politics in Latin America.* New York: Monthly Review Press, 1972).

————. *World Accumulation, 1492–1789.* New York: Monthly Review Press, 1979.

————. *Dependent Accumulation and Underdevelopment.* New York: Monthly Review Press, 1979.

Genovese, E. D. *The World the Slaveholders Made.* New York: Pantheon, 1969.

Gibson, C. *The Aztecs Under Spanish Rule.* Stanford, Calif.: Stanford University Press, 1964.

————. *Spain in America.* New York: Harper & Row, 1966.

Parry, J. H. *The Age of Reconnaissance: Discovery, Exploitation and Settlement 1450 to 1650.* London: George Weidenfeld & Nicolson, 1963.

Riley, C. L., ed. *Man Across the Sea: Problems of Pre-Columbian Contacts*. Austin: University of Texas Press, 1971.

Sheridan, R. B. *Sugar and Slavery: An Economic History of the British West Indies 1623–1775*. Baltimore: Johns Hopkins University Press, 1974.

Stein, S. J., and Stein, B. H. *The Colonial Heritage of Latin America*. London: Oxford University Press, 1970.

Van Sertima, I. *They Came Before Columbus*. New York: Random House, 1977.

Wachtel, N. *The Vision of the Vanquished: The Spanish Conquest of Peru Through Indian Eyes 1530–1570*. New York: Barnes & Noble, 1977.

Wallerstein, I. *The Modern World System: Capitalist Agriculture and Origins of the European World Economy in the Sixteenth Century*. New York: Academic Press, 1974.

Chapter 5

Amin, S. "Underdevelopment and Dependence in Black Africa—Origins and Contemporary Forms," *Journal of Modern African Studies* X (1972):503–24.

Beachey, R. W. *The Slave Trade of Eastern Africa*. Rex Collings, 1976.

————. *The Slave Trade of Eastern Africa: A Collection of Documents*. Rex Collings, 1976.

Curtin, P. D. *The Atlantic Slave Trade: A Census*. Madison: University of Wisconsin Press, 1969.

Davidson, B. *The African Slave Trade*. Boston: Little, Brown, 1961.

Goody, J. *Technology, Tradition, and the State in Africa*. London: Oxford University Press, 1971.

Hopkins, A. G. *An Economic History of West Africa*. New York: Columbia University Press, 1973.

July, R. W. *Precolonial Africa: An Economic and Social History*. New York: Charles Scribner's Sons, 1975.

Kilson, M. L., and Rotberg, R. I., eds. *The African Diaspora: Interpretive Essays*. Cambridge, Mass.: Harvard University Press, 1976.

Klein, M. A., and Johnson, G. W., eds. *Perspectives on the African Past*. Boston: Little, Brown, 1972.

Levtzion, N. *Ancient Ghana and Mali*. London: Methuen, 1973.

Oliver, R., and Fage, J. D., eds. *The Cambridge History of Africa*, 8 vols. Cambridge: Cambridge University Press, 1975 ff.

Reynolds, E. *Trade and Economic Change on the Gold Coast 1807–1874*. London: Longman, 1974).

————. *Stand the Storm: African Slavery and the Slave Trade*. London: Oxford University Press, forthcoming.

Rodney, W. *How Europe Underdeveloped Africa*. Washington, D.C.: Howard University Press, 1974.

Chapter 6

Ashton, E. *A Social and Economic History of the Near East in the Middle Ages*. Berkeley: University of California Press, 1976.

Barkan, O. L. "The Price Revolution of the Sixteenth Century: A Turning Point in the Economic History of the Near East," *International Journal of Middle East Studies* VI (Jan. 1975):3–28.

Cook, M. A., ed. *Studies in the Economic History of the Middle East*. London: Oxford University Press, 1970.

Ergil, D., and Rhodes, R. I. "The Impact of the World Capitalist System on Ottoman Society," *Islamic Culture* 48 (Apr. 1974):77–91.

Gibb, H. A. R., and Bowen, H. *Islamic Society and the West*, Pt. I, II. London: Oxford University Press, 1950, 1957.

Inalcik, H. *The Ottoman Empire: The Classical Age 1300–1600*. New York: Praeger, 1973.

Issawi, C., ed. *The Economic History of the Middle East 1800–1914*. Chicago: University of Chicago Press, 1966.

Review. "The Ottoman Empire and the World Economy," a series of articles on this subject, II (Winter 1979):389–451.

Sousa, N. *The Capitulatory Regime of Turkey*. Baltimore: Johns Hopkins University Press, 1933.

Stavrianos, L. S. *The Balkans Since 1453*. New York: Rinehart, 1958.

Stoianovich, T. "Conquering Balkan Orthodox Merchant," *Journal of Economic History* XX (June 1960):234–313.

Sunar, I. *State and Society in the Politics of Turkey's Development*. Ankara, 1974.

Chapter 7

Boxer, C. R. *The Portuguese Seaborne Empire 1415–1825*. New York: Alfred A. Knopf, 1969.

Hudson, G. F. *Europe and China*. Boston: Beacon Press, 1961.

Lach, D. F. *Asia in the Making of Europe*. Chicago: University of Chicago Press, 1965 ff.

Meilink-Roelofsz, M. A. P. *Asian Trade and European Influence in the Indonesian Archipelago Between 1500 and About 1630*. The Hague: Martinus Nijhoff, 1962.

Musselman, G. *The Cradle of Colonialism*. New Haven, Conn.: Yale University Press, 1963.

Panikkar, K. M. *Asia and Western Dominance*. New York: John Day, 1954.

Parry, J. H. *The Age of Reconnaissance*. London: George Weidenfeld & Nicolson, 1963.

Pearson, M. N. *Merchants and Rulers in Gujarat*. Berkeley: University of California Press, 1976.

Sansom, G. B. *The Western World and Japan*. New York: Alfred A. Knopf, 1951.

Simkin, C. G. F. *The Traditional Trade of Asia*. London: Oxford University Press, 1968.

Steensgaard, N. *The Asian Trade Revolution of the Seventeenth Century*. Chicago: University of Chicago Press, 1974.

Chapter 8

Clairmonte, F. *Economic Liberalism and Underdevelopment*. London: Asia Publishing House, 1960.

Fieldhouse, D. K. *The Colonial Empires: A Comparative Study from the Eighteenth Century*. London: George Weidenfeld & Nicolson, 1966.

Gallagher, J., and Robinson, R. "The Imperialism of Free Trade," *Economic History Review* VI (1953):1–15.

Hannerty, P. *Imperialism and Free Trade: Lancashire and India in the Mid-Nineteenth Century*. Vancouver: University of British Columbia Press, 1976.

Hobsbawm, E. J. *The Age of Revolution: Europe from 1789 to 1848*. London: George Weidenfeld & Nicolson, 1962.

———. *The Age of Capital: 1848–1875*. London: George Weidenfeld & Nicolson, 1975.

Huttenback, R. A. *Racism and Empire: White Settlers and Colored Immigrants in the British Self-Governing Colonies 1830–1910*. Ithaca, N.Y.: Cornell University Press, 1976.

Semmel, B. *The Rise of Free Trade Imperialism*. Cambridge: Cambridge University Press, 1970.

Chapter 9

Beckford, G. L. *Persistent Poverty: Underdevelopment in Plantation Economies in the Third World*. London: Oxford University Press, 1972.

Davis, D. B. *The Problem of Slavery in Western Culture*. Ithaca, N.Y.: Cornell University Press, 1966.

———. *The Problem of Slavery in the Age of Revolution, 1770–1823*. Ithaca, N.Y.: Cornell University Press, 1976.

Dean, W. *Rio Claro: A Brazilian Plantation System 1820–1920*. Stanford, Calif.: Stanford University Press, 1976.

Ferns, H. S. *Britain and Argentina in the Nineteenth Century*. Oxford: Clarendon Press, 1960.

Frank, A. G. *Lumpenbourgeoisie, Lumpendevelopment*. New York: Monthly Review Press, 1972.

Furtado, C. *Economic Development of Latin America*. Cambridge: Cambridge University Press, 1970.

Humphreys, R. A., and Lynch, J., eds. *The Origins of the Latin American Revolutions, 1808–1826*. New York: Alfred A. Knopf, 1965.

Lang, J. *Conquest and Commerce: Spain and England in the Americas*. New York: Academic Press, 1975.

Lynch, J. *The Spanish American Revolutions, 1808–1826*. New York: W. W. Norton, 1973.

Platt, D. C. M. *Latin America and British Trade, 1806–1914*. New York: Barnes & Noble, 1973.

Rennie, Y. F. *The Argentina Republic*. Oxford: Clarendon Press, 1945.

Stein, S. J., and Stein, B. H. *The Colonial Heritage of Latin America*. London: Oxford University Press, 1970.

Chapter 10

Dike, K. O. *Trade and Politics in the Niger Delta 1830–1885*. Oxford: Clarendon Press, 1956.

Klein, M. A., and Johnson, C. W., eds. *Perspectives on the African Past*. Boston: Little, Brown, 1972.

Oliver, R., and Fage, J. D., eds. *The Cambridge History of Africa*, 8 vols. Cambridge: Cambridge University Press, 1975 ff.

Perham, M., and Simmons, J. *African Discovery: An Anthology of Exploration*. London: Faber & Faber, 1942.

Reynolds, E. *Trade and Economic Change on the Gold Coast, 1807–1874*. London: Longman, 1974.

Rodney, W. *How Europe Underdeveloped Africa*. Washington, D.C.: Howard University Press, 1974.

Schiffers, H. *The Quest for Africa: Two Thousand Years of Exploration*. London: Oldhams, 1957.

Chapter 11

Blaisdell, D. C. *European Financial Control of the Ottoman Empire*. New York: Columbia University Press, 1929.

Clark, E. C. "Ottoman Industrial Revolution," *International Journal of Middle East Studies* V (1974):65–76.

Cook, M. A., ed. *Studies in the Economic History of the Middle East*. London: Oxford University Press, 1970.

Issawi, C., ed. *The Economic History of the Middle East 1800–1914*. Chicago: University of Chicago Press, 1966.

———. *The Economic History of Iran, 1800–1914*. Chicago: University of Chicago Press, 1971.

Kazemzadeh, F. *Russia and Britain in Persia, 1864–1914*. New Haven, Conn.: Yale University Press, 1968.

Keddie, N. R. *Religion and Rebellion in Iran: The Tobacco Protest of 1891–1892*. London: Frank Cass, 1966.

———. "The Economic History of Iran, 1800–1914, and Its Political Impact: An Overview," *Iranian Studies* (Spring and Summer 1972):58–78.

Lambton, A. K. S. *Landlord and Peasant in Persia*. London: Oxford University Press, 1953.

Landes, D. *Bankers and Pashas*. Cambridge, Mass.: Harvard University Press, 1958.

Owen, E. R. J. *Cotton and the Egyptian Economy 1820–1914*. London: Oxford University Press, 1969.

Polk, W. R., and Chambers, R. L., eds. *Beginnings of Modernization in the Middle East: The Nineteenth Century.* Chicago: University of Chicago Press, 1968.

Radwan, S. *Capital Formation in Egyptian Industry and Agriculture 1882–1967.* London: Ithaca Press, 1974.

Richards, A. R. "Primitive Accumulation in Egypt, 1798–1882," *Review* I (Fall 1977):3–49.

Sunar, I. *State and Society in the Politics of Turkey's Development.* Ankara, 1974.

Tignor, R. L. *Modernization and British Colonial Rule in Egypt 1828–1914.* Princeton, N.J.: Princeton University Press,. 1966.

Ward, R. E., and Rustow, D. A. *Political Modernization in Japan and Turkey.* Princeton, N.J.: Princeton University Press, 1964.

Warriner, D. *Land and Poverty in the Middle East.* London: Oxford University Press, 1948.

Chapter 12

Bagchi, A. K. *Private Investment in India 1900–1939.* Cambridge: Cambridge University Press, 1972.

Clairmonte, F. *Economic Liberalism and Underdevelopment.* London: Asia Publishing House, 1960.

Gough, K., and Sharma, H. P., eds. *Imperialism and Revolution in South Asia.* New York: Monthly Review Press, 1973.

Harnetty, P. *Imperialism and Free Trade: Lancashire and India in the Mid-Nineteenth Century.* Vancouver: University of British Columbia Press, 1972.

Kessinger, T. G. *Vilyatpur 1848–1968: Social and Economic Change in a North Indian Village.* Berkeley: University of California Press, 1974.

Leach, E., and Mukherjee, S. N., eds. *Elites in South Asia* (Cambridge University Press, 1970).

Mukherjee, R. *The Rise and Fall of the East India Company,* new ed. New York: Monthly Review Press, 1974.

Murphey, R. *The Outsiders: The Western Experience in India and China.* Ann Arbor: University of Michigan Press, 1977.

Panikkar, K. M. *Asia and Western Dominance.* New York: John Day, 1954.

Thorner, D., and Thorner, A. *Land and Labour in India.* London: Asia Publishing House, 1962.

Whitcombe, E. *Agrarian Conditions in Northern India. Vol. I: The United Provinces Under British Rule, 1860–1900.* Berkeley: University of California Press, 1972.

Zinkin, M. *Asia and the West.* London: Chatto & Windus, 1951.

Chapter 13

Baran, P. A., and Sweezy, P. *Monopoly Capital.* New York: Monthly Review Press, 1966.

Brown, M. Barratt, *After Imperialism.* London: Merlin Press, 1970.

Beckford, G. L. *Persistent Poverty: Underdevelopment in Plantation Economies of the Third World.* London: Oxford University Press, 1972.

Clairmonte, F. *Economic Liberalism and Underdevelopment.* London: Asia Publishing House, 1960.

Hobsbawm, E. J. *Industry and Empire: An Economic History of Britain Since 1750.* London: George Weidenfeld & Nicolson, 1967.

Huttenback, R. A. *Racism and Empire: White Settlers and Colored Immigrants in the British Self-governing Colonies 1830–1910.* Ithaca, N.Y.: Cornell University Press, 1976.

Mandel, E. *Marxist Economic Theory,* 2 vols. London: Merlin Press, 1962.

Owen, R., and Sutcliffe, B., eds. *Studies in the Theory of Imperialism.* London: Longman, 1972.

Chapter 14

Cartey, W., and Kilson, M., eds. *The Africa Reader: Colonial Africa.* New York: Vintage Books, 1970.

Crowder, M. *West Africa Under Colonial Rule.* Evanston, Ill.: Northwestern University Press, 1968.

———. *West African Chiefs.* New York: Africana, 1970.

———. *West African Resistance.* New York: Africana, 1970.

Duignan, P., and Gann, L. H., eds. *Colonialism in Africa 1870–1960,* 5 vols. Cambridge: Cambridge University Press, 1969–75.

Gann, L. H., and Duignan, P. *The Burden of Empire: An Appraisal of Western Colonialism South of the Sahara.* New York: Praeger, 1967.

Isaacman, A. F. *The Tradition of Resistance in Mozambique.* London: William Heinemann, 1976.

Rotberg, R. I., and Mazrui, A. A., eds. *Protest and Power in Black Africa.* London: Oxford University Press, 1970.

Wolff, R. D. *The Economics of Colonialism: Britain and Kenya, 1870–1930.* New Haven, Conn.: Yale University Press, 1974.

Chapter 15

Chesneau, J. *Peasant Revolts in China 1840–1949.* London: Thames & Hudson, 1973.

Elvin, M. *The Pattern of the Chinese Past.* Stanford, Calif.: Stanford University Press, 1973.

Fairbank, J. K., Reischauer, E. O., and Craig, A. M. *East Asia: A Modern Transformation.* Boston: Houghton Mifflin, 1965.

Feuerwerker, A. *China's Early Industrialization.* Cambridge, Mass.: Harvard University Press, 1958.

———. *Rebellion in Nineteenth-Century China.* Ann Arbor: Michigan Papers in Chinese Studies, No. 21, 1975.

Franke, W. *A Century of Chinese Revolution 1851–1949.* London: Basil Blackwell & Mott, 1971.

Hao Yen-p'ing, *The Comprador in Nineteenth-Century China: Bridge Between East and West.* Cambridge, Mass.: Harvard University Press, 1970.

Jen Yu-wen, *The Taiping Revolutionary Movement.* New Haven, Conn.: Yale University Press, 1973.

Moulder, F. V. *Japan, China, and the Modern World Economy: Toward a Reinterpretation of East Asian Development ca. 1600 to ca. 1918.* Cambridge: Cambridge University Press, 1977.

Murphey, R. *The Outsiders: The Western Experience in India and China.* Ann Arbor: University of Michigan Press, 1977.

Perkins, D. H., ed. *China's Modern Economy in Historical Perspective.* Stanford, Calif.: Stanford University Press, 1975.

Selby, J. *The Paper Dragon: An Account of the China Wars, 1840–1900.* New York: Praeger, 1968.

Spence, J. *To Change China: Western Advisers in China 1620–1960.* Boston: Little, Brown, 1967.

Teng, S. Y. *The Taiping Rebellion and the Western Powers.* London: Oxford University Press, 1971.

Wolf, E. R. *Peasant Wars of the Twentieth Century.* New York: Harper & Row, 1969.

Workman, F., Jr. *The Fall of Imperial China.* New York: The Free Press, 1975.

Chapter 16

Balzak, S. S., et al., eds. *Economic Geography of the U.S.S.R.* New York: Macmillan, 1961.

Blackwell, W. L., ed. *Russian Economic Development from Peter the Great to Stalin.* New York: Franklin Watts, 1974.

Crisp, O. *Studies in the Russian Economy Before 1914.* New York: Harper & Row, 1976.

Crouzet, F., et al., eds. *Essays in European Economic History, 1789–1914.* London: Edward Arnold, 1969.

Falkus, M. E. *The Industrialization of Russia 1700–1914.* New York: Macmillan, 1972.

Maynard, J. *Russia in Flux.* New York: Macmillan, 1941.

McKay, J. P. *Pioneers for Profit: Foreign Entrepreneurship and Russian Industrialization, 1885–1913.* Chicago: University of Chicago Press, 1970.

Von Laue, T. H. *Sergei Witte and the Industrialization of Russia.* New York: Columbia University Press, 1963.

————. *Why Lenin? Why Stalin?* Philadelphia: J. B. Lippincott, 1964.

Wallace, D. M. *Russia on the Eve of War and Revolution.* New York: Vintage Books, 1961.

Chapter 17

Craig, A. *Choshu in the Meiji Restoration*. Cambridge, Mass.: Harvard University Press, 1961.

Halliday, J. *A Political History of Japanese Capitalism*. New York: Pantheon Books, 1975.

Lockwood, W. W. *The Economic Development of Japan*. Princeton, N.J.: Princeton University Press, 1954.

Maulder, F. V. *Japan, China, and the Modern World Economy: Toward a Reinterpretation of East Asian Development ca. 1600 to ca. 1918*. Cambridge: Cambridge University Press, 1977.

Moore, B., Jr. *Social Origins of Dictatorship and Democracy*. Boston: Beacon Press, 1966.

Nakamura, J. I. *Agricultural Production and the Economic Development of Japan, 1873–1922*. Princeton, N.J.: Princeton University Press, 1966.

Norman, E. H. *Japan's Emergence as a Modern State: Political and Economic Problems of the Meiji Period*. New York: Institute of Pacific Relations, 1940.

Sansom, G. B. *The Western World and Japan*. New York: Alfred A. Knopf, 1950.

Smith, T. C. *Political Change and Industrial Development in Japan: Government Enterprise, 1868–1880*. Stanford, Calif.: Stanford University Press, 1955.

——. *The Agrarian Origins of Modern Japan*. Stanford, Calif.: Stanford University Press, 1959.

Ward, R. E., and Rostow, D., eds. *Political Modernization in Japan and Turkey*. Princeton, N.J.: Princeton University Press, 1968.

Chapter 18

GENERAL

Moore, Barrington. *Social Origins of Dictatorship and Democracy*. Boston: Beacon Press, 1966.

Wolf, E. R. *Peasant Wars of the Twentieth Century*. New York: Harper & Row, 1969.

BLACK RESISTANCE IN THE AMERICAS

Foner, R. S. *History of the Black Americans*. Westport, Conn.: Greenwood Press, 1975.

Foner, L., and Genovese, E. D., eds. *Slavery in the New World: A Reader in Comparative History*. Englewood Cliffs, N.J.: Prentice-Hall, 1969.

Genovese, E. D. *From Rebellion to Revolution*. Baton Rouge: Louisiana State University Press, 1979.

James, C. L. R. *The Black Jacobins*, 2nd rev. ed. New York: Vintage Books, 1963.

RESISTANCE IN CUBA AND THE PHILIPPINES

Foner, P. S. *The Spanish-Cuban-American War and the Birth of American Imperialism*, 2 vols. New York: Monthly Review Press, 1972.

Francisco, L. "The First Vietnam: The Philippine-American War of 1899," *Bulletin of Concerned Asian Scholars* V (Dec. 1973):2–16.

Pomeroy, W. J. *American Neo-Colonialism: Its Emergence in the Philippines and Asia*. New York: International Publishers, 1970.

Schirmer, D. B. *Republic or Empire: American Resistance to the Philippine War*. Cambridge, Mass.: Schenkman, 1972.

Wolff, L. *Little Brown Brother*. Garden City, N.Y.: Doubleday, 1960.

RUSSO-JAPANESE WAR AND THE 1905 RUSSIAN REVOLUTION

Harcave, S. *First Blood: The Russian Revolution of 1905*. New York: Macmillan, 1964.

Mehlinger, H. D., and Thompson, J. M. *Count Witte and the Tsarist Government in the 1905 Revolution*. Bloomington: Indiana University Press, 1972.

Spector, I. *The First Russian Revolution: Its Impact on Asia*. Englewood Cliffs, N.J.: Prentice-Hall, 1962.

Walder, D. *The Short Victorious War: The Russo-Japanese Conflict 1904–5*. New York: Harper & Row, 1974.

PERSIAN REVOLUTION

Browne, E. G. *The Persian Revolution of 1905–1909*. Cambridge: Cambridge University Press, 1910.

Kazemzadeh, F. *Russia and Britain in Persia, 1864–1914: A Study in Imperialism*. New Haven, Conn.: Yale University Press, 1968.

Lambton, A. K. S. "Secret Societies and the Persian Revolution of 1905–6," *St. Antony's Papers*, No. 4, *Middle Eastern Affairs*, No. 1. Carbondale: Southern Illinois University Press, n.d., pp. 43–60.

————. "Persian Political Societies 1906–11," *St. Antony's Papers*, No. 16, *Middle Eastern Affairs*, No. 3. Carbondale: Southern Illinois University Press, n.d., pp. 41–89.

Shuster, W. M. *The Strangling of Persia*. New York: Century, 1912.

YOUNG TURK REVOLUTION

Ahmed, F. *The Young Turks: The Committee of Union and Progress in Turkish Politics 1908–1914*. Oxford: Clarendon Press, 1969.

Ergil, D. "A Reassessment: The Young Turks, Their Politics and Anti-Colonial Struggle," *Balkan Studies* XVI (1975):26–72.

Ergil, D., and Rhodes, R. I. "Western Capitalism and the Disintegration of the Ottoman Empire," *Economy and History* XVIII (1975):41–60.

Sousa, N. *The Capitulatory Regime of Turkey*. Baltimore, Md.: Johns Hopkins University Press, 1933.

CHINESE REVOLUTION

Esherick, J. W. "1911: A Review," *Modern China* II (Apr. 1976):141–84.
Sheridan, J. E. *China in Disintegration: The Republican Era in Chinese History, 1912–1949.* New York: The Free Press, 1975.
Wakeman, F., Jr. *The Fall of Imperial China.* New York: Free Press, 1975.
Wright, M. C., ed. *China in Revolution: The First Phase, 1900–1913.* New Haven, Conn.: Yale University Press, 1968.
Wu Yu-chang, *The Revolution of 1911: A Great Democratic Revolution of China.* Peking: Foreign Languages Press, 1962.
Young, E. P. "Nationalism, Reform, and Republican Revolution: China in the Early Twentieth Century," in J. B. Crowley, ed., *Modern East Asia: Essays in Interpretation.* New York: Harcourt, Brace & World, 1970.

MEXICAN REVOLUTION

Cockcroft, J. D. *Intellectual Precursors of the Mexican Revolution, 1900–1913.* Austin: University of Texas Press, 1968.
———— et al. *Dependence and Underdevelopment: Latin America's Political Economy.* Garden City, N.Y.: Anchor Books, 1972.
Hansen, R. D. *The Politics of Mexican Development.* Baltimore, Md.: Johns Hopkins University Press, 1971.
Ruiz, R. E. *The Great Rebellion: Mexico 1905–1924.* New York: W. W. Norton, 1980.
Russell, P. *Mexico in Transition.* Austin, Texas: Colorado River Press, 1977.
Womack, J., Jr. *Zapata and the Mexican Revolution.* New York: Alfred A. Knopf, 1969.

AFRICAN RESISTANCE

Asante, S. K. B. *Pan-African Protest: West Africa and the Italo-Ethiopian Crisis, 1934–1941.* London: Longman, 1977.
Rotberg, R. I., and Mazrui, A. A. *Protest and Power in Black Africa.* London: Oxford University Press, 1970.

Chapter 19

Amin, S. *Unequal Development.* New York: Monthly Review Press, 1976.
Bairoch, P. *The Economic Development of the Third World Since 1900.* Berkeley: University of California Press, 1975.
Barnet, R. J., and Muller, R. E. *Global Reach: The Power of the Multinational Corporations.* New York: Simon & Schuster, 1974.
Burbach, R., and Flynn, P. *Agribusiness in the Americas.* New York: Monthly Review Press, 1980.
Carnoy, M. *Education as Cultural Imperialism.* New York: David McKay, 1974.

Chaliand, G. *Revolution in the Third World: Myths and Prospects.* New York: Viking Press, 1977.

Chomsky, N., and Herman, E. S. *The Political Economy of Human Rights,* 2 vols. Boston: South End Press, 1979.

Frobel, F. *The New International Division of Labor.* Cambridge: Cambridge University Press, 1980.

George, S. *How the Other Half Dies: The Real Reasons for World Hunger.* London: Penguin Books, 1976.

————. *Feeding the Few: Corporate Control of Food.* Washington, D.C.: Institute for Policy Studies, 1978.

Klare, M. T. *War Without End.* New York: Vintage Books, 1972.

————. *Supplying Repression: U. S. Support for Authoritarian Regimes Abroad.* Washington, D.C.: Institute for Policy Studies, 1979.

Lappé, F. M., and Collins, J. *Food First: Beyond the Myth of Scarcity.* Boston: Houghton Mifflin, 1977.

Lernoux, P. *Cry of the People.* Garden City, N.Y.: Doubleday, 1980.

Magdoff, H., and Sweezy, P. M. *The End of Prosperity: The American Economy in the 1970s.* New York: Monthly Review Press, 1977.

Myrdal, G. *The Challenge of World Poverty.* London: Allen Lane, 1970.

Radosh, R. *American Labor and United States Foreign Policy.* New York: Random House, 1969.

Schiller, H. I. *Mass Communications and American Empire.* Boston: Beacon Press, 1971.

————. *Communication and Cultural Domination.* White Plains, N.Y.: International Arts & Sciences Press, 1976.

————. "Computer Systems: Power for Whom and for What?" *Journal of Communication* 28 (Autumn 1978):184–93.

Smith, A. *The Geopolitics of Information: How Western Culture Dominates the World.* London: Oxford University Press, 1980.

Vallianatos, E. G. *Fear in the Countryside: The Control of Agricultural Resources in the Poor Countries by Non-Peasant Elites.* Cambridge, Mass.: Ballinger, 1976.

Chapter 20

Bettelheim, C. *Class Struggles in the USSR: First Period 1917–1923.* New York: Monthly Review Press, 1976.

————. *Class Struggles in the USSR: Second Period 1923–1930.* New York: Monthly Review Press, 1978.

Carr, E. H. *A History of Russia: The Bolshevik Revolution 1917–1923.* New York: Macmillan, 1951.

Claudin, F. *The Communist Movement,* 2 vols. New York: Monthly Review Press, 1975.

d'Encausse, H. C., and Schram, S. R. *Marxism and Asia.* London: Allen Lane, Penguin Books, 1969.

Levin, N. G., Jr. *Woodrow Wilson and World Politics.* London: Oxford University Press, 1968.

Lewin, M. *Russian Peasants and Soviet Power*. New York: W. W. Norton, 1968.

Mayer, A. J. *Politics and Diplomacy of Peacemaking: Containment and Revolution at Versailles 1918–1919*. New York: Alfred A. Knopf, 1967.

Silverlight, J. *The Victor's Dilemma: Allied Intervention in the Russian Civil War*. New York: Weybright and Talley, 1970.

Wilber, C. K. *The Soviet Model and Underdeveloped Countries*. Chapel Hill: University of North Carolina Press, 1969.

Chapter 21

CHINA

Bianco, L. *Origins of the Chinese Revolution 1915–1949*. Stanford, Calif.: Stanford University Press, 1971.

Clubb, O. E. *Twentieth Century China*. New York: Columbia University Press, 1964.

Guillermaz, J. *A History of the Chinese Communist Party, 1921–1949*. London: Methuen, 1972.

Isaacs, H. R. *The Tragedy of the Chinese Revolution*, 2nd rev. ed. New York: Atheneum, 1968.

Sheridan, J. E. *China in Disintegration. The Republican Era in Chinese History, 1912–1949*. New York: The Free Press, 1975.

INDIA

Gandhi, M. K. *An Autobiography*. Boston: Beacon Press, 1957.

Hiro, D. *Inside India Today*. London: Routledge and Kegan Paul, 1976.

Nehru, J. *The Discovery of India*. New York: John Day, 1946.

Segal, R. *The Crisis of India*. London: Penguin Books, 1965.

Thorner, D., and Thorner, A. *Land and Labour in India*. Bombay: Asia Publishing House, 1962.

Wiser, W., and Wiser, C. *Behind Mud Walls 1930–1960*. Berkeley: University of California Press, 1964.

MIDDLE EAST

Abu-Lughod, I., ed. *The Transformation of Palestine*. Evanston, Ill.: Northwestern University Press, 1971.

Cohen, A. *Israel and the Arab World*. New York: Funk & Wagnalls, 1970.

Halpern, B. *The Idea of the Jewish State*. Cambridge, Mass.: Harvard University Press, 1961.

Lambton, A. K. S. *Landlord and Peasant in Persia*. London: Oxford University Press, 1953.

Lesch, A. M. *Arab Politics in Palestine 1917–1939: The Frustration of a National Movement*. Ithaca, N.Y.: Cornell University Press, 1979.

Lewis, B. *The Emergence of Modern Turkey*. London: Oxford University Press, 1961.

Radwan, S. *Capital Formation in Egyptian Industry and Agriculture 1882–1967*. London: Ithaca Press, 1974.

Sluglett, P. *Britain in Iraq 1914–1922.* London: Ithaca Press, 1976.
Sunar, I. *State and Society in the Politics of Turkey's Development.* Ankara, 1974.

AFRICA

Brett, E. A. *Colonialism and Underdevelopment in East Africa: The Politics of Economic Change 1919–1939* (New York: NOK Publishers, 1973).
Chinweizu, *The West and the Rest of Us.* New York: Vintage Books, 1975.
Gann, L. H., and Duignan, P. *Colonialism in Africa 1870–1960,* 5 vols. Cambridge: Cambridge University Press, 1969–75.
Gutkind, P. C. W., and Wallerstein, I. *The Political Economy of Contemporary Africa.* Beverly Hills, Calif.: Sage Publications, 1976.
Hopkins, A. G. *An Economic History of West Africa.* New York: Columbia University Press, 1973.
Rodney, W. *How Europe Underdeveloped Africa.* Washington, D.C.: Howard University Press, 1974.
Wallerstein, I. *The Road to Independence: Ghana and the Ivory Coast.* La Haye: Mouton, 1964.

LATIN AMERICA

Blanksten, G. I. *Peron's Argentina.* New York: Russell & Russell, 1953.
Furtado, C. *Economic Development of Latin America.* Cambridge: Cambridge University Press, 1970.
Hansen, R. D. *The Politics of Mexican Development.* Baltimore, Md.: Johns Hopkins University Press, 1971.
Russell, P. *Mexico in Transition.* Austin, Texas: Colorado River Press, 1977.
Scobie, J. R. *Argentina: A City and a Nation.* London: Oxford University Press, 1964.
Wagley, C. *An Introduction to Brazil.* New York: Columbia University Press, 1963.

Chapter 22

Belden, J. *China Shakes the World.* New York: Monthly Review Press, 1970.
Bianco, L. *Origins of the Chinese Revolution 1915–1949.* Stanford, Calif.: Stanford University Press, 1971.
Gurley, J. *China's Economy and the Maoist Strategy.* New York: Monthly Review Press, 1976.
Meisner, M. *Mao's China: A History of the People's Republic.* New York: The Free Press, 1978.
Milton, D., and Milton, N. *The Wind Will Not Subside: Years in Revolutionary China, 1964–1969.* New York: Pantheon Books, 1976.
Milton, D.; Milton, N.; and Schurmann, F., eds. *People's China.* New York: Vintage Books, 1974.

Selden, M., ed. *The People's Republic of China: A Documentary History of Revolutionary Change*. New York: Monthly Review Press, 1979.

Sheridan, J. E. *China in Disintegration*. New York: The Free Press, 1975.

Snow, E. *Red Star Over China*. New York: Grove Press, 1968.

———. *Red China Today*. New York: Vintage Books, 1971.

Chapter 23

DYNAMICS OF THIRD WORLD POLITICS

Albertini, R. von. *Decolonization: The Administration and Future of the Colonies 1919–1960*. Garden City, N.Y.: Doubleday, 1971.

Barnet, R. D. *Intervention and Revolution: The United States in the Third World*. Cleveland, O.: World, 1968.

Chaliand, G. *Revolution in the Third World: Myths and Prospects*. New York: Viking Press, 1977.

Chomsky, N., and Herman, E. S. *The Political Economy of Human Rights*, 2 vols. Boston: South End Press, 1979.

Horowitz, D. *Imperialism and Revolution*. London: Allen Lane, 1969.

Kolko, G. *The Politics of War*. New York: Random House, 1968.

Payer, C. *The Debt Trap: The IMF and the Third World*. New York: Monthly Review Press, 1974.

Shoup, L. H., and Minter, W., *Imperial Brain Trust*. New York: Monthly Review Press, 1977.

Worsley, P. *The Third World*, 2nd ed. Chicago: University of Chicago Press, 1970.

INDIA

Bettelheim, C. *India Independent*. New York: Monthly Review Press, 1968.

Brecher, M. *Nehru*. London: Oxford University Press, 1959.

Dutt, B. C. *Mutiny of the Innocents*. Bombay: Sindhu, 1971.

Frankel, F. R. *India's Green Revolution*. Princeton, N.J.: Princeton University Press, 1972.

Gough, K., and Sharma, H. P., eds. *Imperialism and Revolution in South Asia*. New York: Monthly Review Press, 1973.

Hiro, D. *Inside India Today*. New York: Monthly Review Press, 1976.

Menon, V. P. *The Transfer of Power in India*. Princeton, N.J.: Princeton University Press, 1957.

Myrdal, G. *Asian Drama: An Inquiry into the Poverty of Nations*, 3 vols. New York: Pantheon Books, 1968.

Weiner, M. *Party Building in a New Nation*. Chicago: University of Chicago Press, 1967.

MIDDLE EAST

Abdel-Fadil, M. *Development, Income Distribution and Social Change in Rural Egypt (1952–1970)*. Cambridge: Cambridge University Press, 1975.

Amin, S. *The Arab Nation.* London: Zed Press, 1978.

Anthony, J. D. *Arab States of the Lower Gulf.* Washington, D.C.: Middle East Institute, 1975.

Graham, R. *Iran: The Illusion of Power.* New York: St. Martin's Press, 1978.

Halliday, F. *Arabia Without Sultans.* London: Penguin Books, 1974.

————. *Iran: Dictatorship and Development.* New York: Viking Press, 1979.

Hussein, M. *Class Conflict in Egypt 1945–1970.* New York: Monthly Review Press, 1973.

Lackner, H. *A House Built on Sand: A Political Economy of Saudi Arabia.* London: Ithaca Press, 1979.

Kazziha, W. W. *Revolutionary Transformation in the Arab World.* New York: Barnes and Noble, 1975.

Mabro, R., and Radwan, S. *The Industrialization of Egypt 1939–1973.* Oxford: Clarendon Press, 1976.

Sunar, I. *State and Society in the Politics of Turkey's Development.* Ankara, 1974.

TROPICAL AFRICA

Bender, G. J. *Angola under the Portuguese.* Berkeley: University of California Press, 1978.

Cabral, A. *Return to the Source.* New York: Monthly Review Press, 1973.

Davidson, B.: *The Liberation of Guiné.* Harmondsworth, Middlx.: Penguin Books, 1969.

————. *Let Freedom Come: Africa in Modern History.* Boston: Little, Brown, 1978.

Davidson, B.; Slovo, J.; and Wilkinson, A. R. *Southern Africa: The New Politics of Revolution.* Harmondsworth, Middlx.: Penguin Books, 1976.

Freyhold, M. von. *Ujamaa Villages in Tanzania: Analysis of a Social Experiment.* New York: Monthly Review Press, 1979.

Gutkind, P. C. W., and Waterman, P., eds. *African Social Studies.* New York: Monthly Review Press, 1977.

Isaacman, A. *A Luta Continua: Creating a New Society in Mozambique* [Southern Africa Pamphlets No. 1]. Fernand Braudel Center, State University of New York at Binghampton, 1978.

Lappé, F. M., and Beccar-Varela, A. *Mozambique and Tanzania: Asking the Big Questions.* San Francisco: Institute for Food and Development Policy, 1980.

Magubane, B. M. *The Political Economy of Race and Class in South Africa.* New York: Monthly Review Press, 1980.

Marcum, J. A. *The Angolan Revolution,* 2 vols. Cambridge, Mass.: MIT Press, 1969–78.

Mondlane, E. *The Struggle for Mozambique.* London: Penguin Books, 1969.

Nkrumah, K. *I Speak of Freedom: A Statement of African Ideology.* New York: Praeger, 1961.

Nyerere, J. K. *Freedom and Socialism*. London: Oxford University Press, 1968.

Seidman, A. *Planning for Development in Sub-Saharan Africa*. New York: Praeger, 1974.

Seidman, A., and Makgetla, N. S. *Outposts of Monopoly Capitalism: Southern Africa in the Changing Global Economy*. Westport, Conn.: Lawrence Hill, 1980.

LATIN AMERICA

Agee, P. *Inside the Company: CIA Diary*. London: Allen Lane, 1975.

Chilcote, R. H., and Edelstein, J. C., eds. *Latin America: The Struggle with Dependency and Beyond*. New York: John Wiley & Sons, 1974.

Cockcroft, J. D.; Frank, A. G.; and Johnson, D. L. *Dependence and Underdevelopment: Latin America's Political Economy*. Garden City, N.Y.: Doubleday, 1972.

Dominguez, J. I. *Cuba: Order and Revolution*. Cambridge, Mass.: Harvard University Press, 1978.

Furtado, C. *Economic Development of Latin America: A Survey from Colonial Times to the Cuban Revolution*. Cambridge: Cambridge University Press, 1970.

————. *Obstacles to Development in Latin America*. Garden City, N.Y.: Doubleday, 1970.

Langguth, A. J. *Hidden Terrors: The Truth about U.S. Police Operations in Latin America*. New York: Pantheon Books, 1978.

Lernoux, P. *Cry of the People*. Garden City, N.Y.: Doubleday, 1980.

Petras, J. *Latin America: From Dependence to Revolution*. New York: John Wiley & Sons, 1973.

Petras, J., and Morley, M. *The United States and Chile*. New York: Monthly Review Press, 1975.

Philip, G. D. E., *The Rise and Fall of the Peruvian Military Radicals, 1968–1976*. London: Athlone Press, 1978.

SOUTHEAST ASIA

Chomsky, N., and Herman, E. S. *The Political Economy of Human Rights*, 2 vols. Boston: South End Press, 1979.

Committee of Concerned Asian Scholars. *Indochina Story*. New York: Bantam Books, 1976.

Fall, B. B., ed. *Ho Chi Minh on Revolution: Selected Writings, 1920–66*. New York: Praeger, 1966.

Kahin, G. M., and Lewis, J. E. *The United States in Vietnam*, rev. ed. New York: Delta, 1969.

Kissinger, H. *White House Years*. Boston: Little, Brown, 1979.

Lebra, J. C. *Japanese-Trained Armies in Southeast Asia*. New York: Columbia University Press, 1977.

Pentagon Papers, Senator Gravel Edition, 4 vols. Boston: Beacon Press, 1971.

Porter, G. *A Peace Denied*. Bloomington: Indiana University Press, 1976.
———. *Cambodia: Starvation and Revolution*. New York: Monthly Review Press, 1976.
———. *Vietnam: The Definitive Documentation of Human Decisions*. Pine Plains, N.Y.: Earl M. Coleman Enterprises, 1980.
Shawcross, W. *Sideshow: Kissinger, Nixon and the Destruction of Cambodia*. New York: Simon & Schuster, 1979.

SOUTH AFRICA

Carter, G. M. *Which Way Is South Africa Going?* Bloomington: Indiana University Press, 1980.
Cervenka, Z., and Rogers, B. *The Nuclear Axis: Secret Collaboration Between West Germany and South Africa*. New York: Times Books, 1978.
Davidson, B., et al. *Southern Africa: The New Politics of Revolution*. Harmondsworth, Middlx.: Penguin Books, 1976.
Ehrensaft, P. "Polarized Accumulation and the Theory of Economic Dependence: The Implications of South African Semi-Industrial Capitalism," in P. C. W. Gutkind and I. Wallerstein, eds., *The Political Economy of Contemporary Africa*. Beverly Hills, Calif.: Sage, 1976, pp. 58–89.
First, R., et al. *The South African Connection: Western Investment in Apartheid*. Harmondsworth, Middlx.: Penguin Books, 1973.
Houghton, D. H. *The South African Economy*. London: Oxford University Press, 1973.
Serfontein, J. H. P. *Brotherhood of Power: An Exposé of the Secret Afrikaner Broederbond*. Bloomington: Indiana University Press, 1978.

ISRAEL

Begin, M. *The Revolt*. Los Angeles: Nash, 1972.
Ben-Gurion, D. *Rebirth and Destiny of Israel*. New York: Philosophical Library, 1954.
Chomsky, N. *Peace in the Middle East?* New York: Pantheon Books, 1969.
Cohen, A. *Israel and the Arab World*. New York: Funk & Wagnalls, 1970.
Davis, U. *Israel: Utopia Incorporated*. London: Zed Press, 1977.
El-Asmar, F. *To Be an Arab in Israel*. London: Frances Pinter, 1975.
Hirst, D. *The Gun and the Olive Branch*. London: Faber & Faber, 1977.
Jiryis, S. *The Arabs in Israel*. New York: Monthly Review Press, 1976.
Safran, N. *Israel: The Embattled Ally*. Cambridge, Mass.: Harvard University Press, 1978.
Said, E. W., *The Question of Palestine*. New York: Times Books, 1980.
Stevens, R. P., and Elmessiri, A. M. *Israel and South Africa*. New York: New World Press, 1976.
The Colonization of the West Bank Territories by Israel: Hearings before the Subcommittee on Immigration and Naturalization of the Committee on the Judiciary, United States Senate, 95th Cong., 1st sess. (Oct. 17, 18, 1977). Washington, D.C.: U.S. Government Printing Office, 1978.

Chapter 24

Barnet, R. J. *The Lean Years: Politics in the Age of Scarcity.* New York: Simon & Schuster, 1980.

Caldwell, M. *The Wealth of Some Nations.* London: Zed Press, 1977.

Chomsky, N., and Herman, E. S. *The Political Economy of Human Rights,* 2 vols. Boston: South End Press, 1979.

Heilbroner, R. *An Inquiry into the Human Prospect.* New York: W. W. Norton, 1974.

———. *Business Civilization in Decline.* New York: W. W. Norton, 1976.

———. *Beyond Boom and Crash.* New York: W. W. Norton, 1978.

Henderson, H. *Creating Alternative Futures.* New York: Berkley, 1978.

Kohr, L. *The Breakdown of Nations.* New York: E. P. Dutton, 1975.

Lappé, F. M., and Collins, J. *Food First: Beyond the Myth of Scarcity.* Boston: Houghton Mifflin, 1977.

Rifkin, J. *Entropy: A New World View.* New York: Viking Press, 1980.

Sweezy, P. M. *Post-Revolutionary Society.* New York: Monthly Review Press, 1980.

Stavrianos, L. S. *The Promise of the Coming Dark Age.* San Francisco: W. H. Freeman, 1976.

Stokes, B. *Local Responses to Global Problems: A Key to Meeting Basic Human Needs.* Worldwatch Paper No. 17, Feb. 1978.

Wallerstein, I. *The Capitalist World-Economy.* Cambridge: Cambridge University Press, 1979.

Zwerdling, D. *Democracy at Work: A Guide to Self-Management Experiments in the United States and Europe.* Washington, D.C.: Association for Self-Management, 1978.

The Third World: Premises of U.S. Policy. San Francisco: Institute for Contemporary Studies, 1978.

About the Author

Born in Vancouver, B.C., in 1913, L. S. Stavrianos received his B.A. from the University of British Columbia and his M.A. and Ph.D. from Clark University. At present he is Adjunct Professor of History at the University of California, San Diego, and lives in La Jolla. He is also Professor Emeritus, Northwestern University, and has taught at Queens University, Canada, and Smith College.

Honors awarded to Dr. Stavrianos include a Guggenheim Fellowship, a Ford Faculty Fellowship and a Rockefeller Foundation Fellowship. He has been a Fellow at the Center for Advanced Study in the Behavioral Sciences and done research in world history under grants from the Carnegie Corporation in New York.

Previously published books include *The Promise of the Coming Dark Age, The World to 1500, The World Since 1500, A Global History, The Balkans Since 1453, Greece: American Dilemma and Opportunity* and *Balkan Federation: A History of the Movement toward Balkan Unity in Modern Times.*

Index